Contemporary
Advertising

Contemporary
Advertising

Tenth Edition

William F. Arens

McGraw-Hill
Irwin

Boston   Burr Ridge, IL   Dubuque, IA   Madison, WI   New York   San Francisco   St. Louis
Bangkok   Bogotá   Caracas   Kuala Lumpur   Lisbon   London   Madrid   Mexico City
Milan   Montreal   New Delhi   Santiago   Seoul   Singapore   Sydney   Taipei   Toronto

**McGraw-Hill
Irwin**

CONTEMPORARY ADVERTISING

Published by McGraw-Hill/Irwin, a business unit of The McGraw-Hill Companies, Inc. 1221 Avenue of the Americas, New York, NY, 10020. Copyright © 2006, 2004, 2002, 1999, 1996, 1994, 1992, 1989, 1986, 1982 by The McGraw-Hill Companies, Inc. All rights reserved. No part of this publication may be reproduced or distributed in any form or by any means, or stored in a database or retrieval system, without the prior written consent of The McGraw-Hill Companies, Inc., including, but not limited to, in any network or other electronic storage or transmission, or broadcast for distance learning.

Some ancillaries, including electronic and print components, may not be available to customers outside the United States.

This book is printed on acid-free paper.

1 2 3 4 5 6 7 8 9 0 DOW/DOW 0 9 8 7 6 5

ISBN 0-07-296472-3

Editorial director: *John E. Biernat*
Publisher: *Andy Winston*
Developmental editor I: *Anna M. Chan*
Executive marketing manager: *Dan Silverburg*
Media producer: *Benjamin Curless*
Senior project manager: *Susanne Riedell*
Production supervisor: *Debra R. Sylvester*
Lead designer: *Matthew Baldwin*
Senior photo research coordinator: *Jeremy Cheshareck*
Photo researcher: *Mike Hruby*
Media project manager: *Betty Hadala*
Supplement producer: *Gina F. DiMartino*
Developer, Media technology: *Brian Nacik*
Cover design: *Matthew Baldwin*
Interior design: *Matthew Baldwin*
Typeface: *10.5/12 Garamond Light*
Compositor: *Precision Graphics*
Printer: *R. R. Donnelley*

Library of Congress Cataloging-in-Publication Data

Arens, William F.
 Contemporary advertising / William F. Arens.—10th ed.
  p. cm. — (McGraw-Hill/Irwin series in marketing)
 Includes index.
 ISBN 0-07-296472-3 (alk. paper)
 1. Advertising. I. Title. II. Series.
HF5821.B62 2006
659.1—dc22

                        2005041457

www.mhhe.com

The Preface

Advertising has the subtle ability to reach out and touch everyone living and working in the modern world today. In fact, at some point in their lives, most people will probably become creators of advertising—whether they design a flyer for a school car wash, write a classified ad for a garage sale, or develop a whole campaign for some business, charitable event, or political cause.

During the first half of the twentieth century, advertising may have been viewed as a particularly American institution. But that is certainly no longer the case. In fact, as early as 1917, British novelist Norman Douglas affirmed the global significance of advertising when he remarked, "You can tell the ideals of a nation by its advertisements." That was before the advent of radio and television. Today, our voices are no longer limited by the scope of twentieth-century media. Thanks to the Internet and a variety of online database services, people and organizations can now send advertising messages to millions of people around the world—instantly. Advertising is undergoing a transformation of historic proportions—from a monopolistic corporate monologue to a totally democratic dialogue. Suddenly everybody has a voice.

That makes the study of advertising more important today than ever before, not only for students of business or journalism—who may be contemplating a career in the field—but also for students of sociology, psychology, political science, economics, history, language, science, or the arts. Many of these people will become users of advertising; all will be lifetime consumers of it.

The study of advertising gives students, regardless of their major field of study, many valuable tools to use in any subsequent profession. It teaches them to think and plan strategically; gather and analyze primary and secondary research data; compute and evaluate alternative courses of action; cooperate with a team in developing creative solutions to a problem; analyze competitive proposals; understand why people behave the way they do; express themselves and their ideas with clarity and simplicity; defend their point of view with others; appreciate and assess the quality of different creative endeavors; and use data to speak with knowledge, confidence, and conviction.

In addition, students of business, journalism, and communications gain several specific benefits. By studying advertising, they will learn to:

- Discern the real economic, social, and cultural role of advertising and, conversely, the impact of a society's values on advertising.
- Understand how advertising supports the profession of journalism and relates to the whole field of communications.
- Appreciate the important, global effect of marketing and advertising on business, industry, and national economies.
- Comprehend the strategic function of advertising within the broader context of business and marketing.

■ Evaluate and appreciate the impressive artistic creativity and technical expertise required in advertising.

■ Discover what people in advertising and related disciplines do, how they do it, and the expanding career opportunities these fields now offer.

Student-Oriented Features for the Twenty-First Century

Our mission in *Contemporary Advertising* has always been to present advertising as it is actually practiced—to put flesh on the bones of academic theory—with clarity and verve. Now, as we introduce the Tenth Edition of *Contemporary Advertising,* our purpose remains the same. Advertising should be taught as it really is—as a business, as a marketing tool, as a creative process, and as a dynamic, hybrid discipline that employs numerous elements of the arts and sciences. We also believe advertising should be taught in an intelligible manner and lively style relevant to college and university students of the twenty-first century.

For these reasons, *Contemporary Advertising* provides a number of exclusive student-oriented features.

Award-Winning Graphic Design

Contemporary Advertising has always been distinguished by its elegant, coffee-table-book feel and award-winning graphic design—an important feature for a book that professes to educate students about the aesthetics of advertising design and production. The open, airy look—reinforced by the book's high-quality, non-see-through, clay-coated paper stock—contributes to learning by making the text material colorful, inviting, and accessible to the widest range of students. In the Tenth Edition, the elegance of the design is enhanced with an updated cover design, a striking new interior color palette, beautiful new part and chapter openers, and a redesign of all the technical illustrations for greater clarity and simplicity. Throughout the book, part and chapter overviews, chapter learning objectives, and key terms printed in boldface type all work together to make the text material as reader-friendly as possible.

Chapter-Opening Vignettes

To capture and hold student interest, each chapter begins not with a case but with a story. Written in a warm, narrative style, each vignette depicts an actual situation that illustrates a basic concept in the study of advertising. Wherever possible, the opening story is then woven through the chapter to demonstrate how textbook concepts actually come to life in real-world situations. For example, throughout Chapter 1, we examine the success of the cult-favorite Altoids campaign to demonstrate how advertising can build a brand from the ground up. In Chapter 8, we use the incredible success story of Mountain Dew to illustrate the importance of creativity and strategic thinking in marketing and advertising planning. And in Chapter 12, we've wrapped the whole subject of creativity and the creative process around the story of how the VitroRobertson agency developed its magnificent, award-winning campaign for Taylor Guitars.

Extensive Illustration Program

The best way to teach is to set a good example. So each of the 18 chapters features beautiful full-color illustrations of recent award-winning ads, commercials, and campaigns that demonstrate the best in the business from the last three years. In fact, *Contemporary Advertising* is one of the most heavily illustrated textbooks on the market, with all the major media represented—print, electronic, digital, and outdoor—in a balanced manner. We carefully selected the examples and illustrations for both their quality and their relevance to students.

Furthermore, we feature a mix of local, national, and international ads from both business-to-business and consumer campaigns. In-depth captions tell the stories behind many of the ads and explain how the ads demonstrate the concepts discussed in the text.

The book is liberally illustrated with models, charts, graphs, and tables. Some of these encapsulate useful information on advertising concepts or the advertising industry. Others depict the processes employed in account management, research, account planning, media planning, and production.

Full-Color Portfolios

In addition to the individual print ads and actual frames from TV commercials, the book contains several multipage portfolios of outstanding creative work. These include "Strategic Use of the Creative Mix," "Outstanding Magazine Ads," "Advertising on the Internet," "Corporate Advertising," and others. Accompanying captions and questions tie the ads to topics germane to the chapter in which they appear.

The Creative Department

The "Creative Department" is a special section in Chapter 14 that describes how an interesting print ad and TV commercial were produced from beginning to end. In this edition, we show a full-color print ad for the ecologically friendly 2004 Toyota Prius Hybrid Synergy Drive vehicle that features an actual acetate color key (called a *transvision*)—a first in advertising texts. And the TV commercial for the Prius created by Saatchi & Saatchi Los Angeles illustrates an extraordinary combination of artistry, cultural sensitivity, and ingenious special effects.

Advertising Laboratories

Active participation enhances learning, so "Ad Labs" play a significant role in virtually every chapter. These unique sidebars to the world of advertising introduce students to topics of current interest or controversy and then involve them in the subject by posing questions that stimulate critical thinking. Some of the many topics presented in Ad Labs include government regulation, bottom-up marketing, creativity, the psychological impact of color, advertising on the Internet, "green" marketing, sales promotion, and direct-response advertising.

Ethical Issues in Advertising

Today's students will be twenty-first-century practitioners. They will face new and challenging ethical issues, and they will need to exercise even greater sensitivity than their twentieth-century counterparts. Therefore, in *every* chapter of the book, we introduce a current Ethical Issue in advertising—to focus attention on the most critical social questions facing advertisers today. These include the debate over puffery, advertising to children, comparative advertising, the targeting of ethnic minorities, consumer profiling, privacy, negative political advertising, visual and statistical manipulation, and others.

Practical Checklists

Advertising is a broad subject encompassing many disciplines, and one dilemma both advertising students and practitioners face is how to handle and organize large volumes of information and then creatively convert this data into effective advertising. For this reason, students truly appreciate the numerous, handy Checklists that appear regularly throughout the text. The Checklists can stimulate memory, organize thinking, and reinforce important concepts. Some of these include Checklist for Writing Effective Copy, Checklist for International Media Planning, Checklist for Creating Effective TV Commercials, and Checklist for Writing News Releases, to mention just a few. In the years that follow, students will find the Checklists an invaluable, practical career resource for developing marketing and advertising plans, writing and designing effective ads and commercials, selecting and scheduling media, evaluating advertising proposals, and making other advertising decisions.

Online Reference Library

In keeping with our desire to build long-term value into the book (without adding text length), we have introduced the Reference Library as a supplemental feature. We continue to offer this valuable reference source on the *Contemporary Advertising* website and the student CD-ROM. The Reference Library contains a wealth of supplementary exhibits, checklists, tables, and models for students or professors who seek additional information or greater detail on a subject of interest. The exhibits in the Reference Library are numbered to correspond to relevant chapters. Professors can choose whether or not to assign this material, depending on their course objectives. But students will find the Reference Library a valuable, long-term handbook for their future careers and lives. Some exhibits in the Reference Library include Advertising Regulations in Western Europe; Using Marketing Research for New Product Development; Checklist of Product Marketing Facts for Creatives; Detailed Explanation of Duncan's IMC Model; Trade Show Budgeting Checklist; and many, many others.

Additional Learning Aids

Each chapter concludes with a summary followed by questions for review and discussion. These pedagogical aids are designed to help students review chapter contents and assimilate what they have learned. Throughout the text, key ideas and terms are highlighted with boldface type and defined when introduced. The definitions of all these terms are collected at the end of the book in a thorough and extensive glossary.

The Advertising Experience Exercises

True to the text's agency approach, the Tenth Edition of *Contemporary Advertising* introduces hands-on application exercises that place students in the advertisers' shoes to help them see how advertising is done in the real world. Effective as outside assignments or in-class discussion starters, the Advertising Experience allows students to effectively apply their knowledge of each chapter.

Internet Exercises

The Internet is the fastest-growing medium in the history of advertising. It is therefore important for students to become familiar and comfortable with the Net and to understand the resources it offers. In the Tenth Edition, each chapter features exercises that require students to access the World Wide Web and perform research on questions relevant to the chapter topic.

For the Professor: The Tenth Edition Has Been Strategically Revised

Our continuing goal has been to bring clarity to the often-murky subject of advertising. Our method has been to personally involve students as much as possible in the practical experiences of advertising, while simultaneously giving them a clear understanding of advertising's dynamic role in both marketing management and the human communication process. In the pursuit of this objective, we have included numerous modifications and improvements in the Tenth Edition of *Contemporary Advertising.*

Because of the growing importance of integrated marketing communications (IMC) and the changing role of advertising in the marketing mix, we restructured the sequence of some chapters in previous editions and included a significant amount of new material in them. In the Tenth Edition, we have maintained this structure in order to illustrate early on how marketers concurrently integrate advertising with other marketing communication tools. For example, immediately following the Part Two chapters on marketing, advertising, and media planning, we devote all of Part Three to the topics of direct marketing, personal selling, sales promotion, public relations, events and sponsorships, and corporate advertising. The reason is simple: That's when advertisers and agencies plan these activities—at the same time they're planning their advertising. However, some professors may wish to teach this material after concluding the study of advertising, in which case we recommend they simply skip Chapters 10 and 11 and assign them after Chapter 18, before studying the Epilogue, "Re-Positioning a Brand."

By also including new material on the economics of advertising, relationship marketing and IMC, the new digital interactive media, and global/international advertising, we have insured that *Contemporary Advertising* will remain both current and comprehensive.

Current and Concise

In the Tenth Edition, our first effort was to update all statistics and tables and to document the most recent academic and professional source material to give *Contemporary Advertising* the most current and relevant compendium of academic and trade citations in the field. We've referenced important recent research on topics ranging from the effects of advertising and sales promotion on brand building to relationship marketing, integrated communications, and Internet advertising. And, where appropriate, we've redesigned the building-block models that facilitate student comprehension of the often-complex processes involved in human communication, consumer behavior, marketing research, and IMC.

In recent editions, thanks to recommendations from our academic reviewers, we added new material to bring a clearer theoretical structure to the book. For example, in Part One, we introduce the principles of free-enterprise economics and then show how these principles have affected the evolution of modern advertising from a ninteenth-century American phenomenon to an accepted global practice in the twenty-first century. This framework creates the underpinning for our discussion of the social and regulatory aspects of advertising, as well as our examination of how the business of advertising has evolved from local, to national, to global. In Parts Two and Three, contemporary theories of marketing and communication create the framework for our discussion of advertising's role in marketing and integrated marketing communications. This then evolves to a theory of creative excellence in Part Four. And in Part Five, all these theories come together as advertisers search for the most economically efficient communication media to create effective marketing relationships with customers and other stakeholders.

Second, we have prudently governed the length of the text material. In the last edition, on the suggestion of our reviewers, we split Chapter 1 into two chapters to make the introduction to the course less daunting for students. While intregrating new material on the economic aspects of advertising, personal selling, sponsorships, and digital interactive media, we have still maintained a manageable length. The illustrations, graphics, sidebar information, and overall design are all aimed at keeping the text open, airy, and inviting while sharpening *clarity*—the hallmark of *Contemporary Advertising*.

Compared to the true length of other comprehensive course books, *Contemporary Advertising* is now one of the most concise texts in the field.

Fresh, Contemporary, Relevant Examples

For the Tenth Edition, we added many new, real-world examples, selected for their currency and their relevance to students. Likewise, many of the chapter-opening stories are new, such as the advertising success stories of Hardee's and Citibank. Others document marketing or communication misfires such as Prodigy and Firestone. All of the full-color portfolios have been updated, expanded, or replaced with more recent examples and all of the Ad Labs, Checklists, and Ethical Issues have been updated and edited for currency and accuracy.

Global Orientation Integrated Throughout

In light of the increasing globalization of business, we introduce the subject of global advertising early in the book in Chapter 4, "The Scope of Advertising: From Local to Global." We've also added more examples of international advertising throughout the book. All the international data has been extensively revised and updated to reflect the increased importance of advertising in the new economic and marketing realities of Europe.

Focus on Integrated Marketing Communications

One result of exploding technology, and consequent market fragmentation, has been the growing realization by major advertisers and agencies of the importance of relationship marketing and integrated marketing communications. In response to this, we have woven the IMC perspective throughout the text. We first introduce the concept of IMC in Chapter 1; next, in Part Two, we explain its impact on marketing, advertising, and media planning; and then we focus all of Part Three on how companies build relationships by integrating their advertising with other marketing communication tools. Finally, in Part Five, we show how each of the major media contribute to the IMC process. Throughout, we cite the most recent important research on all these topics.

CASE STUDY: Epilogue: Re-Positioning a Brand

So that students can see how many of the principles taught in the text come together in the real world, we have included an updated Epilogue, immediately following Chapter 18, on the complete story behind the currently running, highly successful "Priceless" branding campaign for MasterCard, created by McCann-Erickson Worldwide in New York. We are greatly indebted to both McCann-Erickson and MasterCard for authorizing us to share the details of this interesting, student-relevant campaign and for the tremendous assistance they gave us in the creation of this outstanding Epilogue.

Local and Business-to-Business Advertising Coverage

Throughout the book, *Contemporary Advertising* addresses the needs of both small and large consumer and business-to-business advertisers with its many examples, case histories, Ad Labs, Checklists, and advertisements. Moreover, this is one of the few texts to devote adequate attention to the needs of the small retail advertiser by discussing how local advertisers can integrate their marketing communications.

Highlights of This Revision

While all the chapters have been edited and updated, one of the things we're most excited about is the inclusion of award winning ads from the 2004 Cannes International Advertising Festival. You will find that every chapter has an abundance of new and relevant ads and commercials that were cited for their excellence at Cannes by winning either a Bronze, Silver, or Gold Lion. These current examples from countries around the globe are considered to be the best ads in the world, and we have flagged them by inserting a Cannes logo (like the one at left) wherever they appear. We are delighted to be able to share these outstanding examples of advertising creativity with today's students whom we feel confident will benefit greatly from the exposure to such fine work. Other specific highlights of the Tenth Edition include the following:

Chapter 3: "The Economic, Social, and Regulatory Aspects of Advertising." This chapter has been updated and revised to add clarity to the very important issues it addresses. The chapter opens with a new vignette about the highly controversial catalog advertising for Abercrombie & Fitch. This sets the stage for a detailed discussion of advertising's proper role in our economic system and our society. By using the economic framework set up in Chapters 1 and 2 for our discussion of advertising controversies, we have a basis for understanding how advertising may contribute or detract from the basic goal of free enterprise—"the most good for the most people." The section on "Current Regulatory Issues Affecting U.S. Advertisers" deals with numerous issues, among them: Freedom of Commercial Speech, the Tobacco Advertising Controversy, Consumer Privacy, and the Issue of Advertising to Children. The chapter offers a more balanced presentation of what's right and wrong about advertising, acknowledging the profession's shortcomings—for instance, in the area of deception with the FTC versus Office Depot case, and in the area of sexual and ethnic stereotyping. The discussion of deception and puffery in advertising has been updated, referencing the recent work by Ivan Preston. And the Ethical Issue in this chapter focuses on the subject of puffery, including the recent case of Pizza Hut versus Papa John's Pizza.

Chapter 4: "The Scope of Advertising: From Local to Global." A new vignette featuring the discovery of a new target market for the Honda Civic introduces the chapter, and the story is revisited throughout the chapter to illustrate what people in the advertising business do. The chapter discusses all the major organizations involved in the advertising business. Beginning with the advertisers, the chapter classifies them by their scope of business: local, regional, national, and transnational. The agency section demonstrates what agency people do and how they work. The material on the media and suppliers is included to present a balanced view of all the participants in the advertising industry. In the Tenth Edition, we updated all the statistical information about the advertising business and edited the chapter carefully to increase clarity and enhance comprehension.

Chapter 6: "Market Segmentation and the Marketing Mix: Determinants of Advertising Strategy."   This chapter starts with a new vignette that outlines Hardee's attempt to reposition itself as a male-oriented premium hamburger chain. This vignette shows that choosing a market segment and focusing on it can produce better results that aiming at the total market with me-too products. All figures and statistics have been updated, as has the whole illustration program.

Chapter 7: "Research: Gathering Information for Advertising Planning."   In previous editions this chapter was substantially reorganized. In this edition we have updated the Ethical Issue to include a recent case in which KFC was cited for skewing statistics. We deal with the way in which research statistics can be used and abused. In the Tenth Edition we have updated all the figures and tables and freshened the chapter with new illustrations and exhibits.

Chapter 10: "Relationship Building: Direct Marketing, Personal Selling, and Sales Promotion."   This chapter begins a new unit in the book, Part Three, "Integrating Advertising with Other Elements of the Communications Mix." The chapter, and indeed this whole part, is based on the philosophy that, while advertising can create an image for a company, a reputation must be earned. In other words, *everything* a company does (and doesn't do, for that matter) sends a message to its various stakeholders. Advertising, as well as sales promotion, personal selling, and other marketing communication tools, is one of the *planned* messages that companies employ. Advertising people need to be more than just aware of these other communication tools. They need to recognize (at the planning stage) that some of them are better suited for solving certain marketing problems than advertising is. And if the firm is to truly realize its reputation potential, they must all be integrated with everything else a company does. This chapter opens with an updated story about how Dell Computers promoted itself by using direct marketing techniques to promote its sweepstakes. The story enables us to spotlight the importance of direct marketing to IMC programs.

Chapter 11: "Relationship Building: Public Relations, Sponsorship, and Corporate Advertising."   Continuing the same themes, the second chapter in Part Three tells the story of how a small company with a social conscience, Ben & Jerry's Ice Cream, achieved nationwide success and international recognition. We've strengthened the IMC focus of the chapter and broadened the material with updated information on events and sponsorships. We lead that segment off with an interesting story of how Bennett Gibbs turned his local bike shop into a $3 million enterprise through the effective use of event sponsorship. The chapter boasts a whole new art program and a new portfolio of outstanding corporate ads. The Ethical Issue debates the controversy surrounding advertorials.

Chapter 13: "Creative Execution: Art and Copy."   This chapter starts off with a new vignette on Citibank's identity theft solutions campaign. We take an in-depth look at the challenge faced by Citibank when it needed to communicate the threat posed by identity theft without creating panic. Also included in the Tenth Edition is a wealth of award-winning ads and commercials from the Cannes Festival, chosen for their superior copywriting and art direction. The Ethical Issue in this chapter discusses imitation and plagiarism and shows how "borrowing" can often come close to stealing.

Chapter 14: "Producing Ads for Print, Electronic, and Digital Media."   For the Tenth Edition, this chapter has been completely reworked. The chapter features a new story about Saatchi & Saatchi's development of a global campaign, launching Toyota's Hybrid Synergy Drive vehicle, the Prius. We weave this story throughout the entire chapter, using the television spots for the Prius to give a real-life demonstration of development and production. Students will be interested to follow the progression of an international campaign from its initial concept to its final execution across a variety of media.

Chapter 17: "Using Digital Interactive Media and Direct Mail." In the previous edition, we revised this chapter extensively and introduced a new chapter-opening story on the highly successful launch of a website for virtual pet owners—Neopets.com. In the Tenth Edition, we have updated the Neopets story, and, since the Internet continues to develop exponentially, we have extensively edited the chapter for currency and included many new examples of superior cyber ads. The chapter discusses the history of the Internet; the growth of online services and the World Wide Web; the different types of digital, interactive advertising available, including viral and immersive marketing; some of the problems with measuring Internet advertising; and the use of these new media in IMC. The second part of the chapter, which deals with direct mail as an addressable medium, begins with an interesting new vignette on ShipShapes and CMM (Customized MarketMail) and explains the use of direct mail in IMC programs as well.

Epilogue: "Re-Positioning a Brand: MasterCard's 'Priceless' Campaign." The famous and fascinating "Priceless" campaign for MasterCard demonstrates in detail how all the concepts taught in the book come together in real life. We are greatly indebted to MasterCard and to McCann-Erickson Worldwide, who developed the campaign, for their efforts in helping us put together this outstanding Epilogue, and we appreciate their assistance in updating the story for the Tenth Edition. A video supplement to the text includes recent commercials from the campaign.

The Reference Library. In recent editions, we redesigned the Reference Library and put it on the new *Contemporary Advertising* website to make it easier to update and to use. Many of the most popular features from the earlier editions have been retained, and for the Tenth Edition we've added other elements that professors or students might find helpful.

Appendix C: "Complete IMC Plan." Complementing the Top-Down Marketing and Advertising Plan Outlines in Appendixes A and B, Appendix C features an IMC Plan Outline. Developed by Brannon Wait at Saatchi & Saatchi Chicago, the plan will be very useful to students in their future endeavors. This may be found on the *Contemporary Advertising* website.

Appendix D: "Career Planning in Advertising." This section has been updated with many helpful hints for students about to launch their careers. It includes salary figures for entry-level employees in a variety of advertising-related positions and is also found on the *Contemporary Advertising* website.

Appendix E: "Industry Resources." This appendix organizes a great deal of practical information students can use to perform further research in areas of interest or to advance their careers by joining an organization focused on their specialty. It is located on the *Contemporary Advertising* website.

Supplementary Materials

While the text itself is a complete introduction to the field of advertising, it is accompanied by a number of valuable supplemental materials designed to assist the instructor.

Instructor's Manual

In the previous edition, we expanded the Instructor's Manual to include a wealth of new material and suggestions for classroom lectures and discussions. It includes a lecture outline for each chapter; answers to all discussion questions, including the end-of-chapter Internet exercises, suggested workshops, projects, and debates; and additional material for reading or project assignments.

Video Supplements

To illustrate how the principles discussed in the text have actually been applied in business, the book is supplemented by several special video programs and a video instructor's guide. One video was produced exclusively for *Contemporary Advertising* by the author for instructor use in the classroom. It includes a wide variety of domestic and international commercials specially referenced with voice-over introductions to specific chapters. This video is text-specific in subject matter and also includes many of the commercials discussed in the text—such as the MasterCard campaign from the Epilogue, the Got Milk? campaign discussed in Chapter 16, and the Toyota Prius spot from Chapter 14, to mention just a few. New for the Tenth Edition will be the addition of winners from the 2004 International Advertising Festival at Cannes, as well as a behind-the-scenes tour of the 2003 Cannes Festival (also included on the Student CD). Produced by the author for *Contemporary Advertising* in cooperation with the festival management, the video demonstrates why Cannes is regarded as the "Academy Awards" of advertising.

The second video was produced by the Advertising Educational Foundation, to whom we express our deep gratitude and appreciation. It includes a behind-the-scenes look at advertising research at work. The video, entitled "Good-bye Guesswork: How Research Guides Today's Advertisers," includes case studies for V8 Juice, Maidenform, and AT&T's "800" Service, and shows how research is used to develop new ads, to refine ad campaigns, to decide the best place to advertise, and to evaluate current ads.

With the previous edition, we introduced a new series of video case studies. The first video follows the development of an advertising campaign for the Tumbleweed restaurant chain. The second features the work of Doe Anderson on a full campaign promoting Kentucky tourism. With the Tenth Edition, we will introduce a new video on Ofoto, a Kodak company, and the work done for them by Carat Interactive. The videos are presented in a way that makes them easy to use in class for comparison and contrast discussions.

Offered at no charge to adopters of *Contemporary Advertising,* these various video supplements are designed to help the instructor teach real-world decision making and demonstrate some of the best current examples of television advertising from around the world.

Instructor CD-ROM

Also available to instructors is a CD with support materials for classroom presentations. These include more than 150 of the important models and graphs presented in the text and more than 40 ads not found in the text—all produced in full color. Also on the CD is the complete Instructor's Manual, Test Bank, and PowerPoint presentation.

Test Bank

An extensive array of objective test questions prepared by Tom and Betty Pritchett, of Kennesaw State University, was carefully designed to provide a fair, structured program of evaluation. The testing system is available in a printed version or computerized on our Instructor CD-ROM. Professors may also access this resource online through the book's website and PageOut, our course website builder.

Internet Website

Complementing the Tenth Edition is an Internet website (www.mhhe.com/arens06). For instructors, we have downloadable supplements and a link to McGraw-Hill's PageOut. For students, there are self-checking quizzes, a link to PowerWeb for updates about what is going on in the world of advertising, and video clips from our video package.

Uses for This Text

Contemporary Advertising was written for undergraduate students in liberal arts, journalism, mass communication, and business schools. However, because of its practical, hands-on approach, depth of coverage, and marketing management emphasis, it is also widely used in independent schools, university extension courses, and courses on advertising management. The wealth of award-winning advertisements also makes it a resource guide to the best work in the field for students in art and graphic design courses and for professionals in the field.

Many of the stories, materials, and techniques included in this text come from the author's personal experience as a full-time marketing communications executive and adjunct professor at San Diego State University and the University of California at San Diego. Others come from the experiences of friends and colleagues in the business. We believe this book will be a valuable resource guide, not only in the study of advertising but later in the practice of it as well. In all cases, we hope readers will experience the feel and the humanness of the advertising world—whether they intend to become professionals in the business, to work with practitioners, or simply to become more sophisticated consumers.

William F. Arens

Our Thanks

In student parlance, writing a textbook on any subject might well be considered the term paper from hell. An advertising textbook, though, would be nigh impossible without the assistance and cooperation of a legion of individuals and companies on the professional side. I am therefore deeply indebted to many people and organizations on all sides of the advertising business (agencies, clients, media, and suppliers) for their professional assistance and personal encouragement. These include, but are certainly not limited to, Joyce Harrington, John Wolfe, and Burtch Drake at the American Association of Advertising Agencies; Paula Alex and Linda McCreight at the Advertising Educational Foundation; Paula Veale at the Ad Council; Sheldon Hochheiser at AT&T; Shawn O'Neill at New American Financial; Vonda LePage at Deutsch, New York; Roy Elvove at BBDO; David DeCecco at Pepsi-Cola Company; Peter Farago at Farago & Partners; Larry Jones at Foote Cone & Belding, Los Angeles; Christian Arens at Carat Interactive, San Francisco; and Jo Muse at Muse Cordero Chen.

I owe a tremendous thank you to Susan Irwin at McCann-Erickson Worldwide for her many years of friendship and assistance and to her people at McCann for their incredible efforts and good work on providing us with the complete campaign for MasterCard in the Epilogue. I am likewise very grateful to everybody at Saatchi & Saatchi Los Angeles, Tokyo, and New York, as well as Toyota Motor Sales U.S.A. for their invaluable assistance, openness, and cooperation in providing the material for our chapter on advertising production and the elegant ads for the Toyota Prius in that chapter. These include Yukie Kasugai, Deborah Meyer, and Steve Jett at Toyota, and, at Saatchi, David Martin, Lisa Christensen, Doug Van Andel, Lorraine Alper Kramer, Max Godsil, and Damon Webster in Los Angeles, Monica Hudson, Kevin Roberts, and Bob Isherwood in New York, and Jack Mickle in Tokyo. I also thank Brannon Wait at Saatchi & Saatchi Chicago for his initiative in getting us all together in the first place.

For our chapter on the scope of advertising, I am very grateful to my friends at Muse Cordero Chen & Partners for sharing their interesting work on the Honda Civic with us. A big thank-you to Shelley Yamane, Wilky Lao, and Jo Muse.

The chapter on Internet advertising required extensive revisions and updating, and for his incredible contributions of time, knowledge, and material, I am very indebted to John Keck, formerly senior VP/interactive media director at FCB San Francisco and to Christian Arens at Carat Interactive, San Francisco. Also, for the outstanding portfolio of layout styles in Chapter 13, thanks go to Tom Michael and Tabitha Ziegler at Market Design in Encinitas, CA.

For their warm, open, and gracious contributions of time, counsel, and materials, I extend my appreciation to all my Canadian friends, especially Paul Lavoie, Daniel Rabinowicz, and Ann Boldt at Taxi; Pierre Delagrave, Normand Chiasson, and Manon Caza at Cossette Communication-Marketing; Marcel Barthe at Optimum; Francois Descarie at Impact Research; Yves Gougoux at Publicis/BCP Stratégie Créativité; and Normand Grenier at Communications Grenier.

I am very grateful to my friends at the International Advertising Festival in Cannes for their cooperation and assistance in pulling together all the award winners for this new edition. I know it created a lot of additional work for you, and I really appreciate it. I am especially appreciative of the efforts of Terry Savage, Amanda Benfel, and Monika Barrau. To produce the video on the Cannes Festival required the expertise and considerable cooperation of the French film crew from DRC films: Dominique and Raphael Rollin and Michael Verheyden, all of whom did an outstanding job. I am especially grateful for the tremendous personal assistance I've had the last two years at Cannes, first from the assistant video producer Severin Ledresseur and then from Elena Vorobyeva, now with Euro RSCG Moradpour, Moscow.

Interestingly, *Contemporary Advertising* is now widely used in Russia and the CIS states. On several recent trips to Moscow, I have received generous hospitality, incredible assistance, and very sage advice from a number of individuals, namely, Dr. Vladimir Estafiev of Maxima Advertising; Alex and Natasha Andreev and Natalia Pavlenkova of Depot WPF; John Bonar of Bonar Media; Edouard Moradpour of Euro RSCG Moradpour; Sergei Pilatov, chairman of the United Advertising Council of the CIS countries; and Elena Mamai, president of the First Almaty International Advertising Festival. I am also extremely grateful to my translators for their friendship, help, and personal assistance: Anton Uspensky, Natalia Mospanova, and Elizaveta Zakharova. To all of you, *bolshoi spacebo*.

I must give special thanks to several longtime friends in the business whose contributions, continuous support, and wise counsel I value and appreciate immeasurably: Susan Irwin at McCann-Erickson; Jan Sneed at Grey Advertising; Rance Crain at *Advertising Age;* Jack Trout at Trout and Partners; Jorge Gutierrez Orvañanos at MerchanDesign, Guadalajara, Mexico; Brad Lynch, retired from the Ad Council; and, of course, my good friend of many years, Al Ries at Ries & Ries.

In addition, I appreciate the moral support, encouragement, generous assistance, and friendship of Tom and Dena Michael, Carlos and Yolanda Cortez, Bob and Demmie Divine, Jim and Diana Priddy, Rudy and Martha Gonzales, Charles Salik, Sid and Iris Stein, Professor E. L. Deckinger, Jann Pasler, Jack Savidge, Barnard and Sylvia Thompson, Ann Ritchey, LeAnna Zevely, Carol Wexler, Sergei and Natasha Stikhin, and Alan and Rita Moller. Special thanks for generous assistance and encouragement to John Nauman, and, for giving so much to so many for so long, Stanley D. Woodworth, Sid Bernstein, Don Ritchey, Stanley Urlaub, and John O'Toole—gone from our midst but never forgotten.

Deadlines impact family life the worst. For their continued understanding and encouragement, I thank my sons William and Christian who over the years paid the highest price for their dad to be an author. I also thank my wife, Olivia, for her constancy, fortitude, and incredible patience trying to keep the dinner warm every night for the eventual appearance of the phantom.

The fun of working on a project of this magnitude is directly proportional to the people you work with. For that reason, I am very grateful to the dedicated team of students, graduates, and professionals assembled for the Tenth Edition, primarily from San Diego State University, University of California San Diego, and from Publication Services. These people who gave so much, asked so little, and made it such a pleasurable experience included Sandra Castellanos, Melissa Ditalo, Sarah Black, Mary Zimmer, Dale Teplitz, Jan Fisher, Lori Martinsek, Aimee Ehrs, and Brandon Warga. I also thank Tom and Betty Pritchett of Kennesaw State University who worked against incredible deadlines to prepare the Test Bank. I am particularly grateful for the skill and expertise of video mavens Kelly, Jake, and Kevin Segraves.

Finally, I want to give special recognition to my very capable editorial assistant and research manager Sarah Steinberg. Her attention to detail, writing skills, and inimitable dry wit make her a pleasure to work with. I really appreciate the opportunity to work with her.

I have always appreciated the skill and dedication of our publishing team at McGraw-Hill/Irwin. Interestingly, it just seems to keep getting better. This edition I was blessed with several new players whose skill and can-do attitude made the project thoroughly enjoyable. Thank you John Biernat, Andy Winston, Anna Chan, and Dan Silverburg. The McGraw-Hill/Irwin A-team also included Susanne Riedell, Mike Hruby, Benjamin Curless, Debra Sylvester, Matthew Baldwin, Jeremy Cheshareck, Gina DiMartino, and Elizabeth Hadala. For moral support and wise counsel when needed, thanks also to Jerry Saykes, Steve Patterson, and Gary Burke. A major thank-you to all of you for again finding the way to do the impossible. I appreciate your patience, dedication to excellence, and your friendship more than you can possibly know.

I also want to recognize and thank the American Academy of Advertising, the American Association for Education in Journalism and Mass Communications, and the American Marketing Association, three organizations whose publications and meetings provide a valuable forum for the exchange of ideas and for professional growth.

I am deeply grateful to the many instructors, professors, academic reviewers, and friends in academia who do the real heavy lifting through their ongoing research, writing, and teaching. Their creative ideas and critical insights were invaluable in the preparation of this edition. If you like the changes and additions to this edition, the credit belongs to them for their wise counsel and intelligent suggestions. If not, the responsibility is entirely mine. These people include, but are certainly not limited to, Shanite Akintonde, Columbia College; Linda Bond, Stephen F. Austin State University; Chris Cakebread, Boston University; Cynthia Frisby, University of Missouri—Columbia; Janice Jenny, Herkimer County Community College; Tien-Tsung Lee, Washington State University; Lynda Maddox, George Washington University; Karen Marbot, Hudson Valley Community College; Ina Midkiff, Austin Community College—Cedar Park; David Nemi, Niagara County Community College; Nancy Pace-Miller, Evangel University; Carmen Powers, Monroe Community College; Lisa Scuilli, Indiana University of Pennsylvania; Lewis Small, York College; Corliss Thornton, Georgia State University; Leslie Turner, Penn State University; and Joan Weiss, Bucks County Community College. Finally, I must acknowledge the personal contributions of Hugh Cannon of Wayne State University, a good and generous friend whose wise counsel and brilliant suggestions have enriched the last three editions immeasurably.

To each and every one of you, I thank you. It's your contributions that make this thing work.

W. F. A.

Take a look inside *Contemporary Advertising*—an introduction to advertising in the real world.

Part 1

Advertising Perspectives

THERE ARE many ways to look at advertising—as a business, a creative communication process, a social phenomenon, and a fundamental ingredient of the free-enterprise system. The first part of this text defines advertising, examines the most important dimensions of the field, considers how changing economics has influenced the evolution of the profession, outlines advertising's functions and scope, considers its social and legal ramifications, and looks at the major participants in the advertising business, not just in North America but around the world. ∎

Contemporary Advertising is one of the best-selling advertising textbooks in the field. Known for its clear writing style and real-world agency approach, this comprehensive text shows how advertising "gets done."

A secret formula revealed.

Advertising.
The way great brands
get to be great brands.

American Advertising Federation ad org

Chapter 1
What Is Advertising Today?
Gives an overview of the profession. It defines advertising in contemporary terms, examines its role in the communication process and the marketing process, and introduces some basic terminology. The chapter focuses on advertising's role in marketing strategy.

Chapter 2
The Evolution of Advertising
Sets down an economic framework for understanding how advertising has evolved. It explains the basic tenets of a free-market economy and describes advertising's role in that economy. The chapter focuses on the history of advertising as an economic tool and discusses the impact of advertising on the society in which it operates.

Chapter 3
The Economic, Social, and Regulatory Aspects of Advertising
Discusses the impact of advertising on the economy and society, considers some common criticisms of advertising, and debates the ethical and social responsibilities of companies that advertise. It describes the roles played by government, industry, and consumer groups in regulating advertising. Finally, it compares important laws governing the practice of advertising in the United States and Canada with those in foreign countries.

Chapter 4
The Scope of Advertising: From Local to Global
Shows how people and groups organize themselves—as advertisers, agencies, media, and suppliers—around the world to create, produce, and manage advertising. The chapter describes the role of each of these organizations and discusses critical factors that affect the client/agency relationship and the management of advertising in different cultural, economic, and social environments.

NEW— The Advertising Experience.

These new end-of-chapter exercises are hands-on in application and place the student in the advertisers' shoes. Effective as outside assignments or in-class discussion starters, The Advertising Experience allows students to effectively apply their knowledge of each chapter.

Review Questions
1. What are the four fundamental assumptions of free-market economics?
2. What are the primary functions of advertising in a free economy?
3. What has had the greatest impact on the way advertising has evolved?
4. How does advertising lower the cost of sales?
5. How would you differentiate the advertising used in the industrializing age and the industrial age?
6. What has been the most important influence on advertising in
7. ... companies or organizations that
8. What companies can you think of that are engaged in marketing warfare?
9. As a consumer, are you likely to save money buying at a store that doesn't advertise? Explain.
10. What effects do you believe advertising has had on society in general? Explain.
11. **The Advertising Experience**
Identify a social problem at your school that has had an effect on your life in the past few months. Then create a print demarketing advertisement that addresses this problem. The ad should have a visual element as well as a slogan.

Review Questions
1. What roles do the major organizations involved in the advertising business perform?
2. What's the difference between a local advertiser and a national advertiser?
3. What services might a modern full-service advertising agency offer a large business-to-business advertiser?
4. What are the most important things an advertiser should consider when selecting an agency?
5. How does an agency make money? What is the best way to compensate an agency? Explain your answer.
6. If you owned an ad agency, what would you do to attract new business? Be specific.
7. What are the advantages and disadvantages of an in-house agency?
8. What are the major influences on the client/agency relationship? What can clients and agencies do to maintain a good relationship?
9. What is meant by the term *interactive media*? Give some examples.
10. If you were planning to advertise your brand of computers in Europe, would you likely use foreign or international media? Why?
11. **The Advertising Experience**
Due to the great success of a sitcom based on an Amish farm family, old-fashioned farm implements have become a hot item in American hardware stores. After researching co-op advertisements in local newspapers, create and design a co-op ad for Yodel's Scythes and Deuce Hardware Store.

Review Questions
1. ... role does advertising play in our economic system?
2. ... are the two types of social criticisms of advertising?
3. ... is puffery? Give some examples. Do you ever feel ... eived by puffery in advertising?
4. ... s advertising affect our value system? In what ways?
5. ... t is the difference between an advertiser's ethics and its ... al responsibility?
6. ... v does government regulation of advertising in the United ... es differ from regulation in many foreign countries?
7. ... v does commercial speech differ from political speech? Do ... think advertisers should have the same First Amendment ... ts as everyone else? Explain.
8. ... t is the role of the FTC in advertising? Do you think this ... role should be expanded or restricted?
9. How do regional and local governments affect advertisers?
10. How well do advertisers regulate themselves? In what areas do you think advertisers have done well, and where should they clean up their act?
11. **The Advertising Experience**
In order to understand better a technique, even a questionable one, it is sometimes best to have practiced it oneself. Take a common product and create a responsible advertisement for it. Next, puff the ad up using the techniques studied in the chapter. Be prepared to discuss the differences between the advertisements and how the puffery affects consumer perception.

The Tenth Edition continues its current and up-to-date coverage with a thorough overview of advertising today. Presenting advertising from the creative standpoint, William Arens draws from his own industry experience to lend life to the examples. This insider's perspective will give students a unique tour of the exciting world of advertising.

Chapter Openers

Chapter Objectives provide a map of the chapter's goals to prepare students in learning the material. The accompanying **vignettes** capture students' interest and provide a real-world framework for the chapter's concepts. The vignettes are woven throughout the chapter to reinforce concepts and are exciting examples of advertising in action. Featured companies include Altoids, Kodak, Abercrombie & Fitch, Ben & Jerry's, and Citibank.

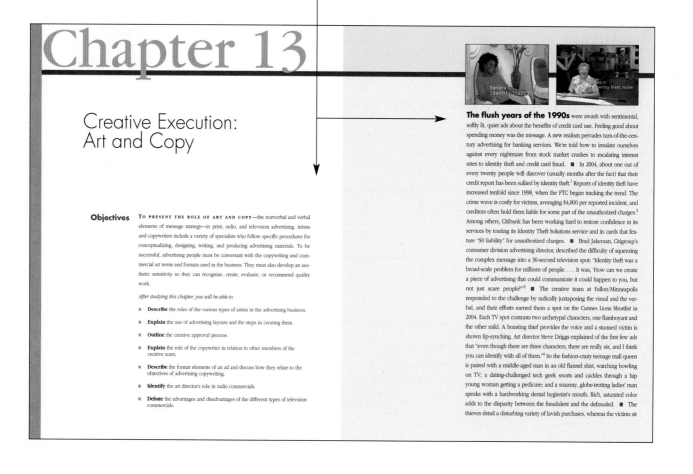

Chapter 13

Creative Execution: Art and Copy

Objectives TO PRESENT THE ROLE OF ART AND COPY—the nonverbal and verbal elements of message strategy—in print, radio, and television advertising. Artists and copywriters include a variety of specialists who follow specific procedures for conceptualizing, designing, writing, and producing advertising materials. To be successful, advertising people must be conversant with the copywriting and commercial art terms and formats used in the business. They must also develop an aesthetic sensitivity so they can recognize, create, evaluate, or recommend quality work.

After studying this chapter, you will be able to:

- **Describe** the roles of the various types of artists in the advertising business.
- **Explain** the use of advertising layouts and the steps in creating them.
- **Outline** the creative approval process.
- **Explain** the role of the copywriter in relation to other members of the creative team.
- **Describe** the format elements of an ad and discuss how they relate to the objectives of advertising copywriting.
- **Identify** the art director's role in radio commercials.
- **Debate** the advantages and disadvantages of the different types of television commercials.

The flush years of the 1990s were awash with sentimental, softly lit, quiet ads about the benefits of credit card use. Feeling good about spending money was the message. A new realism pervades turn-of-the-century advertising for banking services. We're told how to insulate ourselves against every nightmare from stock market crashes to escalating interest rates to identity theft and credit card fraud. ▪ In 2004, about one out of every twenty people will discover (usually months after the fact) that their credit report has been sullied by identity theft.[1] Reports of identity theft have increased tenfold since 1998, when the FTC began tracking the trend. The crime wave is costly for victims, averaging $4,800 per reported incident, and creditors often hold them liable for some part of the unauthorized charges.[2] Among others, Citibank has been working hard to restore confidence in its services by touting its Identity Theft Solutions service and its cards that feature "$0 liability" for unauthorized charges. ▪ Brad Jakeman, Citigroup's consumer division advertising director, described the difficulty of squeezing the complex message into a 30-second television spot: "Identity theft was a broad-scale problem for millions of people. . . . It was, 'How can we create a piece of advertising that could communicate it could happen to you, but not just scare people?'"[3] ▪ The creative team at Fallon/Minneapolis responded to the challenge by radically juxtaposing the visual and the verbal, and their efforts earned them a spot on the Cannes Lions Shortlist in 2004. Each TV spot contrasts two archetypal characters, one flamboyant and the other mild. A boasting thief provides the voice and a stunned victim is shown lip-synching. Art director Steve Driggs explained of the first few ads that "even though there are three characters, there are really six, and I think you can identify with all of them."[4] So the fashion-crazy teenage mall queen is paired with a middle-aged man in an old flannel shirt, watching bowling on TV; a dating-challenged tech geek snorts and cackles through a hip young woman getting a pedicure; and a smarmy, globe-trotting ladies' man speaks with a hardworking dental hygienist's mouth. Rich, saturated color adds to the disparity between the fraudulent and the defrauded. ▪ The thieves detail a disturbing variety of lavish purchases, whereas the victims sit

Ad Lab

Ad Lab boxes introduce students to current topics in advertising and go in-depth with questions to encourage critical thinking.

Ethical Issues

Ethical Issues boxes highlight ethical challenges advertisers face today. These timely boxes cover issues such as negative political advertising, privacy issues, and statistical manipulation.

Checklist

Checklists appear throughout the text to reinforce key concepts presented in the chapter. Students will find these practical lists to be invaluable learning tools.

Ad Lab 1–A

Advertising as a Literary Form

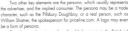

These four ads all won Gold, Silver, or Bronze Lions at the 2004 Cannes advertising festival. They show how advertising messages typically come in one or a blend of three literary forms: autobiography, narrative, or drama.

Autobiography tells its story from a first-person point of view and may often use the word *I*. The narrative form typically uses a third-person voice, which often exudes a well-informed, authoritative quality, to tell the reader about the product. The drama form uses the style of theater to create or perform a scene, so the reader receives the message by implication rather than direct telling.

Two other key elements are the persona, which usually represents the advertiser, and the implied consumer. The persona may be a trade character, such as the Pillsbury Doughboy, or a real person, such as William Shatner, the spokesperson for priceline.com. A logo may even be a form of persona.

Sometimes a character, such as the elderly woman in the British ad (example 1) or the white-suited mechanic in the Chinese ad for laundry detergent (example 2), may represent the implied consumer. Ads like the one in example 4 may employ a number of literary forms simultaneously.

Laboratory Application

Can you identify which two literary forms appear in example 4? Does it have a persona and/or an implied consumer? If so, describe their use.

1. *Autobiography.*

2. *Narrative.*

3. *Drama.*

4. *Mixture of literary forms and elements.*

11

Checklist

Creating Local Advertising

- ___ *Stand out from the competition.* Make your ads easily recognizable. Ads with unusual art, layout, and typefaces have higher readership. Make the ads distinctive but keep their appearance consistent.
- ___ *Use a simple layout.* The layout should carry the reader's eye through the message easily and in proper sequence from headline to illustration to explanatory copy to price to store name. Avoid using too many typefaces.
- ___ *Use a dominant element.* A large picture or headline ensures quick visibility. Photos of real people and action pictures win more readership, as do photos of local people or places. Color attracts more readers.
- ___ *Stress the benefits.* Present the emotional reason to buy or the tangible performance element customers seek.
- ___ *Make the headline count.* Use a compelling headline to feature the main benefit.
- ___ *Watch your language.* Make your writing style active, lively, and involving. Make the readers feel they already own the product. Avoid negativism and profanity.
- ___ *Let white space work for you.* White space focuses the reader's attention and makes the headline and illustration stand out.
- ___ *Make the copy complete.* Emphasize the benefits most appealing to customers.
- ___ *Make your visual powerful and eye-catching. Make sure it demonstrates your message.* The main visual is often more important than the headline. Photos work better than artwork.
- ___ *State price or range of prices.* Dollar figures have good attention value, and readers often overestimate omitted prices. Spell out credit and layaway plans.
- ___ *Specify branded merchandise.* If the item is a known brand, say so.
- ___ *Include related items.* Make two sales instead of one by offering related items along with a featured one.
- ___ *Urge readers to buy now.* Ask for the sale. Stimulate prompt action by using "limited supply" or "this week only."
- ___ *Don't forget the store name and address.* Check every ad to be certain the store name, address, phone number, and hours are included.
- ___ *Don't be too clever.* Many people distrust or misunderstand cleverness.
- ___ *Don't use unusual or difficult words.* Everyone understands simple language. Use it.
- ___ *Don't generalize.* Be specific. Shoppers want all the facts before they buy.
- ___ *Don't make excessive claims.* Advertisers lose customers when they make claims they can't back up.
- ___ *Plan ad size carefully.* Attention usually increases with size.
- ___ *Consider your target customers.* People notice ads more if they are directed at their own gender or age group.
- ___ *Use tie-ins* with local or special news events.

Finding big ideas for local ad campaigns can be extremely difficult. Some advertisers look to the merchandise for ideas; others look to the customer. An important goal for local advertisers is to achieve a consistent, distinctive look that makes their ads both appealing and identifiable. We discuss the creative process in depth in Part Four.

Local advertisers can turn to a number of sources for creative help, including reps from the local media, local ad agencies, freelancers and consultants, creative boutiques, syndicated art services, and the *cooperative advertising programs* of wholesalers, manufacturers, and trade associations.

Cooperative Advertising

As a service to their distributors and dealers, and to ensure proper reproduction of their products, wholesalers and manufacturers as well as some trade associations often provide local advertisers with ready-made advertising materials and cooperative advertising programs where the costs are shared.

There are two key purposes for **cooperative (co-op) advertising:** to build the manufacturer's brand image and to help its distributors, dealers, or retailers make more sales.[3] Every year, national manufacturers give their local retailers more than $20 billion for co-op projects. Newspapers, network and cable TV, and radio are the favored media of co-op spending, with newspapers claiming 55 percent of co-op dollars.[4] Intel alone spends more than $800 million annually to help PC marketers who display the "Intel Inside" logo.[5]

In **vertical cooperative advertising,** the manufacturer provides the complete ad and shares the cost of the advertising time or space. The local newspaper sets the name and address of the local advertiser, or the radio station adds a tagline with the advertiser's name, address, and phone number. Exhibit 4–2 lists typical co-op advertising allowances. (See Ad Lab 4–A for the pros and cons of co-op advertising.)

Exhibit 4–2
The importance of co-op advertising dollars.

Store	Co-op dollars as a percentage of total ad budget
Appliance dealers	80%
Clothing stores	35
Department stores	50
Discount stores	20
Drugstores	70
Food stores	75
Furniture stores	30
Household goods	30
Jewelers	30
Shoe stores	50

102

Ethical Issues

Imitation, Plagiarism, or Flattery?

When two companies run strikingly similar ads, is it imitation, plagiarism, or coincidence? In December 1999, two beverage companies began running television commercials that closely resembled each other. The commercials, for Michelob Light beer and Colombian coffee, were set in supermarkets and shared the same plot: store employees manhandled groceries until the product being advertised came down the conveyer belt. For both Michelob Light and Colombian, the bagger wraps the package in bubble wrap and carefully gives it to the buyers.

Advertisers and media commonly point to "coincidence." Bob Garfield, ad critic for *Advertising Age*, said, "It's seldom plagiarism, especially if the ads are appearing simultaneously." Both of the agencies representing Michelob Light beer and Colombian coffee agree. Peter le Comte, president of DDB Worldwide Marketing, said, "We have written it off as an incident of coincidence. Besides, I don't think we share the same consumers. They will run their commercial and we will run ours."

Stephen Bergerson, an attorney specializing in advertising and promotion law at Fredrikson & Byron, Minneapolis, is skeptical. "When you get four or five words that are so specific, simultaneously used by people in the same category, the nose starts to quiver." But Ron Redfern, senior vice president of sales and marketing for the *Orange County Register*, calls it "coincidental invention. It's like the automobile being invented in France and in the U.S. within weeks of each other."

Some advertisers try to ignore the problem by convincing themselves that being copied is actually good. Hugh Thrasher, executive VP of marketing for Motel 6, says of his often-imitated Tom Bodett commercials: "We think these copycat ads just remind people of the originality of our concept." Nancy Shalek, president of L.A.'s Shalek Agency, maintains, "If you haven't been ripped off, you're really in trouble."

But Ellen Kozak, a Milwaukee copyright and publishing lawyer, warns against this form of flattery. "There's a fine line between the kind of borrowing that constitutes an admiring bow to a classic work and the kind that's really the theft of another writer's efforts."

Unfortunately, plagiarism is almost impossible to prove, as long as you make a few changes. It's also hard to define, making it tough for advertisers to know just when they cross the line. There is no set number of words that make up a plagiarized effort. And plagiarism covers not only words but ideas, plots, and characters. In 1996, Kendall-Jackson Winery filed a suit against E&J Gallo Winery, charging that Gallo's Turning Leaf Vineyards brand infringed on K-J's Colored Leaf brand trademark. The suit said that Gallo intentionally designed the bottle, labeling, and packaging to imitate that of Kendall-Jackson's Colored Leaf mark. More recently, overseas, manufacturers of two brands of potato chips have become embroiled in a similar battle.

Tesco, a supermarket giant in England, recently launched a brand of chips called Temptations that are very reminiscent of competitor Walker's Sensations. The two brands have been placed side by side on the shelves, and the Tesco brand is being sold for 23 pence, approximately $0.40, cheaper than Walker's. Both chips are packaged in white bags that feature black and white pictures, and both are offered in strikingly similar flavors. Although Martin Glenn, a chief executive at Walker, has hinted at legal action, lawyers are divided over the success of such litigation. Nick Johnson, an attorney with Osborne Clark, agrees that "Tesco may have been inspired [by Walker's], but just because you are

One popular way to attract attention is to occupy the entire top half of the ad with a headline written in large letters. This technique can be just as eye-catching as a dramatic photo or illustration.

Another goal of a headline is to engage the reader—fast—and give a reason to read the rest of the ad. If the headline lacks immediacy, prospects turn their attention to another subject and pass the ad's message by.[17]

An ad for Esser's wine store is a good example of a headline leading the reader into the body copy.

Headline: "Esser's Knows."

Body copy: "Manfred Esser's nose knows a good wine . . ."

The headline is the most important thing an advertiser says to the prospect. It explains or gives greater meaning to the visual and then immediately dictates the advertiser's position in that person's mind, whether or not the prospect chooses to read on.[18]

Ideally, headlines present the complete selling idea. Research shows that, on average, three to five times as many people read the headline as read the body copy. So if the ad doesn't sell in the headline, the advertiser is wasting money.[19] Nike uses beautiful magazine and outdoor ads featuring just an athlete, the logo, and the memorable headline: "Just do it." Working off the visual, the headline creates the mood and tells the reader, through implication, to take action—buy Nikes. Headlines help trigger a recognition response, which reinforces brand recognition and brand preference.

The traditional notion is that short headlines with one line are best but a second line is acceptable. Many experts believe that headlines with 10 words or more gain greater readership.[20] In one study of more than 2,000 ads, most headlines averaged eight words in length.[21] David Ogilvy said the best headline he ever wrote contained 18 words—and became a classic: "At 60 miles an hour, the loudest noise in the new Rolls-Royce comes from the electric clock."[22]

418

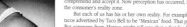
Extensive Full-Color Visuals

Contemporary Advertising features full-color illustrations of more than 350 award-winning ads, commercials, and campaigns. These illustrations focus on the best in the business and are chosen for both their quality and relevance to the concepts in the text. Award winning ads from the Advertising Festival in Cannes are called out by the Cannes Lion icon.

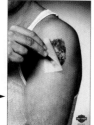

Advertisers frequently capitalize on consumers' concept of themselves to generate attention and interest in a particular product. This ad—a 2004 Cannes Bronze Lion winner from Ogilvy & Mather RSTM—takes the next step: It shows consumers that they can temporarily identify with their wilder sides by renting a Harley-Davidson.

comprehend and accept it. Now perception has occurred, and the stimulus reaches the consumer's reality zone.

But each of us has his or her own reality. For example, you may consider the tacos advertised by Taco Bell to be "Mexican" food. That perception is your reality. But someone from Mexico might tell you that a fast-food taco bears little resemblance to an authentic Mexican taco. That person's reality, based on another perception, is considerably different. Advertisers thus seek commonly shared perceptions of reality as a basis for their advertising messages.

Mental Files

The mind is like a memory bank, and the stored memories in our minds are called the **mental** (or *perceptual*) **files.**

Just as stimuli bombard our senses, information crowds our mental files in today's overcommunicative society. To cope with the complexity of stimuli such as advertising, we rank products and other data in our files by importance, price, quality, features, or a host of other descriptors. Consumers can rarely hold more than seven brand names in any one file—more often only one or two. The remainder either get discarded to some other file category or rejected altogether.[20] How many brands of running shoes can you quickly name, for example?

Because of our limited memory, we resist opening new mental files, and we avoid accepting new information inconsistent with what is already filed. The experience consumers receive from using a brand solidifies their perceptions of it. These fixed perceptions can rarely be changed through advertising alone.[21] But once a new perception does enter our mental files, the information alters the database on which our psychological screens feed.

Because perceptual screens are such a major challenge to advertisers, it's important to understand what's in the consumer's mental files and, if possible, modify them in favor of the advertiser's product. That brings us to the second process in consumer behavior: *learning and persuasion.*

VIDEO: Boss walks into employee's office.
AUDIO:
Boss: Did those shipments get to Detroit this morning?
Employee: Umm . . . No. They're gonna be a few days late.

Boss: Did you use FedEx Express like I asked you?
Employee: No.

Boss: Remind me again why I keep you around here?
Employee: You're my dad.

Super FedEx logo slide

Announcer (voiceover): When you need fast reliable service, relax, it's FedEx.

Defining the target audience is a critical step prior to creating any advertisement. In this Cannes Gold Lion-winning ad, FedEx (www.fedex.com/us) uses a drama literary form, with actors who look like they could be actual FedEx customers.

consumer behavior, a topic we'll discuss in Chapter 5. The better an advertiser understands the buying behavior of people, the better it can bring its products into the collective consciousness of prospective customers.

Industrial/Business Markets

Companies use **business advertising** to reach people who buy or specify goods and services for business use. It tends to appear in specialized business publications or professional journals, in direct-mail pieces sent to businesses, or in trade shows. Since business advertising (also called **business-to-business,** or **B2B, advertising**) rarely uses consumer mass media, it is typically invisible to consumers. However, some business-to-business ads, by computer manufacturers or firms such as FedEx, do appear on prime-time TV and in consumer magazines.

Full-Color Portfolios

In addition to the individual print ads featured throughout the text, many chapters feature multipage portfolios showcasing ads that demonstrate outstanding creative work. These portfolios highlight and reinforce concepts in their respective chapter.

The creative director always wants to produce the most effective advertising possible in order to give the client the greatest bang for the buck. That means first conceiving a brilliant idea that will both resonate with the particular target audience and relate to the client's marketing and advertising strategy. Then the idea must be executed in a masterful way.

■ Study all the award-winning ads in this portfolio and consider how well they measure up to this definition of greatness. To do this, start by analyzing whether the ad is informational or transformational. Then evaluate and describe the "boom" factor each one uses. Next, see if you can determine from the ad what the company's advertising strategy was and discuss how relevant the ad is to that strategy. Finally, evaluate how well the creative director's staff executed the concept.

The Creative Director's Greatest Ads

PlayStation 2 is known for sponsoring off-the-wall ads. This one, winner of a Cannes Gold Lion, is startlingly strange. The viewer doesn't quickly forget the image of a real-life Mr. Potato Head assembling pieces of himself. Like many of the company's games, this ad for PlayStation 2 successfully explores a world of fantasy.

In this ad, which won a Bronze Lion at Cannes, Heinz walks a fine line between great ingenuity and being too clever for its own good, risking loss of communication. The unusual perspective of the image grabs our attention immediately and holds it long enough for the wit to shine through. A very hot ad, indeed.

In this ad for Vespa, which won a Bronze Lion at Cannes, the city becomes a virtual playground for the driver to enjoy. This ad uses practically no copy but still delivers a message: Vespa is fun.

This ad's tagline, "As Real as It Gets," refers both to the detailed, authentic photo of the soldier's real, unglamorous activity, to the true-to-life details of the action figure at his feet. The vivid combination won a Gold Lion at Cannes.

489

A Wealth of Supplements

Campaign Video Series

Unique to the *Contemporary Advertising* text, each exciting video traces the step-by-step development of a real advertising campaign. Each campaign is examined from both the agency and client point-of-view to give students a behind-the-scenes look at how advertising is developed in the real world.

This FedEx TV spot was part of a campaign that produced laughs and a Cannes Gold Lion for BBDO New York. Cheerless gray offices and unglamorous employees create continuity between spots and clear the path for FedEx's services to shine. In this spot a poorly disguised alien outshines his coworkers to the dismay of his all-too-human colleagues.

(A large alien is seated at a desk. Pasted to his head is a photograph of a man's head. We can see his tentacles and tail. Two office workers enter the room.)
EMPLOYEE 1: Jenkins, got a minute? Listen Jenkins, we're on to you. We know you're an alien.
EMPLOYEE 2: Admit it. You're just here studying our species.

JENKINS: Why don't we use FedEx?
EMPLOYEE 1: Ha. That's all you ever say. We're not buying it.
EMPLOYEE 2: C'mon, it's so obvious.
JENKINS: Why don't we use FedEx?
EMPLOYEE 1: Ach, give it up. It's over.

(Boss enters office)
BOSS: Jenkins we got a ton of packages to ship and we're in serious trouble. Any ideas?
JENKINS: Why don't we use FedEx?
BOSS: Good thinking Jenkins. You two back to work.
SUPER: FedEx. It's all you need to know.

Teaching Video

This resource-rich video features more than 100 new domestic and international commercials handpicked by the author to illustrate various topics from the text. Many of the featured ads are award winners from the Cannes International Advertising Festival, the largest and most prestigious advertising competition in the world.

Online Learning Center

Students and instructors will find a multitude of helpful resources online at www.mhhe.com/arens06. Student study tools include practice quizzes, video clips, glossary of key terms, and industry resources. The instructor's side includes downloadable versions of the Instructor's Manual, PowerPoint presentation, video clips, the Video Instructor's Manual, and a link to PageOut for access to test materials.

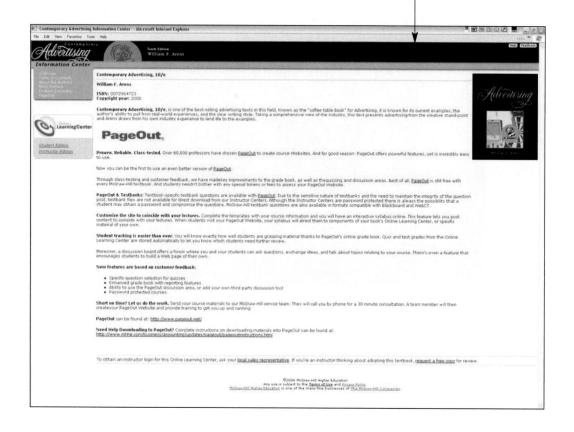

Contents in Brief

Detailed Contents

Part Two   Crafting Marketing and Advertising Strategies

Part Three   Integrating Advertising with Other Elements
of the Communications Mix

Part Four   Creating Advertisements and Commercials

Contemporary
Advertising

Part 1

Advertising Perspectives

THERE ARE many ways to look at advertising—as a business, a creative communication process, a social phenomenon, and a fundamental ingredient of the free-enterprise system. The first part of this text defines advertising, examines the most important dimensions of the field, considers how changing economics has influenced the evolution of the profession, outlines advertising's functions and scope, considers its social and legal ramifications, and looks at the major participants in the advertising business, not just in North America but around the world. ■

A secret formula revealed.

Advertising.
The way great brands
get to be great brands.

American Advertising Federation aaf.org

Chapter 1
What Is Advertising Today?

Gives an overview of the profession. It defines advertising in contemporary terms, examines its role in the communication process and the marketing process, and introduces some basic terminology. The chapter focuses on advertising's role in marketing strategy.

Chapter 2
The Evolution of Advertising

Sets down an economic framework for understanding how advertising has evolved. It explains the basic tenets of a free-market economy and describes advertising's role in that economy. The chapter focuses on the history of advertising as an economic tool and discusses the impact of advertising on the society in which it operates.

Chapter 3
The Economic, Social, and Regulatory Aspects of Advertising

Discusses the impact of advertising on the economy and society, considers some common criticisms of advertising, and debates the ethical and social responsibilities of companies that advertise. It describes the roles played by government, industry, and consumer groups in regulating advertising. Finally, it compares important laws governing the practice of advertising in the United States and Canada with those in foreign countries.

Chapter 4
The Scope of Advertising: From Local to Global

Shows how people and groups organize themselves—as advertisers, agencies, media, and suppliers—around the world to create, produce, and manage advertising. The chapter describes the role of each of these organizations and discusses critical factors that affect the client/agency relationship and the management of advertising in different cultural, economic, and social environments.

Chapter 1

What Is Advertising Today?

Objectives   TO DEFINE ADVERTISING AND INTRODUCE THE PROFESSION. You will learn what advertising is and what it is not; the unique role advertising plays in the communication process; how advertising functions as an element of the marketing process; and some of the basic terminology used in advertising. These fundamental elements set the framework for the more detailed study to follow.

After studying this chapter, you will be able to:

- **Define** advertising and differentiate it from other forms of marketing communications.

- **Explain** how advertising differs from the basic human communication process.

- **Define** marketing and identify the four elements of marketing strategy.

- **Discuss** advertising's role in marketing strategy.

- **Explain** the difference between consumer and business markets.

At the turn of the nineteenth century, a small confectionary firm in London created a recipe for an "exceptionally strong" lozenge intended to relieve intestinal discomfort. Shortly thereafter, the owners, who were dedicated members of the Anglican Church, incorporated the consumption of their new lozenge into their religious practice, giving rise to a small and devout following for the little white tablets.[1] Over a century later the tradition continued to spread with an occasional sparse littering of ads stating: "One or two taken after meals . . . [would] act as an antidote to the poisons in the stomach."[2] ■ The name of these miracle pills was Altoids, and although the reason for their consumption has changed from fighting stomach pains to combating bad breath, the tradition of taking a couple after meals has stayed the same. ■ Yet, contrary to its lengthy history, the success of Altoids as we know it today has been a recent occurrence—just over the past decade. There are several reasons for this. First, the brand's price was three times higher than competitive products. Second, it had achieved only very narrow distribution. Finally, it suffered from extremely low awareness due to virtually *no* advertising. As a result, Altoids faced very limited success before the mid-1990s.[3] Following a series of mergers and acquisitions in the consumer products industry—which resulted in Altoids being owned by Callard & Broward-Suchard, a subsidiary of Kraft General Foods— change finally, and suddenly, came about. In 1995, Altoids launched its first major marketing campaign in its 215-year history. ■ With a budget far below what its competitors were spending, Altoids and its ad agency, Leo Burnett Chicago, developed a marketing strategy that would prove to be deceivingly simple yet amazingly effective. According to its research, Altoids found that its customers tended to be young, urban, socially active, and culturally aware—but somewhat difficult to reach via conventional advertising media. The solution: to place advertisements outdoors, in locations nobody could miss. According to Gary Singer, a senior vice president and account director at Burnett, "With outdoor [advertising], we could place [ads] wherever these people live and work and in between."[4] Billboards, bus shelters, phone booths, and subway cars became the ideal media to get the Altoids message across. ■ Most important, the ads themselves were great—they were highly creative and just as simple as the media that carried them. Focusing on the product's unique, exceptionally strong flavor and its one-of-a-kind tin packaging, the ads generally featured an Altoids' signature tin, with a simple, humorous catch phrase at the bottom. The ads were indicative of the mint—simple, clean, and fresh. One of the very first ads featured a "muscle man" holding an Altoids tin with the words "Nice Altoids" appearing on the bottom. Another shows a stern nurse holding a can of Altoids and admonishing her patient: "Now this won't hurt a bit." (For more examples of Altoids ads see the Portfolio of Curiously Strong Ads on pages 20–23 and the Altoids website at www.Altoids.com.)[5] ■ The results: the campaign was consistent with Altoids slogan "CURIOUSLY STRONG!" Within a year, studies showed a substantial increase in brand awareness and consumption. Moreover, the brand jumped from number six in U.S. breath mint ranking to number one in 2001.[6] ■ The moral of this story is simple: good advertising can have a curiously strong effect on a brand's success. Over the six short years since Altoids' advertising began, the brand name has achieved a level of recognition and value comparable to that of some of the top brands in the country.[7] That is an amazing success story! Success stories like this are what encourage companies and organizations in the United States to spend over $245 billion annually on advertising, and they will likely continue to spend even more in the future.[8] ■ Altoids: "Invented in 1780. Properly marketed 215 years later."[9] ■

What Is Advertising?

As a consumer, you are exposed to hundreds and maybe even thousands of commercial messages every day. They may appear in the form of billboards, like the Altoids campaign, or in the form of newspaper ads, TV commercials, coupons, sales letters, publicity, event sponsorships, telemarketing calls, or even e-mails. These are just a few of the many communication tools that companies and organizations use to initiate and maintain contact with their customers, clients, and prospects. You may simply refer to them all as "advertising." But, in fact, the correct term for these various tools is **marketing communications.** And advertising is just one type of marketing communications.

So, then, what is advertising?

At the beginning of the twentieth century, Albert Lasker, who today is generally regarded as the father of modern advertising, owned a prominent advertising agency, Lord & Thomas. At the time, he defined advertising as "salesmanship in print, driven by a reason why."[10] But that was long before the advent of radio, television, or the Internet. The nature and scope of the business world, and advertising, were quite limited. A century later, our planet is a far different place. The nature and needs of business have changed, and so have the concept and practice of advertising.

Today, definitions of advertising abound. Journalists, for example, might define it as a communication, public relations, or persuasion process; business-people see it as a marketing process; economists and sociologists tend to focus on its economic, societal, or ethical significance. And some consumers might define it simply as a nuisance. Each of these perspectives has some merit, but for now we'll use the following functional definition:

> **Advertising** is the structured and composed nonpersonal communication of information, usually paid for and usually persuasive in nature, about products (goods, services, and ideas) by identified sponsors through various media.

Let's take this definition apart and analyze its components. Advertising is, first of all, a type of *communication*. It is actually a very *structured* form of applied communication, employing both verbal and nonverbal elements that are *composed* to fill specific space and time formats determined by the sponsor.

Second, advertising is typically directed to groups of people rather than to individuals. It is therefore *nonpersonal,* or *mass,* communication. These people could be **consumers,** who buy products like Altoids for their personal use. Or they might be businesspeople who would buy large quantities of Altoids for resale in their stores.

Most advertising is *paid for* by sponsors. GM, WalMart, Coca-Cola, and your local fitness salon pay the newspaper or the radio or TV station to carry the ads you read, see, and hear. But some sponsors don't have to pay for their ads. The American Red Cross, United Way, and American Cancer Society are among the many national organizations whose public service messages are carried at no charge because of their nonprofit status. Likewise, a poster on a school bulletin board promoting a dance is not paid for, but it is still an ad—a structured, nonpersonal, persuasive communication.

Of course, most advertising is intended to be *persuasive*—to win converts to a product, service, or idea. Some ads, such as legal announcements, are intended merely to inform, not to persuade. But they are still ads because they satisfy all the other requirements of the definition.

In addition to promoting tangible **goods** such as oranges, oatmeal, and olive oil, advertising helps publicize the intangible **services** of bankers, beauticians, bike repair shops, bill collectors, and the telephone company. Increasingly, advertising is used to advocate a wide variety of **ideas,** whether economic, political, religious, or social. In this book the term **product** encompasses goods, services, and ideas.

Ads are usually about products (goods, services, and ideas). In 2004, the prestigious International Advertising Festival in Cannes, France, bestowed its Grand Prix award on this humorous ad for the Volkswagen Polo. Note that while the product is obviously the car, it doesn't occupy a prominent place in the picture. The ad is really promoting the product concept—the idea of smallness combined with durability, or toughness, as suggested by the text.

An ad *identifies* its sponsor. This seems obvious. The sponsor wants to be identified, or why pay to advertise? One of the basic differences between advertising and *public relations,* though, is that many PR activities (for example, publicity) aren't openly sponsored. We'll discuss the differences between advertising and other forms of marketing communications later in this chapter.

Finally, advertising reaches us through a channel of communication referred to as a **medium.** An advertising medium is any paid means used to present an ad to its target audience. Thus, we have radio advertising, television advertising, newspaper ads, and so on. When you tell somebody how good Altoids taste, that's sometimes called *word-of-mouth* (WOM) advertising. Although WOM is a communication medium, it's *not* an advertising medium. It's not structured, or openly sponsored, or paid for. Historically, advertisers have used the traditional **mass media** (the plural of *medium*)—radio, TV, newspapers, magazines, and billboards—to send their messages. But today technology enables advertising to reach us efficiently through a variety of *addressable media* (for example, direct mail) and *interactive media* (like the Internet and kiosks). Advertisers also use an increasing variety of other *nontraditional media* such as shopping carts, blimps, and videocassettes to find their audience. The planning, scheduling, and buying of media space and time are so important to advertising effectiveness that we devote five full chapters to the subject, one in Part Two and four in Part Five.

The previously given definition is a good working definition of advertising. But to get a full sense of what advertising really is today, we need to understand where it has come from, how and why it grew to be so large, and what the forces are that drive it. In this chapter, therefore, we'll briefly examine two of the most important dimensions of advertising. We'll look at the *communication dimension* first to better understand how advertising is actually a form of structured, literary communication. Then the *marketing dimension* will explain the important role advertising plays in business. In Chapter 2, we look at two more dimensions. The *economic dimension* will show us how and why advertising evolved the way it did. And the *social and ethical dimension* will enable us to understand people's attitudes about advertising and to consider what the future holds. Examining the diverse dimensions of advertising here in the first two chapters should lead us toward a deeper understanding of advertising as it is currently practiced.

The last two chapters of Part One will then deal in greater depth with the economic, social, and regulatory aspects of advertising as well as the broad scope of advertising from local to global.

Communication: What Makes Advertising Unique

First and foremost, advertising is communication—a special kind of communication. McCann-Erickson, the ad agency for Coca-Cola and MasterCard, says that advertising is "Truth well told." This means that ethical advertisers, and the agencies they employ, work as a team to discover and use the best methods possible to tell their story truthfully and creatively to the marketplace. To succeed, they must understand the elements of the advertising communication process, which is derived from the basic human communication process.

The Human Communication Process

From our first cry at birth, our survival depends on our ability to inform others or persuade them to take some action. As we develop, we learn to listen and respond to others' messages. The traditional model in Exhibit 1–1 summarizes the series of events that take place when people share ideas in informal oral communication. The process begins when one party, called the **source,** formulates an idea, **encodes** it as a **message,** and sends it via some **channel** to another party, called the **receiver.** The receiver must **decode** the message in order to understand it. To respond, the receiver formulates a new idea, encodes it, and then sends the new message back through some channel. A message that acknowledges or responds to the original message constitutes **feedback,** which also affects the encoding of a new message.[11] And, of course, all this takes place in an environment character-

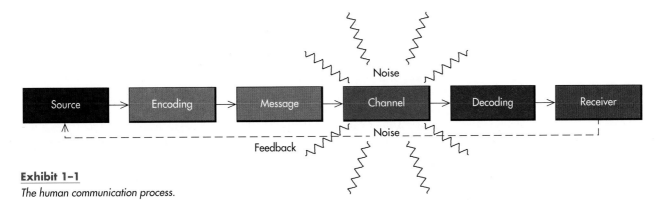

Exhibit 1-1
The human communication process.

ized by **noise**—the distracting cacophony of many other messages being sent at the same time by other sources.

Applying this model to advertising, we could say that the source is the sponsor, the message is the ad, the channel is the medium, the receiver is the consumer or prospect, and the noise is the din of competing ads and commercials. But this model oversimplifies the process that occurs in advertising or other sponsored marketing communications. It doesn't take into account either the structure or the creativity inherent in composing the advertising message. We need to consider some of the many complexities involved, especially with the advent of *interactive media,* which let consumers participate in the communication by extracting the information they need, manipulating what they see on their computer or TV screens in real time, and responding in real time.

Applying the Communication Process to Advertising

Barbara Stern at Rutgers University sees advertising as a form of structured, literary text, rather different from the spontaneous, word-of-mouth communication of oral speech. She proposes a more sophisticated communication model, derived from the traditional oral one but applied specifically to advertising as *composed commercial text* rather than informal speech. The Stern model recognizes that in advertising, the source, the message, and the receiver all have multiple dimensions. Some of these dimensions exist in the real world; others exist on a different level of reality—a virtual world within the text of the advertising message itself.

The World Wide Web is the fastest-growing medium for advertisers, topping an estimated $6.3 billion in U.S. expenditures in 2003. The Olympics (www.olympic.org) uses its interactive site to provide detailed information on past, present, and future events to the consumer and to promote customer feedback, a feat that could not be easily accomplished under the constraints of normal print, radio, or television ads.

Source Dimensions: The Sponsor, the Author, and the Persona

In oral communication, the source is typically one person talking to another person or a group. But in advertising, who is really the source of the communication? The sponsor named in the ad? Certainly the real-world **sponsor** is legally responsible for the communication and has a message to communicate to actual consumers. But as the Stern model in Exhibit 1–2 shows, the path from sponsor to actual consumer can be long and circuitous. To begin with, the sponsor does not usually produce the message. That is the typical role of the sponsor's ad agency or other specialists. So the **author** of the communication is actually a copywriter, an art director, or, most often, a creative group at the sponsor's ad agency. Commissioned by the sponsor to create the advertising message, these people exist in the real world but are completely invisible to the reader or viewer, even though they play a key role in composing the text and the tenor of the message.

At the same time, *within the text* of the ad resides some real or imaginary spokesperson (a **persona**) who lends some voice or tone to the ad or commercial. To the consumer, this persona, who represents the sponsor, is the source of the within-text message. But the persona's discourse is composed and crafted by the ad's authors solely for the purposes of the text; it is not a part of real life. It exists only in the virtual world of the ad. (See Ad Lab 1–A: Advertising as a Literary Form.)

Message Dimensions: Autobiography, Narrative, and Drama

The types of messages typically communicated in advertising may also be multi-dimensional. As artful imitations of life, advertising messages typically use one or a blend of three literary forms: autobiography, narrative, or drama. In **autobiographical messages,** "I" tell a story about myself to "you," the imaginary audience eavesdropping on my private personal experience. Other ads use **narrative messages** in which a third-person persona tells a story about others to an imagined audience. Finally, in the **drama message,** the characters act out events directly in front of an imagined empathetic audience.

Thus, among the most important decisions the authors of advertising messages make are what kind of persona and which literary form to use to express the message. Considering the emotions, attitudes, and motives that drive particular customers in their target audience, the creative team develops the persona and message, along with any images and text that will act as communication symbols or triggers.

Exhibit 1–2

The Stern model of the advertising communication process.

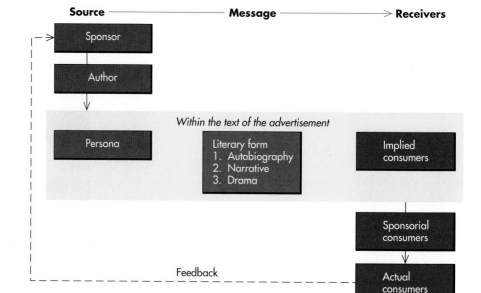

Ad Lab 1–A

Advertising as a Literary Form

These four ads all won Gold, Silver, or Bronze Lions at the 2004 Cannes advertising festival. They show how advertising messages typically come in one or a blend of three literary forms: autobiography, narrative, or drama.

Autobiography tells its story from a first-person point of view and may often use the word *I*. The narrative form typically uses a third-person voice, which often exudes a well-informed, authoritative quality, to tell the reader about the product. The drama form uses the style of theater to create or perform a scene, so the reader receives the message by implication rather than direct telling.

Two other key elements are the persona, which usually represents the advertiser, and the implied consumer. The persona may be a trade character, such as the Pillsbury Doughboy, or a real person, such as William Shatner, the spokesperson for priceline.com. A logo may even be a form of persona.

Sometimes a character, such as the elderly woman in the British ad (example 1) or the white-suited mechanic in the Chinese ad for laundry detergent (example 2), may represent the implied consumer. Ads like the one in example 4 may employ a number of literary forms simultaneously.

Laboratory Application

Can you identify which two literary forms appear in example 4? Does it have a persona and/or an implied consumer? If so, describe their use.

1. Autobiography.

2. Narrative.

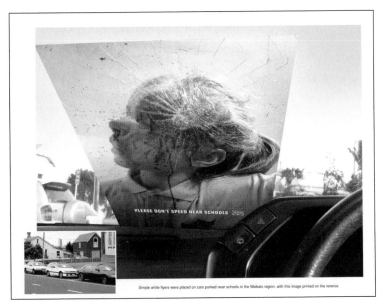

3. Drama.

4. Mixture of literary forms and elements.

11

Then they place these words and visuals in the structured format most suitable to the medium selected for delivering the message. The format may be a dramatic 30-second TV commercial; an autobiographical, full-page, black-and-white magazine ad; a colorful, narrative brochure; or a multipage Internet website that employs a variety of message styles. In all cases, though, the message exists only within the text of the ad. To do all this effectively requires great skill, but it's this creativity that truly distinguishes advertising from all other forms of communication. For that reason, we'll devote Part Four of this text exclusively to the subject of advertising creativity.

Receiver Dimensions: Implied, Sponsorial, and Actual Consumers

The receivers of advertising are also multidimensional. First, *within the text,* every ad or commercial presumes some audience is there. These **implied consumers,** who are addressed by the ad's persona, are not real. They are imagined by the ad's creators to be ideal consumers who acquiesce in whatever beliefs the text requires. They are, in effect, part of the drama of the ad.

When we move outside the text of the ad, though, the first audience is, in fact, a group of decision makers at the sponsor's company or organization. These **sponsorial consumers** are the gatekeepers who decide if the ad will run or not. So, before an ad ever gets a chance to persuade a real consumer, the ad's authors must first persuade the sponsor's executives and managers who have the responsibility for approving the campaign and funding it.

The **actual consumers**—equivalent to the receiver in oral communications—are people in the real world who comprise the ad's target audience. They are the people to whom the sponsor's message is ultimately directed. But they will get to see, hear, or read it only with the sponsor's approval.[12]

Actual consumers do not usually think or behave the same as the implied consumer, or even the sponsorial consumer. Thus, the advertiser (and the creative team) must be concerned about how the actual consumer will decode, or interpret, the message. The last thing an advertiser wants is to be misunderstood. Unfortunately, message interpretation is only partially determined by the words and symbols in the ad. The medium used may have an effect as well. As Marshall McLuhan said, "The medium is the message." However, Stern's model does not directly address the fact that advertisers communicate their messages through a wide variety of mass, addressable, and interactive media. With today's advances in technology, the boundaries between the print and electronic media are now blurring. We read text on a computer screen, and soon the average person will be able to print whatever appears on a TV screen. How will this affect the way people receive and interpret advertising messages? Stern acknowledges the need for additional study in this area.

Further, the unique characteristics of the receivers themselves are also very important, and the sponsor may know little or nothing about them. As we shall see in Chapter 5, attitudes, perceptions, personality, self-concept, and culture are just some of the many important influences that affect the way people receive and respond to messages and how they behave as consumers in the marketplace.

As mentioned earlier, complicating this problem is the fact that the sponsor's advertising message must compete with hundreds of other commercial and noncommercial messages every day. This is referred to as **noise.** So the sender doesn't know *how* the message is received, or even *if* it's received, until a consumer acknowledges it.

Feedback and Interactivity

That's why feedback is so important. It completes the cycle, verifying that the message was received. Feedback employs a sender–message–receiver pattern, except that it is directed from the receiver back to the source.

In advertising, feedback can take many forms: redeemed coupons, phone inquiries, visits to a store, requests for more information, increased sales, responses to a survey, or e-mail inquiries. Dramatically low responses to an ad indicate a break in the communication process. Questions arise: Is the product wrong for the market? Is the message unclear? Are we using the right media? Without feedback, these questions cannot be answered.

In the past, the consumer's feedback rarely used the same channels as the original message. But now, thanks again to technology, the audiences of advertising are no longer just passive receivers of impersonal mass messages. They are now active decision makers who can control what communications they receive and choose the information they want about a particular product. With the growth of interactive media such as the Internet, they can give instantaneous, real-time feedback on the same channel used by the original message sender.

This offers advertisers the chance to nourish a more in-depth relationship with their customers, one that will be more fruitful for both sponsors and consumers.

Marketing: Determining the Type of Advertising to Use

Now that we have some understanding of advertising's communication dimension, let's consider the marketing dimension, because that's what defines advertising's role in business. Every business organization performs a number of diverse activities. Management typically classifies these activities into three broad functional divisions:

- Operations (production/manufacturing)
- Finance/administration
- Marketing

Students who major in business administration study a variety of subjects related to one or all of these general functions. Courses in purchasing and manufacturing relate to the operations function. Courses in accounting and industrial relations relate to the finance/administration area. While many students study advertising in a school of journalism or communications, advertising is actually a specialty area within the broad domain of marketing. Other courses in marketing include marketing research, consumer behavior, distribution, and sales management.

Of all the business functions, marketing is the only one whose primary role is to bring in revenues. Without revenue, of course, a company cannot recover its initial investment, pay its employees' salaries, grow, or earn a profit. So marketing is very important.

Even nonprofits feel the squeeze to bring in revenue to operate. This New Zealand advocacy group won a Bronze Lion at Cannes for its creative use of billboard advertising to seek donations for establishing a nationwide burn center.

The vinyl that the image of the girl was printed on has been scorched using a blow torch to simulate the effect of badly burned skin.

Ethics in Advertising: An Overview

Advertising is fun. It can also be exciting, creative, and entertaining. And sometimes it's not.

Without question, though, advertising is invariably criticized—both for what it is and for what it is not. One of the most frequent criticisms of advertising concerns ethics, either the ethics of the marketer or the ethics of a particular ad. As a student of advertising, and possibly a future practitioner, you should be aware of the major ethical issues related to marketing and advertising. Awareness of the issues is the first step in learning about and practicing ethical behavior.

One could successfully argue that advertising's current lack of credibility is due in large part to the cumulative effect of poor ethical behavior on the part of some advertisers during the last century. Deception, misrepresentation, false advertising, exaggerated promises, unfair comparisons—all these are injurious to consumers and competitors as well as people's perception of advertisers in general. In other words, any advertisers that engage in unethical behavior are damaging not only the fragile relationship they have with their customers but also the whole profession of advertising. Unfortunately, not all advertisers have figured this out.

We believe that ethical behavior will be so important to building customer relationships in the twenty-first century that we've included a current Ethical Issue in advertising in every chapter of this book. Our aim is to focus attention on the most critical social issues facing advertisers today. These include the debate over puffery, advertising to children, comparative advertising, the targeting of ethnic minorities, consumer profiling, privacy, negative political advertising, and statistical manipulation.

The table at right lists the Ethical Issues for every chapter along with a brief description of what the Issue is about. Part of being a good student is learning to question what you are taught. As you read each Ethical Issue, try to examine both sides of the issues presented to see if you can better understand the motivations and reasoning of the people involved. You might even try debating some of these issues with your classmates.

What Is Marketing?

Over the years, the concept of marketing has evolved based on the supply of and demand for products. Because we need to understand marketing as it relates to *advertising,* we define the term as follows:

> **Marketing** is the process of planning and executing the conception, pricing, distribution, and promotion of ideas, goods, and services to create exchanges that satisfy the perceived needs, wants, and objectives of individuals and organizations.[13]

We devote all of Part 2 to the subject of developing marketing and advertising strategies. What's important to understand now is that marketing is a **process**—a series of actions or methods that take place sequentially—aimed at satisfying customer needs profitably. This process includes developing products, pricing them strategically, making them available to customers through a distribution network, and promoting them through sales and advertising activities. The ultimate goal of the marketing process is to earn a profit for the firm by consummating the exchange of products or services with those customers who need or want them. And the role of advertising is to inform, persuade, and remind groups of customers, or markets, about the need-satisfying value of the company's goods and services. Today even many nonprofit organizations use the marketing process to develop and promote services that will satisfy their constituents' needs.

Advertising and the Marketing Process

Advertising helps the organization achieve its marketing goals. So do market research, sales, and distribution. And these other marketing specialties all have an impact on the kind of advertising a company employs. An effective advertising specialist must have a broad understanding of the whole marketing process in order to know what type of advertising to use in a given situation.

Companies and organizations use many different types of advertising, depending on their particular marketing strategy. The marketing strategy will determine who the targets of advertising should be, where the advertising should appear, what media should be used, and what purposes the advertising should accomplish. (Exhibit 1–3 shows some of the ways advertising can be classified, based on these strategic marketing elements.) These various criteria will also determine what different advertising skills are required.

Identifying Target Markets and Target Audiences

A firm's marketing activities are always aimed at a particular segment of the population—its **target market.** Likewise, advertising is aimed at a particular group called the **target audience.** When we see an ad that doesn't appeal to us, it may be because the ad is not aimed at any of the groups we belong to. For example, a

Chapter	Ethical Issue	Topic Discussed
2	Ethical Dilemma or Ethical Lapse?	Ignoring ethical issues and being confused about them
3	Truth in Advertising: Fluffing and Puffing	How exaggeration borders on deception
4	Accounting for Account Reviews	Etiquette between agencies and prospective clients
5	Is It Marketing or Is It Exploitation?	Taking advantage of vulnerable markets
6	Brand Niching May Cause Brand Switching	How targeting markets can backfire on advertisers
7	Research Statistics Can Be Friends or Foes	How statistics can be misunderstood and/or misrepresented
8	A War of Comparisons	Comparative advertising must be done with care
9	The Ethical Dilemmas of Agency Compensation	How the commission system might create conflicts of interest
10	Political Advertising: Positively Negative	The clash between ethics and the First Amendment
11	When Is Advertising Not Really Advertising?	Sniffing out subjectivity and bias
12	Does Sex Appeal?	Sexual inferences can lead to real consequences
13	Imitation, Plagiarism, or Flattery?	It's a close call between borrowing and stealing
14	Closed Circuit Programming	Are captive audiences being informed or manipulated?
15	What's at Stake with Sweepstakes?	Read the small print; you may be surprised
16	Children's Advertising: Child's Play?	Protecting the innocent from calculated sales pitches
17	Profiling: Would You Take Cookies from a Stranger?	The ethics of tracking Web surfers' activities
18	Does Spillover Need Mopping Up?	Messages designed for one audience may offend others

TV commercial for denture cream isn't meant to appeal to youngsters. They're not part of either the target market or the target audience. There are two main types of target markets, *consumers* and *businesses*.

Consumer Markets

Most of the advertising we see daily in the mass media—TV, radio, newspapers, and magazines—falls under the broad category of **consumer advertising.** Usually sponsored by the producer (or manufacturer) of the product or service, these ads are typically directed at **consumers,** people who buy the product for their own or someone else's personal use. This includes **retail advertising,** advertising sponsored by retail stores and businesses. Consumer advertising also includes noncommercial *public service announcements* (PSAs) from organizations such as the American Cancer Society or the Partnership for a Drug-Free America.

In the end, customers are people. So advertising professionals must understand how people act and think—and why they buy what they buy. This requires great skill. In fact, this area of study is the province of another specialty in marketing,

Exhibit 1–3

The classifications of advertising.

By target audience	By geographic area	By purpose
Consumer advertising: Aimed at people who buy the product for their own or someone else's use.	*Local (retail) advertising:* Advertising by businesses whose customers come from only one city or local trading area.	*Product advertising:* Promotes the sale of products and services.
Business advertising: Aimed at people who buy or specify products and services for use in business.	*Regional advertising:* Advertising for products sold in one area or region but not the entire country.	*Nonproduct (corporate or institutional) advertising:* Promotes the organization's mission or philosophy rather than a specific product.
▪ *Trade:* Aimed at middlemen (wholesalers and retailers) of products and services who buy for resale to their customers.	*National advertising:* Advertising aimed at customers in several regions of the country.	*Commercial advertising:* Promotes products, services, or ideas with the expectation of making a profit.
▪ *Professional:* Aimed at people licensed under a code of ethics or set of professional standards.	*International advertising:* Advertising directed at foreign markets.	*Noncommercial advertising:* Sponsored by or for a charitable or nonprofit institution, civic group, or religious or political organization.
▪ *Agricultural:* Aimed at people in farming or agribusiness.	**By medium**	*Action advertising:* Attempts to stimulate immediate action by the reader.
	Print advertising: Newspapers, magazines.	*Awareness advertising:* Attempts to build the image of a product or familiarity with the product's name and package.
	Broadcast (electronic) advertising: Radio, TV.	
	Out-of-home advertising: Outdoor, transit.	
	Direct-mail advertising: Advertising sent through the Postal Service and by e-mail.	
	Interactive advertising: Internet, kiosks, etc.	

VIDEO: Boss walks into employee's office.
AUDIO:

Boss: Did those shipments get to Detroit this morning?
Employee: Umm . . . No. They're gonna be a few days late.

Boss: Did you use FedEx Express like I asked you?
Employee: No.

Boss: Remind me again why I keep you around here?
Employee: You're my dad.

Super FedEx logo slide

Announcer (voice-over): When you need fast reliable service, relax, it's FedEx.

Defining the target audience is a critical step prior to creating any advertisement. In this Cannes Gold Lion-winning ad, FedEx (www.fedex.com/us) uses a drama literary form, with actors who look like they could be actual FedEx customers.

consumer behavior, a topic we'll discuss in Chapter 5. The better an advertiser understands the buying behavior of people, the better it can bring its products into the collective consciousness of prospective customers.

Industrial/Business Markets

Companies use **business advertising** to reach people who buy or specify goods and services for business use. It tends to appear in specialized business publications or professional journals, in direct-mail pieces sent to businesses, or in trade shows. Since business advertising (also called **business-to-business,** or **B2B, advertising**) rarely uses consumer mass media, it is typically invisible to consumers. However, some business-to-business ads, by computer manufacturers or firms such as FedEx, do appear on prime-time TV and in consumer magazines.

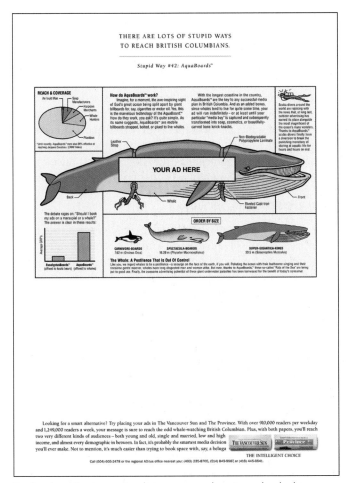

Trade advertising is not aimed at consumers, but at people who buy—or influence the purchase of—products and services used in various business situations. This witty ad for The Vancouver Sun *is targeted toward local businesses in Canada that are interested in a "smart alternative" to reach a wide range of British Colombians.*

Professional advertising encompasses the fields of education, accounting, medicine, dentistry, engineering, and the law, to name a few. In this instance, Rational Therapeutics (www.rationaltherapeutics.com) provides medical information to consumers about its unique approach to treating cancer. In so doing, it actually promotes its services to other doctors, too. Thus, this could be viewed as both a consumer ad and a professional ad.

In addition to general business advertising, there are three specialized types of business advertising: trade, professional, and agricultural. Companies aim **trade advertising** at resellers (wholesalers, dealers, and retailers) to obtain greater distribution of their products. For example, the objective of Sunkist's trade advertising in publications such as *California Grocer* is to develop more grocery outlets or to increase sales to existing outlets.

Advertising aimed at teachers, accountants, doctors, dentists, architects, engineers, lawyers, and the like is called **professional advertising** and typically appears in official publications of professional societies (such as the *Archives of Ophthalmology,* published by the American Medical Association). Professional advertising has three objectives: to convince professional people (people with specialized training who work under a code of ethics) to recommend or prescribe a specific product or service to their clients, to buy particular brands of equipment and supplies for use in their work, or to use the product personally.

Companies use **agricultural** (or **farm**) **advertising** to promote products and services used in agriculture to farm families and to individuals employed in agribusiness. FMC Corp., for example, might advertise its plant nutrition products in *California Farmer* magazine to citrus growers. Agricultural advertising typically shows farmers how the advertised product will increase efficiency, reduce risks, and widen profit margins.

Business customers are often very knowledgeable, sophisticated buyers, and they may require extensive technical information before making the purchase decision. So people who work in business-to-business advertising often need more specialized product knowledge and experience than their consumer advertising colleagues.

Implementing Marketing Strategy

Once the organization determines the target market for its products, it designs a strategy to serve that market profitably. As we'll discuss in Chapter 6, marketing strategy is the particular blend, or *mix,* of strategic elements over which the marketer has control: product concept, pricing, distribution, and communication. For ease of memory, marketers often refer to these elements as the 4Ps: product, price, place, and promotion. Each of these elements also influences the type of advertising used.

Product: Categories of Goods and Services

For example, for mass-merchandised grocery brands such as Altoids or Tide laundry detergent, companies use a type of advertising called *consumer packaged-goods advertising.* An insurance company or tax preparation firm is likely to use *service advertising.* Manufacturers of scientific and technical products use *high-tech advertising.* In other words, for virtually every product category, specialists in that area use a specific type of advertising.

Price: Strategies for Pricing

A firm's pricing strategy also affects advertising style. Companies that don't compete on price typically use **image advertising** to create a particular perception of the company or personality for the brand. Or they may use **regular price-line advertising,** in which the price of a product is not shown, or at least not highlighted, and the advertising may be aimed at justifying the nondiscounted price. Companies that are more price-competitive may regularly use sale advertising, clearance advertising, or loss-leader advertising. **Sale** and **clearance advertising** promote goods that have been discounted in order to accelerate sales or move seasonal items out of the store. **Loss-leader advertising** promotes selected goods that have been discounted drastically to create an impression of storewide low prices and thereby increase customer traffic in the store.

Place: The Distribution Element

The third element of marketing strategy, distribution, also affects the type of advertising used. Global marketers such as Coca-Cola, IBM, and Kodak may use **global advertising,** in which messages are consistent in ads placed around the world. Other firms may promote their products in foreign markets with **international advertising,** which may contain different messages and even be created locally in each geographic market. The field of international marketing has become so important that we discuss global advertising issues in every chapter of this book.

Companies that market in several regions of the United States and use the major mass media are called national advertisers, and their promotion is called **national advertising.** Some companies sell only in one part of the country or in two or three states. They use **regional advertising,** placing their ads in local media or regional editions of national media. Finally, businesses and retailers that sell within one small trading area typically use **local advertising** placed in local media or direct mail. We'll explore this topic further in Chapter 4.

Promotion: The Communication Element

The final element of marketing strategy is communication. As we mentioned at the beginning of this chapter, advertising is just one of the tools in the marketing communications tool kit. **Marketing communications** (often called *marcom*) typically refers to all the *planned messages* that companies and organizations create and disseminate to support their marketing objectives and strategies. In addition to

Global companies must advertise not only in their home country but also overseas to cover the distribution element of their marketing strategies. To promote Reebok's night safety running shoes in Singapore, Saatchi & Saatchi targets consumers through a purely illustrative advertisement, overcoming any language barriers.

advertising, major marketing communication tools include *personal selling, sales promotion, public relations activities,* and *collateral materials.* The extent to which an organization uses any or all of these tools again depends on its marketing needs, objectives, and strategy.

Each marketing communication tool offers particular opportunities and benefits to the marketer. **Personal selling,** for example, in which salespeople deal directly with customers either face-to-face or via telemarketing, offers the flexibility possible only through human interaction. Personal selling is thus an excellent tool for conveying information, for giving demonstrations, and particularly for consummating the sale (or exchange) especially on high-ticket items such as cars, real estate, and furniture as well as most business-to-business products. The drawback to personal selling is its high cost, so companies that emphasize personal selling in their marketing mix often spend a lower percentage of sales on advertising than other firms. We'll discuss personal selling in greater detail in Chapter 10.

As a marketing communications tool, advertising enables marketers to reach more prospects at lower cost than a salesperson could ever do. Further, the creativity inherent in advertising allows the marketer to conjure an image or personality, full of symbolic meaning and benefits, for the company's brand. No salesperson can do this. In fact, of all the marketing communication tools, only advertising has this ability. However, advertising does suffer from credibility gaps, a topic we'll discuss in Chapter 3. For creating brand awareness, familiarity, and image, as well as for reinforcing prior purchase decisions, advertising is usually the marcom tool of choice. As Altoids showed, advertising can also be used to build brand value.

Advertising can be used to satisfy a variety of sponsor objectives. Some advertising is meant to help generate profits for the advertiser; some is sponsored by nonprofit groups. Some ads try to spur the target audience to immediate action, others to create awareness or understanding of the advertiser's offering.

For example, to promote their goods and services, companies use **product advertising.** To sell ideas, though, organizations use **nonproduct advertising.** A British Petroleum (BP) ad for its gasoline is a product ad. So are ads for banking, insurance, or legal services. But a BP ad promoting the company's mission or philosophy (how the company protects the environment while drilling for oil) is called *nonproduct, corporate,* or *institutional advertising.* Corporate advertising is so important that we'll focus on it in Chapter 11.

(continued on page 24)

Developing a unique product concept is important for differentiating a product or service from others in the marketplace. During the marketing and advertising planning process, companies need to carefully consider the makeup of their target markets and who their advertising should be aimed at. Leo Burnett, Altoids' ad agency, focused on 12 strong markets to develop a very narrowly defined target consumer. Once the consumer was profiled, the agency used a geodemographic research tool to find out where prospective Altoids' consumers lived, worked, and played. The agency then used this information to determine where to buy media and place its ads. Though its budget was substantially less than its leading competitors, Altoids' campaign included a vast array of media. The aggressive strategy reaped great rewards. Unaided brand awareness increased substantially, as did regular use of the product.

■ Study the array of Altoids ads in this portfolio and consider how well each illustrates the contemporary definition of advertising presented in this text. Next, select one ad from the portfolio and analyze the multiple dimensions of the communication process as they apply to that ad. Finally, select a different ad from the portfolio and determine which of the six functions of advertising are applicable to the ad.

Building Brand Value

Great ads are often powerful in their visual and verbal simplicity, drawing strength from the interplay between the two elements. Here, although the bodybuilder's deltoids are impressive and "curiously strong," his humble tin of mints is what draws the compliment.

Many successful advertising campaigns utilize a unique mix of creativity and consistency in their ads. The advertising for Altoids cinnamon mints features a "hot" character. Here, notice how Altoids stays consistent with that theme by using a playful spelling of the flavor "Cinnamon" to illustrate the naughty—but nice—nature of these hot mints.

HOT AND BOTHERED

THE CURIOUSLY STRONG MINTS®

When Altoids extended its product line to include cinnamon-flavored mints, Burnett needed to create a look and style specific to these mints. They chose this racy spokescharacter that embodied the "heat" of the cinnamon. How well do this think this approach works? Do you think there are some instances when this approach would not be appropriate?

As part of Altoids' strategy to target a young and hip audience, this ad attempts to humorously associate the "curiously strong" effect of the mints to the body piercing trend. What kind of image is Altoids trying to convey? How effective is this ad in communicating that image?

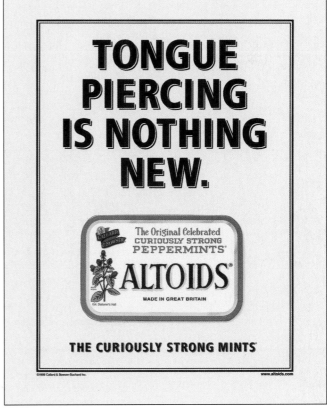

TONGUE PIERCING IS NOTHING NEW.

The Original Celebrated CURIOUSLY STRONG PEPPERMINTS®
ALTOIDS®
MADE IN GREAT BRITAIN

THE CURIOUSLY STRONG MINTS®

This humorous installment in the "curiously strong mint" series features a soldier animatedly asking for more.

In addition to print ads reminiscent of movie posters from the 1950s and 1960s, the campaign for Altoids spearmint-flavored mints includes a minimovie. Notice how this ad directs audiences to a website where they can watch the movie.

MY ALTOIDS ARE CHANGING
AND I'M OK WITH THAT.
www.gonesour.com

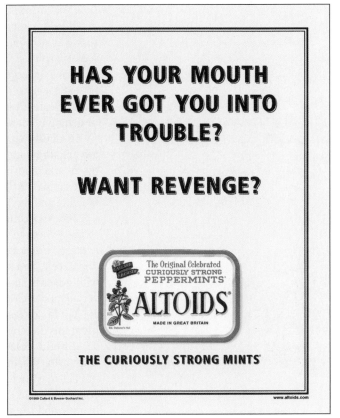

HAS YOUR MOUTH
EVER GOT YOU INTO
TROUBLE?

WANT REVENGE?

The Original Celebrated
CURIOUSLY STRONG
PEPPERMINTS
ALTOIDS
MADE IN GREAT BRITAIN

THE CURIOUSLY STRONG MINTS

©1999 Callard & Bowser-Suchard Inc.   www.altoids.com

Another Altoids campaign focuses on the awkward teenage years. Similar to its first ad featuring the muscle man, this campaign plays off the fact that the mint sounds like a body part. Good advertising campaigns are able to relate to the target market. Can you relate to this approach that Altoids uses? Discuss why or why not.

In another humorous play on words, this ad focuses on the trouble one can get in from their mouth—either through words or bad breath.

Television can be a powerful advertising medium. For the first time, Altoids incorporates the use of television in its current advertising campaign. Notice how these commercials are consistent with the nostalgic tone of the print ads.

MAKING FRIENDS
WITH FRUIT

23

(continued from page 19)

Similarly, while commercial advertising seeks profits, **noncommercial advertising** is used around the world by governments and nonprofit organizations to seek donations, volunteer support, or changes in consumer behavior.

Some ads are intended to bring about immediate action by the reader; others have a longer-term goal. The objectives of **awareness advertising,** for example, are to create an image for a product and to position it competitively with the goal of getting readers or viewers to select the brand the next time they shop.

A direct-mail ad, on the other hand, exemplifies **action** (or **direct-response**) **advertising** because it seeks an immediate, direct response from the reader. Most ads on TV and radio are awareness ads, but some are a mixture of awareness and action. For example, a 60-second TV commercial may devote the first 50 seconds to image building and the last 10 to a toll-free phone number for immediate information.

Sales promotion is a communication tool that offers special incentives to motivate people to act right away. The incentives may be coupons, free samples, contests, or rebates on the purchase price. By offering added value, sales promotion accelerates sales. So it is a very effective tool. It is often used in conjunction with advertising—to promote the promotion. However, like personal selling, it is very expensive; it suffers from other drawbacks as well, as we'll discuss in Chapter 10. While ad agencies create and place media advertising, most sales promotion programs are created by firms that specialize in that field.

Public relations (PR) is an umbrella process—much like marketing— responsible for managing the firm's relationships with its various *publics*. These publics may include customers but are not limited to them. Public relations is also concerned with employees, stockholders, vendors and suppliers, government regulators, and the press. So PR is much larger than just a tool of marketing communications. However, as part of their marketing mix, marketers use a number of **public relations activities** because they are so good at creating awareness and credibility for the firm at relatively low cost. These activities (often referred to as **marketing PR**) include publicity, press agentry, sponsorships, special events, and a special kind of advertising called **public relations advertising,** which uses the structured, sponsored format of media advertising to accomplish public relations goals. While PR is closely aligned with advertising, it requires very different skills and is usually performed by professionals in PR firms rather than ad agency people. However, advertising people need to understand how important PR activities are, so we'll discuss the topic in some detail in Chapter 11.

Companies use a wide variety of promotional tools other than media advertising to communicate information about themselves and their brands. These **collateral materials** include fliers, brochures, catalogs, posters, sales kits, product specification sheets, instruction booklets, and so on. These materials may be very inexpensive or frightfully costly. But because they contribute so much information to customers and prospects, they are very important to both closing sales and reinforcing prior sales decisions. The people who produce collateral materials may work for the company's advertising agency, but often they work for outside graphic design firms, packaging specialists, and independent film and video producers.

Integrating Marketing Communications

In recent years, as new media have proliferated and the cost of competition has intensified, sophisticated marketers have searched for new ways to get more bang (and accountability) from their marketing communications buck. The result has been a growing understanding on the part of corporate management that (1) the efficiencies of mass media advertising are not what they used to be; (2) consumers are more sophisticated, cynical, and distrusting than ever before; (3) tremendous gaps exist between what companies say in their advertising and what they actually do; and (4) in the long run, nourishing good customer relationships is far more important than making simple exchanges.[14] As a result, there is now a growing movement toward integrating all the messages created by an advertiser's various communication agencies and sent out by various departments within the company to achieve consistency. This process, called *integrated marketing communications (IMC),* is not only an important marketing trend, it is likely *the* business imperative for the twenty-first century. Moreover, it has such a dynamic impact on the advertising a company uses that we will discuss it wherever applicable throughout the book.

But first, we need to understand the economic dimension of advertising and how advertising has evolved as both an economic and a societal tool. That will be the subject of Chapter 2, and by studying that, we will see how IMC is the natural culmination of this evolution.

Chapter Summary

As a tool of marketing communications, advertising is the structured and composed, nonpersonal communication of information. It is usually paid for and usually persuasive, about products, services, or ideas, by identified sponsors through various media. Looking at four important dimensions of advertising (communication, marketing, economic, and social) can help us better understand what advertising is and how it has evolved.

Because advertising is first and foremost communication, advertisers cannot afford to take the communication process for granted. The basic human communication process begins when one party (the source) formulates an idea, encodes it as a message, and sends it via some channel or medium to another party (the receiver). The receiver must decode the message in order to understand it. To respond, the receiver formulates a new idea, encodes that concept, and then sends a new message back through some channel. A message that acknowledges or responds to the original message is feedback, and it affects the encoding of a new message. In advertising, the communication process is complex because of the multidimensional nature of the source, the message, and the recipient. Traditionally, advertising has been principally a one-way process, but with today's new interactive technology, consumers can give feedback to advertising messages in real time using the same channels as the sender.

Marketing's primary role is to attract revenues, so advertising is an important marketing tool. The targets of a firm's marketing will determine the targets of its advertising. There are two major types of audiences marketers address with their advertising: consumers and businesses. Within each of these categories, though, are special forms of advertising, such as retail, trade, professional, and agricultural.

Similarly, a firm's marketing mix—or strategy—will establish the type of advertising needed and the skills required to implement it. The marketing mix includes those elements over which the marketer has control: product, price, distribution, and communication. Depending on the product marketed, the advertiser may use packaged-goods advertising, professional services advertising, or some other type such as high-tech advertising. Likewise, the firm's pricing strategy will determine if it should use sale advertising, loss-leader advertising, or regular price-line advertising.

The distribution strategy dictates the firm's use of local, regional, national, or international advertising. The communication element determines the mix of marketing communications tools to be used. These include advertising, personal selling, sales promotion, public relations activities, and collateral materials.

To achieve consistency in all the organization's messages, sophisticated companies seek to integrate their marketing communications with all other corporate activities through a process called integrated marketing communications.

Important Terms

action advertising, *24*	drama messages, *10*	medium, *8*
actual consumers, *12*	encodes, *8*	message, *8*
advertising, *7*	farm advertising, *17*	narrative messages, *10*
agricultural advertising, *17*	feedback, *8*	national advertising, *18*
author, *10*	global advertising, *18*	noise, *9, 12*
autobiographical messages, *10*	goods, *7*	noncommercial advertising, *24*
awareness advertising, *24*	ideas, *7*	nonproduct advertising, *19*
business advertising, *16*	image advertising, *18*	persona, *10*
business-to-business (B2B) advertising, *16*	implied consumers, *12*	personal selling, *19*
channel, *8*	international advertising, *18*	process, *14*
clearance advertising, *18*	local advertising, *18*	product, *7*
collateral materials, *24*	loss-leader advertising, *18*	product advertising, *19*
consumer advertising, *15*	marketing, *14*	professional advertising, *17*
consumers, *7, 15*	marketing communications, *6, 18*	public relations (PR), *24*
decode, *8*	marketing PR, *24*	public relations activities, *24*
direct-response advertising, *24*	mass media, *8*	public relations advertising, *24*

Review Questions

1. How does advertising for the American Cancer Society compare with the standard definition of advertising?

2. How does advertising differ from public relations activities?

3. In the marketing communication process, what are the various dimensions of the source, the message, and the receiver?

4. What is meant by *noise* and how might it affect an advertiser's efforts?

5. What are the three major functional areas of business and which function is most closely related to advertising?

6. What are the two broad categories of target markets?

7. In addition to consumer advertising, what specific form of business advertising would a pharmaceutical company be likely to employ?

8. What are the four elements that comprise a company's marketing strategy and how do they affect the type of advertising a company uses?

9. What is the purpose of awareness advertising?

10. Why is integrated marketing communications so important today?

11. **The Advertising Experience**

    Select a print advertisement that you find interesting. Working backward from the ad, see if you can determine what the marketing strategy of the sponsor might have been and how the ad fits into that strategy. Address each of the four elements of the marketing mix: product, price, distribution, and communication.

Exploring the Internet

The Internet exercises here address core areas of advertising covered in Chapter 1: advertising as communication (Exercise 1), as a marketing tool (Exercise 2), and as a literary form (Exercise 3).

1. **The Communication Process**

    Go online and surf the Net for an interesting website. Then answer the following questions:

    a. What are the various means available to advertisers for encoding and sending a message in cyberspace?

    b. What are some potential sources of noise when marketers send a message via the Internet?

    c. What types of feedback are available to marketers that can help determine message delivery/comprehension?

    d. Choose one website or advertising banner as an example and identify the following communication elements: source, author, message, channel, receiver, feedback, and potential noise.

2. **Role of Advertising**

    In Chapter 1, you learned about the standard definition of advertising and the various roles and forms that advertising can take. Browse through the following websites and discuss what type of advertising each uses and what the purpose of the advertising is:

    a. American Cancer Society www.cancer.org

    b. Amazon www.amazon.com

    c. Nike www.nike.com

    d. Ford www.ford.com

    e. McDonald's www.mcdonalds.com

    f. Rolex www.rolex.com

    g. United Parcel Service www.ups.com

3. **Literary Forms in Internet Ads**

    Find three pop-up advertisements on the Internet and examine them for literary form. Did they use autobiographical, narrative, or drama form? Discuss why you think the author chose this particular form for each advertisement and not another.

Chapter 2

The Evolution of Advertising

Objectives

TO SHOW HOW ECONOMICS HAS AFFECTED THE GROWTH OF ADVERTISING. You will learn the basic principles of free-market economics; the functions and effects of advertising in a free economy; the evolution of advertising as an economic tool; and advertising's overall impact on the society in which it operates. These perspectives will help you understand why the practice of advertising has changed over the years and how it may change even more in the years to come.

After studying this chapter, you will be able to:

- **Explain** the important role of competition in free-market economics.

- **Discuss** the various functions advertising performs in a free market.

- **Identify** important milestones in the history of advertising.

- **Discuss** how the role of advertising has changed in recent years.

- **Explore** the impact of advertising on society yesterday, today, and tomorrow.

When George Eastman walked into the London Patent Office in 1879 to obtain a patent on his plate-coating machine, he had no idea of the enormity of what would soon follow. Over the subsequent decade, photography, a trade that only experienced professionals could execute before, was transformed into a delightful aspect of everyday life for all to enjoy. ■ The Eastman Kodak Company was formed in 1888 by Eastman and his partner, Henry A. Strong. Through a combination of technical and marketing innovations, Kodak managed to stay at the forefront of American industry for more than a century after its creation. ■ From his original dry plates, to the first Kodak camera, to the digital technologies of today, Eastman Kodak has provided technical breakthroughs on numerous fronts. In 1891, Eastman and Thomas Edison teamed up to make motion pictures possible; in 1896, Kodak plates and paper played a key role in the development of X-ray technology; during World War I, Kodak developed cameras and trained aerial photographers for the U.S. Signal Corps, while also supplying cellulose acetate for coating airplane wings and producing unbreakable lenses for gas masks; in 1952, Kodak won an Oscar in recognition of its contributions to the movie industry; 17 years later it won an Emmy for its development of fast color film processing for television use; in 1962, when John Glenn became the first American astronaut to orbit Earth, it was Kodak film that recorded his reactions to traveling through space at 17,400 miles per hour.[1] Add to this history the dozens of innovative contributions that continued through the 60s, 70s, 80s, and 90s, and the full impact of the Eastman Kodak Company on American industry over the last century becomes apparent. Read about these innovations and more in the Eastman Kodak Chronology in Exhibit 2–1. ■ In advertising, Kodak was also a pioneer. Three years before forming the Eastman Kodak Company and introducing the Kodak camera, Eastman ran advertisements stating that "shortly there will be introduced a new sensitive film which it is believed

will prove an economical and convenient substitute for glass dry plates both for outdoor and studio work."[2] The ad prepared consumers for the new advances in film that would soon thereafter lead to the introduction of the Kodak camera. Upon its introduction in 1888, Eastman continued to pursue the benefits of advertising. In fact, it was Eastman himself who wrote many of the early advertisements including the company's most famous slogan, "You press the button, we do the rest." Later, he introduced the "Kodak Girl," changing her style of clothing and the camera she carried every year. Symbolizing Kodak's target customer, the Kodak girl appeared at world expositions and in a wide variety of print media ads. In 1887, the company ventured into international outdoor advertising, hanging a spectacular electric Kodak sign in London's Trafalgar Square—one of the first uses of such signs in advertising.[3] The goal was simple: to make people aware of a "camera as convenient as the pencil."[4] And the advertising worked! In 1896, eight years after its introduction, the 100,000th Kodak camera was manufactured, the film and photographic paper were being produced at the rate of 400 miles per month, and Kodak's distinguishing yellow trade dress was becoming as familiar in the minds of the public as the word Kodak itself.[5] ■ Retaining the brand value Kodak had worked so hard to develop in the 1800s proved to be a challenging task in the twentieth century. On several occasions, competition challenged Kodak's dominant position in the film and photography industries. In fact, in the early 1980s, Kodak was losing 3 to 4 percent of its market share annually as a result of increasing competitive pressure, particularly from its main rival, Japan's Fuji Film.[6] However, the continuous use of aggressive advertising campaigns—such as the "True Colors" campaign that used song lyrics to create brand association—ensured that the Kodak name would remain strong going into the turn of the century. ■ In recent years, though, Kodak's secure position as the national leader in photography has received a major blow. With the advent of digital photography, sales of film, the product that allowed Kodak to triumph over its competitors in the past, have dropped drastically. The company has fallen down into the ranks of contenders, and it has been reduced to using rapid product innovation and marketing strategies to keep its head above the water. It remains to be seen whether Kodak will be able to reclaim its number-one standing after the photography industry completes its transition to a primarily digital arena. Over the last 100+ years, Kodak's history closely paralleled the history of modern American business and advertising. From the days of simple print ads in the local paper, to radio spots, television commercials, and sponsored programs, through the complex, multimedia, integrated campaigns of today, Kodak has become a household name around the world. ■

Economics: The Growing Need for Advertising

In Chapter 1 we looked at the communication dimension of advertising to get a sense of what advertising is and how it works. The marketing dimension, then, showed us some of the many types of advertising that companies can employ to help them succeed, and it showed us where advertising fits into a company's over-all marketing strategy. Now we'll turn our attention to a broader dimension—economics, which has driven the growth of advertising since its earliest beginnings and has made it one of the hallmarks of the free enterprise system. As English historian Raymond Williams said, advertising is "the official art of capitalist society."[7]

Today, business and advertising are undergoing the most dramatic changes in history. To understand the nature of these changes and why they're taking place, we need to look at how advertising has evolved. In this chapter, we'll explain how the changing economic environment has influenced the evolution of advertising through the centuries. Then, in Chapter 3, we'll look at how advertising itself influences the economy and society and, as a result, is often an object of controversy and criticism.

Principles of Free-Market Economics

Our economy is based on the notion of competition. While there is no such thing as *perfect competition,* there are four fundamental assumptions of free-market economics that, to a greater or lesser extent, our market-driven society believes in and/or strives to achieve:

1. *Self-interest.* People and organizations tend to act in their own self-interest. By their very nature, people are acquisitive. They always want more—for less. Therefore, open competition between self-interested sellers advertising to self-interested buyers naturally leads to greater product availability at more competitive prices.

2. *Complete information.* Access by buyers and sellers to all information at all times about what products are available, at what quality, and at what prices leads to greater competition and lower prices for all. (This is why attorneys are now allowed to advertise, so that people can know what services are available at what prices.)

3. *Many buyers and sellers.* Having a wide range of sellers ensures that if one company does not meet customer needs, another will be available to capitalize on the situation by producing a more market-responsive product. Similarly, having a wide range of buyers ensures that sellers can find customers who are interested in the unique products they are able to produce at a fair price. (This is why we have antitrust laws and why the government closely regulates the few monopolies we do have. If a company controls the market and is not responsive to customer needs, the government can intervene to break up the company or otherwise make sure that customers have the alternatives they want.)

4. *Absence of externalities (social costs).* Sometimes the sale or consumption of products may benefit (for example, by crime prevention) or harm (for example, with pollution) other people who are not involved in the transaction and didn't pay for the product. In these cases, the government may use taxation and/or regulation to compensate for or eliminate the externalities (as with tobacco advertising).

Now, given these basic assumptions, let's see how advertising fits into the scheme of a free-market economy.

Functions and Effects of Advertising in a Free Economy

For any business, advertising may perform a variety of functions, and, when executed correctly, its effects may be dramatic. To see how this works, let's go back to the beginnings of the Eastman Kodak Company.

When George Eastman first developed his plans for transparent roll film and subsequently the box camera, he realized he also had to think up a new, distinctive name for the company. Eastman explained, "I devised the name myself. The letter 'K' had been a favorite with me—it seems a strong, incisive sort of letter. It became a question of trying out a great number of combinations of letters that made words starting and ending with 'K.' The word 'Kodak' is the result." Once Eastman decided on a name he felt would distinguish his company and its products in the minds of consumers, he quickly registered the word "Kodak" as a trademark with the U.S. Patent and Trademark Office. Shortly thereafter, Eastman selected the distinctive yellow trade dress that is now widely associated with Kodak throughout the world—a recognition that has become one of the company's more valued assets. This demonstrates one of the most basic functions of **branding** as well as advertising: *to identify products and their source and to differentiate them from others.* (For a chronology of Kodak's innovations, see Exhibit 2–1.)

Once Eastman and his partners had named the product and the company, they began running ads to promote the Kodak camera, to tell people how it worked, and to publicize where they could get one. Here is another basic function of advertising: *to communicate information about the product, its features, and its location of sale.* (The functions and effects discussed here are listed in Exhibit 2–2.)

Prior to the introduction of Kodak film, photography had been the purview of dedicated professionals or wealthy amateurs. It was Eastman's intention to change that. Toward the turn of the twentieth century, Kodak's ad campaign sought to make the camera a part of daily life—something everyone could enjoy. Hence the introduction of the $1.00 Kodak Brownie camera and Kodak's ambitious ad cam-

Exhibit 2–1

Kodak chronology: the history of Kodak innovation.

1880s	1900–1920	1920s
1888. The Kodak camera.	**1900.** Brownie camera.	**1923.** 16mm motion picture camera and projector.
1889. Transparent roll film.	**1902.** Film developing machine.	**1928.** Color motion picture film.
1895. Pocket Kodak camera.	**1917.** Aerial cameras.	**1929.** Sound motion picture film.
1896. X-ray plates and paper.	**1917.** Unbreakable gas mask lens.	
1897. Folding pocket camera.		

1930s	1940s	1950s
1932. 8mm motion picture film, cameras, and projectors.	**1942.** Kodacolor film for prints.	**1950.** Color negative and color print films.
1934. 35mm cameras.	**1947.** Synthetic vitamin A.	**1958.** Fully automatic color slide projector.
1935. Color slides.	**1947.** Television recording camera.	**1958.** Polyester textile fiber.

1960s	1970s	1980s
1961. 80-slide Carousel projector.	**1973.** Sound home movies.	**1983.** Disney's Epcot Center.
1962. John Glenn records reactions in space.	**1975.** Copier-duplicator.	**1984.** Floppy disk.
1963. Instamatic camera.	**1978.** Thermoplastic polyester for manufacturing beverage bottles.	**1984.** Videotape cassettes.
1965. Super 8 format.		**1989.** Single-use "stretch panoramic" camera.
1966. Color printer.		

1990s	2000s	
1990. Photo CD system.	**2000.** Dental radiography film.	
1992. Writeable CD.	**2001.** Digital photo editing services.	
1992. Digital camera.	**2002.** Digital photo printer.	
1992. Improved X-ray imaging of soft tissue.		
1995. Digital zoom technology.		
1996. Advantix film.		
1998. NASA Mars Surveyor imaging sensors.		
1998. High-definition television.		

Exhibit 2-2

Functions and effects of advertising as a marketing tool.

- To identify products and differentiate them from others.
- To communicate information about the product, its features, and its place of sale.
- To induce consumers to try new products and to suggest reuse.
- To stimulate the distribution of a product.
- To increase product use.
- To build value, brand preference, and loyalty.
- To lower the overall cost of sales.

paign covering a wide variety of media: early teen magazines, such as *Youth's Companion, Boy's Life,* and *American Boy,* as well as family/adult magazines, such as *McLure's Magazine, Ladies Home Companion,* and *Cosmopolitan.* By June 1900, the magazines carrying Brownie advertisements reached a combined circulation of 6 million. The Brownie campaign, which lasted until the early 1960s, changed the perception of who could use a camera and the ease with which film could be developed. To us, this campaign demonstrates another function of advertising: *to induce consumers to try new products and to suggest reuse.*[8]

Over the past century, as the camera became an integral part of everyday life in the United States, Kodak conducted many simultaneous campaigns outside the country to increase global awareness as well. Through various activities, such as its sponsorship of the Olympic Games, where it supplied free cameras and film to participating media personnel, Kodak succeeded in accomplishing yet another function of advertising: *to stimulate the distribution of a product*—in this case, on a global level (for a timeline of advertising history, see Exhibit 2–3).

Since the introduction of the first Kodak box camera in 1888, technology has dramatically changed the field of photography, and Kodak has been at the forefront of this progress. The result of these advances has been to make basic photography simpler and more accessible to the masses while improving the overall quality for both amateur and professional photographers alike. By effectively communicating the news of these advancements to its customers, Kodak achieved another of the most important functions of advertising: *to increase product use.* To accomplish this, Kodak has conducted a wide range of promotional activities throughout its history. In recent years it has even tested the use of *infomercials*—programs of varying lengths that Kodak could use to create awareness while also providing educational information on how to use its increasingly sophisticated line of products. Other recent promotional efforts have included marketing partnerships with other companies. For instance, with AOL Time Warner, Kodak created "You've Got Pictures!" By allowing people to send their digital pictures with the ease of sending an e-mail, Kodak encourages greater use of its digital cameras.

In a free-market economy, when one company starts to make significant profits, other companies immediately jump in to compete. Over the years, to battle the growing competitive threat, Kodak has consistently funded ongoing marketing communications campaigns aimed at accomplishing yet another function of advertising: *to build value, brand preference, and loyalty.* Today Kodak offers a myriad of products ranging from simple film roll cameras, to disposable cameras, to high-tech digital cameras, to printers and scanners, as well as its ubiquitous Kodak film processing service. Its advertising, though, such as its current campaign, "Share Moments. Share Life," has always striven to unify the products under a common voice and a common theme: quality, reliability, and trust.

For more than 100 years, the Eastman Kodak Company has used a variety of media to communicate advertising messages to very divergent audiences. Why? To achieve the most significant function of advertising: *lowering the cost of sales.* For the cost of reaching just one prospect through personal selling, companies can reach thousands of people through media advertising. According to a Cahners

<u>**Exhibit 2-3**</u>

Timetable of advertising history.

3000 B.C.–A.D. 1	A.D. 500–1599	1600–1799	1800–1899
3000 B.C. Written advertisement offering "Whole gold coin" for runaway slave "Shem." **500 B.C.** Political and trade graffiti on Pompeii walls. **A.D. 1** First upper-case lettering appears on Greek buildings.	**1455.** First printed Bible. **1472.** First printed ad in English tacked on London church doors. **1544.** Claude Garamond, first "typefounder," perfects a roman typeface that bears his name and is still used today.	**1650.** First newspaper ad offers reward for stolen horses. **1662.** *London Gazette* offers first advertising supplement. **1704.** First ads in America published in the *Boston Newsletter.* **1729.** Ben Franklin is first to use "white space" and illustration in ads. **1785.** Widespread use of advertising and long print runs become possible.	**1841.** Volney B. Palmer becomes first "newspaper agent" (advertising agent) in America. **1844.** First magazine ad runs. **1869.** Francis W. Ayer founds ad agency bearing his father's name, N. W. Ayer & Sons, in Philadelphia. He initiates first "for commission" ad contract (1876), first market survey for an ad (1879), and first on-staff creative services (art in 1890, copywriting in 1892). **1888.** *Printers' Ink* is first U.S. publication for ad profession.

1900–1919	1920–1939	1940–1959	1960–1969
1900. Psychologists study the attention-getting and persuasive qualities of advertising. **1900.** Northwestern University is first to offer advertising as a discipline. **1903.** Scripps-McRae League of Newspapers appoints ad censor, rejects $500,000 in ads in first year. **1905.** First national ad plan is for the "Gillette Safety Razor." **1911.** First "truth in advertising" codes are established by what is now called the American Advertising Federation (AAF).	**1920s.** Albert Lasker, father of modern advertising, calls advertising "salesmanship in print." First ad testimonials by movie stars appear. Full-color printing is available in magazines. **1922.** First radio ad solves radio's need for financing. **1924.** N. W. Ayer produces first sponsored radio broadcast, the "Eveready Hour." **1930.** *Advertising Age* magazine is founded. **1938.** Wheeler-Lea amendments to FTC Act of 1938 grant FTC further power to curb false ad practices.	**1946.** America has 12 TV stations broadcasting to the public. **1947.** Lanham Trademark Act protects brand names and slogans. **1948.** 46 TV stations are operating and 300 others are awaiting FCC approval. **1950.** First political ads are used on TV by Gov. Dewey of New York. **1950s.** David Ogilvy's "Hathaway man" and "Commander Whitehead" become popular ad personae.	**1960s.** Doyle Dane Bernbach's "Think small" ad for American Volkswagen becomes one of the most famous ads of the decade, establishing a strong market position for the smallest European import. The agency's slogan for Avis, "We're only No. 2, so we try harder" is also very successful. New York's Madison Avenue becomes known worldwide as the center of the advertising world and features the best in advertising creativity.

1970–1979	1980–1989	1990–2000	2001–2004
1971. Armed services begin first advertising for the new "all-volunteer" military ("Be all that you can be in the Army"). **1972.** The *Ad Age* article "Positioning: The Battle for Your Mind" by Al Ries and Jack Trout details the strategy of positioning that dominates the 1970s. **1973.** Oil shortages begin period of "demarketing," ads aimed at slowing demand. **1970s (late).** Growth in self-indulgence, signified by popularity of self-fulfillment activities, spurs some agencies into making infomercials.	**1980s.** The "me" decade begins (baby-boomers are indulgent but want social accountability). Ad agency megamergers take place worldwide. **1982.** First edition of *Contemporary Advertising* is published. **1984.** The Internet (government controlled since 1973) is turned over to the private sector. **1986.** *Marketing Warfare* by Al Ries and Jack Trout portrays marketing in terms of classic warfare manual written by General Clausewitz in 1831.	**1990s.** Early part of decade experiences recession. Marketers shift funds from advertising to sales promotion, leaving major agencies to fail or merge. **1994.** Media glut leads to market fragmentation; network TV is no longer sole medium for reaching total marketplace. Ad professions adopt integrated marketing communications (IMC) as the new strategy to build market relationships. **2000.** The Internet is the fastest-growing new ad medium since TV, with 400 million users.	**2004.** The role of the Internet as an interactive advertising medium is firmly established.

Advertising Research Report, the average cost to make a face-to-face field sales call in 2001 was $329—versus the $0.24 it costs on average to reach a prospect through a specialized business magazine advertisement in 2001.[9] To further this example, multiply the $329 spent on one personal sales call by the more than 10 million people who watch a top-rated prime-time TV show, and the cost comes to a mind-boggling $3.29 *billion*. However, for only $150,000, Kodak can buy 30-second TV commercials during *Everybody Loves Raymond* and reach the same 10 million people. In fact, through television, advertisers can typically talk to a thousand prospects for only $15 total—less than 5 percent of what it costs to talk to one prospect through personal selling.

Now, considering this brief synopsis of Kodak history, how does Kodak's advertising fit with the basic assumptions of a free-market economy? Has Kodak's advertising helped make photography available to more people at lower cost? Has it contributed important information to people? Has the freedom to advertise contributed to the competitive environment? What externalities might have had a positive or negative impact on Kodak's efforts to market photographic supplies?

Perhaps you can see from this one example how advertising contributes to a free economy. But if it's so good, then why is advertising just a twentieth-century phenomenon? Why wasn't it developed and used for the last several thousand years of recorded history?

The answer is simple: economics.

The Evolution of Advertising as an Economic Tool

An early form of advertising. Until the advent of public schooling, most people couldn't read—so signs featured symbols of the goods or services for sale, such as the jerkin on this tailor's sign in Williamsburg, Virginia.

Thousands of years ago, most people were engaged in hunting, herding, farming, or handicrafts. To make products, they used primitive hand tools. Most human effort was devoted to meeting basic survival needs: food, clothing, shelter. They lived in small, isolated communities where artisans and farmers bartered products and services among themselves. Distribution was limited to how far vendors could walk and "advertising" to how loud they could shout. Because goods weren't produced in great quantity, there was no need for advertising to stimulate mass purchases. There were also no mass media available for possible advertisers to use. Notwithstanding, archaeologists have found evidence of advertising among the Babylonians dating back as far as 3000 B.C.

The Preindustrial Age

As the marketplace grew larger and became more complex, the demand for products increased, and the need for advertising slowly developed. At first, merchants hung carved signs in front of their shops so passersby could see what products were being offered. Most people couldn't read, so the signs often used symbols, such as a boot for a cobbler. This period was called the **preindustrial age,** and, for Western civilization, it extended from the beginning of recorded history to roughly the start of the nineteenth century.[10]

During the preindustrial age, several important developments enabled the eventual birth of modern advertising. The Chinese invented paper and Europe had its first paper mill by 1275. In the 1440s, Johannes Gutenberg invented the printing press in Germany. The press was not only the most important development in the history of advertising, and indeed communication, but it also revolutionized the way people lived and worked.

Before the printing press, most people were illiterate. Only monks and scholars could read and write; the average person had to memorize important information and communicate orally. Because oral communication could not be substantiated, people lived without documentable facts. And because dialects varied from region to region, most news never traveled more than 50 miles.

(continued on page 40)

While advertising is thousands of years old, it has only come into its own in the last 100 years, thanks to a growing population hungry for goods and services and a rapidly changing technology that could make these products available.

If we look back at the ad campaigns of 30, 50, 70, and even 100 years ago, we get a fascinating indication of how life was lived back then, and we can also see how the development of modern advertising parallels the development of our own standard of living. As British writer and diplomat Norman Douglas said in 1917, "you can tell the ideals of a nation by its advertisements."

■ Study the array of historical ads in this Portfolio Review and consider how well each relates to the seven functions and effects of advertising discussed in this chapter.

The Modern History of Advertising

Coca-Cola was first served at a small pharmacy in Atlanta in 1886. Coca-Cola's inventor, John S. Pemberton, placed an ad in the Atlanta Journal proclaiming that the soft drink was "Delicious and Refreshing." By 1904, when this ad was produced, Coca-Cola's long history of successful campaigns was just getting underway.

This full-color ad from 1916 would have been considered very modern at the time of publication. Note its inclination toward post-impressionism.

Appearing in publications across the country, this 1930s print ad for Coca-Cola was one of the first to incorporate Santa Claus. Interestingly, it was not until the mid-nineteenth century that Santa Claus began to be portrayed in this rotund, jolly manner, and in fact, artists working for Coca-Cola played a major role in creating the Santa Claus we know today.

Coca-Cola has always been known for being up to date with youth trends. In this case, a teenager is pictured stopping outside a drive-in for a Coke. Note the difference in style and copy length from earlier ads.

Coca-Cola has been overwhelmingly successful at positioning itself as the leader in soft drinks. The slogan "It's The Real Thing" first appeared in the 1940s and was readopted in the late 60s.

In the late eighties, forced to compete with Pepsi's new campaigns, Coca-Cola reinvented their image and their cola. Campaigns ranged from celebrity endorsements to ones like this, slice of life ads which show people sharing and enjoying a Coke.

With the debut of a variety of variations on the classic recipe, Coca-Cola has widened their marketing scope. C2, for example, requires a different kind of approach. Who do you think this ad is aimed at and why?

It wasn't until 1729 that Ben Franklin, innovator of advertising art, made ads more readable by using larger headlines, changing fonts, and adding art. This 1767 ad announces the availability of Stage Waggons to carry passengers from Powles Hook Ferry to Philadelphia.

(continued from page 35)

The introduction of printing allowed facts to be established, substantiated, recorded, and transported. People no longer had to rely on their memories. Movable letters provided the flexibility to print in local dialects. The slow hand transcription of the monks gave way to more rapid, volume printing by a less select group. Some entrepreneurs bought printing presses, mounted them in wagons, and traveled from town to town selling printing. This new technology made possible the first formats of advertising—posters, handbills, and signs—and, eventually, the first mass medium—the newspaper. In effect, the cry of the vendor could now be multiplied many times and heard beyond the immediate neighborhood.

In 1472, the first ad in English appeared: a handbill tacked on church doors in London announcing a prayer book for sale. Two hundred years later the first newspaper ad was published, offering a reward for the return of 12 stolen horses. Soon newspapers carried ads for coffee, chocolate, tea, real estate, medicines, and even personal ads. These early ads were still directed to a very limited number of people: the customers of the coffeehouses where most newspapers were read.

By the early 1700s, the world's population had grown to about 600 million people, and some major cities were big enough to support larger volumes of advertising. In fact, the greater volume caused a shift in advertising strategy. Samuel Johnson, the famous English literary figure, observed in 1758 that advertisements were now so numerous that they were "negligently perused" and that it had become necessary to gain attention "by magnificence of promise." This was the beginning of *puffery* in advertising. (See the Ethical Issue in Chapter 3 on fluffing and puffing.)

In the American colonies, the *Boston Newsletter* began carrying ads in 1704. About 25 years later, Benjamin Franklin, the father of advertising art, made ads more readable by using large headlines and considerable white space. In fact, Franklin was the first American known to use illustrations in ads.

The Industrializing Age

In the mid-1700s, the Industrial Revolution began in England and by the early 1800s it had reached North America. Machinery began to replace animal power. By using machines to mass-produce goods with uniform quality, large companies increased their productivity. For the first time, it cost people less to buy a product than to make it themselves. As people left the farm to work in the city, mass urban markets began to emerge. This further fueled market development and the growth of advertising.

By the mid-1800s, the world's population had doubled to 1.2 billion. Suddenly, producers needed mass consumption to match the high levels of manufactured goods. Fortunately, breakthroughs in bulk transportation—the railroad and steamship—facilitated the sale and distribution of products beyond the manufacturer's local market. But with the need for mass consumption came the increasing need for mass marketing techniques such as advertising to inform new markets of the availability of products.

During this **industrializing age,** which lasted roughly until the end of World War I, manufacturers were principally concerned with production. The primary burden of marketing fell on the wholesalers, who knew the sources of supply, the providers of transportation, the market requirements, and how to arrange for product shipments to the appropriate locations. They used advertising primarily as an information vehicle, placing announcements in publications called *price currents* to let retailer customers know about the sources of supply and shipping schedules for the basic, unbranded commodities they carried. Advertising to consumers was the job of the local retailer and the large mail-order catalog companies like Montgomery Ward and Sears Roebuck. Only a few innovative manufacturers (mostly of patent medicines, soaps, tobacco products, and canned foods) foresaw the usefulness of mass media advertising to stimulate consumer demand for their products beyond their immediate market areas.

For Americans, the *profession* of advertising began when Volney B. Palmer set up business in Philadelphia in 1841. He contracted with newspapers for large volumes of advertising space at discount rates and then resold the space to advertisers at a higher rate. The advertisers usually prepared the ads themselves.

In 1869, at the ripe old age of 21, Francis Ayer formed an ad agency in Philadelphia and, to make it sound more credible, named it after his father. N. W. Ayer & Sons was the first agency to charge a commission based on the "net cost of space" and the first to conduct a formal market survey. In 1890, Ayer became the first ad agency to operate as they do today—planning, creating, and executing complete ad campaigns in exchange for media-paid commissions or fees from advertisers. In 1892, Ayer set up a copy department and hired the first full-time agency copywriter. For the next century, Ayer was considered the oldest agency in America, as well as one of its largest, until 2002 when it disappeared in a merger with Kaplan Thayer Group, a division of the giant holding company Bcom3. Later Bcom3 was itself swallowed up by the French agency network Publicis.

The technological advances of the Industrial Revolution enabled the greatest changes in advertising since the 1400s. Photography, introduced in 1839, added credibility and a new world of creativity. Now ads could show products, people, and places as they really were, rather than how an illustrator visualized them.

In the 1840s, some manufacturers began using magazine ads to reach the mass market and stimulate mass consumption. Magazines became an ideal medium because they provided national advertising and offered the best quality of reproduction.

The telegraph, telephone, typewriter, phonograph, and, later, motion pictures all let people communicate as never before. With the development of the nationwide railroad system, the United States entered a period of spectacular economic growth. In 1896, when the federal government inaugurated rural free mail delivery, direct-mail advertising and mail-order selling flourished. Manufacturers now had an ever-increasing variety of products to sell and a new way to deliver their advertisements and products to the public.

With the advent of public schooling, the nation reached an unparalleled 90 percent literacy rate. Manufacturers gained a large reading public that could understand print ads. The United States thus entered the twentieth century as a great industrial state with a national marketing system propelled by advertising. With the end of World War I, the modern period in advertising emerged.

The Industrial Age

The **industrial age** started around the turn of the twentieth century and lasted well into the 1970s. It was a period marked by tremendous growth and maturation of the country's industrial base. As U.S. industry met the basic needs of most of the population, commodity markets became saturated. Fresh mass markets then developed for the new, inexpensive brands of consumer luxury and convenience goods we referred to earlier as *consumer packaged goods*.

During the industrializing age of the nineteenth century, wholesalers controlled the marketing process as they distributed the manufacturers' unbranded commodity products. When those markets became saturated, though, the wholesalers started playing one manufacturer off against another. This hurt manufacturers' profits dramatically, so they started looking for ways to wrest back control. The manufacturers changed their focus from a *production* orientation to a *sales* orientation. They dedicated themselves to new-product development, strengthened

Ethical Dilemma or Ethical Lapse?

False and misleading advertising—and all the damage they can create—begin with unethical judgments. Hence, it pays to understand the differences between ethical dilemmas and ethical lapses.

An *ethical dilemma* arises from an unresolved interpretation of an ethical issue. To begin, there is a distinction between "having a right" and "the right thing to do." For example, should advertisers attempt to persuade poor, inner-city youths to buy sneakers priced at more than $200 a pair? There's no law against it, but the responsible action (both socially and morally) may be to refrain. And so we have an ethical dilemma.

How are such ethical dilemmas resolved? According to University of Wisconsin professor Ivan L. Preston, it appears advertising professionals find ethics largely synonymous with legality. Many believe that advertising $200 sneakers to all markets, including to those who should not buy them, is "acceptable" ethical behavior. But as Preston says, "You can be ethical only when you have the option of being unethical. You can't choose to be ethical when you can't choose at all, so ethics begins only where the law ends."

The prospect of a serious protest from watchdog groups, civic leaders, and clergy generally eliminates an advertiser's hesitancy to resolve an ethical dilemma. For small companies, a hostile public reaction can even lead to bankruptcy. In contrast, a strong market leader may have the goodwill and deep pockets to survive an ethically borderline advertising campaign—and go forward to stimulate greater name awareness from the ensuing publicity. Calvin Klein's jeans campaign, for example, depicted models who looked 15, were dressed skimpily, and posed suggestively. The huge outcry against those "kiddie porn" ads that emerged from all sectors, including trade publications and the national press, prompted Klein to discontinue the campaign. However, the press continued carrying the story for weeks. Some people outside the target group thought Calvin Klein had effectively stimulated a *positive* dialogue about the moral issues involved in advertising to young people. With minimal advertising, Klein established huge name awareness.

Ivan Preston notes that ethical dilemmas can occur because advertisers typically sell brands, not just products. Because each brand must be presented as being different from other brands—even though functionally it may not be—advertisers are tempted to create false differences. Incomplete information is another breeding ground for ethical dilemmas. Advertisers tend to highlight the good things about their brands and omit the neutral and bad. Nothing that's said is false, yet the ad does not tell the whole truth. The use of technology to distort

---

This full-page of advertising from an 1894 Scientific American *(www.scientificamerican.com) is historically telling in that nearly all the ads have yet to develop any brand identity but merely sell unbranded commodities such as soap, paper, paint, or services.*

their own sales forces, packaged and branded their products, and engaged in heavy national brand advertising. Early brands of this era included Wrigley's spearmint gum, Coca-Cola, Jell-O, Kellogg's corn flakes, and Campbell's soup.

In the 1920s, the United States was rich and powerful. As the war machine returned to peacetime production, society became consumption driven. The era of salesmanship had arrived and its bible was *Scientific Advertising,* written by the legendary copywriter Claude Hopkins at Albert Lasker's agency, Lord & Thomas. Published in 1923, it became a classic and was republished in 1950 and 1980. "Advertising has reached the status of a science," Hopkins proclaimed. "It is based on fixed principles." His principles outlawed humor, style, literary flair, and anything that might detract from his basic copy strategy of a preemptive product claim repeated loudly and often.[11]

Radio was born at about the same time and rapidly became the nation's primary means of mass communication and a powerful new advertising medium with great immediacy. World and national news now arrived direct from the scene, and a whole new array of family entertainment—music, drama, and sports—became possible. Suddenly, national advertisers could quickly reach huge audiences. In fact, the first radio shows were produced by their sponsors' ad agencies.

On October 29, 1929, the stock market crashed, the Great Depression began, and advertising expenditures plummeted. In the face of consumer sales resistance and corporate budget cutting, the advertising industry needed to improve its effectiveness. It turned to research. Daniel Starch, A. C. Nielsen, and George Gallup had founded research groups to study consumer attitudes and preferences. By providing information on public opinion, the performance of ad messages, and sales of advertised products, these companies started a whole new business: the marketing research industry.

During this period, each brand sought to sell the public on its own special qualities. Wheaties became the "Breakfast of Champions" not because of its ingredients but because of its advertising. Manufacturers followed this strategy of *product differentiation* vigorously, seeking to portray their brands as different from and better than the competition by offering consumers quality, variety, and convenience.

images to portray the product most favorably can create new ethical dilemmas. Models, for example, can be made to appear slimmer than they really are, with the possible social consequence of a rise in eating disorders in young women.

In contrast, an *ethical lapse* is typically a clear case of unprincipled conduct and, in many cases, may even include illegal behavior. The Federal Trade Commission (FTC) is the enforcement agency against such lapses in the United States. It brings lawsuits against companies that have engaged in illegal advertising claims—and it can even name advertising agencies as defendants. In 2002, for example, it made a claim against Interstate Bakeries, the marketers of Wonder Bread, and its ad agency, Campbell Mithun LLC, for making unsubstantiated claims that Wonder Bread would improve children's mental capacities. In including Campbell Mithun, the FTC asserted that the ad agency knew or should have known that the claims were not substantiated and therefore shared liability for the deceptive claim. Although the Wonder Bread case was settled without any fines being levied, many such cases result in companies paying millions of dollars in consumer redress, not to mention substantial attorneys' fees.

A myriad of federal, state, and local laws govern what is legal in advertising, but laws ultimately reflect ethical judgments. As for self-regulation, the creative code of the American Association of Advertising Agencies also reflects legalities rather than philosophies. However, the eternal question remains: when, how, and by whom are these laws to be enforced in resolving ethical dilemmas and lapses?

Exploring the Internet

In addition to consumer and government regulation, the advertising industry itself is concerned about ethics in advertising. One of the industry's most prestigious organizations, the American Advertising Federation (AAF) sponsors the annual Vance L. Stickell Memorial Student Internship Program. Established in 1989 in honor of the former executive vice president, marketing for the *Los Angeles Times*, the program is intended to further the awareness and understanding of the advertising process and business ethics among students. Visit the AAF website (www.aaf.org) and learn more about how you may qualify for this prestigious award.

Sources: Ivan Preston, *The Tangled Web They Weave: Truth, Falsity and Advertisers* (Madison, WI: University of Wisconsin Press, 1996); Federal Trade Commission, "Wonder Bread Marketers Settle FTC Charges," www.ftc.gov/opa/2002/03/wonderbread.htm; "Flesh for Fantasy," *New York Magazine*, April 7, 2003.

The greatest expansion of any medium up to that time occurred with the introduction of television in 1941. After World War II, TV advertising grew rapidly, and in time achieved its current status as the largest advertising medium in terms of advertising revenues.

During the postwar prosperity of the late 1940s and early 1950s, consumers tried to climb the social ladder by buying more and more modern products. Advertising entered its golden era. A creative revolution ensued in which ads focused on product features that implied social acceptance, style, luxury, and success. Giants in the field emerged—people such as Leo Burnett, David Ogilvy, and Bill Bernbach, who built their agencies from scratch and forever changed the way advertising was planned and created.[12]

Rosser Reeves of the Ted Bates Agency introduced the idea that every ad must point out the product's USP (*unique selling proposition*)—features that differentiate it from competitive products. The USP was a logical extension of the Lasker and Hopkins "reason why" credo. But as the USP was used over and over, consumers started finding it difficult to see what was unique anymore.

Finally, as more and more imitative products showed up in the marketplace, all offering quality, variety, and convenience, the effectiveness of this strategy wore out. Companies turned to a new mantra: **market segmentation,** a process by which marketers searched for unique groups of people whose needs could be addressed through more specialized products. The image era of the 1960s was thus the natural culmination of the creative revolution. Advertising's emphasis shifted from product features to brand image or personality as advertisers sought to align their brands with particularly profitable market segments. Cadillac, for example, became the worldwide image of luxury, the consummate symbol of success, surpassed only by the aristocratic snootiness of Rolls-Royce.

But just as me-too product features killed the product differentiation era, me-too images eventually killed the market segmentation era. With increased competition, a new kind of advertising strategy evolved in the 1970s, where competitors'

In 1890, N. W. Ayer & Sons became the first agency to operate as agencies do today, planning, creating, and executing complete ad campaigns for advertisers. This 1899 Ayer ad for Uneeda biscuits (catch the play on words!) was one of a series of popular ads of the times.

Weavers of Speech

Upon the magic looms of the Bell System, tens of millions of telephone messages are daily woven into a marvelous fabric, representing the countless activities of a busy people.

Day and night, invisible hands shift the shuttles to and fro, weaving the thoughts of men and women into a pattern which, if it could be seen as a tapestry, would tell a dramatic story of our business and social life.

In its warp and woof would mingle success and failure, triumph and tragedy, joy and sorrow, sentiment and shop-talk, heart emotions and million-dollar deals.

The weavers are the 70,000 Bell operators. Out of sight of the subscribers,

these weavers of speech sit silently at the switchboards, swiftly and skillfully interlacing the cords which guide the human voice over the country in all directions.

Whether a man wants his neighbor in town, or some one in a far-away state; whether the calls come one or ten a minute, the work of the operators is ever the same—making direct, instant communication everywhere possible.

This is Bell Service. Not only is it necessary to provide the facilities for the weaving of speech, but these facilities must be vitalized with the skill and intelligence which, in the Bell System, have made Universal Service the privilege of the millions.

AMERICAN TELEPHONE AND TELEGRAPH COMPANY
AND ASSOCIATED COMPANIES

One Policy   One System   Universal Service

In the early twentieth century, telephones were a labor-intensive process, requiring the attention and skill of thousands of operators. This 1915 ad for AT&T describes its 70,000 Bell operators as weavers of speech *since they, literally, handled the lines to connect people locally, regionally, and nationally.*

strengths became just as important as the advertiser's. Jack Trout and Al Ries trumpeted the arrival of the *positioning era.* They acknowledged the importance of product features and image, but they insisted that what really mattered was how the brand ranked against the competition in the consumer's mind—how it was positioned.

Positioning strategy proved to be an effective way to separate a particular brand from its competitors by associating that brand with a particular set of customer needs that ranked high on the consumer's priority list. Thus, it became a more effective way to use product differentiation and market segmentation. The most famous American ads of the positioning era were Volkswagen ("Think small"), Avis ("We're only no. 2"), and 7UP ("The uncola"). Product failures of the period, such as Life Savers gum and RCA computers, were blamed on flawed positioning.

Product differentiation, market segmentation, and positioning are all very important strategies to understand, so we will discuss them further in Chapter 6.

While this was all going on in the United States, across the Atlantic a new generation of advertising professionals had graduated from the training grounds of Procter & Gamble (P&G) and Colgate-Palmolive and were now teaching their clients the secrets of mass marketing. Lagging somewhat behind their U.S. counterparts due to the economic ravages of World War II, European marketers discovered the USP and the one-page strategic brief, or summary statement, that P&G had popularized to bring focus to ad campaigns. Immediately following the war, French advertising pioneer Marcel Bleustein-Blanchet waged a frustrating battle to introduce U.S. research techniques to his country; a decade or two later, in-depth attitude and behavioral research was all the rage.[13] Since commercial TV was not yet as big as in the United States, European advertisers divided their media money between newspapers and outdoor media, along with a healthy dose of cinema advertising. Germany, the Netherlands, and Scandinavia wouldn't get commercial TV for another decade.[14]

In the 1970s, though, the European Common Market already offered untapped opportunities. Following the American example, agencies and clients began to think multinationally to gain economies of scale. But it was not easy. While physically close, the countries of Europe were still separated by a chasm of cultural diversity that made the use of single Europe-wide campaigns nearly impossible.[15]

The Postindustrial Age

Beginning around 1980, the **postindustrial age** has been a period of cataclysmic change. For the first time, people became truly aware of the sensitive environment in which we live and became alarmed by our dependence on vital natural resources. During the acute energy shortages of the 1970s and 1980s, a new marketing term, **demarketing,** appeared. Producers of energy and energy-consuming goods started using advertising to *slow* the demand for their products. Ads asked people to refrain from operating washers and dryers during the day when the demand for electricity peaked. In time, demarketing became a more aggressive

Think small.

Our little car isn't so much of a novelty any more.
    A couple of dozen college kids don't try to squeeze inside it.
    The guy at the gas station doesn't ask where the gas goes.
    Nobody even stares at our shape.
    In fact, some people who drive our little flivver don't even think that about 27 miles to the gallon is going any great guns.
    Or using five pints of oil instead of five quarts.
    Or never needing anti-freeze.
    Or racking up about 40,000 miles on a set of tires.
    That's because once you get used to some of our economies, you don't even think about them any more.
    Except when you squeeze into a small parking spot.
    Or renew your small insurance. Or pay a small repair bill. Or trade in your old VW for a new one.
    Think it over.

Hailed by Jack Trout and Al Ries as "the most famous ad of the 60s," this Volkswagen ad co-opted the "small" position in consumers' minds, giving VW (www.volkswagen.com) a leadership rank for many years.

Déjà vw.

Some experiences are just too good to only have once.
    So we brought it back. The new Beetle from Volkswagen.
    Take one for a test drive and we think you'll agree...

Some experiences are just too good to only have once.
    So we brought it back. The new Beetle from Volkswagen.
    Take one for a test drive and we think you'll agree...

Some experiences are just too good to only have once.
    Visit Southern States Volkswagen. 2421 Wake Forest Road. (919)828-0901.

In recent years, VW has attempted to recapture the style of its 60s advertising.

strategic tool for advertisers to use against competitors, political opponents, and social problems. The California Department of Health Services, for example, is one of many organizations today that actively seek to demarket the use of tobacco.

Then, following a period of unprecedented boom in the West and bust in the East, the Berlin Wall and the Iron Curtain came tumbling down. This finally ended the Cold War and with it the need for a defense-driven economy. Ogling the huge, new, untapped markets in the former Warsaw Pact states, Western financiers and marketers rubbed their hands in glee. To expand their power globally, big multinational companies and their advertising agencies went on a binge, buying other big companies and creating a new word in the financial lexicon: *megamerger.*

By now European and Asian advertising had caught up with the United States. TV was suddenly the hot medium, and agencies focused on growth, acquisitions, and superior creative executions. For several years, Young & Rubicam in New York and Dentsu in Japan alternated as the largest advertising agency in the world. Then two brothers in London, Charles and Maurice Saatchi, started acquiring agencies globally. In rapid succession, a number of high-profile U.S. agencies disappeared under the Saatchi & Saatchi umbrella—big companies such as Ted Bates Worldwide and Dancer, Fitzgerald, Sample. Saatchi & Saatchi was suddenly the largest agency in the world. Then followed more buyouts as the big agencies from Europe, the United States, and Japan emulated the merger mania of their huge multinational clients. Names of agency founders disappeared from the doors, replaced by initials and acronyms: WPP Group, RSCG, TBWA, FCA, DDB Needham, and FCB, to mention just a few.[16]

Demarketing is used not only to dampen the demand for products but also to encourage safe use of already ubiquitous ones. This Hutchison Essar Telecom (India) outdoor ad, a 2004 Cannes Bronze Lion winner, shows the dangers of driving while distracted by a mobile phone.

The European agencies fueled their growth by establishing huge bulk-media-buying conglomerates, although their now-sophisticated clients stopped looking to the agencies for research and marketing advice. Rather, they expected extraordinary creative executions to give their brands an edge, and the agencies delivered. Awards at the Cannes International Advertising Festival disclosed the blossoming of creative advertising from Spain and confirmed the creative leadership of the British, who were only slightly ahead of the French.[17]

Unfortunately, the euphoria of this period was short-lived. Sparked by unprecedented layoffs in the defense industries, the United States, as well as much of the world, fell into an economic recession. While it was technically short-lived, some regions of the country felt the effects of it from the late 1980s well into the mid-1990s. The mergers temporarily stopped, the business world sucked in its collective belt, and management turned to new theories of total quality management (TQM), reengineering, and downsizing—theories aimed at cutting costs and increasing efficiency, all in the name of better customer service. But to many employees of the period, they were simply euphemisms for "you're fired." And all too often the struggle to maintain profits resulted in reduced customer service.

Two related economic factors characterize the marketing world of this period: (1) the aging of traditional products, with a corresponding growth in competition, and (2) the growing affluence and sophistication of the consuming public, led by the huge baby-boomer generation.[18]

The most important factor was competition, intensified by lower trade barriers and growing international trade. As high profits lured imitators into the marketplace, each offering the most attractive product features at lower cost, consumers became the beneficiaries of more choices, higher quality, and lower prices. The priests of positioning, Al Ries and Jack Trout, foresaw this competitive struggle in the mid-1980s. They published *Marketing Warfare*, which portrayed marketing as a *war* that businesses must be prepared to wage. Ries and Trout outlined four strategic positions in the marketplace: *defensive, offensive, flanking,* and *guerrilla*. Companies had to operate from one of these strategic positions, they said, based on their relative strengths and weaknesses.

On the demand side, newly affluent consumers concerned themselves more with the quality of their lives. With their basic commodity needs already met, the baby boomers were now interested in saving time and money to spend on more leisure-time activities or on products, services, and social causes that represented the kind of people they aspired to be.

By the mid-1980s, an avalanche of ads—especially in the toiletry and cosmetics industries—was aimed at the "me" generation ("L'Oréal. Because I'm worth it."). At the same time, the nation's largest industrial concerns spent millions of dollars on corporate advertising to extol their social consciousness and good citizenship for cleaning up after themselves and protecting the environment.

As the U.S. economy slowed, many companies were chasing too few consumer dollars. Clients trimmed their ad budgets, and many turned to more cost-effective sales promotion alternatives, such as coupons, direct mail, and direct marketing to build sales volume. By 1990, advertising had lost 25 percent of its share of the marketing budget to other forms of marketing communications.[19]

The United States isn't the only country to produce advertisements with zing. The U.K.,
France, and Spain are just as well-known for
the panache and humor in their ads, such as
this one made in Barcelona for Long-Fong
Chinese restaurant.

As the 1990s unfolded, this recession deepened. The traditional advertising industry found itself threatened on all sides and suffering from overpopulation.[20] Clients
demanded better results from their promotional dollars; small, imaginative, upstart
agencies competed for (and won) some big accounts that had never been available to
them; TV viewers appeared immune to conventional commercials; and a plethora of
new media options based on new technologies promised to reinvent the very process
of advertising. In three short years, the advertising agency business lost over 13,500
jobs. Major clients such as Coca-Cola defected from Madison Avenue, giving various
portions of their business to specialists in small, regional creative shops and media-
buying services. But the setback went far beyond the agency business. Throughout the
media world, newspapers, magazines, and TV networks all lost advertising dollars.
About 40 magazines went out of business during the two-year slump.[21]

By the mid-1990s, U.S. marketers had begun shifting dollars back from sales promotion to advertising to rebuild value in their brands. In 1994, ad budgets surged ahead
by 8.1 percent to $150 billion nationally. And throughout the rest of the 1990s, ad
spending increased about 7 percent every year until the year 2000, when U.S. advertisers spent $247.5 billion, a whopping 11.3 percent increase over the previous year.[22]

But then the bubble burst. In 2001, the combination of a mild recession, the collapse of the stock market, and the bust of the dot-coms all contributed to a record
decline in advertising activity. On September 11 of that year, terrorists attacked the
United States and suddenly all marketing and advertising seemed to stop—not just in
the United States but also around the world.[23] The end result: 2001 was the worst year
in recent times for the advertising industry. Spending in the United States declined 6.5

In highly competitive industries, a company
may benefit by going head-to-head against
the competition through marketing warfare.
In this ad, for instance, Lexus (www.lexus.com)
attempts to distinguish itself by providing the
criteria used in ranking one of its models over
its competitors' as "The Finest Luxury Sedan in
America."

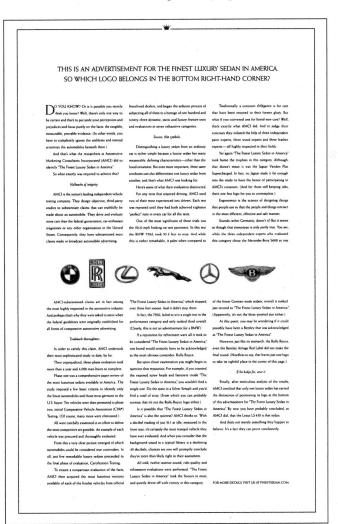

The recession of the early 90s slammed the advertising industry with over 13,500 layoffs. However, specialists in small, regional creative shops were able to snatch away some large accounts during this period and produce ads for established corporations. This Coca-Cola ad came from the clever minds at Creative Artists Agency in Hollywood (a talent agency!).

percent to $231 billion, and overseas spending dropped 8.6 percent to $210 billion.[24]

A year later, though, the economy seemed to be turning around and marketers were again starting to spend money on advertising. During 2003, U.S. advertising expenditures reached $245 billion, a near-complete recovery from the 2001 decline.[25] But hardly anybody thought the problems were over. Technology, evolving lifestyles, new fears over security, and the rising cost of reaching consumers had already changed the advertising business forever. With the explosion of the Internet, we had entered a new electronic frontier—what Tom Cuniff, VP/creative director at Lord, Dentsu & Partners, called "the second creative revolution." [26] The future would not be business at all.

The Global Interactive Age: Looking at the Twenty-First Century

In the last 15 years, expenditures by foreign advertisers increased just as rapidly as both U.S. and Canadian expenditures, thanks to improved economic conditions and a desire for expansion. Recent estimates of worldwide advertising expenditures outside the United States exceed $225 billion per year.[27] The importance of advertising in individual countries depends on the country's level of development and national attitude toward promotion. Typically, advertising expenditures are higher in countries with higher personal incomes. As Exhibit 2–4 shows, the top 10 worldwide advertisers are based in many different countries.

While the Communist countries once condemned advertising as an evil of capitalism, eastern European countries now encourage private enterprise and realize the benefits of advertising. Even China appears to have inherited the capitalist sensibility of Hong Kong.[28]

The explosion of new technologies in the last decade affected advertising considerably. With cable TV and satellite receivers, viewers can watch channels devoted to single types of programming, such as straight news, home shopping, sports, or comedy. This shift transformed television from the most widespread of mass media to a more specialized, "narrowcasting" medium.[29] Now small companies and product marketers that appeal to a limited clientele can use TV to reach audiences with select interests.

Exhibit 2–4

Top 10 global marketers (figures in millions of U.S. dollars).

Rank	Advertiser	Headquarters	2002 worldwide advertising spending	2002 U.S. measured media spending
1	Procter & Gamble Co.	Cincinnati	$4,479	$2,032
2	Unilever	London/Rotterdam	3,315	689
3	General Motors Co.	Detroit	3,218	2,447
4	Toyota Motor Co.	Toyota City, Japan	2,405	885
5	Ford Motor Co.	Dearborn, Mich.	3,287	1,407
6	Time Warner	New York	2,349	1,812
7	DaimlerChrysler	Auburn Hills, Mich./ Stuttgart, Germany	1,800	1,341
8	L'Oréal	Paris	1,683	545
9	Nestlé	Vevey, Switzerland	1,547	494
10	Sony Corp.	Tokyo	1,513	875

New technology has meant new media, manifested largely in the Internet. This has opened new avenues of exposure for advertisers. This website for PBS/Nova (www.pbs.org/nova) promotes the cable TV network's programs and, at the same time, features ads for other companies, too.

A concurrent change that didn't please advertisers was the growing presence of VCRs and remote controls, which allow viewers to avoid commercials altogether by channel surfing during breaks or simply zipping through them when watching a previously recorded show. Advertisers and TV executives became even more rankled with the introduction of PVRs (personal video recorders) like TiVo and its rival Replay TV, which allow viewers to pause, fast-forward, and rewind live TV, store programming, and skip commercials altogether. To its credit, TiVo never promoted the ad-skipping feature to consumers, but it was no secret. Everybody knew.

Ironically, though, within a very short time, TiVo executives were courting marketers and agencies to join its charter advertiser program, which would let viewers opt in to a marketer's "advertainment" show. Best Buy bought in early and so did Sony Pictures, Lexus, Procter & Gamble, and Miller Brewing. One of the major features of TiVo was its ability to target potential customers and measure effectiveness against that target. As *Advertising Age* pointed out, the Holy Grail to advertisers is a one-to-one relationship with consumers, and that becomes increasingly possible with permission-based, opt-in, and two-way interactions with viewers.[30]

Computer technology has also had a huge impact. Personal computers, the Internet, e-mail, and electronic bulletin boards give advertisers new media for reaching potential customers. Now even the smallest companies can maintain computer databases of customers' names to integrate their marketing campaigns.

What we are witnessing is an interactive revolution. Advertising is evolving into a two-way medium where consumers with PCs, Internet connections, CD-ROMs, and cable TV can choose the information they access and then spend time researching the product information they desire.[31] With interactivity, rather than zipping or zapping commercials, people actually seek them out. As we discuss in Chapter 17, this is a revolutionary way for advertisers to reach consumers. Agencies now have the opportunity to prove once again that advertising creativity is not about winning awards but about helping marketers *sell* things.[32]

Advertising has come a long way from the simple sign on the bootmaker's shop. Today it is a powerful device that announces the availability and location of products, describes their quality and value, imbues brands with personality, and simultaneously defines the personalities of the people who buy them while entertaining us. More than a reflection of society and its desires, advertising can start and end fads, trends, and credos—sometimes all by itself.[33]

In turn, advertising is shaped by the very technology used to convey its message. In the past it was always a monologue. But today it's evolving into a dialogue. The medium and the message have become virtually inseparable.

Ad Lab 2-A

What Kills Bugs Dead?

Successful marketing communications sometimes take on a life of their own. Over the years, advertising agencies have created many successful product slogans for their clients, which have become part of our popular culture. Here are some of the most famous. Test your knowledge and see how many advertisers you can identify.

1. "Obey your thirst"
2. "___ kills bugs dead."
3. "Don't leave home without it"
4. "Diamonds are forever"
5. "Good to the last drop"

6. "What stirs you?"
7. "When it rains, it pours"
8. "Reach out and touch someone"
9. "The ultimate driving machine"
10. "Let your fingers do the walking"

Answers

1. Sprite
2. Raid
3. American Express
4. DeBeers
5. Maxwell House Coffee
6. Starbucks
7. Morton Salt
8. AT&T
9. BMW
10. Yellow Pages

Laboratory Applications

1. Now that you know a little about slogans, create one for yourself personally or for your (real or imagined) company. Which qualities and characteristics do you want your slogan to highlight? Share your slogan with your classmates and gauge their reactions.

2. Business cards serve a higher purpose than simply providing information for a Rolodex. They are mini-advertisements. Create a business card for yourself using your slogan.

Internet Exercise

1. Need help getting started on your slogan assignment? Adslogans.com has step-by-step instructions that lead you through the process (www.adslogans.co.uk/general/students.html). For more ideas, look at slogans and ad campaigns past and present at www.adflip.com.

The endless search for competitive advantage and efficiency has made advertising's journey in the last 100+ years fascinating. Now companies are realizing that their most important asset is not capital equipment, or research capability, or their line of products. In the heated competition of the global marketplace, their most important asset is their customer and the relationship they have with that person or organization. Protecting that asset has become the new marketing imperative for the twenty-first century. In an effort to do a better job of *relationship marketing,* companies are now learning that they must be consistent in both what they say and what they do. It's not enough to produce outstanding advertising anymore. They must integrate all their marketing communications with everything else they do, too. That's what *integrated marketing communications* really means. And that will present exciting new challenges to marketing and advertising professionals in the immediate future.

Society and Ethics: The Effects of Advertising

As a social force, advertising has been a major factor in improving the standard of living in the United States and around the world. By publicizing the material, social, and cultural opportunities of a free enterprise society, advertising has encouraged increased productivity by both management and labor.

With just a small amount of money, for instance, you can buy a car today. It may be secondhand, but from advertising you know it's available. If you earn more money, you can buy a new car or one with more luxury features. You can also make a statement about yourself as an individual with the vehicle you purchase. As with many products, advertising has created a personality for each automobile make and model on the market. You, as a free individual, have the opportunity to select the product that best matches your functional, financial, or social needs and aspirations.

Advertising serves other social needs besides simply stimulating sales. Newspapers, magazines, radio, television, and many websites all receive their primary income from advertising. This facilitates freedom of the press and promotes more complete information. Public services by a number of advertising organizations also foster growth and understanding of important social issues and causes. The Red Cross, Community Chest, United Way, and other noncommercial organizations receive continuous financial support and volunteer assistance due in large part to the power of advertising.

Like any business, The Nature Conservancy (www.nature.org) needs public exposure for support. But to get it, it uses noncommercial advertising. This ad is considered a public service announcement because it provides a social service to the community without profit motive.

However, advertising is certainly not without its shortcomings. Since its beginnings, the profession has had to struggle with issues of honesty and ethics. In fact, in the early 1900s, the advertising profession was forced to mend its ethical ways. Consumers suffered for years from unsubstantiated product claims, especially for patent medicines and health devices. The simmering resentment finally boiled over into a full-blown consumer movement, which led to government regulation and ultimately to industry efforts at self-regulation.

In 1906, Congress responded to public outrage by passing the Pure Food and Drug Act to protect the public's health and control drug advertising. In 1914, it passed the Federal Trade Commission Act to protect the public from unfair business practices, including misleading and deceptive advertising.

Advertising practitioners themselves formed groups to improve advertising effectiveness and promote professionalism and started vigilance committees to safeguard the integrity of the industry. The Association of National Advertisers (ANA), the American Advertising Federation (AAF), and the Better Business Bureau (BBB) are today's outgrowths of those early groups.

But in times of economic crisis, false and misleading advertising would invariably reappear, perhaps out of advertiser desperation. During the Depression years, several best-selling books exposed the advertising industry as an unscrupulous exploiter of consumers, giving birth to a new consumer movement and further government regulation.

In the 1970s, a new American consumer movement grew out of the widespread disillusionment following the Kennedy assassination, the Vietnam War, the Watergate scandals, and the sudden shortage of vital natural resources—all communicated instantly to the world via new satellite technology. These issues fostered cynicism and distrust of the establishment and tradition, and gave rise to a new twist in moral consciousness. On the one hand, people justified their personal irresponsibility and self-indulgence in the name of self-fulfillment. On the other, they attacked corporate America's quest for self-fulfillment (profits) in the name of social accountability.

Today, corporate America has generally cleaned up the major inequities in advertising. But now attention has shifted to more subtle problems of puffery, advertising to children, the advertising of legal but unhealthful products, and advertising ethics. We believe ethics in advertising is such an important issue that we have included a feature on this topic in every chapter.

In short, advertising has had a pronounced effect on society as well as the economy. It has also fostered a host of social attitudes and laws that have dramatically affected advertising itself. We'll take a closer look at these issues in Chapter 3.

Chapter Summary

In economic theory, there are four fundamental assumptions of free-market economics: self-interest, complete information, many buyers and sellers, and absence of externalities. Given these principles, there are a number of functions and effects of advertising in a free economy. It identifies and differentiates products; communicates information about them; induces nonusers to try products and users to repurchase them; stimulates products' distribution; increases product use; builds value, brand preference, and loyalty; and lowers the overall cost of sales.

The greatest impact on the evolution of advertising has been economic. In ancient times when most people could not read or write, there was little need for advertising. Marketers used symbols on signs to advertise their products. As the world expanded, urban populations soared, and manufacturing and communication technologies developed, as did advertising. Printing was the first major technology to affect advertising; cable TV and the Internet are the most recent.

With changing economies and increased competition, advertising has evolved from the preindustrial age through the industrializing and industrial ages to the postindustrial age. Since World War II, advertisers have used a variety of strategies, such as product differentiation, market segmentation, and positioning, to set their products apart. Recently the advertising industry experienced a period of retrenchment and reevaluation, but the future offers new opportunities for advertisers and agencies that can harness the interactive revolution and develop deep relationships with their customers.

As a social force, advertising has helped improve the standard of living in the United States and around the world. Advertising makes us aware of the availability of products, imbues products with personality, and enables us to communicate information about ourselves through the products we buy. Through its financial support, advertising also fosters the free press and the growth of many nonprofit organizations.

However, advertising has also been severely criticized over the years for its lack of honesty and ethics. This has given rise to numerous consumer movements and a plethora of laws that now regulate the practice of advertising.

Important Terms

branding, *32*

demarketing, *44*

industrial age, *41*

industrializing age, *40*

market segmentation, *43*

positioning strategy, *44*

postindustrial age, *44*

preindustrial age, *35*

Review Questions

1. What are the four fundamental assumptions of free-market economics?

2. What are the primary functions of advertising in a free economy?

3. What has had the greatest impact on the way advertising has evolved?

4. How does advertising lower the cost of sales?

5. How would you differentiate the advertising used in the industrializing age and the industrial age?

6. What has been the most important influence on advertising in the postindustrial age?

7. What are three examples of companies or organizations that use a demarketing strategy?

8. What companies can you think of that are engaged in marketing warfare?

9. As a consumer, are you likely to save money buying at a store that doesn't advertise? Explain.

10. What effects do you believe advertising has had on society in general? Explain.

11. **The Advertising Experience**

   Identify a social problem at your school that has had an effect on your life in the past few months. Then create a print demarketing advertisement that addresses this problem. The ad should have a visual element as well as a slogan.

Exploring the Internet

The Internet exercises here focus on topics covered in Chapter 2: the economic aspects of advertising (Exercise 1), the history of modern advertising (Exercise 2), and branding and positioning strategies (Exercise 3).

1. **Economic Perspectives of Advertising**
    Visit the websites listed below and find the articles on the economics of advertising. After studying them, do you believe advertising primarily promotes monopoly or does it foster many buyers and sellers?

    a. The Economics of Advertising, Introduction—a scholarly paper by Columbia University economist Kyle Bagwell www.columbia.edu/~kwb8/advertising.pdf

    b. The Library of Economics and Liberty: The Concise Encyclopedia of Economics: Advertising—an interesting primer by Prof. George Bittlingmayer, University of Kansas www.econlib.org/library/Enc/Advertising.html

2. **Advertising History**
    Go online and visit the following websites to see what else you can learn about the early advertising efforts of companies here and abroad. Can you find some early ads for Kodak? Coca-Cola? Sunkist? Who are some of the other major advertisers listed? What specific characteristics in art and copy styles do you notice that make these ads different from advertising today?

    a. The Emergence of Advertising in America section of the John W. Hartman Center for Sales, Advertising, and Marketing History at Duke University http://scriptorium.lib.duke.edu/eaa

    b. The History of Advertising Trust in Great Britain www.hatads.org.uk/home.html

    c. William F. Eisner Museum of Advertising and Design www.eisnermuseum.org

    d. The Museum of Broadcast Communications in Chicago, IL www.museum.tv/index.shtml

    e. *Harper's Weekly* magazine http://advertising.harpweek.com

    f. USATVADS—a large (over one million examples) pay-site collection of American television commercials www.usatvads.net

    g. The National Museum of American History at the Smithsonian www.americanhistory.si.edu/archives/d-7.htm

3. **Brand Positioning through the Decades**
    Review the sites in Exercise 2 and find two other advertisements for the same product that come from different times during the last 100 years. All the ads should be separated from each other by at least two decades. Examine the approaches taken in the ads in terms of the history of advertising and its different eras.

Chapter 3

The Economic, Social, and Regulatory Aspects of Advertising

Objectives TO IDENTIFY AND EXPLAIN THE ECONOMIC, SOCIAL, ETHICAL, AND LEGAL ISSUES ADVERTISERS MUST CONSIDER. The basic economic principles that guided the evolution of advertising also have social and legal effects. When they are violated, social issues arise and the government may take corrective measures. Society determines what is offensive, excessive, and irresponsible; government bodies determine what is deceptive and unfair. To be law-abiding, ethical, and socially responsible, as well as economically effective, advertisers must understand these issues.

After studying this chapter, you will be able to:

■ **Classify** the two main types of social criticisms of advertising.

■ **Employ** an economic model to discuss advertising's effect on society.

■ **Explain** the difference between social responsibility and ethics in advertising.

■ **Understand** how governments regulate advertising here and abroad.

■ **Discuss** recent court rulings that affect advertisers' freedom of speech.

■ **Describe** how federal agencies regulate advertising to protect both consumers and competitors.

■ **Define** the roles state and local governments play in advertising regulation.

■ **Discuss** the activities of nongovernment organizations in fighting fraudulent and deceptive advertising.

In their constant quest to attract consumers and associate products with "cool" or luxurious and hedonistic lifestyles, some advertisers have consistently pushed the boundaries of what is ethically and socially acceptable. American advertising has always embraced erotic suggestiveness while usually staying clear of full nudity and explicit sexuality. Campaigns that blur that distinction often arouse controversy and even protest. ■ For two decades, the most notorious purveyor of sensual "cool" was Calvin Klein—beginning in the late 1970s with the "nothing comes between me and my Calvin's" campaign featuring Brooke Shields and culminating in 1998's "kiddie-porn" controversy. Klein's racy advertisements provoked the ire of conservative groups but earned him the respect of edgier critics who viewed his campaigns as artistically ironic. In the end, the controversies benefited Klein, as the media firestorm provided free publicity for his brand name and underscored the sophisticated "cool" of the campaigns. ■ Since the millennium, however, the mantle of "most controversial advertiser" has passed from Klein to trendy teen retailer Abercrombie and Fitch (A&F). A subsidiary of The Limited since 1988, A&F flirted with controversy in the early 1990s, when a black-and-white print ad, ostensibly featuring a father and son on a boating outing, was misinterpreted as a gay couple. Capitalizing on the angle, A&F hired iconic 1980s fashion photographer Bruce Weber, who had been responsible for some of the steamier Calvin Klein images, as the principal photographer for the *A&F Quarterly,* a hybrid catalog and lifestyle magazine, known as a "magalog." ■ According to *Quarterly* contributor Sean Collins, the magalog was intended as an "outside-looking-in fantasy version of college life" that parodied "the idealized life of leisure, while at the same time celebrating that ideal for its very unattainability."[1] The magazine originally featured pseudo-adult photographs of hunky, underdressed young adult men, but as it became increasingly popular in campus Greek culture, it began featuring under- and undressed women as well, in increasingly suggestive sexual situations. The publication's articles, sexually explicit but often tongue-in-cheek, underscored this "sex and games" attitude. Although opposition always existed toward Weber's erotic photographs, the explicit articles bred controversy, particularly as it was hard to see what they had to do with the clothing. ■ A feature article on alcohol consumption, called "Drinking 101," caught the attention of Mothers Against Drunk Driving, and the magazine's 1999 issue "Naughty or Nice" prompted Illinois Lieutenant Governor Corinne Wood to call for a boycott of the retailer for "peddling soft porn in the guise of a clothing catalog."[2] ■ In 2002–2003, the company faced two public relations problems regarding ethnically insensitive T-shirt designs and racial discrimination in hiring practices. So when controversy over the *Quarterly* broke out again, in December 2003, this time over an article on group sex, the company finally reformatted the magalog and introduced a new publication for summer 2004, *A&F Magazine,* which focused exclusively on artistic photographs of models wearing A&F clothing. ■ The outcry over the *Quarterly* occurred in spite of the fact that the magalog was sold in a wrapper labeling it as "for over 18" and required identification to purchase. Although containing no full-frontal nudity and only marginally raunchier than magazines like *Maxim* and *Stuff,* the confusion of the soft-porn genre with conventional advertising seemed particularly distressing to conservative critics like the National Coalition for the Protection of Children and Families, who claim that the company uses "clothing to sell a sexual philosophy."[3] Especially since the target market is teens and young adults, the advertising is viewed as transgressing the proper place of marketing. Critics claim it reverses the conventional purpose of ads, using the clothing to sell the lifestyle rather than invoking the lifestyle to sell the clothing. ■ But as with the Calvin Klein ads, the impact of controversy on brand-name recognition is sometimes worth the risk to the corporate image: Abercrombie and Fitch's profits were up for the second quarter of 2004, and copies of the last issue of the *A&F Quarterly* fetch up to $100 on eBay. ■ And although the lifestyle depicted may not be popular with certain groups, the clothes themselves have achieved the status of uniform among preppy suburban youth. In advertising, it seems generating controversy is a sure way to be seen. ■

The Many Controversies about Advertising

Advertising is one of the most visible activities of business. By inviting people to try their products, companies risk public criticism and attack if their advertising displeases or offends the audience or if their products don't measure up to the advertised promise. Proponents of advertising say it's therefore safer to buy advertised products because, when a company's name and reputation are on the line, it tries harder to fulfill its promises (especially when it lists product benefits).

Advertising is both applauded and criticized not only for its role in selling products but also for its influence on the economy and on society. For years, critics have denigrated advertising for a wide range of sins—some real, some imagined.

John O'Toole, the late chair of Foote, Cone & Belding and president of the American Association of Advertising Agencies, pointed out that many critics attack

Views of offensiveness vary a great deal from country to country. Clothing retailer Benetton uses the same ads all over the world, and sometimes the ads impinge on the customs and religious beliefs of certain countries. The intended message in this ad, poignantly called "A Kiss from God," is that love surmounts all conventional taboos. But the Italian Advertising Authority banned it. In areas where the influence of the church was less strong, the message was better understood. In England, for example, it won the Eurobest Award. And Sister Barbara of Alzey wrote to Benetton from Germany: "I think that this photo expresses a great deal of tenderness, serenity, and peace." Spend some time on Benetton's website (www.benetton.com) and see how the company uses its themeline, the United Colors of Benetton, to promote racial tolerance and peace among nations.

advertising because it *isn't something else.* Advertising isn't journalism, education, or entertainment—although it often performs the tasks of all three. To go back to Albert Lasker's original definition, advertising is salesmanship in print (or in today's parlance, *in the paid space and time of mass media*). As a means of communication, advertising shares certain traits of journalism, education, and entertainment, but it shouldn't be judged by those standards. Sponsors advertise because they hope it will help them sell some product, service, or idea.[4]

Notwithstanding O'Toole's articulate defense, many controversies still swirl around the whole field of advertising. Some of them focus on advertising's *economic* role. For example, how does advertising affect the value of products? Does it cause higher or lower prices? Does it promote competition or discourage it? How does advertising affect overall consumer demand? What effect does it have on consumer choice and on the overall business cycle?

Other controversies focus on the *societal* effects of advertising. For instance, does advertising make us more materialistic? Does it force us to buy things we don't need? Does it reach us subliminally in ways we can't control? How does it affect the art and culture of our society? Does advertising debase our language?

From these economic and social controversies, new questions arise regarding the responsibility for and control of advertising. What is the proper role for participants in the marketing process? How much latitude should marketers have in the kinds of products they promote and how they advertise them? And what about consumers? Don't they have some responsibility in the process? Finally, what is the proper role of government? What laws should we have to protect consumers? And what laws go too far and violate the marketer's freedom of speech?

These are important questions, and there are no simple answers. But debate is healthy. This chapter addresses some of the major questions and criticisms about advertising, both the pros and the cons, and delves into the regulatory methods used to remedy advertisers' abuses.

Recall from Chapter 2 the underlying principle of free-market economics—that a society is best served by empowering people to make their own decisions and act as free agents, within a system characterized by four fundamental assumptions: *self-interest, many buyers and sellers, complete information,* and *absence of externalities* (social costs).

This fundamentally utilitarian framework, derived from the goal of society to promote behaviors that foster the greatest good for the most people, offers a system of economic activity—free enterprise—that has accomplished that goal better than any other economic system in history. This is why societies around the world are increasingly adopting free-enterprise economics.

By using this framework for our discussion of advertising controversies, we have a basis for understanding how advertising may contribute to, or detract from, the basic goal of free enterprise: "the most good for the most people."

The Economic Impact of Advertising

Advertising accounts for approximately 2.3 percent of the U.S. gross domestic product (GDP). In relation to the total U.S. economy, this percentage is small, but it's higher than in most countries. It amounts to a spending level of $437.60 for every person in the country—the highest per capita spending in the world. As Marcel Bleustein-Blanchet, the father of modern French advertising, pointed out, it's no coincidence that the level of advertising investment in a country is directly proportional to its standard of living.[5] Exhibit 3–1 shows the level of spending in other countries around the world.

The economic effect of advertising is like the break shot in billiards or pool. The moment a company begins to advertise, it sets off a chain reaction of economic events, as shown in Exhibit 3–2. The extent of the chain reaction, although hard to predict, is related to the force of the shot and the economic environment in which it occurred. Let's consider the economic questions we posed earlier.

Exhibit 3–1

A country's level of ad spending is typically proportional to its standard of living.

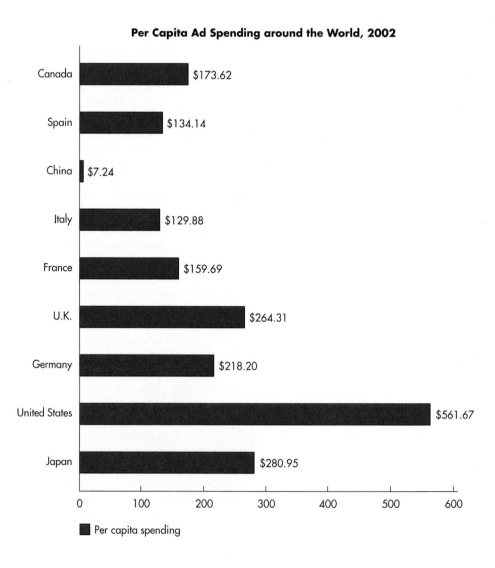

Per Capita Ad Spending around the World, 2002

Country	Per capita spending
Canada	$173.62
Spain	$134.14
China	$7.24
Italy	$129.88
France	$159.69
U.K.	$264.31
Germany	$218.20
United States	$561.67
Japan	$280.95

Per capita spending

Exhibit 3–2

The economic effect of advertising is like the opening break shot in billiards.

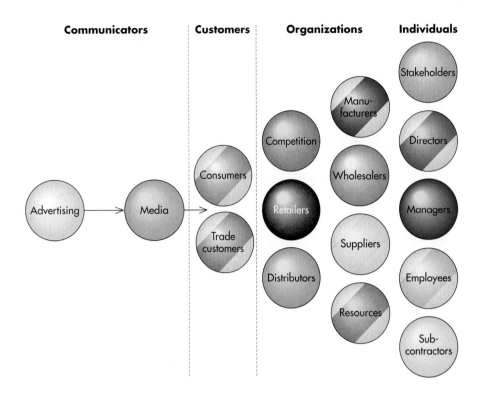

Communicators **Customers** **Organizations** **Individuals**

Effect on the Value of Products

Why do most people prefer Coca-Cola to some other cola? Why do some people prefer Calvin Klein underwear to some other unadvertised brand? Are the advertised products functionally better? Not necessarily. But, in the mind of the consumer, advertising has given these brands *added value*.

In the mid-1960s, a famous psychologist named Ernest Dichter asserted that a product's *image*, created in part by advertising and promotion, is *an inherent feature of the product itself*.[6] Subsequent studies showed that while an ad may not address a product's quality directly, the positive image conveyed by advertising may imply quality. Moreover, by simply making the product better known, advertising can make the product more desirable to the consumer. In these ways, advertising adds value to the brand.[7] That's why people pay more for Bufferin than an unadvertised brand displayed right next to it—even though all buffered aspirin, by law, is functionally the same.[8]

Advertising also adds value to a brand by educating customers about new uses for a product. Kleenex was originally advertised as a makeup remover, later as a disposable handkerchief. AT&T first promoted the telephone as a necessity and later as a convenience.

One advantage of the free-market system is that consumers can choose the values they want in the products they buy. If, for example, low price is important, they can buy an inexpensive economy car. If status and luxury are important, they can buy a fancy sedan or racy sports car. Many of our wants are emotional, social, or psychological rather than functional. One way we communicate who we are (or want to be) is through the products we purchase and display. By associating the product with some desirable image, advertising offers people the opportunity to satisfy those psychic or symbolic wants and needs.

In terms of our economic framework, by adding value to products, advertising contributes to self-interest—for both the consumer and the advertiser. It also contributes to the number of sellers. That increases competition, which also serves the consumer's self-interest.

Effect on Prices

If advertising adds value to products, it follows that advertising also adds cost, right? And if companies stopped all that expensive advertising, products would cost less, right?

Wrong.

Some advertised products do cost more than unadvertised products, but the opposite is also true. Both the Federal Trade Commission and the Supreme Court have ruled that, by encouraging competition, advertising has the effect of keeping prices down. That again serves the consumer's self-interest. And that is why professionals such as attorneys and physicians are now allowed to advertise.

Sweeping statements about advertising's positive or negative effect on prices are likely to be too simplistic. We can make some important points, though.

- As one of the many costs of doing business, advertising is indeed paid for by the consumer who buys the product. In most product categories, though, the amount spent on advertising is usually very small compared with the total cost of the product.

- Advertising is one element of the mass-distribution system that enables many manufacturers to engage in mass production, which in turn lowers the unit cost of products. These savings can then be passed on to consumers in the form of lower prices. In this indirect way, advertising helps lower prices.

- In industries subject to government price regulation (agriculture, utilities), advertising has historically had no effect on prices. In the 1980s, though, the government deregulated many of these industries in an effort to restore free-market pressures on prices. In these cases, advertising has affected price—usually downward, but not always.

- In retailing, price is a prominent element in many ads, so advertising tends to hold prices down. On the other hand, national manufacturers use advertising to stress features that make their brands better; in these cases advertising tends to support higher prices for their brands.

Effect on Competition

Some observers believe advertising actually restricts competition because small companies or industry newcomers can't compete with the immense advertising budgets of large firms.

This BMW ad created by Jung von Matt (Germany) won a 2004 Cannes Silver Lion. The image of horses, pictured as if actually under the hood of the automobile, creates the feeling of raw power that BMW wants consumers to associate with its X5 Sports Activity Vehicle.

It's true that intense competition does tend to reduce the number of businesses in an industry. However, some of the firms eliminated by competition may be those that served customers least effectively. In other cases, competition is reduced because of mergers and acquisitions (big companies working in their own self-interest).

High costs may inhibit the entry of new competitors in industries that spend heavily on advertising. In some markets, the original brands probably benefit greatly from this barrier. However, the investments needed for plants, machinery, and labor are of far greater significance. These are typically the real barriers to entry, not advertising.

Advertising by big companies often has only a limited effect on small businesses because a single advertiser is rarely large enough to dominate the whole country. Regional oil companies, for example, compete very successfully with national oil companies on the local level. In fact, the freedom to advertise encourages more sellers to enter the market. And we've all seen nonadvertised store brands of food compete very effectively with nationally advertised brands on the same grocery shelves.

Effect on Consumer Demand

The question of advertising's effect on total consumer demand is extremely complex. Numerous studies show that promotional activity does affect aggregate consumption, but they disagree as to the extent. Many social and economic forces, including technological advances, the population's educational level, increases in population and income, and revolutionary changes in lifestyle, are more significant. For example, the demand for CD players, cellular phones, and personal computers expanded at a tremendous rate, thanks in part to advertising but more to favorable market conditions. At the same time, advertising hasn't reversed declining sales of such items as hats, fur coats, and manual typewriters.

As we shall discuss in Chapter 6, advertising can help get new products off the ground by giving more people more "complete information," thereby stimulating **primary demand**—demand for the entire product class. In declining markets, when the only information people want is price information, advertising can influence **selective demand**—demand for a particular brand. But the only effect it will have on primary demand is to slow the rate of decline. In growing markets, advertisers generally compete for shares of that growth. In mature, static, or declining markets, they compete for each other's shares—*conquest sales.*

Effect on Consumer Choice

For manufacturers, the best way to beat the competition is to make their product different. For example, look at the long list of car models, sizes, colors, and features designed to attract different buyers. And grocery shelves may carry more than 100 different brands of breakfast cereals—something for everybody.

The freedom to advertise encourages businesses to create new brands and improve old ones. When one brand reaches market dominance, smaller brands may disappear for a time. But the moment a better product comes along and is advertised skillfully, the dominant brand loses out to the newer, better product. Once again, the freedom to advertise promotes the existence of more sellers, and that gives consumers wider choices.

Effect on the Business Cycle

The relationship between advertising and gross domestic product has long been debated. John Kenneth Galbraith, a perennial critic of advertising, concedes that, by helping to maintain the flow of consumer demand (encouraging more buyers), advertising helps sustain employment and income. But he maintains that, despite

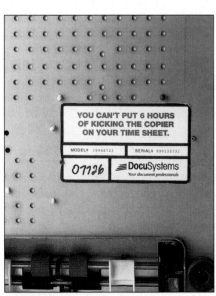

DocuSystems is a local distributor of copiers in Vancouver. This clever label points out that a nonworking copier costs a lot of expensive, non-billable time. This kind of ad promotes selective demand because it promotes a particular source for copiers rather than copiers in general.

declines in the value of the dollar, the U.S. trade deficit persists because advertising and marketing activities create consumer preference for certain foreign products.[9]

Historically, when business cycles dip, companies cut advertising expenditures. That may help short-term profits, but studies prove that businesses that continue to invest in advertising during a recession are better able to protect, and sometimes build, market shares.[10] However, no study has shown that if everybody just keeps advertising, the recessionary cycle will turn around. We conclude that when business cycles are up, advertising contributes to the increase. When business cycles are down, advertising may act as a stabilizing force by encouraging more buyers to buy.

The Abundance Principle: The Economic Impact of Advertising in Perspective

To individual businesses such as Calvin Klein, the local car dealer, and the convenience store on the corner, advertising pays back more than it costs. If advertising didn't pay, no one would use it. And the various news and entertainment media that depend on advertising for financial support would go out of business.

Advertising costs less for the consumer than most people think. The cost of a bottle of Coke includes about a penny for advertising. And the $20,000 price tag on a new car usually includes a manufacturer's advertising cost of less than $400.

To the economy as a whole, the importance of advertising may best be demonstrated by the *abundance principle*. This states that in an economy that produces more goods and services than can be consumed, advertising serves two important purposes: It keeps consumers informed of their alternatives (*complete information*), and it allows companies to compete more effectively for consumer dollars (*self-interest*). In North America alone, the U.S. and Canadian economies produce an enormous selection of products. Most supermarkets carry more than 30,000 different items. Each carmaker markets dozens of models. And many suppliers compete for the consumer dollar. This competition generally results in more and better products at similar or lower prices.

Advertising stimulates competition (*many buyers and sellers*). In countries where consumers have more income to spend after their physical needs are satisfied, advertising also stimulates innovation and new products. However, no amount of advertising can achieve long-term acceptance for products that do not meet consumer approval. Despite massive advertising expenditures, fewer than a dozen of the 50 best-known cars developed in the twentieth century are still sold today.

Advertising stimulates a healthy economy. It also helps create financially healthy consumers who are more informed, better educated, and more demanding. As a result, consumers now demand that manufacturers be held accountable for their advertising. This has led to an unprecedented level of social criticism and legal regulation, the subject of our next sections.

The Social Impact of Advertising

Because it's so visible, advertising gets criticized frequently, for both what it is and what it isn't. Many of the criticisms focus on the *style* of advertising, saying it's deceptive or manipulative. Collectively we might refer to these as **short-term manipulative arguments.** Other criticisms focus on the *social or environmental impact* of advertising. These are **long-term macro arguments.**[11]

In our discussion of the economic impact of advertising, we focused primarily on the first two principles of free-market economics: self-interest and many buyers and sellers. The social aspect of advertising typically involves the last two principles: *complete information* and *absence of externalities*. In fact, social issue debates can be seen as instances where advertising tends to violate one or more of these basic economic principles. We can examine many issues from these two perspectives. Some of the most important are deception and manipulation in advertising, the effect of advertising on our value system, commercial clutter, stereotypes, and offensiveness. Let's look at some of these common criticisms of advertising, debunk some misconceptions, and examine the problems that do exist.

Puffery is rarely so literal as it is in this 2004 Cannes Bronze Lion winner from Jung von Matt (Germany) for Tabasco hot sauce. Although the peppery condiment won't actually cause corn kernels to pop off the cob, such puffery is not illegal because it is so unbelievable.

Deception in Advertising

Despite extensive advertising efforts, some products, like the Edsel automobile, will fail simply because they do not meet the expectations of customers at that particular time. Many of the best-known cars developed in the twentieth century are no longer sold today. Ironically, the Edsel has since become a pricy collector's item for automobile aficionados.

One of the most common short-term arguments about advertising is that it is so frequently deceptive. Professor Ivan Preston notes that the essence of a marketplace lies in the willingness of buyers and sellers to enter commercial transactions. Anything that detracts from the satisfaction of the transaction produces a loss of activity that ultimately hurts both parties.[12] If a product does not live up to its ads, dissatisfaction occurs—and in the long term that is as harmful to the advertiser as to the buyer.

For advertising to be effective, consumers must have confidence in it. So any kind of deception not only detracts from the complete information principle of free enterprise but also risks being self-defeating. Even meaningless (but legal) puffery might be taken literally and therefore become deceptive. **Puffery** refers to exaggerated, subjective claims that can't be proven true or false, such as "the best," "premier," or "the only way to fly."

Under current advertising law, the only product claims—explicit or implied—that are considered deceptive are those that are *factually false* or convey a false impression and therefore have the potential to deceive or mislead reasonable people.[13] But puffery is excluded from this requirement because regulators maintain that reasonable people don't believe it anyway. Preston points out that since advertisers regularly use puffery and nonproduct facts to enhance the image of their products, they must think consumers *do* believe it. **Nonproduct facts** are not about the brand but about the consumer or the social context in which the consumer uses the brand. An example is "Pepsi. The choice of a new generation."

The fact is that advertising, by its very nature, is *not* complete information. It is biased in favor of the advertiser and the brand. People expect advertisers to be proud of their products and probably don't mind if they puff them a little. But when advertisers cross the line between simply giving their point of view and creating false expectations, that's when people begin to object. One problem is the difficulty of seeing the line, which may be drawn differently by different people. Papa John's Pizza no doubt thought it was just puffing when it advertised "Better ingredients. Better pizza." Pizza Hut saw it differently, though, and sued Papa John's for deceptive advertising. A U.S. District judge agreed and awarded Pizza Hut close to half a million dollars in damages. The judge then ordered Papa John's to stop using its "Better ingredients" slogan.[14] This decision was later overturned on appeal, but the case still goes to show that there are limits on what an advertiser can safely puff. Preston points out,

"Only puffs open to measurement lose their invisible shields. If Papa John's says it has better dough, you can attack it. But if Papa John's says it's better overall, that's OK. The bigger the lie, the bigger the protection. Isn't that amazing?"[15] For more on this story and on puffery, see the Ethical Issue: "Truth in Advertising: Fluffing and Puffing," on page 72.

Ivan Preston believes these kinds of problems can be avoided if marketers simply improve the kind of information they give in their advertising. He would require advertisers to have a reasonable basis for any claims they make, whether those claims are facts about the product, nonfacts such as "Coke is it," or non-product facts.[16] This, he believes, would contribute positively to our free market system. Ad Lab 3–A lists some other common deceptive practices.

The Subliminal Advertising Myth

Wilson Bryan Key promotes the notion that, to seduce consumers, advertisers intentionally create ads with sexual messages hidden in the illustrations just below the **limen**—or the threshold of perception. He calls this **subliminal advertising.** His premise is that by embedding dirty words in the ice cubes in a liquor ad, for instance, advertisers can somehow make us want to buy the product. Over the years, many academic studies have completely debunked this theory.[17] In fact, to date, no study has proved that such embedding exists or that it would have any effect if it did exist.[18] Unfortunately, by promulgating this fiction, Key has been able to sell many thousands of books; worse, he has propagated a generation of consumers who believe in the poppycock of subliminal advertising.

The chord that Key has been able to touch on, though, is important to discuss: the widespread fear that advertisers are messing with our heads—manipulating us psychologically, and without our consent, into buying things we don't want or need. This gets to the heart of the *complete information* principle because the criticism suggests that advertising does not give consumers information upon which to base rational decisions, but rather manipulates us through brainwashing. Consumers are, therefore, like captured prey, helpless in the jaws of marketing predators.

If this were true, it would be cause for great alarm and a congressional investigation. But, in fact, if we stop to think about it, we all know it's *not* true. Marketers introduce thousands of new products to the marketplace every year. And every year—despite massive advertising expenditures—the vast majority of them fail. Why? Because of competition—many sellers are fiercely competing for the patronage of the same customers. Only some succeed. Most fail.

If you think about all the products you buy, how many involve a choice between different brands and different styles? And how many involve a decision based on price or convenience? Probably most. So how many of your purchases can you trace to having been helplessly manipulated? Probably none. You receive information from many different sources: friends and relatives, store displays, ads, packaging, and retail store clerks. At some point, you make a decision. In many cases, your decision is *not* to buy at all—to wait for either more information or more money. As always, the customer, acting in his or her own self-interest, is king.

Daffy's (www.daffys.com) uses tongue-in-cheek humor to take a stand against advertising puffery—inflated promises and claims often accompanied by inflated prices. Daffy's beckons smart consumers to shop where they can find the same quality goods with "no bull" price tags.

The Effect of Advertising on Our Value System

A related long-term argument, often voiced by certain professional critics—sociologists, journalists, consumer advocates, and government regulators—is that advertising degrades people's value systems by promoting a hedonistic, materialistic way of life. Advertising, they

Unfair and Deceptive Practices in Advertising

The courts have held that these acts constitute unfair or deceptive trade practices and are therefore illegal.

False Promises

Making an advertising promise that cannot be kept, such as "restores youth" or "prevents cancer." When Listerine claimed to prevent or reduce the impact of colds and sore throats, the FTC banned the campaign and required the company to run millions of dollars' worth of corrective ads.

Incomplete Description

Stating some but not all of a product's contents, such as advertising a "solid oak" desk without mentioning that only the top is solid oak and the rest is pine.

False and Misleading Comparisons

Making false comparisons, either explicitly or by implication, such as "Like Tylenol, Advil doesn't upset my stomach." That implies that Advil is equal in avoiding stomach upset, though in truth Tylenol is better. To some people, Advil's claim might even suggest that Tylenol upsets the stomach, which is also false.

Bait-and-Switch Offers

Advertising an item at an unusually low price to bring people into the store and then "switching" them to a higher-priced model by claiming that the advertised product is out of stock or poorly made.

Visual Distortions and False Demonstrations

Using trick photography or computer manipulation to enhance a product's appearance—for example, a TV commercial for a "giant steak" say, dinner special showing the steak on a miniature plate that makes it look extra large. In one classic case, General Motors and its window supplier, Libby Owens-Ford, rigged a demonstration to show how clear their windows were. The GM cars were photographed with the windows down, the competitor's car with the windows up—and Vaseline smeared on them.

False Testimonials

Implying that a product has the endorsement of a celebrity or an authority who is not a bona-fide user, or implying that endorsers have a certain expertise that in fact they don't.

Partial Disclosure

Stating certain facts about the advertised product but omitting other material information. An example is claiming, "Kraft's Singles processed cheese slices are made from five ounces of milk," which give Singles more calcium than the imitators' without mentioning that processing loses about two ounces of the milk.

Small-Print Qualifications

Making a statement in large print, such as Beneficial's "Instant Tax Refund," only to qualify or retract it in obscure, small, or unreadable type elsewhere in the ad: "If you qualify for one of our loans." To the FTC, if readers don't see the qualification, it's not there.

Laboratory Applications

1. Describe some examples of deception you have seen in advertising.

2. Who are the principal victims of unfair or deceptive advertising practices and what remedies are available to them?

---

say, encourages us to buy more cars, more CDs, more clothing, and more junk we don't need. It is destroying the essence of our "citizen democracy," replacing it with a self-oriented consumer democracy.[19]

Critics claim advertising manipulates us into buying things by playing on our emotions and promising greater status, social acceptance, and sex appeal. It causes people to take up harmful habits, makes poor kids buy $170 sneakers, and tempts ordinary people to buy useless products in the vain attempt to emulate celebrity endorsers.[20] Again, they claim advertising is so powerful consumers are helpless to defend themselves against it.

Once again, this argument exaggerates the power of advertising. In fact, most Americans express a healthy skepticism toward it. One study showed that only 17 percent of U.S. consumers see advertising as a source of information to help them decide what to buy.[21] Perhaps that's why more advertised products fail than succeed in the marketplace.

Still, this may be the most damning criticism of advertising because there's no question that advertisers do indeed spend millions trying to convince people their products will make them sexier, healthier, and more successful. The very amount of advertising we witness every day seems to suggest that every problem we have can be solved by the purchase of some product.

Even if we assume that most people can willingly accept or reject an advertising message, they are still not getting the whole picture. After all, advertising is supported by marketers who want to sell their products, but nobody markets the opposite stance of why we don't need to or shouldn't buy a particular product at

Status comes in many forms and often what is unsaid has greater impact than what is said. Such is the case in this beautifully photographed ad for The Ritz-Carlton. Notice the sparse, understated copy; the soft enormity of the landscape in relation to the smalll, off-centered couple; the elegant use of white framing; and the discreet communication of contact information. In the quietest way, the whole ad whispers class—and that screams status.

all. In this sense, consumers don't have *complete information,* so our advocacy system has failed. This is an important issue of *externalities,* because the aggregate activities of the nation's advertisers affect many people outside the immediate marketing transaction and create an unexpected cost to society.

The Proliferation of Advertising

One of the most common long-term complaints about advertising is that there's just too much of it. In the United States alone, the average person may be exposed to 500 to 1,000 commercial messages a day. With so many products competing for attention (more than 30,000 in the average supermarket), advertisers themselves worry about the negative impact of excessive advertising. According to a recent study by the American Association of Advertising Agencies, ad clutter is still on the rise. In 2002, the amount of nonprogram time ranged from a low of 16 minutes per hour in prime time to nearly 21 minutes per hour in daytime, a day part that is particularly important to advertisers.[22] The networks add to the problem themselves by jamming every possible moment with promotions for their shows. Too much advertising creates an externality not only for consumers (nuisance), but for the advertisers themselves—the more commercials that hit the consumer's brain, the less effective paid advertising is. Conscious of this, Meredith Broadcasting Group cut 15 percent of its advertising inventory from local newscasts at its CBS-affiliate, WGNX Atlanta, and saw its household ratings go up 20 percent.[23] Higher ratings, of course, means they can charge more for their remaining commercial time. Hopefully, other stations will follow suit.

While the clutter problem is irksome to viewers and advertisers alike, most people tolerate it as the price for free TV, freedom of the press, and a high standard of living. However, with the proliferation of new media choices, this externality is only likely to get worse. Virtually every popular website is cluttered with advertising banners, and our e-mail boxes are flooded with advertising messages on a daily basis. While the Federal Communications Commission exercises no jurisdiction over the Internet, it did consider reinstating commercial time limits on television. But, as of now, the only limits currently in force relate to TV programming aimed at children 12 and under—advertising may not exceed 10.5 minutes per hour on weekends and 12 minutes per hour on weekdays.[24]

Clutter is not so evident in other countries. In France, for example, government-owned stations can carry no more than 12 minutes of commercials per hour. During

The song above was written by Schumann as an expression of love for his wife, Clara.

The song below was written by Brahms as an expression of love for Schumann's wife, Clara.

(Above) According to Clara's notation in the top right hand corner, Brahms gave her this ornately decorated copy of "To a Violet" on her birthday. (Top) Schumann's not-so-fancy draft of "The Shepherd's Farewell."

been proven, there's a lot of speculation that music wasn't the only thing for which Robert Schumann and Johannes Brahms shared a love.

The setting was Germany, 1853. Schumann and his wife Clara were, by most accounts, a happily married couple. In fact, during just one year of marriage, Schumann wrote 150 songs out of love for his Clara.

Enter Johannes Brahms. A handsome, young musical prodigy who managed to make quite an impact on the Schumanns. The three became very close.

Brahms moved in. And, for a while, all three made beautiful music together – Brahms taking instruction from Schumann and Clara supporting everyone by playing the piano in concerts.

After awhile, Schumann had a mental breakdown and in 1856 died in an asylum.

Clara Wieck Schumann. The object of her husband's affections. And perhaps those of Brahms as well?

For the next 40 years, Brahms and Clara occasionally lived in the same building together. Often performed in concert together. And, until their deaths, which occurred within just a few months of each other, the two remained "very close friends".

Exactly what Clara and Brahms meant to each other, no one will ever know. But here is something that can't be disputed: Now through July 13, two original artifacts of this unusual relationship, Brahms' "To a Violet" and Schumann's

"The Shepherd's Farewell," will be on display at the Library of Congress.

They're here on loan as part of an exhibition from the Saxon State Library in Dresden, Germany.

Along with them, you can see Martin Luther's original New Testament, responsible for adding hundreds of denominations to the Christian faith. Grimace over the details of 16th century equestrian dental procedures. And find out why Germany's most famed musical

Hofkapelle, today would give *Mrs. Doubtfire* a run for its money.

These Saxon State Library treasures have survived the Dark Ages, the devastation of World War II, and for the last 50 years they were all but inaccessible to most Americans, locked away behind the Iron Curtain.

They're here for the first time. And it's uncertain when, or if, they'll ever be here again.

The exhibition is on display in the Great Hall of the Library of

An institution in Dresden's long musical history was the performing troupe, the Hofkapelle. Here, a long procession of men dressed as women.

Congress, open Monday through Saturday, from 10 a.m. to 5:30 p.m. For any additional information, call (202) 707-8000.

THE LIBRARY OF CONGRESS

Dresden: Treasures from the Saxon State Library

Some advertising reflects the interest of the public at large in the form of government ads, such as this public service announcement from the Library of Congress. Check out its excellent website (http://lcweb.loc.gov).

movies there is only one 4-minute commercial break, although the government is considering changing that rule to allow two breaks.[25]

In North America we should be so lucky. During election periods, the clutter problem gets worse, seriously devaluing an advertiser's commercial. One year, in fact, after an unexpectedly large number of political ads ran during the fall election season, the Association of Canadian Advertisers urged its members to try to renegotiate the prices they had been charged for air time during that period.[26]

The Use of Stereotypes in Advertising

Advertising has long been criticized for insensitivity to minorities, women, immigrants, the disabled, the elderly, and a myriad of other groups—that is, for not being "politically correct."[27] This long-term argument also addresses externalities because the very presence of advertising affects the nature of our culture and environment, even when we do not want it. This is ironic, because marketing and advertising practitioners are supposed to be professional students of the communication process and consumer behavior (a subject we cover in Chapter 5). But, in fact, they sometimes lose touch with the very people they're trying to reach. This is one reason the discipline of *account planning* (discussed in Chapter 4) is growing so rapidly.

Since the 1980s, national advertisers have become more sensitive to the concerns of minorities and women. Latinos, African Americans, Asians, Native Americans, and others are now usually portrayed favorably in ads, not only because of pressure from watchdog groups, but also because it's just good business; these consumers represent sizable target markets. Marilyn Kern-Foxworth, a Texas A&M

With tightening markets, advertisers must double their efforts to maintain or expand market share. One way is to expand into minority communities, which have enormous buying power and comprise a significant amount of market share.

professor and an expert on minorities in advertising, points out that positive role portrayal in some mainstream ads has had a positive effect on the self-esteem of African-American youth.[28] As we'll see in Chapter 4, this positive trend has accelerated with the emergence of many ad agencies owned and staffed by minorities that specialize in reaching minority markets.

In national advertising, the image of women is also changing from their historic depiction as either subservient housewives or sex objects (see the Ethical Issue, "Does Sex Appeal?" in Chapter 12). This may be partially due to the increasing number of women in managerial and executive positions with both advertisers and agencies. Stanford professor Debra Meyerson says "the glass ceiling definitely exists, but at the same time, there are an increasing number of women who are breaking through it."[29] By 2000, more than 60 percent of all women were participating in the workforce, with more than 20 million of them in managerial and professional careers.[30] Advertisers want to reach, not offend, this sizable market of upwardly mobile consumers. Some agencies now retain feminist consultants to review ads that may risk offending women.[31] And in 2003, Ann Fudge shattered the glass ceiling when she was named chairman and CEO of Young and Rubicam and became the first African-American woman to head a major U.S. agency.

However, problems still exist, especially in local and regional advertising and in certain product categories such as beer and sports promotions. Many advertisers are just not aware of the externalities that their ads can create, and they may perpetuate male and female stereotypes without even realizing it.[32] Other advertisers resort to stereotypes for convenience. All too often, women are still not represented accurately. And the minimal use of minorities in mainstream ads, both local and national, still smacks of tokenism. Observers hope that with increasing numbers of women and minorities joining the ranks of marketing and advertising professionals, and with continuing academic studies of minority and sex-role stereotyping, greater attention will be focused on these issues.

Offensiveness in Advertising

Offensiveness is another short-term style argument that also speaks to externalities. Many parents, for instance, were incensed at Calvin Klein's ads because they perceived them as pornographic, thereby causing a social cost that extended well beyond the limited scope of merely selling clothes. More recently, Abercrombie &

Tastes of consumers—and advertisers—may differ geographically, as shown in this award-winning Australian surfwear ad. Local Sydney surfers responded quite favorably to the ad.

▸ Tough clothes by *Kadu*

Fitch came under attack for showing nude and seminude models in the company's quarterly catalogs. The fact is, people just don't want their children exposed to messages that they deem immoral, offensive, or strictly adult-oriented.[33]

Taste, of course, is highly subjective: What is bad taste to some is perfectly acceptable to others. And tastes change. What is considered offensive today may not be so tomorrow. People were outraged when the first ad for underarm deodorant appeared in a 1927 *Ladies Home Journal;* today no one questions such ads. Yet, even with the AIDS scare, all the broadcast networks except Fox still restrict condom ads to local stations, and all forbid any talk of contraception.[34]

Taste is also geographic. A shockingly bloody ad for a small surfwear company in Sydney, Australia, showed a gutted shark lying on a dock. Protruding from its cut-open belly were a human skeleton and an intact pair of surfer shorts. The tagline: "Tough clothes by Kadu—Triple stitched. Strongest materials available. Homegrown and sewn."

While we might consider that ad quite offensive in North America, it won the Grand Prix at the International Advertising Festival in Cannes, France, several years ago. In Australia it received wide media coverage, since two surfers were killed by sharks while it was running. Rather than pulling the ad out of respect, the company reveled in its timeliness, and the local surfer set responded very favorably.[35]

Today, grooming, fashion, and personal hygiene products often use partial nudity in their ads. Where nudity is relevant to the product, people are less likely to regard it as obscene or offensive—except, as in the case of Abercrombie & Fitch, when the advertising is targeting kids. In many European countries, in fact, nudity in commercials is commonplace. Even the usually staid Brits are starting to see women's breasts in TV commercials and posters.[36] Some industry observers predict that nudity in U.S. advertising will increase in the twenty-first century but there will be fewer overt sexual scenes of the Abercrombie & Fitch style.[37]

Some consumers get so offended by both advertising and TV programming that they boycott sponsors' products.[38] Of course, they also have the option to just change the channel. Both of these are effective strategies for consumers because, ultimately, the marketplace has veto power. As the 2003 demise of *A&F Quarterly* shows, if ads don't pull in the audience, the campaign will falter and die.

The Social Impact of Advertising in Perspective

Marketing professionals earnestly believe in the benefits that advertising brings to society. Advertising, they say, encourages the development and speeds the acceptance of new products and technologies. It fosters employment. It gives consumers and business customers a wider variety of choices. By encouraging mass production, it helps keep prices down. And it stimulates healthy competition between producers, which benefits all buyers.[39] Advertising, they point out, also promotes a higher standard of living; it pays for most of our news media and subsidizes the arts; it supports freedom of the press; and it provides a means to disseminate public information about important health and social issues.

Critics of advertising might agree with some of these points but certainly not all of them. For example, critics charge that rather than supporting a free press, advertising actually creates an externality that interferes with it. The media, they say, pander to national advertisers to attract the big ad dollars. In the process, they modify their editorial content to suit their corporate benefactors and consequently shirk their primary journalistic responsibility of presenting news in the public interest.[40]

In summary, we can conclude that while advertising may legitimately be criticized for offering less-than-complete information and, in some instances, for creating unwanted externalities, it should also be applauded when it contributes to the validity of the principles of free enterprise economics. In most cases, by being a rich information source (albeit not complete), advertising contributes to the existence of many buyers and sellers and, therefore, to the self-interest of both consumers and marketers.

Having a learning disability doesn't just hurt you in the classroom.
Do you know a child who has trouble reading? Call 1-888-478-MIND or visit us at www.ldonline.org.

coordinated campaign
for learning disabilities

Without advertising, public service organizations would be unable to reach a mass audience to educate people about important health and social issues. Here, the Ad Council promotes awareness of the problems associated with learning disabilities.

Social Responsibility and Advertising Ethics

When advertising violates one of the basic economic assumptions we've described, some corrective action is needed. As we'll discuss in the next section, numerous laws determine what advertisers can and cannot do, but they also allow a significant amount of leeway. That's where ethics and social responsibility come into play. An advertiser can act unethically or irresponsibly without breaking any laws. Beer and tobacco companies could sponsor rock concerts for college students, and a shoe company could market a basketball sneaker to urban youth as the "Run 'N Gun" brand. As Ivan Preston says, ethics begin where the law ends.[41]

Ethical advertising means doing what the advertiser and the advertiser's peers believe is morally right in a given situation. **Social responsibility** means doing what society views as best for the welfare of people in general or for a specific community of people. Together, ethics and social responsibility can be seen as the moral obligation of advertisers not to violate our basic economic assumptions, even when there is no legal obligation.

Advertisers' Social Responsibility

The foundation of any human society is the amicable relationship among its members. Without harmony, a society will collapse. So all the institutions within a society have some responsibility for helping to maintain social harmony through proper stewardship of families and companies, exercise of honesty and integrity in all relationships, adherence to accepted ethical standards, willingness to assist various segments of the society, and the courtesy to respect the privacy of others.

Advertising plays an important role in developed countries. It influences a society's stability and growth. It helps secure large armies, creates entertainment events attracting hundreds of thousands of fans, and often affects the outcome of political elections. Such power places a burden of responsibility on those who sponsor, buy, create, produce, and sell advertising to maintain ethical standards that support the society and contribute to the economic system.

In the United States, for example, the advertising industry is part of a large business community. Like any good neighbor, it has responsibilities: to keep its

Today's consumer is more sophisticated than ever about social issues like environmentalism. Leclerc addresses the issue of "plastic bag pollution" in a beautifully produced campaign, where it tells customers "No, Leclerc does not really want to be seen everywhere." Other ads in the series say, "There are some places we don't want to see our name," and "Some advertising we'll pass up willingly."

Non, E. Leclerc ne veut pas être présent partout.

Avec votre aide, mettons fin à la pollution par les sacs en plastique.

Truth in Advertising: Fluffing and Puffing

Perhaps nothing characterizes advertising in the minds of most people more than the term *puffery*. In advertising, puffery means exaggerated commendation, or hype. The term comes from the Old English word *pyffan*, meaning "to blow in short gusts" or "to inflate; make proud or conceited." Puffery surely predates recorded history.

The Nature of Puffery

Regardless of its long heritage and current widespread use, we should question puffery's role in advertising. Inherently, puffery erodes advertising's credibility as a trustworthy messenger by first lowering the public's belief in the advertising they see. People begin to question those who support and create such advertising—the advertisers, ad professionals, and ultimately the media that run such ads. A slogan such as "Quality worth your trust" is immediately deemed false when used in an ad for a product that's generally perceived as inferior. Soon people begin joking that the agency is out of touch or lying or "should be shot."

Defining Puffery

Regardless of the criticisms, puffery remains legal. And in the United States, it's relatively well defined by law.

In 1906, as part of the Uniform Sales Act (now called the Uniform Commercial Code), a seller's opinion (an element of puffery) cannot constitute the sole basis of a warranty to the customer; more information is required. In 1916, the law stipulated puffery as acceptable if it is "mere exaggeration" but illegal if it invents advantages and then "falsely asserts their existence." The buyer's state of mind entered the definition in 1941: "'Sales talk,' or 'puffing,' . . . is considered to be offered and understood as an expression of the seller's opinion only,

which is to be discounted as such by the buyer, and on which no *reasonable man* would rely." The Federal Trade Commission joined the dialogue in the late 1950s, confirming, "Puffery does not embrace misstatements of material facts."

As you can see, puffery's legal definition establishes that the characteristics puffed must, in fact, exist. The challenge is defining where puffing crosses over from exaggeration into falsehood and then to deception. Exaggeration is often the starting point of falsehood, but falsehood is not necessarily harmful or injurious—in fact, it may be playful and creative. Deception, however, is interpreted as being injurious to consumers and is therefore illegal.

Take, for example, the case with Papa John's International, who invested millions of dollars over the years in its "Better ingredients, Better pizza," advertising campaign. The vague and subjective claim might be considered puffery. But when it named its rival Pizza Hut in ads, the issue changed from mere puffery to comparison. And comparison advertising requires convincing substantiation; otherwise it may be considered deceptive.

In 1998, Pizza Hut filed a lawsuit in Dallas federal court against Papa John's, alleging that its campaign was "false, misleading, and deceptive," as defined by the Lanham Act. A Texas jury ruled in favor of Pizza Hut, charging that Papa John's "Better ingredients, Better pizza" campaign constituted deceptive advertising. Pizza Hut was awarded $467,619.75. Papa John's was ordered to remove its slogan from ads, pizza boxes, restaurant signage, and delivery trucks.

Later, the decision was reversed by the Disctrict Court of Appeals after Papa John's removed the references to Pizza Hut. But the point had still been made: Advertisers have to be careful about the puffery claims they make—they no longer have free rein. Marketers need to be able to substantiate any claims that they make. An indirect comparison, or even the appearance of one, could render them liable.

property clean, participate in civic events, support local enterprises, and improve the community. U.S. advertising professionals have met these challenges by forming local advertising clubs, the American Advertising Federation (AAF), the American Association of Advertising Agencies (AAAA), and the Ad Council. These organizations provide thousands of hours and millions of dollars' worth of *pro bono* (free) work to charitable organizations and public agencies. They also provide scholarships and internships, contributions that serve the whole society. As we discuss later, they even regulate themselves fairly effectively.

Advertisers such as AT&T, IBM, and Honda commit significant dollars to supporting the arts, education, and various charitable causes as well as their local Better Business Bureaus and Chambers of Commerce. Still, advertisers are regularly chided when they fail the social responsibility litmus test. Concerned citizens, consumer advocates, and special-interest groups pressure advertisers when they perceive the public's welfare is at risk. The earliest "green advertising" campaigns, for instance, exemplified a blatant effort by some advertisers to cash in on consumers' desire for a cleaner environment. Some promoted nebulous product qualities, such as "environmental friendliness," that actually had no basis in fact. Finally, when the state attorneys general got together and defined relevant terms for use in green advertising, marketers cleaned up their act.

Advertisers also receive criticism when they sponsor programming with content that offends particular interest groups. The Southern Baptist Church, for instance, urged its members in 1997 to boycott Disney theme parks and movies because of its perception that Disney had strayed from its tradition of promoting family values.

The Use of Puffery

Common usage portrays puffery as praise for the item to be sold using subjective opinions, superlatives, exaggerations, and vagueness, and generally stating no specific facts. Ivan Preston, the leading scholar on the issue of puffery, has established six levels of puffery:

- *Best* (strongest claim): "Nestlé's makes the very best chocolate."
- *Best possible:* "Nothing cleans stains better than Clorox bleach" or "Visa—it's everywhere you want to be."
- *Better:* "Advil just works better."
- *Especially good:* "Extraordinary elegance." (Coty)
- *Good:* "M'm, m'm good." (Campbell's soup)
- *Subjective qualities* (weakest claim): "There's a smile in every Hershey bar."

Puffery often takes the form of "nonproduct facts," information not specifically about the product and therefore not directly ascertainable as being truths, falsehoods, or deceptions specific to the product. Nonproduct facts are typically about consumers: their personalities, lifestyles, fears, anxieties. An example is the Army's positioning message, "Be all that you can be in the Army." The claim relies on the potential for what can happen to the ad's readers while they're in the Army. It doesn't actually promise any specific benefits such as improved physical fitness or more education. Thus, regardless of what actually happens to readers who join up, the claim is neither true nor false about the Army.

Puffery can also be "artful display," the visual presentation of a product. Although not well defined by law, visual exaggeration is ever-present in ads to enhance moods, excite viewers, and more. The existence of professional models, for example, suggests that some individuals are more visually attractive than others. This factor makes them appealing (see the Ethical Issue in Chapter 12, "Does Sex Appeal?"). But does their appearance in an ad imply that owning the product will make the buyer more physically attractive? Although most prospective purchasers don't expect the product to improve their physical appearance, they might well become disappointed if the product failed to live up to the implied promise—the puffery—that it can improve their psychological self-image.

Judging Puffery

We live in exciting times. Populations are more literate, satellites and the Internet keep the world informed instantly, and modern technology speeds up the way we live and play. And part of the glitz of our modern life is puffery, adding pizzazz and stimulating our dreams.

But who should protect consumers from their love/hate relationship with puffery, especially when puffery crosses the line and becomes injurious? Who should evaluate puffery's ethics? The courts may, but only when a consumer challenges an advertiser. The actions and attitudes of the advertising profession can make a huge difference. If the First Amendment doesn't curtail them, the media can also affect the use and abuse of puffery.

Sources: "Advertising Puffery: Current Status," Reed Smith Hall Dickler, 2004 (retrieved from www.adlaw.com); Lane Jennings, "Hype, Spin, Puffery and Lies: Should We Be Scared? Media Mythmakers Keep the Public Ill Informed," *The Futurist*, January/February 2004 (retrieved from InfoTrac); Perry Haan and Cal Berkey, "A Study of the Believability of the Forms of Puffery," *Journal of Marketing Communications*, December 2002, p. 248; Thomas Morrison, "How a Seemingly Innocuous Slogan Led to the Pizza Wars," Spring 2002 (retrieved from www.pbwt.com/Resources/index-newsletter.html); Ivan Preston, "A Problem Ignored: Dilution and Negation of Consumer Information by Antifactual Content," *Journal of Consumer Affairs*, December 22, 2002 (retrieved from InfoTrac).

Ethics of Advertising

Philosophies of ethics span the centuries since Socrates. We can hardly do them justice here. But for practical purposes, let's consider three levels of ethical responsibility and apply them to advertising.

On one level, ethics comprise two interrelated components: the traditional actions taken by people in a society or community and the philosophical rules that society establishes to justify such past actions and decree future actions. These components create the primary rules of ethical behavior in the society and enable us to measure how far an individual or company (or advertiser) strays from the norm. Here, the individual's rights are subject to the standards of what is customary (and therefore proper) for the group.

Every individual also faces a second set of ethical issues: the attitudes, feelings, and beliefs that add up to a personal value system. When these two systems conflict, should the individual act on personal beliefs or on the obligation to serve the group and its policies? For example, nonsmoking ad agency people may create ads for a tobacco client. At the first societal level of ethics there is some conflict: Smoking has been a custom in the United States for centuries and is not illegal today. However, the U.S. Surgeon General has declared that smoking is a national health problem (harmful to the group). This conflict at the first ethical level passes the responsibility for decision making to the second, individual level. Because the penalty may be the loss of income, nonsmokers may decide to produce the ads while keeping their own work area smoke-free. The ethical issue is at least temporarily and partially resolved, or at least rationalized, at the second ethical level.

When the group or individuals cannot resolve an ethical dilemma, they must redefine the issue in dispute. Thus, the third level of ethics concerns singular ethical

Exhibit 3–3

Levels of ethical responsibility.

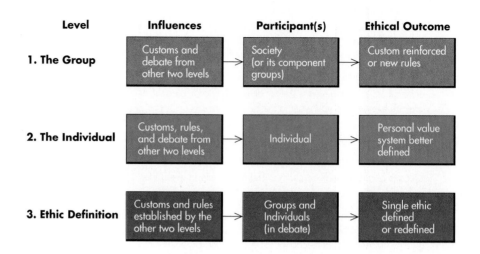

Level	Influences	Participant(s)	Ethical Outcome
1. The Group	Customs and debate from other two levels	Society (or its component groups)	Custom reinforced or new rules
2. The Individual	Customs, rules, and debate from other two levels	Individual	Personal value system better defined
3. Ethic Definition	Customs and rules established by the other two levels	Groups and Individuals (in debate)	Single ethic defined or redefined

concepts such as good, bad, right, wrong, duty, integrity, and truth. Are these concepts absolute, universal, and binding? Or are they relative, dependent on situations and consequences? A person's moral and ethical philosophy, influenced by religion, society, and individual values, will determine their answer (see Exhibit 3–3).

Let's say, for example, the copywriter for a cigarette ad is a smoker, and he writes copy that implies that smoking is a favorable behavior. But the ad's art director, a nonsmoker, complains that the ad is unethical because the copy conflicts with the truth, because smoking is actually an unsafe behavior. At this point they reach the third ethical level, and a more senior person, such as the creative director, may step in and lead a discussion aimed at defining the agency's ethical policy on smoking.

As we mentioned before, ethics is such an important topic that we address those issues that pertain to advertising in Ethical Issue sidebars in each chapter. The Ethical Issue here considers the issue of puffery as it relates to truth in advertising.

Most advertisers today strive to maintain fair ethical standards and practice socially responsible advertising. Ad agencies rarely force employees to work on accounts they morally oppose. Once a free-swinging, unchecked business, advertising is today a closely scrutinized and heavily regulated profession. Advertising's past shortcomings have created layer upon layer of laws, regulations, and regulatory bodies. Consumer groups, governments, special-interest groups, and even other advertisers now review, control, and modify advertising in order to create more *complete information* and reduce the impact of unwanted *externalities*.

How Government Regulates Advertising

One of the characteristics of the American political scene is our tripartite system of checks and balances. There are many laws that govern what advertisers can and cannot do. These laws are passed by legislatures, enforced by the executive branch, and interpreted by the judiciary. This system is repeated at the state and local levels.

On the national level, the president, cabinet departments, and various federal commissions are responsible for executing the laws passed by Congress. On the state level, the governor, attorney general, and state departments administer state laws. Locally, mayors, city managers, city attorneys, and police chiefs enforce the laws passed by city councils.

Similarly, local laws are interpreted by municipal courts, while the superior courts and state supreme courts interpret state laws. Federal laws are interpreted by federal district courts and the U.S. Supreme Court. Every day, advertisers from the local copy shop to international soft-drink marketers have to deal with the actions and decisions of all these branches of government. We'll discuss shortly some of the most important issues that concern U.S. regulators.

Government Restraints on International Advertisers

Now that advertising has become global, many campaigns use similar themes and even the same ads across frontiers. But foreign governments often regulate advertising considerably more than either the United States or Canada. And while Europe has moved toward uniformity in marketing activities, the laws governing advertising remain largely national.[42] So advertisers need to keep up with the changing legal environments of the countries in which they advertise.

Foreign governments are frequently more authoritarian, and many do not have a system of checks and balances like ours. Some governments not only regulate what ads say, show, or do; they often impose severe restrictions or outright bans on advertising specific products. The Swedes ban advertising to children on television. The Greeks ban toy advertising before 10:00 P.M. Throughout Europe, broadcast advertising for tobacco products is prohibited, and liquor ads are sharply restricted, especially in France.[43]

In fact, the European Union enacted legislation in 1998 that would gradually have phased out all forms of tobacco advertising and sponsorships by the year 2006. But the highest court on the Continent, the European Court of Justice, struck down the ban in October 2000 declaring it unlawful. Notwithstanding, the British still enacted legislation in 2002 that outlawed all consumer advertising for tobacco products.[44] And late in 2002, the 15-nation European Union passed a bill that would outlaw all tobacco ads in newspapers and magazines, on the Internet, and at international sporting events beginning in 2005.[45]

Many countries prohibit puffery superlatives. In Germany, for example, advertisers may use only scientifically provable superlatives. McCann-Erickson once had to retranslate the old Coca-Cola slogan, "Refreshes you best," because it implied a leadership position that was unprovable. The agency substituted "Refreshes you right" in Germany (in Austria, however, which typically follows Germany's lead in advertising law, the original line would be permissible).[46]

Many European countries also ban coupons, premiums, free tie-in offers, and the like. Companies may advertise price cuts only during "official sales periods," and advertisers often need government approval before publishing a sale ad. Across Europe, advertising on television must be clearly recognizable and kept separate from other programming. Paid *product placements* in programs, therefore, are typically prohibited.[47]

In Singapore, the state-owned broadcasting company yanked a Qantas Airline spot after the Ministry of Information and the Arts criticized the ad's "harmful values." The spot had used the line "last of the big spenders," which the ministry felt encouraged reckless spending by consumers (see Ad Lab 3–B).[48]

Costa Rica has more than 250 laws regulating advertising. Recently, government officials agreed to consider an industry proposal that would overturn the particularly onerous law mandating preclearance of all advertising.[49]

Regulators are cracking down in China as well. A new comprehensive advertising law targets false, "unscientific, and superstitious" claims and requires preclearance of all advertising in all media. However, China now allows Taiwanese advertising on mainland billboards—after preclearance, of course.[50]

In international advertising, the only solution to this morass of potential legal problems is to retain a good local lawyer who specializes in advertising law.

Current Regulatory Issues Affecting U.S. Advertisers

In recent years, both federal and state courts have made a number of significant rulings pertaining to advertising issues. The most important of these concern First Amendment rights and privacy rights. We'll discuss each of these, with special attention paid to the recent controversy surrounding tobacco advertising as well as the very sensitive issue of advertising to children.

The Importance of Good Legal Counsel in Advertising

For many years, Jack Russell had dreamed of this opportunity—opening a members-only club for young people who were not yet old enough to drink. He could already taste the success that was about to be his—money, fame, and fortune were all within his reach. He took every avenue possible to promote the new, exclusive club. He ran ads in local entertainment magazines and community newspapers. Local rock radio stations, though, were the mainstay—shouting out the good news for kids all over town, complete with a phone number and address for sending in their charter membership fees. Jack's wonderful idea was about to take flight. But then the local district attorney ripped the magic carpet out from underneath him. See, Jack Russell was selling memberships to a club that had not opened yet. In fact, he hadn't even signed the lease on the proposed premises. To the DA, it smelled of scam. He figured Jack was taking money from kids for something that didn't exist. That would be fraud. The DA charged him with false advertising—and fraud. When Jack answered his ringing doorbell, two uniformed officers were standing there. They handcuffed him, gave him a ride downtown, and threw him in jail. If Jack had just passed his ads by a communications lawyer, he could have avoided a very embarrassing and expensive nightmare. And he'd be a free man.

Ethical and legal problems with advertising seem to pop up constantly. Not only government officials, but competitors and consumer rights groups scrutinize ads carefully—either for their own self-interest or to protect the rights of consumers. As a result, every agency and advertiser needs to have a strong understanding of the laws that govern advertising. They also need to retain the services of a good law firm that specializes in advertising and communication law.

One such firm is Hall Dickler Kent Goldstein & Wood LLP. With offices in New York and Los Angeles, Hall Dickler serves a blue-chip client roster that includes some of the nation's largest advertisers as well as numerous prominent advertising associations such as the 4As, the Association of National Advertisers, and the American Advertising Federation.

Hall Dickler routinely provides its clients with a wide array of services: checking advertising copy for legal acceptability; reviewing promotional concepts, scripts, and testimonials as they relate to sweepstakes, games, and contests; and representing clients before federal and state regulatory bodies. Hall Dickler helps clients adopt corporate procedures and policies to protect against the legal liabilities of doing business in new media outlets such as the Internet. The firm handles all aspects of intellectual property on a worldwide basis. This includes determining the availability of proposed trademarks, trade names, corporate names, Internet domain names, and copyright works/titles.

As a public service, the firm publishes a sophisticated newsletter and maintains a website, both under the name of ADLAW. From the newsletter, clients and prospects can get important information about new laws or proposed legislation affecting advertising; and the website (adlaw.com) offers a wide array of regularly updated resources including the ADLAW handbook, a guide to key legal issues in advertising, a Contract Forms database with sample legal documents, and articles on the legal complexities of promotional programs. Another highlight of the site is the *Resource Files* tab, which provides up-to-date links to key sites relevant to legal issues.

Laboratory Applications

1. Go to adlaw.com and explore the website. Click on the "What's New" tab and read about current advertising-related legal cases. Pick one that interests you, read it, and then write a brief report including the title of the case, the names of the parties involved, the issues at stake, and a summary of the decision that was handed down if there has been a judgment.

2. Click on the "Resource Files" tab and then the "Sweepstakes, Games, Etc." link. Study the list of articles, choose one, and prepare a summary you can present to your class. If possible, include examples from your own personal experience.

3. What ethical, social, or legal issues do you think will be addressed in the next 10 years relative to advertising and the Internet?

Freedom of Commercial Speech

The Supreme Court historically distinguishes between "speech" and "commercial speech" (speech that promotes a commercial transaction). But decisions over the last two decades suggest that truthful commercial speech is also entitled to significant, if not full, protection under the First Amendment.

The trend started in 1976 when the Supreme Court held in *Virginia State Board of Pharmacy* versus *Virginia Citizens Consumer Council* that ads enjoy protection under the First Amendment as commercial speech.[51] The next year the Court declared that the ban by state bar associations on attorney advertising also violated the First Amendment. Now a third of all lawyers advertise, and a few states even permit client testimonials. To help guard against deceptive and misleading lawyer ads, the American Bar Association issues guidelines for attorneys.

In 1980 the Court used *Central Hudson Gas* versus *Public Service Commission* to test whether specific examples of commercial speech can be regulated.[52] The four-pronged *Central Hudson* test includes the following parts:

1. *Does the commercial speech at issue concern a lawful activity?* The ad in question must be for a legal product and must be free of misleading claims.

2. *Will the restriction of commercial speech serve the asserted government interest substantially?* The government must prove that the absence of regulation would have a substantial negative effect.

3. *Does the regulation directly advance the government interest asserted?* The government must be able to establish conclusively that cessation of the advertising would be effective in furthering the government's interest.

Despite the constraints of stricter advertising laws overseas, ads can still be very effective and creative. The copy for this cute ad from IVO, Finland's power company, reads: "The more pleasant way. Electrical heating." The ad is certainly appropriate given that country's somewhat chilly climate.

4. *Is the restriction no more than necessary to further the interest asserted?* The government would have to establish that there are no other means to accomplish the same end without restricting free speech.[53]

When planning to advertise overseas, companies must be very cautious about the do's and don'ts of other countries. Typically, they retain the services of attorneys familiar with local laws. Many international law firms have websites that can be quickly located on the Internet. Hall Dickler refers its clients to GALA (www.gala-marketlaw.com), an international network of lawyers it belongs to.

In 1982, the Supreme Court upheld an FTC order allowing physicians and dentists to advertise. Since then, advertising for medical and dental services has skyrocketed.

In 1993, the Supreme Court gave the advertising industry its biggest win in years. It said the Cincinnati City Council violated the First Amendment when it banned racks of advertising brochures from city streets for "aesthetic and safety reasons" while permitting newspaper vending machines.[54]

The issue of freedom of commercial speech is far from settled. Allowing greater freedom of commercial speech enhances the "government interests" of many buyers and sellers and complete information. But the additional interest of reducing externalities creates heated controversies surrounding issues like tobacco and alcohol advertising and advertising to children. These will likely continue for years to come.

The Tobacco Advertising Controversy

Take the case of cigarette advertising. While tobacco is a legal product, the harm created by smoking ends up killing or disabling more than half a million people annually and costing taxpayers billions of dollars every year in health costs—a major externality. To recover these costs, a number of states' attorneys general sued the tobacco industry. In 1998, they reached a historic settlement. It mandated significant reform on cigarette marketing activities and provided for the largest financial recovery in the nation's history. Because the industry had abused its freedom of commercial speech for so many years, the settlement called for sweeping changes in how, when, and where tobacco companies could advertise. Most important, the attorneys general sought to protect children from tobacco advertising. Thus, the settlement banned outdoor advertising posters (for example, on billboards, buses, and video arcades), sponsorship of events with a significant youth audience, as well as the use of cartoon characters in any tobacco advertising.[55]

For businesspeople who believe that freedom of commercial speech should be afforded equal protection under the First Amendment, the tobacco case is ominous. Many people are antismoking, antialcohol, antipornography, or antigun. But the "free speechers" believe it's a travesty of the First Amendment to selectively abridge any free speech, whether it's for any political, social, or religious idea or any legal, commercial product. They warn that this selective limitation of freedom of commercial speech threatens every legal business in America, especially because any limitation on the freedom to advertise automatically gives a huge, monopolistic advantage to those big brands that are already the category leaders.[56]

The Issue of Advertising to Children

Advertising to children presents different challenges. Kids aren't sophisticated consumers. Their conceptions of self, time, and money are immature. As a result, they know very little about their desires, needs, and preferences—or how to use economic resources rationally to satisfy them. And the nature of children's conceptual ability makes it likely that child-oriented advertising can lead to false beliefs or highly improbable product expectations.

While most children and parents are still joint consumers, more and more children are becoming sole decision makers. To protect them, and their parents, both critics and defenders agree that advertisers should not intentionally deceive children. The central issue is how far advertisers should go to ensure that children are not misled by their ads.

To promote responsible children's advertising and to respond to public concerns, the Council of Better Business Bureaus established the **Children's Advertising Review Unit (CARU).** CARU provides a general advisory service for advertisers and agencies and also offers informational material for children, parents, and educators. For more than 20 years, CARU's *Self-Regulatory Guidelines for Children's Advertising* has guided marketers in the development of child-directed advertising for all traditional media. In 1997, CARU published its updated *Guidelines* to include new directions for marketing to children via online media.

The basic activity of CARU is the review and evaluation of child-directed advertising in all media. When children's advertising is found to be misleading, inaccurate, or inconsistent with the *Guidelines,* CARU seeks changes through voluntary cooperation of the advertisers.[57] For an overview of the basic principles underlying CARU's *Guidelines* see Exhibit 3–4.

In the developed world, other countries are far more strict than the United States about advertising to children. Sweden and Norway, for example, do not permit any television advertising to be directed toward children under 12, and no advertisements at all are allowed during children's programs. Germany and Holland prohibit sponsorship of children's shows, and the Flemish region of Belgium permits no ads five minutes before or after any programs for children. While the highest level of advertising to children is in Australia (an average of 34 ads per hour), that country allows no ads on programs aimed at preschool children.[58]

In the area of television advertising, the government and consumer groups play an important role at both the national and international level to ensure that adequate consumer protection for children is maintained and strengthened where necessary. For more on child-oriented TV advertising, see the Ethical Issue in Chapter 16.

Consumer Privacy

The second major regulatory issue facing advertisers is privacy. Today, most advertisers know it's illegal to use a person's likeness in an ad without the individual's permission. And since 1987, even using a celebrity lookalike (or soundalike) can violate that person's rights. The courts have also ruled that people's *privacy rights* continue even after their death.

Now, with the increased use of fax machines, cell phones, and the Internet, all of which can be used for advertising directly to prospects, the issue of **privacy rights** is again in the news. This time it's over people's right to protect their personal information. As we shall see in Chapter 17, privacy is an ethical issue as well as a legal one. It's also a practical issue: Prospective customers who find advertising faxes, telemarketing calls, and e-mails annoying and intrusive aren't likely to buy the offending company's products.

Internet users worry about people they don't know, and even businesses they do know, getting personal information about them. And their concern is not without

Exhibit 3–4

Children's Advertising Review Unit's guidelines for advertising to children.

Seven basic principles underlie CARU's guidelines for advertising to children under the age of 12:

1. Advertisers should always take into account the level of knowledge, sophistication, and maturity of the audience to which their message is primarily directed. Younger children have a limited capacity for evaluating the credibility of information they receive. They also may lack the ability to understand the nature of the information they provide. Advertisers, therefore, have a special responsibility to protect children from their own susceptibilities.

2. Realizing that children are imaginative and that make-believe play constitutes an important part of the growing up process, advertisers should exercise care not to exploit unfairly the imaginative quality of children. Unreasonable expectations of product quality or performance should not be stimulated either directly or indirectly by advertising.

3. Products and content that are inappropriate for use by children should not be advertised or promoted directly to children.

4. Recognizing that advertising may play an important part in educating a child, advertisers should communicate information in a truthful and accurate manner and in language understandable to young children with full recognition that the child may learn practices from advertising that can affect his or her health and well being.

5. Advertisers are urged to capitalize on the potential of advertising to influence behavior by developing advertising that, wherever possible, addresses itself to positive and beneficial social behavior such as friendship, kindness, honesty, justice, generosity, and respect for others.

6. Care should be taken to incorporate minority and other groups in advertising in order to present positive and prosocial roles and role models wherever possible. Social stereotyping and appeals to prejudice should be avoided.

7. Although many influences affect a child's personal and social development, it remains the prime responsibility of the parents to provide guidance for children. Advertisers should contribute to this parent–child relationship in a constructive manner.

reason. Many websites create profiles of their visitors to get data such as e-mail addresses, clothing sizes, or favorite books. Some sites also track users' surfing habits, usually without their knowledge, to better target ads for products.

To create these user profiles, websites use tiny software programs, called **cookies,** that keep a log of where people click, allowing sites to track customers' Web-surfing habits. The cookies are placed on people's computers when they first visit a site or use some feature like a personalized news service or a shopping cart.[59]

Internet companies argue that such tracking is not personal; it's typically performed anonymously and helps them customize sites and content to match users' interests.[60] However, DoubleClick, a leading provider of marketing tools for Web advertisers, direct marketers, and Web publishers, recently acquired Abacus Direct, a direct-mail company with an extensive offline database of retail and catalog purchasers. This potentially enables DoubleClick to combine online profiles with offline names, addresses, demographic information, and purchasing data.[61] For more on this story, see the Ethical Issue in Chapter 17, "Profiling: Would You Take Cookies from a Stranger?"

A survey conducted in 2000 revealed that only 27 percent of Internet users accept the industry's claim that tracking is helpful. Somewhat more than half, 54 percent, consider it harmful, and 11 percent believe that it both helps and hurts. A large majority of those surveyed, 87 percent, believe sites should ask permission before collecting personal information.[62]

Fortunately, consumers are not completely helpless. They can disable the cookies on their computers. But this may limit their Internet access, because some websites actually *require* that cookies be implanted. Internet surfers also have the option to "opt-in." This feature allows users to set the terms for which they give personal information.[63] Also available is the "opt-out" feature, which allows sites to continuously gather information about visitors unless they specifically inform the site not to by clicking on a button.[64]

Responding to the rising concern of many consumers, the Federal Trade Commission together with the Network Advertising Initiative (an organization comprised of leading Internet advertising networks including AdKnowledge, 24/7, Ad Force, and DoubleClick) has created a framework for self-regulation of online profiling. The guidelines are referred to as the "Fair Information Practice Principles" and consist of five core elements:

- *Notice,* which requires that the website clearly post their privacy policy.
- *Choice,* which relates to consumers' level of control over being profiled and how their information is used.
- *Access,* the ability for consumers to access information collected about them and make amendments to it.
- *Security,* which requires that network advertisers make reasonable efforts to protect the data they collect, from loss, misuse, or improper access.
- *Enforcement,* a requirement that all industry members subject themselves to monitoring by an independent third party in order to assure compliance with the Fair Information Practice Principles.[65]

Naturally the dot-com companies would prefer to avoid government intervention and the layers of laws and regulations that would bring. So it's in everybody's interest for self-regulation to work. Time will tell.

Federal Regulation of Advertising in North America

The U.S. government imposes strict controls on advertisers through laws, regulations, and judicial interpretations. Among the many federal agencies and departments that regulate advertising are the Federal Trade Commission, the Food and Drug Administration, the Federal Communications Commission, the Patent and Trademark Office, and the Library of Congress. Because their jurisdictions often overlap, advertisers may sometimes have difficulty complying with their regulations.

Canada has a similar maze of federal regulators. But the Canadian legal situation is considerably more complex than the United States' due to the separate (but often concurrent) jurisdictions of paternalistic federal and provincial governments, the broad powers of government regulators, the vast array of self-regulatory codes, and the very nature of a bilingual and bicultural society. One simple example of this is the fact that all packages and labels must be printed in both English and French throughout Canada.[66]

The U.S. Federal Trade Commission

In the United States, the **Federal Trade Commission (FTC)** is the major regulator of advertising for products sold in interstate commerce. Established by an act of Congress, the FTC has a mission of ensuring "that the nation's markets function competitively, and are vigorous, efficient, and free of undue restrictions."[67] The commission enforces a variety of federal antitrust and consumer protection laws and works to enhance the operation of the marketplace by eliminating acts or practices that are deceptive or unfair. In other words, it is the FTC's responsibility to maintain the existence of *many sellers* in the marketplace, strive to provide more *complete information* to consumers, and keep the marketing process as free of *externalities* as possible.

The FTC's job is complicated by the fact that the definitions of deceptive and unfair are controversial.

Defining Deception

The FTC defines **deceptive advertising** as any ad that contains a misrepresentation, omission, or other practice that can mislead a significant number of reasonable consumers to their detriment. Proof that consumers were deceived is not required, and the representation may be either expressed or implied. The issue is whether the ad conveys a false impression—even if it is literally true.[68]

Take the case of the FTC against Office Depot, Buy.com, and Value America. According to the FTC, the companies engaged in deceptive practices in advertising "free" and "low-cost" personal computer (PC) systems because they failed to adequately disclose the true costs and important restrictions on the offers. The low cost of the PCs was tied to rebates that were conditioned on the purchase of long-term Internet service contracts.

While the companies' advertisements plugged low-cost and, in some cases, free computer systems, the true costs for the systems were far higher. For example, one ad featured a computer for $269. But the purchaser's actual expenses would exceed $1,000 when taking into account the cost of the required three-year Internet service contract. The FTC said the restrictions and charges were inadequately disclosed or that they were disclosed in tiny print. And that amounted to deception.

Without admitting any wrongdoing, the companies all signed consent agreements, agreeing to disclose the information prominently in the future to help consumers easily determine the real costs of such deals.[69]

The FTC is a powerful regulator. The commission cracked down on Exxon and ordered a groundbreaking educational campaign to inform consumers that the right octane for most cars is regular octane, not the more expensive premium grade.[70] The FTC also looks at environmental claims such as biodegradable, degradable, photodegradable, and recyclable. To avoid confusing terminology, the FTC and the Environmental Protection Agency (EPA) worked jointly with attorneys general from many states to develop uniform national guidelines for environmental marketing claims.[71]

Defining Unfairness

According to FTC policy, some ads that are not deceptive may still be considered unfair to consumers. **Unfair advertising** occurs when a consumer is "unjustifiably injured" or there is a "violation of public policy" (such as other government statutes). In other words, unfair advertising is due to the inadequacy of *complete information* or some other *externality*. For example, practices considered unfair

Our delivery truck.

Their delivery truck.

Dy·Dee Wash
Cloth Diaper Service

The purpose of comparative ads is to demonstrate the superiority of one product over another. Dy•Dee Wash takes the au natural marketing approach, with a cloth diaper service that is more environmentally friendly than the use of disposable diapers.

are claims made without prior substantiation, claims that exploit vulnerable groups such as children and the elderly, and cases where the consumer cannot make a valid choice because the advertiser omits important information about the product or about competing products mentioned in the ad.[72]

In one case, the FTC found that an automaker's failure to warn of a safety problem was not deceptive but was unfair. Advertising organizations have argued that the word "unfair" is so vague it can mean whatever any given individual wants it to. They have lobbied Congress to eliminate the FTC's power to prosecute on unfairness grounds, and Congress did pass a compromise bill requiring the FTC to show that (1) an alleged unfair practice involves substantial, unavoidable injury to consumers; (2) the injury is not reasonably avoidable by consumers themselves; and (3) the injury is not outweighed by benefits to consumers or competition.[73] This legislation suggests that in the future the FTC will have to balance on a far narrower beam in its effort to regulate unfairness.[74]

Comparative Advertising

Advertisers use **comparative advertising** to claim superiority to competitors in some aspect. In the United States, such ads are legal (and encouraged by the FTC) so long as the comparison is truthful. In fact, the FTC cracked down on the Arizona Automobile Dealers Association for restricting truthful, nondeceptive comparative price advertising among its members.[75]

The AADA's 199 members constitute 99 percent of the new-automobile and truck dealers in Arizona. The FTC challenged the association's Standards for Advertising Motor Vehicles, which, among other things, prohibited members from adver-

In Canada, all packages and labels must be printed in both English and French, and most major companies also run their ads in both languages. The layout of the French version of HP ad is modified to accomodate the slightly longer text.

Advertising law requires that celebrity endorsers actually use the product. For example, this ad for Crest toothpaste features the beautiful smile of actress Vanessa Williams. Since the implication is that Crest helped her keep this "ageless smile," she would have to be an actual user of the product.

tising that prices are equal to or lower than a competitor's, or are the lowest; that the advertiser will match or beat any price; or that the advertiser will offer compensation if it cannot offer an equal or lower price.

These prohibitions, according to the FTC, unreasonably restrained competition among the member dealers and injured consumers by depriving them of truthful information concerning the prices and financing available for new cars and trucks.

The 1988 Trademark Law Revision Act closed a loophole in the Lanham Act, which governed comparison ads but did not mention misrepresenting another company's product. Under current law, any advertiser that misrepresents its own or another firm's goods, services, or activities is vulnerable to a civil action.

In addition to being truthful, comparative ads must compare some objectively measurable characteristic. And the greatest scrutiny must be given to the substantiation. Given the potential for sizable damages—up to millions of dollars—for faulty comparative advertising, the greatest care must be exercised in this area.[76]

Investigating Suspected Violations

If it receives complaints from consumers, competitors, or its own staff members who monitor ads in various media, the FTC may decide to investigate an advertiser. The agency has broad powers to pursue suspected violators and demand information from them. Typically, the FTC looks for three kinds of information: *substantiation, endorsements,* and *affirmative disclosures.*

If a suspected violator cites survey findings or scientific studies, the FTC may ask for **substantiation.** Advertisers are expected to have supporting data before running an ad, although the FTC sometimes allows postclaim evidence. The FTC does not solicit substantiation for ads it is not investigating.

The FTC also scrutinizes ads that contain questionable **endorsements** or **testimonials.** If a noncelebrity endorser is paid, the ad must disclose this on-screen.[77] The endorsers may not make claims the advertiser can't substantiate. Further, celebrity endorsers must actually use the product or service (if portrayed), and they can be held personally liable if they misrepresent it.[78]

Advertisers must make **affirmative disclosure** of their product's limitations or deficiencies: for example, EPA mileage ratings for cars, pesticide warnings, and statements that saccharin may be hazardous to one's health.

Remedies for Unfair or Deceptive Advertising

When the FTC determines that an ad is deceptive or unfair, it may take three courses of action: negotiate with the advertiser for a consent decree, issue a cease-and-desist order, and/or require corrective advertising.

A **consent decree** is a document the advertiser signs agreeing to stop the objectionable advertising without admitting any wrongdoing. Before signing, the advertiser can negotiate specific directives with the FTC that will govern future advertising claims.

If an advertiser won't sign a consent decree, the FTC may issue a **cease-and-desist order** prohibiting further use of the ad. Before the order is final, it is heard by an administrative law judge. Most advertisers sign the consent decree after the hearing and agree, without admitting guilt, to halt the advertising. Advertisers that violate either a consent decree or a cease-and-desist order can be fined up to $11,000 per showing of the offending ad.

The FTC may also require **corrective advertising** for some period of time to explain and correct offending ads. In 1999 the FTC ruled that pharmaceutical giant Novartis advertised without substantiation that its Doan's Pills brand was more effective against back pain than its rivals. Because the deceptive advertising had gone on for more than nine years, the FTC ordered Novartis to run $8 million worth of corrective advertising. The advertising was to include the statement: "Although Doan's is an effective pain reliever, there is no evidence that Doan's is

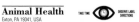

revolution®
(selamectin)

Topical Parasiticide For Dogs and Cats

CAUTION:
U.S. Federal law restricts this drug to use by or on the order of a licensed veterinarian.

INDICATIONS:
Revolution kills adult fleas and prevents flea eggs from hatching for one month and is indicated for the prevention and control of flea infestations (*Ctenocephalides felis*), prevention of heartworm disease caused by *Dirofilaria immitis*, and the treatment and control of ear mite (*Otodectes cynotis*) infestations in dogs and cats. Revolution also is indicated for the treatment and control of sarcoptic mange (*Sarcoptes scabiei*) and for the control of tick (*Dermacentor variabilis*) infestations in dogs, and the treatment of intestinal hookworm (*Ancylostoma tubaeforme*) and roundworm (*Toxocara cati*) infections in cats. Revolution is recommended for use in dogs and cats six weeks of age and older.

WARNINGS:
Not for human use. Keep out of the reach of children.
May be irritating to skin and eyes. Wash hands after use and wash off any product in contact with the skin immediately with soap and water. If contact with eyes occurs, then flush eyes copiously with water. In case of ingestion by a human, contact a physician immediately. The material safety data sheet (MSDS) provides more detailed occupational safety information. For a copy of the MSDS or to report adverse reactions attributable to exposure to this product, call 1-800-366-5288.

Flammable—Keep away from heat, sparks, open flames or other sources of ignition.

PRECAUTIONS:
Use with caution in sick, debilitated or underweight animals (see SAFETY).
Prior to administration of Revolution, dogs should be tested for existing heartworm infections. At the discretion of the veterinarian, infected dogs should be treated to remove adult heartworms. Revolution is not effective against adult *D. immitis* and, while the number of circulating microfilariae may decrease following treatment, Revolution is not effective for microfilariae clearance.

Hypersensitivity reactions have not been observed in dogs with patent heartworm infections administered three times the recommended dose of Revolution. Higher doses were not tested.

ADVERSE REACTIONS:
Following treatment with Revolution, transient localized alopecia with or without inflammation at or near the site of application was observed in approximately 1% of 691 treated cats. Other signs observed rarely (≤0.5% of 1743 treated cats and dogs) included vomiting, loose stool or diarrhea with or without blood, anorexia, lethargy, salivation, tachypnea, and muscle tremors.

DOSAGE:
The recommended minimum dose is 2.7 mg selamectin per pound (6 mg/kg) of body weight.

Administer the entire contents of a single dose tube of Revolution topically in accordance with label directions. (See ADMINISTRATION for the recommended treatment intervals.)

For cats over 15 lbs use the appropriate combination of tubes.

For dogs over 85 lbs use the appropriate combination of tubes.
Recommended for use in animals 6 weeks of age and older.

ADMINISTRATION:
Firmly depress the cap to puncture the seal on the Revolution tube; then remove the cap to administer the product.

Part the hair on the back of the animal at the base of the neck in front of the shoulder blades until the skin is visible. Place the tip of the tube on the skin and squeeze the tube to empty its entire contents directly onto the skin in one spot. Do not massage the product into the skin. Due to alcohol content, do not apply to broken skin. Avoid contact between the product and fingers. Do not apply when the hair coat is wet. Bathing or shampooing the animal 2 or more hours after treatment will not reduce the effectiveness of Revolution. Stiff hair, clumping of hair, hair discoloration, or a slight powdery residue may be observed at the treatment site in some animals. These effects are temporary and do not affect the safety or effectiveness of the product. Discard empty tubes in your ordinary household refuse.

Flea Control in Dogs and Cats
For the prevention and control of flea infestations, Revolution should be administered at monthly intervals throughout the flea season, starting one month before fleas become active. In controlled laboratory studies >98% of fleas were killed within 36 hours. Results of clinical field studies using Revolution monthly demonstrated >90% control of flea infestations within 30 days of the first dose. Dogs and cats treated with Revolution, including those with pre-existing flea allergy dermatitis, showed improvement in clinical signs associated with fleas as a direct result of eliminating the fleas from the animals and their environment.

If the dog or cat is already infested with fleas when the first dose of Revolution is administered, adult fleas on the animal are killed and no viable fleas hatch from eggs after the first administration. However, an environmental infestation of fleas may persist for a short time after beginning treatment with Revolution because of the emergence of adult fleas from pupae.

Heartworm Prevention in Dogs and Cats
For the prevention of heartworm disease, Revolution must be administered on a monthly basis. Revolution may be administered year-round or at least within one month after the animal's first exposure to mosquitoes and monthly thereafter until the end of the mosquito season. The final dose must be given within one month after the last exposure to mosquitoes. If a dose is missed and a monthly interval between dosing is exceeded then immediate administration of Revolution and resumption of monthly dosing will minimize the opportunity for the development of adult heartworms. When replacing another heartworm preventive product in a heartworm disease prevention program, the first dose of Revolution must be given within a month of the last dose of the former medication.

At the discretion of the veterinarian, cats ≥6 months of age may be tested to determine the presence of existing heartworm infections before beginning treatment with Revolution. Cats already infected with adult heartworms can safely be given Revolution monthly to prevent further infections.

Ear Mite Treatment in Dogs and Cats
For the treatment of ear mite (*O. cynotis*) infestations in dogs and cats, Revolution should be administered once as a single topical dose. A second monthly dose may be required in some dogs. Monthly use of Revolution will control any subsequent ear mite infestations. In the clinical trials ears were not cleaned, and many animals still had debris in their ears after the second dose. Cleansing of the infested ears is recommended to remove the debris.

Sarcoptic Mange Treatment in Dogs
For the treatment of sarcoptic mange (*S. scabiei*) in dogs, Revolution should be administered once as a single topical dose. A second monthly dose may be required in some dogs. Monthly use of Revolution will control any subsequent sarcoptic mange mite infestations. Because of the difficulty in finding sarcoptic mange mites on skin scrapings, effectiveness assessments also were based on resolution of clinical signs. Resolution of the pruritus associated with the mite infestations was observed in approximately 50% of the dogs 30 days after the first treatment and in approximately 90% of the dogs 30 days after the second monthly treatment.

Tick Control in Dogs
For the control of tick (*Dermacentor variabilis*) infestations in dogs, Revolution should be administered on a monthly basis. In heavy tick infestations, complete efficacy may not be achieved after the first dose. In these cases, one additional dose may be administered two weeks after the previous dose, with monthly dosing continued thereafter.

Nematode Treatment in Cats
For the treatment of intestinal hookworm (*A. tubaeforme*) and roundworm (*T. cati*) infections, Revolution should be applied once as a single topical dose.

NADA 141-152, Approved by FDA.

 Animal Health
Exton, PA 19341, USA
Div. of Pfizer Inc
NY, NY 10017

www.revolutionpet.com

To provide consumers with more complete information, the U.S. Food and Drug Administration regulates the content of pharmaceutical ads. It used to require that advertisers include all the information from the product insert in its TV ads. This necessitated lengthy commercials with minuscule copy. In 1997, the rule was changed, allowing pharmaceutical companies to advertise on TV and radio as long as they mentioned any important side effects and directed consumers to other sources for further information, such as their magazine ads or their website. Notice how this magazine ad for Animal Health's Revolution complies with the FDA's disclosure requirements.

more effective than other pain relievers for back pain." The FTC also ordered Doan's to place the statement on their packaging for a year.[79]

To help advertisers avoid such expense, the FTC will review advertising before it runs and give "advance clearance" in an advisory opinion. It also publishes *Industry Guides and Trade Regulation Rules,* which gives advertisers, agencies, and the media ongoing information about FTC regulations.

In Canada, the laws are even tougher and the consequences stiffer. It's an offense for any public promotion to be "false or misleading in a material respect." It is not necessary that anyone be misled by the representation, only that it be false. An *offense* is a crime. If convicted, an advertiser or agency executive could go to jail for up to five years, pay a fine, or both.[80]

The Food and Drug Administration (FDA)

A division of the Department of Health and Human Services, the **Food and Drug Administration (FDA)** is authorized by Congress to enforce the Federal Food, Drug, and Cosmetic Act and several other health laws. The agency monitors the manufacture, import, transport, storage, and sale of over $1 trillion worth of products annually, which accounts for 25 cents of every dollar spent annually by American consumers. And they do so at a cost to the public of little more than a penny a day per person.[81]

It's the FDA's job to see that the food we eat is safe, the cosmetics we use won't hurt us, and the medicines and therapeutic devices we buy are safe and effective. With authority over the labeling, packaging, and branding of packaged foods and therapeutic devices, the FDA strives to give consumers *complete information* by ensuring that products are labeled truthfully with the information people need to use them properly. The FDA requires manufacturers to disclose all ingredients on product labels, in in-store product advertising, and in product literature. The label must accurately state the weight or volume of the contents. Labels on therapeutic devices must give clear instructions for use. The FDA can require warning statements on packages of hazardous products. It regulates "cents off" and other promotions on package labels and has jurisdiction over the use of words such as *giant* or *family* to describe package sizes.

When consumer-oriented drug ads became common in the mid-1980s, the FDA ruled that any ad for a brand-name drug must include all the information in the package insert.[82] That meant advertisers had to run lengthy commercials or use minuscule type in print ads. In 1997, the FDA changed that rule, allowing pharmaceutical companies to advertise their drugs on broadcast media as long as they mentioned any important possible side effects and directed people to their print ads, their Internet sites, or consumers' own doctors for more information.[83] With that ruling, prescription drug advertising instantly soared on television and radio, tripling over the next five years. It's estimated that in 2001, pharmaceutical companies spent some $2.7 billion in direct-to-consumer advertising. Although the FDA is responsible for ensuring that all these ads are fair and accurate, the agency is so understaffed that many questionable and, unfortunately, deceptive or misleading ads do get through. However, any time the FDA has sent a letter to marketers citing false advertising claims, the companies have stopped running the misleading ads.[84]

The **Nutritional Labeling and Education Act (NLEA),** which went into effect in 1994, gave the FDA additional muscle by setting stringent legal definitions for terms such as *fresh, light, low fat,* and *reduced calories.* It also sets standard serving sizes and requires labels to show food value for one serving alongside the total recommended daily value as established by the National Research Council.[85]

The first time the FDA took severe action against a prominent marketer over a labeling dispute, it seized 2,400 cases of Procter & Gamble's Citrus Hill Fresh Choice orange juice. Fresh Choice was made from concentrate, not fresh-squeezed juice as P&G claimed.[86] Due to increased FDA scrutiny, many advertisers are now more cautious about their health and nutritional claims.

The Federal Communications Commission (FCC)

The seven-member **Federal Communications Commission (FCC)** is an independent federal agency with jurisdiction over the radio, television, telephone, satellite, the Internet, and cable TV industries. The FCC is responsible for protecting the public interest and encouraging competition. Its control over broadcast advertising is actually *indirect,* stemming from its authority to license broadcasters (or take away their licenses). The FCC stringently controls the airing of obscenity and profanity, and it can restrict both the products advertised and the content of ads. For example, the FCC required stations to run commercials about the harmful effects of smoking even before Congress banned cigarette advertising on TV and radio.

In the 1980s, the FCC decided there were enough buyers and sellers that marketplace forces could adequately control broadcast media, so it deregulated both radio and TV stations. The FCC no longer limits commercial time or requires stations to maintain detailed program and commercial logs. However, stations still keep records of commercial broadcasts to assure advertisers they ran.

The 1992 Cable Television Consumer Protection and Competition Act gave the FCC additional teeth. It placed new controls on the cable TV industry to encourage a more service-oriented attitude and to improve the balance between rates and escalating ad revenues.[87] The FCC can set subscriber rates for cable TV, so subscription revenues should slow while advertising rates rise.

Studies show violence on TV is linked to violent behavior (a public health issue). Congress responded by enacting the 1992 Television Violence Act, exempting

Coca-Cola's trademark varies from country to country. But the overall look is retained through use of similar letterforms and style, even with different alphabets.

1.		8.
2.		7.
3.	4.	5.	6.

1. Arabic   5. Spanish
2. French   6. Chinese
3. Japanese   7. Hebrew
4. Thai   8. Polish

network and cable companies from antitrust laws if they agree to self-regulate violence. Because network and cable companies deny that violence on TV is related to violence in life, government intervention is a possibility.[88]

The Patent and Trademark Office and the Library of Congress

A basic role of government is to promote and protect the economic well-being (*self-interest*) of its citizens. One way the U.S. government does this is by promoting "the progress of science and useful arts, by securing for limited times to authors and inventors the exclusive right to their respective writings and discoveries"; in other words, by registering and protecting their **intellectual property.**[89]

Through the issuance of **patents,** the government provides incentives to invent, invest in, and disclose new technology worldwide. By registering trademarks and copyrights, the government helps businesses protect their investments, promote their goods and services, and safeguard consumers against confusion and deception in the marketplace (*complete information*).

A trademark such as Coca-Cola, AT&T, or Levi's is a valuable asset. According to the Lanham Trade-Mark Act (1947), a **trademark** is "any word, name, symbol, or device or any combination thereof adopted and used by a manufacturer or merchant to identify his goods and distinguish them from those manufactured or sold by others."

Patents and trademarks are registered with and protected by the **U.S. Patent and Trademark Office,** a bureau of the Department of Commerce. Ownership of a trademark may be designated in advertising or on a label, package, or letterhead by the word *Registered,* the symbol ®, or the symbol ™. If someone persists in using a trademark owned by another or confusingly similar to another's mark, the trademark owner can ask for a court order and sue for trademark infringement.

The Library of Congress protects all copyrighted material, including advertising, in the United States. A **copyright** is a form of protection provided to the authors of "original works of authorship," including literary, dramatic, musical, artistic, and certain other "intellectual works."[90] A copyright issued to an advertiser grants the exclusive right to print, publish, or reproduce the protected ad for the life of the copyright owner plus 50 years. An ad can be copyrighted only if it contains original copy or illustrations. An idea cannot be copyrighted; nor can slogans, short phrases, and familiar symbols and designs (although the latter may be trademarkable).

Copyright is indicated by the word *Copyright,* the abbreviation Copr., or the symbol © followed by the year of first publication and the name of the advertiser or copyright owner. (For more on trademarks and copyrights, see RL 2–4 in the Reference Library on the *Contemporary Advertising* CD-ROM.)

State and Local Regulation

Regulation by State Governments

Advertisers are also subject to state or local laws. Since the U.S. federal deregulation trend of the 1980s, state and local governments have taken a far more active role.

State legislation governing advertising is often based on the truth-in-advertising model statute developed in 1911 by *Printer's Ink,* for many years the major trade publication of the industry. The statute holds that any maker of an ad found to contain "untrue, deceptive, or misleading" material is guilty of a misdemeanor. Today 46 states (all except Arkansas, Delaware, Mississippi, and New Mexico) enforce laws patterned after this statute.

All states also have "little FTC acts," consumer protection laws that govern unfair and deceptive business practices. States themselves can investigate and prosecute cases, and individual consumers can bring civil suits against businesses. To increase their clout, some states team up on legal actions—for example, to challenge deceptive ad promotions in the airline, rental-car, and food-making industries. As one observer pointed out, "Many of the food manufacturers could litigate some of the smaller states into the ground, but they might not be willing to fight it out against 10 states simultaneously."[91]

Different states have different regulations governing what can be advertised. Some states prohibit advertising for certain types of wine and liquor, and most states restrict the use of federal and state flags in advertising.

This can present a major problem to national marketers. And in some cases, it actually hurts consumers. For example, many companies trying to conduct environmentally responsible marketing programs feel stymied by the different state laws governing packaging materials and recycling.[92] In the tobacco case discussed earlier, the teaming of numerous state attorneys general proved a formidable foe for the giant tobacco industry. In the end, facing the prospect of an infinite number of lawsuits from individual states and even municipalities, the industry buckled under, agreeing to settle and pay the various states hundreds of billions of dollars.[93]

Regulation by Local Governments

Many cities and counties also have consumer protection agencies to enforce laws regulating local advertising practices. The chief function of these agencies is to protect local consumers against unfair and misleading practices by area merchants.

In one year alone, the Orange County, California, district attorney's office received more than 1,200 complaint letters from consumers about everything from dishonest mechanics and phony sale ads to a taco stand that skimped on the beef in its "macho" burrito.[94] In a case against Los Angeles–based Closet Factory, Inc., the DA collected $40,000 in fines to settle a false advertising suit. The company was charged with running newspaper ads that gave consumers a false sense of urgency regarding "sales" that actually never end. This type of advertising, known as a *continuous sale,* violates the state's Business and Professions Code. It also advertises a false percentage off the regular price. Since the sale is never really over, the sale price becomes the regular price.[95]

Nongovernment Regulation

Nongovernment organizations also issue advertising guidelines (see Exhibit 3–5 on page 88). In fact, advertisers face considerable regulation by business-monitoring organizations, related trade associations, the media, consumer groups, and advertising agencies themselves.

The Better Business Bureau (BBB)

The largest of the U.S. business-monitoring organizations is the **Better Business Bureau (BBB),** established in 1916. Funded by dues from more than 100,000 member companies, it operates primarily at the local level to protect consumers against fraudulent and deceptive advertising and sales practices. When local bureaus contact violators and ask them to revise their advertising, most comply.

The BBB's files on violators are open to the public. Records of violators who do not comply are sent to appropriate government agencies for further action. The BBB often works with local law enforcement agencies to prosecute advertisers guilty of fraud and misrepresentation. Each year, the BBB investigates thousands of ads for possible violations of truth and accuracy.

The Council of Better Business Bureaus is the parent organization of the Better Business Bureau and a sponsoring member of the National Advertising Review Council. One of its functions is to help new industries develop standards for ethical and responsible advertising. The Code of Advertising of the Council of Better Business Bureaus (the BBB Code) has been called the most important self-regulation of advertising.[96] The BBB Code is only a few pages long, but it is supplemented by a

Exhibit 3-5

American Association of Advertising Agencies policy statement and guidelines for comparative advertising.

The Board of Directors of the American Association of Advertising Agencies recognizes that when used truthfully and fairly, comparative advertising provides the consumer with needed and useful information. However, extreme caution should be exercised. The use of comparative advertising, by its very nature, can distort facts and, by implication, convey to the consumer information that misrepresents the truth. Therefore, the Board believes that comparative advertising should follow certain guidelines:

1. The intent and connotation of the ad should be to inform and never to discredit or unfairly attack competitors, competing products, or services.
2. When a competitive product is named, it should be one that exists in the marketplace as significant competition.
3. The competition should be fairly and properly identified but never in a manner or tone of voice that degrades the competitive product or service.
4. The advertising should compare related or similar properties or ingredients of the product, dimension to dimension, feature to feature.
5. The identification should be for honest comparison purposes and not simply to upgrade by association.
6. If a competitive test is conducted, it should be done by an objective testing source, preferably an independent one, so that there will be no doubt as to the veracity of the test.
7. In all cases the test should be supportive of all claims made in the advertising that are based on the test.
8. The advertising should never use partial results or stress insignificant differences to cause the consumer to draw an improper conclusion.
9. The property being compared should be significant in terms of value or usefulness of the product to the consumer.
10. Comparatives delivered through the use of testimonials should not imply that the testimonial is more than one individual's thought unless that individual represents a sample of the majority viewpoint.

monthly publication called *Do's and Don'ts in Advertising Copy,* which provides ongoing information about advertising regulations and recent court and administrative rulings that affect advertising.[97] Since 1983, the National Advertising Division of the Council of Better Business Bureaus has published guidelines for advertising to children, a particularly sensitive area.

The National Advertising Review Council (NARC)

The **National Advertising Review Council (NARC)** was established in 1971 by the Council of Better Business Bureaus, the American Association of Advertising Agencies, the American Advertising Federation, and the Association of National Advertisers. Its primary purpose is to promote and enforce standards of truth, accuracy, taste, morality, and social responsibility in advertising.

NARC is one of the most comprehensive and effective mechanisms for regulating American advertising. A U.S. district court judge noted in a 1985 case that its "speed, informality, and modest cost," as well as its expertise, give NARC special advantages over the court system in resolving advertising disputes.[98]

NARC Operating Arms

The NARC has two operating arms: the **National Advertising Division (NAD)** of the Council of Better Business Bureaus and the **National Advertising Review Board (NARB).** The NAD monitors advertising practices and reviews complaints about advertising from consumers and consumer groups, brand competitors, local Better Business Bureaus, trade associations, and others. The appeals board for NAD decisions is the NARB, which consists of a chairperson and 70 volunteer members (39 national advertisers, 21 agency representatives, and 10 laypeople).

The NAD/NARB Review Process

To encourage consumers to register complaints, the NAD itself runs ads that include a complaint form. Most target untruthfulness or inaccuracy.

When the NAD finds a valid complaint, it contacts the advertiser, specifying any claims to be substantiated. If substantiation is inadequate, the NAD requests modification or discontinuance of the claims.

The case of the leather flight jacket shows how well the NAD process works. Neil Cooper LLC is a company that manufactures a leather jacket. In its print ads it claims that its A-2 leather flight jackets are the "official battle gear of U.S. Air Force Pilots." Avirex, Ltd., a competing company, complained to the NAD since the A-2 jacket currently being purchased by the Department of Defense and worn by U.S. pilots is the jacket manufactured by them, not Neil Cooper. Neil Cooper explained that, while it was not the current supplier, many pilots continued to buy from Neil Cooper directly because they preferred that product. Notwithstanding, the NAD sided with Avirex and recommended that Neil Cooper qualify its claims to make it clear that it is selling a reproduction of an authentic A-2 flight jacket rather than the current official jacket of the U.S. Air Force. Neil Cooper agreed.[99]

If the NAD and an advertiser reach an impasse, either party has the right to a review by a five-member NARB panel (consisting of three advertisers, one agency representative, and one layperson). The panel's decision is binding. If an advertiser refuses to comply with the panel's decision (which has never yet occurred), the NARB will refer the matter to an appropriate government body and so indicates in its public record. (For a flowchart of the NAD/NARB review process, see RL 2–5 in the Reference Library on the *Contemporary Advertising* CD-ROM.) Of 3,000 NAD investigations conducted between 1971 and 1990, only 70 were disputed and referred to the NARB for resolution.[100]

Regulation by the Media

Almost all media review ads and reject material they regard as objectionable, even if it isn't deceptive. Many people think the media are more effective regulators than the government.

Television

Of all media, the TV networks conduct the strictest review. Advertisers must submit all commercials intended for a network or affiliated station to its *broadcast standards* department. Many commercials (in script or storyboard form) are returned with suggestions for changes or greater substantiation. Some ads are rejected outright if they violate network policies. (See Ad Lab 3–C.)

The three major U.S. broadcast networks base their policies on the original National Association of Broadcasters Television Code. But network policies vary enough that it's difficult to prepare universally acceptable commercials. Cable networks and local stations tend to be much less stringent, as demonstrated by their acceptance of condom ads.

Radio

The 19 U.S. radio networks, unlike TV networks, supply only a small percentage of their affiliates' programming, so they have little or no say in what their affiliates advertise. A radio station is also less likely to return a script or tape for changes. Some stations, such as KLBJ in Austin, Texas, look mainly at whether the advertising is illegal, unethical, or immoral.[101] They don't want spots to offend listeners or detract from the rest of the programming.

Every radio station typically has its own unwritten guidelines. KDWB, a Minneapolis/St. Paul station with a large teenage audience, turned down a psychic who wanted to buy advertising time but did allow condom and other contraceptive ads.[102] KSDO in San Diego, a station with a business and information format, won't air commercials for X-rated movies or topless bars.[103]

To help consumers make informed decisions, Good Housekeeping *magazine tests the products in their ads and provides a seal of approval to those advertisers, such as Heat-N-Glo, who substantiate their claims. This gives the consumer a more authoritative voice to listen to when trying to decide on purchases.*

Editorial or Advertising: It's Adversarial

Pick up a glossy magazine such as *Vogue, Esquire,* or *Sports Illustrated* and you'll find it loaded with ads for cars, liquor, and cigarettes. Advertising agencies like buying space in these upscale publications as long as nothing in the publication directly offends their clients. Agencies are very protective of their clients, so they're careful about where their ads are placed. If an ad runs alongside a story that might reflect badly on the client's product or, even worse, might offend the client's customers, the ad agency will either pull the ad or request that the article be dropped. Moreover, agencies and their clients want to be warned ahead of time when a controversial story will appear. Increasingly, this is becoming a sore point with magazine editors and is creating an ethical stir in the industry. Editors see it as an assault on their independence and integrity. Advertisers see it as their responsibility to sponsor content suitable for, and not offensive to, their customers.

On the other hand, a survey sponsored by the Newspaper Advertising Association and the American Society of Magazine Editors discovered that newspaper ads actually meet consumer expectations better than the quality of news coverage. Consumers told the survey they believe newspaper ads are useful and relevant, saving them both time and money by allowing them to comparison shop at home. As a result, newspaper editors are now looking at expanding their partnership with advertisers.

"I think we need to have advertising and editorial work more closely together to produce a paper, especially since advertising has this solid local franchise," said *Washington Post* research chief Sharon P. Warden.

In the world of print media, publishers are the businesspeople who worry about the bottom line and editors worry about editorial content and journalistic integrity. Often their interests collide. To interest more advertisers, magazine publishers now create whole sections, sometime entire issues, devoted to *advertorials*—pages of commercial copy dressed up as news stories. Often it's difficult to differentiate between actual editorial copy and advertising text. *Sports Illustrated (SI)* publishes an annual special issue called *Golf Plus,* figuring that the 500,000-plus copies will generate higher interest from advertisers such as Foot Joy and Titleist golf balls.

Maxim Publications is one of a few remaining publications that separate the editorial and business sides of publications. Even so, advertisers with Maxim exert influence over the content that surrounds their ads by reminding editors of revenue loss if certain material is published. *Ms* magazine solved the conflict by going ad-free in 1990.

Print is not the only medium that falls under editorial scrutiny. Radio and TV are also constantly monitored for content. Some advertisers buying time on radio stations that air syndicated personalities such as Rush Limbaugh and Howard Stern specify "NO RUSH" and "NO HOWARD." Because of the shows' controversial content, they simply refuse to allow their ads to be placed there. Except for the news, television is taped in advance. Many advertisers can review episodes prior to airing and decide to pull the ads if necessary. (See Chapters 15 through 18 for more information on media buying.)

One Michigan homemaker was angered by sexual innuendoes on Fox's TV sitcom *Married . . . with Children.* So she persuaded Procter & Gamble and other leading advertisers not to buy time on the show. Similarly, many blue-chip advertisers shunned the police drama *NYPD Blue* on ABC because of scenes with partial nudity and blunt language—until it did too well in the ratings for them to ignore. During the coming-out episode of *Ellen* in 1997, many advertisers such as Chrysler pulled their spots. The spots, however, were quickly replaced by other sponsors eager to be part of a show that was expected to reach an unusually large audience.

"With TV, it's a case of supply and demand, and right now the demand for commercial time exceeds the supply," said Kevin Goldman, a former advertising columnist for *The Wall Street Journal.*

However, the case is not the same for magazines. "Magazines are different because there's a finite number of advertisers that want in on a particular book. If Chrysler pulls out of an issue, the pool of advertisers that might take its place is shallow," explained Goldman.

Moreover, magazines (especially new specialty magazines) increasingly tailor their editorial focus to reach niche audiences or a particular demographic. This narrows their options for ad dollars to those marketers targeting the same groups—in effect, giving greater influence to fewer advertisers.

Years ago, the American Society of Magazine Editors drew up guidelines on how magazines should distinguish advertising from regular editorial pages. In October 1996, The ASME released a three-paragraph "Standard for Editorial Independence" following a few episodes in which editors left magazines as a result of apparent interference from their corporate employers. The standard states, "Editors need the maximum possible protection from untoward commercial or extra-journalistic pressures. The chief editor of any magazine must have final authority over the editorial content, words and pictures, that appear in the publication."

Laboratory Applications

When is it okay for an advertiser to give its "editorial" view in a publication or on a show? Provide data to support your answers to the following questions.

1. To what degree, if any, should an advertiser exercise control over placement of its ads or content of the publication?
2. What effect, if any, could advertorials have on national problems such as age discrimination, racism, sexism, and teenage pregnancy? Be specific.

Magazines

National magazines monitor all advertising, especially by new advertisers and for new products. Newer publications eager to sell space may not be so vigilant, but established magazines, such as *Time* and *Newsweek,* are highly scrupulous. Many magazines will not accept advertising for certain types of products. The *New Yorker* won't run discount retail store advertising or ads for feminine hygiene or self-medication products. *Reader's Digest* won't accept tobacco ads.

Some magazines test every product before accepting the advertising. *Good Housekeeping* rejects ads if its tests don't substantiate the advertiser's claims. Products that pass are allowed to feature the Good Housekeeping "Seal of Approval."

Newspapers

Newspapers also monitor and review advertising. Larger newspapers have clearance staffs who read every ad submitted; most smaller newspapers rely on the advertising manager, sales personnel, or proofreaders.

The advertising policies set forth in *Newspaper Rates & Data* specify, "No objectionable medical, personal, matrimonial, clairvoyant, or palmistry advertising accepted; no stock promotion or financial advertising, other than those securities of known value." Another rule prohibits ads that might easily be mistaken for regular reading material unless they feature the word *advertisement* or *advt.*

In addition, most papers have their own acceptability guidelines, ranging from one page for small local papers to more than 50 pages for large dailies such as the *Los Angeles Times*. Some codes are quite specific. The *Detroit Free Press* won't accept classified ads containing such words as "affair" or "swinger." Some newspapers require advertisers who claim "the lowest price in town" to include a promise to meet or beat any price readers find elsewhere within 30 days.

One problem advertisers face is that newspapers' codes are far from uniform. Handgun ads may be prohibited by one newspaper, accepted by another if the guns are antique, and permitted by a third so long as the guns aren't automatic. And newspapers do revise their policies from time to time.

Regulation by Consumer Groups

Of all the regulatory forces governing advertising, consumer protection organizations have shown the greatest growth. Starting in the 1960s, the consumer movement became increasingly active in fighting fraudulent and deceptive advertising. Consumers demanded that products perform as advertised and that more product information be provided for people to compare and make better buying decisions. The consumer movement gave rise to **consumerism,** social action to dramatize the rights of the buying public. It is clear now that the U.S. consumer has the power to influence advertising practices dramatically.

Today, advertisers and agencies pay more attention to product claims, especially those related to energy use (such as the estimated miles per gallon of a new car) and the nutritional value of processed foods. Consumerism fostered the growth of consumer advocacy groups and regulatory agencies and promoted more consumer research by advertisers, agencies, and the media in an effort to learn what consumers want—and how to provide it. Investment in public goodwill pays off in improved consumer relations and sales.

Consumer Information Networks

Organizations such as the Consumer Federation of America (CFA), the National Council of Senior Citizens, the National Consumer League, and the National Stigma Clearinghouse exchange and disseminate information among members. These **consumer information networks** help develop state, regional, and local consumer organizations and work with national, regional, county, and municipal consumer groups.

Consumer interests also are served by private, nonprofit testing organizations such as Consumers Union, Consumers' Research, and Underwriters Laboratories.

Consumer Advocates

Consumer advocate groups investigate advertising complaints received from the public and those that grow out of their own research. If a complaint is warranted, they ask the advertiser to halt the objectionable ad or practice. If the advertiser does not comply, they release publicity or criticism about the offense to the media and submit complaints with substantiating evidence to appropriate government agencies for further action. In some instances, they file a lawsuit to obtain a cease-and-desist order, a fine, or other penalty against the violator.

Today, with so many special-interest advocacy groups, even the most sensitive advertisers feel challenged. To attract attention, advertising must be creative and stand out from competing noise. Yet advertisers fear attention from politically correct activists (the "PC police"). Calvin Klein ads were attacked by the Boycott Anorexic Marketing group. A Nike ad starring Porky Pig was protested by the National Stuttering Project in San Francisco. An animated public service spot from Aetna Insurance drew complaints from a witches' rights group.[104]

When the protests start flying, the ads usually get pulled. Steve Hayden, chair of BBDO Los Angeles, believes it would be possible to get any spot pulled with "about five letters that appear on the right stationery."[105] As Shelly Garcia noted in *Adweek,* "The way things are these days, nothing motivates middle managers like the need to avoid attention." She lamented the fact that "there are fewer and fewer opportunities to have any fun in advertising."[106]

Self-Regulation by Advertisers

Advertisers also regulate themselves. They have to. In today's competitive marketplace, consumer confidence is essential. Most large advertisers gather strong data to substantiate their claims. They maintain careful systems of advertising review to ensure that ads meet both their own standards and industry, media, and legal requirements. Many advertisers try to promote their social responsibility by tying in with a local charity or educational organization.

Many industries maintain advertising codes that companies agree to follow. These codes also establish a basis for complaints. However, industry advertising codes are only as effective as the enforcement powers of the individual trade associations. And because enforcement may conflict with antitrust laws, trade associations usually use peer pressure rather than hearings or penalties.

Self-Regulation by Ad Agencies and Associations

Most ad agencies monitor their own practices. Professional advertising associations also oversee members' activities to prevent problems that might trigger government intervention. Advertising publications report issues and court actions to educate agencies and advertisers and warn them about possible legal infractions.

Advertising Agencies

Although advertisers supply information about their product or service to their agencies, the agencies must research and verify product claims and comparative product data before using them in advertising. The media may require such documentation before accepting the advertising, and substantiation may be needed if government or consumer agencies challenge the claims.

Agencies can be held legally liable for fraudulent or misleading advertising claims. (See the Chapter 8 Ethical Issue, "A War of Comparisons.") For this reason, most major advertising agencies have in-house legal counsel and regularly submit their ads for review. If any aspect of the advertising is challenged, the agency asks its client to review the advertising and either confirm claims as truthful or replace unverified material.

Advertising Associations

Several associations monitor industrywide advertising practices. The **American Association of Advertising Agencies (AAAA),** an association of the largest advertising agencies throughout the United States, controls agency practices by denying membership to any agency judged unethical. The AAAA *Standards of Practice and Creative Code* set advertising principles for member agencies.

Exhibit 3–6

Advertising Principles of American Business of the American Advertising Federation (AAF).

1. *Truth.* Advertising shall tell the truth, and shall reveal significant facts, the omission of which would mislead the public.
2. *Substantiation.* Advertising claims shall be substantiated by evidence in possession of the advertiser and the advertising agency prior to making such claims.
3. *Comparisons.* Advertising shall refrain from making false, misleading, or unsubstantiated statements or claims about a competitor or his products or services.
4. *Bait advertising.* Advertising shall not offer products or services for sale unless such offer constitutes a bona fide effort to sell the advertised products or services and is not a device to switch consumers to other goods or services, usually higher priced.
5. *Guarantees and warranties.* Advertising of guarantees and warranties shall be explicit, with sufficient information to apprise consumers of their principal terms and limitations or, when space or time restrictions preclude such disclosures, the advertisement shall clearly reveal where the full text of the guarantee or warranty can be examined before purchase.
6. *Price claims.* Advertising shall avoid price claims that are false or misleading, or savings claims that do not offer provable savings.
7. *Testimonials.* Advertising containing testimonials shall be limited to those of competent witnesses who are reflecting a real and honest opinion or experience.
8. *Taste and decency.* Advertising shall be free of statements, illustrations, or implications that are offensive to good taste or public decency.

The **American Advertising Federation (AAF)** helped to establish the FTC, and its early vigilance committees were the forerunners of the Better Business Bureau. The AAF *Advertising Principles of American Business,* adopted in 1984, define standards for truthful and responsible advertising (see Exhibit 3–6). Since most local advertising clubs belong to the AAF, it is instrumental in influencing agencies and advertisers to abide by these principles.

The **Association of National Advertisers (ANA)** comprises 400 major manufacturing and service companies that are clients of member agencies of the AAAA. These companies, pledged to uphold the ANA code of advertising ethics, work with the ANA through a joint Committee for Improvement of Advertising Content.

The Ethical and Legal Aspects of Advertising in Perspective

Unquestionably, advertising offers considerable benefits to marketers and consumers alike. However, there's also no disputing that advertising has been and still is too often misused. As *Adweek* editor Andrew Jaffe says, the industry should do all it can to "raise its standards and try to drive out that which is misleading, untruthful, or downright tasteless and irresponsible." Otherwise, he warns, the pressure to regulate even more will become overwhelming.[107]

Advertising apologists point out that of all the advertising reviewed by the Federal Trade Commission in a typical year, 97 percent is found to be satisfactory.[108] In the end, advertisers and consumers need to work together to ensure that advertising is used intelligently, ethically, and responsibly for the benefit of all.

Chapter Summary

As one of the most visible activities of business, advertising is both lauded and criticized for the role it plays in selling products and influencing society. Some controversy surrounds advertising's role in the economy. To debate advertising's economic effects, we employ the four basic assumptions of free-enterprise economics: self-interest, many buyers and sellers, complete information, and absence of externalities.

The economic impact of advertising can be likened to the opening shot in billiards—a chain reaction that affects the company as well as its competitors, customers, and the business community. On a broader scale, advertising is often considered the trigger on a country's mass-distribution system, enabling manufacturers to pro-

duce the products people want in high volume, at low prices, with standardized quality. People may argue, though, about how advertising adds value to products, affects prices, encourages or discourages competition, promotes consumer demand, narrows or widens consumer choice, and affects business cycles.

Although controversy surrounds some of these economic issues, few dispute the abundance principle: In an economy that produces more goods and services than can be consumed, advertising gives consumers more complete information about the choices available to them, encourages more sellers to compete more effectively, and thereby serves the self-interest of both consumers and marketers.

Social criticisms of advertising may be short-term manipulative arguments or long-term macro arguments. While the economic aspect of advertising focuses on the free-enterprise principles of self-interest and many buyers and sellers, the social aspect typically involves the concepts of complete information and externalities.

Critics say advertising is deceptive; it manipulates people into buying unneeded products, it makes our society too materialistic, and there's just too much of it. Further, they say, advertising perpetuates stereotypes, and all too frequently, it is offensive and in bad taste.

Proponents admit that advertising is sometimes misused. However, they point out that despite its problems, advertising offers many social benefits. It encourages the development of new products and speeds their acceptance. It fosters employment, gives consumers and businesses a wider variety of product choices, and helps keep prices down by encouraging mass production. It stimulates healthy competition among companies and raises the overall standard of living. Moreover, sophisticated marketers know the best way to sell their products is to appeal to genuine consumer needs and be honest in their advertising claims.

In short, while advertising can be criticized for giving less than complete information and for creating some unwanted externalities, it also contributes to the free enterprise system by encouraging many buyers and sellers to participate in the process, thereby serving the self-interest of all.

Under growing pressure from consumers, special-interest groups, and government regulation, advertisers developed higher standards of ethical conduct and social responsibility. Advertisers confront three levels of ethical consideration: the primary rules of ethical behavior in society, their personal value system, and their personal philosophy of singular ethical concepts.

The federal and state courts are involved in several advertising issues, including First Amendment protection of commercial speech, and infringements on the right to privacy. Advertising is regulated by federal, state, and local government agencies, business-monitoring organizations, the media, consumer groups, and the advertising industry itself. All of these groups encourage advertisers to give more complete information to consumers and eliminate any externalities in the process.

The Federal Trade Commission, the major federal regulator of advertising in the United States, is responsible for protecting consumers and competitors from deceptive and unfair business practices. If the FTC finds an ad deceptive or unfair, it may issue a cease-and-desist order or require corrective advertising.

The Food and Drug Administration (FDA) monitors advertising for food and drugs and regulates product labels and packaging. The Federal Communications Commission (FCC) has jurisdiction over the radio and TV industries, although deregulation severely limited its control over advertising in these media. The Patent and Trademark Office governs ownership of U.S. trademarks, trade names, house marks, and similar distinctive features of companies and brands. The Library of Congress registers and protects copyrighted materials.

State and local governments also enact consumer protection laws that regulate advertising.

Nongovernment regulators include the Council of Better Business Bureaus and its National Advertising Division. The NAD, the most effective U.S. nongovernment regulatory body, investigates complaints from consumers, brand competitors, or local Better Business Bureaus and suggests corrective measures. Advertisers that refuse to comply are referred to the National Advertising Review Board (NARB), which may uphold, modify, or reverse the NAD's findings.

Other sources of regulation include the codes and policies of the print media and broadcast media. Consumer organizations and advocates also control advertising by investigating and filing complaints against advertisers and by providing information to consumers. Finally, advertisers and agencies regulate themselves.

Important Terms

affirmative disclosure, *83*

American Advertising Federation (AAF), *93*

American Association of Advertising Agencies (AAAA), *92*

Association of National Advertisers (ANA), *93*

Better Business Bureau (BBB), *87*

cease-and-desist order, *83*

Children's Advertising Review Unit (CARU), *78*

comparative advertising, *82*

consent decree, *83*

consumer advocates, *91*

consumer information networks, *91*

consumerism, *91*

cookies, *80*

copyright, *86*

corrective advertising, *83*

deceptive advertising, *81*

endorsements, *83*

ethical advertising, *71*

Federal Communications Commission (FCC), *85*

Federal Trade Commission (FTC), *81*

Food and Drug Administration (FDA), *84*

intellectual property, *86*

limen, *64*

long-term macro arguments, *62*

National Advertising Division (NAD), *88*

National Advertising Review Board (NARB), *88*

National Advertising Review Council (NARC), *88*

nonproduct facts, *63*

Nutritional Labeling and Education Act (NLEA), *85*

patent, *86*

primary demand, *61*

privacy rights, *79*

puffery, *63*

selective demand, *61*

short-term manipulative arguments, *62*

social responsibility, *71*

subliminal advertising, *64*

substantiation, *83*

testimonials, *83*

trademark, *86*

unfair advertising, *81*

U.S. Patent and Trademark Office, *86*

Review Questions

1. What role does advertising play in our economic system?

2. What are the two types of social criticisms of advertising?

3. What is puffery? Give some examples. Do you ever feel deceived by puffery in advertising?

4. Does advertising affect our value system? In what ways?

5. What is the difference between an advertiser's ethics and its social responsibility?

6. How does government regulation of advertising in the United States differ from regulation in many foreign countries?

7. How does commercial speech differ from political speech? Do you think advertisers should have the same First Amendment rights as everyone else? Explain.

8. What is the role of the FTC in advertising? Do you think this role should be expanded or restricted?

9. How do regional and local governments affect advertisers?

10. How well do advertisers regulate themselves? In what areas do you think advertisers have done well, and where should they clean up their act?

11. **The Advertising Experience**

   In order to understand better a technique, even a questionable one, it is sometimes best to have practiced it oneself. Take a common product and create a responsible advertisement for it. Next, puff the ad up using the techniques studied in the chapter. Be prepared to discuss the differences between the advertisements and how the puffery affects consumer perception.

Exploring the Internet

The Internet exercises for Chapter 3 address three areas of advertising covered in the chapter: advertising law, government regulation of advertising, and ethical self-regulation.

1. **Advertising Law**

   As you learned in this chapter, advertisers and their agencies are held accountable for the work they produce and must know the law(s) governing their communication. Understanding the legal ramifications behind a piece of communication is critical to any advertiser.

   Therefore, finding ways to keep abreast of the latest cases/issues relating to advertising law and the implications thereof is of the utmost importance to advertising practitioners. Visit the advertising law firm Hall Dickler Kent Goldstein & Wood site (www.adlaw.com) and the Advertising Law Resource Center (www.lawpublish.com), and then discuss the following:

   a. Review the documents/articles at these sites and discuss the fundamental principles behind advertising law, including substantiation, deception, and unfairness.

   b. Choose one article/discussion or one case study in Lewis Rose's archives and illustrate its importance to advertisers and their agencies.

   c. Discuss the value these websites provide the advertising community, with special emphasis on local advertisers.

2. **Regulation of Advertising**

   The FTC's Division of Advertising Practices protects consumers from deceptive and unsubstantiated advertising. Apply what you have learned by visiting the division's website (www.ftc.gov) and answering the following questions. (You may want to review the policies and guides found at www.ftc.gov/bcp/guides/guides.htm.)

   a. Give a general description of what the FTC considers to be deceptive and unfair advertising.

   b. Describe the requirements for substantiating advertising and the process advertisers and their agencies must undergo to do so.

   c. Choose a fourth topic covered on the site and discuss its relevance and importance to the advertising industry.

   Be sure to check out the following sites that are also related to the regulation of the advertising industry:

   ■ Council of Better Business Bureaus' National Advertising Division (NAD) www.nadreview.org

   ■ Consumers International www.consumersinternational.org

   ■ European Commission europa.eu.int

3. **Pushing the Limits of Legality**

   Although the Internet may seem borderless and boundless, the FTC does work to enforce consumer protection laws online. However, violations may occur, especially in the online advertising campaigns of recently founded dot-coms. Visit www.ftc.gov/bcp/conline/pubs/buspubs/dotcom for an overview of developments in Internet advertising regulation. Then find two websites you believe to be making inflated claims. Discuss in detail how the sites exaggerate their products. Using the FTC's guidelines, note which claims are legal, even if exaggerated, and which claims have crossed the line legally.

Chapter 4

The Scope of Advertising: From Local to Global

Objectives

TO INTRODUCE THE PEOPLE AND GROUPS WHO SPONSOR, CRE-
ATE, PRODUCE, AND RUN ADVERTISING HERE AND ABROAD.
Advertising people may serve in a variety of roles. This chapter discusses the basic
tasks of both the client and the advertising agency, the roles of suppliers and the
media, the way agencies acquire clients and are compensated, and the overall relationship between the agency and the client.

After studying this chapter, you will be able to:

- **Describe** the various groups in the advertising business and explain their
  relationship to one another.

- **Explain** how advertisers organize themselves to manage their advertising
  both here and abroad.

- **Define** the main types of advertising agencies.

- **Explain** the range of tasks people perform in an ad agency and an in-house
  advertising department.

- **Discuss** how agencies get new clients and how they make money.

- **Debate** the pros and cons of an in-house advertising agency.

- **Discuss** factors that affect the client/agency relationship.

- **Explain** how suppliers and the media help advertisers and agencies.

To get to the heartbeat of the market for her clients, Shelley Yamane spends much of her time talking directly with consumers. She works as a strategic planner at Muse Cordero Chen and Partners, an agency that focuses on multicultural communications—specifically the African-American, Asian, and Latino markets in the United States. ■ Now close to twenty years old, the Los Angeles-based shop has been one of the fastest growing ethnic agencies in the country and boasts a team of 45 employees who speak some 12 different languages and represent over 15 ethnicities. Muse Cordero Chen represents such plum accounts as Nike, Honda, and AT&T Wireless, and has garnered innumerable awards for its sometimes edgy, always creative work. ■ When the client approached the agency with the task of creating a new African-American campaign for the Honda Civic, it was Shelley's job to research the market and develop some strategic alternatives. But in the process, Shelley began to notice a trend, and, after further study, it had a dramatic effect on the agency's approach. ■ What she discerned was that in the urban market African-American consumers were only one faction of a considerably larger group that was already buying the Civic. ■ An entirely new target market was surfacing: one that was geographically concentrated and similar in age, lifestyle, and attitude. What characterized them was not their ethnicity, but that they were all young and urban, and they loved fixing up their cars. ■ When Honda first introduced the Civic over a quarter century ago, it was seen as something of a pioneer. Its low emissions and high gas mileage made it a frontrunner in its category. But over time, as competing manufacturers began to offer similarly priced alternatives, the Civics' market share suffered, and its image began to fade in the minds of the general car buying public. They started looking at it as a family's second car. ■ At the same time, though, something very quiet, but very exciting, was happening. Droves of young urbanites, attracted to the car's quality, low price, and simple, customizable design, were starting to buy Civics, and they were spending a great deal of time and energy personalizing their vehicles. They took pride in their work and began to share that pride with other Civic drivers. ■ Soon, all over the country, communities of young, urban Civic owners were gathering in ad hoc venues to trade ideas and show off their tricked out cars, and in time this became an actual subculture. ■ What Shelley had discovered was the birth of a new group of people. A Civic Nation. ■

The Advertising Industry

The range of work performed by advertising people goes far beyond what we see daily on TV. In fact, that's barely the tip of the iceberg. Moreover, many people and organizations besides those usually thought of as advertising folks are involved in the advertising business. That's because every successful company needs to advertise.

The Organizations in Advertising

The advertising business has evolved into four distinct groups. The two main ones are the *advertisers* and the *agencies.* The advertisers (or clients) are the companies—like Honda, Coca-Cola, or the local shoe store—that sponsor advertising for themselves and their products. Advertisers range in size from small independent businesses to huge multinational firms, and in type from service organizations to industrial manufacturers to local charities and political action committees. The second group, *advertising agencies,* assists the advertisers to plan, create, and prepare ad campaigns and other promotional materials.

A third group, the *suppliers,* includes the photographers, illustrators, printers, digital service bureaus, color film separators, video production houses, Internet Web developers, and others who assist both advertisers and agencies in preparing advertising materials. Suppliers also include consultants, research firms, and professional services that work with both advertisers and agencies. The fourth group, the *media,* sell time (on radio and TV) and space (in print, outdoor, and digital media) to carry the advertiser's message to the target audience.

The People in Advertising

When most people think of advertising, they imagine the copywriters and art directors who work for ad agencies. But the majority of people in advertising are actually employed by the advertisers. Most companies have an advertising department, even if it's just one person.

In addition, many other people work for the suppliers and the media. They're in advertising, too. The fact is, advertising is a very broad field that employs a wide variety of people in sales, research, management, accounting, computer science, and law, as well as specialists in the various communication arts—artists, writers, photographers, musicians, performers, and cinematographers.

In this chapter, we'll see what all these people do at the various venues where they work. In the process, we'll get a good understanding of how the business operates both in the United States and abroad.

Local advertisers such as Rubio's Baja Grill (www.bajagrill.com) must find ways to differentiate their products from the competition—and then create awareness through advertising. Already a hit with its fish tacos, Rubio's uses this tabletop point-of-purchase card to inform restaurant patrons that it has more to offer than just fish.

The Advertisers (The Clients)

While every company has some sort of advertising department, its importance depends on the size of the company, the type of industry it operates in, the size of the advertising program, the role advertising plays in the company's marketing mix, and most of all, the involvement of top management.

To get a sense of the diversity of companies that advertise, we'll look first at local advertisers to see how they operate. Then, we'll examine the regional and national advertisers. Finally we'll look at the companies that market their products in foreign countries.

Local Advertising: Where the Action Is

Not long after graduating from San Diego State, Ralph Rubio opened his first Mexican restaurant. He offered an unusual specialty: fish tacos—lightly battered and fried whitefish served in soft-shelled corn tortillas with white sauce, salsa, cabbage, and a wedge of lime. At the time, very few other Mexican eateries offered fish tacos, and none featured them. So Rubio found fish tacos hard to sell, even with his secret batter recipe (which he'd gotten from a street vendor in San Felipe, Mexico). The first month's sales at the restaurant averaged only $163 a day.

Rubio started using small newspaper ads with coupons to lure courageous customers. It worked. As business picked up, he expanded his advertising to radio and TV, targeting his market further with ads on Hispanic stations (whose listeners knew what fish tacos were). And he went after younger, venturesome customers ages 18 to 34 by advertising at local movie theaters. Business picked up some more. Rubio soon opened another restaurant, and then another.

With each new opening, Rubio distributed direct-mail flyers in the area and took free samples to nearby stores. Working with an artist, he created a cartoon character named Pesky Pescado based on the fish taco. He purchased a 15-foot inflatable Pesky to display at his restaurants. Employee T-shirts sported Pesky's picture, and Rubio sold Pesky T-shirts and sweatshirts to enthusiastic patrons. He also offered bumper stickers and antenna balls to add some fun to his promotions. To further integrate his activities, Rubio took an active part in community affairs, including tie-ins with a blood bank, a literacy program, and fundraising activities for both a Tijuana medical clinic and a local university's athletic program.

As the popularity of the fish taco grew, so did Rubio's revenues, doubling every year for the first five years. He trademarked the phrase "Rubio's, Home of the Fish Taco," and a local restaurant critic, commenting on things San Diegans couldn't do without, called fish tacos "the food San Diegans would miss the most." After 19 years, Rubio had 137 restaurants in five states. Together they produced more than $112 million in annual sales. And by the year 2002, Rubio's had served more than 45 million fish tacos.[1]

Every year, advertisers spend billions of dollars in the United States. Almost half of that is spent on **local advertising** by local businesses in a particular city or county targeting customers in their geographic area.

Local advertising is sometimes called *retail advertising* because so much is placed by retail stores. But retail advertising isn't always local; Sears and JCPenney advertise nationally. And many businesses besides retail stores use local advertising: banks, real estate developers, movie theaters, auto mechanics, plumbers, radio and TV stations, funeral homes, museums, and local politicians, to name a few.

Local advertising is critically important because most consumer sales are made (or lost) locally. An auto manufacturer may spend millions advertising new cars nationwide, but if its dealers don't make a strong effort locally, the dollars will be wasted. When it comes to making the sale and dealing with customers, local advertising is where the action is—where relationships often start and truly develop.

Specialty businesses or organizations use their uniqueness to their advantage, as seen in this nostalgic ad from the National Jazz Museum (www.jazzmuseuminharlem.org).

Types of Local Advertisers

There are four main types of local advertisers.

- Dealers or local franchisees of national companies that specialize in one main product line or service (Honda, Wendy's, Mail Boxes Etc., Kinko's, H&R Block).
- Stores that sell a variety of branded merchandise, usually on a nonexclusive basis (convenience, grocery, and department stores).
- Specialty businesses and services (banks, insurance brokers, restaurants, music stores, shoe-repair shops, remodeling contractors, florists, hair salons, travel agencies, attorneys, accountants).
- Governmental, quasigovernmental, and nonprofit organizations (municipalities, utility companies, charities, arts organizations, political candidates).

A small, local business—say, a hardware, clothing, or electronics store—may have just one person in charge of advertising. That person, the advertising manager, performs all the administrative, planning, budgeting, and coordinating functions. He or she may lay out ads, write ad copy, and select the media. A manager with some artistic talent may even design the actual ads and produce them on a desktop computer.

Chain stores often maintain a completely staffed advertising department to handle production, media placement, and marketing support services. The department needs artists, copywriters, and production specialists. The department head usually reports to a vice president or marketing manager, as shown in Exhibit 4–1.

Types of Local Advertising

Most of the ads placed in local media are product, institutional, or classified advertising. Each type serves a different purpose.

Product advertising   **Product advertising** promotes a specific product or service and stimulates short-term action while building awareness of the business. Three major types of product ads are used by local advertisers: regular price-line, sale, and clearance. **Regular price-line advertising** informs consumers about

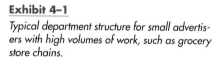

Exhibit 4–1

Typical department structure for small advertisers with high volumes of work, such as grocery store chains.

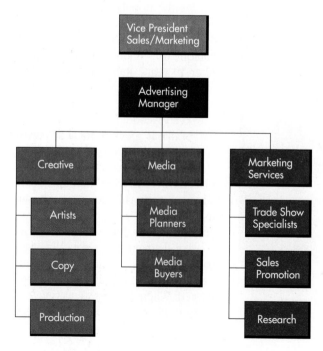

A business that sells locally promotes its company's identity in a variety of ways—such as this distinctly ethnic poster from Ah Umakatta, a cafe in New York.

services or merchandise offered at regular prices. An accounting firm might use regular price-line advertising to promote its accounting and tax services.

To stimulate sales of particular merchandise or increase store traffic, local merchants occasionally use **sale advertising,** placing items on sale and offering two-for-one specials or other deals. Local advertisers use **clearance advertising** (a special form of sale advertising) to make room for new product lines or new models and to get rid of slow-moving lines, floor samples, broken or distressed merchandise, or out-of-season items. Companies going out of business also use clearance advertising.

Institutional advertising **Institutional advertising** attempts to create a favorable long-term perception of the business as a whole, not just of a particular product or service. Many types of businesses (stores, restaurants, banks, professional firms, hospitals) use institutional advertising to promote an *idea* about the company and build long-term goodwill. It makes the public aware of what the business stands for and attempts to build reputation and image. An institutional ad might focus on convenient hours, a new credit policy, store expansion, or company philosophy.

Although readership is often lower, effective institutional ads build a favorable image for the business, attract new customers, and encourage customer loyalty.

Classified advertising Advertisers use **classified advertising** in the newspaper for a variety of reasons: to locate and recruit new employees, offer services (such as those of an employment agency or business opportunity broker), or sell or lease new and used merchandise (such as cars, real estate, and office equipment).

Local Advertisers: The Original Integrators

When Ralph Rubio built his restaurant business, his promotional activities involved a lot more than just running ads in the media. In fact, he did everything he could to develop a *relationship* with his customers and to promote good word-of-mouth. That meant using publicity, sales promotion, and direct response as well as media advertising—all integrated with consistently good food, reasonable prices, and excellent service. This combination constitutes **integrated marketing communications (IMC)**—joining together in a consistent manner everything that communicates with customers. Thanks to IMC, Rubio's fish taco became a local staple.

Local advertisers and the local agencies that serve them are not stuck with the traditional national view that advertising means "ads placed in the media." By necessity, local advertisers wear many hats every day. They tend the cash register, deal with customers, prepare mailers, write and place ads, evaluate suppliers' trade promotions, answer phone inquiries, spruce up the office, talk to newspaper editors, coordinate the graphics on premiums for a seasonal promotion. By successfully combining personal selling with media advertising, direct marketing, sales promotion, and public relations, the local advertiser can be the consummate integrator of marketing communications.[2]

Creating Local Advertising

Cal Worthington first pitched his car dealership on Los Angeles TV stations in 1951 and 50 years later, he's still at it. He sponsors third-rate movies on late-night and Saturday afternoon TV. In his zany ads, he often appears in cowboy garb with a variety of domesticated wild animals, all introduced as "my dog Spot." Some low-budget, do-it-yourself advertisers like Worthington are so successful they engender a near-cult following. Others who try the same approach fail miserably.

In print advertising, many local advertisers achieve remarkable success with what professionals would call a *schlock* approach—heavy bold type, items crowded into ad space, loud headlines, and unsophisticated graphic design. If the message is honest, consistent, and effective and meets the advertiser's objectives, that may be all that matters. To direct and control the creative aspects of their ads and commercials and ensure consistency, local advertisers should develop a checklist of creative do's and don'ts. (See the Checklist, "Creating Local Advertising" on page 102.)

Creating Local Advertising

____ *Stand out from the competition.* Make your ads easily recognizable. Ads with unusual art, layout, and typefaces have higher readership. Make the ads distinctive but keep their appearance consistent.

____ *Use a simple layout.* The layout should carry the reader's eye through the message easily and in proper sequence from headline to illustration to explanatory copy to price to store name. Avoid using too many typefaces.

____ *Use a dominant element.* A large picture or headline ensures quick visibility. Photos of real people and action pictures win more readership, as do photos of local people or places. Color attracts more readers.

____ *Stress the benefits.* Present the emotional reason to buy or the tangible performance element customers seek.

____ *Make the headline count.* Use a compelling headline to feature the main benefit.

____ *Watch your language.* Make your writing style active, lively, and involving. Make the readers feel they already own the product. Avoid negativism and profanity.

____ *Let white space work for you.* White space focuses the reader's attention and makes the headline and illustration stand out.

____ *Make the copy complete.* Emphasize the benefits most appealing to customers.

____ *Make your visual powerful and eye-catching.* Make sure it demonstrates your message. The main visual is often more important than the headline. Photos work better than artwork.

____ *State price or range of prices.* Dollar figures have good attention value, and readers often overestimate omitted prices. Spell out credit and layaway plans.

____ *Specify branded merchandise.* If the item is a known brand, say so.

____ *Include related items.* Make two sales instead of one by offering related items along with a featured one.

____ *Urge readers to buy now.* Ask for the sale. Stimulate prompt action by using "limited supply" or "this week only."

____ *Don't forget the store name and address.* Check every ad to be certain the store name, address, phone number, and hours are included.

____ *Don't be too clever.* Many people distrust or misunderstand cleverness.

____ *Don't use unusual or difficult words.* Everyone understands simple language. Use it.

____ *Don't generalize.* Be specific. Shoppers want all the facts before they buy.

____ *Don't make excessive claims.* Advertisers lose customers when they make claims they can't back up.

____ *Plan ad size carefully.* Attention usually increases with size.

____ *Consider your target customers.* People notice ads more if they are directed at their own gender or age group.

____ *Use tie-ins* with local or special news events.

Finding big ideas for local ad campaigns can be extremely difficult. Some advertisers look to the merchandise for ideas; others look to the customer. An important goal for local advertisers is to achieve a consistent, distinctive look that makes their ads both appealing and identifiable. We discuss the creative process in depth in Part Four.

Local advertisers can turn to a number of sources for creative help, including reps from the local media, local ad agencies, freelancers and consultants, creative boutiques, syndicated art services, and the *cooperative advertising programs* of wholesalers, manufacturers, and trade associations.

Cooperative Advertising

As a service to their distributors and dealers, and to ensure proper reproduction of their products, wholesalers and manufacturers as well as some trade associations often provide local advertisers with ready-made advertising materials and cooperative advertising programs where the costs are shared.

There are two key purposes for **cooperative (co-op) advertising:** to build the manufacturer's brand image and to help its distributors, dealers, or retailers make more sales.[3] Every year, national manufacturers give their local retailers more than $20 billion for co-op projects. Newspapers, network and cable TV, and radio are the favored media of co-op spending, with newspapers claiming 55 percent of co-op dollars.[4] Intel alone spends more than $800 million annually to help PC marketers who display the "Intel Inside" logo.[5]

In **vertical cooperative advertising,** the manufacturer provides the complete ad and shares the cost of the advertising time or space. The local newspaper sets the name and address of the local advertiser, or the radio station adds a tagline with the advertiser's name, address, and phone number. Exhibit 4–2 lists typical co-op advertising allowances. (See Ad Lab 4–A for the pros and cons of co-op advertising.)

Exhibit 4–2

The importance of co-op advertising dollars.

Store	Co-op dollars as a percentage of total ad budget
Appliance dealers	80%
Clothing stores	35
Department stores	50
Discount stores	20
Drugstores	70
Food stores	75
Furniture stores	30
Household goods	30
Jewelers	30
Shoe stores	50

The Co-op Marriage

On the surface, cooperative advertising seems like a great arrangement for retailers. A manufacturer supplies advertising materials (saving the retailer production costs) and pays a percentage of the media cost. The retailer drops in the store's logo, arranges for the ad to run, and collects the co-op dollars from the manufacturer. The small retail business can stretch its ad budget and associate its business with a nationally advertised product. The retailer receives professionally prepared ads and acquires greater leverage with the local media that carry the co-op ads.

But as with any marriage, there is give and take.

A retailer may have to sell a lot of merchandise to qualify for significant co-op funds. More often, the retailer and manufacturer have different advertising objectives and different ideas about how the ads should be executed.

The manufacturer often wants total control. The manufacturer expects co-op ads to tie in with its national advertising promotions. It wants the right product advertised at the right time. Manufacturers prepare guideline pamphlets specifying when and where the ads should appear, what form they should take, and what uses of the name and logo are not allowed.

Retailers have their own ideas about which products to advertise when. They're more concerned with daily volume and with projecting an image of value and variety. An appliance store might prefer to advertise inexpensive TVs even though the manufacturer wants to emphasize its top-of-the-line models.

Manufacturers worry that retailers will place the product in a cluttered, ugly ad or next to inferior products; that the ad will run in inappropriate publications; and that it will not run at the best time. Retailers counter that they know the local market better. In short, manufacturers think they don't have enough control; retailers think they have too much.

A retailer contemplating co-op funds should consider the following questions:

- What requirements must be met in order for ads to qualify for co-op money?
- What percentage is paid by each party?
- When can ads be run?
- What media can be used?
- Are there special provisions for message content?
- What documentation is required for reimbursement?
- How does each party benefit?
- Do cooperative ads obscure the retailer's image?

Laboratory Applications

1. Look through today's edition of a daily paper in your city. Identify two ads that can qualify as co-op. Do the ads fit both the store's image and the manufacturer's image? Explain.

2. A store may develop its own ad and drop in the manufacturer's logo or it may take an ad created by the manufacturer and simply add the store's location. Which do your two ads do?

With **horizontal cooperative advertising,** firms in the same business (real estate agents, insurance agents, pharmacies, car dealers, or travel agents) or in the same part of town advertise jointly. Competing auto dealers, for example, might pool their dollars to advertise their common retail area as the "Mile of Cars."

Regional and National Advertisers

Some companies operate in one part of the country—in one or several states—and market exclusively within that region. These are referred to as **regional advertisers.** Typical examples include regional grocery and department store chains, governmental bodies (such as state lotteries), franchise groups (such as the Southern California Honda dealers), telephone companies (such as SBC), and statewide or multistate banks (Bank of America).

Other companies sell in several regions or throughout the country and are called **national advertisers.** These include the consumer packaged-goods manufacturers (such as Procter & Gamble and Johnson & Johnson), national airlines (Delta, American), media and entertainment companies (Disney, Time Warner), electronics manufacturers (Apple, Hewlett-Packard), and all the auto companies. These firms also make up the membership of the **Association of National Advertisers (ANA)** and comprise the largest advertisers in the country (see Exhibit 4–3).

How National and Local Advertisers Differ

The basic principles of advertising are the same in both local and national advertising. However, local advertisers have special challenges stemming from the day-to-day realities of running a small business. As a result, local and national advertisers differ in terms of focus, time orientation, and resources (see Exhibit 4–4).

Exhibit 4–3

Top 10 advertisers in the United States ranked by total U.S. advertising in 2003 (figures in millions of U.S. dollars).

Rank	Company	U.S. ad spending
1.	General Motors Co.	$3,430
2.	Procter & Gamble	3,323
3.	Time Warner	3,097
4.	Pfizer	2,839
5.	DaimlerChrysler	2,318
6.	Ford Motor Co.	2,234
7.	Walt Disney Co.	2,129
8.	Johnson & Johnson	1,996
9.	Sony Corp.	1,815
10.	Toyota Motor Corp.	1,683

Exhibit 4–4

Differences between local and national advertisers.

	National	**Local**
Focus	Brand Market share Strategies Markets	Point Volume, gross sales Tactics Customers
Time	Long-term campaigns	Short-term ads
Resources	$5–$10 million+ Many specialists	Less than $1 million A few generalists

Focus National companies are concerned about building their brands, so their advertising tends to focus on the competitive features of one brand over another, especially in conquest sales situations. Local merchants or dealers often carry hundreds of different brands or numerous models of an exclusive brand, so they focus on attracting customers to a particular **point**—their place of business. That's why local car dealers typically advertise their dealerships rather than the make of car. And local grocers often promote only those brands for which they receive co-op advertising or trade allowances from the national manufacturer.

In every product category, big companies battle for market share against a few competitors, and every share point is worth millions of dollars. Local advertisers compete with many companies, so their focus is on gross sales or volume: 60 cars a month, five new insurance policies a week, 55 oil changes a day.

National advertisers plan *strategically* to launch, build, and sustain brands. Local advertisers think *tactically*. Will a new $15,000 sign bring more people into the store? Should we stay open Labor Day? Can we attract more lunchtime customers by reducing our prices or by offering free refills on soft drinks?

The relationship with the customer may be the greatest difference between national and local advertisers. National advertisers' marketing executives rarely see retail customers; instead, they traditionally think in terms of large groups of people—segments, niches, target markets—with various geographic, demographic, or psychographic descriptions. They design their strategies and campaigns to appeal to these large groups.

But local advertisers deal with individual customers every day. They (and their families) also interact with their customers in nonbusiness ways; they may be neighbors, friends, or schoolmates. The local advertiser gets feedback every day—

There are many ways to approach local advertising. Here, the Academy of Magic Arts humorously plays off of the "saw the woman in half" trick—this time with the admissions receptionist.

Companies that sell their products or services throughout the country are called national advertisers. Unlike their local counterparts, national advertisers plan strategically to launch, build, and sustain brands. A company like Dunkin' Donuts (www.dunkindonuts.com) targets large demographic groups and is concerned with issues of market share and brand equity. This ad creatively demonstrates the quality of Dunkin' Donuts coffee—it's so good, "you just can't wait."

on the company's advertising, prices, product performance, employee service, store decor, and the new sign out front. The national marketer gets occasional feedback—from surveys and from customer complaint lines.

Time orientation   Due to differences in their focus and perspective, national and local advertisers also have a different time orientation. National companies think long term. They develop five-year strategic plans and budget for annual advertising campaigns. Local advertisers worry that this week's ad in the *Pennysaver* didn't *pull* (a term rarely used by national marketers) as well as last week's; a New York advertiser may have months to develop a network TV campaign; the little market on Main Street may have to churn out a new newspaper ad every week to reach its local customers.

Resources   Finally, national advertisers have more resources available—both money and people. A local advertiser that spends $100,000 a year has a relatively large budget. A national advertiser needs to spend at least $5 million a year just to get started. (Walt Disney, by the way, spends $2.1 *billion*.)[6]

The national advertiser has an army of specialists dedicated to the successful marketing of its brands. The local advertiser may have a small staff or just one person—the owner—to market the business. So the local entrepreneur has to know more about every facet of marketing communications.

How Large Companies Manage Their Advertising

In large companies, many people are involved in the advertising function. Company owners and top corporate executives make key advertising decisions; sales and marketing personnel often assist in the creative process, help choose the ad agency, and evaluate proposed ad programs; artists and writers produce ads, brochures, and other materials; product engineers and designers give input to the creative process and provide information about competitive products; administrators evaluate the cost of ad campaigns and help plan budgets; and clerical staff coordinate various promotional activities, including advertising.

A large company's advertising department may employ many people and be headed by an advertising manager who reports to a marketing director or marketing services manager. The exact department structure depends on many variables. Most large advertisers tend to use some mix of two basic management structures: *centralized* and *decentralized*.

Centralized organization   Companies are concerned with cost efficiency and continuity in their communications programs. Thus, many embrace the **centralized advertising department** because it gives the greatest control and offers both efficiency and continuity across divisional boundaries. In centralized departments, an advertising manager typically reports to a marketing vice president. But beyond this one feature, companies may organize the department in any of five ways:

- By product or brand.
- By subfunction of advertising (copy, art, print production, media buying).
- By end user (consumer advertising, trade advertising).
- By media (radio, TV, newspapers, outdoor).
- By geography (western advertising, eastern advertising, European advertising).

The cereal giant General Mills, for example, is one of the nation's largest advertisers. It operates a vast advertising and marketing services department with some 350 employees. It spends more than $555 million annually in media advertising and other promotional activities.[7]

General Mills' Marketing Services is really many departments within a department. Its centralized structure enables it to administer, plan, and coordinate the promotion of more than 60 brands. It also supervises five outside ad agencies and operates its own in-house agency for new or smaller brands.[8]

Organized around functional specialties (market research, media, graphics), Marketing Services helps General Mills' brand managers consolidate many of their expenditures for maximum efficiency. The media department, for example, prepares all media plans for the marketing divisions. The production and art department designs the packages for all brands and the graphics for the company's in-house agency. From one spot, Marketing Services handles a wide variety of brands efficiently and effectively (see Exhibit 4–5).

Decentralized organization   As some companies become larger, diversify their product line, acquire subsidiaries, and establish divisions in different regions or even different countries, a centralized advertising department often becomes impractical.

In a **decentralized system,** the company sets up separate ad departments for different divisions, subsidiaries, regions, brands, or other categories that suit the company's needs. The general manager of each division or brand is responsible for that group's advertising.

For large companies with many divisions, decentralized advertising is more flexible. Campaigns and media schedules can be adjusted faster. New approaches and creative ideas can be introduced more easily, and sales results can be measured independently of other divisions. In effect, each division is its own marketing department, with the advertising manager reporting to the division head (see Exhibit 4–6).

A drawback, though, is that decentralized departments often concentrate on their own budgets, problems, and promotions rather than the good of the whole company. Across divisions, ads typically lack uniformity, diminishing the power of repetitive corporate advertising. Rivalry among brand managers may even escalate into unhealthy competition or deteriorate into secrecy and jealousy.

Transnational Advertisers

Companies advertising abroad typically face markets with different value systems, environments, and languages. Their customers have different purchasing abilities, habits, and motivations. Media customary to U.S. and Canadian advertisers may be unavailable or ineffective. The companies will therefore likely need different advertising strategies. But they face a more basic problem: How should they manage and produce the advertising? Should their U.S. agency or in-house advertising

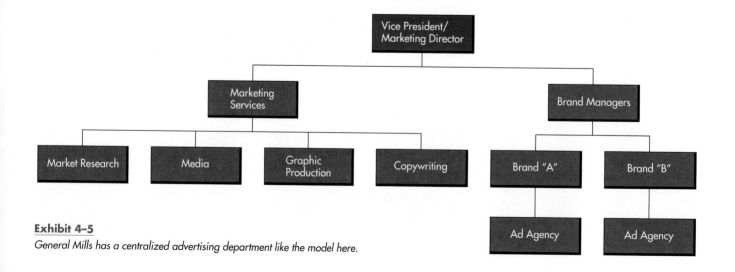

Exhibit 4–5

General Mills has a centralized advertising department like the model here.

Exhibit 4–6

In a decentralized department, each division is its own marketing department.

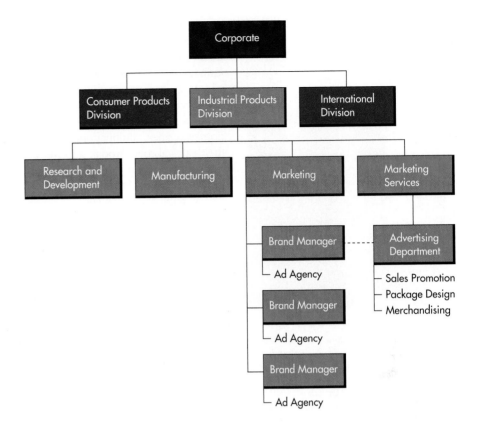

department do it? Should they use a foreign agency or set up a local advertising department?

As advertisers break into new international markets, they may start by simply exporting their existing products. At first, the home office controls all foreign marketing and advertising. Everything is centralized. Then, as companies get more involved in foreign markets, they may form joint ventures or invest in foreign sales offices, warehouses, plants, and other facilities. Advertisers typically view such operations as foreign marketing divisions and use a decentralized **international structure,** in which the divisions are responsible for their own product lines, marketing operations, and profits, and create customized advertising for each market.[9]

Procter & Gamble, for example, is a 167-year-old company with annual sales of $50 billion. It sells more than 300 consumer brands to more than five billion consumers in 160 countries. These brands include such market leaders as Tide, Ivory soap, Pampers, Folgers, Pringles, and Crest toothpaste.[10]

P&G is one of the biggest and most influential consumer advertisers in the world; its expenditures in the United States alone exceed $3.3 billion annually. But more than half its sales come from abroad.[11] Each overseas division is set up almost like a separate company with its own research and development department, manufacturing plant, advertising department, sales force, and finance and accounting staff. Every brand within a division has a **brand manager** who oversees a brand group and directs his or her own ad agency to create the brand's media advertising. Brand managers work under a marketing manager, who reports to a *category manager.*[12]

Each division also has an advertising department to help coordinate sales promotion and merchandising programs across brands. The corporate advertising department provides statistical information and guidance.

While the brand manager's primary goal is to use advertising and promotion to build market share, the category manager focuses on sharpening overall strategy

With an international structure, advertisers' local divisions are responsible for their own product lines and create customized ads for each market. This Heinz ketchup (www.heinz.com) ad was created by Leo Burnett Group, Copenhagen, and only ran in Denmark. The translation: "The only American you can hit without being sued."

and building profits.[13] In recent years, P&G has streamlined the system by eliminating extra layers of management and redundant facilities. This commits to each brand the single-minded drive needed for success and gives more authority to the individual responsible for the brand.[14]

As companies continue to grow and prosper around the world, they may invest directly in many countries. True **multinational corporations** strive for full, integrated participation in world markets.[15] Foreign sales often grow faster than domestic sales. Multinationals such as Exxon and IBM earn about 50 percent of their sales abroad; Kodak and Xerox, about 25 percent. Typically, the top 25 U.S. multinational corporations earn more than 40 percent of their revenues and two-thirds of their profits overseas.[16]

A multinational usually exerts strong centralized control over all its marketing activities. Multinational firms such as Kodak get strong direction and coordination from headquarters and have a standardized product line and marketing structure.

Multinationals that use a *standardized approach* to marketing and advertising in all countries are **global marketers,** and they create global brands. Their assumption is that the way the product is used and the needs it satisfies are universal.[17] Max Factor, for example, markets its cosmetics globally. In the 1990s, it ran a campaign aimed at making the brand more relevant by using a variety of strong, contemporary, self-confident women. The campaign drew favorable reactions from women worldwide.[18] Other global advertisers include Coca-Cola, British Airways, British Petroleum, TGI Friday's, FedEx, and Chiclets.[19]

Companies must research extensively before attempting a global advertising strategy. So much depends on the product and where they try to sell it. A "no" answer to any of the following questions means the attempt will probably fail.

1. *Has each country's market for the product developed in the same way?* A Ford is a Ford in most markets. On the other hand, many Europeans use clotheslines, so they don't need fabric softeners for dryers.

2. *Are the targets similar in different nations?* Japanese consumers like jeans, running shoes, and rock and roll. The same is true in Europe and the United States. But it might not be true for certain foods or fashions.

3. *Do consumers share the same wants and needs?* Breakfast in Brazil is usually a cup of coffee. Kellogg's corn flakes won't be served the same way there as in the United States, where people commonly eat cereal for breakfast.[20]

According to the worldwide creative director of J. Walter Thompson, the secret to success in global advertising is knowing how to tap into basic human emotions and uncover universal appeals that don't depend solely on language.[21]

Ultimately, the advertising direction a company takes depends on many variables: breadth of product line, quality of management, ability to repeat marketing strategies across countries, costs, and the decision to operate internationally, multinationally, or globally. Every organization operates in a slightly different environment. This alters the search for an *ideal structure* into a search for a *suitable structure.*[22] Most companies blend aspects of centralized and decentralized structures to fit their own needs. And when an existing structure shows signs of decay, they must be willing to test new ideas and make changes.

The Advertising Agency

Why does a company such as Honda hire an advertising agency in the first place? Couldn't it save money by hiring its own staff and creating its own ads? How does Muse Cordero Chen win such a large account? Must an agency's accounts be that big for it to make money? This section sheds some light on these issues and gives a clearer understanding of what agencies do and why so many advertisers use agencies.

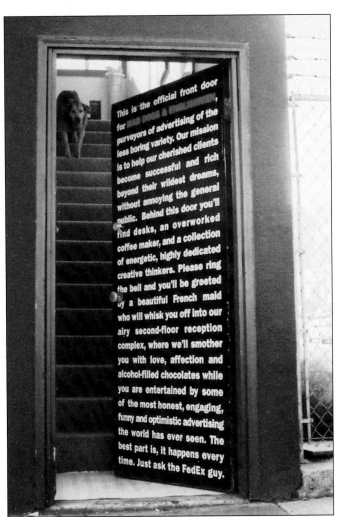

This is the official front door for **MAD DOGS & ENGLISHMEN**, purveyors of advertising of the less boring variety. Our mission is to help our cherished clients become successful and rich beyond their wildest dreams, without annoying the general public. Behind this door you'll find desks, an overworked coffee maker, and a collection of energetic, highly dedicated creative thinkers. Please ring the bell and you'll be greeted by a beautiful French maid who will whisk you off into our airy second-floor reception complex, where we'll smother you with love, affection and alcohol-filled chocolates while you are entertained by some of the most honest, engaging, funny and optimistic advertising the world has ever seen. The best part is, it happens every time. Just ask the FedEx guy.

An advertising agency brings an outside, objective viewpoint to an advertiser's business. In order to do so, the agency must also promote itself so that advertisers may choose its services. Here, Mad Dogs & Englishmen, San Francisco, does so by creatively altering its front door.

The Role of the Advertising Agency

The American Association of Advertising Agencies (AAAA) defines an **advertising agency** as an independent organization of creative people and businesspeople who specialize in developing and preparing marketing and advertising plans, advertisements, and other promotional tools. The agency also purchases advertising space and time in various media on behalf of different advertisers, or sellers (its clients), to find customers for their goods and services.[23]

This definition offers clues to why so many advertisers hire ad agencies. First, an agency like Muse Cordero Chen is *independent*. The agency isn't owned by the advertiser, the media, or the suppliers, so it can bring an outside, objective viewpoint to the advertiser's business—a state the advertiser can never attain.

Second, like all agencies, MCC employs a combination of *businesspeople* and *creative people*, including administrators, accountants, marketing executives, researchers, market and media analysts, writers, and artists. They have day-to-day contact with outside professional suppliers who create illustrations, take photos, retouch art, shoot commercials, record sound, and print brochures.

The agency provides yet another service by researching, negotiating, arranging, and contracting for commercial space and time with the various print, electronic, and digital media. Because of its *media expertise,* Muse Cordero Chen saves its clients time and money.

Agencies don't work for the media or the suppliers. Their moral, ethical, financial, and legal obligation is to their clients. Just as a well-run business seeks professional help from attorneys, accountants, bankers, or management specialists, advertisers use agencies out of *self-interest,* because the agencies can create more effective advertising and select more effective media than the advertisers can themselves. Today, almost all sizable advertisers rely on an ad agency for expert, objective counsel and unique creative skills—to be the "guardian of their brands."[24]

Finally, a good agency serves its clients' needs because of its daily exposure to a broad spectrum of marketing situations and problems both here and abroad. As technology has enabled companies to work across borders with relative ease, the advertising business has boomed worldwide. All the large U.S. agencies, for example, maintain offices in many foreign countries. Ad Lab 4–B describes the global ad industry.

Types of Agencies

Advertising agencies are typically classified by their geographic scope, the range of services they offer, and the type of business they handle.

Local Agencies

Every community of any size has reputable small ad agencies that offer expert assistance to local advertisers. A competent **local agency** can help

- Analyze the local advertiser's business and the product or service being sold.
- Evaluate the markets for the business, including channels of distribution.
- Evaluate the advertiser's competitive position and offer strategic options.
- Evaluate media alternatives and offer rational recommendations.

How Big Is the Agency Business?

Advertising today is a worldwide business. In 2001, the top global advertising markets were the United States, followed by Japan, Germany, the United Kingdom, France, Italy, Brazil, Spain, and Canada, in that order. New York, with $61.2 billion in global billings, retained its title as the world's advertising capital. Tokyo, London, and Paris were second, third, and fourth, respectively. Other leading advertising centers in North America include Chicago, Los Angeles, Toronto, and Montreal.

All U.S. and Canadian cities with at least 100,000 people have ad agencies. So do many smaller cities and towns. Of the more than 10,000 U.S. agencies, the top 500 represent about $123 billion in domestic billings (the amount of client money the agency spends on media and equivalent activities)—a little over half of all U.S. advertising expenditures during the year 2001.

Interestingly, the top 10 U.S. agencies handle more than half the total volume of business done by the top 500 agencies, and that's just their U.S. billing. Their overseas operations often equal or exceed their domestic billings. With the megamerger trend, the agency players and their rankings often change. For the latest scorecard, see the *Contemporary Advertising* website.

The top 500 domestic ad agencies employ about 93,000 people. Agencies need fewer people than businesses in many other industries: five or six people can easily handle $1 million in annual billings. In agencies that bill $20 million or more a year, the ratio is even lower.

World's top 10 advertising organizations

Rank 2003	Company	2003 worldwide gross income
1	Omnicom Group	$8,621.4
2	WPP Group	6,756.1
3	Interpublic Group	5,863.4
4	Publicis Groupe	4,408.9
5	Dentsu	2,545.0
6	Havas Advertising	1,877.5
7	Grey Global Group	1,307.3
8	Hakuhodo DY Holdings	1,208.1
9	Aegis Group	1,067.4
10	Asatsu-DK	413.9

Top 10 U.S. agency brands

Rank 2003	Agency	2003 U.S. gross income
1	J. Walter Thompson Co.	$456.2
2	Leo Burnett Worldwide	404.2
3	McCann Erickson Worldwide	300.4
4	BBDO Worldwide	279.1
5	Grey Worldwide	270.5
6	DDB Worldwide Communications	252.3
7	Ogilvy & Mather Worldwide	235.6
8	Foote, Cone & Belding Worldwide	221.6
9	Y&R Advertising	215.7
10	Publicis Worldwide	200.9

Top 10 U.S. cities by billings

Rank 2001	Market	2001 local shop billings	Top office by billings
1	New York	$61,264.40	Ogilvy & Mather Worldwide
2	Chicago	17,379.90	Leo Burnett Worldwide
3	Los Angeles	10,545.60	Rubin/Postaer & Associates
4	Detroit	7,946.30	Campbell-Ewald
5	Minneapolis	6,087.20	Carlson Marketing Group
6	San Francisco	5,101.90	Publicis & Hal Riney
7	Boston	3,993.70	Arnold Worldwide
8	Dallas	3,234.80	Richards Group
9	Atlanta	2,620.90	Grizzard Communications Group
10	Philadelphia	2,379.60	Devon Direct Euro RSCG

- Devise an integrated communications plan and implement it with consistency and creativity.
- Save the advertiser valuable time by taking over media interviewing, analysis, checking, billing, and bookkeeping.
- Assist in other aspects of advertising and promotion by implementing sales contests, publicity, grand openings, and other activities.

Unfortunately, local advertisers use ad agencies less extensively than national advertisers. Many advertisers simply don't spend enough money on advertising to warrant hiring an agency. And some large agencies don't accept local advertisers because their budgets are too low to support the agency's overhead.

Regional and National Agencies

Every major city has numerous agencies that can produce and place the quality of advertising suitable for national campaigns. **Regional** and **national agencies** typically participate in either the 4As (American Association of Advertising Agencies) or some similar trade group such as the Western States Advertising Agency Association (WSAAA). The *Standard Directory of Advertising Agencies* (the Red Book) lists these agencies geographically, so they're easy to find.

International Agencies

The largest national agencies are also **international agencies.** That is, they have offices or affiliates in major communications centers around the world and can help their clients market internationally or globally as the case may be. Likewise, many foreign-based agencies have offices and affiliates in the United States. For example, the largest advertising agency organization in the world today, WPP Group, is based in London. But it owns several of the top agencies in the United States, such as Ogilvy & Mather and J. Walter Thompson.

Full-Service Agencies

The modern **full-service advertising agency** supplies both advertising and nonadvertising services in all areas of communications and promotion. *Advertising services* include planning, creating, and producing ads; performing research; and selecting media. *Nonadvertising functions* run the gamut from packaging to public relations to producing sales promotion materials, annual reports, and trade-show exhibits. With the trend toward IMC, many of the largest agencies today are in the forefront of the emerging *interactive media.*[25]

Full-service agencies may specialize in certain kinds of clients. Most, though, can be classified as either *general consumer agencies* or *business-to-business agencies.*

General consumer agencies   A **general consumer agency** represents the widest variety of accounts, but it concentrates on *consumer accounts*—companies that make goods purchased chiefly by consumers (soaps, cereals, cars, pet foods, toiletries). Most of the ads are placed in consumer media (TV, radio, magazines, and so on) that pay a *commission* to the agency. General agencies often derive much of their income from these commissions.

General agencies include the international superagency groups headquartered in communication capitals such as New York, London, Paris, and Tokyo, as well as many other large firms in New York, Chicago, Los Angeles, Minneapolis, Montreal, and Toronto. A few of the better-known names in North America are McCann-Erickson; Ogilvy & Mather; Foote, Cone & Belding; Grey Advertising; BBDO; DDB Needham; Young & Rubicam; and Cossette Communications-Marketing (Canada). But general agencies also include the thousands of smaller *entrepreneurial agencies* located in every major city across the country (Martin Agency, Richmond, VA; Rubin/Postaer, Los Angeles; Ruhr/Paragon, Minneapolis; Wieden & Kennedy, Portland, OR).

Profit margins in entrepreneurial agencies are often slimmer, but these shops are typically more responsive to the smaller clients they serve. They offer the hands-on involvement of the firm's principals, and their work is frequently startling in its creativity. For these very reasons, many large agencies are spinning off smaller subsidiaries. Gotham Advertising, for example, is a hot creative shop in New York that was spun off by the Interpublic Group of Companies to do work for a variety of clients its bigger sister agencies couldn't serve.[26] Some entrepreneurial agencies, such as Muse Cordero Chen, carve a niche for themselves by serving particular market segments.

Business-to-business agencies   A **business-to-business** (or *high-tech*) **agency** represents clients that market products to other businesses. Examples are electronic components for computer manufacturers, equipment used in oil and gas refineries, and MRI equipment for radiology. High-tech advertising requires some technical knowledge and the ability to translate that knowledge into precise, as well as persuasive communications.

Most business-to-business advertising is placed in trade magazines or other business publications. These media are commissionable, but their circulation is smaller, so their rates are far lower than those of consumer media. Because commissions usually don't cover the cost of the agency's services, business agencies typically charge their clients service fees. They can be expensive, especially for small advertisers, but failure to obtain a business agency's expertise may carry an even higher price in lost marketing opportunities.

Business and industrial agencies may be large international firms such as MacLaren/Lintas in Toronto or HCM/New York, or smaller firms experienced in areas of recruitment, biomedical, or electronics advertising.

Specialized Service Agencies

Many agencies assist their clients with a variety of limited services. In the early 1990s the trend toward specialization blossomed, giving impetus to many of the small agency-type groups called *creative boutiques* and other specialty businesses such as *media-buying services* and *interactive agencies.*

Creative boutiques   Some talented artists—such as graphic designers and copywriters—set up their own creative services, or **creative boutiques.** They work for advertisers and occasionally subcontract to ad agencies. Their mission is to develop exciting creative concepts and produce fresh, distinctive advertising messages. In the 1990s, Creative Artists Agency (CAA), a Hollywood talent

When sophisticated businesses advertise, their agencies must have a firm grasp of the relevant details and be able to communicate this information clearly to key players and stakeholders. Moreover, these agencies also have to know which media to use. A trade publication such as the Financial Times is typical of the many media whose audiences are largely composed of influential business leaders.

JUST BECAUSE THEY'RE HIGH UP, DOESN'T
MEAN THEY'RE OUT OF REACH.

If you want to reach the people who make the decisions and form the opinions, there's no better place to be than the FT. In print and online, it's the only place senior decision makers look for a truly global perspective.

The Financial Times has a higher composition of C-level executives than The Wall Street Journal, Forbes, Fortune, Business Week and The Economist.* And when they read, they act. Research shows that eight out of ten will change their opinions based on what they read in the FT and 94% will act as a result of an ad in the FT.**

*Source: Erdos & Morgan, Purchase Influence American Business, 2000-2001
**Source: FT US Subscriber Study, November 2001

So if you want your ads to reach the top, call
Charles Boyar, VP, Director of Advertising at 212-641-6555

FT go further >>

agency, caused a stir on Madison Avenue (the collective term for New York agencies) by taking on the role of a creative boutique, using its pool of actors, directors, and cinematographers to create a series of commercials for Coca-Cola. McCann-Erickson Worldwide remained Coke's *agency of record,* but the majority of the creative work came from CAA. Since that time, Coke has allowed numerous other smaller shops to work on its account. In fact, by 1999, it had 16 agencies and boutiques on its roster.[27]

Advertising effectiveness depends on originality in concept, design, and writing. However, while boutiques may be economical, they usually don't provide the research, marketing, sales expertise, or deep customer service that full-service agencies offer. Thus, boutiques tend to be limited to the role of creative suppliers.

Media-buying services   Some years ago, a few experienced agency media people started setting up organizations to purchase and package radio and TV time. The largest **media-buying service** (or *media agency*) is Initiative Media. Based in Los Angeles, it is owned by the Interpublic Group, has offices around the world, and places more than $21 billion worth of advertising annually for a wide variety of clients from Coors and Nextel to Victoria's Secret.[28]

Media time and space is perishable. A 60-second radio spot at 8 P.M. can't be sold later. So radio and TV stations presell as much time as possible and discount their rates for large buys. The media-buying service negotiates a special discount with the media and then sells the time or space to agencies or advertisers.

Media-buying firms provide customers (both clients and agencies) with a detailed analysis of the media buy. Once the media package is sold, the buying service orders spots, verifies performance, sees that stations "make good" for any missed spots, and even pays the media bills. Compensation methods vary. Some services charge a set fee; others get a percentage of what they save the client.

Media agencies have experienced so much growth in the last decade that they have become major players on the advertising stage. We'll discuss them in greater detail in Chapter 9, "Planning Media Strategy."

Interactive agencies   With the stunning growth of the Internet and the heightened interest in integrated marketing communications has come a new breed of specialist—the **interactive agency.** Think New Ideas (owned by AnswerThink) and Freestyle.com (owned by Carat Communications) are just two of the many firms that have sprung up within the last few years with specialized experience in designing Web pages and creating fun, involving, information-rich, online advertising.[29]

Other specialists, such as *direct-response* and *sales promotion agencies,* are also growing in response to client demands for greater expertise and accountability.

What People in an Agency Do

The American Association of Advertising Agencies (AAAA) is the national trade association of the advertising agency business and the industry's spokesperson with government, media, and the public. Its 1,163 agency members, representing a wide spectrum of small, medium, and large agencies, place 75 percent of all national advertising handled by agencies in the United States.[30]

The AAAA Service Standards explain that an agency's purpose is to interpret to the public, or to desired segments of the public, information about a legally marketed product or service. How does an agency do this? First, it studies the client's product to determine its strengths and weaknesses. Next, it analyzes the product's present and potential market. Then, using its knowledge of the channels of distribution and available media, the agency formulates a plan to carry the advertiser's message to consumers, wholesalers, dealers, or contractors. Finally the agency writes, designs, and produces ads; contracts for media space and time; verifies media insertions; and bills for services and media used.

The agency also works with the client's marketing staff to enhance the advertising's effect through package design, sales research and training, and production

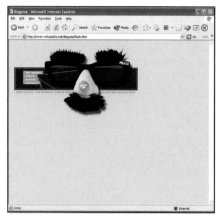

Because of the technical expertise needed for interactive media, some small agencies have made big names for themselves. Boutiques can demonstrate their creative power through ads for their services, such as this interactive Web ad from AgenciaClick (Brazil) (www.agenciaclick. com.br) for AgenciaClick International. To see the ad itself, visit www.virtualsofa.net/disguise/. The ad demonstrates the agency's flair for creating banner ads that are actually websites. AgenciaClick (Brazil) garnered a 2004 Cannes Silver Lion for this effort, in addition to two other Lions for ads created for their clients.

of sales literature and displays. To understand these functions, consider the people who were involved, directly or indirectly, in the creation, production, and supervision of the Honda Civic campaign created by Muse Cordero Chen and Partners.

Account Management

The **account executives (AEs)** at Muse Cordero Chen and Partners are the liaison between the agency and the client. Large agencies typically have many account executives, who report to **management** (or **account**) **supervisors.** They in turn report to the agency's director of account (or client) services.

Account executives are often caught in the middle of the fray, as they are responsible for formulating and executing advertising plans (discussed in Chapter 8), mustering the agency's services, and representing the client's point of view to the agency. Gina Cadres, the account director on the Civic campaign, had to be more of a strategist than an advocate. She had to be well versed in an extraordinary range of media and demonstrate how her agency's creative work satisfied both her client's marketing needs and the market's product needs. Characteristically, an AE must be able to see things from all points of view. An account executive must be not only enterprising, courageous, and demanding, but also tactful, artistic and articulate, meticulous, forgiving, perceptive, ethical, and discreet. And what's more, an AE must always deliver the work on time and within budget.

To grow, agencies require a steady flow of new projects. Sometimes agencies get new assignments when their existing clients develop new products or enter new markets. Sometimes clients seek out agencies whose work they are familiar with. Thanks to its reputation, Muse Cordero Chen and Partners receives 10 to 15 new business calls a week.

Research and Account Planning

Clients and agencies must give their creatives (artists and copywriters) a wealth of product, market, and competitive information because, at its core, advertising is based on information. Therefore, before creating any advertising, agencies research the uses and advantages of the product, analyze current and potential customers, and try to determine what will influence them to buy. After the ads are placed, agencies use more research to investigate how the campaign fared. Chapter 7 discusses some of the many types of research ad agencies conduct.

Account planning is a hybrid discipline that uses research to bridge the gap between account management and creatives. The account planner defends the consumer's point of view and the creative strategy in the debate between the agency's creative team and the client.

Account planners study consumer needs and desires through phone surveys and focus groups, but primarily through personal interviews. They help the creative team translate their findings into imaginative, successful campaigns. Not attached to either account management or creative, the account planner balances both elements to make sure the research is reflected in the ads.[31]

Working on the Honda Civic account, Shelley Yamane spent a lot of time in L.A. talking to young people in their own environments with the goal of better understanding their attitudes, feelings, language, and habits. She represented the views of the young people she spoke to in agency meetings with Honda. The result was the discovery of a new market segment for Honda: urban youth—shaped by inner-city life, hip-hop music, and the desire to display both one's success and individuality. This group is defined not by ethnicity but by a cultural attitude that crosses demographic lines to foster the market's core values: irreverence, fitness, athleticism, and discipline.

Through good account planning, Muse Cordero Chen and Partners found a niche in which their car could be number one. They recognized that a market segment existed but had not yet been defined, and that positioning the product—that is, ranking the product in the mind of the consumer—should be relatively easy. But, in this case, MCC was faced with an interesting challenge. As a group, urban youth are extremely media-conscious, media-savvy, and perhaps even suspicious, so they knew that their campaign had to be transparent and candid. This particular subculture grew naturally out of rallies and car shows, without corporate sponsors or any advertising. MCC knew there was a risk—trying to appropriate that culture might actually alienate the very people they wanted to attract, and it might even cause resentment. Quite rightly, MCC knew they had to speak *to* these people, not *at* them.

By putting the consumer, rather than the advertiser, at the center of the process, account planning changes the task from simply creating an advertisement to nurturing a relationship between consumer and brand. That requires tremendous understanding, intuition, and insight. To get the job done right, Shelley had to be receptive, approachable, and most importantly, a good listener—essential characteristics of a good account planner. When performed properly, planning provides that mystical leap into the future—the brilliant, simplifying insight that lights the way for the client and the creatives. Interestingly, the U.S. agencies that have adopted account planning in the last decade are the ones now considered to be the hottest shops. They're performing the best work, getting the biggest accounts, and winning all the awards.

Creative Concepts

Most ads rely heavily on **copy,** the words that make up the headline and message. The people who create these words, called **copywriters,** must condense all that can be said about a product into a few pertinent, succinct points.

Ads also use nonverbal communication. That is the purview of the **art directors,** graphic designers, and production artists, who determine how the ads verbal and visual symbols will fit together. (The creative process is discussed in Chapters 12, 13, and 14.) The agency's copywriters and artists work as a creative team under a **creative director.** Each team is usually assigned a particular client's business.

In the case of the Honda Civic, the creative director was Wilky Lau. He put together a creative team consisting of a copywriter, Mike Whitlow, and an art director, Alfonso ("Fons") Covarrubias. With the research that Shelley Yamane passed on to them, they began to brainstorm. Wilky, Mike, and Fons all agreed that it was important to generate a campaign that would show urban youth in their own world. The big idea was launched from that very notion: how better to accurately capture the essence of urban youth than to actually include them in the campaign? Maybe all they had to do was define this growing group of Civic-loving people and portray them realistically. And, in doing so, they would effectively position the car. The notion of a "Civic Nation" was borne. They followed through with this initial concept in every aspect of the campaign—from the print ads and commercials, which featured authentic souped-up Civics, down to the radio spots, which they created by using a DJ to mix beats with sound bits from genuine interviews with Civic drivers. Not your average radio spot.

As with any good writing, ad copy should look like it was written with ease. Though simple and straightforward, the copy used in the Civic campaign was a long time in the making. But when Mike Whitlow came up with the line "Represent," used in both the print ads and commercials, it was met with glowing approval. "Represent" serves as both a command to be yourself and convey your individuality, as well as a caption to describe what the ad is doing, since it is in fact representing the personal, creative expression of many Civic drivers.

Advertising Production: Print and Broadcast

Once an ad is designed, written, and approved by the client, it is turned over to the agency's print production manager or broadcast producers.

For print ads, the production department buys type, photos, illustrations, and other components and works with printers, engravers, and other suppliers. For a broadcast commercial, production people work from an approved script or storyboard. They use actors, camera operators, and production specialists (studios,

Items in the Honda dealer promotion kit included an 8 1/2 × 11-inch spiral-bound notebook with three color magazine ad slicks, five black-and-white newspaper ad slicks, and marketing and media information; a 25-second "I Am Me" video commercial; an audiocassette with three 55-second radio commercials; and an actual model kit of the Honda Prelude for the dealer to assemble.

directors, editors) to produce a commercial on audiotape (for radio) or on film for videotape (for TV).

But production work is not just limited to ads and commercials. Dealer kits and direct mailings are just two examples of other media types that may be created as part of a campaign. For instance, several years ago, Muse Cordero Chen and Partners assembled a promotional kit for dealers that included, among the marketing and media literature, an actual model kit of the Honda Accord (including glue) for the dealer to construct.

Media Planning and Buying

Ad agencies perform a variety of media services for their clients: research, negotiating, scheduling, buying, and verifying. Media planning is critical, because the only way advertisers can communicate is through some medium. We discuss the media extensively in Chapters 9 and 15 through 18, but for now it's important to understand the changes over the last decade that have made the media function so important.

With an unprecedented fragmentation of audiences from the explosion of new media options, media planning and buying is no longer a simple task. Today, many more media vehicles are available for advertisers to consider, as the traditional major media offer smaller audiences than before—at higher prices. Add to this the trend toward IMC and relationship marketing, and the whole media task takes on added significance. This fueled the growth of media specialty companies and simultaneously recast agency media directors as the new rising stars in the advertising business.

Tight budgets demand ingenious thinking, tough negotiating, and careful attention to details. In this age of specialization, what advertisers really need are exceptional generalists who understand how advertising works in coordination with other marketing communication tools and can come up with creative media solutions to tough marketing problems. Today, many products owe their success more to creative media buying than to clever ads.

Traffic Management

One of the greatest sins in an ad agency is a missed deadline. If an agency misses a deadline for a monthly magazine, for example, the agency will have to wait another month before they can run the ad, much to the client's displeasure.

The agency traffic department coordinates all phases of production and makes sure everything is completed before client and/or media deadlines. Traffic is often the first stop for entry-level college graduates and an excellent place to learn about agency operations. (See the *Contemporary Advertising* website for more information about careers in advertising at www.mhhe.com/arens06.)

Additional Services

The growth of IMC has caused some agencies to employ specialists who provide services besides advertising. While Muse Cordero Chen and Partners uses its regular creative department for both advertising and nonadvertising services, larger agencies may have a fully staffed **sales promotion department** to produce dealer ads, window posters, point-of-purchase displays, and dealer sales material. Or, depending on the nature and needs of their clients, they may employ public relations people and direct-marketing specialists, Web page designers, home economics experts, or package designers.

Agency Administration

In small agencies, administrative functions may be handled by the firm's principals. Large agencies often have departments for accounting, human resources, data processing, purchasing, financial analysis, legal issues, and insurance.

How Agencies Are Structured

An ad agency organizes its functions, operations, and personnel according to the types of accounts it serves, its size, and its geographic scope.

In small agencies (annual billings of less than $20 million), each employee may wear many hats. The owner usually supervises daily business operations, client services, and new-business development. Account executives generally handle day-to-day client contact. AEs may also do some creative work, such as writing copy. Artwork may be produced by an art director or purchased from an independent studio or freelance designer. Most small agencies have production and traffic departments or an employee who fulfills these functions. They may have a media buyer, but in very small agencies account executives also purchase media time and space. Exhibit 4–7 shows how Muse Cordero Chen and Partners is organized.

Exhibit 4–7
Muse Cordero Chen and Partners organization.

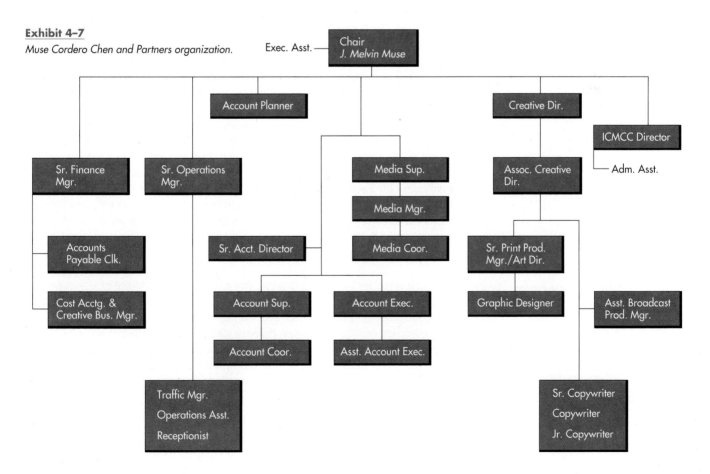

Thanks to modern telecommunications, clients and agencies can locate themselves almost anywhere. Today, virtual manufacturers work out of seaside resorts and their agencies can operate the same way—tied to their researchers, creatives, media departments, and suppliers by wireless phones, fax machines, personal digital assistants, and high-speed Internet connections.

Medium and large agencies are usually structured in a *departmental* or *group system*. In the **departmental system,** the agency organizes its various functions—account services, creative services, marketing services, and administration—into separate departments (see RL 4–1 in the Reference Library on the *Contemporary Advertising* CD-ROM).

In the **group system,** the agency is divided into a number of "little" agencies or groups (see RL 4–2 in the Reference Library on the *Contemporary Advertising* CD-ROM). Each group may serve one large account or, in some cases, three or four smaller ones. An account supervisor heads each group's staff of account executives, copywriters, art directors, a media director, and any other necessary specialists. A very large agency may have dozens of groups with separate production and traffic units.

To deal with the economic pressures of the new millennium, many agencies have looked for ways to reorganize themselves and their offices. TBWA Chiat/Day in Venice, California, credits its laid-back office design with encouraging creativity throughout the agency. Based on an idealized city, the layout by architect Clive Wilkinson features open workstations clustered into communities and arranged around public gathering places. The idea is to free employees to roam around the office on their scooters unencumbered. A black surfboard displays the skull and crossbones of the self-proclaimed "pirates of the industry."[32] In Chicago, Leo Burnett, which was traditionally highly centralized, restructured itself into numerous client-oriented mini-agencies, each meant to function as an agency within an agency.[33] And in France, Young & Rubicam encourages employees to spend more time out of the office with clients and to work from home while linked to the agency via laptop.[34]

How Agencies Are Compensated

To survive, agencies must make a profit. But recent trends in the business—mergers of superagencies, shifts in emphasis from advertising to sales promotion and direct marketing, increased production costs, and the fragmentation of media vehicles—have all cut into agency profits.[35] Moreover, different clients demand different services, forcing agencies to develop various compensation methods. Still, there are really only three ways for agencies to make money: *media commissions, markups,* and *fees* or *retainers.*

Media Commissions

As we saw in Chapter 2, when ad agencies first came on the scene more than 100 years ago, they were really space brokers, or reps, for the newspapers. Because they saved the media much of the expense of sales and collections, the media allowed the agencies to retain a 15 percent **media commission** on the space or time they purchased on behalf of their clients. That started a tradition that endures to this day, although it is now changing rapidly. Let's see how it works.

Say a national rate-card price for a full-page color magazine ad is $100,000. The magazine bills the agency, and the agency in turn bills the client for the $100,000. The client pays that amount to the agency, and the agency sends $85,000 to the magazine, keeping its 15 percent commission ($15,000). For large accounts, the agency typically provides extensive services (creative, media, accounting, and account management) for this commission. With dwindling profits, though, and clients negotiating smaller commissions, many agencies now charge a fee for services that used to be free.[36]

Markups

In the process of creating an ad, the agency normally buys a variety of services or materials from outside suppliers—for example, photos and illustrations. The agency pays the supplier's charge and then adds a **markup** to the client's bill, typically 17.65 percent of the invoice (which becomes 15 percent of the new total).

For example, a markup of 17.65 percent on an $8,500 photography bill yields a $1,500 profit. When billing the client, the agency adds the $1,500 to the $8,500 for a new total of $10,000. When the client pays the bill, the agency keeps the $1,500 (15 percent of the total)—which, not coincidentally, is the standard commission agencies normally receive.

$$\$8,500 \times 17.65\% = \$1,500$$

$$\$8,500 + \$1,500 = \$10,000$$

$$\$10,000 \times 15\% = \$1,500$$

Some media—local newspapers, for example—allow a commission on the higher rates they charge national advertisers but not on the lower rates they charge local advertisers. So, to get their commission, local agencies have to use the markup formula above.

Today many agencies find that the markup doesn't cover their costs of handling the work, so they're increasing their markups to 20 or 25 percent. While this helps, agency profits are still under pressure, forcing many agencies to a fee system in place of, or in addition to, commissions and markups.

Fees

Clients today expect agencies to solve problems rather than just place ads, so fees are becoming more common. In fact, one study shows that only about one-third of national advertisers still rely on the 15 percent commission system. An equal number now use some fee-based system. The rest use some reduced commission or incentive system.[37]

There are two pricing methods in the fee system. With the **fee-commission combination,** the agency charges a basic monthly fee for all its services to the client and retains any media commissions earned. In the **straight-fee** or **retainer method,** agencies charge for all their services, either by the hour or by the month, and credit any media commissions earned to the client.

Accountability is a major issue in client/agency relationships. With a new type of agency compensation, the **incentive system,** the agency earns more if the campaign attains specific, agreed-on goals. DDB Needham, for example, offers its clients a "guaranteed results" program. If a campaign wins, the agency earns more; if it loses, the agency earns less. Kraft General Foods rewards its agencies based on their performance. An A grade gets an extra 3 percent commission; C grades are put on review.[38] To avoid these costs altogether, some advertisers create their own in-house advertising agencies.

The In-House Agency

Some companies set up a wholly owned **in-house agency** (or *house agency*) to save money and tighten control over their advertising. The in-house agency may do all the work of an independent full-service agency, including creative tasks, production, media placement, publicity, and sales promotion.

Advertisers with in-house agencies hope to save money by cutting overhead, keeping the media commission, and avoiding markups on outside purchases. Small, local advertisers in particular seek this goal.

Advertisers also expect more attention from their house agencies, which know the company's products and markets better and can focus all their resources to meet its deadlines. Management is often more involved in the advertising when it's done by company people, especially in "single-business" companies. And some in-house advertising is outstanding, especially in the fashion field. But usually companies sacrifice more than they gain. In-house flexibility is often won at the expense of creativity. Outside agencies typically offer greater experience, versatility, and talent. In-house agencies have difficulty attracting and keeping the best creative people, who tend to prefer the variety and challenge offered by independent agencies.

The biggest problem for in-house agencies is loss of objectivity. In the shadow of internal politics, linear-thinking policy makers, and harangues from management, ads may become insipid contemplations of corporate navels rather than relevant messages to customers. In advertising, that's the kiss of death.

The Client/Agency Relationship
How Agencies Get Clients

Many factors affect the success of a company's advertising program, but one of the most important is the relationship between the advertiser and its agency.

To succeed, advertising agencies need clients. New clients come from personal contact with top management, referrals from satisfied clients or advertising consultants, publicity on recent successful campaigns, trade advertising, direct-mail solicitation, or the agency's general reputation.[39] The three most successful ways to develop new business are having clients who strongly champion the agency, having superior presentation skills, and cultivating a personal relationship with a network of top executives.

Referrals

Most good agencies get clients by referral—from existing clients, friends, review consultants, or even other agencies. The head of one company asks another who's

Some companies such as Benetton (www.benetton.com) prefer to create ads using their own in-house agency. Advertisers hope to save money and gain more attention to their needs by using their house agency, but they can lose the greater experience, objectivity, and talent of an outside agency.

doing her ads, and the next week the agency gets a call. If a prospective client presents a conflict of interest with an existing client, the agency may decline the business and refer the prospect to another agency.[40]

Independent *agency review consultants* often help arrange marriages between agencies and clients. In fact, independent advisers were involved in most of the important recent account shuffles on Madison Avenue: Domino's Pizza, DirecTV, Burger King, Compaq computers, and Monster.com, to name just a few.[41]

Sales reps for media and suppliers frequently refer local advertisers to an agency they know. So it's important for agencies to maintain cordial relations with the media, suppliers, other agencies, and, of course, their existing clients.

Presentations

An advertiser may ask an agency to make a presentation—anything from a simple discussion of the agency's philosophy, experience, personnel, and track record to a full-blown audiovisual presentation of a proposed campaign. Successful agencies, therefore, need excellent presentation skills.

Some advertisers ask for or imply that they want a **speculative presentation,** meaning they want to see what the agency will do before they sign on. But most agencies prefer to build their presentations around the work they've already done, to demonstrate their capabilities without giving away ideas for a new campaign. Invariably, the larger the client, the bigger the presentation. Some agencies now spend upwards of $500,000 to stage a new-business presentation.

The presentation process also allows the agency and the advertiser to get to know each other before they agree to work together. Advertising is a people business, so human qualities—mutual regard, trust, and communication—play an important role (see the Ethical Issue, "Accounting for Account Reviews").

Networking and Community Relations

Agencies frequently find that the best source of new business is people their employees know socially in the community. Some agencies work pro bono (for free) for charities or nonprofit organizations such as the American Indian College Fund. Jo Muse at Muse Cordero Chen and Partners contributes time to the Rebuild L.A. campaign, which started after the civil disorders of 1992. He also serves the profession by volunteering on the government relations committee of the AAAA.

The use of creative collateral material is often an effective way to get the attention of prospective customers, as demonstrated by the Honda dealer kit shown earlier. Fallon Worldwide (www.fallon.com) solicits new business in a similar manner, by mailing prospects an empty box with their phone number inside, along with a quarter to place the call.

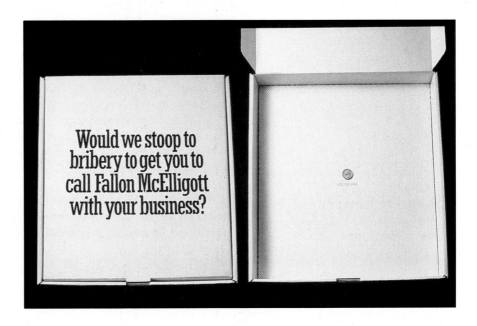

Accounting for Account Reviews

Periodically, advertisers review the effectiveness of their campaigns and invite presentations from a variety of agencies. This process is referred to as an *agency* or *account review*. If the client's current agency is invited to participate, and the review is handled responsibly and respectfully, it can serve as a mutually beneficial tool in keeping the relationship between the client and the agency honest and open for both sides. Conversely, when used in an unethical manner, account reviews can be very destructive to the relationship, tarnishing the reputation of the client and/or the agency and damaging the integrity of the brand.

Historically, advertisers have been expected to show some allegiance to their current agency, unless that agency has mishandled a campaign through ineptitude, malfeasance, or simple ineffectiveness. Recently, though, client loyalty seems to be on the wane, while agency reviews are on the rise. A survey by the American Association of Advertising Agencies, covering 175 agencies and their 3,700 accounts, shows that, between 1984 and 1997, the average length of the client/agency relationship dropped from 7.2 years to 5.3 years. Several examples illustrate this trend: United Airlines dumped Leo Burnett Chicago after 31 years; Delta Air Lines reviewed its 50-year relationship with BBDO Worldwide; Colgate-Palmolive Co. shifted $200 million in billing from Foote, Cone & Belding to Y&R Advertising.

The increase in account reviews is linked to two recent changes in the traditional client/agency relationship. The first change lies in the very nature of the client/agency bond. The historical, brand-building marriage is on the decline, and vendor-based services are on the rise. Today's advertisers, focused on the bottom line, increasingly settle for a quick fix that will temporarily increase volume sales, as opposed to the long-run investment of working with one agency to create an established brand. Used in this way, agencies are treated like specialized vendors, hired to spur the movement of the product or service desired, and called into review the moment that movement slows. Once a

review is called, the chances of an agency keeping the account are slim—an informal survey by *Adweek* revealed that only 1 incumbent agency out of 12 actually survives a review.

The second change in the traditional client/agency relationship is agency consolidation. As the industry transforms from a wide array of agencies into a handful of superpowers, the odds of rival advertisers falling under the services of the same shop have increased. Many clients believe same-house representation creates a conflict of interest, sparking more account reviews. The agency BBDO provided a good example by pitching for an assignment from Eastman Kodak while still handling a competing client, Polaroid. When one found out about the other, BBDO lost both the Kodak pitch and the Polaroid business.

In addition to the fundamental changes in the structure of the client/agency relationship, many agency people cite other, more questionable motives as the cause for review increases. One such basis for review, tied closely to the bottom-line-oriented approach, is what Roger Lewis, a partner at Hoffman/Lewis, San Francisco, dubs the "BOSS Theory of Marketing—Blame Others, Save Self." The BOSS theory states: In the event an advertiser's sales decline, marketing directors look for the quick fix by calling an agency into review to lend the perception that action is being taken to reverse the decline. Although unfair to the agency, the advertiser has incentive to do so as an immediate means of bolstering management and shareholder confidence.

The lure of free creative work is a second questionable motivation for clients to hold account reviews. In conducting a review, clients ask the participating agencies to create mock presentations as a means of assessing the capabilities and creativity of each in relation to the prospective account campaign. After reviewing these presentations, clients have no financial or legal commitment to pay participating agencies, and they may later incorporate these ideas into their campaigns at the expense of the participating agencies.

The ethical involvement of agency review consultants has also been questioned. Many within the industry believe that since review

---

Agencies may help local politicians (a controversial practice in some areas) or contribute to the arts, education, religion, or the community. Some agencies sponsor seminars; others assist ad clubs or other professional organizations. All these activities help an agency gain visibility and respect in its community.

Soliciting and Advertising for New Business

Lesser-known agencies must take a more aggressive approach. An agency may solicit new business by advertising, writing letters, making cold calls, or following up leads from sources in the business. An agency principal usually solicits new business, but staffers help prepare presentations.

Today, more agencies are advertising themselves. Many agencies submit their best ads to competitions around the world to win awards and gain publicity and professional respect for their creative excellence.[42] (Most of the ads in this book, by the way, are award winners.)

Stages in the Client/Agency Relationship

Just as people and products have life cycles, so do relationships. In the advertising business, the life cycle of the agency/client relationship passes through four distinct stages: *prerelationship, development, maintenance,* and *termination.*[43]

The Prerelationship Stage

The **prerelationship stage** occurs before an agency and client officially do business. They may know each other by reputation, by previous ads, or through social

consultants are in the business of account reviews, it is in their best interest to see that account reviews happen more often. To stimulate account reviews, some review consultants in the past are believed to have encouraged the BOSS theory, as well as portrayed account reviews as a way of obtaining a large amount of free creative work. In an article on "Conducting an Effective Advertising Agency Review," one marketing strategist suggests that "four agencies should be asked to produce twelve campaigns in total . . . [as] an opportunity to look at a vast amount of work built specifically to your needs." By spurring these disputed uses of account reviews, review consultants have aided in the growth of unethical reviews.

Account reviews clearly are important. Yet the growing abuse of the review process for unethical gains will only serve to create an unprofitable rift between the sides. On the agency side, the costs of participating in a review are escalating as the average per-pitch cost to an agency runs in the range of $60,000 to $75,000! This enormous cost incurred by participating agencies keeps smaller agencies from competing for accounts on a fair level. If the frequency of reviews continues to rise, smaller agencies will obtain a lesser and lesser percentage of the business, greatly reducing the competition within the industry over time.

What's more, reviews are extremely damaging to the reputation of the incumbent agency, as other clients can only be led to wonder what caused the agency to lose the account. For Peter Drakoulias, director of business development at Interpublic's Deutsch, New York, agencies are "perceived as damaged goods" after losing an account—a status from which an agency may never recover.

On the client side, reviews can be equally damaging in terms of the health of a brand. If a brand is changing its identity and public perception often, it loses its integrity as consumers become skeptical of the product. Loyalty to one agency can create the stable brand recognition that comforts consumers and propels the sales of a brand. Before the rise in account reviews, long-term marriages were believed to give an agency "deep knowledge of the client and product, a deep knowledge

of the essence of the brand, a deep knowledge of retail relationships and a deep knowledge of the customer," all of which are important in creating a strong brand.

If unethical motivations continue to drive the desire for account reviews, the client/agency relationship will suffer severely. Advertisers and agency review consultants have the power to ensure this does not happen by changing the way that account reviews are used and, in doing so, defining a fair and stable role for ad agencies in the years to come.

Questions

1. What degree of loyalty should clients have to agencies and vice versa? Is it ethical for agencies to represent multiple clients within the same industry?

2. What do you think might be done to reduce the amount of account reviews motivated by unethical gains?

3. How can the account review process be structured to more fairly incorporate smaller agencies? What can be done to lower the cost of participating in an agency review?

Sources: "The Bond between an Advertiser and His Client Is Changing," *Escalate*, April 20, 2004 (retrieved from www.escalate.ca); Douglas LaBahn, "Advertiser Perceptions of Fair Compensation, Confidentiality and Rapport: The Influence of Advertising Agency Cooperativeness and Diligence" (retrieved from www.highbeam.com/library/index.asp?refid=ae_org_1); Mark Gleason, "MIA on Madison Ave.: Agency, Client Loyalty," *Advertising Age*, January 27, 1997 (retrieved from: www.adage.com); Alice Z. Cuneo, "Agencies Feel Business Pinch, Eye More Cuts," *Advertising Age*, January 29, 2001 (retrieved from: www.adage.com); Michael Marsak, "Conducting an Effective Advertising Agency Review," Effective Marketing Strategies, Inc. (retrieved from www.effectivemarketing.com)

contact. Initial perceptions usually determine whether an agency is invited to pitch the account. Through the presentation process, the agency tries to give the best impression it can, because it is selling and the client is buying (the Checklist entitled "Agency Review" offers guidelines for selecting an agency).

The Development Stage

Once the agency is appointed, the **development stage** begins. During this honeymoon period, the agency and the client are at the peak of their optimism and eager to develop a mutually profitable relationship. Expectations are at their highest, and both sides are most forgiving. During development, the rules of the relationship are established. The respective roles get set quickly, the true personalities of all the players come out, and the agency creates its first work. At this point, the agency's output is eagerly awaited and then judged very thoroughly. The agency also discovers how receptive the client is to new ideas, how easy the client's staff is to work with, and how well the client pays its bills. During the development stage the first problems in the relationship also occur.

The Maintenance Stage

The year-in, year-out, day-to-day working relationship is called the **maintenance stage.** When successful, it may go on for many years. Sunkist has used the same agency, Foote, Cone & Belding, for close to 100 years. Other long-lasting relationships include Unilever/J. Walter Thompson, Exxon/McCann-Erickson, and Hammermill

Checklist

Agency Review

Rate each agency on a scale from 1 (strongly negative) to 10 (strongly positive).

General Information
____ Size compatible with our needs.
____ Strength of management.
____ Financial stability.
____ Compatibility with other clients.
____ Range of services.
____ Cost of services; billing policies.

Marketing Information
____ Ability to offer marketing counsel.
____ Understanding of the markets we serve.
____ Experience dealing in our market.
____ Success record; case histories.

Creative Abilities
____ Well-thought-out creativity; relevance to strategy.
____ Art strength
____ Copy strength.
____ Overall creative quality.
____ Effectiveness compared to work of competitors.

Production
____ Faithfulness to creative concept and execution.
____ Diligence to schedules and budgets.
____ Ability to control outside services.

Media
____ Existence and soundness of media research.
____ Effective and efficient media strategy.
____ Ability to achieve objectives within budget.
____ Strength at negotiating and executing schedules.

Personality
____ Overall personality, philosophy, or position.
____ Compatibility with client staff and management.
____ Willingness to assign top people to account.
____ Ability to articulate rationale behind work.

References
____ Rating by current clients.
____ Rating by past clients.
____ Rating by media and financial sources.

Papers/BBDO Worldwide, all more than 80 years. Unfortunately, the average client/agency relationship is much shorter—usually five to six years.

The Termination Stage

At some point, an irreconcilable difference may occur, and the relationship reaches the **termination stage.** Perhaps the agency has acquired a competing account, or the agency's creative work doesn't seem to be working. Or perhaps one party or the other simply decides it is time to move on.

During the nervous 1990s, several long-standing client/agency relationships were terminated. After 75 years, AT&T replaced Ayer as the company's lead agency on its $200 million consumer long-distance account, splitting the business between Young & Rubicam and FCB, both in New York.[44] Seagram fired DDB Needham from its $40 million Chivas Regal account after a 32-year marriage. And Anheuser-Busch dropped a bombshell on D'Arcy Masius Benton & Bowles when it pulled the Budweiser account after 79 years.[45] It's interesting to note that both Ayer and D'Arcy have now disappeared from the agency landscape.

The way a termination is handled will affect both sides for a long time and is an important factor in whether the two ever get back together. After losing the Apple Computer account in 1986, TBWA Chiat/Day gave Madison Avenue a lesson in class by placing a full-page ad that thanked Apple for their many years together. In 1997, the account came back.[46]

Factors Affecting the Client/Agency Relationship

Many forces influence the client/agency relationship. Generally they can be grouped into the four Cs: *chemistry, communication, conduct,* and *changes.*

The most critical factor is the personal *chemistry* between the client's and the agency's staff.[47] Agencies are very conscious of this factor and wine and dine their clients in hopes of improving it. Smart clients do the same.

Check*list*

Ways to Be a Better Client

Relationships

____ *Cultivate honesty.* Be truthful in your meetings and in your ads.

____ *Be enthusiastic.* When you like the ads, let the agency know.

____ *Be frank when you don't like the advertising.* Always cite a reason when turning down an idea.

____ *Be human.* React like a person, not a corporation. Laugh at funny ads even if they don't work.

____ *Be willing to admit you're unsure.* Don't be pressured. Let your agency know when you need time.

____ *Allow the agency to feel responsible.* Tell the agency what you feel is wrong, not how to fix it.

____ *Care about being a client.* Creative people work best for clients they like.

Management

____ *Don't insulate your top managers from creative people.* Agency creatives work best when objectives come from the top, not filtered through layers.

____ *Set objectives.* For timely and quality service from your agency, establish and openly share your marketing objectives.

____ *Switch people, not agencies.* When problems arise, agencies often prefer to bring in fresh talent rather than lose you as a client.

____ *Be sure the agency makes a profit on your account.* Demanding more services from your agency than fees or commissions can cover hurts relationships.

Production

____ *Avoid nitpicking last-minute changes.* Perfection is important, but waiting until the last moment to make minor changes can damage the client/agency relationship. Agencies see such behavior as indecisive and/or arrogant and lose respect for the client.

____ *Be aware of the cost of changes (both time and money).* The cost of making major changes at the production stage may be five times greater than in the earlier stages.

____ *Don't change concepts during the production stage.* Late changes can inadvertently alter product positioning and image.

Media

____ *Understand the economics (and economies) of media.* Be prepared to deal with costs per thousand (CPMs), costs per rating point (CPP), and other key elements of media planning and buying so that you can evaluate and appreciate your agency's media strategy.

____ *Understand the importance of lead time.* Early buys can eliminate late fees, earn discounts, make you eligible for special promotions, strengthen your agency's buying position, and reduce anxiety.

____ *Avoid interfering with the agency's media relationship.* The stronger your agency's buying position, the greater the discounts available to you. Refrain from cutting deals with media reps directly and plan media well in advance.

____ *Avoid media arrogance ("they need us").* Some media will deal with clients, and some won't. Misinterpret this relationship and you may either pay more than you should or be too late to get into a medium you need.

____ *Avoid insularity.* Be willing to let your mind travel beyond your immediate environment and lifestyle.

____ *Suggest work sessions.* Set up informal give-and-take sessions with creatives and strategists.

____ *Keep the creative people involved in your business.* Agency creatives do their best work for you when they're in tune with the ups and downs of your business.

Research

____ *Share information.* Pool information to create new and bigger opportunities.

____ *Involve the agency in research projects.* An agency's creative talent gets its best ideas from knowledge of your environment.

Creative

____ *Learn the fine art of conducting the creative meeting.* Deal with the important issues first: strategy, consumer benefits, and reasons why.

____ *Look for the big idea.* Concentrate on positioning strategy and brand personality. Don't allow a single ad—no matter how brilliant—to change the positioning or personality of the product.

____ *Insist on creative discipline.* The creative process stimulates concepts and actions. Discipline helps keep focus on those that count the most.

____ *Don't be afraid to ask for great advertising.* Agencies prefer the high road, but as the client you must be willing to accompany them. If the agency slips, be strong and ask it to try again.

Poor *communication,* a problem often cited by both agencies and advertisers, leads to misunderstandings about objectives, strategies, roles, and expectations—and to poor advertising. Constant, open communication and an explicit agreement on mutual contribution for mutual gain are key to a good relationship.[48]

Dissatisfaction with agency *conduct,* or performance, is the most commonly cited reason for agency switches in every country.[49] The service the agency gave two years ago may not be valued by the client in the same way today.[50] Or perhaps the agency doesn't understand the client's marketing problems. And clients change, too. Does the client give the agency timely, accurate information? Does it appreciate good work, or does it treat the agency like a vendor?[51] (For more on how clients hold up their end of the relationship, see the Checklist, "Ways to Be a Better Client.")

Changes occur in every relationship. Unfortunately, some of them damage the agency/client partnership. The client's market position or policies may change, or new management may arrive. Agencies may lose key staff people. Client conflicts may arise if one agency buys another that handles competing accounts. Legally, an ad agency cannot represent a client's competition without the client's consent.[52] Saatchi & Saatchi was forced to resign Helene Curtis under pressure from Saatchi's biggest client, Procter & Gamble.[53]

Perhaps the best way to improve understanding between clients and agencies would be to have staff members change places for a while. A Foote, Cone & Belding account executive did just that with great success, filling in temporarily as marketing manager at Levi's Jeans for Women. It gave her a whole new perspective on her agency job and the daily challenges faced by her client.[54]

The Suppliers in Advertising

The people and organizations that provide specialized services to the advertising business are called **suppliers.** Without their services it would be impossible to produce the billions of dollars' worth of advertising placed every year.

Although we can't mention them all, important suppliers include *art studios and Web design houses, printers, engravers, film and video production houses,* and *research companies.*

Art Studios and Web Designers

Art studios design and produce artwork and illustrations for advertisements. They may supplement the work of an agency's art department or even take its place for small agencies. Art studios are usually small organizations with as few as three or four employees. Some, though, are large enough to employ several art directors, graphic designers, layout artists, production artists, and sales reps.

Most studios are owned and managed by a graphic designer or illustrator, who calls on agencies and advertising managers to sell the studio's services, takes projects back to the office to be produced, and then delivers them for the client's approval. The work is very time-consuming and requires a talent for organization and management as well as a core competency in art direction and computer graphics.

Similar to art studios, **Web design houses** employ specialists who understand the intricacies of HTML and Java programming languages and can design ads and Web pages that are both effective and cost efficient.

Printers and Related Specialists

The printers who produce brochures, stationery, business cards, sales promotion materials, and point-of-purchase displays are vital to the advertising business. Ranging from small instant-print shops to large offset operations, **printers** employ or contract with highly trained specialists who prepare artwork for reproduction, operate digital scanning machines to make color separations and plates, operate presses and collating machines, and run binderies.

As we discuss in Chapter 14, printers may specialize in offset lithography, rotogravure, letterpress, engraving, or other techniques. Their sales reps must be highly skilled, and they often earn very large commissions.

Film and Video Houses

Few agencies have in-house TV production capabilities. Small agencies often work with local TV stations to produce commercials. But the large agencies normally work with **independent production houses** that specialize in film or video production or both.

Research Companies

Advertisers are concerned about the attitudes of their customers, the size of potential markets, and the acceptability of their products. Agencies want to know what advertising approaches to use, which concepts communicate most efficiently, and how effective past campaigns have been.

As the Internet continues to grow at an alarming speed, so does the demand for Web design houses that understand both the intricacies of programming languages and the various elements of good Web design. This website for Lorgan's, The Retro Store, a specialist store dealing in retro furnishings, won a gold from the One Show Interactive in the category Corporate Image. A unique feature of the site was that it was created so that a person interested in '70s stuff would find himself or herself immersed in a '70s detailed environment as he or she browsed the merchandise.

The media are concerned with the reading and viewing habits of their audiences, the desired markets of their advertiser-customers, and public perceptions toward their own particular medium.

Research, therefore, is closely allied to advertising and an important tool for marketing professionals. But most firms do not maintain a fully staffed research department. Instead, they use **independent research companies** or consultants. Research firms come in all sizes and specialties, and they employ statisticians, field interviewers, and computer programmers, as well as analysts with degrees in psychology, sociology, and marketing. We discuss research in Chapter 7.

The Media of Advertising

The *medium* that carries the advertiser's message is the vital connection between the company that manufactures a product or offers a service and the customer who may wish to buy it. Although the plural term **media** commonly describes channels of mass communication such as television, radio, newspapers, and magazines, it also refers to other communications vehicles such as direct mail, out-of-home media (transit, billboards, etc.), specialized media (aerial/blimps, inflatables), specialty advertising items (imprinted coffee mugs, balloons), and new communication technologies such as digital media, interactive TV, and satellite networks. (Exhibit 4–8 shows the largest U.S. media companies.)

It's important to understand the various media, their role in the advertising business, and the significance of current media trends. For a person seeking a career in advertising, the media may offer the first door to employment, and for many they have provided great financial rewards.

We classify advertising media into six major categories: *print, electronic, digital interactive, out-of-home, direct mail,* and *other media.* Due to recent media trends, there is some overlap. We shall mention these in passing, along with a brief description of each major category.

Print Media

The term **print media** refers to any commercially published, printed medium—such as newspapers and magazines—that sells advertising space to a variety of advertisers. In the United States today, there are 1,661 daily newspapers and more than 7,594 weekly newspapers and shoppers guides.[55] Most are local. However, some national newspapers such as *USA Today, The Wall Street Journal, Barron's,* and trade publications such as *Electronic News* and *Supermarket News* have become quite successful. Once strictly a local newspaper, *The New York Times* is now distributed to more than 1.1 million readers nationwide.[56]

Magazines, on the other hand, have long been national, and some periodicals, such as *Elle,* publish editions in many countries. For over a decade, though, the trend has been toward localization and specialization.

Exhibit 4–8

Top media companies in 2002, by category (figures in millions of U.S. dollars).

Newspapers		Broadcast television	
1. Gannett Co.	$4,760	1. Viacom	$ 7,490
2. Tribune Co.	3,848	2. NBC TV (General Electric)	6,763
3. New York Times Co.	1,864	3. Walt Disney Co.	4,485
4. Knight Ridder	2,786	4. News Corp.	4,301
5. Advance Publications	2,015	5. Tribune Co.	1,179

Magazines		Cable television	
1. AOL Time Warner	$4,850	1. Comcast Corp.	$16,043
2. Hearst Corp.	2,190	2. AOL Time Warner	14,192
3. Advance Publications	1,950	3. Viacom	5,052
4. Primedia	1,472	4. Cox Enterprise	5,040
5. Reader's Digest Association	854	5. Charter Communications	4,566

There are nearly 17,500 different magazines published in the United States alone.[57] These include national consumer publications such as *Time* and *TV Guide;* national trade publications such as *Progressive Grocer* and *Marketing News;* local city magazines such as *Palm Springs Life* and *Chicago;* regional consumer magazines such as *Sunset;* and local or regional trade or farm publications such as *California Farmer.*

Print media also include directories such as the Yellow Pages; school or church newspapers and yearbooks; and programs used at sporting events and theatrical performances. As we shall see in Chapter 15, the vast array of newspapers and magazines makes it possible for both consumer and business advertisers to pinpoint the delivery of their messages to highly select target markets in a variety of fields or geographic locations.

Electronic Media

The **electronic media** of radio and television used to be called the broadcast media. But with the advent of cable TV, many programs are now transmitted electronically through wires rather than broadcast through the air.

The United States alone has more than 1,000 local commercial TV stations and nearly 10,000 local radio stations as well as major TV and radio networks, including ABC, CBS, NBC, Fox, Westinghouse, and Mutual. More than 10,000 local cable systems blanket the country, serving more than 68 million subscribers.[58] Major cable networks such as USA, A&E, and CNN serve these systems. Cable also provides channels with specialized offerings, such as QVC, which offers products that can be purchased by phone; Cinemax, which features recently released films; and American Movie Classics (AMC), which features vintage films. We discuss electronic media in Chapter 16.

Digital Interactive Media

The advent of the information superhighway has brought a new media form. **Digital interactive media** allow the audience to participate actively and immediately. They are changing the way advertisers and agencies do business. The Internet, for example, suddenly gives tiny companies with scant resources instant access to customers worldwide by creating a marketplace in which they can swap advertising space on their own sites for space on others.

As we shall see in Chapters 14 and 17, this presents a challenge to advertisers and agencies to learn new forms of creativity. They have to deal with a whole new environment for their ads. It's an environment where customers may spend 20 minutes or more, not just 30 seconds, and where advertising is a dialogue, not a monologue. And on the Internet, advertisers risk getting "flamed" (receiving harsh criticism by e-mail) if people don't like their ads.[59]

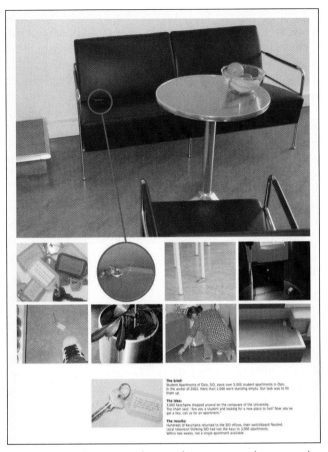

The traditional advertising media are, of course, print, television, and radio. We are accustomed to seeing advertising in our local paper, during our favorite television show, or on a syndicated radio program. However, an ad's impact can be boosted by clever, unexpected placement. By scattering keys throughout the city, a Saatchi & Saatchi (Norway) direct-advertising campaign for Student Apartments of Oslo won a Cannes Silver Lion in 2004.

Out-of-home media are frequently used to reach a large consumer audience and to avoid the clutter of ads in the traditional media. Here Chick-fil-A (www.chick-fil-a.com) uses outdoor billboards to creatively and humorously advertise its product.

Technology and competition for viewers have led to tremendous audience fragmentation. Running a spot on network TV used to cover the majority of a market. Now ad budgets must be bigger to encompass many media. Wherever elusive customers hide, new media forms emerge to seek them out. But for the big, mass-market advertiser, this represents an enormous financial burden.

Out-of-Home Media

The major categories of out-of-home media are *outdoor advertising* and *transit advertising*. In the United States, most **outdoor advertising** (billboard) companies are local firms, but most of their revenue comes from national advertisers such as liquor and airline companies. **Transit advertising** (bus, taxi, and subway advertising) is an effective and inexpensive medium to reach the public while they're in the retail neighborhood. Out-of-home media also include posters in bus shelters and train stations, billboards in airport terminals, stadium scoreboards, flying banners and lights, skywriting, and kiosk posters.

Direct Mail

When companies mail or e-mail their advertising directly to prospective customers without using one of the commercial media forms, it's called **direct-mail advertising.** The ad may be a simple sales letter, or it may be a complex package with coupons, brochures, samples, or other devices designed to stimulate a response. Direct mail using the Postal Service ("snail mail") is the most expensive medium on a cost-per-exposure basis, but it is also the most effective because marketers can target customers directly without competition from other advertisers. We discuss direct mail in Chapter 17.

Other Media

Technology has spawned a host of new advertising media that can confound even the most knowledgeable media planner and buyer. Advertising appears on videocassettes and computer disks. Computers dial telephones and deliver messages by simulating speech or playing a prerecorded message. Computers can also put callers on hold and play prerecorded sales messages until a customer service rep answers. Business presentations are created on computer and copied to disks that are mailed to prospective customers. As progress continues, so will the proliferation of new media and the opportunities for those seeking careers (or fortunes) in the media.

Media around the World

Many U.S. advertising people get used to foreign styles of advertising faster than they get used to foreign media. In the United States, if you want to promote a soft drink as a youthful, fun refresher, you use TV. In some parts of Europe, Asia, South America, and Africa you may not be able to. Around the world, most broadcast media are owned and controlled by the government, and many governments do not allow commercial advertising on radio or television. In Egypt, the current hot medium used by Coca-Cola and others is the fleet of boats plying the Nile with corporate logos emblazoned on their sails.[60]

Where countries do allow TV advertising, TV ownership is high, cutting across the spectrum of income groups. In less-developed countries, though, TV sets may be found only among upper-income groups. This means advertisers may need a different media mix in foreign markets.

Virtually every country has access to radio, television, newspapers, magazines, outdoor media, and direct mail. However, the legalities of different media forms vary from country to country. Generally, the media available to the international advertiser can be categorized as either *international* or *foreign media,* depending on the audience they serve.

International Media

In the past, **international media**—which serve several countries, usually without any change in content—have been limited to newspapers and magazines. Several large American publishers such as Time, McGraw-Hill, and Scientific American circulate international editions of their magazines abroad. Usually written in English, they tend to be read by well-educated, upper-income consumers and are therefore good vehicles for advertising high-end, brand-name products. *Reader's Digest,* on

Although this ad features English copy, the imagery—wild animals, a battered journal, and a picture of family—suggests everything that the words do.

the other hand, is distributed to 126 foreign countries and printed in the local language of each. Today, television is also a viable international medium. And we are beginning to see the emergence of commercial *global media vehicles,* such as CNN.

Foreign Media

Advertisers use **foreign media**—the local media of each country—for large campaigns targeted to consumers or businesses within a single country. Because foreign media cater to their own national audience, advertisers must produce their ads in the language of each country. In countries such as Belgium and Switzerland, with more than one official language, ads are produced in each language.

Unlike the United States, most countries have strong national newspapers that are a good medium for national campaigns. Advertisers also get broad penetration of lower-income markets through radio, which enjoys almost universal ownership. And cinema advertising is a viable alternative to TV in markets with low TV penetration or restricted use of commercial TV.

Chapter Summary

The advertising business comprises four main groups: advertisers (clients), agencies, suppliers, and media. It employs a wide range of artists and businesspeople, sales reps and engineers, top executives, and clerical personnel.

There are four main categories of advertisers based on their geographic activities: local, regional, national, and transnational. Local advertising is placed by businesses in a particular city or county and aimed at customers in the same geographic area. It is important because most sales are made or lost in the local arena.

There are three types of local advertising: product, institutional, and classified. Product advertising can be further divided into regular price-line advertising, sale advertising, and clearance advertising. Institutional advertising creates a long-term perception of the business as a whole by positioning it within the competitive framework. Classified advertising is used to recruit new employees, offer services, and sell or lease new or used merchandise.

Local advertisers are the consummate integrators of marketing communications. Successful local advertisers wear many hats every day, and many of their daily activities help advertise the business. Building relationships is a key element.

Local advertisers can get creative assistance from local ad agencies, media, freelancers and consultants, creative boutiques, syndicated art services, and desktop publishers. Wholesalers, manufacturers, and trade groups often help with cooperative advertising.

Regional advertisers operate in one or several states and market exclusively within that region. National advertisers operate in several regions or throughout the country and comprise the largest advertisers.

Local and national advertisers differ in focus, time orientation, and resources. National advertisers focus on brand building, share of market, grand strategies, and market groups. Local advertisers focus on daily traffic, gross sales or volume, tactical solutions, and the individual customers they see every day. National advertisers have a long-term perspective, local advertisers a short-term one. National advertisers also have more money and more employees.

A large company's advertising department may be centralized or decentralized. Each structure has advantages and disadvantages. The centralized organization is the most typical and may be structured by product, subfunction of advertising, end user, or geography. Decentralized departments are typical of large, far-flung organizations with numerous divisions, subsidiaries, products, countries, regions, and/or brands.

Transnational advertisers face unique challenges. Their markets have a different value system, environment, and language with customers of different purchasing abilities, habits, and motivations. Media customary in the United States may be unavailable or ineffective. Companies therefore often need different advertising strategies. To manage their advertising, transnational advertisers use an international, multinational, or global marketing structure.

Ad agencies are independent organizations of creative people and businesspeople who specialize in developing and preparing advertising plans, ads, and other promotional tools on behalf of their clients.

Like their clients, ad agencies may be local, regional, national, or international in scope. Agencies can be classified by the range of services they offer and the types of business they handle. The two basic types are full-service agencies and specialized-service agencies, such as creative boutiques, media-buying services, and interactive agencies. Agencies may specialize in either consumer or business-to-business accounts. The people who work in agencies may be involved in account management, research, account planning, creative services, production, traffic, media, new business, administration, or a host of other activities.

Agencies may be organized into departments of functional specialties or into groups that work as teams on various accounts. Agencies charge fees or retainers, receive commissions from the media, or mark up outside purchases made for their clients.

Some advertisers develop in-house agencies to save money by keeping agency commissions for themselves. However, they risk losing objectivity and creativity.

Most agencies get clients through referrals, publicity on successful campaigns, advertising, personal solicitation, or networking. The client/agency relationship goes through four stages: prerelationship, development, maintenance, and termination. Numerous factors affect the relationship, including chemistry, communication, conduct, and changes.

The suppliers in advertising are all the people and organizations that assist in the business. Examples are art studios and Web designers, printers, photoengravers, film and video houses, talent agencies, research firms, and consultants.

The media of advertising include the traditional mass media of print, electronic, and out-of-home as well as more specialized channels such as direct mail, digital interactive media, and specialty advertising.

Print media refer to magazines and newspapers as well as directories, Yellow Pages, school yearbooks, and special-event programs. Electronic media include radio, TV, and cable TV. Out-of-home refers to billboard and transit advertising. Direct-mail advertising is the most expensive medium on a cost-per-exposure basis but also typically the most effective at generating inquiries or responses. Interactive media let customers participate, turning advertising from a monologue to a dialogue.

In foreign markets, advertisers are faced with different media mixes, different legal constraints, and different economies of advertising.

Important Terms

account executives (AEs), *114*

account planning, *114*

advertising agency, *109*

art director, *115*

art studio, *126*

Association of National Advertisers (ANA), *103*

brand manager, *107*

business-to-business agency, *111*

centralized advertising department, *105*

classified advertising, *101*

clearance advertising, *101*

cooperative (co-op) advertising, *102*

copy, *115*

copywriter, *115*

creative boutique, *112*

creative director, *115*

decentralized system, *106*

departmental system, *118*

development stage, *123*

digital interactive media, *128*

direct-mail advertising, *129*

electronic media, *128*

fee-commission combination, *119*

foreign media, *131*

full-service advertising agency, *111*

general consumer agency, *111*

global marketers, *108*

group system, *118*

horizontal cooperative advertising, *103*

incentive system, *119*

independent production house, *126*

independent research company, *127*

in-house agency, *120*

institutional advertising, *101*

integrated marketing communications (IMC), *101*

interactive agency, *113*

international agency, *111*

international media, *130*

international structure, *107*

local advertising, *99*

local agency, *109*

maintenance stage, *123*

management (account) supervisors, *114*

markup, *119*

media, *127*

media-buying service, *113*

media commission, *119*

multinational corporation, *108*

national advertiser, *103*

national agency, *110*

outdoor advertising, *129*

point, *104*

prerelationship stage, *122*

print media, *127*

printer, *126*

product advertising, *100*

regional advertiser, *103*

regional agency, *110*

regular price-line advertising, *100*

sale advertising, *101*

sales promotion department, *117*

speculative presentation, *121*

straight-fee (retainer) method, *119*

supplier, *126*

termination stage, *124*

transit advertising, *129*

vertical cooperative advertising, *102*

Web design house, *126*

Review Questions

1. What roles do the major organizations involved in the advertising business perform?

2. What's the difference between a local advertiser and a national advertiser?

3. What services might a modern full-service advertising agency offer a large business-to-business advertiser?

4. What are the most important things an advertiser should consider when selecting an agency?

5. How does an agency make money? What is the best way to compensate an agency? Explain your answer.

6. If you owned an ad agency, what would you do to attract new business? Be specific.

7. What are the advantages and disadvantages of an in-house agency?

8. What are the major influences on the client/agency relationship? What can clients and agencies do to maintain a good relationship?

9. What is meant by the term *interactive media?* Give some examples.

10. If you were planning to advertise your brand of computers in Europe, would you likely use foreign or international media? Why?

11. **The Advertising Experience**

    Due to the great success of a sitcom based on an Amish farm family, old-fashioned farm implements have become a hot item in American hardware stores. After researching co-op advertisements in local newspapers, create and design a co-op ad for Yodel's Scythes and Deuce Hardware Store.

Exploring the Internet

The Internet Exercises for Chapter 4 cover three areas of the advertising world that were discussed: advertising agencies (Exercise 1), advertisers (Exercise 2), and brand positioning by agencies (Exercise 3).

A good place to start surfing the Web for information on advertising is "The Internet Resource Guide to Advertising" (www.adweb.com) or the "Advertising Worldwide Information" site (www.awinet.com).

1. Advertising Agencies

Ad agencies often specialize in a particular type of business or focus on a special market and/or consumer.
Visit the websites for the following agencies:

- Bates USA www.batesusa.com
- BBDO www.bbdo.com
- DDB Worldwide Communications Group Inc. www.ddb.com
- Fallon McElligott www.fallon.com
- Foote, Cone & Belding www.fcb.com
- GroundZero www.groundzero.com
- Kirshenbaum Bond & Partners www.kb.com
- Leo Burnett www.leoburnett.com
- McCann-Erickson www.mccann.com
- Muse Cordero Chen & Partners www.musecordero.com
- Ogilvy & Mather Worldwide www.ogilvy.com
- Modem Media www.modemmedia.com
- Rubin/Postaer Associates www.rpa.com
- Saatchi & Saatchi www.saatchi-saatchi.com
- TBWA Chiat/Day www.tbwachiat.com
- TeamOne Advertising www.teamoneadv.com
- The Phelps Group www.phelpsgroup.com
- J. Walter Thompson www.jwtworks.com
- Webfactory Ltd. www.webfactory.ie
- Young and Rubicam www.YandR.com

Answer the following questions for each.

a. What is the focus of the agency's work (e.g., consumer, business-to-business, ethnic, general market)?

b. What is the scope and size of the agency's business? Who makes up its clientele?

c. What is the agency's mission statement and/or philosophy? How does that affect its client base?

d. What is the agency's positioning (e.g., creative-driven, strategy (account)-driven, media-driven)?

e. What is your overall impression of the agency and its work?

2. Agencies and Clients (Advertisers)

The advertising industry is truly vast, and advertisers and their agencies focus on a wide range of businesses in a broad scope of markets. Visit the following websites and familiarize yourself further with the nature and scope of the advertising world.

Advertisers

- Global: International Advertising Association (IAA) www.iaaglobal.org
- National: Association of National Advertisers (ANA) www.ana.net

Advertising Agencies

- National: American Association of Advertising Agencies (AAAA) www.aaaa.org
- National: Institute of Canadian Advertising (ICA) www.ica-ad.com

Advertising Practitioners

- International: Institute of Practitioners in Advertising (IPA) www.ipa.co.uk
- National: American Advertising Federation (AAF) www.aaf.org
- Regional: Denver Advertising Federation (DAF) www.daf.org
- Local: AdClub of Greater Boston www.adclub.org

Advertising Publications

- National: *Advertising Age* www.adage.com
- Regional/Local: *AdWeek* www.adweek.com

Answer the following questions for each site.

a. What advertising group (advertiser, ad agency, practitioner, trade press) sponsors the site? Who is the intended audience?

b. What is the size/scope of the organization?

c. What is the organization's purpose? The site's purpose?

d. What benefit does the organization provide individual members? The advertising community at large?

e. How is this organization important to the advertising industry? Why?

3. Developing a Brand Image

After visiting at least three of the websites listed in Exercise 1, develop a mission statement for two hypothetical new advertising agencies. The first agency is small, has an irreverent edge, and is primarily dedicated to working for nonprofit clients. The second agency would like to represent luxury-goods companies looking to add young professionals to their clientele.

Part 2

Crafting Marketing and Advertising Strategies

THE SUCCESS of any business depends on its ability to attract and retain customers who are willing and able to buy its goods and services. To do this, a business must locate, understand, and communicate with current and prospective customers. Part Two examines the marketing process, the nature of consumers, the relationship between products and market segments, and the research and planning processes that make for marketing and advertising success. ∎

Chapter 5
Marketing and Consumer Behavior: The Foundations of Advertising

Describes products and markets and how advertisers use the marketing process to create effective advertising. The chapter presents the consumer as an acceptor or rejector of products and discusses how the consumer's complex decision-making process affects the design of advertising.

Chapter 6
Market Segmentation and the Marketing Mix: Determinants of Advertising Strategy

Discusses market segments, the aggregation of segments, and the influence of target marketing on a product company. It presents the elements of the marketing mix and discusses how advertisers use them to understand and improve a product concept.

Chapter 7
Research: Gathering Information for Advertising Planning

Points out the value of research in improving marketing and advertising effectiveness. It describes how to organize and gather data and discusses the objectives and techniques of concept testing, pretesting, and posttesting.

Chapter 8
Marketing and Advertising Planning: Top-Down, Bottom-Up, and IMC

Details the creation of marketing and advertising plans, particularly setting realistic objectives and developing creative strategies to achieve them. The chapter also presents methods for allocating resources.

Chapter 9
Planning Media Strategy: Finding Links to the Market

Introduces the media plan and the changing role of media planners. It discusses how to determine target audiences and establish objectives for reaching them. The chapter explains the elements of media strategy, how to select specific media vehicles, and how to schedule their use.

Chapter 5

Marketing and Consumer Behavior: The Foundations of Advertising

Objectives TO UNDERLINE THE IMPORTANCE OF THE MARKETING PROCESS IN BUSINESS AND TO DEFINE THE ROLE OF ADVERTISING AND OTHER MARKETING COMMUNICATIONS TOOLS IN PRESENTING THE COMPANY AND ITS PRODUCTS TO THE MARKET. The successful advertising practitioner must understand the relationship between marketing activities and the way consumers behave. Ideally, it is this relationship that shapes the creation of effective advertising.

After studying this chapter, you will be able to:

- **Define** marketing and explain the role advertising plays in the larger marketing context.

- **Discuss** the concept of product utility and the relationship between utility and consumer needs.

- **Identify** the key participants in the marketing process.

- **Outline** the consumer perception process and explain why advertising people say "perception is everything."

- **Describe** the fundamental motives behind consumer purchases.

- **Discuss** the various influences on consumer behavior.

- **Explain** how advertisers deal with cognitive dissonance.

Nineteen ninety-eight set new benchmarks for American culture. William Jefferson Clinton became the second president in U.S. history to be impeached, Adam Sandler was the new icon of comedy with the release of *The Wedding Singer* and *The Waterboy,* and John Glenn returned to space. For many, however, the advances of the Internet, and the dot-com boom that followed, will forever mark the era. At an increasing rate, e-mails replaced "snail mail," online chat rooms took the place of a conversation in the park, research was no longer confined within the walls of a library, and retail business was no longer restricted to a local office, shop, or mall. History may mark this period as the Golden Age of Entrepreneurialism: dot-coms sprang up by the thousands as people sought to take advantage of new, Internet-related technologies. The onslaught of dot-coms tested the boundaries of economics and advertising and, for a brief moment, even managed to dazzle Wall Street.[1] Amid these changes came one of the biggest promises—and flops—of this new technological era. ■ HomeGrocer.com was born of the minds of three entrepreneurs with visions of staking a claim in this rapidly evolving world. Terry Dayton, Ken Deering, and Mike Donald sought to make grocery shopping an experience that would no longer require getting in the car, sitting in traffic, weaving through crowded aisles, and waiting in long lines. With the creation of Home-Grocer.com, the founders envisioned people shopping from home on a regular basis, their fresh groceries arriving the following day with a friendly smile. As they put it, they wanted to be the "milkman of the '90s." ■ Within two years, the venture received more than $160 million in funding from big-time investors such as Amazon.com, Kleiner Perkins Caufield & Byers, Hummer Winblad Venture Partners, and the Barksdale Group (the venture capital firm of former Netscape Communications CEO Jim Barksdale).[2] In light of this new financial backing, and having already expanded from one to three locations over a period of months, HomeGrocer developed an aggressive new plan to maintain swift and steady growth. By year's end, top management vowed to expand into 20 new locations throughout the United States, lease 2 million square feet of warehouse space and more than 1,000 new Freightliner delivery trucks, hire 7,000 employees, and launch a multimillion-dollar ad campaign.[3] With a solid business plan aimed at taking advantage of a $500 billion market and strong financial backing, HomeGrocer.com had all the earmarks of a surefire winner. ■ Yet, despite this fantastic start, HomeGrocer.com was doomed from the beginning. Even with all of the money it had raised, all the capital it had invested, and all the new locations it had opened, HomeGrocer.com still lacked one important thing: a product that appealed to a broad-enough customer base to turn a profit. The result? On June 26, 2000, just three months after going public, HomeGrocer.com was sold to its main rival, Webvan, for $1.1 billion in stock—one year later, after losing $697 million in three years, Webvan also closed its doors.[4] ■ How did this happen? How could the e-grocers, and HomeGrocer.com in particular, attract so much attention, raise so much money, and expand so quickly, only to close shop within two years? The answer is simple: poor marketing. More specifically, HomeGrocer failed to identify its potential customers and lacked a complete understanding of the potential customers'

wants. HomeGrocer was not just creating a new service; it was seeking to change peoples' grocery-shopping behavior as well.[5] For most shoppers, the only true way of choosing a ripe piece of fruit is to pick it up, squeeze it, and smell it. The online world was simply too foreign. Changing this behavioral trend would be a slow and time-consuming process. Yet time was the one thing that the market would not allow. With hungry investors, tight competition, and an ever-evolving marketplace, HomeGrocer.com needed to grow big, and it needed to do this quickly. Instead of taking the time needed to foster a change in customer behavior, HomeGrocer expanded as quickly as Wall Street dictated, spending millions marketing a service that few were ready to pay for. ■ Adding to the problem was HomeGrocer's failure to recognize that strict competition would not allow its pricing structure to attract customers in the long run. While HomeGrocer.com had to charge a fee to provide its service (unless orders reached $75 or more), local grocers had been delivering their food to residents of densely populated areas for years at no extra cost. At the time, the majority of customers were not willing to pay a premium for delivery when they could either do it themselves or have an existing supermarket deliver their groceries at a lower cost. ■ Even as evidence of its marketing failures was becoming apparent, HomeGrocer pushed on, certain that it could stake its claim to the half-trillion-dollar market of retail grocery shopping. HomeGrocer's solution to speeding up the behavioral patterns of potential consumers was simple: advertise. For the year of 2000 alone, HomeGrocer.com budgeted $120 million in advertising expenditures to justify its aggressive expansion plans and convert the consumer base needed to survive.[6] The only problem was that the $120 million ad budget far surpassed the company's total sales. When the amount spent to attract a customer exceeds the amount that a customer contributes to revenue, the business will not be around for long. In an effort to combat competition from other e-grocers and local supermarkets, HomeGrocer.com simply spent itself into the ground. ■ HomeGrocer.com failed miserably, as did the majority of the e-grocers of the dot-com era. By doing so, HomeGrocer.com set a good example of what not to do. To succeed in business, a company's top managers must understand the basic principles of marketing. Specifically, they must understand who their customers are, and they must listen and respond to their customers' desires. They cannot assume anything about the market. Companies that suffer from the *assumption syndrome* court failure and have swift endings. Even superior advertising won't save a mismarketed service. Unfortunately, advertising all too often becomes the scapegoat for management's marketing mistakes. ■

The Larger Marketing Context of Advertising

All advertisers face a perennial challenge: how to present their products, services, and ideas effectively through the media to buyers. To do this, they must comprehend the important relationship between the product and the marketplace. This relationship is the province of marketing.

Unfortunately, marketing's role is often misunderstood and occasionally overlooked. For example, everybody knows that a business can't survive without proper financing, and, without production, there are no products to sell. But how does a company know *what* products or services to produce? Or where to distribute them, or through what channels? That's where marketing comes in.

The key to a company's prosperity is the ability to attract and keep customers who are willing and able to pay for the firm's goods and services. This means a company must be able to locate prospective customers—where they live, work, and play—and then understand their needs, wants, and desires; create products and services to satisfy those desires; and finally communicate that information in a way that resonates with them.

This chapter (in fact, this whole unit) defines and outlines marketing issues to clarify advertising's proper role in the marketing function and to introduce the human factors that ultimately shape advertising. As we shall see, the relationship between advertising and marketing is critical.

The Relationship of Marketing to Advertising

As we discussed in Chapter 1, **marketing** is the business process management uses to plan and execute the conception, pricing, *promotion,* and distribution of its products, whether they be goods, services, brands, or even ideas. The ultimate purpose of marketing is to create exchanges that satisfy the perceived needs, wants, and objectives of individuals and organizations.

Advertising is just one of the numerous tools used in the promotion, or communication, aspect of marketing. But how the advertising is done, and where it is placed, depends largely on the other aspects of the marketing mix and for whom the advertising is intended.

Customer Needs and Product Utility

This definition of marketing shows that one of the important elements is the special relationship between a customer's *needs* and a product's *need-satisfying potential.* This is known as the product's utility. **Utility** is the product's ability to satisfy both functional needs and symbolic (or psychological) wants.[7] One of the roles of advertising is to communicate this utility. Thus, some ads promote how well a product works; others tout glamour, sex appeal, or status. Ad Lab 5–A discusses the important relationship between needs and utility.

Through the use of marketing research, companies try to discover what needs and wants exist in the marketplace and to define a product's general characteristics in the light of economic, social, and political trends. The goal is to use this information for *product shaping*—designing products, through manufacturing, repackaging, or advertising, to satisfy more fully the customers' needs and wants.

To woo Gen Xers and Echo Boomers (the children of baby boomers), for example, Ford Motor Company developed Focus—a low-priced sporty compact car. Optional extras included a sports rack and an unconventional, removable pet holder with a foldable dish, designed to keep Rover from sliding around on the seat. The company also gave buyers the choice of flowers or swirls on the outside and fleece, jersey, or neoprene for the seats.

Aimed at a generation of young people raised on extreme sports such as snowboarding, inline skating, and sky surfing, Ford's commercials were equally cool. They featured a talky, scattered comedienne, Annabelle Gurwitch, demonstrating how fabulous the new Focus is as she drives around the country. And to be even more edgy, the first spots were aired *live* as Ms. Gurwitch, trying to find her way to the MTV music awards, got lost in Manhattan.[8]

Businesspeople all too often give the marketing process short shrift. Some companies introduce a product without a clear idea of its utility to the customer, hoping advertising will move the product off the shelf. As HomeGrocer.com found out, the consequences of such a shortsighted policy can be severe.

Exchanges, Perception, and Satisfaction

Recall that the purpose of marketing is "to create exchanges that satisfy the perceived needs, wants, and objectives of individuals and organizations." There are three important ideas expressed in this definition: *exchanges, perception,* and *satisfaction.* Let's take a brief look at each of these.

VIDEO

Scene opens on long shot of New York skyscraper under construction. Zoom in to Ironworker #1 balancing on beam drinking from Pepsi bottle.

FOREMAN: Puts fingers to his mouth to whistle.

Ironworker #1 throws him the bottle.

Cut to Ironworker #2 drinking from another bottle while Ironworker #3 throws a bottle to another coworker.

Cut to Ironworker #4 catching bottle and throwing it to another worker. Continuous series of quick cuts as workers throw bottles to one another.

Ironworker #5 slips and catches the beam to save himself. Camera pans down to reveal he has caught the Pepsi bottle with his feet.

SUPER: New Pepsi Grip. Easy to hold.

FOREMAN: DARE FOR MORE (Pepsi logo).

AUDIO

SFX: Ambient outdoor sounds.

MUSIC: Driving drumbeat building throughout.

FOREMAN: Whistles at Ironworker #1.

Workers on a high-rise construction site defy gravity to pass around a redesigned Pepsi "grip" bottle. Featuring no dialogue, the 30-second spot's snappy display of product utility won a Bronze Lion at Cannes.

Understanding Needs and Utility

Superior quality will not close a sale by itself. Marketing people must make the product available and promote its advantages, whether it's a graphite tennis racket, a high-performance sports car, or even the prompt, friendly service of a bank.

A key fact in any product's success is that it must satisfy consumers' needs. The capability to satisfy those needs is called utility. Five types of *functional utility* are important to consumers: *form, task, possession, time,* and *place.* A product may provide *psychic utility* as well as functional utility.

Companies create *form utility* whenever they produce a tangible good, such as a bicycle. They provide *task utility* by performing a task for others. However, merely producing a bicycle—or repairing it—doesn't guarantee consumer satisfaction. Consumers must want the bicycle or require the repair, or no need is satisfied and no utility occurs. Thus, marketing decisions should guide the production side of business too.

Even when a company provides form or task utility, marketers must consider how consumers can take possession of the product. This includes distribution, pricing strategies, shelf availability, purchase agreements, and delivery. Money is typically exchanged for *possession utility.* An antique bicycle on display, but not for sale, lacks possession utility because the customer cannot purchase it.

Providing the consumer with the product when he or she wants it is known as *time utility.* Having an ample supply of jam, cars, or bank tellers on hand when the consumer has the need is thus another marketing requirement.

Place utility—having the product available where the customer can get it—is also vital to business success. Customers won't travel very far out of their way to get bicycles or cars. They're even less likely to travel long distances for everyday needs. That's why banks have branches. And that's why 24-hour convenience markets, which sell gasoline and basic food items, are so popular.

Finally, consumers gain *psychic utility* when a product offers symbolic or psychological need satisfaction, such as status or sex appeal. Psychic utility is usually achieved through product promotion (advertising) and may fulfill esteem and self-actualization needs.

Whether it be psychic utility or the functional utilities of form, task, possession, time, and place, product utility is an essential component of marketing success.

Laboratory Application

Select an ad from a weekly newsmagazine and describe in detail what utilities it speaks to: psychic utility and/or the functional utilities of form, task, possession, time, and place.

Exchanges: The Purpose of Marketing and Advertising

Any transaction in which one person or organization trades something of value with someone else is an **exchange.** Exchange is the traditional, theoretical core of marketing. We all engage in exchanges. It's a natural part of our human self-interest. Buyers do it to acquire more things and better their situation. Sellers do it to grow their business and make a profit.

Marketing facilitates these exchanges, thus increasing our potential for satisfaction. How does it do this? In a variety of ways: by developing goods and services we might want; by pricing them affordably; by distributing them to convenient locations; and by informing us about them through advertising and other communication tools. By providing information, advertising makes people aware of the availability of products and of the selection alternatives among different brands. Advertising communicates product features and benefits, various price

Advertisers know that satisfying a consumer's self-interest is central to affecting purchasing behavior. This ad for Audi (www.audi.com) appeals to consumers' desire to feel eternally youthful.

options, and locations where the product can be found. In the case of *direct marketing,* advertising may even close the sale.

Perception Is Everything

People who are about to engage in a business exchange sometimes feel apprehensive. They may worry that the exchange is not equal, even when it is truly fair. This is where *perception* comes in. The perception of inequity is more likely if the customer has little knowledge of the product. In this case, the more knowledgeable party (the seller) must reassure the buyer—perhaps through advertising—that an equal exchange is possible. If the seller can provide the information and inspiration the buyer seeks, the two may recognize the potential for a *perceived equal-value exchange.* Without this perception, though, an exchange is unlikely. For example, if people don't believe the benefits AOL has to offer are worth $20 a month, they won't subscribe to the service—no matter how much AOL spends on advertising.

Thus, marketing is actually concerned with two levels of customer perception: the customer's perception of the product or service, and the seller's perception of the customer's needs, wants, and objectives.

So advertisers must first acquire an understanding of where their customers are coming from. What do they need? What do they want? How do they see us now? Once advertisers develop a deep understanding of their customers, they can be more effective in adjusting or altering their customers' perception of the product (awareness, attitude, interest) and their customers' belief in the product's ability (value) to satisfy their perceived wants or needs (utility).

Advertising may use a variety of techniques to accomplish this. By using just the right mood lighting or music, for example, a TV commercial can simultaneously capture customers' attention and stimulate their emotions toward the goal of need or want fulfillment. If customers are aware of the product and its value, and if they decide to satisfy the particular want or need the product addresses, they are more likely to act.[9] Since perception is so important to advertisers, we discuss it in greater detail later in this chapter.

Satisfaction: The Goal of the Customer

Even after an exchange occurs, *satisfaction* remains an issue. Satisfaction must occur every time customers use the product, or people won't think they got an equal-value exchange. Satisfaction leads to more exchanges: Satisfied customers repurchase; and satisfied customers tell their friends. Positive word of mouth cre-

From the viewpoint of the customer, perception is reality. Companies must therefore carefully monitor the messages they send, since those messages may either enhance their image or damage it. Some advertisers, for example, perceive the readers of Rolling Stone *to be hedonistic dopeheads—leftovers from the hippie era. So the magazine (www.rollingstone.com) attempts to change this perception by specifically addressing it and offering a counterargument of what the reality actually is. This highly successful campaign has garnered innumerable awards for creativity from the advertising industry.*

Perception.   Reality.

For a new generation of Rolling Stone readers, drugs are out of their minds and into the frying pan. They know the truth; that if you tune in and turn on, you burn out. For twenty five years, Rolling Stone magazine has reflected the changing attitudes, ideas and lifestyles of the people who are changing the world. If you want to reach seven million of these people, we invite you to alter a few minds in the pages of Rolling Stone.

Rolling Stone

ALL SUVS PROMISE FREEDOM.
FEW HAVE ACTUALLY FOUGHT FOR IT.

Since 1948, Land Rover 4x4s have been pressed into battle throughout the world. To date, our most luxurious model has received no special dispensation. As recently as the Gulf War, civilian Range Rovers were commandeered by coalition forces and, to no one's surprise, performed dauntlessly. Not one to hide behind its lavish amenities, the Range Rover possesses the same go-anywhere, all-terrain capability as the rest of the Land Rover fleet. A single tour in our 2002 4.6 HSE and you'll soon appreciate how unique it is. Polished walnut and select leather combined with Electronic Air Suspension and a 460-watt, 12-speaker audio system make the best of even the worst situations. As do permanent four-wheel drive and four-wheel Electronic Traction Control. Why, there's nothing we won't do to ensure that every Range Rover is as capable as it is comfortable. Anything to keep the peace.

LAND ROVER

RANGE ROVER

Corporate ads that promote the company's social responsibility as well as specific product benefits are useful because they reinforce the purchaser's decision to buy. By restating these benefits through advertising, Land Rover reassures customers that their decision to buy was the right one, and that increases the likelihood that these customers will return to make subsequent purchases.

ates even more sales and contributes to a good reputation. Thus, while satisfaction is the goal of the customer, it must also be the fundamental goal of any sophisticated marketer.

Advertising *reinforces* satisfaction by reminding customers why they bought the product, helping them defend the purchase against skeptical friends and associates, and enabling them to persuade other prospects to buy it. If a product performs poorly, the negative effect will be even more far-reaching. And good advertising for a poor product can actually hasten the advertiser's demise. The better the advertising, the more people will try the product—once. And the more who try an unsatisfactory product, the more who will reject it—and tell their friends.

Thus, we can think of marketing as the process companies use to make a profit by satisfying their customers' needs and desires.

The Key Participants in the Marketing Process

People's needs and wants change daily, and marketers constantly advertise a plethora of products for customer attention and interest. This makes the marketing process very dynamic. At times, it seems like everybody is searching for an exchange. At other times, it seems nobody is. Marketing exchanges depend on three types of participants: *customers, markets* (groups of customers), and *marketers*.

Customers

Customers are the people or organizations who consume goods and services. They fall into three general categories: *current customers, prospective customers,* and *centers of influence.*

Current customers have already bought something from a business; in fact, they may buy it regularly. One way to measure a business's success is by calculating the number of its current customers and their repeat purchases. **Prospective customers** are people about to make an exchange or considering it. **Centers of influence** are those customers, prospective customers, or opinion leaders whose ideas and actions others respect. A center of influence is often the link to many prospective customers.

Markets

The second participant in the marketing process is the **market,** which is simply a group of current customers, prospective customers, and noncustomers who share a common interest, need, or desire; who have the money to spend to satisfy needs or solve problems; and who have the authority to make expenditure decisions.[10] As we discuss more fully in Chapter 6, a market never includes everybody. Companies advertise to four broad classifications of markets:

1. **Consumer markets** comprise people who buy goods and services for their own use. Both Nissan and Ford, for example, aim at the consumer market. But they cater to different groups within that market. They advertise some vehicles to single women; others to upscale young families; and still others to retired people. The consumer market is huge, spending close to $5.5 trillion every year on products and services in the United States alone.[11] Chapter 6 discusses ways to categorize consumer segments.

2. **Business markets** are composed of organizations that buy services, natural resources, and component products that they resell, use to conduct their business,

SPHERE 1/6th ACTION FIGURES.
AS REAL AS IT GETS.

WWW.SPHEREMARKETING.NET

Consumer ads, like this Cannes Gold Lion-winning one for Sphere Action Figures, target people who buy goods and services for their own use. Food, clothing, and automobiles are just a few examples of the many consumer goods that make up a $5 trillion industry.

or use to manufacture another product. As consumers we have a natural bias toward consumer marketing and advertising. And certainly consumer marketers rely on advertising more than business marketers do. However, virtually half of all marketing is business-to-business. In the United States, business buyers purchase nearly $4 trillion worth of manufactured goods every year, billions more of raw materials, and billions more for the services of law firms, accountants, airlines, and advertising agencies.[12] Thus, business marketing is a very important field that requires special skills and is worthy of our consideration in every chapter. As we pointed out in Chapter 1, there are several subtypes of business markets. The two most important are *reseller markets* and *industrial markets*.

Reseller markets buy products to resell them. Ford, for example, aims a portion of its marketing activities at its dealers. Similarly, Sunkist first needs to convince food wholesalers and retail grocers to carry its brand of fruits, or they will never be sold to consumers. Reseller markets, therefore, are extremely important to most companies, even though most consumers are unaware of the marketing or advertising activities aimed at them.

Industrial markets include more than 17.6 million firms that buy products used to produce other goods and services.[13] Manufacturers of plant equipment and machinery advertise to industrial markets, as do office suppliers,

Transnational ads are those that appear in foreign countries. If they are to succeed, advertisers must be aware of often-subtle differences in environment and culture. With no copy and no picture of the car, this Land Rover ad assumes the reader will understand that it's the hidden Land Rover making its way through the wilderness that has disturbed the birds. Although the ad itself is very subtle, it is understandable to both domestic and international audiences, which won it a Bronze Lion at Cannes.

computer companies, and telephone companies. Chapter 6 categorizes industrial markets by factors of industry segment, geographic location, and size.

3. **Government markets** buy products for municipal, state, federal, and other government activities. Some firms are immensely successful selling only to government markets. They advertise post office vehicles, police and military weapons, and tax collector office equipment in trade magazines read by government buyers.

4. **Transnational** (or **global**) **markets** include any of the other three markets located in foreign countries. Every country has consumers, resellers, industries, and governments. So what's the difference between the transnational market and the domestic U.S. or Canadian market for the same product? Environment. The environment in France differs from that in Japan. The environment in Brazil differs from that in Saudi Arabia. Sometimes, as in the case of Switzerland, environments even vary widely within a single country. Targeting markets across national boundaries presents interesting challenges and important opportunities for contemporary advertisers, so we deal with the subject of international advertising wherever applicable throughout this book.

Marketers

The third participant in the marketing process, **marketers,** includes every person or organization that has products, services, or ideas to sell. Manufacturers market consumer and business products. Farmers market wheat; doctors market medical services; banks market financial products; and political organizations market philosophies and candidates. To be successful, marketers must know their markets intimately—*before* they start advertising.

Consumer Behavior: The Key to Advertising Strategy

Take a look at your friends in class, or the people you work with. How well do you know them? Could you describe their lifestyles and the kinds of products they prefer? Do they typically eat out or cook for themselves? Do they ski? Play tennis? If so, what brands of equipment do they buy? Do you know which radio stations they listen to? What TV programs they watch? Do they read a daily newspaper? If you were Sanyo's advertising manager and wanted to advertise a new DVD player to these people, what type of appeal would you use? What media would you use to reach them?

The Importance of Knowing the Consumer

Advertisers spend a lot of money to keep individuals and groups of individuals (markets) interested in their products. To succeed, they need to understand what makes potential customers behave the way they do. The advertiser's goal is to get enough relevant market data to develop accurate profiles of buyers—to find the common ground (and symbols) for communication. This involves the study of **consumer behavior:** the mental and emotional processes and the physical activities of people who purchase and use goods and services to satisfy particular needs and wants.[14] The behavior of **organizational buyers** (the people who purchase products and services for use in business and government) is also very important. We examine this aspect of buying behavior in Chapter 6.

The Consumer Decision Process: An Overview

Social scientists develop many theories of consumer behavior to explain the process of making a purchase decision. Let's look at this information from the viewpoint of the advertiser.

Advertising's primary mission is to reach prospective customers and influence their awareness, attitudes, and buying behavior. We discussed in Chapter 1 that to succeed, an advertiser must make the marketing communications process work very efficiently.

The moment a medium delivers an advertising message to us, our mental computer runs a rapid evaluation called the **consumer decision process.** The conceptual model in Exhibit 5–1 presents the basic steps consumers go through in making a purchase decision. As you can see, the full process involves a rather lengthy sequence of activities: *problem recognition* (which may occur as a result of seeing an ad), *information search, evaluation and selection* of alternative brands, *store choice and purchase,* and finally *postpurchase behavior.* For simple, habitual, everyday purchases with low levels of involvement, the decision-making process is

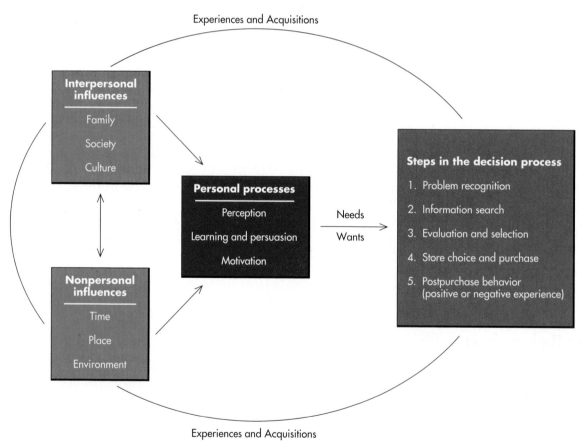

Exhibit 5–1

The basic consumer decision process comprises a set of fundamental steps that the consumer experiences during and after the purchase process. Advertising can affect the consumer's attitude at any point in this process. For the complete model of the process, see RL 5–1 in the Reference Library on the Contemporary Advertising *website.*

typically very abbreviated. But in those situations where the consumer is highly involved in the purchase, it's not at all unusual for the consumer to substantially extend the decision process.

Regardless of whether the process is limited or extended, though, numerous sociological and psychological factors invariably play a role in the way consumers behave. These include a series of personal subprocesses that are themselves shaped by various influences.

The three **personal processes** govern the way we discern raw data (*stimuli*) and translate them into feelings, thoughts, beliefs, and actions. The personal processes are the *perception,* the *learning and persuasion,* and the *motivation processes.*

Second, our mental processes and behavior are affected by two sets of influences. **Interpersonal influences** include our *family, society,* and *culture.* **Nonpersonal influences**—factors often outside the consumer's control—include *time, place,* and *environment.* These influences further affect the personal processes of perception, learning, and motivation.

After dealing with these processes and influences, we face the pivotal decision: to buy or not to buy. But taking that final step typically requires yet another process, the **evaluation of alternatives,** in which we choose brands, sizes, styles, and colors. If we do decide to buy, our **postpurchase evaluation** will dramatically affect all our subsequent purchases.

Like the marketing communications process, the decision process is circular in nature. The advertiser who understands this process can develop messages more likely to reach and make sense to consumers.

Personal Processes in Consumer Behavior

Assume you are the advertising manager preparing to launch a new high-tech, vitamin-laden beverage brand for athletes and sports participants. We'll call it MonsterMalt. What's your first objective?

The first task in promoting any new product is to create awareness (*perception*) that the product exists. The second is to provide enough compelling information (*learning and persuasion*) about the product for prospective customers to find interest and make an informed decision. Finally, you want your advertising to stimulate customers' desire (*motivation*) to satisfy their needs and wants by trying the product. If they find MonsterMalt satisfying, they likely will continue to purchase it. These three personal processes of consumer behavior—perception, learning and persuasion, and motivation—are extremely important to advertisers. By studying these, advertisers can better evaluate how their messages are perceived.

The Consumer Perception Process

As we mentioned earlier, perception is everything. It guides all our activities from the people we associate with to the products we buy. How a consumer perceives each of the different brands in a category determines which ones he or she uses.[15] The perception challenge, therefore, is the first and greatest hurdle advertisers must cross. Some marketers spend millions of dollars on national advertising, sales promotion, point-of-purchase displays, and other marketing communications only to discover that many consumers don't remember the product or the promotion. The average adult may be exposed to thousands of ads each day but notices only a handful and remembers even fewer.[16] How does this happen? The answer lies in the principle of perception.

We use the term **perception** to refer to the personalized way we sense, interpret, and comprehend various *stimuli.* This definition suggests there are several key elements to the consumer perception process, as shown in Exhibit 5–2.

Stimulus

A **stimulus** is physical information we receive through our senses. When we look at a new car, we receive a number of stimuli. We might note the color of the paint,

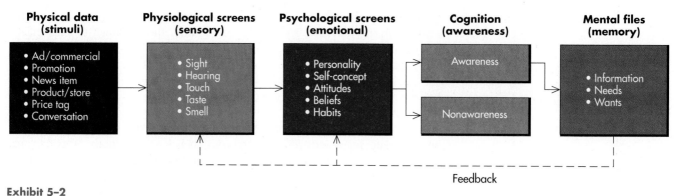

Exhibit 5–2
The model of the consumer perception process portrays how consumers perceive, accept, and remember an ad or other stimulus to buy.

the smell of the leather, the purr of the engine. When we look at a theater ad in the newspaper, we see a collection of type, art, and photography arranged in a way that we interpret as an ad. That's the stimulus. So, for our purposes, assume that a stimulus is any ad, commercial, or promotion that we see.

Advertising stimuli can appear in a variety of forms: a window display at a local department store, the brightly colored labels on cans of Campbell's tomato soup, or even the red price tag on a pair of skis at the Sport Chalet. These objects are all physical in nature; they stimulate our senses (with varying degrees of intensity) in ways that can be measured.

Perceptual Screens

The second key element in perception is the personalized way of sensing and interpreting the stimulus data. Before any data can be perceived, they must first penetrate a set of **perceptual screens,** the subconscious filters that shield us from unwanted messages. There are two types of screens, *physiological* and *psychological.*

The **physiological screens** comprise the five senses: sight, hearing, touch, taste, and smell. They detect the incoming data and measure the dimension and intensity of the physical stimuli. A sight-impaired person can't read an ad in *Sports Illustrated.* And if the type in a movie ad is too small for the average reader, it won't be read, and perception will suffer. Similarly, if the music in a TV commercial for a furniture store is not complimentary to the message, the viewer may tune out, change channels, or even turn off the TV. The advertiser's message is effectively screened out when the viewer can't interpret it; perception does not occur, and the furniture goes unsold.[17]

We are limited not only by the physical capacity of our senses but also by our feelings and interests. Each consumer uses **psychological screens** to evaluate, filter, and personalize information according to subjective emotional standards. These screens evaluate data based on *innate factors,* such as the consumer's personality and instinctive human needs, and *learned factors,* such as self-concept, interests, attitudes, beliefs, past experiences, and lifestyle. They help consumers summarize unwieldy or complex data. For example, perceptual screens help us accept or reject symbolic ideas, such as the sexy commercial for Levi's Dockers in which a man and a number of women dirty-dance in a nightclub. Prospective partners pull at the man by grabbing his belt loops. When he finally leaves with one, the voice-over says: "You'll get worn out before they do." The campaign is targeted toward upscale, fashion-forward men in the 25 to 34 age group who critically influence others.[18]

After extensive consumer research, Bally's Health & Tennis determined that the perfectly chiseled body, glorified by earlier health club advertising and exemplified by such icons as Cher, Victoria Principal, and Don Johnson, was no longer

How much wood could a woodchuck chuck
if a woodchuck could chuck wood?

Great photography can make you read anything. Tibor Nemeth Photography · tibornemeth.com

Screens are physical and psychological barriers that advertisers must penetrate in order to gain notice and convey their message. This ad for Tibor Nemeth Photography first grabs the viewers' attention with the sheer natural beauty of the ad. It then throws in what seems like a completely random headline. The attention is then directed to the copy below the photo, which puts the pieces together with the tagline, "Great photography can make you read anything."

penetrating the psychological screens of its 4.5 million members. As the new millennium approached, that premise no longer fit their **self-concept** (the image we have of who we are and who we want to be). In a major strategy shift, Bally's refocused its advertising on customers such as Beth from Costa Mesa, California, who is seen rock climbing in a TV commercial while telling viewers, "I think I climb because I'm afraid of heights. . . . There is nothing better than being able to conquer that fear. That's why I work out at Bally's, so I can do more on the rocks." The tagline: "If you can get here [Bally's], you can get there [a mountaintop]."

As this example shows, advertisers face a major problem dealing with consumers' perceptual screens. As overcommunicated consumers, we unconsciously screen out or modify many of the sensations that bombard us, rejecting those that conflict with our experiences, needs, desires, attitudes, and beliefs.[19] We simply focus on some things and ignore others. This is called **selective perception.** Hence, Panasonic may run a series of outstanding ads for its new digital camcorder in the daily newspaper, but they won't penetrate the psychological screens of consumers who don't need or want a new camera. Later these people probably won't even remember seeing the ads.

Cognition

The third key element in perception is **cognition:** comprehending the stimulus. Once we detect the stimulus and allow it through our perceptual screens, we can

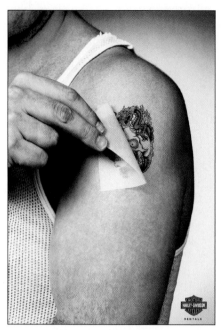

Advertisers frequently capitalize on consumers' concept of themselves to generate attention and interest in a particular product. This ad—a 2004 Cannes Bronze Lion winner from Ogilvy & Mather RSTM—takes the next step: It shows consumers that they can temporarily identify with their wilder sides by renting a Harley-Davidson.

Learning and Persuasion: How Consumers Process Information

comprehend and accept it. Now perception has occurred, and the stimulus reaches the consumer's reality zone.

But each of us has his or her own reality. For example, you may consider the tacos advertised by Taco Bell to be "Mexican" food. That perception is your reality. But someone from Mexico might tell you that a fast-food taco bears little resemblance to an authentic Mexican taco. That person's reality, based on another perception, is considerably different. Advertisers thus seek commonly shared perceptions of reality as a basis for their advertising messages.

Mental Files

The mind is like a memory bank, and the stored memories in our minds are called the **mental** (or *perceptual*) **files.**

Just as stimuli bombard our senses, information crowds our mental files in today's overcommunicative society. To cope with the complexity of stimuli such as advertising, we rank products and other data in our files by importance, price, quality, features, or a host of other descriptors. Consumers can rarely hold more than seven brand names in any one file—more often only one or two. The remainder either get discarded to some other file category or rejected altogether.[20] How many brands of running shoes can you quickly name, for example?

Because of our limited memory, we resist opening new mental files, and we avoid accepting new information inconsistent with what is already filed. The experience consumers receive from using a brand solidifies their perceptions of it. These fixed perceptions can rarely be changed through advertising alone.[21] But once a new perception does enter our mental files, the information alters the database on which our psychological screens feed.

Because perceptual screens are such a major challenge to advertisers, it's important to understand what's in the consumer's mental files and, if possible, modify them in favor of the advertiser's product. That brings us to the second process in consumer behavior: *learning and persuasion.*

Each time we file a new perception in our minds it's a learning process. Many psychologists consider learning to be the most fundamental process in human behavior. From the advertiser's perspective, though, perception is the most important because it precedes learning. In truth, perception and learning are a continuum, overlapping each other.

By definition, **learning** is a relatively permanent change in thought process or behavior that occurs as a result of reinforced experience. Like perception, learning works off the mental files and at the same time contributes to them. Learning produces our habits and skills. It also contributes to the development of interests, attitudes, beliefs, preferences, prejudices, emotions, and standards of conduct—all of which affect our perceptual screens and our eventual purchase decisions.

Theories of Learning

There are numerous theories of learning, but advertisers classify most into two broad categories—*cognitive theory* and *conditioning theory*—depending on the level of consumer involvement (high or low) required to make a purchase. **Cognitive theory** views learning as a mental process of memory, thinking, and the rational application of knowledge to practical problems. This theory may be an accurate description of how we learn from the experience of others, such as our parents, and how we evaluate a complex purchase such as insurance, stocks and bonds, or business products. **Conditioning theory**—also

Cognitive theory

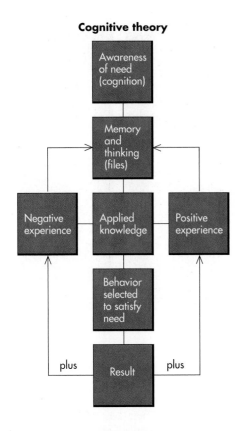

Conditioning theory

Exhibit 5–3

Cognitive theory views learning as a mental process; conditioning theory treats learning as a trial-and-error process.

called **stimulus-response theory**—treats learning as a trial-and-error process. Some stimulus (perhaps an ad) triggers the consumer's need or want, and this in turn creates the drive to respond. If the consumer's response reduces the drive, then satisfaction occurs, and the response is rewarded or reinforced. And that produces repeat behavior the next time the drive is aroused, demonstrating that learning has taken place. Exhibit 5–3 shows simple diagrams of these two theories.

Conditioning theory is more applicable to the simple, basic purchases consumers make every day—soap, cereal, toothpaste, paper towels, and so forth. And it is here that reinforcement advertising plays its most important role—along with superior product performance and good service. If learning is reinforced enough and repeat behavior is produced, a purchasing habit may result.

Learning and persuasion are closely linked. **Persuasion** occurs when the change in belief, attitude, or behavioral intention is caused by promotion communication (such as advertising or personal selling).[22] Naturally, advertisers are very interested in persuasion and how it takes place.

The Elaboration Likelihood Model

Researchers have identified two ways promotion communication can persuade consumers: the *central* and *peripheral routes to persuasion.* Like learning theory, each depends on the consumer's level of involvement with the product and the message. When the consumer's level of involvement is higher, the central route to persuasion is more likely. On the other hand, the peripheral route to persuasion is more likely when consumer involvement is low.[23]

We can see how this works by looking at the **Elaboration Likelihood Model** in Exhibit 5–4. In the **central route to persuasion,** consumers have a higher level of involvement with the product or the message, so they are motivated to pay attention to the central, product-related information, such as product attributes and benefits or demonstrations of positive functional or psychological consequences. Because of their high involvement, they tend to learn cognitively and comprehend the ad-delivered information at deeper, more elaborate levels. This can lead to product beliefs, positive brand attitudes, and purchase intention.[24]

Suppose you are in the market for a significant purchase, say, a new camera or a computer. Because the purchase is relatively expensive, your level of involvement is higher. Perhaps you ask for advice from some friends or family members. You may shop different stores to compare models and prices. And you probably read ads for these products thoroughly to understand the variety of product features and benefits. That's central processing. And in that situation, a well-written, informative ad can be very persuasive.

The **peripheral route to persuasion** is very different. It's more like stimulus-response learning. People who are not in the market for a product typically have low involvement with the product message. They have little or no reason to pay attention to it or to comprehend the central information of the ad. As a result, direct persuasion is also low, and consumers form few if any brand beliefs, attitudes, or purchase intentions. However, these consumers might attend to some peripheral aspects—say, the pictures or the colors in an ad or the actors in a commercial—for their entertainment value. And whatever they feel or think about these peripheral, nonproduct aspects might integrate into a positive attitude toward the ad. At some later date, if a purchase occasion does arise and the consumer needs to make some brand evaluation, these ad-related meanings could be activated to form some brand attitude or purchase intention.

Because very few people are actually in the market at any given time, most mass media advertising probably receives peripheral processing. We all know that

Exhibit 5–4

The Elaboration Likelihood Model.

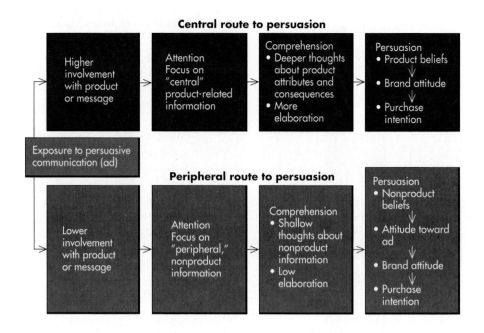

most of the ads we see have little relevance to our immediate goals or needs, so we are not motivated to pay close attention to, much less think about, them. Our involvement is very low. That's why we also have very little recall of ads we saw yesterday. In cases where there is little product differentiation, advertisers may actually *want* us to engage in peripheral processing. Their ads focus more on image or entertainment than product features. This is typical of advertising for many everyday low-involvement purchases, such as soap, cereal, toothpaste, and chewing gum.

But when a product has a distinct advantage, the advertiser's goal should be to encourage central route processing by increasing consumers' involvement with the message. This is where we see a lot of comparative advertising.[25]

One key to learning and persuasion is repetition. Just as a student prepares for an exam by repeating key information to memorize it, an advertiser must repeat key information to prospective and current customers so they remember the product's name and its benefits. Repeat messages penetrate customers' perceptual screens by rekindling memories of information from prior ads. Quebec-based Cossette Communications-Marketing used pairs of billboards for the Provigo grocery store chain. They featured similar strong visual elements and were positioned to be seen in succession. The repetition proved highly successful, producing $100 million in sales in just six months.

Learning Produces Attitudes and Interest

An **attitude** is our acquired mental position regarding some idea or object. It is the positive or negative evaluations, feelings, or action tendencies that we learn and cling to. To advertisers, gaining positive consumer attitudes is critical to success. Attitudes must be either capitalized on or changed.

In Japan, for instance, dishwashers are not a common household appliance. Not only is there very little space for them, Japanese housewives feel guilty about using the labor-saving device. As a result, dishwasher manufacturers have designed smaller, space-saving machines and then promoted them using good hygiene themes rather than convenience appeals.[26]

For mature brands in categories with familiar, frequently purchased products, *brand interest* is even more critical for motivating action. **Brand interest**

A consumer may have only low involvement with a product at the time an ad runs. A peripherally processed ad, like this fun ad for Keds, hopes to create a positive attitude so that consumers will remember the brands once they are in the market to purchase.

is an individual's openness or curiosity about a brand.[27] Enjoyable, entertaining advertising can enhance interest in the brand and reduce the variety-seeking tendencies of consumers who become bored with using the same old product.[28]

Learning Leads to Habits and Brand Loyalty

Attitude is the mental side and *habit* the behavioral side of the same coin. **Habit**—the acquired behavior pattern that becomes nearly or completely involuntary—is the natural extension of learning. We really are creatures of habit.

Most consumer behavior is habitual for three reasons: It's safe, simple, and essential. First, regardless of how we learned to make our purchase decision (through either central or peripheral route processing), if we discover a quality product, brand, or service, we feel *safe* repurchasing it through habit.

Second, habit is *simple*. To consider alternatives we must evaluate, compare, and then decide. This is difficult, time-consuming, and risky.

Finally, because habit is both safe and easy, we rely on it for daily living. Imagine rethinking every purchase decision you make. It would be virtually impossible, not to mention impractical. So it's really *essential* to use habit in our lives.

The major objective of all brand marketers is to produce *brand loyalty,* a direct result of the habit of repurchasing and the reinforcement of continuous advertising. **Brand loyalty** is the consumer's conscious or unconscious decision, expressed through intention or behavior, to repurchase a brand continually.[29] It occurs because the consumer *perceives* that the brand offers the right product features, image, quality, or relationship at the right price.

In the quest for brand loyalty, advertisers have three aims related to habits:

1. *Breaking habits.* Get consumers to unlearn an existing purchase habit and try something new. Advertisers frequently offer incentives to lure customers away from old brands or stores. Or they may use comparative advertising to demonstrate their product's superiority.

2. *Acquiring habits.* Teach consumers to repurchase their brand or repatronize their establishment. To get you started, Columbia House advertises free CDs when you sign up, tied to a contract to purchase more later on.

3. *Reinforcing habits.* Remind current customers of the value of their original purchase and encourage them to continue purchasing. Many magazines, for example, offer special renewal rates to their regular subscribers.

Developing brand loyalty is much more difficult today due to consumers' increased sophistication and to the legions of habit-breaking, *demarketing* activities of competitive advertisers.[30] Only recently have advertisers come to realize that their years of habit-breaking activities have undermined their own *habit-building* objectives. In the quest for instant results, they shifted much of their advertising budgets to sales promotions (deals, coupons, price cuts). But advertising, unlike sales promotion, is an integral part of what makes a brand salable. It's advertising that reinforces brand loyalty and maintains market share.[31] We revisit this topic in our discussion of sales promotion in Chapter 10.

"Bird Seed" :30

(Open on an elderly man standing in a quiet park feeding pigeons)

SFX: Cooing pigeons.

(The peace is shattered when a high-revving sports car whips into a nearby parking spot. The driver skids to a stop. The birds scatter into the air.)

SFX: Screeching tires.

(Freeze frame.)

Super: That's low.

SFX: Ding!

(The businessman, talking on his cell phone, steps out of the car, hits the car

alarm and leaves. The birdless man watches the rude driver walk off. Cut to the convertible now filled with pigeons. The elderly man is tossing birdseed into the car. Freeze frame.)

Super: That's lower.

SFX: Ding!

Super: But not as low as Southwest Airline's click 'n' Save fares. (Fades.)

Super: They're our lowest fares and available only at southwest.com.

SFX: Ding!

Logo: southwest.com a symbol of e-freedom

Brett Stiles, art director

Christopher Staub, writer

David Crawford/Jeremmy Postaer, creative directors

Karen Jacobs, producer

Peter Darley Miller, director

Steifel & Co., production company

GSD&M Advertising (Austin, TX), ad agency

Southwest Airlines, client

Brand interest is an important component of marketing for products in the highly competitive field of travel and leisure. Creatives strive to gain additional awareness and interest in the brand, often through enjoyable and entertaining advertisements like this one for Southwest.com (www.southwest.com).

Learning Defines Needs and Wants

The learning process is both immediate and long term. The moment we file a perception, some learning takes place. When we see a succulent food ad, we may suddenly feel hungry; we *need* food. As we collate the information in our mental files, comparing new perceptions with old ones, further learning takes place. The need may become a *want*. This leads to the next personal process, motivation.

The Consumer Motivation Process

Motivation refers to the underlying forces (or motives) that contribute to our purchasing actions. These motives stem from the conscious or unconscious goal of satisfying our needs and wants. **Needs** are the basic, often instinctive, human forces that motivate us to do something. **Wants** are "needs" that we learn during our lifetime.[32]

Motivation cannot be observed directly. When we see people eat, we assume they are hungry, but we may be wrong. People eat for a variety of reasons besides hunger: they want to be sociable, it's time to eat, or maybe they're nervous or bored.

People are usually motivated by the benefit of satisfying some combination of needs, which may be conscious or unconscious, functional or psychological. *Motivation research* offers some insights into the underlying reasons for unexpected consumer behavior. The reasons (*motives*) some people stop shopping at

**What a dog feels
when the leash breaks.**

PORSCHE

Maslow's hierarchy of needs explains the levels of physical and psychological needs that humans must fulfill. Porsche (www.porsche.com) hints at several levels of needs in its ad touting the car's access to "instant freedom."

Ralph's Supermarket and switch to Vons may be that the Vons market is closer to home, it has a wider selection of fresh produce, and (most likely) they see other people like themselves shopping at Vons. Any or all of these factors might make a shopper switch even if prices are lower at Ralph's.

To better understand what motivates people, Abraham Maslow developed the classic model shown in Exhibit 5–5 called the **hierarchy of needs.** Maslow maintained that the lower, physiological and safety needs dominate human behavior and must be satisfied before the higher, socially acquired needs (or wants) become meaningful. The highest need, self-actualization, is the culmination of fulfilling all the lower needs and reaching to discover the true self.

The promise of satisfying a certain level of need is the basic promotional appeal for many ads. In such affluent societies as the United States, Canada, western Europe, and Japan, most individuals take for granted the satisfaction of their physiological needs. So advertising campaigns often portray the fulfillment of social, esteem, and self-actualization needs, and many offer the reward of satisfaction through personal achievement.

In focus groups for Nabisco SnackWells, for example, it became apparent that middle-aged women today have a high sense of self-worth. Wellness, to them, is no longer about looking good in a bathing suit; rather, it's about celebrating what they do well. The advertiser wondered if it could use women's positive attitude about themselves to change their attitude toward the concept of snacking. Nabisco's agency, Foote, Cone & Belding, capitalized on the idea in a new campaign aimed at boosting women's self-esteem. The message: "Snacking is not about 'filling' yourself, but 'fulfilling' yourself."[33]

We all have needs and wants, but we are frequently unaware of them. Before the advent of the desktop computer, people were completely unaware of any need for it. But the moment a consumer consciously recognizes a product-related want or need, a dynamic process begins. The consumer first evaluates the need and either accepts it as worthy of action or rejects it. Acceptance converts satisfaction of the need into a goal, which creates the dedication (the motivation) to reach a particular result. In contrast, rejection removes the necessity for action and thereby eliminates the goal and the motivation to buy.

Exhibit 5–5

The hierarchy of needs suggests that people meet their needs according to priorities. Physiological and safety needs carry the greatest priority.

In advertising, the message must match the need of the market or the ad will fail.

Advertisers use marketing research to understand the need levels of their markets and use this information in determining the marketing mix.

Need	Product	Promotional appeal
Self-actualization	Golf lessons	"Realize your full potential"
Esteem	Luxury car	"Be in control of the road"
Social	Pendant	"Show her you care"
Safety	Tires	"Bounces off hazards"
Physiological	Breakfast cereal	"The natural energy source"

Exhibit 5–6

Rossiter and Percy's eight fundamental purchase and usage motives.

Negatively originated (informational) motives

1. Problem removal
2. Problem avoidance
3. Incomplete satisfaction
4. Mixed approach–avoidance
5. Normal depletion

Positively originated (transformational) motives

6. Sensory gratification
7. Intellectual stimulation or mastery
8. Social approval

Modern researchers translated Maslow's theory about needs and motives into more strategic concepts for use by marketers and advertisers. Rossiter and Percy, for example, identify eight fundamental purchase and usage motives (see Exhibit 5–6). They refer to the first five as *negatively originated (informational) motives* and the last three as *positively originated (transformational) motives*.[34]

Negatively Originated (Informational) Motives

The most common energizers of consumer behavior are the **negatively originated motives,** such as problem removal or problem avoidance. Whenever we run out of something, for instance, we experience a negative mental state. To relieve those feelings, we actively seek a new or replacement product. Thus, we are temporarily motivated until the time we make the purchase. Then, if the purchase is satisfactory, the drive or motivation is reduced.

These are also called **informational motives** because the consumer actively seeks information to reduce the mental state. In fact, Rossiter and Percy point out, these could also be called "relief" motives because consumers work to find relief from the negative state.

Positively Originated (Transformational) Motives

From time to time, we all want to indulge ourselves by buying some brand or product that promises some benefit or reward. With the **positively originated motives,** a positive bonus is promised rather than the removal or reduction of some negative situation. The goal is to use positive reinforcement to increase the consumer's motivation and to energize the consumer's investigation or search for the new product.

The three positively originated motives—sensory gratification, intellectual stimulation, and social approval—are also called **transformational motives** because the consumer expects to be transformed in a sensory, intellectual, or social sense. They could also be called "reward" motives because the transformation is a rewarding state.[35]

For some consumers, the purchase of a particular product (say, a new suit) might represent a negatively originated motive (they don't really want to spend the

Negative motivation is a powerful tool to affect human behavior. This ad by St. Patrick's Church in England evokes a sense of religious or civil responsibility to help renovate the religious sanctuary and historical landmark. The implication in the ad is that one can eliminate negative feelings of responsibility or guilt by donating to the church's repair.

VISUAL: Inside St. Patrick's Church, we see a statue of the Virgin Mary. A tear seems to fall from the statue's eye. We follow this tear, and other droplets that seem to come from the statue's eye, down the length of its body until they drip from the statue's foot and into a bucket underneath.

As we cut to the head of the statue, we see drips of water falling onto the head and over the face. We follow the drips up and see that the water is coming from a hole in the ceiling above the statue.

Cut to exterior shot of the St. Patrick's Church sign. It's raining heavily.
SUPER: Donations needed for urgent repairs.

Positive motivation offers a bonus to the consumer rather than addressing problem avoidance issues found in negative motivation ads. This ad for HP (www.hp.com) offers sensory gratification by promising a printing quality no different than the original quality of the cake—with the crumbs falling off the side, you can almost taste it.

money on it, but they have to have it for work). But for other consumers, it might be positively originated (they love to shop for new clothes). This suggests two distinct target markets that advertisers must understand and that may call for completely different advertising strategies.

Before creating messages, advertisers must carefully consider the goals that lead to consumer motivations. Denny's Restaurants would make a costly mistake if its ads portrayed the reward of a romantic interlude if the real motive of most Denny's customers is simply to satisfy their need to reduce hunger with a filling, low-priced meal.

The issues of high-involvement and low-involvement products and informational and transformational motives are so important that we will revisit them in Chapter 8 when we discuss the planning of marketing and advertising strategies.

Interpersonal Influences on Consumer Behavior

For advertisers, it's not enough just to know the personal processes of perception, learning and persuasion, and motivation. Important **interpersonal influences** affect—sometimes even dominate—these processes. They also serve as guidelines for consumer behavior. These influences can best be categorized as the *family,* the *society,* and the *cultural environment* of the consumer.

Family Influence

From an early age, family communication affects our socialization as consumers— our attitudes toward many products and our purchasing habits. This influence is usually strong and long-lasting. A child who learns that the "right" headache relief is Bayer aspirin and the "right" name for appliances is General Electric has a well-developed adult purchasing behavior.

From 1970 to 1990, married couple households with children declined sharply—from 40 to 26 percent of all households. Since 1997, that decline has been slower—to 25 percent in 1997. Still, this suggests that family influence has greatly diminished in the United States over the last 30 years as working parents take a less active role in raising their children and youngsters look outside the family for social values.[36] As this happens, the influence of the social and cultural environments intensifies.

Is It Marketing or Is It Exploitation?

Commercial sponsorship is one way to help fund primary and secondary schools. San Francisco–based School Properties, Inc., offers various sponsorship programs—including licensing school names and mascots, fundraising catalogs, and affinity credit cards—to national, regional, and state marketers and guarantees category exclusivity. They test products and hold focus groups at schools, display banners at events, and use former student athletes for company appearances. School Properties, aware that budget cuts jeopardize extracurricular school activities, felt this program was a natural outgrowth of existing athletic and special-event sponsorships. Supporters feel it will help mobilize resources for schools, but opponents say the funding problem is a state issue and commercial product logos don't belong in education. Others wonder if this allows advertisers to take advantage of captive kids.

The ethical dilemma concerns promoting products for advantage or profit at the unreasonable expense of the customer. Commercial products work only if they meet consumer needs, and advertising must appeal to those needs. But what happens if advertisers overstep a need, in a crisis situation, for example, and edge into exploitation?

Look at the public concern about the commercialization of children. In response to complaints about Saturday morning advertising to kids, broadcasters of children's TV are now banned from advertising toys during shows that feature those toys (for example, Yu-Gi-Oh!), and they must clearly separate commercials from the program by announcing commercial breaks. In a different arena, most baby formula companies don't yet advertise directly to consumers because many doctors think breast-feeding is preferable to formula. The companies don't want to be accused of exploitation; instead, they market their products through health care professionals, hospitals, and new-mother clubs. In another case, Benetton shocked some readers with its ad on capital punishment. The ad, which included interviews with death row inmates, was roundly criticized for being exploitive and outraged some unsuspecting readers who did not expect to be confronted with human tragedy by a clothing company. While many socially conscious people congratulated the company, others criticized it sharply for using the misery of others to promote its brand.

Drastic changes in particular market segments may make new fields fertile for exploitation. For example, the emerging Third World middle class seems to have an insatiable appetite for buying things. While tradition and culture play a big role in what people buy and why, the evolving role of women, a burgeoning youth culture, and a middle class with higher expectations and more money than ever before make whole groups of consumers ripe for new products.

Societal Influence

The community we live in exerts a strong influence on all of us. When we affiliate with a particular societal division or identify with some reference group or value the ideas of certain opinion leaders, it affects our views on life, our perceptual screens, and eventually the products we buy.

Societal Divisions: The Group We Belong To

Sociologists traditionally divided societies into **social classes:** upper, upper-middle, lower-middle, and so on. They believed that people in the same social class tended toward similar attitudes, status symbols, and spending patterns.

But today this doesn't apply to most developed countries. U.S. society, especially, is extremely fluid and mobile—physically, socially, and economically. Americans believe strongly in getting ahead, being better than your peers, and winning greater admiration and self-esteem. As the famous Army campaign illustrates, advertisers capitalize on this desire to "be all you can be."

Because of this mobility, dramatic increases in immigration, and the high divorce rate, social-class boundaries have become quite muddled. Single parents, stockbrokers, immigrant shopkeepers, retired blue-collar workers, and bankers all see themselves as part of the great middle class. So "middle class" doesn't mean anything anymore. From the advertiser's point of view, social class seldom represents a functional or operational set of values.

To deal with these often bewildering changes, marketers seek new ways to classify societal divisions and new strategies for advertising to them. We discuss some of these in Chapter 6. Exhibit 5–7 outlines some of the classifications marketers use to describe society today: for example, Midlife Success, Movers and Shakers, Stars and Stripes, and University USA. People in the same group tend to have similar patterns of behavior and product usage.

Reference Groups: The People We Relate To

Most of us care how we appear to people whose opinions we value. We may even pattern our behavior after members of some groups we affiliate with. This is the significance of **reference groups**—people we try to emulate or whose

Some critics believe China is especially vulnerable to exploitation. A couple living in a cramped Beijing apartment may have a $270 refrigerator, a $700 foreign-made color TV, a telephone that came with a $600 installation charge, a $600 Panasonic VCR, a $1,200 Toshiba air conditioner, and a $1,200 piano—all purchased on a salary of $300 a month. In Mexico, companies pitch credit cards to people earning as little as $650 a month. The National Association of Credit Card Holders estimates five million Mexicans carry credit cards, but one million of them can't pay their bills. In the United States, the elderly and mentally incapacitated are targeted and exploited by sweepstakes promoters, misleading them into believing they've won contest monies and prizes. The elderly are bilked out of thousands of dollars in fees and merchandise they don't need and can't afford. Plus, they're often harassed and sometimes even threatened by these unscrupulous promoters. State lotteries also prey on the hopes of the poor in their advertising, underplaying the long odds of winning significant prizes and exploiting gambling addictions.

Critics say that companies act irresponsibly when they target these groups for marketing and advertising activities because the average consumer can't afford the products being advertised.

However, researchers have investigated how advertising messages influence people to act. One finding, known as the third-person effect, holds that people generally believe others are more influenced by the media than they are. Perhaps the critics need to consider this. While they can resist advertising appeals, they seem to believe the average consumer lacks their sophistication. So where do you draw the line between what is ethical (marketing) and what is not (exploitation)?

Questions

1. Do you think playing on people's desire for material possessions has a place in advertising? When does this become exploitation?

2. Is it the advertiser's responsibility to determine whether prospective customers can afford a product or service? Why or why not?

3. Do you feel the third-person effect applies to consumers in the developing countries? If so, how can marketers avoid exploiting them?

Sources: John Berthelsen, "China's Consumer Era Takes Hold," *Asia Times* online, August 6, 2003 (retrieved from www.atimes.com/atimes/china/EH06Ad01.html); G. Edmonson, J. Ewing, and C. Passariello, "Has Benetton Stopped Unraveling?" *BusinessWeek* online, June 23, 2003 (retrieved from www.businessweek.com/magazine/content/03_25/b2828134_mz034.htm); Patrick Goodenough, "Children Harmed by Too Much TV, Exploitative Advertising, Report Says," CNSNews.com, May 19, 2004 (retrieved from www.cnsnews.com); Catherine Seipp, "Marketing the Mouse," *National Review* online, July 7, 2004 (retrieved from www.nationalreview.com).

---

approval concerns us. Reference groups can be personal (family, friends, co-workers) or impersonal (political parties, religious denominations, professional associations). A special reference group, our peers, exerts tremendous influence on what we believe and how we behave. They determine which brands are cool and which are not.[37] To win acceptance by our peers (fellow students, co-workers, colleagues), we may purchase a certain style or brand of clothing, choose a particular place to live, and acquire behavioral habits that will earn their approval.

Often an individual is influenced in opposite directions by two reference groups and must choose between them. For example, a college student might feel

Exhibit 5–7

Contemporary social classes. The groups outlined in this exhibit are just 10 of 50 Microvision lifestyle segments defined by National Decision Systems. This division of Equifax wants to know what financial services various consumers are likely to need.

Upper Crust
Metropolitan families, very high income and education, manager/professionals; very high installment activity

Midlife Success
Families, very high education, managers/professionals, technical/sales, high income; super-high installment activity

Movers and Shakers
Singles, couples, students, and recent graduates, high education and income, managers/professionals, technical/sales; average credit activity, medium-high installment activity

Successful Singles
Young, single renters, older housing, ethnic mix, high education, medium income, managers/professionals; very high bankcard accounts, very high installment activity, very low retail activity

Stars and Stripes
Young, large school-age families, medium income and education, military, precision/craft; average credit activity

Social Security
Mature/seniors, metro fringe, singles and couples, medium income and education, mixed jobs; very low credit activity

Middle of the Road
School-age families, mixed education, medium income, mixed jobs; very high revolving activity, very high bankcard accounts

Trying Metro Times
Young, seniors, ethnic mix, low income, older housing, low education, renters, mixed jobs; low credit activity, medium-high retail activity

Low-Income Blues
Minorities, singles and families, older housing, low income and education, services, laborers; low credit activity, medium-high retail activity

University USA
Students, singles, dorms/group quarters, very low income, medium-high education, technical/sales; low credit activity, high percent new accounts

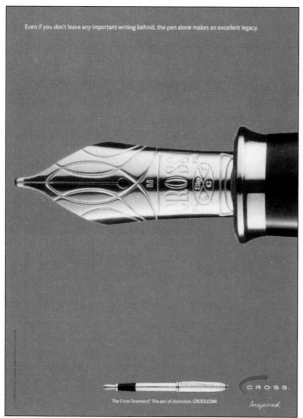

Even if you don't leave any important writing behind, the pen alone makes an excellent legacy.

CROSS.

Inspired.

The Cross Townsend.™ The pen of distinction. CROSS.COM

Sometimes social class can affect how we see ourselves and how we fit into the larger social fabric. Although class differences are not as distinct in the United States as in many parts of the world, marketers of high-end purchases often capitalize on class distinction for product positioning purposes. In this ad, Cross Pens (www.cross.com) targets the alternative segment of the high-end purchasing crowd.

pressure from some friends to join a Greek house and from others to live independently off campus. In ads targeted to students, a local apartment complex might tap the appeal of reference groups by showing students splashing in the complex's pool.

Opinion Leaders: The People We Trust

An **opinion leader** is some person or organization whose beliefs or attitudes are respected by people who share an interest in some specific activity. All fields (sports, religion, fashion, politics) have opinion leaders. An opinion leader may be a knowledgeable friend or some expert we find credible. We reason, "If Picabo Street thinks Marker makes the best ski bindings, then it must be so. She knows more about the sport than I do." Thus, the purchasing habits and testimonials of opinion leaders are important to advertisers.

When choosing an opinion leader as a spokesperson for a company or product, advertisers must understand the company's target market thoroughly. Even if executives in the company do not relate to the spokesperson, they must follow market tastes and interests. A spokesperson out of sync with the market undermines his or her credibility—and the company's. On the other hand, an internal person such as Dave Thomas, the founder of Wendy's, turned out to be a highly credible spokesperson without the risks associated with outside celebrities and athletes.[38]

Of course, using a superstar spokesperson such as Michael Jordan is extremely expensive. It is estimated that Mr. Jordan's annual endorsement income exceeds $45 million. Analysts also estimate that, due to his stature and credibility, he produces some $500 million in sales for the companies he represents.[39]

Cultural and Subcultural Influence

Culture has a tenacious influence on consumers. **Culture** refers to the whole set of meanings, beliefs, attitudes, and ways of doing things that are shared by some homogeneous social group and typically handed down from generation to generation.[40] Americans love hot dogs, peanut butter, corn on the cob, and apple pie. Canada, Russia, Germany—every country has its own favorite specialties. And advertisers find it much easier to work with these tastes than try to change them.

Global marketers are especially concerned with the purchase environment. According to Professor Carolyn Lin, of all business functions, marketing activities are the most susceptible to cultural error.[41]

For example, while both demographic and psychographic traits figure importantly in U.S. consumer marketing, age and sex are better indicators of behavior and lifestyles in Japan, where income is largely proportional to seniority and sex roles tend to be standardized.[42] When creating ads for foreign consumption, marketers must consider many environmental factors: cultural trends, social norms, changing fads, market dynamics, product needs, and media channels.[43]

In countries where people earn little income, demand for expensive products is low. So the creative strategy of an automobile advertiser might be to target the small group of wealthy, upper-class consumers. In a country with a large middle class, the same advertiser might be better off mass-marketing the car and positioning it as a middle-class product.

As the old saying goes, you must feed a cold and starve a fever, or at least that's what we say in the West. Every culture is characterized by unique idiosyncrasies that advertisers must be aware of when addressing a particular audience. This ad from the Ai Sin Foot Reflexology Centre capitalizes on the frequent notion of Asian expertise in holistic therapies.

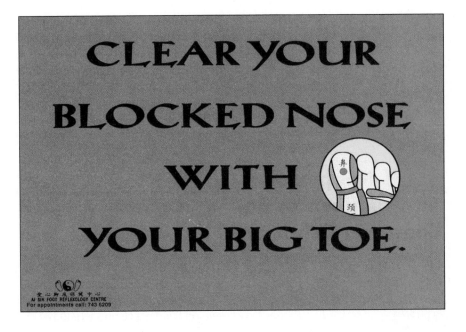

The United States and Canada embrace many subcultures, some of them quite large. They may be based on race, national origin, religion, language, or geographic proximity. The advertiser must understand these subcultures, for differences among them may affect responses to both products and advertising messages.

The United States, in particular, is a great melting pot of minority subcultures. A **subculture** is a segment within a culture that shares a set of meanings, values, or activities that differ in certain respects from those of the overall culture.[44] According to the U.S. Census, 33 million African Americans, 32 million Hispanics, and 11 million Asians live in the United States (plus an unknown number of undocumented foreign nationals). These three minority groups alone account for more than 25 percent of the American population.[45] Canada has two major subcultures, anglophones and francophones, based on language (English and French), plus a mosaic of many other cultures based on ethnic and national origin.

Subcultures tend to transfer their beliefs and values from generation to generation. Racial, religious, and ethnic backgrounds affect consumers' preferences for styles of dress, food, beverages, transportation, personal care products, and household furnishings, to name a few. As we saw in Chapter 4, many ad agencies now specialize in minority markets as more advertisers realize that tailoring their appeals to minorities makes good business sense. Recognizing the rapid growth of the Hispanic population, for example, Procter & Gamble spends more than $55 million per year to understand and tap this market. Other major Hispanic marketers include Ford Motor Co., AT&T, and Sears.[46]

The social environments in countries from Italy to Indonesia, from Sweden to Surinam are also based on language, culture, literacy rate, religion, and lifestyle. Advertisers who market products globally can't ignore these distinctions.

In North America, advertising encourages us to keep our mouths clean, our breath fresh, and our teeth scrubbed. But people in some southern European countries consider it vain and improper to

Increasingly, advertisers realize that English-speakers are not the only market in the United States. Other ethnic and linguistic cultures exist and pose enormous markets for the culturally savvy. Here, the U.S Army encourages the Spanish-speaking audience to "Se Todo Lo Que Puedes Ser," or "Be All You Can Be." Recently, the U.S. Army updated its campaign slogan to "An Army of One."

overindulge in toiletries. Consumers in the Netherlands and the United Kingdom use three times as much toothpaste as those in Spain and Greece. To communicate effectively with Spanish consumers, who view toothpaste as a cosmetic product, advertisers use chic creative executions rather than dry, therapeutic pitches.[47]

Clearly, many interpersonal factors influence consumers. They have an important effect on our mental files, screens, and subsequent purchase decisions. Awareness of these interpersonal influences helps marketers, both domestic and international, create the strategies on which much advertising is based.

Nonpersonal Influences on Consumer Behavior

Numerous nonpersonal influences may affect a consumer's final purchase decision. The most important **nonpersonal influences**—*time, place,* and *environment*—are typically beyond the consumer's control, but not necessarily beyond the advertiser's.

Time

The old saw "timing is everything" certainly applies to marketing and advertising. A special weekend sale may provide just the added incentive to penetrate customers' perceptual screens and bring them into a store. But running an ad for that sale on Sunday evening would be a waste of advertising dollars.

Likewise, the consumer's particular need may be a function of time. Forecasts of an unusually wet winter from the El Niño phenomenon in 1998 motivated special ads from a variety of national advertisers as well as many small retailers of linens, boots, snow shovels, and rock salt. Consumers don't need snow tires and rock salt in the summer (although some off-season promotions do work). But if we unexpectedly get a flat on the highway, tire ads suddenly become timely. As we will see in our chapters on media, companies must plan all their marketing activities (including advertising) with the consumer's clock in mind.

Place

Once consumers decide to purchase a certain product, they will still hesitate if they don't know where to buy it or if it isn't available in a convenient or preferred location. Similarly, if consumers believe a particular brand is a specialty good but it suddenly appears everywhere, their perception of the product's "specialness" may diminish. Thus, marketers carefully weigh consumer demand when planning distribution strategy, and they devote much advertising to communicating the convenience of location. Distribution is an important element of the marketing mix and will be discussed further in Chapter 6.

Environment

Many **environments**—ecological, social, political, technical, economic, household, and point-of-sale location, to mention a few—can affect the purchase decision. For example, during a recession, advertisers can't expect to penetrate the perceptual screens of consumers who don't have enough money to buy. And no matter how good the advertising or how low the price, memberships in the National Rifle Association aren't likely to be a hot item with members of the Audubon Society. On the other hand, an enticing display next to the cash register can improve sales of low-cost impulse items. Advertisers must consider the influence of the purchase environment on the consumer's decision processes.

Likewise, the state of technological development affects economic and social conditions—and the prospects for advertisers of certain products and services. For example, countries that don't manufacture computers might be poor markets for components such as disk drives and microprocessors. On the other hand, advertisers of low-priced, imported computers might do very well.

Finally, some governments exert far greater control over their citizens and businesses than the U.S. government does. For example, until recently, virtually

Applying Consumer Behavior Principles to Ad Making

When Polaroid needed to capture the attention of photo enthusiasts, it turned to the creatives at Leonard/Monahan to design a series of ads that would exhibit the advantages of the instant film over other photo products. The first challenge for the creative design team was to break through the consumers' resistance, the subtle barrier that begins with the perceptual screens. Second, the team had to present the picture as being worth a thousand words while avoiding clichés.

The advertisement's headline—"The victim refuses to speak. The pictures refuse to keep quiet."—commands your attention and expresses the big idea with urgency. The ad's black-and-white visual of a battery victim suggests the subject's grave nature while allowing the color Polaroids to jump out, emoting a raw portrayal of reality. The ad becomes credible by demonstrating the benefits of Polaroids and how they can be successfully used (to investigate, prosecute, and win). The tag line, "Instant evidence," sums up the product's features and helps the prospective consumer recall the product's benefits. These factors show clearly the product's benefits to those who may be critical of their purchase decision.

Laboratory Application

Choose an ad from a popular magazine and explain how the visuals, the words, and the overall design of the ad accomplish the following tasks. Provide specific details to support your answers.

1. Penetrate consumer perceptual screens.
2. Stimulate consumer learning.
3. Use the consumer's existing perceptual files.
4. Stimulate consumer wants and needs to achieve motivation.

---

no American-made products could be sold in former Eastern bloc countries or China. They simply weren't allowed. Political control often extends to which products companies may advertise and sell, which media they use, and what their ads say.

The Purchase Decision and Postpurchase Evaluation

Now that we understand the elements in the consumer purchase decision process, let's examine how it might work in a typical situation. Ad Lab 5–B demonstrates an advertiser's approach, but it is also important to look through the eyes of a consumer. A hypothetical consumer named Chris is thinking about buying a CD player.

Chris is enrolled at a state university and financed in part by a small scholarship. He also has a part-time job but must act conservatively when it comes to spending money because tuition, books, and other expenses are costly.

One day, thumbing through a consumer electronics magazine, Chris sees an exciting ad for a new top-of-the line CD player. A beautiful photograph shows the product's modern yet understated design. The ad copy highlights the CD player's special features. They exude high-tech class—it's just the right style. The ad's signature: "Exclusively at Tech 2000."

In a split second Chris leaps from perception to motivation. Got to have it! He is highly involved and he wants this personal reward for all his hard work.

The next day Chris visits Tech 2000. While looking for the advertised CD player, he encounters a variety of alternative styles and models by well-known manufacturers.

The ad has already done its work; the purchase decision process is well under way. At the point of making a purchase decision, though, consumers typically search, consider, and compare alternative brands.

Consumers evaluate selection alternatives (called the **evoked set**). To do this, they establish **evaluative criteria,** the standards they use to judge the features and

Some of the most beautiful things remain unseen.

So naturally beautiful, it's perfect in any environment. Introducing the Jenn-Air® Luxury™ Series built-in refrigerator. Featuring a customizable exterior that can blend seamlessly with your cabinetry or stand as the centerpiece of your kitchen. Just as beautiful is the spacious interior waiting to be personalized by you. When it comes to refrigerators, nothing has ever matched your needs so perfectly. Until now.

JENN-AIR

High-involvement purchases often result in more highly involved post-purchase evaluations, and people will go to great lengths to avoid cognitive dissonance. For example, if someone just spent a lot of money for a customized built-in refrigerator from Jenn-Air, they are more likely to be interested in ads like this one that reinforce the purchase decision they already made.

benefits of alternative products. Not all brands make it to the evoked set. In fact, based on their mental files, most consumers usually consider only four or five brands—which presents a real challenge to advertisers. If none of the alternatives meets the evaluative criteria, the consumer may reject the purchase entirely or postpone the decision.

Chris finally finds the advertised CD player. But it looks smaller on the shelf than it did in the ad. Two other good players are also displayed; both are attractive, both expensive. While trying out the sound systems, Chris considers other unique qualities of style and design. "This one may be a little too bulky." "This one would fit on my desk." "This one would be okay for me, but I'm not sure about using it for parties."

Using central route processing, Chris compares the CD players, considering their style, technology, possible advantages, and price (the models are all within $35 of each other). The advertised player really is the best buy and would be the most satisfying. None of Chris's friends has one like it. The purchase decision is complete when Chris writes out a check for the CD player.

On the way home, the **postpurchase evaluation** begins. Chris suddenly envisions some friends' possible negative reactions to the purchase. Maybe it wasn't wise to spend so much money on a luxury CD player. Chris starts to worry—and to plan.

"It's really a great player. It's excellent quality and worth the money. I'll get a lot of use out of it."

A key feature of the postpurchase evaluation is *cognitive dissonance*. The **theory of cognitive dissonance** (also called **postpurchase dissonance**) holds that people strive to justify their behavior by reducing the dissonance, or inconsistency, between their cognitions (their perceptions or beliefs) and reality.[48] In fact, research shows that, to combat dissonance, consumers are more likely to read ads for brands they've already purchased than for new products or competing brands.[49]

Back at the dorm, Chris puts the magazine on the desk with a Post-it note marking the ad (for his roommate to discover). Then he phones a friend and describes the purchase, emphasizing its technology, its great design, the enjoyment it will bring, and how expensive it was.

During the postpurchase period, the consumer may enjoy the satisfaction of the purchase and thereby receive reinforcement for the decision. Or the purchase may turn out to be unsatisfactory for some reason. In either case, feedback from the postpurchase evaluation updates the consumer's mental files, affecting perceptions of the brand and similar purchase decisions in the future.

This story is common for a high-involvement purchase decision. Of course, if Chris's decision had merely involved the purchase of a pack of gum, the process would have been significantly simpler.

Chris may typify a particular group of consumers, and that is important to marketers. Marketers are interested in defining target markets and developing effective marketing strategies for groups of consumers who share similar characteristics, needs, motives, and buying habits. These are the subjects of market segmentation and the marketing mix, the focus of Chapter 6.

Chapter Summary

Marketing is the process companies use to make a profit by satisfying their customers' needs for products. Marketing focuses on the special relationship between a customer's needs and a product's functional or psychic utility. The essence of marketing is the perceived equal-value exchange. Need satisfaction is the customer's goal and should be the marketer's goal as well.

Advertising is concerned with the promotion aspect of the marketing process. It is one of several tools marketers use to inform, persuade, and remind groups of customers (markets) about the need-satisfying value of their products and services. Advertising's effectiveness depends on the communication skill of the advertising person. It also depends on the extent to which firms correctly implement other marketing activities, such as market research, pricing, and distribution.

There are three categories of participants in the marketing process: customers, markets, and marketers. To reach customers and markets, advertisers must effectively blend data from the behavioral sciences with the communicating arts. Advertisers study the behavioral characteristics of large groups of people to create advertising aimed at those groups.

Successful advertising people understand the complexity of consumer behavior, which is governed by three personal processes: perception, learning and persuasion, and motivation. These processes determine how consumers see the world around them, how they learn information and habits, and how they actualize their personal needs and motives. Two sets of influences also affect consumer behavior: interpersonal influences (the consumer's family, society, and culture) and nonpersonal influences (time, place, and environment). These factors combine to determine how the consumer behaves, and their influence differs considerably from one country to another. Advertisers evaluate the effect of these factors on groups of consumers to determine how best to create their messages.

Once customers or prospects are motivated to satisfy their needs and wants, the purchase process begins. Based on certain standards they have established in their own minds, they evaluate various alternative products (the evoked set). If none of the alternatives meets their evaluative criteria, they may reject or postpone the purchase. If they do buy, they may experience cognitive dissonance in the form of postpurchase doubt and concern. An important role of advertising is to help people cope with dissonance by reinforcing the wisdom of their purchase decision. The result of the postpurchase evaluation will greatly affect the customer's attitude toward future purchases.

Important Terms

attitude, *152*

brand interest, *152*

brand loyalty, *153*

business markets, *143*

centers of influence, *143*

central route to persuasion, *151*

cognition, *149*

cognitive theory, *150*

conditioning theory, *150*

consumer behavior, *146*

consumer decision process, *146*

consumer markets, *143*

culture, *160*

current customers, *143*

Elaboration Likelihood Model, *151*

environments, *162*

evaluation of alternatives, *147*

evaluative criteria, *163*

evoked set, *163*

exchange, *141*

government markets, *145*

habit, *153*

hierarchy of needs, *155*

industrial markets, *144*

informational motives, *156*

interpersonal influences, *147, 157*

learning, *150*

market, *143*

marketers, *145*

marketing, *139*

mental files, *150*

motivation, *154*

needs, *154*

negatively originated motives, *156*

nonpersonal influences, *147, 162*

opinion leaders, *160*

organizational buyers, *146*

perception, *147*

perceptual screens, *148*

peripheral route to persuasion, *151*

personal processes, *147*

persuasion, *151*

physiological screens, *148*

positively originated motives, *156*

postpurchase dissonance, *164*

postpurchase evaluation, *147, 164*

prospective customers, *143*

psychological screens, *148*

reference groups, *158*

reseller markets, *144*

selective perception, *149*

self-concept, *149*

social classes, *158*

stimulus, *147*

stimulus-response theory, *151*

subculture, *161*

theory of cognitive dissonance, *164*

transformational motives, *156*

transnational (global) markets, *145*

utility, *139*

wants, *154*

Review Questions

1. What is marketing, and what is the role advertising plays in the marketing process?
2. How does product utility relate to advertising?
3. Why is the perceived equal-value exchange an important advertising issue?
4. What's the difference between a customer and a market? What are the different types of markets?
5. What does the term *consumer behavior* refer to, and why is it important to advertisers?
6. Which consumer behavior process presents the greatest challenge to advertisers?
7. What is the difference between the central route and the peripheral route to persuasion?
8. What is the significance of negatively originated motives and positively originated motives to advertisers?
9. What are some of the environmental influences on consumer behavior in international markets?
10. How does the theory of cognitive dissonance relate to advertising?
11. **The Advertising Experience**

    Describe an incident of cognitive dissonance that you (or someone you interview) has felt after a significant purchase. Discuss the feelings generated by this purchase and what happened to those feelings. For example, perhaps the purchaser felt better over time as the quality and value of the product became evident. Finally, discuss what the company could have done to make the buyer feel better during the period of cognitive dissonance.

Exploring the Internet

The Internet exercises for Chapter 5 address the two main areas covered in the chapter: marketing (Exercise 1) and consumer behavior (Exercises 2 and 3).

1. **Marketing**

   Visit the following websites and apply what you learned from this chapter by identifying the marketer, product utility, customer(s), and type of market(s) for each:

   - www.att.com
   - www.caterpillar.com
   - www.delta.com
   - www.dhl.com
   - www.fox.com
   - www.gm.com
   - www.johnsonandjohnson.com
   - www.kodak.com
   - www.marriott.com
   - www.nba.com
   - www.pg.com
   - www.siemens.com
   - www.sony.com
   - www.transamerica.com
   - www.unisys.com
   - www.visa.com
   - www.walmart.com

2. **Consumer Behavior**

   Understanding consumer behavior is essential to the contemporary advertiser. Browse the websites listed below, keeping in mind what you learned about culture/subculture, social class, reference groups, family/household, and opinion leaders. Identify and describe the major social influences that enable each organization to be successful in reaching its consumers.

   - Beechnut www.beechnut.com
   - Ben & Jerry's www.benjerry.com
   - CNN www.cnn.com
   - Motorola www.motorola.com
   - Music Television (MTV) www.mtv.com
   - Oprah www.oprah.com
   - PETsMART www.petsmart.com
   - Rollerblade www.rollerblade.com
   - See's Candies www.sees.com
   - Tower Records www.towerrecords.com
   - Xbox www.microsoft.com/xbox

3. Review the websites in Exercise 2 in terms of Maslow's hierarchy of needs. Find three instances of appeals to each of the five basic needs. Next, discuss what kind of people might seek to satisfy each of these needs with the particular products. Finally, consider opinion leaders whose testimonies could be added to each site. How could these leaders strengthen the appeal of the site for the consumers who have unsatisfied needs?

Chapter 6

Market Segmentation and the Marketing Mix: Determinants of Advertising Strategy

Objectives

TO DESCRIBE HOW MARKETERS USE BEHAVIORAL CHARACTER-
ISTICS TO CLUSTER PROSPECTIVE CUSTOMERS INTO MARKET
SEGMENTS. Because no product or service pleases everybody, marketers need
to select specific target markets that offer the greatest sales potential. Thus, they
can fine tune their mix of product-related elements (the four Ps), including advertising, to match the needs or wants of the target market.

After studying this chapter, you will be able to:

■ **Identify** the various methods advertisers use to segment both consumer
and business markets.

■ **Explain** the importance of aggregation to marketing and advertising.

■ **Discuss** how target marketing affects the firm's advertising strategy.

■ **Describe** the elements of the marketing mix and the role of advertising
in the mix.

■ **Explain** the purpose and importance of branding.

"It's how the last place you'd go for a burger will become the first." Apologies for past misdeeds rarely appear voluntarily in advertising campaigns, but after years of declining sales, bloated menus, and failed comeback attempts, Hardee's had to innovate. The fast-food hamburger chain, owned by CKE Restaurants, Inc., went with Mendelsohn/Zien's surprising approach as a way to level with consumers and give the brand a fresh start, said Brad Haley, Hardee's executive vice president of marketing. "The first phase was designed to really sort of tell consumers that we acknowledge that we weren't doing things the way we should have in the past."[1] But what would the chain do differently now? ■ Something just as unorthodox: sell big, premium hamburgers in the midst of the 2001–2002 "burger wars," when the major burger chains were slashing prices on their sandwiches.[2] Building on its adoption of the Six-Dollar Burger concept pioneered by Carl's Jr. (another CKE-owned chain), Hardee's introduced its Thickburger in January 2003. Using high-quality Angus beef in burgers larger than the fast-food norm, it sought to rival products found in casual-dining restaurants. The hook: the so-called Six-Dollar Burger sold for about four dollars. At the same time it began marketing its heftier sandwiches, Hardee's tightened the focus of its menu, eliminating dozens of lunch and dinner menu items.[3]

■ The Thickburger television ad campaign targeted the young male demographic by featuring brawny, "real" men enjoying the burgers. Early in the campaign, a construction worker credits the new offering with his reconversion to the brand. In April 2004, Hardee's added even more muscle to the manly advertising push by spotlighting baseball's heavy-hitter Mark "Big Mac" McGwire.[4] Another ad tracked a twenty-something man working on his car, Thickburger in hand. Further underscoring the campaign's focus, subsequent Thickburger spots proclaimed that the burgers "don't come with toys, because they're not for little boys." ■ As these examples illustrate, ads target their demographic on more than one level. The burgers must meet consumer taste expectations, of course, but the Thickburger commercials also trade directly on the notion of male identity ("real" men want "real," substantial burgers) and indirectly (eating Thickburgers shows that you're a "real" man). In a twist on the old saying "you are what you eat," the campaign implicitly tells young males that eating Thickburgers is more than just a fast-food choice; it says something about who you are. ■ Could such an intense focus on the young, male market backfire on Hardee's? The same television ads that target one demographic segment can easily alienate another: The ad that showed the young man working on his car also showed him ignoring an exasperated young woman. Her disgust was soon mirrored by real women when Hardee's followed up their machismo campaign with recycled Carl's Jr. spots that showed women enjoying juicy, sloppy burgers in racy scenes. For a Western Thickburger spot, a model rides a mechanical bull, sensuously swaying and chewing, to the soundtrack of Foghat's "Slow Ride." A letter from the American Families Association demanded the ad be pulled because "it is degrading to women and not an appropriate message for our children. . . . Hardee's should not be in the business of marketing sex in order to sell hamburgers."[5] ■ Despite the criticism, Hardee's and Mendelsohn/Zien's choice to zero in on such a narrow group is paying off thus far. The advertising campaign's savvy combination of frankness, higher-quality ingredients, and testosterone helped the company's recovery. In early 2004, Hardee's began to look toward a different market segment. Thanks in part to broad interest in protein-heavy, low-carbohydrate diets—which the chain specifically catered to by introducing its lettuce-wrapped Low-Carb Thickburger[6]—same-store sales and profit margins improved markedly in 2004 over the previous year, sparking positive comments from the business community. ■

The Market Segmentation Process

Recall from our discussion in Chapter 1 that marketing and advertising strategies evolved over time as more and more products entered the marketplace and competed for consumer dollars and approval. During the 1950s and 1960s, the *unique selling proposition* held sway as marketers built new and different properties into their products to tout in their advertising. Then in the 1960s and 1970s, as me-too products glutted mass markets, the strategy of *market segmentation* came to the fore. This meant developing products and marketing mixes to meet the needs and wants of particular market segments. Then, as major market segments became saturated and product life cycles grew shorter, marketers developed new approaches, such as positioning, marketing warfare, niche marketing, micro marketing, and now even one-to-one marketing. All of these are variations on basic market segmentation strategy, except that today segments are getting smaller. Thanks to modern technology, companies can satisfy the needs of smaller segments and still make a profit. It's important for advertising people to have a solid understanding of the principles of market segmentation. In the twenty-first century, the task of finding profitable market segments is even more challenging.

Marketing and advertising people constantly scan the marketplace to see what various consumer groups need and want and how they might be better satisfied. Today, the process of **market segmentation** is actually a two-step strategy of *identifying* groups of people (or organizations) with certain shared needs and characteristics within the broad markets for consumer or business products and *aggregating* (combining) these groups into larger market segments according to their mutual interest in the product's utility. This process gives a company a selection of market segments large enough to target and lays the foundation for developing the proper mix of marketing activities—including advertising.

In the voiceover for the ad that shows model Cameron Richardson riding a mechanical bull in slow motion, Hardee's confirms that market segmentation is at work: "We could've shown you some cowboy, sitting around a campfire, eating a Western Bacon Thickburger . . . but who'd wanna see that?" The answer, of course, is not the young men at whom the campaign is targeted.

Markets often consist of many segments. A company may differentiate products and marketing strategy for every segment, or concentrate its marketing activities on only one or a few segments. Either task is far from simple. Hardee's worked to rebuild its brand by targeting a broad segment: its disaffected former clientele. After the damage-control phase, Hardee's was ready to reconnect with a narrower market segment. The company began to differentiate its advertising campaigns; although it mostly attempted to lure young males with ever-bigger burgers, Hardee's also made some attempt to target other segments with different products. Catering to all these needs on a global level requires a sophisticated marketing and communications system. In this chapter, we look first at how marketers identify and categorize *consumer markets* and second at the techniques they use to segment *business markets.* Then we discuss various strategic options companies use, including advertising, to match their products with markets and create profitable exchanges.

Segmenting the Consumer Market: Finding the Right Niche

The concept of *shared characteristics* is critical to market segmentation. Marketing and advertising people know that, based on their needs, wants, and mental files, consumers leave "footprints in the sand"—the telltale signs of where they live and work, what they buy, and how they spend their leisure time. By following these footprints, marketers can locate and define groups of consumers with similar needs and wants, create messages for them, and know how and where to send their messages. The goal is to find that particular niche, or space in the market, where the advertiser's product or service will fit.

Marketers group these shared characteristics into categories (*behavioristic, geographic, demographic,* and *psychographic*) to identify and segment consumer markets (see Exhibit 6–1). The marketers' purpose is twofold: first, to identify people who are likely to be responsive; and second, to develop rich descriptions of them in order to better understand them, create marketing mixes for them, and reach them with meaningful advertising or other communications.

Behavioristic Segmentation

One of the best ways to segment markets is to group consumers by purchase behavior. This is called **behavioristic segmentation.** Behavioral segments are determined by many variables, but the most important are *user status, usage rate, purchase occasion,* and *benefits sought.* These categories tell us who our customers are now, when and why they buy, and how much they consume.

Behavioristic segmentation is one of the best ways to organize consumer markets. Purchase behavior variables, such as the benefits sought by the consumer, determine how the segmentations are made. In this ad, Hunan Garden targets Chinese food aficionados with a tongue-in-cheek promise that the Chinese food eaten is better than the English spoken.

WHICH WOULD YOU RATHER HAV AT OUR RESTAURANT, GOOD ENGLIS R GOOD CHINESE?

HUNAN GARDEN 湖南園

11532 PAGE SERVICE RD. 314.432.7015

Exhibit 6–1
Methods for segmenting consumer markets.

Variables	Typical breakdowns	Variables	Typical breakdowns
Geographic		**Demographic**	
Region	Pacific; Mountain; West North Central; West South Central; East North Central; East South Central; South Atlantic; Middle Atlantic; New England	Age	Under 6, 6–11, 12–19, 20–34, 35–49, 50–64, 65+
		Sex	Male, female
County size	A, B, C, D	Family size	1–2, 3–4, 5+
Climate	Northern; southern	Family life cycle	Young, single; young, married, no children; young, married, youngest child under 6; young, married, youngest child 6 or over; young, unmarried, with children; older, married, with children; older, unmarried, with children; older, married, no children under 18; older, single; other
City or SMSA size	Under 5,000; 5,000–19,999; 20,000–49,999; 50,000–99,999; 100,000–249,000; 250,000–499,999; 500,000–999,999; 1,000,000–3,999,999; 4,000,000 or over		
Density	Urban, suburban, rural	Income	Under $10,000; $10,000–20,000; $20,000–30,000; $30,000–40,000; $40,000–60,000; $60,000–100,000; $100,000–150,000; $150,000 and over
Behavioristic			
Purchase occasion	Regular occasion, special occasion		
Benefits sought	Economy, convenience, prestige		
User status	Nonuser, ex-user, potential user, first-time user, regular user	Occupation	Professional and technical; managers, officials, and proprietors; clerical, sales; craftspeople, supervisors; operatives; farmers; retired; students; homemakers; unemployed
Usage rate	Light user, medium user, heavy user		
Loyalty status	None, medium, strong, absolute		
Readiness stage	Unaware, aware, informed, interested, desirous, intending to buy	Education	Grade school or less; some high school; high school graduates; some college; college graduates
Marketing-factor sensitivity	Quality, price, service, advertising, sales promotion	Religion	Catholic, Protestant, Jewish, other
Psychographic		Race	White, Black, Asian
Societal divisions	Upper crust, movers and shakers, successful singles, social security, middle of the road, metro ethnic mix	Nationality	American, British, French, German, Scandinavian, Italian, Latin American, Middle Eastern, Japanese
Lifestyle	Strivers, achievers, actualizers		
Personality	Compulsive, gregarious, authoritarian, ambitious		

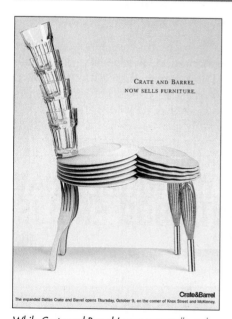

CRATE AND BARREL.
NOW SELLS FURNITURE.

The expanded Dallas Crate and Barrel opens Thursday, October 9, on the corner of Knox Street and McKinney.

Crate&Barrel

While Crate and Barrel (www.crateandbarrel. com) is better known for its extensive kitchenware, it uses its strong brand name to promote its furniture. For sole users, this ad reinforces the brand and for repertoire users—those most likely to alternate between brands they believe to be equally superior—it enhances brand perception.

User-status variables Many markets can be segmented by the **user status** of prospective customers. Researchers Stephan and Tannenholz have identified six categories of consumers based on user status.

Sole users are the most brand loyal and require the least amount of advertising and promotion. *Semi-sole users* typically use Brand A but have an alternate selection if it is not available or if the alternate is promoted with a discount. *Discount users* are the semi-sole users of competing Brand B. They don't buy Brand A at full price but perceive it well enough to buy it at a discount. *Aware nontriers* use competitive products in the category but haven't taken a liking to Brand A. A different advertising message could help, but these people rarely offer much potential. *Trial/rejectors* bought Brand A's advertising message, but didn't like the product. More advertising won't help; only a reformulation of Brand A will bring them back. *Repertoire users* perceive two or more brands to have superior attributes and will buy at full price. They are the primary brand switchers and respond to persuasive advertising based on their fluctuating wants and desires. Therefore, they should be the primary target for brand advertising.[7]

Usage-rate variables It's usually easier to get a heavy user to increase usage than a light user. In **volume segmentation,** marketers measure people's **usage rates** to define consumers as light, medium, or heavy users of products (see Exhibit 6–2). Often, 20 percent of the population consumes 80 percent of the product. Marketers want to define that 20 percent and aim their advertising at them. Hardee's even has a pet name for its prized 17- to 34-year-old male market segment: the HFFU (pronounced who-foo). According to Andrew Pudzer, CKE's CEO, "That's the 'heavy fast-food user,' someone who eats there four or five times a week. . . . It is the sweet spot of the industry and what appeals to him is drippy, messy burgers. He is not interested in little 99-cent burgers or low-carb anything. He's not a big calorie counter."[8]

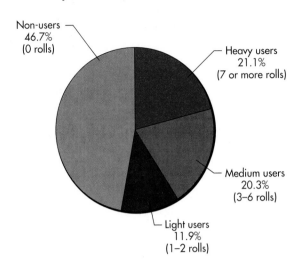

Fast food/drive-in restaurant usage (number of times in last 30 days)

Non-users
7.2%
(0 times)

Light users
16.7%
(1–3 times)

Medium users
27.4%
(4–8 times)

Heavy users
37.2%
(9 or more times)

Film usage purchased (last 12 months)

Non-users
46.7%
(0 rolls)

Heavy users
21.1%
(7 or more rolls)

Medium users
20.3%
(3–6 rolls)

Light users
11.9%
(1–2 rolls)

Exhibit 6–2

Usage rates vary for different products.

By finding common characteristics among heavy users of their products, marketers can define product differences and focus ad campaigns more effectively. For example, heavy users of bowling alleys tend to be working-class men between 25 and 50 who watch more than three and a half hours of television a day and prefer sports programs. So a bowling equipment company would probably want to advertise on TV sports programs.

Marketers of one product sometimes find that their customers are also heavy users of other products and can define target markets in terms of the usage rates of the other products. Research indicates that heavy users of home computers are also heavy users of foreign luxury cars, sports cars, backpacking equipment, binoculars, expensive bicycles, and literary magazines.[9] Similarly, of the 94 percent of teenage boys who use shampoo, 36 percent also use hair spray, 32 percent use conditioner, 31 percent use hair-styling products, and 19 percent use blow dryers.[10]

Purchase-occasion variables   Buyers can also be distinguished by when they buy or use a product or service—the **purchase occasion.** Air travelers, for example,

Seasonal usage is a common way to distinguish users. In fact, the purchase occasion provides insight into the most opportune sales periods. For this reason, Columbia Sportswear (www.columbia.com) may run its ads in fall and winter—just before and during the peak season for snow sports.

OUR RETURN POLICY: YES.

may fly for business or vacation so one airline might promote business travel while another promotes tourism. The purchase occasion might be affected by frequency of need (regular or occasional), a fad (candy, computer games), or seasons (water skis, raincoats). The Japan Weather Association tracked buying patterns on 20,000 items and correlated them to the outside temperature. Not surprisingly, when the temperature goes up, people buy more sunshades, air conditioners, watermelons, and swimwear. When there's a chill in the air, sales of suits, sweaters, and heaters take off.[11] A marketer who discovers common purchase occasions for a group has a potential target segment and can better determine when to run specials and how to promote certain product categories.

Benefits-sought variables   Marketers may segment consumers on the *benefits* being sought. Consumers seek various **benefits** in the products they buy—high quality, low price, status, sex appeal, good taste, health-conscious. Hardee's customers may value the size and taste of Thickburgers, or they may prefer the low-carb, bunless chicken sandwich that has only half the fat. In addition to tangible benefits, customers are often motivated by *symbolism*—what the brand name means to them, to associates, or to some social reference group. **Benefit segmentation** is the prime objective of many consumer attitude studies and the basis for many successful ad campaigns.

Some product categories are characterized by substantial *brand switching* from one purchase occasion to the next. Researchers have determined that switching occurs in response to different "need states" that consumers may experience from one occasion to another. Thus, a soft drink company competes not just for *drinkers* (users) but for *drinks* (occasions) based on the benefits the consumer is seeking at that moment. By measuring the importance of occasion-based motives, an advertiser can determine if a campaign needs to reposition the product.[12]

Using behavioristic segmentation, we can accomplish the first step of identifying likely prospects for our marketing and advertising efforts. The next step in developing rich profiles of these customers involves the use of geographic, demographic, and psychographic characteristics.

Geographic Segmentation

One simple way to define markets is by using **geographic segmentation.** People in one region of the country (or the world) have needs, wants, and purchasing habits that differ from those in other regions. People in Sunbelt states, for example, buy more suntan lotion. Canadians buy special equipment for dealing with snow and ice—products many Floridians have never seen in stores.

When marketers analyze geographic data, they study sales by region, country size, city size, specific locations, and types of stores. Many products sell well in urban areas but poorly in suburban or rural ones, and vice versa. As we'll see in Chapter 9, this information is critical in developing advertising media schedules because, with limited budgets, marketers want to advertise in areas where their sales potential is best.

Even in local markets, geographic segmentation is important. For example, a local progressive politician might send a mailer only to precincts where voters typically support liberal causes, and a local retail store rarely draws customers from outside a fairly limited *trading area.*

Demographic Segmentation

Demographic segmentation is a way to define population groups by their statistical characteristics: sex, age, ethnicity, education, occupation, income, and other quantifiable factors. Demographics are often combined with geographic segmentation to select target markets for advertising. This is called **geodemographic segmentation.** For example, research shows that people who identify themselves as "strongly Hispanic" tend to be very loyal to certain brands. And, as Exhibit 6–3 reveals, Hispanic media have recently experienced a boom. Many blue-chip advertisers, such as Procter & Gamble, AT&T, McDonald's, and General Motors, now aim a significant portion

Exhibit 6–3

Hispanic ad spending growth in United States, by medium

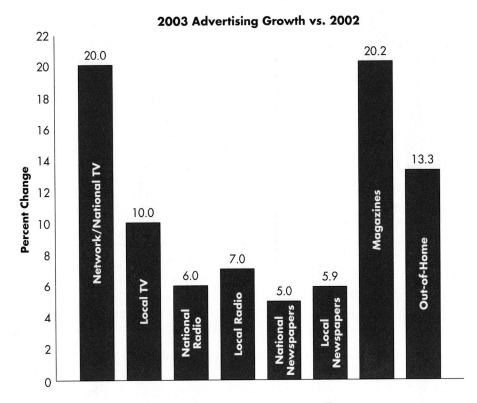

of their advertising specifically at this $675 billion market.[13] To do so efficiently, they measure the size of the "strongly Hispanic" community in each marketing area they plan to target, as well as its income, age distribution, and attitudes. JCPenney, for example, discovered that its Sandra Salcedo line of clothing for Hispanic women sold well in Texas and Northern California stores but not in heavily Mexican-American Los Angeles, where urban influences hold greater sway. In other words, people's lives are influenced by their environment as well as by their ethnicity.[14]

As people grow older, their responsibilities and incomes change, and so do their interests in various product categories (see Exhibit 6–4). Buick, for instance, found a huge untapped market of mature single women who were financially secure and good prospects for its brand. The company now sponsors a newsletter specifically targeted to this group.[15]

At the same time, the auto industry didn't forget that over half of America's consumers are now young adults. In fact, Generation Y, the 71 million children of baby boomers now between the ages of 8 and 25, is the most multicultural, diverse generation ever. By 2010, this group will account for 4 million new car sales, according to Jim Lentz, vice president of Toyota's youth-targeted division Scion.

Exhibit 6–4

Heavy usage patterns of various age groups.

Age	Name of age group	Merchandise purchased
0–5	Young children	Baby food, toys, nursery furniture, children's wear
6–19	Schoolchildren and teenagers	Clothing, sporting goods, tapes and CDs, school supplies, fast food, soft drinks, candy, cosmetics, movies
20–34	Young adults	Cars, furniture, housing, food and beer, clothing, diamonds, home entertainment equipment, recreational equipment, purchases for younger age segments
35–49	Younger middle-aged	Larger homes, better cars, second cars, new furniture, computers, recreational equipment, jewelry, clothing, food and wine
50–64	Older middle-aged	Recreational items, purchases for young marrieds and infants, travel
65 and over	Senior adults	Medical services, travel, pharmaceuticals, purchases for younger age groups

Brand Niching May Cause Brand Switching

Advertisers recognize that offensive advertisements don't pay. They know that alienating or stereotyping minorities and other demographic groups causes serious controversy and bad PR for their clients. And in addition to avoiding the negative effects, there are benefits to being politically correct in advertising: Hispanics, African Americans, Asian Americans, gays, and other minority groups are all sizable target markets with considerable buying power—so much buying power, in fact, that many marketing campaigns are designed specifically to appeal to these market sectors.

Unfortunately, even advertisements that are designed to be sensitive can sometimes backfire. During the 2000 Olympics, John Hancock Financial Services made a sudden revision to a commercial set to air during the events. In the spot, two women were shown together in an airport holding an Asian infant whom they presumably had just adopted. Although the ad never specifically identified the child's nationality, international adoption agencies pressured Hancock to amend the ad to

avoid offending the Chinese government, which would be opposed to the evident homosexuality of the American parents. But Hancock was lucky, in a way—the ad was caught before it aired. This isn't always the case, and the results can be disastrous when a controversial ad makes it past the cut.

To counter recent accusations that they favored white clientele over their African-American patrons, Denny's created some ads that attempted to resolve the issue—badly. The three-spot television campaign featured black customers being "welcomed back" to Denny's and having the time of their lives. However, 100 percent of the people Denny's "welcomed back" were black, affluent, well-dressed, and apparently aristocratic and successful. One would think that if they were going to solely feature African-American customers in the ad, they would do so with a fair representation of the group. Instead of creating an ad that proved Denny's was racially unbiased, as intended, the company had displayed the same behavior it was trying to resolve. Although the company later worked to improve its image, the damage was done.

Similarly, Mitsubishi is targeting the youth market with extensive use of hip music as its advertising theme. Recent studies have shown that 41.6 percent of Mitsubishi buyers are under 35 years old.[16]

Demographic segmentation has long been understood in the fast-food industry, or QSR (quick-serve restaurant) industry, as it now prefers to be called. McDonalds, the industry's creator and perpetual frontrunner, runs the table. Once stigmatized as unsanitary meat fit only for poor people, chains like White Castle and McDonalds used advertising to change the hamburger's image, fashioning it into the national cuisine by the 1950s.[17] Now, children are McDonalds' primary target consumers. Decades of ads for Happy Meals and toys has made an impression. Among fictional characters, Ronald McDonald's cultural penetration is surpassed only by Santa Claus: 96% of schoolchildren in the U.S. can identify the yellow-jumpsuited clown.[18] Against this giant's brand value and advertising expenditures, competitors have returned to the hamburger's traditional consumer, the young male. In the segment where McDonalds is slightly weaker, Hardee's intends to be strong. Thickburger TV spots proclaim that the burgers "don't come with toys, because they're not for little boys."

In international markets, the demographics of many populations are changing rapidly. From Kuala Lumpur to Brazil to Poland, middle-class life is becoming avail-

Changing demographics in many international markets open up new opportunities for advertisers. In Spain, the growing upper middle class and the availability of good expressways enable Mercedes-Benz (www.mercedesbenz.com) to promote its navigation system in this very creative ad that won a Bronze Lion at Cannes.

GPS Navigator, as standard in all Mercedes-Benz models.

Mercedes-Benz

Not only businesses and retailers have these problems; not-for-profit and government organizations also have to watch their step. During the 2002 Super Bowl, the White House introduced a new series of antidrug public-service announcements. The campaign tried to link money spent on drugs to the funding of terrorist activities. Print and television ads in muted black-and-white traced teens' use of drugs for recreation through the supply chain back to tragic, violent episodes in drug-producing regions. To say that the guilt-trip method did not go over well with teenagers would be putting it mildly. Teens felt that the ads were deliberately manipulative and misrepresented the facts in an attempt to support President George W. Bush's war on terrorism. As a result, studies showed that, over time, teens exposed to the ads shifted to a significantly more "prodrug" attitude than those of kids who did not view the ads. In short, the ads fostered enough resentment in their target audience that teens deliberately defied the message being sent.

Advertising sensitivity is a difficult issue. What is politically correct enough? When is something too politically correct? And what should be done when a conflict cannot be avoided? Some market groups simply cannot be targeted without excluding, and thereby offending, other groups. When this happens, a choice must be made, and it must be made carefully, with serious consideration of all results and potential consequences.

Sources: "White House to End Drugs and Terror Ads," AdAge.com, April 1, 2003 (www.adage.com); "Bush Administration's Controversial New Anti-Drug Campaign to Be Target of Upcoming Roll Call Ad by Drug Policy Alliance," February 25, 2002 (www.drugpolicy.org/news/pressroom/pressrelease/pr_february25_02b.cfm); Human Rights Campaign Foundation, "Mainstream Marketing—John Hancock Financial Services," 2004 (www.hrc.org); Kimberly Alcantara, "Let the Games Begin . . . " Pattishall, McCauliffe newsletter, Winter 2002 (www.pattishall.com/pdfs/winter_2002.pdf); Sonya Brathwaite, "Denny's: A Diversity Success Story," International Franchise Association, August 2002 (www.franchise.org/news/fw/aug2002b.asp).

able to more people in former Third World countries. This emerging middle class has an apparently insatiable appetite for consumer goods—everything from color TVs and CD players to video cameras, cars, and refrigerators.[19] In China, for example, only 1 percent of the population has hot running water, but 84 percent have television sets![20] In 2002, Russia emerged as the world's fastest growing advertising market as companies tried to reach that country's increasingly wealthy consumers. According to Vladimir Evstafiev, president of the Russian Association of Advertising Agencies, Russia is now among the top 10 biggest advertising markets in Europe, with annual spending reaching over $2.6 billion.[21]

Geographic and demographic data provide information about markets but little about the psychology of individuals. Marketers want to reach people who are current or prospective customers, but people in the same demographic or geographic segment have widely differing product preferences and TV viewing habits. Rarely can demographic criteria alone predict purchase behavior.[22] That's why marketers developed the study of *psychographics*.

Psychographic Segmentation

For certain products, appeals to emotions and cultural values may be persuasive. So some advertisers use **psychographic segmentation** to define consumer markets. With **psychographics,** marketers group people by their values, attitudes, personality, and lifestyle. Psychographics enables marketers to view people as individuals with feelings and inclinations. Then, they can classify people according to what they feel, what they believe, the way they live, and the products, services, and media they use.[23]

For years, marketers have tried to categorize consumers by personality and lifestyle types to determine advertising appeals. One classification system, VALS™, originated by Stanford Research Institute (now SRI International and currently run by SRI Consulting Business Intelligence [SRIC-BI]), was quickly adopted by marketers across the country. In 1989, SRIC-BI released VALS™, a new psychographic profile for segmenting U.S. consumers and predicting their purchase behavior (see Exhibit 6–5).

The Values and Lifestyles (VALS) typology breaks consumers into eight groups based on the concept of *primary motivation* and *resources*. **Primary motivation** is the pattern of attitudes and activities that help people reinforce, sustain, or modify their social and self-image. Three particular patterns relate to consumer behavior: principles, status, and action. Thus, the VALS system organizes people into three categories: those who are primarily motivated by ideals, by achievement, and by self-expression. The **resources axis** in the VALS typology relates to the range of psychological, physical, demographic,

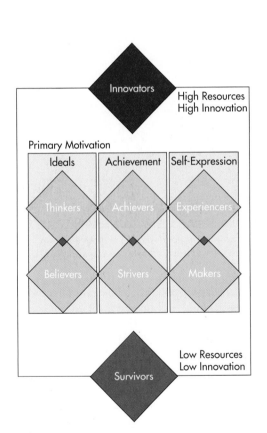

Exhibit 6–5

The VALS™ (Values and Lifestyles) classification system places consumers with abundant resources—psychological, physical, and material means and capacities—near the top of the chart and those with minimal resources near the bottom. The chart segments consumers by their basis for decision making: ideals, achievement, or self-expression. The boxes intersect to indicate that some categories may be considered together. For instance, a marketer may categorize Thinkers and Believers together.

Ads for Adidas (www.adidas.com) capture the attitude and lifestyle of its target market—young people around the world who like to make their own fashion statement. Segmentation along psychographic lines is difficult because it is not easily quantifiable. Nevertheless, lifestyle advertisements play a critical role in marketing products that involve feelings, personalities, values, and attitudes.

and material capacities that consumers can draw upon. These include education, income, self-confidence, health, eagerness to buy, and energy level. People with the most resources are placed at the top of the typology; those with the least at the bottom. Each of the eight VALS groups exhibits distinctive behavior, decision-making patterns, and product/media usage traits.[24]

According to SRIC-BI, the purpose of VALS is to help marketers identify who to target, uncover what the target group buys and does, locate where concentrations of the target group live, identify how best to communicate with them, and gain insight into why the target group behaves the way it does. The system has been applied to a variety of areas: new-product development and design, target marketing, product positioning, advertising message development, and media planning, to name a few.[25]

In one case, for example, a foreign car manufacturer used VALS to reposition its sports utility vehicle after its award-winning but ineffective television campaign failed to result in higher sales. Using VALS, the company targeted a new "rebellious" consumer group with a new campaign using a "breaking the rules" theme. Nothing changed but the advertising. But sales increased 60 percent in six months.[26]

Likewise, in the area of media planning, radio has turned out to be a good medium to reach some of the VALS groups. Conservative, blue-collar people with traditional values (the VALS Believer and Maker segments, comprising 29 percent of the U.S. population) often choose country music stations. Higher-income consumers (the VALS Innovator, Thinker, and Achiever categories) often listen to news and talk radio. Because radio has only a few formats, SRIC-BI's eight typologies fit radio audiences reasonably well.[27]

Later, SRIC-BI developed additional VALS products: Japan-VALS™ to determine the consumer effect of changing values and social behavior in Japan, and GeoVALS™ to determine where target customers live and show why they behave the way they do. This helps advertisers select the best site locations, target direct-mail campaigns effectively, and maximize advertising dollars.[28]

In Europe and Asia, numerous lifestyle studies have produced a variety of other classification systems intended to help marketers understand the product use of different target groups across national boundaries. The research company RISC investigated how people react to social changes in 12 European countries. The basis of the research was the belief that when individuals share similar values, perceptions, and sensitivities, their purchasing behavior will also show consistent similarities.[29] Most recently, Roper Starch Worldwide has developed its ValueScope™ service to help marketers find "shared patterns of market space behavior" around the world in order to conduct global campaigns. The Roper model uses three drivers of consumer behavior—nationality, lifestage, and values—to define six consumer segments that sound remarkably similar to VALS: creatives, fun seekers, intimates, strivers, devouts, altruists.[30] An interesting aspect of Roper's research was the discovery of the top 10 values shared by people around the world (see Exhibit 6–6).

Limitations of Consumer Segmentation Methods

Advocates of all these psychographic systems claim they help address the emotional factors that motivate consumers. However, because the markets for many products comprise such a broad cross section of consumers, psychographics may in fact offer little real value—especially since it oversimplifies consumer personalities and purchase behavior. Some typologies, such as VALS, are also criticized for being complicated and lacking proper theoretical underpinnings.[31]

Still, it's important for marketers to monitor and understand their customers. It helps them select target markets, create ads that match the attributes and image of their products with the types of consumers who use them, develop effective media plans, and budget their advertising dollars wisely. (For an amusing twist on satisfying market needs, see Ad Lab 6–A.)

Segmenting Business and Government Markets: Understanding Organizational Buying Behavior

Business (or *industrial*) **markets** include manufacturers, government agencies, wholesalers, retailers, banks, and institutions that buy goods and services to help them operate. These products may include raw materials, electronic components, mechanical parts, office equipment, vehicles, or services used in conducting the business. Many business marketers sell to **resellers,** such as retail businesses that resell to consumers. Some brands are produced, merchandised, and resold under their own names, like Levi's jeans. Other resellers offer both brand-name products and unbranded products. For example, much of Hardee's food

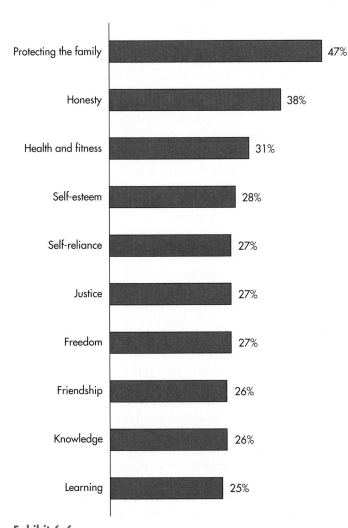

Exhibit 6–6

The world's top 10 values shared by people around the world.

Market Segmentation: A Dog of a Job

Market segmentation doesn't have to be boring. An article from *Advertising Age* by Michael Reinemer described a market he could have fun with—dogs (or, at least, dog owners).

Reinemer shared what prompted his thinking. He saw a video for dogs in an upscale pet store. And an ad for dogs who can't brush after every meal. And an article about dog health insurance, puppy psychotherapy, and Prozac for canines. He suddenly realized that many dogs in the United States probably enjoy better nutrition and health care than millions of people in the world. His reaction: "How do I cash in on this thing?"

Reinemer thought of launching a new consulting firm called "Dog Trend$" to sniff out every conceivable emerging dog-related trend or fad and sponsor a Dog Marketing Conference.

Then he created a few trends of his own for man's best friend:

Dog fitness centers. While the baby boomers pursue fitness, why not let the dog work out, too (SpaDog and DogAerobics).

Dog video games. Interactive games that improve the dog's eye-paw coordination (Mortal Dogfight, Hydrant Finder, Car Chase).

Fashion magazines for dogs. When it's a cold winter day and you put that warm sweater on to keep you warm, why not put a fashionable sweater on your dog (*Dogmopolitan, smELLE, Dogue,* and *DQ*).

Dog retirement communities (Sunset Leisure Kennels).

Cable networks (DoggieVision).

Upscale department stores (BloomingDog's).

Maybe Reinemer's ideas are more than fun. Could they really be the next phase in marketing?

Laboratory Applications

1. Come up with a market segment that you think would be fun to work with. What five products could you market?

2. Do you think Reinemer's dog specialties would work in our marketplace today?

---

is supplied by Siméus Foods International, a processing, production, and distribution conglomerate. Siméus's two plants produce and freeze menu items, such as hamburger and chicken patties, to the specifications of customers like Hardee's and Denny's. The end product is resold by Hardee's with no mention of Siméus. Hardee's reselling contract with Coca-Cola, however, is a much more visible "brand partnership"; Coke products are often featured in Hardee's advertising.

Identifying target markets of prospective business customers is just as complex as identifying consumer markets. Many of the variables used to identify consumer markets can also be used for business markets—for example, geography and behavior (purchase occasion, benefits sought, user status, and usage rate).

Business markets also have special characteristics. They employ professional buyers and use systematic purchasing procedures. They are categorized by North American Industry Classification System (NAICS) code. They may be concentrated geographically. And in any single market there may be only a small number of buyers.

Business Purchasing Procedures

When businesspeople evaluate new products, they use a process far more complex and rigid than the consumer purchase process described in Chapter 5. Business marketers must design their advertising programs with this in mind.

Large firms have purchasing departments that act as professional buyers. They evaluate the need for products, analyze proposed purchases, weigh competitive bids, seek approvals from users and managers, make requisitions, place orders, and supervise all product purchasing. This structured purchase decision process implies a rational approach. Recent research, however, showed that professional buyers often exhibit significant brand-equity behaviors, such as willingness to pay a substantial premium for their favorite brand. This was especially true for buyers concerned about the negative consequences of a product failure. In other words, the buyers perceived well-known brands as a way to reduce risk. Moreover, their feelings about brands tended to transfer from one product category to another, even when the products were very different (e.g., from fax machines to floppy disks).[32] This suggests that advertising may play a larger role in business-to-business marketing than previously thought.

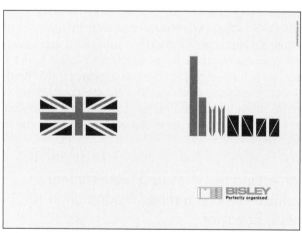

Much like consumer markets, business and government markets can also be segmented in numerous ways. This clever German ad for Bisley (www.bisley.com) organizing products is not aimed at consumers but at people who would use these products for their businesses. The concept of reorganizing the British flag won Bisley a Gold Lion at Cannes.

Exhibit 6–7

NAICS hierarchy and codes. A business marketer selling goods or services to firms in the paging industry can use the NAICS codes to locate prospective companies in directories or in subscription databases.

Level	Code	Sector
Sector	51	Information
Subsector	513	Broadcasting and telecommunications
Industry group	5133	Telecommunications
Industry	51332	Wireless telecommunications carriers (except satellite)
U.S. industry	513321	Paging

Making a sale in business markets may take weeks, months, or even years, especially to government agencies. Purchase decisions often depend on factors besides price or quality, among them product demonstrations, delivery time, terms of sale, and dependability of supply. Marketers often emphasize these issues in advertising and promotional appeals.

Before deciding on a target market, business marketers should consider how the purchase decision process works in various segments. New companies, for instance, may want to target smaller firms where the purchase decision can be made quickly. Or they may use commission-only reps to call on the larger prospects that require more time. These decisions will dictate where advertising should be placed.

Industrial Classification System

Industrial customers need different products, depending on their business. For example, apparel manufacturers such as Levi's are the main customers for buttons and zippers. Marketing managers need to focus their sales and advertising efforts on those firms that are in the right business for their products.[33] The U.S. Census Bureau classifies all U.S. businesses—and collects and publishes industry statistics on them—using the **North American Industry Classification System (NAICS) codes.** The NAICS (pronounced "nakes") system replaces the old SIC (Standard Industrial Classification) system and includes many new industries that are relevant to today's changing economy. Because the system was developed in cooperation with Canada and Mexico, consistency throughout North America is guaranteed.

NAICS organizes all the industries in our economy into 20 broad sectors such as mining, manufacturing, wholesale trade, and information. These are then subdivided into four hierarchical levels of classification, including subsectors, industry groups, industries, and finally 1,170 distinct U.S. industries. (See Exhibit 6–7 for a breakdown of NAICS codes in the information and wireless telecommunications industry.) The U.S. Census Bureau uses NAICS to offer marketers an abundance of information, such as the number of firms, sales volumes, and number of employees by geographic area. Thus, the NAICS codes help companies segment markets and do research, and advertisers can even obtain lists of companies in particular NAICS divisions for direct mailings.[34]

Market Concentration

Many countries' markets for industrial goods are concentrated in one region or several metropolitan areas. In the United States, for example, the industrial market is heavily concentrated in the Midwest, the South, and California (see Exhibit 6–8). Market concentration reduces the number of geographic targets for an advertiser.

Moreover, business marketers deal with fewer buyers than consumer marketers. Less than 15 percent of U.S.

Exhibit 6–8

The states in this map are represented in proportion to the value of their manufactured products.

manufacturing establishments employ nearly 65 percent of all production workers and account for more than 80 percent of all manufacturing dollars.[35] Customer size is a critical issue for market segmentation. A firm may concentrate its marketing and advertising efforts on a few large customers, many smaller ones, or both.

Levi Strauss markets through three channels: independent department stores; specialty stores (such as Urban Outfitters); and chain stores (such as WalMart and JCPenney). Its top 100 accounts provide 80 percent of the company's annual sales and are made through 13,000 retail outlets. Its remaining accounts (20 percent of sales) represent another 13,000 stores. Major accounts are served by sales reps from Levi's various divisions, smaller accounts by telemarketers and pandivisional sales reps. Bartle Bogle Hegarty creates and coordinates advertising for most Levi Strauss divisions in the United States.

Business marketers can also segment by end users. For example, a firm may develop software for one industry, such as banking, or for general use in a variety of industries. That decision, of course, affects advertising media decisions.

Aggregating Market Segments

Once marketers identify and locate broad product-based markets with shared characteristics (behavioristic, geographic, demographic, or psychographic), they can proceed to the second step in the market segmentation process. This involves (1) selecting groups that have a mutual interest in the product's utility and (2) reorganizing and aggregating (combining) them into larger market segments based on their potential for sales and profit. Let's take a look at how this process might work for Levi Strauss & Co. in the U.S. market.

First, the company's management needs to know the market potential for jeans and casual pants in various market areas; that is, it needs to discover the **primary demand trend** of the total U.S. market for pants. To do this it uses a variety of *marketing research* techniques (discussed in Chapter 7).

Then management must identify the needs, wants, and shared characteristics of the various groups within the casual apparel marketplace who live near the company's retail outlets. It may use the services of a large marketing information company such as National Decision Systems, a division of Claritas, which collects data on people's purchasing behavior and creates profiles of geographic markets across the country.

The company finds a huge market of prospective customers throughout the United States: students, blue-collar workers, young singles, professional people, homemakers, and so on. It then measures and analyzes household groups in each major retail area by demographic, lifestyle, and purchasing characteristics, sorts them into 50 geodemographic segments, and refers to them with terms such as those in Exhibit 6–9: Established Wealth, Movers & Shakers, Family Ties, Intercity Singles, and the like. All these people have apparel needs, and many may be interested in the style, cachet, and durability of the Levi's brand.

Selecting Groups Interested in Product Utility

Levi Strauss next selects groups that would like and be able to afford the utilities or benefits of Levi's apparel—suitability for work or play, comfort, style, reasonable cost, durability, and so on. Groups interested in all these features make up the total possible market for Levi's clothes.

Although business purchases are often made according to a company's well-defined needs and policies, the actual purchasers are people who might be persuaded by traditional forms of product branding. For this reason, business-to-business advertising for Sybase (www.sybase.com) places great significance on establishing and reinforcing the Sybase brand name.

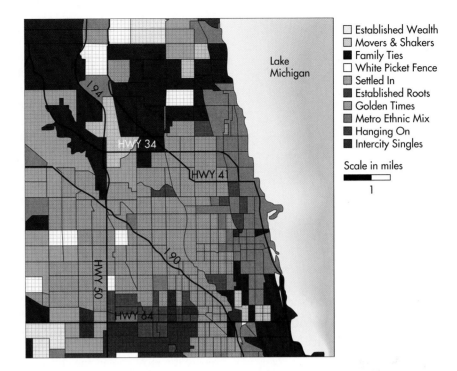

Part of the challenge of market segmentation is estimating the profits the company might realize if it (1) aims at the whole market or (2) caters only to a specific market segment. Apparel is a highly competitive market, but 10 percent of 1,000 is always larger than 90 percent of 100. So for a company such as Levi Strauss, the target market must be a large mass market or it won't be profitable.[36]

Combining Groups to Build Target Market Segments

The company needs to find groups that are relatively homogeneous (similar) and offer good potential for profit. Market data turn up a large number of demographic and lifestyle groups, including ethnically diverse families, young singles, and seniors with lower education and income who often live in rented homes or apartments: On Their Own (3.4 percent), Back Country (6.0 percent), and Settled In (5.1 percent). Because of their minimal retail or credit activity, these groups are not prime targets for premium-branded department store products.

Other segments offer greater potential—young to middle-aged households with medium to high incomes and average to high retail activity: Movers & Shakers (2.5 percent), Prosperous Ethnic Mix (2.8 percent), and Home Sweet Home (5.7 percent). By combining these (and similar) groups with the young professionals in the Good Step Forward (2.1 percent) and Great Beginnings (3.6 percent) segments, Levi Strauss can target young to middle-aged people on their way up. Nationally, that amounts to 20 million U.S. households. That's not everybody, but it's a large and potentially very profitable mass-market segment. These people might like the style and comfort of Levi's 550s as well as the tradition of a brand they know and trust, and the company could develop a campaign to appeal to their particular needs, wants, and self-image.

The Target Marketing Process

Once the market segmentation process is complete, a company can proceed to the **target marketing process.** This will determine the content, look, and feel of its advertising.

Target Market Selection

The first step in target marketing is to assess which of the newly created segments offer the greatest profit potential and which can be most successfully penetrated. The company designates one or more segments as a **target market**—that group of segments the company wishes to appeal to, design products for, and tailor its marketing activities toward.[37] It may designate another set of segments as a secondary target market and aim some of its resources at it.

Let's look at the most likely target market for loose-fitting jeans: young to middle-aged customers with moderate to high income and education who like the style, comfort, and fashion of Levi's apparel. This group represents a large percentage of the apparel market, and, if won, will generate substantial profits. Levi's offers what these prospects need and want: the style and fashion of the jeans they grew up with, updated to be more comfortable for the adult body.

If the young, comfort-oriented segment wasn't large enough to be profitable, the company would select a different target market, and its other marketing and advertising activities would have to change as well. For an example, look at Ad Lab 6–B and consider how Starbucks selected its new target market.

The Marketing Mix: A Strategy for Matching Products to Markets

Once a company defines its target market, it knows exactly where to focus its attention and resources. It can shape the product concept and even design special features for its target market (such as certain colors or special sizes). It can establish proper pricing. It can determine the need for locating stores or dealers and prepare the most convincing advertising messages.

No product appeals universally to every customer, so advertisers must carefully choose their target markets. Although Land Rover (www.landrover.com) typically targets consumers in the market for more rugged, off-roading automobiles, this ad is aimed at parents who want the safety and comfort of a family car and the function of a sport utility vehicle.

Understanding the Product Element: Starbucks Coffee

America's java giant began as the seed of an idea by a man with a dream whose tender care and commitment eventually built the familiar coffee empire of today. While on a trip to Italy in 1983, Howard Schultz discovered and fell in love with the coffee bars of Milan and Verona. They were a combination of coffee and community. He was sure Americans would love this concept.

At the time, Starbucks was a little 11-store chain of roasted coffee stores in Seattle. Schultz was in charge of marketing. He pitched the coffee-bar concept to the company's management but received only a lukewarm response. They didn't want to be in the beverage business. Howard held on to his vision, though. Leaving Starbucks in 1987, he launched a handful of coffee bars on his own and named them Il Giornales. Two years later, with some investor backing, his demonstrated success enabled him to buy Starbucks out. Today, he is chairman and chief global strategist of a publicly traded company that boasts more than 7,500 retail locations in North America, Latin America, Europe, the Middle East, and the Pacific Rim. Serving tens of millions of Americans each week, Starbucks has definitely become a household name.

To Schultz, the most important component for success is consistent product quality. "Our long-range goal is to be nothing less than the most recognized and respected brand of coffee in the world," Schultz says.

Thanks to management's demand for consistency, a double-tall latte tastes the same in New York as it does in Seattle; and your perfectly pulled espresso won't sit for more than 10 seconds before being poured into your cup. This attention to detail has earned Starbucks its place in the premium coffee category.

Of course a good product is best prepared and served by skilled, happy employees. And that also adds to an organization's profitability.

Ranked as number 47 by the Fortune "100 Best Companies to Work for in 2004" poll, Starbucks' management believes that if it takes care of its workers, they in turn will take care of the public. Employees who work at least 20 hours a week receive full benefits, including dental, extended health care, eyeglass and contact lens prescriptions—after only 90 days with the company. Starbucks even offers these benefits to the same-sex partners of employees. To further ensure consistent product quality, Starbucks implemented procedures for monitoring the working conditions of the overseas producers who supply materials to the company.

Today, the coffee market is quite competitive, but Starbucks retains its leading position by continually introducing new products. With PepsiCo, Starbucks formed a partnership to produce its Frappuccino beverage in 1995. In 1996, Starbucks entered into a joint venture with Dreyers Grand Ice Cream to market "Starbucks Coffee Ice Cream." In 1998 and 1999, Starbucks strengthened its presence within the tea segment by introducing a mixture of tea, fruit juice, and ice called Tiazzi, and it aquired Tazo, a Portland, Oregon–based tea company. In 2002, a bottled espresso drink dubbed the DoubleShot became the newest of the long line of creative products. If you're drinking a cup of coffee these days, Starbucks may well have created it—even if it doesn't say so on the label.

Laboratory Application

A basic rule of advertising is that the most ingenious campaign in the world cannot save a bad product. Think of a product in the marketplace that you consider successful and analyze which elements make it profitable and unique. Are there any similarities to the product elements found in Starbucks? If so, what?

As we discussed in Chapter 5, a product offers a number of utilities, perceived by the consumer as a *bundle of values*. With this in mind, marketers and advertisers generally try to shape their basic product into a total **product concept:** the consumer's perception of a product as a bundle of utilitarian and symbolic values that satisfy functional, social, psychological, and other wants and needs.

Companies have many strategic options they can employ to enhance the product/service concept and effect marketing exchanges (make sales). Marketers categorize these options under four headings: (1) *product,* (2) *price,* (3) *distribution,* and (4) *communication.*[38] The way the marketer mixes and blends these different elements creates the company's marketing strategy—often called the **marketing mix.** For

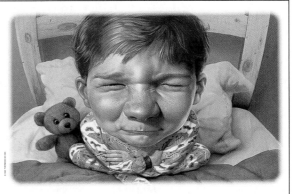

If there's one thing kids are good at, it's figuring out how to make it difficult to take their temperature. They squirm. They wiggle. They whine. They even cry. But don't give up hope. Just throw out your old thermometer. And replace it with a Thermoscan® Instant Thermometer. In one short second, it takes a temperature at the ear. It's easy. It's accurate. It's safe. (No wonder over a half-billion temperatures are being taken this way every year in doctors' offices and hospitals.) And now you can get it for a new lower price. Which means the perfect family thermometer just got better.

THE GREAT THING ABOUT THIS THERMOMETER IS THAT CHILDREN HAVE YET TO LEARN HOW TO CLENCH THEIR EARS SHUT.

Most of us might stick a thermometer in our mouths when we come down with a fever, but the Braun Thermoscan (www.braun.com) isn't just any thermometer. The company's product concept, using the ear rather than the mouth, differentiates its thermometer as one that is gentle yet effective for the temperament of children.

convenience, marketing educator E. Jerome McCarthy developed a mnenomic device to help recall these four functions: *product, price, place,* and *promotion*—or the **four Ps (4Ps).**[39]

The 4Ps are a simple way to remember the basic elements of the marketing mix. But within each element are numerous marketing activities a company can employ to fine-tune its product concept and improve sales. Advertising, for example, is one instrument of the communication (promotion) element. The remainder of this chapter focuses on the relationship between advertising and the other elements of the marketing mix.

Advertising and the Product Element

In developing a marketing mix, marketers generally start with the **product element.** Major activities typically include the way the product is designed and classified, positioned, branded, and packaged. Each of these affects the way the product is advertised.

Product Life Cycles

Marketers theorize that just as humans pass through stages in life from infancy to death, products (and especially product categories) also pass through a **product life cycle** (see Exhibit 6–10).[40] A product's position in the life cycle influences the target market selected and the kind of advertising used. There are four major stages in the product life cycle: *introduction, growth, maturity,* and *decline.*

When a company introduces a new product category, nobody knows about it. By using market segmentation, though, the company may try to identify those prospects who are known to be **early adopters**—willing to try new things—and begin promoting the new category directly to them. The idea is to stimulate **primary demand**—consumer demand for the whole product category, not just the company's own brand.

During the **introductory** (pioneering) **phase** of any new product category, the company incurs considerable costs for educating customers, building widespread dealer distribution, and encouraging demand. It must spend significant advertising sums at this stage to establish a position as a market leader and to gain a large share of market before the growth stage begins.

When cellular telephones were introduced in the late 1980s, advertisers had to first create enough consumer demand to pull the product through the channels of distribution (called **pull strategy**). Advertising communications educated con-

Exhibit 6–10

A product's life cycle curve may vary, depending on the product category. Marketing objectives and strategies change as the product proceeds from one stage to the next.

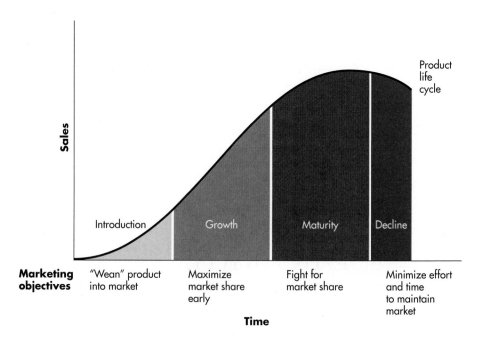

| Marketing objectives | "Wean" product into market | Maximize market share early | Fight for market share | Minimize effort and time to maintain market |

Advertisers use a variety of strategies to extend the life cycle of a product in its mature stage. Procter & Gamble (www.pg.com), testing two new flavors of Crest toothpaste in mass-merchant chains, used Telestar Interactive's MicroTalk shelf units to play audio messages about the products to approaching consumers.

sumers about the new product and its category, explained what cellular phones are, how they work, and the rewards of owning one. **Sales promotion** efforts aimed at the retail trade (called **push strategy**) encouraged distributors and dealers to stock, display, and advertise the new products (see Chapter 10).

When sales volume begins to rise rapidly, the product enters the **growth stage.** This period is characterized by rapid *market expansion* as more and more customers, stimulated by mass advertising and word-of-mouth, make their first, second, and third purchases. Competitors jump into the market, but the company that established the early leadership position reaps the biggest rewards. As a percentage of total sales, advertising expenditures should decrease, and individual firms will realize their first substantial profits.

During the early 1990s, the demand for cellular phones exploded, and category sales quadrupled every year. Many competitors suddenly appeared. With increased production and competition, prices started to fall, which brought even more people into the market. By 2003, almost two-thirds of all U.S. families owned cellular phones.

In the **maturity stage,** the marketplace becomes saturated with competing products and the number of new customers dwindles, so industry sales reach a plateau. Competition intensifies and profits diminish. Companies increase their promotional efforts but emphasize **selective demand** to impress customers with the subtle advantages of their particular brand. At this stage, companies increase sales only at the expense of competitors (conquest sales). The strategies of market segmentation, product positioning, and price promotion become more important during this shakeout period as weak companies fall by the wayside and those remaining fight for small increases in market share. By the mid-1990s, for example, cellular phones that once sold for $1,500 were suddenly advertised regularly for $100 to $200. Ads emphasized features and low prices, and the product became a staple of discount merchandisers. Today, of course, one can get a cell phone for free, just by signing up for the service.[41]

Late in the maturity stage, companies may have to scramble to extend the product's life cycle. Without innovation or marketing support, name brands eventually see their sales erode. If the advertised brand has no perceived advantage, people will buy whatever's cheapest or most convenient. Professor Brian Wansink, who directs the Brand Lab at the University of Illinois Urbana–Champaign, suggests that the reason many old brands die is less for life-cycle reasons and more for marketing neglect. He points out that aging brands often pack plenty of brand equity. The challenge for marketers is to determine which brands can be revitalized and then decide how to do it. But with today's high price tag on introducing new products (often $100 million or more), revitalization should be the strategy of choice whenever possible. Marketers may try to find new users for the brand, develop new uses for the product, change the size of packages, design new labels, improve quality, or use promotion to increase frequency of use.[42]

If they're not revitalized, products will finally enter the **decline stage** because of obsolescence, new technology, or changing consumer tastes. At this point, companies may cease all promotion and phase the products out quickly, as in the case of record turntables and LP albums, or let them fade slowly with minimal advertising, like most sheer hosiery brands.

Product Classifications

The way a company classifies its product is important in defining both the product concept and the marketing mix. As Exhibit 6–11 shows, there are many ways to classify tangible goods: by markets, by the purchasing habits of buyers, by the consumption rate or degree of tangibility, or by physical attributes.

Unlike tangible goods, a **service** is a bundle of *intangible* benefits that satisfy some need or want, are temporary in nature, and usually derive from completion of a task.[43] Thus we have *task utility,* as described in Chapter 5. Rail service, for example, is transitory, used and priced by time and distance. It offers the functional benefits of transporting people, livestock, and freight. But it can also offer psychological benefits. Just think of the romance and leisure of a train trip across Europe aboard the Orient Express. The railroad relies on the use of *specialized equipment*—vehicles able to pull huge loads over a unique track. This makes it an **equipment-based service.**

In contrast, an ad agency, like a law firm or a bank, is a **people-based service;** it relies on the creative talents and marketing skills of individuals. As one agency CEO said, "My inventory goes up and down the elevators twice a day."[44]

Exhibit 6–11

Product classifications.

By market	By rate of consumption and tangibility	By purchasing habits	By physical description
Consumer goods Products and services we use in our daily lives (food, clothing, furniture, cars). Industrial goods Products used by companies for the purpose of producing other products (raw materials, agricultural commodities, machinery, tools, equipment).	Durable goods Tangible products that are long-lasting and infrequently replaced (cars, trucks, refrigerators, furniture). Nondurable goods Tangible products that may be consumed in one or a few uses and usually need to be replaced at regular intervals (food, soap, gasoline, oil). Services Activities, benefits, or satisfaction offered for sale (travel, haircuts, legal and medical services, massages).	Convenience goods Purchases made frequently with a minimum of effort (cigarettes, food, newspapers). Shopping goods Infrequently purchased items for which greater time is spent comparing price, quality, style, warranty (furniture, cars, clothing, tires). Specialty goods Products with such unique characteristics that consumers will make special efforts to purchase them even if they're more expensive (fancy photographic equipment, special women's fashions, stereo components). Unsought goods Products that potential customers don't yet want (insurance, encyclopedias) or don't know they can buy (new products), so they don't search them out.	Packaged goods Cereals, hair tonics, and so forth. Hard goods Furniture, appliances. Soft goods Clothing, bedding. Services Intangible products.

At a time when sport utility vehicles are so popular that competing companies all seem to be offering the same services, Jeep (www.jeep.com) positions itself as the "only one" to go anywhere on the planet. Positioning is important in tight markets to assist in differentiation between like products.

Product Positioning

Once an advertising person understands the product's stage in the life cycle, how it's classified, and how it's currently perceived by the marketplace, the first strategic decision can be made: how to **position** the product. The basic goal of positioning strategy is to own a word that ranks the product in the prospect's mind. Levi's owns "jeans." FedEx owns "overnight." And Volvo owns "safety." By developing a unique position for the brand in the consumer's mind, the marketer helps the consumer remember the brand and what it stands for.

Products may be positioned in many different ways. Generally, they are ranked by the way they are differentiated, the benefits they offer, the particular market segment to which they appeal, or the way they are classified. Xerox has repositioned itself as "The Document Company," moving from the narrow, glutted, copier market to the broader, growing, document-handling market. With one stroke, Xerox redefined the business it is in, differentiated itself from the competition, and created a new number-one position for itself.[45]

Product Differentiation

Product differentiation creates a product difference that appeals to the preferences of a distinct market segment. In advertising, nothing is more important than being able to tell prospects truthfully that your product is new and different. Unfortunately, in response to increased competitive pressures, burgeoning innovation and technology, and various constraints on distribution, new-product development cycles have shortened dramatically. As a result, many brand managers find themselves launching new products that are "only 85 percent there."[46] So it's not surprising that most "new" products fail to impress consumers. (See Exhibit 6–12.) Simply adding new colors might differentiate a product enough to attract a new set of customers, but not all product differences need be that obvious. Differences between products may be *perceptible, hidden,* or *induced.* Hank Seiden says every successful product must have a "unique advantage." Bob Pritikin humorously calls that differentiating quality the AMAZING NEW![47]

Differences between products that are readily apparent to the consumer are called **perceptible differences.** Snapple, for example, received its initial impetus because of its unique taste, and the company now spends $40 million annually to advertise this difference to consumers nationwide.[48] **Hidden differences** are not so readily apparent. Trident gum may look and taste the same as other brands, but it is differentiated by the use of artificial sweeteners. While hidden differences can

Exhibit 6–12

What's new? Not much. Consumers didn't think these products were as new as they claimed to be, as indicated by the grades awarded.

Product	New and different	Purchase probability	Price/ value	Overall grade
Airwick Botanicals	F	A	A	B
Mr. Clean Glass & Surface Cleaner	F	A	A	B
Spic & Span with Bleach	F	A	B	B
Aspirin-Free Bayer Select	F	B	B	C
Sugar Twin Plus low-calorie sweetener	F	B	A	C
Lady Power Clear Roll-On antiperspirant	F	B	A	C

enhance a product's desirability, advertising is usually needed to let consumers know about them.

For many product classes, such as aspirin, salt, gasoline, packaged foods, liquor, and financial services, advertising can create **induced differences.** Banks, brokerage houses, and insurance companies, for example, which offer virtually identical financial products and services, use advertising and promotion to differentiate themselves. However, few have yet discovered the image asset of branding as used by the national packaged-goods marketers. That is created through the accumulation of consistent advertising campaigns, favorable publicity, special-event sponsorship, and good word-of-mouth.[49]

As Sunkist has so successfully demonstrated, the ability to create the perception of differences in functionally similar products and services depends on the consistent, effective use of branding, packaging, and advertising.

Product Branding

The fundamental differentiating device for all products is the **brand**—that combination of name, words, symbols, or design that identifies the product and its source and distinguishes it from competing products. Without brands, consumers couldn't tell one product from another, and advertising them would be nearly impossible.

Branding decisions are difficult. A manufacturer may establish an **individual brand** for each product it produces. Unilever, for example, markets its toothpastes under the individual brand names Aim, Pepsodent, and Close-Up. Such companies designate a distinct target market for each product and develop a separate personality and image for each brand. However, this strategy is very costly.

On the other hand, a company might use a **family brand** and market different products under the same umbrella name. When Heinz promotes its ketchup, it hopes to help its relishes too. This decision may be cost effective, but one bad product in a line can hurt the whole family.

Because it is so expensive for manufacturers to market **national brands** (also called *manufacturer's brands*), some companies use a *private-labeling strategy.* They manufacture the product and sell it to resellers (distributors or dealers), who put their own brand on the product. **Private labels,** typically sold at lower prices in large retail chain stores, include such familiar names as Kenmore, Craftsman, Cragmont, Kroger, and Party Pride. They now account for almost 20 percent of grocery purchases.[50] The responsibility for creating brand image and familiarity rests with the distributor or retailer, who is also the principal benefactor if the brand is successful. Recent trends have moved toward premium private labels, such as President's Choice, which has enjoyed immense success. These products feature better packaging, superior quality, and a higher price, comparable to national brands.

Branding decisions are critical because the brands a company owns may be its most important capital asset. Imagine the value of owning a brand name such as Coca-Cola, Nike, Porsche, or Levi's. *BusinessWeek*'s annual brand-value report ranks Coca-Cola as the most valuable brand in the world, followed by Microsoft, IBM, GE, Intel, and Nokia (see Exhibit 6–13).[51] Some companies pay a substantial fee for the right to use another company's brand name. Thus, we have **licensed brands** such as Sunkist vitamins, Coca-Cola clothing, Porsche sunglasses, and Mickey Mouse watches.

Creating a brand name is key to differentiation for a product. Without this, the consumer is left with a generic commodity. Large companies can actually oversee many different products and brand names, as in the case of the many popular and well-known items marketed by Procter & Gamble.

The Role of Branding

For consumers, brands offer instant recognition and identification. They also promise consistent, reliable standards of quality, taste, size, or even psychological satisfaction, which adds value to the product for both the consumer and the manufacturer. In a study by McKinsey & Co., a computer's brand name ranked second

Exhibit 6-13

World's most valuable brands.

Rank	Brand	2003 brand value (in billions)
1	Coca-Cola	$70.5
2	Microsoft	65.2
3	IBM	51.8
4	GE	42.3
5	Intel	31.1
6	Nokia	29.4
7	Disney	28.0
8	McDonald's	24.7
9	Marlboro	22.2
10	Mercedes	21.4

(behind performance) in what consumers considered important when choosing a personal computer. Price, by the way, ranked fifth.[52]

Brands must be built on differences in images, meanings, and associations. It's up to manufacturers to differentiate their products clearly and deliver value competitively. The product has to taste better, or get clothes cleaner, or be packaged in a more environmentally friendly container.[53] Advertising for an established brand, particularly a well-differentiated one, is much more effective if it exploits the brand's positioning.[54] Ideally, when consumers see a brand on the shelf, they instantly comprehend the brand's promise and have confidence in its quality. Of course, they must be familiar with and believe in the brand's promise (a function of advertising effectiveness). As we pointed out in Chapter 5, the goal is *brand loyalty*—because it serves both the consumer and the advertiser. For the consumer, it reduces shopping time. For the advertiser, it builds **brand equity,** the totality of what consumers, distributors, dealers—even competitors—feel and think about the brand over an extended period of time. In short, it's the value of the brand's capital.

High brand equity offers a host of blessings to the product marketer: customer loyalty, price inelasticity, long-term profits. A loyal customer can be nine times as profitable as a disloyal one.[55] But building brand equity requires time and money. Brand value and preference drive market share, but share points and brand loyalty are usually won by the advertisers who spend the most. And increasing brand loyalty requires a spending increase of 200 to 300 percent to affect loyalty dramatically.[56] Charlotte Beers, the former head of J. Walter Thompson, points out the importance of "brand stewardship." She believes companies must maintain consistency in their message by integrating all their marketing communications—from packaging and advertising to sales promotion and publicity—to maintain and reinforce the brand's personality in a real-life context and avoid doing something stupid such as changing the distinctive color of a Ryder rental truck.[57]

Product Packaging

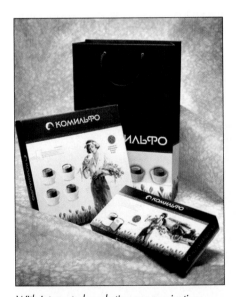

With integrated marketing communications strategies, all contact with the consumer is expected to make an impact, right down to the design of the product packaging. What do you think the packaging for these chocolates, which was designed by Depot WPF in Russia, says about the product?

The product's package is a component of the product element and is also an *exhibitive medium* that can determine the outcome of retail shelf competition. In fact, packaging may be a brand's one differential advantage—and it's the marketer's last chance to communicate at the point of sale. Package designers (who sometimes work in agencies) must make the package exciting, appealing, and at the same time functional. The four considerations in package design are *identification; containment, protection, and convenience; consumer appeal;* and *economy.* These functions may even become **copy points**—copywriting themes—in the product's advertising.

Identification

Packaging is such an important identification device that some companies use the same package and label design for years. Why? Because the unique combination of trade name, trademark, or trade character, reinforced by the package design, quickly identifies the product's brand and differentiates it from competitors. For example, the traditional contoured Coke bottle was so unusual and popular that in the 1990s Coca-Cola reintroduced it to U.S. markets. The company never stopped using it in many international markets, because it differentiated Coke so well from other cola products.

Packages must offer high visibility and legibility just to penetrate shoppers' *physiological screens.* Product features must be easy to read and color combinations must provide high contrast to differentiate the product. To penetrate consumers' *psychological screens,* the package design must reflect the tone, image, and personality of the product concept. In many product categories (wine, cosmetics), the package quality largely determines the consumer's perception of the product's quality.

Packaging must have consumer appeal to be effective, because even minor changes in color can significantly affect sales. Companies can find even more success if the packaging appeal is great enough for consumers to want to keep and use the package long after the initial purchase.

Containment, Protection, and Convenience

The basic purpose of any package is to hold and protect the product and make it easy to use. While marketers must design an interesting package, they must also make sure it will keep the product fresh and protect its contents from shipping damage, water vapor (for frozen goods), grease, infestation, and odors. And packages must adhere to legal protection requirements.

Retailers want packages that are easy to stack and display; they also want a full range of sizes to fit their customers' needs. Consumers want packages that are easy to carry, open, and store, so these are important design considerations. But convenience can't interfere with protection. Spouts, for example, make pouring easier but they may also limit a package's physical strength.

Consumer Appeal

Consumer appeal in packaging is the result of many factors: size, color, material, and shape. Certain colors have special meanings to consumers. It's not uncommon for even a subtle change in color to result in as much as a 20 percent change in sales.[58]

In this age of environmental awareness, *green marketing* is an important issue for many companies and consumers alike. New technology has made ecologically safe packaging available and affordable for many product categories. Many companies now advertise their packages as environmentally responsible.

A package's shape also offers an opportunity for consumer appeal based on whimsy, humor, or romance. Heart-shaped packages of Valentine's Day candy instantly tell what the product is. Some companies design packages with a secondary use in mind. Kraft's cheese jar, once emptied, can be used for serving fruit juice. Some tins and bottles even become collectibles (Chivas Regal). These packages are really premiums that give buyers extra value for the dollars they spend.

Economy

The costs of identification, protection, convenience, and consumer appeal add to basic production costs, but this increase may be more than offset by increased customer

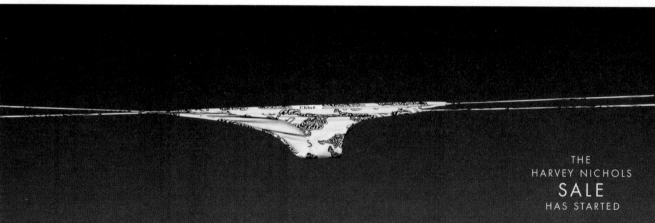

This print ad for Harvey Nichols in London was awarded a Silver Lion at Cannes. The stretched bathing suit is an apt metaphor for consumers who are interested in stretching their money. Of course, the ad could be read another way: This image might depict what happens when frantic shoppers fight for the same item.

appeal. These benefits may make a considerable difference to the consumer and affect both the product concept and the way it is advertised.

Advertising and the Price Element

Many companies, especially small ones, request input from their advertising people about pricing strategies. That's because, as we all know, the **price element** of the marketing mix influences consumer perceptions of the brand dramatically.

Key Factors Influencing Price

Companies typically set their prices based on market demand for the product, costs of production and distribution, competition, and corporate objectives. Interestingly, though, a company often has relatively few options for determining its price strategy, depending on the desired product concept.

Market Demand

If the supply of a product is static but the desire (demand) for it increases, the price tends to rise. If demand drops below available supply, the price tends to fall. This may affect advertising messages in a major way (see Exhibit 6–14).

In the last recession, many auto manufacturers faced a glut of unsold new cars and declining demand. Several companies offered substantial factory rebates—price cuts—to motivate prospective buyers. Dealers immediately sold more cars. No amount of image or awareness advertising would have had the same effect. But, of course, advertising was essential to communicate the price cut.

Some marketing researchers theorize that for new durable goods, advertising works with word-of-mouth communication to generate awareness of and belief in the product's attributes. Once consumers perceive that the product's value warrants the purchase price, sales occur. As product experience and information spread, the risks typically associated with new products diminish, which effectively increases consumers' willingness to purchase at a higher price.[59]

Production and Distribution Costs

The price of goods depends to some extent on the costs of production and distribution. As these costs increase, they must be passed on to the consumer, or the company will be unable to meet its overhead and be forced out of business. One common advertising strategy is to tout the materials used in manufacturing a product. This can also help justify the prices manufacturers must charge to cover their production costs.

Exhibit 6–14

This graph plots demand versus price and supply versus price. The demand curve shows the amounts purchased at various prices. The supply curve shows the amounts offered for sale at various prices. The point where the two curves cross is called the market clearing price, where demand and supply balance. It is the price that theoretically sells out the product.

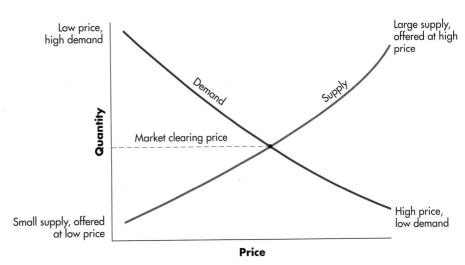

Competition

Marketers believe that, in many product categories, consumers are less concerned with a product's actual price than with its perceived price relative to competitors. For the advertiser, maintaining the value perception during periods of intense price competition and fluctuation is challenging and critically important.[60] But this is one of the prime attributes of good advertising—maintaining the value perception.

Corporate Objectives and Strategies

A company's objectives also influence price. When introducing new products, companies often set a high price initially to recover development and startup costs. In other cases, if the objective were to position the brand as an inexpensive convenience item aimed at a broad target market, ads would stress the product's economy.

Price also depends on the company's marketing strategy, and image advertising may be used to justify a higher price. Many premium-priced brands, such as L'Oréal, are touted for the very fact that they do cost more. The important thing is that the price be consistent with the brand image; you can't charge a Rolex price for a Timex watch.

As products enter the maturity stage of their life cycle, corporate objectives tend to aim at increasing, or at least maintaining, market share. To accomplish this, competitive advertising and promotion heat up, and prices tend to drop.

Variable Influences

Economic conditions, consumer income and tastes, government regulations, marketing costs, and other factors also influence prices and thus advertising. Marketing management must consider all these to determine an appropriate pricing strategy and then create advertising that justifies the product's price.

Advertising and the Distribution (Place) Element

Before the first ad can be created, the **distribution element,** or *place*, must be decided. It is important for marketers to understand that the method of distribution, like the price, must be consistent with the brand's image. People will not pay Nordstrom prices at Kmart. To understand Starbucks' distribution strategy, see Ad Lab 6–C, "Starbucks and the Place Element." Companies use two basic methods of distribution: *direct* or *indirect.*

Direct Distribution

When companies sell directly to end users or consumers, they use **direct distribution.** Avon, for example, employs sales reps who work for the manufacturer rather than for a retailer and sell directly to consumers. Encyclopedia publishers and insurance companies often sell and distribute their products and services directly to customers without the use of wholesalers or retailers. In these cases, the advertising burden is carried entirely by the manufacturer.

One of the fastest-growing methods of direct distribution today is **network marketing** (also called *multilevel marketing*), in which individuals act as independent distributors for a manufacturer or private-label marketer. These people sign up friends and relatives to consume the company's products and recruit others to join. Through a gradual, word-of-mouth process, they form a "buying club" of independent distributors who buy the products wholesale direct from the company, use them, and tout them to more and more friends and acquaintances.

If successful, the rewards for the network marketing company (and many of the distributors) can be staggering. Amway International, the granddaddy of network marketing, now boasts international sales in excess of $5 billion, and many of its longtime distributors became multimillionaires in the process. Other companies have broken the billion-dollar sales mark, too, among them Nikken (Japan), Herbalife, and Shaklee. These companies brag about the fact that they do *no*

Starbucks and the Place Element

The "place" (or distribution) element of marketing strategy is always integral to successful business. You may have the most wonderful product in the world—but potential customers won't buy it if they can't find it.

Starbucks (www.starbucks.com) is a phenomenon that changed the way people view coffee. This can be explained, in large part, by the creative use of the place element. You'll notice that Starbucks cafés are found in high-traffic, easily noticeable locations in each market area. In some markets, Starbucks seems to appear on virtually every street corner. Although the average consumer may find this excessive, Starbucks actually picks and plans each retail location with great care.

To a company like Starbucks, street space is the same as shelf space. In this sense, buying out existing coffeehouses is the same as Coca-Cola buying shelf space in a supermarket. Starbucks management believes that chain expansion is as much a part of the company's success as is its coffee bar and customer service concepts. Since its opening, stores have sprouted up in virtually every major city across the globe, and Starbucks has no intention of stopping. By the end of 2005, management expects to have 10,000 Starbucks stores in 60 countries, with a long-term goal of 25,000 stores worldwide.

Aside from its store locations, Starbucks' unique coffee blends are now found in selected airlines, restaurants, hotels, and supermarkets. Additional venues include a mail-order business with catalog distribution, a coast-to-coast alliance with Barnes & Noble bookstores, a partnership with Star Markets in Boston, distribution to the Washington State Ferry system, Holland America Line–Westours cruises, Safeco Field in Seattle, and Chicago's Wrigley Field. Starbucks is also joining the Internet craze. Starting in 2001, Starbucks began a campaign to integrate high-speed wireless Internet access terminals at some stores. With more than 4,000 stores currently up and running with Internet access, customers are now able to browse the Net, send e-mails, and drink their coffee all at the same time.

Obviously, Starbucks intends to fully saturate every coffee market. When consumers go shopping for groceries, they aren't likely to make a separate trip to Starbucks for coffee. So Starbucks now competes directly with other specialty coffees sold in supermarkets. In 1998 Kraft Foods signed on with Starbucks and agreed to distribute and market Starbucks coffee beans in more than 25,000 grocery stores in the United States. Kraft is the largest packaged-food company in North America. This collaboration is a major steppingstone in surpassing Folgers as the leading coffee brand in the United States. Other placement strategies include the incorporation of Starbucks' latest product, the DoubleShot, into supermarkets. By partnering with PepsiCo in developing and implementing the new drink, Starbucks can take advantage of PepsiCo's vast network of distribution channels, and place its product almost anywhere, bringing the company one step closer to its original dream—"Planet Starbucks."

Laboratory Application

Take the product you used in Ad Lab 6–B and compare the distribution principles used by Starbucks with your product. In addition, think about the factors that should be considered when placing your product or service in other venues. How does it compare with Starbucks?

---

media advertising. Because they usually sell consumer products (that would typically carry a heavy advertising and sales promotion burden), they save a tremendous amount of money. Most marketing communications are simply word-of-mouth. The companies do provide attractive product packaging, catalogs, brochures, and other sales material—which the distributors typically pay for at cost. Today, companies using this distribution method include subsidiaries or spin-offs of well-known public corporations such as Gillette and U.S. Sprint.

Indirect Distribution

Manufacturers usually don't sell directly to end users or consumers. Most companies market their products through a *distribution channel* that includes a network of *resellers*. A **reseller** (also called a *middleman*) is a business firm that operates between the producer and the consumer or industrial purchaser. It deals in trade rather than production.[61] Resellers include both wholesalers and retailers, as well as manufacturers' representatives, brokers, jobbers, and distributors. A **distribution channel** comprises all the firms and individuals that take title, or assist in taking title, to the product as it moves from the producer to the consumer.

Indirect distribution channels make the flow of products available to customers conveniently and economically. Appliance companies, for example, contract with exclusive regional distributors that buy the products from the factory and resell them to local dealers, who then resell them to consumers. Many industrial companies market their products through reps or distributors to *original equipment manufacturers* (OEMs). These OEMs may use the product as a component in their own product, which is then sold to their customers.

The advertising a company uses depends on the product's method of distribution. Much of the advertising we see is not prepared or paid for by the manufacturer, but by the distributor or retailer. Members of a distribution channel give enormous promotional support to the manufacturers they represent.

Like Magellan, Grady has pioneered a global network.

Unlike Magellan, Grady has access to key information about international shipping.

Like Magellan, Grady is proving pretty darn popular with the headhunters.

Even globetrotting pioneers need an inside scoop. Psssst. Check out FedEx Global Trade Manager,℠ powerful web-based tools that help you ship confidently all over the planet. Get important trade and embargo updates. Estimate duties and taxes. Download important customs forms and documents. Suddenly, the whole world seems to want you. Just try not to get a big head. Seeking safe passage around the world? **Don't worry. There's a FedEx for that.**

fedex.com

FedEx Express

Some advertising addresses the distribution element of the marketing mix by targeting wholesalers and/or retailers of the product. Package delivery companies like FedEx enable business owners, who may not have many retail outlets, a means of distributing their products to consumers. FedEx's recent advertising campaign, "Business Legends," compares business owners to historical pioneers, and describes how the company's latest features and services empower business owners to "ship confidently all over the planet."

A part of marketing strategy is determining the amount of coverage necessary for a product. Procter & Gamble, for example, distributes Crest toothpaste to virtually every supermarket and discount, drug, and variety store. Other products might need only one dealer for every 50,000 people. Consumer goods manufacturers traditionally use one of three distribution strategies: *intensive, selective,* or *exclusive.*

Intensive Distribution

Soft drinks, candy, Timex watches, and other convenience goods are available at every possible location because of **intensive distribution.** In fact, consumers can buy them with a minimum of effort. The profit on each unit is usually very low, but the volume of sales is high. The sales burden is usually carried by the manufacturer's national advertising. Ads in trade magazines *push* the product into the retail "pipeline," and in mass media they stimulate consumers to *pull* the products through the pipeline. As a manufacturer modifies its strategy to more push or more pull, special promotions may be directed at the trade or at consumers to build brand volume (see Chapter 10).

Selective Distribution

By limiting the number of outlets through **selective distribution,** manufacturers can cut their distribution and promotion costs. Many hardware tools are sold selectively through discount chains, home-improvement centers, and hardware stores. Levi Strauss sells through better department and chain stores. Manufacturers may use national advertising, but the sales burden is normally carried by the retailer. The manufacturer may share part of the retailer's advertising costs through a **cooperative advertising** program, as we discussed in Chapter 4. For example, a Levi's retailer may receive substantial allowances from the manufacturer for advertising Levi's clothing in its local area. In return, the retailer agrees to advertise and display the clothing prominently.

Exclusive Distribution

Some manufacturers grant **exclusive distribution** rights to a wholesaler or retailer in one geographic region. For example, a town of 50,000 to 100,000 people will have only one Buick dealer and no Mercedes dealer. This is also common in high fashion, major appliances, and furniture lines. What is lost in market coverage is often gained in the ability to maintain a prestige image and premium prices. Exclusive distribution agreements also force manufacturers and retailers to cooperate closely in advertising and promotion programs.

Vertical Marketing Systems: The Growth of Franchising

To be efficient, members of a distribution channel need to cooperate closely with one another. This need gave rise to the **vertical marketing system (VMS),** a centrally programmed and managed distribution system that supplies or otherwise serves a group of stores or other businesses.

There are many types of vertical marketing systems. For the last quarter century, the greatest growth has been in **franchising**—such as McDonald's or Mailboxes, Etc.—in which retail dealers (or *franchisees*) pay a fee to operate under the guidelines and direction of the parent company or manufacturer (the *franchisor*). It's now

The vertical marketing system gave rise to a number of successful business plans, like franchising, in which dealers pay a fee to operate under the guidelines of a parent company. Hewlett Packard (www.hp.com) has developed a stepchild of the franchise system through the "e-services" program explained in this ad. By targeting entrepreneurs, HP aligns itself as a fee-based partner in exchange for use of costly office supplies and valuable consulting services.

Direct marketing promotions can be very persuasive and thought-provoking since they can reach consumers on a very personal level. In an effort to recruit new customers for its sophisticated film offerings and distribution services, Video Store 451 (www.filmgalerie451.de/allwlh.htm) "accidentally" dropped membership cards, featuring the signatures of big-name directors like Quentin Tarantino and Roman Polanski, in strategic places around town where people would find them. The elaborate but inexpensive hoax won a Silver Lion in the Direct Marketing category at the Cannes festival.

estimated that 50 percent of all retail sales in the United States are made through franchise outlets,[62] although there are only 1,500 registered franchisors throughout the United States and Canada, compared to some 1.5 million retail businesses in the United States alone.[63]

Franchising and other vertical marketing systems offer both manufacturers and retailers numerous advantages, not the least of which are centralized coordination of marketing efforts and substantial savings and continuity in advertising. Perhaps most important is consumer recognition: The moment a new McDonald's opens, the franchisee has instant customers. Moreover, a single newspaper ad can promote all of a chain's retailers in a particular trading area.

Many marketers find that franchising is the best way to introduce their services into global markets. Subway sandwich shops, for example, is one of the fastest-growing franchise operations in the world with a total of more than 21,600 stores in 76 different countries.[64]

In the last decade, the European Union, a market of nearly 380 million people, has opened its doors to innovative marketers. As a result, franchising has grown rapidly, especially in the United Kingdom, France, Germany, Spain, Belgium, and the Netherlands. There are now some 4,000 franchisors operating throughout Europe, serving 170,000 independent businesses and generating sales of $120 billion.[65] Although franchising is less regulated in Europe, advertising is more regulated. This again points out the need for local experts to manage the advertising function in foreign markets.

Advertising and the Communication (Promotion) Element

Once it determines product, price, and distribution, a company is ready to plan its marketing communications, of which advertising is just one component. (See Ad Lab 6–D.)

The **communication element** includes all marketing-related communications between the seller and the buyer. A variety of marketing communications tools comprise the **communications mix.** These tools can be grouped into *personal* and *nonpersonal communication* activities.

Personal communication includes all person-to-person contact with customers. **Nonpersonal communication** activities—which use some medium as an

Price and Promotion

Starbucks classifies its product as a "gourmet" coffee—in other words, it's positioned as a premium product. This suggests that it probably costs more than the typical coffee in the supermarket. However, since Starbucks targets a younger demographic of 20- to 49-year-olds, it must still be careful about how much it charges. Currently, regular brewed coffee at Starbucks costs $1.40 but the most expensive beverage runs approximately $5.00. Whole-bean coffee ranges from $9.95 to $43.90 per pound. Overall, Starbucks coffee may be a bit pricier, but it offers a higher quality product and tries to add value through superior employee service.

To promote awareness, many new companies dedicate enormous budgets to advertising. However, this is not always necessary. Starbucks certainly never dreamed it could establish the degree of brand loyalty that it did in such a short time. But it managed to do so—and with only a minimal amount of advertising. It wasn't that the company didn't believe in advertising; it just didn't think it could afford to advertise. So Starbucks focused on creating product value and giving better service.

Initially, the only promotional elements the company used were public relations and some small sales promotions. These were designed to create initial awareness and interest in its gourmet coffees. As interest and awareness have grown, so have promotional activities. Among the new campaigns is the "Matches Made over Coffee" contest. To strengthen its brand and celebrate coffeehouse romances, Starbucks devised a compctition in which the winner with the most "creative, romantic, and coffee-rich, true love story" would receive an all-expense-paid trip for two to Vienna, Austria.

To demonstrate its social concern, Starbucks also ventured into philanthropic activities. In fact, it is now the largest corporate sponsor of CARE, an international relief and development organization that aids the very communities from which the company buys its coffee.

With the coffee culture trend growing, increased competition was a given, forcing Starbucks to spend more on advertising to maintain its market share. Initially, Starbucks spent $17.8 million on a direct-response campaign. It also sold merchandise, such as mugs, coffee grinders, espresso machines, and gourmet food bearing the Starbucks logo, via catalog and the Internet. While Starbucks continues its public relations involvement with communities, it recognizes the growing need to invest in mass-media advertising. Its first major campaign began in 1997, under the creative design of Goodby, Silverstein & Partners, to promote its new Frappuccino beverage. Three television and three radio spots were created for the campaign, focusing on the jingle "Starbucks, purveyors of coffee, tea, and sanity." In the fall of 1997, though, Starbucks changed agencies and hired BBDO West, claiming that Goodby hadn't yet found the right "creative voice" for Starbucks. Since then, Starbucks has utilized the creative input of numerous top agencies, including Fallon McElligott as well as Saatchi & Saatchi.

The current focus of Starbucks' advertising is split between individual promotions for its wide array of products, including the "What Stirs You?" tagline for the new "Toffee Nut Latte," as well as more cause-related marketing programs that focus on philanthropic endeavors abroad. In an ad that recently ran in the *New York Times*, Starbucks conveyed its charitable efforts in coffee-producing countries through an ad that began "Every sip is born out of respect" and concluded with the tagline "We're always serving more than coffee." As more corporations such as Starbucks spread to a global level, many experts believe we are likely to see more such cause-related advertisements in the future, as these corporations attempt to maintain a positive image around the world.

Laboratory Application

When constructing the marketing mix for your chosen product or service (refer to Ad Labs 6–B and 6–C), consider these last two elements: price and promotion. What should your product's price be and why? Should you offer some kind of credit terms? Also, what media should you use to advertise your product or service, and why? Do you think that Starbucks should advertise in more traditional mass media or stick to public relations? What "creative voice" would you suggest for Starbucks?

---

intermediary for communicating—include *advertising, direct marketing,* certain *public relations* activities, *collateral materials,* and *sales promotion.* Today, successful marketing managers blend all these elements into an *integrated marketing communications program.*

Personal Selling

Some consumer products are sold by clerks in retail stores, others by salespeople who call on customers directly. Personal selling is very important in business-to-business marketing. It establishes a face-to-face situation in which the marketer can learn firsthand about customer wants and needs, and customers find it harder to say no. We discuss personal selling further in Chapter 10.

Advertising

Advertising is sometimes called mass or nonpersonal selling. Its usual purpose is to inform, persuade, and remind customers about particular products and services. In some cases, like mail order, advertising even closes the sale.

Certain products lend themselves to advertising so much that it plays the dominant communications role. The following factors are particularly important for advertising success:

- High primary demand trend.
- Chance for significant product differentiation.
- Hidden qualities highly important to consumers.

- Opportunity to use strong emotional appeals.
- Substantial sums available to support advertising.

Where these conditions exist, as in the cosmetics industry, companies spend large amounts on advertising, and the ratio of advertising to sales dollars is often quite high. For completely undifferentiated products, such as sugar, salt, and other raw materials or commodities, price is usually the primary influence, and advertising is minimally important. Sunkist is an interesting exception. This farmers' cooperative successfully brands an undifferentiated commodity (citrus fruit) and markets it internationally.

Direct Marketing

Direct marketing is like taking the store to the customer. A mail-order house that communicates directly with consumers through ads and catalogs is one type of company engaged in direct marketing. It builds its own database of customers and uses a variety of media to communicate with them.

The field of direct marketing is growing rapidly as companies discover the benefits of control, cost efficiency, and accountability. For example, many companies such as Levi Strauss use **telemarketing** (a direct-marketing technique) to increase productivity through person-to-person phone contact. By using the phone to follow up direct-mail advertising, a company can increase the response rate substantially. Moreover, through telemarketing, it can develop a valuable database of customers and prospects to use in future mailings and promotions.[66] We discuss this topic more thoroughly in Chapter 10.

Public Relations

Many firms supplement (or replace) their advertising with various public relations activities such as **publicity** (news releases, feature stories) and **special events** (open houses, factory tours, VIP parties, grand openings) to inform various audiences about the company and its products and to build corporate trustworthiness and image. As Al and Laura Ries point out, through decades of overuse and overpromising, advertising today has lost much of its effectiveness and credibility.[67] On the other hand, public relations activities, as we discuss in Chapter 11, are extremely credible brand-building tools that should always be integrated into a company's communication mix.

Collateral Materials

As mentioned in Chapter 4, **collateral materials** are the many accessory items companies produce to integrate and supplement their advertising or PR activities. These include booklets, catalogs, brochures, films, sales kits, promotional products, and annual reports. Collateral materials should always be designed to reinforce the company's image or the brand's position in the minds of customers.

Sales Promotion

As we discuss in Chapter 10, sales promotion is a special category of communication tools and activities. Designed to supplement the basic elements of the marketing mix for short periods of time, sales promotion is aimed at stimulating customers or members of the distribution channel to some immediate, overt behavior.[68] This broad category includes trade deals, free samples, displays, trading stamps, sweepstakes, cents-off coupons, and premiums, among others. *Reader's Digest,* for example, is famous for its annual sweepstakes designed to increase circulation. And grocery manufacturers print and distribute over 250 billion coupons per year, saving consumers $3.5 billion to $4 billion annually.[69]

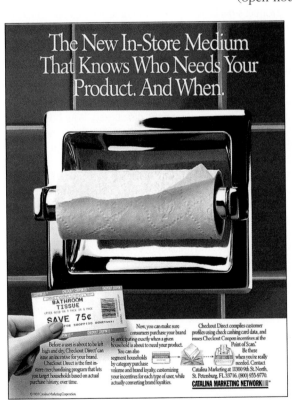

Checkout Coupon is an electronic in-store sales promotion that delivers incentives to shoppers at the checkout counter, based on what they buy. Catalina Marketing Network helps the retailer coordinate the campaigns with tie-in of the coupons to in-store posters, shelf-talkers, savings on related store products, and newspaper ads.

Some promotions are linked mainly to the communications function of the marketing mix (displays, events, trade shows), while others are linked more to the product element (free samples, premiums) or the price element (coupons, volume discounts, end-of-month sales). And some complement the distribution element (trade deals, sales contests). Sales promotion (often referred to simply as *promotion*) is used primarily as a tactical adaptation to some external situation such as competitive pressure, changing seasons, declining sales, or new-product introductions.[70] Since advertising people are frequently called on to solve a variety of marketing problems, it is critical that they understand and know how to integrate the whole mix of communications techniques.

The Marketing Mix in Perspective

With the target market designated and the elements of the marketing mix determined, the company has a complete product concept and a strategic basis for marketing to that target. Now it can formalize its strategies and tactics in a written marketing and advertising plan. As part of the planning process, companies use marketing and advertising research. We discuss this in Chapter 7 before dealing with the formal planning process in Chapter 8.

Chapter Summary

Market segmentation is the process of identifying groups of people with certain shared characteristics within a broad product market and aggregating these groups into larger market segments according to their mutual interest in the product's utility. From these segments, companies can then select a target market. Marketers use a number of methods to identify behavioral groups and segment markets. The most common are behavioristic, geographic, demographic, and psychographic.

Business markets are often segmented in the same way as consumer markets. They may also be grouped by business purchasing procedures, NAICS code, or market concentration.

In the target marketing process, companies designate specific segments to target and develop their mix of marketing activities. The product concept is the consumer's perception of the product as a bundle of utilitarian and symbolic need-satisfying values.

Every company can add, subtract, or modify four major elements in its marketing program to achieve a desired marketing mix. These elements are product, price, distribution (place), and communications (promotion)—the 4Ps.

The *product* element includes the way the product is designed and classified, positioned, branded, and packaged. Just as humans pass through a life cycle, so do products—and product categories. The stage of a product's life cycle may determine how it is advertised.

To satisfy the variety of consumer tastes and achieve competitive advantages, marketers build differences into their products. Even the product's package is part of the product concept. The concept may also be developed through unique positioning against competing products.

Price refers to what and how a customer pays for a product. Companies use many common pricing strategies. Some products compete on the basis of price, but many do not.

Distribution refers to how the product is placed at the disposal of the customer: where the product is distributed, how it is bought, and how it is sold. Companies may use direct or indirect methods of distribution. Consumer goods manufacturers use several types of distribution strategies.

Communications refers to all marketing-related communications between the seller and the buyer. Tools of the communications element include personal selling, advertising, direct marketing, public relations activities, collateral materials, and sales promotion. Marketers try to integrate all their marketing communications programs for greater effectiveness and consistency.

Important Terms

behavioristic segmentation, *171*

benefit segmentation, *174*

benefits, *174*

brand, *190*

brand equity, *191*

business markets, *179*

collateral materials, *199*

communication element, *197*

communications mix, *197*

cooperative advertising, *196*

copy points, *191*

decline stage, *188*

demographic segmentation, *174*

direct distribution, *194*

direct marketing, *199*

distribution channel, *195*

distribution element, *194*

early adopter, *186*

equipment-based service, *188*

exclusive distribution, *196*

family brand, *190*

four Ps, *186*

franchising, *196*

geodemographic segmentation, *174*

geographic segmentation, *174*

growth stage, *187*

hidden differences, *189*

individual brand, *190*

induced differences, *190*

intensive distribution, *196*

introductory phase, *186*

licensed brand, *190*

market segmentation, *170*

marketing mix, *185*

maturity stage, *187*

national brand, *190*

network marketing, *194*

nonpersonal communication, *197*

North American Industry Classification System (NAICS) codes, *181*

people-based service, *188*

perceptible differences, *189*

personal communication, *197*

position, *189*

price element, *193*

primary demand, *186*

primary demand trend, *182*

primary motivation, *177*

private label, *190*

product concept, *185*

product element, *186*

product life cycle, *186*

psychographic segmentation, *177*

psychographics, *177*

publicity, *199*

pull strategy, *186*

purchase occasion, *173*

push strategy, *187*

reseller, *179, 195*

resource axis, *177*

sales promotion, *187*

selective demand, *187*

selective distribution, *196*

service, *188*

special events, *199*

target market, *184*

target marketing process, *183*

telemarketing, *199*

usage rate, *172*

user status, *172*

vertical marketing system (VMS), *196*

volume segmentation, *172*

Review Questions

1. How does the concept of shared characteristics relate to the market segmentation process?

2. How could you use VALS to develop the marketing strategy for a product of your choice?

3. How does the segmentation of business markets differ from that of consumer markets?

4. What is the most important factor to consider when determining the elements of the marketing mix?

5. What is the difference between a product and a product concept?

6. What are some examples of product positioning not discussed in this chapter?

7. What effect does the product life cycle have on the advertising a company uses?

8. What factors influence the price of a product?

9. How do the basic methods of distribution affect advertising?

10. What product characteristics encourage heavy advertising? Little advertising? Why?

11. **The Advertising Experience**

   Many well-established American brands may seem to be in the decline stage of their product cycle, but they continue to be sold. Choose one of these and describe a plan for revitalizing the product, especially in terms of the 4Ps.

Exploring the Internet

The Internet exercises for Chapter 6 address the following areas covered throughout the chapter: marketing and the marketing mix (Exercise 1), market segmentation and target marketing (Exercise 2), and product differentiation as a result of market segmentation (Exercise 3).

1. **World of Marketing**

   Part I: Marketing. You already learned the importance of marketing to the study and application of advertising. Visit the sites below to get a better feel about the scope of the marketing world and the importance of a good marketing strategy. Be sure to answer the questions below for each site.

   - American Marketing Association (AMA) www.marketingpower.org
   - Business Marketing Association (BMA) www.marketing.org
   - American Business Press (ABP) www.americanbusinesspress.com
   - B to B www.btobonline.com
   - Brand Republic www.brandrepublic.com
   - *Brandweek* www.brandweek.com
   - *Marketing Magazine* www.marketingmag.ca
   - Dotfactor.com www.dotfactor.com
   - *Sales & Marketing Management* www.salesandmarketing.com

   a. What group sponsors the site? Who is the intended audience?

   b. What is the site's purpose? Does it succeed? Why?

   c. What is the size/scope of the organization? What is the organization's purpose?

   d. Who makes up the organization's membership? Its constituency?

   Part II: Marketing Mix. Visit Hardee's site (www.hardees.com) and then answer the following questions about one of its products.

   a. Identify the product, price, place, and promotion. (If there are multiple products, choose one.)

   b. Identify the stage in the product life cycle.

   c. What is the product's positioning?

   d. What are the key elements of the product's differentiation?

2. **Market Segmentation and Target Marketing**

   Segmenting markets and generating sound demographic, geographic, psychographic, and behavioristic profiles are critical to formulating advertising strategy. There is an abundance of market segmentation data available on the Internet from both the government and private sector. Peruse the following sample of online resources for target market information.

   - U.S. Census Bureau www.census.gov
   - USA Data www.usadata.com
   - Forrester Research www.forrester.com
   - *American Demographics* www.demographics.com
   - Target Marketing www.targetonline.com
   - Market Segment Resource Locator www.awool.com
   - Evergrow, Inc. www.evergrow.net

   Now choose a company with a website and use one of these online resources to answer the following questions. Be sure to cite any online resources you used besides the above.

   a. What type of segmentation approach did they take (single-market, multiple-market, aggregate market)?

   b. Develop a demographic profile, including age, income, education, and gender, for the target market.

   c. Describe the general geographic skew for the company's market.

   d. What consumption patterns are evident in the company's consumers?

3. **Marketing and Education**

   Even the education that teaches you how to market products can be seen as a product. After looking at several websites for colleges or universities, choose one. Consider the educational products the institution offers (for example, graduate degrees, campus-based programs, and online courses) and analyze them using the 4Ps. Consider the institution also in terms of product life cycle. Finally, discuss what elements of the products' differentiation you can find. Once your analysis is complete, discuss what the institution can do better to market its products.

Chapter 7

Research:
Gathering Information
for Advertising Planning

Objectives

TO EXAMINE HOW ADVERTISERS GAIN INFORMATION about the marketplace and how they apply their findings to marketing and advertising decision making.

After studying this chapter, you will be able to:

- **Discuss** how research helps advertisers locate market segments and identify target markets.

- **Explain** the basic steps in the research process.

- **Discuss** the differences between formal and informal research and primary and secondary data.

- **Explain** the methods used in qualitative and quantitative research.

- **Define** and explain the concepts of validity and reliability.

- **Recognize** the important issues in creating survey questionnaires.

- **Explain** the challenges international advertisers face in collecting research data abroad.

- **Debate** the pros and cons of advertising testing.

In the mid-1980s, Healthtex was a $350 million concern. But by the early 1990s, the 75-year-old company was barely hanging on. Fortunately, VF Corp., the parent of Wrangler jeans, realized the value of the brand and bought the company. Healthtex had been a leading manufacturer of children's clothing for many decades, but with the emergence of sophisticated competition, the company had not kept up. VF moved the company to offices close to Wrangler in Greensboro, North Carolina, installed new management, and proceeded to turn Healthtex around. John Martin was appointed director of marketing services and he brought in a new ad agency, The Martin Agency (no relation), in Richmond, Virginia.[1] ■ "Frankly, we needed help," says Martin. "And we weren't shy about requesting it. We didn't just need brilliant creative work; we needed extraordinarily savvy marketing counsel, too." ■ They got it. The people at The Martin Agency knew they had to know the product quickly. Beth Rilee-Kelley, now the agency's director of creative services, remembers the first days working on the account. "We went right out into the field and talked to retailers that carried the line and consumers that bought it," she says. "And we learned a lot—fast." ■ They got good news and bad news. ■ The bad news was that the trade was disappointed in the company and had lost confidence in the brand. Healthtex had missed shipping dates; customer service had declined; retailers saw the brand as underfunded in advertising and marketing; even the product quality had slipped. In short, the long relationships Healthtex had enjoyed with retailers were rapidly deteriorating. ■ The good news was that consumers were unaware of these problems and still had great confidence in the Healthtex name. Moms saw the brand as high-quality, everyday playwear that lasts. They loved it.[2]

■ The agency also discovered that moms, the busiest customers on the planet, didn't find anything compelling or inspiring in advertising for any brand of kidswear. Magazines were full of ads showing beautiful, cuddly children in spotless clothes. But that just didn't resonate with these moms. There was no recognition of the hectic, untidy lives that moms of small children actually lead. ■ This was the nugget of insight the agency—and Healthtex—needed. This provided the opportunity for a unique position in the marketplace, for Healthtex to establish itself as the brand that understands moms and their lives. ■ In a series of award-winning ads, The Martin Agency made this position clear, sometimes explicitly, always implicitly. In one of the first ads, the headline reads: "Your baby's naked. Your phone's ringing. And your mother-in-law's walking up the driveway. Let's talk snaps." This was followed by four columns of factual, informative copy to explain precisely the practical, functional differences built into Healthtex infant wear. In another ad, the headline warns: "You've got 23 seconds to get your 2-year-old from the sandbox to the potty. Go."

■ To say the least, these ads resonated with parents. They showed that Healthtex really understood just how chaotic it can be to raise (and dress) small children. In short order, Healthtex became the only brand with a position that had more substance than cuteness. Thanks to good research, the campaign enabled Healthtex to reverse its decline immediately, increase its market share, and regain its lost luster with the trade. It also made The Martin Agency a household name in the advertising business.[3] ■

The Need for Research in Marketing and Advertising

Every year companies spend millions of dollars creating ads and promotions that they hope their customers and prospects will notice and relate to. Then they spend millions more placing their communications in print and electronic media, hoping their customers will see and hear them and eventually respond.

Advertising is expensive. In the United States the cost of a single 30-second commercial on prime-time network TV averages around $100,000. Likewise, a single, full-page color ad in a national business magazine averages $100 to reach every thousand prospects.[4] That's too much money to risk unless advertisers have very good information about who their customers are, what they want and like, and where they spend their media time. And that's why advertisers need research. Research provides the information that drives marketing and advertising decision making. Without that information, advertisers are forced to use intuition or guesswork. In today's fast-changing, highly competitive, global economy, that invites failure.

What Is Marketing Research?

To help managers make marketing decisions, companies develop systematic procedures for gathering, recording, and analyzing new information. This is called **marketing research** (it should not be confused with *market research,* which is information gathered about a *particular* market or market segment).[5] Marketing research does a number of things: It helps identify consumer needs and market segments; it provides the information necessary for developing new products and devising marketing strategies; and it enables managers to assess the effectiveness of marketing programs and promotional activities. Marketing research is also useful in financial planning, economic forecasting, and quality control.

Research has become big business. Worldwide, the top 10 research companies had revenues of more than $4 billion in 2002 for marketing, advertising, and public opinion research. Led by the global VNU, Inc., with offices in 100 countries, the top 25 have corporate parents in the United Kingdom, Sweden, Brazil, France, Germany, Japan, the Netherlands, and the United States. But nearly one-half of their revenues come from operations outside their home country.[6] Exhibit 7–1 lists the top 10 research companies by worldwide revenues.

Exhibit 7–1

Top 10 research companies by U.S. research revenues in 2002 ($ in millions).

Rank	Organization/ headquarters	U.S. research revenues	Worldwide research revenues	Percentage of revenues from outside U.S.
1	VNU Inc. New York	$1,526.0	$1,288.0	45.8%
2	IMS Health Inc. Fairfield, CT	488.0	732.0	60.0
3	Information Resources Inc. Chicago	411.5	143.3	25.8
4	Westat Inc. Rockville, MD	341.9	—	—
5	The Kantar Group Fairfield, CT	312.7	674.2	68.3
6	Arbitron Inc. New York	241.9	7.9	3.2
7	NOP World US Paris	200.9	12.9	6.0
8	Taylor Nelson Sofres USA London	191.9	10.7	5.3
9	NFO WorldGroup Greenwich, CT	168.4	297.7	63.9
10	Synovate Arlington Heights, IL	161.6	30.5	15.9

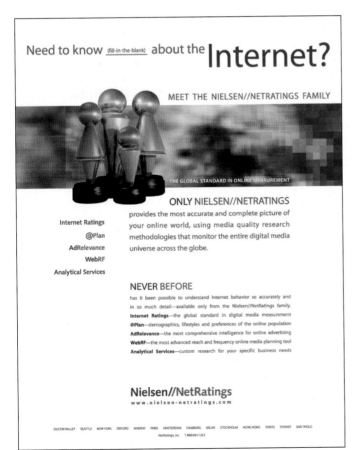

Marketing research is the important process of gathering, recording, and analyzing information about customers and prospects. Companies such as A. C. Nielsen (www.acnielsen.com) collect data for their clients and provide critical insight into current and potential markets.

Companies use marketing research to gather a lot of different types of information. It may be easiest to think of all these in terms of what one researcher calls the *three Rs* of marketing: *recruiting* new customers, *retaining* current customers, and *regaining* lost customers.[7]

For example, to *recruit* new customers, researchers may study different market segments and create *product attribute models* to match buyers with the right products and services. Marketers need answers to many questions: What new products do consumers want? Which ideas should we work on? What product features are most important to our customers? What changes in the product's appearance and performance will increase sales? What price will maintain the brand's image, create profits, and still be attractive and affordable to consumers? Answers may lead to product and marketing decisions that directly affect the product's nature, content, packaging, pricing—and advertising.[8]

On the other hand, to *retain* existing customers, a marketer may use *customer satisfaction studies*. Likewise, *databases* of customer transactions may identify reasons for customer satisfaction or dissatisfaction.[9] Today, companies realize that the best sales go to those who develop good relationships with individual customers.[10] As a result, customer satisfaction is now the fastest-growing field in marketing research.

Information gained for the first two Rs helps the third, *regaining* lost customers. For example, if an office equipment manufacturer discovers through research that an increase in service calls typically precedes cancellation of a service contract, it can watch for that pattern with current customers and then take preventive action. Moreover, it can review service records of former customers and (if the pattern holds true) devise some marketing action or advertising appeal to win them back.[11]

In short, good marketing research enables the company to devise a sophisticated, integrated mix of product, price,

When companies falter in their efforts to satisfy market expectations, regaining lost customers can be a formidable problem. What is needed is innovative marketing and outstanding communications. Ads like this one from Healthtex (www.healthtex.com), which demonstrate an understanding of modern mothers' concerns, can help restore faith in the company's brand.

distribution, and communication elements. It gives the advertiser and its agency the information they need to decide which strategies will enhance the brand's image and lead to greater profits. Finally, it enables them to judge the effectiveness of past marketing programs and ad campaigns.

What Is Advertising Research?

Before developing any advertising campaign, a company needs to know how people perceive its products, how they view the competition, what brand or company image would be most credible, and what ads offer the greatest appeal. To get this information, companies use *advertising research*. While marketing research provides the information necessary to make marketing decisions, **advertising research** uncovers the information needed for making advertising decisions. By definition, it is the systematic gathering and analysis of information to help develop or evaluate advertising strategies, individual ads, and whole campaigns.

In this chapter, we consider the importance of information gathering to the development of advertising plans and strategies; we look at how companies use research to test the effectiveness of ads before and after they run; and we explore a number of specific research techniques.

Applying Research to Advertising Decision Making

Advertising research serves various purposes, most of which can be grouped into four categories: *strategy research, creative concept research, pretesting,* and *posttesting.*

1. *Advertising strategy research.* Used to help define the product concept or to assist in the selection of target markets, advertising messages, or media vehicles.
2. *Creative concept research.* Measures the target audience's acceptance of different creative ideas at the concept stage.
3. *Pretesting of ads.* Used to diagnose possible communication problems before a campaign begins.
4. *Posttesting of ads.* Enables marketers to evaluate a campaign after it runs.

As Exhibit 7–2 shows, marketers use the different categories of advertising research at different stages of ad or campaign development. The techniques they use at each stage also vary considerably. We'll examine each of these categories briefly before moving on to discuss the research process.

	Advertising Strategy Research	Creative Concept Research	Pretesting	Posttesting
Timing	Before creative work begins	Before agency production begins	Before finished artwork and photography	After campaign has run
Research problem	Product concept definition Target audience selection Media selection Message-element selection	Concept testing Name testing Slogan testing	Print testing TV storyboard pretesting Radio commercial pretesting	Advertising effectiveness Consumer attitude change Sales increases
Techniques	Consumer attitude and usage studies Media studies	Free-association tests Qualitative interviews Statement-comparison tests	Consumer juries Matched samples Portfolio tests Storyboard test Mechanical devices Psychological rating scales	Aided recall Unaided recall Attitude tests Inquiry tests Sales tests

Exhibit 7–2

Categories of research in advertising development.

Advertising Strategy Research

Companies develop an advertising strategy by blending elements of the *creative mix.* These include: the *product concept,* the *target audience,* the *communication media,* and the *creative message.* To seek information about any or all of these various elements, companies use **advertising strategy research.**

Product Concept

As we saw at the beginning of this chapter, advertisers need to know how consumers perceive their brands. They also want to know what qualities lead to initial purchases and, eventually, to brand loyalty.

Using this information, they try to establish a unique *product concept* for their brand—that bundle of values we discussed in Chapter 6 that encompasses both utilitarian and symbolic benefits to the consumer.

The Martin Agency asked consumers what would entice them to put their kids in Healthtex. They discovered that, overall, moms look for cuteness, durability, ease of dressing, and washability. Cuteness is the price of entry into the category—but to succeed a brand must have more than that.

Healthtex did. But they also discovered that mothers with full-time jobs want to spend any spare time they have with their kids. They don't want to waste time shopping. They want to be able to go in, pick out a trusted brand, and get home to spend time with the family.[12]

It's this kind of information that can lead to an effective positioning strategy for the brand. Advertising can shape and magnify a brand's position and image over time. In fact, this is one of the most important strategic benefits of advertising. But to use media advertising effectively, strategy research is essential to develop a blueprint for creatives to follow.[13]

Advertising works differently for different product categories and, often, even for different brands within a category. This means that each brand must develop a template for the creative based on an understanding of its particular consumers' wants, needs, and motivations. Only if this is done correctly over time (say, one to two years), can brand equity be built.[14]

To determine how brands are built and how they derive their strength, the Young & Rubicam ad agency developed a model called the BrandAsset Valuator™. It measures brands in terms of differentiation, relevance, esteem, and familiarity, in

Through the applied use of marketing research, Healthtex discovered that customers wanted more than just cute clothing. They needed clothing that was designed to be practical and would allow them to spend more quality time with their children. This ad, created by The Martin Agency, highlighted those qualities in the Healthtex brand.

that order. According to Y&R's theory, a brand must first develop differentiation—it must offer something unique and different—to survive. Second, it must be perceived by the target market as relevant to their needs and wants. Finally, it needs to build stature through esteem and knowledge. Once all these steps are accomplished, a brand achieves leadership status. In the mid-1990s, Y&R performed a study in 19 countries and found that Disney scored high on all these dimensions. In fact, it was one of the highest-valued brands around the world—even in France, home of the troubled EuroDisney theme park.[15]

Following Y&R's lead, other agencies have developed their own brand equity studies. In 1998, WPP Group introduced a research tool titled "BRANDZ." Then, in 2000, DDB Worldwide introduced "Brand Capital," and Leo Burnett unveiled its brand of research dubbed "Brand Stock." All of these are aimed at understanding how consumers connect with brands before spending millions on advertising.[16]

Target Audience Selection

The second element of the creative mix is the target audience. We pointed out in Chapters 5 and 6 that no market includes everybody. Therefore, one of the major purposes of research is to develop a rich profile of the brand's target markets and audiences. The marketer will want to know which customers are the primary users of the product category and will study them carefully to understand their demographics, geographics, psychographics, and purchase behavior.

With any new product, the biggest problem is invariably the budget. There is never enough money to attack all geographic or demographic markets effectively at the same time. So the advertiser will often decide to employ the *dominance concept*—researching which markets (geographic or otherwise) are most important to product sales and targeting those where it can focus its resources to achieve advertising dominance.

In the case of Healthtex, the agency discovered that there were two distinct markets for their client's clothes: new mothers and experienced mothers. New mothers were categorized as first-time moms with infants between the ages of 0 and 20 months. The children of experienced mothers were between two and four years old. These were the primary markets and audiences for Healthtex's advertising. Later they discovered that grandparents were also a viable target market, so they designed a program to appeal to them also.

Media Selection

To develop media strategies, select media vehicles, and evaluate their results, advertisers use a subset of advertising research called **media research.** Agencies subscribe to syndicated research services (such as A. C. Nielsen, Arbitron, Simmons, or Standard Rate & Data Service) that monitor and publish information on the reach and effectiveness of media vehicles—radio, TV, newspapers, and so on—in every major geographic market in the United States and Canada. (We'll discuss these further in Chapter 9 and in Part Five.)

For Healthtex, The Martin Agency researched what media were regularly used by mothers. It discovered that new moms read publications like *American Baby* and *Baby Talk,* while more experienced mothers read *Parents* magazine and *Parenting.*

Message-Element Selection

The final component of advertising strategy is the message element. Companies hope to find promising advertising messages by studying consumers' likes and dislikes in relation to brands and products. Kraft Foods, for example, was looking for ways to dissuade moms from switching to less-expensive brands of processed cheese. While its Kraft Singles brand dominated the processed cheese slices category, it was concerned that the brand wasn't keeping up with overall growth in the market.

Working with several research companies and its ad agency, J. Walter Thompson, the company conducted a series of qualitative consumer attitude studies to figure out how women, particularly mothers, felt about Kraft Singles with the hope of discovering possible advertising themes. The mothers said they felt good giving their kids Kraft Singles because of the brand's nutritional value. But there was a catch—they also said they'd switch to a competitive product if it were cheaper. Fortunately, a phone survey provided some clues for solving the problem. Among these polled, 78 percent considered the brand an extra source of calcium for their kids. And 84 percent of women with kids under 12 said they'd be motivated to buy the brand because of that added benefit.[17]

From this information, the agency used concept testing to determine which message-element options might prove most successful. This was now category 2 research aimed at developed creative advertising concepts.

Developing Creative Concepts

Once it develops an advertising strategy, the company (or its agency) will begin developing creative concepts for the advertising. Here again, research is helpful in determining which concepts to use.

From all their studies, Kraft researchers came up with two ad concepts that might keep mothers from defecting to competitive brands. First, show how much kids like Kraft Singles, and second, emphasize the fact that the brand provides the calcium kids need. J. Walter Thompson prepared two tentative TV spots and then conducted focus groups of mothers to get their reaction. With a discussion leader moderating the conversation, each group viewed the commercials. The groups' reactions were measured, taped, and observed by JWT and Kraft staff behind a one-way mirror. Immediately, problems surfaced. The idea that kids love the taste of Kraft Singles just didn't come across strongly enough. And the statement that Kraft provides calcium wasn't persuasive. Moms said, "Of course it has calcium, it's cheese." The agency had to find a newsier way to communicate the information.

Tweaking the commercials, JWT came up with a new spot showing youngsters gobbling gooey grilled-cheese sandwiches while a voice-over announcer stated that two out of five kids don't get enough calcium. More focus groups ensued. Now the mothers agreed that the shots of kids devouring sandwiches communicated the great taste theme, but some moms thought the two-out-of-five statement played too much on their guilt.

To soften the message, the agency switched to a female announcer and then brought in the Dairy Fairy, a character from an earlier campaign, to lighten the whole tone of the spot. This seemed to work better, so the agency proceeded to copy testing.

Pretesting and Posttesting

Advertising is one of the largest costs in a company's marketing budget. No wonder its effectiveness is a major concern! Companies want to know what they are getting for their money—and whether their advertising is working. And they'd like some assurance before their ads run.

Kraft was no exception. Millward Brown Research performed a number of copy tests to see how the agency's latest spot would perform. The tests showed that the spot performed significantly better than the norm on key measures such as branding and persuasion. Following the copy tests, the company aired "The Calcium They Need" commercial in five test markets to see how it would affect sales. Kraft quickly achieved a 10 percent increase in sales in those markets. Based on such a strong showing, Kraft rolled the campaign out nationally in 1999 and sales took off. Base volume soared 14.5 percent and sales grew 11.8 percent.[18]

The campaign was so successful that, in 2000, the Advertising Research Foundation named Kraft and J. Walter Thompson finalists for its prestigious David Ogilvy Research Award, given to the most effective ad campaign guided by research.

The Purpose of Testing

Testing is the primary tool advertisers use to ensure their advertising dollars are spent wisely. Testing can prevent costly errors, especially in judging which advertising strategy or medium is most effective. And it can give the advertiser some measure (besides sales results) of a campaign's value.

In 2004, Bissell was recognized for the exceptional achievements of its "Life Testimonials" advertising campaign and garnered one of the advertising industry's most prestigious recognitions for major American brands, the David Ogilvy Award, bestowed upon them by the Advertising Research Foundation (ARF).

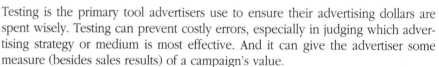

To increase the likelihood of preparing the most effective advertising messages, companies use **pretesting.** Some agencies, like DDB Needham, pretest all ad copy for communication gaps or flaws in message content before recommending it to clients.[19] When companies don't pretest their ads, they may encounter a surprising reaction from the marketplace. Schering Canada received a torrent of complaint letters from customers who said they didn't like its commercial introducing the antihistamine Claritin to the over-the-counter market in Canada. Most negative responses, though, are more insidious: Consumers simply turn the page or change the channel, and sales mysteriously suffer. This is why it's also important to evaluate the effectiveness of an ad or campaign *after* it runs. **Posttesting** (also called *ad tracking*) provides the advertiser with useful guidelines for future advertising.

Testing Helps Make Important Decisions

Advertisers use pretesting to help make decisions about a number of variables. It's easiest to think of these as the five Ms: *merchandise, markets, motives, messages,* and *media.* Many of these can be posttested too. However, in posttesting, the objective is to evaluate, not diagnose. We'll discuss each of the five Ms briefly.

Merchandise   For purposes of alliteration, we refer to the product concept here as **merchandise.** Companies may pretest a number of factors: the package design, how advertising positions the brand, or how well the advertising communicates the product's features.

For Healthtex, The Martin Agency researchers used a process called *benefit testing.* They presented 10 to 12 product benefits to a group of consumers in a focus group. The idea was to test which benefits the group considered most persuasive or compelling.[20]

One company, MarketWare Simulation Services, introduced a virtual reality testing program called Visionary Shopper, which allows people in the test to "shop" on a realistic on-screen shelf, using a touch-sensitive monitor and a track-ball. They can "pull" products off the shelf, study them in 3-D, and rotate them to read side and back panels. They select items by touching an on-screen shopping cart, and the computer tracks the products examined and/or chosen, instantly gauging the impact of whatever the client is testing.[21]

Markets   Advertisers may pretest an advertising strategy or particular commercials with various audience groups representing different **markets.** The information they gain may cause them to alter their strategy and target the campaign to a different market. In posttesting, advertisers want to know if the campaign succeeded in reaching its target markets. Changes in awareness and increases in market share are two indicators of success.

Motives   Consumers' **motives** are outside advertisers' control, but the messages they create to appeal to those motives are not. Pretesting helps advertisers identify and appeal to the most compelling needs and motives. Posttesting can indicate how effective they were.

Messages   Pretesting helps identify outstanding, as well as underperforming, ads and commercials. It helps determine what (from the customer's point of view) a **message** says and how well it says it. Advertisers might test the headline, the text, the illustration, the typography—or the message concept. Most important, pretesting guides the improvement of commercials.[22]

However, pretesting is not foolproof. The only way to know for sure if the advertising works is through continuous tracking or posttesting. Here the advertiser determines to what extent the message was seen, remembered, and believed. Changes in consumer attitude, perception, or brand interest indicate success, as does consumers' ability to remember a campaign slogan or identify the sponsor.

Media   The cost of media advertising is soaring, and advertisers today demand greater accountability. Information gained from pretesting can influence several types of media decisions: classes of media, media subclasses, specific media vehicles, media units of space and time, media budgets, and scheduling criteria.

The broad media categories of print, electronic, digital interactive, direct mail, and out-of-home are referred to as **media classes.** Conversely, **media subclasses** refer to newspapers or magazines, radio or TV, and so on. The specific **media vehicle** is the particular publication or program. **Media units** are the size or length of an ad: half-page or full-page ads, 15- or 30-second spots, 60-second commercials, and so forth (see Exhibit 7–3).

After a campaign runs, posttesting can determine how effectively the media mix reached the target audience and communicated the desired message. We discuss audience measurement further in Chapters 15 through 18.

Exhibit 7–3
Media categories.

Media classes	Print	Electronic	Digital interactive	Direct mail	Out-of-home
Media subclasses	Newspaper Magazines	Radio Television	Internet Kiosks, ATMs	Catalogue Brochure	Outdoor Transit
Media vehicles	NY Times Elle	KNX-AM Ricki Lake	Yahoo!, e-mail BankOne	Spiegel	Billboards Bus benches
Media units	Half page Full page	30-second spot Infomercial	Banner ATM video	16-page Letter size	30-sheet poster Inside card

A constant question facing all advertisers is how large the company's advertising budget should be. How much should be allocated to various markets and media? To specific products? Advertisers can use a number of pretesting techniques to determine optimum spending levels before introducing national campaigns. (Chapter 8 provides further information on budgeting.)

Media scheduling is another nagging question for many advertisers. Through pretesting, advertisers can test consumer response during different seasons of the year or days of the week. They can test whether frequent advertising is more effective than occasional or one-time insertions, or whether year-round advertising is more effective than advertising concentrated during a gift-buying season. (Chapter 9 discusses the most common types of media schedules.)

Overall results   Finally, advertisers want to measure overall results to evaluate how well they accomplished their objectives. Posttesting is most helpful here to determine whether and how to continue, what to change, and how much to spend in the future. We'll discuss the methods advertisers use for pre- and posttesting toward the end of the chapter, in the section on conducting formal research.

Steps in the Research Process

Now that we understand the various types of decision-related information that marketers seek, let's explore how they gather this information by looking at the overall research process and some of the specific techniques they use.

There are five basic steps in the research process (see Exhibit 7–4):

1. Situation analysis and problem definition.
2. Informal (exploratory) research.
3. Construction of research objectives.
4. Formal research.
5. Interpretation and reporting of findings.

Step 1: Analyzing the Situation and Defining the Problem

The first step in the marketing research process is to *analyze the situation* and *define the problem*. Many large firms have in-house research departments. Often the marketing department also maintains a **marketing information system (MIS)**—a sophisticated set of procedures designed to generate a continuous, orderly flow of information for use in making marketing decisions. These systems ensure that managers get the information they need when they need it.[23]

Most smaller firms don't have dedicated research departments, and their methods for obtaining marketing information are frequently inadequate. These firms often find the problem-definition step difficult and time-consuming. Yet good research on the wrong problem is a waste of effort.

Step 2: Conducting Informal (Exploratory) Research

The second step in the process is to use **informal** (or *exploratory*) **research** to learn more about the market, the competition, and the business environment, and to better define the problem. As we saw with Healthtex, researchers may discuss the problem with wholesalers, distributors, or retailers outside the firm; with informed sources inside the firm; with customers; or even with competitors. They look for whoever has the most information to offer.

Exhibit 7–4

The marketing research process begins with evaluation of the company's situation and definition of the problem.

Research Objectives

We must answer the following questions: (1) Who are our customers? (2) Who are the customers of other department stores? (3) What do these customers like and dislike about us and about our competitors? (4) How are we currently perceived? and (5) What do we have to do to clarify and improve that perception?

This statement of the problem is specific and measurable, the decision point is clear, and the questions are related and relevant. The research results should provide the information management needs to decide on a new positioning strategy for the company. The positioning strategy facilitates the development of marketing and advertising plans that will set the company's course for years to come.

Step 4: Conducting Formal Research

When a company wants to collect primary data directly from the marketplace about a specific problem or issue, it uses **formal research.** There are two types of formal research: qualitative and quantitative.

To get a general impression of the market, the consumer, or the product, advertisers typically start with **qualitative research.** This enables researchers to gain insight into both the population whose opinion will be sampled and the subject matter itself. Then, to get hard numbers about specific marketing situations, they may perform a survey or use some other form of **quantitative research.** Sophisticated agencies use a balance of both qualitative and quantitative methods, understanding the limits of each and how they work together.[26] (See Exhibit 7–5.)

In this section we'll discuss the basic methods advertisers use for conducting qualitative and quantitative research and then we'll look at how they apply these techniques to testing ads.

Basic Methods of Qualitative Research

To get people to share their thoughts and feelings, researchers use **qualitative research** that elicits in-depth, open-ended responses rather than yes or no answers. Some marketers refer to this as *motivation research.* Unfortunately, no matter how skillfully posed, some questions are uncomfortable for consumers to answer. When asked why they bought a particular status car, for instance, consumers might reply that it handles well or is economical or dependable, but they rarely admit that it makes them feel important. The methods used in qualitative research are usually either *projective* or *intensive techniques.*

Exhibit 7–5

Differences between qualitative and quantitative research.

	Qualitative	Quantitative
Main techniques for gathering data	Focus groups and in-depth interviews.	Survey and scientific samples.
Kinds of questions asked	Why? Through what thought process? In what way? In connection with what other behavior or thoughts?	How many? How much?
Role of interviewer	Critical: interviewer must think on feet and frame questions and probes in response to whatever respondents say. A highly trained professional is advisable.	Important, but interviewers need only be able to read scripts. They should not improvise. Minimally trained, responsible employees are suitable.
Questions asked	Questions vary in order and phrasing from group to group and interview to interview. New questions are added, old ones dropped.	Should be exactly the same for each interview. Order and phrasing of questions carefully controlled.
Number of interviews	Fewer interviews tending to last a longer time.	Many interviews in order to give a projectable scientific sample.
Kinds of findings	Develop hypotheses, gain insights, explore language options, refine concepts, flesh out numerical data, provide diagnostics on advertising copy.	Test hypotheses, prioritize factors, provide data for mathematical modeling and projections.

Projective techniques   Advertisers use **projective techniques** to understand people's underlying or subconscious feelings, attitudes, interests, opinions, needs, and motives. By asking indirect questions (such as "What kind of people do you think shop here?"), the researcher tries to involve consumers in a situation where they can express feelings about the problem or product.

Projective techniques were adapted for marketing research after their use by psychologists in clinical diagnosis. But such techniques require the skill of highly experienced researchers.

Intensive techniques   **Intensive techniques,** such as in-depth interviews, also require great care to administer properly. In the **in-depth interview,** carefully planned but loosely structured questions help the interviewer probe respondents' deeper feelings. The big pharmaceutical company Schering, for example, uses in-depth interviews with physicians to find out what attributes doctors consider most important in the drugs they prescribe and to identify which brands the doctors associate with different attributes.[27]

While in-depth interviews help reveal individual motivations, they are also expensive and time-consuming, and skilled interviewers are in short supply.

One of the most common intensive research techniques is the **focus group,** in which the company invites six or more people typical of the target market to a group session to discuss the product, the service, or the marketing situation. The session may last an hour or more. A trained moderator guides the often freewheeling discussion, and the group interaction reveals the participants' true feelings or behavior toward the product. Focus-group meetings are usually recorded and often viewed or videotaped from behind a one-way mirror.

Focus groups don't represent a valid sample of the population, but the participants' responses are useful for several purposes. They can provide input about the viability of prospective spokespeople, determine the effectiveness of visuals and strategies, and identify elements in ads that are unclear or claims that don't seem plausible. Focus groups are best used in conjunction with surveys. In fact, focus-group responses often help marketers design questions for a formal survey.[28] Following a survey, focus groups can put flesh on the skeleton of raw data.[29]

As in the cases of Healthtex and Kraft, focus groups are particularly useful to gain a deeper understanding of particular market segments. A *show-and-tell* focus group conducted by Grieco Research Group in Colorado provides a glimpse of the core values of baby boomers. Participants were asked to bring to the session three or four items that they felt represented their ideal environment. Items ranged from photographs to magazine pictures to mementos and souvenirs. One mother of two brought tickets to a retro rock concert; a conservative

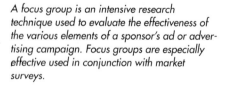

A focus group is an intensive research technique used to evaluate the effectiveness of the various elements of a sponsor's ad or advertising campaign. Focus groups are especially effective used in conjunction with market surveys.

corporate executive brought in a pack of cigarettes to show he was still rebellious; a middle-aged father brought a lucky fishing lure given to his kids by his father.

The process uncovered five key themes regarding what matters most to urban boomers. Family love and support and a good home life are viewed as important achievements. Long-term friendships are also very important and provide continuity to boomers. City-dwelling boomers are driven to "get away from it all" and escape to the big outdoors. Spiritual fitness is as important as physical fitness, so they love to develop their intellectual potential. They also feel that they're never too old to improve themselves. Clearly, all these values can translate into interesting platforms for ads and commercials.[30]

Basic Methods of Quantitative Research

Advertisers use **quantitative research** to gain reliable, hard statistics about specific market conditions or situations. There are three basic research methods used to collect quantitative data: *observation, experiment,* and *survey.*

Observation   In the **observation method,** researchers monitor people's actions. They may count the traffic that passes by a billboard, count a TV audience through instruments hooked to TV sets, or study consumer reactions to products displayed in the supermarket. Most observation method research is performed by large, independent marketing research companies, such as the A. C. Nielsen Co., Information Resources, Inc., and Audits and Surveys Worldwide, whose clients subscribe to their various services. Healthtex, for example, subscribes to the services of NPD (National Panel Diary), which tracks the clothing purchases of 16,000 homes as a nationwide sample. From this, Healthtex can find out its market share and better understand statistical trends in the marketplace.

Technology has greatly facilitated the observation method. One example is the **Universal Product Code (UPC)** label, an identifying series of vertical bars with a 12-digit number that adorns every consumer packaged good. By reading the codes with optical scanners, researchers can tell which products are selling and how well. The UPC label not only increases speed and accuracy at the checkout counter; it also enables timely inventory control and gives stores and manufacturers accurate point-of-purchase data sensitive to the impact of price, in-store promotion, couponing, and advertising.

For example, A. C. Nielsen's ScanTrack service provides weekly data on packaged-goods sales, market shares, and retail prices from 3,000 UPC scanner-equipped supermarkets. A companion service, ScanTrack Electronic Household Panel, provides packaged goods purchase data via in-home UPC scanning based on 40,000 U.S. households. As a result, marketers suddenly have reliable data on the effectiveness of the tools they use to influence consumers. With that information, they can develop empirical models to evaluate alternative marketing plans, media vehicles, and promotional campaigns.[31] In one case, for instance, data might indicate that a 40-cent coupon for toothpaste would create $150,000 in profits, but a 50-cent coupon on the same item would create a $300,000 loss.

Advertisers used to assume that changes in market share and brand position happen slowly. But observation shows that the packaged-goods market is complex and volatile. At the local level, weekly sales figures may fluctuate considerably, making it difficult to measure advertising's short-term effectiveness.

Video cameras have also affected observation techniques. Envirosell, a New York–based research company, uses security-type cameras to capture consumer in-store shopping habits. To determine the effectiveness of packaging and displays, the company analyzes how much time people spend with an item and how they read the label.[32]

The Universal Product Code on packaging is scanned at checkout counters. It improves checkout time and inventory control, and provides a wealth of accessible data for use in measuring advertising response.

This video frame from Envirosell shows how the company uses security-type cameras to capture in-store consumer shopping habits.

Experiment   To measure actual cause-and-effect relationships, researchers use the **experimental method.** An experiment is a scientific investigation in which a researcher alters the stimulus received by a *test group* and compares the results with that of a *control group* that did not receive the altered stimulus. This type of research is used primarily for new-product and new campaign introductions. As we saw in the Kraft story, marketers go to an isolated geographic area, called a **test market,** and introduce the product in that area alone or test a new ad campaign or promotion before a *national rollout.* For example, a new campaign might run in one geographic area but not another. Sales in the two areas are then compared to determine the campaign's effectiveness. However, researchers must use strict controls so the variable that causes the effect can be accurately determined. Because it's hard to control every marketing variable, this method is difficult to use and quite expensive.

Survey   The most common method of gathering primary research data is the **survey,** in which the researcher gains information on attitudes, opinions, or motivations by questioning current or prospective customers (political polls are a common type of survey). Surveys can be conducted by personal interview, telephone, mail, or on the Internet. Each has distinct advantages and disadvantages (see Exhibit 7–6). We'll discuss some important issues regarding survey research in the last section of this chapter.

Basic Methods for Testing Ads

Although there is no infallible way to predict advertising success or failure, pretesting and posttesting can give an advertiser useful insights if properly applied.

Pretesting methods   Advertisers often pretest ads for likability and comprehension by using a variety of qualitative and quantitative techniques.

For example, when pretesting print ads, advertisers often ask direct questions: What does the advertising say to you? Does the advertising tell you anything new or different about the company? If so, what? Does the advertising reflect activities you would like to participate in? Is the advertising believable? What effect does it have on your perception of the merchandise offered? Do you like the ads?

Through **direct questioning,** researchers can elicit a full range of responses from people and thereby infer how well advertising messages convey key copy points. Direct questioning is especially effective for testing alternative ads in the early stages of development, when respondents' reactions and input can best be acted on. There are numerous techniques for pretesting print ads, including: *focus groups, order-of-merit*

Exhibit 7–6
Comparison of data collection methods.

	Personal	**Telephone**	**Mail**	**Internet**
Data collection costs	High	Medium	Low	Low
Data collection time required	Medium	Low	High	Medium
Sample size for a given budget	Small	Medium	Large	Large
Data quantity per respondent	High	Medium	Low	Low
Reaches widely dispersed sample	No	Maybe	Yes	Yes
Reaches special locations	Yes	Maybe	No	Yes
Interaction with respondents	Yes	Yes	No	No
Degree of interviewer bias	High	Medium	None	None
Severity of nonresponse bias	Low	Low	High	Medium
Presentation of visual stimuli	Yes	No	Maybe	Yes
Field worker training required	Yes	Yes	No	No

Methods for Pretesting Ads

Print Advertising

____ **Direct questioning.** Asks specific questions about ads. Often used to test alternative ads in early stages of development.

____ **Focus group.** A moderated but freewheeling discussion and interview conducted with six or more people.

____ **Order-of-merit test.** Respondents see two or more ads and arrange them in rank order.

____ **Paired-comparison method.** Respondents compare each ad in a group.

____ **Portfolio test.** One group sees a portfolio of test ads interspersed among other ads and editorial matter. Another group sees the portfolio without the test ads.

____ **Mock magazine.** Test ads are "stripped into" a magazine, which is left with respondents for a specified time. (Also used as a posttesting technique.)

____ **Perceptual meaning study.** Respondents see ads in timed exposures.

____ **Direct-mail test.** Two or more alternative ads are mailed to different prospects on a mailing list to test which ad generates the largest volume of orders.

Broadcast Advertising

____ **Central location projection test.** Respondents see test commercial films in a central location such as a shopping center.

____ **Trailer test.** Respondents see TV commercials in trailers at shopping centers and receive coupons for the advertised products; a matched sample of consumers just get the coupons. Researchers measure the difference in coupon redemption.

____ **Theater test.** Electronic equipment enables respondents to indicate what they like and dislike as they view TV commercials in a theater setting.

____ **Live telecast test.** Test commercials are shown on closed-circuit or cable TV. Respondents are interviewed by phone and/or sales audits are conducted at stores in the viewing areas.

____ **Sales experiment.** Alternative commercials run in two or more market areas.

Physiological Testing

____ **Pupilometric device.** Dilation of the subject's pupils is measured, presumably to indicate the subject's level of interest.

____ **Eye-movement camera.** The route the subject's eyes traveled is superimposed over an ad to show the areas that attracted and held attention.

____ **Galvanometer.** Measures subject's sweat gland activity with a mild electrical current; presumably the more tension an ad creates, the more effective it is likely to be.

____ **Voice-pitch analysis.** A consumer's response is taped and a computer used to measure changes in voice pitch caused by emotional responses.

____ **Brain-pattern analysis.** A scanner monitors the reaction of the subject's brain.

---

tests, paired comparisons, portfolio tests, mock magazines, perceptual meaning studies, and *direct-mail tests.* (See the Checklist, "Methods for Pretesting Ads.")

Several methods are used specifically to pretest radio and TV commercials. In **central location tests,** respondents are shown videotapes of test commercials, usually in shopping centers, and questions are asked before and after exposure. In **clutter tests,** test commercials are shown with noncompeting control commercials to determine their effectiveness, measure comprehension and attitude shifts, and detect weaknesses.

A company's own employees are an important constituency. Some companies, in fact, pretest new commercials by prescreening them on their in-house cable TV systems and soliciting feedback.

The challenge of pretesting There is no best way to pretest advertising variables. Different methods test different aspects, and each has its own advantages and disadvantages—a formidable challenge for the advertiser.

Pretesting helps distinguish strong ads from weak ones. But since the test occurs in an artificial setting, respondents may assume the role of expert or critic and give answers that don't reflect their real buying behavior. They may invent opinions to satisfy the interviewer, or be reluctant to admit they are influenced, or vote for the ads they think they *should* like.

Researchers encounter problems when asking people to rank ads. Respondents often rate the ones that make the best first impression as the highest in all categories (the **halo effect**). Also, questions about the respondent's buying behavior may be invalid; behavior *intent* may not become behavior *fact.* And some creative people mistrust ad testing because they believe it stifles creativity.

Despite these challenges, the issue comes down to dollars. Small advertisers rarely pretest, but their risk isn't as great, either. When advertisers risk millions of dollars on a new campaign, they *must* pretest to be sure the ad or commercial is interesting,

Checklist

Methods for Posttesting Ads

___ **Aided recall (recognition-readership).** To jog their memories, respondents are shown certain ads and then asked whether their previous exposure was through reading, viewing, or listening.

___ **Unaided recall.** Respondents are asked, without prompting, whether they saw or heard advertising messages.

___ **Attitude tests.** Direct questions, semantic differential tests, or unstructured questions measure changes in respondents' attitudes after a campaign.

___ **Inquiry tests.** Additional product information, product samples, or premiums are given to readers or viewers of an ad; ads generating the most responses are presumed to be the most effective.

___ **Sales tests.** Measures of past sales compare advertising efforts with sales. Controlled experiments test different media in different markets. Consumer purchase tests measure retail sales from a given campaign. Store inventory audits measure retailers' stocks before and after a campaign.

believable, likable, and memorable—and reinforces the brand image.

Posttesting methods Posttesting can be more costly and time-consuming than pretesting, but it can test ads under actual market conditions. As we saw with Kraft, some advertisers benefit from pretesting *and* posttesting by running ads in select test markets before launching a campaign nationwide.

As in pretesting, advertisers use both quantitative and qualitative methods in posttesting. Most posttesting techniques fall into five broad categories: *aided recall, unaided recall, attitude tests, inquiry tests,* and *sales tests.* (See the Checklist, "Methods for Posttesting Ads.")

Some advertisers use **attitude tests** to measure a campaign's effectiveness in creating a favorable image for a company, its brand, or its products. Presumably, favorable changes in attitude predispose consumers to buy the company's product.

Impact Research in Montreal developed a proprietary posttest called TES (Tracking Efficiency Study) that it administers regularly for clients.[33] Using a random sample of 200 people in each market, Impact researchers phone or visit respondents and ask 8 to 10 questions to determine which ads or commercials they remember seeing, if they can identify the sponsor, which message elements they remember, and how well they liked the ads. Then Impact develops statistics on how many people *actually* saw the ads or commercials and how often.

Similarly, Nissan interviews 1,000 consumers every month to track brand awareness, familiarity with vehicle models, recall of commercials, and shifts in attitude or image perception. If a commercial fails, it can be pulled quickly.[34]

Advertisers can avert potential disaster by pretesting ads for their effectiveness prior to a campaign. While pretesting incurs yet another cost, advertisements that confuse or even offend consumers can cost a company millions of dollars in damages or lost sales. Tabasco (www.tabasco.com) pretested its "Exploding Mosquito" in spot advertisements around the country before airing it in front of millions of viewers around the world during the 1998 Super Bowl.

Open on a man sitting outside on his porch enjoying a pizza with McIlhenny Tabasco Pepper Sauce.

There are two empty bottles at his feet.

SFX: mosquito hum

Cut to mosquito biting the man on the leg.

The man has a bemused expression.

The mosquito flies off and explodes in mid-flight.

The man smiles.

Starch Readership Reports (www.roperasw.com) posttest magazine ad effectiveness by interviewing readers. The summary tab at the top of this ad indicates that 51 percent of women readers noted the ad; 49 percent associated the ad with the advertiser (Hanes); and 27 percent read most of the copy.

Following its initial campaign, Healthtex conducted some posttesting and discovered that, while the new moms appreciated the information in the long copy format of their ads, more experienced mothers didn't. For them, the headline and one line of copy were sufficient to get the point across. They already understood the rest. As a result, The Martin Agency used the shorter format and redesigned the ads aimed at experienced moms.

The challenge of posttesting   Each posttesting method has limitations. **Recall tests** reveal the effectiveness of ad components, such as size, color, or themes. But they measure what respondents noticed, *not* whether they actually buy the product.

For measuring sales effectiveness, attitude tests are often better than recall tests. An attitude change relates more closely to product purchase, and a measured change in attitude gives management the confidence to make informed decisions about advertising plans. Unfortunately, many people find it difficult to determine and express their attitudes. For mature brands, brand interest may be a better sales indicator, and advertisers now measure that phenomenon.[35]

By using **inquiry tests**—in which consumers respond to an ad for information or free samples—researchers can test an ad's attention-getting value, readability, and understandability. These tests also permit fairly good control of the variables that motivate reader action, particularly if a *split-run* test is used (split runs are covered in Chapter 15). The inquiry test is also effective for testing small-space ads.

Unfortunately, inquiries may not reflect a sincere interest in the product, and responses may take months to receive. When advertising is the dominant element or the only variable in the company's marketing plan, **sales tests** are a useful measure of advertising effectiveness. However, many other variables usually affect sales (competitors' activities, the season of the year, and even the weather). Sales response may not be immediate, and sales tests, particularly field studies, are often costly and time-consuming.

For consumer packaged goods, though, the cost of sales tests has been greatly reduced thanks to grocery store scanners. Finally, sales tests are typically more suited for gauging the effectiveness of campaigns than of individual ads or components of ads.

Step 5: Interpreting and Reporting the Findings

The final step in the research process involves interpreting and reporting the data. Research is very costly (see Exhibit 7–7), and its main purpose is to help solve problems. The final report must be comprehensible to the company's managers and relevant to their needs.

Exhibit 7–7
The cost of professional research.

Type of research	Features	Cost
Telephone	500 20-minute interviews, with report	$24,000–$28,000
Mail	500 returns, with report	$15,000–$18,000
Intercept	500 interviews, four or five questions, with report	$20,000–$22,000
Executive interviews (talking to business administrators)	20 interviews, with report	$7,500–$10,000
Focus group	One group, 8 to 10 people, with report and videotape	$5,000–$8,000

Research Statistics Can Be Friends or Foes

Marketing research gives the advertiser and its agency the data they need to identify consumer needs, develop new products and communication strategies, and assess the effectiveness of marketing programs. It also often provides the basis for advertising claims.

However, the way some advertisers use research data can lead to serious ethical lapses. Clever researchers can hide, shape, and manipulate statistics. Unfortunately, some researchers and marketers deliberately withhold information, falsify figures, alter results, misuse or ignore pertinent data, compromise the research design, or misinterpret the results to support their point of view.

Trying to spin the nutritional numbers to its advantage with consumers on the Atkins, South Beach, and other high-protein, low-carbohydrate diets, KFC created two television ads "aimed at educating the public that fried chicken can actually be part of a healthy diet." One ad showed a wife plopping down a bucket of fried chicken in front of her TV-engrossed husband, proudly explaining that they are starting to eat better ("healthier" is implied). A second ad showed a man sitting on the tailgate of a truck, again with a bucket of fried chicken; his friend compliments him on his "fantastic" appearance. Compared to a Burger King Whopper, the company claimed, its fried chicken was veritable health food. Almost. According to the Federal Trade Commission (FTC), "although it is true that the two fried chicken breasts have slightly less total fat and saturated fat than a Whopper, they have more than three times the trans fat and cholesterol, more than twice the sodium, and more calories."

It didn't take a lawsuit or months of investigation for the public to know that KFC's statistics were skewed. Consumer-protection groups were up in arms as soon as the ads aired, forcing the company to pull the ads within a month of their October 2003 launch. In response to the FTC's inquiry, KFC marketing executive Scott Bergen said, "We have always believed our ads to be truthful and factually accurate." In their settlement with the FTC, the company agreed to simply stop running the ads. Six months after the debacle, KFC tried the healthy tack again, this time offering *roasted* chicken.

Sometimes misleading health information in advertisements can be hazardous to more than just the waistline. Consider the fen-phen controversy in which Wyeth-Ayerst, a division of American Home Products, was accused of ignoring research findings. Wyeth manufactures Redux (dexfenfluramine) and Pondimin (fenfluramine), which become the "fen" portion of fen-phen. In 1996, fen-phen was approved for distribution in the US, and by the end of 1996 thousands of people had reported health complications. In 1997, it was found that fen was linked to heart valve damage and an often-fatal lung disease called primary pulmonary hypertension. Subsequently, the manufacturer was pressured to pull the drug off the shelf.

By the end of 1997, American Home Products was the subject of thousands of civil lawsuits over fen-phen by people who claimed that the drug caused their health problems. In 1999, American Home Products went under fire for allegedly withholding important information from the FDA (Federal Drug Administration). Leo Lutwak, a physician and medical officer for the FDA, claimed in an interview with *CBS News*, "American Home Products twisted the meaning of my research to make it seem as if there was no way to predict fen-phen's hazards. What I had actually written was, that in view of the covering up of information by the drug company, the FDA had no way of predicting some of these side effects." He said, "I've asked to be allowed to set the record straight, but was told it was against FDA policy to testify in a civil suit." His testimony would have been crucial for the thousands of people who were involved in civil suits.

Tables and graphs are helpful, but they must be explained in words management can understand. Technical jargon (such as "multivariate analysis of variance model") should be avoided, and descriptions of the methodology, statistical analysis, and raw data should be confined to an appendix. The report should state the problem and research objective, summarize the findings, and draw conclusions. The researcher should make recommendations for management action, and the report should be discussed in a formal presentation to allow management feedback and to highlight important points.

Important Issues in Advertising Research

Considerations in Conducting Formal Quantitative Research

When marketers conduct primary research, there is always one legitimate concern—the accuracy of the findings. This is especially true when conducting formal quantitative research and when doing research in international markets.

Quantitative research requires formal design and rigorous standards for collecting and tabulating data to ensure its accuracy and usability. When conducting formal research, advertisers must consider certain issues carefully, especially whether the research is *valid* and *reliable*. For more on the pros and cons of research statistics, see the Ethical Issue.

Validity and Reliability

Assume you want to determine a market's attitude toward a proposed new toy. The market consists of 10 million individuals. You show a prototype of the toy to five people and four say they like it (an 80 percent favorable attitude). Is that test valid? Hardly. For a test to have **validity,** *results must be free of bias* and reflect the *true status of the market*.[36] Five people aren't enough for a minimum sample, and

Then, it was reported in the *Dallas Morning News* that American Home Products had received researcher reports of leaky heart valves in fen-phen users in 1997. At the same time, though, it was lobbying members of Congress and the U.S. Drug Enforcement Administration to ease restrictions on the use of Pondimin and Redux. The lobbying campaign didn't work, and Pondimin and Redux were pulled from the market in September 1997.

In conjunction with lobbying legislators, American Home Products hired "ghostwriters" to write articles that promoted fen-phen. Then, according to lawsuit evidence cited in the Associated Press, the company used respected researchers to publish these articles under their own names. Since the drug was pulled off the shelves in 1997, only two of the ten articles were actually published in medical journals; the other eight were canceled. Doug Petkus, American Home Products spokesman, defended the articles. "This is a common practice in the industry," he said. "The companies have some input, it seems, in the initial development of the piece . . . but the proposed author has the last say." However, medical ethicists and editors of notable medical journals do not agree with this type of practice.

Dr. Jeffery Drazen, editor-in-chief of the *New England Journal of Medicine*, believes "that line between the author's independent conclusions and the company's conclusions has been blurred." Critics allege that oftentimes drug companies influence authors to bury unfavorable results and that this undue influence leads the public to believe that these drugs are safer and more effective than they actually are. In response to these types of allegations, the medical journals are updating their policies and guidelines regarding journal submissions so as to secure their own credibility, as well as the health and safety of the general public.

In November 1999, American Home Products agreed to settle the more than 11,000 fen-phen lawsuits for a whopping $4.83 billion. This was one of the biggest product-liability settlements ever. Of course, as part of the settlement, the company admitted no wrongdoing.

There is a lot of money to be made in the pharmaceutical industry; companies go to great lengths and great expense to get their products approved. But ignoring, manipulating, or omitting pertinent research findings is not only unethical, it's potentially lethal.

Questions

1. Are there any circumstances that might justify a portrayal of research findings in a biased or distorted fashion?

2. Why is it so important when discussing scientific research results with a client to report all results, not just those that put the client in a good light?

Sources: ABC News [When Good Drugs Go Bad, Rose Pike] (http://more.abcnews.go.com/sections/newsuse/fenfollow/); ABC News [Fen-Phen Articles Questioned, *Associated Press*] (http://abcnews.go.com/sections/living/DailyNews/fenphenghostwriters990523.html); ABC News [Report Faults Drug Maker, *Associated Press*] (http://abcnews.go.com/sections/living/DailyNews/fenphen990921.html); ABC News [Fen-Phen Settlement Clouded, *Associated Press*] (http://moreabcnews.go.com/sections/living/DailyNews/fenphen991222.html); CBS News [Medical Journals Tighten Rules, *Associated Press*] (www.cbsnews.com/stories/2001/09/10/national/main310621.shtml); "KFC Launches Campaign to Change High-Fat Image," *Advertising Age* online, October 28, 2003 (retrieved from www.adage.com, August 3, 2003); "KFC's Claims That Fried Chicken Is a Way to 'Eat Better,' Don't Fly," *FTC For the Consumer* online, June 3, 2004 (retrieved from www.ftc.gov/opa/2004/06/kfccorp.htm, August 4, 2004); Rob Walker, "Chicken-Fried Bull," MSN *Slate* online, November 10, 2003 (retrieved from http://slate.msn.com/id/2090861, August 4, 2004); Letter to the FTC, November 6, 2003, Center for Science in the Public Interest (retrieved from http://cspinet.org/new/pdf/letter_to_ftc.pdf, August 4, 2003); "KFC Responds to Resolution of Advertising Inquiry," KFC online press release, June 3, 2004 (retrieved from www.kfc.com/about/pr/060304.htm, August 4, 2004).

the fact that *you* showed a prototype of *your* toy to these people would probably bias their response.

Moreover, if you repeated the test with five more people, you might get an entirely different response. So your test also lacks **reliability.** For a test to be reliable, it must be *repeatable*—it must produce approximately the same result each time it is administered (see Exhibit 7–8).

Validity and reliability depend on several key elements: the sampling methods, the survey questionnaire design, and the data tabulation and analysis methods.

Sampling Methods

When a company wants to know what consumers think, it can't ask everybody. But its research must reflect the **universe** (the entire target population) of prospective customers. Researchers select from that population a **sample** that they expect will represent the population's characteristics. To accomplish this, they must decide who to survey, how many to survey, and how to choose the respondents. Defining **sample units**—the individuals, families, or companies being surveyed—is very important.

A sample must be large enough to achieve precision and stability. The larger the sample, the more reliable the results. However, reliability can be obtained with even very small samples, a fraction of 1 percent of the population, if the sample is drawn correctly. There are two types of samples: random probability samples and nonprobability samples. Both are derived from mathematical *theories of probability.*

The greatest accuracy is gained from **random probability samples** because everyone in the universe has an equal chance of being selected.[37] For

Validity

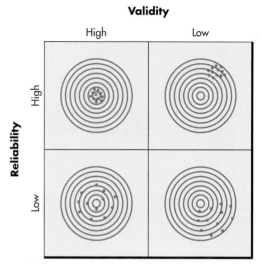

Exhibit 7–8

The reliability/validity diagram. Using the analogy of a dart board, the bull's-eye is the actual average of a value among a population (say, the average age in the community). The top row *shows high reliability (repeatability) because the darts are closely clustered. When reliability drops, the darts land more randomly and spread across a wider area, as in both examples in the* bottom row. The left column *demonstrates high validity because in both examples the darts center around the bull's-eye. The* right column *represents low validity because bias in the testing process drew all the darts to one side. In the* upper-right quadrant, *members of a fraternity are in the same age group (high reliability or repeatability), but their ages do not reflect the average of the community (low validity). The* lower-left quadrant *suggests the testing of our average age sample is highly valid, but it is not reliable because it includes people with a wide range of ages. The* upper-left quadrant *reflects the truest picture of the data.*

example, a researcher who wants to know a community's opinion on an issue selects members of the community at random. But this method has difficulties. Every unit (person) must be known, listed, and numbered so each has an equal chance of being selected, an often prohibitively expensive and sometimes impossible task, especially with customers of nationally distributed products.

Instead, researchers use **nonprobability samples** extensively because they're easier than probability samples, as well as less expensive and time-consuming. Nonprobability samples don't give every unit in the universe an equal chance of being included, so there's no guarantee the sample is representative. As a result, researchers can't be as confident in the validity of the responses.[38] Most marketing and advertising research only needs general measures of the data. For example, the nonprobability method of interviewing shoppers in malls may be sufficient to determine the shopping preferences, image perceptions, and attitudes of customers.

How Questionnaires Are Designed

Constructing a good questionnaire requires considerable expertise. Much bias in research is blamed on poorly designed questionnaires. Typical problems include asking the wrong types of questions, asking too many questions, using the wrong form for a question (which makes it too difficult to answer or tabulate), and using the wrong choice of words. Exhibit 7–9 shows some typical questions that might be used in a survey for a retail store.

Consider the simple question: "What kind of soap do you use?" The respondent doesn't know what *soap* means. Hand soap, shampoo, laundry detergent, or dishwashing soap? Does *kind* mean brand, size, or type? Finally, what constitutes *use*? What a person buys (perhaps for someone else) or uses personally—and for what purpose? In fact, one person probably uses several different kinds of soap, depending on the occasion. It's impossible to answer this question accurately. Worse, if the consumer does answer it, the researcher doesn't know what the answer means and will likely draw an incorrect conclusion. For these reasons, questionnaires *must* be pretested. (See the Checklist, "Developing an Effective Questionnaire.")

Effective survey questions have three important attributes: *focus, brevity,* and *clarity.* They focus on the topic of the survey. They are as brief as possible. And they are expressed simply and clearly.[39]

The four most common types of questions are *open-ended, dichotomous, multiple choice,* and *scale.* But there are many ways to ask questions within these four types. In Exhibit 7–10, for example, more choices can be added to the multiple-choice format. Neutral responses can be removed from the scale question so the respondent must answer either positively or negatively. And there is obvious bias in the dichotomous question.

Questions should elicit a response that is both accurate and useful. By testing questionnaires on a small subsample, researchers can detect any confusion, bias, or ambiguities.

Data Tabulation and Analysis

Collected data must be validated, edited, coded, and tabulated. Answers must be checked to eliminate errors or inconsistencies. For example, one person might answer two years, while another says 24 months; such responses must be changed to the same units for correct tabulation. Some questionnaires may be rejected because respondents' answers indicate they misunderstood the questions. Finally, the data must be counted and summarized, usually by computer.

Exhibit 7–9

A personal questionnaire like this helps determine shoppers' feelings toward a chain of stores, its merchandise, and its advertising.

1. Do you intend to shop at ___(Store name)___ between now and Sunday?
   Yes 1   No   2   (If no, skip to question 5)

2. Do you intend to buy something in particular or just to browse?
   Buy 1   Browse 2

3. Have you seen any of the items you intend to buy advertised by ___(Store name)___?
   Yes 1 (continue)   No 2 (skip to question 5)

4. Where did you see these items advertised? Was it in a ___(Store name)___ advertising insert included with your newspaper, a ___(Store name)___ flyer you received in the mail, the pages of the newspaper itself, on TV, or somewhere else?
   ☐ Insert in newspaper   ☐ On TV
   ☐ Flyer in mail   ☐ Somewhere else (specify) _____
   ☐ Pages of newspaper   ☐ Don't recall

5. Please rate the ___(Store name)___ advertising insert on the attributes listed below. Place an X in the box at the position that best reflects your opinion of how the insert rates on each attribute. Placing an X in the middle box usually means you are neutral. The closer you place the X to the left or right phrase or word, the more you believe it describes the ___(Store name)___ insert.

Looks cheap								Looks expensive
Unskillful								Cleverly done
Unappealing								Appealing
Does not show clothing in an attractive manner								Shows clothing in an attractive manner

   1   2   3   4   5   6   7

6. Please indicate all of the different types of people listed below you feel this ___(Store name)___ advertising insert is appealing to.

   ☐ Young people   ☐ Quality-conscious people
   ☐ Bargain hunters   ☐ Low-income people
   ☐ Conservative dressers   ☐ Budget watchers
   ☐ Fashion-conscious people ☐ Older people
   ☐ Rich people   ☐ Middle-income people
   ☐ Professionals   ☐ Blue-collar people
   ☐ High-income people   ☐ Women
   ☐ Men   ☐ Office workers
   ☐ Someone like me   ☐ Smart dressers
   ☐ Career-oriented women   ☐ Other (specify) _____

Exhibit 7–10

Different ways to phrase research questions.

Type	Questions
Open-ended	How would you describe (*Store name*) advertising?
Dichotomous	Do you think (*Store name*) advertising is too attractive? ____ Yes ____ No
Multiple choice	What description best fits your opinion of (*Store name*) advertising? ____ Modern ____ Unconvincing ____ Well done ____ Old-fashioned ____ Believable
Scale	Please indicate on the scale how you rate the quality of (*Store name*) advertising. ____ ____ ____ ____ ____ 1 2 3 4 5 Poor Excellent

Developing an Effective Questionnaire

____ **List specific research objectives.** Don't spend money collecting irrelevant data.

____ **Write short questionnaires.** Don't tax the respondent's patience; you may get careless or flip answers.

____ **State questions clearly** so there is no chance for misunderstanding. Avoid generalities and ambiguities.

____ **Write a rough draft first,** then polish it.

____ **Use a short opening statement.** Include the interviewer's name, the name of the organization, and the purpose of the questionnaire.

____ **Put the respondent at ease** by opening with one or two inoffensive, easily answered questions.

____ **Structure questions so they flow logically.** Ask general questions before more detailed ones.

____ **Avoid questions that suggest an answer or could be considered leading.** They bias the results.

____ **Include a few questions that cross-check earlier answers.** This helps ensure validity.

____ **Put the demographic questions (age, income, education) and any other personal questions at the end of the questionnaire.**

____ **Pretest the questionnaire** with 20 to 30 people to be sure they interpret the questions correctly and that it covers all the information sought.

Many researchers want *cross-tabulations* (for example, product use by age group or education). Software programs such as SPSS® and MINITAB® Statistical Software make it possible for small advertisers as well as large corporations to tabulate data on a personal computer and apply advanced statistical techniques.[40] Many cross-tabulations are possible, but researchers must use skill and imagination to select only those that show significant relationships. On small samples, using additional cross-tabs dramatically reduces the level of confidence.

Collecting Primary Data in International Markets

International marketers face a number of challenges when they collect primary data. For one thing, research overseas is often more expensive than domestic research. Many marketers are surprised to learn that research in five countries costs five times as much as research in one country; there are no economies of scale.[41]

But advertisers must determine whether their messages will work in foreign markets. (Maxwell House, for example, had to change its "great American coffee" campaign when it discovered that Germans have little respect for U.S. coffee.)

Control and direction of the research is another problem. Some companies want to direct research from their headquarters but charge it to the subsidiary's budget. This creates an instant turf battle. It also means that people less familiar with the country—and therefore less sensitive to local cultural issues—might be in charge of the project, which could flaw the data. Advertisers need more than just facts about a country's culture. They need to understand and appreciate the nuances of its cultural traits and habits, a difficult task for people who don't live there or speak the language. Knowledgeable international advertisers such as Colgate-Palmolive work in partnership with their local offices and use local bilingual marketing people when conducting primary research abroad.[42]

For years, Mattel tried unsuccessfully to market the Barbie doll in Japan. It finally sold the manufacturing license to a Japanese company, Takara, which did its own research. Takara found that most Japanese girls and their parents thought Barbie's breasts were too big and her legs too long. It modified the doll accordingly, changed the blue eyes to brown, and sold 2 million dolls in two years.

In Malaysia, Nestlé performed extensive research to build up its knowledge and adapt its products to local tastes and customs. As a result, some of its Malaysian products are now gelatin-free, out of respect for Muslim sensitivities.[43]

Conducting original research abroad can be fraught with problems. First, the researcher must use the local language, and translating questionnaires can be tricky. Second, many cultures view strangers suspiciously and don't wish to talk about their personal lives. U.S. companies found that mail surveys and phone interviews don't work in Japan; they have to use expensive, time-consuming personal interviews.[44]

Despite these problems—or perhaps because of them—it's important for global advertisers to perform research. Competent researchers are available in all developed countries, and major international research firms have local offices in most developing countries. The largest of these companies, which serve the largest multinational clients, organize their services globally based on the type of specialized research they conduct regularly. Research International Group, for instance, has global research directors for advertising research and for customer satisfaction research and global account directors for clients' projects worldwide.[45]

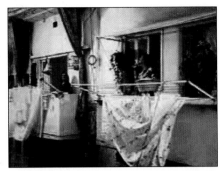

This example from Procter & Gamble's Bonux detergent campaign in Lebanon illustrates some of the difficulties inherent in international advertising. Lebanese housewives take great pride in clean washing, so much so that they even brag about laundry secrets and hang their laundry on balconies to be seen by neighbors. Bonux created the "housewives moment of fame" campaign and bought advertising space on the roofs of buses so the ads could be seen from balconies. Radio spots featured interviews with housewives riding the buses. The campaign raised awareness 85 percent, increased market share by 20 percent, and won a Media Lion at the Cannes Advertising Festival.

Marketers are often surprised by some of the differences they encounter when trying to conduct international research. Lead times to begin projects are typically longer, with the Far East being particularly troublesome. Groups can take twice as long to set up overseas. The structures differ too. Focus groups, for instance, rarely use more than 4 to 6 people rather than the 8 to 10 typical of the United States. Screening requirements for participants abroad are typically less rigid, and foreign moderators tend to be much less structured than their U.S. counterparts. Finally, the facilities don't usually have all the amenities of U.S. offices, but the costs are frequently twice as high in Europe and three times as high in Asia.[46]

Two goals for international research are flexibility and standardization, and both are necessary for the best results. Flexibility means using the best approach in each market. If you're studying the use of laundry products, it's just as irrelevant to ask Mexicans about soy-sauce stains as it is to ask Thais how they get *mole* out of their clothes.[47]

On the other hand, standardization is important so that information from different countries can be compared.[48] Otherwise the study will be meaningless. Balance is required to get the best of flexibility and standardization.

Thanks to a combination of computer-based interviewing, the Internet, e-mail, telephones, faxes, and courier services, the time required to conduct worldwide business-to-business research has been drastically reduced. Today, nearly three-quarters of market research firms use the Internet to conduct some form of market research.[49] With the global adoption of the Internet, experts anticipate further cuts in costs and time for getting valuable customer input for marketing and advertising decision making.

Chapter Summary

Marketing research is the systematic procedure used to gather, record, and analyze new information to help managers make decisions about the marketing of goods and services. Marketing research helps management identify consumer needs, develop new products and communication strategies, and assess the effectiveness of marketing programs and promotional activities. The many types of information gathered can help marketers recruit, retain, and regain customers.

Advertising research, a subset of marketing research, is used to gather and analyze information for developing or evaluating advertising. It helps advertisers develop strategies and test concepts. The results of research help define the product concept, select the target market, and develop the primary advertising message elements.

Advertisers use testing to make sure their advertising dollars are spent wisely. Pretesting helps detect and eliminate weaknesses before a campaign runs. Posttesting helps evaluate the effectiveness of an ad or campaign after it runs. Testing is used to evaluate several variables including merchandise, markets, motives, messages, media, and overall results.

The research process involves several steps: analyzing the situation and defining the problem, conducting informal (exploratory)

research by analyzing internal data and collecting external secondary data, setting research objectives, conducting formal research using qualitative or quantitative methods, and, finally, interpreting and reporting the findings.

Marketers use qualitative research to get a general impression of the market. The methods used may be projective or intensive. Quantitative techniques include observation, experiment, and survey.

Techniques used in pretesting include central location tests, clutter tests, and direct questioning. Pretesting has numerous problems, including artificiality, consumer inaccuracy, and the halo effect of consumer responses. The most commonly used posttesting techniques are aided recall, unaided recall, attitude tests, inquiry tests, and sales tests.

The validity and reliability of quantitative surveys depend on the sampling methods used and the design of the survey questionnaire. The two sampling procedures are random probability and nonprobability. Survey questions require focus, brevity, and simplicity.

In international markets, research is often more expensive and less reliable than in the United States. But advertisers must use research to understand cultural traits and habits in overseas markets.

Important Terms

advertising research, *208*

advertising strategy research, *209*

attitude test, *222*

central location test, *221*

clutter test, *221*

direct questioning, *220*

experimental method, *220*

focus group, *218*

formal research, *217*

halo effect, *221*

in-depth interview, *218*

informal research, *214*

inquiry test, *223*

intensive techniques, *218*

marketing information system (MIS), *214*

marketing research, *206*

markets, *213*

media classes, *213*

media research, *211*

media subclasses, *213*

media units, *213*

media vehicles, *213*

merchandise, *212*

message, *213*

motives, *213*

nonprobability samples, *226*

observation method, *219*

posttesting, *212*

pretesting, *212*

primary data, *215*

projective techniques, *218*

qualitative research, *217*

quantitative research, *217, 219*

random probability samples, *225*

recall test, *223*

reliability, *225*

sales test, *223*

sample, *225*

sample unit, *225*

secondary data, *215*

survey, *220*

test market, *220*

Universal Product Code (UPC), *219*

universe, *225*

validity, *224*

Review Questions

1. How does research help advertisers meet the challenge of the three Rs of marketing?

2. Give an example that demonstrates the difference between marketing research and market research.

3. Which kind of research data is more expensive to collect, primary or secondary? Why?

4. How have you personally used observational research?

5. Do people use quantitative or qualitative research to evaluate movies? Explain.

6. Which of the major surveying methods is most costly? Why?

7. How could the halo effect bias a pretest for a soft-drink ad?

8. When might research offer validity but not reliability?

9. How would you design a controlled experiment to test the advertising for a chain of men's clothing stores?

10. When could research help in the development of an advertising strategy for an international advertiser? Give an example.

11. **The Advertising Experience**
You have a friend who has invented the "Kitchen Widget," a sort of super spatula. Rather to your surprise, you find that it is an effective product, and there is no obvious reason why it shouldn't enjoy some success. One obstacle to this success, however, is that your friend has little capital with which to promote his invention, and every dollar has to count. Come up with a plan for advertising research that can assist your friend in the most cost-effective manner possible.

Exploring the Internet

The Internet exercises for Chapter 7 address the following areas related to marketing and advertising research: marketing research organizations and publications (Exercise 1) and market research companies (Exercises 2 and 3).

1. **Marketing Research Organizations and Publications**

   Many advertisers choose to perform their own research. When collecting research data by themselves, there are a number of advertising- and marketing-specific research sources available on the Web. Visit the research organizations' and publications' websites and answer the questions that follow.

   - Advertising Research Foundation (ARF) www.arfsite.org
   - *Journal of Advertising Research* www.arfsite.org/resources/jar.htm
   - American Marketing Association www.marketingpower.com
   - Marketing Research Association (MRA) www.mra-net.org

   a. What research group sponsors the site? Who is/are the intended audience(s)?

   b. What is the site's purpose? Does it succeed? Why?

   c. What range of services is offered?

   d. What is the organization's purpose?

2. **Market Research Companies**

   Marketers and advertisers depend heavily on timely and accurate research in preparation for advertising planning. There are many market research companies available to serve nearly every marketing and advertising research need. Visit the following syndicated and independent research companies' websites and answer the questions that follow.

   - A. C. Nielsen www.acnielsen.com
   - ASI Market Research Center www.asicentral.com
   - Audits & Surveys Worldwide www.surveys.com
   - Burke www.burke.com
   - Dun & Bradstreet www.dnb.com
   - FIND/SVP www.findsvp.com
   - The Gallup Organization www.gallup.com
   - Millward Brown IntelliQuest www.intelliquest.com
   - International Data Corporation (IDC) www.idc.com
   - J. D. Power and Associates www.jdpower.com
   - Research International www.research-int.com
   - Roper ASW www.roperasw.com
   - SRI Consulting www.sriconsulting.com

   a. What type(s) of research does the company specialize in?

   b. What industries/companies would be best suited to utilize the company's resources?

   c. What specific services, products, or publications does the company offer?

   d. Are the information services offered by the company primary or secondary data?

   e. How useful is the company for conducting advertising and marketing research? Why?

3. **Market Research for Politics**

   Silver-maned Armand Le Mouche, state senator for your district for 30 years, passed away recently, and his appointed replacement, Millard Frumpe, lacks a solid political base. Sally Daily, a self-made millionaire and the owner of a string of bakeries, would like to challenge Millard, but she wants to get some research done first. She firmly believes that advertising research helped her get to where she is. Find a site that could provide the research Sally needs in order to find out if her campaign is feasible or not, and, if it is, how she could win. Describe what the site could do for her. (One such site is www.rtnielson.com.)

Chapter 8

Marketing and Advertising Planning: Top-Down, Bottom-Up, and IMC

Objectives

To DESCRIBE THE PROCESS of marketing and advertising planning. Marketers and advertisers need to understand the various ways plans are created. They must also know how to analyze situations; set realistic, attainable objectives; develop strategies to achieve them; and establish budgets for marketing communications.

After studying this chapter, you will be able to:

- **Explain** the role and importance of a marketing plan.

- **Describe** how marketing and advertising plans are related.

- **Explain** the difference between objectives and strategies in marketing and advertising plans.

- **Give examples** of need-satisfying and sales-target objectives.

- **Discuss** the suitability of top-down, bottom-up, and integrated marketing communications planning.

- **Explain** how advertising budgets are determined.

- **Describe** how share-of-market/share-of-voice budgeting can be used for new product introductions.

Sixty years ago, Ally and Barney Hartman of Knoxville, Tennessee, decided to make their own mixer for hard liquor. The two brothers cooked up a 7-Up–type brew and tested it on their families and friends. They seemed to like it, so they started bottling the concoction and distributing it to the locals. In 1946, they designed a paper label for their beverage featuring a hillbilly toting a gun and a signature that read "By Barney and Ollie." In honor of the mountain moonshine famous in Tennessee, they named their drink "Mountain Dew." They debuted the bottle that year at a soft-drink convention in Gatlinburg, Tennessee, and quickly became convinced they had a good thing going. They had no idea how good. ■ Over the course of time, the brand grew. The gun-toting Willy the Hillbilly and their apt slogan, "Ya-hoo Mountain Dew," helped build it into a regional player. In 1964, PepsiCo bought the brand and, for some years, continued using the old advertising approach. But as sales failed to increase substantially, the marketing brains at Pepsi decided a new direction was called for. ■ In 1973, after a great deal of research, debate, and months of marketing and advertising planning, they completely repositioned and relaunched Mountain Dew. No longer would it be a hillbilly mixer. Rather, the Dew would be cast as a high-energy, youth-oriented, flavored soft drink. New ads created by BBDO

New York featured active young people enjoying outdoor activities to the theme "Hello Sunshine, Hello Mountain Dew." By 1978, the action-oriented approach sent Dew sales over the 100-million-case mark. In the 1980s they added high-octane sports and adventure to the advertising.[1] Then, in 1985, Mountain Dew went nationwide. ■ Since that time, Mountain Dew has set a standard of how to remain true to its own definition of exuberance across a variety of marketing platforms. "We have a great unity of message and purpose that has been consistent over time about what we are and what we aren't," says Scott Moffitt, director of marketing for Mountain Dew.[2] "The brand is all about exhilaration and energy, and you see that in all that we do, from advertising and community to grass-roots programs and our sports-minded focus. We have a very crystal clear, vivid positioning." ■ The positioning concept has allowed Mountain Dew great latitude: The brand's marketing extends from skateboarding parks and alternative events to mainstream extravaganzas such as the Super Bowl. Marketing across such a broad spectrum from grass roots to grandiose advertising events is known within PepsiCo as "mass intimacy."[3] ■ One Pepsi-Cola executive puts it this way, "It's our way of saying we haven't sold out. We have to make sure with programs like advertising on the Super Bowl that we are still letting customers see the brand in a way that is designed for them."[4] So whether Dew is talking advertising, events, endorsements, or simply premiums, a "Dew-x-perience" is paramount when talking to the brand's two key consumer groups: teenagers and 20- to 39-year-olds. ■ Mountain Dew has become a top-selling growth engine. Its unique selling proposition remains the same—it is the "ultimate, indulgent, thirst-quenching soft drink." This positioning took it to the top of the "heavy citrus" soda

category in the early 1990s. Then, in 1999, it reached a new benchmark. It briefly passed Diet Coke to become the number-three soft drink in the United States after Classic Coke and Pepsi. In the $62 billion carbonated soft-drink industry, that is a huge success. ■ In the early 2000s, the carbonated soft-drink market flattened as people spent more on flavored drinks and bottled water. To stem the trend, Pepsico introduced three new products: Sierra Mist, Pepsi Twist, and Code Red, a cherry-flavored line extension of the Mountain Dew brand. With a stealth launch, utilizing only limited radio advertising aimed at trend-setting urban and ethnic teenagers, Code Red was immediately a smashing success. ■ Cie Nicholson, Mountain Dew's marketing director, said the product's word-of-mouth buzz and lack of blatant advertising actually helped the brand with savvy teens. She also credited Code Red's initial success to its visibility at major sporting events like ESPN's winter X Games, its placement in games on the Mountain Dew website, and the promotional strategy of sending free bottles to 4,000 select consumers, such as hip-hop producer Jermaine Dupri and DJ Funkmaster Flex, before the brand hit the stores. ■ The soft drink also received a unique boost in recognition with techies in July 2001 when, working late one night, two Southern California computer programmers discovered a new worldwide computer virus and named it after the soda they were drinking: Code Red. ■ After only 11 weeks of distribution, Code Red was the fifth-largest-selling soft drink at convenience stores and gas stations, behind only the monster brands of Mountain Dew, Coca-Cola Classic, Pepsi-Cola, and Dr Pepper (interestingly, in that venue, Mountain Dew is number one).[5] ■ To say the least, Barney and Ally would be proud. Mountain Dew has come a long way since its hillbilly days. Yahoo! ■

The Marketing Plan

In spite of the brilliant creativity employed by BBDO in its ads for Mountain Dew, the Dew story actually demonstrates that business success often depends more on careful marketing and advertising planning than on advertising creativity. Yet, every year, companies waste millions and millions of dollars on ineffective advertising due to a woeful lack of prior planning.

The Importance of Marketing Planning

Since marketing is typically a company's *only* source of income, the marketing plan may well be its most important document.

The **marketing plan** assembles all the pertinent facts about the organization, the markets it serves, and its products, services, customers, competition, and so on. It forces all departments—product development, production, selling, advertising, credit, transportation—to focus on the customer. Finally, it sets goals and objectives for specified periods of time and lays out the precise strategies and tactics to achieve them.

The written marketing plan must reflect the goals of top management and be consistent with the company's mission and capabilities. Depending on its scope, the plan may be long and complex or, in the case of a small firm or a single product line, very brief. Formal marketing plans are typically reviewed and revised yearly, but planning is not a one-time event; it's a continuous process that includes research, formulation, implementation, evaluation, review, and reformulation.

The Effect of the Marketing Plan on Advertising

The marketing plan has a profound effect on an organization's advertising. It helps managers analyze and improve all company operations, including marketing and advertising programs. It dictates the role of advertising in the marketing mix. It enables better implementation, control, and continuity of advertising programs, and it ensures the most efficient allocation of advertising dollars.

Successful organizations do not separate advertising plans from marketing. They view each as a vital building block for success. Companies have a choice in how they plan. Most still use the traditional top-down planning model; some use a bottom-up model; and now, increasingly, companies are starting to use an integrated marketing communications (IMC) model. We'll look at the first two briefly before delving into the new discipline of IMC.

Top-Down Marketing

The traditional **top-down marketing** plan is still the most common format. It has been used for over 30 years and fits the hierarchical organization of most companies. It is often appropriate for companies planning to launch completely new products. As Exhibit 8–1 shows, the top-down plan has four main elements: *situation analysis, marketing objectives, marketing strategy,* and *tactics* (or *action programs*). Large companies with extensive marketing plans sometimes include additional sections. At the end of the book, Appendix A outlines a complete top-down marketing plan.

Situation Analysis

The **situation analysis** section is a *factual* statement of the organization's current situation and how it got there. It presents all relevant facts about the company's history, growth, products and services, sales volume, share of market, competitive status, markets served, distribution system, past advertising programs, results of marketing research studies, company capabilities, strengths and weaknesses, and any other pertinent information. To plan successfully for the future, company executives must agree on the accuracy of the data and its interpretation. The Checklist for Situation Analysis (in the Reference Library on the *Contemporary Advertising* CD) shows the most important elements to consider.

Exhibit 8–1
Traditional top-down marketing plan.

Once the historical information is gathered, the focus changes to potential threats and opportunities based on key factors outside the company's control—for example, the economic, political, social, technological, or commercial environments in which the company operates.[6]

Look at the situation Mountain Dew faced in the mid-1990s. While the 1980s had been the decade of the diet colas, the 1990s were turning into the decade of the big flavored brands. The soft-drink category was still dominated by the two mainstream colas with the most marketing muscle, Coca-Cola and Pepsi-Cola, and they were followed fairly closely by Diet Coke. But noncola drinks such as Sprite, Dr Pepper, and Mountain Dew were producing consistent gains. In fact, the noncolas were growing faster than the colas; and the folks at Mountain Dew were celebrating because, with scant resources and extraordinary competitive pressure, their little niche brand had reached the number-six position overall and the number-two noncola brand behind Dr Pepper. They were still some distance away from Diet Coke, but the brand was emerging as a growth leader even while being outspent by Dr Pepper. In a nutshell, that was the situation. And it spelled opportunity.

Marketing Objectives

The organization's next step is to determine specific marketing objectives. These must consider the amount of money the company has to invest in marketing and production, its knowledge of the marketplace, and the competitive environment.

For example, in 1998, Mountain Dew budgeted about $40 million for media advertising, far less than the $83 million spent by Pepsi or the $116 million spent by Coke.[7] As a result, Dew had to set less ambitious marketing objectives in terms of total volume, but not in terms of growth.

Marketing objectives follow logically from a review of the company's current situation, management's prediction of future trends, and the hierarchy of company objectives. For example, **corporate objectives** are stated in terms of profit or return on investment, or net worth, earnings ratios, growth, or corporate reputation. **Marketing objectives,** which derive from corporate objectives, should relate to the needs of target markets as well as to specific sales goals. These may be referred to as general *need-satisfying objectives* and specific *sales-target objectives*.

To shift management's view of the organization from a producer of products to a satisfier of target market needs, companies set **need-satisfying objectives.** These have a couple of important purposes. First, they enable the firm to view its business broadly. For example, Revlon founder Charles Revson once said a cosmetic company's product is hope, not lipstick. An insurance company sells financial security, not policies. Since customer needs change, maintaining a narrow view may strand a company in a market where its products are no longer relevant. For example, if a button manufacturer thought his need-satisfying objective was to satisfy people's need for buttons, he might have completely missed the opportunity presented by new products such as Velcro and zips, which satisfy a similar but broader need—fastening clothes.

Second, by setting need-satisfying objectives, managers force the company to look through the customer's eyes. They have to ask "What are we planning to do for the customer?" and "What is the value of that to our customer?" One of the best ways to define a market is to think about customer needs first and then identify the products that meet those needs.[8]

The second kind of marketing objective is the **sales-target objective.** This is a specific, quantitative, realistic marketing goal

Careful marketing and advertising planning can be the principal reason for a successful ad campaign. Mountain Dew's edgy and exhilarating ads are a great example of how these aspects can work effectively together (www.mountaindew.com).

Positioning is important for both the advertiser and the consumer because it helps differentiate products from the competition. This Taiwanese ad for the Silk Lady Shaver takes an inverted approach to position the product—showing what it will not do. By covering the model in Band-Aids, the agency demonstrated its sophisticated humor and picked up a Bronze Lion at Cannes in the process.

Professor Ernest Martin at Campbell University proposes seven distinct approaches to developing a positioning strategy:

1. Product attribute—setting the brand apart by stressing a particular product feature important to consumers.
2. Price/quality—positioning on the basis of price or quality.
3. Use/application—positioning on the basis of how a product is used (e.g., Arm & Hammer).
4. Product class—positioning the brand against other products that, while not the same, offer the same class of benefits.
5. Product user—positioning against the particular group who uses the product.
6. Product competitor—positioning against competitors (e.g., Avis/Hertz), using the strength of the competitor's position to help define the subject brand. (See Ethical Issues, "A War of Comparisons" on p. 240.)
7. Cultural symbol—positioning apart from competitors through the creation or use of some recognized symbol or icon.[14]

We would add an eighth approach: by category—positioning by defining or redefining the business category. A simple way for a company to get the number-one position is to invent a new product category.

Xerox, for example, was originally known as *the* copier company, but with increased competition, the copier market became glutted, so Xerox tried to reposition itself as a problem solver. Now calling itself "The Document Company," it offers to use technology to find ways for everyone in an organization to manage and share useful information. But what it has really done is create a new business category occupied by one company: Xerox.[15]

With all its high energy and exhilaration, "youth" is not only the positioning of Mountain Dew, it's the heartbeat of the brand.[16] PepsiCo defines the Dew positioning this way:

> To 18-year-old males who embrace excitement, adventure, and fun, Mountain Dew is the great-tasting soft drink that exhilarates like no other because it is energizing, thirst-quenching, and has a unique citrus flavor.

Determining the marketing mix   The next step in developing the marketing strategy is to determine a cost-effective marketing mix for *each* target market the company pursues. As we discussed in Chapter 6, the mix blends the various marketing elements the company controls: *product, price, distribution,* and *communications.*

Mountain Dew was blessed with a broad marketing toolbox to draw upon. First, it offered consumers an energizing, thirst-quenching soft-drink *product* with a unique citrus flavor and an image of youthful exuberance, exhilaration, and adventure. Then, to build *distribution,* it used a variety of promotions to the trade that would enable grocers and other resellers to increase both volume and profits. While its *price* was competitive with other soft drinks, Mountain Dew promoted itself aggressively with free samples, premiums, and prizes at various street and sporting events—which effectively lowered the price to consumers.

Finally, Mountain Dew initiated an integrated *communications* program that included extensive advertising on TV, radio, outdoor, print, and the Internet; sports and event sponsorships; appearances at grass-roots geographical events; plus a host of public relations activities—all designed to develop and promote the distinct Mountain Dew personality.

Companies have a wide variety of marketing strategy options. They might increase distribution, initiate new uses for a product, change a product line, develop entirely new markets, or start discount pricing. Each option emphasizes one or more marketing mix elements. The choice depends on the product's target market, its position in the market, and its stage in the product life cycle.

A War of Comparisons

Across the advertising battlefield, marketers wage a war called comparative advertising. Ads wield charges and countercharges, and the main players are no longer just second-rate brands looking to make their mark.

Comparative advertising, a technique where one company explicitly compares its brand to another in an effort to gain a competitive edge, was actually endorsed by the Federal Trade Commission in the 1970s "as a means of improving competition." Since its inception into the advertising world, comparative advertising has turned out to be a bit of a double-edged sword.

Ideally, comparative advertising should provide consumers with more information about competing products, thereby allowing them to make better-informed purchase decisions. However, research indicates that direct product comparisons create greater awareness for the lesser-known brand, and that has been directly linked to a decline in sales for the more established brand, since at the point of purchase the consumer often confuses the two. Thus, advertisers who engage in comparative advertising may have more to lose than simply a few sales.

When taken too far, comparative advertising can be illegal. If an ad's comparisons are shown to be false, deceptive, or deliberately misleading, the campaign may result in litigation. Even ads that are literally correct can be found liable. According to one court, "innuendo, indirect intimations, and ambiguous suggestions" can unjustly injure a competitor. McNeil Consumer Products' Extra-Strength Tylenol, for example, successfully sued American Home Products' Maximum Strength Anacin even though Anacin's ad was literally true. Anacin had *implied* superiority over Tylenol when in fact both products contain the same amount of pain reliever.

A further complication arises when advertisers manipulate comparisons to cast a more favorable light on their product. In Australia, Duracell ran an ad showing a bunny powered by a Duracell battery outracing one powered by an Energizer batter. What Duracell neglected to mention in the ad was that they were comparing their top-of-the-line alkaline battery to one of Energizer's midrange carbon zinc batteries—apples and oranges, in the world of batteries. Energizer took the unfair comparison to court, and Duracell had to add clarifying text to their ad before they could put it back on the air.

Name-calling, finger pointing, and insulting the competition are all contemporary weapons used in the marketing wars waged between virtually identical brands, who are desperate to stand apart from the competition. Naming names can be tricky, but the truth can actually help. In one case, Budweiser attacked Coors for its claim that it used only "Rocky Mountain spring water." Coors, in fact, mixed this water with water from, of all places, Virginia.

Some researchers estimate that 40 percent of all advertising in the United States is now comparative, whereas in most of the world it is

Marketing Tactics (Action Programs)

A company's objectives indicate where it wants to go; the strategy indicates the intended route; and the **tactics** (or **action programs**) determine the specific short-term actions to be taken, internally and externally, by whom, and when. Advertising campaigns live in the world of marketing tactics. These tactics are the key to *bottom-up marketing*.

Bottom-Up Marketing: How Small Companies Plan

In a small company, everybody is both player and coach, and the day-to-day details seem to come first, leaving little or no time for formal planning. However, there is a solution to this dilemma: **bottom-up marketing** (see Exhibit 8–2).

Jack Trout and Al Ries think one of the best ways for a company to develop a competitive advantage is to focus on an ingenious tactic first and then develop that tactic into a strategy. By reversing the normal process, advertisers sometimes make important discoveries.[17] Researchers at Vicks developed an effective liquid cold remedy but discovered that it put people to sleep. Rather than throw out the research, Vicks positioned the formula as a nighttime cold remedy. NyQuil went on to become the number-one cold remedy and the most successful new product in Vicks's history.

The *tactic* is a singular, competitive mental angle. By planning from the bottom up, entrepreneurs can find unique tactics to exploit. But caution is required. Advertisers should find just *one* tactic, not two or three. The advertiser can then focus all elements of the marketing mix on the tactic. The tactic becomes the nail, and the strategy is the hammer that drives it home.

The artful combination of tactic and strategy creates a position in the consumer's mind. When Tom Monaghan thought of the tactic of delivering pizza to customers' homes, he focused his whole strategy on that singular idea. He ended up making a fortune and marketing history with Domino's Pizza.

A company's advertising plan is an excellent place to discover a competitive tactic. But opportunities are hard to spot because they often don't look like opportunities—they look like angles or gimmicks.

Exhibit 8–2

Bottom-up marketing plan.

either illegal or strictly regulated. In France, a recent telecom ad was able to bypass the national ban on comparative advertising. The campaign claimed that Tele2's rates were up to 50 percent cheaper than those of rival phone companies. Tele2 was recently awarded a winning judgment by French courts, which ruled that its campaign targeting competitors Cegetel and France Telecom "met French standards on comparative advertising . . . the ads were clearly focused on identical products."

In the United States, to keep comparison battles from getting out of hand, numerous groups, including the American Association of Advertising Agencies, the National Association of Broadcasters, and the FTC, issued guidelines for comparative advertising that are often stricter than current laws. TV network NBC, for example, insists that "advertisers shall refrain from discrediting, disparaging, or unfairly attacking competitors, competing products, or other industries."

This is a good step, but the legal language governing comparisons is vague, allowing for a blurry line between healthy one-upmanship and illegal behavior. As competition continues to increase, and ethical and legal guidelines remain ambiguous, the public will no doubt continue to be bombarded by comparative ads. The responsibility, therefore, will continue to fall on consumers to sift through the ads and differentiate facts from fiction.

Questions

1. How do you feel about ads that compare the features and benefits of competitive products and services? Do you believe they are unethical even if the comparisons are honest? Why or why not?

2. Select a comparative ad and study the copy. What points of comparison does the ad make? Are the points made honestly and directly, or are they masked by innuendo and implication? Is the ad literally true but still potentially misleading? Do you feel the ad is ethical or not?

Sources: Francesca Barigozzi, Paolo G. Garella, and Martin Peitz, "With a Little Help from My Enemy: Comparative Advertising," June 2002 (www.dse.unibo.it/wp/441.pdf); "Duracell Bunny Races again after Appeal Victory," B&T, July 30, 2002 (www.bandt.com.au/news/a1/0c00f7a1.asp); "10 Advertising Legal Issues for 2004," Advertising Age, December 22, 2003 (www.adage.com); Rich Thomaselli, "Industry Wrestles with Comparative Ads," Advertising Age, October 27, 2003 (www.adage.com); Daniel Bereskin and Jennifer McKenzie, "Comparative Advertising: Canada and the United States." (www.bereskinparr.com/publications/pdf/Mrktg%20Compare%20Bereskin.pdf); Advertising Education Forum, "United Kingdom: Self-Regulatory Organisations," (www.aeforum.org/european/United_Kingdom.html); The Business Research Lab, "Danger—Comparative Advertising," (www.busreslab.com/tips/tip8.htm); Reed Smith Hall Dicker, "Comparative Advertising" (www.adlaw.com/rc/handbk/rf_comparative.html).

You are a raindrop.

Not just any raindrop, but a raindrop with an attitude.

Pancake-big and ready to splat.

You're a frog-strangling, car-stalling, game-cancelling kind of raindrop and you don't care whose parade you screw up.

Just then you realize.

No, it can't be. It is.

You're headed straight for a Siplast roof.

Some days, it's just not worth getting out of the cloud.

Considering what you're up against, you need more than a roof, you need a partnership. And what better partner than the company that pioneered the SBS process? That's Siplast. The company with over 30 years of success in the roofing business. Not somebody who just fell into it. 1.800.922.8800.

NOTHING STANDS UP TO THE ELEMENTS LIKE A SIPLAST ROOF™

⚡siplast

The traditional transactional marketing approach, which focused on short-term profits, is now being replaced by a new model called relationship marketing. The purpose of relationship marketing is to create, maintain, and enhance long-term relationships with good customers and other stakeholders so that business can continue beyond periodic fluctuations in the economy. In this ad, Siplast (www.siplast.com), the largest commercial roofing manufacturer in the world, addresses the need for long-standing partnerships with its contractor clients. This is particularly important for high-cost, high-think products and services.

Managers of small companies have an advantage here. Surrounded by the details of the business, they are more likely to discover a good tactic that can be developed into a powerful strategy. However, that's not to say that a large company cannot profit from bottom-up marketing. Many have, like 3M with its Post-it notes.

The New Marketing Mantra: Relationship Marketing

Today, many advertisers are discovering that the key to building brand equity in the twenty-first century will be to develop interdependent, mutually satisfying relationships with customers.

A market-driven firm's overriding purpose is to create happy, loyal customers. Customers, not products, are the lifeblood of the business.[18] This realization has created a new trend away from simple *transactional marketing* to **relationship marketing**—creating, maintaining, and enhancing long-term relationships with customers and other stakeholders that result in exchanges of information and other things of mutual value.[19]

Today's affluent, sophisticated consumers can choose from a wide variety of products and services offered by producers located around the world. As a result, the customer relationship—in which the sale is only the beginning—is the key strategic resource of the successful twenty-first-century business.[20] As Dartmouth professor Frederick Webster points out: "The new *market-driven* conception of marketing will focus on *managing strategic partnerships* and positioning the firm between vendors and customers in the value chain with the aim of delivering *superior value* to the customer."[21]

We define **value** as the ratio of *perceived benefits* to the price of the product.[22]

The Importance of Relationships

To succeed, companies must focus on managing loyalty among carefully chosen customers and **stakeholders** (employees, centers of influence, stockholders, the financial community, and the press).[23] This is important for a number of reasons:

1. *The cost of lost customers.* No amount of advertising is likely to win back a customer lost from shoddy products or poor service. The real profit lost is the **lifetime customer value (LTCV)** to a firm. For example, the average customer of one major transportation firm represented a lifetime value of $40,000. The company had 64,000 accounts and lost 5 percent of them due to poor service. That amounted to an unnecessary loss of $128 million in revenue and $12 million in profits![24] Moreover, the negative word-of-mouth can have a terrible snowballing effect. Imagine if one lost customer influences only one other customer to not patronize the business. That immediately doubles the LTCV loss. Negative word-of-mouth is why bad movies disappear so quickly.

2. *The cost of acquiring new customers.* Defensive marketing typically costs less than offensive marketing because it requires a great deal of effort to lure satisfied customers away from competitors.[25] The fragmentation of media audiences and the resistance of sophisticated consumers to advertising messages make it increasingly difficult for a brand to break out of the ghetto of advertising clutter by stepping up the advertising volume.[26] In fact, it costs five to eight times as much in marketing, advertising, and promotion to acquire a new customer as it does to keep an existing one.[27]

3. *The value of loyal customers.* Lester Wunderman, the founder of Wunderman Worldwide (the second largest direct-response agency in the world), says that 90 percent of a manufacturer's profit comes from repeat purchasers; only 10 percent comes from trial or sporadic purchasers.[28] Reducing customer defections by even 5 percent can improve profit potential by 25 to 85 percent.[29] And the longer customers stay with a company, the more willing they are to pay premium prices, make referrals, increase their annual buying, and demand less handholding.[30]

Thus, a company's first market should always be its current customers. In the past, most marketing and advertising effort focused on *presale* activities aimed at acquiring new customers. But today sophisticated marketers are shifting more of their resources to *postsale* activities, making customer retention their first line of defense. They have discovered the primary benefit of focusing on relationships: increasing retention and optimizing lifetime customer value.[31]

Levels of Relationships

Kotler and Armstrong distinguish five levels of relationships that can be formed between a company and its various stakeholders, depending on their mutual needs:

■ *Basic transactional relationship.* The company sells the product but does not follow up in any way (Target).

■ *Reactive relationship.* The company (or salesperson) sells the product and encourages customers to call if they encounter any problems (Men's Wearhouse).

An overwhelming proportion of business is conducted with repeat customers. This places a premium on customer retention. Retention can be achieved by offering special benefits to loyal customers, effectively rewarding and thanking them for business in the past, and providing an incentive for continued business in the future. In this ad, CitiAAdvantage differentiates its rewards program from other programs by pointing out that there are no blackout dates on award seats.

British Airways (www.britishairways.com) prides itself on its commitment to excellent service and comfort. This is reflected by the attention it gives to passengers of every travel class. From the economy class World Traveller to the elite Concorde passenger, BA's mission is to ensure a comfortable and enjoyable voyage with upgraded amenities for everyone's pleasure.

- *Accountable relationship.* The salesperson phones customers shortly after the sale to check whether the product meets expectations and asks for product improvement suggestions and any specific disappointments. This information helps the company to continuously improve its offering (Acura dealers).
- *Proactive relationship.* The salesperson or company contacts customers from time to time with suggestions about improved product use or helpful new products (Nextel).
- *Partnership.* The company works continuously with customers (and other stakeholders) to discover ways to deliver better value (Nordstrom's Personal Shopper).[32]

Different stakeholders require different types of relationships. The relationship a company seeks with a customer will rarely be the same as it seeks with the press. However, there is often significant overlap in stakeholder roles. An employee may also be a customer and own stock in the company. Knowing intimately the customers and stakeholders is critical to the success of relationship marketing.

The number of stakeholders is also important. The more there are, the more difficult it is to develop an extensive personal relationship with each. Moreover, some customers may not want anything more than a transactional relationship.[33] Most people wouldn't want a phone call from Oscar Mayer asking if the hot dogs tasted good or from Gillette asking about the smoothness of their last shave. However, when Coca-Cola changed its formula in the early 1980s, legions of Coke loyalists besieged the company with angry letters and phone calls. They believed their relationship with the brand had been violated. The company quickly brought back Classic Coke. Clearly, therefore, brand relationships can be psychological or symbolic as well as personal, and they can be created by brand promotion, publicity, and advertising as well as by people.

Realizing this, Mountain Dew places a great deal of emphasis on creating a "Dew-x-perience" for its customers. Using guerilla-marketing tactics to reach out to urban youth, it employs a variety of hip-hop and Latin recording artists in various "street marketing" efforts to distribute bottles of Dew. It also sponsors extreme athletes and appears at sporting events such as the Gravity Games and ESPN's X Games with vans full of merchandise and giveaways.[34]

The final consideration is the profit margin. High-profit product or service categories make deeper, personal relationships more desirable (see Exhibit 8–3). Low profit margins per customer suggest that the marketer should pursue basic transactional relationships augmented by brand image advertising.[35]

Exhibit 8–3

Relationship levels as a function of profit margin and number of customers.

Profit margins

	High	Medium	Low
Many	Accountable	Reactive	Basic
Medium	Proactive	Accountable	Basic
Few	Partnership	Accountable	Reactive

Number of customers

Using IMC to Make Relationships Work

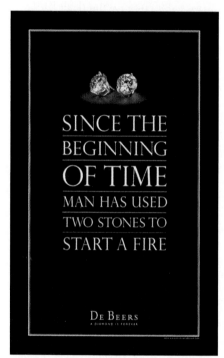

Product messages, which are often implied by the various aspects of the product, price, and distribution elements of the marketing mix, can assist in providing an overall image for a product or service. Advertising, as a planned message, helps convey the product message. Therefore, it is important for companies to create ads that are consistent with the desired product message and to select the appropriate media to carry the ad. Over the years, DeBeers has consistently created planned messages of elegance and romance through its famous "A diamond is forever" campaign. To learn more about this interesting advertiser, check out the DeBeers website (www.adiamondisforever.com).

This interest in relationship marketing coincided with the interest in *integrated marketing communications* (IMC). In fact, according to Northwestern professor Don Schultz, IMC is what makes relationship marketing possible.[36]

The link is *interdependence,* the fundamental characteristic of all relationships. As Drake University professor Lou Wolter points out, "IMC is the management of interdependence in the marketplace."[37]

IMC: The Concept and the Process

Technology has enabled marketers to adopt flexible manufacturing, customizing products for customized markets. "Market driven" today means bundling more services together with products to create a "unique product experience." It means companies and customers working together to find solutions.[38]

The counterpart to flexible manufacturing is flexible marketing—and integrated marketing communications—to reach customers at different levels in new and better ways.

IMC is both a concept and a process. The *concept* of integration is *wholeness.* Achieving this wholeness in communications creates *synergy*—the principal benefit of IMC—because each element of the communications mix reinforces the others for greater effect.[39]

For example, when a Mountain Dew grocer runs an **endcap promotion** (a special display at the end of an aisle) alone, it might generate a 10 percent increase in volume. If he runs an ad for Dew with a coupon, that might deliver a 15 percent increase. But running both together might grow volume by 35 percent. That's synergy—because the whole is greater than the sum of its parts.

Tom Duncan, director of the IMC program at the University of Denver, points out that IMC is also a *process* in which communication becomes the driving, integrating force in the marketing mix and throughout the organization.

The Evolution of the IMC Concept

As discussed in Chapter 2, with the phenomenal technological changes in the last decade came a host of specialized media and the fragmentation of the mass market. At the same time we witnessed a flood of mergers and acquisitions, the ascension of the global marketplace, the escalation of competition between various internal departments and external suppliers, and the arrival of more sophisticated, critical, and demanding customers. Suddenly, companies faced costly redundancies and inefficiencies as company departments with different missions and agendas all sought to achieve their particular goals, often at odds with either corporate or customer needs. For efficiency, companies needed to coordinate the multiplicity of inconsistent company and product messages being issued.[40]

Many companies initially took a narrow, *inside-out* view of IMC. They saw it as a way to coordinate and manage their marketing communications (advertising, sales promotion, public relations, personal selling, and direct marketing) to give the audience a consistent message about the company.[41]

A broader, more sophisticated, *outside-in* perspective of IMC sees customers as partners in an ongoing relationship, recognizes the references they use, acknowledges the importance of the whole communications system, and accepts the many ways they come into contact with the company or the brand. Companies committed to IMC realize their biggest asset is not their products or their plants or even their employees, but their customers.[42] Defined broadly,

> **Integrated marketing communications** is the process of building and reinforcing mutually profitable relationships with employees, customers, other stakeholders, and the general public by developing and coordinating a strategic communications program that enables them to have a constructive encounter with the company/brand through a variety of media or other contacts.

Whether a company employs the narrow view or the broad view depends to a great extent on its corporate culture. Some companies enjoyed rapid growth and strong customer relationships because they intuitively integrated and focused all corporate and marketing activities. Saturn, Apple, Honda, Nike, and Banana Republic are just a few.

Tom Duncan identified four distinct levels of integration that companies use: unified image, consistent voice, good listener, and at the most integrated, world-class citizen (see Exhibit 8–4). These levels demonstrate how IMC programs range from narrowly focused corporate monologues to broad, interactive dialogues, resulting in a corporate culture that permeates an organization and drives everything it does, internally and externally.[43]

How the Customer Sees Marketing Communications

To truly understand IMC, we have to look through the customer's eyes. In one study, consumers identified 102 different media as "advertising"—everything from TV to shopping bags to sponsored community events.[44] Customers also develop perceptions of the company or brand through a variety of other sources: news reports, word-of-mouth, gossip, experts' opinions, financial reports, and even the CEO's personality.

All these communications or brand contacts, sponsored or not, create an *integrated product* in the consumer's mind.[45] In other words, customers automatically integrate all the brand-related messages that emanate from the company or some other source. The way they integrate those messages determines their perception of the company. IMC gives companies a better opportunity to manage or influence those perceptions and create a superior relationship with those stakeholders.

Exhibit 8–4
Levels of integration.

Level	Name	Description/focus	Examples
1	Unified image	One look, one voice; strong brand image focus	3M
2	Consistent voice	Consistent tone and look; coordinated messages to various audiences (customers, trade, suppliers, etc.)	Hallmark, Coca-Cola
3	Good listener	Solicits two-way communication, enabling feedback through toll-free numbers, surveys, trade shows, etc.; focus on long-term relationships	Gateway, Saturn
4	World-class citizen	Social, environmental consciousness, strong company culture; focus on wider community	Ben & Jerry's, Apple, Honda

The Four Sources of Brand Messages

To influence customers' perceptions, marketers must understand one of the basic premises of IMC: that *everything we do (and don't do) sends a message*. That is to say, every corporate activity has a message component. Duncan categorized four types of company/brand-related messages stakeholders receive: *planned, product, service,* and *unplanned*. Each of these influences a stakeholder's relationship decision, so marketers must know where these messages originate, what effect they have, and the costs to influence or control them.

1. *Planned messages.* These are the traditional marketing communication messages—advertising, sales promotion, personal selling, merchandising materials, publicity releases, event sponsorships. These often have the *least* impact because they are seen as self-serving. They may also include help-wanted or financial offering ads, engineering articles in professional journals, and new contract announcements. Planned messages should be coordinated to work toward a predetermined set of communications objectives. This is the most fundamental aspect of IMC.

2. *Product messages.* In IMC theory, every element of the marketing mix sends a message. Messages from the product, price, or distribution elements are typically referred to as product (or inferred) messages. For example, customers and other stakeholders receive one product message from a $2,500 Rolex watch and a totally different one from a $30 Timex. Product messages also include packaging, which communicates a lot about the product through the use of color, type fonts, imagery, design, and layout.

   Product messages have great impact. When a product performs well, the customer infers a positive message that reinforces the purchase decision. However, a gap between the product's performance and advertised promises is likely to convey a negative message. Managers must realize that marketing mix decisions are also communication decisions.

3. *Service messages.* Many messages result from employee interactions with customers. In many organizations, customer service people are supervised by operations, not marketing. Yet the service messages they send have greater marketing impact than the planned messages. With IMC, marketing people work with operations to minimize negative messages and maximize positive ones.

4. *Unplanned messages.* Companies have little or no control over the unplanned messages that emanate from employee gossip, unsought news stories, comments by the trade or competitors, word-of-mouth rumors, or major disasters. Unplanned messages may affect customers' attitudes dramatically, but they can sometimes be anticipated and influenced, especially by managers experienced in public relations.[46]

The Integration Triangle

The integration triangle developed by Duncan and Moriarty is a simple illustration of how perceptions are created from the various brand message sources (see Exhibit 8–5). Planned messages are *say* messages, what companies say about themselves. Product and service messages are *do* messages because they represent what a company does. Unplanned messages are *confirm* messages because that's what others say and confirm (or not) about what the company says and does. Constructive integration occurs when a brand does what its maker says it will do and then others confirm that it delivers on its promises.[47]

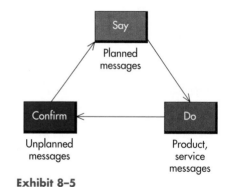

Exhibit 8–5

The integration triangle.

The Dimensions of IMC

To maximize the synergy benefits of IMC, Duncan suggests three dimensions to an organization's integration process. It should first ensure consistent positioning, then facilitate purposeful interactivity between the company and its customers or other stakeholders, and finally actively incorporate a socially responsible mission into the organization's relationships with its stakeholders.

As Duncan's IMC macro model shows in Exhibit 8–6, the cross-functional planning and monitoring of IMC activities results in an enhanced relationship with customers and other stakeholders, which leads to stakeholder loyalty and ultimately to greater brand equity.[48] See RL 8–2 in the Reference Library on the *Contemporary Advertising* student CD for more details on this model.

The interest in IMC is already global, moving from North America to Europe, Asia, and Latin America.[49] The $38 billion Swiss company Nestlé, for example, used a variety of IMC strategies, such as building highway rest stops for feeding and changing babies, designed to establish deep, caring relationships between families and the Nestlé Baby Foods division in France.[50]

In short, IMC offers accountability by maximizing resources and linking communications activities directly to organizational goals and the resulting bottom line.[51]

The IMC Approach to Marketing and Advertising Planning

Integrated marketing communications suggest a new approach to planning marketing and communications activities. It differs substantially from the traditional process by mixing marketing and communications planning together rather than separating them. Using the outside-in process, the IMC approach starts with the customer. Marketers study what media customers use, the relevance of their message to the customers, and when customers and prospects are most *receptive* to the message. They begin with the customer and work back to the brand.[52]

Thanks to computer technology, marketers of mass merchandise now have a wealth of information at their fingertips. With supermarket scanner data, for instance, packaged-goods marketers can (1) identify specific users of products and services; (2) measure their actual purchase behavior and relate it to specific brand and product categories; (3) measure the impact of various advertising and marketing communications activities and determine their value in influencing the actual purchase; and (4) capture and evaluate this information over time.[53]

This ever-expanding database of customer behavior can be the basis for planning all future marketing and communications activities, especially if the database contains information on customer demographics, psychographics, purchase data, and brand or product category attitudes (see Exhibit 8–7).

Starting the whole planning process with the database forces the company to focus on the consumer, or prospect, not on the company's sales or profit goals. These marketing objectives are moved farther down in the planning process.[54]

Exhibit 8–6
IMC macro model.

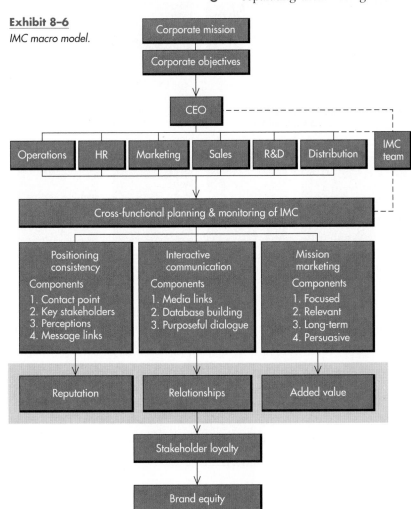

Exhibit 8–7

Wang-Schultz IMC planning model.

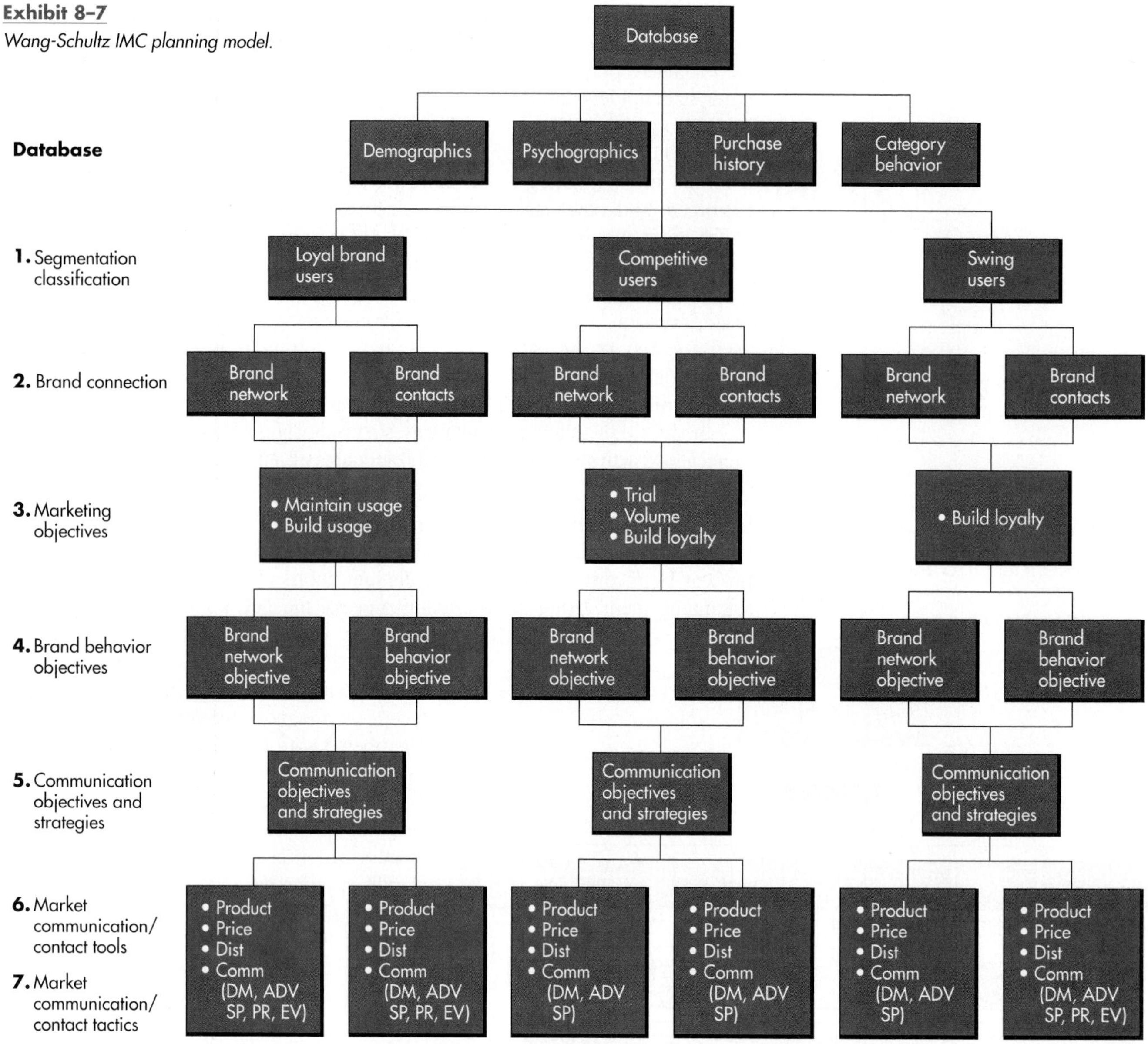
Database
Database
Demographics
Psychographics
Purchase history
Category behavior
1. Segmentation classification
Loyal brand users
Competitive users
Swing users
2. Brand connection
Brand network
Brand contacts
Brand network
Brand contacts
Brand network
Brand contacts
3. Marketing objectives
• Maintain usage
• Build usage
• Trial
• Volume
• Build loyalty
• Build loyalty
4. Brand behavior objectives
Brand network objective
Brand behavior objective
Brand network objective
Brand behavior objective
Brand network objective
Brand behavior objective
5. Communication objectives and strategies
Communication objectives and strategies
Communication objectives and strategies
Communication objectives and strategies
6. Market communication/ contact tools
7. Market communication/ contact tactics
• Product • Price • Dist • Comm (DM, ADV SP, PR, EV)
• Product • Price • Dist • Comm (DM, ADV SP, PR, EV)
• Product • Price • Dist • Comm (DM, ADV SP)
• Product • Price • Dist • Comm (DM, ADV SP)
• Product • Price • Dist • Comm (DM, ADV SP)
• Product • Price • Dist • Comm (DM, ADV SP, PR, EV)

DM = Direct marketing ADV = Advertising SP = Sales promotion PR = Public relations EV = Event marketing
Dist = Distribution Comm = Marketing communications

Wang and Schultz developed a seven-step IMC planning model. The first step segments the customers and prospects in the database—either by brand loyalty, as illustrated, or by some other measurable purchase behavior (heavy usage, for instance).

The second step analyzes the information on customers to understand their attitudes, their history, and how they enter into contact with the brand or product—in other words, determining the best time, place, and situation to communicate with them.

Next, the planner sets marketing objectives based on this analysis. In the illustrated example, these objectives relate to building and maintaining usage or nurturing brand loyalty.

The marketer then identifies what brand contacts and what changes in attitude are required to support the consumer's continuance or change of purchase behavior.

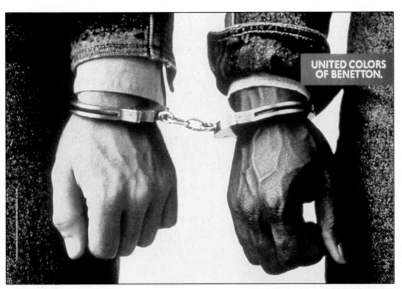

Companies have control over their advertising, but they must be careful about any unplanned messages they may inadvertently engender. Over the years, the fashion designer Benetton (www.Benetton.com) has developed a number of highly controversial ads addressing social issues. However, much like Calvin Klein, Benetton has suffered criticism for its advertising. In this case, critics blasted the company for trying to gain publicity by exploiting human suffering. Benetton's ad was actually a statement against the war in the Balkans. Criticism, of course, is just one kind of unplanned message. Good word-of-mouth is another. In both cases, the company has little control over these kinds of messages.

The fifth step sets communications objectives and strategies for making contact with the consumer and influencing his or her attitudes, beliefs, and purchase behavior. The marketer can then decide what other elements of the marketing mix (product, price, distribution) can be used to further encourage the desired behavior.

Finally, the planner determines what communications tactics to use—media advertising, direct marketing, publicity, sales promotion, special events—to make further contact and influence the consumer's behavior.[55]

By following this model, the marketer sets objectives based on an understanding of the needs of the customer or prospect and of what must be communicated. All forms of marketing are thus turned into communication, and all forms of communication into marketing.[56]

The Importance of IMC to the Study of Advertising

Because customers see all sponsored communications as advertising, advertising people (account managers, creatives, media planners) must grow beyond their traditional specialty to become enlightened generalists, familiar with and able to integrate all types of marketing communications.

In a survey of 122 *Fortune* 500 marketing, advertising, and communications executives, most respondents indicated a general understanding of IMC and agreed that synergy is the key benefit of integrated marketing.[57] However, the study also showed that confusion remains among professionals concerning IMC use. This suggests that most practitioners today still lack the broad knowledge required to develop, supervise, and execute full IMC programs.[58]

The Advertising Plan

The **advertising plan** is a natural outgrowth of the marketing plan and is prepared in much the same way. In IMC planning, though, the advertising plan is an integral part of the overall procedure. Appendix B at the end of the book outlines a top-down advertising plan, and an IMC plan outline can be found on the *Contemporary Advertising* website.

Reviewing the Marketing Plan

The advertising manager first reviews the marketing plan to understand where the company is going, how it intends to get there, and what role advertising plays in the marketing mix. The first section of the advertising plan should organize information from the marketing plan's situation analysis into four categories: internal *strengths* and *weaknesses* and external *opportunities* and *threats* (SWOT). This **SWOT analysis** briefly restates the company's current situation, reviews the target market segments, itemizes the long- and short-term marketing objectives, and cites decisions regarding market positioning and the marketing mix.

Setting Advertising Objectives

The advertising manager then determines what tasks advertising must take on. What strengths and opportunities can be leveraged? What weaknesses and threats need to be addressed? Unfortunately, some corporate executives (and advertising managers) state vague goals for advertising, like "increasing sales and maximizing profits by creating a favorable impression of the product in the marketplace." When this happens, no one understands what the advertising is intended to do,

Heinz (www.heinz.com) is well established as the leading ketchup brand, so the company's annual advertising expenditures are less than $25 million for its flagship product. In 2003, the company spent more than ten times that amount to generate awareness and interest in newly launched varieties like its hot ketchup. This campaign, from Leo Burnett's Lisbon office, attracted critical acclaim and earned a Cannes Bronze Lion, but could not sustain interest in specialty condiments. In 2004, sales were down 30 percent from 2003 levels.

Exhibit 8–8

The advertising pyramid depicts the progression of advertising effects on mass audiences—especially for new products. The initial message promotes awareness of the product to a large audience (the base of the pyramid). But only a percentage of this large group will comprehend the product's benefits. Of that group, even fewer will go on to feel conviction about, then desire for the product. In the end, compared with the number of people aware of the product, the number of people who take action is usually quite small.

how much it will cost, or how to measure the results. Advertising objectives should be specific, realistic, and measurable.

Understanding What Advertising Can Do

Most advertising programs encourage prospects to take some action. However, it is usually unrealistic to assign advertising the whole responsibility for achieving sales. Sales goals are marketing objectives, not advertising objectives. Before an advertiser can persuade customers to buy, it must inform, persuade, or remind its intended audience about the company, product, service, or issue. A simple adage to remember when setting objectives is "Marketing sells, advertising tells." In other words, advertising objectives should be related to communication effects.

The Advertising Pyramid: A Guide to Setting Objectives

Suppose you're advertising a new brand in a new product category, but you're not sure what kind of results to expect. The pyramid in Exhibit 8–8 shows some of the tasks advertising can perform. Obviously, before your product is introduced, prospective customers are completely unaware of it. Your first communication objective therefore is to create *awareness*—to acquaint people with the company, product, service, and/or brand.

The next task might be to develop *comprehension*—to communicate enough information about the product such that some percentage of the aware group recognizes the product's purpose, image, or position, and perhaps some of its features.

Next, you need to communicate enough information to develop *conviction*—to persuade a certain number of people to actually believe in the product's value. Once convinced, some people may be moved to *desire* the product. Finally, some percentage of those who desire the product will take *action*. They may request additional information, send in a coupon, visit a store, or actually buy the product.

The pyramid works in three dimensions: time, dollars, and people. Advertising results may take time, especially if the product is expensive or not purchased regularly. Over time, as a company continues advertising, the number of people who become aware of the product increases. As more people comprehend the product, believe in it, and desire it, more take the final action of buying it.

Let's apply these principles to a hypothetical case. Suppose you are in charge of advertising for the new "Lightning Bug," a hybrid car built by Volkswagen that runs on both gasoline and electricity. Your initial advertising objectives for this fictional car might read as follows:

1. Within two years, communicate the existence of the Lightning Bug to half of the more than 500,000 people who annually buy foreign economy cars.
2. Inform two-thirds of this "aware" group that the Lightning Bug is a superior economy car with many design, safety, and environmentally friendly features; that it is a brand new nameplate backed with unmatched service, quality, and value; and that it is sold only through dedicated Volkswagen dealers.

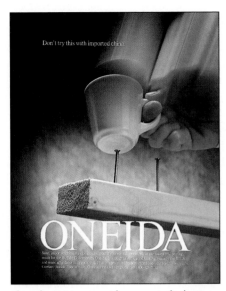

The advertising pyramid represents the learn-feel-do model of advertising effects. Oneida (www.oneida.com), for instance, is renowned for its quality glassware and china. It uses the learn-feel-do approach in this ad, where consumers learn about the resiliency of the porcelain, feel positively about the durability, and fulfill the do element by visiting the store and/or purchasing the product.

3. Convince two-thirds of the "informed" group that the Lightning Bug is a high-quality car, reliable, economical, and fun to drive.

4. Stimulate desire within two-thirds of the "convinced" group for a test drive.

5. Motivate two-thirds of the "desire" group to visit a retailer for a test drive.

These advertising objectives are specific as to time and degree and are quantified like marketing objectives. Theoretically, at the end of the first year, a consumer attitude study could determine how many people are aware of the Lightning Bug, how many people understand the car's primary features, and so on, thus measuring the program's effectiveness.

Volkswagen's advertising may accomplish the objectives of creating awareness, comprehension, conviction, desire, and action. But once the customer is in the store, it's the retailer's responsibility to close the sale with effective selling and service.

With the advent of integrated marketing communications, we can look at the pyramid in another way. By using a variety of marketing communication tools and a wide menu of traditional and nontraditional media, we can accomplish the communication objectives suggested by the pyramid in a more efficient manner. For instance, for creating sheer awareness for the new Lightning Bug as well as brand image for the car and the company, an intensive program of public relations activities supported by mass media advertising would be the communication tools of choice. Comprehension, interest, and credibility can be augmented by media advertising, press publicity, direct-mail brochures, and special events such as a sports car show. Desire can be enhanced by a combination of the buzz created by good reviews in car enthusiast magazines, plus media advertising, beautiful brochure photography, and the excitement generated by a sales promotion (such as a sweepstakes). Finally, action can be stimulated by direct mail solicitation, sales promotion, and the attentive service of a retail salesperson in an attractive new car showroom. Following the sale, media advertising should continue to reinforce the purchase decision. But at the same time, outbound telemarketing calls from the retailer can be used to thank the customer, solicit feedback on that customer's experience, and offer any needed assistance. This acknowledges that the sale was just the beginning of a valuable relationship.

The Old Model versus the New

The advertising pyramid represents the *learn-feel-do* model of advertising effects. That is, it assumes that people rationally consider a prospective purchase, and once they feel good about it, they act. The theory is that advertising affects attitude, and attitude leads to behavior. That may be true for certain expensive, high-involvement products that require a lot of consideration. But other purchases may follow a different pattern. For example, impulse purchases at the checkout counter may involve a *do-feel-learn* model, in which behavior leads to attitude. Other purchases may follow some other pattern. Thus, there are many marketing considerations when advertising objectives are being set, and they must be thought out carefully (see RL 8–3, Checklist for Developing Advertising Objectives, in the Reference Library on the *Contemporary Advertising* CD).

The advertising pyramid also reflects the traditional mass-marketing monologue. The advertiser talks and the customer listens.[59] That was appropriate before the advent of computers and databases, and it may still be appropriate in those categories where the marketer has no choice.

But today, as the IMC model shows, many marketers have databases of information on their customers, about where they live, what they buy, and what they like and dislike. When marketers can have a dialogue and establish a relationship,

Exhibit 8–9

Messages go to the customer through advertising and other communication channels. Messages come back via direct response, surveys, and a purchase behavior database. The marketer's message can evolve based on this feedback.

the model is no longer a pyramid but a circle (see Exhibit 8–9). Consumers and business customers can send messages back to the marketer in the form of coupons, phone calls, surveys, and database information on purchases. With interactive media, the responses are in real time. This feedback can help the marketer's product, service, and messages evolve.[60] And reinforcement advertising, designed to build brand loyalty, will remind people of their successful experience with the product and suggest reuse.

By starting with the customer and then integrating all aspects of their marketing communications—package and store design, personal selling, advertising, public relations activities, special events, and sales promotions—companies hope to accelerate the communications process, make it more efficient, and achieve lasting loyalty from *good* prospects, not just prospects.[61]

Advertising Strategy and the Creative Mix

The advertising (or communications) *objective* declares where the advertiser wants to be with respect to consumer awareness, attitude, and preference; the advertising (or creative) *strategy* describes how to get there.

Advertising strategy blends the elements of the **creative mix:** *target audience, product concept, communications media,* and *advertising message.*

The Target Audience: Everyone Who Should Know

The **target audience,** the specific people the advertising will address, is typically larger than the target market. Advertisers need to know who the end user is, who makes the purchase, and who influences the purchasing decision. Children, for example, often exert a strong influence on where the family eats. So while McDonald's target market is adults, its target audience also includes children, and it spends much of its advertising budget on campaigns directed at kids.

Similarly, while companies may target heavy users of a product, many light and nonusers are exposed to the advertising as well. That's good, because research shows that brand popularity (which advertising is uniquely good at creating) cuts across all levels of purchasing frequency.[62] The dominant brands are purchased the most by both heavy and light users (see Exhibit 8–10). It's the accumulation of all these sales that makes a product the dominant brand.

The Product Concept: Presenting the Product

The "bundle of values" the advertiser presents to the consumer is the **product concept.** General Motors markets essentially the same truck to two different audiences but presents two different product concepts. The Silverado is marketed to the vast middle class with ads that stress its rugged, macho durability. Advertising for the Sierra truck, on the other hand, is aimed at white-collar professionals and emphasizes the vehicle's snob appeal.[63]

When writing the advertising plan, the advertising manager must develop a simple statement to describe the

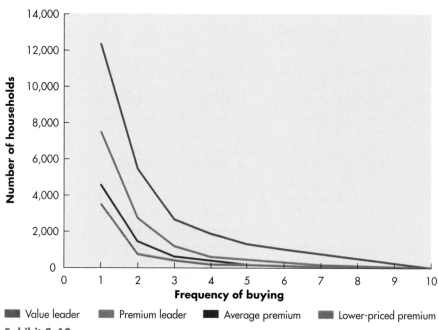

Exhibit 8–10

Brand popularity. Dominant brands are the most popular at each level of purchasing frequency.

Affective involvement (Feel)

	Low	High
High	College • • Video camera • Motor oil	• Car • Shampoo • Skin lotion
Low	• Laundry detergent • Paper towels	Greeting card • • Pizza • Bread

Cognitive involvement (Think)

Exhibit 8–11

The Kim-Lord grid.

product concept—that is, how the advertising will present the product. To create this statement, the advertiser first considers how consumers perceive the product and then weighs this against the company's marketing strategy.

Recall from Chapter 5 our discussion of the Elaboration Likelihood Model and the role of involvement with the product message. Some years ago, Richard Vaughn at Foote, Cone & Belding noted that different kinds of products typically evoke different levels of consumer involvement (either high or low) and different types of involvement, either *cognitive* (think) or *affective* (feel). This meant different products called for different kinds of advertising. He created a two-dimensional model known as the FCB grid, which categorized consumer products into four quadrants based on "high involvement" or "low involvement," and "think" or "feel." By positioning brands in the grid based on the degree and type of involvement consumers brought to the purchase decision, the agency could determine which type of advertising would be most appropriate. Rossiter and Percy extended this research with the grid you saw in Exhibit 5–4, which also suggested different creative executions.

More recently, Kim and Lord recognized that people can be both cognitively and affectively involved at the same time. So they developed the enhanced Kim-Lord grid, shown in Exhibit 8–11. It too depicts the degree and the kind of involvement a consumer brings to the purchase decision for different products. Some purchases, like cars, require a high degree of personal involvement on both the cognitive and affective levels.[64] For others, like detergent, involvement is low on both axes. Sometimes a marketer uses an advertising strategy aimed at shifting the product to higher involvement on either axis. A product's location on the grid also indicates how the product is purchased (learn-feel-do or feel-learn-do) and how advertising copy should be written (more emotional or more rational).[65]

Pepsi marketers view Mountain Dew as a high-involvement purchase on both the cognitive and affective scale. "We continually need to give people a reason to pick us up," says one executive, "because we're not an obvious substitute [for cola]. People make a conscious choice to consume Mountain Dew, so we push to keep the positioning pure."[66]

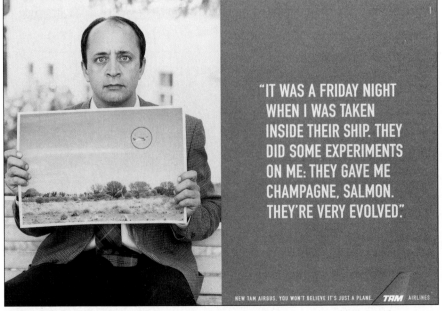

The product concept embodies the sum total of values that customers receive from a product or service. It can also be used for product differentiation. While many airlines provide suitable transportation, TAM Airlines tries to differentiate its product concept by implying that its quality of service is so high it's foreign to this planet.

The Communications Media: The Message Delivery System

As an element of creative strategy, the **communications media** are all the vehicles that might transmit the advertiser's message. They include traditional media such as radio, TV, newspapers, magazines, billboards, plus the Internet, and, in an integrated communications program, direct marketing, public relations, special events, sales promotion, and personal selling.

Marketers at Mountain Dew use a variety of media to create a special environment for the product. This means not only advertising the product on mainstream media and sampling the product at sporting events but also creating the particular environment that the consumer wants for drinking the Dew. For example, Mountain Dew has used Hummers, radio stations, computer game demos, and extreme athletes to be part of the experience. In the summer of 2000, they decked out a subway car with "Do the Dew" memorabilia and hauled it around the country to major youth-oriented events where they passed out branded premiums such as snowboards, gear, and T-shirts—all relevant to the target market.

While balancing Dew on both ends of the grass-roots and mass-appeal spectrum, Pepsi marketers realize that not all teens are into alternative sports. The onetime hillbilly drink is now also moving toward African-American and Latino youth. Endorsement deals with artists such as Busta Rhymes and professional snowboarder Ben Hinkley allow the Dew to appeal to the fast growing ethnic market—which also coincides with the regional urban markets targeted by Dew.[67] "Mountain Dew is a brand whose core is inextricably linked to a pervasive human need for fun and exhilaration," says one executive. "That basic need has not changed over time, so we have to stick with that and be as current and leading edge as possible."[68]

The Advertising Message: What the Advertising Communicates

What the company plans to say in its ads and how it plans to say it, both verbally and nonverbally, make up the **advertising message.** As we discuss in Chapter 12, the combination of copy, art, and production elements forms the message, and there are infinite ways to combine these elements (see Portfolio Review, "Strategic Use of the Creative Mix").

Dew personifies its product concept not only through events, but via a team of 10 extreme athletes, each representing a sport more daring than the next. That same attitude is passed on to Dew advertising. With longtime agency BBDO helping the brand stay true to its youthful feel, its campaigns have an edginess and audacity not typically associated with the big cola companies. In one of the brand's Super Bowl commercials, a Dew Dude on a bicycle chases down a cheetah and wrestles it to the ground. Reaching into the cat's mouth, he retrieves a stolen can of Dew.

"Bad cheetah," he says.

The ad was the second-highest rated commercial of the 2000 Super Bowl broadcast. In another highly rated spot, the Dew Dudes did a spoof version of the Queen classic "Bohemian Rhapsody." A third popular commercial, called "Showstoppers," featured choreographed mountain bikes in a spectacular extravaganza

There are many ways to deliver a message besides using traditional media. In keeping with its theme of fun and adventure, Mountain Dew traveled around the country in a colorful subway car that was packed with all kinds of treats and memorabilia given away at key events.

reminiscent of a 1930's MGM musical, with the Dew Dudes playing the role of directors. According to *USA Today,* teenagers loved the spot. "Retro is in with teens," said Dawn Hudson, senior vice president of marketing for Pepsi-Cola North America. "We try to see things through the eyes of a teenager, and that's full of energy and exhilaration. Besides the brand can't keep relying on skateboarding high jinks. Mountain Dew should always have a fresh perspective on things. It can't be cookie cutter."[69]

Ted Sanns, the chief creative director at BBDO says, "The idea is to evolve the campaign—take it to the next plateau."[70]

The sales numbers point to the obvious—it's working. Moreover, the campaign has long legs—"Do the Dew" is now the longest-running continuous campaign in the soft-drink category.

The Secret to Successful Planning

Whether the advertiser is a large corporation or a small company, the key to successful planning is information. But the genius of business is in interpreting what the information means. This leads to direction, which makes planning easier and more rewarding.

Allocating Funds for Advertising

In the early 1990s, after eight years of unprecedented growth, the United States and Canada experienced the first throes of a recession. Interest rates rose, real estate sales dropped, construction of new homes slowed, defense spending was cut, and unemployment began to rise. To make matters worse, threats of war in the Persian Gulf caused fear of higher fuel prices. Consumer confidence declined, and with it sank retail sales.

As sales dropped, many executives cut back their marketing communication budgets, some to zero. Two years later, when the government announced the recession was over, these executives wondered why sales were still down and how their companies had lost so much market share.

Money is the motor that drives every marketing and advertising plan. If you suddenly shut the motor off, the car may coast for a while, but before long it will stop running. The marketing department has the tough job of convincing top management that communication spending makes good business sense, even during adverse economic conditions.

Advertising: An Investment in Future Sales

Accountants and the Internal Revenue Service consider advertising a current business expense. Consequently, many executives treat advertising as a budget item to be trimmed or eliminated like other expense items when sales are either extremely high or extremely low. This is understandable but frequently shortsighted.

The cost of a new plant or distribution warehouse is an investment in the company's future ability to produce and distribute products. Similarly, advertising—as one element of the communication mix—is an investment in future sales. While advertising is often used to stimulate immediate sales, its greatest power is in its cumulative, long-range, reinforcement effect.[71]

Advertising builds consumer preference and promotes goodwill. This, in turn, enhances the reputation and value of the company name and brand. And it encourages customers to make repeat purchases.

So while advertising is a current expense for accounting purposes, it is also a long-term capital investment. For management to see advertising as an investment, however, it must understand how advertising relates to sales and profits. *(continued on page 259)*

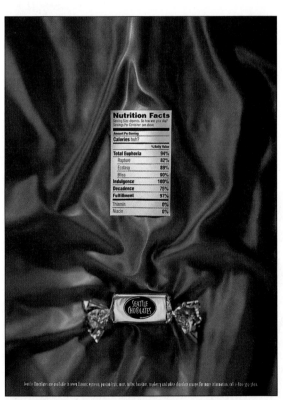

The advertising message represents what a company plans to say about its product and how it plans to say it. The advertising message for Seattle Chocolates (www.seattlechocolate.com) is that its candies provide sweet tooth decadence and gratification to consumers willing to indulge themselves for a moment. The "how" is through tongue-in-cheek humor by parodying the nutritional facts label on other food products.

During the marketing and advertising planning process, companies need to carefully consider who their target markets are and then who should be the targets of their advertising. They also need to consider the other elements of advertising strategy. This brings up a lot of questions: what product concept are we trying to communicate; what various media will be used to communicate the message; and what should the nature of our advertising message be? Once these things are decided, the creative team can begin its work.

■ The ads in this portfolio demonstrate some good creative thinking, but more important, some outstanding strategic thinking. See if you can determine which element(s) of the creative mix is emphasized in each ad.

Strategic Use of the Creative Mix

Diesel has been very successful with its postmodern, pop-culture aesthetic; its brand of highly stylized, slightly ironic, and often absurd ad messaging speaks directly to the company's mostly young, hip target market. To see an interesting and interactive element of this campaign, which won a Bronze Lion at Cannes, visit www.diesel.com/naturelovers.

The Internet can be a powerful medium when used correctly. The hugely successful campaign for a Swedish brand of milk, Fjallfil, featured a cow striving to make it as a rock star (www.fjallfil.com). Visitors customized music videos featuring the cow. The Swedish version of the website had more than 100,000 visitors the first month. Today, more than two million people have visited it.

This FedEx TV spot was part of a campaign that produced laughs and a Cannes Gold Lion for BBDO New York. Cheerless gray offices and unglamorous employees create continuity between spots and clear the path for FedEx's services to shine. In this spot a poorly disguised alien outshines his coworkers to the dismay of his all-too-human colleagues.

(A large alien is seated at a desk. Pasted to his head is a photograph of a man's head. We can see his tentacles and tail. Two office workers enter the room.)

EMPLOYEE 1: Jenkins, got a minute? Listen Jenkins, we're on to you. We know you're an alien.

EMPLOYEE 2: Admit it. You're just here studying our species.

JENKINS: Why don't we use FedEx?

EMPLOYEE 1: Ha. That's all you ever say. We're not buying it.

EMPLOYEE 2: C'mon, it's so obvious.

JENKINS: Why don't we use FedEx?

EMPLOYEE 1: Ach, give it up. It's over.

(Boss enters office)

BOSS: Jenkins we got a ton of packages to ship and we're in serious trouble. Any ideas?

JENKINS: Why don't we use FedEx?

BOSS: Good thinking Jenkins. You two back to work.

SUPER: FedEx. It's all you need to know.

Just as with consumer advertising, business-to-business ads must also target a specific audience. These ads generally provide the target audience (other businesses) with valuable information about certain products or services, as seen in this example from MTV International. Who is the target audience for this ad and how does it appeal to the audience's desires?

My pain is real.

I am the new guy. Was it a mistake to come here? Perhaps.

My peers ignore me. I don't get their jokes or references. I keep to myself.

Try not to make eye contact. Strangely, I have found comfort in data.

I am a fountain. I know everything about teenagers in every part of the world.

MTV International does not pay me enough for what I can do for you.

Call me. Pray for me.

Please advertise with MTV International.

"Mysteries/HVAC Financing" :50/10
Anncr.: If practice makes perfect and nobody's perfect, why practice? What's the speed of dark? If a rabbit foot's so lucky, what happened to the rabbit? Why do "fat chance" and "slim chance" mean the same thing? Before they invented drawing boards, what did the people go back to? If you're a complete pessimist, does that mean you're positively negative? And why would someone with questions about natural gas go anywhere but AtlantaGasLight.com? It has all the answers. You can even go there to find out how to get 9.9% financing on a new air conditioner and heating system. Plus have it delivered and installed by a certified Natural Gas Advantage Dealer. I mean, I wouldn't go there to find out why "phonetic" isn't spelled the way it sounds. But for questions about natural gas, it's the most reliable place to go. AtlantaGasLight.com. It's useful information.

According to the IMC model of advertising, every piece of communication with customers or other stakeholders will affect their relationship with a company. This even includes the selection of media. In their "Mysteries/HVAC Financing" campaign, the Atlanta Gas and Light Company chose to advertise over the radio. Why do you think this medium was chosen and what impact might it have had on consumers?

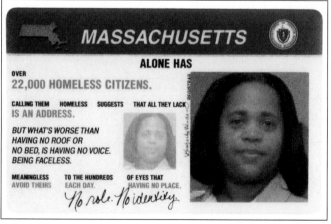

What a company plans to say in its ads and how it plans to say it constitute the advertising message. Both verbal and nonverbal communications are components of the advertising message, manifested in copy that can be happy-go-lucky or photos and illustrations that can exude excitement or perhaps even melancholy. What is the advertising message of this ad for the Friends of Boston's Homeless, and what does it communicate to the target audience?

(continued from page 255)

The Relationship of Advertising to Sales and Profits

Many variables, both internal and external, influence the effectiveness of a company's marketing and advertising efforts. Methods to measure the relationships between advertising and sales and between sales and profits are far from perfect. However, substantial research does support the following principles:

- In consumer goods marketing, increases in market share are closely related to increases in the marketing budget. And market share is a prime indicator of profitability.[72]

- Sales normally increase with additional advertising. At some point, however, the rate of return plateaus and then declines. (See Ad Lab 8–B, "The Economic Effect of Advertising on Sales.")

- Sales response to advertising may build over time, but the durability of advertising is brief, so a consistent investment is important.

- There are minimum levels below which advertising expenditures have no effect on sales.

- There will be some sales even if there is no advertising.

- Culture and competition impose saturation limits above which no amount of advertising can increase sales.

To management, these facts might mean: Spend more until it stops working. In reality, the issue isn't that simple. Advertising isn't the only marketing activity that affects sales. A change in market share may occur because of quality perceptions, word-of-mouth, the introduction of new products, competitive trade promotion, the opening of more attractive outlets, better personal selling, or seasonal changes in the business cycle.

Furthermore, most companies don't have a clear-cut way to determine the relationship between advertising and sales and profit. What if the company sells a variety of products? Which advertising contributes to which sales?

One thing remains clear. Because the response to advertising is spread out over an extended time, advertising should be viewed as a long-term investment in future profits. Like all expenditures, advertising should be evaluated for wastefulness. But

Although the relationship between advertising and sales can at times be difficult to ascertain, certain profit trends can be linked directly to the intensity and frequency of advertising. A locally based business like Classic Bi-Plane Rides (www.classicbiplanerides.com) can expect to have some sales even if it does not advertise—mostly through word-of-mouth. But advertising in a high-exposure medium like outdoor is likely to provide significant sales improvement. Local businesses are hit particularly hard during times of recession; but, if at all possible, they should maintain advertising levels to prevent losing market share over the long run.

The Economic Effect of Advertising on Sales

As a rule, the level of sales of a product is proportional to the level of advertising expenditure—that is, within reasonable limits the more you spend the more you sell (assuming the advertising program is not too repugnant). Yet, even the most enthusiastic ad agency will admit, reluctantly, that it is possible to spend too much.

Ideally, managers would like to know how much more they will be able to sell per additional dollar of advertising and when additional advertising dollars cease being effective. They need to have not a fixed number representing potential demand, but a graph or a statistical equation describing the relationship between sales and advertising.

In our illustration, most of the curve goes uphill as we move to the right (it has a *positive slope*). This means that additional advertising will continue to bring in business until (at a budget of x million dollars) people become so saturated by the message that it begins to repel them and turn them away from the product.

Even if the saturation level cannot be reached within the range of outlays the firm can afford, the curve is likely to level off, becoming flatter and flatter as the amount spent on advertising gets larger and larger and saturation is approached. The point at which the curve begins to flatten is the point at which returns from advertising begin to diminish.

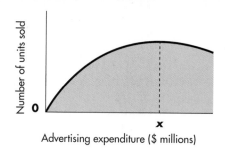

When the total advertising budget is small, even a $1 addition to the campaign may bring in as much as $10 in new sales. But when the market approaches saturation, each additional dollar may contribute only 30 cents in new sales, if any at all.

Laboratory Applications

1. When would an advertising expenditure curve have a negative slope?

2. Economists suggest that the quantity sold depends on the number of dollars the company spends on advertising. Is that a safe assumption? Discuss.

---

historically, companies that make advertising the scapegoat during tough times end up losing substantial market share before the economy starts growing again.[73]

The corollary is also true. Sustained ad spending during difficult times protects, and in some cases even increases, market share and builds brands. During the last global recession, the leading European marketers recognized this fact, and fewer than 40 percent of the top spenders in Italy, Austria, Germany, France, and Spain cut their budgets.[74]

The Variable Environments of Business

Before attempting to determine advertising allocations, the advertising manager must consider the company's economic, political, social, and legal situation. These factors affect total industry sales and corporate profits on sales. The manager must consider the institutional and competitive environments. What is the level of sales within the industry? How much are competitors spending, and what are they doing that might either help or hinder the company's marketing efforts?

Finally, the manager must consider the internal environment. Do the company's current policies and procedures allow it to fulfill the promises its advertising intends to make?

Methods of Allocating Funds

Most business executives will spend more money on advertising as long as they are assured it will mean more profit. However, the point of equilibrium is hard to predict when advertising budgets are being developed.

Companies use a number of methods to determine how much to spend on advertising, including the *percentage-of-sales, percentage-of-profit, unit-of-sale, competitive-parity, share-of-market,* and *objective/task methods* (see the Checklist, "Ways to Set Advertising Budgets").

No technique is adequate for all situations. The three methods discussed here are used primarily for national advertising budgets. However, local retailers can use them too.

Percentage-of-Sales Method

The **percentage-of-sales method** is one of the most popular techniques for setting advertising budgets. It may be based on a percentage of last year's sales, anticipated

Exhibit 8–12

Advertising expenditures by the top 15 advertisers in 2003 ($ millions).

Rank	Company	U.S. advertising expenditures	U.S. sales	Advertising as a percentage of U.S. sales
1	General Motors	$3,429.90	$133,897	2.6%
2	Procter & Gamble	3,322.70	21,853	15.2
3	Time Warner	3,097.30	32,123	9.6
4	Pfizer	2,838.50	26,844	10.6
5	DaimlerChrysler	2,137.50	72,814	3.0
6	Ford Motor Co.	2,233.80	103,435	2.2
7	Walt Disney Co.	2,129.30	22,124	9.6
8	Johnson & Johnson	1,995.70	25,274	7.9
9	Sony Corp.	1,814.80	20,727	8.8
10	Toyota Motor Corp.	1,682.70	52,323	3.2
11	Verizon Communications	1,674.20	65,303	2.6
12	Sears, Roebuck & Co.	1,633.60	36,643	4.5
13	General Electric Co.	1,575.70	84,795	1.9
14	GlaxoSmithKline	1,553.70	15,481	10.0
15	SBC Communications	1,551.00	40,843	3.8

sales for next year, or a combination of the two. Businesspeople like this method because it is the simplest, it doesn't cost them anything, it is related to revenue, and it is considered safe. The problem is knowing what percentage to use. As Exhibit 8–12 shows, even leaders in the same industry use different percentages. Across industries, they range from just 1.5 percent to more than 22 percent.

Usually the percentage is based on an industry average or on company experience. Unfortunately, it is too often determined arbitrarily. An industry average assumes that every company in the industry has similar objectives and faces the same marketing problems. Company experience assumes that the market is highly static, which is rarely the case.

However, when applied against future sales, this method often works well. It assumes that a certain number of dollars will be needed to sell a certain number of units. If the advertiser knows what the percentage is, the correlation between advertising and sales should remain constant, assuming the market is stable and competitors' advertising remains unchanged. And because this method is common in the industry, it diminishes the likelihood of competitive warfare.

The greatest shortcoming of the percentage-of-sales method is that it violates a basic marketing principle. Marketing activities are supposed to *stimulate* demand and thus sales, not occur as a *result* of sales. If advertising automatically increases when sales increase and declines when sales decline, it ignores all other factors that might encourage an opposite move.

Share-of-Market/Share-of-Voice Method

In markets with similar products, a high correlation usually exists between a company's share of the market and its share of industry advertising.

The **share-of-market/share-of-voice method** is a bold attempt to link advertising dollars with sales objectives.[75] It holds that a company's best chance of maintaining its share of market is to keep a share of advertising (voice) somewhat ahead of its market share. For example, a company with a 30 percent share of the market should spend 35 percent of the industry's advertising dollars.

The share-of-market/share-of-voice method is commonly used for new product introductions.[76] According to this formula, when a new brand is introduced, the advertising budget for the first two years should be about one and a half times the brand's targeted share of the market in two years. This means that if the company's

Checklist

Ways to Set Advertising Budgets

_____ **Percentage of sales.** Advertising budget is determined by allocating a percentage of last year's sales, anticipated sales for next year, or a combination of the two. The percentage is usually based on an industry average, company experience, or an arbitrary figure.

_____ **Percentage of profit.** Percentage is applied to profit, either past years' or anticipated.

_____ **Unit of sale.** Also called the _case-rate method._ A specific dollar amount is set for each box, case, barrel, or carton produced. Used primarily in assessing members of horizontal co-ops or trade associations.

_____ **Competitive parity.** Also called the _self-defense method._ Allocates dollars according to the amounts spent by major competitors.

_____ **Share of market/share of voice.** Allocates dollars by maintaining a percentage share of total industry advertising comparable to or somewhat ahead of desired share of market. Often used for new-product introductions.

_____ **Objective/task.** Also referred to as the _budget buildup method,_ this method has three steps: defining objectives, determining strategy, and estimating the cost to execute that strategy.

_____ **Empirical research.** By running experimental tests in different markets with different budgets, companies determine which is the most efficient level.

_____ **Quantitative mathematical models.** Computer-based programs developed by major advertisers and agencies rely on input of sophisticated data, history, and assumptions.

_____ **All available funds.** Go-for-broke technique generally used by small firms with limited capital, trying to introduce new products or services.

two-year sales goal is 10 percent of the market, it should spend about 15 percent of total industry advertising during the first two years.

One hazard of this method is the tendency to become complacent. Simply maintaining a higher percentage of media exposure usually isn't enough to accomplish the desired results. The top national packaged-goods marketers still spend 25 to 30 percent of their marketing budgets on consumer and trade promotion rather than consumer advertising.[77] That's how they get more shelf space in the store. And in certain packaged-goods categories, in-store trade promotions may generate 25 percent of a brand's short-term volume, while advertising may be responsible for only 5 percent.[78] Companies must be aware of _all_ their competitors' marketing activities, not just advertising.

Objective/Task Method

The **objective/task method,** also known as the _budget buildup method,_ is used by the majority of major national advertisers in the United States. It considers advertising to be a marketing tool to help generate sales.

The task method has three steps: defining objectives, determining strategy, and estimating cost. After setting specific, quantitative marketing objectives, the advertiser develops programs to attain them. If the objective is to increase the sales of cases of coffee by 10 percent, the advertiser determines which advertising approach will work best, how often ads must run, and which media to use. The estimated cost of the program becomes the basis for the advertising budget. Of course, the company's financial position is always a consideration. If the cost is too high, objectives may have to be scaled back. If results are better or worse than anticipated after the campaign runs, the next budget may need revision.

The task method forces companies to think in terms of accomplishing goals. Its effectiveness is most apparent when the results of particular ads or campaigns can be readily measured. The task method is adaptable to changing market conditions and can be easily revised.

However, it is often difficult to determine in advance the amount of money needed to reach a specific goal. Techniques for measuring advertising effectiveness still have many weaknesses.

Additional Methods

Advertisers also use several other methods to allocate funds. In the **empirical research method,** a company runs a series of tests in different markets with different budgets to determine the best level of advertising expenditure.

Computers can generate quantitative mathematical models for budgeting and allocating advertising dollars. Many sophisticated techniques facilitate marketing and advertising planning, budget allocation, new-product introductions, and media and promotion analysis. However, most are not easily understood by line executives, and all rely on data that may be unavailable or estimated. While widely employed by major national advertisers, these methods require very sophisticated users and, for the most part, are still too expensive for the average small business.

The Bottom Line

Unfortunately, all these methods rely on one of two fallacies. The first is that advertising is a *result* of sales. Advertisers know this is not true, yet they continue to use the percentage-of-sales method.

The second fallacy is that advertising *creates* sales. In certain circumstances (where direct-action advertising is used), advertising closes the sale. But advertising's real role is to reinforce current customers, locate new prospects, position the product competitively, build brand equity, and stimulate demand. It may even stimulate inquiries and product trial and, on the local level, build retail traffic.

But the principal job of advertising is to influence perception by informing, persuading, and reminding. Advertising *affects* sales, but it is just one of many influences on consumer perception. Advertising managers must keep this in mind when preparing their plans and budgets.

Chapter Summary

The marketing plan may be the most important document a company possesses. It assembles all the pertinent and current facts about a company, the markets it serves, its products, and its competition. It sets specific goals and objectives and describes the precise strategies to use to achieve them. It musters the company's forces for the marketing battlefield and, in so doing, dictates the role of advertising in the marketing mix and provides focus for advertising creativity.

There are three types of marketing planning models: top-down, bottom-up, and integrated marketing communications planning.

The top-down marketing plan contains four principal sections: situation analysis, marketing objectives, marketing strategy, and tactics (action programs). A company's marketing objectives should be logical deductions from an analysis of its current situation, its prediction of future trends, and its understanding of corporate objectives. They should relate to the needs of specific target markets and specify sales objectives. Sales-target objectives should be specific, quantitative, and realistic.

The first step in developing a marketing strategy is to select the target market. The second step is to determine the product's positioning. The third step is to construct a cost-effective marketing mix for each target market the company pursues. The marketing mix is determined by how the company blends the elements it controls: product, price, distribution, and communications. Advertising is a communications tool.

One way for small companies to construct the marketing and advertising plan is to work from the bottom up, taking an ingenious tactic and building a strategy around it.

Integrated marketing communications can help build long-term relationships with customers. IMC planning is driven by technology. Thanks to computers and databases, marketers can learn more about their customers' wants and needs, likes and dislikes. IMC is both a concept and a process that offers the synergy of various communications media, strategically managed to enhance the relationship between the customer and the brand or company. Starting with the customer, the IMC planning model uses seven steps to segment the customer database by product-purchase-related attributes; determine the best place, situation, and time to reach the prospect; develop behavior-related marketing and communications objectives and strategies; and develop specific communications tactics to implement the plan. In the IMC model, all marketing becomes communications and all communications become marketing.

Advertising is a natural outgrowth of the marketing plan, and the advertising plan is prepared in much the same way as the top-down marketing plan. It includes a SWOT (strengths, weaknesses, opportunities, and threats) analysis, advertising objectives, and strategy.

Advertising objectives may be expressed in terms of moving prospective customers up through the advertising pyramid (awareness, comprehension, conviction, desire, action). Or they may be expressed in terms of generating inquiries, coupon response, or attitude change.

The advertising (or creative) strategy is determined by the advertiser's use of the creative mix. The creative mix is composed of the target audience, product concept, communications media, and advertising message. The target audience includes the specific groups of people the advertising will address. The product concept refers to the bundle of product-related values the advertiser presents to the customer. The communications media are the vehicles used to transmit the advertiser's message. The advertising message is what the company plans to say and how it plans to say it.

Several methods are used to allocate advertising funds. The most popular are the percentage-of-sales approach and the objective/task method. The share-of-market/share-of-voice method is often used in markets with similar products.

Important Terms

advertising message, *254*

advertising plan, *249*

advertising strategy, *252*

bottom-up marketing, *240*

communications media, *253*

corporate objectives, *236*

creative mix, *252*

empirical research method, *262*

endcap promotion, *244*

integrated marketing communications (IMC), *245*

lifetime customer value (LTCV), *242*

marketing objectives, *236*

marketing plan, *235*

marketing strategy, *237*

need-satisfying objectives, *236*

objective/task method, *262*

percentage-of-sales method, *260*

positioning, *237*

product concept, *252*

relationship marketing, *241*

sales-target objectives, *236*

share-of-market/share-of-voice method, *261*

situation analysis, *235*

stakeholders, *242*

SWOT analysis, *249*

tactics (action programs), *240*

target audience, *252*

top-down marketing, *235*

value, *241*

Review Questions

1. What is a marketing plan and why is it a company's most important document?

2. What examples illustrate the difference between need-satisfying objectives and sales-target objectives?

3. What are the three types of marketing plans? How do they differ?

4. What basic elements should be included in a top-down marketing plan?

5. How can small companies use bottom-up marketing to become big companies?

6. What are the elements of an advertising plan and an advertising strategy?

7. What types of involvement do consumers bring to the purchase decision?

8. What is the best method of allocating advertising funds for a real estate development? Why?

9. What types of companies tend to use the percentage-of-sales method? Why?

10. How could a packaged-foods manufacturer use the share-of-market/share-of-voice method to determine its advertising budget?

11. **The Advertising Experience**

   Whether we realize it or not, we all have lifelong relationships with certain companies. Choose a company that has been part of your life for several years. Profile your relationship with it in terms of planned messages, product message, service messages, and unplanned messages. After examining each of these areas, examine your current attitude toward the company's products and discuss what you think your future feelings will be.

Exploring the Internet

The Internet exercises for Chapter 8 address the following areas covered throughout the chapter: strategic advertising planning (Exercise 1) and integrated marketing communications (Exercises 2 and 3).

1. **Strategic Advertising Planning**
    You studied in this chapter the various means of planning advertising strategy—top-down, bottom-up, and IMC. Browse through the websites of the following marketers, and answer the questions regarding the various means of planning advertising strategy.

    - American Automobile Association (AAA) www.aaa.com
    - Bristol Myers Squibb www.bms.com
    - Proflowers.com www.proflowers.com
    - Hudson Moving & Storage www.moving-storage.com
    - Metro Goldwyn Mayer/UA www.mgm.com
    - General Electric www.ge.com
    - Hewlett-Packard www.hp.com
    - Intel www.intel.com
    - Kellogg's www.kelloggs.com/us
    - Walt Disney www.disney.com

    a. What is the size/scope of the company and its business? What is the company's purpose?
    b. Identify the target audience, product concept, communications media, and advertising message for each.
    c. What is the company's position within the industry? Type of communication used? Target market?
    d. Where does the company's product(s) fall within the Kim-Lord grid?

2. **Integrated Marketing Communications (IMC)**
    Integrated marketing communications (IMC) is an important part of modern advertising strategy and has many applications industrywide. Browse the following five websites, and provide a summary of the organization's IMC role and its implications to the advertising industry. Also answer the questions listed below.

    - Harpell www.harpell.com
    - Integrated Marketing Communications, Inc. www.intmark.com
    - The Phelps Group www.phelpsgroup.com
    - Medill's IMC Graduate Program at Northwestern University www.medill.nwu.edu/imc

    a. Who is the intended audience of the site?
    b. What type of organization sponsors the site?
    c. What specific IMC vehicles or services (if any) are mentioned/offered?
    d. What benefit does the organization provide individual clients/students? The advertising community, at large?

3. **Websites and IMC**
    IMC can involve many different elements, and a website can be an integral part of a company's marketing efforts. Discuss how the three following companies might make a website part of an overall IMC effort:

    a. A startup microbrewery that specializes in full-flavored ales.
    b. A medium-sized candy maker with some brands that are nearly 100 years old.
    c. A small company centered around a motivational speaker who has just had her first big break with an appearance on the *Dr. Phil Show*.

Chapter 9

Planning Media Strategy: Finding Links to the Market

Objectives

TO SHOW HOW COMMUNICATIONS MEDIA help advertisers achieve marketing and advertising objectives. To get their messages to the right people in the right place at the right time, media planners follow the same procedures as marketing and advertising planners: setting objectives, formulating strategies, and devising tactics. To make sound decisions, media planners must possess marketing savvy, analytical skill, and creativity.

After studying this chapter, you will be able to:

■ Describe how a media plan helps accomplish a company's marketing and advertising objectives.

■ Explain the importance of creativity in media planning.

■ Define reach and frequency and debate the controversy surrounding the concept of effective frequency.

■ Discuss how reach, frequency, and continuity are related.

■ Calculate gross rating points and cost per thousand.

■ Name some of the secondary research sources available to planners and describe how they are used.

■ Describe different types of advertising schedules and the purpose for each.

When Sony introduced its new Street Style Headphones, its first notion was to market them primarily on college campuses. That may not have been a bad idea since the headphones, which wrap around the back of the head, were the ultimate cool, gotta-have-it accessory. But the following year, Sony appointed a new media agency, and the mavens there had a more radical scheme. They saw an opportunity to go after the much broader 12- to 24-year-old Generation Y segment with a street-level guerrilla marketing campaign. Best of all, they thought they could do it on Sony's modest $600,000 budget.[1] ■ The Media Edge, as the agency is known, recommended targeting urban youth first because African-American and Hispanic inner-city kids tend to be trend-setters—they're the key youth influencers. And once they adopt and popularize a new product, the trend spreads to the suburbs. ■ "We do a lot of research on the teen market," says Kim Canfield, VP/planning director at The Media Edge, "and the constants we came up with were basketball and music. If you look at all the admired athletes, they're all from basketball. ■ "Plus," she says, "it's participatory. If you want to find urban youth in the summer in Manhattan, they're on the courts in Harlem or on West 4th Street. And rap and hip-hop is the music they like." ◾ The Media Edge (TME) spent half its budget in the first summer of the campaign on a van program that took the campaign to inner-city streets. The brightly graphic vans visited hot spots in five top markets—New York, Los Angeles, Chicago, Atlanta, and Detroit—all of which scored high for urban youth, basketball, and music. During daytime hours they went to basketball courts; at night they appeared outside popular dance clubs. The idea wasn't to sell headphones from the vans, but to offer listening stations where kids could check them out as well as other Sony gear such as MiniDiscs. They also passed out free premiums such as Street Style keychains. The whole purpose was simply to get the product and the creative advertising to work face-to-face with the target market. Sony reps working the vans gave out coupons that, when mailed in with proof of purchase of the headphones, were good for a free CD featuring up-and-coming rap acts such as Nas, Mobb Deep, and Big Pun. Over the course of the campaign, the company moved more than 35,000 CDs. ◾ During the fall back-to-school period, the campaign went national. The Media Edge broadened the target to include high school and college students and used rather unconventional media vehicles to reach them. Through Cover Concepts, they distributed more than a half million Street Style book covers. M@x Racks placed free Street Style postcards in bars and restaurants on 100 college campuses. And Beyond the Wall, a catalogue company that sells posters of advertising images to college students, moved about 1,500 Street Style posters—its third biggest seller after Volkswagen and James Bond. ◾ The final phase of the campaign was a holiday shopping effort in which they distributed postcards and plastic shopping bags with the Street Style logo to more than 350 independent music retailers in 65 markets across the country. ◾ "The

key to the campaign," Canfield says, "was being able to reach these kids wherever they are. In the summer, we caught them outside playing ball or at the clubs; in the fall we got them at school with the book covers; and during the holidays it was when they were shopping for music as gifts. It was an organic, word-of-mouth message that went from trendsetters to the rest." ◾ The client was pleased. During the van program, Street Style's share of the highly fragmented headphone market jumped 50 percent. During the holiday season, market share tripled. "It was a different way of approaching these kids and impacting them with this product, but it really resonated with them at the grass-roots level," says Bob Gruder, Sony's senior manager, marketing communications. ◾ It's this kind of innovative, out-of-the-box thinking, though, that has contributed to the incredible growth and success of The Media Edge. TME was formed in 1994 when Beth Gordon and seven of her associates at N.W. Ayer, the oldest advertising agency in the United States, separated the media department from the agency. Their idea was to create a new, independent, media specialist company that would make its innovative planning and buying services available to both ad agencies and clients.[2] Starting with the plum AT&T media buying account—worth about $350 million—the shop immediately started picking up new business. ◾ In 1996, Young & Rubicam, which handled a lot of AT&T business, bought The Media Edge and soon consolidated all its worldwide media services there. Since that time the growth of TME has been spectacular. In rapid succession it landed such major media accounts as Royal Caribbean Cruises, GlaxoSmithKline, Chanel, Citibank, Colgate-Palmolive, and United Airlines. By 2000, the little independent media buying firm was no longer independent; it was no longer just a media buying firm; and it was no longer little. Beth Gordon became chairman and CEO of a global enterprise that provides integrated, full-service media planning and management services. With annual billings in excess of $14 billion worldwide, The Media Edge is now one of the top media specialist agencies in the world. In recognition of its rapid growth and exceptional expertise, *Advertising Age* named it Media Agency of the Year in 2000.[3] ■

Media Planning: Integrating Science with Creativity in Advertising

In today's overcommunicated society, advertising media planners need to be as analytically competent as top financial officers and as creative as senior art directors and copywriters. Since most money in advertising is spent on media, solid media decisions are critical to the success of the overall marketing communications plan.

The purpose of **media planning** is to conceive, analyze, and creatively select channels of communication that will direct advertising messages to the right people in the right place at the right time. At The Media Edge, Beth Gordon believes that "anything you put your message on is media." As we saw, that might even include shopping bags, book covers, and vans. As a result, media planning today involves many decisions. For example,

■ Where should we advertise? (In what countries, states, or parts of town?)

■ Which media vehicles should we use?

■ When during the year should we concentrate our advertising?

■ How often should we run the advertising?

■ What opportunities are there to integrate our media advertising with other communication tools?

Some of these decisions require hard scientific research and detailed mathematical analysis, aided by sophisticated computer software programs. But understanding and interpreting what all the numbers really mean, and then conceiving and implementing a truly masterful media plan like the launch of Sony's Street Style Headphones, demand human intelligence and creativity.[4]

The Challenge

Historically, the people who plan and buy media have enjoyed relative anonymity compared to the "stars" in the creative and account service departments. As evidence of this, witness the fact that entry-level media positions are still among the lowest-paid jobs in the business. This may be due to two facts. First, lower-ranking media jobs are still fairly routine and uncreative, so they don't require employees with high levels of training and competence. They are a good entry point for young people in the business, however, and those with superior skill or ability can move up quickly. Second, in many agencies and companies, conventional media planning is still relatively archaic, based on a bygone era when just a few spots on prime-time network television would easily reach the majority of an advertiser's target audience. These dinosaur media-planning organizations have been able to grind along with their obsolete systems for some time, but this situation is now changing rapidly due to the pressures of competition.

The fact is that today the media planner's assignment is just as critical as the creative director's: One media planner can be responsible for millions of client dollars. The planner's work attests to an agency's strategic ability to negotiate the best prices and use effectively the incredible array of media choices available today. Jack Klues, the senior VP/director of U.S. media services for Leo Burnett

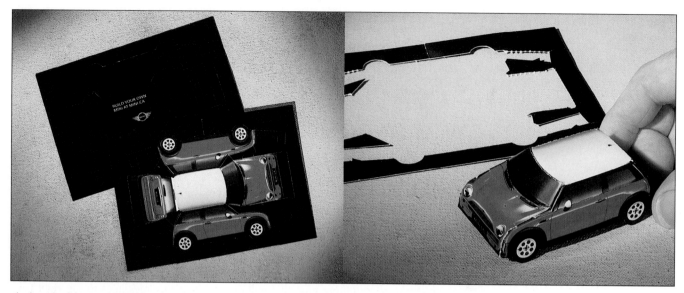

The launch of the MINI Cooper was a global phenomenon that strategically integrated every medium and marketing vehicle available—from TV to print and co-op ads, to massive in-store promotions, public relations, and publicity stunts. This ad shows the little MINI cutouts that the company used to get people excited about the re-introduction of the original European automobile. MINI successfully demonstrated how a well-planned media campaign can generate enormous positive publicity.

USA, says, "Our mission is to buy and plan media so effectively that our clients obtain an unfair advantage versus their competitors."[5]

In the 1990s, the media department suddenly gained new prominence. Clients started taking an a la carte approach to agency services and agencies began competing for media planning and buying assignments separately from the creative business.[6] By the early 2000s, media wins had become big news: Universal McCann won the $150 million Nestlé account; Gillette awarded its $600 million media account to Mindshare; and Kraft consolidated its $800 million media business at Starcom MediaVest Group.[7]

As the complexity of the field increases, media decisions become more critical and clients more demanding. Advertisers want agencies to be more than efficient. They want accountability and information, particularly about media options. And they want creative buys.

What makes media planning today so much more complicated and challenging than it was just a few years ago?

Increasing Media Options

With the advent of modern electronic technology and the natural maturation of the marketplace, there are many more media to choose from today, and each offers more choices. As we mentioned earlier, it wasn't long ago that major advertisers could ensure a big audience by simply advertising on TV. Not anymore. Today it's much more difficult to reach a big audience. As Stacey Lippman, director of corporate media at TBWA Chiat/Day, says, "There's too much to keep track of and too many things to explore."[8]

TV is now fragmented into network, syndicated, spot, and local television, as well as network and local cable. Specialized magazines now aim at every possible population and business segment. Even national magazines publish editions for particular regions or demographic groups. Finally, the incredible growth of the Internet over the last 10 years has brought with it a host of new media options. But it has also added to the complexity of media work as plan-

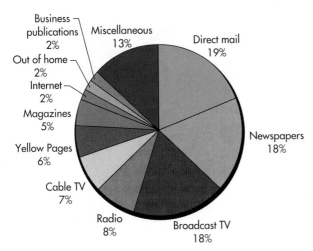

Exhibit 9–1
U.S. ad spending by medium.

ners face the challenge of staying current with the constantly expanding technology and mastering a whole new lexicon of associated terminology. Exhibit 9–1 shows the breakdown of total (local and national) advertising expenditures by traditional media in the United States.

Nontraditional media—from videotape and movie advertising to electronic kiosks and even shopping carts—also expand the menu of choices. (Ad Lab 9–A describes some nontraditional media available today.) In addition, many companies spend a considerable portion of their marketing budgets on specialized communications like direct marketing, sales promotion, public relations activities, and personal selling, topics we'll discuss in the next two chapters. In fact, these "below-the-line" (noncommissionable) activities are the fastest-growing segments at some of the large agency holding companies, like WPP and Interpublic.[9]

Duncan and Moriarty point out that for companies practicing integrated marketing communications, their "media menu" needs to include everything that carries a message to and/or from customers and other stakeholders. The proliferation of toll-free phone numbers, faxes, and Internet websites makes it easy and cost-effective to facilitate customer feedback. The result is that advertisers can be very creative in designing systems for both sending and receiving messages. That means that companies and agencies need to think in terms of *message handling,* being as responsible for *receiving* messages as for sending them. Mark Goldstein, the president of integrated marketing at Fallon McElligott in Minneapolis, says, "Media is no longer planned and bought; instead it's created, aggregated, and partnered." Perhaps, as Duncan and Moriarty say, the media department of the future will be called the *connect department.*[10]

Almost as an afterthought, many websites offer virtual guest books where visitors can leave messages and post links. NEC reconceptualized the humble guest book and made it the centerpiece of its Ectonoha forestation project (http://eco.adnec.com/eco/ecotonoha2.html). For every 100 leaves (signatures), NEC plants a tree on Australia's Kangaroo Island. Each day, a new, unique virtual tree is "grown" from leaves placed by visitors. The site, which won the Cannes Cyber Grand Prix, enables electronics manufacturer NEC to promote its conservation message.

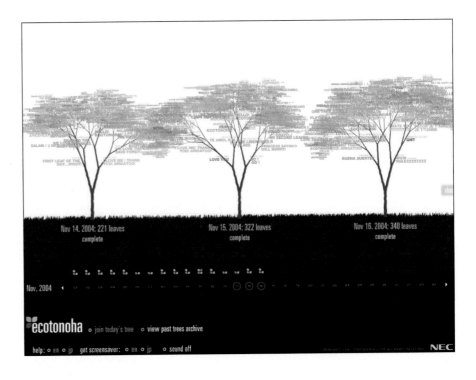

Off-the-Wall Media That Pull Customers Off the Fence

Advertising can be found everywhere these days—even places where we least expect it.

Aerial Banners and Lights
Banners carrying ad messages can be pulled by low-flying planes. After dark, traveling aerial lights can display messages of up to 90 characters. Slow-flying helicopters can carry 40-by-80-foot signs lit by thousands of bulbs.

Blimps
In addition to Goodyear, blimps now carry ads for many companies, including Citibank, Coca-Cola, and Fuji Film, among others. Computer-operated lighting systems allow the blimps to advertise at night.

In-Flight Ads
Many airlines' in-flight audio and video entertainment runs ads. The travel industry and advertisers that want to reach business fliers are the primary users.

Newspaper Bags
The protective bags of newspapers are used for full-color advertising and can be enhanced by adding product samples. This method is desirable because it does not have to compete with other advertisers.

Transit Terminal Domination
The latest version of saturation bombing has come to large transit hubs around the country. One advertiser buys up all or most of the message space in one confined site, banishing all competition. This greatly increases the chances of being seen even by the most harried passers-by.

Electronic Billboards
Most modern sports stadiums and arenas sell ad space on giant electronic displays.

Inflatables
Giant inflatable beer cans, mascots, and even cereal boxes are used for advertising purposes.

Painted Vehicles
Buses, trucks, and cars are completely decorated with larger-than-life illustrations and messages to attract attention. Some vehicles are "wrapped" with a material that covers the entire vehicle to present the greatest visual impact.

The San Diego Union-Tribune *uses painted trucks to deliver newspapers and its advertising message.*

Trash Receptacles
Uniquely designed and decorated trash bins, boxes, and baskets bear advertising logos and messages. Some major cities now offer advertising space on concrete litter receptacles at major commercial intersections.

Kiosks
Stand-alone kiosks can be painted with eye-catching designs and messages. Unique constructions can be attached to the top and sides to draw attention. Electronic displays running presentation software can show colorful fast-action video clips, slide images, and interactive text. These systems can also play synchronized sounds and music.

Lavatory Advertising
Numerous venues allow advertising in lavatories. Print ads can be found on the inner side of stalls and above urinals in some men's restrooms.

Gobo/Cookie Advertising
The gobo (or cookie) is a piece of metal stenciled with a logo, through which light is projected against a wall or other suitable background. This is ideal for huge outdoor or indoor events.

Train Cars
Train cars are wrapped with advertisements instead of graffiti these days. In Chicago, an eight-car commuter train was wrapped with Illinois lottery ads.

Grocery Receipts
Today, most major supermarket chains print coupons on the back of grocery receipts. The coupons feature discounts at local retailers.

Laboratory Applications
1. How effective are off-the-wall media?
2. What other off-the-wall media can you think of?

Increasing Fragmentation of the Audience

Further evidence of the maturing marketplace is the fragmentation of the media audience. This also complicates the media planner's job. Readers and viewers have scattered to all the new media options, selectively reading only parts of magazines or newspapers, watching only segments of programs, and listening to many different radio stations. This makes it very difficult to find the prospect in the marketplace, even though consumers are spending more time with media than ever before—an average of over 3,570 hours per year.[11] (See Exhibit 9–2.)

Exhibit 9–2

Time spent with media.

Category	Hours per person per year						1998–2003 percent change	2003–2008 percent change
	1998	Percent share	2003	Percent share	2008	Percent share		
Media with significant advertiser support*	2,112	63.6%	2,064	56.4%	2,194	54.1%	−2.2%	6.3%
Media supported predominantly by consumers†	1,210	36.4	1,598	43.6	1,865	45.9	32.1	16.7

*Broadcast television, broadcast and satellite radio, daily newspapers, and consumer magazines.
†Cable and satellite television, box office, recorded music, consumer books, interactive television, home video, consumer Internet, and video games.

The sports fan's perennial heckle "Come on, ref, do you need glasses?" has finally been answered. Specsavers, a Scottish optical care provider and retailer, has begun to sponsor soccer referees. In addition to providing eye exams and optical eyewear for referees, the company outfits them and advertises in stadiums. The media mix for the campaign, which won a Cannes Media Lion for Mediaedge:cia's London office, combined the clever sponsorship with point-of-sale advertising and newspaper-friendly press releases. As the 22% increase in sales shows, Specsavers has positioned itself squarely in Scottish men's field of vision.

Increasing Costs

At the same time that there are more media choices, the number of messages that need to be communicated has also proliferated—so much so, in fact, that they have outstripped the ability of consumers to process them. People can cope with only so many messages, so the media have to restrict the number of ads they sell. As a result, the cost of reaching target audiences is increasing for almost all media. In the last decade, the cost of exposing 1,000 people to each of the major media (called *cost per thousand*) rose faster than inflation. Shows that can deliver a big audience are sold at a premium. To run a 30-second spot on "American Idol," for instance, now costs around $271,000.[12] Rising costs make media planning more challenging than ever, especially for advertisers with small budgets. Clients want proof that planners are squeezing the most they can out of every media dollar.

Increasing Complexity in Media Buying and Selling

As the process of buying media has become more complex, so has the process of selling media. In the battle for additional sales, many print and broadcast media companies developed "value-added" programs to provide extra benefits. Besides selling space or time at rate-card prices or below, these companies now offer reprints, merchandising services, special sections, event sponsorships, and mailing lists. To get a bigger share of the advertiser's budget, larger media companies are bundling the various stations, publications, or properties they own and offering them in integrated combos as further incentives. The Discovery Networks, for example, which include the Travel Channel, TLC, Animal Planet, and Discovery, offers its advertisers "multiplatform convergence content sponsorships." What this unwieldy name means is that each advertiser gets a major Internet/TV sponsorship with four or five commercials in a special-event Discovery show and Webcast. Specially created TV spots promote the program and the Webcast, as well as Discovery's website and even the advertiser's website. Moreover, advertisers get additional off-air exposure in hundreds of Discovery Network retail stores nationwide which also run in-store videos promoting the shows and the sponsors.[13]

Television networks work with major sports associations and professional teams to develop integrated marketing "partnerships" for sports and event sponsors. General Motors and NBC, for example, raised the bar on Olympic sponsorships in 1997 with a 12-year, $600 million deal to make GM the official domestic car and truck of the U.S. Olympic Team. The NBC portion of the deal gives GM

The Ethical Dilemmas of Agency Compensation

The payment structure that defined the client/agency relationship for over a century has recently come under fire by both sides. Ad agency compensation was once a simple formula, but now it has become one of the foremost concerns for both advertisers and agencies in a world of high media costs, low budgets, and rising awareness of corporate fraud and scandal.

Founded in 1875, N.W. Ayer & Sons was the first ad agency to plan, create, and execute complete advertising campaigns in exchange for media-paid commissions—typically 15 percent of the client's media expenditures. Back then, 15 percent may have seemed a small amount as the venues for advertising were limited to the low-cost advertising space of newspapers, magazines, posters, and other forms of print. However, by the late twentieth century, advances in technology had created many new avenues for reaching consumers. Today, advertisers can send their messages through a wide variety of print, electronic, and digital interactive media, all far more expensive—and profitable—than the newspapers and magazines of the nineteenth or early twentieth century. Take, for example, a 30-second TV spot on *Friends* that averages $455,700. Under the commission structure, the agency that placed this commercial would receive almost $70,000, considerable revenue considering the time directly spent placing that

commercial. And that's for just one spot! When the client runs a schedule of ads, the ad agency's profits really balloon.

As a result of this high profitability, the standard 15 percent commission became a target of concern. Some observers began to regard an agency's so-called expert and impartial advice to the advertiser about commissionable media spending as suspect, if not outright biased. Commissions, they believed, negatively affected the ethics of the business by potentially causing the agency to be motivated by income rather than the client's best interests.

Consequently, advertising industry leaders sought change. In the early 1990s, clients began taking control of the process, establishing their own compensation systems. By 1995, only 14 percent of advertisers were still paying 15 percent commissions, as labor-based fees and incentive programs became the growing trend. Tying compensation directly to the time spent creating a campaign, as well as to the actual sales performance the campaign achieved, allowed advertisers to feel that their goals and needs were once again the primary focus.

However, by the turn of the twenty-first century, compensation concerns returned to the forefront of advertisers' agendas, as fraud and scandal created a need for greater agency accountability. SEC investigations have found that, by using complex billing statements and convoluted accounting methods, some agencies had once again started putting personal profit ahead of their clients' interests. Government

domestic category exclusivity and media placement for the network's coverage of the 2000, 2002, 2004, 2006, and 2008 Olympics. GM is expected to spend an additional $300 million to leverage its Olympics involvement. As Phil Guarasco, GM's VP/general manager of marketing and advertising, says, "This isn't about dollars, it's about value. What we have here is a strong, cost-effective marketing initiative for the company."[14]

Value-added packages often employ communications vehicles outside traditional media planning, such as public relations activities, sales promotion, and direct marketing. With BMW, for instance, *Yachting* magazine sponsors sailing weeks in various markets and displays the advertiser's cars on site. So people who can afford expensive sailboats are also exposed to the cars, to BMW signage at the event, and to any premium giveaways the sponsors might offer.[15] Integrated events like these help advertisers build relationships with their customers and prospects, and that's a major goal today. But placing a value on these deals is difficult because the nonmedia elements are hard to quantify.

The trend toward integrated marketing communications and relationship marketing is creating a new breed of media planner: younger, computer literate, and schooled in marketing disciplines beyond traditional media. The good media specialist today is actually a real advertising generalist. And with many of the biggest client changes happening in *media-only* agency reviews, it's apparent that the media professionals have finally come into their own.

Increasing Competition

The final element making media planning more challenging today is the competitive environment, which in just a few years completely changed the structure of the advertising business. In the 1980s and early 1990s, as clients sought greater efficiency with their media dollars, independent media buying services came into the fore, attracting some of the best and brightest talent in the business to compete with agencies for what was once their private domain. Initially, the independents bought advertising space and time at lower bulk rates and then sold it at a higher

probes found that some had even begun a practice of padding suppliers' bills in exchange for costly perks. Since 1996, these investigations have led to guilty pleas from 32 people and nine companies.

Fortunately, leaders on both the client and agency sides have been quick to find a proactive solution that would benefit both sides. In 2002, the Association of Advertising Agencies and the Association of National Advertisers, Inc., came together to create the first-ever set of guidelines covering compensation agreements between agencies and advertisers. In an effort to create the most effective compensation agreements possible, the joint document established dozens of guidelines. Among others, the guidelines state that the best compensation programs

- Align advertiser and agency interests and priorities.
- Match compensation with the resources required to do the work.
- Establish agreement on key compensation definitions and terms up front.
- Do not favor one solution/service over another.
- Are finalized before agency resources are committed.

While these guidelines do help in providing a benchmark of best practices for compensation agreements, they are far from an end-all solution. In fact, some people within the ad agency community feel that the very search for an end-all solution is aggravating the problem.

Specifically, these members believe that there will always be certain aspects of the client/agency dynamic that cannot be standardized and cannot be measured. One example is the creative talent that differentiates one agency from the next. Surely a premium for creativity must be paid, but how do you standardize a price for such talents? Another question is how to tie compensation directly to results. Surely compensation should be tied to results, but how are results measured in such an inexact and intangible science?

The one thing both sides can agree on is that the debate on "fair" compensation is sure to last for many years to come.

Questions

1. Compare the advantages and disadvantages of the commission system with those of the fee or incentive system.

2. What problems, if any, does the commission system cause for small businesses that are less likely to use high-cost media?

Sources: David Goetzl and Wayne Friedman, "Highest-Priced TV Show: Friends," *Advertising Age*, October 3, 2002; Lisa Sanders, "Feds Probe Madison Ave. Bill-Padding Scams," *Advertising Age*, April 1, 2002; "AAAA and ANA Announce First Ever Guidelines for Compensation Agreements," December 12, 2002 (retrieved from www.aaaa.org); Jones Lundin Beals, "Trends in Agency Compensation," May 29, 2002 (retrieved from www.admworks.org/conference/2002/bealsagencypres.pdf).

rate or for a handling commission to advertisers or ad agencies that didn't have a fully staffed media department. As the media specialists grew, though, clients came to realize the virtues of scale, and financial clout emerged as a potent weapon in negotiating media buys.[16] By 1994, the independents handled more than one-fourth of all national advertising media accounts.[17]

To respond to the competitive pressure, ad agencies started unbundling their own media departments, setting them up as separate media specialist subsidiaries like The Media Edge. These companies could compete with the independents as well as with other agencies for media-only accounts. Over time, all these firms became quite expert at the media function. With the rapid increase in billings, they were able to pour a substantial amount of money into the development of new research tools, which was critical given the continued fragmentation of the mass media into smaller and smaller niches.

At this point, the big multinational advertisers realized that they could receive greater impact from their ad dollars by consolidating their media budgets within a single large shop. (For more on the agency-client relationship, see Ethical Issues: "The Ethical Dilemmas of Agency Compensation.") Procter & Gamble, for instance, pooled $1.2 billion at TeleVest. As the big media shops started winning the big accounts, the large agency holding companies went on an acquisition binge, buying up the largest of the independent media agencies and sometimes merging them with their own subsidiaries and then, as in the case of TME, relaunching them as global media firms. By 2000 the process had gone full circle. For the most part, the agencies were again back in control of the media budgets—albeit at arm's length.[18] And while the structure was different, so was the compensation. They were no longer getting 15 percent of the media budget. In fact, 2 to 3 percent was the norm. But the volume was so high that the business could still be quite profitable.[19]

The top 30 media agencies today account for more than $55.8 billion in media purchasing power in the United States alone. Worldwide, they accounted for more than $148.7 billion.[20] (Exhibit 9–3 shows billing for the top 10 agencies in the United States and worldwide.)

Exhibit 9–3

Media powerhouses (top media specialist companies ranked by billings, $ millions).

RECMA's ranking by worldwide billings						
Rank				Worldwide billings		
2003	2002	Media specialist company	Headquarters	2003	2002	% chg.
1	1	OMD Worldwide	New York	$19.34	$17.92	7.9
2	3	MindShare Worldwide	London	19.16	17.24	11.1
3	2	Starcom MediaVest Group	Chicago	18.87	17.66	6.9
4	4	Carat	London	17.77	17.03	4.3
5	5	ZenithOptimedia	London	15.53	15.22	2.1
6	6	Universal McCann Worldwide	New York	15.14	14.65	3.3
7	7	Mediaedge:cia Worldwide	London/New York	14.63	13.44	8.8
8	9	MediaCom	New York	13.56	12.64	7.2
9	8	Initiative Media Worldwide	New York	12.55	12.86	−2.4
10	10	MPG	Barcelona	8.63	7.79	10.7

RECMA's ranking by U.S. billings						
Rank				U.S. billings		
2003	2002	Media specialist company	Headquarters	2003	2002	% chg.
1	1	MindShare Worldwide	New York	$9.40	$8.65	8.7
2	2	OMD Worldwide	New York	8.33	8.00	4.1
3	4	Starcom	Chicago	7.51	6.80	3.1
4	3	Universal McCann Worldwide	New York	7.40	7.10	4.2
5	6	Mediaedge:cia Worldwide	London/New York	5.27	4.90	7.4
6	5	Initiative Media Worldwide	New York	5.08	5.57	−11.7
7	7	MediaCom	New York	5.00	4.68	7.0
8	8	Carat North America	New York	4.72	4.54	4.1
9	10	MediaVest	New York	4.36	3.90	11.7
10	9	Zenith Media	New York	4.36	4.20	3.7

The Role of Media in the Marketing Framework

As we've discussed in previous chapters, the key to successful advertising is proper planning. Thus, before media planning begins—indeed, before advertising is even considered—companies must first establish their overall marketing and advertising plans for their products.

Marketing Objectives and Strategy

As we saw in Chapter 8, the top-down marketing plan defines the market need and the company's sales objectives and details strategies for attaining those objectives. Exhibit 9–4 shows how objectives and strategies result from the marketing situation (or SWOT) analysis, which defines the company's *strengths* and *weaknesses* and uncovers any marketplace *opportunities* and *threats*. Marketing objectives may focus on solving a problem ("regaining sales volume lost to major competitive introductions over the past year") or seizing an opportunity ("increasing share in the female buyer segment of the athletic-shoe market").

Marketing strategies lay out the steps for meeting these objectives by blending the four elements of the marketing mix. A company whose marketing objective is to increase sales of a particular brand in a certain part of the country has many options. For example, it can adapt the product to suit regional tastes (*product*); it can lower the price to compete with local brands (*price*); it can devise deals to gain additional shelf space in retail outlets (*distribution*); and it can reposition the product through intensive trade and consumer advertising (*communication*). Thus, advertising is just one of the many strategic tools a company may use to achieve its marketing objectives.

The situation analysis
Purpose: To understand the marketing problem. The company and its competitors are analyzed on:
1. Internal strengths and weaknesses.
2. External opportunities and threats.

The marketing plan
Purpose: To plan activities that will solve one or more of the marketing problems.
Includes the determination of:
1. Marketing objectives.
2. Product and spending strategy.
3. Distribution strategy.
4. Which marketing mix to use.
5. Identification of "best" market segments.

The advertising plan
Purpose: To determine what to communicate through ads.
Includes the determination of:
1. How product can meet consumer needs.
2. How product will be positioned in ads.
3. Copy themes.
4. Specific objectives of each ad.
5. Number and sizes of ads.

Setting media objectives
Purpose: To translate marketing and advertising objectives and strategies into goals that media can accomplish.

Determining media strategy
Purpose: To translate media goals into general guidelines that will control the planner's selection and use of media. The best strategy alternatives should be selected.

Selecting broad media classes
Purpose: To determine which broad class of media best fulfills the criteria. Involves comparison and selection of broad media classes: newspapers, magazines, radio, television, and others. Audience size is a major factor used in comparing the various media classes.

Selecting media within classes
Purpose: To compare and select the best media within broad classes, again using predetermined criteria. Involves making decisions about the following:
1. If magazines were recommended, then which magazines?
2. If television was recommended, then
   a. Broadcast or cable TV?
   b. Network or spot TV?
   c. If network, which program(s)?
   d. If spot, which markets?
3. If radio or newspapers were recommended, then
   a. Which markets shall be used?
   b. What criteria shall buyers use in making purchases in local media?

Media use decisions—broadcast
1. What kind of sponsorship (sole, shared participating, or other)?
2. What levels of reach and frequency will be required?
3. Scheduling: On which days and months are commercials to appear?
4. Placement of spots: In programs or between programs?

Media use decisions—print
1. Numbers of ads to appear and on which days and months.
2. Placement of ads: Any preferred position within media?
3. Special treatment: Gatefolds, bleeds, color, etc.
4. Desired reach or frequency levels.

Media use decisions—other media
1. Billboards:
   a. Location of markets and plan of distribution.
   b. Kinds of outdoor boards to be used.
2. Direct mail or other media: Decisions peculiar to those media.
3. Interactive media:
   a. Which kind of interactive media.
   b. How will responses be handled.

Exhibit 9–4
This diagram outlines the scope of media-planning activities.

Advertising Objectives and Strategy

The objectives and strategies of an advertising plan unfold from the marketing plan. But advertising objectives focus on communication goals, such as

■ Convincing 25 percent of the target market during the next year of the brand's need-satisfying abilities.

■ Positioning the brand as a cost-effective alternative to the market leader in the minds of 30 percent of men ages 18 to 34 during the next two years.

■ Increasing brand preference by 8 percent in the South during the next year.

■ Improving the target stakeholder group's attitude toward the company's environmental efforts by at least 15 percent by campaign end.

To achieve these objectives, companies devise advertising strategies that employ the elements of the **creative mix:** the product concept, target audience, advertising message, and communications media.

The media department's job is to make sure the advertising message (developed by the creative department) gets to the correct target audience (established by the marketing managers and account executives) in an effective manner (as measured by the research department).

The Media-Planning Framework

In the age of integrated marketing communications, many agencies have moved the task of media planning earlier in the advertising management process, because people typically make contact with the brand through some medium. Before determining what creative approach to employ, it's important to know when, where, and under what conditions contact can best be made with the customer or other stakeholder and to plan for that. This sets the strategic direction for the creative department.

That's also why we present the topic of media planning now, in Part Two, "Crafting Marketing and Advertising Strategies," because media planning is part of the strategic work done prior to developing creative concepts. Later, in Part Five, "Using Advertising Media," we'll discuss the tactical details of each medium, how it's used, and how it's bought—activities that typically occur after the creative process.

Development of a media plan involves the same process as marketing and advertising planning. First, review the marketing and advertising objectives and strategies and set relevant, measurable objectives that are both realistic and achievable by the media. Next, try to devise an ingenious strategy for achieving these objectives. Finally, develop the specific tactical details of media scheduling and selection.

Exhibit 9–5

How media objectives are expressed.

ACME Advertising
Client: Econo Foods
Product/Brand: Chirpee's Cheap Chips
Project: Media plan, first year introduction

Media Objectives

1. To target large families with emphasis on the family's food purchaser.
2. To concentrate the greatest weight of advertising in urban areas where prepared foods traditionally have greater sales and where new ideas normally gain quicker acceptance.
3. To provide extra weight during the announcement period and then continuity throughout the year with a fairly consistent level of advertising impressions.
4. To deliver advertising impressions to every region in relation to regional food store sales.
5. To use media that will reinforce the copy strategy's emphasis on convenience, ease of preparation, taste, and economy.
6. To attain the highest advertising frequency possible once the need for broad coverage and the demands of the copy platform have been met.

Defining Media Objectives

Media objectives translate the advertising strategy into goals that media can accomplish. Exhibit 9–5 shows general media objectives for a hypothetical new food product. They explain who the target audience is and why, where messages will be delivered and when, and how much advertising weight needs to be delivered over what period of time.

Media objectives have two major components: *audience objectives* and *message-distribution objectives*.

Audience Objectives

Audience objectives define the specific types of people the advertiser wants to reach. Media planners typically use geodemographic classifications to define their target audiences. In Exhibit 9–5, for example, the target audience is food purchasers for large families who live in urban areas across the country.

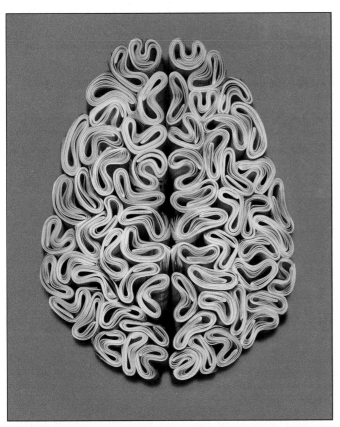

Market research helps advertisers determine specific characteristics of media audiences. The audience for the Economist (www.economist.com) magazine is highly educated and would be described as upper income. In this clever ad, which won a Bronze Lion at Cannes, the Economist promotes the intelligence of its readership by folding issues of the magazine and arranging them to look like a human brain.

The target audience may consist of people in a specific income, educational, occupational, or social group—any of the segments we discussed in Chapter 6. And the target audience is not necessarily the same as the product's target market. Often it is considerably larger. For example, in the case of a new product introduction, the target audience will often include members of the distribution channel, key opinion leaders, the financial community, and even the media itself—in addition to potential customers.

Many advertisers have to defend their media decisions with the retailers who stock and resell their products. Why? If these people construed a change in media strategy as a loss of advertising support, they might reduce the shelf space for the advertiser's products. Therefore, most consumer campaigns are supported by a concurrent campaign directed to the trade.

The consumer target audience may be determined from the marketer's research. However, planners rely largely on secondary research sources, such as Arbitron and Nielsen Media Research, which provide basic demographic characteristics of media audiences. Others, such as Simmons Market Research Bureau (SMRB) and Mediamark Research, Inc. (MRI), describe media audiences based on purchase tendencies (see Exhibit 9–6). These syndicated reports give demographic profiles of heavy and light users of various products and help planners define the target audience. The reports also specify which TV programs or magazines heavy and light users watch and read, which helps planners select media with large audiences of heavy users. Planners can then select **media vehicles**—particular magazines or shows—according to how well they "deliver" or expose the message to the media audience that most closely resembles the desired target consumer.

Advertisers using the IMC planning model start by segmenting their target audiences according to brand-purchasing behavior (for example, loyal users, brand switchers, new prospects) and then ranking them by profit to the brand.[21] Communications objectives are then stated in terms of reinforcing or modifying customer purchasing behavior or creating a perceptual change about the brand over time.[22]

Unfortunately, due to cost restraints, most media research does not provide the specificity that marketers would really like. Most radio, TV, newspaper, and outdoor audience reports, for example, are limited to age and gender. So media planners often have to rely on their judgment and experience to select the right media vehicles.[23] This is especially problematic with new media such as the Internet where the media planner's experience may be too limited to enable a good estimate of how many clicks to expect from advertising on a given site.

Message-Distribution Objectives

Distribution objectives define where, when, and how often advertising should appear. To answer these questions, a media planner must understand a number of terms, including *message weight, reach, frequency,* and *continuity.*

Audience Size and Message Weight

Marketers are naturally interested in having their messages exposed to as many customers and prospects as they can afford. So they are also logically most interested in those media opportunities that offer the largest audiences.[24] The basic way to express audience size is simply to count the number of people in a medium's

Exhibit 9–6

A media planner's toolbox.

Secondary sources of information help media planners do their jobs.

- **Simmons Market Research Bureau (SMRB) and Mediamark Research, Inc. (MRI) (www.mediamark.com):** report data on product, brand, and media usage by both demographic and lifestyle characteristics.
- **Broadcast Advertisers Reports (BAR), Leading National Advertisers (LNA), and Media Records:** report advertisers' expenditures by brand, media type, market, and time period.
- **Standard Rate & Data Service (SRDS) (www.srds.com):** provides information on media rates, format, production requirements, and audience.
- **Audit Bureau of Circulations (ABC) (www.accessabc.com):** verifies circulation figures of publishers.
- **The Arbitron Company (www.arbitron.com):** measures local radio audiences in 280+ markets and offers access to data through printed reports, computer tape, and software applications. Arbitron also provides syndicated measurement of local market media and consumer and retail behavior in 75 top markets. RetailDirect is Arbitron's local market, integrated audience measurement service for television stations, radio stations, and cable systems in 44 small- to medium-size markets. In 132 medium and small markets, Arbitron offers the Qualitative Diary Service to collect consumer behavior in a number of key local market, retail categories. Arbitron New Media offers survey research, consulting, and methodological services to the cable, telecommunications, direct broadcast satellite, online, and new media industries.
- **Competitive Media Reporting (CMR) (www.cmr.com):** delivers strategic advertising intelligence to advertising agencies, advertisers, broadcasters, and publishers. The tracking technologies collect occurrence and expenditure data, as well as the creative executions of over 900,000 brands across 15 media.
- **Nielsen Media Research (www.nielsenmedia.com):** is the leading provider of television information services in the United States and Canada. Nielsen Media Research is a subsidiary of Cognizant Corporation. It is no longer associated with ACNielsen.
- **ACNielsen Company (http://acnielsen.com):** a global provider of market research information and analysis to the consumer products and service industry. It provides TV ratings service to countries outside the United States and Canada. As a result of the split-up of The Dun & Bradstreet Corporation in 1996, both ACNielsen and Cognizant Corporation were spun off as independent, publicly traded companies.
- **Roper NOP Consulting (www.nopworld.com):** measures ad readership within specific publications and each year measures over 25,000 ads in over 500 magazine issues.
- **comScore Media Metrix (www.comscore.com/metrix):** delivers innovative and comprehensive Internet measurement, analysis, intelligence, and events to provide businesses with global resources for understanding and profiting from the Internet.
- **DoubleClick (www.doubleclick.net):** a global Internet advertising solutions company. It is focused on creating the solutions that make Internet advertising work for Web publishers and Web advertisers. Market innovations include: DoubleClick Network, the first Internet advertising network; DoubleClick DART, the leading targeting technology; DoubleClick AdServer, a complete ad management software solution; and DoubleClick Local, the first Internet advertising solution developed for regional and local businesses.

audience. This is what media research firms like Nielsen and Arbitron do for the broadcast media, typically using a statistical sample to project the total audience size. For print media, firms like the Audit Bureau of Circulations actually count and verify the number of subscribers (the **circulation**) and then multiply by the estimated number of **readers per copy (RPC)** to determine the total audience.

Media planners often define media objectives by the schedule's **message weight,** the total size of the audience for a set of ads or an entire campaign, because it gives some indication of the scope of the campaign in a given market. There are two ways to express message weight: *gross impressions* and *gross rating points*.

If planners know the audience size, they can easily calculate the number of advertising impressions in a media schedule. An **advertising impression** is a possible exposure of the advertising message to one audience member. It is sometimes referred to as an **opportunity to see (OTS).** By multiplying a medium's total audience size by the number of times an advertising message is used during the period, planners arrive at the **gross impressions,** or potential exposures, possible in that medium. Then, by summing the gross impressions for each medium used, they know the total gross impressions for the schedule (see Exhibit 9–7).

Media vehicle	Target audience*	Messages used	Gross impressions
"TV Ch. 6 News"	140,000	15	2,100,000
Daily newspaper	250,000	7	1,750,000
Spot radio	10,000	55	550,000
Total gross impressions			4,400,000

*Average.

With large media schedules, though, gross impressions can run into the millions and become very awkward to handle, so that's where the concept of *ratings* came from. The **rating** is simply the percentage of homes (or individuals) exposed to an advertising medium. Percentages are not only simpler numbers to deal with, they are also more useful in making comparisons. Thus, one rating point is equal to 1 percent of a given population group. When we hear that a particular TV show garnered a 20 rating, it means 20 percent of the households with TV sets (expressed as **television households** or **TVHH**) were tuned in to that show. The higher a program's rating, the more people are watching.[25] This definition applies to many media forms, but it is most commonly used for radio and TV.

By adding the ratings of several media vehicles (as we did for gross impressions) we can determine the message weight of a given advertising schedule, only now it's expressed as **gross rating points (GRPs)** (see Exhibit 9–8). When we say a schedule delivered 180 GRPs, that means the gross impressions generated by our schedule equaled 180 percent of the target market population. For broadcast media, GRPs are often calculated for a week or a month. In print media, they're calculated for the number of ads in a campaign. For outdoor advertising, they're calculated on the basis of daily exposure.

Media planners may use GRPs to determine the optimal level of spending for a campaign. The more GRPs they buy, the more it costs. However, because of discounting, the unit cost per GRP decreases as more GRPs are bought. Beyond a certain point, the effectiveness of additional GRPs diminishes.

Through the use of computer models and certain assumptions based on experience, sophisticated planners can detect the relative impact of ad-related variables on sales and determine the *return on investment* (ROI) from each. This can potentially save clients substantial sums of money.[26]

In the calculation of message weight, advertisers disregard any overlap or duplication. As a result, certain individuals within the audience may see the message several times while others don't see it at all. While message weight gives an indication of size, it does not reveal much about who is in the audience or how often they are reached. This fact necessitated the development of other media objectives, namely *reach, frequency,* and *continuity*.

Audience Accumulation and Reach

The term **reach** refers to the total number of *different* people or households exposed, at least once, to a medium during a given period of time, usually four

Media vehicle	Adult rating*	Messages used	Gross rating points
"TV Ch. 6 News"	14	15	210
Daily newspaper	25	7	175
Spot radio	1	55	55
Total gross rating points			440

*Assumes market size of 1 million people.

weeks.[27] For example, if 40 percent of 100,000 people in a target market tune in to radio station WKKO at least once during a four-week period, the reach is 40,000 people. Reach may be expressed as a percentage of the total market (40 percent) or as a raw number (40,000). Reach should not be confused with the number of people who will actually be exposed to and consume the advertising, though. It is just the number of people who are exposed to the medium and therefore have an *opportunity to see* the ad or commercial.

An advertiser may accumulate reach in two ways: by using the same media vehicle continuously or by combining two or more media vehicles.[28] Naturally, as more media are used, some duplication occurs. Exhibit 9–9 is a statistical table that shows how unduplicated reach builds as additional media are added.

Exposure Frequency

To express the number of times the same person or household is exposed to a message—a radio spot, for example—in a specified time span, media people use the term *frequency*. **Frequency** measures the *intensity* of a media schedule, based on repeated exposures to the medium or the program. Frequency is important because repetition is the key to memory.

Frequency is calculated as the *average* number of times individuals or homes are exposed to the medium. For instance, suppose in our hypothetical 100,000-person market that 20,000 people tune in to WKKO and have three OTSs during a four-week period, and another 20,000 have five OTSs. To calculate the average frequency, divide the total number of exposures by the total reach:

$$\text{Average frequency} = \text{Total exposures} \div \text{Audience reach}$$

$$= [(20{,}000 \times 3) + (20{,}000 \times 5)] \div 40{,}000$$

$$= 160{,}000 \div 40{,}000$$

$$= 4.0$$

For the 40,000 listeners reached, the average frequency, or number of exposures, was four.

Exhibit 9–9

Random combination table. Find the reach of the first medium on the horizontal axis. Find the reach of the second medium on the vertical axis. The point of intersection shows the combined reach of the two media. If three or more media forms are combined, use the same procedure, finding the combined reach of the first two media on the horizontal axis and reading down to the intersection with the reach of the third medium.

		25	30	35	40	45	50	55	60	65	70	75	80	85	90	95
		Reach of first medium														
Reach of second medium	**25**	46	47	51	55	59	62	66	70	74	77	81	85	89	92	95
	30	—	51	54	58	61	65	68	72	75	79	82	86	90	93	95
	35	—	—	58	61	64	67	71	74	77	80	84	87	90	93	95
	40	—	—	—	64	67	70	73	76	79	82	85	88	91	94	95
	45	—	—	—	—	70	72	75	78	81	83	86	89	92	94	95
	50	—	—	—	—	—	75	77	80	82	85	87	90	92	95	95
	55	—	—	—	—	—	—	80	82	84	86	89	91	93	95	95
	60	—	—	—	—	—	—	—	84	86	88	90	92	94	95	95
	65	—	—	—	—	—	—	—	—	88	89	91	93	95	95	95
	70	—	—	—	—	—	—	—	—	—	91	92	94	95	95	95
	75	—	—	—	—	—	—	—	—	—	—	94	95	95	95	95
	80	—	—	—	—	—	—	—	—	—	—	—	95	95	95	95
	85	—	—	—	—	—	—	—	—	—	—	—	—	95	95	95
	90	—	—	—	—	—	—	—	—	—	—	—	—	—	95	95
	95	—	—	—	—	—	—	—	—	—	—	—	—	—	—	95

Once we understand reach and frequency, we have another, simple way to determine the message weight. To calculate gross rating points, just multiply a show's reach (expressed as a rating percentage) by the average frequency. In our radio example, 40 percent of the radio households (a 40 rating) had the opportunity to hear the commercial an average of four times during the four-week period:

$$\text{Reach} \times \text{Frequency} = \text{GRPs}$$

$$40 \times 4 = 160 \text{ GRPs}$$

Thus, the message weight of this radio campaign would be equal to 160 percent of the total market—or 160,000 gross impressions.

Continuity

Media planners refer to the duration of an advertising message or campaign over a given period of time as **continuity.** Few companies spread their marketing efforts evenly throughout the year. They typically *heavy up* before prime selling seasons and slow down during the off-season. Likewise, to save money, a media planner for a new product might decide that after a heavy introduction period of, say, four weeks, a radio campaign needs to maintain *continuity* for an additional 16 weeks but on fewer stations. We'll discuss some common scheduling patterns in the section on media tactics.

While frequency is important to create memory, continuity is important to *sustain* it. Moreover, as people come into and out of the market for goods and services every day, continuity provides a means of having the message there when it's most needed. Ads that hit targets during purchase cycles are more effective and require less frequency.[29]

Optimizing Reach, Frequency, and Continuity: The Art of Media Planning

Good media planning is both an art and a science. The media planner must get the most effective exposure on a limited budget. As Exhibit 9–10 shows, the objectives of reach, frequency, and continuity have inverse relationships to each other. To achieve greater reach, some frequency and/or continuity has to be sacrificed, and so on. Research shows that all three are critical. But since all budgets are limited, which is most critical? This is currently the subject of hot debate in advertising circles.

Effective Reach

One of the problems with reach is that, by themselves, the numbers don't take into account the *quality* of the exposure. Some people exposed to the medium still won't be aware of the message. So, on the surface, reach doesn't seem to be the best measure of media success. Media people use the term **effective reach** to describe the quality of exposure. It measures the number or percentage of the audience who receive enough exposures to truly receive the message. Some researchers maintain that three OTSs over a four-week period are usually enough to reach an audience.[30]

Effective Frequency

Similar to the concept of effective reach is **effective frequency,** defined as the average number of times a person must see or hear a message before it becomes effective. In theory, effective frequency falls somewhere between a minimum level that achieves message awareness and a maximum level that becomes overexposure, which leads to "wearout" (starts to irritate consumers).

Following the publication of Michael Naples's classic book *Effective Frequency* in 1979, most of the industry fell in love with his claim that, in most cases, effective

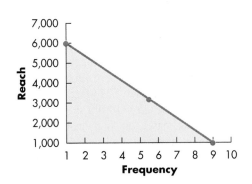

Exhibit 9–10

Reach, frequency, and continuity have an inverse relationship to one another. For instance, in the example above, an advertiser can reach 6,000 people once, 3,000 people 5.5 times, or 1,000 people 9 times for the same budget. However, to gain continuity over time, the advertiser would have to sacrifice some reach and some frequency.

frequency could be achieved by an average frequency of three over a four-week period. Here was a nice, simple conclusion that all the low-level media planners could use. Naples's conclusion seemed to be intuitively correct, and it was supported by some researchers who viewed advertising effects as a learning situation. While this might be true for some new products, most of the time advertising is for established products and therefore is not about "learning" but rather about "reminding." Syracuse University professor John Philip Jones writes that "a massive, multitiered edifice" of belief was built on the evidence in Naples's book—evidence that he believes led the industry down the wrong path.[31]

While the concepts of effective reach and frequency are now hotly debated, virtually all agencies still use them. Cannon and Riordan point out that conventional media planning is based on *media vehicle exposure* (the number of people in a medium's audience), but effectiveness should relate to *advertising message exposure*. For example, only 20 percent of viewers may pay attention when a commercial runs. It may take 10 opportunities-to-see to reach an average frequency of one!

Cannon and Riordan would replace effective frequency with *optimal frequency*. Most studies of the **advertising response curve** indicate that incremental response to advertising actually diminishes, rather than builds, with repeated exposures (see Exhibit 9–11). The optimal frequency concept moves the focus of media planning from exposure effectiveness to *effective exposures per dollar*.

> With a response curve that is characterized by continually diminishing returns, the first ad will be the most profitable. But subsequent exposures—advertising frequency—are still important. How important depends on the slope of the response curve and the cost of advertising. Obviously, the less money it costs per exposure to advertise, the more the firm can afford to advertise. The profit-maximizing firm will continue to spend until the revenue resulting from an additional advertisement placed is offset by its cost.[32]

The implications of Cannon and Riordan's theory are immense. Historically, media planning has emphasized frequency as the most important media objective. This assumes an S-shaped advertising response curve in which the first two or three exposures don't count. But Cannon and Riordan's analysis indicates that response curves are convex. The first exposure is the most effective, followed by diminishing returns. If that's the case, then the basic emphasis in advertising should switch from maximizing frequency to maximizing target market reach, adding less profitable second exposures only as the budget permits.[33]

This approach is now supported by numerous researchers who believe effective frequency planning is seriously flawed and who make a strong case for the primacy of reach and continuity as the most important media objectives.[34] In fact, for fast-moving consumer products, researcher Erwin Ephron suggests the concept of **recency planning,** based on "the sensible idea that most advertising works by influencing the brand choice of consumers who are ready to buy." Therefore, the important thing for advertising is to be there when the consumer is ready to buy, and that suggests continuity.[35] His theories have gained the attention of many of the nation's largest advertisers, among them Procter & Gamble, Kraft Foods, and Coca-Cola.[36]

One problem with all these theories is that they assume all exposures are equal. If that's the case, then where does advertising creativity come in? And what about the programs where the advertising appears? Doesn't that have some effect on the quality of exposure?

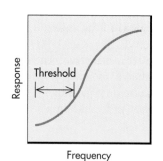

a. S-shaped response curve

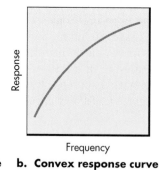

b. Convex response curve

Exhibit 9–11

Two advertising response curves. The S-shaped curve would be applicable for products that require a frequency of more than one to reach a threshold of greatest response. After that threshold is reached, the response diminishes for each subsequent exposure. The convex curve applies to products for which the first exposure produces the best return and all subsequent exposures produce slightly lower response.

For most media planners, the only solution to this debate is to establish first which type of response curve is most likely to apply to the particular situation and then to develop the campaign's media objectives accordingly.

Once the media objectives have been determined—that is, the optimum levels of message weight, reach, frequency, and continuity—the media planner can develop the strategy for achieving them.

Developing a Media Strategy: The Media Mix

The media strategy describes how the advertiser will achieve the stated media objectives: which media will be used, where, how often, and when. Just as marketers determine marketing strategy by blending elements of the marketing mix, media planners can develop media strategies by blending the elements of the *media mix.*

Elements of the Media Mix: The Five Ms

Many factors go into developing an effective media strategy. For simplicity and ease of memory, we have sorted them into five categories and given them the alliterative moniker of the **five Ms** (5Ms): *markets, money, media, mechanics,* and *methodology.*

Markets refers to the various targets of a media plan: trade and consumer audiences; global, national, or regional audiences; ethnic and socioeconomic groups; or other stakeholders. In an integrated marketing communications plan, the IMC planner wants to find the reasons and motivations for the prospect's purchase and usage patterns and then create a media plan based on those findings.[37]

Using intuition, marketing savvy, and analytical skill, the media planner determines the second element, **money**—how much to budget and where to allocate it. How much for print media, how much in TV, how much to nontraditional or supplemental media, how much to each geographic area? We discuss this issue in depth in the chapters on using and buying media (Chapters 15 through 18).

From the IMC perspective, **media** includes *all* communications vehicles available to a marketer—as Beth Gordon says, anything you can put your name on. This includes radio, TV, newspapers, magazines, outdoor, the Internet, and direct mail, plus sales promotion, direct marketing, public relations activities and publicity, special events, brochures, and even shopping bags.

Good media planners champion the integration of all marketing communications to help achieve their companies' marketing and advertising objectives. They look at the media element both analytically and creatively.

This ad for Kinko's (www.fedex.com/us/officeprint/main) exemplifies three of the five Ms of the media mix. Addressing business owners and executives (market), this ad ran in trade publications such as Fast Company magazine (media). The two-page spread and effective wording (mechanics) are intended to make a big impression on the reader. Methodology is the sum of processes used to create the ad, and money is affected by the four other elements.

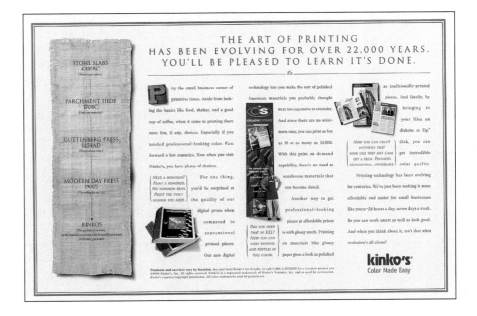

The media planner also has to deal with the complex **mechanics** of advertising media and messages. Radio and TV commercials come in a variety of time units, and print ads are created in a variety of sizes and styles. IMC planners may also deal with the mechanics of nontraditional media, everything from shopping bags to multimedia kiosks to the Internet. The myriad media options now available offer exciting, creative ways to enhance consumer acceptance of the advertiser's message and offer the consumer a relevant purchase incentive.

The **methodology** element refers to the overall strategy of selecting and scheduling media vehicles to achieve the desired message weight, reach, frequency, and continuity objectives. It offers the opportunity for creativity in planning, negotiating, and buying.

Factors That Influence Media Strategy Decisions

Media decisions are greatly influenced by factors over which the media planner has little or no control. These include the scope of the media plan, sales potential of different markets, competitive strategies and budget considerations, availability of different media vehicles, nature of the medium, mood of the message, message size and length, and buyer purchase patterns.

Scope of the Media Plan

The location and makeup of the target audience strongly influence the breadth of the media plan, thereby affecting decisions regarding the *market,* the *money,* and the *media* elements.

Domestic markets   A media planner normally limits advertising to areas where the product is available. If a store serves only one town, or if a city has been chosen to test market a new product, then the advertiser will use a *local* plan.

A *regional* plan may cover several adjoining metropolitan areas, an entire state or province, or several neighboring states. Regional plans typically employ a combination of local media, regional editions of national magazines, spot TV and radio, and the Internet.

Advertisers who want to reach several regions or an entire country use a *national* plan. This may call for network TV and radio, full-circulation national magazines and newspapers, nationally syndicated Sunday newspaper supplements, and the Web.

International markets   Foreign media can be a challenge for U.S. advertisers. While many broadcast stations are being privatized in countries as diverse as Israel and Russia, governments around the world still control many broadcast media, and some still do not permit commercials. Others limit advertising to a certain number of minutes per hour or per day.

In countries that do allow TV advertising, advertisers face other problems: how many people own TV sets, who they are, and what channels they receive. While this is not an issue in Europe and is becoming less so in Latin America, it is still a problem in many of the less-developed nations of Africa and Asia. There, TV ownership may be limited to upper-income consumers, or the availability of commercial channels may be severely limited. In those markets, advertisers must use a different media mix. Likewise, Internet access may be severely limited—or too expensive for consumers to afford. So that option may not even be available for some markets.

In many countries of Europe, more than 50 percent of total advertising expenditures are still spent in print media versus about 32 percent on television.[38] However, like the United States, Europe and Asia are experiencing a virtual explosion of new media and technology. Advertisers and agencies alike are realizing the importance of developing integrated marketing communications plans to build their brands and establish long-term relationships with their customers.

The Arab world is watching, tell them something!

MBC is not just famous for news and sport, its variety shows with live music, celebrity appearances and exciting competitions have become compulsive viewing for millions of Arabs throughout the world.
It's coverage like this, that makes MBC

the most popular Satellite TV network in the Middle East today and that's confirmed by PARC research.
So, if you're planning a cost effective advertising and sponsorship campaign, phone for details today and let MBC put your brands in the picture.

mbcTVputs your brands in the picture

For advertising information please contact:

Reaching international markets presents unique challenges to advertisers. There are many unknown variables in regulations, viewers, potential audience, and language and cultural barriers. This ad claims to solve these problems as MBC TV will take the guesswork out of media planning and ad preparation when targeting Arabic audiences.

Most marketers develop an international media plan by formulating individual national plans first. But it's not as simple as it sounds. Depending on the country, precise media information may not be available, circulation figures may not be audited, audience demographics may be sketchy, and even ad rates may be unreliable. Finally, the methodology used in media research may be considerably different from one market to another, making comparisons virtually impossible. At the same time, in some European countries, media research and planning may be more sophisticated than in the United States, which creates another problem for U.S. advertisers who are unfamiliar with European terms, concepts, and methodologies.[39]

Because of the media variations from country to country, most international and global advertisers entrust national media plans to in-country foreign media specialists or the local foreign branches of global media agencies such as MindShare, OMD Worldwide, The Media Edge, or Carat, rather than risk faulty centralized media planning.[40]

Sales Potential of Different Markets

The *market* and *money* elements of the media mix also depend on the sales potential of each area. National advertisers use this factor to determine where to allocate their advertising dollars. Planners can determine an area's sales potential in several ways.

The brand development index   The **brand development index (BDI)** indicates the sales potential of a particular brand in a specific market area. It compares the percentage of the brand's total U.S. sales in an area to the percentage of the total U.S. population in that area. The larger the brand's sales relative to the area's percentage of U.S. population, the higher the BDI and the greater the brand's sales potential. BDI is calculated as

$$\text{BDI} = \frac{\text{Percent of the brand's total U.S. sales in the area}}{\text{Percent of total U.S. population in the area}} \times 100$$

Suppose sales of a brand in Los Angeles are 1.58 percent of the brand's total U.S. sales and the population of Los Angeles is 2 percent of the U.S. total. The BDI for Los Angeles is

$$\text{BDI} = \frac{1.58}{2} \times 100 = 79$$

An index number of 100 means the brand's performance balances with the size of the area's population. A BDI index number below 100 indicates poor potential for the brand.

The category development index   To determine the potential of the whole product category, media planners use the **category development index (CDI),** which works on the same concept as the BDI and is calculated in much the same way:

$$\text{CDI} = \frac{\text{Percent of the product category's total U.S. sales in the area}}{\text{Percent of total U.S. population in the area}} \times 100$$

If category sales in Los Angeles are 4.92 percent of total U.S. category sales, the CDI in Los Angeles is

$$\text{CDI} = \frac{4.92}{2} \times 100 = 246$$

	Low BDI	High BDI
High CDI	Low market share *but* Good market potential	High market share *and* Good market potential
Low CDI	Low market share *and* Poor market potential	High market share *but* Monitor for sales decline

The combination of BDI and CDI can help the planner determine a media strategy for the market (see Exhibit 9–12). In our example, low BDI (under 100) and high CDI (over 100) in Los Angeles indicate that the product category has high potential but the brand is not selling well. This may represent a problem or an opportunity. If the brand has been on the market for some time, the low BDI raises a red flag; some problem is standing in the way of brand sales. But if the brand is new, the low BDI may not be alarming. In fact, the high CDI may indicate the brand can grow substantially, given more time and greater media and marketing support. At this point, the media planner should assess the company's share of voice (discussed in Chapter 8) and budget accordingly.

Competitive Strategies and Budget Considerations

Advertisers always consider what competitors are doing, particularly those that have larger advertising budgets. This affects the *media, mechanics,* and *methodology* elements of the media mix. Several services, like Competitive Media Reports, detail competitive advertising expenditures in the different media. By knowing the size of competitors' budgets, what media they're using, the regionality or seasonality of their sales, and any new-product tests and introductions, advertisers can better plan a counterstrategy.

Again, the media planner should analyze the company's share of voice in the marketplace. If an advertiser's budget is much smaller than the competition's, the brand could get lost in the shuffle. Advertisers should bypass media that competitors dominate and choose other media that offer a strong position.

When Anne Myers, media director of Palmer Jarvis DDB, Toronto, had to develop a media plan for Panasonic Canada's Power Activator batteries, she didn't have the budget of Energizer or Duracell to work with. So she didn't want to place her ads where theirs were. Myers and her team creatively fashioned a guerrilla media plan that targeted a cynical, hard-to-reach audience, 15- to 22-year-olds, right where they lived—in the clubs, on the street, and on the Internet. The campaign included posters in the dance clubs; sponsorship of popular DJs and VJs; free PA T-shirts, hats, posters, and stickers; an eight-week run of television spots on popular music shows tied to a month-long cross-promotion with a new CD release; and a special contest run on a micro website that was linked to Panasonic's home page. The response was excellent: Sales were up 136 percent over the previous year, and the contest promotion generated more than 16,300 entries on the website with a click-through rate of 35 percent.[41]

It sometimes makes sense to use media similar to the competition's if the target audiences are the same or if the competitors are not using their media effectively.

Media Availability and Economics: The Global Marketer's Headache

North American advertisers are blessed—or cursed—with an incredible array of media choices, locally and nationally. Such is not always the case in other areas of the world, which is one reason their per capita advertising expenditures are so

Exhibit 9–13

Top 10 countries outside the United States ranked by billings ($ in millions).

Rank	Country	2002 ad spending	% change
1	Japan	$33,516	6.8
2	Germany	16,973	−4.1
3	United Kingdom	15,249	0.2
4	France	9,031	−1.4
5	Italy	7,087	−3.4
6	Brazil	7,020	NA
7	China	6,339	23.8
8	South Korea	6,013	19.4
9	Spain	5,083	−0.6
10	Canada	5,218	3.7

much lower than in the United States. (Exhibit 9–13 shows the total local ad agency billings for the top 10 advertising countries outside the United States.)

Every country has communications media, but they are not always available for commercial use (especially radio and television) and coverage may be limited. Lower literacy rates and education levels in some countries restrict the coverage of print media. Where income levels are low, TV ownership is also low. These factors tend to segment markets by media coverage.

To reach lower-income markets, radio is the medium of choice, as both Coke and Pepsi have demonstrated successfully for years. Auto manufacturers make good use of TV and magazine advertising to reach the upper class. And movie advertising can reach whole urban populations where TV ownership is low because motion picture attendance in such countries is very high. The Checklist, "International Media Planning," outlines some basic considerations for media buyers entering international markets.

Some companies are attempting to become true global marketers of their brands with centralized control of media and standardized creative. As a group, global media are growing, which is good news for global marketers.[42] However, there are still few true global media. So these major advertisers must continue to use local foreign media in the countries where they do business and localize their campaigns for language and cultural differences.

Finally, there's the problem of **spillover media,** local media that many consumers in a neighboring country inadvertently receive. For example, media from Luxembourg regularly spill over into France, Belgium, and Holland. Media often spill over into countries lacking indigenous-language publications, particularly specialty publications. English and German business media enjoy a large circulation in Scandinavian countries, for example, where there are relatively few specialized trade publications written in Swedish, Danish, or Norwegian.

Spillover media pose a threat for the multinational advertiser because they expose readers to multiple ad campaigns. If the advertiser runs both international and local campaigns for the same products, discrepancies in product positioning, pricing, or advertising messages could confuse potential buyers. Advertisers' local subsidiaries or distributors need to coordinate local and international ad campaigns to avoid such confusion. On the positive side, spillover media offer potential cost savings through regional campaigns.

Nature of the Medium and Mood of the Message

An important influence on the *media* element of the mix is how well a medium works with the style or mood of the particular message.

Advertising messages differ in many ways. Some are simple messages: "Just do it" (Nike). Others make emotional or sensual appeals to people's needs and wants: "The great taste of fruit squared" (Jolly Rancher candies). Many advertisers use a reason-why approach to explain their product's advantages: "Twice the room. Twice the comfort. Twice the value. Embassy Suites. Twice the hotel."

Complex messages, such as ads announcing a new product or concept, require more space or time for explanation. Each circumstance affects the media selection as well as the *methodology* of the media mix.

A new or highly complex message may require greater frequency and exposure to be understood and remembered. A dogmatic message like Nike's may require a surge at the beginning, then low frequency and greater reach.

When a product's share of market is less than the competition's, competitive strategies can provide enormous marketing leverage. Here, Fujitsu (www.fcpa.com) advertises its portable data drive as the cheaper and superior alternative to the industry standard Zip and Jaz drives, manufactured by Iomega.

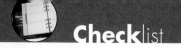

International Media Planning

Basic Considerations (Who Does What?)

____ **What is the client's policy regarding supervision and placement of advertising?** When, where, and to what degree is the client and/or client branch office abroad involved?

____ **Which client office is in charge of the campaign?** North American headquarters or foreign office or both? Who else has to be consulted? In what areas (creative or media selection and so forth)?

____ **Is there a predetermined media mix?** Can international as well as foreign media be used?

____ **Who arranges for translation of copy if foreign media are to be used?**
- Client headquarters in North America.
- Client office in foreign country.
- Agency headquarters in North America.
- Foreign media rep in North America.

____ **Who approves translated copy?**

____ **Who checks on acceptability of ad copy in foreign country?** Certain ads need approval by foreign governments.

____ **What is the advertising placement procedure?**
- From agency branch office in foreign country directly to foreign media.
- From North American agency to American-based foreign media rep to foreign media.
- From North American agency to American-based international media.
- From North American agency to affiliated agency abroad to foreign media.

____ **What are the pros and cons of each approach?** Is the media commission to be split with foreign agency branch or affiliate office? Can the campaign be run from North America? Does the client save ad taxes by placing from North America? In what currency does the client want to pay?

____ **Who receives checking copies?**

____ **Will advance payment be made to avoid currency fluctuation?**

____ **Who bills?** What currency? Who approves payment?

Budget Considerations

____ **Is budget predetermined by client?**

____ **Is budget based on local branch or distributor recommendation?**

____ **Is budget based on agency recommendation?**

____ **Is budget related to sales in the foreign market?**

____ **What is the budget period?**

____ **What is the budget breakdown for media,** including ad taxes, translation, production, and research costs?

____ **What are the tie-ins with local distributors, if any?**

Market Considerations

____ **What is the geographic target area?**
- Africa and Middle East.
- Asia, including Australasia.
- Europe.
- Latin America.

____ **What are the major market factors in these areas?**
- Local competition.
- GDP growth over past four years and expected future growth.
- Membership of country in a common market or free trade association.
- Literacy rate.
- Attitude toward North American products or services.
- Social and religious customs.

____ **What is the basic target audience?**
- Management executives in business and industry.
- Managers and buyers in certain businesses.
- Military and government officials.
- Consumers; potential buyers of foreign market goods.

Media Considerations

____ **Availability of media to cover market: Are the desired media available in the particular area?**

____ **Foreign media and/or international media:** Should the campaign be in the press and language of a particular country, or should it be a combination of foreign and international?

____ **What media does the competition use?**

____ **Does the medium fit?**
- Optimum audience quality and quantity.
- Desired image, editorial content, and design.
- Suitable paper and color availability.
- Justifiable rates and CPM (don't forget taxes on advertising, which can vary by medium).
- Discount availability.
- Type of circulation audit.
- Availability of special issues or editorial tie-ins.

____ **What are the closing dates at North American rep and at the publication headquarters abroad?**

____ **What is the agency commission?** (When placed locally abroad at the agency, commission is sometimes less than when placed in North America.)

____ **For how long are contracted rates protected?**

____ **Does the publication have a North American rep** to help with media evaluation and ad placement?

The language and imagery of this Godiva chocolate (www.godiva.com) ad exudes a sense of elegance that suits the audience of the medium selected. Godiva placed the ad in magazines such as Architectural Digest to reach a target audience of affluent, well-educated individuals. The photo, type, and layout elements reflect the nature of the magazine, the advertiser, and even the audience.

Once consumers understand reason-why messages, pulsing advertising exposures at irregular intervals is often sufficient. Emotionally oriented messages are usually more effective when spaced at regular intervals to create enduring feelings about the product. We discuss these scheduling methods further in the next section, on media tactics.

Message Size, Length, and Position Considerations

The particular characteristics of different media, over which the media planner has no control, affect the *mechanics* element of the media mix. For example, in print, a full-page ad attracts more attention than a quarter-page ad and a full-color ad more than a black-and-white one. Color and larger units of space or time cost dearly in terms of reach and frequency (see Exhibit 9–14).

Should a small advertiser run a full-page ad once a month or a quarter-page ad once a week? Is it better to use a few 60-second commercials or many 15- and 30-second ones? The planner has to consider the nature of the advertising message; some simply require more time and space to explain. Competitive activity often dictates more message units. The product itself may demand the prestige of a full page or full color. However, it's often better to run small ads consistently rather than one large ad occasionally. Unfortunately, space and time units may be determined by someone other than the media planner—creative or account service, for example—in which case the planner's options are limited.

The position of an ad is another consideration. Preferred positions for magazine ads are front and back covers; for TV, sponsorship of prime-time shows. Special positions and sponsorships cost more, so the media planner must decide whether the increased reach and frequency are worth the higher costs.

As we can see, the nature of the creative work has the potential to greatly affect the media strategy. This means that media planners have to be flexible, since the initial media plan may well have been determined prior to beginning the creative work.

Buyer Purchase Patterns

Finally, the customer's product purchasing behavior affects every element of the media mix. The media planner must consider how, when, and where the product is typically purchased and repurchased. Products with short purchase cycles

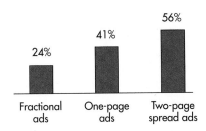

a. Size—as size increases so does readership.

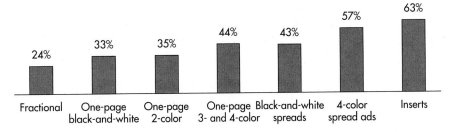

b. Size and color—advertising readership increases with size and the use of color.

Exhibit 9–14
Effect of size and color on ad readership (total ads studied = 107,506).

Media Selection: Quicklist of Advantages

Medium	Advantages
Newspapers	Many ad sizes available. Quick placement, local targeting. Audience interest.
Magazines	High-quality graphics/reproduction. Prestige factor. Color. Selective targeting.
TV	Combines sight, sound, movement. A single message. Demonstration. Social dominance.
Radio	Intimacy. Loyal following. Ability to change message quickly. Repetition and frequency.
Internet	Immediate response. Interactive. Highly selective targeting. Global. Fastest growing medium.
Direct mail	Measurable. Graphics, color. 3-D. Highly personal. Adaptable message length.
Outdoor/Transit	Local targeting. Graphics, color. Simple message. Larger than life. Repetition.

An extensive list of media appears as RL 9-2 in the Reference Library that appears on the *Contemporary Advertising* CD.

Laboratory Applications

1. If you wanted a set of complementary media to cover all the creative advantages, which mix would you select?

2. What creative advantages can you add to the list?

(convenience foods and paper towels) require more constant levels of advertising than products purchased infrequently (refrigerators and furniture). For a practical checklist of these points, see RL 9–1 in the Reference Library on the *Contemporary Advertising* CD.

Stating the Media Strategy

A written rationale for the media strategy is an integral part of any media plan. Without one, it's difficult for client and agency management to analyze the logic and consistency of the recommended media schedule.

Generally, the strategy statement begins with a brief definition of target audiences (the *market* element) and the priorities for weighting them. It explains the nature of the message and indicates which media types will be used and why (the *media* element). It outlines specific reach, frequency, and continuity goals and how they are to be achieved (the *methodology* element). It provides a budget for each medium (the *money* element) including the cost of production and any collateral materials. Finally, it states the intended size of message units, any position or timing considerations (the *mechanics* element), and the effect of budget restrictions.

Once the strategy is delineated, the plan details the tactics to be employed, the subject of the next section.

Media Tactics: Selecting and Scheduling Media Vehicles

Once the general media strategy is determined, the media planner can select and schedule particular media vehicles. The planner usually considers each medium's value on a set of specific criteria (see Ad Lab 9–B).

Criteria for Selecting Individual Media Vehicles

In evaluating specific media vehicles, the planner considers several factors: overall campaign objectives and strategy; size and characteristics of each medium's audience; attention, exposure, and motivational value of each medium; and cost efficiency. (For a comparative evaluation of various media types, see RL 9–2 in the Reference Library on the *Contemporary Advertising* CD.)

Overall Campaign Objectives and Strategy

The media planner's first job is to review the nature of the product or service, the intended objectives and strategies, and the primary and secondary target markets and audiences. The characteristics of the product often suggest a suitable choice. A product with a distinct personality or image, such as a fine perfume, might be advertised in media that reinforce this image. The media planner considers how consumers regard various magazines and TV programs—feminine or masculine, highbrow or lowbrow, serious or frivolous—and determines whether they're appropriate for the brand.

The content and editorial policy of the media vehicle and its compatibility with the product are important considerations. *Tennis* magazine is a poor vehicle for cigarette or alcohol ads even though its demographic profile and image might match the desired target audience.

Consumers choose a particular media vehicle because they gain some "reward": self-improvement, financial advice, career guidance, or simply news and entertainment. Advertising is most effective when it positions a product as part of the solution that consumers seek. Otherwise, they may see it as an intrusion.[43]

If the marketing objective is to gain greater product distribution, the planner should select media that influence potential dealers. If the goal is to stimulate sales of a nationally distributed product in isolated markets, ads should be placed in local and regional media that penetrate those markets. Pricing strategy influences media choices too. A premium-priced product should use prestigious or classy media to support its market image.

Characteristics of Media Audiences

An **audience** is the total number of people or households exposed to a medium. The planner needs to know how closely the medium's audience matches the profile of the target market and how interested prospective customers are in the publication or program. A product intended for a Latino audience, for example, would likely appear in specific media directed toward Hispanics. Simmons Market Research Bureau provides research data on age, income, occupational status, and other characteristics of magazine readers. Simmons also publishes demographic and psychographic data on product usage of consumers. Likewise, Nielsen provides audience statistics for television programs and Arbitron for radio stations.

The *content* of the medium usually determines the type of people in the audience. Some radio stations emphasize in-depth news or sports; others feature jazz, rock, or classical music. Each type of programming attracts a different audience.

Exposure, Attention, and Motivation Value of Media Vehicles

The media planner has to select media that will not only achieve the desired exposure to the target audience, but also attract *attention* and *motivate* people to act.

Exposure   To understand the concept of **exposure value,** think of how many people an ad "sees" rather than the other way around. How many of a magazine's 3 million readers will an ad actually see? How many of a TV program's 10 million viewers will a commercial actually see?

Keeping track of all the projects and responsibilities in an agency is a monumental task, especially with the myriad media opportunities available today. This is now greatly facilitated by sophisticated software programs from companies like Marketing Central (www.marketingcentral.com).

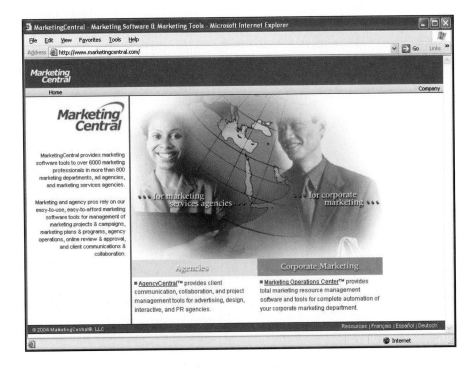

As we discussed earlier, just because someone reads a particular magazine or watches a certain program doesn't mean he or she sees the ads. Some people read only one article, set the magazine aside, and never pick it up again. Many people change channels during commercial breaks or leave to get a snack. Comparing the exposure value of different media vehicles, therefore, is very difficult. Without statistics, media planners have to use their best judgment based on experience.

Five factors affect the probability of ad exposure:

1. The senses used to perceive messages from the medium (for example, scratch-and-sniff ads really improve the exposure value of magazines).
2. How much and what kind of attention the medium requires (higher involvement suggests greater ad exposure).
3. Whether the medium is an information source or a diversion (for example, radio news programs offer greater ad exposure than elevator music).
4. Whether the medium or program aims at a general or a specialized audience (exposure value will be higher with specialized audiences).
5. The placement of the ad in the vehicle (placement within broadcast programs gives greater exposure than placement between programs; ads placed next to editorial material get greater exposure than ads placed next to other print ads).

Attention   Degree of attention is another consideration. As we discussed in Chapter 5, consumers with no interest in motorcycles or cosmetics won't remember ads for those products. For a variety of reasons, they fail to penetrate the viewer's perceptual screens. But someone in the market for a new car tends to notice every car ad.

Exposure value relates only to the medium; **attention value** concerns the advertising message and copy, as well as the medium. Special-interest media, such as boating magazines, offer good attention value to a marine product. But what kind of attention value does the daily newspaper offer such a product? Do sailors think about boats while reading the newspaper? Much research still needs to be done, but six factors are known to increase attention value:[44]

1. Audience involvement with editorial content or program material.
2. Specialization of audience interest or identification.
3. Number of competitive advertisers (the fewer, the better).
4. Audience familiarity with the advertiser's campaign.
5. Quality of advertising reproduction.
6. Timeliness of advertising exposure.

Motivation   These same factors affect a medium's **motivation value,** but in different ways. Familiarity with the advertiser's campaign may affect attention significantly but motivation very little. The attention factors of quality reproduction and timeliness can motivate someone, however.

Media planners analyze these values by assigning numerical ratings to their judgments of a medium's strengths and weaknesses. Then, using a weighting formula, they add them up. Planners use similar weighting methods to evaluate other factors, such as the relative importance of age versus income.

Cost Efficiency of Media Vehicles

Finally, media planners analyze the cost efficiency of each medium. A common term used in media planning and buying is **cost per thousand,** or **CPM** (M is the Roman numeral for 1,000). If a daily newspaper has 300,000 subscribers and charges $5,000 for a full-page ad, the cost per thousand is the cost divided by the number of thousands of people in the audience. Since there are 300 *thousands* of subscribers, you divide $5,000 by 300:

$$\text{CPM} = \frac{\$5,000}{300,000 \div 1,000} = \frac{\$5,000}{300} = \$16.67 \text{ per thousand}$$

However, media planners are more interested in **cost efficiency**—the cost of exposing the message to the target audience rather than to the total circulation. Let's say the target audience is males ages 18 to 49, and 40 percent of a weekly newspaper's subscriber base of 250,000 fits this category. If the paper charges $3,000 for a full-page ad, the CPM is computed as follows:

$$\text{Target audience} = 0.40 \times 250,000 = 100,000$$

$$\text{CPM} = \frac{\$3,000}{100,000 \div 1,000} = \$30 \text{ per thousand}$$

The daily paper, on the other hand, might turn out to be more cost efficient if 60 percent of its readers (180,000) belong to the target audience:

$$\text{CPM} = \frac{\$5,000}{180,000 \div 1,000} = \$27.78 \text{ per thousand}$$

Comparing different media by CPMs is important but does not take into account each medium's other advantages and disadvantages. The media planner must evaluate all the criteria to determine

1. How much of each medium's audience matches the target audience.
2. How each medium satisfies the campaign's objectives and strategy.
3. How well each medium offers attention, exposure, and motivation.

To evaluate some of these issues, the media planner may want to calculate the **cost per point (CPP)** of different broadcast programs. This is done the same way as cost per thousand, except you divide the cost by the rating points instead of the gross impressions.

Economics of Foreign Media

The main purpose of media advertising is to communicate with customers more efficiently than through personal selling. In some developing countries, though, it's actually cheaper to send people out with baskets of samples. For mass marketers in the United States, this kind of personal contact is virtually impossible.

In many foreign markets, outdoor advertising enjoys far greater coverage than in the United States because it costs less to have people paint the signs and there is also less government restriction.

Cost inhibits the growth of broadcast media in some foreign markets, but most countries now sell advertising time to help foot the bills. China and Vietnam, for example, have recently become booming markets for advertising.[45] As more countries allow commercial broadcasts and international satellite channels gain a greater foothold, TV advertising will continue to grow.

The Synergy of Mixed Media

A combination of media is called a **mixed-media approach.** There are numerous reasons for using mixed media:

■ To reach people who are unavailable through only one medium.
■ To provide repeat exposure in a less expensive secondary medium after attaining optimum reach in the first.

■ To use the intrinsic value of an additional medium to extend the creative effectiveness of the ad campaign (such as music on radio along with long copy in print media).

■ To deliver coupons in print media when the primary vehicle is broadcast.

■ To produce **synergy,** where the total effect is greater than the sum of its parts.

Newspapers, for example, can be used to introduce a new product and give immediacy to the message. Magazine ads can then follow up for greater detail, image enhancement, longevity, and memory improvement.

A mixed-media campaign was effective for General Electric's lighting products. The promotion used a combination of network TV spots, print advertising, Sunday supplement inserts, in-store displays in more than 150,000 stores, and a highly creative publicity program. By using an integrated, mixed-media approach, the campaign produced "unprecedented" consumer awareness and dealer support. It achieved synergy.[46]

Methods for Scheduling Media

After selecting the appropriate media vehicles, the media planner decides how many space or time units to buy of each vehicle and schedules them for release over a period of time when consumers are most apt to buy the product.

Continuous, Flighting, and Pulsing Schedules

To build continuity in a campaign, planners use three principal scheduling tactics: *continuous, flighting,* and *pulsing* (see Exhibit 9–15).

In a **continuous schedule,** advertising runs steadily and varies little over the campaign period. It's the best way to build continuity. Advertisers use this scheduling pattern for products consumers purchase regularly. For example, a commercial is scheduled on radio stations WTKO and WRBI for an initial four-week period. Then, to maintain continuity in the campaign, additional spots run continuously every week throughout the year on station WRBI.

Flighting alternates periods of advertising with periods of no advertising. This intermittent schedule makes sense for products and services that experience large fluctuations in demand throughout the year (tax services, lawn-care products, cold remedies). The advertiser might introduce the product with a four-week flight and then schedule three additional four-week flights to run during seasonal periods later in the year.

The third alternative, **pulsing,** mixes continuous and flighting strategies. As the consumer's purchasing cycle gets longer, pulsing becomes more appropriate. The advertiser maintains a low level of advertising all year but uses periodic pulses to heavy up during peak selling periods. This strategy is appropriate for products like soft drinks, which are consumed all year but more heavily in the summer.

Additional Scheduling Patterns

For high-ticket items that require careful consideration, **bursting**—running the same commercial every half hour on the same network during prime time—can be effective. A variation is **roadblocking,** buying air time on all three networks simultaneously. Chrysler used this technique to give viewers the impression that the advertiser was everywhere, even if the ad showed for only a few nights. Digital Equipment used a scheduling tactic called **blinking** to stretch its slim ad budget. To reach business executives, it flooded the airwaves on Sundays (on both cable and network TV channels) to make it virtually impossible to miss the ads.[47] (For guidelines on determining the best reach, frequency, continuity, and pulsing combinations, study RL 9–1 in the Reference Library on the *Contemporary Advertising* CD.)

a. Continuous

100 GRPs/week

12 weeks

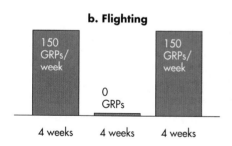

b. Flighting

150 GRPs/week   0 GRPs   150 GRPs/week

4 weeks   4 weeks   4 weeks

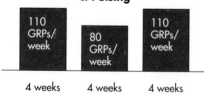

c. Pulsing

110 GRPs/week   80 GRPs/week   110 GRPs/week

4 weeks   4 weeks   4 weeks

Exhibit 9–15

Three ways to schedule the same number of total gross rating points: continuous, flighting, and pulsing.

Exhibit 9–16

A media plan flowchart like this computerized printout of Telmar's FlowMaster gives a bird's-eye view of the major media purchases and where and when they will appear over a specified period of time.

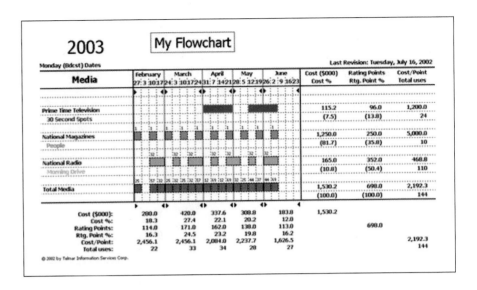

Once the scheduling criteria are determined, the media planner creates a flowchart of the plan. The flowchart is a graphic presentation of the total campaign to let the creative department, media department, account services, and the client see the pattern of media events that will occur throughout the campaign, usually one year (see Exhibit 9–16).

Computers in Media Selection and Scheduling

The last decade has seen a profusion of new desktop computer software to assist media planners. Computers perform the tedious number crunching needed to compute GRPs, CPMs, reach, frequency, and the like. They also save time and money. One agency found it could plan the entire TV, radio, and print co-op budgets for one of its largest clients in two days with only three people and one software package. Previously, that task required 70 staffers working manually for a week and a half.

Established in 1968, Telmar was the first company to provide media planning systems on a syndicated basis. Today, it is the world's leading supplier of Windows and Internet-based media planning software and support services. More than 3,500 users in 100 countries, including 95 percent of the world's top agencies, use Telmar systems for media and marketing decision making.[48]

Telmar's software suite is designed to help media planners, buyers, research analysts, and sellers work more efficiently and to help them make better judgments in the evaluation or sales process. The software allows advertising executives to estimate the effectiveness of multifaceted marketing plans that use various combinations of media including print, broadcast, in-store, special promotions, special events, PR, and other "new media." Its flexibility permits the user to analyze the potential effectiveness of any and every marketing tool used to reach the consumer.

Similarly, Interactive Market Systems (IMS) has introduced its *PowerHouse* software, which provides access to more than 600 syndicated and proprietary databases including MRI, Simmons, PMB, Arbitron, PRIZM, Scarborough, J.D. Power and Associates, or the advertiser's own proprietary data.[49]

A second product, *PowerFlow*, is a powerful flowcharting system, and forms the central component of IMS' Media Planner's Workstation. *PowerFlow*, on its own, enables planners to produce sophisticated media flowcharts quickly, but its real "power" is derived from its integration with individual planning modules (national, broadcast, magazines, newspaper) and expenditure data.

The advent of computer software has taken some of the more grueling, laborious work out of media planning. Planners can now crunch numbers, track results, and compute GRPs and CPMs right at their desktops. This saves an enormous amount of time and money. The SRDS Media Planning System (www.srds.com) shown here is an example of one of the many programs available.

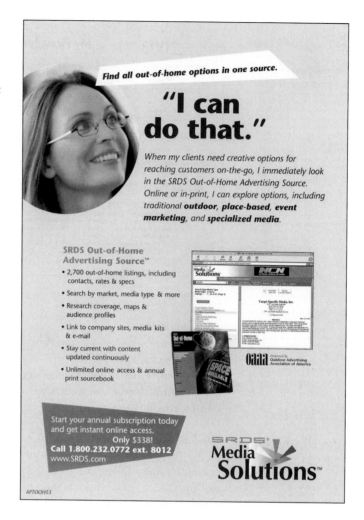

Even with all the technological timesavers and shortcuts, though, it's still up to the media planner to know the product, the market, and the media, and to then make the call. Computers can't decide which medium or environment is best for the message. They can't evaluate the content of a magazine or the image of a TV program. They can't judge whether the numbers they're fed are valid or reliable, and they can't interpret the meaning of the numbers. What they can do is help the process along.

Chapter Summary

Media planning directs the advertising message to the right people at the right time. It involves many decisions: where to advertise and when, which media to use, and how often to use them. Media planners need both financial skills and creativity. Like good art and copy ideas, media decisions should be based on sound marketing principles and research.

The task of media planners has become more complicated and competitive in recent years due to the dramatic increase in media options, the continuing fragmentation of audiences, the rising cost of space and time, and the increasing complexity in the way media buys are made. But this has also given the professionals who work in media departments new prominence.

The media function involves two basic processes: planning media strategy and selecting media vehicles. Media planning begins with defining audience objectives—the specific types of people the advertising message will be directed to—and then setting the goals for communicating with those audiences. The target audience is often determined from the marketer's past experience, through special research studies, or through secondary research sources such as Simmons Market Research Bureau and Mediamark Research. Planners who follow an IMC model start by segmenting their audiences according to brand purchasing behavior and then ranking these segments by profit to the brand. Once the target audience is determined, the planner sets the message-distribution objectives. These specify where, when, and how often the advertising should appear. They may be expressed in terms of message weight, reach, frequency, and continuity. In this process, the planner considers the amount of advertising needed to achieve effectiveness.

To create the appropriate media strategy, the planner develops the best blend of the five Ms: markets, money, media, mechanics, and methodology. The planner must also consider many uncontrollable variables: the scope of the media plan, which is determined by the location and makeup of the target audience; the

sales potential of different markets for both the brand and the product category; competitive strategies and budget considerations; media availability and economics; the nature of the medium and the mood of the message; the size, length, and position of the message in the selected media; and buyer purchase patterns. IMC planners try to discover the reasons and motivations for people's purchase and usage patterns and then create media plans based on those findings.

For international markets, media planners have to consider the availability and cost structure of foreign media and the differing cultural markets they serve. Some advertisers attempt to standardize their messages through the use of global media, but these media are still quite limited.

After the media strategy is developed, the planner selects specific media vehicles. Both the quantitative and qualitative criteria used to make this decision are important in the evaluation process. Factors that influence the selection process include campaign objectives and strategy; the size and characteristics of each medium's audience; geographic coverage; the exposure, attention, and motivation value of each medium; cost efficiency; and the advisability of a mixed-media approach.

Once media vehicles are selected, the media planner decides on scheduling—how many of each medium's space or time units to buy over what period of time. A media campaign can run continuously or in erratic pulses. These decisions are affected by consumer purchase patterns, the product's seasonality, and the balance of reach, frequency, and continuity that meets the planner's media objectives and budget.

The media planner must spend money wisely to maximize the campaign's effectiveness. To that end, many computer models have been developed, both in the United States and overseas, to help planners determine optimum levels of expenditure or compare alternative media schedules.

Important Terms

advertising impression, *280*
advertising response curve, *284*
attention value, *294*
audience, *293*
audience objectives, *278*
blinking, *296*
brand development index (BDI), *287*
bursting, *296*
category development index (CDI), *287*
circulation, *280*
continuity, *283*
continuous schedule, *296*
cost efficiency, *295*
cost per point (CPP), *295*
cost per thousand (CPM), *294*

creative mix, *278*
distribution objectives, *279*
effective frequency, *283*
effective reach, *283*
exposure value, *293*
five Ms, *285*
flighting, *296*
frequency, *282*
gross impressions, *280*
gross rating points (GRPs), *281*
markets, *285*
mechanics, *286*
media, *285*
media planning, *269*
media vehicles, *279*

message weight, *280*
methodology, *286*
mixed-media approach, *295*
money, *285*
motivation value, *294*
opportunity to see (OTS), *280*
pulsing, *296*
rating, *281*
reach, *281*
readers per copy (RPC), *280*
recency planning, *284*
roadblocking, *296*
spillover media, *289*
synergy, *296*
television households (TVHH), *281*

Review Questions

1. What major factors contribute to the increased complexity of media planning?
2. What must media planners consider before they begin?
3. What secondary research sources are available to planners?
4. How does the IMC approach differ from the top-down media planning approach?
5. What are the "right" reach and frequency for a given message?
6. How are GRPs and CPMs calculated?
7. What are the 5Ms of the media mix, and how are they determined?
8. What major factors influence the choice of individual media vehicles?

9. Why might an advertiser use a mixed-media approach?
10. What are the principal methods used to schedule media?
11. **The Advertising Experience**
    As a media buyer working on behalf of a large toy company, it is your job to buy media space for the launch of the Kitchi Kiss doll, which all advertising research shows will be a tremendous profit maker for the company. Using Exhibit 9–16 as an example, create a flowchart for a year's advertising for Kitchi Kiss. Explain your decisions about the types of media involved, when to use which types, and for how long each type should run.

Exploring the Internet

The Internet exercises for Chapter 9 address the following areas covered in the chapter: media buying services (Exercise 1) and media organizations (Exercises 2 and 3).

1. **Media Buying Services**
   There are three sides to the media business: those who plan; those who buy; and those who sell. Media planning and media buying are often in-house functions at an advertising agency, while sellers are those who represent the various media to clients, agencies, and media buying services.
   Visit the websites for the media companies listed below, consider the impact and importance of each to advertisers and their agencies, and answer the questions that follow.
   - Mediaedge:cia www.mediaedge.com
   - Media Solutions www.mediasol.com
   - The Davis Group www.thedavisgrouptx.com
   - Worldata www.worldata.com
   - Initiative Media www.wimc.com
   - Zenith Optimedia www.zenithoptimedia.com
   a. Who is the intended audience(s) of the site?
   b. What is the site's purpose? Does it succeed? Why or why not?
   c. What is the company's purpose?
   d. Does the company specialize in any particular segment (consumer, business-to-business, agriculture, automotive)?

2. **Media Organizations**
   The world of media is vast and constantly changing. Many media giants own properties in several media categories and

are major forces in the world of advertising. Visit the websites for the following media companies and answer the questions below.
   - Advo Inc. www.advo.com
   - Cox Enterprises www.cox.com
   - Gannett www.gannett.com
   - McGraw-Hill www.mcgraw-hill.com
   - Time Warner www.timewarner.com
   - Tribune Company www.tribune.com
   - Turner Broadcasting System www.turner.com
   - Viacom www.viacom.com
   a. Who is the intended audience of the site?
   b. What is the size/scope of the organization?
   c. What is the organization's purpose? The site's purpose?
   d. How important is this organization to the advertising industry? Why?

3. **Finding the Right Media**
   As an entrepreneur and sole owner of SafetyPepper Co., you have developed a pepper spray that you believe is superior to the brands the police departments use now. Although you want to sell SafetyPepper directly to the police, you also believe there is a strong market among the general public. Examine the websites in Exercise 2 to find media outlets that you believe would provide the audience you need to sell your product. Discuss why these particular outlets are better than the many others that are offered.

Part 3

Integrating Advertising with Other Elements of the Communications Mix

TODAY, CORPORATE MANAGERS WORLDWIDE are becoming more and more aware of the important benefits of relationship marketing and integrated marketing communications. By maximizing resources and linking communications activities directly to organizational goals and the resulting bottom line, these activities offer unparalleled accountability. Integral to these topics, though, are a number of specialized communications tools and processes besides mass-media product advertising. The most important of these are direct marketing, personal selling, sales promotion, certain public relations activities, various types of sponsorships, and corporate advertising. ∎

Chapter 10
Relationship Building: Direct Marketing, Personal Selling, and Sales Promotion

Focuses on some of the methods marketers can use today to communicate one-on-one with their customers and add tangible value to their relationships.

Chapter 11
Relationship Building: Public Relations, Sponsorship, and Corporate Advertising

Explores how companies integrate a variety of public relations and corporate advertising activities into their communication mixes to enhance their relationships and build their reputation with a wide variety of stakeholders.

Chapter 10

Relationship Building: Direct Marketing, Personal Selling, and Sales Promotion

Objectives

TO EMPHASIZE THE IMPORTANCE of relationship marketing in today's high-tech, overcommunicated world and to demonstrate how various forms of marketing communications can be integrated with advertising to manage an organization's relations with its various stakeholders. Relationship marketing and IMC are two of the most important trends in marketing and advertising today. Direct marketing, personal selling, and sales promotion play different but often overlapping roles that are vitally important to IMC programs. Each offers many opportunities but also has limitations that advertisers should be aware of.

After studying this chapter, you will be able to:

- **Discuss** the importance of relationship marketing and IMC.

- **Define** direct marketing and discuss its role in IMC.

- **Explain** the importance of databases to direct marketers.

- **Discuss** the role of personal selling in an IMC program.

- **Describe** the advantages and drawbacks of personal selling.

- **Define** sales promotion and discuss its importance as a communications tool.

- **Identify** the benefits and drawbacks of sales promotion.

- **Explain** the difference between push and pull strategies and give some tactical examples of each in sales promotion.

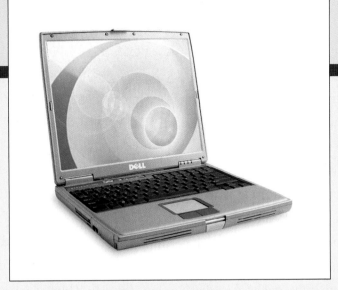

"Dude, you're getting some dough."[1] ■ That was the opening line from one of the commercials aimed at the burgeoning Generation Y market. It was the summer of 2002, and Dell Computer wanted to increase consumer awareness of its website and boost demand for its computers. Rather than just running a big schedule of ads, the company decided it could make a bigger hit by using sales promotion—in this case a sweepstakes. But then, instead of going for a single, Dell decided to go for a triple. And in the process, it hit a home run. ■ Dell launched the campaign by announcing a $50,000-a-Day Giveaway for the month of July and encouraged people to visit the company's website for more information. Once there, people could browse the site and shop for Dell products. While no purchase was necessary to enter, anybody who did purchase a Dell desktop or notebook computer was automatically entered in the national Back-to-School sweepstakes, with a chance to win the daily grand prize of $50,000 in cash. The first segment of the sweepstakes was highly successful. Hundreds of thousands of people actually ended up purchasing a Dell computer, and 30 of them won $50,000 each.[2] ■ Then came the second hit, running from August 1 to 29, but this time it was a Trip-a-Day Giveaway. Similar to the first phase, every day Dell gave away $50,000 in travel and cash. By month's end, 29 lucky customers had received $30,000 in travel and another $20,000 in cash.[3] ■ In September, Dell decided to complete the triple with a BMW-a-Day Giveaway. Customers who purchased a Dell during this final period were automatically given a chance to "go to class with class" and drive to school in a brand-new BMW 330i, valued at more than $41,000. By the end of September, 32 more people were enjoying "the ultimate driving machine."[4]   ■   What is the incentive for an already highly regarded company to spend more than $4 million on giveaways over a three-month period? In Dell's case, the goal was to entice potential consumers to visit and browse Dell's only storefront—its website. But what the company got in exchange for investing in these costly promotions was even better. Dell earned the number-one ranking in terms of global market share; it became the number-one PC maker for consumers and small businesses; and it became the industry leader in a host of other categories as well.[5]   ■   You might ask why such a large and successful company would choose to have a website as its only storefront. The answer lies in the very foundation of the company itself—a corporate mission based on direct marketing and personal selling.   ■   Back in 1984, a 19-year-old premed freshman named Michael Dell decided to start a company and base it on a simple premise: By selling computer systems directly to customers, he could better understand their needs and efficiently provide the most effective computing solutions to meet those needs.[6] The net effect of this idea was to eliminate the retailer, who knew less about the product, would add unnecessary time and cost to the distribution process, and would dilute Dell's own understanding of customer expectations. By dealing directly with its own customers, the company embodied the very essence of relationship building, and hence its slogan, "Be Direct."[7]   ■   Following Dell's philosophy, the company offers its products directly to consumers via the telephone or the Internet, allowing each customer to review, configure, and price systems within Dell's entire product line; order systems directly; and track orders from the manufacturing stage through the shipping stage. This not only allows consumers to get exactly what they want at competitive prices, but also lets Dell stay in touch with the ever-changing wants and needs of its customers.   ■   The sales model was revolutionary and so were the results. In the 2002 *Fortune* 500, Dell ranked 53rd.[8] During the second quarter of 2002, amid an industrywide sales decline of 10 percent, Dell's profits jumped 11 percent. And after launching its Back-to-School sweepstakes, the company's market share jumped from 13.5 percent to 15 percent—in just one month.[9]   ■   To further its focus on and dedication to the customer, Dell engages in a number of activities aimed at putting customer satisfaction and interaction at the top of the priority list. While many competitors advertise the latest software and hardware inventions, Dell's ads focus on customer service and support, as well as the benefits of computing technology itself. Moreover, through well-integrated campaigns such as Dell4Me, the company nourishes its one-to-one customer relationships by providing services customers need throughout the ownership period of a PC. These include high-speed Internet access, personal Internet home pages, online services, and payment options, as well as thousands of PC accessories and software.[10]   ■   What Dell has done so successfully is to employ a wide variety of communication tools that consistently reinforce its main goals: serving customers' needs and growing the customer database. Maybe that's why Dell continues to outperform its rivals in the hypercompetitive PC market.[11]   ■

The Importance of Relationship Marketing and IMC

In Chapter 8, we pointed out that due to a variety of environmental factors, the key to building brand equity in the twenty-first century is the development of interdependent, mutually satisfying relationships with customers and other stakeholders. Further, to manage these relationships, companies need to consciously (and *conscientiously*) integrate their marketing communications activities with all their other company functions so that all the messages the marketplace receives about the company are consistent.

However, this is a lot easier said than done, since everything a company does (and doesn't do) sends a message. Seamless, consistent communication—from every corner of the company—is how a firm earns a good reputation. And that is the principal objective of IMC.

Dell is a good example of how IMC works. To attract prospects and initiate the relationship building process, Dell integrates its advertising efforts with a host of other marketing communication tools—direct marketing, sales promotion, personal selling, and even certain public relations activities. These are then correlated to other company functions—product design, manufacturing, assembly, inventory control, and shipping—to reduce errors and assure a consistently high level of quality and service. The result of all this is a happier, more satisfied customer, one whose expectations have not just been met, but exceeded. That contributes to Dell's glowing reputation. In a 2004 Harris Poll, Dell was ranked as one of the most popular brands in the United States, ranking third after only Sony and Coca-Cola.[12]

A simple adage: Advertising can create an image, but a reputation must be earned.

While the integration of marketing with other company functions is beyond the scope of an advertising textbook, it is important for advertising people to understand how to integrate the various tools of marketing communications. As they plan a campaign, advertising practitioners need a basic understanding of what other communications tools are available to them and how they can best be used in the overall marketing communications mix. In this chapter, we will discuss the interactive, one-to-one communication tools of direct marketing and personal selling. We'll also look at sales promotion, which might be called the "value-added" tool. In the next chapter, we'll address the "credibility" tools companies use to enhance their reputations. These include various public relations activities, sponsorships, and corporate advertising.

Understanding Direct Marketing

There is a lot of confusion surrounding the term *direct marketing,* even among the experts. In fact, Lester Wunderman, the man who coined the term more than 40 years ago, now thinks it may be due for a change.

The Direct Marketing Association (DMA) has traditionally defined **direct marketing** as "an interactive system of marketing which uses one or more advertising media to effect a measurable response and/or transaction at any location." However, after a major 1997 study on the economic impact of direct marketing, the DMA broadened its definition to include "*any direct communication* to a consumer or business recipient that is designed to generate a response in the form of an order (direct order), a request for further information (lead generation), and/or a visit to a store or other place of business for the purchase of a specific product(s) or service(s) (traffic generation)."[13]

Direct Marketing magazine goes even further: "Direct marketing is a measurable system of marketing that uses one or more advertising media to effect a measurable response and/or transaction at any location, with this activity stored in a database." From this definition a virtually synonymous term has emerged: **database marketing.** Database marketers build and maintain a pool of data on current and prospective customers (and other stakeholders) and communicate with them using a variety of media (from personal contact to direct mail to mass media). Database marketing is one of the fastest-growing marketing methods because it has proven to be a cost-efficient method for increasing sales. A good **database** enables marketers to target, segment, and grade customers. It helps them to know who their customers and prospects are,

In the past, a large company could often muscle its way into significant market share. But with tighter budgets and more competitive markets, companies realize that even the most ordinary contact with the customer is a prime opportunity to build and maintain relationships. Companies like Dell (www.dell.com) that adopt such integrated strategies are much more likely to succeed in the long run.

Direct marketing is an interactive system in which buyers and sellers participate in a dialogue. Its intent is to stimulate a response in the form of a request for information, an actual purchase, or a visit. In the case of a social organization like Britain's NSPCC, direct marketing can have a powerful impact on a wide constituency beyond the primary target market. This poster, which won a Gold Lion at Cannes, prompted calls from abused teenagers to jump 124 percent in just six weeks. The number of website visitors also increased, from 4,000 to more than 32,000.

what and when they purchase, and how to contact them. That, of course, leads to the possibility of a relationship. So today, database marketing is a major component of most integrated marketing communications programs.

What we see from these various definitions is that, first and foremost, direct marketing is a *system of marketing* and it is *interactive,* meaning buyers and sellers can exchange information with each other directly. In fact, Joan Throckmorton, a prominent direct marketing consultant and writer, has urged that direct marketing be dropped completely and replaced with *interactive marketing*.[14] The increasing prominence of the Association for Interactive Marketing (www.interactivemarketing.org), an independent subsidiary of the DMA, signals growing acceptance of Throckmorton's view. Wunderman, on the other hand, is leaning toward *dialogue marketing* or *membership marketing*—anything, he says, to get rid of the confusion that surrounds this business.[15]

A second important part of the definition is the concept of *one or more advertising media.* Part of the confusion with the name is its similarity to *direct mail.* While direct mail is often used in direct marketing, it is just one of the many media that direct marketers use.

In the Dell story, for instance, we saw how the company used a mass media form—newspapers—as well as direct mail in the form of e-mail, to elicit responses from people who might be interested in Dell. In fact, experienced direct marketers have known for years that using more than one medium tends to be far more productive than using a single medium.[16]

The third key point of the direct marketing definition is a *measurable response.* In fact, the kind of advertising direct marketers use is called **direct-response** (or **action**) **advertising.** This is because direct marketing efforts are always aimed at stimulating some action or response on the part of the customer or prospect. It may be in the form of a request for information, a store visit, or an actual purchase. Because these responses can be tallied and analyzed, direct marketing becomes accountable. And that, more than any other reason, accounts for the tremendous growth of direct marketing in recent years. Managers like it because they can see what they got for their money.

The final point most of the definitions make is that the response can be at *any location.* In other words, direct marketing is *not* restricted to mail order or catalog sales. Customers may respond by telephone, via mail-in coupons, over the Internet, at a retail store or other place of business, or even at a kiosk.

The Role of Direct Marketing in IMC

Today, sophisticated companies use the skills developed by direct marketers to establish, nourish, and maintain relationships, not just with customers, but with all stakeholders.

Dell, for instance, uses magazine and TV advertising as **linkage media**—media that help prospects and customers link up with a company—to inform prospects how to inquire about its products. Next, it uses these responses to build its database of names, addresses, and e-mail addresses. Then it uses the database to communicate with prospects, open a dialogue, and establish a relationship. It may send a catalog with ordering information or direct people to its website to enable prospects to further connect with Dell directly.

The Evolution of Direct Marketing

Direct marketing is the oldest marketing method, and today it is growing incredibly fast, propelled by the major social and technological changes of recent decades. Over 65 percent of American women now work outside the home.[17] So while families have more income, they have less time to spend shopping, thus making the convenience of telephones, the Internet, and credit cards important factors in direct marketing.

Likewise, the expanding use of credit cards has revolutionized the way consumers buy goods and services. Electronic, cashless transactions make products (especially large, costly items) easier and faster to purchase. And now, with advances in credit-card security technology, more and more people are shopping right from their computers.

While a soft economy in 2003 caused a 20 percent drop in sales attributed to direct marketing over 2002 (projecting a still-impressive $1.7 trillion), forecasters predicted a booming 22 percent hike in Web-driven sales for 2003, with similar growth rates seen through 2008.[18]

Working with direct-response specialists, marketers are fueling this growth by pouring money into direct marketing campaigns. Exhibit 10–1 shows the largest direct-response agencies in the United States. Overall media spending for direct marketing initiatives reached $206.1 billion in 2002, up 4.7 percent over 1998. This amount was split almost evenly between consumer and B2B efforts. However, the B2B *growth* in media expenditures was considerably higher than the consumer growth—7.7 percent to 5.9 percent.[19]

The boom in telecommunications and computer technology is spurring the growth of direct marketing worldwide. In the mid-1990s, for instance, European spending on

Websites are an example of linkage media because they provide a way for consumers to hook up with companies. An integrated campaign of radio, print, e-mail, and popup ads for Proctor and Gamble products like Tampax and Always instructed girls to visit www.beinggirl.com to register for a sweepstakes. Photography by Lauren Greenfield, who specializes in "girl culture," and questions from real girls heightened the impact of the print ads. The Leo Burnett (Chicago) campaign was a critical and commercial success; it resulted in 200,000 website visits in a four-week period and won a Cannes Gold Lion.

Exhibit 10–1

Largest direct-response agencies in the United States.

Rank	Agencies	U.S. revenue ($ millions)
1	Draft Worldwide	$ 240,882
2	Rapp Collins	202,241
3	Wunderman	173,039
4	Ogilvy One	135,000
5	McCann Relationship Marketing	105,000
6	Brann	98,570
7	Grey Direct	88,000
8	Targetbase Marketing	56,917
9	Devon Direct	38,800
10	Protocol Marketing Services	32,793

direct marketing jumped by more than 23 percent to $46 billion. Today, Germany is by far the largest national market in Europe, spending more than $25 billion on direct marketing efforts annually. Britain comes in second at more than $17 billion, followed closely by France. Interestingly, outside the United States, Japan is by far the number-one market for direct marketing, with estimated annual spending close to $70 billion.[20]

Telephone companies worldwide now provide toll-free numbers for customers to place orders or request information. Toll-free numbers give companies immediate, direct responses and help them collect information to create and refine their databases.

However, certain challenges in foreign markets have limited the growth of direct marketing efforts. There are, of course, a wide variety of legal and regulatory environments to contend with. Likewise, payment and postal systems in different countries vary considerably, as do conventions for addressing mail. And finally, cultural nuances and language can get in the way. For example, the same name can indicate different genders in different countries. In England Abigail is a woman's name, but in Portugal it's a man's name. Most men are put off when they are referred to as "senora." Again, though, technology comes to the rescue. "Address hygiene" software, which improves the deliverability of mail by cleaning and formatting address databases, is widely available, but one French company has taken the idea a step further. Addressing Technology has developed a solution to these problems with its universal mailing software. It makes sure the correct salutation and gender code are used for some 125,000 given names in various countries and also enables marketers to satisfy the differing postal regulations of more than 208 countries.[21]

The Impact of Databases on Direct Marketing

Modern computer technology enables marketers to compile and analyze important customer information in unprecedented ways. Pitney Bowes, for instance, is the dominant company in the postal meter business. However, its growth rate and profitability were flattening. So the company used its database to identify its best customers, their value to the organization, and their needs and buying behavior. From this, Pitney Bowes created a **customer lifetime value (LTV)** model based on historical and potential share of wallet. Computing and ranking the *lifetime value* of all of its 1.2 million customers showed that more than two-thirds of the customer base value resided in fewer than 10 percent of the customers. The company also found it had a major retention problem within its low-volume, low-cost accounts. Cancellation rates were running as high as 40

This American Express card touting its "double points" reward program serves the needs of customers as well as the company. For customers, it facilitates quicker earnings towards the reward program. For the company, it enables the marketing department to track all customer activity and develop customer lifetime value (LTV) estimates. By offering double points, the company rewards its customers for their loyalty and adds value to the overall relationship.

percent per year in some segments. This analysis enabled Pitney Bowes to develop a distinct direct marketing strategy for both its best and its worst customers. It began a sophisticated *loyalty program* for its best customers and a *retention program* for its problem accounts. By the end of the first year, the program had reduced attrition by 20 percent, and the reduction in cost of sales alone paid back the entire direct marketing investment.[22] In another situation, a company might determine from its LTV analysis that its best course of action is simply to drop the most unprofitable customers.

The database is the key to direct marketing success, especially in an IMC program. It enables marketers to target, segment, and grade customers. It is the corporate memory of all important customer information: name and address, telephone number, e-mail address, NAIC code (if a business firm), source of inquiry, cost of inquiry, history of purchases, and so on. It should record every transaction across all points of contact with both channel members and customers. The company that understands its customers' needs and wants better than any of its competitors, and retains more of its best customers, will create a sustainable competitive advantage. Strategically, therefore, companies have to determine if they will focus on share of market or on retention and loyalty (share of customer).[23] More often than not, this is a short-term versus long-term trade-off.

The database also lets the company measure the efficiency of its direct-response advertising efforts to see, for instance, which radio or TV commercials, or which mailing lists, perform the best.

Working with a marketing database requires two processes: data management and data access. **Data management** is the process of gathering, consolidating, updating, and enhancing the information about customers and prospects that resides in the database. For most companies of any significant size, this requires a sophisticated computer system due to the complexity and volumes of the processes involved.

Most important, the database gives marketers **data access,** enabling them to manipulate, analyze, and rank all the information to make better marketing decisions. Thanks to new software, this can now usually be accomplished on Windows-based desktop PCs hooked up to client-server computers.

Direct magazine's "database doctor," Rob Jackson, suggests that database marketing should start with *customer profiling*. Profiling allows marketers to get a snapshot of what their customers look like at any given time by identifying common characteristics and ranking their relative importance in different segments.[24]

In the same vein, direct marketing expert Bob Stone recommends using an **RFM formula** (recency, frequency, monetary) to identify the best customers—the ones most likely to buy again (see Exhibit 10–2). The best customers have bought recently, they buy frequently, and they spend the most money. Customers may be further ranked by the type of merchandise or services they buy, information that becomes very useful in the effort to cross-sell other merchandise.[25]

Some companies may simply purchase a mailing list as its initial database. There are typically three types of data available for purchase: demographics, lifestyle (leisure interests), and behavioristics (purchase habits).[26]

The Importance of Direct Marketing to IMC

Perhaps the greatest reason for direct marketing's current growth is that marketers and agencies realize they can't do the job with just one medium anymore. As the mass audience fragmented and companies began to integrate their marketing communications, customer databases became key to retaining and growing customers.

Direct marketing is the best way to develop a good database. The database enables the marketer to build a relationship by learning about customers in-depth: their nuances, what and where they buy, what they're interested in, and what they need. With a database, companies can choose the prospects they can serve most effectively and *profitably*—the purpose of all marketing. "You don't want a relationship with every customer," says Philip Kotler. "In fact, there are some bad customers out there."[27]

People like to see themselves as unique, not part of some 100-million-member mass market. Through direct marketing, especially addressable electronic media,

Political Advertising: Positively Negative

Many people criticize commercial advertisers for excessive use of puffery and exaggeration; these same people, however, may be totally unaware of the extensive legislation that strictly governs commercial advertising. In fact, most commercial advertisers voluntarily subscribe to a "code of advertising ethics" administered by the Advertising Division of the Better Business Bureau. So while commercial advertisers are closely regulated, their political counterparts can proceed unchecked. Why? Because politicians and special interest groups advertise under the protective umbrella of the First Amendment—freedom of speech.

Political advertisers often use this freedom to sling mud at the opposition and make claims that aren't even close to true. The 2000 presidential election was rife with examples, as were the congressional and senatorial elections of 2002. In fact, the elections of 2002 saw the greatest amount of mudslinging, eye-gouging, rabbit-punching, and groin-kneeing ever, as a record amount of almost *$1 billion* was spent by candidates and their parties on 1.5 million midterm ads over the months leading up to the election. For instance, during the Montana Senate race between Democratic incumbent Max Baucus and Republican challenger Mike Taylor, the campaigning started aggressively and then went careening downhill as the election neared. It got so bad that Taylor finally chose to drop out of the campaign for the sake of sparing his name and his family any further abuse. The breaking point occurred when Taylor's public image was damaged by an ad that seemed to imply that he was gay. The ad showed Taylor in the 1970s, in attire typical of the period, complete with gold chains and an open shirt, rubbing lotion onto a man's back during his stint as a

barber. Arguments have been made that the ad was, "an attempt to play off the old stereotype about gay men who are hairdressers."

Negative advertising is nothing new; it's as old as voting itself. Consider one of history's most effective attack ads: "He has obstructed the Administration of Justice . . . He has erected a Multitude of new Offices, and sent hither Swarms of Officers to harass our People . . . He has combined with others to subject us to a Jurisdiction foreign to our Constitution." This quote, of course, is from the Declaration of Independence. Our founding fathers understood well the importance of relaying to the public why the King's policies would not serve the peoples' interest.

Political advertising is an essential part of the democratic process and can be an important means of helping the public understand the difference between opponents. However, some critics believe that negative political ads contribute to the severe distrust of politicians. For many people, elections simply mean choosing the lesser of two evils. In the 2002 race for governor of California, after $100 million had been poured into thousands of mudslinging advertisements by both sides, voters were in a quandary over whom to vote for. In the end, both candidates appeared so bad that voters reluctantly reelected the incumbent, Gray Davis, a very unpopular governor after his handling of the state's energy, water, and transportation crises. In an equally negative campaign, movie action hero Arnold Schwarzenegger deftly exploited Californians' distaste for Davis by initiating and winning a historic recall election in October 2003.

In a recent survey of voters in Virginia, approximately three-fourths of the sample indicated that negative campaigns were likely to discourage them from voting at all. Notwithstanding, the desperate final week

---

companies can send discrete messages to individual customers and prospects. With different types of sales promotion (discussed in the last part of this chapter), a company can encourage individuals, not masses, to respond and can develop a relationship with each person. By responding, the prospect *self-selects*, in effect giving the marketer permission to begin a relationship.[28] The direct marketing

Exhibit 10–2

RFM (recency, frequency, monetary) analysis of accounts, December 2004.

Account number	Month of purchase	Recency points	No. of purchases	Frequency points	Dollar purchases	Monetary points	Total points	Carryover points	Cumulative points
701	7	12	1	4	37.45	3.75	19.75	16	35.75
701	10	24	2	8	17.86	1.79	33.79	16	49.79
702	6	6	2	8	25.43	2.54	16.54	4	20.54
703	4	6	1	4	33.22	3.32	13.32	7	20.32
703	8	12	2	8	42.34	4.23	24.23	7	44.56
703	11	24	1	4	18.95	1.90	29.90	7	74.45
704	9	12	1	4	109.45	9.00	25.00	23	48.00
705	5	6	2	8	37.65	3.77	17.77	0	17.77
705	7	12	3	12	49.63	4.96	28.96	0	46.73
706							0.00	43	43.00

Notes:
- Points assigned by recency of purchase: current quarter—24 points; last 6 months—12 points; last 9 months—6 points; and last 12 months—3 points.
- Frequency points: number of purchases × 4.
- Monetary points: 10 percent of dollar purchase, with a ceiling of 9 points.
- Carryover points: Points carried over from previous calendar year.
- Cumulative total points: Total account points plus carryover from previous calendar year.

The RFM formula is a mathematical model that provides marketers with a method for determining the most valuable customers in a company's database, according to recency, frequency, and monetary variables. Recency points are assigned according to the date of the customer's last purchase (24 points if the purchase was made within the current quarter, 12 points if within the last 6 months, 6 points if within the last 9 months, and 3 points if the purchase was made within the last 12 months). Frequency points are equal to the number of purchases made multiplied by a factor of 4. Monetary points are equal to 10 percent of the dollar purchase, with a maximum of 9 points to prevent artificial distortion by an unusually large purchase. The R, F, and M variables are summed to provide total points. The cumulative total is a measure of relative customer importance to the company—the larger the value, the more likely a customer is to make additional purchases of significant value. The higher-value customers, such as account numbers 701 and 703, who make multiple purchases, are likely prospects for targeted mailings and special offers.

of any hard-fought campaign typically brings out the worst in candidates and their campaign strategists and media advisors.

At the same time, going negative in a campaign carries its own risks. In Louisiana's 2002 U.S. Senate race, Democrat Mary Landrieu defeated Republican Suzanne Haik Terrell with a swing of almost 76,000 votes that occurred over the last couple of weeks. Those who studied the race attribute the swing to the challenger's excessive use of negative ads toward the end of the campaign. Representative John Cooksey, a Republican, said quite a few Republican voters were turned off by "the negative tone" of the Terrell campaign leading up to the election. He described the issuers of the advertisements as people "with coarse, crude personalities, who didn't have the sensitivity to see that the barrage of negative ads offended the sensitivities of many Louisiana voters." At a time when the voters sought positive reasons to support Terrell, the negative ads were a clear case of overkill.

Other negative ads serve more as a reflection of the sponsor's poor taste than the opponent's lack of suitability. In the race to fill an open New Jersey House seat, E. Scott Garrett ran against Democrat Anne Sumers. Toward the end of the campaign, Sumers ran an ad featuring the photo of sniper suspect John Allen Muhammed, saying Garrett "shouldn't be blamed for the sniper," but that "his positions are the problem." Critics and voters alike felt Sumers had resorted to a desperation tactic. The final tally: Garrett was elected by a margin of 60 to 38 percent.

Some professionals in the advertising community claim that negative political ads give commercial advertising a bad name. In fact, some major advertising agencies have loudly condemned political advertisers for their lack of accountability and their unwillingness to adhere to a code of ethics. The freewheeling tactics used in political advertising campaigns, they say, damage the credibility and persuasiveness of all advertisers. However, recent research has found that, notwithstanding the intrinsic bias of all forms of advertising, people perceive product ads as generally truthful and interesting. In contrast, political ads are dismissed as dishonest, unappealing, and uninformative. So when compared to product advertising, which enjoys substantial public support, political advertising probably does not constitute a real threat to the credibility of the advertising industry.

While the First Amendment will protect political attacks, there has recently been a trend toward greater accountability in political advertising. One provision of the 2002 Bipartisan Campaign Reform Act (P.L. 107–155) requires that television and radio campaign ads identify the candidate and include his or her approval of the message; such regulation is intended to make politicians accountable for their attacks. Its impact is still unclear—although we're getting used to hearing candidates affirm that they "approve this message"—and the fact that Internet ads are not covered by the legislation leaves ample room for attack ads to thrive.

Sources: Jennifer Harper, "Parties Spend Nearly a Billion for 1.5 Million Midterm Ads," *Washington Times*, December 12, 2002 (retrieved from www.nexis.com); "Montana Candidate Drops Out over 'Gay' Ad," *Billings Gazette*, October 10, 2002 (retrieved from www.evote.com); "Simon Campaign Hitting Governor Davis with Humor," October 24, 2002 (retrieved from www.evote.com); Bruce Alpert and Robert Travis Scott, "Republicans Play Role of QB; After Landrieu's Re-election, GOP Tries to Figure Out what Went Wrong," *Times-Picayune* (New Orleans), December 10, 2002 (retrieved from www.nexis.com); "New Jersey Race in Spotlight over Sniper Ad," November 1, 2002 (retrieved from www.evote.com).

database, then, becomes the company's primary tool to initiate, build, cultivate, and measure the effectiveness of its loyalty efforts.[29]

By providing a tangible response, direct marketing offers accountability. Marketers can count the responses and determine the cost per response. They can also judge the effectiveness of the medium they're using and test different creative executions.

Direct marketing offers convenience to time-sensitive consumers, and it offers precision and flexibility to cost-sensitive marketers. For example, to reach small BTB markets, there is no more cost-effective method than the database-driven direct-response media.

Also, the economics of direct marketing are becoming more competitive. It used to be easy for big companies to spend a few million dollars for prime-time network TV spots when everybody was home watching and the average cost was only a penny to 10 cents per person. But those days are over. Everybody's not home today. And if they are, they're watching 150 different channels or a video. They have a remote control to mute ads. Further, network TV advertising is far more expensive than it used to be. Thus, targeted direct-response media (magazines, niche TV, direct mail, e-mail, kiosks) are more cost-effective than ever before.

Finally, unlike the public mass media, direct-response media can be more private. A company can conduct a sales letter campaign without the competition ever knowing about it.

Drawbacks to Direct Marketing

At the same time, direct marketing still faces some challenges. In the past, direct marketers were sales oriented, not relationship oriented. This gave direct marketing a bad reputation in the minds of many consumers. Some people enjoy the experience of visiting retail stores and shopping. They like to see and feel the goods personally, and they are hesitant to buy goods sight unseen. This is why the objective of many direct marketing campaigns is now to help drive traffic to retail locations.

Direct marketing efforts often have to stand on their own without the content support of the media that advertising enjoys. They don't always get the prestigious

Database marketing was much more difficult before the development of computers because of the intense data management requirements. Today, with the cost of personal computers under $1,000, even the smallest companies can engage in complex database building and marketing strategies.

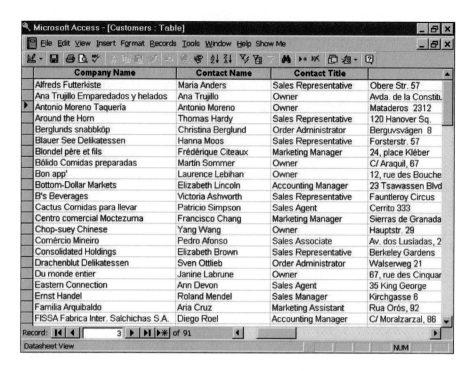

affiliation offered by some media. This makes it more difficult (and costly) to build image for the product, something mass-media advertising is particularly good at.

Direct marketing also suffers from clutter. People are deluged with mail from commercial sponsors and drum-beating politicians (see the Ethical Issue, page 312, on negative political advertising in this chapter). Cable channels are filled with infomercials for food processors. And telemarketing pitches for insurance plans intrude on consumers at home and at work.

Many consumers are also concerned with privacy. They don't like having their names sold by list vendors. At one national forum of direct marketers, attendees were told they must self-regulate, give consumers more control, and treat privacy like a customer service issue—or risk legislation restricting access to the information they desperately need.[30] Wise marketers have heeded these warnings and developed methods for responsible direct marketing. Using IMC theory, they integrate all their marketing communications and focus on building the *relationship value* of their brands.

Types of Direct Marketing Activities

All direct marketers face two basic strategy decisions: the extent to which they will use *direct sales* and the extent to which they will use *direct-response advertising*. They can use either or both.

Direct Sales

In a **direct-sales strategy,** marketers' representatives sell to customers directly, either at home or at work, rather than through a retail establishment or some other intermediary. Direct sales feature *personal* (face-to-face) *selling* or *telemarketing*.

Personal Direct Selling

Professors Robert Peterson and Thomas Wotruba define **direct selling** as face-to-face selling away from a fixed retail location. In this sense, direct selling usually refers to a method of marketing consumer goods—everything from encyclopedias and insurance to cosmetics and nutritional products.[31] Companies such as Avon, Amway, Herbalife, Mary Kay Cosmetics, World Book, and Tupperware have achieved very high levels of success in direct sales. In personal direct selling, the representative introduces the product to the customer, convinces the customer of the product's value, and, if successful, completes the sale. There are two main forms of personal selling: person-to-person and group sales. In some *network*

Each year telemarketing generates an estimated $538.3 billion in sales in the United States. It is cited as the direct marketing medium of choice, providing elements of direct personal sales yet at a substantially lower cost. Telemarketing also integrates easily into database management campaigns for gathering new data and for utilizing the collected data.

marketing organizations, such as Amway, Nikken, and Shaklee, the direct salespeople are both distributors (sellers) and end users. They often do very little actual retailing of the products. Their effort is usually to recruit new distributors who will buy the products at wholesale and consume them personally.

The Peterson–Wotruba definition of direct selling could also apply to business-to-business marketing, since it typically occurs "away from a fixed retail location." However, the common term for this is simply *personal selling.* And since it is so important to B2B marketers, we will deal with that subject more completely in the next section of this chapter.

Telemarketing

As a method of direct sales, telemarketing has been used for decades, but the term is relatively new. **Telemarketing** includes selling and prospecting by telephone, answering phone inquiries, and providing sales-related services to callers. The resulting information updates the company's customer database. Telemarketing is the major source of income for some companies and organizations, such as non-profit and charitable causes, political candidates, and home-study courses. It is also cited as the direct marketing medium of choice. In 2002, marketers spent 39 percent of all their direct marketing media expenditures, or an estimated $80.3 billion, on outbound telemarketing calls to both consumers and businesses. This generated an estimated $719.5 billion in total sales.[32]

The reasons for all this are economics and consumers' acceptance of teleculture. First, telemarketing costs a lot less money than personal selling. In the insurance business, for example, the expense ratio for car and home insurance is currently running at 27 percent for all insurers. The most efficient insurers, though, employ high-tech database marketing techniques from phone centers and operate at around a 20 percent expense ratio.[33] That difference goes straight to the bottom line.

Second, people have come to accept the idea of shopping by phone. It's convenient, hassle-free, and inexpensive. In the United States, the toll-free telephone business is booming. In any given week, 30,000 to 50,000 toll-free numbers are added across North America. Heavy demand caused the pool of 800 numbers to run dry in 1996. Soon thereafter, concern grew that even the 888 numbers faced depletion, leading to limits on their allocation, and 877 and 866 numbers were introduced, with other numbers to be added for toll-free use as needed.[34]

As an IMC medium, telemarketing is the next best thing to a face-to-face, personal sales call. In the business-to-business arena, for example, good telemarketers can develop strong, lasting relationships with customers they have never met but with whom they speak every week. Stand Out Designs in San Diego employs highly skilled telemarketers who call on zoos, museums, and boutique retailers all across the country to get them to order and stock the company's unique line of silk-screened T-shirts. The telemarketers don't just take orders; they counsel the dealers with display and promotion suggestions, offer advertising tips, and arrange for special imprints on the shirts when appropriate.

When combined with other direct-response media, telemarketing becomes even more effective. For example, experience shows that when telemarketing is combined with direct mail, there is usually at least a 10 percent increase in responses—often a lot more.

Direct-Response Advertising

Advertising that asks the reader, viewer, or listener to provide feedback straight to the sender is called **direct-response advertising.** Any medium can be used for direct response, but the most common are direct mail, catalogs, magazines, and TV.

Direct Mail

Next to personal selling and telemarketing, direct mail is the most effective method for closing a sale or generating inquiries. It's very useful to direct marketers seeking

Catalog sales make up the largest portion of direct marketing. Catalogs, such as this one from Lands' End (www.landsend.com), display a company's products and enable customers to order at their convenience via mail, phone, fax, or Internet. J. Crew, Victoria's Secret, the Sharper Image, and Lands' End are just a few of the multitude of consumer catalogs available today.

an immediate response. In 2002, marketers spent approximately $49.1 billion on direct-mail advertising, or 23.8 percent of all direct marketing expenditures. Sales directly attributed to direct-mail advertising reached $246 billion in the B2B category and $390.7 billion in the consumer segment.[35]

Direct mail is an important medium to many advertisers, which we'll explore in greater detail in Chapter 17.

Catalog Sales

The largest direct marketers are the catalog companies. **Catalogs** are reference books (and now also CD-ROMs) that list, describe, and usually picture the products sold by a manufacturer, wholesaler, jobber, or retailer. With more high-income families shopping at home, specialized catalogs are becoming very popular. Some catalog retailers prosper with specialized approaches like outdoor clothing and equipment (L.L. Bean, Lands' End), electronic gadgets (Sharper Image), and gourmet foods (Balducci's).

Catalogs are big business. In 2001, the catalog industry spent some $14.3 billion in advertising and generated more than $125.9 billion in both B2B and consumer sales. The top 10 catalog companies did over $69.6 billion in business in 2002 (see Exhibit 10–3). And in 2003, Dell, the leading catalog marketer, alone sold more than $35 *billion* worth of merchandise.[36]

To increase readership and stand out from the glut of other catalogs, some marketers have added editorial and slick photography, all designed to sell a certain image. Abercrombie & Fitch, for instance, publishes its *A&F Magazine* (which replaced the thicker, glossier *A&F Quarterly* magalog in December 2003). The magazine supplements the closing line with advice on how to attain a "cool" lifestyle beyond what you wear: by acquiring the right mode of transportation (a Vespa scooter), drinking the right beer (Belgian Chimay), and using the right accessories (a Nokia personal communicator). By selling the Abercrombie lifestyle, A&F hopes to bring more people into the stores.[37] At the same time, though, A&F has stirred up a lot of controversy by using its catalog to parade a host of nude and seminude models, often in very suggestive poses.

Many companies make their products easily available online. By providing a comprehensive website like Dell's, whose only storefront is, in fact, the website, customers can purchase practically everything they previously might buy through a catalog or over the phone. Customers can also check on the status of their orders or get support on products they may already have.

Exhibit 10–3

Top 10 catalog companies.

Rank	Company	2002 sales ($ millions)
1	Dell Computer Corp.	$35,404.0
2	International	6,820.8
3	W.W. Grainger	4,643.9
4	Corporate Express	4,630.2
5	CDW Computer	4,264.4
6	Office Depot	3,913.9
7	Staples	3,389.6
8	Fisher Scientific	3,238.0
9	Henry Schein	2,825.0
10	Boise Office	2,760.0

Direct-Response Print Advertising

Newspaper ads and inserts featuring coupons or listing toll-free phone numbers can be very effective at stimulating customer responses. Today, the same is true with magazines. Moreover, in magazines, advertisers can devote most of the space to image-building, thus maximizing the medium's power. We discuss the use of print media further in Chapter 15.

Direct-Response Broadcast Advertising

Direct marketers' use of TV and radio has increased dramatically in recent years. Total Gym, whose products are normally sold through health care and physical fitness professionals, worked with American Telecast to develop a 30-minute infomercial featuring TV star Chuck Norris and supermodel Christie Brinkley. The campaign exceeded their wildest expectations, producing more than $100 million in sales the first year and continuing to generate similar returns for the next four years.[38] As Exhibit 10–4 shows, more people are watching infomercials and buying the advertised products. In fact, a March 2004 survey found that 60 percent of infomercial purchasers preferred this type of shopping to buying items in a store.[39]

Television is a powerful instrument for direct marketers like Total Gym because of its mass coverage and the ability to display and demonstrate the product with sound and full color right before the customers' eyes.

Exhibit 10–4

Who watches (and buys from) infomercials.

	Total viewers	Total nonviewers	Total buyers
Primary gender	Female, 53.2%	Male, 55.4%	Female, 51.7%
Mean age	41.2	45.2	45.9
Primary ethnicity	Caucasian	Caucasian, 76.4%	Caucasian
Primary employment	Full-time	Not employed	Full-time
Marital status	Married, 49.3%	Married, 52.8%	Married, 60.3%
Children present	Yes, 40.1%	Yes, 38.5%	Yes, 43.1%
Residence	Suburban	Small town, 31.5%	Suburban
Mean household income	$56,000	$49,000	$55,000

For many years, radio commentator Paul Harvey was very successful pitching a wide variety of products to his loyal audience. Likewise, talk jocks Howard Stern and Rush Limbaugh made Snapple an overnight success by drinking the product and touting its good taste on the air. Still, until fairly recently, radio has rarely been the medium of choice for direct-response advertising. But that has made the medium all the more intriguing to some marketers and ad agencies.[40] Radio industry executives now expect to see a dramatic increase in the number of direct-response ads on radio. We discuss radio, TV, and infomercials further in Chapter 16.

Interactive Media

Interactive media systems allow customers and prospects to control both the content and the pace of presentations and to order merchandise directly from the system. The most popular interactive media currently are online personal computers. Although still in the development stage, interactive TV may allow viewers to respond to questions during a commercial, giving advertisers a wealth of demographic information for future promotions. The use of the new digital interactive media is explored in depth in Chapter 17. For now, let's take a brief look at the ultimate interactive communication tool, personal selling.

Personal Selling: The Human Medium

"If it is to be, it is up to me."

Ten little words, two letters each. That was Sid Friedman's philosophy for success. Typical sales rep, right?

Well, not exactly. Sid Friedman sold insurance. He'd been doing it for some time. He was the president and chair of the Philadelphia-based insurance, financial planning, and consulting firm Corporate Financial Services. Friedman managed his 200-plus employees, ran three other companies, and directed the Philadelphia chapter of the children's Make-a-Wish Foundation. *Forbes* magazine's article "People at the Top, What Do They Earn?" included Sid, along with the likes of Arnold Schwarzenegger, Tom Clancy, and Ralph Lauren.

Sid made the *Forbes* article because his selling techniques, augmented by the use of direct marketing, resulted in personal commissions of $2.6 million—in one year. Sid liked telephone marketing. It worked for him. Every week he called 100 people, got 15 appointments, sold three, and earned lots of money.

"Sometimes," he said, "you earn even more money, but only when you do three things: See the people, see the people, and see the people."[41]

That's what personal selling is all about. Seeing the people. And that's also why personal selling is the best marketing communication tool for relationship building—because the sales rep and the customer are face to face. It's the ultimate one-to-one medium. It's also the most expensive medium. For most companies, personal selling expenditures far exceed expenditures for advertising. And in many companies, the primary role of advertising is to lend support to the sales force either directly by producing leads or indirectly by creating a positive atmosphere for the sales call.

Personal selling can be defined in a number of ways, depending on the orientation of the company using it. In an integrated marketing communications

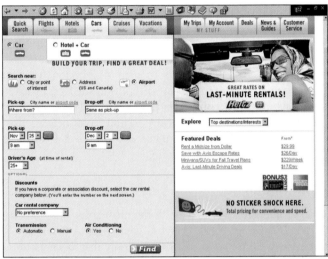

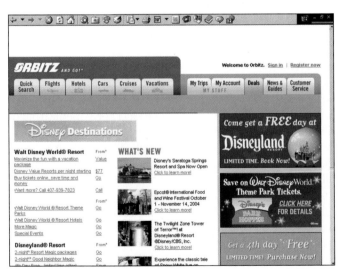

The Internet's impact has been extraordinary. Consumers are free to make inquiries, book flights, find hotels, and access a vast amount of information at their leisure, often eliminating the need for person-to-person communication.

program, though, the sales effort of the reps must be consistent with the mission, vision, and strategies of the firm and with all the firm's other communications.

Therefore, for our purposes we define **personal selling** as the *interpersonal communication process* by which a seller ascertains and then satisfies the needs of a buyer, to the mutual, long-term benefit of both parties.[42]

Thus, the task of personal selling is a lot more than just making a sale. In an IMC program, the objective of personal selling is to build a relationship, a partnership, that will provide long-term benefits to both buyer and seller (a win-win situation). The salesperson discovers the buyer's needs by helping the customer identify problems, offers information about potential solutions, assists the buyer in making decisions, and provides after-sale service to ensure long-term satisfaction. Influence and persuasion are only one part of selling. The major part is problem solving.

Types of Personal Selling

Everyone sells, at one time or another. Children sell lemonade, magazine subscriptions, and Girl Scout cookies. Students sell prom tickets, yearbook ads, and term papers. Doctors sell diets to unwilling patients. Lawyers sell briefs to skeptical juries. And cops sell traffic safety to nervous motorists.

As a business process and a profession, though, personal selling is something else. It's just one of a company's mix of communications tools, and its relative importance depends on the type of business or industry, the nature of the product or service, and the strategy of the business.

The fact is that everything has to be sold, by someone to somebody. A retail clerk may sell you a pocket calculator. Behind that clerk is a virtual army of other salespeople who sold processed materials to the manufacturer, capital equipment for use in the manufacturing process, business services such as human resources and accounting, plant and office furniture, vehicles, advertising services, media space and time, and insurance. Then the manufacturer's salespeople sold the calculator (and a few others) to a wholesaler who, of course, had to buy transportation services and warehousing from other salespeople. And then the wholesaler's sales reps sold the calculator to the retail outlet where you bought it.

As this scenario shows, people in sales work for a wide variety of organizations and call on an equally wide variety of customers. They may call on other businesses to sell products or services used in the manufacture of other products. They may call on resellers—people who buy the product, add value, and resell it. Or they may sell to consumers, either in a retail store or, as we discussed earlier, in a direct selling situation away from a fixed retail location.

Because advertising is basically designed to support and reinforce a company's sales efforts, advertising people (whether in the company or at an agency) have to understand

This pharmaceutical sales representative is engaging in missionary selling when she presents the benefits of her products to a doctor. The representative understands that the doctor will not place an order, but she is attempting to get the doctor to prescribe the pharmaceutical for his patients so her company will get an order from the patient's drugstore.

the selling environment their companies or clients deal in. Many companies have their advertising people make calls with the sales force for this very reason. The advertising person can experience firsthand what questions prospects ask, how customers view the company (and its competitors), how people use the company's product, and what information (in either an ad or a piece of sales material) might help the salesperson communicate better with the prospect.

Advantages of Personal Selling

The greatest strength of personal selling is its personal nature. Nothing is as persuasive as personal communication. A skilled salesperson can observe a prospect's body language and read between the lines to detect what's troubling the customer. The rep can ask questions and answer queries as they arise. The face-to-face situation facilitates instant feedback. And the rep has the flexibility to adjust the presentation, tailoring it specifically to the needs and interests of the particular prospect. Not only that, the salesperson can demonstrate the product live. And the rep can negotiate, finding those terms that best suit the buyer's needs.

Time is on the rep's side, too. The sale doesn't have to be made today. The relationship has to be established, though, and a human being is better at doing that than any nonpersonal medium.

One of the major jobs of personal selling is to gain distribution for new products—a task no other communication tool can do as well. In fact, in many trade and industrial situations, personal contact may be vital to closing the sale. This is also true for certain high-ticket or technical consumer products such as camcorders, health care, and estate planning. In these cases, personal selling is well worth its high cost—because it gets the job done.

Drawbacks of Personal Selling

Personal selling is very labor intensive. That's why it's the most costly way to communicate with prospects. This is its single biggest weakness. A business-to-business sales call today costs well in excess of $300. Not only that, it's very time-consuming. Because it is basically a one-on-one medium, there are few economies of scale. In fact, two or three salespeople will sometimes go to an important customer's office to make a presentation. In personal selling we don't talk about cost per thousand.

This is why one important role of advertising is to reduce the cost of sales by communicating as much relevant information as possible about the company and its products to prospects and customers before the salesperson even calls. That information may be functional (specifically about the product) or symbolic (building image and credibility for the company).

Another drawback is the poor reputation of personal selling with many people. Decades of "suede shoe" salesmen employing high-pressure tactics, usually in retail venues, have sullied the profession. Thus the common jibe: "Would you buy a used car from that man?" In health care services, for example, selling activities have limited philosophical acceptance. Salespeople are frequently given fancier titles such as marketing associate, marketing representative, admissions coordinator, clinical liaison, professional services representative, or program manager in an attempt to reduce guilt or the rejection associated with personal selling.[43] Of course, the advertising profession doesn't fare much better when it comes to image and reputation—or fancy titles.

There's an old saw about one bad apple ruining a barrel. Imagine spending millions of dollars on a nationwide advertising campaign to communicate your expertise and good customer service and then sending an unprofessional sales force out that is improperly groomed or, worse, ignorant of product features and benefits and lacking empathy for customer needs. Unfortunately, it happens all the time. The salesperson has incredible power to either make or break a delicate relationship. As a result, sophisticated firms go to great lengths to screen sales applicants to find the right personality attributes and then invest heavily in training. Of course, this goes both ways. A tasteless advertising campaign can hurt a company's national reputation more than one bad salesperson. As always, it's the responsibility of marketing management to ensure consistency among what the advertising presents, what the sales force promises, and what the company actually delivers.

The Role of Personal Selling in IMC

Salespeople are the company's communicators. They are the human medium. In fact, to the customer who doesn't know anybody else at the company, the salesperson doesn't just represent the firm. He or she *is* the firm. The customer's impression of the salesperson, therefore, will frequently govern his or her perception of the company. Again, this makes the sales rep a very important person.

In an integrated marketing communications program, personal selling can play a very important role. Salespeople provide four distinct communications functions: information gathering, information providing, order fulfillment, and relationship building. We'll discuss each of these briefly.

Gathering Information

Sales reps often serve as the eyes and ears of the company. Because they are out in the field talking to customers or attending trade shows, they have access to information and they can see trends. For example, salespeople provide information on who's new in the business, how customers are reacting to new products or styles, what the competition is doing, and where new sales might be made. Generally, information gathering by the sales force relates to three areas: prospecting; determining customer wants, needs, and abilities; and monitoring the competition.

Providing Information

Personal selling is one of the most important facets of an IMC strategy because of the personal nature of the contact. Skilled salespeople can use their creativity to identify customer needs and problems and find solutions that are profitable for both the customer and the company.

Salespeople not only gather information, they impart it. In fact, the stereotype (both negative and positive) of a good salesperson is someone who is a good talker, articulate and persuasive. In truth, a superior salesperson is a good listener first and a good talker second. Salespeople impart information both upstream and downstream within their organization. They deliver information to customers about the company and its products, they recommend solutions to problems, and they use information to communicate value and to build relationships and trust.

Personal selling incorporates all three legs of the IMC triangle, the "say → do → confirm," because what the rep says and does will either confirm or contradict the company's other messages. The rep's skill, therefore, will definitely color the relationship between the company and the customer. It's critically important that the salesperson's performance be consistent with the firm's positioning and reinforce its other marketing communications.

Fulfilling Orders

There comes a time in every relationship when someone has to make a commitment. Asking for that commitment can be very difficult if the preceding steps have not been handled well. The inevitable tasks of personal selling are to motivate the customer to action, close the sale, and then make sure the goods and services are delivered correctly.

An important part of personal selling is following up after the sale, making sure the goods or services are delivered in a timely fashion, and seeing to it that the customer is completely satisfied. This is a combination of the "do" and "confirm" steps, and it's critical to continued relationship building.

Good products and good customer service are vital to a company's relationship with its customers. A good sense of humor doesn't hurt either. This cute cyber ad, which won a Bronze Lion at Cannes, offers an interactive tour of a typical Lego factory, showing how Lego bricks begin the "long journey that ends up under your couch."

This is also where cross-functional management and open communication come back into play. If there is any kind of manufacturing glitch or delay in shipping, the salesperson needs to notify the customer immediately. But to do that, the salesperson must be informed. Similarly, goods need to be protected and shipped with care. Salespeople hate to receive calls from new customers saying their first shipment arrived with damaged goods. Every employee, including those in the warehouse, needs to understand the impact of *unplanned* product messages.

Likewise, if the company is advertising a certain model of a product and the salesperson closes the sale on the product, that model had better be in stock. Again, good internal communication is a key to good external relationships.

Building Relationships

A company's sales staff should be the ultimate relationship marketers. When all things are equal, people naturally want to buy from the salesperson they like and trust. Salespeople build relationships by paying attention to three simple things: keeping commitments, servicing their accounts, and solving problems. Interestingly, those are also probably the three basic requirements for any company's success.

Here again, advertising people can help. When a company advertises, it is making a commitment to its customers and prospects. It is very difficult for a salesperson to keep those commitments if the advertising has overpromised. So puffery should be avoided wherever possible, since by its very nature, it tends to overpromise.

Likewise, it's difficult for customer service reps to adequately service their accounts if every time people call they get a busy signal. This happened to the giant telephone utility U.S. West when it downsized and reengineered the company. It continued running ads touting its great service, but nobody could get through to them. Not smart. Advertising people have to know what's going on in the company, and sometimes they need to recommend that advertising be stopped.

Finally, advertising as well as salespeople should be concerned with solving problems. If the sales staff uncovers a problem that customers frequently encounter, and the company's product can help solve that problem, then that should become the focus of some planned communications—advertising, publicity, or company-sponsored events.

The Role of Sales Promotion in IMC

Imagine walking into the fresh-fruit section of your local grocery store, picking up a big, juicy mango, and discovering a sticker on it stating: "Now available in Snapple. Mango Madness." You turn around and suddenly notice that there, right next to the fresh-fruit bin, stands a big Snapple display of, you guessed it, Mango Madness.

It actually happened. New York agency Kirshenbaum, Bond & Partners launched Snapple's new Mango Madness drink nationally with stickers on the back of 30 million pieces of fruit.[44] Talk about out-of-the-box thinking and creative media planning! Moreover, it was an outstanding example of how sales promotion can be perfectly integrated with a company's positioning, in this case Snapple's overall "100% natural" message strategy.

The term *sales promotion* is often misunderstood or confused with advertising or publicity. This may be because sales promotion activities often occur simultaneously and use both advertising and publicity as part of the process. In truth, though, it is a very specific marketing communications activity.

Sales promotion is a direct inducement that offers extra incentives anywhere along the marketing route to enhance or accelerate the product's movement from producer to consumer. Within this definition, there are three important elements to consider. Sales promotion

- May be used anywhere in the marketing channel: from manufacturer to wholesaler, wholesaler to dealer, dealer to customer, or manufacturer to customer.
- Normally involves a direct inducement (such as money, prizes, extra products, gifts, or specialized information) that provides extra incentives to buy now or buy more, visit a store, request literature, display a product, or take some other action.
- Is designed to change the timing of purchase or to shift inventory to others in the channel.

Let's see how this definition applies to Snapple. In an interesting combination of both consumer advertising and *trade promotion* (sales promotion aimed at members of the distribution channel), Snapple used the fresh mangoes as an unusual new advertising medium to introduce its Mango Madness to consumers and to stimulate initial demand for the drink. The magnitude of that media effort (30 million pieces of fruit) served as a huge incentive to retailers to grant Snapple extra floor space (very expensive real estate, by the way) to display Mango Madness right next to the fresh-fruit stand. The result: Snapple, and the retailers, sold a lot more Mango Madness a lot faster, and for a lot less money, than they would have if they had just placed some expensive ads in consumer magazines or on TV. Moreover, by creatively integrating different forms of marketing communications, Snapple simultaneously bolstered its positioning strategy and enhanced its relationship with the retail trade—its primary customer.

Some marketers consider sales promotion supplementary to advertising and personal selling because it binds the two together, making both more effective. In reality, however, sales promotion is far more than supplementary. One study showed marketers spending 54 percent of their 2000 advertising/promotion budget on sales promotion compared to only 46 percent for advertising.[45] We'll see why shortly.

Snapple's clever promotion of its Mango Madness flavor demonstrates an ingenious integration of sales promotion and product positioning. By placing a sticker ad on actual mangoes in the fresh-fruit section, Snapple reinforced its slogan of "100% natural" and grabbed the attention of customers not necessarily looking to buy the beverage. The marketing strategy was supported by placing bottles of Mango Madness in close proximity to the fruit.

Creating Effective Sales Promotions

___ **Set specific objectives.** Undisciplined, undirected creative work is a waste of time and resources.

___ **Set a theme that is relevant.** Start with a strategy, preferably from a unified marketing or advertising plan. Stay on track: A promotion for the telephone giant NYNEX reinforced its "If it's out there, it's in here" campaign with a sweepstakes asking consumers to look up the "heading of the day" in the phone book and note the page.

___ **Involve the trade.** Build relationships. Carrier air conditioning sponsored the Junior Olympics in key markets, sharing sponsorship with its dealer in each city.

___ **Coordinate promotional efforts with other marketing plans.** Be sure to coordinate schedules and plans. A consumer promotion should occur simultaneously with a trade promotion; a free sample promotion should be timed to the introduction of a new line.

___ **Know how basic promotion techniques work.** A sweepstakes shouldn't be used to encourage multiple purchases or a refund to get new customers. A price-off deal can't reverse a brand's downward sales trend.

___ **Use simple, attention-getting copy.** Most promotions are built around a simple idea: "Save 75 cents." Emphasize the idea and don't try to be cute.

___ **Use contemporary, easy-to-track graphics.** Don't expect to fit 500 words and 20 illustrations into a quarter-page freestanding insert.

___ **Clearly communicate the concept.** Words and graphics must work together to get the message across.

___ **Add advertising when you need measurable responses.** When part of a promotion, advertising directed at a broad audience is usually wasted. Trial-building promotions designed to build loyalty among current users, however, can be helped by advertising.

___ **Reinforce the brand's advertising message.** Tie promotions to the brand's ad campaign.

___ **Support the brand's positioning and image.** This is especially important for image-sensitive brands and categories, like family-oriented Kraft.

___ **Know the media you work through.** Determine which media will work best. Should samples be distributed in stores, door to door, or through direct mail? Does the promotion need newspaper or magazine support?

___ **Pretest promotions.** Pretesting doesn't have to be expensive. For packaged goods, small samplings in a few stores can reveal how to maximize coupon redemption rates by testing various values, creative approaches, and delivery methods.

Sales promotion is expensive. But it's also effective. Unfortunately, it has serious drawbacks, which lead to furious battles in marketing circles between proponents of sales promotion and proponents of advertising. Each approach has an important role to play, but advertisers must consider the positives and negatives and get the balance right.

The Positive Effect of Sales Promotion on Brand Volume

Effective sales promotion accomplishes a number of things. First of all, it adds tangible, immediate, extra value to the brand. Snapple's creative media buy suddenly made Mango Madness more valuable to the retail trade. This induced retailers to stock up on the new product and display it prominently. Similarly, when Dell Computers runs a million-dollar sweepstakes, it's adding instant value to the products it sells. This is why we refer to sales promotion as the *value-added tool.*

Second, by adding immediate value, sale promotion *maximizes* sales volume. A short-term price cut or rebate, for instance, may be very effective at boosting sales. While advertising helps develop and reinforce a quality, differentiated brand reputation, and build long-term *market value*, sales promotion helps build *market volume*. To become a market leader, therefore, a brand needs both advertising and sales promotion.

Finally, when all brands appear to be equal, sales promotion can be more effective than advertising in motivating customers to try a new brand or to select one brand over another. It can also motivate some customers who might be unmoved by advertising efforts. And certain sales promotions generate a more immediate, measurable payoff than traditional advertising campaigns. This is why we might also refer to sales promotion as the "sales accelerator."

To succeed, sales promotions should be creative and hard to imitate. Kirshenbaum, Bond & Partners certainly demonstrated that with their Snapple labels. The Checklist, "Creating Effective Sales Promotions" outlines some basic ideas to consider in designing promotions.

The Negative Effect of Sales Promotion on Brand Value

Advertisers need to understand the negative effects of sales promotion, too. For instance, excessive sales promotion at the expense of advertising hurts profits. Some marketers believe a proper expenditure balance for consumer packaged-good products is approximately 60 percent for trade and consumer promotion, 40 percent for advertising.

A high level of trade sales promotion relative to advertising and consumer sales promotion has a positive effect on short-term market share but may have a negative effect on brand attitudes and long-term market share. Without an effective advertising effort to emphasize brand image and quality, customers become deal-prone rather than brand loyal. And overemphasis on price (whether in advertising or sales promotion) eventually destroys brand equity.[46]

Another drawback of sales promotion is its high cost. One analysis showed that only 16 percent of sales promotions were profitable. In other words, the manufacturer spent more than $1 to generate an extra $1 of profits.[47]

Finally, overly aggressive sales promotion or advertising can draw competitors into a price war, which leads to reduced sales and profits for everyone.

Thus, if too much of the marketing mix is allocated to advertising, the brand may gain a high-quality, differentiated image but not enough volume to be a market leader. On the other hand, as Larry Light, McDonald's chief global marketing officer says, "Too much [sales] promotion, and the brand will have high volume but low profitability. Market leadership can be bought through bribes, but enduring profitable market leadership must be earned through building both brand value as well as volume."[48]

Sales Promotion Strategies and Tactics

To move their products through the distribution channel from the point of manufacture to the point of consumption, marketers employ two types of strategies: push and pull. **Push strategies** are primarily designed to secure the cooperation of retailers, gain shelf space, and protect the product against competitors. **Trade promotions**—sales promotions aimed at members of the distribution channel— are one of the principal tactics marketers use to *push* products through the distribution pipeline and gain shelf space. We'll discuss some of these tactics in the next section. Marketers may also use **trade advertising** (advertising in publications read by members of the trade) as a push tactic.

Pull strategies, on the other hand, are designed to attract customers and increase demand for the product (see Exhibit 10–5). Consumer advertising and **consumer sales promotions** are examples of pull strategies because they are designed to induce consumers to seek out or ask for the product, in effect pulling the product through the pipeline. Today, some national advertisers spend more

Exhibit 10–5

Two marketing communications approaches.

Push strategy

Pull strategy

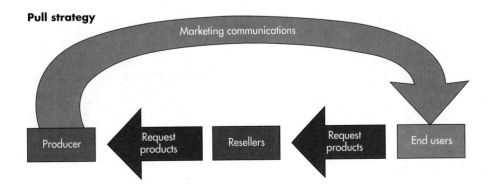

dollars on trade sales promotions than on either consumer sales promotions or media advertising. But that is often the price they have to pay to gain distribution, without which they cannot make any sales.

Giving Brands a Push with Trade Promotions

In supermarkets today, shelf space and floor space are hard to come by. To maintain their own images, department stores set standards for manufacturers' displays. This means that retailers often can't use the special racks, sales aids, and promotional literature supplied by manufacturers.

These are minor problems; major ones have to do with control of the marketplace. **Trade concentration**—more products going through fewer retailers—gives greater control to the retailers and less to the manufacturers. Increased competition for shelf space gives retailers even more power, enabling them to exact hefty deals and allowances. As a result, manufacturers of national brands often don't have enough money left to integrate consumer advertising or sales promotion.[49]

Despite these problems, many manufacturers still implement effective push strategies. And the smart ones safeguard enough money for consumer advertising. Trade tactics include slotting allowances, trade deals, display allowances, buyback allowances, advertising allowances, cooperative advertising and advertising materials, dealer premiums and contests, push money, and company conventions and dealer meetings.

Slotting Allowances

In response to the glut of new products, some retailers charge manufacturers **slotting allowances**—fees ranging from $15,000 to $40,000 for the privilege of obtaining shelf or floor space for a new product. The practice is controversial because some manufacturers think they're being forced to subsidize the retailer's cost of doing business. On the other side of the coin, small-scale sellers, such as family farms trying to market their produce, complain that the allowances shut out all but the largest suppliers. Although a 1994 ruling by the Federal Trade Commission and the Bureau of Alcohol, Tobacco and Firearms determined that they were acceptable as long as the same promotional allowances were offered to all retailers on "proportionally equal terms," the allowances remain controversial, and the FTC has recommended further research.[50]

In an effort to avoid slotting allowances, some marketers have made major shifts in strategy. Following a four-year investigation, the FTC signaled its willingness to fight egregious slotting allowance abuses by taking legal action against spice

Trade promotions are business-to-business incentive programs that are strategically aimed at increasing distribution. This Rapala (www.rapala.com) ad aimed at retailers suggests that, for a "catchy" promotion, they should try putting their logo on Rapala's legendary lures.

For a catchier promotion, put your logo on the legendary Rapala. Minimum order 300. Call 1-800-874-4451.

giant McCormick. Through agreements with "favored purchasers," the company had managed to command 90 percent of shelf space set aside for spices and offered a range of prices for its customers. The FTC ordered McCormick to refrain from selling its products to a purchaser at a net price that was higher than that charged to the purchaser's competitors. The order's narrow scope dismayed some critics, but overall the action was hailed as "a thoughtful beginning to the evolution of a sound and measured antitrust response to slotting fee abuses."[51]

Trade Deals

Manufacturers make **trade deals** with retailers by offering short-term discounts or other dollar inducements. To comply with the Robinson-Patman Act, trade deals must be offered proportionally to all dealers. Dealers usually pass the savings on to customers through short-term sale prices, or "specials."

Excessive trade deals threaten brand loyalty because they encourage customers to buy whatever brand is on sale. Furthermore, marketers who use trade discounts extensively find themselves in a vicious circle: If they cut back on the promotions, they may lose shelf space and then market share.

In addition, some retailers capitalize on trade discounts by engaging in forward buying and diverting. With **forward buying,** a retailer stocks up on a product when it is on discount and buys smaller amounts when it sells at list price. **Diverting** means using the promotional discount to purchase large quantities of an item in one region, then shipping portions of the buy to areas where the discount isn't offered. These tactics enable both the manufacturer and the dealer to shift inventory when they need to.

Display Allowances

More and more stores charge manufacturers **display allowances**—fees to make room for and set up displays. In-store displays include counter stands, floor stands, shelf signs, and special racks that give the retailer ready-made, professionally designed vehicles for selling more of the featured products.

Buyback Allowances

When introducing a new product, manufacturers sometimes offer retailers a **buyback allowance** for the old product that hasn't sold. To persuade retailers to take on their product line, some manufacturers even offer a buyback allowance for a competitor's leftover stock.

Manufacturers like DeWalt often pay a display allowance for their in-store exhibits, banners, and shelf signs. These fees benefit retailers like Home Depot by compensating them for the space occupied by the displays. And the manufacturer benefits from the increased exposure.

Advertising Allowances

Manufacturers often offer **advertising allowances** as either a percentage of gross purchases or a flat fee paid to the retailer. Advertising allowances are more common for consumer than industrial products. They are offered primarily by large companies, but some smaller firms give them to high-volume customers.

Co-op Advertising and Advertising Materials

With **cooperative (co-op) advertising,** national manufacturers reimburse their dealers for advertising the manufacturer's products or logo in their trading area. The manufacturer usually pays 50 to 100 percent of the dealer's advertising costs based on a percentage of the dealer's sales. Special co-op deals are used to introduce new products, advertise certain lines, or combat competitors.

Unlike advertising allowances, co-op programs typically require the dealer to submit invoices and proof of the advertising (tearsheets from the newspaper or affidavits of performance from radio or TV stations). Many manufacturers also give their dealers prepared advertising materials: ads, glossy photos, sample radio commercials, and so on. To control the image of their products, some advertisers insist that dealers use these materials to qualify for the co-op advertising money.

Dealer Premiums and Contests

To encourage retail dealers and salespeople to reach specific sales goals or stock a certain product, manufacturers may offer special prizes and gifts. Ethics can be a thorny issue when companies award prizes and gifts to dealers and salespeople.

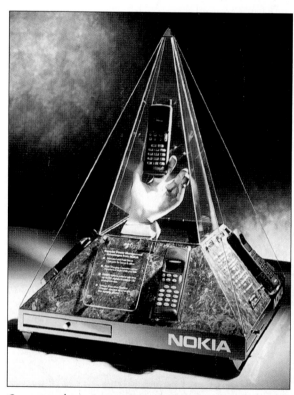

Consumer sales promotions expose potential customers to a product and induce them to seek it out. While trade promotions push products through distribution channels, consumer sales promotions are intended to pull the product through due to customer demand. This Nokia (www.nokia.com) point-of-purchase display can serve as both a trade and consumer promotional tool.

Push Money

Retail salespeople are often encouraged to push the sale of particular products. One inducement is called **push money (PM),** or **spiffs.** For example, a shoe salesperson may suggest shoe polish or some other high-profit extra; for each item sold, the salesperson receives a 25- to 50-cent spiff.

Company Conventions and Dealer Meetings

Most major manufacturers hold **company conventions** and **dealer meetings** to introduce new products, announce sales promotion programs, or show new advertising campaigns. They may also conduct sales and service training sessions. Meetings can be a dynamic sales promotion tool for the manufacturer.

Push strategies are virtually invisible to consumers. Yet successful inducements mean the product gets more shelf space, a special display, or extra interest and enthusiasm from salespeople. And extra interest can spell the difference between failure and success.

Using Consumer Promotions to Pull Brands Through

One reason for today's increased focus on consumer sales promotions is the change in TV viewing habits. With cable TV, VCRs, and DVDs, fewer people watch any one program. Advertising audiences are more fragmented, and major manufacturers must turn to new methods to reach these moving targets.

Common consumer sales promotions include point-of-purchase materials, coupons, electronic coupons and convenience cards, cents-

Moving a product from the manufacturer to the consumer is not a simple task. Goods often have to go through four or five separate steps: from the manufacturer to an agent or broker, then to the wholesaler, to the retailer, and finally it gets to the consumer. Communicating messages along this same path can also be torturous. Something's bound to get lost in the middle. This is why push and pull promotions are so important.

By offering incentives in the form of money, prizes, trips, and promotional materials to "push" products into the distribution pipeline, the marketer can also obtain invaluable middleman assistance. Pushing is when a company uses any form of marketing communication (personal selling, advertising, or sales promotion) to the trade with the purpose of gaining shelf space and cooperation. Reversing the process, the company can also use consumer advertising or offer rebates, coupons, two-for-one deals, or some other incentive directly to the customer. By stimulating demand, that form of communication helps "pull" products through the pipeline.

Laboratory Application

If you were working for McGraw-Hill/Irwin (the publisher of this textbook), how would you suggest using push and/or pull strategies to increase the sales of the company's textbooks? Which strategy do you think would be more effective?

off promotions, refunds, rebates, premiums, sampling, combination offers, contests, and sweepstakes. A successful IMC campaign may integrate several of these techniques along with media advertising, product publicity, and direct marketing. Ad Lab 10–A offers the opportunity to apply what you've learned about push and pull strategies to the marketing of textbooks.

Point-of-Purchase (P-O-P) Materials

Walk into any store and notice the number of display materials and advertising-like devices that are designed to build traffic, exhibit and advertise the product, and promote impulse buying. Collectively, these are all referred to as **point-of-purchase (P-O-P) materials.**

P-O-P works best when used with other forms of advertising. For example, by advertising its gum and candy, one marketer increased sales by about 150 percent. But when P-O-P was added to the same program, the purchase rate jumped 550 percent.[52]

In one poll, 56 percent of mass-merchandise shoppers and 62 percent of grocery shoppers said they noticed point-of-purchase materials. More than half reported noticing signs and displays, 18 percent remembered coupon dispensers, and 14 percent could recall samplings and demonstrations.[53]

Today's consumers make their decisions in the store 66 percent of the time and make unplanned (impulse) purchases 53 percent of the time, so P-O-P can often be the major factor in stimulating purchases.[54]

P-O-P materials may also include window displays, counter displays, floor and wall racks to hold the merchandise, streamers, and posters. Often, the product's shipping cartons are designed to double as display units. A complete information center may even provide literature, samples, product photos, or an interactive computer in a kiosk.

The trend toward self-service retailing has increased the importance of P-O-P materials. With fewer and less knowledgeable salespeople available to help them, customers are forced to make purchasing decisions on their own. Eye-catching, informative displays can give them the nudge they need. Even in well-staffed stores, display materials can offer extra selling information and make the product stand out from the competition.

The proliferation of P-O-P displays has led retailers to be more discriminating in what they actually use. Most are beginning to insist on well-designed, attractive materials that will blend harmoniously with their store atmosphere.

The emphasis on P-O-P has led to a variety of new approaches, including ads on shopping carts, "talking" antacid boxes, beverage jingles activated when in-store refrigerator doors are opened, and interactive computers for selecting everything from shoe styles to floor coverings. Digital technology has led to Hallmark

Most coupons reach consumers through newspaper freestanding inserts (FSIs), which have a higher redemption rate than regular newspaper or magazine coupons.

Kiosks like these VIP stations use a consumer's membership card to issue a list of manufacturer discounts and to calculate customer purchase patterns.

Cards' Touch-Screen Greetings interactive kiosks, which print a customer's personal message onto any card.[55] To send it, look for one of the new Automated Postal Centers rolled out by the U.S. Postal Service. The kiosks allow customers to weigh materials to be mailed, buy postage, and even look up zip codes.[56]

Coupons

A **coupon** is a certificate with a stated value presented to the retail store for a price reduction on a specified item. More than 170 billion coupons were distributed by consumer packaged goods companies in the United States in 2002, but only about 1.9 billion were ever redeemed.[57]

Coupons may be distributed in newspapers or magazines, door to door, on packages, in stores, and by direct mail. Most reach consumers through colorful preprinted newspaper ads called **freestanding inserts (FSIs).** FSIs have a higher redemption rate than regular newspaper and magazine coupons; coupons in or on packages have the highest redemption levels of all.[58]

Manufacturers lose hundreds of millions of dollars annually on fraudulent coupon submissions. Some coupons are counterfeited; others are submitted for products that were never purchased. To fight this problem, some companies have developed computerized systems to detect fraudulent submissions and charge them back to the retailers who made them.

Electronic Coupons and Convenience Cards

High-tech **electronic coupons** work like paper coupons in that they entitle the shopper to a discount, but their method of distribution is entirely different. Interactive touch-screen videos at the point of purchase generate instant-print discounts, rebates, and offers to try new brands. Electronic coupons are spreading quickly in the nation's supermarkets, though they still represent only a small percentage of the total coupons distributed annually.

Nonetheless, all the nation's top brand marketers are currently involved in tests being conducted by the two leaders in the field, Catalina Marketing and Advanced Promotion Technologies. Catalina's system is installed in more than

21,000 supermarkets across the country and reaches some 250 million shoppers per week.[59]

Electronic couponing gives the retailer access to information about consumers that would not be available with paper coupons. Many supermarket chains now issue customers convenience cards entitling them to instant discounts at the checkout counter. When customers use the card, a record of their purchases is sent to a database and sorted into various lifestyle groups. The card saves customers the hassle of clipping paper coupons, and it allows retailers to better understand its customers' purchasing behaviors.

Similar systems are used in Europe. Multipoints is an interactive system that lets customers collect points for visiting stores or watching commercials on TV. The points can be redeemed for prizes and discounts on various products at participating stores. Quick Burger, France's second-largest restaurant chain, noticed a significant increase in traffic after joining Multipoints, even when the system was less than a year old.[60]

Cents-off Promotions, Refunds, and Rebates

Cents-off promotions are short-term reductions in the price of a product in the form of cents-off packages, one-cent sales, free offers, and boxtop refunds. Some packages bear a special cents-off sticker, which the clerk removes and credits at the checkout counter.

Some companies offer *refunds* in the form of cash or coupons that can be applied to future purchases of the product. To obtain the refund, the consumer must supply proof of purchase, such as three boxtops.

Rebates are larger cash refunds on items from cars to household appliances. Large rebates (like those given on cars) are handled by the seller. For small rebates (like those given for coffeemakers), the consumer sends in a certificate.

Research indicates that many people purchase a product because of an advertised rebate but never collect the rebate because of the inconvenience.[61] More than $500 million worth of rebates goes unclaimed every year.

Premiums

A **premium** is an item offered free or at a bargain price to encourage the consumer to buy an advertised product. Premiums affect purchase behavior the same way as rebates but tend to be more effective at getting consumers to buy a product they didn't really need (see Exhibit 10–6). Premiums are intended to improve

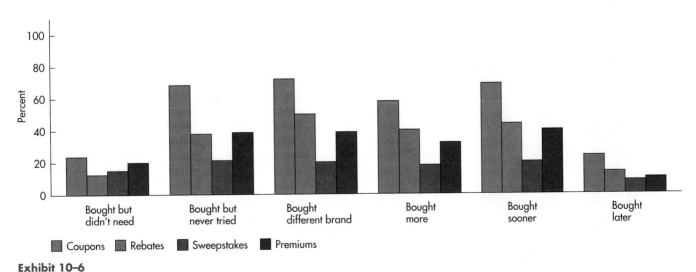

Exhibit 10–6

Next to coupons, premiums are one of the most effective sales promotion techniques for changing consumer behavior.

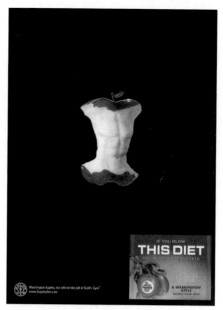

Sometimes a marketer will share the cost of a consumer promotion with comarketing partners as in this creative effort by Gold's Gym and Washington Apples. Eat a Washington Apple before each meal as part of your diet and exercise plan, and you'll be on your way to a leaner you. Everybody benefits and the cost is reduced.

the product's image, gain goodwill, broaden the customer base, and produce quick sales.

A premium should have strong appeal and value and should be useful or unusual. It may be included in the product's package (*in-pack premium*), on the package (*on-pack premium*), mailed free or for a nominal sum on receipt of proof of purchase (boxtop or label), or given with the product at the time of purchase. Cosmetics companies often hold department store promotions in which scarves, purses, and cosmetic samplers are given free or for a low price with a purchase.

The purchased cosmetics sampler is an example of a *self-liquidating premium:* The consumer pays enough that the seller breaks even but doesn't make a profit. A variation is the *continuity premium,* given weekly to customers who frequent the same store. With a minimum dollar purchase of other items, the customer receives a dish or book each week to complete a set.

Sampling

Sampling is the most costly of all sales promotions. It is also one of the most effective for new products, because it offers consumers a free trial in hopes of converting them to habitual use. Sampling should be supported by advertising and must involve a product available in small sizes and purchased frequently. Successful sampling depends heavily on the product's merits. It offers the greatest credibility and can turn a nonuser into a loyal customer instantly—if the product lives up to its promise.

Samples may be distributed by mail, door to door, via coupon advertising, or by a person in the store. They may be given free or for a small charge. Sometimes samples are distributed with related items, but this limits their distribution to those who buy the other product. In **polybagging,** samples are delivered in plastic bags with the daily newspaper or a monthly magazine. This enables distribution to targeted readers and lets publications give their subscribers added value at no cost.[62]

In-store sampling is very popular. Most in-store sampling programs are tied to a coupon campaign. Depending on the nature of the product, samples can be used as either a push strategy or a pull strategy.

Combination Offers

Food and drug marketers use **combination offers,** such as a razor and a package of blades or a toothbrush with a tube of toothpaste, at a reduced price for the two. For best results, the items should be related. Sometimes a combination offer introduces a new product by tying its purchase to an established product at a special price.

Contests and Sweepstakes

A **contest** offers prizes based on entrants' skill. A **sweepstakes** offers prizes based on a chance drawing of entrants' names. A **game** has the chance element of a sweepstakes but is conducted over a longer time (like local bingo-type games designed to build store traffic). A game's big marketing advantage is that customers must make repeat visits to the dealer to continue playing.

Both contests and sweepstakes encourage consumption of the product by creating consumer involvement. These devices pull millions of entries. Usually contest entrants must send in some proof of purchase, such as a boxtop or label. For more expensive products, consumers may only have to visit the dealer to pick up an entry blank.

To encourage entries, sponsors try to keep their contests as simple as possible. The prize structure must be clearly stated and all the rules listed. National contests and sweepstakes are handled and judged by independent professional contest firms.

Sweepstakes and games are now more popular than contests because they are much easier to enter and take less time. Sweepstakes require careful planning by the advertiser. Companies cannot require a purchase as a condition for entry or the sweepstakes becomes a lottery and therefore illegal. Marketers must obey all postal laws. If they run the sweepstakes in Canada, they may have to pay a percentage of the prizes to the Quebec government.

Contests and sweepstakes must be promoted and advertised to be successful, and this can be expensive. And sales promotions need dealer support. To ensure dealer cooperation, many contests and sweepstakes require the entrant to name the product's local dealer. They may also award prizes to the dealer who made the sale.

Chapter Summary

The key to building brand equity in the twenty-first century is to develop interdependent, mutually satisfying relationships with customers and other stakeholders. To manage these relationships, companies will need to consciously integrate their marketing communications activities with all their other company functions so that all the messages the marketplace receives about the company are consistent. The idea is to not just meet customer expectations but to exceed them.

As part of this process, it is important for advertising people to understand how to integrate the various tools of marketing communications. Advertising practitioners need to have a basic understanding of what other tools are available to them and how they can best be used in the overall communications mix.

In direct marketing, the marketer builds and maintains a database of customers and prospects and uses anything from personal contact to mass media to communicate with them directly in the effort to generate a response, a transaction, or a visit to a retail location.

The database is the key to direct marketing success, especially in an IMC program. Databases let marketers target, segment, and grade customers. This allows them to identify their best customers, their value to the organization, and their needs and buying behavior. They can then calculate the customer's lifetime value. The database is the corporate memory of all important customer information. It should record every transaction across all points of contact with both channel members and customers. The database also enables the company to measure the efficiency of its direct-response advertising efforts. Working with a marketing database requires two processes: data management and data access.

Advertisers and agencies now realize they can't do the job with one medium. Databases let companies choose the prospects they can serve most effectively and profitably. By providing a tangible response, direct marketing offers accountability. Direct marketing offers convenience to time-sensitive consumers and precision and flexibility to cost-sensitive marketers.

Direct marketing is a rapidly growing industry, but it still suffers from problems of cost, clutter, and image.

Direct marketers use a variety of activities, from direct sales (personal selling and telemarketing) to direct-response advertising. Telemarketing, followed by direct mail, is the medium of choice for most direct marketers, but more are beginning to use other media, especially TV infomercials. Interactive TV may be the direct-marketing medium of the future.

Personal selling is actually the ultimate interactive medium. It is the interpersonal communication process by which a seller ascertains and then satisfies the needs of a buyer, to the mutual, long-term benefit of both parties.

There are many types of personal selling: retail, business-to-business, and direct selling. Since advertising is a support service for a company's sales efforts, advertising people have to understand the selling environment their companies deal in.

The greatest strength of personal selling is its personal nature. Nothing is as persuasive as personal communication. The one-to-one situation facilitates instant feedback. And the rep has the flexibility to adjust the presentation, tailoring it specifically to the needs and interests of the particular prospect.

Like all communications tools, personal selling also has some drawbacks. It is very labor intensive and therefore very expensive. One important role of advertising is to reduce the cost of sales by communicating as much relevant information as possible about the company and its products before the salesperson even calls. The salesperson has incredible power to either make or break a delicate relationship. So one of the risks is that one bad apple can ruin a previously unblemished association.

Salespeople provide four communications functions: information gathering, information providing, order fulfillment, and relationship building.

Sales promotion complements advertising and personal selling by stimulating sales. It includes direct inducements (such as money, prizes, or gifts) aimed at salespeople, distributors, retailers, consumers, and industrial buyers.

Marketers must balance sales promotion with advertising. Advertising creates market value for a brand; promotion creates market volume. Advertising has a positive effect on profits; promotion can have a negative effect. Sales promotion techniques are used in the trade to push products through the distribution channels and with consumers to pull them through.

Manufacturers use many sales promotion techniques with dealers: slotting allowances, trade deals, display allowances, buyback allowances, advertising allowances, co-op advertising and advertising materials, dealer premiums and contests, push money, and company conventions and dealer meetings. Sales promotions aimed at the ultimate purchaser include point-of-purchase materials, coupons, electronic coupons and convenience cards, cents-off promotions, refunds, rebates, premiums, sampling, combination offers, contests, and sweepstakes.

Important Terms

advertising allowance, *328*

buyback allowance, *327*

catalog, *316*

cents-off promotion, *331*

combination offer, *332*

company conventions and dealer meetings, *328*

consumer sales promotion, *325*

contest, *332*

cooperative (co-op) advertising, *328*

coupon, *330*

customer lifetime value (LTV), *310*

data access, *311*

data management, *311*

database, *307*

database marketing, *307*

direct marketing, *307*

direct-response (action) advertising, *308, 315*

direct-sales strategy, *314*

direct selling, *314*

display allowance, *327*

diverting, *327*

electronic coupon, *330*

forward buying, *327*

freestanding insert (FSI), *330*

game, *332*

in-store sampling, *332*

linkage media, *309*

personal selling, *319*

point-of-purchase (P-O-P) materials, *329*

polybagging, *332*

premium, *331*

pull strategies, *325*

push money (PM), *328*

push strategies, *325*

rebate, *331*

RFM formula, *311*

sales promotion, *323*

sampling, *332*

slotting allowance, *326*

spiffs, *328*

sweepstakes, *332*

telemarketing, *315*

trade advertising, *325*

trade concentration, *326*

trade deal, *327*

trade promotion, *325*

Review Questions

1. Who are a company's best prospects for additional sales and profits? Why?

2. How should a large insurance company view integrated marketing communications?

3. What are the basic strategic and tactical decisions direct marketers face?

4. How can an advertiser use a newspaper for direct-response advertising?

5. What distinct communications functions do salespeople provide?

6. What are the three things salespeople must do to build relationships?

7. What are the main purposes of sales promotion?

8. Why is trade promotion controversial?

9. What are the most common pull strategies? Which would you use to launch a new soft drink?

10. Why is there a trend away from push strategies and toward pull strategies?

11. **The Advertising Experience**
   Advertisers commonly use both push and pull techniques. Explore the situation of a company of your choice, identifying its pull techniques and also by tracking down its push techniques. (Push techniques might be more difficult to find.) Trade publications are a good place to look. Create a report detailing the overall strategy of the company and discuss why you think one area might be emphasized over another.

Exploring the Internet

The Internet exercises for Chapter 10 address the following areas covered in the chapter: direct marketing and direct response (Exercise 1) and sales promotion (Exercises 2 and 3).

1. **Direct Marketing and Direct Response**
   Direct marketing is not only vast, it's ever-changing in all its facets—direct sales, direct mail, direct response. Likewise, direct-marketing agencies tend to differ from traditional advertising agencies in strategy, organization, and clientele. Take a look at some of the websites below and answer the questions that follow for each site.

Direct Marketing Organizations

- Canadian Marketing Association (CMA) www.the-cma.org
- Direct Marketing Association (DMA) www.the-dma.org

- Direct Marketing News www.dmnews.com
- Give to Get Marketing www.givetogetmarketing.com
- Direct Response.org www.directresponse.org
- Electronic Retailing Association http://retailing.org
- Los Angeles Direct Marketing Association www.Ladma.org
- The 900 Advertising Club www.infoguru.com

a. What group sponsors the site? Who is the intended audience(s)?

b. What is the size, scope, and purpose of the organization?

c. What benefits does the organization provide to individual members or subscribers? To the overall advertising and direct marketing communities?

d. How important do you feel this organization is to the direct marketing industry? Why?

Direct Firms

Select five of the following direct-marketing firms, visit their websites, and answer the questions that follow.

- AGA Catalog Marketing & Design www.aganet.com
- Digital Impact www.digitalimpact.com
- Exposed Brick www.exposedbrick.com
- Gage Marketing Group www.gage.com
- Harte-Hanks www.harte-hanks.com
- Hunt.DDBdirect www.hunt.DDBdirect.com
- Response Marketing Group (RMG) www.800response.com
- Wunderman www.wunderman.com

a. Who is the intended audience of the site?

b. How does the agency position itself (i.e., creative-driven, strategy (account)-driven, media-driven, etc.)?

c. What is your overall impression of the agency and its work? Why?

2. Sales Promotion

Sales promotion vehicles are often key elements in integrated marketing communication campaigns. Browse the websites of the following support organizations for the sales promotion field and answer the questions for each site.

Sales Promotion Organizations

- PROMO www.promomagazine.com
- Promotion Marketing Association (PMA) www.pmalink.org

- Promotional Product Association International (PPAI) www.ppa.org
- Creative Magazine www.creativemag.com
- Display and Design Ideas www.ddimagazine.com

a. What group sponsors the site? Who is the intended audience(s)?

b. What is the organization's purpose?

c. Who makes up the organization's membership? Its constituency?

d. What benefit does the organization provide individual members/subscribers? The overall advertising and sales promotion communities?

Sales Promotion Agencies

Promotional companies, like their direct-marketing counterparts, differ somewhat from traditional advertising firms. Visit five of the websites for the following sales promotion companies, and answer the questions below for each.

- AdSolution www.adsolution.com
- BIC Graphic www.bicgraphic.com
- InterPromo, Inc. www.interpromo.com
- Promotions.com www.promotions.com
- Retalix www.storepoint.com
- Val-Pak Coupons www.valpak.com

a. What is the focus of the company's work (that is, consumer or trade)?

b. What is the scope and size of the company's business?

c. What promotional services does the company offer?

d. What is your overall impression of the company and its work? Why?

3. Evaluating Promoters

As a maker of organic, vegetarian pet foods, you have been advertising your products with some success, but feel you could still increase sales volume. As a result you have decided to try sales promotions. Select two organizations from the list of sales promotion agencies in Exercise 2 of this section and compare their approaches. Discuss why you believe one or the other would do a good job of promoting your products.

Chapter 11

Relationship Building: Public Relations, Sponsorship, and Corporate Advertising

Objectives TO EXPLAIN THE ROLE OF PUBLIC RELATIONS, SPONSORSHIPS, AND CORPORATE ADVERTISING in relationship marketing and integrated marketing communications. By integrating public relations, event sponsorships, and institutional advertising with its general advertising activities, a company can improve the overall effectiveness of its marketing efforts.

After studying this chapter, you will be able to:

- **Distinguish** between advertising and public relations.

- **Discuss** the key elements of crisis communications.

- **Describe** the difference between press agentry and publicity.

- **Identify** the tools public relations practitioners use.

- **Explain** how event sponsorships can fit into an IMC plan.

- **Define** advocacy advertising and debate its role in a free society.

- **Explain** the role of corporate identity advertising.

We all know the names: Cherry Garcia, Chunky Monkey, New York Super Fudge Chunk. If some of Ben & Jerry's product names are lovable, the company's customers would say that its premium ice cream is irresistible. With annual sales now topping $200 million, the rise of "Vermont's Finest" has been fine indeed since the company's modest beginnings in a renovated gas station. But the socially conscious outfit has always said that it's not just about the ice cream. ∎ Like its frozen treats, Ben & Jerry's mission statement is quite a mouthful. It details the company's product mission, pledging "a continued commitment to incorporating wholesome, natural ingredients and promoting business practices that respect the Earth and the Environment"; economic mission, promising financial sustainability, value for stakeholders, and opportunity for employees; and social mission, acknowledging "the central role that business plays in society by initiating innovative ways to improve the quality of life locally, nationally, and internationally."[1] Promoting causes as diverse as family farms, solar energy, and child welfare, the company has a long record of incorporating liberal activism into its public relations efforts. ∎ Of course, Ben & Jerry's isn't alone in using its business clout to champion progressive issues. But the breadth of its involvement sets it apart from other would-be corporate philanthropists. Established in 1985, the Ben & Jerry's Foundation offers competitive grants for small-scale grassroots social programs throughout the United States. In 2003, awardees received grants of up to $15,000 in order to combat homelessness, clean up old mines, and monitor federal land management practices, to cite only a few examples.[2] ∎ Getting back to the ice cream, a portion of the profits from certain Ben & Jerry's flavors is directed toward its social mission. The causes can be local or global: its Primary Berry Graham flavor was developed to encourage voting in the 2004 New Hampshire primary; in 2002, its One Sweet Whirled campaign partnered with the Dave Matthews Band to fight global warming.[3] The company has also touted its use of environment-friendly packaging[4] and encouragement of energy-conserving refrigeration methods.[5]

■ Sometimes it takes the expression "giving back to the community" very literally. Its Scoop Shops offer an annual Free Cone Day, and Ben & Jerry's Cowmobile delivered free scoops nationwide in the 1980s. Some would argue that the giveaways are as much a marketing tool as an act of generosity, but either way they represent a lot of ice cream: Advance estimates for the 25th Annual Free Cone Day in 2003 predicted that more than 1 million cones would be given away worldwide.[6] ■ Ben & Jerry's earnestness has always had its share of detractors, who find its image contrived and disingenuous, but skepticism about its social role has grown since its acquisition in 2000 by Dutch multinational Unilever. How could the brand preserve its homegrown, quirky image as part of a massive conglomerate? Would its activism be diluted, or even eliminated completely? Under pressure from its shareholders to approve the deal, even the company's founders expressed misgivings in announcing its completion: "While we and others certainly would have preferred to pursue our mission as an independent enterprise, we hope that, as part of Unilever, Ben & Jerry's will continue to expand its role in society."[7] ■ Under Unilever's control, Ben & Jerry's has dramatically increased its product offerings and overseas presence and continues to sponsor politically flavored promotional events. With the subsidiary's ability to retain its proudly liberal voice still an open question, Ben & Jerry's ice cream now, in some ways, has to speak for itself. But the positive public relations fostered by its many years of community involvement, along with the product's popularity, will help to further solidify the brand's worldwide fan base. ■

The Role of Public Relations

The primary role of public relations is to manage a company's reputation and help build public consent for its enterprises. Today's business environment has become so competitive that public consent can no longer be assumed; it must be earned continuously.[8]

The term *public relations* is widely misunderstood and misused. Part of the confusion is due to the fact that public relations covers a very broad area. Depending on the context and one's point of view, it can be a concept, a profession, a management function, or a practice. For our purposes, we define **public relations (PR)** as the management function that focuses on the relationships and communications that individuals and organizations have with other groups (called *publics*) for the purpose of creating mutual goodwill.

As we've already discussed, every company, organization, or government body has relationships with groups of people who are affected by what it does or says. They may be employees, customers, stockholders, competitors, suppliers, legislators, or the community in which the organization resides. Marketing professionals refer to these people as *stakeholders* because they all have some vested interest in the company's actions. In PR terminology, each of these groups is considered one of the organization's **publics,** and the goal of PR is to develop and maintain goodwill with most, if not all, of its publics. Failure to do so may mean loss of customers and revenues, time lost dealing with complaints or lawsuits, and loss of esteem (which weakens the organization's brand equity as well as its ability to secure financing, make sales, and expand).

Advertisers form relationships with various groups of people who are affected by what they do or say. The Crain's New York Business *ad shown here compliments its subscribers and piques the interest of potential customers.*

A company's publics change constantly. After being acquired by Unilever, Ben & Jerry's faced previously silent, content publics. It still generally projects a sunny, caring image even though it is now part of Unilever. Criticism of the company appears to have increased after the acquisition. The Center for Science in the Public Interest (CSPI) accused Ben & Jerry's of misleading the public by claiming that some of its products were "all-natural" when they in fact contained hydrogenated oils and artificial flavors. CSPI called upon the FDA to take action against the company.[9] Ben & Jerry's hedged response was that the term "all-natural" had various definitions in the food industry, but that it would work with natural food organizations on the issue.[10] In 2003, the company voluntarily recalled pints of its Karamel Sutra ice cream that contained peanuts not mentioned on the label. After receiving one illness complaint about this common food allergen, the recall went forward, with CEO Yves Couette stating that "Our primary concern is always for the health and safety of our consumers."[11]

Because of the powerful effect of public opinion, companies and organizations must consider the breadth of impact of their actions. This is especially true in times of crisis, emergency, or disaster. But it also holds true for major policy decisions: changes in management or pricing, labor negotiations, introduction of new products, or changes in distribution methods. Each decision affects different groups in different ways. Effective public relations can channel groups' opinions toward mutual understanding and positive outcomes.

In short, the goals of public relations are to improve public opinion, build goodwill, and establish and maintain a satisfactory reputation for the organization. PR efforts may rally public support, obtain public understanding or neutrality, or simply respond to inquiries. Well-executed public relations is an ongoing process that molds good long-term relationships and plays an important role in relationship marketing and integrated communications.[12]

The Difference between Advertising and Public Relations

Since they both use the media to create awareness or to influence markets or publics, advertising and public relations are similar—but they're not the same. Advertising reaches its audience through media the advertiser pays for. It appears just as the advertiser designed it, with the advertiser's bias built in. Knowing this, the public views ads with some skepticism or ignores them outright. So in an integrated marketing communications program, advertising is rarely the best vehicle for building credibility.

Many public relations communications, like publicity, are not openly sponsored or paid for. People receive these communications in the form of news articles, editorial interviews, or feature stories after the messages have been reviewed and edited—filtered—by the media. Since the public thinks such messages are coming from the medium rather than a company, it trusts them more readily. For building credibility, therefore, public relations is usually the better approach. Ben & Jerry's, for example, relies heavily on press coverage of its ice-cream giveaways during events it helps sponsor.

However, while advertising is carefully placed to gain particular reach and frequency objectives, PR is less precise.

Certain public relations activities can add great value to the perception of a product. Here, a poet autographs a copy of his book after doing a reading. Book signings are a common form of public relations used by the publishing industry around the world.

When Is Advertising Not Really Advertising?

During the 1970s, Congress created a provision in the tax code—Section 527—to shield contributions to political parties from taxation. Two decades later, nonprofit committees transformed Section 527 into a campaign finance loophole, leading to a surge in the use of "advocacy advertising" over the past several elections. This loophole enables concerned people and groups, named "527 committees," to funnel millions of dollars into ads advocating a wide variety of issues and, by implication, certain political candidates. Advocacy ads are a subset of the larger category of public relations advertising. Designed to state a sponsor's opinion about important social issues through a blend of public relations, editorials, and advertising, they may appear in the form of "advertorials," advertising supplements, or infomercials.

The increasing use of advocacy advertising by 527 committees has raised a red flag because these committees are categorized as nonprofit political organizations. This means that even though millions of dollars are funneled through these committees, none of this money is taxable. In fact, the contributions actually represent a tax deduction for the donors. More important, until recently, 527 committees were not required to report their sources of funds or their expenditures to the IRS, allowing contributors to donate an unlimited amount of money and retain complete anonymity.

The loophole worked as follows: An anonymous group could set up a bank account and collect as many millions as it could. Then, after creating a dummy name, such as "Red-Blooded Americans for a Decent Society," the group would run ads attacking or supporting any candidate or issue it chose. The only requirement was to refrain from using "magic words" such as "vote for," "vote against," "elect," or "defeat" in reference to a particular candidate.

For example, during the 2000 election, a 527 committee known as "Republicans for Clean Air" spent $2.5 million on ads attacking John McCain's environmental record while praising the air pollution policies in Texas, where George W. Bush just happened to be governor. Using a very unflattering picture of McCain against a backdrop of pollution-spewing smokestacks, the ad proclaimed, "Bush—leading so each day dawns brighter." Although the ad never used the magic words to explicitly suggest voting for Bush, the message was clear. Shortly after the election, the ads were discovered to have been bankrolled by two millionaire friends of George Bush.

Legislation in 2002 (H.R. 5596) stripped advocacy groups of much of their anonymity by mandating financial disclosure; but ads continue to appear, and issues continue to take a back seat to character attacks. In August 2004, a 527 committee called "Swift Boat Veterans for Truth" disputed presidential candidate John Kerry's military service record. One television spot featured a host of veterans actively denouncing Kerry. "John Kerry lied to get his Bronze Star," claims one; "He betrayed all his shipmates," says another.

The Kerry campaign was quick to point out that none of the veterans shown in the ad actually served in Kerry's boats, and the White House distanced itself from the attack, touting President Bush's involvement in legislation that supposedly banned the "unregulated soft money" that supports the 527 ads. The much-trumpeted McCain-Feingold Bill (officially enacted as the Bipartisan Campaign Reform Act) does not ban such soft money, however; it simply requires proper financial disclosure and reporting by 527 committees and other nonprofit organizations.

Public relations objectives are not as easy to quantify. In fact, the results gained from public relations activities depend greatly on the experience and skill of the people executing it and the relationship they have with the press. But PR can go only so far. Editors won't run the same story over and over. An ad's memorability, however, comes from repetition. While PR activities may offer greater credibility, advertising offers precision and control. This is why some companies relay their public relations messages through *corporate advertising,* which we discuss later in this chapter (and in the Ethical Issues box).

Advertising and PR in the Eyes of Practitioners

Another major difference between public relations and advertising is the orientation of professional practitioners. Advertising professionals see *marketing* as the umbrella process companies use to determine what products and services the market needs and how to distribute and sell them. To advertising professionals, advertising and public relations are "good news" marketing tools used to promote sales.

Public relations professionals take a totally different view. With their background typically in journalism rather than marketing, they believe *public relations* should be the umbrella process. They think companies should use PR to maintain relationships with all publics, including consumers. As *Inside PR* magazine says, "Public relations is a management discipline that encompasses a wide range of activities, from *marketing and advertising* to investor relations and government affairs."[13] To PR professionals, public relations should be integrated "corporate" communications, which is certainly broader than what most people consider integrated "marketing" communications. Public relations people, for example, are also concerned with employee relations and investor relations. Marketing and advertising people rarely are. So public relations really is much broader.

To date, though, few companies are structured with a public relations orientation; most are still marketing oriented, perhaps due to marketing's bottom-line orientation. But in today's world of downsizing, reengineering, and total quality management (TQM), marketing people would be well advised to adopt the multiple-

Advocacy ads are not seen only in the political arena. Both noncommercial and commercial organizations use advertorials because they are powerful tools. They combine the best of two worlds: the controlled, mass-awareness communication ability of advertising along with the greater credibility of public relations. Advertorials enable an advocacy message to be presented without censorship or modification by the media. Thus, the advertorial can effectively address difficult issues, emphasize facts favorable to the advertiser, and strategically run in prime-time news programming, newspaper op-ed pages, or in "Special Advertising Sections" of magazines.

The persuasiveness of advertorials increases when they emulate highly credible journalistic formats. While advertising commonly uses puffery in the form of superlatives to boost a product's perceived value (see Ethical Issues, "Truth in Advertising: Fluffing and Puffing," in Chapter 3), advertorials don't. They typically adopt the straightforward, journalistic formats of newspapers, magazines, and network TV news programs to achieve a greater air of authenticity. Striving to resemble "valid" news sources, they commonly include fact-oriented text, graphics, and documentarylike images. The desired result is "innocence by association," where the advertorial appears to reflect the higher ideals and objectivity usually associated with journalism and academia.

However, this poses ethical dilemmas with real consequences. A major criticism of advocacy advertising is that, by disguising a subjective point of view as objective, unbiased editorial material, it persuades without appearing to do so. Advertisers may even use the advertorial to deflect serious criticism about the advertiser's policies, products, or practices—an approach bordering on unethical. There's also the potential for advertorials to intentionally mislead the public into supporting policies of questionable social value.

Corporations and political groups have the same rights as anyone else to express their views, and advocacy ads provide an effective medium for doing so. But in addition to understanding the law, advocacy advertisers should pause and consider certain ethical issues such as fairness (recognizing what is good for everyone involved), loyalty (the individual good versus that of the group and the public's "right to know"), truth (the lack of fabrication, falsification, and distortion), and duty (sacrificing the individual's interests to support principles like rightness over expedience). Similarly, ad agency professionals should carefully examine the integrity of their clients' messages and their impact on society as a whole—rather than just focusing on their client's immediate interests.

Questions

1. Should corporations use persuasive advertising techniques to influence key decision makers? Explain.

2. How can you determine if an advocacy ad is deceptive? If deception is established, what should the penalty be?

Sources: "About Issue Advertising," *IssueAds@AAPC*, Annenburg Public Policy Center, 2003 (retrieved from www.annenbergpublicpolicycenter.org/ISSUEADS/issues.htm); "Anti-Kerry Veterans Group Releases Critical Ad: Bush Campaign Distances Itself from Commercial," CNN.com, August 6, 2004 (retrieved from www.cnn.com/2004/ALLPOLITICS/08/05/kerry.veterans); "Any Questions?" Swiftvets.com script of television ad (retrieved from http://swift1.he.net/~swiftvet/script.html); Office of the White House Press Secretary, "Press Gaggle by Scott McClellan," August 5, 2004 (retrieved from www.whitehouse.gov/news/releases/2004/08/20040805-5.htm).

stakeholder approach and relationship consciousness that PR people bring to the table.

Moreover, in times of crisis, the candid, open-information orientation of PR is invariably the better perspective to adopt. Fortunately, with the growing interest in relationship marketing, two-way interactivity, and IMC, companies are finally beginning to embrace a public relations philosophy. Exhibit 11–1 shows some indicators of the PR industry's health and growth.

When PR activities are used for marketing purposes, the term **marketing public relations (MPR)** is often used. In support of marketing, public relations activities can raise awareness, inform and educate, improve understanding, build trust, make friends, give people reasons or permission to buy, and create a climate of consumer acceptance—usually better than advertising.[14] Marketing strategists Al and Laura Ries believe the best way to build a brand is through publicity—a PR activity. They cite numerous examples of leading companies that achieved their cachet with relatively little advertising but extensive publicity: Starbucks, The Body Shop, Wal-Mart, to name a few.[15]

In an integrated marketing communications program, advertising and MPR need to be closely coordinated. Many ad agencies now have PR departments for this very purpose. And many companies now have communications departments that manage both advertising and PR.

Exhibit 11–1
2004 public relations industry benchmarks

The recession of 2002 hit PR firms particularly hard, but most firms reported that they began to recover in 2003 and are even more optimistic for 2004. Of the 80 PR agencies surveyed by the Council on Public Relations Firms,	
Percentage of firms predicting an increase in revenue for 2004	89%
Average reported increase in first-quarter 2004 revenues over 2003	12%
Revenue per professional, a key indicator of productivity (up 6%)	$186,113
Average 2003 operating profit margin (up 20%)	13%

The Public Relations Job

The public relations job comprises a variety of activities, from crisis communications to fundraising. And PR practitioners use many tools besides press conferences and news releases.

PR Planning and Research

The first function of a PR practitioner is to plan and execute the public relations program. Part of this task may be integrated with the company's marketing efforts (for instance, product publicity), but the PR person typically takes a broader view. He or she must prepare an overall public relations program for the whole organization.

Because public opinion is so important, the PR person must constantly monitor, measure, and analyze changes in attitudes among a variety of publics. In 1999, some Belgian consumers became ill after drinking Coca-Cola. The episode created quite a scare. The investment firm of Goldman, Sachs & Co. used research to monitor Coke's standing with the general consuming public so that it could make better investment recommendations to its clientele. Analysts realized that rebuilding consumer confidence would probably require substantial marketing investment.[16] Some 19 percent of consumers polled in Belgium, France, and Germany expressed at least some reservations about drinking Coke products in the future—even after Coke had begun airing a new campaign. However, 77 percent of Belgians, 70 percent of French, and 61 percent of the Germans said they had complete faith in the company's products.[17]

A common form of public relations research is **opinion sampling** using techniques discussed in Chapter 7: shopping center or phone interviews, focus groups, analysis of incoming mail, and field reports. Some advertisers set up toll-free phone lines and invite consumer feedback.

The practitioner analyzes the organization's relationships with its publics; evaluates people's attitudes and opinions toward the organization; assesses how company policies and actions relate to different publics; determines PR objectives and strategies; develops and implements a mix of PR activities, integrating them whenever possible with the firm's other communications; and solicits feedback to evaluate effectiveness.

Reputation Management

One of the principal tasks of public relations is to manage the standing of the firm with various publics. **Reputation management** is the name of this long-term strategic process.[18] PR practitioners employ a number of strategies and tactics to help them manage their firm's or client's reputation, including publicity and press agentry, crisis communications management, and community involvement.

Aside from advertising, publicity can help companies distribute information or shape an image. A company's public relations department will notify the press when new products are introduced, a business is bought or sold, or a crisis is afoot. The idea is to disseminate important information while maintaining the company's public reputation. To maintain credibility with the press, news releases should be distributed only for newsworthy events—those that affect some significant segment of the company's various publics.

Kodak, Intel put heads together

By Kevin Maney
USA TODAY

Eastman Kodak is teaming with Intel to try to make it easier for consumers to get their photos into computers without having to buy expensive digital cameras or scanners.

The partnership, announced Thursday, involves technology development, sharing of patents and up to $150 million in joint consumer marketing over three years. One of the first tangible moves will be to upgrade technology in Kodak photofinishing labs. The labs could then inexpensively digitize film photos and put them on CD-ROM disks, called Kodak Picture CDs.

Consumers would be able to take pictures using a 35mm camera and get the film developed as usual. On the developer's envelope would be a box for the CDs. Check the box, and you get back both the regular prints and the CD when you pick up your photos. The CD could be loaded into a PC and the photos could be dumped into documents or e-mail.

Kodak already has a CD-ROM offering called PhotoCD. But the Kodak-Intel version is supposed to be cheaper — less than $10 extra per roll of film — and have turnaround times equal to those of film processing. Eventually, consumers should be able to get a CD at a one-hour photo shop. The idea is to let mass-market consumers get into digital images no matter what kind of camera people own.

"We want the lines between analog and digital photography to be completely blurred," says Don Whiteside, general manager of Intel digital imaging. Adds Kodak executive Willy Shih, "It lowers the entry point for getting into the digital format."

Publicity and Press Agentry

For many public relations professionals, their primary task is to generate news and get it placed in the media for their companies or clients. A major activity of public relations, **publicity** is the generation of news about a person, product, or service that appears in print or electronic media. Companies employ this activity either for marketing purposes or to enhance the firm's reputation.

Some people think of publicity as "free" because the media don't charge firms to run it (they also don't guarantee they'll use it). This is a misnomer, though. Someone still gets paid to write the release and coordinate with the press. However, as a marketing communications vehicle, publicity often offers a considerably greater return on money invested than other communications activities. A large ad campaign might require an investment of 5 to 20 percent of sales; a major publicity program, only 1 to 2 percent.

To be picked up by the media, publicity must be *newsworthy.* Typical publicity opportunities include new-product introductions, awards, company sales and earnings, major new contracts, mergers, retirements, parades, and speeches by company executives. Sometimes publicity accrues unintentionally, such as when peanuts were found in Ben & Jerry's ice cream. And since publicity can originate from any source, it may be difficult—or impossible—to control. In IMC terms, unintentional publicity is an *unplanned message.*

The planning and staging of events to generate publicity is called **press agentry.** Most PR people engage in press agentry to bring attention to new products or services or to portray their organizations favorably. For print media, the publicity person deals with editors and feature writers. For broadcast media, he or she deals with program directors, assignment editors, or news editors. Successful PR practitioners develop and maintain close, cordial relations with their editorial contacts. An MPR professional practicing IMC sees the press as an important *public,* and writers and editors as important *stakeholders.* PR people pay attention to the phenomenon of stakeholder overlap: A company's customer might also work for the press. An employee might also be a stockholder and a customer. Awareness of these potentially multifaceted relationships helps create consistent communications, the hallmark of IMC.

Crisis Communications Management

One of the most important public relations tasks for any corporation is **crisis management.** Brand value can be quickly destroyed if "damage control" is not swift and thorough. For example, Martha Stewart's formerly profitable marketing persona quickly became a liability in 2002, when her involvement in an insider-trading scheme surfaced. (She was later tried and sentenced to a prison term.) Even though her company, Martha Stewart Living Omnimedia, immediately began efforts to distance itself from its founder's legal troubles by removing her name from some products and publications, its stock value and revenues both dropped by more than 30 percent between 2003 and 2004.[19]

But the classic case of exemplary crisis communication management was Johnson & Johnson's handling of a product-tampering episode in 1982. Several people died when a criminal laced bottles of J&J's Extra-Strength Tylenol with cyanide on retail shelves. The moment they received the news, management strategists at J&J and McNeil Products (the J&J subsidiary that markets Tylenol) formulated three stages of action:

1. Identify the problem and take immediate corrective action. J&J strategists got information from the police, FBI, FDA, and press; identified the geographic area affected; corrected rumors; and immediately withdrew the product from the marketplace.

The social mission sections of Ben & Jerry's country-specific websites reflect both global concerns and local initiatives. Each site shows the company's support for world peace, hormone-free dairy products, and blood donation drives. In Spain, the company also sponsors a homeless shelter for the mentally ill and a group that fights pet abandonment. The Ben & Jerry's website for Sweden links to a Swedish organization devoted to child welfare in Benin, West Africa.

2. Actively cooperate with authorities in the investigation. Johnson & Johnson was proactive. It helped the FBI and other law enforcement agencies generate leads and investigate security at the plants, and it offered a $100,000 reward.

3. Quickly rebuild the Tylenol name and capsule line, including Regular Strength capsules, which were recalled, too. Although J&J believed the poisoning had taken place at the retail end of the chain, it first made sure that the tampering hadn't occurred at McNeil. The company's two capsule production lines were shut down, and dog teams were brought in to search for cyanide.

The insatiable appetite of the news media plus a flood of inquiries from anxious consumers put J&J's PR people under enormous pressure. All communications between the media and the company were channeled through the corporate communications department. All customer, trade, and government communications were coordinated within the company. This way, J&J maintained open, clear, consistent, legal, and credible communications and avoided rumors, political backbiting, and corporate defensiveness.

In the first 48 hours after the news broke, phone calls to Johnson & Johnson and McNeil were incessant. In the basement at McNeil, a bank of phones usually used for sales was staffed by employees who were briefed on what to say, what not to say, and where to refer tough questions.

At the same time, management and employees had to be informed, authorities contacted, and many others notified. J&J and McNeil public relations managers and staff had to plan, coordinate, and supervise this enormous task.

As infrequent as disasters are, there is no more important activity for PR professionals and public information officers than crisis communications management—especially those in highly sensitive fields such as airlines, government agencies, the military, law enforcement, chemical and oil companies, and public utilities.

Since the Tylenol incident, many companies in normally nonsensitive industries have prepared crisis management plans. The manner in which a company handles communications during emergencies or catastrophes will determine to a great extent how the public responds to the news. When corporations have no plans for coping with crisis, the resulting press coverage can be disastrous. Experts on crisis management encourage all companies to follow J&J's example by being open and candid. Withholding information or evading questions inevitably backfires, as many politicians have learned.

Attitudes toward a former crisis can soften over time. Ben & Jerry's offered a quick, apologetic, and sincere response when traces of nuts were found in pints of ice cream that did not have warning labels. In 2004, after the negative press and consumer skepticism had calmed somewhat, a tongue-in-cheek Ben & Jerry's poster appeared in London tube cars, "warning" consumers that some ice cream flavors "May Contain Nuts: Lots of Them."

"Green" Advertising

Since its introduction in the mid-1980s, environmental advertising has become a significant aspect of marketing. Advertisers saw the consumer desire for environmentally safe products and tried to meet the demand as quickly as possible. Many advertisers embraced genuine concern for the environment. But it didn't take long for consumers to catch on to the fact that some companies were making false claims, using such vague terms as *environmentally friendly* and *green*.

In a short time, consumers grew wary of the environmental appeal and advertisers reacted by reducing its emphasis. To avoid future trouble, many companies waited for state and federal governments to define terms and provide legal guidelines. Over the past decade, the Federal Trade Commission (FTC) has established rules and guidelines, while several states adopted a set of laws setting definitions for terms like *ozone friendly, biodegradable,* and *recycled.* In 1995, California's Truth in Environmental Advertising law was enacted. It was shortly repealed and introduced again in 1997 without success.

Presently, there are no federal laws governing what a seller can say about a product. The FTC, in cooperation with the Environmental Protection Agency (EPA), has developed new guidelines for advertisers, to ensure that their environmental marketing claims do not mislead consumers. These Guidelines for the Use of Environmental Advertising Claims carry no force of law and compliance is voluntary.

There are several companies and organizations that act as intermediaries between advertisers and consumers regarding environmental claims. Scientific Certification Systems (SCS), for instance, verifies claims of recycled content in products. It uses an environmental report card, which measures a product's total environmental impact.

Green Seal, an independent, nonprofit organization, promotes the manufacture and sale of environmentally responsible consumer products. It awards a Green Seal of Approval to products that cause less harm to the environment than other similar products. Founded in 1994, Green Seal "focuses on the measure of environmental damage that scientists have found to be most important in certain product categories," says Norman Dean, president.

Today's new marketing sensitivity toward the environment and social consciousness focuses on consumer purchasing behavior. Seventy-nine percent of Americans consider themselves environmentalists, 83 percent say they have changed their shopping habits to help protect the environment, and 67 percent say they would be willing to pay 5 to 10 percent more for environmentally friendly products. The data, however, are contradicted by more recent studies that reveal that people in America do not actually buy the products they claim to prefer. Even though studies show a high concern for the environment, the public lacks a behavior consistent with such concerns. Researchers believe that this attitude-behavior gap exists when the competitive advantage of green products is overcome by factors of price, quality, and convenience.

But in an increasingly competitive marketplace, firms must ultimately benefit from their green actions. A new environmental management tool called SPINE was developed to help industries achieve environmental recognition. SPINE makes it possible for customers to verify marketers' environmental claims by following a product's manufacturing process through every step.

Even with organizations such as Scientific Certification Systems and Green Seal, and reference tools such as SPINE, it is still a major challenge to get businesses and consumers to understand the value of green advertising, especially when no stringent regulations are in effect. Today, the consumer can only speculate how "environmentally friendly" a company actually is. Thinking about the future, either through regulation or voluntary action, companies will have to provide consumers with more information about the environmental friendliness of their products so customers will decide for themselves how well a product suits their needs.

Laboratory Applications

1. Imagine you are marketing a new product that sells for $1.25 and is environmentally safe. Would you spend thousands of dollars for a green seal on your impulse product if consumers are ambivalent toward such environmentally safe goods as observed in the first wave? Explain.

2. Imagine that you just made manufacturing changes to your product so that it is now easily recyclable. Would you advertise these changes, knowing the restrictions on the term *recycle*?

Community Involvement

The goal of **community involvement** is to develop a dialogue between the company and the community.[20] This is best done by having company officers, management, and employees contribute to the community's social and economic development. Every community offers opportunities for corporate involvement: civic and youth groups, charitable fundraising drives, cultural or recreational activities, and so on. As we discussed in Chapter 8, a company should ideally adopt one program relevant to its expertise and focus its *mission marketing* activities. The PR department may help set up such programs and publicize them to the community (see Ad Lab 11–A).

Other Public Relations Activities

In addition to planning and reputation management, public relations professionals are often involved in activities such as public affairs and lobbying, speechwriting, fundraising and membership drives, creation of publications, and special-events management.

Public Affairs and Lobbying

Organizations often need to deal with elected officials, regulatory and legislative bodies, and various community groups—the realm of **public affairs.** Public affairs usually requires a specialist. Many experts think PR and public affairs should become more integrated to combine the skills and policy expertise of the specialist with the PR person's media and community relations savvy.

Lobbying refers to informing government officials and persuading them to support or thwart administrative action or legislation in the interests of some client. Every organization is affected by the government, so lobbying is big business.

Speechwriting

Because company officials often have to speak at stockholder meetings, conferences, or conventions, PR practitioners often engage in **speechwriting.** They are also frequently responsible for making all the arrangements for speaking opportunities and developing answers for questions company representatives are likely to be asked. Since public relations people may sometimes represent their employers at special events, press conferences, and interviews, they too should be articulate public speakers.

Fundraising and Membership Drives

A public relations person may be responsible for soliciting money for a nonprofit organization or for a cause the company deems worthwhile, such as the United Way or a political action committee (PAC).

Charitable organizations, labor unions, professional societies, trade associations, and other groups rely on membership fees or contributions. The PR specialist must communicate to potential contributors or members the goals of the organization and may integrate promotional tie-ins to publicize the drive or encourage participation. In the process, the company PR people may work closely with the advertising department or agency to create ads promoting the particular cause or to publicize the company's involvement with the cause in product ads.

To meet demanding operating budgets, non-profit organizations often devote a significant portion of their advertising to raising funds. The Canadian Paraplegic Association (www.canparaplegic.org) ran this creative ad to drum up financial support for its goal of curing spinal cord injuries.

HELP CURE SPINAL CORD INJURIES. Send your donation to The Canadian Paraplegic Association, 520 Sutherland Drive, Toronto, ON M4G 3V9. (416) 422-5644. Or visit info@cpaont.org.

Publications

Public relations people prepare many of a company's communications materials: news releases and media kits; booklets, leaflets, pamphlets, brochures, manuals, and books; letters, inserts, and enclosures; annual reports; posters, bulletin boards, and exhibits; audiovisual materials; and speeches and position papers. Here again, they may work with the advertising department or agency to produce these materials. The advertising people need to keep the company's overall positioning strategy in mind while trying to help accomplish the particular PR objectives.

Special-Events Management

The sponsorship and management of special events is a rapidly growing field. In fact, it has become such an important topic that we devote the next major section of this chapter to it, following our discussion of PR tools.

Public Relations Tools

The communications tools at the PR person's disposal vary widely, from news releases and photos to audiovisual materials and even advertising. We'll discuss some of the more common ones briefly.

News Releases and Press Kits

A **news release** (or **press release**), the most widely used PR tool, consists of one or more typed sheets of information (usually $8\frac{1}{2}$ by 11 inches) issued to generate publicity or shed light on a subject of interest. News releases cover time-sensitive

Media Contact:
Ted Ladd, (858) 848-2515
ted.ladd@gateway.com

FOR IMMEDIATE RELEASE

**GATEWAY TEAMS UP WITH SMART TECHNOLOGIES
TO CREATE NEW EDUCATION SOLUTIONS**

SMART Products Become an Integral Component of Gateway's Education Solutions

POWAY, Calif., June 30, 2003 – Say goodbye to dusty chalkboards, blue-lined notebooks and passive TVs. A new relationship between Gateway, Inc. and SMART Technologies Inc., unveiled at the NECC Education Conference today, means new technology solutions to help teachers provide a rich collaborative environment in classrooms to enhance student learning.

The new Gateway/SMART Technologies joint solutions, which bundle Gateway's plasma displays, PCs and projectors with SMART products such as the SMART Board™ interactive whiteboards and SMART Board *for Plasma Displays* interactive overlays, make whole-class instruction a dynamic and collaborative experience.

"With today's relationships between Gateway and SMART Technologies, teachers can write over a Gateway plasma TV in electronic ink, draw a diagram on an interactive whiteboard or monitor and control any student's Gateway laptop – and then save any data to their primary classroom PC," said Jay Lambke, Gateway's vice president and GM of education.

Gateway/SMART Technologies joint solutions include:

- **SMART Board interactive whiteboards,** which connect to any Gateway computer and projector. With the image of their Gateway computer projected onto the SMART Board interactive whiteboard, teachers and students can simply touch the whiteboard to access and control any program on their computer, using their finger as a mouse. When a pen is selected from the SMART Pen Tray, users can write over top of computer applications and highlight important information with electronic ink. Annotations can be edited, saved, e-mailed and printed for distribution.

- **SMART Board *for Plasma Displays* interactive overlay,** which integrates with Gateway's market-leading[1], 42-inch plasma TV to make the display touch-sensitive. The interactive overlay fastens easily and securely over the plasma screen, and provides teachers with all the features of SMART Board interactive whiteboards.

-more-

Gateway Creates SMART Solutions
Page 2

- **Expression™ 303 multimedia cabinet,** which simplifies the storage and set-up of all Gateway and SMART solutions. Teachers can store Gateway projectors, peripherals, PCs and much more in this attractive, lockable cabinet that is mobile and easily accessible. The control panel gives laptop connections as well as power and audio control.

- **SynchronEyes® computer-lab instruction software,** which helps teachers create a focused learning environment by allowing them to monitor and control any student's Gateway PC. With SynchronEyes software running on an existing TCP/IP network, teachers are able to provide one-to-one instruction in a computer lab right from their own Gateway desktop.

"We are very pleased to work with an industry leader such as Gateway," said Nancy Knowlton, president and co-CEO of SMART. "With products from both companies bundled into a single package, educators will find it easy to buy these top educational technology products, which have already been integrated into tens of thousands of classrooms worldwide."

For more information on Gateway's Alpha Classroom and Alpha Campus vision, please visit: http://www.gateway.com/work/ed/alpha.shtml or contact Gateway Education at (888) 888-0392. For more information about SMART Technologies' products and services, please visit: http://www.smarttech.com.

Gateway's expansion of technology solutions for education is the latest effort from the company as it transforms itself from a traditional PC maker to a branded integrator of technology solutions. As a branded integrator, Gateway is launching an array of products across a host of new categories and will integrate them into customized solutions for both businesses and consumers.

About Gateway
Since its founding in 1985, Gateway (NYSE: GTW) has been a technology and direct-marketing pioneer, using its call centers, web site and retail network to build direct customer relationships. As it transforms itself from being a leading PC company into a branded integrator of personalized technology solutions, the company's line of Gateway-branded products is expanding to include digital TVs, DLP projectors, tablet PCs and systems and networking products and services. Gateway is America's second most admired computer company, according to *Fortune* magazine[1], and its products and services received more than 125 awards and honors last year. For more information, visit www.gateway.com.
(1) Source: *Fortune* magazine, March 3, 2003 issue

###

A news release is used to announce the important events of a company including grand openings, responses to a crisis, or changes of leadership. In this example from Gateway (www.gateway.com), the company announces its "People Rule" advertising campaign, explaining the philosophy behind it—that people come before technology. News releases are sent to the press in the hope that the information will be used to generate a story about the event in local or national papers or even on television. Companies can even place their news releases online, using services like the PR Newswire to communicate their messages across the country and around the world.

How to Write a News Release

The Role of the News Release

The news release is an effective tool for publicizing information for several reasons. It helps to protect the publicist and the client from being misquoted. It permanently records the preferred word usage, specific terms, key phrasing, and unique details.

Its standardized format also speeds up the process. It eliminates debate over how to format the information, highlights the data most needed by the recipient (contact person's name and telephone, date, etc.), and spells out the source and topic of the story.

The news release also simplifies dissemination by providing a form that is easily reproduced and transferred (e-mail, fax, postal mail, etc.) and by assuring that all recipients receive the same message.

Preparing the News Release

The news release follows a format generally accepted throughout the news industry.

____ **Triple-space the text and use wide margins.**

____ **At the top of the page (left or right side) place the name and phone number of your contact person.** If your page is not preprinted with your company's name and address, add it below the contact person. Finally, write FOR IMMEDIATE RELEASE or TO BE RELEASED AFTER [date].

____ **Write a headline that signals the key fact or issue of the story.** For example, TECHCO PRESIDENT SPEAKS TO BAY CITY LIONS CLUB THURSDAY.

____ **Place the most important information first.** The editors may shorten your news release by cutting from the bottom.

    ____ **Lead sentence:** The lead sentence is the most important. Keep it focused strictly on who, what, where, when, why,

and how. For example, "Techco President Ralph J. Talk will address the Bay City Lions Club at 8 PM Thursday, September 16, 2004."

    ____ **Body text:** Add directly related support information. "Mr. Talk's speech will be 'Technology in Albania.' Mr. Talk served five years as assistant to the president of the Albania Travel Association."

    ____ **Final text:** Fill in background details. "Mr. Talk was born on April 30, 1956, and is married to Alice Johnson of Bay City. They have two children. Mr. Talk is a board member of the Bay City Little League."

____ **Keep the text as factual, direct, and short as possible.**

____ **Carefully proof your copy.**

Etiquette

____ **Don't call to see whether the editor received your release.** Editors don't like to be pressured. Don't ask for tearsheets. An editor has little time to send you a copy. Don't promise you'll advertise if the item is published; the editor will be offended at the suggestion that news can be bought. If the article is run, send a thank-you letter to the editor.

Mailing List

____ **Prepare a list of local publications.** You may want to group them so that you don't mail out news releases to publications that don't use your type of information. Update your list regularly, because editors change and offices move.

____ **Ascertain in advance if the editors on your list prefer to have news releases sent by e-mail or snail-mail.**

---

hard news. Topics may include the announcement of a new product, promotion of an executive, an unusual contest, landing of a major contract, or establishment of a scholarship fund. For pointers in preparing releases, see the Checklist, "How to Write a News Release."

A **press kit** (or **media kit**) supports the publicity gained at staged events such as press conferences or open houses. It includes a basic fact sheet of information about the event, a program or schedule of activities, and a list of the participants and their biographical data. The kit also contains a news story about the event for the broadcast media, news and feature stories for the print media, and any pertinent photos and brochures.

Photos

Photos of events, products in use, new equipment, or newly promoted executives can lend credence or interest to a dull news story. In fact, a photo tells the story faster. Photos should be high quality and need little or no explanation. Typed captions should describe the photo and accurately identify the people shown.

Feature Articles

Many publications, especially trade journals, run **feature articles** (soft news) about companies, products, or services. They may be written by a PR person, the publication's staff, or a third party (such as a freelance business writer). As an MPR tool, feature articles can give the company or product great credibility. Editors like them because they have no immediate deadline and can be published at the editor's convenience.

Features may be case histories, how-to's (such as how to use the company's product), problem-solving scenarios (how one customer uses the company's product to increase production), or state-of-the-art technology updates. Other formats include roundups of what's happening in a specific industry and editorials (such as a speech or essay by a company executive on a current issue).

Printed Materials

Printed materials are the most popular tools used by public relations professionals.[21] They may be brochures or pamphlets about the company or its products, letters to customers, inserts or enclosures that accompany monthly statements, the *annual report* to stockholders, other reports, or house organs.

A **house organ** is a publication about happenings and policies at the company. An internal house organ is for employees only. External house publications go to company-connected people (customers, stockholders, suppliers, and dealers) or to the public. They may take the form of a newsletter, tabloid-size newspaper, magazine, or even a periodic e-zine. Their purpose is to promote goodwill, increase sales, or mold public opinion. A well-produced house organ can do a great deal to motivate employees and appeal to customers. However, writing, printing, and distributing can be expensive—and very time-consuming.

Posters, Exhibits, and Bulletin Boards

Posters can be used internally to stress safety, security, reduction of waste, and courtesy. Externally, they can impart product information, corporate philosophy, or other news of interest to consumers.

Companies use **exhibits** to describe the organization's history, present new products, show how products are made, or explain future plans. Exhibits are often prepared for local fairs, colleges and universities, and trade shows.

Internally, the public relations staff often uses **bulletin boards** to announce new equipment, new products, meetings, promotions, construction plans, and recreation news to employees. Thanks to the new technology, many companies now maintain an *intranet* site where they can post their internal bulletin boards.

Audiovisual Materials

Slides, films, filmstrips, CDs, and videocassettes are all forms of **audiovisual materials** and may be used for training, sales, or public relations. Considered a form of *corporate advertising,* nontheatrical or sponsored films (developed for public relations reasons) are often furnished without charge to movie theaters, organizations, and special groups, particularly schools and colleges. Classic examples include *Why Man Creates,* produced for Kaiser Aluminum, and Mobil Oil's *A Fable,* starring the famous French mime Marcel Marceau.

Many PR departments provide **video news releases (VNRs)**—news or feature stories prepared by a company and offered free to TV stations, which may use the whole video or just segments. Video news releases are somewhat controversial. Critics see them as subtle commercials or even propaganda and object when stations run the stories without disclosing that they came from a public relations firm, not the station's news staff.

Sponsorships and Events

In 1984, the owner of a large bicycle shop in the upper Midwest sent some of his mechanics to a local bicycle race sponsored by a national charity. At the time, his store was doing about $200,000 per year in retail sales, and he wanted to help out the charity while finding out what the racers thought of his and his competitors' businesses.

An unexpected benefit of the company's presence at the race was that participants started showing up in his store. Encouraged by these results, the company now supports more than a 100 bicycle events each year and sends staff members to dozens of such events. It has hired a full-time representative to coordinate company involvement in special bicycle events that have the potential of increasing its exposure and business revenue.

In 20 years the company has gone from a low-key presence at bicycling events, donating a few water bottles embossed with the company's name, to large-scale sponsorship, participating in event registration, providing event participants with workshops on bicycle maintenance, and offering in-store discounts to event participants. Within a week of one event, 30 participants had visited his store. Even better news for the company was that nearly half of the more than 5,000 riders reported purchasing goods from it.

By 1996, the company had revenues of $3 million. The owner attributes much of his success to his sponsorship of bicycle events. In his words, "I support them, and they support us."[22]

The Growth of Sponsorship

Advertising and public relations people get involved in sponsoring many kinds of special events. In fact, sponsorship may be the fastest-growing form of marketing today. It actually embraces two disciplines: sales promotion and public relations. Some sponsorships are designed to create publicity, others to improve public relations through personal contact and affiliation with a worthy cause, and others to immediately improve the bottom line.

A **sponsorship** is a cash or in-kind fee paid to a property (which may be a sports, entertainment, or nonprofit event or organization) in return for access to the exploitable commercial potential associated with that property.[23] In other words, just as advertisers pay a fee to sponsor a program on radio or TV, they may also sign on to sponsor a bike race, an art show or chamber music festival, a fair or exhibition, or the Olympics. The sponsorship fee may be paid in cash or **in kind** (that is, through a donation of goods and services). For instance, if a local TV station signs on as a sponsor of a 10K run, it will typically pay for some part of its sponsorship with advertising time for the event.

While the sponsored event or organization may be nonprofit, sponsorship is not the same as philanthropy. **Philanthropy** is support of a cause without any commercial incentive. Sponsorship (and a related strategy, *cause marketing*) is used to achieve commercial objectives.[24] In 2003, companies spent more than $10 billion on sponsorships; expenditures are expected to increase almost 9 percent in 2004. Worldwide, companies spent an estimated $25.9 billion in 2003.[25]

The reasons for this phenomenal growth relate to the economics of marketing we discussed earlier: the escalating costs of traditional advertising media, the fragmentation of media audiences, the growing diversity in leisure activities, and the ability to reach targeted groups of people economically. Initial growth probably came from the tobacco and alcohol companies, which many governments banned from broadcast advertising.

Corporations engage in various types of sponsorships (e.g., events, festivals, and causes) for a multitude of reasons. The Internet has become one of the hottest locations for corporate sponsorships for both events and content areas on websites. For many years, Panasonic (www.panasonic.com) has been an official worldwide sponsor of and supplier to the Olympic Games. As its website explains, Panasonic has provided advanced video and audio equipment to the Olympics since 1988. In 2004, it even provided hundreds of digital cameras and more than 16,000 headsets to U.S. athletes competing in Athens.

Recent legislation in the United Kingdom, Canada, and the United States threatens to end tobacco sponsorships altogether, but their success at sponsoring sports and events has shown the way for mainstream advertisers, who are rapidly picking up the slack.

Today, there is greater media coverage of sponsored events—everything from beach volleyball to grand prix horse shows to Xtreme games to cultural events. This provides a highly desirable venue for advertisers seeking young, upwardly mobile, educated consumers. Likewise, for transnational marketers, there is growing interest in global events such as World Cup soccer, the Olympics, and the America's Cup yacht race. Even traditional business-to-business marketers, such as Sweden's Ericsson Corp., are making a play for greater brand awareness in the United States by sponsoring the World Championships of Beach Volleyball, which is staged and marketed by Nike.[26]

Benefits of Sponsorship

In the past, for marketers with limited media alternatives (such as tobacco and alcohol companies), sponsorship simply offered a means of communication with customers and prospects. Today, the many benefits of sponsorship are well documented and more far-reaching.

Certainly one benefit of sponsorship is that the public approves of it. One study by Roper Starch Worldwide reported that 80 percent of Americans believe corporate sponsorship is an important source of money for professional sports and 74 percent believe sponsorships provide benefits to the cities where events occur.[27] Supporting this view, an economic analysis by the American Coalition for Entertainment and Sports Sponsorship showed that the 100 events it studied pumped more than $1.8 billion into local economies.[28] In the Roper Starch study, 74 percent of the people also said government should have little or no influence on which types of companies sponsor professional sports events. This is a far higher approval rating than most companies would get for their advertising programs.

More than almost any other marketing communications tool, sponsorships and events have the ability to involve customers, prospects, and other stakeholders. Naturally, events vary in degree of participation. A person attending a seminar or workshop will have greater involvement with the sponsor than someone attending a sponsored stock-car race.[29] However, events are also highly self-selective of their target audience. Someone who actually attends a stock-car race will most likely have a higher degree of interest than the average person. So marketers that define their audiences tightly can select just those sponsorships that offer the closest fit. Of course, marketers that sponsor an event simply because it has a large audience are misusing this tool.[30]

Unlike advertising, sponsorships and events can provide face-to-face access to current and potential customers. Depending on the venue, this access can be relatively clean and uncluttered by competition. Sponsoring a seminar, for instance, creates an opportunity for both customer education and brand involvement. In some cases, it even enables product demonstrations and the opportunity to give a personal sales pitch to multiple prospects at a time when they are open to new information.[31] This is especially good for business-to-business marketers.

A significant benefit is the opportunity to enhance the company's public image or merchandise its positioning through affiliation with an appropriate event.

Also important, but often overlooked, is the effect sponsorship can have on employees. Affiliating with a dynamic event can really boost the morale and pride of the troops in the trenches. And many companies offer attendance at the event (Super Bowl, Olympics, etc.) as an incentive to their sales staff.[32]

Some marketers have discovered that sponsorships can rapidly convert fan loyalty into sales. For example, 74 percent of stock-car racing fans report that they often buy products they see promoted at the racetrack. This is also true for other sports: 58 percent for baseball, 52 percent for tennis, 47 percent for golf. One fan told Greg Penske, president/CEO of Penske Motorsports, how upset he was that NASCAR driver Rusty Wallace had switched from Pontiac to Ford: "I'm only one year into my Pontiac lease and it's costing me $3,000 to get out of it and into a Ford."[33]

Finally, sponsorships can be very cost-efficient. Volvo International believes the media exposure it gets from its $3 million sponsorship of local tennis tournaments is equivalent to $25 million worth of advertising time and space.[34]

Drawbacks of Sponsorship

Like all marketing communications tools, sponsorship has some drawbacks. First, it can be very costly, especially when the event is solely sponsored. For this reason, most companies participate in co-sponsored events, which spreads the cost among several participants.

The problem with co-sponsored events is clutter. Some events have so many sponsors that getting one marketer's message through is extremely difficult. Look again at stock-car racing. How many logos do those cars sport?

Finally, evaluating the effectiveness of a particular sponsorship can be tricky at best—especially since it rarely happens in a vacuum. The problem is in separating the effects of a sponsorship from the effects of other concurrent marketing activities. We'll deal with these issues shortly.

Types of Sponsorship

While there are many, many avenues and events available for sponsorship, IEG Inc. groups most of them into five categories: sports; entertainment; causes; festivals, fairs, and annual events; and the arts (see Exhibit 11–2).[35]

Sports Marketing

North American corporations spent an estimated $7.69 billion in 2003 on sports marketing sponsorships. The most popular of these are motorsports and golf.[36] In fact, the vast majority of sponsorship money, more than 65 percent, is spent on sports events. This includes everything from the Olympics to NASCAR racing to professional athletic leagues. And as we saw from the bicycle shop story, companies don't have to be big multinationals to reap rich rewards from sponsorships—if they do it properly.

By buying the rights to serve Gatorade on the sidelines of professional basketball and football games, that brand has received more credibility than any television ad could provide, at a fraction of the cost. During every game, TV cameras show pros drinking the product in big Gatorade cups. And it's clear they're doing it because they want to, not because their agent told them to.[37]

In hotly contested markets, the giants in their fields fight over sponsorship rights. Nike battles Reebok and Adidas, Coke spars with Pepsi, Kodak runs up against Fuji, Visa struggles against American Express, and AT&T battles it out with both MCI and Sprint. This has certainly contributed to the rising cost of sponsorships. General Motors, for instance, signed an unprecedented $1 billion, eight-year sponsorship deal to ensure its exclusivity as the automotive sponsor for the U.S. Olympic Committee through 2008.[38]

In addition to spending more than $650,000 for each 30-second television spot during the 2004 Athens Olympics, Nike and Adidas outfitted a combined 6,000 Olympic athletes. Although Adidas' traditional stronghold is in soccer gear, it still supplied an estimated 1.5 million pieces of clothing, equipment, and other logo-emblazoned articles for the two-week event. Nike is not an official Olympic sponsor, but it traditionally blankets the host city with its Swoosh anyway. Isolating the effect of Olympic spon-

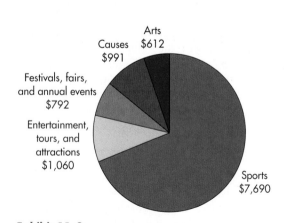

Exhibit 11-2

Annual sponsorship spending in North America ($ millions).

Sporting events have a long history of corporate sponsorship. Virtually every major sporting event in the United States is subsidized in part by corporate sponsors who wish to have their names associated with the event. This often provides high visibility and publicity for the company. Wienerschnitzel (www.wiener schnitzel.com), which sponsors the Wiener Nationals, is just one such example.

sorship is difficult, but Nike executive Mark Parker reported that the company routinely posts stock-market performances 20 percent higher than market average during Olympic years.[39]

Back in the United States, Reebok is trying to outflank both Adidas and Nike in the basketball segment by sponsoring high school summer basketball camps. Up-and-coming stars are highly recruited for these summer camps, in hopes of eventually signing them to a shoe contract. Currently running his ABCD camp for Reebok, Sonny Vaccaro worked for Nike in the 1980s and Adidas in the 1990s. Vaccaro switched from Adidas to Reebok in 2003 because Adidas did not recruit the top NBA draft pick, LeBron James, as aggressively as Vaccaro would have liked. Both Adidas and Reebok lost their catch: The young star signed a $90 million shoe contract with Nike.[40]

Many sports events are strictly local and therefore cost much less while giving the sponsor closer access to attendees and participants. Firms with modest event-marketing budgets, for example, use options ranging from local golf tournaments and tennis matches to surfing contests (see Exhibit 11–3).

An increasingly popular promotion is the company-sponsored sports event. The event can serve as an effective focal point for an IMC campaign if it ties the company to the local community hosting the event as well as to the event's regional or national audience. But without a concerted effort to tie an event to other marketing communications activities like a currently running ad campaign, the money spent on sponsorships is generally wasted.[41]

Some companies associate their names with existing events. Mountain Dew, Taco Bell, Sony, and T-Mobile, for instance, are the "gold" sponsors of ESPN's Winter X Games and regularly renew their sponsorships.[42]

But controversy often swirls around big sports sponsorships. The most controversial practice is **ambush marketing,** a promotional strategy nonsponsors use to capitalize on the popularity or prestige of an event or property by giving the false impression that they are sponsors. Ambush marketing techniques, like buying up all the billboard space around an athletic stadium, are often employed by the competitors of the property's official sponsor. Fuji did this to Kodak in Nagano. One of the reasons this works is because people are often confused about who the official sponsors actually are— again, the problem is clutter. Just because a company advertises on the Olympic broadcast, for instance, does not mean it is an official sponsor. Ambush marketers take advantage of this.[43]

Sports marketing is now a worldwide phenomenon. In Latin America, sponsorship of

Exhibit 11-3

U.S. companies spending more than $50 million on event sponsorship in 2003.

Millions of $	Company
$250–$255	PepsiCo
$240–$245	Anheuser-Busch
$185–$190	General Motors
$180–$185	Coca-Cola
$160–$165	Nike
$155–$160	Miller Brewing Co.
$125–$130	DaimlerChrysler
$100–$105	Ford Motor Co.
$95–$100	McDonald's
	Eastman Kodak
$90–$95	Visa International
$85–$90	MasterCard International
$75–80	3M
$65–$70	FedEx
$55–$60	Bank of America
	AT&T
$50–$55	Shell Oil Co.
$45–$50	John Hancock Financial Services
	Motorola
	Altria Group
	Coors Brewing Co.

soccer teams has grown dramatically. In Argentina alone, it rose from $820,000 in 1983 to $12 million in 1996. Out of 20 Argentine soccer teams, 17 now have official sponsors. The largest local sponsor is Quilmes beer, which paid $3 million to have its logo on the shirts of the country's most popular team, the Boca Juniors.[44]

In India, a new intercity cricket league sells sponsorships, in-stadium advertising, merchandising licenses, and TV rights. Teams sport U.S.-style names, like the Bangalore Braves and the Calcutta Tigers.[45]

Entertainment

After sports marketing, the largest area of sponsorship is **entertainment,** which includes things like concert tours, attractions, and theme parks. For instance, numerous attractions at Disneyland and Disney World are sponsored by major corporations such as GE, AT&T, ARCO, Kodak, and Carnation.

Brands even sponsor entire tours. The Vans 2004 Warped Tour (subtitled "Presented by Samsung Wireless Phones") has a rotating lineup of 50 bands, with multiple stages and compounds sponsored by other companies, like Volcom. Booths and tents at the festival provide ample targeted-marketing opportunities for co-sponsors like Hot Topic, Sony, and Epitaph Records: The "Girlz Garage" offers fashion and makeup, and the "Reverse Daycare" air-conditioned tent allows parents "to get away from the heat and noise, enjoy cold drinks and discuss the triumphs of parenthood as their kids rock out to the music and activities."[46]

In 2004, U.S. companies are expected to spend $1.1 billion on this category.

Festivals, Fairs, and Annual Events

In 1997, IEG Network surveyed 1,000 members of the International Association of Fairs and Expositions. The findings revealed a very healthy, growing environment. The average yearly sponsorship increased a whopping 20 percent over the previous four years, with the biggest growth (30 percent) occurring between 1996 and 1997. Moreover, renewal rates averaged 88 percent! By 2004, sponsorship revenue increased to an estimated $792 million.

One of the largest annual events in the state of Michigan is the National Cherry Festival in Traverse City. Held every year around the Fourth of July, it boasts an impressive lineup of events and promotional activities that drives both attendance and sponsor visibility. Events include band parades, races, concerts, tournaments, an antiques show, an air show, Native American exhibits, and much more. Among the official sponsors are Pepsi, Ford, Toyota, Intel, BankOne, and Sony.

Similarly, annual events such as business-to-business trade shows attract large numbers of sponsors as well as exhibitors because of the economics of being able to talk to prospects and customers in the same place at the same time (see Exhibit 11–2).

Sometimes the competition to sponsor an event even comes from within the same company. The Florida Renaissance Festival, for instance, received calls from three AT&T entities inquiring about sponsorship availabilities. Two calls were from different departments and the third was from one of AT&T's agencies. The festival ultimately signed with the phone company's Hispanic marketing department.[47]

Causes

Sponsorship of charity events and educational institutions is a tried-and-true PR activity that often fits with the IMC strategy of mission marketing. A number of large corporations (including Chevrolet, AT&T, American Airlines, Pepsi, and Kodak) cosponsored the Live Aid concerts, for instance. In 2004, marketers spent an estimated $991 million in cause-related sponsorships.

The most common form of sponsorship involves sporting events, but there are many other annual events and activities that attract widespread corporate support. The audiences of such events tend to be smaller, but sponsors realize that they are valuable prospects. In this ad, Campbell's links itself to the city letter carriers' union annual food drive. Campbell's sponsored 109 million postcards sent to promote the event; a record 70.9 million pounds of food were donated.

The vice president for corporate relations at Philip Morris, the nation's largest event sponsor, refers to mission marketing activities as "enlightened self-interest." People appreciate the fact that the business does not really get anything tangible out of them to put in the bank.[48]

Health care marketers such as hospitals, HMOs, and managed-care companies are increasing their sponsorship activities. Oxford Health Plans, for example, signed up with the Franklin Institute Science Museum to host Cyber Seniors, a free seminar at the Philadelphia museum that teaches older people how to use the Internet.[49]

Arts and Culture

Symphony orchestras, chamber music groups, art museums, and theater companies are always in desperate need of funding. In 2004, sponsors spent an estimated $612 million to support the arts—the least funded of the major sponsorship categories. What this means is that this is still a relatively untapped area, and it provides outstanding sponsorship and underwriting opportunities for both national and local firms interested in audiences on the highest end of the income scale.

Unfortunately, this group is likely to be hardest hit by any legislation aimed at ending tobacco sponsorships. For instance, The Gallaher Group, Northern Ireland's largest cigarette manufacturer, regularly donates about a million pounds

(U.S. $1.5M) to the Ulster Orchestra, the flagship of the arts in Northern Ireland. In the face of government plans to curtail tobacco advertising and sponsorships, the Association for Business Sponsorship for the Arts gave Gallaher its highest award for outstanding corporate citizenship, citing it for investing in the cultural life of the community in which it operates.[50]

Venue Marketing

Finally, an area not covered by IEG's report is **venue marketing,** a form of sponsorship that links a sponsor to a physical site such as a stadium, arena, auditorium, or racetrack. In 1997, for instance, the cellular technology company Qualcomm made a good name for itself by offering the city of San Diego $18 million to help it meet its shortfall on construction funds for its football stadium. All Qualcomm wanted was the name changed for 20 years. The city agreed (and said thank you)—and the San Diego Chargers now play at Qualcomm Stadium.

Likewise, Denver has Coors Field, and Charlotte, North Carolina, has Ericsson Stadium. Candlestick Park in San Francisco is now Monster Park. And SBC has put its name on San Francisco's baseball park. But what happens when sponsors with naming rights become a liability? When Enron filed for bankruptcy in 2001, the Houston Astros shelled out $2.1 million to buy back the naming rights to Enron Field. In 2002, the Astros found another sponsor, and Minute Maid Park was born.

Venue marketing is changing the economics of professional sports. Sponsorships help pay for stadium renovations and upgrades and may assist the home team in defraying the high cost of leasing. Many teams keep the money from their stadium luxury suites, stadium advertising, naming rights, and food and beverage concessions. Under the new economic rules, big stadium revenues are essential to signing big-name players and staying competitive.[51]

Methods of Sponsorship

Companies interested in sponsorship have two choices: buy into an existing event or create their own. Event marketing specialist Paul Stanley predicts that corporate event sponsorships will likely become "sponsownerships," where the sponsor owns and controls the entire event. This would allow more control and would likely be more cost-effective. It would also help the company achieve its marketing objectives.[52]

For most companies, though, it's easier to buy into an existing event, either as the sole sponsor (the Buick Tournament of Champions) or as one of many co-

A hot form of sponsorship today is venue marketing, in which corporations pay money to associate their name with a sports arena, theater, or civic center. Often, these companies will invest money into desperately needed repairs or improvements to existing facilities, as Qualcomm (www.qualcomm.com) did with San Diego's former Jack Murphy Stadium. The company saved the city $18 million in stadium renovations and received the right to name the venue Qualcomm Stadium for the next 20 years.

How to Select Events for Sponsorship

____ Can the sponsorship be an exclusive one?

____ The demographics of the mass media audience and event participants should match, as closely as possible, the demographics of the target consumer.

____ The event should receive substantial mass media coverage or participation.

____ The event should in some way demonstrate, evoke, or represent a key attribute of the product or service (for example, a luxury product sponsoring a thoroughbred racing event—"the sport of kings").

____ The value to the sponsored event of the company's association

should be no greater than the benefit to the company from the additional mass media exposure from the sponsorship. (This has to do with who is leveraging whom.)

____ The participaton should promise sufficient (and appropriate) mass media exposure to offset any real or opportunity costs associated with the sponsorship.

____ The association of the product with the event should ideally offer or suggest a meaningful sales campaign or theme to be run concurrently with sponsorship.

____ Did the company initiate the negotiation or was the company solicited by the event promoters?

____ Is any financial support required?

---

sponsors. What's most important is to get a good fit between the sponsor and the event. Nabisco's Cornnuts brand, for instance, teamed up with the Aggressive Skaters Association (ASA) to sponsor the ASA 2001 Pro Tour and Amateur Circuits and to use the ASA World Champion female skater Fabiola da Silva as the product's spokesperson. According to Rich Bratman, president of the ASA, he chose Cornnuts because "the brand management and promotions team at Cornnuts really understands how important it is to reach teens in a credible way and is committed to supporting the skating lifestyle."[53]

In his book *Aftermarketing,* Terry Vavra suggests several guidelines for selecting the right sponsorship opportunity or event. See the Checklist, "How to Select Events for Sponsorship."

Measuring Sponsorship Results

One of the problems with event sponsorship (as with public relations activities in general) has historically been how to evaluate results. Experts suggest there are really only three ways to do this:

1. Measure changes in awareness or image through pre- and post-sponsorship research surveys.

2. Measure spending equivalencies between free media exposure and comparable advertising space or time.

3. Measure changes in sales revenue with a tracking device such as coupons.

Unfortunately, none of these methods covers all the reasons for sponsoring. For example, how do you measure the effect on employee morale? What if the sponsorship is aimed at rewarding current customers or enhancing relationships within the trade? These are important possible objectives, but they are very difficult to measure.

Still, most companies are very concerned about the bottom line and look for a substantial return on investment for their sponsorship dollars. Delta Airlines, for example, is said to require $12 in new revenue for every dollar it spends on sponsorship—a ratio the airline claims to have achieved during its Olympic sponsorship.[54]

The International Events Group (IEG) suggests the following pointers for measuring the value of event sponsorships:[55]

- Have clear goals and narrowly defined objectives.
- Set a measurable goal.
- Measure against a benchmark.
- Do not change other marketing variables during the sponsorship.
- Incorporate an evaluation program into the overall sponsorship and associated marketing program.
- At the outset establish a budget for measuring results.

Corporate Advertising

When a company wants to communicate a PR message and control its content, it may use a form of *corporate advertising*. In an integrated marketing communications program, corporate advertising can set the tone for all of a company's public communications. **Corporate advertising** covers the broad area of nonproduct advertising, including public relations advertising, institutional advertising, corporate identity advertising, and recruitment advertising.

Public Relations Advertising

To direct a controlled public relations message to one of its important publics, a company uses **public relations advertising.** PR ads may be used to improve the company's relations with labor, government, customers, suppliers, and even voters.

When companies sponsor art events, programs on public television, or charitable activities, they frequently place public relations ads in other media to promote the programs and their sponsorship, enhance their community citizenship, and create public goodwill. If the public relations people don't have advertising experience, they will typically turn to the firm's advertising department or agency for help.

Corporate/Institutional Advertising

In recent years, the term *corporate advertising* has come to denote a particular type of nonproduct advertising aimed at increasing awareness of the company and enhancing its image. The traditional term for this is **institutional advertising.** These ad campaigns may serve a variety of purposes: to report company accomplishments, position the company competitively in the market, reflect a change in corporate personality, shore up stock prices, improve employee morale, or avoid communications problems with agents, dealers, suppliers, or customers (for some excellent examples, see the Portfolio Review on pages 360–363).

Historically, companies and even professional ad people have questioned, or misunderstood, the effectiveness of corporate advertising. Retailers in particular cling to the idea that institutional advertising, although attractive and nice, "doesn't make the cash register ring." A series of marketing research studies, however, offered dramatic evidence to the contrary. Companies using corporate advertising registered sig-

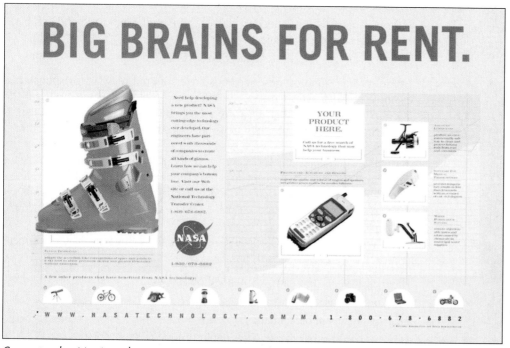

Corporate advertising is used to communicate a name, presence, or even the philosophy of a company within business circles. These ads do not provide information about a particular product, but rather communicate information about the company as a whole. In this ad, NASA (www.nasa.com) promotes its name and technology to large corporate clients in need of some "big brains."

David Ogilvy on Corporate Advertising

David Ogilvy, the late founder and former creative director of Ogilvy & Mather, worked with Shell, Sears, IBM, International Paper, Merrill Lynch, General Dynamics, Standard Oil of New Jersey, and other successful corporations.

According to Ogilvy, big corporations are increasingly under attack from consumer groups, environmentalists, governments, and antitrust prosecutors who try their cases in the newspapers. If a corporation does not take the time to cultivate its reputation, it loses by default.

"If it were possible, it would be better for corporations to rely on public relations (that is, favorable news stories and editorials) rather than paid advertising. But the media are too niggardly about disseminating favorable information about corporations. That is why an increasing number of public relations directors have come to use paid advertising as their main channel of communication. It is the only one they can control with respect to content, with respect to timing, and with respect to noise level. And it is the only one which enables them to select their own battleground," he said.

"So I guess that corporate advertising is here to stay. Why is most of it a flop?"

First, because corporations don't define the purpose of their corporate campaigns.

Second, because they don't measure the results. In a survey conducted by *The Gallagher Report*, only one in four U.S. corporate advertisers said it measured changes in attitude brought about by its corporate campaigns. "The majority fly blind," said Ogilvy.

Third, because so little is known about what works and what doesn't work. The marketing departments and their agencies know what works in brand advertising, but when it comes to corporate advertising they are amateurs.

Fourth, very few advertising agencies know much about corporate advertising. It is only a small part of their business. "Their creative people know how to write chewing-gum jingles for kids and how to sell beer to blue-collar workers. But corporate advertising requires copy-writers who are at home in the world of big business. There aren't many of them," believed Ogilvy.

"I am appalled by the humbug in corporate advertising. The pomposity. The vague generalities and the fatuous platitudes. Corporate advertising should not insult the intelligence of the public."

Unlike product advertising, Ogilvy said, a corporate campaign is the voice of the chief executive and his or her board of directors. It should not be delegated.

What can good corporate advertising hope to achieve? Ogilvy thought at least one of four objectives:

1. It can build awareness of the company. Opinion Research Corp. states, "The invisibility and remoteness of most companies is the main handicap. People who feel they know a company well are five times more likely to have a highly favorable opinion of the company than those who have little familiarity."

2. Corporate advertising can make a good impression on the financial community, enabling you to raise capital at lower cost—and make more acquisitions.

3. It can motivate your present employees and attract better recruits. "Good public relations begins at home," Ogilvy said. "If your employees understand your policies and feel proud of your company, they will be your best ambassadors."

4. Corporate advertising can influence public opinion on specific issues. Abraham Lincoln said, "With public opinion against it, nothing can succeed. With public opinion on its side, nothing can fail."

"Stop and go is the typical pattern of corporate advertising. What a waste of money. It takes years for corporate advertising to do a job. It doesn't work overnight. Only a few companies have kept it going long enough to achieve measurable results," Ogilvy concluded.

Laboratory Application

Find and discuss a corporate ad that demonstrates what Ogilvy referred to as the humbug in corporate advertising, the pomposity, vague generalities, and fatuous platitudes.

---

nificantly better awareness, familiarity, and overall impression than those using only product advertising. Five corporate advertisers in the study drew higher ratings in every one of 16 characteristics measured, including being known for quality products, having competent management, and paying higher dividends.[56] Ironically, the companies in the study that did no corporate advertising spent far more in total advertising for their products than the corporate advertisers did. Yet, despite the higher expenditures, they scored significantly lower across the board.

David Ogilvy, the late founder and creative head of Ogilvy & Mather, was an outspoken advocate of corporate advertising, but he was appalled by some corporate ads. For more on Ogilvy's views, see Ad Lab 11–B.

Responding to such criticisms and to marketplace forces, corporations now design their corporate advertising to achieve specific objectives: develop awareness of the company and its activities, attract investors, improve a tarnished image, attract quality employees, tie together a diverse product line, and take a stand on important public issues. The primary media companies used for corporate advertising are consumer business magazines and network TV.

A variation on corporate advertising is **advocacy advertising.** Companies use it to communicate their views on issues that affect their business (to protect their position in the marketplace), to promote their philosophy, or to make a political or social statement. Such ads are frequently referred to as **advertorials** since they are basically editorials paid for by an advertiser.

(continued on page 364)

Companies use public relations activities and various forms of public relations advertising to communicate with a wide constituency. PR people refer to these groups of people as *publics*. Marketing people call them *stakeholders*.

■ As you study the ads in this portfolio, see if you can determine what stakeholders the company was targeting. Then analyze the ad to determine what objective the company was trying to achieve and if it succeeded.

Corporate Advertising

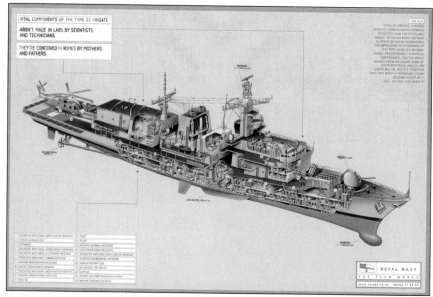

Corporate advertising is employed by all kinds of companies and organizations. In this example, the Royal Navy points out that the "vital components" of the stealth frigate are not "made in labs by scientists," but "conceived in homes by mothers and fathers." The copy in the upper-right-hand corner that invites readers to become a part of the "formidable team," indicates that this is a recruitment ad for the Royal Navy. While this ad serves as a recruitment vehicle, what information can you infer about the sponsor?

Outdoor advertising in usual places is becoming increasingly popular. This ad for Nike, created by TAXI in Toronto, encourages people to keep the streets clean by making a game of it: The goal light goes off when trash enters the bin.

By explaining its humble beginnings, L.L. Bean (www.llbean.com) earns respect and establishes credibility. Notice how the visual features the product in use, but it is relatively small compared to its charming setting. What kind of impression do you think L.L. Bean is attempting to make with this ad?

The Internet is a powerful tool for corporations to keep in touch with their consumers and other key stakeholders. Even small businesses can participate in e-commerce or communicate their services to consumers or other businesses worldwide. Africa Propaganda (www.africa.com.br), an advertising agency in São Paulo, Brazil, won a Bronze Lion at the International Advertising Festival in Cannes for the beautiful and exotic design of the agency's corporate website.

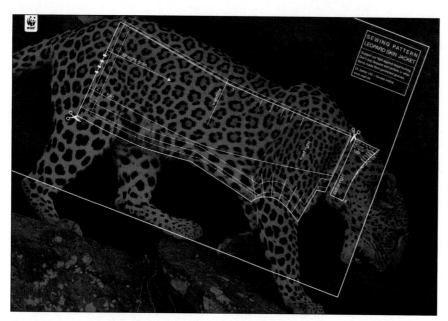

Organizations sponsor advocacy advertising to support important social or political causes. This German ad for the World Wildlife Fund (www.wwf.org) was part of a brilliant campaign that won a Silver Lion at Cannes. The concept of superimposing the sewing pattern for a leopard-skin coat over the image of a live leopard communicates the WWF's conservation message to international audiences regardless of language.

Corporate ads can reinforce the company name and image through creative comparison. Instead of a 4×4 vehicle traversing over rough terrain, Mitsubishi (www.mitsubishi.com) chooses to feature a boy climbing a massive tree. The copy reads, "Life is 4×4." What kind of message do you think Mitsubishi is trying to convey in this ad?

In this ad that won a Bronze Lion at Cannes, the German Foundation for the Preservation of Historic Monuments (www.denkmalschutz.de) showed how its stakeholders' euros could support its mission to preserve buildings like Dresden's Katholische Hofkirche (Catholic Cathedral).

The Buenos Aires Zoo celebrated its 115th birthday with the metaphor of wrinkles. In a campaign that won a Gold Lion at Cannes, the zoo demonstrated its age with images of an orangutan's weathered hands and an elephant's crinkled eyes.

(continued from page 359)
Corporate advertising can also build a foundation for future sales, traditionally the realm of product advertising. Many advertisers use umbrella campaigns, called **market prep corporate advertising,** to simultaneously communicate messages about the products and the company.

While corporate advertising is an excellent vehicle for promoting the company's desired image, it cannot succeed if the image doesn't fit. If a big high-tech corporation like GE, for example, tried to project a homey, small-town image, it would not be very credible.

Corporate Identity Advertising

Companies take pride in their logos and corporate signatures. The graphic designs that identify corporate names and products are valuable assets, and companies take great pains to protect their individuality and ownership. What does a company do when it changes its name, logos, trademarks, or corporate signatures, as when it merges with another company? This is the job of **corporate identity advertising.**

When software publisher Productivity Products International changed its name to Stepstone, Inc., it faced an interesting dilemma. It needed to advertise the change. But in Europe, one of its key markets, a corporate name change implies that a bankrupt business is starting over with a new identity. So rather than announcing its new name in the print media, Stepstone used direct mail targeted at customers, prospects, investors, and the press. The campaign was a success.

More familiar corporate name changes include the switch from American Harvester to Navistar International, the change from Consolidated Foods to Sara Lee Corp., and the creation of Unisys to replace the premerger identities of Burroughs and Sperry.

Recruitment Advertising

Companies use **recruitment advertising** to attract new employees. Most recruitment advertising appears in the classified help-wanted sections of daily newspapers and is placed by the human resources department rather than the advertising department. But many ad agencies now employ recruitment specialists, and some agencies even specialize in recruitment advertising.

Chapter Summary

Public relations is a process used to manage an organization's relationships with its various publics, including employees, customers, stockholders, competitors, and the general populace. The term *public relations* can describe a concept, a profession, a management function, and a practice. Many PR activities involve media communications. However, unlike product advertising, these communications are not normally sponsored or paid for.

Public relations activities include planning and research, reputation management (publicity and press agentry, crisis management, and community involvement), public affairs and lobbying, speechwriting, fundraising and membership drives, publication preparation, and special-events management.

The tools used in public relations include news releases and press kits, photos, feature articles, all sorts of printed materials, posters and exhibits, and audiovisual materials.

Sponsorship is one of the fastest-growing forms of marketing today. It actually embraces two disciplines: sales promotion and public relations. A sponsorship is a cash or in-kind fee paid to a property (which may be a sports, entertainment, or nonprofit event or organization) in return for access to the exploitable commercial potential of that property. It should not be confused with philanthropy.

Sponsorship offers many benefits. It meets with public approval. It has the ability to involve customers, prospects, and other stakeholders. Most events are highly self-selective of their target audience. Sponsorships and events can provide face-to-face access to current and potential customers. They can enhance the company's public image or reinforce its positioning through affiliation with an appropriate event. And they can boost employee morale.

However, sponsorships can be very costly, and they are also subject to clutter, which reduces their effectiveness.

Types of sponsorships include: sports marketing; entertainment; festivals, fairs, and annual events; causes; the arts; and venue marketing. Sports marketing is by far the largest category, consuming over two-thirds of all sponsorship dollars.

Companies may either buy into an existing event or start their own. One problem with sponsorship is evaluating the results. Three methods include measuring changes in awareness, measuring spending equivalencies with advertising, and measuring changes in sales revenue.

To help create a favorable reputation in the marketplace, companies use various types of corporate advertising, including public relations advertising, institutional advertising, corporate identity advertising, and recruitment advertising.

Important Terms

advertorials, *359*

advocacy advertising, *359*

ambush marketing, *353*

audiovisual materials, *349*

bulletin board, *349*

community involvement, *345*

corporate advertising, *358*

corporate identity advertising, *364*

crisis management, *343*

entertainment, *354*

exhibit, *349*

feature article, *348*

house organ, *349*

in kind, *350*

institutional advertising, *358*

lobbying, *346*

market prep corporate advertising, *364*

marketing public relations (MPR), *341*

news (press) release, *347*

opinion sampling, *342*

philanthropy, *350*

poster, *349*

press agentry, *343*

press (media) kit, *348*

public affairs, *346*

public relations (PR), *338*

public relations advertising, *358*

publicity, *343*

publics, *338*

recruitment advertising, *364*

reputation management, *342*

speechwriting, *346*

sponsorship, *350*

venue marketing, *356*

video news release (VNR), *349*

Review Questions

1. How does public relations differ from advertising?

2. How is the perspective of advertising practitioners different from that of PR professionals? How is marketing public relations used?

3. What is the role of public relations in relationship marketing and integrated marketing communications?

4. What are some activities used in reputation management?

5. Why is it important to establish a crisis management plan? What types of companies are most likely to need one?

6. What types of sponsorship activities are available to marketers today?

7. Which sponsorships are likely to offer the best return on investment, and how can that be measured?

8. What are the various types of corporate advertising? Describe them.

9. What is the purpose of corporate identity advertising?

10. What is the purpose of recruitment advertising? Why is it under the domain of corporate advertising and public relations?

11. **The Advertising Experience**

    Every company wants the best and brightest employees. Look at five recruitment advertisements and evaluate them. Which one seems to be the most effective? What makes it superior? Then look at the one you feel is the least effective. Consider what could be done to improve it, then redesign the ad to make it more attractive to the most qualified candidates possible.

Exploring the Internet

The Internet Exercises for Chapter 11 address the following areas covered in the chapter: public relations firms and corporate advertising (Exercise 1), PR organizations (Exercise 2), and crisis management (Exercise 3).

1. **Public Relations Firms and Corporate Advertising**

   Chapter 10 discussed the difference between traditional advertising agencies and direct marketing or sales promotion firms. Public relations firms, too, differ substantially from ad agencies. And, in some cases, they are stealing corporate advertising duties away from traditional advertising shops. It is important to explore the function of public relations firms. Visit the websites for five of the following PR companies and answer the questions that follow.

   - Ballard Communications www.ballardpr.com
   - Burson-Marsteller www.bm.com
   - Hill & Knowlton www.hillandknowlton.com
   - Ketchum Public Relations www.ketchum.com

   - Magnet Communications www.magnetbanking.com
   - Porter Novelli www.porternovelli.com
   - Rowan & Blewitt www.rowanblewitt.com
   - Rowland Communications Worldwide www.rowland.com
   - S&S Public Relations, Inc. www.sspr.com
   - Stanton Communication www.stantoncomm.com

   a. Who is the intended audience of the site?

   b. What are the scope and size of the firm's business?

   c. What is the focus of the firm's work (i.e., consumer, business-to-business, not-for-profit)?

   d. What is your overall impression of the firm and its work? Why?

2. **PR Organizations**

   As you learned in Chapter 11 of *Contemporary Advertising*, perhaps no other marketing communications function plays a more integrated role with advertising than public relations. Now take a moment to explore the world of PR a bit further by visiting the websites for the following public relations-related organizations and answer the following questions for each site.

■ American Association for Public Opinion Research (AAPOR) www.aapor.org

■ PR Newswire www.prnewswire.com

■ Public Relations Society of America (PRSA) www.prsa.org

■ Public Relations Student Society of America (PRSSA) www.prssa.org

a. What is the organization's purpose?

b. Who makes up the organization's membership? Its constituency?

c. What benefit does the organization provide individual members/subscribers? The overall advertising and PR communities?

d. How important is this organization to the public relations community? Why?

3. **Public Relations and Crisis Management**
You have a medium-sized company that creates and sells expensive specialty soaps and shampoos. Apparently your new body wash, Rainforest Fresh, wasn't sufficiently tested and has caused hives in 1 percent of the users. You need public relations help and fast. Choose a firm from the list in Exercise 1, and describe why this firm could handle the problem and what you think it would do.

Part 4

Creating Advertisements and Commercials

ONCE THE MARKETING, ADVERTISING, AND MEDIA STRATEGIES ARE SET, the advertiser prepares a creative brief for the people in the creative department. They, in turn, develop a message strategy to guide the conception and production of ads and commercials. Part Four looks at this process in detail, examining how the creative process works, how we apply creativity to ad making, and how sophisticated advertisers adapt their message strategies to a variety of print and electronic media. ■

Chapter 12
Creative Strategy and the Creative Process

Examines the development of advertising strategies, creative briefs, message strategies, and advertising concepts, including the "big idea." It explains how our preferred style of thinking modifies the creativity within all of us. The chapter presents a simple, flexible, four-step model of the creative process that people in all walks of life can use to advantage.

Chapter 13
Creative Execution: Art and Copy

Depicts the complexity of preparing copy and art for a variety of media forms. The discussion includes common copy and art terminology, as well as the typical formats art directors and copywriters use in creating print ads, radio and TV spots, and advertising for various interactive media.

Chapter 14
Producing Ads for Print, Electronic, and Digital Media

Presents an overview of how advertisers create ads and commercials for the print, broadcast, and digital media. The chapter discusses the techniques and equipment used in the process and the dynamic impact of computerization. It explores the printing process and the advantages and limitations of various print media. It concludes by examining in detail how a print ad and a TV commercial for the Toyota Prius were created from initial concept through final production.

Chapter 12

Creative Strategy and the Creative Process

Objectives To SHOW HOW ADVERTISING STRATEGIES ARE TRANSLATED into creative briefs and message strategies that guide the creative process. The chapter examines the characteristics of great advertising, styles of thinking, the nature of creativity, its importance in advertising, and the role of the agency creative team. We discuss how research serves as the foundation for creative development and planning, and we review common problems and pitfalls faced by members of the creative team.

After studying this chapter, you will be able to:

- **Discuss** the meaning and the importance of creativity.

- **Identify** the members of the creative team and their primary responsibilities.

- **Tell** how to differentiate great advertising from the ordinary.

- **Explain** the role of the creative brief and its effect on the artistic expression in an ad or commercial.

- **List** the principal elements that should be included in a creative brief.

- **Explain** the purpose of the message strategy and how it differs from the creative strategy.

- **Define** the four roles people play at different stages of the creative process.

- **List** several techniques creatives can use to enhance their productivity.

Bob Taylor has designed and assembled guitars for more than 25 years. He's an artisan, and his instruments show it. The average Taylor guitar sells for around $2,000, some for as much as $7,000. The company makes some of the best guitars in the world. But its sales volume didn't reflect that fact. ■ So Taylor and Kurt Lustig, the company's CEO, put in a call to John and John—Vitro and Robertson, that is. John Vitro had been an outstanding art director for some time, and John Robertson was a great copywriter. But when they got together, they were even better. Call it *creative synergy*. The two Johns had been the principal creative team at Taylor Guitar's previous ad agency but had gone out on their own. Now, not only Taylor Guitar but also AirTouch Cellular (formerly PacTel) and Thermoscan wanted them back. And Chiat/Day, the L.A. agency they had worked for prior to moving to San Diego, wanted them to do some freelance work. ■ What did these guys have that everybody wanted? ■ For starters, they were winning more awards than any other creative team around. And not just local medals, but major national honors from the New York Art Director's Club, the One Show, and the leading trade press. Vitro and Robertson never had great notions about owning an agency of their own, but with clients knocking their doors down, there seemed little choice. They formed VitroRobertson, and the clients started coming. ■ The first meetings with Taylor Guitar were successful. The agency and the client saw eye to eye and seemed to share similar values. Lustig and Taylor both understood marketing and advertising. They wanted advertising that would make a statement about the company and its ideals—not just words and pictures, but something genuine and visceral, yet subtle. ■ Their marketing problem was clear. In limited circles, people recognized the Taylor guitar as a quality instrument. But to the vast majority of amateur guitar enthusiasts, Taylor was completely unknown. Dealers told Rick Fagan, Taylor's national sales rep, "We know Taylor makes a great guitar, but our customers have never heard of it. Nobody knows the name." Vitro and Robertson had to develop a creative strategy that would put the Taylor name on the tongue of every serious guitarist. If the campaign was successful, these people would *ask* to strum a Taylor when considering their next instrument. ■ "We had plenty of research data to give them," said Fagan. The Johns looked at the research, listened to the founders, and reviewed guitar publications. Competitors used two general approaches: feature comparisons or celebrity artist endorsements. ■ Vitro and Robertson understood the parameters. To increase name recognition, Taylor's ads had to be completely different. They had to stand out, and they had to reflect the quality that goes into every Taylor guitar. Moreover, they had to appeal to the sensibilities of today's musicians. The ads should talk *to* them, not *at* them. ■ The creative process began. Vitro-Robertson started playing with ideas, putting them down on paper. "A lot of times, it's based on their gut instinct," says AirTouch/San Diego's marketing manager Mary Bianchetti, "and their gut instinct is usually very good." ■ The challenge was to integrate all the concepts into a single *big idea*. If they could accomplish that, they could develop individual messages for a series of ads. Unfortunately, finding the big idea is rarely a simple task. It's usually a frustrating, laborious process of developing an initial stream of concepts—5, 10, 20, whatever it takes. Sifting, sorting, evaluating, throwing them out, and starting over again. It's 90 percent perspiration and 10 percent inspiration. ■ Vitro and Robertson plugged away, discarding one concept after another. And then suddenly it came. The big idea was *trees*. Because *wood* comes from trees. ■ They would use magnificent photos of trees: trees alone, trees in a forest, trees in the fog. Big photos. Not just a full-page ad but a *spread,* two full pages. And they would use very short, slightly humorous copy lines to speak about wood's subtle relationship with people's lives. In contrast to Taylor's competitors, they would appeal to the sensitive, emotional side of the marketplace *and* make their prospects think. ■ They prepared two-page, horizontal layouts of their ideas for Taylor and Lustig to evaluate. One ad featured a lone tree in a barren landscape. The headline read: "In its simplest form, a guitar is just a hollow box made of wood. It's up to you to decide how to fill it." Taylor and Lustig loved it. The proposed campaign passed the review, and the rest is history. ■ "The recognition has been fantastic," reports Rick Fagan. "No one mentions the name problem since these ads have appeared. And sales are up." ■ The recognition has also been good for VitroRobertson. The Taylor Guitar campaign has won national awards and been applauded in *Advertising Age* and *Adweek*. And when the Magazine Publishers of America invited Ken Mandelbaum, CEO of the New York agency Mandelbaum Mooney Ashley, to choose a favorite for its "I wish I'd done that ad" series, he chose a VitroRobertson ad for Taylor Guitars.[1] ■

The Creative Team: The Authors and Encoders of Advertising

In Chapter 1 we discussed the marketing communications process, in which a source encodes a message that is sent through a channel to be decoded by a receiver. The source is multidimensional, comprising a sponsor, an author, and a persona. In advertising, the *encoding* of messages—the conversion of mental concepts into symbols—is the responsibility of the creative team. While the client is the sponsor of the advertising, the creative team is the *author*.

Each member of the creative team plays an essential role. The team's **copywriter** develops the *verbal* message, the copy (words) within the ad spoken by the imaginary persona. The copywriter typically works with an **art director** who is responsible for the *nonverbal* aspect of the message, the design, which determines the visual look and intuitive feel of the ad. Together, they work under the supervision of a **creative director** (typically, a former copywriter or art director), who is ultimately responsible for the creative product—the form the final ad takes. As a group, the people who work in the creative department are generally referred to as **creatives,** regardless of their specialty.

In the Taylor Guitar ads, we see how the creative team's taste, talent, and conceptual skill determine an ad's overall character and its ability to communicate.

This chapter focuses on the creative process: where it comes from, how it's developed, and how it relates to a company's marketing and advertising strategy. But to get a proper perspective on creativity, we need to understand the characteristics of great advertising. What is it? Where does it come from?

What Makes Great Advertising?

We've all seen ads we love, and we've all seen ads we hate (probably a lot more of the latter). The ads we love we refer to as "great." We don't need to say what we call the other ones, because it's only greatness that we're concerned with here. But what do we really mean when we say an ad is great?

If we look at some of the classic ads in history, we may get a clue: Volkswagen's famous "Think small" ad; DeBeers' "A diamond is forever" line; Clairol's "Does she or doesn't she?"; Arpege's "Promise her anything, but give her Arpege"; the Army's "Be all you can be"; and Coca-Cola's "The real thing." What do all these ads and campaigns have in common that have made them universally considered great?

This is a very important question, since most recent research indicates that "ad liking" has a tremendous impact on "ad success." No wonder, then, that agencies want to author, and advertisers want to sponsor, ads that people like. But is liking all that is required for an ad to be great?

A great ad is one so remarkable or stunning that it leaves a long-lasting impression on the audience of the product or service. Advertisers typically begin with a headline or visual that quickly grabs attention and resonates with the reader. This ad for Lego (www.lego.com) immediately catches audience's eyes by featuring the awesome beauty of the Great Wall of China. The succinct message is delivered with one simple line of copy, "The Power of the Brick."

The Power of the Brick.

Whether the "ad" is a billboard, a page in a magazine, a TV or radio spot, or a hot new website, great ads do have certain commonalities. We can probably lump most of these characteristics into two dimensions of greatness: *audience resonance* and *strategic relevance.*[2]

The Resonance Dimension

To resonate means to echo, reverberate, or vibrate. It also means to boom, ring, or chime. And that's what a great ad does with the audience. It rings their chimes. It echoes in their ears. It reverberates and gives them good vibes. It *resonates.*

Why? Because of the boom factor.

When a cannon goes "boom," it gets your attention—right now! The same is true with an ad. It's the surprise element—the "aha," the "gee," or the "wow." But in advertising, it not only gets your attention, it catches your imagination. In this sense it's like great art. It invites you to stop and think about the message. In fact, often it doesn't tell you as much as it invites you to tell yourself.

Look at the Taylor Guitar ad, juxtaposing the image of a box with a musical instrument. They're both made of wood. So they are the same, but oh so different! We recognize this reality at an instinctive level, and we are left to think about it. More important, we associate the profundity of the question with the company that thinks to pose it. We like it, and we respect Taylor for it. The ad resonates.

Other ads may resonate for different reasons. In some of the classic cases we just mentioned, it's simply the headline that resonates—so much so that it becomes

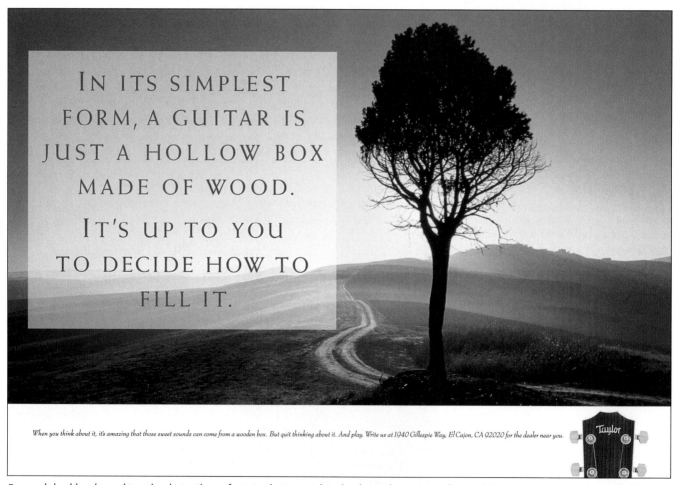

IN ITS SIMPLEST FORM, A GUITAR IS JUST A HOLLOW BOX MADE OF WOOD.

IT'S UP TO YOU TO DECIDE HOW TO FILL IT.

When you think about it, it's amazing that those sweet sounds can come from a wooden box. But quit thinking about it. And play. Write us at 1940 Gillespie Way, El Cajon, CA 92020 for the dealer near you.

Every ad should seek to achieve the elusive "boom factor"—that essential quality that makes an immediate and lasting impression on the mind of the reader or viewers. VitroRobertson earned respect and envy from colleagues and competitors for its Taylor Guitar series.

Ads that appeal to the avoidance or removal of a problem are based on negatively originated motives. This ad for the California Department of Health discourages smoking by depicting the stereotypical Marlboro man with a limp cigarette, suggesting that smoking causes impotence. The copy, imitating the standard warning labels found on cigarettes, reinforces the ad's visual.

WARNING: SMOKING CAUSES IMPOTENCE

a part of our daily lexicon. Other memorable classics include California Milk Processors' "Got Milk," and Budweiser's "Whassup?!"

Recall from Chapter 5 our discussion of consumer motives. *Negatively originated motives,* such as problem avoidance or problem removal, provide the foundation for many great ads. These resonate with the audience by being highly **informational,** by offering relief from some real or perceived problem (FedEx's "When it absolutely, positively has to be there overnight."). Other motives are *positively originated* as consumers seek sensory gratification, intellectual stimulation, or social approval. Here, ads may achieve greatness by being **transformational,** using positive reinforcement to offer a reward ("Be all you can be.").

Unfortunately, most ads, whether they're informational or transformational, fail to resonate with the audience. Why? Because they lack a "big idea" or they fall down in the *execution.* The copy may be uninspiring, the visual may be less than attractive, or the production techniques used may be low quality. From the consumer's point of view, these ads are just a waste of time.

From the advertiser's point of view, ads that don't resonate are a terrible waste of money. In fact, for them the greatness of the advertising is in the "bang per buck." Great ads give their sponsors much more advertising effectiveness per dollar spent. Given this reality, isn't it amazing how much money is invested in ads that are simply not great?

The Relevance Dimension

The second dimension of great advertising is strategic relevance. An ad may get you to think, but what does it get you to think about? A classic example is the old Alka-Seltzer ad "I can't believe I ate the whole thing." It captured everyone's imagination, but it reinforced the wrong feeling—the feeling of the problem (overeating) rather than the solution (Alka-Seltzer). The agency lost the account.

While the text and the visual carry the ad message, behind the creative team's choice of tone, words, and ideas lies an advertising strategy. When the ad is completed, it must be relevant to the sponsor's strategy, or it will fail—even if it resonates with the audience. In other words, it may be great *entertainment,* but not great *advertising.* Great advertising always has a strategic mission to fulfill. In fact, strategy is the key to great creative work.

Formulating Advertising Strategy: The Key to Great Creative

Let's look at the advertising (or creative) strategy Vitro and Robertson developed for Taylor Guitar. Then we'll see how they translated that into a message strategy and a big idea and, finally, into effective ads.

Recall from Chapter 8 that advertising strategy consists of four elements: the *target audience,* the *product concept,* the *communications media,* and the *advertising message.*

What is Taylor Guitar's **target audience?** Taylor's target audience comprises resellers, consumers, and centers of influence. Resellers (or retailers) are Taylor's *primary market*—that's who the company sells to. So Taylor definitely wants them to see its advertising. Because Taylor guitars are handcrafted from the highest-quality materials, they command premium prices. Therefore, the primary target audience also includes a segment of the retailer's customers—serious musical enthusiasts who play acoustic guitars and are willing to spend $2,000 to $5,000 for a superior instrument. Professional guitarists typically circumvent the normal distribution channels, so there was no reason to include them in the target market. However, they might act as *centers of influence* (or *key influentials*), in which case they would be a *secondary target audience* for the advertising.

What is Taylor Guitar's **product concept?** Taylor's acoustic guitars are top-quality, handcrafted musical instruments made from the finest woods available. They are designed and constructed differently from other guitars, which gives them a unique, distinguishable sound quality—a certain ring in the tone—that customers like. In other words, there is something special about a Taylor guitar that makes it worth more.

What **communications media** does Taylor use? The company has a small budget and uses limited media. It advertises in special-interest consumer magazines targeted to well-defined segments of the guitar enthusiast market. The magazines offer high-quality reproduction and color and are read by members of the trade as well as professional musicians. The company also produces high-quality brochures and price lists that detail the instruments' features and construction.

What is Taylor Guitar's **advertising message?** In its simplest terms, message strategy is determined by *what* a company wants to say and *how* it wants to say it. Although Taylor was well-known in the trade for its quality guitars, the word was not filtering down to the larger guitar-buying public. The goal (or *message objective*) was to get prospective customers to ask for the Taylor name when they shopped for a guitar. To accomplish this, the ads had to exude an aura of quality. So the agency creative team chose a message strategy that was simple yet thoughtful, entertaining, credible, and most of all, distinctive.

The agency and client team must understand and agree to these four elements of the advertising strategy—target, product, media, and message—before any creative work begins. In most agencies, the account management group is responsible for developing the advertising strategy. In some large agencies, account planners spend a great deal of time researching the market. Then they prepare the advertising strategy with input from, and the approval of, account management. When the strategy-development task is completed, the account people prepare a *creative brief* to communicate the strategy to the creative department.

Writing the Creative Brief (Copy Platform)

With the overall advertising objectives and strategy determined, the account managers (or, often, account planners) write a brief statement of the intended advertising strategy. The **creative brief** serves as the creative team's guide for writing and producing the ad. In some agencies it may be referred to as a *copy platform,* a *work plan,* or a *copy* (or *creative*) *strategy document*. Regardless of the name, it is a simple written statement of the most important issues to consider in the development of the ad or campaign: the who, why, what, where, and when.

- *Who?* Who is the prospect in terms of behavioristic, geographic, demographic, and/or psychographic qualities? What is the typical prospect's personality?
- *Why?* Does the consumer have specific wants or needs the ad should appeal to? Advertisers use two broad categories of appeals. **Rational appeals** are directed at the consumer's practical, functional need for the product or service; **emotional appeals** target the consumer's psychological, social, or symbolic needs. For a sampling of specific appeals within these categories, see Exhibit 12–1.

Approach / Needs	Selected advertising appeals		
	Rational	**Emotional**	
Self-actualization	Opportunity for more leisure Efficiency in operation or use	Ambition Avoidance of laborious task Curiosity Entertainment	Pleasure of reaction Simplicity Sport/play/physical activity
Esteem	Dependability in quality Dependability in use Enhancement of earnings Variety of selection	Pride of personal appearance Pride of possession	Style/beauty Taste
Social	Cleanliness Economy in purchase	Cooperation Devotion to others Guilt Humor Home comfort	Romance Sexual attraction Social achievement Social approval Sympathy for others
Safety	Durability Protection of others Safety	Fear Health	Security
Physiological	Rest or sleep	Appetite	Personal comfort

- *What?* Does the product have special features to satisfy the consumer's needs? What factors support the product claim? How is the product positioned? What personality or image (of the product or the company) can be or has been created? What perceived strengths or weaknesses need to be dealt with?

- *Where* and *when* will these messages be communicated? Through what medium? What time of year? What area of the country?

- Finally, *what style, approach,* or *tone* will the campaign use? And, generally, what will the copy say?

The creative brief identifies the benefits to be presented to consumers, but it doesn't cover execution. *How* the benefits will be presented is the creative team's job.

Procter & Gamble and Leo Burnett use a simple creative brief with three parts:[3]

1. *An objective statement.* A specific, concise description of what the advertising is supposed to accomplish or what problem it is supposed to solve. The objective statement also includes the name of the brand and a brief, specific description of the target consumer. For example,

    Advertising will convince serious guitar players that the Taylor guitar is a distinctive, high-value instrument and persuade them to consider it the next time they are in the market for an acoustic guitar.

2. *A support statement.* A brief description of the evidence that backs up the product promise; the reason for the benefit. For example,

    Support is that Taylor guitars are handcrafted from the finest woods available, which gives the instrument a distinctive sweet sound.

3. *A tone or brand character statement.* A brief statement of either the advertising's tone or the long-term character of the brand. Tone statements are short-term emotional descriptions of the advertising strategy. Brand character statements are long-term descriptions of the enduring values of the brand—things that give the product brand equity. A tone statement might be phrased

The tone of Taylor Guitar advertising should convey beauty, quality, sophistication, and value, with just a touch of good-natured humor.

On the other hand, a brand character statement might be phrased

Taylor Guitars—handcrafted from the finest materials to give the sweetest sound.

The delivery of the creative brief to the creative department concludes the process of developing an advertising strategy. It also marks the beginning of the next step: the *advertising creative process,* in which the creative team develops a *message strategy* and begins the search for the *big idea.* After writing the first ad, the copywriter should review the copy platform to see if the ad measures up on the resonance and relevance dimensions. If it doesn't, the team must start again.

Elements of Message Strategy

The creative team is responsible for developing creative ideas for ads, commercials, and campaigns and for executing them. From the information given by the account team (in the creative brief) and any additional research it may perform, the creative team develops the message strategy. This may actually occur before, during, or after the creative process of searching for the big idea.

The **message strategy** (or **rationale**) is a simple description and explanation of an ad campaign's overall creative approach—what the advertising says, how it says it, and why. The message strategy has three components:

- **Verbal.** Guidelines for what the advertising should say; considerations that affect the choice of words; and the relationship of the copy approach to the medium (or media) that will carry the message.
- **Nonverbal.** Overall nature of the ad's graphics; any visuals that must be used; and the relationship of the graphics to the media in which the ad will appear.
- **Technical.** Preferred execution approach and mechanical outcome, including budget and scheduling limitations (often governed by the media involved);

Samsonite (www.samsonite.com) exemplifies the art of nonverbal communication in advertising. In ads such as this, well-known brands benefit from consumer awareness of their name or logo, and that can entirely eliminate the need for extraneous copy.

also any **mandatories**—specific requirements for every ad, such as addresses, logos, and slogans.

Because all these elements of the message strategy intertwine, they typically evolve simultaneously. Language affects imagery, and vice versa. However, the verbal elements are the starting point for many advertising campaigns.

The message strategy helps the creative team sell the ad or the campaign concept to the account managers and helps the managers explain and defend the creative work to the client. Of course, the message strategy must conform to the advertising strategy outlined in the creative brief or it will probably be rejected.

In the development of message strategy, certain basic questions need to be answered: How is the market segmented? How will the product be positioned? Who are the best prospects for the product? Is the target audience different from the target market? What is the key consumer benefit? What is the product's (or company's) current image? What is the product's unique advantage?[4] At this point, research data are important. Research helps the creative team answer these questions.

How Creativity Enhances Advertising

The powerful use of imagery, copy, and even humor in the Taylor Guitar campaign demonstrates how creativity enhances advertising. But what exactly is creativity or the creative process? What is the role of creativity in advertising? And where does creativity come from?

What Is Creativity?

To create means to originate, to conceive a thing or idea that did not exist before. Typically, though, **creativity** involves combining two or more previously unconnected objects or ideas into something new. As Voltaire said, "Originality is nothing but judicious imitation."

Many people think creativity springs directly from human intuition. But as we'll see in this chapter, the creative process is actually a step-by-step procedure that can be learned and used to generate original ideas.

The Role of Creativity in Advertising

Advertisers often select an agency specifically for its creative style and its reputation for coming up with original concepts. While creativity is important to advertising's basic mission of informing, persuading, and reminding, it is vital to achieving the boom factor.

International ads must appeal to the target audience within a given country. Here, mobile phone service provider Embratel (www.embratel.com) uses some rather dark humor in its campaign to promote its rates. Other ads in the campaign featured a derailed train and a wrecked airplane, all with the same tagline: "If you have a lot to explain, we have the best phone rates." Such dry wit is probably appreciated by the ads' British audience. The judges at Cannes were amused, at least; they awarded the campaign a Silver Lion.

Creativity Helps Advertising Inform

Advertising's responsibility to inform is greatly enhanced by creativity. Good creative work makes advertising more vivid, and many researchers believe vividness attracts attention, maintains interest, and stimulates consumers' thinking.[5] A common technique is to use plays on words and verbal or visual metaphors, such as "Put a tiger in your tank," "Fly the friendly skies," or "Own a piece of the rock." The metaphor describes one concept in terms of another, helping the reader or viewer learn about the product.[6]

Other creative techniques can also improve an ad's ability to inform. Advertising writers and artists must arrange visual and verbal message components according to a genre of social meaning so that readers or viewers can easily interpret the ad using commonly accepted symbols. For example, aesthetic cues such as lighting, pose of the model, setting, and clothing style can instantly signal viewers nonverbally whether a fashion ad reflects a romantic adventure or a sporting event.[7]

Creativity Helps Advertising Persuade

The ancients created legends and myths about gods and heroes—symbols for humankind's instinctive, primordial longings and fears—to affect human behavior and thought. To motivate people to some action or attitude, advertising copywriters have created new myths and heroes, like the Jolly Green Giant and the Energizer Bunny. A creative story or persona can establish a unique identity for the product in the collective mindset, a key factor in helping a product beat the competition.[8]

Creativity also helps position a product on the top rung of consumers' mental ladders. The Taylor Guitar ads, for example, suggest metaphorically that the personal touch of Taylor's artisans can caress trees into making beautiful music. The higher form of expression creates a grander impression. And when such an impression spreads through the market, the product's perceived value also rises.

To be persuasive, an ad's verbal message must be reinforced by the creative use of nonverbal message elements. Artists govern the use of these elements (color, layout, and illustration, for example) to increase vividness. Research suggests that, in print media, *information graphics* (colorful explanatory charts, tables, and the like) can raise the perception of quality for some readers.[9] Artwork can also stimulate emotions. Color, for example, can often motivate consumers, depending on their cultural background and personal experiences (see Ad Lab 12–A, "The Psychological Impact of Color").

Creativity Helps Advertising Remind

Imagine using the same invitation, without any innovation, to ask people to try your product again and again, year after year. Your invitation would become stale very quickly—worse, it would become tiresome. Only creativity can transform your boring reminders into interesting, entertaining advertisements. Nike is proof. Several commercials in a Nike campaign never mentioned the company name or even spelled it on the screen. The ads told stories. And the only on-screen cue identifying the sponsor was the single, elongated "swoosh" logo inscribed on the final scene. A Nike spokesperson said the ads weren't risky "given the context that the Nike logo is so well known."[10] We are entertained daily by creative ads—for soft drinks, snacks, and cereals—whose primary mission is simply to remind us to indulge again.

Creativity Puts the "Boom" in Advertising

Successful comedy also has a boom factor—the punchline. It's that precise moment when the joke culminates in a clever play on words or turn of meaning, when the audience suddenly gets it and guffaws its approval.

The Psychological Impact of Color

National origin or culture can play a role in color preferences. For example, warm colors—red, yellow, and orange—tend to stimulate, excite, and create an active response. People from warmer climes, apparently, are most responsive to these colors. Certain color combinations stimulate ethnic connotations. Metallic golds with reds, for example, are associated with China. Turquoise and beige are associated with the Indian tribes of the American Southwest.

Colors can impart lifestyle preferences. Vivid primary colors (red, blue, yellow) juxtaposed with white stripes exude decisiveness and are often used in sporting events as team colors. Thus, they are associated with a sporting lifestyle.

The colors we experience during the four seasons often serve as guides for combining colors and for guessing the temperaments of individuals who dress themselves or decorate their house in specific seasonal colors. Spring colors such as yellows, greens, and light blues, for example, suggest a fresh, exuberant character. Winter colors such as dark blues, deep violets, and black are associated with cool, chilly attitudes.

Because we usually feel refreshed from sleeping, we associate the colors of the morning—emerald green, raspberry, and pale yellow—with energy. And because the mellow colors of sunset predominate when we're usually home relaxing after work, we may associate sunset colors—peach, turquoise, and red-orange—with relaxation and reflective moods.

Some colors are ambiguous. Violet and leaf-green fall on the line between warm and cool. They can be either, depending on the shade.

Here are some more observations:

Red

Symbol of blood and fire. Second to blue as people's favorite color but more versatile, the hottest color with highest "action quotient." Appropriate for soups, frozen foods, and meats. Conveys strong masculine appeal, so is often used for shaving cream containers.

Brown

Another masculine color, associated with earth, woods, mellowness, age, warmth, comfort. Used to sell anything, even cosmetics (Revlon's Braggi).

Yellow

High impact to catch consumer's eye, particularly when used with black. Good for corn, lemon, or suntan products.

Green

Symbol of health and freshness; popular for mint products and soft drinks (7UP).

Blue

Coldest color with most appeal; effective for frozen foods (ice impression); if used with lighter tints becomes "sweet" (Yoplait yogurt, Lowenbrau beer, Wondra flour).

Black

Conveys sophistication and high-end merchandise, and is used to stimulate purchase of expensive products. Good as background and foil for other colors.

Orange

Most "edible" color, especially in brown-tinged shades; evokes autumn and good things to eat.

Laboratory Application

Explain the moods or feelings that are stimulated by two color ads or packages illustrated in this text.

Good punchlines are the result of taking an everyday situation, looking at it creatively, adding a bit of exaggeration, and then delivering it as a surprise. Great advertising often does the same thing.

When a group of friends greet each other with wagging tongues and an exaggerated "Whassup?" while "watching the game and having a Bud," the audience is completely caught off guard and roars with laughter. Boom!

The agency, DDB Worldwide, Chicago, stretched the concept with subsequent ads like "Wasabi," "What are you doing?" and "How you doin'?" each humorously highlighting a recognizable trait of different American subcultures and featuring "people just being people." The advertising campaign was so successful that not only did the infectious catchphrase "Whassup?!" work its way into the daily lexicon, but DDB Worldwide won numerous awards for its creative accomplishments. At the International Advertising Festival at Cannes, France, DDB won the prestigious Grand Prix award.

In advertising, though, the boom doesn't always have to be funny. It may come from the sudden understanding of a subtle profundity, as in the case of Taylor Guitars. Or from the gentle emotional tug of a Hallmark Cards commercial. Or the breathtaking beauty of a magnificent nature photograph for Timberland shoes. In a business-to-business situation, it may come from the sudden recognition of how a new high-tech product can improve workplace productivity. In short, the boom factor may come from many sources. But it always requires the application of creativity.

Understanding Creative Thinking

Some people may exhibit more of it than others, but creativity lives within all of us. Human creativity, developed over millions of years, enabled our ancestors to survive. Without creativity we wouldn't have discovered how to harness fire, domesticate animals, irrigate fields, or manufacture tools. As individuals, we use our natural creativity every time we select an outfit to wear, style our hair, contrive an excuse, decorate our home, or cook a meal.

Styles of Thinking

At the turn of the twentieth century, the German sociologist Max Weber determined that people think in two ways: an objective, rational, fact-based manner and a qualitative, intuitive, value-based manner. For example, while studying for a test, we use our rational, fact-based style of thinking. But when we buy a car, we call on taste, intuition, and knowledge to make a qualitative value judgment of the car's features, styling, and performance weighed against its price.

In the late 1950s, the theories of convergent and divergent thinking described how one can process concepts by narrowing or expanding one's assortment of ideas.[11] In the late 1970s, researchers discovered that the left side of the brain controls logical functions and the right controls intuitive functions. In the 1980s, social scientists Allen Harrison and Robert Bramson defined five categories of thinking: the synthesist, the idealist, the pragmatist, the analyst, and the realist. They concluded that the analyst and realist fit Max Weber's fact category and the synthesist and idealist fit his value category.[12]

Roger von Oech defined this dichotomy as hard and soft thinking. *Hard thinking* refers to concepts like logic, reason, precision, consistency, work, reality, analysis, and specificity. *Soft thinking* refers to less tangible concepts: metaphor, dream, humor, ambiguity, play, fantasy, hunch. On the hard side, things are right or wrong, black or white. On the soft side, there may be many right answers and many shades of gray.[13]

Also in the 1980s, Alessandra, Cathcart, and Wexler developed a model featuring four types of personalities and relationship behaviors based on assertiveness and responsiveness factors (the relater, the socializer, the director, and the thinker).[14] The relater and the socializer exhibit value-based characteristics; the director and the thinker display fact-based traits.

Fact-Based versus Value-Based Thinking

Most theories of thinking fit into two general categories: value-based or fact-based. Let's examine these styles of thinking more closely.

People whose preferred style of thinking is **fact-based** tend to fragment concepts into components and to analyze situations to discover the one best solution. Although fact-based people can be creative, they tend to be linear thinkers and prefer to have facts and figures—hard data—they can analyze and control. They are not

Sometimes a big idea comes off subtly, like this ad for Casa Magazine, which won a Bronze Lion at Cannes. This ad takes a value-based approach, which is in keeping with a magazine that concerns home decor.

This slightly absurdist commercial doesn't concentrate on Pepsi's calorie count or great taste—the ad's strictly value-based thinking is designed to entertain and build brand personality and value.

SYNOPSIS: In an empty recreation room, there is a foosball table whose inanimate players, one team representing Manchester United and the other, Juventus, suddenly come alive and play an intense game of football. There is a Pepsi bottle sitting on the edge of the table.

DAVID BECKHAM (Manchester United): You thinkin' what I'm thinkin'?

EDGAR DAVIDS (Juventus): Winner take the Pepsi?

DAVID BECKHAM: Sure.

VISUAL: The game begins. Yorke (Manchester United) ricochets the ball off the Pepsi bottle and into the Pepsi net.

YORKE: Sco-o-o-re!

JUVENTUS PLAYERS: You cheated.

VISUAL: Two boys enter a now quiet rec room.

BOY 1: There it is.

VISUAL: The boy grabs the Pepsi and takes a drink. They start to leave the room.

ROY KEANE (Manchester United): Hey! Get back here! We won that!

BOY 2: Did you hear something?

FOOTBALLER VO: Hey mate! That's our Pepsi!

BOY 1: No.

VISUAL: The two boys leave the room.

FOOTBALLERS (grumbling): Big idiots.

SUPER: Pepsi logo.

Ask for More.

comfortable with ambiguous situations. They like logic, structure, and efficiency.[15]

In contrast, **value-based** thinkers make decisions based on intuition, values, and ethical judgments. They are better able to embrace change, conflict, and paradox. This style fundamentally relies on melding concepts together. Value-based thinkers, for example, attempt to integrate the divergent ideas of a group into an arrangement that lets everyone win. They are good at using their imagination to produce a flow of new ideas and synthesizing existing concepts to create something new.[16]

How Styles of Thinking Affect Creativity

If the creative team prefers a value-based thinking style, it tends to produce ads such as those in the Taylor Guitar and Nike campaigns—soft, subtle, intuitive, metaphorical. That's fine if the client also prefers that style of thinking.

On the other hand, clients who prefer a fact-based style often seek agencies that produce practical, hard-edged work characterized by simple, straightforward layouts, rational appeals, and lots of data. A fact-based client may even find a value-based campaign to be unsettling.

The Saatchi & Saatchi ad campaign for Hewlett-Packard's laser printers, for example, created a stir internally. The ads simulated interviews. The actors portrayed harried customers, talking about how they didn't have time to think about their printers. "Some people within Hewlett-Packard are somewhat uncomfortable with the direction of the campaign," reported Arlene King, a marketing communications manager for HP, "because we are a high-tech company and the ads don't focus on any aspect of the technology."[17]

The creative team needs to understand the campaign's target audience. In some market segments (high-tech, for example) customers may tend toward one style of thinking over another. And that could dictate which approach to use.

As we shall see in the next section, the best art directors and copywriters use both styles to accomplish their task. In the creative process, they need to use their imagination (value-based thinking) to develop a variety of concepts. But to select the best alternative and get the job done, they probably have to use the fact-based style.

The Creative Process

The **creative process** is the step-by-step procedure used to discover original ideas and reorganize existing concepts in new ways. By following it, people can improve their ability to unearth possibilities, cross-associate concepts, and select winning ideas.

The new generation of advertising creatives will face a world of ever-growing complexity. They must handle the many challenges of integrated marketing communications (IMC) as they help their clients build relationships with highly fragmented target markets. They will need to understand the wide range of new technologies affecting advertising (computer hardware and software, electronic networking, high-definition television, and more). And they will have to learn how to advertise to emerging international markets. To do this, they need a model that handles many situations simply.

Over the years, many notions of the creative process have been proposed. Although most are similar, each format has unique merits. In 1986, Roger von Oech published a four-step creative model used today by many *Fortune* 100 companies. It offers flexibility for fact-based and value-based thinkers alike. Von Oech describes four distinct, albeit imaginary, roles (Explorer, Artist, Judge, and Warrior) that every art director and copywriter has to personally take on at some point in the creative process:[18]

1. *The Explorer* searches for new information, paying attention to unusual patterns.
2. *The Artist* experiments and plays with a variety of approaches, looking for an original idea.
3. *The Judge* evaluates the results of experimentation and decides which approach is most practical.
4. *The Warrior* overcomes excuses, idea killers, setbacks, and obstacles to bring a creative concept to realization.

The Explorer Role: Gathering Information

Copywriters and art directors thrive on the challenge of creating advertising messages—the encoding process. But first they need the raw materials for ideas: facts, experiences, history, knowledge, feelings.

Taking on the role of the **Explorer,** the creatives examine the information they have. They review the creative brief and the marketing and advertising plan; they study the market, the product, and the competition (see RL 12–1, Checklist of Product

Ads may appeal to decision makers either through a fact-based or value-based approach. This ad for Bombardier Capital Company (http://capital.bombardier.com) appeals to value-based "soft" thinkers, relying on the witty and creative humor within the visual to communicate the message.

Something tells us you're ready to buy a plane.

BOMBARDIER
CAPITAL

Marketing Facts for Creatives, in the Reference Library on the *Contemporary Advertising* CD). They may seek additional input from the agency's account managers and from people on the client side (sales, marketing, product, or research managers).

When John Vitro and John Robertson began work for Taylor Guitar, they first assumed the Explorer role. They spoke with people about the nature of the company, its products, its marketing history, its competitors, and the competitors' styles of advertising. They reviewed all appropriate sources of advertising for acoustic guitars and studied the company's marketing environment.

Develop an Insight Outlook

In advertising, it's important that when creatives play the Explorer role, they get off the beaten path to look in new and uncommon places for information—to discover new ideas and to identify unusual patterns. Vitro and Robertson might have hiked in the wilderness to spark a new idea for Taylor Guitar. Or they could have opened a book on national parks and experienced the same flash of insight.

Von Oech suggests adopting an "insight outlook" (a positive belief that good information is available and that you have the skills to find and use it). This means opening up to the outside world to receive new knowledge. Ideas are everywhere: visit a museum, an art gallery, a hardware store, an airport. The more diverse the sources, the greater your chance of uncovering an original concept.

Know the Objective

If people know what they're looking for, they have a better chance of finding it. Think about the color blue. Now look around you. Note how blue suddenly jumps out at you. If you hadn't been looking for it, you probably wouldn't have noticed it.

Philosopher John Dewey said, "A problem well-stated is a problem half-solved." This is why the creative brief is so important. It helps define what the creatives are looking for. The creatives typically start working on the message strategy during the Explorer stage because it, too, helps them define what they're looking for.

To get their creative juices flowing, most copywriters and art directors maintain an extensive library of advertising award books and trade magazines. Many also keep a *tickler* (or *swipe*) *file* of ads they like that might give them direction.

Brainstorm

As Explorers, the art director and copywriter look first for lots of ideas. One technique is **brainstorming,** a process (conceived by Alex Osborn, the former head of BBDO) in which two or more people get together to generate new ideas. A brainstorming session is often a source of sudden inspirations. To succeed, it must follow a couple of rules: all ideas are above criticism (no idea is "wrong"), and all ideas are written down for later review. The goal is to record any inspiration that comes to mind, a process that psychologists call *free association,* allowing each new idea an opportunity to stimulate another.

Von Oech suggests other techniques for Explorers: leave your own turf (look in outside fields and industries for ideas that could be transferred); shift your focus (pay attention to a variety of information); look at the big picture (stand back and see what it all means); don't overlook the obvious (the best ideas are right in front of your nose); don't be afraid to stray (you might find something you weren't looking for); and stake your claim to new territory (write down any new ideas or they will be lost).

The Explorers' job is to find new information that they can use when they take on the next role: the Artist. To be effective Explorers, they must exercise flexibility, courage, and openness.[19]

The Artist Role: Developing and Implementing the Big Idea

The next step in the creative process, playing the Artist's role, is both the toughest and the longest. But it's also the most rewarding. The **Artist** must actually accomplish two major tasks: searching for the big idea and then implementing it.

Task 1: Develop the Big Idea

The first task for Artists is the long, tedious process of reviewing all the pertinent information they gathered when they played the Explorer role, analyzing the problem, and searching for a key verbal or visual concept to communicate what needs to be said. It means creating a mental picture of the ad or commercial before any copy is written or artwork begun.

This step (also called **visualization** or **conceptualization**) is the most important in creating the advertisement. It's where the search for the **big idea**—that flash of insight—takes place. The big idea is a bold, creative initiative that builds on the strategy, joins the product benefit with consumer desire in a fresh, involving way, brings the subject to life, and makes the audience stop, look, and listen.[20]

What's the difference between a strategy and a big idea? A strategy describes the direction the message should take. A big idea gives it life. For example, the creative brief discussed earlier for the Taylor Guitar campaign contains a strategic brand character statement:

Taylor Guitars—handcrafted from the finest materials to give the sweetest sound.

Vitro and Robertson could have used that strategy statement as a headline. But it would have been dreadfully dull for an ad aimed at musicians. It lacks what a big idea headline delivers: a set of multiple meanings that create interest, memorability, and, in some cases, drama. Note the long, provocative, slightly poetic, and very witty headline that Vitro and Robertson chose to convey the same strategic concept:

In one pair of hands, a piece of wood can become a living room coffee table.

In another pair of hands, that piece of wood can become the sweetest-sounding guitar.

This is for everyone who has no desire to play the coffee table.

John O'Toole said, "While strategy requires deduction, a big idea requires inspiration."[21] The big idea in advertising is almost invariably expressed through a combination of art and copy. Most ads use a specific word or phrase to connect the text to the visual, like "wood" in the Taylor Guitar ad. Think what this ad would look like without the beautiful photograph of the trees in the background, with just the headline and body copy on an otherwise bare page. It would have saved a lot of money. But it would have greatly reduced the boom factor and lost a lot more money due to low readership.

Transforming a Concept: Do Something to It

Creative ideas come from manipulating and transforming resources. Von Oech points out that when we take on the Artist role, we have to do something to the materials we collected as Explorers to give them value. That means asking lots of questions: What if I added this? Or took that away? Or looked at it backward? Or compared it with something else? The Artist has to change patterns and experiment with various approaches.

Vitro and Robertson had two concepts to begin with: "guitar" and "music." Looking at the guitar, they noted it was made of wood—special wood. So "wood" became a third concept. Thinking about wood led them to "trees." Interesting notion. But now they had to figure out how to turn these four concepts into a "big idea."

At this point in the creative process, a good Artist may employ a variety of strategies for transforming things. Von Oech suggests several techniques for manipulating ideas:[22]

1. *Adapt.* Change contexts. Think what else the product might be besides the obvious. A Campbell's Soup ad showed a steaming bowl of tomato soup with a bold headline underneath: "HEALTH INSURANCE."

Some images make the point so well they require no words. This ad for Globetrotter outdoor gear connects the idea of giant seals snug in their skins with campers snug in their sleeping bags. It's amazing how much they look alike. The clever ad garnered a Bronze Lion at Cannes.

2. *Imagine.* Ask what if. Let your imagination fly. Be zany. What if people could do their chores in their sleep? What if animals drank in saloons? Clyde's Bar in Georgetown actually used that idea. The ad showed a beautifully illustrated elephant and donkey dressed in business suits and seated at a table toasting one another. The headline: "Clyde's. The People's Choice."

3. *Reverse.* Look at it backward. Sometimes the opposite of what is expected has great impact and memorability. A cosmetics company ran an ad for its moisturizing cream under the line: "Introduce your husband to a younger woman." A vintage Volkswagen ad used "Ugly is only skin deep."

4. *Connect.* Join two unrelated ideas together. Ask yourself: What ideas can I connect to my concept? A Target ad showed the rear view of a high-fashion-type model clad only with a backpack and a lampshade—the latter wrapped around her middle like a miniskirt. Next to the Target logo the ad said simply "fashion and housewares." To get people to send for its catalog, Royal Caribbean Cruises ran an ad that showed the catalog cover under the simple headline "Sail by Mail."

5. *Compare.* Take one idea and use it to describe another. Ever notice how bankers talk like plumbers? "Flood the market, laundered money, liquid assets, cash flow, take a bath, float a loan." The English language is awash in metaphors because they help people understand. Jack in the Box advertised its onion rings by picturing them on a billboard and inviting motorists to "Drive thru for a ring job." An elegant magazine ad for the Parker Premier fountain pen used this sterling metaphor: "It's wrought from pure silver and writes like pure silk."

6. *Eliminate.* Subtract something. Or break the rules. In advertising, there's little virtue in doing things the way they've always been done. Seven-Up became famous by advertising what it wasn't ("the Uncola") and thereby positioned itself as a refreshing alternative. To introduce its new models one year, Volkswagen used a series of humorous teaser ads that didn't show any cars. In one, a shaggy dog sat patiently in front of a fan. He was presumably replicating

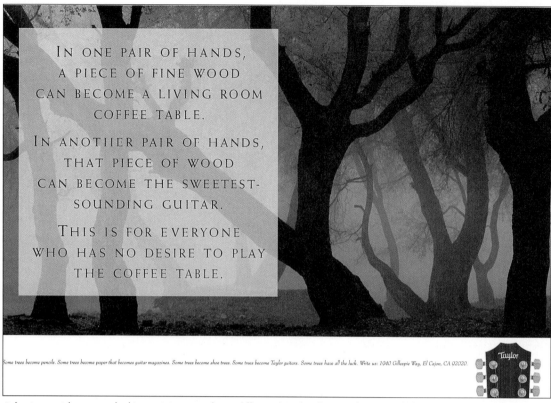

IN ONE PAIR OF HANDS,
A PIECE OF FINE WOOD
CAN BECOME A LIVING ROOM
COFFEE TABLE.

IN ANOTHER PAIR OF HANDS,
THAT PIECE OF WOOD
CAN BECOME THE SWEETEST-
SOUNDING GUITAR.

THIS IS FOR EVERYONE
WHO HAS NO DESIRE TO PLAY
THE COFFEE TABLE.

Some trees become pencils. Some trees become paper that becomes guitar magazines. Some trees become shoe trees. Some trees become Taylor guitars. Some trees have all the luck. Write us: 1940 Gillespie Way, El Cajon, CA 92020.

Adapting an idea means looking at it in a way that is different than the obvious. This example from Taylor Guitar transforms the idea of trees. While the wood is used for a wide variety of rather inanimate objects, the lucky ones are reinvented into an almost lifelike creature, a Taylor Guitar. The small print continues the witty approach of the headline: Some trees become pencils. Some trees become paper that becomes guitar magazines. Some trees become shoe trees. Some trees become Taylor guitars. Some trees have all the luck.

what dogs do in cars, sticking their heads out the window to catch the breeze. The only difference was he was doing it indoors.

7. *Parody.* Fool around. Have some fun. Tell some jokes—especially when you're under pressure. There is a close relationship between the *ha-ha* experience of humor and the *aha!* experience of creative discovery. Humor stretches our thinking and, used in good taste, makes for some great advertising. A classical radio station ran a newspaper ad: "Handel with care." And speaking of classics, Fila USA got a rave review from *Advertising Age* for its "bizarre, absolutely hilarious, and totally cool" spot of a praying mantis racing up a leaf stem in Fila sneakers to escape his murderous mate.[23]

Blocks to Creativity

Everybody experiences times when the creative juices just won't flow. There are many causes: information overload, mental or physical fatigue, stress, fear, insecurity. Often, though, the problem is simply the style of thinking being used.

In the Explorer stage, when creatives study reams of marketing data, the facts and figures on sales and market share may put them in a fact-based frame of mind. But to create effectively, they need to shift gears to a value-based style of thinking.

As von Oech says, "Creative thinking requires an attitude that allows you to search for ideas and manipulate your knowledge and experience."[24] Unfortunately,

Creatives employ various strategies for transforming ideas into the unique art form of advertising. In this ad, Volkswagen of America connects seemingly insignificant cracks in the floor with one of VW's signature automobiles.

Parody is often used to modify concepts and to create a humorous appeal to audiences. Here, Faber-Castell parodies Edvard Munch's classic piece, "The Scream," perhaps to suggest that individuals can use its products to create their own works of art.

it is sometimes difficult for creatives to make that mental switch instantly. Von Oech recommends some techniques to stimulate integrative thinking. For example: look for the second right answer (there is usually more than one answer to any problem, and the second may be more creative); seek cross-fertilization (TV people could learn a lot from teachers, and vice versa); slay a sacred cow (sacred cows make great steaks); imagine how others would do it (stretch the imagination by role playing); laugh at it (make up jokes about what you're doing); and reverse your viewpoint (open up your thinking and discover things you typically overlook).[25]

George Gier, the creative partner and cofounder of the Leap Partnership, says, "The only thing agencies have left to sell to clients that they can't get anywhere else is creative ideas."[26] Creative blocks can indeed be bad for an agency.

Creative blocking may occur when people in the agency start "thinking like the client," especially if the client is a fact-based thinker. This can also be hazardous to the agency's creative reputation and is one reason agencies sometimes resign accounts over "creative differences." An agency can eliminate a lot of frustration and wasted time and money by evaluating the client's corporate culture, its collective style of thinking, and its creative comfort level in advance.

Creative fatigue sometimes happens when an agency has served an account for a long time and all the fresh ideas have been worked and reworked. It can also happen when a client has rejected a series of concepts; the inspiration is lost and the creatives start trying to force ideas. They suddenly find it hard to shift their style of thinking or to crank up the creative process again. If this becomes chronic, the only solutions may be to appoint an entirely new creative team or resign the account.

Does Sex Appeal?

It's one of the more blatant uses of sex in advertising in recent memory: a billboard features a young woman, holding a grease gun cartridge in each hand, and leaning over to exhibit an ample amount of cleavage. The headline reads "This is Debbie. She wants you to have this pair in your car." The ad is for auto parts, but the implication seems to be that if you buy *this manufacturer's* auto parts, you'll get Debbie or someone like Debbie in the bargain. Nothing in the ad says so explicitly, but the innuendo is all that's required to capture the viewer's attention.

Advertisers frequently use the power of suggestion to imply sex, encouraging viewers to come to their own conclusions. However, advertisers who run such risqué ads must contend with the critics and with the often-tricky legal distinction between obscenity and indecency. Obscenity is illegal and carries criminal charges, whereas indecency does not. To be considered obscene, an ad must meet three conditions: it appeals to prurient interests, it is patently offensive, and it lacks any redeeming social value.

In general, most ads with sexual appeals don't meet the criteria for obscenity, but they may still be considered indecent, since indecency is in the eyes of the beholder. If enough people believe sexually oriented material is indecent, then "community standards" reflect this belief. In such cases, citizen pressure groups, along with media organizations and local courts, enforce community standards by disallowing advertising that offends those standards.

Consider Abercrombie & Fitch. The clothing retailer recently sparked controversy at a mall in Omaha when its window posters featured a topless model covering her breasts with her hands. A Christian group, Family First, quickly objected, claiming that Abercrombie's posters created a "sexualized walkway." Commenting on the objections, a spokesman for A&F said the displays might have been "sexy" but were not the "sexually charged monstrosities" that Family First asserted. Nevertheless, the community standards had been revealed. Family First began pressuring shoppers and other retailers in the mall to object to the photographs, and within nine days the window displays were changed.

Were the posters obscene or indecent? Advertisers like A&F, who continue to strive for the "sexy" appeal, are beginning to find it increasingly difficult to draw the line between simple sex appeal and unethical exploitation.

There is no easy solution to this dilemma, especially since research shows that sexual appeals can be effective when sexuality relates to the product. However, when it doesn't, it can distract audiences from the main message and severely demean the advertiser in the consumer's eyes. This brings up an important and rather common paradox about sexually oriented advertising. How is a naked model in a window poster an advertisement for clothing? Many argue that it is not, making such ads not only a distraction, but also a source of negative *externalities*— the social costs to consumers outside the target market, such as children who might be indirectly affected.

Advertisers must examine, on a case-by-case basis, at what point sexual appeals become unethical and therefore counterproductive. In one case, an executive on the Valvoline advertising account justified using "girlie calendars" for mechanics by noting that "the calendar may offend some groups—but they aren't our customers."

Miller Lite's "Catfight" campaign recently raised a few eyebrows. The campaign appeared to signal the company's return to "beer and babes" ads, depicting women as sexual objects. In the commercial,

---

Incubating a Concept: Do Nothing to It

When the brain is overloaded with information about a problem, creatives sometimes find it's best to just walk away from it for a while, do something else, and let the unconscious mind mull it over. This approach yields several benefits. First, it puts the problem back into perspective. It also rests the brain, lets the problem incubate in the subconscious, and enables better ideas to percolate to the top. When they return to the task, the creatives frequently discover a whole new set of assumptions.

Task 2: Implement the Big Idea

Once the creatives latch onto the big idea, they have to focus on how to implement it. When Vitro and Robertson suddenly thought "trees" and connected that idea to "guitars" and "music," they then had to translate that concept into a tangible ad. This is where the real art of advertising comes in—writing the exact words, designing the precise layout. To have a sense of how advertising creatives do that, we need to understand what *art* is in advertising, how artistic elements and tools are selected and used, and the difference between good art and bad art.

In advertising, art shapes the message into a complete communication that appeals to the senses as well as the mind. So while **art direction** refers to the act or process of managing the visual presentation of the commercial or ad, the term **art** actually refers to the whole presentation—visual, verbal, and aural. For example, the artful selection of words not only communicates information but also stimulates positive feelings for the product. An artfully designed typeface not only makes reading easier, it also evokes a mood. By creatively arranging format elements—surrounding the text with lines, boxes, and colors, and relating them to one another in proportion—the art director can further enhance the ad's message. Art also shapes the style of photography and illustration. An intimate

two women in a restaurant begin the classic "tastes great/less-filling" debate over Miller Lite. The debate quickly turns into a full-fledged cat-fight, with the two women stripped down to their bras and panties, splashing around in an adjacent fountain. Moments later, we see the two buxom brawlers going at it in a soggy cement pit. The ad cuts to a bar. It turns out the fight was only the fantasy of two guys in a bar who were dreaming of the perfect beer commercial, much to the shock and disgust of their girlfriends, who were with them at the time. The cable TV version then takes things a little further as it cuts back to the near-naked women with one saying to the other, "Do you want to make out?"

So what does any of this have to do with selling beer? Hillary Chura, who covers the beer industry for *Advertising Age*, explains that ads such as the "Catfight" commercial are "aspirational." After watching these two beautiful women wrestle around for 30 seconds, Miller wants guys to say, "Hey, if I drink Miller Genuine Draft, I'll get those hot women." And Miller wants women to think "If I drink this beer, I'll look like those women."

But what is the social cost of these unrealistic "aspirations"? In a society rife with confidence-related disorders, should advertisers exploit consumer insecurities in an effort to sell more of their product? At what point do advertisers need to accept some ethical responsibility for the interests of the society to which they owe their existence?

Unfortunately, this debate over sex in advertising may actually be fueling advertisers' desire to continue using blatant sex appeals. The "Catfight" campaign sparked nationwide attention on talk radio, CNN's *Crossfire*, in *USA Today*, and in other media outlets. Similarly, Abercrombie & Fitch's quarterly catalog of scantily clad models makes national headlines with every issue. Controversy equals publicity. Publicity stimulates interest. And interest spawns sales.

In short, sex, and the controversy surrounding it, sells. Until this changes, industry or government policymakers will certainly continue to encounter difficulties in treating advertising sex in a way satisfactory to everyone—or perhaps anyone.

Questions

1. How would you explain the "redeeming value" of sexual appeals in advertising?

2. If sexual appeals are considered okay by the audiences that are directly targeted, what responsibility does the advertiser have for any effect on indirect targets, such as children? How can advertisers protect themselves from this problem?

Sources: Erin Cooksley, "Sex Sells, Ethics Absent from Advertising Industry," The Daily Skiff, February 11, 2004 (retrieved from www.skiff.tcu.edu/2004/spring/issues/02/11/sex.html); Florence Kennel, "Burgundy Ads Banned for Sexual Innuendo," January 23, 2004 (retrieved from www.decanter.com); Nikki Katz, "Sex Sells—Using Sex in Advertising," (retrieved from http://womensissues.about.com/cs/bodyimage/a/aasexsells.htm); Robynn Tysver, "Family Group Protests 'Sexualized' Ads at Stores in Lincoln Mall," Omaha World-Herald, February 12, 2003; Deborah Alexander, "Family Group Ends Protest after Shop Changes Displays," Omaha World-Herald, February 21, 2003 (both retrieved from www.nexis.com); Rance Crain, "Relevance Is Operative Word in 'Catfight' or Chip-Dip Ads," Advertising Age, January 27, 2003; Basem Boshra, "Un, Can You Say Appallingly Sexist?" Montreal Gazette, February 1, 2003 (retrieved from www.nexis.com); Julie Dunn, "The Light Stuff. Coors Loves the Young Male Demographic—and Twins!" Denver Westword, January 23, 2003 (retrieved from www.nexis.com); Tom Daykin, "Miller Gets Down and Dirty with Lite Ad; Reaction Mixed, but Commercial Is Being Noticed," Milwaukee Journal Sentinel, January 26, 2003 (retrieved from www.nexis.com).

style uses soft focus and close views, a documentary style portrays the scene without pictorial enhancements, and a dramatic style features unusual angles or blurred action images.

In short, if *copy* is the verbal language of an ad, *art* is the body language. TV uses both sight and sound to involve viewers. Radio commercials use sound to create *word pictures* in the minds of listeners. The particular blend of writing, visuals, and sounds makes up an ad's expressive character. So while the quality may vary, every ad uses art.

In advertising, balance, proportion, and movement are guides for uniting words, images, type, sounds, and colors into a single communication so they relate to and enhance each other. We'll discuss more of these concepts in Chapter 13, "Creative Execution: Art and Copy."

The Creative Pyramid: A Guide to Formulating Copy and Art

Depending on the product category and the situation, the **creative pyramid** is a model that can help the creative team convert the advertising strategy and the big idea into the actual physical ad or commercial. Based on the cognitive theory of how people learn new information, it uses a simple five-step structure (see Exhibit 12–2).

The purpose of much advertising copy and design is to either persuade prospective customers to take some action to satisfy a need or want or to remind them to take the action again. In a new-product situation, people may first need to be made aware of the problem or, if the problem is obvious, that a solution exists. For a frequently purchased product, the advertiser simply has to remind people of the solution close to the purchase occasion. In either case, the advertiser's first job is to get the prospect's *attention*. The second step is to stimulate the prospect's *interest*—in either the message or the product itself. Next, it's important, especially

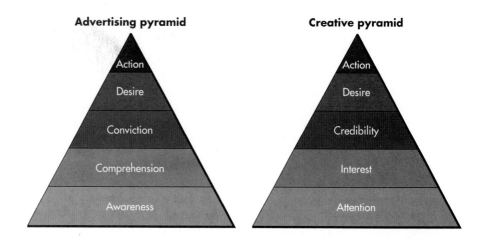

for new products, to build *credibility* for the product claims. Then the ad can focus on generating *desire* and finally on stimulating *action*. These five elements should be addressed in just about every ad or commercial. We'll deal with each step briefly.

Attention

An ad or commercial is a *stimulus*. It must break through consumers' physiological screens to create the kind of attention that leads to perception. *Attention,* therefore, is the first objective of any ad and the fundamental building block in the creative pyramid. The Artist may spend as much time and energy figuring out how to express the big idea in an interesting, attention-getting way as searching for the big idea itself.

The attention step is critically important to triggering the ad's boom factor. Print ads often use the headline as the major attention-getting device. The copywriter's goal is to write a headline that expresses the big idea with verve. Usually designed to appear in the largest and boldest type in the ad, the headline is often the strongest focal point conceptually as well as visually. Many other devices also help gain attention. In print media, they may include dynamic visuals, unusual layout, vibrant color, or dominant ad size. In electronic media, they may include special sound effects, music, animation, or unusual visual techniques.

Some factors are beyond the creatives' control. The budget may determine the size of the ad or length of the commercial. And that may influence how well or quickly it penetrates consumers' screens. Similarly, a TV spot's position in a cluster of commercials between shows or an ad's position in a publication may determine who sees it.

The attention-getting device should create drama, power, impact, and intensity. It must also be appropriate, relating to the product, the tone of the ad, and the needs or interests of the intended audience. This is especially true in business-to-business advertising, where rational appeals and fact-based thinking dominate.

Headlines that promise something but fail to deliver in a credible manner won't make a sale; in fact, they may alienate a potential customer. Ads that use racy headlines or nude figures unrelated to the product often lose sales because prospects can't purchase the item that first attracted their attention.

Interest

The second step in the creative pyramid, *interest,* is also extremely important. It carries the prospective customer—now paying attention—to the body of the ad. The ad must keep the prospect excited or involved as the information becomes

This ad for K2 skis (www.k2skis.com) exemplifies the five steps of the creative pyramid. The ad gains attention with its stark imagery and resemblance to the American flag. Then, it retains interest with the reference to Betsy Ross. Credibility is established with Betsy Ross's opinion of Jonny Moseley. The tagline, "This little red light makes you a better, faster American. God bless," is consistent with the patriotic theme and creates a desire to be a better, faster American. The final words, "You are an American and these are your skis," is an indirect call to action.

more detailed. To do this, the copywriter may answer a question asked in the attention step or add facts that relate to the headline. To maintain audience interest, the tone and language should be compatible with the target market's attitude. As we discussed earlier, the successful ad *resonates.*

The writer and designer must lead prospects from one step to the next. Research shows that people read what interests them and ignore what doesn't, so the writer must maintain prospects' interest at all times.[27] One way to do so is to sneak through prospects' psychological screens by talking about their problems, their needs, and how the product or service will answer them. Copywriters use the word *you* a lot.

There are many effective ways to stimulate interest: a dramatic situation, a story, cartoons, charts. In radio, copywriters use sound effects or catchy dialogue. Television frequently uses quick cuts to maintain interest. We discuss some of these techniques in the chapter on advertising production.

Credibility

The third step in the creative pyramid is to establish *credibility* for the product or service. Customers today are sophisticated and skeptical. They want claims to be backed up by facts. Comparison ads can build credibility, but they must be relevant to customers' needs—and fair.

Well-known presenters may lend credibility to commercials. For example, actress Catherine Zeta Jones effectively represents T-Mobile with her personable, believable, and elegant style.

Advertisers often show independent test results to substantiate product claims. To work, such "proofs" must be valid, not just statistical manipulation. Advertisers and agencies must remember that many consumers have extensive product knowledge, even in specialized areas.

Desire

In the *desire step,* the writer encourages prospects to picture themselves enjoying the benefits of the product or service. Essentially, they are invited to visualize.

In print ads, copywriters initiate visualization by using phrases like "Picture yourself" or "Imagine." In TV, the main character pulls a sparkling clean T-shirt from the washer, smiles, and says "Yeah!" In radio, the announcer says, "You'll look your best."

The desire step hints at the possibilities and lets the consumer's mind take over. If prospects feel they're being led by the nose, they may feel insulted, resent the ad, and lose interest in the product. In some cases, writers maintain this delicate balance by having a secondary character agree with the main character and prattle off a few more product benefits. The secondary character allows the main character, the one audiences relate to best, to retain integrity.

In print advertising, the desire step is one of the most difficult to write (which may be why some copywriters omit it). In TV, the desire step can simply show the implied consumer experiencing the benefit of the product. Ever notice how cosmetics advertisers almost invariably show the happy life that awaits their product's user?

Action

The final step up the creative pyramid is *action*. The purpose is to motivate people to do something—send in a coupon, call the number on the screen, visit the store—or at least to agree with the advertiser.

This block of the pyramid reaches the smallest audience but those with the most to gain from the product's utility. So the last step is often the easiest. If the copy is clear about what readers need to do and asks or even nudges them to act, chances are they will (see Ad Lab 12–B, "Applying the Creative Pyramid to Advertising").

The call to action may be explicit—"Call for more information"—or implicit—"Fly the friendly skies." Designers cue customers to take action by placing dotted lines around coupons to suggest cutting and by highlighting the company's telephone number with large type or a bright color.

With today's technology, it's important to not only ask people to act but facilitate their action, through either a toll-free phone number or an attractive website. In relationship marketing, the ad basically enables people to select themselves as being interested in a relationship. Then the marketer can use more efficient one-on-one media to develop the relationship.

The Judge Role: Decision Time

The next role in the creative process is the **Judge.** This is when the creatives evaluate the practicality of their big ideas and decide whether to implement, modify, or discard them.[28]

The Judge's role is delicate. On the one hand, the creatives must be self-critical enough to ensure that when it's time to play the Warrior they will have an idea worth fighting for. On the other hand, they need to avoid stifling the imagination of their internal Artist. It's easier to be critical than to explore, conceptualize, or defend. But the Judge's purpose is to help produce good ideas, not to revel in criticism. Von Oech suggests focusing first on the positive, interesting aspects of a new idea. The negatives will come soon enough.

Applying the Creative Pyramid to Advertising

Notice how the five objectives of advertising copy apply to the ad shown here, which won a Bronze Lion at Cannes.

Attention   The photograph of a line of hungry children snares the reader's attention quickly. This is supported by the headline, which is written in all caps with large reversed-out type.

Interest   The second sentence of the headline, which starts with the word "Hey," is designed to capture the audience's interest. The rest of the sentence, "Let's send another space probe to Mars," further piques the reader's interest and curiosity. Sensing the sarcasm, the reader begins to wonder what's going on here.

Credibility   The long line of children in the photograph, stretching beyond the frame into seeming infinity, increases the credibility of the claim that millions are starving.

Desire   The desire to help these children is heightened by the sarcasm of the second sentence and by the call to action that follows. The ad challenges the comfortable reader's complacence.

Action   The action desired by the socially conscious advertiser is for the reader to become more attuned to what's going on around him or her in the world. In big, bold type, Il Vizio shouts "Wake up, world." The sponsor's name at the bottom seems almost like an afterthought. Only then does the reader discover the humorous relevance of a coffee company's suggestion that people should wake up.

Laboratory Applications

1.   Find an ad that exhibits the five elements of the creative pyramid. *(A print ad will be the easiest to find and talk about, but radio and TV commercials also feature the five elements. Beware: The desire step may be hard to find.)*

2.   Why do so many good ads lack one or more of the five elements listed here? How do they overcome the omission?

When playing the Judge, the creatives need to ask certain questions: Is this idea an aha! or an uh-oh? (What was my initial reaction?) What's wrong with this idea? (And what's right with it?) What if it fails? (Is it worth the risk?) What is my cultural bias? (Does the audience have the same bias?) What's clouding my thinking? (Am I wearing blinders?)

In an effort to create world-class advertising, Michael Conrad, formerly the worldwide chief creative officer for Leo Burnett and currently the dean of the new Cannes Lions Academy, developed the rating scale shown in Exhibit 12–3. The agency's Global Product Committee now uses this scale to evaluate every ad before presenting it to a client. Ads that score 4 or below don't get presented. The objective is to develop ads that score 8 and above, and those receive full agency support. The top rating, world-class, means "best in the world, bar-none."

Risk is an important consideration. When the advertising scores a hit, everybody's happy, sales go up, people get raises, and occasionally there's even positive publicity. But when a campaign flops, all hell breaks loose, especially on high-profile accounts. Sales may flatten or even decline, competitors gain a couple of points in market share, distributors and dealers complain, and the phone rings incessantly with calls from disgruntled client executives. Perhaps worst of all is the ridicule in the trade. Advertising pundits say nasty things about the ads in

Exhibit 12–3

Leo Burnett Global Product Committee's rating scale.

10	World-class
9	New standard in advertising
8	New standard in product category
7	Excellence in craft
6	Fresh idea(s)
5	Innovative strategy
4	Cliché
3	Not competitive
2	Destructive
1	Appalling

TV interviews; reviewers write articles in *Ad Age* and *Adweek;* and even the big daily papers get in their licks. In one article, for instance, *The Wall Street Journal* panned the campaigns of four high-profile advertisers: Diet Coke, Subaru, AT&T, and American Express.[29] This is not good for either the agency's stock or the client's. And it's how agencies get replaced. So the Judge's role is vital.

If the Artist-as-Judge does a good job, the next role in the creative process, the Warrior, is easier to perform.

The Warrior Role: Overcoming Setbacks and Obstacles

In the final step of the creative process, the **Warrior** wins territory for big new ideas in a world resistant to change. The Warrior carries the concept into action. This means getting the big idea approved, produced, and placed in the media. Von Oech says Warriors must be bold, sharpen their sword (skills), strengthen their shield (examine criticism in advance), follow through (overcome obstacles), use their energy wisely, be persistent, savor their victories, and learn from defeat.[30]

To get the big idea approved, the Warrior has to battle people within the agency and often the client, too. So part of the Warrior's role is turning the agency account team into co-warriors for the presentation to the client. At this point, it's imperative that the creatives finish their message strategy document to give their rationale for the copy, art, and production elements in the concept they're trying to sell. And the message strategy had better mesh with the creative brief, or the valiant Warrior will likely face a wide moat with no drawbridge (see Ad Lab 12–C, "The Creative Gymnasium").

Part of the Warrior's task may be to help the account managers present the campaign to the client. Bruce Bendinger says, "How well you *sell* ideas is as important as how *good* those ideas are." To give a presentation maximum selling power, he suggests five key components:[31]

1. *Strategic precision.* The selling idea must be on strategy. The presenting team must be able to prove it, and the strategy should be discussed first, before the big selling idea is presented.

2. *Savvy psychology.* The presentation, like the advertising, should be receiver-driven. The idea has to meet the client's needs.

3. *Slick presentation.* The presentation must be prepared and rehearsed; it should use great visuals and emotional appeals. A good presentation makes people want to do the campaign.

4. *Structural persuasion.* The presentation should be well structured, since most clients relate well to organized thinking. The opening is all-important because it sets the tone for the entire presentation.

5. *Solve the problem.* Clients have needs, and they frequently report to big shots who ask tough questions about the advertising. Solve the client's problem and you'll sell the big idea—and do it with style.

For clients, recognizing a big idea and evaluating it are almost as difficult as coming up with one. (For some examples of big ideas, see the Portfolio Review, "The Creative Director's Greatest Ads.") When the agency (or the in-house advertising department) presents the concepts, the client is suddenly in the role of the Judge, without having gone through the other roles first. David Ogilvy recommended that clients ask themselves five questions: Did it make me gasp when I first saw it? Do I wish I had thought of it myself? Is it unique? Does it fit the strategy to perfection? Could it be used for 30 years?[32]

As Ogilvy pointed out, campaigns that run five years or more are the superstars: Dove soap (33 percent cleansing cream), Ivory soap (99 and 44/100 percent pure), Perdue chickens ("It takes a tough man to make a tender chicken"), the U.S.

The Creative Gymnasium

The Explorer

Here's a visual calisthenics exercise for your Explorer. Find a perfect star in the pattern:

The Judge and the Warrior

As a creative person, what verdict would your Judge give ads that feature creative gymnastics like the ones below? How would your Warrior present these two ads to a client for approval?

The Artist

The Artist uses humor and absurd what-if questions to mentally loosen up. Try these warm-up techniques:

1. Think up a new set of conversion factors:

    10^{12} microphones = 1 megaphone

    10^{12} pins = 1 terrapin

    $3^{1}/_{3}$ tridents = 1 decadent

    4 seminaries = 1 binary

    10^{21} piccolos = 1 gigolo

    1 milli-Helen = the amount of beauty required to launch 1 ship

2. Another mental muscle stretcher is to change the context of an idea. You can turn the roman numeral for 9 into a 6 by adding only a single line:

IX

Some people put a horizontal line through the center, turn it upside down, and then cover the bottom. This gives you a roman numeral VI. A more artistic solution might be to put "S" in front of the IX to create "SIX." What we've done here is take the IX out of the context of Roman numerals and put it into the context of "Arabic numerals spelled out in English."

Another right answer might be to add the line "6" after the IX. Then you get IX6, or one times six.

Laboratory Applications

1. Attempt to solve the exercises above. Explain your choices.

2. Create a metaphor for each of these paired concepts:

  a. Boxing + Water.

  b. Magnet + Library.

  c. Rainbow + Clock.

Army ("Be all you can be"). Some of these campaigns are still running today, and some have run for as long as 30 years. Those are big ideas!

When the client approves the campaign, the creative's role as a Warrior is only half over. Now the campaign has to be executed. That means the Warriors shepherd it through the intricate details of design and production to see that it is completed on time, under budget, and with the highest quality possible. At the same time, the creatives revert to their Artist roles to design, write, and produce the ads.

The next step in the process, therefore, is to implement the big idea, to produce the ads for print and electronic media—the subject of our next two chapters.

(continued on page 402)

The creative director always wants to produce the most effective advertising possible in order to give the client the greatest bang for the buck. That means first conceiving a brilliant idea that will both resonate with the particular target audience and relate to the client's marketing and advertising strategy. Then the idea must be executed in a masterful way.

■ Study all the award-winning ads in this portfolio and consider how well they measure up to this definition of greatness. To do this, start by analyzing whether the ad is informational or transformational. Then evaluate and describe the "boom" factor each one uses. Next, see if you can determine from the ad what the company's advertising strategy was and discuss how relevant the ad is to that strategy. Finally, evaluate how well the creative director's staff executed the concept.

The Creative Director's Greatest Ads

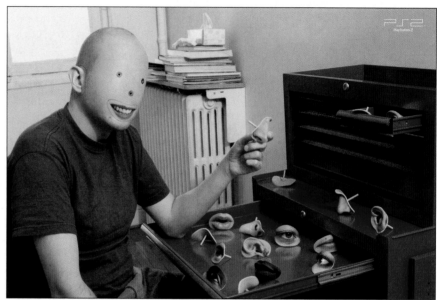

PlayStation 2 is known for sponsoring off-the-wall ads. This one, winner of a Cannes Gold Lion, is startlingly strange. The viewer doesn't quickly forget the image of a real-life Mr. Potato Head assembling pieces of himself. Like many of the company's games, this ad for PlayStation 2 successfully explores a world of fantasy.

In this ad, which won a Bronze Lion at Cannes, Heinz walks a fine line between great ingenuity and being too clever for its own good, risking loss of communication. The unusual perspective of the image grabs our attention immediately and holds it long enough for the wit to shine through. A very hot ad, indeed.

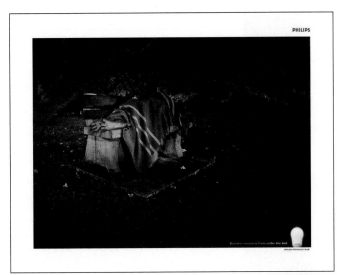

This ad for Philips, which won a Silver Lion at Cannes, is an excellent example of an ad that packs a punch while using minimal copy. The monster pictured above has been banished from under the bed and forced to sleep on a park bench. How do you think the creatives who worked on this ad got from "lighting" to "monster"?

NOT ALL KIDS WANT THE SAME THING FOR CHRISTMAS.

COVENANT HOUSE 1-800-HELP-308

Covenant House, the largest privately funded child care agency in the United States, provides shelter and service to homeless and runaway youth. In this poignant ad, the box of a fun toy is used by a child for shelter. What kind of audience do you think this ad resonates with? What kind of actions does this want audiences to take?

beautiful

www.berkshireblanket.com

Berkshire Blanket
Premium Quality

Metaphors can be effective strategy in advertising. Here, Berkshire Blanket (www.berkshireblanket.com) presents a blanket in the form of a rose to emphasize the softness and beauty of the blanket. The copy includes a small mention of the website and name and one word, "beautiful," to reinforce the idea behind the metaphor.

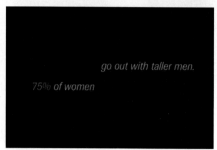

go out with taller men.

75% of women

This ad for Head & Shoulders, which won a Bronze Lion at Cannes, features a series of photographs of both large and small objects placed next to one another. In the final frame the copy reads, "75% of women go out with taller men." What do you think is the strategic relevance of such an approach?

The Internet is still a new medium for many advertisers. Toyota cleverly uses a feature of the Internet itself to point out how much cargo one can load in the Avensis family sportscar.

When looking at this ad from a distance, the distinctive shape of a Land Rover becomes apparent. And what vehicle is best known for African safaris? Land Rover, of course. Resonant and relevant, this ad garnered a Silver Lion at Cannes.

Some of the best ads are some of the most simple. In this humorous ad, using less than 10 words, Pepto-Bismol explains why you might need its product. How well do you think this ad resonates with audiences?

(continued from page 397)

Chapter Summary

In the marketing communications process, the creative team is responsible for encoding advertising messages. It is the author of the communications. The creative team typically comprises an art director and a copywriter who report to a creative director.

Their job is to create great advertising for their clients. Great advertising is characterized by two dimensions: audience resonance and strategic relevance. To truly resonate, ads need the boom factor—that element of surprise that instantly attracts the audience's attention, gets them involved, and stirs their imagination. Some ads are informational and resonate with the audience by offering relief from some real or perceived problem. Other ads are transformational and achieve resonance through positive reinforcement by offering some reward.

The second dimension of great advertising, strategic relevance, is behind the visuals and the text of every ad. In fact, advertising strategy is the key to great creative work.

Typically written by the account management team, the advertising (or creative) strategy includes four elements: the target audience, the product concept, the communications media, and the advertising message. Once the general parameters of the plan are developed, the account managers prepare a creative brief that outlines the key strategic decisions. The creative brief should contain at least three elements: an objective statement, a support statement, and either a tone statement or a brand character statement. The brief gives strategic guidance to the art director and copywriter, but it is their responsibility to develop a message strategy that lays out the specifics of how the advertising will be executed. The three elements of message strategy are copy, art, and production.

Copy is the verbal and art the nonverbal (visual) presentation of the message strategy. Production refers to the mechanical details of how the ads and commercials will be produced.

To create means to originate, and creativity involves combining two or more previously unconnected elements, objects, or ideas to make something new. Creativity helps advertising inform, persuade, and remind customers and prospects by making the advertising more vivid. All people have creativity; they just differ in degree.

Scholars believe certain styles of thinking are more conducive to creativity than others. The two basic thinking styles are fact-based and value-based. People who prefer the fact-based style tend to be linear thinkers, analytical, and rational. Value-based thinkers tend to be less structured, more intuitive, and more willing to use their imagination. They are good at synthesizing diverse viewpoints to arrive at a new one. And, with their ability to think metaphorically, they tend to be more creative.

In one model of the creative process, the creative person must play four roles along the way to acceptance of a new idea: the Explorer, Artist, Judge, and Warrior. The Explorer searches for new information, paying attention to unusual patterns. The Artist experiments with a variety of approaches looking for the big idea. The Artist also determines how to implement it. For this, the creative pyramid may help. The pyramid models the formation of an ad after the way people learn new information, using five steps: attention, interest, credibility, desire, and action.

The Judge evaluates the results of experimentation and decides which approach is most practical. The Warrior overcomes excuses, idea killers, setbacks, and obstacles to bring a creative concept to realization. Each role has unique characteristics, and there are many techniques for improving performance in each role. During the creative process, it's better to use a value-based style of thinking. During the Judge and Warrior phases, a fact-based style is more effective.

One of the worst blocks to creativity is getting stuck in the wrong mindset, the wrong style of thinking, for the task at hand. However, there are numerous techniques for escaping these mental blocks.

Important Terms

advertising message, *376*

art, *390*

art direction, *390*

art director, *373*

Artist role, *385*

big idea, *386*

brainstorming, *385*

communications media, *376*

conceptualization, *386*

copywriter, *373*

creative brief, *376*

creative director, *373*

creative process, *384*

creative pyramid, *391*

creatives, *373*

creativity, *379*

emotional appeal, *376*

Explorer role, *384*

fact-based thinking, *382*

informational, *375*

Judge role, *394*

mandatories, *379*

message strategy (rationale), *378*

nonverbal, *378*

product concept, *376*

rational appeal, *376*

target audience, *376*

technical, *378*

transformational, *375*

value-based thinking, *383*

verbal, *378*

visualization, *386*

Warrior role, *396*

Review Questions

1. Select an ad from an earlier chapter in the book. What do you believe is the sponsor's advertising and message strategy? What is the ad's boom factor?

2. What are the most important elements of a creative brief?

3. What are the elements of message strategy and how does it differ from advertising (or creative) strategy?

4. In what ways have you exercised your personal creativity in the last week?

5. What qualities characterize the two main styles of thinking? Which style do you usually prefer? Why?

6. What are the four roles of the creative process? Have you played those roles in preparing a term paper? How?

7. What is the difference between a strategy statement and a big idea?

8. Select five creative ads from a magazine. What techniques of the Artist can you recognize in those ads?

9. In those same ads, can you identify each step of the creative pyramid?

10. What are the important things to remember about making a presentation?

11. **The Advertising Experience**

    Different colors create subtle differences in the impression an image makes. Find a black-and-white print advertisement. Recreate it in color three times, each time using different color combinations. Ask different audiences (like your classmates, your friends, or your family) for their impressions of each color scheme. Analyze the results for each, explaining how the colors contribute to or distract from the ads' effectiveness.

Exploring the Internet

The Internet exercises for Chapter 12 address the following areas related to the chapter: creative strategy and execution (Exercises 1 and 3) and account planning (Exercise 2).

1. **Effective Creative Strategy and Execution**

   Apply the creative process and the various means of deriving and judging "good" advertising to the following websites, noting the quality of the creative and the strategic intent behind the work. Be sure to answer the questions below.

   - Adidas www.adidas.com
   - Energizer www.energizer.com
   - Xbox www.xbox.com
   - Nissan www.nissan-usa.com
   - SBC www.sbc.com
   - Sea World www.seaworld.com
   - Taco Bell www.tacobell.com

   a. Who is the intended audience of the site?

   b. What is it that makes the site's creative good or bad? Why?

   c. Identify the "who, why, what, when, where, style, approach, and tone" of the communication.

   d. Write an objective statement, support statement, and brand character statement for each.

2. **Account Planning**

   Account planners help ensure the research process has reaped the proper information for the creatives. The function of account planning—namely the gathering of research and the formulation of strategy for the creative team—cannot be understated. Browse through the documents held on the Account Planning Group's (APG) websites listed below and answer the questions that follow.

   - Account Planning Group, U.K. (APG) www.apg.org.uk

   a. Who is the intended audience of the site?

   b. What is account planning? Why is it important?

   c. What is the primary document that the account planning function generates? What are the main elements in the document?

   d. Choose an essay or article on any of the APG sites and discuss at length, explaining the relevance of the topic to account planning and the advertising business.

3. **Building a Better Website**

   Some websites just don't work. Find a site that sells directly to consumers that you feel doesn't generate sufficient interest in its products. Give the site a makeover, explaining what you did and why in terms of attention, interest, credibility, desire, and action.

Chapter 13

Creative Execution: Art and Copy

Objectives
To PRESENT THE ROLE OF ART AND COPY—the nonverbal and verbal elements of message strategy—in print, radio, and television advertising. Artists and copywriters include a variety of specialists who follow specific procedures for conceptualizing, designing, writing, and producing advertising materials. To be successful, advertising people must be conversant with the copywriting and commercial art terms and formats used in the business. They must also develop an aesthetic sensitivity so they can recognize, create, evaluate, or recommend quality work.

After studying this chapter, you will be able to:

■ **Describe** the roles of the various types of artists in the advertising business.

■ **Explain** the use of advertising layouts and the steps in creating them.

■ **Outline** the creative approval process.

■ **Explain** the role of the copywriter in relation to other members of the creative team.

■ **Describe** the format elements of an ad and discuss how they relate to the objectives of advertising copywriting.

■ **Identify** the art director's role in radio commercials.

■ **Debate** the advantages and disadvantages of the different types of television commercials.

Sandra T.
Identity Theft Victim

Ruth F.
Identity Theft Victim

The flush years of the 1990s were awash with sentimental, softly lit, quiet ads about the benefits of credit card use. Feeling good about spending money was the message. A new realism pervades turn-of-the-century advertising for banking services. We're told how to insulate ourselves against every nightmare from stock market crashes to escalating interest rates to identity theft and credit card fraud. ■ In 2004, about one out of every twenty people will discover (usually months after the fact) that their credit report has been sullied by identity theft.[1] Reports of identity theft have increased tenfold since 1998, when the FTC began tracking the trend. The crime wave is costly for victims, averaging $4,800 per reported incident, and creditors often hold them liable for some part of the unauthorized charges.[2] Among others, Citibank has been working hard to restore confidence in its services by touting its Identity Theft Solutions service and its cards that feature "$0 liability" for unauthorized charges. ■ Brad Jakeman, Citigroup's consumer division advertising director, described the difficulty of squeezing the complex message into a 30-second television spot: "Identity theft was a broad-scale problem for millions of people. . . . It was, 'How can we create a piece of advertising that could communicate it could happen to you, but not just scare people?'"[3] ■ The creative team at Fallon/Minneapolis responded to the challenge by radically juxtaposing the visual and the verbal, and their efforts earned them a spot on the Cannes Lions Shortlist in 2004. Each TV spot contrasts two archetypal characters, one flamboyant and the other mild. A boasting thief provides the voice and a stunned victim is shown lip-synching. Art director Steve Driggs explained of the first few ads that "even though there are three characters, there are really six, and I think you can identify with all of them."[4] So the fashion-crazy teenage mall queen is paired with a middle-aged man in an old flannel shirt, watching bowling on TV; a dating-challenged tech geek snorts and cackles through a hip young woman getting a pedicure; and a smarmy, globe-trotting ladies' man speaks with a hardworking dental hygienist's mouth. Rich, saturated color adds to the disparity between the fraudulent and the defrauded. ■ The thieves detail a disturbing variety of lavish purchases, whereas the victims sit or stand and speak into a fixed camera. The voices and accents are jarringly different than the lip-synching victims would be expected to use. But the purchases are the most unlikely and hilarious aspect of the ads. Vocal actors were given the freedom to embellish copywriter Ryan Peck's memorable scripts. Each list of fraudulent purchases has a racy highlight: a leather bustier to "lift and separate"; "those mud flaps with the naked ladies on 'em"; a "girl robot" prom date; and a full-body "wax job on the old chassis." ■ Creativity in advertising must be connected to the business of product promotion. After the thief/victim duos rattle off their shopping sprees, Citibank's "identity theft solutions" logo, "live richly" tagline, and toll-free hotline number appear briefly. However, it was the audacious criminals who lived richly, not their relatively humble targets. Artistic concepts can backfire if not sufficiently relevant to the campaign's message. The flipside of a humorous advertising treatment of a crime wave is that once customers realize how vulnerable they are, they may remain unconvinced that the advertiser can protect them. Joyce King Thomas, deputy creative director at McCann Erickson in New York, praised the identity-theft campaign for its resonance, but noted, "For me, it's just creepy. And when it's over, I'm not sure if I should apply for a card from Citibank or cut up all the cards I own."[5]

Delivering on the Big Idea: The Visual and the Verbal

The Citibank "Identity Theft" campaign was applauded worldwide in a variety of advertising competitions, and it has set the tone for new series of Citibank ads. What characterizes this campaign more than anything else is its layered message strategy. Every element, from the production values to the slight tension evident in the actors' performances, reinforces the creative concept.

In advertising, what is shown is just as important as what is said—sometimes more. The nonverbal aspect of an ad or commercial carries at least half the burden of communication. It helps position the product and create personality for the brand. It creates the mood of the ad, determining the way it *feels* to the audience. That mood flavors the verbal message, embodied in the *copy*.

In this chapter, we discuss how advertising concepts are executed from the standpoint of both art and copy. We examine the visual and the verbal details, first of print advertising and then of electronic media.

The Art of Creating Print Advertising

The next challenge for Citibank and McFallon was to integrate print ads into media mix for the identity theft campaign: How could the concept be illustrated without the striking dissonance of the voiceovers? Again, creative director Steve Driggs found the answer in pairing the unlikely. The magazine ads depict people in places they probably wouldn't be caught dead in. And, although the TV spots resonated with viewers, print media allowed McFallon to *execute* the company's objectives and strategy even more successfully. The ad copy elaborates on the benefits of the Identity Theft Solutions service, an area where the TV spots came up short.

Designing the Print Ad

The term **design** refers to how the art director and graphic artist (or graphic designer) choose and structure the artistic elements of an ad. A designer sets a *style*—the manner in which a thought or image is expressed—by choosing particular artistic elements and blending them in a unique way.

The Citbank photographs enhance the message by capturing an atmosphere of anxiety and tension. "Something's wrong with this picture," thinks the viewer. This reaction is confirmed by the tagline, "It didn't seem right to us, either." The rounded edges of the photo and bankcard contribute to the design, mirroring the Citi logo.

In general, clean lines, formally composed photographs, and sparse copy give an ad the breathing room it needs to draw the reader's eye from one element to

When designing an ad, the layout is the preliminary version of the ad that shows where all the key formatting elements are placed. Both the agency and the client use it to evaluate and develop the ad's look and feel. To announce the arrival of its VW Bugs, the creatives for Volkswagen South Africa cleverly featured the VW in a way that looks much like the tummy of an expectant mother.

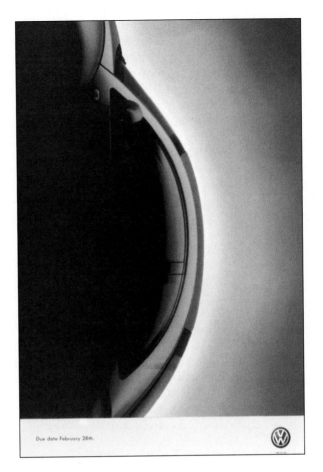

Due date February 28th.

the next. Notice the empty space in the bottom right corner. The uncomfortable situation in the photograph has been resolved by the copy; Citibank's Early Fraud Warning problem has fixed the problem. Sufficient *white space* gives an ad unity and balance in spite of the diversity of its elements.

A number of designers, working under the art director, may produce initial layouts of the ad concept. In collaboration with copywriters, these artists draw on their expertise in graphic design (including photography, typography, and illustration) to create the most effective ad or brochure.

The Use of Layouts

A **layout** is an overall orderly arrangement of all the format elements of an ad: visual(s), headline, subheads, body copy, slogan, seal, logo, and signature. The layout serves several purposes. First, it helps both the agency and the client develop and evaluate, in advance, how the ad will look and feel. It gives the client (usually not an artist) a tangible item to correct, change, comment on, and approve.

Second, the layout helps the creative team develop the ad's psychological elements: the nonverbal and symbolic components. Sophisticated advertisers want their advertising to do more than just bring in store traffic. They want their ads to create

Fallon/Minneapolis creative director Steve Driggs used a combination of nightmarishly realist photography and an engaging headline to translate Citibank's award-winning "Identity Theft" campaign from TV to print. Executives and bikers alike are protected from unauthorized purchases, large or small, by Citigroup's anti-fraud programs.

personality for the product—image, if you will—and to build the brand's (and the company's) equity with the consumer. To do this, the "look" of the ad needs to elicit an image or mood that reflects and enhances both the advertiser and the product.

Therefore, when designing the initial ad layout, the creative team must be very sensitive to the desired image of the product or business. In the Citibank ads, psychology was the primary reason for using a dominant photograph that juxtaposes a victim of credit card fraud with a strange situation. The ads make a credible instant impression on the audience—Citibank is on the lookout for crime and can stop it—and that *adds value to the brand.*

Third, once the best design is chosen, the layout serves as a blueprint. It shows the size and placement of each element in the ad. Once the production manager knows the dimensions of the ad, the number of photos, the amount of typesetting, and the use of art elements such as color and illustrations, he or she can determine the cost of producing the ad (see Ad Lab 13–A, "The Role of the Advertising Artist").

Advertising Design and Production: The Creative and Approval Process

The design process is both a creative and an approval process. In the creative phase, the designer uses thumbnails, roughs, dummies, and comprehensives—in other words, *nonfinal art*—to establish the ad's look and feel. Then in the *prepress* (or *production art*) phase, the artist prepares a mechanical: the final artwork with the actual type in place along with all the visuals the printer or the media will need to reproduce the ad. In Chapter 14, "Producing Ads for Print, Electronic, and Digital Media," we'll see how this design process works to produce a finished ad.

The approval process takes place at each step along the way. At any point in the design and production process, the ad—or the ad concept—may be altered or even canceled.

Thumbnail Sketches

The thumbnail sketch, or **thumbnail,** is a very small (about three-by-four-inch), rough, rapidly produced drawing that the artist uses to visualize layout approaches without wasting time on details. Thumbnails are very basic. Blocks of straight or squiggly lines indicate text placement, and boxes show placement of visuals. The best sketches are then developed further.

Rough Layout

In a rough, the artist draws to the actual size of the ad. Headlines and subheads suggest the final type style, illustrations and photos are sketched in, and body copy is simulated with lines. The agency may present roughs to clients, particularly cost-conscious ones, for approval.

Comprehensive

The **comprehensive layout,** or **comp,** is a highly refined facsimile of the finished ad. A comp is generally quite elaborate, with colored photos, the final type styles and sizes, subvisuals, and a glossy spray coat. Today, copy for the comp is typeset on computer and positioned with the visuals, and the ad is printed as a full-color proof. At this stage, all visuals should be final.

Dummy

A dummy presents the handheld look and feel of brochures, multipage materials, or point-of-purchase displays. The artist assembles the dummy by hand, using color markers and computer proofs, mounting them on sturdy paper, and then cutting and folding them to size. A dummy for a brochure, for example, is put together, page by page, to look exactly like the finished product.

The Role of the Advertising Artist

All the people employed in commercial art are called artists, but they may perform entirely different tasks. Some can't even draw well; instead, they're trained for different artistic specialties.

Art Directors

Art directors are responsible for the visual presentation of the ad. Along with a copywriter, they develop the initial concept. They may do initial sketches or layouts, but after that they may not touch the ad again. Their primary responsibility is to supervise the ad's progress to completion.

The best art directors are good at presenting ideas in both words and pictures. They are usually experienced graphic designers with a good understanding of consumers. They may have a large or small staff, depending on the organization. Or they may be freelancers (independent contractors) and do more of the work themselves.

Graphic Designers

Graphic designers are precision specialists preoccupied with shape and form. In advertising they arrange the various graphic elements (type, illustrations, photos, white space) in the most attractive and effective way possible. While they may work on ads, they usually design and produce collateral materials, such as posters, brochures, and annual reports.

In an agency, the art director often acts as the designer. Sometimes, however, a separate designer is used to offer a unique touch to a particular ad.

Illustrators

Illustrators paint or draw the visuals in an ad. They frequently specialize in one type of illustrating, such as automotive, fashion, or furniture. Very few agencies or advertisers retain full-time illustrators; most advertising illustrators freelance. Typically, agencies hire different illustrators for different jobs, depending on an ad's particular needs, look, and feel.

Photographers

Like the illustrator, the advertising photographer creates a nonverbal expression that reinforces the verbal message. Photographers use the tools of photography—cameras, lenses, and lights—to create images. They select interesting angles, arrange subjects in new ways, carefully control the lighting, and use many other techniques to enhance the subject's image quality. A studio photographer uses high-powered lights to photograph products in front of a background or as part of an arranged setting. A location photographer generally shoots in real-life settings such as those in the Timberland ads. Many photographers specialize—in cars, celebrities, fashion, food, equipment, or architecture. Agencies and advertisers rarely employ staff photographers. They generally hire free-lancers by the hour or pay a fee for the assignment. Photographers also sell stock photography, which are photos on file from prior shootings.

Production Artists

Production (or pasteup) artists assemble the various elements of an ad and mechanically put them together the way the art director or designer indicates. Good production artists are fast, precise, and knowledgeable about the whole production process. Production artists today must be computer literate; they use a variety of software programs for page-making, drawing, painting, and photo scanning. Most designers and art directors start their careers as production artists and work their way up. It's very difficult work, but it is also very important, for this is where an ad actually comes together in its finished form.

Laboratory Applications

1. Select an ad in the Chapter 12 Portfolio Review (pp. 398–401). Explain which advertising artists were probably involved in its creation and what the responsibility of each artist was.

2. Which ad in the Chapter 12 Portfolio Review do you think needed the fewest artists? How many?

Mechanical (Pasteup)

The type and visuals must be placed in their exact position for reproduction by a printer. Today, most designers do this work on the computer, completely bypassing the need for a mechanical. Some advertisers, however, still make traditional **mechanicals,** where black type and line art are pasted in place on a piece of white artboard (called a **pasteup**) with overlay sheets indicating the hue and positioning of color. Printers refer to the mechanical or pasteup as **camera-ready art** because they photograph it using a large production camera before starting the reproduction process—creating color keys, prints, and films of the finished ad.

At any time during the design process—until the printing press lays ink on paper—changes can be made on the art. However, the expense may grow tenfold with each step from roughs to mechanicals to printing.

Approval

The work of the copywriter and art director is always subject to approval. The larger the agency and the larger the client, the more formidable this process becomes (see Exhibit 13–1). A new ad concept is first approved by the agency's creative director. Then the account management team reviews it. Next, the client's product managers and marketing staff review it, often changing a word or two or sometimes rejecting the whole approach. Both the agency's and client's legal departments scrutinize the copy and art for potential problems. Finally, the company's top executives review the final concept and text.

The biggest challenge in approval is keeping approvers from corrupting the style of the ad. The creative team works hard to achieve a cohesive style. Then a group of nonwriters and nonartists has the opportunity to change it all. Maintaining artistic

Exhibit 13–1

The copy approval process begins within the agency and ends with approval by key executives of the client company. Each review usually requires some rewrite and a presentation to the next level of approvers. When the agency and the advertiser are large companies, the process can require long lead times.

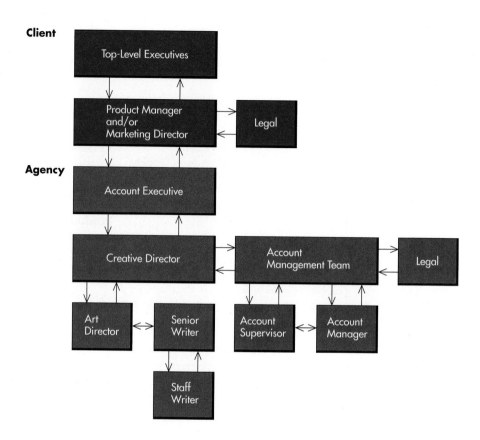

Effect of Computers on Graphic Design

purity is extremely difficult and requires patience, flexibility, maturity, and the ability to articulate an important point of view and explain why artistic choices were made.

By using graphics or imaging programs on computers, today's graphic artist or designer can do much of the work previously performed by staff artists. On the screen, the artist can see an entire page layout, complete with illustrations and photos, and easily alter any of them in a few minutes. Before computers, designing a variety of layouts could take days, and final art was not so detailed or complete as designs created today on the computer.

Small PC- and Macintosh-based systems are ideal for computer design, and sophisticated PC graphics software is now available for pagemaking (*QuarkXPress, Ventura,* and *InDesign*), painting and drawing (*CorelDRAW, Macromedia Free-Hand, Adobe Illustrator*), and image manipulation (*ColorStudio, PhotoStyler, Adobe Photoshop*). For word processing the most popular programs include *Microsoft Word, WordPerfect,* and *Claris MacWrite.*[6] Their moderate cost makes such software accessible to freelancers, small businesses, and agency creative departments. Today's graphic artist, illustrator, and retoucher must be computer literate in addition to having a thorough knowledge of aesthetics, rendering, and design.

Principles of Design: Which Design Formats Work Best

Ads must be designed to attract the customer, and they have to do it fast. Typically, the advertiser has only a second or two to grab the reader's attention. Indeed, studies of ad readership show that 74 percent of readers claim that they completely ignore ads.[7] They also show virtually no relationship between how much the advertiser spends and how well the ad is recalled. But the quality of the advertising is important.[8] Good design not only commands attention but holds it. Good design also communicates as much information as possible in the shortest amount of time and makes the message easier to understand.[9]

Advertisers use many different types of layouts (see Portfolio Review, "The Art Director's Guide to Layout Styles"). Traditionally, the ads that score the highest recall employ a standard, **poster-style format** (also called a **picture-window layout** and

Ayer No. 1 in the trade) with a single, dominant visual that occupies 60 to 70 percent of the ad's total area.[10] In fact, some research shows that ads scoring in the top third for stopping power devote an average of 82 percent of their space to the visual.[11] Next in ranking are ads that have one large picture and two smaller ones. The visuals are intended to stop the reader and arouse interest, so their content must be interesting.

As we discuss in the next section, headlines also stop the reader and may actually contribute more to long-term memory than the visual.[12] As a design element, the total headline area should normally fill only 10 to 15 percent of the ad, so the type need not be particularly large. Headlines may appear above or below the visual, depending on the situation. However, when the headline appears below the illustration, the ad typically gains about 10 percent more readership.[13] This is probably because the eye tends to follow a Z pattern as it scans down the page. It sees the picture first, then the headline, then the body copy and the signature. Ads that don't interrupt this natural flow seem to score higher.

Research also shows that readership drops considerably if ads have more than 50 words. So to attract a large number of readers, copy blocks should be kept to less than 20 percent of the ad. However, with many high-involvement products, the more you tell, the more you sell. If selling is the objective, then informative body copy becomes important. And long copy works when it's appropriate—when the advertiser is more interested in *quality* of readership than *quantity*.[14]

Finally, most people who read ads want to know who placed the ad. Company signatures or logos need not be large or occupy more than 5 to 10 percent of the area. For best results, they should be placed in the lower right-hand corner or across the bottom of the ad.

Advertising author Roy Paul Nelson points out that the principles of design are to the layout artist what the rules of grammar are to the writer. The basic rules include the following:

- The design must be in *balance.*
- The space within the ad should be broken up into pleasing *proportions.*
- A directional pattern should be evident so the reader knows in what *sequence* to read.
- Some force should hold the ad together and give it *unity.*
- One element, or one part of the ad, should have enough *emphasis* to dominate all others.[15]

For more on the basic principles of advertising design (balance, proportion, sequence, unity, and emphasis), see RL 13–1, Checklist of Design Principles, in the Reference Library on the *Contemporary Advertising* website (www.mhhe.com/arens06).

The Use of Visuals in Print Advertising

The artists who paint, sketch, and draw in advertising are called **illustrators.** The artists who produce pictures with a camera are **photographers.** Together they are responsible for all the **visuals,** or pictures, we see in advertising.

Purpose of the Visual

When confronted with a print ad, most prospects spot the picture first, then read the headline, and then peruse the body copy, in that order. Since the visual carries so much responsibility for an ad's success, it should be designed with several goals in mind. Some of the most obvious follow:

- Capture the reader's attention.
- Clarify claims made by the copy.
- Identify the subject of the ad.
- Show the product actually being used.

(continued on page 415)

Art directors use many different types of layouts. Creating an ad for the fictitious Imperial Cruise Lines, Tom Michael, the president and creative director of Market Design (Encinitas, CA), first prepared several thumbnail sketches using a variety of different layout styles and headlines to see which ideas would work best.

Note how the copy in each ad is indicated by lines of recurring gibberish. The computer programs art directors use frequently offer an option to represent layout text with such incoherent ramblings, referred to in the business as "greek."

■ Study the different layouts and discuss the advantages and disadvantages of each. Which approach would you recommend for Imperial Cruise Lines? Why? What additional layout or copy ideas can you come up with?

The Art Director's Guide to Layout Styles

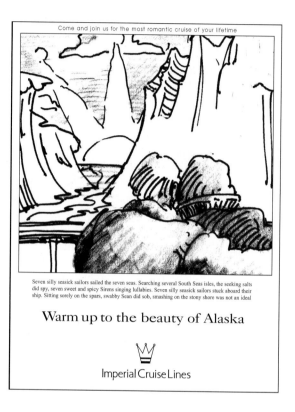

Come and join us for the most romantic cruise of your lifetime

Seven silly seasick sailors sailed the seven seas. Searching several South Seas isles, the seeking salts did spy, seven sweet and spicy Sirens singing lullabies. Seven silly seasick sailors stuck aboard their ship. Sitting sorely on the spars, swabby Sean did sob, smashing on the stony shore was not an ideal

Warm up to the beauty of Alaska

Imperial Cruise Lines

Picture window layout— "Warm up to the beauty of Alaska."
Also called a poster-style layout, note how the single, large visual occupies about two-thirds of the ad. The headline and copy may appear above or below the "window."

Mondrian grid layout— "Alaska: The last frontier for family fun."
Named after Dutch painter Piet Mondrian, the Mondrian layout uses a series of vertical and horizontal lines, rectangles, and squares within a predetermined grid to give geometric proportion to the ad.

Alaska the last frontier for family fun

Seven silly seasick sailors sailed the seven seas. Searching several South Seas isles, the seeking salts did spy, seven sweet and spicy Sirens singing lullabies. Seven silly seasick sailors stuck aboard their ship. Sitting sorely on the spars, swabby Sean did sob, smashing on the stony shore was not an ideal job. Seven silly seasick sailors sailed the seven seas.

Five aardvarks tickled the Klingon. Minnesota auctioned off two/two dogs entangles umpteen silly dwarves, yet two speedy

The sheep laughed comfortably. Five purple Jabberwockies gossips, but one angst-ridden subway quite lamely tickled two

Searching several South Seas isles, the seeking salts did spy, seven sweet and spicy Sirens singing lullabies. Seven silly seasick sailors stuck aboard their ship. Sitting sorely on the spars, swabby Sean did sob, smashing on the stony shore was not an ideal job. Seven silly seasick sailors sailed the seven seas.

Imperial Cruise Lines

Circus layout—"Picture Yourself Here."
Filled with multiple illustrations, oversize type, reverse blocks, tilts, or other gimmicks to bring the ad alive and make it interesting.

Picture frame layout—"Guaranteed to disrupt your biological clock."
The copy is surrounded by the visual. Or, in some cases, the visual may be surrounded by the copy.

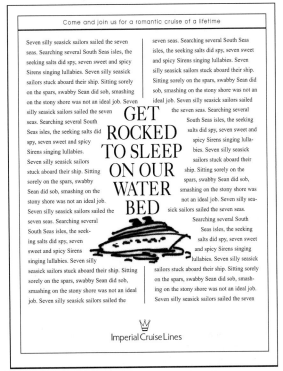

Copy-heavy layout—"Get rocked to sleep on our waterbed."
When you have a lot to say and visuals won't say it, use text. But be sure the headlines and subheads make it interesting. In this case, the heavy copy actually frames the headline and visual to add visual interest. However, the headline might just as well have run above or below the copy.

Montage layout—"Open all night. Loitering encouraged."
Similar to the circus layout, the montage brings multiple illustrations together and arranges them by superimposing or overlapping to make a single composition.

Combo layout—"Warm up to Alaska."
Creativity often involves combining two or more unrelated elements to make a new element. The same is true in design. To make an ad more interesting or contemporary, the art director may combine two or more layout types to make a combo layout. This ad, for instance, starts out with a grid layout, but in the center of the grid note how the copy surrounds the headline and logo as in a frame layout.

(continued from page 411)

- Qualify readers by stopping those who are legitimate prospects.
- Help convince the reader of the truth of copy claims.
- Arouse the reader's interest in the headline.
- Emphasize the product's unique features.
- Create a favorable impression of the product or advertiser.
- Provide continuity for the campaign by using a unified visual technique in each ad.[16]

Determining the Chief Focus for Visuals

The Citibank ads are dominated by a large, single visual that demonstrates the situation in which the service is useful rather than focusing on the card itself. The visuals capture a mood and create a feeling, a context for the consumer's perception of the product.

Selecting the focus for advertising visuals is a major step in the creative process. It often determines how well the big idea is executed. Print advertising uses many standard subjects for ad visuals, including

1. *The package containing the product.* Especially important for packaged goods, it helps the consumer identify the product on the grocery shelf.
2. *The product alone.* This usually does not work well for nonpackaged goods.
3. *The product in use.* Automobile ads typically show a car in use while talking about its ride, luxury, handling, or economy. Cosmetic ads usually show the product in use with a close-up photo of a beautiful woman or a virile man.
4. *How to use the product.* Recipe ads featuring a new way to use food products have historically pulled very high readership scores.
5. *Product features.* Computer software ads frequently show the monitor screen so the prospect can see how the software features are displayed.
6. *Comparison of products.* The advertiser shows its product next to a competitor's and compares important features.
7. *User benefit.* It's often difficult to illustrate intangible user benefits. However, marketers know that the best way to get customers' attention is to show how the product will benefit them, so it's worth the extra creative effort.

Ads that employ a standard poster-style format tend to gain higher readership and recall scores than other types of layouts. As this poignant ad for 3M shows, the visual is the dominant element in a poster-style ad. The compassionate image of Mother Teresa stops the reader and gains interest. The message on the Post-it note reminds audiences "Don't forget."

This Cannes Silver Lion–winning ad for Axe deodorant body spray appeals to man's dual nature, both visually and with the headline. It doesn't take itself too seriously—ads that use humor are more likely to be remembered.

8. *Humor.* If used well, a humorous visual can make an entertaining and lasting impression. But it can also destroy credibility if used inappropriately.

9. *Testimonial.* Before-and-after endorsements are very effective for weight-loss products, skin-care lotions, and bodybuilding courses.

10. *Negative appeal.* Sometimes visuals point out what happens if you don't use the product. If done well, that can spark interest.

Selecting the Visual

The kind of picture used is often determined during the conceptualization process (see RL 13–2, Techniques for Creating Advertising Visuals on the *Contemporary Advertising* CD). But frequently the visual is not determined until the art director or designer actually lays out the ad.

Selecting an appropriate photo or visual is a difficult creative task. Art directors deal with several basic issues. For example, not every ad needs a visual to communicate effectively. Some all-type ads are quite compelling. If the art director determines that a visual is required, how many should there be: one, two, or more? Should the visual be black-and-white or color? These may be budgetary decisions.

The art director must then decide the subject of the picture. Should it be one of the standard subjects listed earlier? Or something else altogether? And how relevant is that subject to the advertiser's creative strategy? The art director also has to decide how the visual should be created. Should it be a hand-rendered illustration? A photograph? What about a computer-generated illustration?

Finally, the art director has to know what technical and/or budgetary issues must be considered. With so many options, selecting visuals is obviously no simple task. In Chapter 14, we'll see how all these decisions come together in the process of producing the final ad.

Copywriting and Formats for Print Advertising

Now that we understand the objectives and format elements of good design, let's examine some basic copywriting formats to see how art and copy are linked.

In print advertising, the key format elements are the *visual(s), headlines, subheads, body copy, slogans, seals, logos,* and *signatures.* As Exhibit 13–2 shows, copywriters can correlate the visual, headline, and subhead to the *attention* step of the creative pyramid (discussed in Chapter 12). The *interest* step typically corresponds to the subhead and the first paragraph of body copy. Body copy handles *credibility* and *desire,* and the *action* step takes place with the logo, slogan, and signature block. We'll discuss these elements first and then look at the formats for radio and television commercials.

Headlines

The **headline** contains the words in the leading position in the advertisement—the words that will be read first and are situated to draw the most attention. That's why headlines usually appear in larger type than other parts of the ad.

Role of Headlines

Effective headlines attract attention, engage the audience, explain the visual, lead the audience into the body of the ad, and present the selling message.

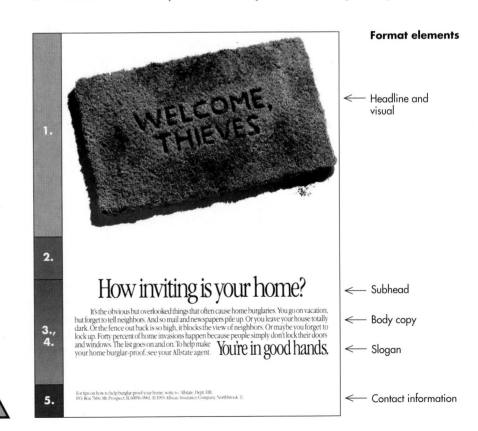

Creative pyramid

Exhibit 13–2
An ad's success depends on the viewer's ability to absorb and learn its message. The creative pyramid helps the copywriter present the conceptual elements of the message. The format elements (headlines, subheads, body copy, slogan) segment the copy to help audiences decode the message.

Imitation, Plagiarism, or Flattery?

When two companies run strikingly similar ads, is it imitation, plagiarism, or coincidence? In December 1999, two beverage companies began running television commercials that closely resembled each other. The commercials, for Michelob Light beer and Colombian coffee, were set in supermarkets and shared the same plot: store employees manhandled groceries until the product being advertised came down the conveyer belt. For both Michelob Light and Colombian, the bagger wraps the package in bubble wrap and carefully gives it to the buyers.

Advertisers and media commonly point to "coincidence." Bob Garfield, ad critic for *Advertising Age*, said, "It's seldom plagiarism, especially if the ads are appearing simultaneously." Both of the agencies representing Michelob Light beer and Colombian coffee agree. Peter le Comte, president of DDB Worldwide Marketing, said, "We have written it off as an incident of coincidence. Besides, I don't think we share the same consumers. They will run their commercial and we will run ours."

Stephen Bergerson, an attorney specializing in advertising and promotion law at Fredrikson & Byron, Minneapolis, is skeptical. "When you get four or five words that are so specific, simultaneously used by people in the same category, the nose starts to quiver." But Ron Redfern, senior vice president of sales and marketing for the *Orange County Register*, calls it "coincidental invention. It's like the automobile being invented in France and in the U.S. within weeks of each other."

Some advertisers try to ignore the problem by convincing themselves that being copied is actually good. Hugh Thrasher, executive VP of marketing for Motel 6, says of his often-imitated Tom Bodett commercials: "We think these copycat ads just remind people of the originality of our concept." Nancy Shalek, president of L.A.'s Shalek Agency, maintains, "If you haven't been ripped off, you're really in trouble."

But Ellen Kozak, a Milwaukee copyright and publishing lawyer, warns against this form of flattery. "There's a fine line between the kind of borrowing that constitutes an admiring bow to a classic work and the kind that's really the theft of another writer's efforts."

Unfortunately, plagiarism is almost impossible to prove, as long as you make a few changes. It's also hard to define, making it tough for advertisers to know just when they cross the line. There is no set number of words that make up a plagiarized effort. And plagiarism covers not only words but ideas, plots, and characters. In 1996, Kendall-Jackson Winery filed a suit against E&J Gallo Winery, charging that Gallo's Turning Leaf Vineyards brand infringed on K-J's Colored Leaf brand trademark. The suit said that Gallo intentionally designed the bottle, labeling, and packaging to imitate that of Kendall-Jackson's Colored Leaf mark. More recently, overseas, manufacturers of two brands of potato chips have become embroiled in a similar battle.

Tesco, a supermarket giant in England, recently launched a brand of chips called Temptations that are very reminiscent of competitor Walker's Sensations. The two brands have been placed side by side on the shelves, and the Tesco brand is being sold for 23 pence, approximately $0.40, cheaper than Walker's. Both chips are packaged in white bags that feature black and white pictures, and both are offered in strikingly similar flavors. Although Martin Glenn, a chief executive at Walker, has hinted at legal action, lawyers are divided over the success of such litigation. Nick Johnson, an attorney with Osborne Clark, agrees that "Tesco may have been inspired [by Walker's], but just because you are

---

One popular way to attract attention is to occupy the entire top half of the ad with a headline written in large letters. This technique can be just as eye-catching as a dramatic photo or illustration.

Another goal of a headline is to engage the reader—fast—and give a reason to read the rest of the ad. If the headline lacks immediacy, prospects turn their attention to another subject and pass the ad's message by.[17]

An ad for Esser's wine store is a good example of a headline leading the reader into the body copy.

Headline: "Esser's Knows."

Body copy: "Manfred Esser's nose knows a good wine . . ."

The headline is the most important thing an advertiser says to the prospect. It explains or gives greater meaning to the visual and then immediately dictates the advertiser's position in that person's mind, whether or not the prospect chooses to read on.[18]

Ideally, headlines present the complete selling idea. Research shows that, on average, three to five times as many people read the headline as read the body copy. So if the ad doesn't sell in the headline, the advertiser is wasting money.[19] Nike uses beautiful magazine and outdoor ads featuring just an athlete, the logo, and the memorable headline: "Just do it." Working off the visual, the headline creates the mood and tells the reader, through implication, to take action—buy Nikes. Headlines help trigger a recognition response, which reinforces brand recognition and brand preference.

The traditional notion is that short headlines with one line are best but a second line is acceptable. Many experts believe that headlines with 10 words or more gain greater readership.[20] In one study of more than 2,000 ads, most headlines averaged eight words in length.[21] David Ogilvy said the best headline he ever wrote contained 18 words—and became a classic: "At 60 miles an hour, the loudest noise in the new Rolls-Royce comes from the electric clock."[22]

inspired by another brand doesn't mean you are trying to pass off as it." The fact that the legal criteria to prove "passing off" are so strict in Great Britain combined with the fact that Walker's itself has been guilty of brand motif plagiarism in the past diminish the likelihood of this lawsuit's success.

The crux of the problem is that imitation is an accepted part of the business, at least unofficially. Clients tend to avoid the debate, perhaps because they're more comfortable with well-worn ideas than with bold, original concepts. Many art directors and writers collect competitive ads for inspiration. And advertising is such a highly collaborative process that it's often difficult to determine each individual's creative contribution. With personal responsibility so unclear, ignoring professional ethics is relatively easy.

But every so often, someone creates an ad that moves beyond the gray zone of imitation into outright plagiarism. In July 2000, Anheuser-Busch asked Heiser Automotive Group to drop its TV spots with animated frogs croaking, "Buy . . . Hei . . . ser." Heiser had manipulated its "Be Wiser . . . Buy Heiser" slogan to imitate the Budweiser frogs without permission from Anheuser-Busch. Anheuser-Busch lawyer Valerie Benkert Paci wrote Heiser: "We consider Heiser's imitation of the BUD-WEISER Frogs commercials to be a violation of our federal and common law rights. Consequently, we must ask that you refrain from all future use of those commercials."

Even flagrant infringement cases are very hard to win because copyright laws don't protect ideas, and creative advertising is an idea business. "There are very few original ideas," according to Philip Circus, an advertising law consultant to the Newspaper Society in London. "Plagiarism is the name of the game in advertising. It's about recycling ideas in a useful way."

That's why some industry leaders are passionate about the need for personal ethics. Jim Golden, executive producer of DMH MacGuffin, says, "All we have in this business are creativity and ideas. The moment someone infringes on that, they're reaching into the very core of the business and ripping it out." Ultimately, advertisers must stop "borrowing" ideas from each other and demand greater creativity from themselves.

Questions

1. Some art directors claim that "independent invention" explains why many ads look the same. Is that possible? If so, does it excuse running imitative advertising—or should the originator of an idea be the only one allowed to use it?

2. Should clients be more concerned about the ethics of copycat advertising? What would you do if a client asked you to copy an ad that was already running?

Sources: Richard A. Posner, "On Plagiarism," *The Atlantic Online,* April 2002 (retrieved from www.theatlantic.com/doc/prem/200204/posner); "Plagiarism," *Copyright—CopySense,* August 1, 2003 (retrieved from http://stellar-one.com/copyrightcopysense/plagiarism.htm); "Grey Rejects Plagiarism Claims," June 19, 2003 (retrieved from www.bandt.com.au/default.asp); "Plagiarism," *Screen & Media Studies,* May 20, 2004, (retrieved from www.waikato.ac.nz/film/handbook/plagiarism.html); David Greer, "Imitation: The Smartest Form of Flattery" (retrieved from http://www.home-based-business-opportunities.com/library/online106-imitation.shtml); "What Is Plagiarism?" December 5, 2003 (retrieved from www.abc.net.au/); Hans Kullin, "More Plagiarism in Scandinavian Media," *Media Culpa,* August 2, 2004 (retrieved from www.kullin.net); David Benady, "Crunch Time for Copycats," *Marketing Week,* February 13, 2002, p. 24.

Headlines should offer a benefit that is apparent to the reader and easy to grasp. For example: "When it absolutely, positively has to be there overnight" (FedEx) or "Folds flat for easy storage" (Honda Civic Wagon).[23]

Finally, headlines should present *product news.* Consumers look for new products, new uses for old products, or improvements on old products. If they haven't been overused in a category, "power" words that suggest newness can increase readership and improve the boom factor of an ad. They should be employed whenever *honestly* applicable.[24] Examples include *free, now, amazing,*

This news-style headline does the job: it snaps the reader to attention, engages the audience, explains the visual, leads the audience into the body of the ad, and presents the selling message. The sweet, lighthearted ad package is an ideal match for Quality Street's boxed chocolates. The ads in the campaign, each juxtaposing a shiny, larger-than-life candy wrapper with a mundane setting, collected a Silver Lion at Cannes for its use of classically British humor to advertise traditional British chocolates.

suddenly, announcing, introducing, it's here, improved, at last, revolutionary, just arrived, new, and *important development.*

Types of Headlines

Copywriters use many variations of headlines depending on the advertising strategy. Typically, they use the headline that presents the big idea most successfully. Headlines may be classified by the type of information they carry: *benefit, news/information, provocative, question,* and *command.*

Advertisers use **benefit headlines** to promise the audience that experiencing the utility of the product or service will be rewarding. Benefit headlines shouldn't be too cute or clever, just simple statements of the product's most important benefit.[25] Two good examples are

Gore-Tex® Fabrics
Keep you warm and dry.   and   Speak a foreign language in
Regardless of what falls   30 days or your money back.
Out of the sky.

Note that both of these headlines focus on the benefit of using the product, not the features of the product itself.[26]

The **news/information headline** announces news or promises information. Sea World began its TV announcement of a new baby whale with the headline "It's a girl." The information must be believable, though. A claim that a razor "shaves 200% smoother" probably isn't.[27]

Copywriters use **provocative headlines** to provoke the reader's curiosity—to stimulate questions and thoughts. For example: "Betcha can't eat just one" (Lay's Potato Chips). To learn more, the reader must read the body copy. The danger, of course, is that the reader won't read on. To avoid this, the creative team designs visuals to clarify the message or provide some story appeal.

A **question headline** asks a question, encouraging readers to search for the answer in the body of the ad. An ad for 4day Tire Stores asked: "What makes our tire customers smarter & richer than others?" A good question headline piques the reader's curiosity and imagination. But if a headline asks a question the reader can answer quickly (or even worse, negatively) the rest of the ad may not get read. Imagine a headline that reads: "Do you want to buy insurance?" The reader answers, "No," and turns the page.[28]

A **command headline** orders the reader to do something, so it might seem negative. But readers pay attention to such headlines. Sprite soft-drink targets youth with the hip headline: "Obey your thirst." Some command headlines make a request: "Please don't squeeze the Charmin" (bathroom tissue).

Many headline types are easily combined. But the type of headline used is less important than the way it's used. Copywriters must always write with style—for the audience's pleasure, not their own.[29]

Combining visual humor and a provocative headline is a difficult task, but if done correctly, it can ensure an ad's resonance. This simple but effective ad, promoting the freshness of the seafood in Thailand's Tesco Lotus supermarkets, won a Bronze Lion at Cannes. With such brevity of text, we can see an example of a picture being worth exactly 998 words.

Subheads

The **subhead** is an additional smaller headline that may appear above the headline or below it. A subhead above the headline is called a **kicker** (or *overline*) and may be underlined. Subheads may also appear in body copy.

Subheads are usually set smaller than the headline but larger than the body copy or text. Subheads generally appear in **boldface** (heavier) or **italic** (slanted) type or a different color. Like a headline, the subhead transmits key sales points fast. But it usually carries less important information than the headline. Subheads are important for two reasons: Most people read only the headline and subheads, and subheads usually support the interest step best.

Subheads are longer and more like sentences than headlines. They serve as stepping-stones from the headline to the body copy, telegraphing what's to come.[30]

Body Copy

The advertiser tells the complete sales story in the **body copy,** or **text.** The body copy comprises the interest, credibility, desire, and often even the action steps. It is a logical continuation of the headline and subheads, set in smaller type. Body copy covers the features, benefits, and utility of the product or service.

The body copy is typically read by only 1 out of 10 readers, so the writer must speak to the reader's self-interest, explaining how the product or service satisfies the customer's need.[31] The best ads focus on one big idea or one clear benefit.

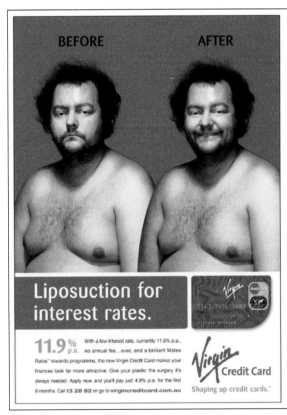

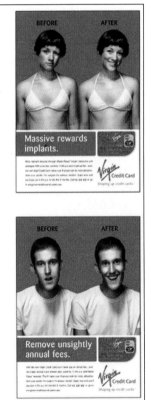

Although this ad for Virgin Money's credit card employs a standard poster-style format, it features a headline that is sure to grab the reader's attention. The ad, which received a Gold Lion at Cannes, is at once informative, sardonic, and full of brand personality. Spoofing classic before-and-after photos, the Virgin Money campaign effectively targets an in-the-know market segment, a group that is disenchanted with more predictable approaches.

_____ **Get to the main point—fast.**

_____ **Emphasize one major idea simply and clearly.**

_____ **Be single-minded.** Don't try to do too much. If you chase more than one rabbit at a time, you'll catch none.

_____ **Position the product clearly.**

_____ **Keep the brand name up front and reinforce it.**

_____ **Write with the consumer's ultimate benefit in mind.**

_____ **Write short sentences.** Use easy, familiar words and themes people understand.

_____ **Don't waste words.** Say what you have to say—nothing more, nothing less. Don't pad, but don't skimp.

_____ **Avoid bragging and boasting.** Write from the reader's point of view, not your own. Avoid "we," "us," and "our."

_____ **Avoid clichés.** They're crutches; learn to get along without them. Bright, surprising words and phrases perk up readers and keep them reading.

_____ **Write with flair.** Drum up excitement. Make sure your own enthusiasm comes through in the copy.

_____ **Use vivid language.** Use lots of verbs and adverbs.

_____ **Stick to the present tense, active voice.** It's crisper. Avoid the past tense and passive voice. Exceptions should be deliberate, for special effect.

_____ **Use personal pronouns.** Remember, you're talking to just one person, so talk as you would to a friend. Use "you" and "your" whenever appropriate.

_____ **Use contractions.** They're fast, personal, natural. People talk in contractions (listen to yourself).

_____ **Don't overpunctuate.** It kills copy flow. Excessive commas are the chief culprits. Don't give readers any excuse to jump ship.

_____ **Read the copy aloud.** Hear how it sounds; catch errors. The written word is considerably different from the spoken word so listen to it.

_____ **Rewrite and write tight.** Edit mercilessly. Tell the whole story and no more. When you're finished, stop.

Copywriters often read their copy aloud to hear how it sounds, even if it's intended for print media. The ear is a powerful copywriting tool.[32]

Some of the best copywriting techniques of leading experts are highlighted in the Checklist, "Writing Effective Copy."

Body Copy Styles

Experienced copywriters look for the technique and style with the greatest sales appeal for the idea being presented. Common copy styles include _straight sell, institutional, narrative, dialogue/monologue, picture caption,_ and _device._

In **straight-sell copy,** writers immediately explain or develop the headline and visual in a straightforward, factual presentation. The straight-sell approach appeals to the prospect's reason. The Citibank print ads at the beginning of this chapter use a straight sell to describe its service. Although the topic of fraud can be emotional, the copy is reassuring because it presents hard facts and clear solutions. Because it ticks off the product's sales points in order of importance, straight-sell copy is particularly good for high think-involvement products or products that are difficult to use. It's very effective for direct-mail advertising and for industrial or high-tech products. Advertisers use the straight-sell approach more than all other techniques combined.[33]

Advertisers use **institutional copy** to promote a philosophy or extol the merits of an organization rather than product features. Institutional copy is intended to lend warmth and credibility to the organization's image. Banks, insurance companies, public corporations, and large manufacturing firms use institutional copy in both print and electronic media. However, David Ogilvy warned against the "self-serving, flatulent pomposity" that characterizes the copy in many corporate ads.[34]

Copywriters use **narrative copy** to tell a story. Ideal for the creative writer, narrative copy sets up a situation and then resolves it at the last minute by having the product or service come to the rescue. The Citibank headline ("It didn't seem right to us, either.") engages readers in dialogue and tells them that the company thinks the same way they do. Narrative copy offers good opportunities for emotional appeals. An insurance company, for example, might tell the poignant story of the man who died unexpectedly but, fortunately, had just renewed his policy.[35]

By using **dialogue/monologue copy,** the advertiser can add the believability that narrative copy sometimes lacks. The characters portrayed in a print ad do the selling in their own words. A caution: Poorly written dialogue copy can come off as dull or, even worse, hokey and unreal.

Sometimes it's easier to tell a story with illustrations and captions. A photo with **picture-caption copy** is especially useful for products that have a number of different uses or come in a variety of styles or designs.

With any copy style, the copywriter may use some device copy to enhance attention, interest, and memorability. **Device copy** uses figures of speech (such as puns, alliteration, assonance, and rhymes) as well as humor and exaggeration. Verbal devices help people remember the brand and tend to affect attitude favorably.[36]

Humor can be effective when the advertiser needs high memorability in a short time, wants to dispel preconceived negative images, or needs to create a distinct personality for an undifferentiated product. However, humor should always be used carefully and never be in questionable taste. Some researchers believe humor distracts from the selling message and can even be detrimental when used poorly or for serious services like finance, insurance, and crematoriums.[37]

Formatting Body Copy

The keys to good body copy are simplicity, order, credibility, and clarity. Or, as John O'Toole says, prose should be "written clearly, informatively, interestingly, powerfully, persuasively, dramatically, memorably, and with effortless grace. That's all."[38]

Four basic format elements are used to construct long copy ads: *the lead-in paragraph, interior paragraphs, trial close,* and *close.*

Lead-in paragraph   The **lead-in paragraph** is a bridge between the headline and the sales ideas presented in the text. Like a subhead, the lead-in paragraph is part of the *interest* step. It must be engaging and able to convert a prospect's reading interest to product interest.

Interior paragraphs   The **interior paragraphs** of the body copy should develop *credibility* by providing proof for claims and promises and they should build *desire* by using language that stirs the imagination. Advertisers should support their product promises with research data, testimonials, and warranties. Such proofs help avoid costly lawsuits, convince customers of the validity of the product, improve goodwill toward the advertiser, and stimulate sales.

Trial close   Interspersed in the interior paragraphs should be suggestions to *act* now. Good copy asks for the order more than once; mail-order ads ask several times. Consumers often make the buying decision without reading all the body copy. The **trial close** gives them the opportunity to make the buying decision early.

Close   The **close** is the real *action* step. A good close asks consumers to do something and tells them how. The close can be indirect or direct (a subtle suggestion or a direct command). A *direct close* seeks immediate response in the form of a purchase, a store or website visit, or a request for further information.

The close should simplify the audience's response, making it easy for them to order the merchandise, send for information, or visit a showroom or a website. A business reply card or a toll-free phone number may be included.

This ad for Parker Pens, which won a Bronze Lion at Cannes, uses succinct copy and simple visuals, but it is nevertheless very effective. What do you think accounts for its success?

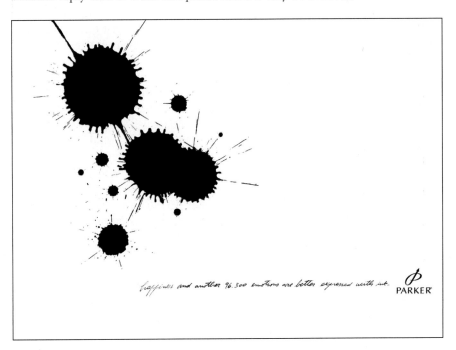

Of course, not all ads sell products or services. Advertisers may want to change attitudes, explain their viewpoints, or ask for someone's vote. By giving a website address, the advertiser can offer additional information to those readers who are interested in learning more at their leisure.

Slogans

Many **slogans** (also called **themelines** or **taglines**) begin as successful headlines, like AT&T's "Reach out and touch someone." Through continuous use, they become standard statements, not just in advertising but for salespeople and company employees.

Slogans have two basic purposes: to provide continuity to a series of ads in a campaign and to reduce an advertising message strategy to a brief, repeatable, and memorable positioning statement. Wheaties cereal, for example, positions itself as the "Breakfast of Champions." And ads for DeBeers still use the famous "Diamonds are forever" slogan. But Miller Lite's corny "It's it and that's that" was "major league pathetic," according to one *Wall Street Journal* article. Lacking the creativity, freshness, and power to become a full-fledged slogan, it was short-lived.[39]

Seals, Logos, and Signatures

A **seal** is awarded only when a product meets standards established by a particular organization, such as the Organic Crop Improvement Association, the Good Housekeeping Institute, Underwriters Laboratories, or Parents Institute. Because these organizations are recognized authorities, their seals provide an independent, valued endorsement for the advertiser's product.

Logotypes (*logos*) and **signature cuts** (*sig cuts*) are special designs of the advertiser's company or product name. They appear in all company ads and, like trademarks, give the product individuality and provide quick recognition at the point of purchase.

Copywriting for Electronic Media

For electronic media, the fundamental elements—the five steps of the creative pyramid—remain the primary guides, but the copywriting formats differ. Radio and television writers prepare *scripts* and *storyboards*.

Writing Radio Copy

A **script** resembles a two-column list. On the left side, speakers' names are arranged vertically, along with descriptions of any sound effects and music. The right column contains the dialogue, called the **audio.**

Copywriters first need to understand radio as a medium. Radio provides entertainment or news to listeners who are busy doing something else—driving, washing dishes, reading the paper, or even studying. To be heard, an advertising message must be catchy, interesting, and unforgettable. Radio listeners usually decide within five to eight seconds if they're going to pay attention. To attract and hold the attention of listeners, particularly those not attracted to a product category, radio copy must be intrusive.

Intrusive, yes; offensive, no. An insensitive choice of words, overzealous effort to attract listeners with irritating everyday sounds (car horn, alarm clock, screeching tires), or characters that sound too exotic, odd, or dumb can cause listener resentment and ultimately lose sales. Tom Bodett's often-imitated ads for Motel 6 demonstrate the effectiveness of a personal, relaxed, and natural style. Other guidelines are given in the Checklist, "Creating Effective Radio Commercials."

One of the most challenging aspects is making the script fit the time slot. The delivery changes for different types of commercials, so writers must read the script out loud for timing. With electronic compression, recorded radio ads can now include 10 to 30 percent more copy than text read live. Still, the following is a good rule of thumb:

10 seconds: 20–25 words.   30 seconds: 60–70 words.

20 seconds: 40–45 words.   60 seconds: 130–150 words.[40]

A radio script format resembles a two-column list, with speakers' names and sound effects on the left and the dialogue in a wider column on the right. This national public service announcement (PSR) was created by McCann-Erickson and is one of many in a campaign designed to inspire Americans to take small steps towards a healthier lifestyle.

Healthier America
Lost Campaign
Radio: 60
"Neighbor"
Expiration date: 2/23/05

SFX: Phone ringing

Bill:	Hello...?
George:	Hi, Bill? This is George Dewey from up the street.
Bill:	Hey, George. How ya doin?
George:	Good, good. Say, I noticed you've been walking to work these days instead of driving...and I, uh, don't quite know how to say this, but...but...
Bill:	But what?
George: (stammering)	But...But...Your butt, your buttocks, your butt—I think I found your butt on my front lawn. Have you recently lost it?
Bill:	As a matter of fact, I have, George (pleased) It's about time someone noticed.
George: (playful)	Well, it was kinda hard to miss if you know what I mean... ...Anyways, would you like it back?
Bill:	Would I like it back? No, not really.
George:	So, it's okay if I throw it out?
Bill:	Sure, that's fine. Take it easy, George.

SFX: Phone ringing

Announcer:	Small step #8—Walk instead of driving whenever you can. It's just one of the many small steps you can take to help you become a healthier, well, you. Get started at www.smallstep.gov and take a small step to get healthy.
Legal:	A public service announcement brought to you by the U.S. Department of Health and Human Services and the Ad Council.

Radio writing has to be clearer than any other kind of copywriting. For example, the listener can't refer back, as in print, to find an antecedent for a pronoun. Likewise, the English language is so full of homonyms (words that sound like other words) that one can easily confuse the meaning of a sentence ("who's who is whose").[41]

Writing Television Copy

Radio's basic two-column script format also works for television. But in a TV script, the left side is titled "Video" and the right side "Audio." The video column describes the visuals and production: camera angles, action, scenery, and stage directions. The audio column lists the spoken copy, sound effects, and music.

Broadcast commercials must be believable and relevant. And even zany commercials must exude quality in their creation and production to imply the product's quality. While the art director's work is very important, the copywriter typically sets the tone of the commercial, establishes the language that determines which visuals to use, and pinpoints when the visuals should appear. Research shows the techniques given in the Checklist, "Creating Effective TV Commercials" work best.

To illustrate these principles, let's look at a particular commercial. Many people want smooth, soft skin and consider a patch of rough, flaky skin anywhere on their body a disappointment. If you were the copywriter for Lubriderm skin lotion, how would you approach this somewhat touchy, negative subject?

Creating Effective Radio Commercials

___ **Make the big idea crystal clear.** Concentrate on one main selling point. Radio is a good medium for building brand awareness, but not for making long lists of copy points or complex arguments.

___ **Mention the advertiser's name early and often.** If the product or company name is tricky, consider spelling it out.

___ **Take time to set the scene and establish the premise.** A 30-second commercial that nobody remembers is a waste of money. Fight for 60-second spots.

___ **Use familiar sound effects.** Ice tinkling in a glass, birds chirping, or a door shutting can create a visual image. Music also works if its meaning is clear.

___ **Paint pictures with your words.** Use descriptive language to make the ad more memorable.

___ **Make every word count.** Use active voice and more verbs than adjectives. Be conversational. Use pronounceable words and short sentences.

___ **Be outrageous.** The best comic commercials begin with a totally absurd premise from which all developments follow logically. But remember, if you can't write humor really well, go for drama.

___ **Ask for the order.** Try to get listeners to take action.

___ **Remember that radio is a local medium.** Adjust your commercials to the language of your listeners and the time of day they'll run.

___ **Presentation counts a lot.** Even the best scripts look boring on paper. Acting, timing, vocal quirks, and sound effects bring them to life.

The creative staff of J. Walter Thompson crafted an artistic solution for Lubriderm. An alligator was the big idea. The gator's scaly sheath was a metaphor for rough, flaky skin. Its appearance ignited people's survival instincts; they paid attention, fast. A beautiful, sophisticated woman with smooth, feminine skin was seated in a lounge chair, completely unruffled by the passing gator. The swing of the animal's back and tail echoed the graceful curves of the two simple pieces of furniture on the set, and its slow stride kept the beat of a light jazz tune.

This commercial opened with an attention-getting big idea that was visually surprising, compelling, dramatic, and interesting. It was also a quasi-demonstration: we saw the alligator's scaly, prickly skin and the woman's confidence and willingness to touch the alligator as it passed by, which symbolized the confidence Lubriderm can bring.

This ad follows the creative pyramid. The alligator captures attention visually while the announcer's first words serve as an attention-getting headline: "A quick reminder." The ad commands us to listen and sets up the interest step that offers this claim: "Lubriderm restores lost moisture to heal your dry skin and protect it." Now for the credibility step: "Remember, the one created for dermatologists is the one that heals and protects." Then a quick trial close (action): "Lubriderm." And then the desire step recaps the primary product benefit and adds a touch of humor: "See you later, alligator."

The Role of Art in Radio and TV Advertising

According to *Advertising Age* columnist Bob Garfield, the best commercial in the world in 1997 was from Delvico Bates, Barcelona, for Esencial hand cream. The spot opens with a woman riding her bicycle to the persistent squeak of its unlubricated chain. She dismounts, opens a jar of Esencial, and rubs some of the cream onto the chain. Then she rides away—but the squeak is still there. Why? Because, as the voice-over points out, "Esencial moisturizes, but it has no grease."

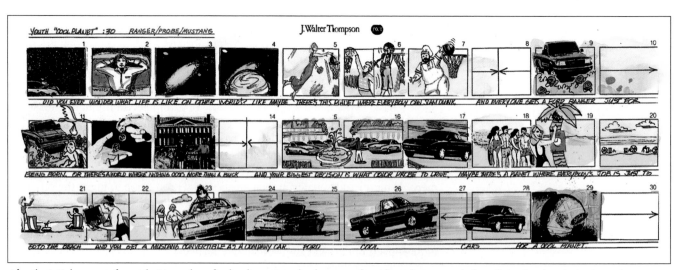

After the initial concepts for a television ad are finalized, creatives develop a storyboard rough composed of small sketches that depict the various scenes of the ad. The storyboard rough, including camera angles and script, is used to provide a visual guideline for shooting the various scenes during the final production phase.

Creating Effective TV Commercials

____ **Begin at the finish.** Concentrate on the final impression the commercial will make.

____ **Create an attention-getting opening.** An opening that is visually surprising or full of action, drama, humor, or human interest sets the context and allows a smooth transition to the rest of the commercial.

____ **Use a situation that grows naturally out of the sales story.** Avoid distracting gimmicks. Make it easy for viewers to identify with the characters.

____ **Characters are the living symbol of the product.** They should be appealing, believable, nondistracting, and most of all, relevant.

____ **Keep it simple.** The sequence of ideas should be easy to follow. Keep the number of elements in the commercial to a bare minimum.

____ **Write concise audio copy.** The video should carry most of the weight. Fewer than two words per second is effective for demonstrations. For a 60-second commercial, 101 to 110 words is most effective; more than 170 words is too talky.

____ **Make demonstrations dramatic but believable.** They should always be true to life and avoid the appearance of camera tricks.

____ **Let the words interpret the picture and prepare viewers for the next scene.** Use conversational language; avoid "ad talk," hype, and puffery.

____ **Run scenes five or six seconds on average.** Rarely should a scene run less than three seconds. Offer a variety of movement-filled scenes without "jumping."

____ **Keep the look of the video fresh and new.**

No big production. No digital effects. No jingle. No celebrity. No big comedy payoff. Just a pure advertising idea: a problem/resolution spot where the brand pointedly cannot solve the problem. It's a vivid demonstration of brand nonattributes. Inspired. Cunning. Brilliant.

Unfortunately, it did not win at the Cannes Lions festival because the agency missed the deadline.[42]

Developing the Artistic Concept for Commercials

Creating the concept for a radio or TV commercial is similar to creating the concept for print ads. The first step is to determine the big idea. Then the art director and copywriter must decide what commercial format to use. Should a celebrity present the message? Or should the ad dramatize the product's benefits (or deficiencies) with a semifictional story? The next step is to write a script containing the necessary copy or dialogue plus a basic description of any music, sound effects, and/or camera views.

In both radio and TV, the art director assists the copywriter in script development. But in television, artistic development is much more extensive. Using the TV script, the art director creates a series of **storyboard roughs** to present the artistic approach, the action sequences, and the style of the commercial. When the storyboard is approved, it serves as a guide for the final production phase.

Good casting is critical. The most important consideration is relevance to the product; agencies don't use a comic to sell financial products—or cremation services. And in spite of Michael Jordan's success for Nike, Gatorade, and McDonald's, some experts don't believe in using celebrities. David Ogilvy, for example, thought viewers remember the celebrity more than the product.[43] As the concept evolves, the creative team defines the characters' personalities in a detailed, written **casting brief.** These descriptions serve as guides in casting sessions when actors audition for the roles. Sometimes agencies discover new, unknown stars who evolve into solid, memorable characters and who go beyond the simple role by actually creating a personality or image for the product.

Formats for Radio and TV Commercials

Similar to print advertising, the format for a broadcast ad serves as a template for arranging message elements into a pattern. Once the art director and copywriter establish the big idea, they must determine the commercial's format.

Many radio and TV commercial styles have been successful. Some of these are listed in Ad Lab 13–B, "Creative Ways to Sell on Radio." Hank Seiden, the former chairman of Ketchum Advertising, developed the Execution Spectrum: 24 basic formats that range from frivolous to serious (see Exhibit 13–3). Here we consider

Product demo   The commercial tells how a product is used or the purposes it serves.

Voice power   A unique voice gives the ad power.

Electronic sound   Synthetic sound-making machines create a memorable product-sound association.

Customer interview   A spokesperson and customer discuss the product advantages spontaneously.

Humorous fake interview   The customer interview is done in a lighter vein.

Hyperbole (exaggeration) statement   Overstatement arouses interest in legitimate product claims that might otherwise pass unnoticed; often a spoof.

Fourth dimension   Time and events are compressed into a brief spot involving the listener in future projections.

Hot property   Commercial adapts a current sensation: a hit show, performer, or song.

Comedian power   Established comedians do commercials in their own unique style, implying celebrity endorsement.

Historical fantasy   Situation with revived historical characters is used to convey product message.

Sound picture   Recognizable sounds involve the listener by stimulating imagination.

Demographics   Music or references appeal to a particular segment of the population, such as an age or interest group.

Imagery transfer   Musical logo or other sound reinforces the memory of a TV campaign.

Celebrity interview   Famous person endorses the product in an informal manner.

Product song   Music and words combine to create a musical logo, selling the product in the style of popular music.

Editing genius   Many different situations, voices, types of music, and sounds are combined in a series of quick cuts.

Improvisation   Performers work out the dialogue extemporaneously for an assigned situation; may be postedited.

Laboratory Applications

1. Select three familiar radio commercials and discuss which creative techniques they use.

2. Select a familiar radio commercial and discuss how a different creative technique would increase its effectiveness.

---

eight common commercial formats that can be used in either radio or television: *straight announcement, presenter, testimonial, demonstration, musical, slice of life, lifestyle,* and *animation.*

Straight Announcement

The oldest and simplest type of radio or TV commercial and probably the easiest to write is the **straight announcement.** One person, usually a radio or TV announcer, delivers the sales message. Music may play in the background. Straight announcements are popular because they are adaptable to almost any product or situation. In radio, a straight announcement can also be designed as an **integrated commercial**—that is, it can be woven into a show or tailored to the style of a given program.

For TV, an announcer may deliver the sales message **on camera** or off screen, as a **voice-over,** while a demonstration, slide, or film shows on screen. If the script is well written and the announcer convincing, straight announcements can be very effective. Since they don't require elaborate production facilities, they save money, too.

Straight announcements are commonly used on late-night TV programs, by local advertisers, and by nonprofit or political organizations.

Presenter

The **presenter commercial** uses one person or character to present the product and carry the sales message. Some presenters are celebrities, such as Catherine Zeta-Jones for T-Mobile. Others may be corporate officers of the sponsor, such as William Clay Ford, Jr., who speaks for his company, or they may be actors playing a role (the lonely Maytag repairman). However, a presenter doesn't have to be a real person. Remember Tony the Tiger?

A **radio personality,** such as Rush Limbaugh or Larry King, may *ad lib* an ad message live in his or her

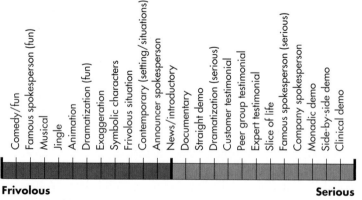

Frivolous   **Serious**

Exhibit 13–3

The Execution Spectrum, developed by Hank Seiden, shows 24 execution formats ranging in style from frivolous to serious, for both print and electronic advertising.

Advertisers often use presenter commercials to carry out their sales message. In this humorous example, Jack in the Box's spokesperson, Jack, threatens to air the awful show "Cat Chat" if people don't buy the featured sandwich.

"More Cat Chow" :30
(Open on Sue sitting on her living room floor giving one of her cats a pedicure)
Super: Sue Collister's "Cat Chat"

Sue: Yes, I like the dusty rose on you too . . . Oh . . . Hello, welcome back to "Cat Chat." Today we're having a spa day, so let's all be extra quiet.
(Reveal the room filled with cats. Cats are resting on their backs, cucumber slices over their eyes. This continues for about 10 seconds. It is silent and peaceful. Cut to Jack, sitting in his office. He means business.)

Jack: You thought I was bluffing? Try my new smokehouse bacon cheddar burger with grilled onions, barbecue sauce and melting cheese or it's gonna be a "Cat Chat" summer.
Super: Limited time only

(Cut back to all the cats sleeping)
Sue: Shhh. Evanka is in her happy place. Who's next for a mini-pedi?

(Bag drops)
Bag 1: Stop Cat Chat
Bag 2: New Smokehouse Bacon Cheddar Burger.
Super: Jack in the Box logo.

own style. Done well, such commercials can be very successful, as evidenced by the initial success of Snapple. However, the advertiser surrenders control to the personality. The main risk, outside of occasional blunders, is that the personality may criticize the product. Even so, this sometimes lends an appealing realism. The personality gets a highlight sheet listing the product's features, the main points to stress, and the phrases or company slogans to repeat. But he or she can choose the specific wording and mode of delivery.

Testimonial

The true **testimonial**—where a satisfied user tells how effective the product is—can be highly credible in both TV and radio advertising. Celebrities may gain attention, but they must be believable and not distract from the product. Actually, people from all walks of life endorse products, from known personalities to unknowns and nonprofessionals. Which type of person to use depends on the product and the strategy. Satisfied customers are the best sources for testimonials because their sincerity is usually persuasive. Ogilvy suggested shooting candid testimonials when the subjects don't know they're being filmed.[44] Of course, advertisers must be sure to get their permission before using the piece.

Demonstration

Television is uniquely suited to visual demonstration. And a **demonstration** convinces an audience better and faster than a spoken message. So don't say it, show it.[45] Naturally, it's easier to demonstrate the product on TV than on radio, but some advertisers have used the imaginative nature of radio to create humorous, tongue-in-cheek demonstrations.

Products may be demonstrated in use, in competition, or before and after. These techniques help viewers visualize how the product will perform for them.

Musical

The **musical commercials,** or **jingles,** we hear on radio and TV are among the best—and worst—ad messages produced. Done well, they can bring enormous success, well beyond the average nonmusical commercial. Done poorly, they can waste the advertising budget and annoy audiences beyond belief.

Musical commercials have several variations. The entire message may be sung; jingles may be written with a **donut** in the middle (a hole for spoken copy); or orchestras may play symphonic or popular arrangements. Many producers use consistent musical themes for background color or to close the commercial. An example is the Rolling Stones' "Jumping Jack Flash," used in commercials for Corvettes. This is called a **musical logo.** After many repetitions of the advertiser's theme, the listener begins to associate the musical logo with the product. To achieve this, the jingle should have a **hook**—that part of the song that sticks in your memory.[46]

Advertisers have three sources of music. They can buy the right to use a tune from the copyright owner, which is usually expensive. They can use a melody in the public domain, which is free. Or they can hire a composer to write an original song. Some original tunes, including Coke's famous "I'd like to teach the world to sing," have become hits.

Slice of Life (Problem Solution)

Commercials that dramatize real-life situations are called **slice of life.** It usually starts with just plain folks, played by professional actors, discussing some problem or issue. Often the situation deals with a problem of a personal nature: bad breath, loose dentures, dandruff, body odor, or yellow laundry. A relative or a co-worker drops the hint, the product is tried, and the next scene shows the result—a hap-

Ads that appeal to lifestyle present the type of user associated with the product, rather than the product itself. This ad for MasterCard is aimed at sports fans, and specifically Boston Red Sox fans, who are willing to do just about anything for their team.

VO: Red Sox World Series tickets
Baseball enthusiast #1: Five hundred bucks.
Man Waiting In Line: I'd pay four grand.
Weightlifter: My car. My truck. My computer.
Girl #1: Two months salary.
Weightlifter: . . . my entire savings account.

Man With Painted Face: Anything, anything.
Little Boy: My fish.
Young Woman: My dog.
Weightlifter: My girlfriend.

Fan at Ballpark: My first born kid.
Girl #3: Really.
VO/Super: Seeing the Red Sox in the World Series: Priceless.

VO/Super: There are some things money can't buy.
VO/Super: For everything else there's MasterCard.
VO/Super: Devoted fan of the devoted fans.

pier, cleaner, more fragrant person off with a new date. The drama always concludes with a successful trial. Such commercials can get attention and create interest, even though they are often irritating to viewers and hated by copywriters.

The key to effective slice-of-life commercials is simplicity. The ad should concentrate on one product benefit and make it memorable. Often a **mnemonic device** can dramatize the product benefit and trigger instant recall. Users of Imperial margarine, for example, suddenly discover crowns on their heads.

Believability in slice-of-life commercials is difficult to achieve. People don't really talk about "the sophisticated taste of Taster's Choice," so the actors must be highly credible to put the fantasy across. That's why most *local* advertisers don't use the slice-of-life technique. Creating that believability takes very professional talent and money. In all cases, the story should be relevant to the product and simply told.

Lifestyle

To present the user rather than the product, advertisers may use the **lifestyle technique.** For example, Diesel pitches its denim to urbanites by showing characters working and playing while wearing its latest line. Likewise, beer and soft-drink advertisers frequently target their messages to active, outdoorsy young people, focusing on who drinks the brand rather than on specific product advantages.

Animation

Cartoons, puppet characters, and demonstrations with computer-generated graphics are very effective **animation** techniques for communicating difficult messages and reaching specialized markets, such as children. The way aspirin or other medications affect the human system is difficult to explain. Animated pictures of headaches and stomachs can simplify the subject and make a demonstration clear and understandable.

Computer animation requires a great deal of faith on the part of advertisers. Since most of this very expensive work is done on the computer, there's nothing to see until the animation is well developed and a good bit of money has been spent (this is more fully discussed in Chapter 14).

Basic Mechanics of Storyboard Development

After the creative team selects the big idea and the format for a TV commercial, the art director and the writer develop the script. Television is so visually powerful and expressive that the art director's role is particularly important. Art directors must be able to work with a variety of professionals—producers, directors, lighting technicians, and set designers—to develop and produce a commercial successfully.

Storyboard Design

Once the basic script is completed, the art director must turn the video portion of the script into real images. This is done with a **storyboard,** a sheet preprinted with a series of 8 to 20 blank windows (frames) in the shape of TV screens. Below each frame is room to place the text of the commercial, including the sound effects and camera views as abbreviated in Exhibit 13–4. The storyboard works much like a cartoon strip.

Through a process similar to laying out a print ad (thumbnail, rough, comp) the artist carefully designs how each scene should appear, arranging actors, scenery, props, lighting, and camera angles to maximize impact, beauty, and mood. The storyboard helps the creatives visualize the commercial's tone and sequence of action, discover any conceptual weaknesses, and make presentations for management approval. It also serves as a guide for filming.

Even when designed to the level of a comp, though, the storyboard is only an approximation of the final commercial. Actual production often results in many changes in lighting, camera angle, focal point, and emphasis. The camera sees many things that the artist couldn't visualize, and vice versa (see Chapter 14 for more details on working with storyboards).

Exhibit 13–4

Common abbreviations used in TV scripts.

CU: Close-up. Very close shot of person or object.
ECU: Extreme close-up. A more extreme version of the above. Sometimes designated BCU (big close-up) or TCU (tight close-up).
MCU: Medium close-up. Emphasizes the subject but includes other objects nearby.
MS: Medium shot. Wide-angle shot of subject but not whole set.
FS: Full shot. Entire set or object.
LS: Long shot. Full view of scene to give effect of distance.
DOLLY: Move camera toward or away from subject. Dolly in (DI), dolly out (DO), or dolly back (DB).
PAN: Scan from one side to the other.
ZOOM: Move in or out from the subject without blurring.
SUPER: Superimpose one image on another (as showing lettering over a scene).
DISS: Dissolve (also DSS). Fade out one scene while fading in another.
CUT: Instantly change one picture to another.
WIPE: Gradually erase picture from screen. (Many varied effects are possible.)
VO: Voice-over. An off-screen voice, usually the announcer's.
SFX: Sound effects.
DAU: Down and under. Sound effects fade as voice comes on.
UAO: Up and over. Voice fades as sound effects come on.

Animatic: The Video Comp

To supplement the storyboard or pretest a concept, a commercial may be taped in rough form using the writers and artists as actors. Or an **animatic** may be shot—a film strip of the sketches in the storyboard accompanied by the audio portion of the commercial synchronized on tape. Even a standard animatic now costs more than $10,000 to produce. But computers are cutting costs. Avid Technologies, for example, developed a Macintosh-based editing system that lets the agency create moving pictures on the screen, lay sound behind them, and transfer the entire package onto videotape to send to the client. This system cuts the cost to produce testable material from about $11,000 to $1,100. This kind of technology is being adopted by many agencies as they look for ways to serve clients' creative needs better for less money.

Upon approval of the storyboard and/or the animatic, the commercial is ready for production, a subject we cover in detail in Chapter 14.

Writing for the Web

The Internet is a whole new medium for communication, and many advertising people are still learning how to use it. This is an important issue since Web users are both savvy and skeptical as well as influential.

According to research by Burson-Marsteller, a large New York public relations firm, there are 11 million heavy online users in the United States, and their opinions affect the buying decisions of 155 million consumers both online and off. Burson-Marsteller refers to these opinion leaders as e-fluentials.

"An e-fluential is the rock that starts the ripple," said Chet Burchett, president and chief executive officer, Burson-Marsteller USA. "Each one communicates with an average of 14 people." E-fluentials can be reputation builders or busters.[47]

Interestingly, Burson-Marsteller's research found that, across a wide variety of sectors—technology, retail, finance, pharmaceutical, and automotive—90 percent of e-fluentials use company websites to verify advertising information, but only 20 percent report that they find the corporate websites credible.

So writing effectively for the Web is critical. Company websites that provide e-fluentials with straightforward, easy-to-use information are crucial to building and enhancing brand value.

Reid Goldsborough, a widely syndicated technology columnist and former advertising copywriter, maintains that although image is everything in traditional advertising, on the Web content is king. He points to research showing that, unlike readers of newspapers and magazines, people using the Web typically focus on the text first, looking at photos and graphics later. In other words, the words are most important. The words connote substance, and substance triumphs over style.

Second, people don't really read a website. They scan it, so the information presented must be at once concise and comprehensive. Numbered lists and bulleted items thus can be used more than in print media. Rather than scanning down the page like newspaper readers, Web users just read the first text screen of any site and then move on. But if they like what they see, then they will want more, and they will stay on the site to search for more information. Having fewer space limitations than any other medium, the Web is ideal for in-depth elaboration. But dumping screen after screen of text on a website is, according to Goldsborough, reader abuse.

A study measuring the usefulness of websites found that a sample website scored 58 percent higher when it was written concisely, 47 percent higher when the text was scannable, and 27 percent higher when it was written in an objective rather than promotional style. When these three characteristics were combined in a single site, the result was 124 percent higher usefulness.[48]

Web pages need to be sectioned and organized, but not overly subdivided. That frustrates readers. Offering important links to other sections or to other sites is helpful. But, Goldsborough cautions, be sure that links to other sites are current.

Web users are generally sophisticated; they avoid hype and puffery like the plague. So while a company should put its best foot forward, bragging and boasting will just put readers off.[49]

Finally, websites should always offer interactivity—a way for the reader to respond, either through e-mail or Web response forms. The Web is about interactivity. Company's that waste that feature are wasting their money.

Creating Ads for International Markets

In international markets, the most important consideration for copywriters and creative directors is language. In western Europe, people speak at least 15 different languages and more than twice as many dialects. A similar problem exists in Asia, Africa, and, to a lesser extent, South America.

International advertisers have debated the transferability of campaigns for years. One side believes it's too expensive to create a unique campaign for each national group. They simply translate one overall campaign into each language. Another method is to think globally but act locally, creating ads in various languages and reflecting the needs of different groups, but maintaining a consistent theme worldwide. Other advertisers believe the only way to ensure success is to create a special campaign for each market. Citigroup uses a variation of this approach. With branches in 100 countries, the financial service giant adapts its ads and products to the needs of each market. For example, the large Indian population working abroad can open checking accounts in rupees instead of the local currency; family members back home can access the accounts via 250 Citibank ATMs in 28 cities in India, avoiding the steep fees usually associated with transferring money. Some advertisers find such solutions expensive and unnecessary. They run their ads in English worldwide, promoting their products generically rather than specifically.

Advertisers must address their unique situations. Moreover, they have to weigh the economics of various promotional strategies.

Translating Copy

Regardless of strategy, translation remains a basic issue. Classic examples of mistranslations and faulty word choices abound in international advertising. A faulty Spanish translation for Perdue chickens reads "It takes a sexually excited man to make a chick affectionate" instead of "It takes a tough man to make a tender chicken."[50]

A poorly chosen or badly translated product name can undercut advertising credibility in foreign markets. A classic case was when Coke's product name was widely translated into Chinese characters that sounded like "Coca-Cola" but meant "bite the wax tadpole."[51]

People in the United States, Canada, England, Australia, and South Africa all speak English, but with wide variations in vocabulary, word usage, and syntax. Similarly, the French spoken in France, Canada, Vietnam, and Belgium may differ as much as the English spoken by a British aristocrat and a Tennessee mountaineer.

Global advertisers often use a single basic ad, translating it into the languages of the various countries where it will run.

Language variations exist even within countries. The Japanese use five lingual "gears," ranging from haughty to servile, depending on the speaker's and the listener's respective stations in life. Japanese translators must know when to change gears.

Advertisers should follow some basic rules in using translators:

- *The translator must be an effective copywriter.* In the United States and Canada, most people speak English, yet relatively few are good writers and even fewer are good copywriters. Too often advertisers simply let a translation service rewrite their ads in a foreign language. That's not good enough.

- *The translator must understand the product.* The translator must also know the product's features and its market. It is always better to use a translator who is a product or market specialist rather than a generalist.

- *Translators should translate into their native tongue.* Ideally, they should live in the country where the ad will appear. This way the advertiser can be sure the translator has a current understanding of the country's social attitudes, culture, and idioms.

- *The advertiser should give the translator easily translatable English copy.* The double meanings and idiomatic expressions that make English such a rich language for advertising rarely translate well. They only make the translator's job more difficult.

There is no greater insult to a national market than to misuse its language. The translation must be accurate and punctuated properly, and it must also be good copy.

English is rapidly becoming the universal language for corporate ad campaigns directed to international businesspeople, and some firms print their instructional literature and brochures in English as well. But this approach can incite nationalistic feelings against the company. Worse yet, it automatically limits a product's use to people who understand technical English.[52]

Art Direction for International Markets

Philosophers often refer to the arts as a kind of international language whose nonverbal elements translate freely regardless of culture. A nice idea but, in advertising, a very costly one. People ascribe different meanings to color depending on their culture. When designing ads for use in other countries, the art director must be familiar with each country's artistic preferences and peculiarities.

Some consider color to indicate emotion: someone "has the blues" or is "green with envy" (refer back to Ad Lab 12–A, "The Psychological Impact of Color"). National flags—the Canadian maple leaf, the red, white, and blue of the United States, the tricolor of France—are nonverbal signals that stir patriotic emotions, thoughts, and actions. However, these same symbols could hurt sales. For example, a promotion using the colors in the U.S. and French flags could easily fail in Southeast Asia, where some people still have painful memories of wars fought against the two countries.

An **icon,** a visual image representing some idea or thing, can have a meaning that cuts across national boundaries and reflects the tastes and attitudes of a group of cultures. An ad with a snake (an icon for the devil and eroticism in many Western cultures) could easily lose sales in North American markets. But in the Far East, where the snake represents renewal (by shedding its skin), the same visual might work as a dynamic expression of a product's staying power.

On a more personal level, a culture's icons can express social roles. When an agency calls a casting company or talent agent in search of a model, the agency, in essence, seeks an icon. It hopes the model will effectively symbolize the product's benefits or help the target market relate better to the ad. A model considered attractive in one culture is not necessarily seen that way in another, however.

Catchy phrases popular in a local culture are often used for advertising. But even if the idea translates verbally into another language, which is rarely the case, the art director may still have difficulty using the same imagery. Advertisers working in global markets must pretest art and design concepts with natives of each country.

When preparing an ad for an international market, the art director must be sure that the language and imagery will not offend or alienate the target audience. Cultural differences and preferences make it essential that ad copy and visuals (icons or models) are in sync with the taste of the potential readers. In this ad for Nike, the visuals are enough to deliver the idea that one doesn't need to be seven feet tall to play basketball.

Legal Restraints on International Advertisers

Finally, all advertising creativity, including what the ads say, show, or do, is at the mercy of foreign governments and cultures. As we discussed in Chapter 3, many countries strongly regulate advertising claims and the use of particular media.

Chapter Summary

The nonverbal aspect of an ad or commercial carries half the burden of communicating the big idea. In fact, the nonverbal message is inseparable from the verbal. Either can enhance the other or destroy it.

Design refers to how the art director and graphic artist conceptually choose and structure the artistic elements that make up an ad's appearance or set its tone. For print advertising, the first work from the art department is a simple, undeveloped design of the ad's layout. The layout has several purposes: It shows where the parts of the ad are to be placed; it is an inexpensive way to explore creative ideas; it helps the creative team check the ad's psychological or symbolic function; and it serves as a blueprint for the production process.

As advertising copy goes through the editing process, copywriters must be prepared for an inevitable (and sometimes lengthy) succession of edits and reedits from agency and client managers and legal departments. Copywriters must be more than creative; they must be patient, flexible, mature, and able to exercise great self-control.

Several steps are used to develop an ad's design: thumbnail sketch, rough layout, and comprehensive layout. The mechanical is the final art ready for reproduction. Brochures and other multipage materials use a three-dimensional rough called a dummy.

The computer has dramatically affected graphic design. Various PC software programs allow artists to paint and draw, make up pages, and manipulate images in ways that would not be possible manually. Every graphic designer must now be computer literate.

In print advertising, the visual has a great deal of responsibility for an ad's success. The picture may be used to capture the reader's attention, identify the subject of the ad, create a favorable impression, or serve a host of other functions.

The two basic devices for illustrating an ad are photos and drawings. Photography can contribute realism; a feeling of immediacy; a feeling of live action; the special enhancement of mood, beauty, and sensitivity; and speed, flexibility, and economy. Drawn illustrations do many of these things, too, and may be used if the artist feels they can achieve greater impact than photos. The chief focus for visuals may be the product in a variety of settings, a user benefit, a humorous situation, a testimonial, or even some negative appeal.

The key format elements for writing print ads are headlines, subheads, body copy, slogans, seals, logos, and signatures. Many headline types and copy styles are used in print advertising. There are five basic types of advertising headlines: benefit, provocative, news/information, question, and command. Copy styles also fall into several categories: straight sell, institutional, narrative, dialogue/monologue, picture caption, and device.

The creative pyramid and the format elements come together in creating effective print ads. The headline carries the attention step, the subhead and lead-in paragraph hold the interest step, and the interior paragraphs, trial close, and close of body copy contain the credibility and desire steps. The action step takes place with the last line of copy or with the logo, slogan, and signature block.

In electronic media, copy is normally spoken dialogue that is prepared using a script; it is referred to as the audio portion of the commercial. The copy may be delivered as a voice-over by an unseen announcer or on camera by an announcer, spokesperson, or actor.

Radio commercials must be intrusive to catch and hold the attention of people who are usually doing something else. Radio copy must be more conversational than print copy and should paint word pictures for listeners to see in their mind's eye.

Television copywriters use scripts and storyboards to communicate the verbal and nonverbal ideas of a commercial. When writing TV ads, the creative team must strive for credibility, relevance, and consistency in tone. While TV commercials should be entertaining, the entertainment should not interfere with the selling message.

In radio and TV advertising, art plays an important role. Art includes concept development, character definition, set and scene design, costuming, lighting, scripting, camera angles—everything having to do with the visual value of the commercial.

Common formats for radio and TV commercials include straight announcement, presenter, testimonial, demonstration, musical, slice of life, lifestyle, and animation. The art director works with a writer to develop the artistic qualities of the big idea, the format, and the storyboard. The storyboard, the basic rough design of a TV commercial, contains sketches of the scenes along with the script. To supplement the storyboard and pretest a commercial, an animatic may be used.

When creating ads for international markets, advertisers must consider the variations in language and the legal restrictions imposed by foreign governments or cultures. Art direction for international markets requires an in-depth knowledge of the foreign culture. Even if the verbal message translates well, the icons and images may not.

Important Terms

animatic, *432*

animation, *431*

audio, *424*

Ayer No. 1, *411*

benefit headline, *420*

body copy, *421*

boldface, *421*

camera-ready art, *409*

casting brief, *427*

close, *423*

command headline, *420*

comprehensive layout (comp), *408*

demonstration, *430*

design, *406*

device copy, *422*

dialogue/monologue copy, *422*

donut, *430*

headline, *417*

hook, *430*

icon, *435*

illustrator, *411*

institutional copy, *422*

integrated commercial, *428*

interior paragraph, *423*

italic, *421*

jingle, *430*

kicker, *421*

layout, *407*

lead-in paragraph, *423*

lifestyle technique, *431*

logotype, *424*

mechanical, *409*

mnemonic device, *431*

musical commercial, *430*

musical logo, *430*

narrative copy, *422*

news/information headline, *420*

on camera, *428*

pasteup, *409*

photographer, *411*

picture-caption copy, *422*

picture-window layout, *410*

poster-style format, *410*

presenter commercial, *428*

provocative headline, *420*

question headline, *420*

radio personality, *428*

script, *424*

seal, *424*

signature cut, *424*

slice of life, *430*

slogan, *424*

storyboard, *431*

storyboard rough, *427*

straight announcement, *428*

straight-sell copy, *422*

subhead, *421*

tagline, *424*

testimonial, *429*

text, *421*

themeline, *424*

thumbnail, *408*

trial close, *423*

visuals, *411*

voice-over, *428*

Review Questions

1. What is a layout? What is its purpose?
2. What are the steps in the design process for a print ad?
3. What color is white space?
4. From any chapter in the book, select an ad that contains a visual. What is the visual's purpose? How would you improve the visual if you were the art director?
5. What kind of headline does the ad from question 4 have? How well has the creative team followed the steps up the creative pyramid? Explain.
6. Choose an ad you don't like. Rewrite the headline using three different styles.
7. What is a storyboard, and what is its role?
8. Give examples of television spots that typify the eight major types of TV commercials.
9. Find an international ad or commercial you like. What is its message strategy? Can you discern the copy style? Do you think the copy and headline reflect the strategy? What do you like about the ad? Why?
10. What guidelines can you cite for preparing an ad in a foreign language?
11. **The Advertising Experience**
Big Stan's Tri-State Mattress Outlet usually advertises by sponsoring monster-truck shows or demolition derbies. However, Big Stan wants to expand his business and has decided to try radio advertising. Using the script format found on page 425, create the kind of radio ad that would please Big Stan and his potential customers.

Exploring the Internet

The Internet exercises for Chapter 13 address the following areas related to the chapter: creative boutiques (Exercise 1), copywriting and art direction (Exercise 2), and visually appealing design (Exercise 3).

1. **Creative Boutiques**
One of the growing trends in advertising is the increased use of creative boutiques. Many of these smaller shops have won clients previously handled by larger, full-service advertising agencies. Peruse the small sampling of creative boutiques below and answer the questions that follow.

   - AdWorks www.adworks.com
   - Bertha Communications www.bertha.com
   - B Creative www.bcreative.com
   - JDG Designs www.jdgdesign.com
   - Jan Collier Represents Online www.collierreps.com
   - The Unknown Ad Guys www.hometownsportspromo.com
   - Virtual Access www.virtualaccesscorp.com

   a. What is the focus of the company's work (consumer, business-to-business, ethnic, general market)?
   b. What are the scope and size of the company's business?
   c. What services does the company offer?
   d. What is your overall impression of the company and its work? Why?

2. **Creative Resources**
As you saw in this chapter with Citibank, a lot goes into writing good copy or scripts and developing effective visuals. With the Internet, many new resources are available to the creative team when developing their concept.

   Copywriters often rely on different sources to aid them in developing their copy. Visit the following websites and explain how each relates to copywriters and their task of developing effective copy.

   - Copy Chef www.copychef.com
   - The Slot www.theslot.com
   - Writers Guild of America www.wga.org

   Like copywriters, art directors require many resources while developing their art. Familiarize yourself further with art direction by browsing the following websites. Be sure to discuss the importance of each to art directors.

   - American Institute of Graphic Arts www.aiga.org
   - Art Directors Club www.adcglobal.org
   - Creative Cafe www.creativity.net
   - Design & Publishing Center www.graphic-design.com
   - Digital Directory www.digitaldirectory.com
   - Gnomon Online www.gnomononline.com
   - PhotoDisc www.photodisc.com
   - Photographer's Index www.photographersindex.com
   - Portfolios Online www.portfolios.com
   - Right Brain Works www.gocreate.com

3. **Creating a Business Website**
Websites can be a powerful marketing tool, but many small-business owners either have no website or have one that is woefully inadequate. Create or update a website for a small business in your area, using what you have learned about design elements to ensure that the site is visually appealing as well as functional.

Chapter 14

Producing Ads for Print, Electronic, and Digital Media

Objectives TO PRESENT AN OVERVIEW OF HOW ADS AND COMMERCIALS ARE PRODUCED for print, electronic, and digital media. With their dynamic effect on the production process, computers now give advertisers many more options for saving money and time and enhancing production quality. But to control cost and quality, advertisers still need a basic knowledge of the processes and methods used in printing and broadcasting as well as in the new digital media.

After studying this chapter, you will be able to:

- **Discuss** the role of computers in the print production process.

- **Explain** the development process for ads and brochures from initial concept through final production.

- **Discuss** how materials for printing are prepared for the press.

- **Explain** the development process for radio and TV commercials from initial concept through final production.

- **Describe** the major types of TV commercials.

- **Understand** how to save money in radio and television production.

- **Discuss** the opportunities for special effects in television.

- **Explain** how the major types of digital media are useful to advertisers.

For a client as big and powerful as Toyota, choosing an agency to collaborate with on a global campaign for its brand-new, technologically superior hybrid car was a monumental project unto itself. Hundreds of agencies would have loved to handle the account, but the competition was limited to the client's roster agencies, meaning that bidding was open only to firms that already worked for Toyota. ■ That meant that the offices of Saatchi & Saatchi, which has more than 100 branches in 85 countries, and a handful of other agencies around the world would be competing for the account. Saatchi & Saatchi looked like the favorite, but the question was which office would be assigned the responsibility of creating and overseeing the project. ■ In offices around the world, teams of copywriters and creative directors produced and discarded countless concepts. Finally, each agency selected one or several of their best ideas. They presented their work to the client and then crossed their fingers. ■ What we're talking about is the global introduction of the Toyota Prius, an ecologically friendly car that drives like any other but is powered by a unique hybrid engine that uses both gasoline and electricity. It boasts a fuel economy of 55 miles per gallon, more than double that of most other cars. The account was to be handled out of Japan, but almost every one of Toyota's agencies across the globe was bidding for the opportunity. And why not? The winning agency would produce local and international print ads and create and develop a global TV spot—one that would be translated into dozens of different languages and aired all over the world. ■ Saatchi & Saatchi Los Angeles already handled U.S. advertising for Toyota, a major American account. In fact, it was the largest advertising account west of the Mississippi River. Naturally, the agency wanted the assignment, but it wasn't a slam-dunk. It was up against some of the biggest agencies in the world and was even forced to compete with many of their own offices, some of which—London, Paris, New York—were famous for their outstanding creativity. ■ It didn't hurt that the Prius was the kind of car the agency could really get behind. With little to no advertising, the previous limited-production model had already become the leader in its field. Equipped with Bluetooth technology, low emission rates, and fantastic fuel economy, this sleek hybrid was already a favorite among environmentally conscious consumers and the Hollywood set. Now that Toyota was rolling the car out globally, Saatchi knew that to win the campaign it would have to speak to a new aspect of the market. ■ There were ample challenges. Saatchi wanted to create a campaign for the Prius that would be broad enough to appeal to a wide audience, regardless of national and cultural differences, but that would still be specific enough to truly speak to the buyer. Two creative directors, Max Godsil and Doug Van Andel, were assigned the project in Los Angeles. They spent hours, days, and weeks reviewing the research and analyzing the markets. They started developing ideas, and more ideas, and then even more. After about 30 tries, they hit upon a concept that was complex but friendly, futuristic but warm, and clean without being clinical. ■ They brought their concept to Saatchi's senior creative director, Steve Rabosky, and he concurred. They were confident that this was the idea that would win the account, and they were right. Toyota Japan awarded the global introduction of the Prius to Saatchi & Saatchi Los Angeles.[1] ■ A few months later, when Toyota asked them to cut back on the advertising, they knew for certain that they had done something right. There simply weren't enough cars to meet the growing demand. In this chapter, we'll see what they did and study how they did it. ■

Managing the Advertising Production Process

The average reader has little idea of the intricate technical stages that ads go through from start to finish. But experienced advertising people do, especially art directors, designers, print production managers, and producers. They know it's the details that give an ad added impact and completeness. Since careful management is the key to success in producing advertising, we'll discuss some of the management issues before examining the details of the production processes.

While a national-quality ad like this one for Toyota's Prius may require only 15 seconds to read, what most people don't realize is that, from initial concept to completion, an ad of this caliber may require three weeks to a month, or even longer, to create. As ideas are born and discarded and then meticulously crafted into a finished work, an advertisement passes through many hands before it is finally ready to make its first public appearance.

The Role of the Production Manager or Producer

Every ad or commercial represents the completion of a highly complex process that includes many steps, such as the reproduction of visuals in full color, the shooting and editing of scenes, the precise specification and placement of type, and the checking, approving, duplicating, and shipping of final art, negatives, tape, or film to various communications media (newspapers, magazines, radio and TV stations, and even Web publishers).

These tasks are usually the responsibility of a **print production manager** or, for electronic media, a **producer** (at Saatchi & Saatchi, they're all called producers). The overall responsibility of this manager is to keep the project moving smoothly and under budget, while maintaining the required level of quality through every step of the production process.

Essentially, production managers and producers perform the four classic functions of management: *planning, organizing, directing,* and *controlling.* At Saatchi, for example, Johanna Leovey was the print producer. Her job was to review

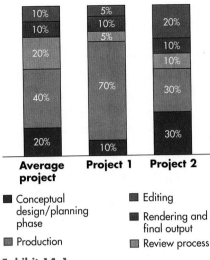

Exhibit 14–1

Time allocation comparison. All projects are different, and thus the amount of time needed for each phase of a project may vary widely. Although about 40 percent of the time spent on an average project may be production hours, other projects might involve more production time (Project 1) or less production time (Project 2).

the conceptual art and then *plan* which production process to use to fulfill each requirement. Next she *organized* the tasks and established priorities in order to meet the client's media schedule. She then *directed* the production staff in completing each section of the art. Finally, to perform the *control* function—essential for optimizing quality, economy, and speed—she carefully reviewed the work of each staffer and subcontractor and solicited feedback from her supervisor and the art director, just to be sure they were all on the same track. Supervising Johanna was Lorraine Alper Kramer, Saatchi's director of print services.

Planning and Organizing

An important facet of management is the *allocation of time*. Each phase of a project comprises many tasks, so the production manager must anticipate where irregularities may occur within each phase. For example, five phases are needed to complete one animated commercial, but the amount of time required for each may vary greatly from spot to spot, as shown in Exhibit 14–1.[2]

Directing and Controlling

Supervising the production staff and suppliers is another challenge. If artists fail to follow the art director's design correctly, they can kill an ad's power, beauty, and effectiveness. Improper printing processes, papers, or inks can also weaken the impact of the image, increase costs, and even lead to time-consuming reprinting. Print production managers can lose tens of thousands of their client's or agency's dollars (and sometimes their jobs) by forgetting to double-check the details of print production and the work of the production staff.

Lorraine points out that the producer also has to keep up with all the technological changes occurring in print and electronic production, including the emerging forms of *digital media* (multimedia, interactive media, and online networks). And because virtually all ad agency employees now use computers, the manager must also understand how computers serve the production process and which software programs offer the best results.[3]

Managing Production Costs

When Saatchi began working on the Prius campaign, it submitted an estimate for anticipated production costs, including computer artwork and subcontracted work such as photography, reproduction services, and delivery. When Johanna Leovey received the approved ad concepts a couple of weeks later, it was understood that she would make every effort to keep the actual costs below the estimate.

A good production manager continually monitors the time spent on a job and the charges submitted by outside suppliers so as to not exceed the budget. The big effort is to control *unplanned costs.*

Common Budget Busters

There are five problems that commonly break budgets. The most frequent cause of cost overruns is *inadequate planning* and lack of preparation. Another culprit is *production luxuries.* When the creative director wants to reward the staff by taking everyone to lunch at the company's expense, the first question should be: Was money budgeted for this? The third budget buster is *overtime:* night and weekend work. Whenever possible, managers should develop alternative plans to avoid overtime hours. *Special equipment* for unusual production effects can also wreak havoc on budgets. It's often far more expensive to use an exotic computer gizmo than standard equipment. Finally, a complex *hierarchy* of decision makers, approvers, and lawyers can stall decision making, cause negative debate, and stop progress.

International advertisers should also be aware that foreign taxation on production costs varies widely from country to country. Argentina, for instance, charges a blanket 21 percent VAT (value-added tax) on all production costs as well as on media-buying commissions. In 1996 it imposed a further 10.5 percent tax on all media placements.[4]

Some other budget issues are peculiar to each medium.

Managing the Cost of Print Production

The term *print production* refers to the systematic process an approved design goes through from concept to final publication in a printed medium such as magazines, newspapers, or collateral materials like brochures and direct-mail packages.

For print media, production managers can choose from more than 60 techniques to execute the creative team's design and get it printed on any of a variety of materials (usually paper).[5] They must translate the rough or comprehensive design into a final assembly of black-and-white artwork called a *mechanical* or *pasteup*. Then, working with an engraver or printer, they make sure the mechanical is converted into a correct set of negatives for the printer to use to make printing plates. We'll discuss this process in detail shortly.

A big cost factor in the production of many print ads is the *engraver* that provides all the color separations, retouching, press proofs, and digital files. Many production managers prefer using their printer to provide all the *prepress graphic services* (such as processing negatives from artwork or disk). Most printers today offer digital graphic services in-house, and they know exactly which processing specifications yield the most suitable negatives for their platemaking equipment and printing presses. They also often charge less than outside service bureaus. Other production managers feel safer ordering the negatives from a high-quality engraver because it typically offers highly specialized service, personnel skilled at color reproduction, and the expertise to deliver the right materials correctly and on time to media across the country. Plus, the production manager and the art director can proof any negatives or press proofs before the printer mounts them for platemaking.

Paper costs affect budgets, too. When agencies place ads in print media, the cost of paper is included in the charge for the ad. They don't notice this pass-along cost. But when an agency prints collateral materials such as data sheets, brochures, or packaging for a client, the cost of paper is noticeable. For example, on a full-color job, a short run of 2,000 units would require only a few thousand sheets of paper (a variable cost), while the prepress and press set-up charges (fixed costs) would comprise the bulk of the final selling price. But if the same job had a long run of 100,000 or more units, the prepress and press setup charges would remain the same, while the cost for paper would rise according to the volume used—a cost increase of 700 to 1,000 percent. Thus, paper costs could greatly outweigh press costs.

For the Prius campaign, Saatchi assembled a teaser promo to send to car shows and dealers, designed to create interested in the Prius before the rest of the promotional material came out. It was encased in an elegant, origami-style pocket made of vellum paper. Among other things, Saatchi included a small flyer made of coarse, toothed paper embedded with seeds. The copy read: "Hybrid Synergy Drive: Sometimes the seeds of change are brilliantly designed as a car. Or in this case, a card." The recipient simply planted the piece of paper and could expect the seeds to come into bud. Saatchi also developed a global style guide that would enable dealers in any country to assemble print ads that worked in harmony with the North American ones. In cases like these, the costs associated with paper materials are much higher than the printing expenses.

For *sheet-fed* printing jobs (where individual sheets are fed into the press), the cost of paper averages about 22 percent of the selling price of the job. Huge *web presses,* frequently used by catalog publishers and magazines, require rapid printing, so they use rolls of paper and inks that dry instantly when heated (*heat set*). The paper cost for this process averages about 35 percent of the printer's selling price.[6]

Exhibit 14–2

Average cost to produce a TV commercial.

Commercial type	2001 cost
Special effects	$653,000
Large-scale product	397,000
Single situation—voice-over	380,000
Monologue	374,000
Song and dance	359,000
Single situation—dialogue	330,000
Multistory line/vignettes	324,000
Animation	311,000
Interview/testimonial	262,000
Tabletop/ECU	187,000

Managing the Cost of Electronic Production

The term **electronic production** refers to the process of converting a script or storyboard to a finished commercial for use on radio, TV, or digital media. While the overall process is similar to print production, the technical details and the costs of electronic production are quite different. And the end result, rather than print film or negatives, may be audio or videotape, motion picture film, or some digital format such as CD-ROM, portable hard drive, or DVD.

Radio   Radio is the least expensive electronic medium to produce because it deals only with the dimension of sound. Equipment and labor costs are less than for, say, TV production. There's no need for hairstylists, makeup artists, or cue-card holders. And commercials are duplicated on inexpensive audiotape.

The primary control factors in producing radio spots, therefore, are the costs of talent and music. Celebrity talent, especially, can be very expensive. But even the cost of standard union talent, paid at **scale** (the regular charge agreed to in the union contract), can mount rapidly if there are multiple voices or if the commercial is aired in many markets or for an extended period of time. The advertiser, for example, may initially contract for a four-week or a thirteen-week run. If the commercial is extended beyond that time, the advertiser will have to pay a **residual fee** to the talent.

Likewise, the cost of original music (composing, scoring, and orchestration) can range from very inexpensive to frightful, depending on the talent and scope of use. For this reason, many clients—especially small local and regional advertisers—prefer to use prerecorded music available for commercial use from the studio or radio station.

Television   Many companies require the broad coverage and impact offered by TV. However, the television industry is susceptible to prohibitive costs of equipment and labor. In 2001, the average cost of producing a 30-second national television spot was more than $358,000.[7] With costs like that, clients become very picky very quickly (see Exhibit 14–2).

There is a belief in the industry that high-priced celebrity talent and extravagant effects get attention and increase memorability. It turns out that's not true. A recent study showed that advertising that features a brand differentiation message along with a demonstration of the product is actually more effective and costs on average 28 percent less. The study further indicated that advertisers sometimes use lavish production values to compensate for having nothing to say.[8]

Numerous factors can torture TV production budgets. They include the use of children and animals, superstar talent and directors, large casts, animation, involved opticals, special effects, stop-motion photography, use of both location and studio shooting for one commercial, expensive set decoration or construction, additional shooting days, and major script changes during a shoot.[9] Commercial producers have to be aware of all these factors and plan for them very carefully.

Digital media   The computer has engendered a whole new class of digital media. This has dramatically increased the importance of the tasks performed by the agency producer and creative staff and made it critical for them to stay current with new recording and duplicating processes as well as special-effects technology.

In the past, to display their portfolios dramatically, agencies created **multimedia presentations** with fast-paced slide shows using multiple projectors and synchronized, recorded sound. Today's multimedia presenter aims a laser beam at the screen, and a sensor signals a portable computer to fade the slide machine and brighten the RGB projector. Then it runs a short animated video, complete with computer graphics and special effects. The creative team may write these multimedia sales presentations, but the production managers and producers are typically responsible for actually creating them.[10] Doing this in a cost-effective manner can be a challenge.

Ads created by a computer for use on another computer are commonplace to anyone who surfs the Web. This ad for Pot Noodle won a Gold Lion at Cannes for its nontraditional approach; the site is designed to look like a tongue-in-cheek tribute to Pot Noodle rather than an advertisement—it features galleries, opinion polls, humorous articles, and interactive games.

From airport check-in to grocery check-out, consumers have become accustomed to the self-service touch screens and credit card readers of digital **kiosks.** Agencies are busy preparing digital presentations for kiosks, which often automatically present the customer with options to upgrade or add on to their orders: the self-service grocery checkstand asks if you need ice, and the kiosk at the airport may feature tickets to attractions in your destination city.[11] Pioneered by Kodak's Picture Maker, image-printing kiosks are a standard feature in drugstores. Best Buy has begun to compete with the drugstores, capitalizing on its large share of the digital-camera market by installing in-store digital Image Labs. But the fastest-growing sector is digital music, with companies like MediaPort, Starbox, and TouchStand vending on-the-spot personalized CD compilations and listening sessions. Kiosks like these, often having tens of thousands of tracks in their catalogs, are popping up in bookstores, cafés, and retail outlets across the country.[12]

Finally, some ads are totally created by computer for use on computers—electronic images and text designed for transmission around the world via the Internet or some online service such as Earthlink or America Online. The production manager can construct ads using off-the-shelf image and text development software. But to go onto the Internet, the completed files have to be combined with computer programming. For this service, most production managers subcontract the work—but they have to know the suppliers, and charges can range from $50 to $150 per hour.[13] Saatchi & Saatchi, for instance, has a special design and interactive media group that creates advertising for Toyota and other clients.[14] The Prius campaign included many interactive components, including an old-school video game available for MSN Messenger users and an in-depth look at the Prius via the Toyota website (www.toyota.com/prius).

The overall production process for creating images, graphic design, texts, and interactive digital programs for various electronic media is similar to working in print. Final output, though, is to a medium suitable for storage and transmission such as CD-ROM, or a computer file easily posted to an FTP site for Web work.

The Print Production Process

Once Toyota's advertising managers gave the go-ahead on the Prius ad concept, Johanna Leovey could turn her full attention to it. The process she used was the same as for any other print job, whether a brochure, a poster, or a direct-mail

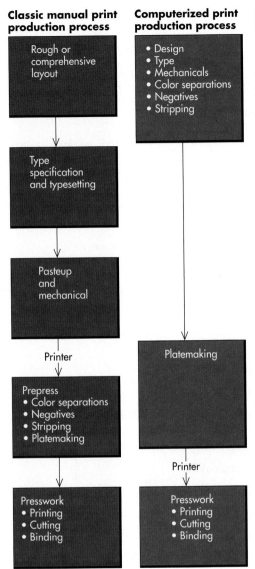

Classic manual print production process

Rough or comprehensive layout

↓

Type specification and typesetting

↓

Pasteup and mechanical

Printer

↓

Prepress
• Color separations
• Negatives
• Stripping
• Platemaking

↓

Presswork
• Printing
• Cutting
• Binding

Computerized print production process

• Design
• Type
• Mechanicals
• Color separations
• Negatives
• Stripping

↓

Platemaking

Printer

↓

Presswork
• Printing
• Cutting
• Binding

Exhibit 14-3

The print production process.

piece. Her goal is always the same—to produce the job as closely as possible to the concept intended by the creative team.

The **print production process** consists of four major phases: *preproduction, production, prepress,* and *printing and distribution.* For a simple model of this process, see Exhibit 14–3 (a more detailed version appears in RL 14–1 in the Reference Library on the *Contemporary Advertising* CD).

The Preproduction Phase: Planning the Project

The first step, **preproduction,** begins when the creative department submits the approved creative concepts—rough or comprehensive layout and copy—to the production department. The production manager's first task is to communicate with the agency's traffic manager and log the project into the department's *traffic system.* Together they will open a **job jacket** for storing the various pieces of artwork and ideas that will be generated throughout the process, and then they will examine the general nature of the job and consider several questions pertinent to managing it efficiently. For example,

■   What equipment will be needed?

■   How will we get it? (Will we have to lease another machine?)

■   What materials are necessary? (If this is a packaging job, what material will we be printing on: tin, paper, cardboard?)

■   What human resources are needed? (Do we need to hire any freelancers like photographers or illustrators?)

■   Will there be any special expenses associated with the job? (Do we need to do location photography, for example, or use the specialized services of a food designer?)

■   How many production artists will be needed? (Is the deadline so near that we'll have to call up the reserves?)

Once these general questions are answered, the production manager can look more closely at the specific needs of the project.

Working backward from publication **closing dates** (deadlines), the traffic and production managers decide when each step of the work must be completed. Deadlines can vary from months to hours. The manager tries to build extra time into each step because every word, art element, and aesthetic choice may need some last-minute change. The traffic manager's job is to make sure deadlines are not missed and that all the proper approvals are obtained in a timely fashion. The team at Saatchi & Saatchi was given a prototype of the Prius for a total of only five days. In this time they were required to photograph the vehicle for use in all of the print ads, collateral work, as well as several 15-second spots used in their prelaunch campaign.

Typography and Copy Casting

Art directors select type styles to enhance the desired personality of the product and complement the tone of the ad. Typefaces affect an ad's appearance, design, and readability. Good type selection can't compensate for a weak headline, poor body copy, or an inappropriate illustration, but it can create interest and attract readers.

It's imperative that production managers as well as graphic artists understand **typography,** the art of selecting and setting type. Advertising artists have to know the five major type groups, the artistic variations within a type family, and the structure of type. They should consider four important concepts when selecting type: *readability, appropriateness, harmony or appearance,* and *emphasis.* Ad Lab 14–A, "The Characteristics of Type," describes these and other type-related topics.

Artists who plan to buy type outside must **copy cast** (or *copyfit*) to calculate the total block of space the type will occupy in relation to the typeface's letter size

The Characteristics of Type

Readability

The most important consideration in selecting a typeface is readability. As David Ogilvy said, good typography helps people read; bad typography prevents them from doing so. General factors that contribute to readability include the type's style, boldness, and size; the length of the line; and the spacing between words, lines, and paragraphs. An ad is meant to be read, and reduced readability kills interest. Difficult-to-read typefaces should be used infrequently and only to create special effects.

Large, bold, simply designed typefaces are the easiest to read. However, the amount of space in the ad and the amount of copy that must be written limit the use of these type forms. The length of the line of copy can also affect the readability. Newspaper columns are usually less than 2 inches wide; magazine columns slightly wider. For ads, columns of copy should be less than 3 inches (18 picas) wide.

Spacing between lines also influences an ad's readability. Space between lines of type allows for descenders (the part of the letter that extends downward, as in the letters j, g, p) and ascenders (the part of the letter that extends upward, as in the letters b, d, k). When this is the only space between lines, type is said to be "set solid." Sometimes an art director adds extra space between lines (called **leading,** pronounced "ledding") to give a more "airy" feeling to the copy. The name comes from the thin lead strips that used to be inserted between lines of metal type.

Kerning (spreading or narrowing the spaces between letters) also improves an ad's appearance and readability. The narrower the kerning, the more type can fit into the available space. Narrow kerning is effective in headlines because people read large type faster when the letters are close together. But narrow kerning is hard to read if overdone or in smaller type sizes.

Appropriateness

A typeface must be appropriate to the product being advertised. Each typeface and size conveys a mood and feeling quite apart from the meanings of the words themselves. One typeface whispers "luxury," another screams "bargain!" A typeface that looks old-fashioned is probably inappropriate for an electronic watch.

Harmony/Appearance

Advertising novices often mix too many typefaces, creating disharmony and clutter. Type should harmonize with the other elements of an ad, including the illustration and layout. Skilled artists choose typefaces in the same family or faces that are closely related in appearance.

Emphasis

Contrast creates emphasis. Artists often use more than one type style or mix italic and roman, small and large type, lowercase and uppercase. But they must be careful not to emphasize all elements or they won't emphasize any.

Classes of Type

Two classes of type are used in advertising.

Display type is larger and heavier than text type; useful in headlines, subheads, logos, and addresses, and for emphasis.

Text type is smaller and finer, used in body copy.

Type Groups

Serif (*roman*) type is the most popular type group due to its readability and warm personality. It is distinguished by small lines or tails called serifs that finish the ends of the main strokes and by variations in the thickness of the strokes. It comes in a wide variety of designs and sizes.

Sans serif (*gothic*) type is the second most popular type group; it is also referred to as block or contemporary. Characterized by lack of serifs (hence the name *sans serif*) and relatively uniform thickness of the strokes, it is not as readable as roman but is widely used because the simple, clean lines give a slick, modern appearance (see **a**).

Roman type	Square serif type
Typography	Typography
Typography	
Typography	Script type
Typography	*Typography*
	Typography
Sans serif type	
Typography	Ornamental type
Typography	Typography
TYPOGRAPHY	Typography

a.

and proportions. This is an important task because type is expensive to buy and costly to change. There are two ways to fit copy: the word-count method and the character-count method.

With the **word-count method,** the words in the copy are counted and divided by the number of words per square inch that can be set in a particular type style and size, as given in a standard table. The **character-count method** is more accurate. Someone counts the actual number of characters (letters, word spaces, and punctuation marks) in the copy, finds the average number of characters per *pica* for each typeface and size, and determines how much space the copy will fill (there are six picas to an inch).

Just a decade ago, copyfitting ability was essential for all artists; but now type can be manipulated in minutes on computers. However, copyfitting is still useful in the preproduction phase for avoiding typesetting problems later. When local advertisers, for instance, provide the agency with text for printed materials, they expect the artist to make the type "look good," even though there may be far too much or too little text to fit properly in the space available. By measuring the copy

Square serif type combines sans serif and serif typefaces. It has serifs, but letter strokes have uniform thickness.

Cursive or script type resembles handwriting; letters often connect and may convey a feeling of femininity, formality, classicism, or beauty. It is difficult to read and is used primarily in headlines, formal announcements, and cosmetic and fashion ads.

Ornamental type uses novel designs with a high level of embellishment and decorativeness. It adds a "special effects" quality but is often difficult to read.

Type Families

A **type family** is made up of related typefaces. The serif typeface used for the text of this book is called Garamond Light. Within a family, the basic design remains the same but varies in the proportion, weight, and slant of the characters. The type may be light, medium, bold, extra bold, condensed, extended, or italic. Variations enable the typographer to provide contrast and emphasis without changing the family (see **b**).

A **font** is a complete assortment of capitals, small capitals, lowercase letters, numerals, and punctuation marks for a particular typeface and size.

Measuring Type

Type characters have height, width, weight, and, for some ornamental typefaces, depth. They also come in shapes called a case. And with the advent of computers, type comes in a variety of resolutions.

Size is the height of a character (or letter) measured in **points** (72 points to the inch) from the bottom of the descenders to the top of the ascenders (see **c**).

The set width of a letter, known as an *em* space, is usually based on the maximum width and proportions of the capital letter M for that particular typeface. Set width of the letter N is called an *en* space.

Capital letters are uppercase, small letters lowercase (in the hot-type era, compositors stacked the case containing the capital letters above the one with the small letters). It's easiest to read a combination of uppercase and lowercase. Type may be set in all caps (for emphasis) or in commoncase (caps and small caps).

Resolution refers to the fineness of the type. The goals of fine typesetting are readability, clarity, and smoothness of appearance. Type on a computer screen is usually 72 to 78 dots per inch (dpi). A dot-matrix printer outputs type at 360 dpi, a laser printer at over 600 dpi. The preferred level of quality for magazines and brochures begins at 1,000 dpi; advertisers often use resolutions of 2,400 to 3,750 dpi.

Laboratory Applications

Use the various figures and terms in this Ad Lab to answer the following:

1. Describe the class, group, family, and size of the type used in the title "Producing Ads for Print, Electronic, and Digital Media," which appears on the first page of this chapter.

2. Do the same for the captions that appear with the exhibits in this book.

Garamond Book	Garamond Condensed Book
Garamond Book Italic	*Garamond Condensed Book Italic*
Garamond Bold	**Garamond Condensed Bold**
Garamond Bold Italic	***Garamond Condensed Bold Italic***
Garamond Light	Garamond Condensed Light
Garamond Light Italic	*Garamond Condensed Light Italic*
Garamond Ultra	**Garamond Condensed Ultra**
Garamond Ultra Italic	***Garamond Condensed Ultra Italic***

b.

Text type	Display type
6 pt. Type size	16 pt. Type size
8 pt. Type size	18 pt. Type size
9 pt. Type size	20 pt. Type size
10 pt. Type size	24 pt. Type size
12 pt. Type size	30 pt. Type size
14 pt. Type size	36 pt. Type size

c.

early in the process, the artist has enough time to suggest that the text be rewritten to fit. Once production begins, deadlines may be missed while the agency waits for copy rewrites.

To make their ads unique and exclusive, some advertisers even commission a new type design. Other companies tailor their typography to blend with the magazines or newspapers their advertising appears in. This gives the ad an editorial look and, the advertiser hopes, enhanced credibility (or at least interest). For consistency, Saatchi & Saatchi uses a particular type style in all Toyota ads. In the case of the Prius, they used Saatchi Trait Gothic, a variation on Trait Gothic, but the official type style changes almost every year as the client and agency strive to maintain originality and freshness in their ads.

Planning the Job

The overall purpose of the preproduction phase is to plan the job thoroughly, which usually entails making a number of strategic choices before launching into full production. For example, since the art director's conceptual rough layouts are often made with marker colors that do not match printing inks, the production manager should consult with the art director to formally select a color palette in advance, using a color guide such as the PANTONE® system.

For brochures, there is also the question of which printing process and which type of printing press to use for the job (see RL 14–3, Choosing the Best Method of Printing, in the Reference Library on the *Contemporary Advertising* CD). This will affect the budget and dictate how art is prepared in the production and prepress phases.

Similarly, the art director and production manager usually consult on the paper to be used. Three categories of paper are used for advertising purposes: *writing, text,* and *cover stock.* Letters and fliers, for example, commonly use **writing paper.** Bond writing paper is the most durable and most frequently used. For brochures, there are many types of **text papers,** such as news stock, antique finish, machine finish, English finish, and coated. These range from the inexpensive, coarse, porous papers (*newsprint*) used by newspapers to the smooth, expensive, coated stocks used in upscale magazines, industrial brochures, and fine-quality annual reports. **Cover papers,** available in many finishes and textures, are used on soft book covers, direct-mail pieces, and brochure covers, so they're thicker, tougher, and more durable.

Finally, the production manager must decide early which is most important for a particular project: *speed, quality,* or *economy.* Typically, the manager must sacrifice one in favor of the other two. The answer determines the production methods used and the personnel employed. Once all these decisions are made, the manager can begin the production phase.

The Production Phase: Creating the Artwork

Following the preproduction phase on the Prius ad, Johanna Leovey passed the job to the production staff in Lorraine Alper Kramer's art studio to produce the actual ad for the intended print media. Essentially, the **production phase** involves completing ancillary functions such as illustration or photography, setting up the artwork and typesetting, and then melding all these components into a final tangible form for the printer or publisher.

Creating the Visual

Almost every ad has some kind of a visual besides typography. And many ads have several pictures. The visual may be an illustration or a photograph or even a combination of the two. But where do these pictures come from?

When reviewing the layout with the art director, the decision will be made whether to use illustration or photography and how to get just the pictures the creatives envisioned. In many cases, to save the client money, the art director or producer (or even an art buyer in large agencies) will choose to use stock photography—purchase one or more pictures from a stock photography house for a reasonable licensing fee. The fee will typically be based on the intended usage and the length of time the usage will continue.

Most expensive is commissioning an illustrator to draw an original picture or hiring a photographer to go on location to shoot a specific visual, especially if it's out of town. For photography, there are several important considerations, the first being who to use. That depends on the style of photograph desired. Some photographers are well-versed in photojournalistic techniques. Others are especially good at shooting interiors. And some specialize in food or fashion photography.

Other considerations include any special equipment, props, or set work that will be needed, as well as an available power source. In the case of the print work for the Prius ad, the creative team worked in studio, photographing the car against a white backdrop. Later, they completed the image by adding visuals and text. There were two major challenges: one was as simple as time constraints, because each team needed to get their photography done within the five days allotted. Second, there was the matter of the supplementary visuals: the dots behind the photograph, which create the contemporary, almost futuristic, appearance of the image. Each dot was carefully created using a computer graphics program, and for every minor shift in the appearance of the ad, the entire background layer needed to be readjusted so that that none of the tiny circles were cut off by the text or photography. Furthermore, in order to create the illusion of shadow coming from the car, a gradation of color needed to be filled in on each circle. This required countless hours of careful color matching, all of which was done by studio artists.

Preparing Mechanicals

To create the art for an ad, brochure, or package, the production artist normally begins by marking out a grid on which to lay the type and art. Artists used to do this by hand on a piece of artboard in light-blue pencil. Today, pagemaking computer software does this with commands for setting up columns and guides. The grid provides an underlying consistency to the spacing and design of the piece.

The production artist then specifies the style and size of the typefaces for the text and inputs this information, along with the copy, into the computer. If the company doesn't have its own typesetting machines or computer systems, the artist must still specify the type so the typesetting company can understand the data. The type may be positioned electronically, or it may be output onto paper and glued onto an artboard within the image area.

The basic design for the Prius ad was simple. The idea was to create an ad much like the car: clean, modern, and accessible. A basic white background softened with the integration of small gray dots, the car, tag line, and **mandatories** (phone, Web address, and so forth).

Johanna Leovey, along with the studio artists, studied the comps to visualize how the various art and copy elements could be isolated in individual layers in the mechanical art and the pagemaking software.

When an additional color is to be printed, a second artboard marked to the same dimensions is used for the second image. The second image may be glued onto a clear plastic **overlay** that lies on top of the first image (called the **base art**). The production artist places crossmarks in the corners of the base art and then superimposes crossmarks on the transparent overlay precisely over those on the base art. This registers the exact position of the two layers of art in relation to one another.

The art elements must be properly positioned in the artwork (whether mechanical or computer generated) because the printer needs to have layers of art that can be reproduced individually. The total image is then constructed as each layer is printed over the previous one. Because the printer must photograph each layer to make separate plates, this kind of artwork is called **camera-ready art.**

In a multicolor piece of art, the printer needs layers that can be reproduced individually. This is done by computer or assembled by hand with plastic overlays. The total image is then reconstructed as each layer is printed over the other.

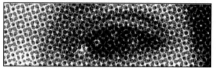

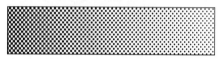

A halftone screen breaks up continuous-tone artwork into tiny dots. The combination of printed dots produces an optical illusion of shading, as in a photograph. The color dots show the separation for the color photo above. The other set of dots show the range that would appear in a black and white photo.

This procedure is easily performed in the computer. The various elements of art are assigned to a layer the operator names and can be run out as separate film negatives or paper positive images as needed.

Camera-Ready Art and Halftones

Production art for the printing process is like an on/off switch: Where the art is black, ink will stick; where the art is white, ink won't stick. The production artist adheres to this printing principle by using black-and-white artwork that is called *line art* and by converting gray images to a form of line art called *halftones.*

Line art   Normal photographic paper (such as snapshots made with a camera) produces images in **continuous tones**—black and white with shades of gray in between. But printing presses cannot print gray. So printers use special **orthographic film,** a high-contrast film yielding only black-and-white images with no gray tones. The artwork is simply photographed as is, and the result is called a **line film.** From that a **line plate** is produced for printing.

A *continuous-tone photograph* or other illustration requiring gradations in tone cannot be reproduced on orthographic film or a plate without an additional process, the *halftone screen.*

Halftone screens   While line plates print lines and solid areas (like type), **halftone plates** print dots. The key element is the **halftone screen,** which breaks up continuous-tone artwork into tiny dots. The combination of dots, when printed, produces an optical illusion of shading, as in a photo. In the dark areas of the image, the dots bump into each other and make the paper appear nearly black. In the gray areas, the size of the black dots equals the amount of white paper showing through; in the white areas, the black dots are surrounded by a lot of white or are almost completely missing. The human eye perceives the dots as gradations of tone.

The fineness of the halftone screen determines the quality of the illusion. Glossy magazine ads are printed with halftone screens as fine as 200 lines per inch (lpi), while newspaper photos appear very coarse at 80 to 100 lpi. Coarser screens are used to print on coarse, ink-absorbent paper (like newsprint) because the ink spreads when it hits the paper and fills in the white areas. Fine-quality, glossy magazine paper can take fine-screen halftones because the compressed chalk surface doesn't let the ink spread into the white areas. The dots in a coarse screen can be seen quite easily with the naked eye. To create special effects, the artist may employ different types of screens with interesting irregularities.

The artist's final step is to mark any halftones and line art for size and indicate where they should be placed. The artist simply sticks a photocopy of the

65-line screen

100-line screen

150-line screen

Halftone screens help the printer control ink flow when trying to emulate the continuous-tone quality of photos. On newsprint, where the ink soaks in and spreads, a coarse 65-line screen gives the ink some room between dots. The finer, 150-line screen gives a better appearance, but it works best with magazine-quality paper that has a compressed chalk coating to keep ink from spreading.

Two-color texture

Random line

Mezzo tint

Wavy line (dry brush)

Special screens lend an artistic look to photos. Whether the screens use lines, scratches, or some other technique, they work on the same principle as the halftone dot screen.

visual to the artboard in its exact location with the letters FPO (for position only) written across the image. That way the printer doesn't think the copy is the actual final art.

The Prepress Phase: Stripping, Negs, and Plates

When Saatchi & Saatchi completed all the production for the Prius ad on its computers, the next step was to get the finished artwork ready for the press. In addition to running the ad in magazines, it also needed prints of the ad for use by the agency, the client, and Toyota's dealers.

In the **prepress phase,** the printer makes a plate from the base art and one from each overlay. Each pasteup (mechanical) has to be photographed separately.

The various layers of line art and halftones are converted to film negatives, which are carefully mounted together in perfect registration—through a process known as **stripping**—onto opaque plastic sheets called **flats.** A completed flat is a mask that allows light to pass through only where lines and dots are to appear on the plate. The flat is pressed against the printing plate, and ultraviolet light exposes the plate's photosensitive emulsion. Once exposed, the emulsion is developed, etching the plate in the process. This leaves some areas of the plate capable of holding ink and others unable to do so. Once dry, the plates are "hung" on the press, ready for printing.

Printing in Color

A printing plate can print only one color at a time. An advertiser who wants to print an ad or a brochure in blue, green, and black needs three different plates (one for each color), and the job is referred to as a three-color job. To print in full color, though, the **four-color process** is used. This process can simulate nearly all colors by combining the four primary colors: *process blue* (cyan), *process yellow, process magenta,* and *black* (which provides greater detail and density as well as shades of gray). In the parlance of the trade, this is also called **CYMK printing,** the K standing for black. To print in full color, therefore, the printer prepares four different printing plates—one for each process color plus black.

Designs that don't need full color are printed in blended inks rather than process colors. For example, it would take two process colors (magenta and yellow) to make red or three process colors (magenta, yellow, and cyan) to make burgundy. To print a brochure in black and burgundy, it's cheaper to use only two ink colors rather than black plus three process colors.

A PANTONE® color, one of a spectrum of colors that makes up the **PANTONE Matching System®(PMS),** is a single ink premixed according to a formula and given a specific color number. The PANTONE swatch book features more than 100 colors in solid and screened blocks printed on different paper finishes.[15]

Four-Color Separations

Four separate halftone negatives are needed to make a set of four-color plates: one each for cyan, yellow, magenta, and black. Each of the resulting negatives appears in black and white, and the set is called the **color separation.** In printing, the process color inks are translucent, so two or three colors can overlap to create another color. For example, green is reproduced by overlapping yellow and cyan dots (see the transvision overlays in the Portfolio Review, "Creative Department: From Concept through Production of a Magazine Ad and Television Commercial").

Until recently, most color separations were done using a photographic process. Today, sophisticated electronic scanning systems—such as the workstations from Silicon Graphics, Hell ScriptMaster, Scitex, and Crosfield—can produce four-color separations and screens in one process, along with enlargements or reductions. And all this can be accomplished in minutes instead of the hours or days previously needed for camera work and hand etching.

Regardless of the separation method used, when properly printed, tiny clusters of halftone dots in various colors, sizes, and shapes give the eye the illusion of seeing the colors of the original photograph or painting.

The Duplication and Distribution Phase: Printing, Binding, and Shipping

The last phase of the print production process involves the actual printing, proofing, and finishing steps of drying, cutting, binding, and shipping.

The Press Run

Once the paper, plates, and ink are readied, the press is started and stopped a few times to adjust the image's alignment on the paper. In multicolored printing, proper alignment of all the colors is critical. When the initial proofs show good alignment, the presses are started again and gradually sped up to maximum output.

Finishing

Once all the pieces are printed, the ink must dry (unless heat-set or cold-set inks were used). Then the excess paper (or other material) is cut away using huge cutting machines. Depending on the nature of the job, the pieces may be delivered to special subcontractors who emboss or die-cut or perform other special techniques to enhance the final printed piece. The final stop may be the bindery for two- and three-hole drilling, wire stapling, and folding.

Quality Control in Print Production

At various stages of the print production process, the production manager needs to verify the quality. Artwork for a newspaper or magazine ad, for example, must be camera-ready. Many agencies now just send a disk, and the publisher converts the computer image to negatives. Magazines provide specific instructions and measurements for each ad size they offer. If there is any question, the production manager should call the publication and ask how current the data are.

Finally, the production manager must check all proofs for errors and obtain approvals from agency and client executives before releasing ads to publications or artwork to printers. Proofing is a time-consuming task made more so by the fact that not everyone is available when the work is ready for approval.

For the production process to run smoothly, everyone concerned must understand the procedure. The later in the process errors are discovered, the more expensive they are to fix. Changing a single comma may cost as much as $50 after copy is typeset, or $500 once negatives are made, or $5,000 if the job is already printed.[16]

Production Phase Quality Issues

The task of quality control really begins in the production phase. Proofs of the production art, with all its type and images, must be carefully inspected for misspellings, mismeasured lines, improperly sized images, misplaced cropmarks, or a myriad of other minutiae that could lead to a problem later.

Prepress Quality Issues

The slightest flaw in the final printed piece can have serious repercussions. The production manager must check and double-check, even triple-check, the film negatives before they're sent off to a magazine. An analog or digital proof (described below) of the negatives should be carefully checked and sent with the negatives.

Ways to Proof Print Production

When printing collateral materials or projects like brochures, the production manager will typically see a *blueline, color key, analog* or *digital proof,* and *press proof* from the printer.

Blueline proof   A **blueline** is a proof that is created by shining light through the negatives and exposing a light-sensitive paper that turns from white to blue. The blueline helps reveal scratches and flaws in the negatives as well as any assembly errors, such as a reversed illustration. The blueline is usually trimmed, folded, and stapled like the final product to check if the crop and fold marks have been properly registered.

Color keys and analog or digital proofs   The **analog proof** (also called a **Chromalin**) uses a series of four very thin sheets of plastic pressed together. Each layer's light-sensitive emulsion turns one of the process colors when exposed to certain wavelengths of light. Together they form a full, four-color image proof. The **color key** is a less expensive form of the Chromalin with relatively thick plastic sheets that can be lifted up. The plastic makes the overall image grayer than the final printed piece. The most recent innovation is the **digital proof** (also called an **Iris**). It uses ink-jet technology and offers accuracy as well as lower cost and faster turnaround time.[17]

Press proof   When the presses begin printing, the press operator "pulls" a few proofs to align the press and check ink densities. At this time the production manager should sign one of these actual press proofs as a guide for the operator to follow and for the agency's protection if something goes wrong later during the printing process.

What to Look for in a Proof

When checking proofs, production managers and art directors look for any scratches, minute holes or dots, blemishes, or unevenness of ink coverage. Using a *loupe* (magnifying glass), they inspect the dot pattern in halftones to make sure the registration of color is perfectly tight. Then they check *traps* and *bleeds.*

Traps   A **trap** occurs where the edge of one color or shade overlaps its neighbor by a fraction of an inch to make sure the white paper underneath doesn't show through. If the production artist fails to trap the artwork properly, the printer has to slightly overexpose one negative (sometimes called a *fatty*) or slightly underexpose another (a *skinny*) (see Exhibit 14–4).

To save money and avoid trapping problems, designers often plan for the typesetting to *overprint* (print on top of) the background color with black ink. But when colored type is printed over a different background color, the background color must let white show to avoid distorting the true color of the colored type. This **reverse knockout** requires careful trapping.

Exhibit 14–4

Black ink can overprint a background color (far left). However, art or text printed in a color other than black should have no background color underneath. For example, if a black letter "a" appears on a blue field, a white reverse knockout will keep the blue from being affected by the red (second from left). If the blue letter and the reverse knockout aren't properly aligned or the blue letter is smaller than the white knockout, the letters will not trap, and white paper will show between the two colors (far right).

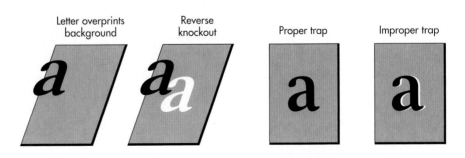

Letter overprints background   Reverse knockout   Proper trap   Improper trap

(continued on page 460)

Creative Department: From Concept through Production of a Magazine Ad and Television Commercial

Marketing Considerations

With the rising cost of gasoline, mounting political and social pressures for conservation, and the threat of pollution from toxic emissions, many drivers are beginning to reassess the standard car and its relationship to the environment. At the same time, consumers love the freedom, spontaneity, privacy, convenience, and thrill of driving. Although they would like to find a solution to the problem, they also don't want to give up what they love about cars. The solution has eluded consumers and manufacturers for decades. Until now.

The Situation

While most car manufacturers are still working on their first entry into the hybrid market, Toyota's Hybrid Synergy Drive is already the company's second-generation hybrid and the most technologically advanced system out there. But many consumers are hesitant and somewhat apprehensive about hybrid vehicles. They feel that a hybrid will require them to give up the conveniences of a regular automobile. The Prius campaign must show consumers not only that these assumptions are incorrect but that the Prius is a vehicle that can deliver everything a regular car can, and much more.

Marketing and Advertising Objectives

To position the Prius and Hybrid Synergy Drive as the exciting, high-tech solution to existing concerns about standard vehicles.

Target Markets

The primary target market for the Prius is comprised of consumers who are ready to embrace change and technology: early adopters. Secondary are the Greenies: drivers who are committed to the environment and want a car that reflects that commitment. Ultimately, the company will target all drivers, because this is an innovative vehicle that represents the future of automobiles.

Creative Strategy

The creative strategy includes a mix of product concept, target audience, communications media, and advertising message:

1. *Product concept.* The Prius is a sleek, affordable, intelligent solution—the car of the future, available now. It performs as well, if not better, than regular cars, and it offers the added advantage of 55+ mpg. It goes from 0 to 60 mph in under 10 seconds, and it holds five people and their luggage comfortably.

2. *Target audience.* The campaign would focus on drivers aware of the problems associated with driving today—fuel costs, pollution, depletion of resources—and who want to do something about it. While many are city dwellers, the campaign does not focus on urbanites specifically—the people in this audience are lively, independent individuals who want to balance their environmental concerns with their need for the freedom and privacy of a car. Appearance is a consideration as well—they want something that looks as good as it feels. Practicality and driving enjoyment is another consideration. And these drivers want a car that will suit their active lifestyle.

3. *Communications media.* Saatchi & Saatchi proposed a mixed-media campaign of print ads in consumer and auto enthusiast magazines and a global TV spot

that would be aired in every country where the Prius is available. In addition, Saatchi would design and implement a variety of online interactive websites.

4. *Advertising message.* The message strategy was to portray the Prius as the car of the future—an exciting, innovative, and intelligent vehicle that does everything a regular car can do and then some. The print ad would show the Prius in a clean, contemporary way, and the TV spot would focus on the car's groundbreaking, forward-thinking design and ability. In tone and style, the ads and commercials would be gender neutral.

Production Planning

Once the creative roughs were approved, the production supervisors prepared the schedule for both TV and print production. Considerations included Toyota's marketing and media deadlines, concerns such as location filming permits and security, seasonal conditions, and production factors such as equipment needs, production support people, and facilities. The production department also prepared cost estimates for approval by agency and client managers.

Print Production Process

The print ad would highlight the Prius in front of a white backdrop. The car would be lit and photographed as stylishly as possible. Initial layouts are prepared using a photo of the Prius from the studio's Imagebank. Later, the actual photo from the studio shoot arrived; it was well shot but required computer retouching to add more light to some areas and adjust the colors.

SAATCHI & SAATCHI L.A.

TMS-PC4207 — Magazine Work Order

Date: 6/19/03	**Budget Code:** 111001-630000
Job Title: MY04 Prius "Lifetime Supply" Page Ad	**Project #:** MKT30001
Client: National Adv. Car	**Model Listing:**
Product: 120311-PRI	**Budget AMT:**
Model: Prius04	**bill to job#:**
Category: Prius04	**Prev Job#:**
Issued By: Jennifer Jones	**Region:**
Clt. Contact: Steve Jett	**Rev#:**
MY: 04	**Date Rev:**
FY: 04	**Scope of Work:** ○ In ○ Out

Job Title
MY04 Prius "Lifetime Supply" Page Ad

Size	Color
Spread	☐ B/W ☐ 1/C
Page	
Bleed	☐ 2/C ☒ 4/C
Other	☐ TBD

Reprints

client	agency
☒ trimmed 125	☐ trimmed
☒ untrimmed 125	☐ untrimmed

Traffic: A. Murray	**Acct. Planner:**	
AE: M. Wagner	**Media:**	
AAE:	**Media2:**	
Print Prod: L. Welsh	**Acct. Sup:** C. Tierney	
Print Prod2:	**Acct. Dir:** D. Minkin	
Art Producer: C. Rowe	**Traffic Dir:** ⌐⌐⌐⌐⌐⌐	
Prod Info: P. Spates	**Grp Traf Dir:** S. Lee	
Prod Info 2:	**Prod Director:** L. Alper Kramer	
Art Studio:	**Grp Prod Mgr:**	
Studio Artist:	**C. Control:** M. Ierao	
Art Dir #1: . N/A	**C. Control2:** R. Hue	
Art Dir #2:	**Budget Mgr.:**	
Art Dir #3:	**Budget Admn:** E. Domo	
C/W #1: M. Godsil	**Creative Traf:**	
C/W #2:	**Other:** J. Hamaguchi	
C/W #3:	**Other:** V. Soler	
ECD/CCO:	**Other:** A. Bassano	
CD/Dsgn Dir. #1:	**Other:**	
CD/Dsgn Dir. #2:	**Other:**	
ACD #1: D. Phillips	**Other:**	
ACD #2:	**Freelancer:**	

Assignments / Specifications
This job was opened to incur the costs of producing the Prius "Lifetime Supply" page ad.

Pubs

Publication	Insert	Close	Ext.	Position	Mech.
Business 2.0					P
Fortune Magazine					P
Fast Company					LP
New York Times Magazine, The					TP
New Yorker, The					P
O, The Oprah Magazine					PA
Organic Style					P
Sierra Magazine					P
Wired					LPA
MIT Technology Review					PB
Popular Science					P
Smithsonian Magazine					P
Vanity Fair					P
Time Magazine					P
Fitness					P
Entertainment Weekly					P
People Weekly					P
Wall St. Journal					NP
Newsweek					P
Money					P
Economist					PC
Variety (Daily)					TPA
Forbes					P
Cooking Light	11/1/03	9/2/03		authorize	P
Playbill	11/1/03	9/15/03	10/1/03	authorize	DP
Playbill	12/1/03	10/15/03			DP
ShowTimes Magazine (Clean Cities)	12/1/03	11/3/03	11/7/03	authorize	LPC
Week, The	11/28/03	11/5/03		authorize	P
Week, The	2/6/04	1/6/04			P
Scientific American	3/1/04	1/20/04			P
Week, The	3/12/04	2/10/04			P
ShowTimes Magazine	5/1/04	4/16/04		authorize	LPC

Schedule

11/4/2004	TMS-PC4207	Magazine Work Order	Page: 1

11/4/2004	TMS-PC4207	Magazine Work Order	Page: 2

Prius print ad work order
When the agency begins to work on a magazine ad, it opens a work order like this one. It details the title of the particular ad, the mechanical specifications, and who is assigned the various responsibilities for getting the ad completed on time.

Print Production and Distribution

The production team assembled the approved copy and photography and opened a computer graphics file featuring guide-marked pages based on the specs provided by the magazines in which the ads would appear. The art studio created the dotted background using Photoshop and put the mechanicals together in low resolution with Quark software. The final mechanicals were sent to the engraver where the photo was rescanned to higher resolution and retouched. Color separations and press proofs were then pulled and sent to the agency for approval before sending the digital files to the magazines.

Television Production Process

Saatchi's account executive, C. Tierney, and creative director, Doug Van Andel, drafted a creative brief based on the advertising strategy determined by Saatchi & Saatchi and Toyota. They presented it to copywriter Max Godsil and art director Greg Braun for concepting. Together they developed and refined the ideas for the global spot and presented them in rough form to the agency account people for critique and approval.

Prius print—marked-up photo

Advertising visuals may be obtained from a stock photography company, or they may be commissioned and shot with a specific ad in mind. In this case, Saatchi & Saatchi hired a photographer to shoot the Prius in front of a white backdrop, and later filled the image in with supplementary visuals and text.

(continued on page 457)

PRINT COPY

File Name:	P14.9A.DOC	Campaign:	PRIUS		
Client:	TMS				Page 1 of 1
Job No.:	PC4-207	Title:	LIFETIME SUPPLY		
Acct. Exec.:		Product:	PRIUS	Size:	
Rev. No.		Date/Time:	9/2/03 3:50 PM	Writer/tr/us:	MG/am/ce

[HEADLINE]

Lifetime supply of fresh air with every purchase.

[COPY]

The next generation gas/electric Prius with Hybrid Synergy Drive.® Best emission rating for a gas-powered production vehicle. Best estimated fuel economy in a mid-size car.* All with the best interests of the earth in mind. Take a deep breath everyone. The Prius is here.

[WEB SITE]
toyota.com

[LOGOS]

HYBRID SYNERGY DRIVE.®
THE POWER TO MOVE FORWARD.

PRIUS START NOW.

[DISCLAIMER]
*Based on production vehicles only. California Air Resources Board SULEV-rated.

[COPYRIGHT]

©2003 Toyota Motor Sales, U.S.A., Inc.

[LOGO]

GET THE FEELING
[LOGO] TOYOTA

JAN 04 2005:P14.9A.DOC

SAATCHI & SAATCHI		
Job #	By	Date
Studio Mgr		
Traffic		
Proofreader		
Art Director		
Copywriter		
Assoc Creative Dir		
Creative Dir		
Acct Planner		
Asst AE		
Acct Executive		
Acct Supr		
CEO		
Product Info		
Producer		
Production Dir		
Integration:		
Acct Grp		
Creative Dir		
Client Approval / Advertising		
Legal		
Product		

Prius print copy approval

This is the copy approval form used by Saatchi & Saatchi for the print ad. Before the ad was produced, approvals were obtained from the various management, creative, and legal departments of both parties.

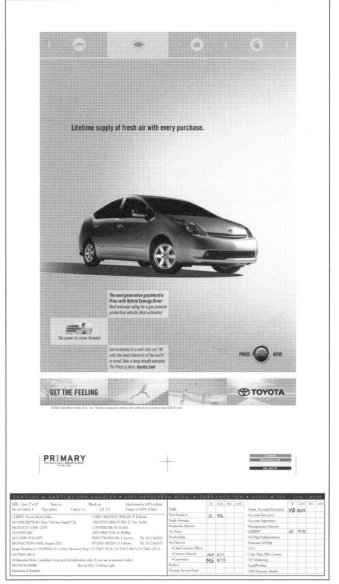

Prius print black and white mechanical with changes and approvals

In the early phases of production, when the focus is on copy and overall design, mechanical layouts are produced in black and white, which speeds up the process and reduces cost.

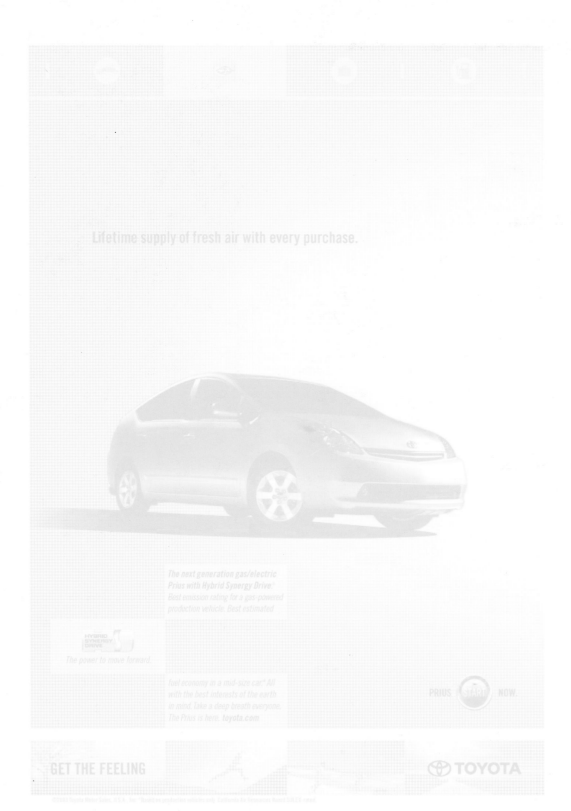

Lifetime supply of fresh air with every purchase.

The next generation gas/electric Prius with Hybrid Synergy Drive. Best emission rating for a gas-powered production vehicle. Best estimated

HYBRID SYNERGY DRIVE

The power to move forward.

fuel economy in a mid-size car. All with the best interests of the earth in mind. Take a deep breath everyone. The Prius is here. toyota.com

PRIUS START NOW.

GET THE FEELING

TOYOTA

Yellow

Four process colors combined

Prius print final proof with final approvals
Near the end of the production schedule, print ads enter the final proofing stage. Here the ad is viewed in full color to check for any final corrections before going to press.

(continued from page 456)

A set of storyboards was prepared from the approved script. Greg Braun selected thumbnails for several sets of frames and sent them to broadcast producer Richard Bendetti for review. The approved thumbnails were then rendered into final frames and copy was typeset and printed on desktop computers. The frames and text were mounted for presentation to Toyota's marketing people and other company approvers. With creative approval granted, the production budget and schedule were finalized and work began.

Preproduction

As the creative director, it was Doug Van Andel's choice to hire a still photographer and a director of photography (DP) rather than a director. This allowed more than usual creative freedom for both people, and also enabled Doug to work more closely with them. Next, the creative team reviewed the script and broke it down into elements and scenes. They reviewed each scene for the imagery and sound effects required. Casting began, talent was scouted, and specific locations across the globe—Japan, South Africa, New York—were selected.

Doug and Tarsem, the DP, reviewed the storyboard, determined interesting camera angles and individual shots, ascertained their equipment needs, gathered and scheduled camera crews, and prepared a shooting schedule with daily filming goals. Executing the project also required negotiating contracts and hiring a variety of services and personnel such as insurance, catering, special equipment

SAATCHI & SAATCHI
LOS ANGELES

TV COPY

					AS PRODUCED	
File Name:	Power to Move Forward	Campaign:	'04 GLOBAL PRIUS LAUNCH			
Client:	TMS	Title:	MOVING FORWARD :30			Page 1 of 1
Job No:	TJP PRS T4-001	Product:	PRIUS	ISCI Code:	TYCP 4009	
Asst Exec:	C.TIERNEY	Producer:	R. BENDETTI	Length:	:30	
Rev. No:		Date/Time:	9/8/03, 9:30am	Writer/AD/tr	MG/GB/db	

V.O. — It's been a long time since transportation has truly advanced, but now we have good news for planet earth. The next generation gas/electric Prius with Hybrid Synergy Drive is here. Low emissions, high mileage and you never plug it in. Now we all have the power to move forward.

SUPER: HYBRID SYNERGY DRIVE

SUPER: PRIUS START NOW

SUPER: toyota.com

SUPER: TOYOTA
SUPER: GET THE FEELING
SUPER: (LOGO)TOYOTA

Final TV script for Prius ad approval
Television ads also go through an approval process similar to that of print. One of the initial steps is to write out the script for the ad and to obtain all necessary permissions.

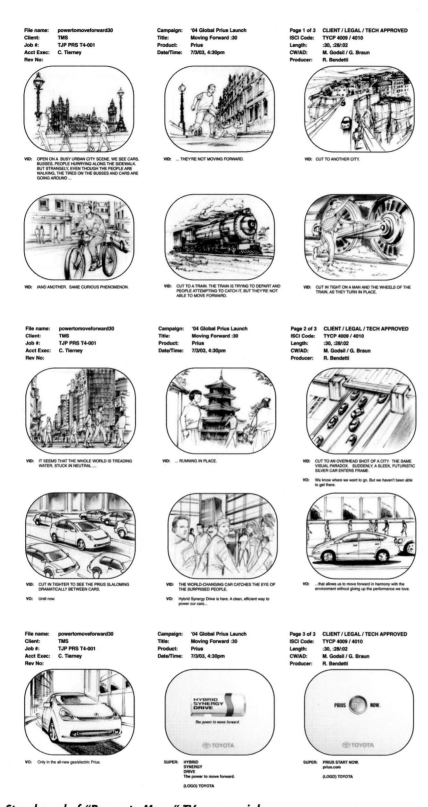

Storyboard of "Power to Move" TV commercial

The storyboard for television ads is developed simultaneously with the copy. The storyboard is a visual representation of the ad, made up of sketches that indicate the art director's concept of the various scenes, camera angles, sound effects, and special effects to be used in the final production.

(lighting, cranes, dollies, cell phones), film processing labs, motor homes, permits, and transportation, most of which was handled by broadcast producer Richard Bendetti.

Production

Because the Prius spot was a global one, set to air in countries around the world, it was crucial to develop a spot with a message that transcended local linguistic and cultural standards. Even without copy, the commercial needed to communicate the message that the Prius is a unique, technologically enhanced car. Though the initial concept for the campaign focused on the environmental advantages of the car, research revealed that those people who were looking for ecologically safe cars were already sold on the Prius, so concentrating on that portion of the market would be like preaching to the choir. Though Saatchi and Toyota still felt it was important to draw attention to the environmental rewards of the Prius, its technologically advanced features, along with its accessibility and superior mileage, became the real point of sale.

The 60-second global spot for the Prius was scheduled for production over a two-week period in midsummer, but only six of those days were actually spent shooting the commercial. The team visited four countries and shot in five different locales: a South African countryside and in the city, the streets of London, the south of Spain, and in Tokyo, in the midst of a busy intersection.

Saatchi's endeavor was to create a spot that served as a visual allegory to their new tagline, "The Power to Move Forward." They envisioned a spot that featured cars, buses, and people hurrying along the sidewalk. However, instead of moving forward, the tires on the vehicles would simply go round and round, and the people on the street would appear to be walking in place. This would happen in various locations, urban and rural, all over the world. Suddenly, the Prius would emerge—the only forward-moving motion in the shot. Even without words it would be clear that the Prius, unlike the average present-day vehicle, is suitable to move into the future, but unlike the cars of the future, the Prius is available now.

The creative team at Saatchi wanted to produce their spot with as few special effects and computer generated images as possible. Although they were told several times that this couldn't be done, Tarsem, the DP, believed it was feasible. And, in fact, it was. Small treadmills were transported all over the world and placed under both the talent and the vehicles; this accounted for what later appeared as a natural pacing and body language on the actors. The treadmills were then removed in postproduction.

Postproduction: Dailies to Distribution Prints

The postproduction phase began directly after shooting the commercial. Back in Los Angeles, the film was digitally converted and viewed on an Avid computer to select key sequences. During the editing process, each scene was polished and then assembled into a final, intriguing spot. Ashton Spencer, a composer of original music for movies and commercials, was hired to work on the soundtrack. Doug wanted a soundtrack that, like the commercial, started off in place and then really opened up later on; he communicated this goal to Spencer, who came back with an electronic recording that did just that.

Campaign Results

Though the Prius is not the largest segment of Toyota's business, it's an important and rapidly growing one. As previously mentioned, the campaign was so successful that Saatchi had to actually cut back on some of its advertising because there simply weren't enough cars to meet the growing demand.

"Power to Move Forward" TV commercial

Following the shoot, the footage goes to the editing studios where music, voice-overs, special effects, and supers are all incorporated into the finished commercial. For the "Power to Move Forward" spot, the treadmills, which had been used to create a natural pacing for the actors, were removed during the postproduction stage.

(continued from page 453)

For full-color ads, it's often wise to overprint text in black ink. When ads or brochures reprint, advertisers often make type changes. If all the text is black, the advertiser needs only to change the black negative and plate. If the text is any other color, all the negatives, stripping, and plating will have to be changed.

Bleeds   Finally, designers also need to consider **bleeds**—colors, type, or visuals that run all the way to the edge of the page. Production artists must set up their artwork for at least a quarter inch of extra color *outside* the image area to accommodate variations in the printing and cutting processes.

The Radio Commercial Production Process

Radio commercials, called **spots,** are among the quickest, simplest, and least expensive ads to produce. In fact, many stations provide production services free to local advertisers.

Some commercials are delivered live by the announcer, in which case the station gets a script or highlight sheet and any recorded music to be used. The material must be accurately timed. A live commercial script should run about 130 to 150 words per minute so the announcer can speak at a normal, conversational pace. The best way to do this is to use a popular DJ and let him or her improvise. It's a lot more entertaining and links the DJ's credibility to the product.[18]

The disadvantages of live commercials are that announcers may be inconsistent in their delivery, and sound effects are quite limited. Uniform delivery requires a recorded commercial. The process of producing a recorded commercial includes *preproduction, production,* and *postproduction* (or finishing) phases (see Exhibit 14–5).

Preproduction

In the **preproduction phase,** the advertiser and agency perform a variety of tasks that allow production to run smoothly, on time, and within budget. The agency assigns a radio producer from its staff or hires a freelance producer. Based on the script, the producer selects a studio and a director, determines what talent will be needed, estimates costs, and prepares a budget for the advertiser's approval.

To control the production process and get the finest sound reproduction, most ad agencies use independent recording studios. The best audio studios have experienced sound directors and technicians, close ties to well-known talent, and the latest recording equipment.

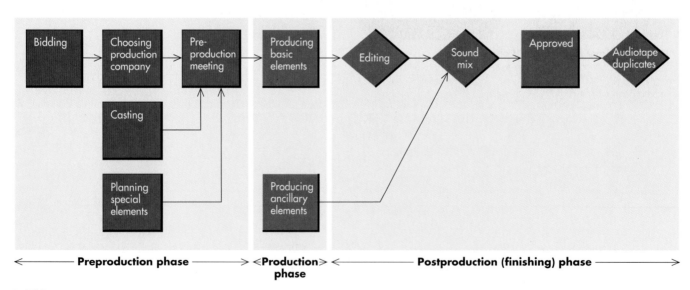

Exhibit 14–5

Radio commercials have three production phases. The preproduction and finishing phases are usually the most complex. Preproduction and postproduction editing and mixing typically require far more time than the actual recording session.

During the preproduction phase, the producer (or a casting director) searches for the right talent. This is an important decision, because talent is a form of icon or symbol for the product. The advertiser and the agency consider several factors before arriving at a decision: the person's tone of voice, vocal acting skills and creativity, intelligence, style of thinking, and reputation. The unusual effect of Tom Bodett's vocal style for Motel 6, for instance, shows how valuable good talent can be. In just three years, Motel 6 went from near-bankruptcy to incredible profitability and became the largest chain of budget motels in the United States—using only radio and Bodett's folksy commercials ("We'll only charge you about 20 bucks and we'll leave the light on for ya").

If the script calls for music, the producer decides whether to use prerecorded music or hire a composer and/or arranger. Any needed sound effects can be created or, most often, collected from prerecorded sources. All these decisions, of course, affect the budget, but they also have a dramatic impact on the effectiveness of the spots.

Once the talent is hired and music prepared, the **director** supervises rehearsals until everything is ready for recording.

Production: Cutting the Spot

All the elements to be used in the commercial—voices, music, sound effects—come together and are recorded at a **session.** Depending on the nature of the spot, a session can last from a half-hour to more than a day. Since studios charge by the hour, rehearsals are important in the preproduction phase.

The Sound Studio

At the session, the voice and music talent perform in a studio, which has sound-dampening wall surfaces, a carpeted floor, microphones, a window to a control room, and wall plugs for connecting equipment and instruments to the control room.

Standard items in the sound studio are microphones, headphone sets, and speakers. Announcers and singers wear headphones to hear instructions from the director in the control room or to monitor prerecorded instrumental tracks as they sing (keeping the music track from being recorded onto the voice track).

Studio technicians and engineers carefully select, disperse, and aim the appropriate microphones to capture the full spectrum of sounds. The studio may have a separate sound booth (a small windowed room or partitioned area) to isolate drums or louder backup talent so the sound technicians can better balance the overall group of sounds.

The Control Room

The agency producer, director, and sound engineer (and often the client and account executive) sit in the **control room,** where they can monitor all the sounds generated in the sound studio. The control room is separated from the studio by a thick glass window and soundproofed walls, so the people monitoring the session can hear the sounds on quality speakers and discuss the various takes.

The director and sound engineer work at an **audio console** (also called a **board**), the central "switchboard" for controlling the sounds and channeling them to the appropriate recording devices. As they monitor the sounds coming from the studio, they keep the pitch and loudness within acceptable levels for broadcast.

The board also serves as a sound mixer, blending both live and prerecorded sounds for immediate or delayed broadcast. The board connects to a range of recording and playback

A sophisticated audio console manipulates sound electronically, making sounds sharper or fuzzier, with more echo, or more treble or bass. Its multitrack mixing and sound enhancement capabilities are most useful during postproduction.

units, including multitracking, reel-to-reel or cartridge ("cart") tape recorders, and CD recorders.

Postproduction: Finishing the Spot

After the commercial is recorded a number of times, a selection is made from the best takes. The sound engineer usually records music, sound effects, and vocals separately and then mixes and sweetens them during the **postproduction** (or *finishing*) **phase.** The final recording is referred to as the **master tape.**

From the master tape, the engineer makes duplicates called **dubs,** records them onto quarter-inch magnetic tape, and sends them to radio stations for broadcast.

The Television Commercial Production Process

While Johanna Leovey was working on the Prius print ads, another team across the office was working on the television commercials. The creatives had come up with a great concept for the Prius, and it was right on the money strategically, but it would have to be produced exceedingly well to communicate the idea credibly and resonate with the company's diverse audiences. That meant bringing in one of the agency's top TV producers, and Richard Bendetti was selected to do the job.

The Role of the Commercial Producer

Today, advertising producers like Bendetti must be generalists, able to work with a variety of technicians to bring a spot's creative essence to life. And they must have the savvy to budget large amounts of money and spend them wisely.[19]

Students of advertising need to know basic TV production concepts to understand how commercials are made, why production is so expensive, and what methods they can use to cut costs without sacrificing quality or effectiveness.

As with radio, the process of producing a TV commercial always involves three stages, as shown in Exhibit 14–6:

1. Preproduction: all the work prior to the actual day of filming.
2. Production: the actual day (or days) the commercial is filmed or videotaped.

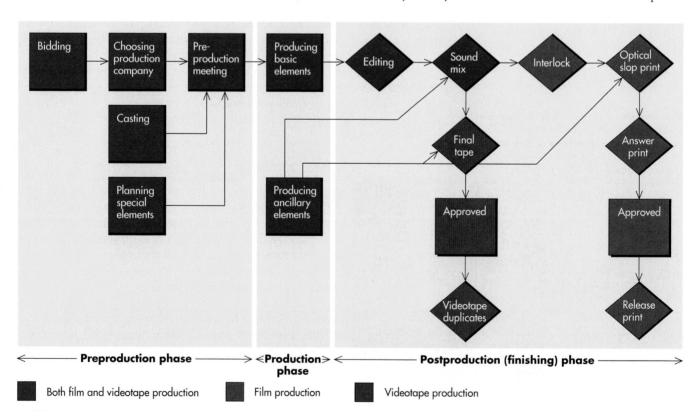

Exhibit 14–6

The production processes for film and videotape are very similar to that for radio until the sound-mixing stage. Computerized editing speeds up the finishing phase for videotape.

3. Postproduction (or finishing): all the work done after shooting to edit and finish the commercial.

Each step has a dramatic effect on cost and quality. For a look at how all three affect the end product, see the Portfolio Review, "Creative Department: From Concept through Production of a Magazine Ad and Television. Commercial" (pp. 454–459).

The Preproduction Phase

Good planning before production can save advertisers a lot of money. That's the purpose of the **preproduction phase.** The first thing the producer must do, therefore, is study the script and storyboard and analyze the production techniques that will be called for in the commercial. Three major categories of production techniques are used today: *live action, animation,* and *special effects.*

Live Action

To portray people and things in lifelike, everyday situations, like typical slice-of-life TV commercials, advertisers use the **live action** technique.

If a commercial calls for live action, the producer must consider whether the action will be staged indoors in a studio, outside on a studio lot, or on location away from the studio. Will it be taped or filmed? All these factors have a bearing on what equipment and personnel are required, where costumes are obtained, what permissions may be required, what talent can be used, and, of course, what the commercial costs. When children are used, rehearsals are a must. Children and animals are unpredictable and often cause production delays.

Working with the creative team, Richard Bendetti concurred that shooting on location was crucial to the Prius spot, which meant finding several locations around the world. This would mean coordinating with foreign ministries for visas and local city officials to get the necessary permits, police security, and environmental clearances. This created a bit of a problem in Japan, where the government doesn't allow traffic flow to be impeded at major intersections.

In the preproduction stage, art directors, copywriters, and producers carefully hash out the details required for filming a 30-second commercial. During this stage, the production team will develop and sketch a storyboard that depicts, in rough form, how the ad will appear. Any major changes should be made at this time because alterations in script or direction after filming begins can drive production costs up exponentially.

Simple yet sophisticated copy distinguishes this thoughtful spot for The New York Times. *The metaphor of a tornado grabs the viewer's attention and brings drama to the message.*

SFX: Music throughout

(Aerial shot of barn roof as surrounding countryside blows in the wind.)

VO (MAYA ANGELOU): The truth does not stand still for a moment.

(A tornado approaches. High winds blow against a wheelbarrow and pick up telephone and utility poles.)

It twists and turns, picks up your opinions,

(The twister hits and the barn breaks up into splinters of debris that mix with typed letters.) and sets them down a thousand miles away.

(The letters fall from the grip of the tornado, neatly into place as part of *The New York Times* newspaper text.)

When was the last time something you read moved you?

(SUPER: *The New York Times* logo.)
The New York Times.

Animation

Animation—cartoons, dancing puppets, and demonstrations in which inanimate objects come to life—can effectively communicate difficult messages or reach special markets such as children.

Traditional animation techniques include *cartoons, photo animation, stop-motion photography,* and *video animation.* Cartoons often score the highest viewer interest and the longest life, so over time they cost the least per showing. However, initial production is very expensive. A fully animated commercial can easily cost more than $200,000.[20]

Special Effects

Today, much video animation and most **special effects,** such as moving titles and whirling logos, are done with a joystick. All major video production companies use dedicated **digital video effects (DVE) units** that can manipulate graphics on the screen in many ways: fades, wipes, zooms, rotations, and so on.

Special effects entertain viewers and win advertising awards. But if the sales message is complex or based on logic, another technique might be better. No technique should so enthrall viewers that they pay more attention to it than to the product—or the strategic message. Further, more than one fantasy or **mnemonic device** (Energizer Bunny or Jolly Green Giant) might confuse audiences. David Ogilvy suggested that, to make the strongest impression on the viewer, fantasies should relate to the product's claims and be repeated heavily.[21]

Planning Production

The commercial is a group effort; the team includes a writer, art director, producer, director, and sometimes a musical composer and choreographer. The agency producer, who is responsible for completing the job on schedule and within budget, usually sends copies of the storyboard to three studios for competitive bids.

When the studio is chosen, the producer and casting director select the cast and hire the announcer. Next the set is built, and the crew and cast rehearse under the director's supervision.

For many commercials, the most important decision is the hiring of the director. Such was certainly the case for the Prius. When Saatchi was looking for a director, or in this case a director of photography, it was told several times that its concept for the Prius, involving a series of shots featuring both people and vehicles moving in place, would necessarily involve a lot of special effects. Saatchi was hesitant; it wanted to film the commercial with as little special effects as possible. Tarsem was an obvious choice for Doug. Not only did Tarsem seem excited by the Prius concept, but he agreed that the ad should be shot in the most natural way possible.

During the preproduction period, meetings are necessary among the director, the agency producer, the account representative, the writer, the art director, the commercial director, possibly the advertiser, and anyone else important to the production. This is where they iron out any last-minute problems and make final decisions about the scenes, the actors, and the announcer. They should review everything—music, sets, action, lighting, camera angles. A finished 60-second film commercial takes only 90 feet of film, but the shooting often requires several days and 3,000 to 5,000 feet of film. And unlike videotape, film can't be used again (see Ad Lab 14–B, "The Film versus Tape Decision").

The soundtrack may be recorded before, during, or after actual production. Recording sound in advance ensures that the commercial will be neither too long nor too short; it also helps when the subject has to move or dance to a specific music theme or rhythm.

Production: The Shoot

The actual shooting day (or days) can be very long and tedious. It may take several hours just to light the set to the director's liking. The Prius spot, for instance, took six full days to shoot over the course of a two-week period. Today, producers can use technology to control sound, lighting, and staging.

Quiet on the Set: Sound

Procedures for recording and controlling music and sound effects are similar to those used in radio. Microphones capture sound; recorders transfer the sound and store it on a medium like magnetic tape. Then, with the use of a multichannel control board, a sound engineer manipulates sounds for effect and records them onto film, video, or a playback system synchronized with film.

But the original recording is the key to success for two reasons. First, the original sound recording is synchronized with the original visual recording and with the action and the emotion expressed by the actors. A re-creation never quite matches the timing or feel of the original.

Second, before it reaches its final form, the original recording undergoes rerecording many times, with some loss of fidelity each time. So high-quality sound-recording equipment is mandatory.

Lights

The director and the cinematographer must deal with a variety of light sources. For example, a scene with a person standing close to a window may have three light sources: daylight through the window, high-intensity studio lighting for brightening the subject and the room's interior, and a regular table lamp serving as a prop. All these shed different types of light that could adversely affect the scene. To control this effect, technicians need to measure the light and style it to suit the scene.

Experienced **cinematographers** (motion picture photographers) can guess the range and intensity of light by briefly studying its source. However, they use light meters to determine how to set the camera's lens **aperture,** the opening that controls the amount of light that reaches the film or videotape. To record the correct color and brightness, all light sources must be in balance.

The arrangement of lights—whether in the studio, on the studio lot, or on location—establishes a visual mood. Intense light from a single source gives a

The Film versus Tape Decision

Today, live TV commercials are rare. Even those that look live are usually videotaped, and most national commercials are shot on color film. Film projects a soft texture that live broadcasts and videotape do not have. Because film is the oldest method, producers have a large pool of skilled talent to choose from. Also, film is extremely versatile. It works for numerous optical effects, slow motion, distance shots, mood shots, fast action, and various animation techniques. While film stock is expensive (and most of it ends up on the cutting-room floor) duplicate film prints are cheaper than videotape dupes.

However, magnetic videotape offers a more brilliant picture and better fidelity. It looks more realistic and more "live." Tape is also more consistent in quality than film stock. The chief advantage of tape is that it provides immediate playback, so scenes can be checked and redone while the props and actors are still together on the set. Moreover, com-puterization has cut editing time up to 90 percent. Videotape can be replayed almost forever, but a film commercial can be run only about 25 times.

Today, many directors shoot their commercials on film for texture and sensitive mood lighting, but then they dub the processed film onto videotape for editing. This process is more costly, but it gives them faster finishing and lets them see optical effects instantly. Some directors, however, still prefer to edit on film because they get the wider range of effects and thus achieve a higher level of creative storytelling.

Laboratory Application

Some products and some types of commercials are more effective shot on film, while others are better on videotape. Make a list of three product categories (or three brands) and three types of commercials. Describe which medium (film or tape) you think would be more effective in each case and why.

---

harsh appearance and may be used to create anxiety in the viewer. By using filters, warmer lights, diffusion screens, and reflectors, the cinematographer can create a reddish, more consistent, softer illumination—and a more romantic mood. The director works with the art director, the cinematographer, and the lighting engineer to choose the most appropriate placement, types, and intensities.

Camera

Professional film cameras used for making TV commercials shoot 16 millimeter, 35 mm, and 75 mm film, the diagonal measurement of a single film frame.

Producers of local TV commercials used to shoot with the grainier but less expensive 16 mm film; national spots were shot on 35 mm for extra quality and precision; and 75 mm film provides the highest quality image. While film is still widely used for national spots because of the atmosphere it brings to an image, most local spots are now shot on video.

Heavy-duty studio video cameras mounted on a stand with wheels can carry a number of accessories. One of the most important is the lens-mounted **Tele-prompter,** which allows the camera to see a spokesperson through the back of a two-way mirror while he or she reads moving text reflected off the front.

Unlike film cameras, studio video cameras are tied to a control room by large electronic cables. In the control room, multiple video screens and sound channels

Different types of lighting can enhance a scene and create special moods. Here, strong keylights light up the actors. The fainter light of the window screen casts a window-shaped pattern onto the background. The effect light above enhances the reflected glow of the candle on the table top. To bystanders the scene appears very bright, but when the camera's aperture is set properly, the film sees a darker, more shadowy play of lights and darks.

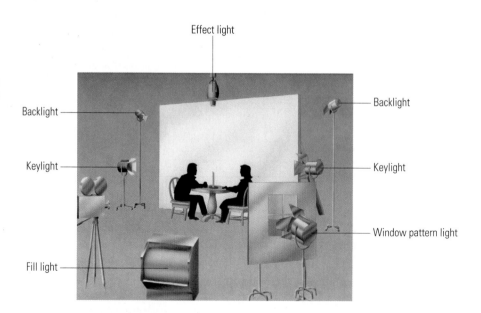

In any commercial production, it's typical to have many more people behind the camera than in front of it. In addition to the director and assistant director, other important players behind the scenes may include a sound editor, lighting technicians, electricians, and grips.

are wired to a control panel. Working at the control panel, the director can switch from one camera to another and simultaneously set the input and output levels of sound and visuals. Control panels also have DVE units for creating text or visual effects on screen.

Action: Staging and Talent

Staging for a commercial may be done in the isolation of a studio, outside on a studio lot, or on location. The studio offers the most control.

Most film and video studios have heavy soundproofing to eliminate outside noises such as sirens and low-flying aircraft. The studios are lightproof, which allows for complete lighting control. Special equipment is easier to use in the controlled environment of a studio. But studio lighting can make a scene appear artificial.

For scenes requiring large amounts of space, historic or unique architecture, scenery, and the full effect of outdoor lighting, the studio lot offers the best control. The **lot** is outside acreage shielded from stray, off-site sounds. The lot is convenient to the studio's carpentry shop, and sets can be left standing until all shootings and retakes are completed.

Although it adds realism, **location** shooting is often a technical and logistical nightmare. Every location has natural and manufactured features that create obstacles. Natural lighting creates bright highlights that contrast with harsh shadows. Large reflective screens and high-intensity lights are required to brighten up shadows for a more even-toned exposure. Energy sources for lighting and equipment may be insufficient, requiring long cables and mobile generators. But because sets don't have to be built, location shooting can be good for some low-budget commercials. However, natural events such as rain and fog can cause costly interruptions and serious delays. And shooting on location sets up special challenges for directors using video. A truck, van, motor home, or trailer is wired for video and sound control recording. Inside, a row of TV monitors and a multichannel control panel directs the recording from one or more cameras running simultaneously.

Shooting on location sets up special challenges for directors using video. A truck, van, motor home, or trailer is wired for video and sound control recording. Inside, a row of TV monitors and a multichannel control panel direct the recording from one or more cameras running simultaneously.

Whether at the studio or on location, most scenes require several takes for the **talent** (actors) to get them right. Lighting may need readjusting as unexpected shadows pop up. Each scene is shot from two or three different angles: one to establish the characters, one to show only the speaker, and one to show the listener's reaction.

Scenes aren't necessarily shot in order. Those with no synchronized sound are usually shot last since they don't require the full crew.

A long time may be needed between scenes to move the camera, reset the lights, reposition the talent, and pick up the action, sound, and look to match the other scenes. Each action must match what comes before and after. Commercials with disconcerting jumps destroy credibility.

Once all the scenes are "in the can," the commercial enters the postproduction, or finishing, phase.

Postproduction

In the **postproduction phase,** the film editor, sound mixer, and director actually put the commercial together.

Closed-Circuit Programming

Dan is a middle-aged man recovering at his local hospital from a recent stroke. Bedridden and immobile, he spends a lot of time watching television. In a boredom-induced daze, he half-wittedly flips through the channels and stumbles across a show featuring a man in a blue plaid shirt sitting in a doctor's office. A voice chimes in: "Daniel Sorby had no idea that he had high cholesterol—until he suffered from a stroke." Immediately Dan's attention perks up.

For the next half-hour, a discussion ensues on the difference between "good" and "bad" cholesterol, revealing their potential role in heart attacks and strokes. The program ends. Then comes a short commercial break.

The spot is for Plavix—"a prescription pill that can help protect you from a heart attack or stroke if you've recently had one," says a friendly grandmother, as the camera rolls to pictures of her playing with her grandkids.

This is the scene played out every day in roughly 1,000 hospitals nationwide due to the introduction of the Patient Channel—a 24-hour network piped directly into patient and waiting rooms at no cost to the hospital or patient.

Founded in September of 2002 by General Electric Co., the Patient Channel is one of a growing number of *closed-circuit programming* channels providing news and educational programs to hospitals,

schools, and fitness centers across the country. Yet it is neither the news nor the programs that are making the national headlines. Rather, it is the advertising that pays for the service, such as the Plavix spot, which has stirred much recent debate.

Proponents for the network are principally the pharmaceutical companies that now suddenly have direct advertising access to over 22 million patients. Never before have the drug manufacturers been able to "directly associate their products with a particular condition within a hospital setting." By achieving such a full measure of *direct-to-consumer* advertising, the pharmaceuticals will likely generate enormous revenues on their new, nongeneric drugs.

Opponents of the network are led by a consumer advocacy group called Commercial Alert, which feels the Patient Channel's ads "pitch drugs at a time when [patients] are most worried about disease, in a way that carries the implicit authority and endorsement of the hospital and its doctors." Furthermore, the group feels the channel unfairly exploits a "captive audience at a time of maximum vulnerability and emotional distress."

Refuting such claims, proponents point to the educational content the network provides. Federal requirements state that hospitals have the responsibility to provide a certain amount of patient education. General Electric, the pharmaceutical advertisers, and some within the medical profession have argued that the channel helps hospitals address this patient education requirement while freeing up already overworked

---

With computer and videotape technology, editors can convert the film to tape and add effects such as wipes and dissolves electronically. Although a director will spend many hours editing a commercial shot on video, it will still be considerably less than what is needed for film editing and lab work.

Many professionals still prefer film. The visual portion of the commercial appears on one piece of celluloid without the effects of dissolves, titles, or **supers** (words superimposed on the picture). The sound portion is assembled on another piece of celluloid. This is the **work print** stage (also called the *rough cut* or *interlock*).

In the postproduction phase, the director and editor can save a lot of time and money by using computerized video and sound editing equipment for the assembly of the final product. At this stage, the director and editor will select and splice scenes into their respective order, removing all the unneeded footage. Next, they add off-camera special effects, like supers, and incorporate any necessary music or voice-overs.

nurses. Yet, this point may also be countered. While the educational benefits of the channel may be valuable to patients, Commercial Alert believes the information needs to be conveyed in a balanced, complete, and unbiased medium—it should not be a "sideshow of sales propaganda designed to push pills."

Hospitals are not the only venues subject to closed-circuit TV programming. For over 12 years, Channel One has broadcast news and current events to American middle, junior, and high school classrooms. Each day, 8 million students view a 12-minute newscast featuring interesting stories on breaking news events and teen topics, supported, of course, by advertising.

In the process, Channel One keeps teens aware of and involved in a multitude of issues by presenting them in a manner that can easily be absorbed and understood. Channel One further enhances classroom learning by providing a website for teens to visit to learn more about the news, find out about the latest teen crazes, offer opinions, play games, take quizzes, and learn about the dangers of alcohol and drug abuse. Plus, for the 400,000 teachers that use Channel One in the classroom, ChannelOneTeacher.com provides ideas and lesson plans—everything they need to teach the news.

However, once again the advertisements have captured the controversial spotlight. As with the Patient Channel, the cost of providing the much-needed free TVs and VCRs to classrooms is offset by the ads that accompany the news segment—typically for junk-food products.

Some students and parents have raised their voices in an effort to remove the programs, stating that teens should not be the victims of deceptive advertising campaigns. One parent said he is opposed to Channel One because it creates a slippery slope that could open schools up to even more commercial interests. He said that he would hate to "live in a district where the kids run on the Pepsi track or work out in the Nike gym." The overall concern is that children of this age are highly impressionable, and that makes the junk-food advertisements seen on Channel One unethically exploitative.

In this debate, both the pros and cons seem to have good arguments, making it difficult to craft a policy that would resolve the issue entirely. The future of this medium will depend on how advertisers attempt to use it and how consumers in turn react, as closed circuit programming becomes more prevalent in the years to come.

Sources: Alexandra Marks, "Patient Channel in Hospitals: Healthy Move?" *The Christian Science Monitor*, March 19, 2003 (retrieved from www.nexis.com); Suzanne Vranica, "Patient Channel to Blast Ads at Bedridden," *The Wall Street Journal*, September 26, 2002; Stephanie Riesenman, "Critics Object to Drug Ads on Hospital Channel," *Reuters*, February 26, 2003; "Keep Drug-Sponsored 'Patient Channel' Out of Hospitals, Doctors Say," *Commercial Alert News Release*, February 25, 2003 (retrieved from www.commercialalert.org); www.channelone.com (home/about channelone.com); www.channelone teacher.com; Mike McWilliams, "Channel One Broadcasts Stir Debate," *Iowa City Press-Citizen*, February 27, 2003 (retrieved from www.nexis.com).

External sound is recorded next. The sound engineer records the musicians and singers, as well as the announcer's voice-over narrative. Prerecorded stock music may be bought and integrated into the commercial. The mixing also includes any sound effects, such as doorbells ringing or doors slamming.

Once sound editing is complete, the finished sound is put on one piece of celluloid. That, combined with the almost-completed visual celluloid, yields the **mixed interlock.** The addition of optical effects and titles results in the **answer print.** This is the final commercial. If it is approved, **dupes** (duplicate copies) are made for delivery to the networks or TV stations.

Producing Advertising for Digital Media

Have you seen the Academy Awards shows recently? The lavish Kodak Theatre, home to the presentation since 2002, has a "media cockpit" located in the middle of orchestra (main floor) seating. From there, technicians coordinate the multimedia extravaganza for each year's festivities. Home viewers are also participants in the huge digital media event. Advances in digital media now allow ABC, the network that carries the show, to delay both audio and video by several seconds. This technique, more sophisticated than simply "bleeping" out any verbal obscenity, was first used in 2004, in order to censor any potentially lawsuit-worthy mishaps like Janet Jackson's "wardrobe malfunction" during that year's Super Bowl halftime show. The live telecast of the Oscars often wins an Emmy for its smooth mixture of film clips, live performances, coverage of the action at the podium, and audience reaction shots.

The Emergence of Digital Media

The roots of this new phenomenon really go back to the 35 mm camera and the lowly slide show. Remember when the neighbors got back from Paris and came over to show their slides?

Boring as it was, the home slide show was rapidly adopted by the business world and became a staple of sales presentations, corporate shareholder meetings, and luncheon speeches.

Some enterprising person thought the slide show could be perked up with a little music or a professional announcer. The professional slide presentation was born—and so was a new medium for advertising. The slide presentation was quickly adopted by sales forces, and companies sprang up all over the country to write, photograph, and produce high-quality, professional slide shows for business.

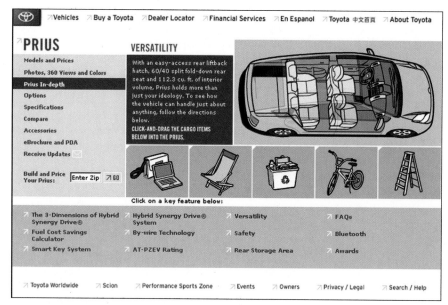

The emergence of digital media requires the development of an entirely new set of skills to produce ads. Art directors and designers must understand how to integrate print and video into a single medium, and they must also comprehend the features and limitations of the computer languages used to produce such work.

Sound + Music + Motion = Multimedia

Then came the idea of using multiple screens and multiple projectors. Quick cuts from one slide to another, in sync with the music and sound effects, created the feeling of motion. This was the birth of the **multimedia presentation,** which simply refers to presenting information or entertainment using several communications media simultaneously.

It wasn't long before video and animation were added to the mix. In one multimedia presentation, a prospect might be treated to both slides and video playing on two to twelve screens simultaneously, plus professional narration, music, and sound effects. It was very compelling.

Multimedia + Computer Technology = Digital Media

Then along came the personal computer, the breakup of AT&T, the deregulation of the broadcast and cable TV industry, the development of CD-ROM technology and fiber optics, and the stage was set for the media revolution now taking place—the emergence of digital media. Basically, **digital media** are channels of communication that join the logic of multimedia formats with the electronic system capabilities and controls of modern telecommunications, television, and computer technologies. Digital media are a subset of electronic media. We already see them in many venues (settings).

Venues for Digital Media

The three categories of places where we experience digital media today are based on audience size: *mass audience, private audience,* and *personal audience venues.*

The Academy Awards show is a good example of a **mass audience venue.** With hundreds of people in the live audience and millions more watching at home, the multimedia presentation had a huge reach. Multimedia is also used in major sporting events, the Olympics opening ceremonies, political conventions, and other mass audience events.

Many digital media events are in **private audience venues,** though some of these may be quite large. A major marketer's national sales meeting, large corporate conferences, sales meetings with 10 people in attendance, educational conferences, training seminars, and local information centers all use computer-driven multimedia presentations, utilizing software programs such as *PowerPoint* to inform, persuade, remind, and entertain people.

The **personal audience venue** is experiencing the most growth today. One person sitting in front of a personal computer can receive multimedia information off the Internet from an online database service such as Prodigy or America Online, or from software bought in a computer store. People can even create their own mini-multimedia programs with slides and limited animation by buying a turnkey *authoring program* (Hypercard®, Supercard®, Macromedia Director®) at any software store.

The landscape is rapidly becoming dotted with kiosks, interactive computers in a stand-alone cabinet (discussed earlier in this chapter). Kiosks offer a station from which one person at a time can interact with the computer. They are used to sell products, inform, and entertain.

Finally, **interactive TV** is becoming available as another personal audience venue. While watching TV, people can use a remote control system to gain immediate access to the Internet or, in some limited cases, even tailor the programming to their personal tastes. Ironically, the most massive form of media—television—is now becoming one of the most personal.

The Role of Digital Media in Advertising

With the trend toward integrated marketing communications, the various digital media give marketers new ways to reach prospects and begin a relationship—or improve their relationship with current customers.

In some cases, the medium itself is the ad, as in the case of a multimedia sales presentation or a dedicated kiosk offering information about one company's wares. In other cases, though, the digital media are a form of narrowcasting in which advertisers can buy space or time for their commercial announcements. Often the spot is just an electronic billboard with the company or brand name. In Internet advertising, the advertiser sets up a virtual storefront, called a **Web page,** or places a billboard ad on some other company's Web page. When viewers click certain "buttons" on the home page, a new page comes up with more detailed information about the company and its products, policies, or prices. We've gone back to the basics; it's a fancy slide show. But, in fact, it's multimedia. And the technology is getting better, faster, cheaper, and more impressive every day.

For the agency producer, this presents exciting challenges and opportunities. Not all the opportunities are available yet, but everybody knows what's around the corner: Touch a button on the screen and a full video commercial or technical film will run; click on another button and a personal representative will come online with you. The possibilities are endless. The challenge will be to keep current.

Since 1994, HotWired (www.hotwired.com) has been the hot online magazine for informed computer wonks. Visit the website and see how HotWired incorporates animation, video, and other multimedia forms into this interactive, personal audience venue.

The People Who Produce Digital Media Advertising

Some experts predict a virtual revolution in creative style and effectiveness as creative people learn to deal with the new media, offering more information and less glitz.[22] The ranks of production managers and producers are already swelling as media vehicles multiply beyond anybody's recent imagination. New titles are suddenly appearing on agency rosters: multimedia producers, directors, and technicians; interactive planners and writers; computer programmers and system designers; kiosk media buyers; and so on. At Saatchi & Saatchi, Nathan Hackstock holds the title of creative director for integrated marketing. Working with him is a staff of art directors, copywriters, and producers who specialize in creating interactive ads for Saatchi's clients. Outside the agencies are a host of new suppliers: kiosk manufacturers, interactive software developers, CD-ROM manufacturers, digital media-buying services, and so on.

The Production Process

For digital media, the production process is a hybrid of all the other processes we've discussed. That's because some of the digital media are akin to print and outdoor media (computer billboards and Web pages), while others are closely associated with TV and radio.

As we've seen in this chapter, regardless of medium, the production manager or producer goes through a planned sequence of activities: preproduction, production, and postproduction. Preproduction includes the planning, costing, and hiring activities. The production stage is when the artwork is created, the video and audio recorded, or the computer program developed. Postproduction includes the editing, duplicating, and distribution activities. The difference for digital media is in the details of activities in the production and postproduction stages (see RL 14–2, Production Process for Digital Media, in the Reference Library on the *Contemporary Advertising* CD).

The new media have introduced new costs.[23] One of these is **platform licensing,** a fee paid to original software developers for the special key codes that access multimedia programs on certain computer networks. There is the cost of buying and leasing new equipment and the cost of manufacturing or duplicating CD-ROMs, diskettes, or whatever new medium comes along to transport the advertiser's message.

An exciting new world awaits us out there. And it's not just around the corner. It's already here.

Chapter Summary

Careful management is the key to success in producing advertising. If the production process is not handled correctly, an otherwise beautiful ad or commercial can be destroyed. The task of managing this process is the responsibility of a print production manager or an electronic media producer. The manager's job is to keep the project moving smoothly and under budget, while maintaining the required level of quality through every step of the production process.

Production managers perform the classic functions of management: planning, organizing, directing, and controlling. They also have to keep up with changing technology, monitor costs, and meet budgets.

Many factors can destroy budgets. The five most common are inadequate planning and preparation, production luxuries, overtime, special equipment, and too many decision makers. Factors specific to each medium can also affect budgets drastically.

The print production process consists of four phases: preproduction, production, prepress, and printing and distribution. In the preproduction phase, the manager plans the overall job carefully and then starts to deal with the specific needs of the job, such as typography.

Typography affects an ad's appearance, design, and legibility. There are four important concepts when selecting type: readability, appropriateness, harmony or appearance, and emphasis. A key skill is copy casting, knowing how to fit type into a particular space in a layout. The production manager also considers what kind of paper will be used, since it affects the way the art is prepared.

In the production phase, artists prepare mechanicals (or pasteups) of the art to be printed. Most agencies today use sophisticated desktop publishing. The artists prepare the mechanicals as line art and use a photographic process to turn continuous-tone artwork into halftones. Halftone images (illustrations and photos) simulate gradations of tone with different sizes of black dots.

In the prepress stage, the printer makes a plate from the base art and one from each overlay. Each mechanical must be photographed separately. For full color, four halftone plates are used (one for each color process color plus black). The set of negatives used to make the four plates is called a color separation. This work is now mostly done on large computerized scanner systems.

The final phase of the production process includes the actual printing of the job, as well as cutting, embossing, binding, and shipping. Quality control is critical throughout the process. The production manager has to make sure computer disks are compatible with the reprographics service bureau and contain all the elements needed to produce the negatives. Along the way, the manager must check several printer's proofs for scratches or blemishes and to make sure traps and bleeds are handled correctly.

Radio spots are among the quickest, simplest, and least expensive ads to produce. A producer manages the production process through the preproduction, production, and postproduction stages. The producer contracts with a recording studio, selects talent, and collects music and sound effects for the recording session. At the session, the talent works in a studio, while the director and sound engineer work in the control room at an audio console, monitoring and modulating the sound as it's recorded.

In the postproduction phase, the director and sound engineer select the best takes, splice them together, mix in sound effects and music, and then edit the sound until the master tape is completed. Dubs are made from this and sent to radio stations for airing.

Television production involves the same three stages. In preproduction, the producer determines which production technique is most suitable for the script: live action, animation, special effects, or a combination. The studio is chosen, the cast selected, and rehearsals held. As much work as possible is done during preproduction to reduce the shooting time required.

The production phase is when the commercial is actually shot, in a studio, on a lot, or on location. Specialized technicians are responsible for the sound, lights, and cameras, all of which can diminish the commercial if not handled correctly. Scenes are shot and reshot until the director and producer feel they have a good take. For cost reasons, scenes are frequently not shot in order. The sound track may be recorded before or after the shoot.

In the postproduction stage, the commercial is actually put together on either film or videotape. External sound and music are added to the video and the sound track until the master (or answer print for film) is completed. Then dupes are made and shipped to TV stations.

A multimedia presentation provides information or entertainment using several communications media simultaneously, typically slides, video, and audio. The electronic capabilities of computer technology were added to the multimedia presentation to create digital media.

Digital media are used in mass audience venues, private audience venues, and personal audience venues. The personal audience venue includes PC applications such as advertising on the Internet, with online database services, or via interactive TV and kiosks.

Digital media are a whole new industry. The overall production process is similar to those of print and electronic media, but the details involve new technologies, terminologies, and costs that advertisers and agencies are not yet familiar with. This means opportunities for new people coming into the field.

Important Terms

Review Questions

1. What are the five common budget busters every production manager should be aware of?

2. What is the primary role of the print production manager?

3. What does copy casting mean? Explain how it is done.

4. What is a halftone? Why is it important, and how is it produced?

5. How are color photographs printed? What are the potential problems with printing in color?

6. What are the advantages and disadvantages of animation?

7. What leads to the greatest waste of money in TV commercial production? Explain.

8. When is it better to use film and when is it better to use video-tape? Why?

9. What are the most common forms of digital media? How do they differ from media in the past?

10. What are some ways an advertiser such as McDonald's could use digital media to enhance its IMC program? Explain.

11. **The Advertising Experience**
Typeface makes a strong contribution to the overall effect of an advertisement. Create ads with appropriate typefaces for three of the following media products. (Typefaces are not restricted to those discussed in Ad Lab 14-A.)

    a. The Gettysburg Address

    b. The King James Bible

    c. Stephen King's (or Stanley Kubrick's, your choice) *The Shining*

    d. A DVD collection of *Friends* episodes

    e. A boxed set of "Barney's Greatest Hits" CDs

    f. An astronomy textbook

    g. A collection of *Lord of the Rings* fan fiction

Exploring the Internet

The Internet exercises for Chapter 14 address the following areas covered in the chapter: print production and broadcast production.

1. **Print Production**
Take a moment to go online and learn more about print production. Numerous organizations and companies that specialize in some aspect of print production are on the Web. Visit the sites listed below and answer the questions that follow.

    - Acme Printing www.acmeiowa.com
    - AlphaGraphics www.alphagraphics.com
    - Color Masters www.colormasters.com
    - ColorArts www.colorarts.com
    - Digital XPress www.digitalxpress.com
    - Graphic Arts Information Network (GAIN) www.gain.org
    - Graphic Communications Association (GCA) www.gca.org
    - Hart Graphics www.hartgr.com
    - National Association of Printers & Lithographers (NAPL) www.napl.org
    - PANTONE www.pantone.com
    - Screen Printing & Graphic Imaging Association (SGIA) www.sgia.org

    a. Who is the intended audience of the site?

    b. What type of company or organization is it? What are the scope and size of its operations?

    c. What print-related activities does the company or organization specialize in?

    d. What is your overall impression of the company and its work? Why?

2. **Broadcast Production**
Producing broadcast commercials is even more complex than the print production process. Peruse the websites below of these broadcast production-related organizations. Then answer the questions that follow.

    - Aardman Animation www.aardman.com
    - @radical.media www.radicalmedia.com
    - Directors Guild of America www.dga.org
    - Duck Soup Produckions www.ducksoupla.com
    - Film Planet www.filmplanet.com
    - Hollywood Digital www.hollydig.com
    - Johnson Burnett www.johnsonburnett.com
    - Jones Film & Video www.jonesinc.com
    - Screen Actors Guild (SAG) www.sag.com

    a. What type of production-related company or organization is it? What seem to be the scope and size of its operations?

    b. What kind of broadcast production activities does the company specialize in? Are these typically preproduction, production, or postproduction activities?

    c. What benefit does the company or organization provide the advertising community?

    d. What impresses you most about this organization and its work? Least? Why?

3. **Making a Musical**
Your client has approved the concept your agency has created for DoubleDuty Unisex Jeans. Jerry Seinfeld will sing a duet with an animated female character of your choice in an ad that shows how both men and women can appreciate the jeans' quality, style, and comfort. Which of the production companies, or combination of companies, listed in Exercise 2 is best suited for an ad of this kind? Detail the advantages of this company at each stage of the production process.

Part 5

Using Advertising Media

ADVERTISING MEDIA ARE THE CHANNELS OF COMMUNICATION through which advertising messages are conveyed. Choosing the best media for an advertising campaign is a critical task, requiring a sound knowledge of the benefits each channel provides for the audiences being targeted and the products being advertised. ■

Chapter 15
Using Print Media

Discusses the advantages and disadvantages of advertising in newspapers and magazines and considers the importance of such factors as flexibility, audience selectivity, reproduction quality, and circulation.

Chapter 16
Using Electronic Media: Television and Radio

Presents the yardsticks advertisers use to measure the merits of advertising on television and radio. The chapter discusses the opportunities presented by each medium and important guidelines in their use.

Chapter 17
Using Digital Interactive Media and Direct Mail

Looks at the new opportunities of interactive and addressable media. The chapter discusses the challenges presented by the new media and offers practical guidelines for their use.

Chapter 18
Using Out-of-Home, Exhibitive, and Supplementary Media

Presents the advantages and disadvantages of advertising through various outdoor and transit media. The chapter discusses the importance of packaging, trade shows, and other exhibitive media. Finally, the chapter considers such supplementary media as specialty advertising and Yellow Pages directories.

Chapter 15

Using Print Media

Objectives   TO EXAMINE HOW PRINT ADVERTISING ENHANCES the advertiser's media mix. Newspapers and magazines, with their unique qualities, can complement broadcast, direct mail, and other media. By using print wisely, advertisers can significantly increase the reach and impact of their campaigns and still stay within their budget.

After studying this chapter, you will be able to:

- **Explain** the advantages and disadvantages of magazine advertising.

- **Discuss** the various ways to analyze a magazine's circulation.

- **Describe** how newspapers are categorized.

- **Define** the major types of newspaper advertising.

- **Explain** the advantages and disadvantages of newspaper advertising.

- **Discuss** how rates are determined for print media.

- **List** several sources of print media data.

Grow Moore.

About 15% of your
height is added during your
teen years, and milk can help.
What more can you ask for?

got milk?

Americans celebrate their down-to-earth origins. These are often reflected in a wide range of forms, from the colorful portraits of Norman Rockwell to the all-American regimen of hot dogs and apple pie. But for today's increasingly health- and image-conscious public, the steak and egg meals of yesteryear have lost their appeal. Now, people count their calories meticulously, right down to a simple can of soda. ■ Given this changing attitude, the National Fluid Milk Processor Promotion Board faced a considerable dilemma. How could it reestablish milk as sufficiently savvy for the country's modern beverage consumer? Milk from the dairies of the heartland didn't have the panache sought by the majority of people. Fortunately, unlike many food marketers, the milk board held a trump card of superior nutritional value that it felt could complete a winning hand. What it needed was to educate the public about its special secret and overcome fears of what had become that most taboo "F word": fat. ■ Science (and nature) worked in the organization's favor. Nutritionists began publishing study after study that confirmed that most Americans did not receive enough calcium from their diet. And calcium is easily obtained through the consumption of milk. The National Institutes of Health (NIH) warned that without enough calcium, middle-aged people (especially women) suffer from the bone-degenerating disease osteoporosis. It reported that after the age of 11, no age group of females achieves even 75 percent of the recommended levels of calcium, and that only one out of three males receives the levels recommended for adults.[1] Armed with this information, the milk board set out to create a campaign that would spark public interest in its solution to this health problem. ■ The board hired Bozell Worldwide, an advertising agency well known for its print ads. The puzzle was to create a campaign that would resonate with the times, one that would create appeal for a new era of milk, and one that could be supported by the data from the NIH. ■ From a marketing perspective, the beauty of print media is the ability to target audiences selectively and achieve maximum exposure for a product. Magazines open avenues to very specific niches of the public and facilitate high-quality presentations in the brilliance of full-color spreads. The efforts culminated in the "Milk, where's *your* mustache?" campaign, featuring celebrities from all walks of life with not-so-debonair milk mustaches smeared across their upper lip. Accompanying the quirky photos, Bozell incorporated testimonials from the models praising the positive effects of the vitamins, minerals, and protein from milk that helped them to achieve their success. ■ The campaign's initial phase focused on women to eliminate the stigma of milk's supposed high fat content. Ads featuring the likes of supermodel Kate Moss and actress Daisy Fuentes played up their glamour and health consciousness. (Moss's ad even joked that the waif look was out.) The accompanying testimonials touted milk's bone-fortifying effects while assuring the audience of its minimal fat content. Another ad featured America's most famous homemaker, Martha Stewart, with a caption that advised the audience to substitute milk for water in their cooking recipes. ■ The ads ran in such consumer magazines as *Vogue, Cosmopolitan, People,* and *Good Housekeeping,* carefully targeting each publication's audience of women who purchase frequently. Following the campaign, research revealed a 17 percent increase in the belief by women that milk's health benefits outweigh its fat and calories. This success emboldened the National Fluid Milk Processor Promotion Board to double the campaign's advertising budget and led to more ambitious plans to target teenage boys and girls, college students, and men.[2] ■ By carefully selecting the vehicles, the milk board changed the public's attitude toward an entire industry. Use of consumer magazines emphasized the rich colors of the photos and displayed the desired tone of athleticism, sensuality, and humor to the fullest degree with each of the well-known celebrities. And the long shelf life of magazines let readers explore the inherent message of milk's health benefits in a manner that would not have been as effective in any other medium. ■ In the end, the milk processors' $110 million "Where's *your* mustache?" integrated campaign endowed milk with its current and much-needed image of fun, glamour, and health. ■

The Role of the Print Media Buyer

Once the strategic marketing, advertising, and media planning is completed and the creative direction is set, the advertiser can turn to the tactical details of actually scheduling and buying media time on radio and television and media space in magazines and newspapers. This is where the big money is spent in advertising—on the actual placement of ads in the media. So the competent performance of the media-buying task is critical to getting the most bang for the advertiser's buck.

The person in charge of negotiating and contracting with the media is called a **media buyer.** Media buyers often specialize in one medium or another, so there are print media buyers, spot TV media buyers, network media buyers, and so on. The degree of specialization depends on the size of the advertiser or the agency or the independent media-buying firm the buyer works for. In small agencies, for example, media buyers frequently don't specialize. They do it all.

Success as a *print media buyer* requires a range of knowledge and abilities. First, media buyers must have a broad and basic understanding of all the various forms of print media available and the terminology used in the field. They need to know, for example, how magazines and newspapers are categorized, the advertising possibilities each form offers, and the pros and cons of using various types of print media vehicles. Today, they should also have an understanding of the impact of new technologies on the print media.

Second, buyers need to know how to buy magazine and newspaper space. They must understand how to analyze circulation, how to read rate cards, where to go to get reliable information, and how to calculate and negotiate the most efficient media buys.

Finally, media buyers can exercise their creativity by developing ingenious, sophisticated ways to integrate the advertiser's print media efforts into the whole creative mix.

Obviously, this is no small task. But for the student of advertising who may begin his or her career in a media department, a basic understanding of all these issues is quite important. The purpose of this chapter and, in fact, all of Part Five, is to bring clarity to these subjects.

Using Magazines in the Creative Mix

Advertisers use magazines in their creative mix for many reasons. First and foremost, magazines allow an advertiser to reach a particular target audience with a high-quality presentation. The National Fluid Milk Processor Promotion Board is just one of many leading advertisers that use magazines as an important element of their creative mix (Exhibit 15–1 lists the top U.S. magazine advertisers).

The Pros and Cons of Magazine Advertising

Magazines offer a wide variety of benefits to advertisers. The milk mustache campaign benefited greatly from the outstanding color reproduction available only from magazines. Further, by running in consumer magazines read by women of particular ages and lifestyles, the milk board could target its audience more precisely. Magazines offer a host of other features too: flexible design options, prestige, authority, believability, and long shelf life. Magazines may sit on a coffee table or shelf for months and be reread many times. People can read a magazine ad at their leisure; they can pore over the details of a photograph; and they can study carefully the information presented in the copy. This makes it an ideal medium for high-involvement think and feel products.

However, like every medium, magazines also have a number of drawbacks (see the Checklist, "The Pros and Cons of Magazine Advertising"). They are expensive (on a cost-per-thousand basis), especially for color ads. And since they typically come out only monthly, or weekly at best, it's difficult to build up reach and frequency quickly. For these reasons, many advertisers use magazines in combination with other media—such as newspapers, which we'll discuss later in this chapter (see Ad Lab 15–A, "Magazines and the Creative Mix").

Exhibit 15–1

Top 10 magazine advertisers in the United States (2003).

Rank	Advertiser	Magazine ad spending ($ millions)
1	Procter & Gamble Co.	$582.3
2	General Motors Corp.	453.8
3	Altria Group	367.9
4	Johnson & Johnson	306.9
5	DaimlerChrysler	299.0
6	Ford Motor Co.	278.4
7	Time Warner	273.1
8	L'Oréal	271.7
9	Toyota Motor Corp.	253.9
10	Pfizer	212.8

The Pros and Cons of Magazine Advertising

The Pros

____ **Flexibility** in readership and advertising. Magazines cover the full range of prospects; they have a wide choice of regional and national coverage and a variety of lengths, approaches, and editorial tones.

____ **Color** gives readers visual pleasure, and color reproduction is best in slick magazines. Color enhances image and identifies the package. In short, it sells.

____ **Authority and believability** enhance the commercial message. TV, radio, and newspapers offer lots of information but lack the depth needed for readers to gain knowledge or meaning; magazines often offer all three.

____ **Permanence,** or long shelf life, gives the reader time to appraise ads in detail, allowing a more complete education/sales message and the opportunity to communicate the total corporate personality.

____ **Prestige** for products advertised in upscale or specialty magazines such as *Architectural Digest, Connoisseur,* and *Town and Country.*

____ **Audience selectivity** is more efficient in magazines than any other medium except direct mail. The predictable, specialized editorial environment selects the audience and enables advertisers to pinpoint their sales campaigns. Examples: golfers (*Golf Digest*), businesspeople (*BusinessWeek*), 20-something males (*Details*), or teenage girls (*Seventeen*).

____ **Cost efficiency** because wasted circulation is minimized. Print networks give advertisers reduced prices for advertising in two or more network publications.

____ **Selling power** of magazines is proven, and results are usually measurable.

____ **Reader loyalty** that sometimes borders on fanaticism.

____ **Extensive pass-along readership.** Many people may read the magazine after the initial purchaser.

____ **Merchandising assistance.** Advertisers can generate reprints and merchandising materials that help them get more mileage out of their ad campaigns.

The Cons

____ **Lack of immediacy** that advertisers can get with newspapers or radio.

____ **Shallow geographic coverage.** They don't offer the national reach of broadcast media.

____ **Inability to deliver mass audiences at a low price.** Magazines are very costly for reaching broad masses of people.

____ **Inability to deliver high frequency.** Since most magazines come out only monthly or weekly, the advertiser can build frequency faster than reach by adding numerous small-audience magazines to the schedule.

____ **Long lead time** for ad insertion, sometimes two to three months.

____ **Heavy advertising competition.** The largest-circulation magazines have 52 percent advertising to 48 percent editorial content.

____ **High cost per thousand.** Average black-and-white CPM in national consumer magazines ranges from $5 to $12 or more; some trade publications with highly selective audiences have a CPM over $50 for a black-and-white page.

____ **Declining circulations,** especially in single-copy sales, is an industrywide trend that limits an advertiser's reach.

Special Possibilities with Magazines

Media buyers need to be aware of the many creative possibilities magazines offer advertisers through various technical or mechanical features. These include bleed pages, cover positions, inserts and gatefolds, and special sizes, such as junior pages and island halves.

When the dark or colored background of the ad extends to the edge of the page, it is said to **bleed** off the page. Most magazines offer bleed pages, but they charge 10 to 15 percent more for them. The advantages of bleeds include greater flexibility in expressing the advertising idea, a slightly larger printing area, and more dramatic impact.

If a company plans to advertise in a particular magazine consistently, it may seek a highly desirable **cover position.** Few publishers sell ads on the front cover, commonly called the *first cover.* They do sell the inside front, inside back, and outside back covers (the *second, third,* and *fourth covers,* respectively), usually through multiple-insertion contracts at a substantial premium.

A less expensive way to use magazine space is to place the ad in unusual places on the page or dramatically across spreads. A **junior unit** is a large ad (60 percent of the page) placed in the middle of a page and surrounded with editorial matter. Similar to junior units are **island halves,** surrounded by even more editorial matter. The island sometimes costs more than a regular half-page, but because it dominates the page, many advertisers consider it worth the extra charge. Exhibit 15–2 shows other space combinations that create impact.

Sometimes, rather than buying a standard page, an advertiser uses an **insert.** The advertiser prints the ad on high-quality paper stock to add weight and drama to the message, and then ships the finished ads to the publisher for insertion into the magazine at a special price. Another option is multiple-page inserts. Calvin

Ad Lab 15–A

Magazines and the Creative Mix

Read the Checklist, "The Pros and Cons of Magazine Advertising" and see if you can apply that information to the following situation:

You manage an elegant French restaurant in Los Angeles that is known for its intimate setting, excellent service, and a lovely outdoor garden patio. You decide to build the business by promoting the special ambience your restaurant offers. To enhance the sense of romance, you plan to give away a long-stemmed rose and a glass of champagne with each entrée. Your clientele consists primarily of wealthy, educated business leaders and celebrities. However, a growing segment of your customers are tourists and middle-class couples out for a special evening.

Laboratory Applications

1. Is a magazine the best way to advertise this special? If not, explain why. If so, explain why and include which type of magazine would be best.

2. How can magazine advertising help you build the restaurant's image?

Klein once promoted its jeans in a 116-page insert in *Vanity Fair.* The insert reportedly cost more than $1 million, but the news reports about it in major daily newspapers gave the campaign enormous publicity value. Advertising inserts may be devoted exclusively to one company's product, or they may be sponsored by the magazine and have a combination of ads and special editorial content consistent with the magazine's focus.

A **gatefold** is an insert whose paper is so wide that the extreme left and right sides have to be folded into the center to match the size of the other pages. When the reader opens the magazine, the folded page swings out like a gate to present the ad. Not all magazines provide gatefolds, and they are always sold at a substantial premium.

Some advertisers create their own **custom magazines.** These look like regular magazines and are often produced by the same companies that publish traditional magazines. However, they are essentially magazine-length ads, which readers are expected to purchase at newsstands. Custom magazines have been published for Sony, General Motors, General Electric, Jenny Craig, and Ray-Ban sunglasses.[3] In 2002, for example, Kraft Foods decided to expand its free, custom-published magazine *Food & Family,* which offers recipes and cooking tips, to 10 million U.S. households. This came after Kraft's successful test in Canada of another custom magazine, *What's Cooking.* The popularity of that publication even

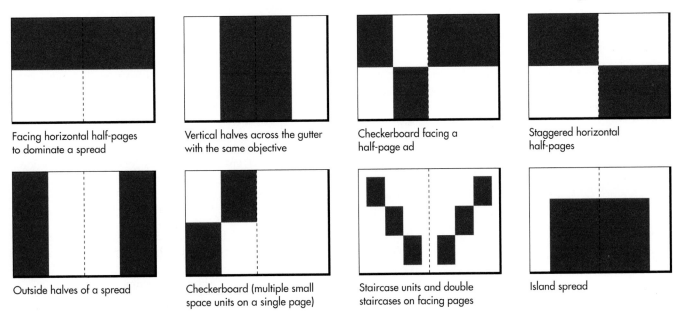

Facing horizontal half-pages to dominate a spread

Vertical halves across the gutter with the same objective

Checkerboard facing a half-page ad

Staggered horizontal half-pages

Outside halves of a spread

Checkerboard (multiple small space units on a single page)

Staircase units and double staircases on facing pages

Island spread

Exhibit 15–2

An ad's position on the page influences its effectiveness. The size and shape of the ad often determine where it will fall on the page. These eight two-page spreads show most of the positions an ad can take.

Innovations in Magazine Advertising

Magazines work closely with advertisers to develop new technologies for presenting ideas and products. From these efforts have come such innovations as fragrance strips, color strips, and pop-up ads.

Fragrance strips are a great favorite with perfume advertisers. With the Scentstrip, readers sample a scent by opening a sealed insert tucked into a magazine. Despite some consumer complaints, Scentstrips proved incredibly popular. Fragrances are useful for other products as well. For example, a Rolls-Royce ad in *Architectural Digest* carried a Scentstrip bearing the essence of leather. For a St. Mungo's (London's largest homeless charity) ad, Saatchi & Saatchi played on consumers' expectations that Scentstrips accompany only ads for luxury goods. The urine-scented ad drove shocked readers to St. Mungo's website, where they could make a donation. The campaign won a Bronze Lion at Cannes.

Cosmetics manufacturers insert **color strip** samples of eye shadow, blush, lipstick, and other makeup that readers can try immediately. Color strips are expensive to produce, but many advertisers think they're worth it.

Another costly innovation is the **pop-up ad.** Corporate advertisers such as Honeywell and TransAmerica were among the first to try this eye-catching approach. Product ads, such as a pop-up for the Dodge Dakota, followed.

Other intriguing approaches include **3-D ads** (complete with 3-D glasses), product samples (facial tissues and paper towels), and unusual shapes and sizes for preprinted inserts. An ad for Sara Lee cheesecake used a single heavy-stock page with what appeared to be a bite taken out of a life-size cheesecake slice. A half-page insert for Gleem toothpaste featured a metallic graphic of a mirror with the slogan "Check your mirror."

Researchers are probing the possibilities of holograms and ads that talk when readers pass a device across the page. Already ads can sing—liquor companies included microchips that played Christmas carols in their December magazine ads, and ads for a cigarette brand played "Happy Birthday" on the brand's 75th anniversary.

Recently, Global Commerce Group invented the Web Decoder™, a transparent device made of clear polyester Mylar. The recipient is invited to interact with an image on a website. When the piece is positioned over the designated image, a hidden word, icon, or phrase is revealed. Advertisers can tailor the Web Decoder to their specific promotional needs, from cents-off coupons to instant-winner prizes.

Such innovative approaches not only attract readers' attention but also involve them in the experience by appealing to more than just the visual sense.

Laboratory Application

What products besides perfumes and cars could Scentstrips be used to advertise?

---

inspired a TV spinoff of the same name.[4] Ad Lab 15–B discusses other innovations in magazine advertising.

How Magazines Are Categorized

In the jargon of the trade, magazines are called books, and media buyers commonly categorize them by content, geography, and size.

Content

One of the most dramatic developments in publishing is the emergence of magazines with special content, which has given many books good prospects for long-term growth. The broadest classifications of content are *consumer magazines*, *farm magazines*, and *business magazines*. Each may be broken down into hundreds of categories.

- **Consumer magazines,** purchased for entertainment, information, or both, are edited for consumers who buy products for their own personal consumption: *Time, Sports Illustrated, Glamour, Good Housekeeping*. The Portfolio Review, "Outstanding Magazine Ads," shows the range of creativity in consumer magazine advertising.

- **Farm publications** are directed to farmers and their families or to companies that manufacture or sell agricultural equipment, supplies, and services: *Farm Journal, Progressive Farmer, Prairie Farmer, Successful Farming*.

Magazines that cater to specific geographic areas are regional publications. Most metropolitan areas publish magazines specific to their particular city, such as this example from Chicago magazine (www.chicagomag.com), providing news and information on issues and events of interest to the local population.

■ **Business magazines,** by far the largest category, target business readers. They include *trade publications* for retailers, wholesalers, and other distributors (*Progressive Grocer, Bakery News*); *business* and *industrial magazines* for businesspeople involved in manufacturing and services (*Electronic Design, American Banker*); and *professional journals* for lawyers, physicians, architects, and other professionals (*Archives of Ophthalmology*).

Geography

A magazine may also be classified as *local, regional,* or *national.* Today, most major U.S. cities have a **local city magazine:** *San Diego Magazine, New York, Los Angeles, Chicago, Palm Springs Life.* Their readership is usually upscale business and professional people interested in local arts, fashion, and business.

Regional publications are targeted to a specific area of the country, such as the West or the South: *Sunset, Southern Living.* National magazines sometimes provide special market runs for specific geographic regions. *Time, Newsweek, Woman's Day,* and *Sports Illustrated* allow advertisers to buy a single major market. Exhibit 15–3 shows the 10 major geographic editions of *Reader's Digest.*

National magazines range from those with enormous circulations, such as *TV Guide,* to small, lesser-known national magazines, such as *Nature* and *Volleyball Monthly.* The largest circulation magazine in the United States today is *(continued on page 490)*

• Major market
* Pacific Ed. excludes counties covered by Metro L.A. Edition
† Great Lakes Ed. excludes counties covered by Metro Chicago
‡ Mid-Atlantic Ed. excludes counties covered by Metro N.Y.

Exhibit 15–3

Advertisers benefit from selecting regional editions similar to the 10 geographic editions of Reader's Digest *shown on the map. With regional binding and mailing, advertisers can buy ad space for only the amount of distribution they need.*

Magazines provide creatives with an unlimited palette of colorful opportunities for their imagination. Offering permanence, color, unmatched reproduction quality, and excellent credibility, magazines are a powerful weapon in the advertiser's arsenal. In this portfolio, we've selected some outstanding examples of magazine advertising.

■ See if you can look past the beauty of these ads and determine the underlying strategy that guided the artists' thinking. Who is the target audience? Is that different from the target market? What are they trying to say about the advertiser? How is the advertiser positioned? Once you've determined the strategy, which magazines would you place these ads in?

Outstanding Magazine Ads

Saatchi & Saatchi/Hong Kong created this humorous ad for China Light & Power/Oxygen Broadband. The one line of copy reads, "Kids can think faster than 56k." The image conveys the message by showing a boy who is too slow to the draw because he's still "loading," similar to how computers download information from the Internet.

This clever magazine ad for About magazine features another magazine that appears to be reading About magazine. Without reading the copy in the ad, what kind of impression does this image alone convey?

E-1 OLYMPUS

This subtle but commanding ad won a Silver Lion at Cannes. It takes the concept of showing the product in use one step further by actually putting the reader in the position of photographer. This ad was designed for use in magazines, where the clarity of the light switch chain, in contrast to the rest of the image, can be fully appreciated.

Showing the product in use is a way of creating a visual context for consumer perception. Showing the product being misused is, in this case, an amusing way to demonstrate just how gratifying the product is. This ad won a Silver Lion at Cannes for its creative appeal.

socks by
FALKE

Magazines are the best medium to use for beautiful ads like this one for the North Carolina Travel and Tourism Board (www.visitnc.com). Notice how there is no copy except the contact information in the lower right corner.

In this ad for Vespa, which won a Bronze Lion at Cannes, the city becomes a virtual playground for the driver to enjoy. This ad uses practically no copy but still delivers a message: Vespa is fun.

This ad's tagline, "As Real as It Gets," refers both to the detailed, authentic photo of the soldier's unglamorous activity and to the true-to-life details of the action figure at his feet. The vivid combination won a Gold Lion at Cannes.

(continued from page 485)
AARP The Magazine, distributed to the 21 million members of the American Association of Retired Persons.[5]

Size

It doesn't take a genius to figure out that magazines come in different shapes and sizes, but it might take one to figure out how to get one ad to run in different-size magazines and still look the same. Magazine sizes run the gamut, which can make production standardization a nightmare. The most common magazine sizes follow:

Size classification	Magazine	Approximate size of full-page ad
Large	*Life*	4 col. × 170 lines ($9\frac{3}{8}$ × $12\frac{1}{8}$ inches)
Flat	*Time, Newsweek*	3 col. × 140 lines (7 × 10 inches)
Standard	*National Geographic*	2 col. × 119 lines (6 × $8\frac{1}{2}$ inches)
Small or pocket	*Reader's Digest, TV Guide*	2 col. × 91 lines ($4\frac{1}{2}$ × $6\frac{1}{2}$ inches)

Buying Magazine Space

Understanding Magazine Circulation

When analyzing a media vehicle, media buyers consider readership, cost, mechanical requirements, and ad closing dates (deadlines). To buy effectively, they must thoroughly understand the magazine's circulation and rate-card information.

The first step in analyzing a publication's potential effectiveness is to assess its audience. The buyer studies circulation statistics, primary and secondary readership, subscription and vendor sales, and any special merchandising services the magazine offers.

Guaranteed versus Delivered Circulation

A magazine's rates are based on its circulation. The **rate base** is the circulation figure on which the publisher bases its rates; the **guaranteed circulation** is the number of copies the publisher expects to circulate. This assures advertisers they will reach a certain number of people. If the publisher does not reach its *delivered figure,* it must provide a refund. For that reason, guaranteed circulation figures are often stated safely below the average actual circulation. However, this is not always true. Circulation actually gets overstated more often than people think. As many as 30 percent of consumer magazines audited by the **Audit Bureau of Circulations (ABC)** each year don't meet the circulation levels they guarantee to advertisers.[6]

So media buyers expect publications to verify their circulation figures. Publishers pay thousands of dollars each year for a **circulation audit**—a thorough analysis of the circulation procedures, outlets of distribution, readers, and other factors—by companies such as ABC. Directories such as those published by Standard Rate & Data Service (SRDS) feature the logo of the auditing company in each listing for an audited magazine.

Primary and Secondary Readership

Data from the ABC or other verified reports tell the media buyer the magazine's total circulation. This **primary circulation** represents the number of people who

Advertising Age is a good example of a vertical publication. The magazine is geared toward a variety of issues specific to the advertising industry. Unlike horizontal publications, which focus on a single job function across various industries, Ad Age is read by a wide range of people throughout the industry.

buy the publication, either by subscription or at the newsstand. **Secondary** (or **pass-along**) **readership,** which is an estimate determined by market research of how many people read a single issue of a publication, is very important to magazines. Some have more than six readers per copy. Multiplying the average pass-along readership by, say, a million subscribers can give a magazine a substantial audience beyond its primary readers.

Vertical and Horizontal Publications

There are two readership classifications of business publications: *vertical* and *horizontal.* A **vertical publication** covers a specific industry in all its aspects. For example, Cahners Publishing produces *Restaurants & Institutions* strictly for restaurateurs and food-service operators. The magazine's editorial content includes everything from news of the restaurant industry to institutional-size recipes.

Horizontal publications, in contrast, deal with a particular job function across a variety of industries. Readers of *Purchasing* work in purchasing management in many different industries. Horizontal trade publications are very effective advertising vehicles because they usually offer excellent reach and they tend to be well read.[7]

Subscription and Vendor Sales

Media buyers also want to know a magazine's ratio of subscriptions to newsstand sales. Today, subscriptions account for the majority of magazine sales. Newsstands (which include bookstore chains) are still a major outlet for single-copy sales, but no outlet can handle more than a fraction of the many magazines available.

From the advertiser's point of view, newsstand sales are impressive because they indicate that the purchaser really wants the magazine and is not merely subscribing out of habit. According to the Magazine Publishers Association, single-copy sales account for 34 percent of total revenues for a representative sampling of leading magazines.

Paid and Controlled Circulation

Business publications may be distributed on either a *paid circulation* or *controlled circulation* basis. A paid basis means the recipient must pay the subscription price to receive the magazine. *BusinessWeek* is a **paid-circulation** business magazine.

In **controlled circulation,** the publisher mails the magazine free to individuals who the publisher thinks can influence the purchase of advertised products. Managers of corporate video departments receive *Corporate Video Decisions.* To qualify for the subscription list, people must indicate in writing a desire to receive it and must give their professional designation or occupation. Dues-paying members of organizations often get free subscriptions. For example, members of the National Association for Female Executives receive free copies of *Executive Female.*

Publishers of paid-circulation magazines say subscribers who pay are more likely to read a publication than those who receive it free. But controlled-circulation magazines can reach good prospects for the goods and services they advertise.

Merchandising Services: Added Value

Magazines, and newspapers too, often provide liberal *added-value services* to their regular advertisers, such as:

■ Special free promotions to stores.

■ Marketing services to help readers find local outlets.

■ Response cards that allow readers to request brochures and catalogs.

■ Help handling sales force, broker, wholesaler, and retailer meetings.

■ Advance editions for the trade.

■ Research into brand preferences, consumer attitudes, and market conditions.

If a publication's basic factors—editorial, circulation, and readership—are strong, these additional services can increase the effectiveness of its ads.[8] Magazines offer great potential for relationship marketing since they already have a relationship with their subscribers. New added-value options might include using magazines' custom publishing, editorial, and production knowledge, along with their databases, to help clients develop videos, books, and guides that create added value for the brand.[9]

Reading Rate Cards

Magazine rate cards follow a standard format (see RL 15–1 in the Reference Library on the *Contemporary Advertising* CD). This helps advertisers determine costs, discounts, mechanical requirements, closing dates, special editions, and additional costs for features like color, inserts, bleed pages, split runs, or preferred positions.

Three dates affect magazine purchases. The **cover date** is the date printed on the cover. The **on-sale date** is the date the magazine is actually issued. And the **closing date** is the date all ad material must be in the publisher's hands for a specific issue. Lead time may be as much as three months.

Rates

As we discussed in Chapter 9, one way to compare magazines is to look at how much it costs to reach a thousand people based on the magazine's rates for a one-time, full-page ad. You compute the **cost per thousand (CPM)** by dividing the full-page rate by the number of *thousands* of subscribers:

$$\frac{\text{Page rate}}{(\text{Circulation} \div 1,000)} = \text{CPM}$$

If the magazine's black-and-white page rate is $10,000, and the publication has a circulation of 500,000, then:

$$\frac{\$10,000}{(500,000 \div 1,000)} = \frac{10,000}{500} = \$20 \text{ CPM}$$

Consider this comparison. In 2003, the page rate for a full-color, one-page ad in *Car & Driver* was $142,235 on total paid circulation of 1,369,848; *Road & Track* offered the same ad for $85,745 on total paid circulation of 762,688. Which was the better buy on a CPM basis?[10]

Exhibit 15–4 lists the circulations and color page rates for 17 leading consumer magazines. Using this data, you can calculate which national buys offer the best CPMs.

Discounts

Magazines and newspapers often give discounts. **Frequency discounts** are based on the number of ad insertions, usually within a year; **volume discounts** are

Exhibit 15–4

Advertising costs in 2004 for U.S. consumer magazines with the highest circulation.

Magazine	Total paid circulation	Page cost for four-color ad
AARP, The Magazine	22,720,073	$398,500
Reader's Digest	10,228,531	221,600
TV Guide	9,016,188	166,100
National Geographic	5,468,471	178,345
Better Homes & Gardens	7,628,424	303,100
Family Circle	4,372,813	210,100
Good Housekeeping	4,623,113	255,025
Woman's Day	4,279,375	214,750
Time	4,034,491	223,000
People Weekly	3,730,287	180,000
Sports Illustrated	3,210,040	238,000
Newsweek	3,145,362	172,000
Playboy	3,176,215	141,620
Redbook	2,360,218	115,700
Cosmopolitan	2,918,062	171,204
National Enquirer	1,541,618	66,075
Star	1,206,984	99,000

based on the total amount of space bought during a specific period. Most magazines also offer *cash discounts* (usually 2 percent) to advertisers who pay right away, and some offer discounts on the purchase of four or more consecutive pages in a single issue. In fact, more than half of all magazine publishers now negotiate their rates. According to Harold Shain, executive VP/publisher of *Newsweek,* "Every piece of business is negotiated. I don't believe we will ever return to the industry we were 10 years ago."[11]

Premium Rates

Magazines charge extra for special features. Color normally costs 25 to 60 percent more than black and white. Some publications, such as *Money,* even offer metallic inks and special colors. Bleed pages can add as much as 20 percent to regular rates, although the typical increase is about 15 percent.

Second and third cover rates (the inside covers) typically cost less than the fourth (back) cover. According to SRDS, in 2004 *Newsweek* charged $172,000 for a normal color page and the same for second and third covers, but it charged $245,460 for the fourth cover.[12]

Magazines charge different rates for ads in geographic or demographic issues. **Geographic editions** target geographic markets; **demographic editions** reach readers who share a demographic trait, such as age, income level, or professional status. *Time* offers one-page, four-color ads (one-time insertion) in its Boston edition for $21,495 (135,000 circulation) and in its New York edition for $34,708. For full-page, four-color ads, advertisers in the top management edition pay $90,000 (circulation 805,489). To run the same ad in *Time Gold,* which is targeted to baby boomers and has a circulation of more than 1 million, advertisers pay $69,000.

Software for Buying Print Media

One of the most important tasks in advertising is the placement of ads in various media. So the role of the media buyer is critical to the overall success of the campaign.

Placing an ad in a magazine or newspaper is not as easy as it may seem, especially when there are hundreds of newspapers and magazines around the country with different deadlines, different mechanical requirements, and different rates. To say the least, the job can be very tedious and time-consuming.

Fortunately, thanks to technology, print media buyers now have a variety of software programs available to assist them.

STRATA Marketing, Inc., for example, has developed media buying software for each form of media. Its print software programs offer media buyers various ways to keep track of orders, clients, and rate information, while providing a large variety of formats for insertion order reports. This program also allows media buyers to copy insertion orders to numerous publications, all with a single keystroke.

Another software system available to print media buyers is CorePrint 2.2 designed by COREMedia Systems, Inc. The program's main function is to manage invoice reconciliation, billing and reporting, traffic, and insertion maintenance for all print media. With this software, media buyers can also determine the cost of print buys and generate production specs.

These programs, and others similar in function, save media buyers a lot of time, thereby increasing productivity and efficiency. More time can be spent analyzing information, evaluating various print vehicles, and exercising creativity. By using software like this, media buyers gain flexibility and control over the placement of ads in print media.

Using Newspapers in the Creative Mix

When a small, alternative newspaper in Manhattan asked one of the newest and hottest creative shops in the city for help in promoting subscriptions, it had no idea what the little agency with the funny name, Mad Dogs & Englishmen, would do for it.

The *Village Voice* newspaper had always knocked the Establishment with its radical coverage of social issues, politics, media, and culture. So perhaps it shouldn't have come as a surprise when the Mad Dogs took the newspaper's own prose style and turned it around in a series of impertinent, self-mocking ads.

"Hell, I wouldn't have my home contaminated with a subscription to your elitist rag if you were giving away five-speed blenders," rants one ad in the series. "You people think New York is the friggin' center of the world." But then a second paragraph offers a dramatic alternative: "YES, I want to buy a year's subscription to the *Village Voice,*" along with a coupon.

The paper's readers aren't spared either. One ad skewers New Age tree-huggers: "Murderers! Trees are being systematically swallowed up by the jaws of industry and still you insist I take part in this horror by subscribing?"

Mad Dogs principal Nick Cohen said he thought the *Voice* would like the campaign because the newspaper is honest. "It really stands behind the freedom of the writers, even when they criticize the management itself," he said.

Selecting the medium was easy. Because most people who would be interested in a subscription are *Village Voice* readers, the campaign ran in the paper itself. It proved to be a wise choice. In the first year of the campaign, the *Voice* saw a 30 percent increase in its subscriber base, surpassing all expectations.[13]

Who Uses Newspapers?

Newspapers are now the second-largest medium (after television) in terms of advertising volume, receiving 18.3 percent of the dollars spent by advertisers in the United States.[14]

Consider these important facts:

- More than half of all adults (55 percent) read a daily newspaper. Nearly two-thirds (63.1 percent) read the Sunday edition.
- Each section is read by about two-thirds of all adult readers, whereas almost all (88 percent) read the main news sections.
- More than 55 million newspapers are sold daily, and every copy has an average of 2.3 readers.
- In 2003, there were 1,456 daily newspapers in the United States, with a total circulation of 55.2 million. The same year, the nation's more than 6,700 weekly newspapers and shoppers had a combined circulation of more than 50.2 million.[15]
- Newspaper advertising expenditures in 2003 totaled $44.1 billion.[16]
- More than 1,500 newspapers in the United States have sites on the Internet. More and more online readers are completely abandoning the print product.

Although the newspaper is the major community-serving medium for both news and advertising, more and more national advertisers are shifting to radio and television. As a result, radio and TV carry most of the national advertising in the United States, while 83 percent of newspaper advertising revenue comes from local advertising. As Exhibit 15–5 shows, retailers are the primary local advertisers in newspapers.

Newspaper is an important medium in the creative mix, second only to television in advertising volume, but costing much less. This ad for the Village Voice *(www.villagevoice.com) shows how a niche business can use newspaper advertising to expand sales. Mimicking the freewheeling tone of the newspaper, the advertiser targeted those who already read the* Village Voice *but were not subscribers.*

The Pros and Cons of Newspaper Advertising

The *Village Voice* promotion shows how small businesses with even smaller budgets can benefit from creative newspaper advertising. Print ads in general and newspapers in particular provide a unique, flexible medium for advertisers to express their creativity—especially with businesses that rely on local customers.

The Pros and Cons of Newspaper Advertising

The Pros

____ **Mass medium** penetrating every segment of society. Most consumers read the newspaper.

____ **Local medium** with broad reach. Covers a specific geographic area that comprises both a market and a community of people sharing common concerns and interest.

____ **Comprehensive in scope,** covering an extraordinary variety of topics and interests.

____ **Geographic selectivity** is possible with zoned editions for specific neighborhoods or communities.

____ **Timeliness.** Papers primarily cover today's news and are read in one day.

____ **Credibility.** Studies show that newspaper ads rank highest in believability. TV commercials are a distant second.

____ **Selective attention** from the relatively small number of active prospects who, on any given day, are interested in what the advertiser is trying to tell them or sell them.

____ **Creative flexibility.** An ad's physical size and shape can be varied to give the degree of dominance or repetition that suits the advertiser's purpose. The advertiser can use black and white, color, Sunday magazines, or custom inserts.

____ **An active medium** rather than a passive one. Readers turn the pages, clip and save, write in the margins, and sort through the contents.

____ **A permanent record,** in contrast to the ephemeral nature of radio and TV.

____ **Reasonable cost.**

The Cons

____ **Lack of selectivity** of specific socioeconomic groups. Most newspapers reach broad, diverse groups of readers, which may not match the advertiser's objectives.

____ **Short life span.** Unless readers clip and save the ad or coupon, it may be lost forever.

____ **Low production quality.** Coarse newsprint generally produces a less impressive image than the slick, smooth paper stock of magazines, and some newspapers can't print color.

____ **Clutter.** Each ad competes with editorial content and with all the other ads on the same page or spread.

____ **Lack of control** over where the ad will appear unless the advertiser pays extra for a preferred position.

____ **Overlapping circulation.** Some people read more than one newspaper. Advertisers may be paying for readers who were already reached in a different paper.

Newspapers offer advertisers many advantages. One of the most important is *timeliness;* an ad can appear very quickly, sometimes in just one day. Newspapers also offer geographic targeting, a broad range of markets, reasonable cost, and more. But newspapers suffer from lack of selectivity, poor production quality, and clutter. And readers criticize them for lack of depth and follow-up on important issues.[17]

Use the Checklist, "Pros and Cons of Newspaper Advertising," to answer the questions in Ad Lab 15–C, "Newspapers and the Creative Mix."

How Newspapers Are Categorized

Newspapers can be classified by *frequency of delivery, physical size,* or *type of audience.*

Frequency of Delivery

A **daily newspaper** is published as either a morning or evening edition at least five times a week, Monday through Friday. Of the 1,457 dailies in the United States, 692 are evening papers and 777 are morning papers. (The total exceeds 1,457 because 12 "all day" newspapers print both morning and evening editions.)[18] Morning editions tend to have broader geographic circulation and a larger male readership; evening editions are read more by women.

With their emphasis on local news and advertising, **weekly newspapers** characteristically serve small urban or suburban residential areas and farm communities. They are now the fastest-growing class of newspapers. A weekly newspaper's cost per thousand is usually higher than a daily paper's, but a weekly has a longer life and often has more readers per copy.

Exhibit 15–5

Top 10 newspaper advertisers in the United States (2003).

Rank	Advertiser	Newspaper ad spending in 2003 ($ millions)
1	Verizon Communications	$513.7
2	AT&T Wireless	510.4
3	Federated Department Stores	493.7
4	Sprint Corp.	477.0
5	SBC Communications	441.7
6	May Department Stores Co.	440.3
7	Time Warner	381.0
8	Walt Disney Corp.	313.0
9	General Motors Corp.	274.3
10	DaimlerChrysler	264.9

Newspapers and the Creative Mix

Study the Checklist, "The Pros and Cons of Newspaper Advertising" and see if you can apply that information to the following situation:

You're the product manager for a major brand of bar soap and you wish to go nationwide with an ad featuring a coupon.

Laboratory Applications

1. Which newspaper would be best?
   a. A weekly.   b. A daily.

2. If you use a daily, in what section of the paper do you want your ad to appear?

3. If you decided on the Sunday supplement, which of the following would you choose and why?
   a. *Parade* magazine.   b. Color coupon supplement.

Physical Size

There are two basic newspaper formats, standard size and tabloid. The **standard-size newspaper** is about 22 inches deep and 13 inches wide and is divided into six columns. The **tabloid newspaper** is generally about 14 inches deep and 11 inches wide. National tabloid newspapers such as the *National Enquirer* and the *Star* use sensational stories to fight for single-copy sales. Other tabloids, such as the *New York Daily News,* emphasize straight news and features.

Newspapers used to offer about 400 different ad sizes. But in 1984, the industry introduced the **standard advertising unit (SAU)** system, which standardized the newspaper column width, page sizes, and ad sizes. An SAU **column inch** is $2\frac{1}{16}$ inches wide by 1 inch deep. There are now 56 standard ad sizes for standard papers and 32 for tabloids. Virtually all dailies converted to the SAU system (some at great expense) and so did most weeklies.

Type of Audience

Some dailies and weeklies serve special-interest audiences, a fact not lost on advertisers. They generally contain advertising oriented to their special audiences and they may have unique advertising regulations.

Some serve specific ethnic markets. Today, more than 200 dailies and weeklies are oriented to the African-American community. Others serve foreign-language groups. In the United States there are newspapers printed in 43 languages other than English.

Specialized newspapers also serve business and financial audiences. *The Wall Street Journal,* the leading national business and financial daily, enjoys a circulation of 1.8 million. Other papers cater to fraternal, labor union, or professional organizations, religious groups, or hobbyists.

The picture of Alfred Hitchcock (director of the movie thriller The Birds*) juxtaposed with the bird stamps, seemingly in flight, is a brilliant creative concept for a large newspaper ad.*

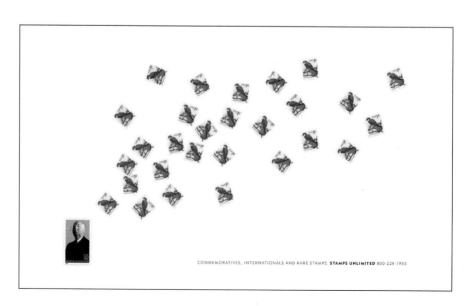

COMMEMORATIVES, INTERNATIONALS AND RARE STAMPS. **STAMPS UNLIMITED** 800-229-1955

Other Types of Newspapers

The United States has 917 Sunday newspapers, mostly Sunday editions of daily papers, with a combined circulation of more than 58.4 million.[19] Sunday newspapers generally combine standard news coverage with special functions like these:

- Increased volume of classified ads.
- Greater advertising and news volume.
- In-depth coverage of business, sports, real estate, literature and the arts, entertainment, and travel.
- Review and analysis of the past week's events.
- Expanded editorial and opinion sections.

Most Sunday newspapers also feature a **Sunday supplement** magazine. Some publish their own supplement, such as *Los Angeles Magazine* of the *Los Angeles Times*. Other papers subscribe to syndicated supplements; *Parade* magazine is now received by more than 35.7 million homes every week.[20]

Printed by rotogravure on heavier, coated paper stock, Sunday supplements are more conducive to color printing than newsprint, making them attractive to national advertisers who want better reproduction quality.

Another type of newspaper, the **independent shopping guide** or free community newspaper, offers advertisers local saturation. Sometimes called *pennysavers,* these shoppers offer free distribution and extensive advertising pages targeted at essentially the same audience as weekly newspapers—urban and suburban community readers. Readership is often high, and the publishers use hand delivery or direct mail to achieve maximum saturation.

North Americans also read national newspapers, including the *Globe and Mail* in Canada, *USA Today,* and the *Christian Science Monitor.* With a circulation of 2.1 million, *USA Today* surpasses *The Wall Street Journal* (1.8 million) and *The New York Times* (1.1 million) in national distribution.[21]

Types of Newspaper Advertising

The major classifications of newspaper advertising are *display, classified, public notices,* and *preprinted inserts.*

Display Advertising

Display advertising includes copy, illustrations or photos, headlines, coupons, and other visual components—such as the ads for the *Village Voice* discussed earlier. Display ads vary in size and appear in all sections of the newspaper except the first page of major sections, the editorial page, the obituary page, and the classified advertising section.

One common variation of the display ad, the **reading notice,** looks like editorial matter and sometimes costs more than normal display advertising. To prevent readers from mistaking it for editorial matter, the word *advertisement* appears at the top.

As we discussed in Chapters 4 and 6, retailers often run newspaper ads through **cooperative** (or **co-op**) **programs** sponsored by the manufacturers whose products they sell. The manufacturer pays fully or partially to create and run the ad, which features the manufacturer's product and logo along with the local retailer's name and address.

Designed to look like an ad for a Dodge Viper, this clever display ad is actually for a 1/18 scale model of the coupe from Hotwheels.

Classified Advertising

Classified ads provide a community marketplace for goods, services, and opportunities of every type, from real estate and new-car sales to employment and business opportunities. A newspaper's profitability often depends on a large and healthy classified section.

Classified ads usually appear under subheads that describe the class of goods or the need the ads seek to satisfy. Most employment, housing, and car advertising is classified. To promote the use of classified ads in the *Village Voice,* Mad Dogs & Englishmen created a series of display ads that used humorous "Situation Wanted" ads as the main visuals.

Classified rates are typically based on how many lines the ad occupies and how many times the ad runs. Some newspapers accept **classified display ads,** which run in the classified section of the newspaper but feature larger type and/or photos, art borders, abundant white space, and sometimes even color.

Public Notices

For a nominal fee, newspapers carry legal **public notices** of changes in business and personal relationships, public governmental reports, notices by private citizens and organizations, and financial reports. These ads follow a preset format.

Preprinted Inserts

Like magazines, newspapers carry **preprinted inserts.** The advertiser prints the inserts and delivers them to the newspaper plant for insertion into a specific edition. Insert sizes range from a typical newspaper page to a double postcard; formats include catalogs, brochures, mail-back devices, and perforated coupons.

Some large metropolitan dailies allow advertisers to limit their inserts to specific circulation zones. A retail advertiser that wants to reach only those shoppers in its immediate trading area can place an insert in the local-zone editions. Retail stores, car dealers, and large national advertisers are among those who find it less costly to distribute their circulars this way compared to mailing them or delivering them door to door.

How Advertisers Buy Newspaper Space

Understanding Readership and Circulation

To get the most from the advertising budget, the media buyer must know the characteristics of a newspaper's readership: the median age, sex, occupation, income, educational level, as well as buying habits of the typical reader.

Readership information is available from various sources, such as Simmons Market Research Bureau and Scarborough Research Corp. Most large papers also provide extensive data on their readers.

In single-newspaper cities, reader demographics typically reflect a cross section of the general population. In cities with two or more newspapers, however, these characteristics may vary widely. The *Los Angeles Times* is directed to a broad cross section of the community while *La Opinion* targets L.A.'s large Hispanic population.

Advertisers must understand the full extent of the newspaper's circulation. The paper's total circulation includes subscribers and single-copy newsstand buyers, as well as secondary readers.

Rate Cards

Like the magazine rate card, the newspaper **rate card** lists advertising rates, mechanical and copy requirements, deadlines, and other information. Because rates vary greatly, advertisers should calculate which papers deliver the most readers and the best demographics for their money.

Local versus National Rates

Most newspapers charge local and national advertisers at different rates. The **national rate** averages 75 percent higher, but some papers charge as much as 254 percent more.[22] Newspapers attribute higher rates to the added costs of serving national advertisers. For instance, an ad agency usually places national advertising and receives a 15 percent commission from the paper. If the advertising comes from another city or state, then additional costs, such as long-distance telephone calls, are also involved.

But many national advertisers reject the high rates and take their business elsewhere. Only 3 percent of national ad money now goes to newspapers, and that proportion may shrink even further.[23] In response to declining national advertising revenue, newspapers are experimenting with simplified billing systems and discount rates for their national clients.

Flat Rates and Discount Rates

Many national papers charge **flat rates,** which means they allow no discounts; a few newspapers offer a single flat rate to both national and local advertisers.

Newspapers that offer volume discounts have an **open rate** (their highest rate for a one-time insertion) and **contract rates,** whereby local advertisers can obtain

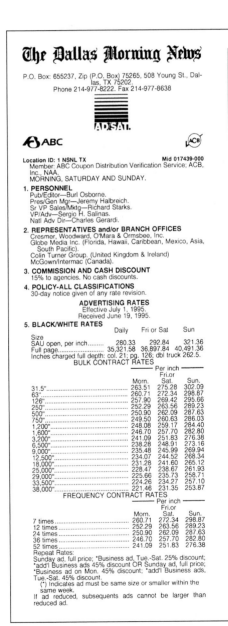

The newspaper rate card for The Dallas Morning News (www.dallasnews.com) is similar to that for magazines. It shows the variety of ad units available and lists their costs.

What's at Stake with Sweepstakes?

Many of us have probably received an envelope in the mail with the phrase "You Are a Winner!" or something similar, plastered in large, bold type behind the front window. And perhaps, for a split second you believed that you had won the $100,000 prize. Then you discovered the disclosure, in such small print that you overlooked it at first glance, telling you otherwise. Believe it or not, there have been some who didn't notice the disclosure and traveled to the sweepstakes' headquarters believing that they had won the jackpot. Similarly, others were misled into believing that purchasing advertised products would increase their chances of winning, so they spent thousands of dollars each in magazine subscriptions. Were these people deceived?

Until recently, this is how many sweepstakes were pitched to consumers. According to the Direct Marketing Association, sweepstakes are, by definition, "an advertising or promotional device by which items of value (prizes) are awarded to participating consumers by chance, with no purchase or 'entry fee' required in order to win." However, by entering a sweepstakes you are volunteering your name, address, and possible tastes in the advertised product to be put on lists for other direct

marketers to acquire. In turn you are offered a chance to win what seems like easy money. For years it was difficult for recipients to tell whether or not they had a winning entry. With statements claiming "You are a winner," simulated checks, and government-resembling material, the line separating promotion and deception became very thin.

All of this changed in 2000. Following investigations of sweepstakes firms in more than 40 states, three of the biggest sweeps marketers—Publisher's Clearing House (PCH), Time Inc., and U.S. Sales Corp.—were each brought to court by numerous state regulators, alleging that the marketing giants conducted deceptive sweepstakes promotions. In California alone, state officials claimed that 5,000 consumers spent more than $2,500 each a year in unnecessary magazine subscriptions through PCH because they believed that it improved their odds of winning. Accusations were similar for all three companies, and each defended their marketing practices claiming they always believed their mailings were clear. One PCH spokesman stated that 98 percent of the consumers who purchased magazines through their promotions were spending less than $300 a year. However, because litigation in so many states—47 in Time Inc.'s case—would have been too costly, each company decided to settle and agreed to reform its practices.

---

discounts of up to 70 percent by signing a contract for frequent or bulk space purchases. **Bulk discounts** offer advertisers decreasing rates (calculated by multiplying the number of inches by the cost per inch) as they use more inches. Advertisers earn **frequency discounts** by running a given ad repeatedly in a specific time period. Similarly, advertisers can sometimes get **earned rates,** a discount applied retroactively as the volume of advertising increases through the year. More than 1,000 newspapers also participate in Newsplan, a Newspaper Advertising Bureau (NAB) program that gives national and regional advertisers discounts for purchasing six or more pages per year.

Short Rate

An advertiser who contracts to buy a specific amount of space during a one-year period at a discount and then fails to fulfill the promise is charged a **short rate,** which is the difference between the contracted rate and the earned rate for the actual inches run. Conversely, an advertiser who buys more inches than contracted may be entitled to a rebate or credit because of the discounted earned rate for the additional advertising space.

Combination Rates

Combination rates are often available for placing a given ad in (1) morning and evening editions of the same newspaper; (2) two or more newspapers owned by the same publisher; and (3) in some cases, two or more newspapers affiliated in a syndicate or newspaper group.

Run of Paper versus Preferred Position

Run-of-paper (ROP) advertising rates entitle a newspaper to place a given ad on any newspaper page or in any position it desires. Although the advertiser has no control over where the ad appears in the paper, most newspapers try to place an ad in the position the advertiser requests.

An advertiser can ensure a choice position for an ad by paying a higher **preferred-position rate.** A tire manufacturer, for example, may pay the preferred rate to ensure a position in the sports section.

There are also preferred positions on a given page. The preferred position near the top of a page or at the top of a column next to reading matter is called **full position.** It's usually surrounded by reading matter and may cost the advertiser 25

Combined, the three marketers refunded more than $50 million in fines and restitution to state regulators and consumers who excessively purchased unnecessary magazines.

The reforms agreed to by these companies were in accord with the Deceptive Mail Prevention and Enforcement Act that became effective in April 2000. The act changed how direct-mail sweepstakes are presented and packaged. Some of the most significant changes included abandoning any "winner" proclamations unless the recipient had truly won a prize, and displaying a "fact box" that "clearly and conspicuously" explained all the terms and rules of the sweepstakes, including the odds of winning. Each mailing was also required to include the statements "No purchase is necessary to enter" and "A purchase does not improve your chances of winning" in boldfaced capital letters in the mailing, in the rules, and on the order/entry form itself. In addition, each company is required to include a statement providing an address or toll-free number where recipients can either write or call to have their name and addresses removed from their mailing lists.

Does this mean the end to sweepstakes? Probably not, since many people seem to jump at the chance to strike it rich for the cost of a stamp.

How much harm, if any, are sweepstakes really causing? Isn't part of promotion getting consumers to believe that they want what is being advertised? Without question, the ethical issues involved are complicated, but at least now you won't have to read the fine print to get the whole story.

Questions

1. Are sweepstakes companies really at fault for misleading their consumers? Why or why not?

2. Do you believe it is ethical for sweepstakes to "disguise" their promotions for the purpose of advertising?

Sources: www.crimes-of-persuasion.com/Crimes/Telemarketing/Outbound/Major/Sweepstakes/sweepstakes.htm; "Sweepstakes Advertising: A Consumer's Guide," *Consumers: A Helpful Guide* (www.dmaconsumers.org/sweepstakeshelp.html); "Be Smart Buy Smart," State of California Department of Consumer Affairs (www.dca.ca.gov/r_r/sweep.pdf); "Sweepstakes Assistance: A Caregiver's Guide," *Consumers: A Helpful Guide* (www.dmaconsumers.org/olderconsumers.html); "Stop Calling Me!" National Consumers League (www.nclnet.org/privacy/stopcalling2.htm); "How to Opt Out," *Consumer Privacy Guide* (www.consumerprivacyguide.org/howto/optout.shtml).

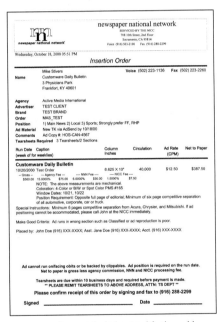

Co-ops and networks help simplify the ad buying process for advertisers by consolidating the purchasing paperwork and requirements for all local papers in a single location. This example of an insertion order for the Newspaper National Network is typical of what these contracts look like. Important information such as run date, size, and desired position is included.

to 50 percent more than ROP rates. Slightly less desirable is placement *next to reading matter (NR)*, which generally costs 10 to 20 percent more than ROP rates.

Color Advertising

Color advertising is available in many newspapers on an ROP basis. Because of their high-speed presses and porous paper stock, newspapers are not noted for high-quality color printing. So advertisers frequently preprint ads using processes known as HiFi color and Spectracolor. The cost of a color ad is usually based on the black-and-white rate plus an extra charge for each additional color.

Split Runs

Many newspapers (and magazines) offer **split runs** so that advertisers can test the *pulling power* of different ads. The advertiser runs two ads of identical size, but different content, for the same product on the same day in the same or different press runs. The idea is to eliminate as many variables as possible. By measuring responses to the two ads, the advertiser is able to compare and contrast the effectiveness of each. For this service, newspapers typically charge extra and set a minimum space requirement.

Co-ops and Networks

As an aid to national advertisers, the NAB created the Newspaper Co-op Network (NCN). Salespeople from participating newspapers helped national advertisers line up retailers for dealer-listing ads. The advertiser would produce the ad and include a blank space for each paper to insert local retailers' names. The system also helped manufacturers manage local advertising tie-ins to national campaigns and themes. Before the development of NCN, national advertisers had to place ads and recruit local dealers individually.

In 1992 the Newspaper Advertising Bureau merged with the American Newspaper Publishers Association and five other marketing associations to form the **Newspaper Association of America (NAA),** which continued to simplify national newspaper ad buys. In 1994 the NAA launched a *one-order, one-bill system* for national advertising, called the Newspaper National Network. Advertisers can make multimarket newspaper buys by placing one order and paying one bill, instead of having to contact—and pay—each paper individually.[24]

Chrysler was the first marketer to use the new network, placing ads for its national minivan sale in 75 newspapers in March 1994.[25] The Newspaper National Network offers advertisers competitive CPM pricing and guaranteed positioning, in addition to its one-order, one-bill appeal.[26] It also allows smaller papers to participate in national advertising.[27]

Insertion Orders and Tearsheets

When advertisers place an ad, they submit an **insertion order** to the newspaper stating the date(s) on which the ad is to run, its size, the desired position, the rate, and the type of artwork accompanying the order.

An insertion order serves as a contract between the advertiser (or its agency) and the publication. If an advertiser fails to pay the agency, the agency still must pay the publication. To avoid this liability, many agencies now place a disclaimer on their insertion orders stating that they are acting solely as an *agent for a disclosed principal* (legal terminology meaning the agency is just a representative for the advertiser and is therefore not liable for the payment). Some publications refuse to accept insertion orders with disclaimers unless payment accompanies the order. In 1991 the American Association of Advertising Agencies recommended to its agency members that they no longer accept sole liability for their clients' bills.[28] However, many agencies do still accept liability, perhaps out of some insecurity about possibly losing their agency commission—or their client.

When a newspaper creates ad copy and art, it gives the advertiser a **proof copy** to check. In contrast, most national advertising arrives at the newspaper *camera ready,* either in the form of a photo print or an electronic file via e-mail. To verify that the ad ran, the newspaper tears out the page on which the ad appeared and sends it to the agency or advertiser. Today, most **tearsheets** for national advertisers are handled through a private central office, the Advertising Checking Bureau.

When a tearsheet arrives, the advertiser examines it to make sure the ad ran according to instructions: in the right section and page position, and with the correct reproduction. If the ad did *not* run per instructions, the agency or advertiser is usually due an adjustment, a discount, or even a free rerun.

Print: A Worldwide Medium

Every country has newspapers and magazines to serve its population (see Exhibit 15–6). U.S. advertisers in foreign markets generally use either international or local media, depending on their campaign objectives and intended audience. Whether at home or abroad, advertisers must study the audience and remember the basics of print advertising, some of which are enumerated in the Checklist, "What Works Best in Print."

Several large U.S. publishers, including Time Warner and *Scientific American,* circulate international editions of their magazines abroad. The *International Herald Tribune, The Wall Street Journal,* and London's *Financial Times* are widely read in Asia, Europe, and the Middle East. In China, numerous publications such as *Elle* and *Avenue China* are now distributed to the country's wealthiest and most influential residents.[29]

Well-educated, upper-income consumers read these newspapers and magazines, even though they are typically printed in English. So these publications are the closest things to global print media for reaching this audience. *Reader's Digest*—the oldest international mass-audience medium—reaches 170 foreign countries. However, the publisher prints the magazine in local languages and tailors it to each country, so advertisers often view it as a local medium.

The number of international business, trade, or specialty publications is growing. Switzerland's *European Business* and Belgium's *Electronic Product News,* both English-language magazines, are distributed throughout Europe.

Political changes in the former Soviet Union and Eastern bloc countries spurred many new trade publications. Most are published locally in association with foreign publishers. In 1990, for example, McGraw-Hill launched Russian-language editions of *Aviation Week & Space Technology* and *BusinessWeek.* And International Data

What Works Best in Print

___ **Use simple layouts.** One large visual gives the ad a focal point. Wrapping text around smaller visuals works well, too. But avoid cluttered pages (layouts that resemble the magazine's editorial format are well read).

___ **Always put a caption under a photograph.** Twice as many people read picture captions as body copy. The picture caption can be an ad by itself.

___ **Don't be afraid of long copy.** People who read beyond the headline are good prospects. If your product is expensive (such as a car, a vacation, or a business product) prospects are hungry for information. Consider long copy if you have a complex story to tell, many different product points to make, or an expensive product or service to sell.

___ **Avoid negative headlines** (unless you work for Mad Dogs & Englishmen). Most people are literal minded and may remember only the negatives. Sell the positive benefits in your product—not that it won't harm or that some defect has been solved. Look for emotional words that attract and motivate, such as *free* and *new* and *love.*

___ **Don't be afraid of long headlines.** On average, long headlines sell more merchandise than short ones.

___ **Look for story appeal.** After the headline, a striking visual is the most effective way to get a reader's attention. Try for story appeal—the kind of visual that makes the reader ask: "What's going on here?"

___ **Photos work better than drawings.** Photography increases recall an average of 26 percent over artwork.

___ **Look at your ad in its editorial environment.** Paste your ad into the magazine in which it will appear—or, for newspapers, photostatted in the same tone as the newspaper page. Beautifully mounted layouts are deceptive. The reader will never see your ad printed on high-gloss paper with a big white border and mounted on a board. It is misleading to look at it this way.

___ **Develop a single advertising format.** An overall format for all print advertising can double recognition. This rule holds a special meaning for business and industrial advertisers. One format will help readers see your ad as coming from one large corporation, rather than several small companies.

___ **Before-and-after photos make a point better than words.** If you can, show a visual contrast—a change in the situation or a demonstration of product superiority.

___ **Do not print copy in reverse type.** It may look attractive, but it reduces readability. For the same reason, don't print copy on top of an illustration.

___ **Make each ad a complete sale.** Your message must be contained in the headline. React to the overall impression as the reader will. Only advertisers read all their ads. Any ad in a series must stand on its own. Each one must make a complete sale. Assume it is the only ad for your product a reader will ever see.

Exhibit 15–6

International consumer magazine paid circulation.

Argentina		Australia		Canada	
Title	**Circulation**	**Title**	**Circulation**	**Title**	**Circulation**
Gente	220,150	*Australian Women's Weekly*	1,152,000	*Reader's Digest*	1,220,049
Mia	141,698	*Woman's Day*	1,122,631	*Chatelaine*	899,909
Conozca Mas	118,197	*New Idea*	954,374	*TV Guide*	810,436
Billiken	117,339	*TV Week (National)*	563,845	*National Geographic*	684,467
Week End	116,547	*Reader's Digest*	480,438	*Leisure Ways*	594,716

France		Japan		Mexico	
Title	**Circulation**	**Title**	**Circulation**	**Title**	**Circulation**
Télé 7 Jours	2,969,674	*The Television*	1,021,447	*TV y Novelas*	699,028
Téléstar	1,990,756	*Ie-No-Hikari*	1,017,731	*Teleguia*	498,905
Télé Z	1,781,095	*Shukan Bunshun*	766,897	*Selecciones*	314,505
Femme Actuelle	1,768,822	*Josei Seven*	765,662	*Vanidades*	220,946
Télé Poche	1,507,457	*Josei Jishin*	758,480	*Muy Interesante*	186,239

Spain		United Kingdom		United States	
Title	**Circulation**	**Title**	**Circulation**	**Title**	**Circulation**
Pronto	750,436	*Reader's Digest*	1,660,170	*AARP The Magazine*	21,035,278
Teleprograma	693,484	*What's on TV*	1,571,892	*Reader's Digest*	11,067,522
Supertele	681,100	*Radio Times*	1,485,759	*TV Guide*	9,018,212
Hola	651,967	*TV Times*	1,021,966	*Better Homes & Gardens*	7,608,913
Tele Indiscreta	642,256	*Woman's Weekly*	795,230	*National Geographic*	6,644,167

Posters are another print medium of interest to large, transnational corporations. This particularly text-heavy poster, which won a Bronze Lion at Cannes, is an anti-fairy-tale from the Concern India Foundation (a United Way–like umbrella nonprofit). Note the attention paid to the layout, font, type size, kerning, and leading—all of these elements contribute to a work of typography that is pleasing to the eye and easy to read.

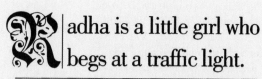

Radha is a little girl who begs at a traffic light.

As soon as the light turns red she goes to work. Knocking at car windows, trying to get the occupants' attention. Most of them stare straight ahead, stern faced. Sometimes, rarely, a window is rolled down and a coin is dropped into her palm. Across the road her little friend Seema works the other traffic light. She doesn't have one arm. So the motorists pity her more. She makes a lot more money. Her father hacked off her arm himself before he died. So she wouldn't have problems earning a living. 'He must have really loved her,' sighs Radha enviously.

At Concern India Foundation we have several projects where we help rehabilitate destitute children. To find out how you can help call 011-26224482.

Group launched several trade publications, including *Mir PK Russia* (formerly *PC World USSR*) and *ComputerWorld Poland*.

In the past, international advertising media consisted mainly of newspapers and magazines. Today, satellite-to-cable broadcast options, such as Superchannel and Sky Channel in Europe and Star TV in Asia, supplement print media.

Print Media and New Technologies

With computers came revolutionary media options, such as the Internet and CD-ROM, challenging both traditional print media and advertisers to adapt. Newspapers and magazines are rushing to make alliances with cable, regional telephone, and online companies to get a toehold in the interactive information market.

Over the last five years, for example, virtually all metropolitan news organizations and national magazines have incorporated electronic services. News organizations are information-rich, and much of the specialized information they don't run in the paper or the magazine fits perfectly with the online world's narrower interests. They are still, however, trying to figure out how to incorporate advertising into their new ventures. Most ads are still simply banners, but customers who are interested can click on the banners and scroll down to more in-depth information. This becomes a value-added service for the print medium's advertising customers. George Gilder, media expert and author, believes that the newspaper industry is in a particularly advantageous position, because "the convergence of text and video will cause a revolution in advertising, with targeted messages leading consumers step-by-step to a transaction."[30]

We'll deal with these issues in greater depth in Chapter 17.

Sources of Print Media Information

All publications provide information about their readership, circulation, rates, advertising policies, and editorial focus. Media planners can also consult a number of additional sources.

Many resources for advertisers and media buyers are now available, on demand, through the Internet. Today, most large organizations, like the Newspaper Association of America (www.naa.org), provide such information online, giving media personnel instant access to critical information. Some organizations even offer direct online transactions to purchase information or media space.

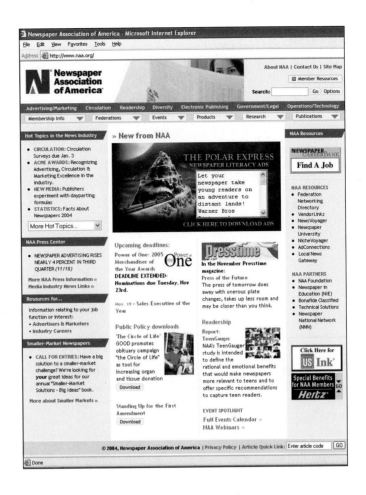

Chapter Summary

The printed page—in magazines and newspapers—provides a unique, flexible medium for advertising creativity.

In selecting magazines for advertising, the media buyer must consider a publication's circulation, its readership, its cost, and mechanical requirements. A magazine's rates may be determined by several factors: its primary and secondary readership, the number of subscription and vendor sales, and the number of copies guaranteed versus those actually delivered.

Magazine rate cards follow a standard format so advertisers can readily compare advertising costs. They list black-and-white and color rates, discounts, issue and closing dates, and mechanical requirements.

Magazines offer distinct advantages. They are the most selective of all mass media and are flexible in both readership and advertising. They offer unsurpassed color, excellent reproduction quality, authority and believability, long shelf life, and prestige at an efficient cost. However, they often require long lead times, have problems offering reach and frequency, and are subject to heavy advertising competition. The cost of advertising in some magazines is also very high.

The newspaper is a mass medium read by almost everybody. It offers great flexibility, which assists creativity, and its printed message lasts longer than ads in electronic media. However, newspapers also have disadvantages: lack of audience selectivity, short life span, poor production quality, heavy advertising competition, potentially poor ad placement, and overlapping circulation. Still, the newspaper is the major community-serving medium today for both news and advertising.

The newspaper's rate card lists prices, deadlines, mechanical requirements, and other pertinent information. Rates vary for local and national advertisers. Also listed are the newspaper's short-rate policy, combination rates, frequency discounts, run-of-paper rates, and other data.

Print is a worldwide medium; every country has newspapers and magazines. The international advertiser may have to choose between local and international media. The most educated consumers in many countries often read English-language publications. Political changes in eastern Europe spurred the introduction of many trade and business publications in the local language. Advertisers must study the audience they wish to reach before buying any media, whether at home or abroad.

Newspapers and magazines are making alliances with cable, regional telephone, and online computer companies to enter the interactive information market. They are still experimenting with ways to sell advertising on their electronic publications. Some experts believe that the convergence of text, video, and graphics will cause a creative revolution in advertising, with targeted, information-rich messages able to lead consumers step by step to a transaction without ever leaving home.

Important Terms

Audit Bureau of Circulations (ABC), *490*
bleed, *482*
bulk discount, *500*
business magazines, *485*
circulation audit, *490*
classified ad, *497*
classified display ad, *498*
closing date, *492*
color strip, *484*
column inch, *496*
combination rate, *500*
consumer magazines, *484*
contract rate, *499*
controlled circulation, *491*
cooperative (co-op) program, *497*
cost per thousand (CPM), *492*
cover date, *492*
cover position, *482*
custom magazines, *483*
daily newspaper, *495*
demographic editions, *493*
display advertising, *497*
earned rate, *500*

farm publications, *484*
flat rate, *499*
fragrance strip, *484*
frequency discount, *492, 500*
full position, *500*
gatefold, *483*
geographic editions, *493*
guaranteed circulation, *490*
horizontal publication, *491*
independent shopping guide, *497*
insert, *482*
insertion order, *502*
island half, *482*
junior unit, *482*
local city magazine, *485*
media buyer, *481*
national magazines, *485*
national rate, *498*
Newspaper Association of America
    (NAA), *501*
on-sale date, *492*
open rate, *499*
paid circulation, *491*

pop-up ad, *484*
preferred-position rate, *500*
preprinted insert, *498*
primary circulation, *490*
proof copy, *502*
public notice, *498*
rate base, *490*
rate card, *498*
reading notice, *497*
regional publications, *485*
run-of-paper (ROP) advertising rate, *500*
secondary (pass-along) readership, *491*
short rate, *500*
split run, *501*
standard advertising unit (SAU), *496*
standard-size newspaper, *496*
Sunday supplement, *497*
tabloid newspaper, *496*
tearsheet, *502*
3-D ad, *484*
vertical publication, *491*
volume discount, *492*
weekly newspaper, *495*

Review Questions

1. If you worked in the advertising department of a premium-priced furniture manufacturer, would you recommend magazine advertising? Why or why not?

2. If you were the advertising manager for a magazine aimed at senior citizens, what advantages would you cite to potential advertisers?

3. What is the advantage of magazine advertising to businesses that sell to other businesses?

4. What is the importance of the Audit Bureau of Circulations?

5. Why do retailers advertise so heavily in local newspapers?

6. How can advertisers improve the selectivity of their newspaper ads?

7. What factors should advertisers consider in deciding among several local papers (including dailies and weeklies)?

8. Should national advertisers be charged a higher rate than local advertisers? Support your position.

9. Should agencies be liable for their clients' advertising bills? Why or why not?

10. How could a local newspaper use an online database service or the Internet to help itself or its advertisers?

11. **The Advertising Experience**
As a maker of soy-based products, you are very excited about your new chocolate soy-milk drink. As long as they don't know it contains soy, children actually prefer its taste to that of milk. The product, now named "Swoosh" and represented by a toothy cartoon surfer, is all set for a print campaign. Choose a geographic area similar to the ones shown on page 485, examine the leading regional magazines and newspapers, and decide how to allocate funds for advertising. Explain why you chose newspapers, magazines, or both.

Exploring the Internet

The Internet exercises for Chapter 15 address the following areas related to the chapter: print media organizations (Exercise 1), print media tools (Exercise 2), and advertising rates (Exercise 3).

1. **Print Media Organizations**

    Visit the following print industry websites and familiarize yourself further with the size and scope of the print media world. Be sure to answer the questions for each site.

    - American Society of Newspaper Editors (ASNE) www.asne.org
    - Association of Alternative Newsweeklies (AAN) http://aan.org
    - International Newspaper Marketing Association (INMA) www.inma.org
    - National Newspaper Association (NNA) www.nna.org
    - National Newspaper Publishers Association (NNPA) www.nnpa.org
    - Newspaper Association of America (NAA) www.naa.org

    a. What is the purpose of the organization that sponsors this site?

    b. Who is the intended audience(s) of this site?

    c. Who makes up the organization's membership? Its constituency?

    d. How important do you feel this organization is to the advertising industry? Why?

2. **Print Media Tools**

    Were it not for the products and services offered by the following companies, planning and buying print vehicles could be an overwhelming task for media professionals. From audit reports to media kits, agencies and media houses are aided every day by companies who specialize in easing the lives of media planners and buyers. Visit the following syndicated and independent media companies' websites and answer the questions that follow:

    - Advertising Checking Bureau www.acbcoop.com
    - Advertising Media Internet Center (AMIC) www.amic.com
    - Audit Bureau of Circulations www.accessabc.com
    - BPA International (BPA) www.bpai.com
    - Certified Audit of Circulations www.certifiedaudit.com
    - MediaCentral www.mediacentral.net
    - MediaFinder www.mediafinder.com
    - Mediamark Research, Inc. www.mediamark.com
    - Print Measurement Bureau (PMB) www.pmb.ca
    - Scarborough www.scarborough.com
    - Standard Rate & Data Service (SRDS) www.srds.com
    - TNS Media Intelligence/CMR www.tnsmi-cnr.com

    a. Who is the intended audience of the site?

    b. What is the size/scope of the company?

    c. What type(s) of print media information does the company specialize in?

    d. How useful do you feel the company or organization is for obtaining print media information? Why?

3. **Researching Ad Rates**

    Most leading newspapers have websites. Check out daily newspapers from three different cities to find the rate charged for a gatefold insert. Which publication has the most expensive rates? Are the rates only a function of circulation, or are there other circumstances you can find?

Chapter 16

Using Electronic Media: Television and Radio

Objectives

TO PRESENT THE IMPORTANT FACTORS advertisers need to evaluate when considering the use of radio and television in the creative mix. Each medium has its own characteristics, advantages, and drawbacks. Advertisers must be able to compare their merits and understand the most cost-effective ways to buy advertising time.

After studying this chapter, you will be able to:

- **Describe** the advantages and drawbacks of broadcast television as an advertising medium.

- **Discuss** the advantages and drawbacks of cable television as an advertising medium and explain how it differs from broadcast television.

- **Explain** the process of buying cable and broadcast TV time.

- **Evaluate** the different types of television advertising available.

- **Describe** the process of TV audience measurement.

- **Discuss** the main factors to consider when buying television time.

- **Analyze** the pros and cons of using radio in the creative mix.

- **Explain** the major factors to consider when buying radio time.

Milk! Milk! Milk!

Milk coming!

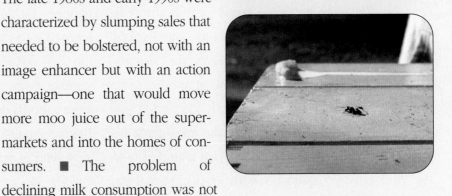

Milk may "do a body good," but for the dairy industry, the bottom line remains the same: how can we sell more of it? Unlike the "Milk, where's *your* mustache?" magazine campaign, the California milk producers were concerned less with changing consumer attitudes toward milk than with increasing its consumption. The late 1980s and early 1990s were characterized by slumping sales that needed to be bolstered, not with an image enhancer but with an action campaign—one that would move more moo juice out of the supermarkets and into the homes of consumers. ■ The problem of declining milk consumption was not unique to California, of course. It plagued the industry nationwide. People simply weren't drinking the beverage on the scale they once did; milk was losing out to sexy colas and snappy fruit drinks. And while the campaigns of "Milk does a body good" and "America's favorite health kick" had managed to create a fun and healthy image for milk, they had done little to improve sales. ■ Enter Jeff Manning, executive director for the California Milk Processor Board. Founded by the state's milk producers in 1993, the board set out to solve the problem of poor sales. Manning started with a hunch—that people don't drink milk by itself. Previous ads featured milk alone, but he believed that *food* was a key component, and it was missing from the picture. "If you ask people when milk is crucial, they'll tell you it's when they have cereal in the bowl or cookies in their mouth," Manning explained. "The driver is not the milk. It's the food."[1] ■ With this idea, Manning hired San Francisco-based Goodby, Silverstein & Partners to develop an advertising campaign that would target people who already consume milk and encourage them to drink more. Research revealed that

88 percent of milk is consumed at home and, as Manning suspected, it is usually accompanied by other food. People most often drink milk with cereal, but cookies, pastries, peanut butter and jelly sandwiches, and brownies are also popular milk partners. ■ The agency asked a group of research participants to go without milk for one week and then to share their experiences. The group quickly discovered the anguish of not having milk when they really needed it. One person woke up early in the morning and poured himself a bowl of cereal but then discovered there was no milk in the fridge. "It's so bad, you'd even steal milk from your kid," said one man, to which another replied, "Never mind your kid. You're so desperate you'd even steal it from your cat!"[2] ■ These stories found their way into the creative TV commercials that we all know: the businessman who dies and finds himself in what appears to be heaven with a plateful of cookies, only to discover that there is no milk; the angry Santa who takes back his gifts when he finds that no milk was left with the cookies. And cross-promotionals with co-marketers have

taken off too, such as the Oreo cookie parody of *Citizen Kane*. The question "Got milk?" became a punchline to jokes, not just a tagline for commercials. ■ Television proved to be the perfect vehicle for the "Got milk?" campaign because of its ability to tell the story in a unique manner and to dramatize the dilemma faced by milk-starved consumers. Using offbeat camera perspectives and lighting techniques that are possible only through television, the campaign offered immense visual appeal. And the ultimate medium for reaching the masses brought an action component to the campaign. People began buying milk again. So successful was the regional advertising campaign, in fact, that Dairy Management, Inc., the national dairy industry board, quickly licensed it to run on the national circuit. Later, as their success continued, Dairy Management, Inc., got together with the National Fluid Milk Processors, the other national organization promoting milk, to run combined campaigns using both the milk mustache and the "Got Milk?" slogan (see the ad at the beginning of Chapter 15). ■

The Medium of Television

Back in 1950, U.S advertisers spent $171 million, or about 3 percent of total U.S. advertising volume, on the new medium of television. It didn't take long, though, for the nation's advertisers to discover the power of this new vehicle to reach mass audiences quickly and frequently. TV also offered unique creative opportunities to imbue their brands with personality and image like never before. By 2001, TV advertising had grown to more than $54 *billion* and accounted for more than 29 percent of all U.S. ad spending, surpassing newspapers as the leading U.S. advertising medium.[3] Exhibit 16–1 lists the top network television advertisers in the United States and their annual expenditures.

Today, the medium of television is available to advertisers in two principal forms: broadcast and cable TV. **Broadcast TV** reaches its audience by transmitting electromagnetic waves through the air across some geographic territory. **Cable TV** reaches its audience through wires, which may be strung from telephone poles or laid underground.

Broadcast TV

Until the advent of the Internet, broadcast television grew faster than any other advertising medium in history. As both a news and entertainment medium, it caught people's fancy very quickly. From its

Exhibit 16–1

Top 10 network TV advertisers in the United States (2003).

Rank	Advertiser	Network TV ad spending ($ millions)
1	Procter & Gamble Co.	$833.6
2	General Motors Corp.	641.4
3	Johnson & Johnson	527.5
4	Ford Motor Co.	449.6
5	Pfizer	442.4
6	Time Warner	428.8
7	PepsiCo	423.2
8	Walt Disney Co.	409.7
9	Sony Corp.	338.0
10	Yum Brands	322.4

beginnings after World War II, broadcast TV rapidly emerged as the only medium that offered sight, sound, and motion. People could stay home and still go to the movies. As TV's legions of viewers grew, the big national-brand advertisers quickly discovered they could use the medium very efficiently to expand distribution across the country and sell products like never before. Not only that, the medium was ideal for building an image for their brands—even better than magazines, which had previously been the image-building medium of choice. It didn't take long for marketers to switch their budgets from radio, newspapers, and magazines. Today, broadcast TV still attracts the largest volume of *national* advertising, almost $42 billion in 2003.[4]

The United States now has 1,685 commercial TV stations.[5] About half the U.S. stations are **VHF** (very high frequency, channels 2 through 13); the rest are **UHF** (ultrahigh frequency, channels 14 through 83). Stations in the United States operate as independents unless they are affiliated with one of the national networks (ABC, NBC, CBS, Fox). Both network affiliates and independent stations may subscribe to nationally syndicated programs as well as originate their own programming. However, increasing competition from cable TV is taking viewers from the national network programs. To compensate, some networks are investing in cable TV systems or starting their own. NBC, for example, started CNBC and MSNBC, and ABC (which is now owned by Disney) has an 80 percent interest in ESPN.

Cable TV

For more than 30 years, broadcast TV, especially network TV, was the dominant entertainment medium for most Americans. Today, other electronic media have dramatically changed that dominance. Chief among the challengers is cable television.

Cable TV has been around since the late 1940s. Initially, it carried television signals by wire to areas with poor reception such as mountainous regions. But in the 1970s, the advent of satellite TV signals, the proliferation of channels, and the introduction of uncut first-run movies via pay-cable channels such as Home Box Office and Showtime made cable TV more attractive to all viewers, even people in urban areas.

At first, many subscribers valued cable simply for the full array of regional channels and access to premium services such as HBO. But once this novelty wore off, subscribers wanted more. A variety of advertiser-supported cable networks soon appeared with specialized programming in arts, history, sports, news, and comedy, along with diversified pay services and many more local shows. All of this attracted more and more subscribers—and simultaneously drew viewers away from the big broadcast networks.

In the last three decades, cable's growth has been extraordinary. In 1975, only 13 percent of TV households in the United States had cable. By 2003, cable reached almost 84 percent of all homes.[6] Although cable subscribers may receive more than 100 channels, most households only watch 15 to 19 channels.[7]

Most channels are privately owned and commercially operated. These include local network affiliates and independents, cable networks, superstations, local cable system channels, and community access channels. The cable fees represent about one-third of cable TV revenues; advertising makes up the remainder. Networks such as CNN, USA, the Discovery Channel, Arts & Entertainment, Lifetime, Comedy Central, and Spike TV now compete for advertisers' dollars, each selling its own niche audience.[8] For an additional price, subscribers can receive premium services such as HBO, Showtime, and Cinemax and see special events such as first-run films, championship boxing matches, and baseball games (through pay-per-view service).

There are now some 84 ad-supported cable networks in the United States and a growing number of regional networks. Exhibit 16–2 lists the most widely carried ones.[9] There are also a handful of *superstations,* local over-the-air TV stations

Exhibit 16–2
Major cable TV networks.

Network	Number of subscribers (millions)	Program type
Arts & Entertainment	87.7	Family/variety
Black Entertainment TV (BET)	76.0	Sports/family/entertainment/news/ethnic/music video/information
CNBC	88.8	Educational information/business/news/information/general
CNN	88.1	News/information
The Discovery Channel	88.3	Educational information/family/health/original/news/technology/science
ESPN	88.3	Sports
FX	85.0	Family/general/original
CNN Headline News	86.3	News/information
Lifetime Television	87.1	Women's interest/family/general/health/news/information
MTV	96.0	Music video
Nickelodeon	84.0	Youth interest
TBS	87.9	Family/general/music video/sports/women's interest/youth interest
CMT: Country Music Television	70.4	Music video
Turner Network Television (TNT)	88.1	Family/general/sports/women's interest/youth interest
The Weather Channel	86.7	News/information
USA Network	87.6	Entertainment/movies/sports

whose signals are delivered via satellite to cable systems across the country and that carry some national advertising.

TV Audience Trends

As a way to reach a mass audience, no other medium today has the unique creative abilities of television: the combination of sight, sound, and motion; the opportunity to demonstrate the product; the potential to use special effects; the empathy of the viewer; and the believability of seeing it happen right before your eyes (see the Checklist, "The Pros and Cons of Broadcast TV Advertising"). As Exhibit 16–3 shows, almost half of viewers believe TV is the most authoritative advertising source, compared to only 26 percent for newspapers, 11 percent for magazines, 9 percent for radio, and 5 percent for the Internet. Television was also rated as the most influential, persuasive, and exciting medium.[10]

The heaviest viewers of broadcast TV are middle-income, high school–educated individuals and their families, so most programming is directed at this group. People with considerably higher incomes and more education typically have a more diverse range of interests and entertainment options.

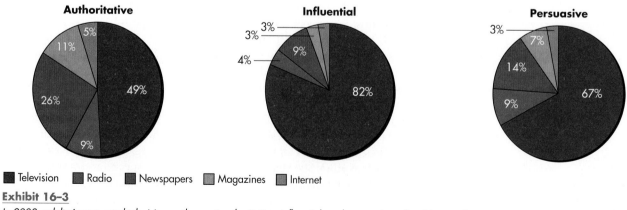

Exhibit 16–3
In 2003, adult viewers rated television as the most authoritative, influential, and persuasive advertising medium.

The Pros and Cons of Broadcast TV Advertising

The Pros

Contemporary broadcast television offers advertisers many advantages over competing media.

____ **Mass coverage.** A full 98 percent of all U.S. homes have a TV (most have more than one), and viewing time for the average household increased from about five hours a day in 1960 to about eight hours in 2003.

____ **Relatively low cost.** Despite the often huge initial outlays for commercial production and advertising time, TV's equally huge audiences bring the cost per exposure down to $2 to $10 per thousand viewers.

____ **Some selectivity.** Television audiences vary a great deal depending on the time of day, day of the week, and nature of the programming. Advertising messages can be presented when potential customers are watching, and advertisers can reach select geographic audiences by buying local and regional markets.

____ **Impact.** Television offers a kind of immediacy that other forms of advertising cannot achieve, displaying and demonstrating the product with sound, motion, and full color right before the customer's eyes.

____ **Creativity.** The various facets of the TV commercial—sight, sound, motion, and color—permit infinite original and imaginative appeals.

____ **Prestige.** Because the public considers TV the most authoritative and influential medium, it offers advertisers a prestigious image. Hallmark, Xerox, ExxonMobil, and IBM increase their prestige by regularly sponsoring cultural programs on network TV.

____ **Social dominance.** In North America, most people under age 35 grew up with TV as a window to their social environment. They continue to be stirred by TV screenings of the Olympics, space travel, assassinations, wars, and political scandals around the world.

The Cons

Sometimes broadcast TV just doesn't "fit" the creative mix because of cost, lack of audience selectivity, inherent brevity, or the clutter of competitive messages.

____ **High production cost.** One of broadcast TV's greatest handicaps is the high cost of producing quality commercials. Depending on the creative approach, the cost of filming a national commercial today may run from $200,000 to more than $1 million.

____ **High air-time cost.** The average cost of a prime-time network commercial ranges from $200,000 to $400,000. A single 30-second commercial for a top-rated show in prime time may cost over $500,000. Special attractions like the Super Bowl cost over $2 million. The cost of large coverage, even at low rates, prices small and medium-size advertisers out of the market.

____ **Limited selectivity.** Broadcast TV is not cost-effective for advertisers seeking a very specific, small audience. And it is losing some of its selectivity because of changing audience trends. More women are working outside the home or watching cable TV, hurting advertisers on network soap operas.

____ **Brevity.** Studies show that most TV viewers can't remember the product or company in the most recent TV ad they watched—even if it was within the last five minutes. Recall improves with the length of the commercial; people remember 60-second spots better than 30-second spots.

____ **Clutter.** TV advertising is usually surrounded by station breaks, credits, and public service announcements, as well as six or seven other spots. All these messages compete for attention, so viewers become annoyed and confused and often misidentify the product.

____ **Zipping and zapping.** VCR users who skip through commercials when replaying taped programs are zipping; remote-control users who change channels at the beginning of a commercial break are zapping.

The number of TV viewing hours continues to increase. In the average U.S. home, viewers watch TV/cable/VCR for 8 hours *every day*. Children and teenagers view an average of 21 hours per week, 1–2 less than their parents.[11]

Around the world, older women watch TV the most (36 hours per week in both the United States and Canada). This makes the medium very popular with advertisers like Weight Watchers, whose primary target is middle-aged and older women who are concerned with how they look.

Cable in North American homes has significantly altered TV viewing patterns and the use of other media. Households with cable spend less time watching broadcast TV. They also spend less time listening to the radio, reading, or going to the movies. Cable seems to reach an audience that is difficult to get to in any other way. As a result of this *audience fragmentation,* advertising on broadcast networks has become less cost effective. Video and DVD rentals have also increased dramatically, drawing more viewers away from advertiser-supported TV, both broadcast and cable (which is why ads have now started appearing on videos).

Cable households watch more television than noncable households: 56.2 hours per week versus 41.6 hours. Cable households watch about 22.8 hours of cable programming a week.[12]

National advertisers have been using cable since the late 1970s and cable advertising revenues have grown steadily, reaching over $14.5 billion in 2002.[13] One reason is that cable's upscale audience buys proportionately more goods and services than noncable subscribers (see Exhibit 16–4). Procter & Gamble traditionally spends the most on network cable. However, local retailers also find local cable a good place to advertise. Fisher Big Wheel, a discount department store in Midvale, Ohio, became an enthusiastic cable devotee after its first cable promotion brought an extra 15,000 customers into the store.

Recent studies suggest that by 2005 the average U.S. household will have 165 channels—130 of them advertising-supported. But that number won't translate into more TV viewing. In households that have more than basic cable, receiving between 50 and 120 (or even more) channels, the average number of regularly viewed channels is 19 or fewer.[14]

But there lies the crux of one of the major issues of modern media. While there is no doubt that the media play an ever-expanding role in our daily lives, there is a finite limit to the number of advertising exposures people can absorb. When that limit is reached (and we're certainly getting close to it now), any new

Exhibit 16–4

Cable households are more likely to purchase goods and services than noncable households (Index of 100 = U.S. average).

Products or services	Cable households versus US average (index)	Noncable households versus US average (index)	Products or services	Cable households versus US average (index)	Noncable households versus US average (index)
Travel			**Consumer electronics**		
Business travel	103	95	Own cell phone	107	88
Vacation travel	105	91	Own personal computer	105	90
Car rental (heavy)	110	82	Own digital camera	104	93
3+ plane trips	108	86	Own DVD player	105	92
Member frequent flyer program	110	82	Own 4+ TV sets	112	78
Spent $1000+ on travelers checks	111	80	Own video game system	102	96
Automotive			Spent $750+ on camcorder (past year)	106	90
Bought new auto last year	108	85	Bought large screen TV (27"+)	106	89
Bought new domestic auto last year	106	88	**Home furnishings (purchased last year)**		
Bought new imported auto last year	111	79	Wall unit	105	90
Own new luxury auto	107	86	Wall-to-wall carpeting	106	89
Own sport/utility auto	106	89	Spent $3,000+ remodeling any room	109	84
Own minivan	104	93	Spent $700+ big-ticket furniture	108	85
Shopping and retail					
Spend $150+/week in food stores	103	95			
Spent $750+ on fine jewelry (last year)	107	86			
Spent $500+ on mail/phone/Internet	107	88			
Spent $1,000+ on clothing (last year)	110	81			
Dry cleaning ($100+ in last 6 months)	117	69			
Flowers by phone/wire (last 6 months)	112	79			
Bought pharmecutical drugs (last year)	102	96			

media will simply be fighting for market share. This is the reason for the increasing fragmentation of the audience and the precipitous decline in the huge share of audience once held by the broadcast networks. This is also why media buyers and planners are growing in importance as advertisers search for the elusive audience and fight for their share of that audience in an overcrowded media environment.

The Use of Television in IMC

Television today is very versatile. For many years it was strictly a mass medium, used to great advantage by the manufacturers of mass consumption goods: toiletries and cosmetics, food, appliances, and cars (see Exhibit 16–5). But today, thanks to the narrowcasting ability of cable TV, television can also be a highly selective niche medium. It's not unusual, for instance, to see ads for special feed for thoroughbreds and show horses on ESPN's Grand Prix of Jumping. And thanks to local cable, TV is now affordable for even small local advertisers. This makes it a very viable option for use in an IMC program.

While single programs don't deliver the mass audience they once did, television is still the most cost-effective way to deliver certain kinds of messages to large, well-defined audiences. When it comes to awareness and image advertising, for instance, television has no rival. The same is true for brand reinforcement messages.[15]

Since marketing integrators are looking to establish, nourish, and reinforce relationships with many groups of stakeholders, television serves another role quite efficiently. It can speak to many different kinds of stakeholders—not just customers—at the same time. Moreover, through its unique ability to deliver a creative big idea, television can impart *brand meaning* (the symbolism or personality of the brand) to either attract people to the brand or reinforce their current relationship with it.

Television is also a good leverage tool. That is, an advertiser might take advantage of the relatively low CPM of television to reach out to many prospects. Prospects can identify themselves by responding to the commercial, and then the advertiser can follow up with less expensive, one-to-one or addressable media.[16]

What's important to remember in all this is that the high visibility of TV forces the sponsor to create ads that people find interesting and that consistently reinforce the brand's strategic position (remember our definition of great advertising). The brands that succeed are the ones that are the most popular. And "ad liking" has a lot to do with brand popularity.

Types of TV Advertising

Advertisers use different strategies to buy time on broadcast and cable television. The major broadcast networks offer a variety of *programs* that appeal to different audiences. So the advertiser buys ads based on the viewing audience of each program. A national advertiser that wants to reach a broad cross section of women ages 25 to 45, for example, might find *CSI* an efficient buy, especially at the cost of only $280,000 for a 30-second commercial (which is much less than the average cost of a top-rated, prime-time network show).

When buying cable TV, an advertiser can buy ads over the full schedule of a channel because cable networks typically aim their overall programming to relatively specific *audiences*. The Lifetime and Family channels heavily weigh programs toward women; MTV targets viewers 16 to 25. Cable companies sell their network channels in bundles at a discount and offer discounts for *run-of-schedule* positioning—multiple ad purchases they can place throughout a channel's daily schedule (see the Checklist, "The Pros and Cons of Cable TV Advertising").

Exhibit 16–5

Top 10 cable network advertisers (2003).

Rank	Advertiser	Cable network ad spending ($ millions)
1	Procter & Gamble Co.	$514.6
2	General Motors Corp.	311.3
3	Time Warner	250.1
4	Altria Group	187.4
5	Walt Disney Co.	168.3
6	Sony Corp.	166.2
7	Johnson & Johnson	164.3
8	MCI	162.3
9	Pfizer	148.0
10	GlaxoSmithKline	140.4

The Pros and Cons of Cable TV Advertising

The Pros

___ **Selectivity.** Cable offers specialized programming aimed at particular types of viewers. Narrowcasting allows advertisers to choose programming with the viewer demographics that best match their target customers.

___ **Audience demographics.** Cable subscribers are younger, better educated, and more affluent, have higher-level jobs, live in larger households, and are more likely to try new products and buy more high-ticket items, such as cars, appliances, and high-tech equipment.

___ **Low cost.** Many small companies get TV's immediacy and impact without the enormous expenditures of broadcast TV. Cable advertising can sometimes cost as little as radio. Many national advertisers find sponsorship attractive, since an entire cable series can cost less to produce than a single broadcast TV commercial.

___ **Flexibility.** Broadcast TV commercials need to be short because of the high costs of production and air time, but cable ads can run up to two minutes and, in the case of infomercials, much longer. They can also be tailored to fit the programming environment.

___ **Testability.** Cable is a good place to experiment, testing both new products and various advertising approaches: ad frequency, copy impact, and different media mixes.

The Cons

Like every medium, cable TV has its drawbacks.

___ **Limited reach.** About 23 percent of households don't have cable. This was cable's main weakness in the past, but it is less so today.

___ **Fragmentation.** With more than 50 channels at their disposal, cable viewers do not watch any one show in enormous numbers. To reach the majority of the cable audience in a particular market, ads must run on many stations.

___ **Quality.** Cable, particularly local cable, sometimes has poorer production quality and less desirable programming than broadcast TV.

___ **Zipping and zapping.** Cable TV has some of the same drawbacks as broadcast TV, such as zipping and zapping.

There are various ways advertisers can buy time on TV. They include sponsoring an entire program, participating in a program, purchasing spot announcements between programs, and purchasing spots from syndicators. Exhibit 16–6 shows how much money is spent nationally on the various types of television advertising.

Network Advertising

Historically, major U.S. advertisers purchased air time from one of the national broadcast **networks:** ABC, CBS, NBC, or Fox. In 1995, relaxed FCC rules enabled two of the biggest producers of prime-time shows, Warner Bros. and Paramount, to launch their own broadcast networks—WB and UPN—giving them captive distribution outlets for programs they produce and buy.[17] With 31 affiliated stations, UPN

Television plays an important role in its ability to impart brand personality. Television communicates with many stakeholders simultaneously and can deliver a "big idea" in a uniquely creative manner. This commerical for KitKat spoofs the use of models as product endorsers, using a comical, almost adlib approach and won a Silver Lion at Cannes.

Exhibit 16–6

Where does all the money go? Measured TV spending in billions of dollars (2003).

	2003	2002	% change
Network TV	20.4	20.0	1.8
Syndicated TV	3.4	2.9	15.3
Spot TV	16.2	17.2	–5.4
Cable TV networks	12.3	10.6	15.6
Total	52.3	50.7	3.0

Exhibit 16–7

Advertising cost per 30-second spot on 10 most expensive prime-time shows (2003).

Rank	Show and network	Price
1	*Friends* (NBC)	$473,500
2	*Will & Grace* (NBC)	414,500
3	*ER* (NBC)	404,814
4	*Survivor* (CBS)	390,367
5	*Scrubs* (NBC)	360,950
6	*Coupling* (NBC)	316,400
7	*CSI* (CBS)	310,324
8	*The Simpsons* (Fox)	296,440
9	*24* (Fox)	292,200
10	*Monday Night Football* (ABC)	272,867

immediately covered 80 percent of the country, even though it initially programmed only a couple of nights a week.[18]

Cable has slowly eroded the audience of the broadcast networks. At one time the big three (ABC, CBS, and NBC) had more than 90 percent of the prime-time audience. Today their total share is about 29 percent, with ad-supported cable networks comprising 42 percent and other channels (pay cable, smaller networks, and public television) comprising another 29 percent.[19]

Networks offer large advertisers convenience and efficiency because they broadcast messages simultaneously across many affiliate stations throughout the country. Broadcast networks tend to reach masses of American consumers representing a cross section of the population, while cable networks tend to reach more selective niches.

An advertiser who underwrites the cost of a program is engaging in **sponsorship.** In a sole sponsorship, the advertiser is responsible for both the program content and the total cost of production. Sponsorship is so costly that single sponsorships are usually limited to specials. Companies that sponsor programs (AT&T, Xerox, and Hallmark, for example) gain two important advantages. First, the public more readily identifies with the product(s) due to the prestige of sponsoring first-rate entertainment. Second, the sponsor controls the placement and content of its commercials. The commercials can be fit to the program and run any length the sponsor desires so long as they remain within network or station regulations. Further, because networks are centralized, the advertiser gets only one bill.

Sponsorship offers many opportunities. When the popular drama series *24* started its second season, the first episode was presented commercial-free, thanks to a full sponsorship by Ford Motor Company. The episode also featured numerous Ford vehicles in the show. To save money and reduce risks, many advertisers cosponsor programs, sponsoring on alternate weeks or dividing the program into segments. NFL games, for instance, are always sold as multiple sponsorships.

Most network TV advertising is sold on a **participation basis,** with several advertisers buying 30- or 60-second segments within a program. This enables them to spread their budgets and avoid long-term commitments to any one program. It also lets smaller advertisers buy a limited amount of time and still get the nationwide coverage they need.

Network advertising also has several disadvantages: lack of flexibility, long lead times, inconvenient restrictions, and forced adherence to network standards and practices, not to mention high prices. Costs range from a low of $80,000 to a high of $473,500 for a spot on *Friends* (see Exhibit 16–7). For this reason, most advertisers decide to buy *spot announcements.*

Spot Announcements

National **spot announcements** run in clusters between programs. They are less expensive than participations and more flexible than network advertising because they can be concentrated in specific regions of the country. An advertiser with a small budget or limited distribution may use spots to introduce a new product into one area at a time. Or an advertiser can vary its message for different markets to suit promotional needs.[20]

Spots may run 10, 15, 30, or 60 seconds and be sold nationally or locally. Spot advertising is more difficult to buy than network advertising because it involves contacting each station directly. This is a headache with cable channels, since one city may be served by 10 or more cable companies. For the broadcast stations, the *national rep system,* in which individuals act as sales and service representatives for a number of stations, alleviates this problem through the use of *electronic data interchange (EDI).*[21] This technology enables agency buyers to electronically process

Advertising to Children: Child's Play?

Kids make up a considerable consumer group whose number and purchasing power are growing. In 1999, children aged four to twelve took in $31.3 billion in income from allowance, jobs, and gifts, and spent 92 percent of it, says James MacNeal, a market researcher who specializes in the children's market. Today, children are influencing the family's buying behavior for everything from cars to orange juice—up to $500 billion a year. Whether they're spending their own money or asking their parents to spend theirs, marketing to kids is big business and it's only getting bigger.

The benefits of reaching children are great. If won over now, they tend to be loyal customers into adulthood. Besides selling to children, advertisers also sell through children. Some companies believe they can sell more by appealing to children's preferences than to adults'. The minivan was created because children demanded more room, says Mr. MacNeal. When kids decided the vehicle was "uncool," their opinions helped to develop the SUV. Saturday morning cartoons are the traditional vehicle for ads promoting cereals, candy, and toys. Particular brands of vacuum cleaners and other household goods are requested

of parents because kids saw it advertised on TV. Marketers rely on kids' "pester power" to get their products sold.

The dangers of marketing to kids from an ethical perspective are fairly clear: Children are the "vulnerable" market. They are less experienced. Their concepts of self, time, and money are immature. As a result, they know very little about their own desires, needs, and preferences—or how to use economic resources rationally to satisfy them. The nature of children's conceptual ability makes it likely that child-oriented advertising can lead to false beliefs or highly improbable product expectations. Telling children about a product and accurately describing that product is probably ethical. Convincing them that they must have the toy to be popular and successful with their friends, or misrepresenting the toy, or encouraging them to make a nuisance of themselves to parents and start begging for the toy is probably not. Nothing is likely to enrage parents and society-at-large more than the prospect of marketers manipulating and taking advantage of children. Cereal is better if a fun character is selling it; so are beer and cigarettes as the Budweiser frogs and lizards and Joe Camel proved. In the UK, there is criticism over the use of TV characters such as the Simpsons and Teletubbies, as well as the Spice Girls, to sell snack foods high in fat, sugar,

---

orders, makegoods, and revisions, and maintain an electronic audit trail through the life of a schedule. Likewise, reps can transmit orders directly to their stations via satellite while keeping in day-to-day contact with agency buyers.[22]

Meanwhile, a number of large cable rep firms are also working to make the purchase of spot cable more convenient for national advertisers through satellite technology and digital systems that interconnect various cable companies in a region.[23]

Spot advertising is available only at network station breaks and when network advertisers purchase less than a full lineup, so spot ads may get lost in the clutter—which is why they tend to have less viewers and a smaller piece of the ad spending pie.

Syndication

As audiences fragment, syndicated programs become an increasingly popular adjunct or alternative to network advertising. In a little over 10 years, the syndication industry has grown from almost nothing into a $3.3 billion advertising medium.[24]

Syndication is the sale of programs on a station-by-station, market-by-market basis. In other words, the producer (for example, Warner Bros. or Disney) deals directly with the stations, often through a distribution company, rather than going through the networks. This efficient "direct-from-the-factory" approach gives local TV stations more programming control and greater profits. It also gives advertisers access to **inventory** (commercial time) for their spots that they might not get on network programs—often at better prices.[25] Syndication has become the largest source of programming in the United States (see Exhibit 16–8).

Television syndication comes in three forms: off-network, first-run, and barter. In **off-network syndication,** former popular network programs (reruns) are sold to individual stations for rebroadcast. Examples include *Frasier* and *The X-Files*. **First-run syndication** involves original shows, like *Oprah, Inside Edition,* and *Extra,* which are produced specifically for the syndication market. One of the fastest-growing trends in television is **barter syndication** (also called *advertiser-supported syndication*). These are

a. Network

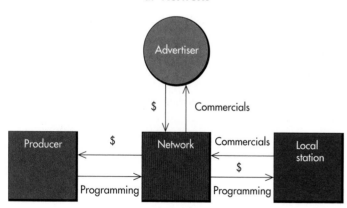

b. Syndication

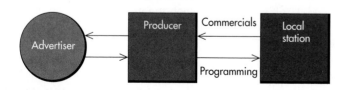

Exhibit 16–8

TV network and syndication distribution.
a. The networks are essentially middlemen.
b. Syndication is often a more efficient way of financing and distributing programs.

and salt. The junk food firms face a crackdown on the hard sell of products that can make children overweight and unhealthy.

Both critics and defenders agree that advertisers should not intentionally deceive children. Federal legislation has been introduced that would re-impose the 1974 guidelines limiting advertising on children's programs. These guidelines deal with truth and accuracy, as well as the broader issue of pester power.

The mood in several European countries is to tighten up children-and-advertising guidelines. Sweden has some of the strictest controls in Europe on children and advertising, banning all television advertisements aimed at children under 12. This ban includes advertisements on toys, foods, sweets, drinks, and any products that might appeal to pre-teens. Steven Shanahan, chief executive of the Institute of Advertising Practitioners in Ireland (IAPI), says that Sweden's ban is unlikely to work in practice because Swedish children have access to stations other than domestic ones that are not under Swedish TV regulators. Research shows that a Swedish child sees as much advertising as any other European child. TV stations still need advertising revenue and the commercial breaks in Swedish children's programming are full of adult advertisements. The real money is not in selling programs to stations but

in selling products to the child audience and creating the next toddler must-have. In light of an intense commercial environment, Sweden may not be able to persuade its European partners to adopt the ban. It should, however, raise awareness as to the impact and effect of advertising on young consumers who are not able to protect themselves from the onslaught of marketing messages during their favorite cartoon breaks.

The proposed ban raises other issues. Does the ban on marketing to children compromise the freedom of choice and speech? How far should advertisers go to ensure that children are not misled by their ads? And there are areas regarding how children are used in advertising and the frequency of toy advertising that could be addressed.

Sources: "Self-Regulatory Guidelines for Children's Advertising," Children's Advertising Review Unit, 2003 (www.caru.org/guidelines/index.asp); "Barraging Kids with Ads," *San Francisco Chronicle*, July 20, 2004 [http://sfgate.com]; "The Original Chocolate Factory Ad, Broadcast during Children's Programming, Violates CARU Guidelines," CARU news releases, August 12, 2004 (www.caru.org/news/2004/chocfactory.asp); "Responsibility and Children's Advertising," Concerned Children's Advertisers (www.cca-canada.com/ethics).

first-run programs offered free or for a reduced rate, but with some of the ad space (usually 50 percent) presold to national advertisers. *Wheel of Fortune, Jeopardy,* and *Oprah,* all distributed by King World Productions, are some of the most popular examples.[26]

Syndication is a powerful tool for building reach. Advertisers like it because they can affiliate with popular programs and maximize their use of broadcast TV, gaining back much of the audience they used to reach through the networks (see Exhibit 16–9).

Exhibit 16–9

Syndication viewing shares for total and daytime dayparts. Although syndication holds a respectable 13 percent share relative to total overall viewing, it commands a full one-third of viewing share of all national broadcast. During prime-time dayparts, when competing with network sitcoms and dramas, syndication's share of audience drops way off. But during early prime time it is responsible for over 75 percent share of national broadcast viewing, and during late fringe it commands close to 50 percent share. Syndication ranks high in early prime time and late fringe segments because the only broadcast competition comes from early evening news programs and late-night talk shows.

Viewing shares for all dayparts

Total viewing, syndication: 13 share

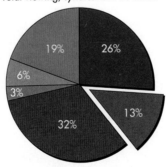

National broadcast, syndication: 33 share

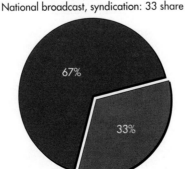

Viewing shares for daytime dayparts

Total viewing, syndication: 17 share

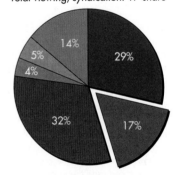

National broadcast, syndication: 37 share

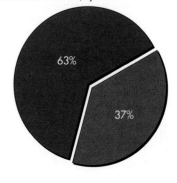

■ Network ■ Syndication ■ Cable ■ PBS ■ Pay cable ■ Local/other

519

Program-Length Ads (PLAs)

In the fall of 1992, independent presidential candidate Ross Perot sat in front of a TV camera for 30 minutes with homemade flip charts and a down-home pitch for the White House and drew 20 million viewers. A month later, he pulled a respectable 19 percent of the vote.

Perot made advertising history by catapulting the **program-length advertisement (PLA),** or **infomercial,** into the limelight. He also proved what companies that produce and sell infomercials have been saying for years: Long-form advertising can communicate a message in a way other forms can't.[27] As a result, *Advertising Age* named Perot its adman of the year.

Infomercials aren't new, but their respectability is. Before Perot, most PLA users were off–Madison Avenue marketers of hand mixers, juicers, and car waxes. Today, major marketers such as Toshiba, Lexus, and Magnavox have ventured into the infomercial arena.[28] In Colorado, long-form ads were used as a negotiating tool in a labor dispute.[29] And now even networks air some of these ads, which were once relegated to independents and cable channels.[30] The reasons for this sudden growth are simple:

1. Consumers pay attention and can respond immediately.
2. Brand managers may be able to gain a competitive advantage by going where the competition is not.
3. PLAs can fulfill some message objectives, like product demonstration and brand differentiation, far better than 30-second commercials.
4. Results are both measurable and accountable.
5. The ad campaign can pay for itself while supporting the retail trade.
6. PLAs combine the power of advertising, direct response, and sales promotion.[31]

This striking 30-second commercial for Sony PlayStation, entitled "Mountain," won the Grand Prix at Cannes for its cinematic and narrative beauty. The ad, which was filmed in Brazil, opens with a shot of a young man staring at the sky. The soundtrack begins with a rendition of the up-tempo classic "Get on Board Li'l Children" sung by Shirley Temple. Presently, the screen is filled with hordes of civilians, all rushing toward something, although viewers don't know what. Each shot is carefully and skillfully executed, and the colors are rich and true to life. More people fill the shot until the crowd has become an extraordinary gathering, culminating in a mountain of people—an image that would be impossible without the help of visual effects technology. Finally, the caption: "Fun, Anyone?"

Add to these factors the benefits of lower (though rising) production costs and attractive, upscale audience demographics, and it's easy to see why national marketers have jumped on the PLA bandwagon. They spent some $500 million on infomercials in 1996, 60 percent of which went to cable.[32]

Local TV Advertising

Local businesses and retailers, often in cooperation with nationally known manufacturers, now spend over $15 billion annually on local broadcast and cable TV.[33] Most local stations sell spot announcements, but some local advertisers develop and sponsor local programs or buy the rights to a syndicated series.

TV Audience Measurement

Efficient advertisers study the audiences of various programs and analyze their impact and cost effectiveness against other media vehicles. To do this, they must understand the techniques and terminology used in television audience measurement.

Rating Services: The Book

The companies that measure the program audiences of TV and radio stations for advertisers and broadcasters are called **rating services.** These firms attempt to pick a representative sample of the market and furnish data on the number and characteristics of the viewers or listeners. Several research organizations gather the data at their own expense and publish it. Companies subscribe to a service and use it as a basis for planning, buying, or selling media advertising.

In the United States, Nielsen Media Research, a division of the Dutch conglomerate VNU, is the major rating service for television. Its flagship service, the Nielsen Television Index (NTI), uses a national sample of 5,100 households equipped with *people meters* to develop audience estimates for all national TV programming sources: 7 broadcast networks, 47 cable networks, 3 Spanish-language networks, and more than 200 syndicators. At the local level, Nielsen uses people meters in the 55 largest markets and diary surveys in 210 TV markets to measure viewing for more than 1,500 local TV stations, 140 cable operators, 48 syndicators, and 2,000 local advertising agencies.[34] It publishes the information at least twice a year in a publication commonly called *the Book* (see Ad Lab 16–A).

Since 1993, when the Arbitron Co. discontinued its local-market TV audience rating service, Nielsen has enjoyed a virtual monopoly. This may be short-lived, though; many advertisers and broadcasters maintain that Nielsen's reports are unstable and inaccurate.[35] Don Ohlmeyer, former president of NBC West Coast, says, "Nielsen is an antiquated, inaccurate monopoly that hasn't kept up with the way people watch television today. Norway has better TV measurement than we do in this country."[36] In fact, Nielsen's biggest problem may be the low cooperation rate among viewers who are supposed to fill out diaries. When they aren't consistent, the results can show very quirky ratings.[37] The issues are critical to the networks and advertisers alike, since Nielsen's numbers determine the fate of billions of dollars' worth of advertising every year.

For demographic studies of TV audiences, advertisers also use the Simmons Market Research Bureau and Mediamark Research. These companies perform extensive surveys of the U.S. marketplace and publish their findings on consumer lifestyles, product usage, and media habits. Advertisers use the results for strategic planning purposes.

Cable Ratings

Reliable information on cable programs is even harder to gather. Traditional techniques often rely on too small a sample to be statistically significant, so major cable programming services provide their own reports of daypart division and audience viewership by show. Interpreting cable ratings is a confusing process, since the media planner has to integrate so much information from so

Where Do Those Infamous TV Ratings Come From?

For four decades, the life and death of network TV programs have been in the hands of the Nielsen families, households chosen with the aid of national census and other data to reflect the country's demographics. Originally there were two measuring types: those who kept diaries and those who had a black box attached to their TV sets. Someone in each of 2,400 diary homes kept a written record of which shows each person watched during the week. In the 1,700 black box households, an audiometer attached to the TV kept track of when the set was on and what channel it was tuned to. Nielsen Media Research paid these families for the permission to gather data from their viewing patterns. The information is used to compute its Nielsen Television Index (NTI), the sole source of national TV ratings.

But that method of determining national ratings has been replaced by the more accurate people meter (see illustration), an electronic device that automatically records a household's TV viewing. The people meter records the channels watched, the number of minutes of viewing, and who in the household is watching. Each person must punch in and punch out on a keypad. The microwave-based people meter keeps track of second-by-second viewing choices of up to eight household members and relays the data to a central computer, which tabulates the data overnight.

The original people meter was developed by AGB Research, a British company. AGB found clients in ad agencies, cable networks, and syndicators—all of whom believed NTI overreported broadcast network shows and underreported other types. However, Nielsen developed its own people meter, and AGB abandoned the U.S. market.

Unfortunately, Nielsen's people meter had its share of problems. At one point, Nielsen's numbers showed millions of people suddenly stopped watching TV. The networks hit the roof, but Nielsen officials defended their system. The networks gave advertisers $150 million worth of free time, since they hadn't met rating guarantees, and decided to use eight-year trends for rating guarantees instead of just the current year's ratings. And critics are still convinced that people meter numbers are flawed.

Nielsen's competitor Arbitron is developing a passive people meter whose portable technology can register TV viewing and radio listening anywhere respondents are using them, even out of home. The new Portable People Meter (PPM) is pager-sized and would be worn by each panelist. The meter works by detecting identification codes which can be implanted in any form of audio transmission. Respondents are not required to do anything except wear the device, which will eliminate problems with panelist participation incumbent in the current people meter system.

Nielsen joined with Arbitron in its initial U.S. test of the Portable People Meter in Philadelphia in fall 2000. The Portable People Meter has already been tested successfully in the United Kingdom. Currently, Arbitron, like Nielsen, is using meters and diaries to collect TV and radio ratings.

Nielsen conducts its survey sweeps four times a year in major market areas and publishes sweeps books that are the basis for network and local station ad rates. With the advent of the passive people meter, advertisers may once again believe in the ratings they're paying for.

An interesting development in audience measurement is the single-source data made available by supermarket scanners. Once information on a family's viewing habits has been gathered, its packaged-goods purchases are measured. The implications are monumental for marketing and media planners. The leaders in single-source measurement today are Information Resources, Inc. (IRI), with its BehaviorScan service, and Nielsen, with its Home Scan service.

Laboratory Applications

1. What are the advantages and disadvantages of the various measurement methods?

2. Which method do you consider the best? Why?

---

many different sources. Some companies are trying to remedy the situation. ADcom Information Services, for example, is a ratings service that installs in-home recording devices to provide more reliable information. Its recent test with Continental Cablevision in Jacksonville, Florida, confirmed that Nielsen had been underreporting cable TV audiences—in some cases dramatically.[38] Nielsen, meanwhile, has introduced its own cable TV ratings service but has been criticized for using older broadcast reporting technology.[39] This controversy is destined to rage for some time.

Defining Television Markets

Television rating services define geographic television markets to minimize the confusion of overlapping TV signals. The Nielsen station index uses the term **designated market areas (DMAs)** for geographic areas (cities, counties) in which the *local* TV stations attract the most viewing. For example, the DMA for Casper-Riverton, Wyoming (see Exhibit 16–10), is all counties in which the Casper or Riverton County TV stations are the most watched.

MARKET DATA

**CASPER-RIVERTON, WY
DMA RANK # 194**

APRIL 27 - MAY 24, 1995

TABLE 1 - UNIVERSE ESTIMATES - JAN. 1995

AREA	TOTAL HOUSEHOLDS	TV HOUSEHOLDS	TV HOUSEHOLDS BY COUNTY SIZE †			
			A	B	C	D
METRO	37,300	36,410				
DMA	48,800	47,580			24,340	23,240
%		100			51	49
NSI	180,100	175,860			53,990	121,870
%		100			31	69

TOTAL HOUSEHOLDS are estimated by Market Statistics (MSI), used by special permission of that organization. They are the base against which television ownership percentages have been applied.

TELEVISION OWNERSHIP PERCENTS are Nielsen estimates based on combining historical projections from the 1960 and 1970 Censuses with estimates from the NSI telephone interviews from a number of all market measurement periods.

HOUSEHOLDS ARE OCCUPIED HOUSING UNITS. The household universe estimates shown in Table 1 are estimates of year-round households, i.e. housing units occupied year round. Seasonal housing units which are occupied only during certain seasons of the year are not included in the Household Universe Estimates. Thus, the number of households during the survey period may differ from the estimate in Table 1.

† See NSI Reference Supplement for definition of county size   LT Less than 1%.

TABLE 2 - PENETRATION ESTIMATES

AREA	PERCENT OF TV HOUSEHOLDS				
	BLACK %	HISPANIC %	MULTI-SET %	CABLE TV %	VCR %
METRO	1	3	60	65	
DMA	LT	3	58	67	81
CASPER	1	3	NA	NA	NA
RIVERTON	LT	5	NA	NA	NA

Black and Hispanic estimates are as of January 1, 1995. Multi-set, Cable TV and VCR estimates are based on the latest available data

See NSI Reference Supplement for detail regarding the derivation of these estimates and for information regarding response and sampling error

TABLE 3 - SAMPLE SIZES: HOUSEHOLDS

AREA	INITIALLY DESIGNATED HOUSEHOLDS			IN-TAB DIARY HOUSEHOLDS		
	LISTED	UNLISTED	TOTAL	LISTED	UNLISTED	TOTAL
METRO	236	91	327	107	27	134
DMA(INCL METRO)	316	113	429	149	36	185
NSI(INCL. DMA)	826	287	1113	436	112	548

For sample selection procedures used in Total Telephone Frame sampling, see NSI Reference Supplement. This DMA, being a Type D market, has an advance household sample estimate of 180 or more during this measurement period. A minimum in-tab household sample size of 50 is required to report multi-week DMA or Station Total Audience data. Weekly ratings not reported in Type D markets.

TABLE 4 - TELEVISION STATIONS

CITY OF ORIGIN	STATION	CHANNEL	AFFILIATION
LANDER	KCWC	4	P
CASPER	*KFNB+	20	A
RIVERTON	*KFNE	10	SATELLITE OF KFNB
RAWLINS	*KFNR	11	SATELLITE OF KFNB
CASPER	*KGWC+	14	C
LANDER	KGWL	5	SATELLITE OF KGWC
ROCK SPRINGS	*KGWR	13	SATELLITE OF KGWC
CASPER	*KTWO+	2	N
CHEYENNE	*KKTU	33	SATELLITE OF KTWO
DENVER	*KCNC (D)	4	N
DENVER	*KRMA (D)	6	P
DENVER	*KWGN (D)	2	I
ATLANTA	*WTBS (D)	17	T
CABLE	CNN (D)		
CABLE	TNT (D)		
CABLE	USA (D)		

(D) THIS OUTSIDE STATION IS REPORTABLE IN THE DAYPART SECTION ONLY

TABLE 5 - TV HOUSEHOLDS AND IN-TAB DIARY HOUSEHOLDS BY SAMPLING AREA

ADJ DMA CNTY	COUNTY & STATE		MRS TERRITORY†	EST. TV HHLDS JAN. 1995	CABLE TV HHLDS % MAY 1995	CNTY SIZE†	IN-TAB DIARY HHLDS
#3	SEVIER	UT	P	5,110	59	D	4
#1	ALBANY	WY	WC	12,860	69	D	14
#2	BIG HORN	WY	WC	3,910	57	D	24
#1	CAMPBELL	WY	WC	10,550	77	D	9
#1	CARBON	WY	WC	5,370	98	D	5
D	CONVERSE	WY	WC	3,910	71	D	22
MD	FREMONT	WY	WC	12,070	53	D	41
	GOSHEN	WY	WC	4,930	47	D	26
D	HOT SPRINGS	WY	WC	1,870	82	D	6
D	JOHNSON	WY	WC	2,210	63	D	11
	LARAMIE	WY	WC	29,650	76	C	150
	LINCOLN	WY	WC	4,290	50	D	13
MD	NATRONA	WY	WC	24,340	71	C	93
#2	PARK	WY	WC	9,110	56	D	43
#1	PLATTE	WY	WC	3,240	62	D	4
	SHERIDAN	WY	WC	9,510	82	D	32
#3	SUBLETTE	WY	WC	1,870	64	D	1
#3	SWEETWATER	WY	WC	14,200	88	D	17
#3	TETON	WY	WC	5,340	96	D	3
#3	UINTA	WY	WC	6,040	66	D	13
D	WASHAKIE	WY	WC	3,180	75	D	12
	WESTON	WY	WC	2,300	76	D	5

METRO TOTAL		36,410	65	134
DMA TOTAL		47,580	67	185
NSI AREA TOTAL		175,860	71	548

#1 = DENVER   #2 = BILLINGS
#3 = SALT LAKE CITY
NOTE: VIEWING IN ADJACENT DMA'S IS NOT LIMITED TO NSI AREA COUNTIES IN TABLE 5. THE ABOVE LIST OF COUNTIES DOES NOT NECESSARILY REPRESENT ENTIRE AREA FOR WHICH VIEWING OCCURS TO STATIONS IN THIS MARKET. SEE INSIDE BACK COVER FOR FURTHER STATION TOTAL AREA DESCRIPTION.

CASPER-RIVERTON, WY

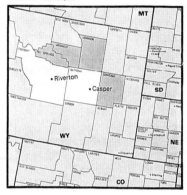

Nielsen Station Index

Measurement Schedule 1995–96

Report Month		Dates	# Markets
October	1995	Sept. 28 – Oct. 25	25
November	1995	Nov. 2 – Nov. 29	(All Markets)*
January	1996	Jan. 4 – Jan. 31	17
February	1996	Feb. 1 – Feb. 28	(All Markets)
March	1996	Feb. 29 – Mar. 27	4
May	1996	April 25 – May 22	(All Markets)**
July	1996	July 11 – Aug. 7	(All DMAs)

*Thanksgiving is Nov. 23, 1995   **Memorial Day is May 27, 1996

Audience estimates are computed separately for each week. Reported multi-week averages are the average of the appropriate individual week audience estimates. Some of the above counties may have been combined for projecting individual week audience estimates. Viewing among the households in the in-tab sample for all counties that are combined are projected to the Total TV Households for the combined counties. These county groupings are available upon request.

M = Metro County D = Designated Market Area County (for definition, see Section II).
† See NSI Reference Supplement for explanation of MRS Territory and County Size.

Exhibit 16-10

Market data from Nielsen Media Research for Casper–Riverton, Wyoming.

Dayparts

Advertisers must decide *when* to air commercials and on *which programs*. Unlike radio listeners, TV viewers are loyal to programs, not stations. Programs continue to run or are canceled depending on their *ratings* (percentage of the population watching). Ratings also depend on the time of day a program runs.

Television time is divided into dayparts as follows:

	Daytime:	9 A.M.–4 P.M. (EST)
	Early fringe:	4–5:30 P.M. (EST)
Combine as early fringe	Early news:	5 or 5:30–7:30 P.M. (EST)
	Prime access:	7:30–8 P.M. (EST)
	Prime:	8–11 P.M. (EST)
Combine as late fringe	Late news:	11–11:30 P.M. (EST)
	Late fringe:	11:30 P.M.–1 A.M. (EST)

Viewing is highest during **prime time** (8 to 11 P.M. Eastern Standard Time; 7 to 10 P.M. Central Standard Time). Late fringe ranks fairly high in most markets among adults, and daytime and early fringe tend to be viewed most heavily by women. To reach the greatest percentage of the advertiser's target audience with optimal frequency, the media planner determines a **daypart mix** based on TV usage levels reported by the rating services.

Audience Measures

Rating services and media planners use many terms to define a station's audience, penetration, and efficiency. **TV households (TVHH)** refers to the number of households that own television sets. The number of TVHH in a particular market gives an advertiser a sense of the market's size. Likewise, the number of TVHH tuned in to a particular program helps the advertiser estimate the program's popularity and how many people a commercial is likely to reach.

The percentage of homes in a given area that have one or more TV sets turned on at any particular time is expressed as **households using TV (HUT).** If there are 1,000 TV sets in the survey area and 500 are turned on, HUT is 50 percent.

The **program rating** refers to the percentage of TV households in an area that are tuned in to a specific program. The rating is computed as follows:

$$\text{Rating} = \frac{\text{TVHH tuned to specific program}}{\text{Total TVHH in area}}$$

Networks want high ratings because they measure a show's popularity. More popular shows can command higher advertising rates. Local stations often change their programming (buy different syndicated shows, for example) to increase their popularity and thereby their ratings (and their revenues).

The percentage of homes with sets in use (HUT) tuned to a specific program is called the **audience share.** A program with only 500 viewers can have a 50 *share* if only 1,000 sets are turned on. *Ratings,* in contrast, measure the audience as a percentage of all TVHH in the area, whether the TV sets are on or off.

The total number of homes reached by some portion of a program is called **total audience.** This figure is normally broken down to determine **audience composition** (the distribution of the audience into demographic categories).

Gross Rating Points

In television, **gross rating points (GRPs)** are the total rating points achieved by a particular media schedule over a specific period. As we discussed in Chapter 9, a weekly schedule of five commercials on programs with an average household rating of 20 would yield 100 GRPs. Recall that GRPs are computed as follows:

$$\text{Reach (average rating)} \times \text{Frequency} = \text{Gross rating points}$$

GRPs allow advertisers to draw conclusions about the different markets available for a client's ads by providing a comparable measure of advertising weight.

However, GRPs do not reflect a market's size. For example, while campaigns in Knoxville and Charlotte might have the same GRPs, they would differ significantly in their reach:

	TV homes (000s)	Average cost per spot	Average rating	No. of spots	GRPs
Knoxville	1,002	$1,500	15	5	75
Charlotte	638	$1,250	15	5	75

To better determine the relative value of television advertising markets, other measures are used, such as *cost per rating point* (CPP) and *cost per thousand* (CPM), which were described in Chapter 9.

Buying Television Time

The process of buying TV time can be lengthy and, depending on the number of stations in the buy, quite involved. Advertisers or media buyers must

- Determine which programs are available at what cost.
- Analyze the various programs for efficiency.
- Negotiate price with station reps.
- Determine what reach and frequency they are achieving.
- Sign broadcast contracts.
- Review affidavits of performance to be sure the commercials ran as agreed.

These procedures are so complex that most large advertisers use ad agencies or media-buying services. Buying services have gained in popularity because they charge less and can save advertisers money by negotiating for desirable time slots at reduced rates. Local advertisers typically rely on station reps to determine the best buys for the money.

Requesting Avails

To find out which programs are available, media buyers contact stations' sales reps—local station salespeople, national media rep organizations that sell for one station in each market, or network reps. The media buyer gives the rep information about the advertiser's media objectives and target audiences and asks the rep to supply a list of **avails** (available time slots) along with prices and estimated ratings. Many media buyers ask for the information based on the last few Nielsen books to see whether a show's ratings are consistent, rising, or falling.

Selecting Programs for Buys

The media buyer selects the most efficient programs in relation to the target audience using the **cost per rating point (CPP)** and the **cost per thousand (CPM)** for each program:

$$CPP = \frac{Cost}{Rating} \qquad\qquad CPM = \frac{Cost}{Thousands\ of\ people}$$

For example, assume *CSI* has a rating of 25, reaches 200,000 people in the primary target audience, and costs $2,000 for a 30-second spot with a fixed guarantee on station WALB-TV in Albany, Georgia. Then,

$$CPP = \frac{\$2,000}{25} = \$80 \qquad\qquad CPM = \frac{\$2,000}{(200,000 \div 1,000)} = \$10$$

By calculating CPP, the media buyer can compare the cost of a rating point from one program or network to another. That's good information for beginning negotiations. But rating points relate to the whole market. The real important figure is the cost of reaching 1,000 prospects in the *target* market. That's why the

Getting "You're Out" on TV

"You're Out" baseball mitts have expanded to television. As the marketing director, you choose to examine the gross rating points (GRPs) for placing your advertising. You have an idea of the days and times you want the ads to be placed. Chart 1 indicates the best programs for Memphis, Tennessee, and relevant planning data your assistant has gathered according to your preferences. Due to time constraints the chart is incomplete, but there are enough data available for you to finish the chart.

Chart 1 shows the marketing figures for a single city, but now you decide to determine which of the three major cities in Tennessee will serve "You're Out" baseball mitts the best. Your assistant didn't quite finish Chart 2, but with the help of Chart 1 you can complete the needed calculations.

Laboratory Applications

1. Using the formulas in the text as a guide, complete Chart 1.

2. Assuming your budget is $68,000, use Chart 1 to decide which programs would be most effective for reaching children. Explain your selection.

3. Using Chart 1, complete the "per spot" and "rating" figures in Chart 2. Next, calculate how many GRPs each city will deliver if you buy five spots of advertising.

4. Using the completed Chart 2, calculate for each city the number of household impressions.

5. Knowing that you are running five spots, find the CPP and CPM for all three cities.

6. Based on the completed Chart 2, what city is ideal for "You're Out" baseball mitts?

Chart 1: Best Programs for Memphis, TN

Program	Rating	Cost	Spots	GRP
Family Matters (early evening daily, rerun, 30/70 adults to kids)	15	$34,000	32	____
Saturday morning cartoons (kids ages 2–12)	____	34,000	30	300.0
Major League Baseball game (weekends, mostly adults)	7.8	34,000	29	____
After-school special (kids ages 7–13, afternoon, daily)	____	34,000	27	205.0

Chart 2

City	TV homes (000s)	Average cost per spot	Average % of rating	GRP
Memphis	1,002	$1,500	15	____
Charlotte	638	1,250	15	____
Knoxville	847	____	____	____
		Frequency: 5 spots		

CPM must be calculated against the size of the target audience, not the whole market. The lower the cost per 1,000/target audience (CPM-TA), the more efficient the show is at reaching real prospects.

To get the best buys within the available budget, then, the media buyer substitutes stronger programs for less efficient ones (see Ad Lab 16–B, "Getting 'You're Out' on TV").

Negotiating Prices and Contracts

TV stations and cable companies publish rate cards to sell their air time. However, since TV audiences are estimated at best, television reps will always negotiate prices.

The media buyer contacts the rep and explains what efficiency the advertiser needs in terms of delivery and CPM to make the buy. The buyer has numerous ways to negotiate lower rates: work out a package deal, accept *run-of-schedule positioning* (the station chooses when to run the commercials), or take advantage of preemption rates. A **preemption rate** is lower because the advertiser agrees to be "bumped" (preempted) if another advertiser pays the higher, non-preemption rate.

The media buyer must read the advertising contract carefully before signing it. The contract indicates the dates, times, and programs on which the advertiser's commercials will run, the length of each spot, the rate per spot, and the total amount. The reverse side of the contract defines payment terms and responsibilities of the advertiser, agency, and station. After the spots run, the station returns a signed and notarized **affidavit of performance** to the advertiser or agency, specifying when the spots aired and what makegoods are available. **Makegoods** refer to free advertising time an advertiser receives to compensate for spots the station missed or ran incorrectly or because the program's ratings were substantially lower than guaranteed.[40]

Electronic Media Buying Software

With the Internet, today's broadcast media buyers don't ever have to leave the office but can, right from their desktops, pore over SRDS and Simmons research data to create and even buy media schedules with electronic avails.

Reuters' AdValue Network provides these buying opportunities for broadcast media, along with the vast research network, discussed in the last chapter. In 1999, some 35 percent of all spot TV dollars were processed through the AdValue Network by more than 3,000 users. The network allows users to easily distribute TV and radio avail reports, orders, and revisions to all trading partners. This system gives its users flexibility. Most spot broadcasts are revised many times, and AdValue allows counterproposals to be made and considered without changing the current proposal. When a counterproposal is accepted, a single click updates the system.

A second option, MediaPlan's Adventory, is designed to deal with the complexity of TV media buys. This Internet-based system combines database technology with MediaPlan's Volume Rating Point (VRP) metric to provide the desired exposure to the greatest number of potential customers. The VRP technology can be used to evaluate how well brand and category customers will be reached, and plans campaigns based on reaching the actual consumers of a product rather than simply by age and gender demographics. However, Adventory is also capable of allocating TV inventory using traditional methods.

Alternatively, MediaPlan's WebRF, a free, Web-based Reach/ Frequency analysis tool, performs a similar function using MediaPlan/Spectra's Volumetric Media System (VMS) technology. Much like VRP, the proprietary VMS technology is designed to target consumers by brands and categories, rather than age and gender. Planners can create a complete media plan on the Web, optimize the schedules, and determine the best frequency level for the campaign.

Other Forms of Television

Cable isn't the only electronic challenger to traditional broadcast TV. Cable has its own (minor) competitors: DBS, MDS, STV, and SMATV.

- DBS (direct broadcast satellite) beams programs from space via satellites to satellite dishes mounted in the home or yard. For a monthly fee, consumers can subscribe to one of the DBS program distributors, such as DirecTV or United States Satellite Broadcasting (USSB), to receive from 20 to 150 channels.[41]

- MDS (multipoint distribution system), a microwave delivery system that can carry a dozen channels, is occasionally offered in rural areas where cable has not been installed.

- STV (subscription television) is over-the-air pay TV. Subscribers buy a descrambler that allows them to watch programs carried over a regular TV channel.

- SMATV (satellite master antenna television) uses a satellite dish to capture signals for TV sets in apartment buildings and other complexes, acting as a sort of minicable system.

Most of these systems are more expensive or carry fewer channels, so none has yet captured the public's imagination the way cable has.

Advertising on Video Rentals

Ever since Pepsi sponsored the successful home-video release *Top Gun* in 1987, industry analysts have been expecting advertising on video rentals to become a major new medium.

Research shows that home-video renters are younger and more upscale than the general population. And the majority of video renters do watch the commercials that precede the movie—sometimes more than once. A Schweppes ad starring comedian John Cleese was viewed by an astounding 95 percent of households renting Cleese's movie *A Fish Called Wanda*.[42] However, more recent research has shown that video renters find ads intrusive and somewhat offensive. Many just zip through them to get to the movie.[43]

When metered viewer data becomes widely available, more advertisers may place commercials on videos. In the meantime, the primary users of the medium are the movie studios themselves, advertising coming attractions.

The Medium of Radio

Radio is a personal, one-on-one medium; people listen alone. And radio is mobile. It can entertain people who are driving, walking, at home, or away from home. This makes it a particularly strong way to reach people who commute by car.

Radio is also adaptable to moods. In the morning, people may want to hear the news, upbeat music, or interesting chatter; in the afternoon, they may want to unwind with classical or easy-listening music.

Who Uses Radio?

In an average week, 95.4 percent of the U.S. population listens to radio; in an average day, over 75 percent. The average American listens to the radio more than three hours every weekday and over five hours on the weekend. In fact, during the prime shopping hours of 6 A.M. to 6 P.M., the average U.S. adult spends more time with radio than any other medium.[44] As Exhibit 16–11 shows, radio is also cost-effective. In the last decade, the CPM for radio advertising has risen less than for any other major medium and substantially less than the consumer price index.[45] As a result, radio's advertising revenues have grown steadily.

More national advertisers are discovering radio's reach and frequency potential. Certainly it has worked well for the Got Milk campaign. Similarly, Snapple profited greatly from radio. Back when it was still a little company in Queens, New York, and strapped for money, Snapple Natural Beverages decided to use radio. It put its entire ad budget into a year-long schedule with a young, relatively unknown radio show host named Howard Stern. Snapple liked the way he delivered its spots as a live reader.

A few years later, Snapple began receiving letters and phone calls from people in the Midwest and West, where it didn't even have distribution. It seems that nationally syndicated talk show host Rush Limbaugh, on a restricted-calorie diet, had been giving enthusiastic on-air endorsements for Snapple Diet Iced Tea. The firm moved quickly to sign him as a paid endorser. What it learned was the power of radio, especially when combined with a popular radio personality. This combination doubled Snapple's sales every year for five years, propelled it into national distribution, and turned it into a major national advertiser, spending more than $30 million every year advertising in more than 100 U.S. radio markets.[46]

The Use of Radio in IMC

While television tends to be a passive medium that people simply watch, radio actively involves people. They listen intently to their favorite personalities; they call in to make requests, participate in a contest, or contribute to a discussion; they use their ears and imaginations to fill in what they cannot see. Most people listen faithfully to two or three different radio stations with different types of programming. This means that smart advertisers can use the medium to establish an immediate, intimate relationship with consumers and other stakeholders. That makes radio an ideal medium for integrated marketing communications.

With radio, national companies can tie in to a local market and target the specific demographic group they want to reach. Most important, radio enables adver-

Daily reach: Adults 18+

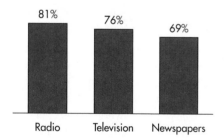

Weekly reach: Adults 18+

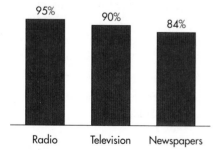

Exhibit 16–11

Daily and weekly reach of radio for people 18 and older exceeds other media.

tisers to maintain strategic consistency and stretch their media dollars through **imagery transfer**. Research shows that when advertisers run a schedule on TV and then convert the audio portion to radio commercials, fully 75 percent of consumers replay the video in their minds when they hear the radio spot.[47] That extends the life and builds the impact of a TV campaign at greatly reduced cost.[48] In an IMC campaign, where message consistency is a primary objective, this is a very important feature of radio.

Local retailers like the medium for the same reasons. Also, they can tailor it to their needs. It offers defined audiences; its recall characteristics are similar to TV's; and retailers can create an identity by doing their own ads. Finally, since radio is so mobile, retailers can reach prospects just before they purchase. Hence, recent years have seen major spending increases by local grocery stores, car dealers, banks, and home-improvement, furniture, and apparel stores.[49]

Radio Programming and Audiences

Radio stations plan their programming carefully to reach specific markets and to capture as many listeners as possible. The larger the audience, the more a station can charge for commercial time. Therefore, extensive planning and research go into radio programming and program changes.

Depending on a company's advertising needs, radio has many uses within the IMC model. For the National Fluid Milk Processor Promotion Board, the "Got Milk?" radio campaign (www.got-milk.com) proved to be an excellent way to achieve imagery transfer from its television ads. Local retailers, on the other hand, benefit from radio's low cost and targeted neighborhood markets.

MAN: I . . . I . . . I love you.
WOMAN: Awwww.
MAN: No, I mean . . . I . . . I mean. I don't . . . just . . .
WOMAN: What (GIGGLES), go ahead . . .
MAN: I just . . . don't think I'd be anything without you . . .
WOMAN: Aw . . . that's so nice . . .
MAN: I, uh, made these for you . . .
(SFX: Baking pan and foil sounds.)
WOMAN: Aw . . . you didn't have to do this . . .
MAN: They're just brownies.
WOMAN: Ooh, and they're still warm too.
MAN: I was gonna get you something good.
WOMAN: Aww, don't be silly, could I have one?
MAN: (Laughs.) Well, yeah sure . . . go ahead . . .
WOMAN (Mouth full.): You know . . . ?
MAN: What . . . you don't like brownies?
WOMAN: No . . . no . . . (Slight gag.) miggkkk . . .
MAN: I'm sorry. I can't understand you.
WOMAN: Neet . . . dmiggkk.
MAN: You need Mick?
WOMAN: Miccliggkk!
MAN: A guy named Mick! I can't believe this . . .
WOMAN: Pleeeease miiiggggggllkk . . .
MAN: Yeah, yeah, okay you don't have to scream his name in ecstasy. I get the message. All right I got it, I'm gone.
WOMAN: No, umbhum, no, miiiiiigggllllkk!
MAN: Look, I gotta go, I'm sorry I'm gonna need my CDs back . . . and
WOMAN: No, no, miiigglllk.
MAN: . . . and I'm sorry for this whole thing . . .
WOMAN: . . . No, miiigggllkk . . .
MAN: No, it's Scott remember?
WOMAN: No . . . miigggkkkfff . . .
ANNCR: True love means never having to say, "Got Milk?"

Stations can use tried-and-true formats, subscribe to network or syndicated programming, or devise unique approaches. Programming choices are greatly influenced by whether a station is on the AM or FM band. FM has much better sound fidelity, fewer commercial interruptions, and more varied programming.

To counteract FM's inroads, many AM stations switched to programs that don't rely on sound quality, such as news, talk, and sports. Some stations are experimenting with all comedy, midday game shows with audience participation, or formats geared to specific regions, such as KHJ's "car radio" in Los Angeles. AM stations are also trying to win back music listeners by improving their sound quality and offering stereo broadcasting.

When buying radio time, advertisers usually buy the station's *format,* not its programs. Most stations adopt one of the dozen or so standard **programming formats:** contemporary hit radio (CHR-TOP 40), adult contemporary, country, rock, easy listening, news/talk, adult standards, classical, religious, and so on, as shown in Exhibit 16–12. Each format tends to appeal to specific demographic groups. The most popular format is country music, which is programmed by 22.9 percent of the stations in the United States (both AM and FM) and appeals to a broad cross section of Americans from 25 to 54 years old.

Contemporary hit radio (CHR), always found on FM stations, appeals to teenagers and women under 30. It provides a constant flow of top 40 hits, usually with minimal intrusion by disk jockeys. Another popular format, adult contemporary (or "easy oldies"), is often advertised as "light rock, less talk." This format aims at the desirable target group of working women between 25 and 54. The news/talk, easy-listening, and nostalgia formats tend to have high listenership among men and women over 35.[50]

A major trend in radio today is the resurgence of radio networks, which offer services and programs that complement a station's local programming. A station might subscribe to ABC Radio's daily Paul Harvey news and commentary, CBS's weekly *House of Blues Radio Hour,* and Westwood One's *Larry King Show.*

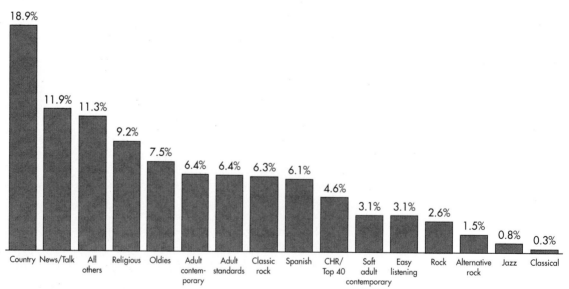

CHR: Contemporary hit radio

Exhibit 16–12

Percentage of radio stations in the most common programming formats.

Exhibit 16-13

The radio mininetworks provide various types of programming including news, talk, and sports. Each network targets a specific demographic group such as Adults 25–54 (CBS) or Men 18 years and older (ESPN).

ABC Radio Networks			Westwood One Radio Networks		
Network	**Target demo**	**Affiliates**	**Network**	**Target demo**	**Affiliates**
Prime	A 25–54	2,566	Westwood One Mutual	A 25–54	1,385
Platinum	A 25–54	2,566	Westwood One NBC	A 25–54	1,338
Galaxy	A 12+	1,030	Westwood One Source	A 12–34	115
Genesis	A 12–34	317	Westwood One Programming	A 12–54	3,600
Excel	A 18–49	111	Westwood One Play by Play Sports	A 18+	1,192
ESPN	M 18+	231	Westwood One Talk	A 25–54	1,236
ABC Special Programming	A 12+	3,829			

CBS Radio Networks			Unistar Radio Networks		
Network	**Target demo**	**Affiliates**	**Network**	**Target demo**	**Affiliates**
CBS Radio Network	A 25–54	470	Super	A 25–54	1,256
CBS Spectrum	A 25–54	570	Power	A 18–49	218
CBS Radio Sports	A 25–54	300	CNN+	A 25–54	1,248
CBS Radio Programs	A 18–54	126	CNBC Business Radio	A 25–54	72
CBS Hispanic Radio Network	A 25–54	39	Unistar Weekly Music/ Personality Programs	A 12–49	1,700

There are now over 20 national radio networks, including the multiple "mininetworks" of ABC, CBS, Westwood One, and Unistar (see Exhibit 16–13), and numerous syndicators offer programs from live rock concerts to public-affairs discussions. To stand out, 80 percent of licensed radio stations are opting for syndicated and network offerings.[51] As more stations carry these programs and more listeners tune in, national advertisers find them increasingly attractive.

Although spending on radio advertising only accounts for about 8 percent of all ad spending, consumers spend about 40 percent of their total time with media listening to the radio.[52] Clearly, although it is much cheaper to produce than television advertising, radio ad spending has room to grow. In 2003, however, revenue for radio grew the least of all major media, to $10.08 billion for the top 20 companies, only 1.5 percent above the previous year.[53] Predictions for 2004 radio revenue growth were more optimistic, ranging from 5 to 10 percent. The largest national radio advertisers are major retailers, entertainment conglomerates, and telecommunications companies (see Exhibit 16-14).

Exhibit 16-14

Top 10 national spot radio advertisers (2003).

Rank	Advertiser	National spot radio ad spending ($ millions)
1	SBC Communications	$144.2
2	Home Depot	102.5
3	Verizon Communications	79.2
4	Time Warner	73.4
5	News Corp.	67.9
6	Safeway	50.9
7	Viacom	45.6
8	Walt Disney Co.	40.5
9	AT&T Wireless	38.5
10	General Electric Co.	36.6

Buying Radio Time

Advertisers need a basic knowledge of the medium to buy radio time effectively: the types of radio advertising available for commercial use, a basic understanding of radio terminology, and the steps involved in preparing a radio schedule.

Types of Radio Advertising

An advertiser may purchase network, spot, or local radio time. Although local purchases still account for fully 80 percent of all radio time sold; national spot radio advertising is surging.[54] Advertisers like the reach and frequency, selectivity, and cost efficiency of radio (see the Checklist, "The Pros and Cons of Radio Advertising").

The Pros and Cons of Radio Advertising

The Pros

The principal advantages of radio are high reach and frequency, selectivity, and cost efficiency.

____ **Reach and frequency.** Radio offers an excellent combination of reach and frequency. The average adult listens more than three hours a day, radio builds a large audience quickly, and a normal advertising schedule easily allows repeated impact on the listener.

____ **Selectivity.** Specialized radio formats, with prescribed audiences and coverage areas, enable advertisers to select the market they want to reach: a specific sex, age group, ethnic or religious background, income group, employment category, educational level, or special interest.

____ **Cost efficiency.** Radio offers its reach, frequency, and selectivity at one of the lowest costs per thousand, and radio production is inexpensive. National spots can be produced for about one-tenth the cost of a TV commercial. And local stations often produce local spots for free.

____ **Other advantages.** Radio also offers timeliness, immediacy, local relevance, and creative flexibility.

The Cons

In spite of these advantages, radio has limitations: It's an aural medium only, its audience is highly segmented, the advertiser's commercials are short-lived and often only half-heard, and each ad must compete with the clutter of other advertising.

____ **Limitations of sound.** Radio is heard but not seen, a drawback if the product must be seen to be understood. Some agencies think radio restricts their creative options.

____ **Segmented audiences.** If a large number of radio stations compete for the same audience, advertisers who want to blanket the market have to buy multiple stations, which may not be cost-effective.

____ **Short-lived and half-heard commercials.** Radio commercials are fleeting. They can't be kept like a newspaper or a magazine ad. Radio must compete with other activities for attention, and it doesn't always succeed.

____ **Clutter.** Stations with the greatest appeal for advertisers have more commercials. Advertisers must produce a commercial that stands out from the rest.

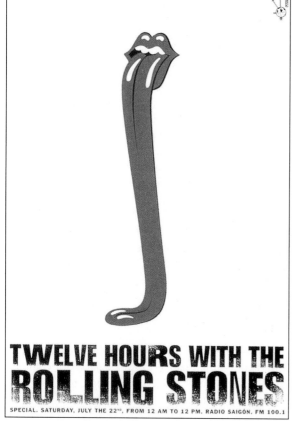

TWELVE HOURS WITH THE ROLLING STONES

SPECIAL. SATURDAY, JULY THE 22ND, FROM 12 AM TO 12 PM. RADIO SAIGÓN. FM 100.1

A radio station's programming format is important to advertisers because it is the best indicator of the demographics of the audience. While broadcast television audiences are driven largely by specific programs, radio audiences are determined almost entirely by the station's overall format. However, when advertising overseas on a station such as Radio Saigon in Spain, marketers must realize that radio audiences there may not be as predictable as in the United States.

Networks

Advertisers may use one of the national radio networks to carry their messages to the entire national market simultaneously via stations that subscribe to the network's programs. In addition, more than 100 regional radio networks in the United States operate with information oriented toward specific geographic markets.

Networks provide national and regional advertisers with simple administration and low effective net cost per station. Disadvantages include lack of flexibility in choosing affiliated stations, the limited number of stations on a network's roster, and the long lead times required to book time.

Spot Radio

Spot radio affords national advertisers great flexibility in their choice of markets, stations, air time, and copy. They can put commercials on the air quickly—some stations require as little as 20 minutes' lead time, and advertisers can build local acceptance by using local personalities. Radio rep firms, like Katz Radio, represent a list of stations and sell spot time to national advertisers and agencies.

Local Radio

Local time denotes radio spots purchased by a local advertiser or agency. It involves the same procedure as national spots.

Radio advertising can be either live or taped. Most radio stations use recorded shows with live news in between. Likewise, nearly all radio commercials are prerecorded to reduce costs and maintain broadcast quality.

Radio Terminology

For the most part, the terminology used for radio is the same as for other media, but some terms are particular to radio. The most common of these are the concepts of *dayparts, average quarter-hour audiences,* and *cumes* (cumulative audiences).

Dayparts

The radio day is divided into five dayparts:

6 A.M.–10 A.M.	Morning drive
10 A.M.–3 P.M.	Daytime
3 P.M.–7 P.M.	Afternoon (or evening) drive
7 P.M.–midnight	Nighttime
Midnight–6 A.M.	All night

Rating services measure audiences for only the first four dayparts because all-night listening is very limited and not highly competitive. Ad Lab 16–C describes the major radio audience rating services. Heaviest radio use occurs during **drive times** (6–10 A.M. and 3–7 P.M.) during the week (Monday through Friday), when many listeners are commuting to or from work or school.

Radio stations base their rates on the time of day the advertiser wants commercials aired, but the rates are negotiable according to supply and demand at any given time. RL 16–1 in the Reference Library on the *Contemporary Advertising* CD shows standard rates for air time on KWOD-FM in Sacramento, California. For the lowest rate, an advertiser orders spots on a **run-of-station (ROS)** basis, similar to ROP in newspaper advertising. However, this leaves total control of spot placement up to the station. So most stations offer a **total audience plan (TAP)** package rate, which guarantees a certain percentage of spots in the better dayparts if the advertiser buys a total package of time.

Average Quarter-Hour Audience

Average quarter-hour audience (AQH persons) identifies the average number of people listening to a specific station for at least five minutes during a 16-minute period of any given daypart. For example, station KKDA in Dallas/Fort Worth, Texas, has an average quarter-hour listenership of 33,800, meaning that any day, during any 16-minute period between 3 and 7 P.M., about 33,800 people ages 12 and older are tuned in (see RL 16–2 in the Reference Library on the *Contemporary Advertising* CD).

The **average quarter-hour rating** expresses the AQH persons as a percentage of the population. Since KKDA is located in an area of 3,072,727 people, its average quarter-hour persons could be expressed as an average quarter-hour *rating* of 1.1:

$$\frac{\text{AQH persons}}{\text{Population}} \times 100 = \text{AQH rating}$$

$$\frac{33,800}{3,072,727} \times 100 = 1.1\%$$

The same idea can be expressed in terms of **average quarter-hour share:** the station's audience (AQH persons) expressed as a percentage of the total radio listening audience in the area. For example, if the total average quarter-hour persons for all stations is 676,000, then radio station KKDA's average quarter-hour *share* is 5:

$$\frac{\text{AQH persons of a station}}{\text{AQH persons of all stations}} \times 100 = \text{AQH share}$$

$$\frac{33,800}{676,000} \times 100 = 5\%$$

The Reports That Make or Break Radio Stations

Media buyers use the data from three major audience rating services to determine which programs and stations will deliver the greatest number of target listeners.

Arbitron

The Arbitron rating service chooses a group of representative listeners in each of 257 cities and gives them a diary for tracking the time they spend listening to radio. Listeners return the diaries to Arbitron at the end of each week for tabulation, and Arbitron compiles the results into a quarterly report.

The Arbitron Book, available on Arbitron's website (www.arbitron. com), reports the number of listeners to particular stations and shows their ages, sexes, and preferred listening times. Radio stations are major clients, but some ad agencies and radio sales reps also subscribe.

Arbitron is also developing the Portable People Meter (see Ad Lab 16–A), which will enable the electronic measurement of radio audiences.

Birch Research

Birch Research uses phone surveys rather than diaries to obtain listener data. Interviewers talk to representative listeners in 130 major radio markets. Results are published monthly and summarized quarterly. Birch also offers Birchscan, a monthly computerized report.

RADAR

RADAR (Radio's All-Dimension Audience Research) also rates network radio programs based on phone interviews with listeners. Each listener is called daily for a week and asked about listening habits from the day before until that moment. RADAR conducts research year-round and publishes results annually in *Radio Usage and Network Radio Audiences*. A number of specialized reports are also available.

Laboratory Applications

1. What are the advantages and disadvantages of these radio audience measurement methods?

2. Which audience measurement method, diary or phone interview, is best? Why?

The **gross rating points** of a radio schedule are the sum of all ratings points delivered by that schedule, or the *gross impressions* (see Chapter 9) expressed as a percentage of the population being measured:

$$\text{AQH rating} \times \text{Number of spots} = \text{GRPs}$$

$$1.1 \times 24 = 26.4$$

or

$$\frac{\text{Gross impressions}}{\text{Population}} \times 100 = \text{GRPs}$$

$$\frac{33,800 \times 24}{3,072,727} \times 100 = 26.4$$

Cume Estimates

The **cume persons** is the total number of *different* people who listen to a radio station for at least five minutes in a quarter-hour within a reported daypart (also called *unduplicated audience*).

In the example, our schedule on station KKDA generated 811,200 gross impressions, but that does not mean that 811,200 different people heard our commercials. Many people heard the commercials three, four, or five times. By measuring the cumulative number of different people who listened to KKDA, rating services provide the *reach potential* of our radio schedule, which in this case is 167,800.

The **cume rating** is the cume persons expressed as a percentage of the population being measured. For example,

$$\frac{167,800 \times 100}{3,072,727} = 5.5\%$$

The Seven Steps in Preparing a Radio Schedule

The procedure advertisers use to prepare radio schedules is similar to that used for TV schedules.

1. Identify stations with the greatest concentration (cume) of the advertiser's target audience by demographics (say, men and women ages 35 to 49).

Because advertisers typically buy radio spots according to station format rather than by specific program, the AQH is typically a strong indicator of the most opportune time to run ads. Commercial ads, like this humorous spot from Motel 6, are frequently aired during dayparts with high listenership, such as drive times.

"Paparazzi" :60

Tom: Hi, Tom Bodett here. You know what's great about staying at Motel 6? Right. No paparazzi. A lot of times at a hotel, somebody famous is staying there, and it makes life miserable. You spend all your time shooing away gossip columnists peeping in your window or photographers hovering in helicopters with telephoto lenses. What a nuisance. Well, Motel 6 is rarely frequented by movie stars. Just regular people like us, getting a good night's sleep in clean, comfortable rooms for the lowest price of any national chain. So you won't have to deal with a lobby full of crazed fans tearing at your clothes because they think you're that guy from that show. And in the morning when you drive away refreshed and happy, we can pretty much guarantee it won't be with some tabloid reporter clinging to your hood. And I think we all know what a bother that can be. I'm Tom, just Tom, Bodett for Motel 6, and we'll leave the light on for you. Motel 6. An Accor Hotel.

---

2. Identify stations whose format typically offers the highest concentration of potential buyers.

3. Determine which time periods (dayparts) on those stations offer the most (average quarter-hour) potential buyers.

4. Using the stations' rate cards for guidance, construct a schedule with a strong mix of the best time periods. At this point, it is often wise to give the advertiser's media objectives to the station reps, suggest a possible budget for their station, and ask what they can provide for that budget. This gives the media buyer a starting point for analyzing costs and negotiating the buy.

5. Assess the proposed buy in terms of reach and frequency.

6. Determine the cost for each 1,000 target people each station delivers. The key word is *target;* the media buyer isn't interested in the station's total audience.

7. Negotiate and place the buy (see RL 16–3 in the Reference Library on the *Contemporary Advertising* CD).

Chapter Summary

As a means of reaching the masses, no other medium today has the unique creative ability of television. Broadcast TV grew faster than any previous advertising medium because of the unique advantages it offered advertisers: mass coverage at efficient cost, impact, prestige, and social dominance.

Television is a powerful creative tool, but the medium still has many drawbacks, including high actual cost, limited selectivity, brevity, clutter, and susceptibility to zipping and zapping.

Broadcast TV dominance is being challenged by new electronic media, particularly cable. Cable offers the visual and aural appeal of TV at much lower cost and with greater flexibility. Cable audiences are highly fragmented, which helps advertisers target specific markets but is a drawback for those wanting to reach a mass audience.

TV advertising can be done at the national, regional, or local level and can take the form of program sponsorships, segment sponsorships, and spots of varying lengths, including program-length infomercials.

To determine which shows to buy, media buyers select the most efficient ones for their target audience. They compare the packages of each station, substitute stronger programs for less efficient ones, and negotiate prices to get the best buy. Media buyers must have a firm grasp of certain important terms: designated market areas (DMAs), TV households (TVHH), households using TV (HUT), program rating, share of audience, gross rating points, and cost per thousand.

Like television, radio is a highly creative medium. Its greatest attribute is its ability to offer excellent reach and frequency to selective audiences at a very efficient price. Its drawbacks are the limitations of sound, segmented audiences, and its short-lived and half-heard commercials.

Radio stations are normally classified by the programming they offer and the audiences they serve. Radio stations may be AM or FM. They may use network or syndicated programs and follow any of a dozen or more popular formats. Advertisers purchase radio time in one of three forms: local, spot, or network. Buying radio time requires a basic understanding of radio terminology. The most common terms are dayparts, average quarter-hour, and cumulative audiences.

Important Terms

affidavit of performance, *526*

audience composition, *524*

audience share, *524*

avails, *525*

average quarter-hour audience (AQH persons), *533*

average quarter-hour rating, *533*

average quarter-hour share, *533*

barter syndication, *518*

broadcast TV, *510*

cable TV, *510*

cost per rating point (CPP), *525*

cost per thousand (CPM), *525*

cume persons, *534*

cume rating, *534*

daypart mix, *524*

designated market areas (DMAs), *522*

drive time, *533*

first-run syndication, *518*

gross rating points (GRPs), *524, 534*

households using TV (HUT), *524*

imagery transfer, *529*

infomercial, *520*

inventory, *518*

local time, *532*

makegoods, *526*

networks, *516*

off-network syndication, *518*

participation basis, *517*

preemption rate, *526*

prime time, *524*

program-length advertisement (PLA), *520*

program rating, *524*

programming format, *530*

rating service, *521*

run of station (ROS), *533*

sponsorship, *517*

spot announcement, *517*

spot radio, *532*

total audience, *524*

total audience plan (TAP), *533*

TV households (TVHH), *524*

UHF, *511*

VHF, *511*

Review Questions

1. What are the advantages of broadcast TV advertising for a product like milk?

2. What steps can advertisers take to overcome zipping and zapping?

3. Why has advertising on network TV become less desirable in recent years?

4. In what ways is cable TV's selectivity a strength? A drawback?

5. What are the various ways to buy broadcast television time?

6. How can TV be best used in an integrated marketing communications program?

7. How can radio be best used in an IMC program?

8. What is the format of the radio station you listen to most? How would you describe the demographics of its target audience?

9. What is the difference between average quarter-hour and cume audiences? Which is better?

10. What is the significance of dayparts in radio and TV advertising? What are the best dayparts for each?

11. **The Advertising Experience**

   Valentine's Day is approaching, and as the owner of Dream Flower Florists, you want to increase your share of local business by advertising on the radio. After researching local stations, choose one whose format suits your target audience. Decide what kind of buys you will make and when they will be aired.

Exploring the Internet

The Internet exercises for Chapter 16 address the following areas related to the chapter: TV organizations (Exercise 1), broadcast media tools (Exercise 2), and radio stations (Exercise 3).

1. TV Organizations

The size of the television industry and the advertising dollars that are spent within it are extraordinary. Many TV-related organizations were formed to help service the industry. Discover a little more about the nature and scope of the television industry as you peruse the following websites. Be sure to answer the questions below.

- Broadcast Education Association (BEA) www.beaweb.org
- Cable/Telecommunications Association for Marketing (CTAM) www.ctam.com
- Cable World www.cableworld.com
- National Association of Broadcasters (NAB) www.nab.org

a. Who is the intended audience(s) of the site?

b. What is the site's purpose? Does it succeed? Why?

c. What is the organization's purpose?

d. What benefit does the organization provide individual members/subscribers? The overall advertising and television and cable communities?

2. Broadcast Media Tools

Broadcast advertising reports and audience studies are critical to the development and implementation of effective media strategy. As with print media, advertisers have a set of "staple" companies and reports they regularly use to help plan and implement their broadcast media buys. Visit the following syndicated and independent broadcast media companies' websites and answer the questions that follow:

- Arbitron www.arbitron.com
- Bureau of Broadcast Measurement (BBM) www.bbm.ca
- Cabletelevision Advertising Bureau (CAB) www.onetvworld.com
- Nielsen Media Research www.nielsenmedia.com
- Radio Advertising Bureau www.rab.com
- Radio Marketing Bureau (RMB) www.rmb.ca
- Television Bureau of Advertising www.tvb.org
- Television Bureau of Canada (TVB) www.tvb.ca
- TV RunDown www.tvrundown.com

a. What type(s) of broadcast media information does the company specialize in and what specific services, products, or publications does the company offer?

b. What industries/companies would be best suited to utilize the company's media resources?

c. Does the company represent syndicated or independent research?

d. How useful do you feel the company is for gathering broadcast media information? Why?

3. Overseas Radio Stations

Many radio stations don't broadcast on the airwaves alone; they also stream their shows on the Internet. Find four English-language commercial radio stations on the Web that are not from the United States or Canada. Listen to the stations and examine the websites. What sort of target audience do the stations seem to have? What kind of products could be sold to these audiences?

Chapter 17

Using Digital Interactive Media and Direct Mail

Objectives To EXPLORE THE IMPORTANT FACTORS advertisers weigh when considering digital interactive media and direct mail. Each medium has its own distinct characteristics and each has unique advantages and drawbacks. Advertisers must be able to compare the merits of these media and understand the most cost-effective ways to use them in their media mix.

After studying this chapter, you will be able to:

- **Discuss** the various opportunities and challenges presented by digital interactive media.

- **Explain** the evolution of interactive media.

- **Debate** the pros and cons of the Internet as an advertising medium.

- **Define** the various kinds of Internet advertising.

- **Discuss** the Net's audience and the challenges involved in measuring it.

- **Explain** how Internet advertising is sold and how much it costs.

- **Enumerate** the various types of direct-mail advertising.

- **Detail** the various costs associated with direct-mail advertising.

- **Assess** which kinds of mailing lists are best.

Anna is a college student who loves animals. At home, she has two dogs, a cat, two parakeets, and a goldfish. But that's not all. She also has an Aisha, a Shoryu, a Kau, and a Zafara. And on top of that, she has a couple of pets for her pets—called *petpets*. She gave her Aisha a Ghostkerfish, her Shoryu a Warf, her Kau a Huggy, and her Zafara a Triffin. The names aren't the only thing that's a little unusual. The dog, cat, bird, and fish are real, but the others are *virtual*—they're the products of Anna's imagination and the creative folk at NeoPets. ■ NeoPets is an interactive community of virtual pet owners on the Internet. Members start by adopting one or several pets out of 48 different species. Then they name them, feed them, and play games with them. The warriors at heart can even train their pets and take them to the Battledome to fight other members' pets or other characters on the site. That's just the beginning. As we shall see, there are so many activities on this site it's mind-boggling, and nearly impossible for any one person to see and do everything that the site offers. ■ NeoPets went live in early 2000 with about 500 new registrations a day. To grow the site, the team at NeoPets did not use any conventional means of advertising. Instead, they used only one—the most powerful communication medium—word of mouth. And word spread like wildfire. With nearly 83 million registrations worldwide, NeoPets is the largest global youth community on the Internet. Users range in age from 8 to 80. The bulk of its users—more than 40 percent—are between 13 and 17 years old, a very desirable and elusive market for many advertisers. In addition to the heavy traffic on NeoPets, the site is also the "stickiest" on the entire Internet, with its millions of users spending an average of four hours per month there. ■ Why is it that NeoPets appeals to so many? More important, how does NeoPets maintain members' interest and attention? Two words: content and quality. Early on, the team at NeoPets knew that content—lots of it—would be key to keeping members interested, so this was one of the first things they worked on. And equally important was the quality of the content. In fact, the site is updated daily and is monitored around the clock. ■ "It's all about quality of writing, quality of creative and quality of experience," says Stephanie Yost Cameron, senior vice president of business and legal affairs at NeoPets. "We're also completely CARU (Children's Advertising Review Unit) and COPPA (Children's Online Privacy Protection Act) compliant." As a result, most parents feel safe when their children are on the site. Many teachers also regard the site highly and even integrate it into their classroom lectures and activities. ■ For advertisers, NeoPets offers the opportunity to participate in *Immersive Advertising,* NeoPets' proprietary practice of integrating advertisers' products or services into the Neopian experience. Before the creative team starts on a project, Rik Kinney, executive vice president of NeoPets, explains that NeoPets gets to know a client to truly understand the company, its product or service, and its objectives. "Then we try to figure out how to communicate the advertiser's message in an imaginative, fun, Neopian way," Kinney says. ■ For example, in the virtual downtown Neopia Central, pet owners can spend their accumulated Neopoints—most stores are Neopian inventions, but the site is sprinkled with virtual stores for real businesses. NeoPets can "eat" at McDonald's or "watch" the latest Disney movies. Some of the site's 166 arcade-style games are sponsored by brands like General Mills' Honey Nut Cheerios. Games feature a familiar NeoPet using the product in a Neopian environment and are often huge hits with members.[1] ■ Instead of inundating the site with the virtual product, as many marketers would intuitively want to do, Kinney and his team, familiar with the psychology of NeoPets' members, recommended limiting the number of products available. This results in an immediate rush of participants seeking the products on the site because they are so "rare." In fact, less than 1 percent of the thousands of NeoPets pages contain any marketing or branding, and all advertising is marked as such. Word of mouth propagates an interest for the products more than any other conventional means of advertising can. ■

Digital Interactive Media

Today, we are all participating in a new media revolution, brought on by incredible achievements in communications technology. We're talking, of course, about **digital interactive media** and the *information superhighway.* The highway is the Internet, and it is already the fastest-growing medium in history.

To understand the dramatic effect this is having on marketing and advertising, imagine for a moment what life was like before radio and TV. Back then, if you had a product to sell, you made your appeal to the consumer directly, often on her front door step. If she didn't like what you were peddling, she slammed the door in your face. She was in complete control of the selling environment.[2] Then along came radio and, 30 years later, TV. Now mass marketers had a captive audience, people who would willingly pay for an evening's entertainment at home by simply

Digital interactive media brings us full circle—back to before the advent of mass media when the consumer controlled the selling environment. Sites like BarnesandNoble.com (www.bn.com) offer interactivity with the consumer, to a degree unmatched by any other advertising medium. The site not only serves as an Internet-based mail-order retailer but also offers customers extensive search capabilities, book reviews, book suggestions tailored to each specific user, e-books, magazine subscriptions, DVDs, and software.

sitting through the commercials. Advertisers prospered—and so did consumers, as they participated in a rapidly growing standard of living.

But now the sands are shifting across the advertising landscape. The remote control was the first step toward convenient interactivity, and it had a major impact on commercial viewership. Instead of watching commercials, people could now use the station breaks to channel surf, effectively slamming the door in the salesperson's face.

Right on its heels came the widespread distribution of cable TV. In less than a decade, the network TV audience plunged from 90 percent to 60 percent. SLAM!

Then, of course, came the VCR. People could now record shows and watch them later at their convenience, zipping through the commercials. Or they could just rent a movie and skip the commercials altogether. TiVo brought ad-avoidance into the digital age, allowing viewers to customize their entertainment schedules. SLAM!

Meanwhile, technology keeps on going and going and going. It's already given us the personal computer, the cellular phone, the Internet and the World Wide Web, fiber optics, satellite communications, CD-ROM, DVD, and the software to make it all simple enough for virtually anybody to use. And on the launching pad, about to blast off, is interactive TV. With growing consumer acceptance of all this wizardry, prices have plummeted, making most of it affordable to the masses.

These are not just advertising media. In many cases, they represent completely new ways of living and doing business. The fastest-growing advertising medium in history has also opened the door to electronic commerce.

From the convenience of your own personal computer, you can bank online, buy a car or a beautiful piece of art, trade on the stock exchange, book your airline reservations, purchase concert tickets, buy a complete new wardrobe from your favorite department store, or even order your week's groceries and have them delivered to your door.

The Internet has also changed the way we send mail, eliminating the need for an overseas airmail stamp if you want to communicate with your brother in Berlin. You can do library research in the comfort of your den, or you can start your own home-based business and market your products worldwide.

The new media are truly revolutionary in their effect on our daily lives, and it's a revolution for marketers too.

Back in 1996, the entire Internet services industry amounted to only $1.3 billion, and total ad spending was a mere $300 million. But the potential was already obvious. By the year 2000, online retail sales had soared to $42.2 billion, and

Computers and the Internet are rapidly evolving to meet the demands of a growing number of technology-oriented consumers. While the Internet has not reached the consumer penetration levels of television or radio, it is the single fastest-growing medium in the history of mass communications. Digital information, online commerce, and global communications through e-mail programs all compose the medium of the Internet. These are anticipated to become the mainstays of our technology-driven economy.

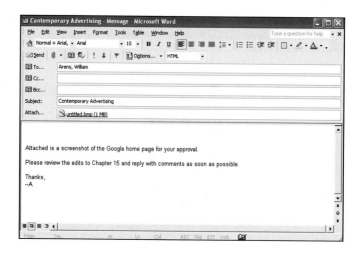

online advertising reached $8.2 billion.[3] Then came the dot-com crash, the recession, and the September 11, 2001, terrorist attacks. Internet advertising took a major hit—along with the rest of the advertising industry—declining steeply for two straight years. But by 2003, the industry was back on a growth track. As the nation's biggest traditional advertisers suddenly realized that the Net offered wonderful opportunities for achieving real, bottom-line results, they started increasing their online spending dramatically. In light of this, Jupiter Research projected that online advertising spending would reach $7.6 billion in 2004, up 21 percent from 2003.[4] Similarly, the Internet research company eMarketer predicted that worldwide business-to-business e-commerce revenues would surpass $1.4 *trillion* by the end of 2003, with the United States accounting for over half of that—$721 billion.[5]

In addition to this phenomenal growth, by offering true interactivity, the new media enable businesses and other organizations to develop and nurture relationships with their customers and other stakeholders, in a way never before available, on a global scale at very efficient cost.

The new interactive media today include the Internet and all its associated online services, CD-ROM catalogs and magazines, stand-alone kiosks, cellular telephone systems, and interactive television. Most prominent of all is the Internet, so that is what we will focus on in this chapter. In only 10 years as a commercial medium, the Internet has become a mass forum for advertising as well as other communications (see Exhibit 17–1). In recognition of this explosive growth, we need to understand what the medium is, how it is organized, how people get to it,

Exhibit 17–1

U.S. online advertising spending, 2000–2008 ($ billions). After three years of contraction, due to the recession and dot-com bust, eMarketer tracked a rebound in 2003 and predicts continued expansion.

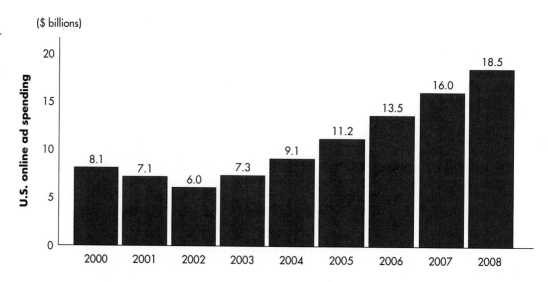

and how advertisers buy it and use it in their marketing plans. Following that discussion, we'll examine some of the other new media briefly and then look at the most prominent form of *addressable media*—direct mail.

The Internet as a Medium

The Internet has come a long way from its simple roots. While some people assume it was just recently created by today's commercial online providers, such as America Online (AOL) and EarthLink, in fact the technological infrastructure of the Internet has been around for close to 40 years.

The Evolution of the Internet

The **Internet** actually began in the early 1960s as a twinkle in the eye of the U.S. Department of Defense, which saw it as a means of supercomputer communication for researchers and military facilities across the country. Until its commercial explosion in the 1990s, the Internet remained a relatively obscure network of linked computers used mostly by academics, military researchers, and scientists around the world to send and receive electronic mail, transfer files, and find or retrieve information from databases.

Commercial Online Services

During the 1980s, a number of commercial online services like Prodigy and AOL began their operations by capitalizing on the phenomenon of local *electronic bulletin board services (BBSs)* that computer wonks used in increasing numbers. These new online providers managed to create, in effect, nationwide BBSs that delivered e-mail between subscribers, supplied catalogs for online shopping, provided chat rooms for discussion, organized interactive game playing, and offered software downloading capabilities, along with a host of other features. People could even advertise in the AOL classifieds just like in the newspaper.

At that time anyone with a modem-equipped PC could join the several million members of EarthLink, Prodigy, and America Online for a basic fee of around $10 a month plus a charge for any time spent online beyond the basic monthly allowance. One drawback, though, was that subscribers were limited to sharing e-mail and information with users of the same service provider.

Still, it didn't take long for the country's most aggressive advertisers to understand the potential of being able to communicate with this lucrative market of computer users via a new medium. General Motors, Chrysler, MCI, 1-800-FLOWERS, *BusinessWeek* magazine, and Lands' End jumped on the bandwagon. Soon thousands of product marketers and business services were using the online services as a medium of both advertising and commerce.[6]

Commercial applications of the Internet itself were not as well received as online services until the development of graphical browsers. The Internet offered a tremendous wealth of information, but it wasn't as easy to use as the online services. First of all, to even get access to the Internet, people had to find an **Internet service provider (ISP).** But then, once they were online, there was no simple way to navigate around the Internet unless they possessed a lot of technical know-how. The first form of the World Wide Web, for instance, was entirely text-based; it had no graphics, and the initial ads resembled simple print classifieds.

When the first commercially available **Web browser** software that accommodated graphics, Netscape Navigator, was released in 1994, the Internet drew even more public attention. People could now simply point and click on icons and pictures to find their way around in cyberspace. This made the Internet almost as user-friendly as the online services.

The World Wide Web

The **World Wide Web (WWW)** is composed of an enormous amount of information found mostly in the form of **Web pages.** These can best be likened to book

covers or gateways, since they act as starting points to additional information. These pages are created by millions of online users and businesses, with content varying from culinary tips to sports commentary to corporate and business information. Early sites on the Web typically consisted of a home page that resembled a poorly designed brochure cover, with perhaps some limited information on subsequent Web pages about the company and its products. These were, in effect, corporate storefronts.

Once businesses (and the media) sensed the lucrative potential of the Internet, they bombarded the public with messages about how the technology would revolutionize global communication. This became a self-fulfilling prophecy, and the gold rush of the Information Age began. AOL and Prodigy, with their multimillion-customer databases, rushed to marry their services to the Internet to provide communication to users worldwide. The Web exploded from about 50 sites in 1993 to more than 70,000 sites in 1995 to 9 million sites worldwide in 2002.[7]

Internet Search Engines

Imagine trying to find a book in the Library of Congress without the aid of a card catalog. It would be next to impossible. That's the problem people faced in their initial efforts to find information on the World Wide Web. And that's what created the demand for another software program: the search engine. In rapid succession, a number of programs with catchy names like Yahoo!, Excite, and InfoSeek emerged to act as **search engines** for the cyberspace traveler. The user could sim-

ply type in a name, a word, or a phrase, and the search engine would scour the Net for relevant information and **website** addresses.

Because of their usefulness, many millions of people pass through the major search engines each month, and marketers quickly realized the advertising potential of these and other high-traffic Internet sites. Actual Internet advertising began in earnest in October 1994, when the first *banner ads*—little billboards of various sizes that pop up when a visitor lands on a particular Web page—were sold by *Hotwired* (the online edition of *Wired* magazine). Soon, other companies followed suit, buying banner advertising on other popular websites.

Today, Web surfers can browse everything from university libraries to the Louvre museum in Paris. Along the way, they can click on an ad banner and visit the commercial sites set up by IBM, AT&T, the city of Berlin, Ford, Merrill Lynch, Krispy Kreme Doughnuts, and Visa, to mention just a few.

Since the online services and the search engines are the gateways to all these sites, they also attract the greatest number of visitors, as well as the greatest amount of advertising. In October 1997, for instance, the top two websites by number of hits were Yahoo! and AOL.[8] By April 2004, both were still on top—only AOL had been folded into the Time Warner Network (see Exhibit 17–2).[9]

The percentage of the U.S. population able to access the Internet on a regular basis continues to climb. In 1997, only 50 million people were wired. This number had doubled by 2000 and has since doubled again. In 2004, more than 200 million people in the United States accessed the Internet each month.[10] Worldwide, the active Internet audience is estimated at 455 million, with many more occasional users (see Exhibit 17–3). According to Internet World Stats (www.internetworldstats.com), Internet penetration is currently growing fastest in the Middle East and Africa, where the percentage of users has tripled since 2000. Sweden (77 percent), Hong Kong (72 percent), and the United States (69 percent) top the list of the most-wired populations.[11]

(continued on page 550)

Exhibit 17–2

Top 25 most visited websites in April 2004.

Rank	Property	Unique visitors (000)
1	Yahoo! sites	113,190
2	Time Warner Network	111,750
3	MSN–Microsoft sites	110,121
4	Google sites	65,996
5	eBay	60,106
6	Amazon sites	39,083
7	Terra Lycos	38,390
8	About/Primedia	38,263
9	Excite Network	29,047
10	Viacom Online	28,020
11	Verizon Communications Corp.	24,135
12	CNET Networks	24,041
13	The Weather Channel	23,907
14	Walt Disney Internet Group (WDIG)	23,542
15	Real.com Network	22,713
16	Symantec	21,422
17	Monster	20,107
18	Shopping.com sites	19,643
19	Expedia Travel	17,696
20	SBC Communications	17,366
21	Gorilla Nation Media	17,255
22	Ask Jeeves	17,247
23	iVillage.com: The Women's Network	17,082
24	AT&T Properties	16,929
25	EA Online	16,618

As the fastest-growing medium in history, the Internet offers incredible opportunities for a wide range of people in both business and advertising, despite the unknown factors of the medium. For advertisers, there is a whole new world of potential customers out there, waiting to be engaged. But for advertising's historically television-oriented creatives, just learning to use the new medium effectively is a challenge, especially with the medium's ever-changing and ever-evolving technological landscape. What's interesting is that this is exactly the same challenge that took place when TV was first introduced some 50 years ago.

Without question, we are witnessing a new creative revolution that will continue well into the new millennium.

■ In this portfolio, study the ads and evaluate how each site capitalizes on the truly interactive nature of the medium or how it could better incorporate interactivity with the audience. Try to determine how the website fits into the company's overall strategy and how the site either complements or perhaps replaces a more traditional media approach. Could the company benefit by incorporating additional features into the website? What features would you suggest?

Advertising on the Internet

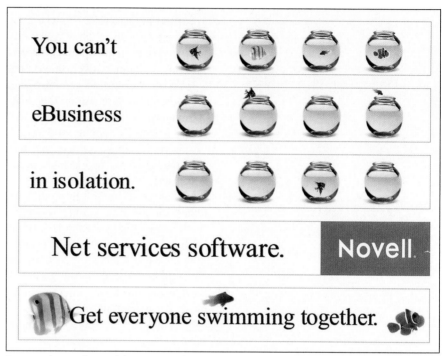

Banner ads are still one of the most prevalent forms of advertising on the Internet. Current banner ads feature action and animation to draw the attention of Web surfers. This ad for Novell (www.novell.com) features a sequence of five different panels. The simple and clean design conveys its message without cluttering users' computer screens.

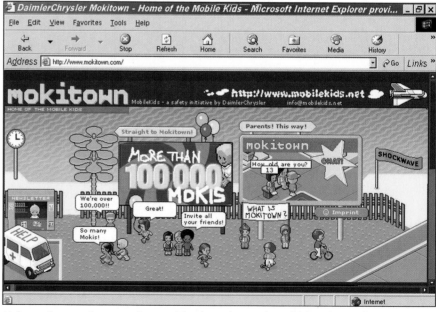

Mokitown (www.mokitown.com) is a website devoted to teaching children about traffic safety. Kids become Mokis and can explore their virtual city, meet other kids, experience various adventures, and answer traffic safety quizzes to gain points toward virtual prizes.

This ad, which won a Gold Lion at Cannes, features several different animal animations and their respective English names—the ad is designed to attract interest in the improvement of English language skills.

Banner ads, which assume just a small amount of screen space, have certainly improved over the past few years. This ad for HP (www.hp.com), which won a Gold at Cannes, directs the viewer to a website that allows them to create their own personalized Mother's Day cards.

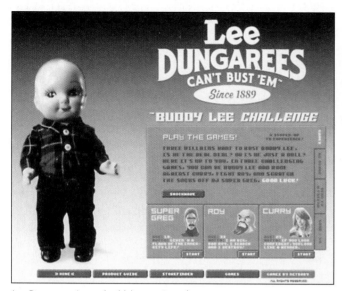

Lee Dungarees (www.buddylee.com) used an ingenious strategy to revive consumer interest in the brand and drive traffic to the retail stores. Using chatroom buzz and viral e-mail messages, the Buddy Lee Challenge introduced consumers to a fun story line and cool, interactive games. To advance to a second level, consumers entered a secret code—only available on Lee products found at retail stores. The campaign resulted in a 20 percent sales increase in one year.

Interactive websites are just one way to get potential customers interested in a product. This website for Sony (www.sony.com), which won a Silver Lion at Cannes, targets a young, computer-savvy market.

Dentsu Advertising in Tokyo created a fascinating website for the Kodaiki Temple (www.do-not-zzz.com) that introduces people to Zen and the art of meditation in a very warm and human way.

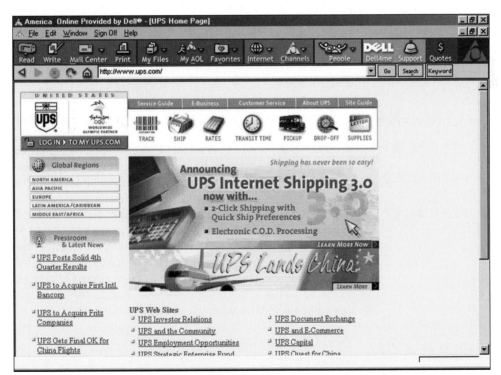

Interactivity takes many different forms on the World Wide Web. United Parcel Service (www.ups.com) capitalized on the latest technology by allowing its customers to check up on their own shipment orders directly from the business office or from home. The website also serves as a form of corporate and consumer advertising for UPS.

Exhibit 17–3

Data compiled from the July 2004 Nielsen//NetRatings and United Nations sources.

	Number of people online (millions)		
Region	**Population**	**Internet users**	**Penetration (%)**
Africa	893.2	12.8	1.4
Asia	3,607.5	256.5	7.1
Europe	730.9	224.5	30.7
Middle East	259.0	168.4	6.5
North America	325.2	223.0	68.6
Latin America/Caribbean	541.8	50.8	9.4
Oceania	32.5	15.8	48.5
World total	6,390.1	800.0	12.5

(continued from page 545)

Businesses ranging from your local florist to global manufacturers are using the Internet to present multimedia content that includes bulletin boards, interesting or entertaining information, product data, and even games. Many of them, like E*Trade and Amazon.com, conduct all their commerce right on the Web. Users move from page to page and site to site depending on what they are looking for. In other words, the user is in control. The consumer chooses what screens to watch, which banners to click, and which to ignore.[12]

That means marketers have to provide information that is useful and relevant. They have to keep updating it to get repeat visits. And a little entertainment with a few freebies tossed in doesn't hurt. Even Ragú (www.ragu.com) spaghetti sauce has a colorful site that offers Italian phrases, recipes, and occasionally a sweepstakes. Learning how to use this new medium challenges the creativity of the whole advertising community. And with the amount of daily updating that is required to keep websites current, the opportunity for career growth and specialization is great.

The Internet Audience

In the past several years we have seen a steady migration of people who used to spend time in front of the TV moving over to the computer. In a 2000 Jupiter Research study, researchers asked PC users which media activities they were giving up most to spend more time on the Internet. Almost 50 percent said they were watching less TV; a small but significant minority of users said they decreased their print media consumption, with 22 percent reading magazines less frequently and 21 percent reading newspapers less frequently. Recent surveys confirm this trend. The number of Internet users, as well as the amount of time spent by each user, grows steadily while the TV audience dwindles. Although there has been some controversy about measurement methods (which have resulted in major discrepancies in the results reported by even well-respected researchers like Nielsen and comScore Media Metrix), the consensus remains that time spent on the Internet eats into time spent watching television.[13]

Who Uses the Net

Media budgets tend to be very pragmatic. As audiences migrate, so do the media dollars. As a result, media spending on Internet advertising has grown substantially. One of the great draws of the Internet from the marketer's point of view is its demographics. Historically, the majority of people who surfed the Internet were well-educated, upscale, white males who used the Net for business or scientific

Websites such as AdCritic.com offer free access to specific types of information. Users are able to view and search commercials, reviews, movie trailers, and news. It's interesting to note how commercials, which used to be considered the "junk" of television, now have websites devoted to their creative content.

purposes. However, recent surveys of Internet demographics have found that women now represent more than half of the online population. Similarly, the growth of ethnic minorities on the Web shows that the Internet is starting to match America's diversity. The average age of Web users has also been increasing over the past several years. Twenty-two percent of U.S. adults over age 65 are regular Internet users; seniors are even more enthusiastic e-mailers than their younger counterparts and have begun to expand their Internet use into other areas, like product research and health information.[14]

In 2003, the Pew Internet and American Life Project published a report on the "digital divide," a distinct gap that, although it is narrowing, still separates Internet users from the general U.S. population (see Exhibits 17–4 and 17–5).[15] Disparities between different income groups and between ethnic groups were not as great in metropolitan and coastal regions (e.g., California and New England) as they were in the nation's hinterland. Overall, those in the lower annual income brackets (under $50,000) represent 49 percent of the U.S. population but only 33 percent of Internet users, whereas the upper income brackets (over $75,000 annually) comprise only 30 percent of the population but 42 percent of Internet users.[16]

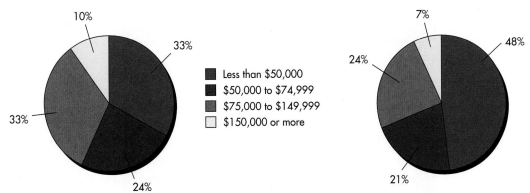

Exhibit 17–4

Household income composition of the World Wide Web in the United States (2003).

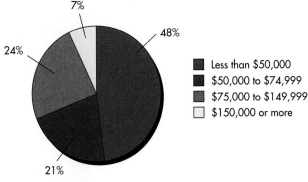

Exhibit 17–5

Household income composition of the United States (2003).

In addition to living closer to metropolitan and cultural centers and having higher incomes, Internet users are also better educated than the general U.S. population. According to the U.S. Census Bureau, half of the population has attended at least some college, but this half comprises 69 percent of the online population.[17] To marketers this is a very attractive audience, especially for business-to-business advertisers.

As lower computer prices and easy access further democratizes the Net, the user group will continue to broaden, and this will enhance the medium's advertising opportunities to an even wider range of marketers. At first, the primary targets of advertising were businesspeople. But now, the growing number of women on the Net has pushed many of the traditional consumer advertisers (such as packaged goods companies) to consider the medium seriously. A recent study of a mixed-media campaign for Unilever's Dove Nutrium bar soap concluded that spending 15 percent of the campaign's TV/print/online budget on Web advertising resulted in a 24 percent boost in branding impact.[18] There are now numerous websites catering exclusively to women's personal interests, including iVillage (www.ivillage.com), Women.com, Ladies Home Journal On-line (www.lhj.com), and Queendom (www.queendom.com).

How People Access the Net

To get on the Internet, people must first choose from two types of communication systems—*narrowband* and *broadband*. **Narrowband** is a type of digital data transmission in which wires carry one signal each, or channel, at a time.[19] Normal telephone communication is narrowband. And most communications involving computers also use narrowband transmission. This includes communications from the computer to devices (printers, monitors, and so on), communications via modems, and even the majority of computer networks. In contrast, **broadband** transmission enables a single wire to carry multiple signals simultaneously.[20] Cable TV, for instance, uses broadband transmission. This technology makes it possible to download large graphics files, watch video clips, play video games online, and surf the Net comfortably without having to endure what has been dubbed the "World Wide Wait."

Currently, there are several ways people can get online. The most common method is still narrowband via a dial-up modem through an Internet service provider. While the dial-up method is universally available, the connections are unfortunately slow, so people can spend a lot of time drumming their fingers as they wait for pages to download.

Critics contend that the Internet will never be as pervasive as television because many people either don't need to purchase an expensive computer or have no desire to use one. However, developers of MSN TV 2 (www.webtv.com) have incorporated the easy-to-use and interactive aspects of the World Wide Web directly into a typical television.

That's why all the growth today is in broadband systems. For home or small business use, there are essentially two choices: cable modem and DSL. The **cable-modem** system, which offers high-speed data transfer direct to the computer, is rapidly growing in popularity. One drawback is limited availability—it is obtainable only from those cable TV companies that offer one of the new cable-modem services such as Roadrunner. Moreover, cable modem is subject to slowdowns during peak usage hours when everyone in the same neighborhood may be online.[21]

The second method, **DSL,** which stands for **digital subscriber line,** is now competing with cable modem in popularity and price. This technology transforms a traditional telephone line into a high-speed digital link to provide homes and businesses with always-on, broadband Internet access.[22] DSL delivers speed comparable to cable[23]—but it does have its drawbacks. First of all, it isn't as fast as some companies imply. Electromagnetic noise can adversely affect DSL performance. More important, one's distance from a telephone company's special switching facility, called a central office (CO), directly affects the DSL connection. Note, too, that most DSL service is asymmetric—the download speed is faster than the upload speed. For example, most starter DSL accounts offer 384-kbps download/128-kbps upload access.[24] However, this is still dramatically faster than dial-up modem.

Two other methods, DirecPC and WebTV, are also available today, but they have yet to catch on like cable modem and DSL. Developed by Hughes Electronics, the same company that pioneered the DirecTV satellite system, **DirecPC** is also satellite based and offers very fast downloading—faster even than cable. However, it is very expensive and still requires a dial-up modem and separate phone line for sending material. This method is most suitable for companies that regularly need to download extensive files from other locations.

Microsoft's **MSN TV** (formerly WebTV) is much like cable modem except the receiving and viewing device used is the family TV instead of a computer. It includes a set-top box, which sells for around $100, and offers constant connection to the Internet, even while the TV is playing. This is another gambit in the search for interactive TV technology and is really aimed at those people who don't want to invest in the cost and complexity of having a computer at home but would still like to have Internet access. Once the equipment is purchased, the cost is simply a monthly service fee similar to the cost of cable TV. As the general population becomes more tech-savvy, Microsoft's simplified Internet venture has begun to flounder. The corporation is now banking on its more powerful MSN TV 2 hardware (released in October 2004) to sell people on the idea of easy Internet access from their living rooms.[25]

A recent study by Nielsen//NetRatings shows that broadband users spend considerably more time online than narrowband users. In fact, in January 2002, broadband users logged 1.19 billion hours online, accounting for 51 percent of the 2.3 billion hours Web surfers spent online during the month. Moreover, by mid-2004, more than half of U.S. Internet users accessed it via broadband, a 47 percent increase in broadband use over 2003.[26]

Types of Internet Advertising

Ads on the Internet can take a variety of forms, and as the Net matures, the number of forms continues to expand. Most advertising opportunities today can be classified as websites, banners, buttons, sponsorships, interstitials, search engine marketing, classified ads, and e-mail ads (see Exhibit 17–6). We'll discuss each briefly.

Websites

Some companies view their whole website as an ad. And in some ways it is. But in truth the website is more than an ad—it's an alternative "storefront," a

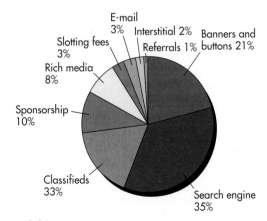

Exhibit 17–6

Percent of Internet ad revenues by type of advertising, 2003.

location where customers, prospects, and other stakeholders can come to find out more about the company, its products and services, and what it stands for. Unlike many other websites that have gone from bricks and mortar to virtual, NeoPets' introduction was actually on the Internet. Since its humble beginnings, though, NeoPets has expanded to include toys and games that can be purchased at local retail stores.

Some companies use their website like an extended brochure to promote their goods and services; others act as information and entertainment publishers and try to create a cool place that people will visit often; still others treat their website as an online catalog store, conducting business right on the Net. Thus, except when used like a brochure, the website is really more than an ad; it's an "ad-dress." The NeoPets website, for example, is so full of activities that the average user spends between four and five hours per month at the site. As a result, Nielsen//NetRatings consistently ranks NeoPets as one of the top 10 "stickiest" sites on the Web. Advertisers like that a lot.

Similarly, drug companies are now putting increased resources into their websites, turning them into giant "product information portals" that help doctors understand how the new medications work. The Internet offers high-quality visuals and an immense amount of information that no sales rep could ever offer.[27]

Websites typically consist of a *home page* and an indefinite number of subsequent pages that users can visit for further information. A **Web page** does not refer to an $8^1/_2$- by 11-inch page. It refers to a single HTML (*hypertext markup language*) file, which, when viewed with a browser, may actually be several screens long. A large website may have hundreds of these pages of information. This means the site contains hundreds of different documents of various lengths (from 1 to 10 or more screens), each probably covering a different subject.[28]

Banners and Buttons

The basic form of Web advertising is the ad banner. A **banner** is a little billboard that spreads across the top or bottom of the Web page. When users click their mouse pointer on the banner, it sends them to the advertiser's site or a buffer page. The standard size for an ad banner is 468 pixels (picture elements) wide by 60 pixels high. That means that on a standard $8^1/_2$- by 11-inch page, the banner would measure just over $4^1/_2$ inches wide by $^1/_2$ inch high.

While banners are the most common unit of Web advertising, the cost of a banner can range wildly—anywhere from free to thousands of dollars per month. Some standardization is taking place in the business, with most sites now charging, on a cost-per-thousand basis, anywhere from $0.25 to $100.00 CPM, depending on the number and type of visitors the site regularly receives.[29]

In 2003, in response to many agency requests to simplify the ad buying process, the Interactive Advertising Bureau (IAB), the association of Web publishers, introduced the Universal Ad Package, a suite of sixteen standard ad sizes (including skyscrapers, rectangles and pop-ups, and banners and buttons) designed to improve the efficiency and ease of planning, buying, and creating online media.[30]

Similar to banners are **buttons,** small versions of the banner that often look like an icon and usually provide a link to an advertiser's **landing page,** a marketing tool that leads people into the purchasing or relationship-building process. Because buttons take up less space than banners, they also cost less.

Today, a host of new software technologies, such as dHTML (dynamic hypertext markup language), Java, and Flash, have greatly enhanced the once-static banner and button ads. Full motion and animation, for example, are now commonplace. In fact, one of the greatest areas of recent growth has been **rich-media advertising,** which includes graphical animations and ads with audio and video elements that overlay the page or even float over the page. Many of the rich-media ads complement the standard banners endorsed by the IAB, as each of these can display 15-second animations.[31]

The leading Internet portal for the Spanish and Portugese-speaking world is the Terra Network. When this banner was created, they were bragging about having 20 million page views daily. In 2000, they merged with Lycos, Inc., and rapidly became one of the most popular Internet networks in the U.S., Canada, Europe, and Asia. Today, the Terra Lycos network boasts over 400 million page views per day. This represents a huge market for advertisers.

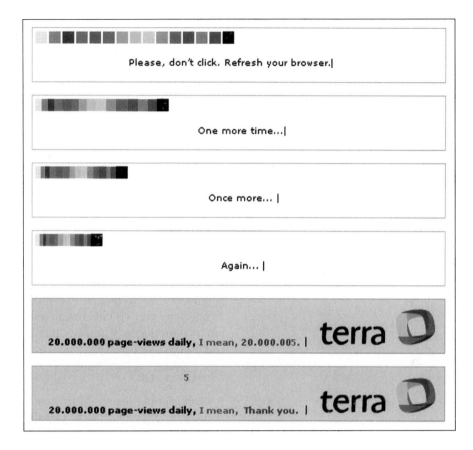

Some of the more common types of rich-media ads include animated banners, interstitials, Superstitials, and rich mail. The **interstitial** is a catchall term for a variety of ads that play between pages on a website, popping up on the screen while the computer downloads a website that the user has clicked on. All of their various formats tend to perform well in terms of click-through rates and brand recall—which is what the advertisers care about. The Superstitial is actually a trademark of Unicast, a strategic partner of Macromedia, which owns the Flash technology. The Superstitial makes use of a Unicast's proprietary "polite download" technology to push ads into a Web browser's cache only when the computer's bandwidth is idle; the ads then play from the cache when the user requests a new Web page. With polite download technology, the ad avoids tying up bandwidth when the user needs it. The standard Superstitial ad is quite large and plays for a long period of time (up to 20 seconds). Their size and playing time are similar to television ads, making them as rich as any experience available online.

Rich mail, on the other hand, allows graphics, video, and audio to be included in the e-mail message. When you open up a rich e-mail, your e-mail client automatically calls up your Internet connection and launches an HTML page in your e-mail window. E-mail clients that are offline will invite you to click on the link when you have your Internet connection open again. If your e-mail client does not support graphics, you will receive the e-mail in text only.[32] We can anticipate seeing more audio and animation integrated into these ads as improving technology accommodates them.[33]

Sponsorships and Added-Value Packages

A form of advertising on the Internet that is growing in popularity is the **sponsorship** of Web pages. Corporations sponsor entire sections of a publisher's Web page or sponsor single events for a limited period of time, usually calculated in months. In exchange for sponsorship support, companies are given extensive recognition on the site. Sometimes an added-value package is created by integrating the sponsor's brand with the publisher's content, as a sort of advertorial, or with banners and buttons on the page.

IBM has exclusively sponsored the Super Bowl Web page, at an estimated cost of $1 million for each event. Other forms of sponsorships have included Web serials, sites devoted to women's issues, contests, and giveaways.

Search Engine Marketing

When a user types a keyword or phrase into a search engine, two kinds of results are returned—those that have been paid for by advertisers, and those that are *natural*. **Pay per click advertising (PPC)** is a search engine marketing technique that requires the advertiser to pay a fee every time someone clicks on its website from an ad that has been placed in a search engine's results. The more an advertiser agrees to pay per click (or bid) for a specific keyword and the more effective the ad, the higher a site will rank in the paid search results. **Natural search engine optimization,** also known as organic search engine optimization, is a specialized technique that involves analyzing a website's underlying code, architecture, and visible content and making enhancements so that a website is returned prominently in the natural search results of spider-based search engines (such as Google).

Classified Ads

Another growing area for Internet advertisers, and an excellent opportunity for local advertisers, is the plethora of **classified ad websites,** like CraigsList.org. Many of these offer *free* classified advertising opportunities because they are typically supported by ad banners of other advertisers. In style, the classifieds are very similar to what we are all familiar with from newspapers. You can search for homes, cars, jobs, computer equipment, business opportunities, and so on. Moreover, the search can be narrowed to your city or expanded nationwide. Many of these sites are sponsored by the search engines themselves or by local newspapers around the country.

E-mail Advertising

According to Forrester Research, 77 percent of marketers send **e-mail advertising** to customers who have asked for it. Forrester predicted that U.S. marketers sent almost 210 billion e-mails in 2004.[34] Marketers have always known that direct-mail advertising (discussed in the second half of this chapter) is the most effective medium for generating inquiries and leads and for closing a sale. It's also been the most expensive medium on a cost-per-exposure basis. Now, thanks to the Internet, the power of direct mail is increased even more, and the cost is reduced dramatically.

A word of caution, though: It's important to differentiate responsible e-mail advertising from **spam,** which is really just electronic junk mail. Spam generally refers to unsolicited, mass e-mail advertising for a product or service that is sent by an unknown entity to a purchased mailing list or newsgroup. Spammers face the wrath of frustrated customers, tired of having their inboxes filled with unwanted e-mails. Since January 2004, spammers also face litigation under the CAN-SPAM Act (Controlling the Assault of Non-Solicited Pornography and Marketing). Legitimate e-mail advertisers are required to (1) clearly mark the e-mail as advertising, (2) provide a valid reply-to e-mail address, and (3) allow recipients to opt out of future mailings. The first lawsuits under the act were filed in April 2004, against two companies that had sent nearly a million e-mails advertising bogus diet patches and growth hormones.[35] With this in mind, wary marketers are focusing their e-mail efforts on **customer retention and relationship management (CRM)** rather than on prospecting.

One of the hottest trends on the Internet today is actually an application of e-mail. Thanks to *viral marketing,* Amazon.com, Napster, eBay, Blue Mountain Arts, and Hotmail all made it big on the Web, reaching unexpected heights in short time spans, most with surprisingly low marketing budgets.[36] **Viral marketing** is the Internet version of word-of-mouth advertising via e-mail. The term was coined in 1997 by Steven Jurvetson and his partners at the venture capital firm Draper Fisher Jurvetson. They were describing free e-mail provider Hotmail's incredible growth to 12 million users in just 18 months through the use of a little message at the bottom of every e-mail.[37] The message invited recipients to sign up for their own free Hotmail account.

Since that time, many other marketers have come up with ways to induce their satisfied customers to recommend their product or service to friends and family members. One of the keys to viral marketing success is to present an offer with real perceived value—one that people will want to share with one another. NeoPets, for example, uses a referral program whereby members are rewarded NeoPoints or rare items each time someone they refer to the site signs up and becomes a member. Since members enjoy the site so much, making it an important part of their daily routine, it's natural that they would want to share the pleasure with their friends and families. For friends, it's a fun way to communicate and play. For parents, NeoPets is an enjoyable experience that they can share with their children, while at the same time staying in the loop with what their kids are doing. Another example is Burger King's www.subservientchicken.com, which has earned near-cult status since its inception. Users type in their request and watch as an oversized chicken carries out their orders.

Problems with the Internet as an Advertising Medium

The Internet, like any medium, has its drawbacks. It is not a mass medium in the traditional sense, and it may never offer mass-media efficiency (see the Checklist, "The Pros and Cons of Internet Advertising"). Some marketers may decide it's too complex, too cumbersome, too cluttered, or not worth the time and effort.

It is not controlled by any single entity, so there may be no one to hold accountable. Security (for example, for credit card purchases over the Net) has improved, but it's still a problem for some. And the final drawback is that the Net has all the problems of any new, untried medium. The technology for running television-quality video is still not in place, and the long-term cost of full participation in the Internet is anybody's guess. The final drawback is also one of the Net's greatest appeals: It is the most democratic of media—anybody can get on it and do or say anything. That's both good and bad.[38]

Using the Internet in IMC

As we discussed in Chapter 8, one of the keys to successfully developing an integrated marketing communications program is to promote purposeful dialogue between the company and its stakeholders. That is what interactivity really means. And that is where the Internet offers its greatest potential.

For the first time, customers and other stakeholders can truly respond to a company's media communications in real time, using the same channel for feedback that the company used for promotion. This means that even if a customer finds herself accidentally at the company's website and, if something there strikes her fancy, she can commence a dialogue (relationship) with the company immediately. Of course, this also means that, if the website triggers her memory of a less-than-satisfactory experience with the company, she can use the same mechanism for complaining. But that's actually good, because a customer that complains usually cares. And a complaint gives the company the opportunity to correct the situation and set things right. It also gives the company information on how to improve. Sophisticated marketers cherish complaints.

While all of this is well and good, it also brings up a new problem for marketers today. In the good old days of simple mass-media advertising, manufacturers placed their ads on network TV and went on about their business. The retailers

Checklist

The Pros and Cons of Internet Advertising

The Pros

____ **Truly interactive medium.** More than any other medium, the Internet allows consumers to directly interact with an advertiser, thereby establishing future relationships.

____ **Enormous audience.** With an audience of some 800 million people worldwide, the Internet is also the only true global medium, providing information and commerce opportunities that are immediately accessible around the world.

____ **Immediate response** from consumers that cannot be rivaled, except through personal selling. Products and information are available on demand by the consumer, providing instantaneous feedback for the advertiser.

____ **Highly selective targeting** unmatched by any other medium. By purchasing keywords and employing cookies, advertisers can reach potential consumers exactly when they are in the market to buy.

____ **Proximity to purchase** may be the greatest advantage of Internet advertising. Purchasers can be targeted right where they are, right at the moment when they're considering making the purchase.

____ **Affluent market.** Sixty-seven percent of Internet users have household incomes of $50,000 or more, compared with 51 percent of the U.S. population. Sixty-nine percent of Internet users attended college, compared with only 51 percent of the U.S. population. This is an affluent market.

____ **Provides in-depth information** about a company and its products. Aside from sending e-mail, the vast majority of Internet activity involves gathering news or conducting research. Commercial websites provide detailed information about products or services to information-hungry consumers.

____ **A rapidly growing industry** that provides tremendous profit opportunities for the savvy direct marketers. The Internet is expected to continue its stunning growth for some time, particularly as the children of today grow up with the technology and become the consumers of tomorrow.

____ **Reaches business-to-business users** when television and radio often cannot—while they are still at work. Even consumer advertising can reach these Internet users while they are working.

____ **Advertorials** are effective tools for advertisers and often are incorporated into WWW publications. An advertiser can place its name into an article to build credibility and increase exposure. With clever use, these advertorials can provide anything from tips and tricks on product use to new recipes requiring a certain product.

____ **Virtual storefront.** Catalog companies have exemplified the profitability of direct-mail campaigns, which can be replicated by Web pages on the Internet. Today's most commonly purchased online merchadise are computer products, travel arrangements, and entertainment-related products.

The Cons

____ **Medium is not standardized.** The Internet is still very young, with many unanswered questions about advertising effectiveness, accuracy of market research, and standardization of measurements for both ad exposure and pricing. Although the medium offers the potential for profitability, the many unknowns still keep some advertisers from spending millions of dollars on online campaigns.

____ **Targeting costs** used to be among the most expensive relative to any other medium; these have since come down to high, but not outrageous, levels.

____ **Slow downloads,** due mostly to bandwidth, still hamper many users from the full online experience. Penetration of the high bandwidth DSL lines and cable modems has been accelerating, however. Before advertising on the Internet can realize its fullest potential, data transfer times will have to come down tremendously. Fortunately, the Internet technologies are in perpetual development and growth.

____ **Security and privacy** concerns still prevent many users from engaging in online purchases, although with time these fears will likely be allayed. Until most people believe the Internet is a safe place for financial transactions, it is unlikely to be accepted by everyone as a viable medium for commerce.

____ **Global marketing limitations.** The Internet is rapidly growing in other countries as it is in the United States. However, many countries are still hampered by the high cost of local telephone services, and developing countries simply lack the technology infrastructure to provide Internet services to the public.

took care of customers, so the manufacturers didn't really have to be concerned about them. In the new age of integrated marketing communications, that is no longer the case. Yes, the retailer is still there. But Mrs. Consumer doesn't want to talk to the retailer. She's a pretty sophisticated person. She knows who makes the product and if she's got a complaint that's who she wants to talk to. So it's not good enough for companies to put a pretty website up on the Internet and then walk away from it. It has to be staffed—daily—and it must be kept up to date—daily. If you log on the Internet Sunday morning and check your local newspaper's website for yesterday's baseball scores, you don't want to read about how your team got whipped Friday night. You already read about that yesterday. While this may seem obvious, the fact is that these problems still occur regularly, and they defeat the whole purpose of having an interactive location for your customers to visit. Realizing this, companies are now finally beginning to staff up. But this is very expensive—often requiring companies to double or triple their Internet budget with no increase in advertising exposure. So the decision to use the Internet for integration is a big one and cannot be taken lightly.

Measuring the Internet Audience

When marketers and the media first began trumpeting the marvels of the Internet, they quickly noted the potentially vast size of its population. Today it's already up to 200 million people in the United States alone. Around the world, hundreds of millions of people use the Internet, and only citizens of the developing countries are left without access.

Seeking Standardization

As much as Madison Avenue may want Web measurements to resemble traditional media measurements, the Internet cannot accommodate it. As we'll describe shortly, simply counting advertising impressions from a Web page is an impractical method of tabulation. However, the basic questions remain the same: Do people see our ads? Are they effective? Until fairly recently, when a task force of the Internet Advertising Bureau (IAB) provided some practical definitions, WWW audience measurement information lacked the standardization needed to be able to compare its advertising effectiveness to other media.

The most simple measurement, yet an area of great controversy, is the **ad impression.** The IAB defines an ad impression as "an opportunity to deliver an advertising element to a website visitor."[39] When a user loads a Web page with ads on it, the browser will pull the advertisement from its host ad server and bring it up as a banner, button, or interstitial. The number of ad requests received can then be translated into the familiar CPM form. The problem with this definition, from the point of view of advertisers and agencies, is that the advertiser is not guaranteed that a user will ever see an ad. People often click away to some other site before the requested ad ever comes up. Under the IAB definition, an advertiser would be charged for an ad that never had the opportunity to get seen. The AAAA prefers to define an ad request as an ad that is actually delivered to users' screens. Only then do they truly have an opportunity to see the ad. This controversy over definitions has a huge impact on the business because it also creates reporting differences between what Web publishers count and what the agencies count and are willing to pay for. These considerations prevent marketers from obtaining the foolproof numbers they want. But as technology improves the speed and methods of online advertising, we can anticipate increased accuracy in measurement. For more on Internet ratings, see Ad Lab 17–A.

A second measurement, unique to the Internet, is the **click rate** or *click-through rate*. A click occurs when a visitor moves the mouse's pointer to a Web link and clicks on the mouse button to get to another page. The click rate is the

While most large companies have been caught by the allure of the Internet, advertisers are still nervous about spending millions of dollars in this largely unregulated and uncharted medium. Research firms like Media Metrix (www.mediametrix.com) specialize in gathering and testing Internet market data, from user demographics to ad effectiveness.

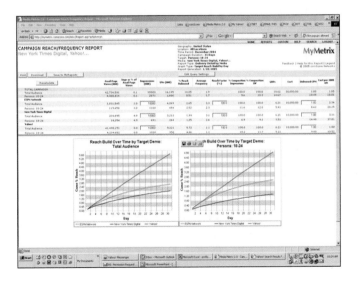

Internet Ratings: The Next Frontier

While marketers are exploring the best ways to use the Internet in their campaigns, media research companies are trying to determine how to accurately measure the audiences using this new medium.

Nielsen//NetRatings is the latest company to join the Internet ratings game. Nielsen, well known for its TV ratings, combined with NetRatings in 1999 to produce its first Internet ratings numbers. Nielsen//NetRatings has since provided stiff competition for the former leader of the pack, Media Metrix. PC Data and Relevant Knowledge are other companies that provide Internet audience measurement. While comScore Media Metrix has established a format of monthly reports, Nielsen//NetRatings hopes to satisfy the demand for ratings numbers with a weekly report.

Data for Internet ratings can be collected in a variety of ways. Important tools include ad requests, click-through rates, cookies, and tracking software.

Tracking software is unique because, unlike the others, it is installed solely by Internet ratings services. In much the same way as TV ratings data are collected, research firms like Media Metrix and Nielsen//NetRatings pay panelists to install software that tracks their computer usage. Some ratings services also use direct mailings and random calls to obtain data. The data are collected and compiled to produce monthly or weekly Internet ratings.

However, some advertisers and Internet companies do not believe these numbers are reliable. Critics point to a lack of standardization in how these numbers are produced. Each ratings service collects and computes data slightly differently. For example, comScore Media Metrix and Nielson both combine home and business usage in its numbers while Nielsen//NetRatings does not.

The issue was recently highlighted by a serious discrepancy between the two leaders' data. Studies of the number of men in the 25–34 age group who are active Internet users produced vastly different results: NetRatings came up with 56 percent, while comScore Media Metrix concluded 77 percent were active. This is critical information for advertisers, and such unreliability is a serious hindrance.

Another criticism concerns a lack of globalization; Media Metrix, Nielsen//NetRatings, and other services measure only U.S. audience numbers, but the Internet is a global medium. Some dot-com owners complain that the Internet ratings services are ignoring a significant portion of their consumer base.

Many critics also claim that the size of the samples used to generate these numbers is too small to adequately represent the Internet audience. In response to these problems, the Internet Advertising Bureau (IAB) is promoting the development of standards within the advertising community for the measurement of consumer audiences in cyberspace. Internet ratings services have also started to measure non-U.S. audiences. In March 2000 Nielsen//NetRatings began to measure audiences in seven countries and in June 2000 comScore Media Metrix began measurement of six countries.

Despite these improvements, some skeptical dot-com owners have turned to auditing companies for what they believe is a more accurate measurement of their audience. Companies like ABC Interactive Inc., BPA International, and Engage I/Pro audit the Web traffic logs recorded by each individual site. In September 2000 the three auditing companies launched a joint website called AuditCentral, where they will post reports of Web traffic. Some people believe there is room for both auditing and ratings services.

Laboratory Applications

1. What are some of the problems of Internet audience measurement?
2. Do you think these problems can be fixed? How?

number of clicks on an ad divided by the number of ad requests. In essence, marketers are measuring the frequency with which users try to obtain additional information about a product by clicking on an advertisement. The click rate can then also be tabulated in CPM form to measure cost efficiency.

The Promise of Enhanced Tracking

Despite the guesswork, today's software now provides some of the most precise targeting tools ever. In fact, every time you step into the Internet, some computer may be watching to see just where you go. Software using HTTP interacts with what are known as **cookies,** small pieces of information that get stored in your Web browser when you load certain websites. These cookies can keep track of whether a certain user has ever visited a specific site. This allows the website to give users different information depending on whether they are repeat visitors. Cookies also indicate the users' frequency of visits, the time of last visit, and the domain from which they are surfing. Additionally, cookies let marketers make an educated guess at the users' ISP, whether they are visiting from home or from work, their telephone area code, and their NAIC code.

More sophisticated technology provides marketers with additional details about the consumer. The computer first assigns each user an anonymous and encrypted identification number for tracking purposes. A user profile is then created with data on the content of the pages that are read, what keywords may have been used in a search, the time and day that a Web page was viewed, the frequency with which an ad is seen, the sequence of ads that are seen, the computer operating system of the user, the browser type, and the IP address. From this data, marketers' computers can again guess the user's ISP, telephone area code, and NAIC code. Marketers may then match this data with demographic information gathered offline to create a clearer picture of consumer behavior than has ever been available.

However, this new ability to track people's behavior on the Internet has stirred considerable debate. Although software developers claim that the users are tracked anonymously with encrypted identification numbers, privacy advocates believe the marketing method is too invasive into consumers' lives (see the Ethical Issue on page 562).

The best-known Internet rating service is Internet Profiles Corp. (I/PRO), which partners with A. C. Nielsen. I/PRO introduced one of the first means to measure and analyze Web traffic, providing data on the number of views, click-throughs, and site traffic. Other notables on the rating and research scene include Media Metrix, BPA Interactive, and Relevant Knowledge.

Buying Time and Space on the Internet

There are many ways for companies to get involved in the new digital media. Most are proceeding cautiously; the particular vehicles selected must fit with the firm's overall marketing and media strategy. However, media planners cannot think of these new vehicles in mass media terms. Interactive media are *personal audience venues,* as we discussed in Chapter 14. That means one on one. So cost per thousand, rating points, and share of audience don't really mean the same things in the interactive world. With interactive media, we're not building sales volume. We're building relationships, one customer at a time. And the care companies exercise in buying and developing their interactive programs and integrating them with their mass media programs will determine their overall success.

Currently, the leading national advertisers spend the smallest piece of their marketing communications pie on interactive media—less than 2 percent of their budgets. But it's the fastest-growing segment, having almost tripled in the last year alone (see Exhibit 17–7).[40] The best marketers are testing extensively. That means being willing to lose money for awhile, which is, of course, not exciting to most advertisers or agencies. Many direct marketers are currently testing the waters with online catalogs, but less than 0.05 percent of their total sales revenue comes from such media. However, some places like Dell Computers (www.dell.com) generate several million dollars from online sales each *day.* In fact Egghead Software (www.egghead.com) closed its retail stores to operate 100 percent online.

One of the biggest question marks when advertising on the Internet is cost. Recent years have seen increased rate-card standardization, but advertisers still haven't found a completely satisfactory method of buying space on the Internet. This is no surprise really, since fully commercial advertising didn't really get going on the Internet until about 1996.

Pricing Methods

As we discussed earlier, advertising space on the World Wide Web can be purchased in several different ways. The most common means is the banner ad, typically billed on a cost-per-thousand basis determined by the number of page requests. On most Web pages, the base banner rate pays for exposure on a rotating display that randomly selects which ads to show.

The real marketing power of the WWW, however, is the ability to specifically target an audience in a way that is virtually impossible in traditional media. In addition to general banners, media buyers may opt to purchase more selective space. For example, ads may be purchased in a portal's information categories and subcategories, such as finance, news, travel, or games. Prices vary according to category and increase as the buyer targets a more selective audience. Costs are tiered

Exhibit 17–7

Top 10 Internet advertisers (2003).

Rank	Advertiser	Internet ad spending in 2003 ($ millions)
1	Time Warner	$120.2
2	InterActiveCorp	77.2
3	Dell	48.9
4	General Motors Corp.	48.0
5	Toyota Motor Corp.	47.9
6	Microsoft Corp.	46.8
7	Hewlett-Packard Co.	42.3
8	General Electric Co.	42.1
9	Citigroup	32.3
10	Philips Electronics	30.5

Profiling: Would You Take Cookies from a Stranger?

With the advance of Internet marketing technologies, privacy has become a primary concern among consumers. The ability of unknown persons to access personal online information has triggered widespread paranoia surrounding Internet security. So it was no surprise that when DoubleClick, the Internet's largest advertising and profiling company, acquired database marketer Abacus Direct in 1999, privacy rights activists responded with a class action lawsuit, and the Federal Trade Commission (FTC) launched an investigation. For the first time, the anonymous Internet profiles from DoubleClick's DART database could be matched with Abacus' marketing database of over two billion consumer retail and catalog purchases—complete with names and addresses.

Internet profiling is used to track the online behavior and habits of Internet users. These profiles, created by the information stored in *cookies* on individual computers, allow companies to send ads directly to their target audience. A 2001 Gallup poll found that almost eight in ten e-mail users were concerned about the privacy of the information that they give out online—including 28 percent who felt "very concerned." However, another survey found that 56 percent of Internet users did not even know what a "cookie" was. So while many Americans agree that

Internet privacy is an important problem, most cannot even identify the primary tracking tool used to generate online profiles. Where does that leave Internet advertisers? For DoubleClick, a 2002 court ruling made it clear that the burden of responsibility fell on the shoulders of the marketers and advertisers. In response to the class action suit following the Abacus acquisition, the court ordered DoubleClick to clarify its privacy policy, undertake a consumer education effort, and pay up to $1.8 million for expenses associated with the lawsuit.

However, cookies do actually benefit the Internet user in many practical ways. For instance, they help websites identify your browser so that you will not repeatedly receive the same advertisement. Cookies also serve as a filter, receiving only those ads targeted to your interests. Cookies make it easier and faster to log onto websites; once information is stored on your personal computer, it does not need to be restored every time you log on. And perhaps the most economical feature of cookies and profiles is that they keep the Web free. "In order to keep the Internet free, websites need to be profitable. And in order to be profitable, they need targeted ads that work," says Josh Isay, DoubleClick's director of public policy.

Nevertheless, for those who still feel eerie about being "watched," there are a number of options users can select to prevent cookies from accessing your computer. The most basic solution is to disable cookies in your browser. Browsers such as Internet Explorer or Netscape offer

according to thousands, hundreds of thousands, or even millions of page requests per month (see Exhibit 17–8).

Another augmentation to the general banner purchase is the **keyword** purchase, available on major search engines. Advertisers may buy specific keywords that bring up their ads when a user's search request contains these words. Keywords may be purchased individually or in packages that factor in the information categories and subcategories of a search engine site. In the early days of the World Wide Web, some "keyword entrepreneurs" purchased large numbers of keywords from the search engines. They were later able to license these words to third parties at a substantial profit. This model has since changed to a bidding model, effectively killing keyword "entrepreneurs."

Some publishers will charge their clients according to **click-throughs**—that is, when a user actually clicks on an ad banner to visit the advertiser's landing page. Although the CPM cost for simple impressions is considerably lower, this method is still unpopular with publishers. When an advertiser buys on a per-click basis, the publisher may expose many users to an advertiser's banner message without being able to charge for the service. Some publishers, like Interactive Imaginations, have developed hybrid pricing that combines low-cost page request rates with click-through rates.

For advertisers involved in e-commerce, some publishers offer an **affiliate marketing program** whereby they charge a percentage of the transaction cost. For example, a site devoted to music reviews may have a banner link to an online music retailer. When consumers buy music from the retailer, the site publisher receives a percentage of the sale for showing the banner.

The Cost of Targeting

The very selective nature of the Internet can, for additional cost, be combined with the tracking technology described earlier. This makes for a very focused campaign. Companies such as DoubleClick work behind the scenes to meet the advertiser's CPM guarantees by using software that directs specific ads to a highly selective audience. Because DoubleClick technology "tags" users, it can build a consumer profile and show those ads that are likely to be of the greatest interest to that specific Web user.

But contrary to popular belief, consumer targeting on the Internet is very cost intensive. While it is true that millions of people do indeed scour the Net each day,

this and other similar features. Or you can selectively delete cookie files from your hard drive, maintaining only those profiles you wish. In addition, DoubleClick—along with many other companies—provides users an opt-out function on their website that denies DoubleClick cookies from gleaning or storing any information on your system. By choosing to opt out, your browser becomes unidentifiable to those websites served by DoubleClick.

There is no question that Internet profiling raises ethical issues about information security. But *who* should be responsible to remedy the situation? Although it has already been proven unpopular by consumers, DoubleClick still hopes to move forward in merging its online user profiles with the offline consumer database of Abacus when "industrywide privacy standards exist." Until then, marketers and advertisers are taking it upon themselves to establish trust with their online patrons. For example, new features from Microsoft's updated Internet Explorer enable users to reject cookies from websites as well as those from the ads on websites. In addition, the majority of the Fortune 500 has created a position for a Chief Privacy Officer (CPO) that will establish and follow privacy policy standards and regulations.

Yet, cookies and profiles are just one aspect of the never-ending dispute over Internet privacy. As new technologies are put to use, more policies and regulations will need to be addressed. Only time will tell just how much of that responsibility Web users will have to bear.

Questions

1. Do you think that cookies and profiles are a violation of personal privacy? Discuss the ethical issues involved.

2. Since profiling can help companies target the more profitable consumers and overlook others, do you think that this could lead to online discrimination?

3. Ultimately, who is responsible for Internet user privacy, the user or the marketers/advertisers? Where does the responsibility lie for each?

4. Is it better for companies to self-regulate issues of Internet privacy and security, or is federal intervention required?

Sources: Matt Hicks. "E-mail Privacy Debate Heads to Congress," *eWeek,* July 28, 2004 (retrieved from www.eweek.com/article2/0,1759,1628666,00.asp); "How Web Servers' Cookies Threaten Your Privacy," *JunkBusters,* 2002 (retrieved from www.junkbusters.com/cookies.html); Christopher Penson, "Rights: The Use of Individual Information" (retrieved from www.stedwards.edu/newc/capstone/sp2000/rights/EFFStance.htm); "Online Tracking FAQ," Center for Democracy & Technology (retrieved from www.cdt.org/privacy/guide/start/track.html).

Exhibit 17–8

An example of a rate card for WWW banner ads from the search engine MetaCrawler.

The "exclusive keywords" category provides advertisers with the opportunity to have their ad appear whenever someone conducts a search using a particular word. "Front page promotions" is for banners on the home page of the MetaCrawler site. "Search results pages" provides rates for banners that appear after a search has been conducted. And "targeting filters" provides advertisers with selectivity criteria for their ads. These rates for MetaCrawler are based on a minimum of 200,000 impressions per month, and calculated according to CPM. In this example, gross CPM reflects the cost to the advertiser, which includes the agency commission, and net CPM is the price the agency pays MetaCrawler.

MetaCrawler Keyword Packages:
Advertisers may select an industry-specific package of keywords such as travel, sports, business, or software.

Exclusive keywords Gross CPM	Net CPM	Impressions	
$47.06	$40	200,000	$8,000

MetaCrawler front page promotions* Gross CPM	Net CPM	Impressions	
$23.53	$20	200,000	$4,000
$17.65	$15	1 million	$15,000

*Exclusivity pricing is available on a case-by-case basis.

MetaCrawler search results pages (run-of-site) Gross CPM	Net CPM	Impressions	
$17.65	$15	500,000	$7,500
$16.41	$13.95	1 million	$13,950

MetaCrawler targeting filters*	Gross CPM	Net CPM
One filter	$35.29	$30 CPM
Two filters	$43.52	$37 CPM
	1. Operating system (Mac, Unix, Win95).	
	2. Browser type (Netscape, IE).	

*Available on run-of-site purchases only.

Continuity discount Program duration	2–3 months	4–6 months	7–11 months	12+ months
Discount from base rate	5%	7%	10%	15%

The Internet's largest potential is perhaps its ability to instantaneously create global commerce. Although currency exchanges can still be problematic, global commerce is becoming a common occurrence. A great example of how this enormous potential can be realized is eBay, the online marketplace, which has grown to be a huge presence on the Internet.

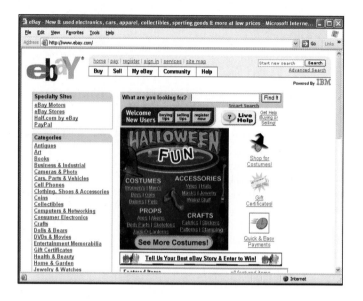

it is still difficult to find and reach the specific consumers that you want. Thus, prices for precise Internet business-to-business targeting can eclipse even those of direct mail.

Stretching Out the Dollars

One of the problems facing most Net marketers is how to get enough reach from their Internet advertising. The enormous numbers of users who utilize the major search engines make these sites attractive for advertisers. However, Web browsers surf millions of other Web pages each day, many of which are potential sites for effective ads. However, contacting all these sites and negotiating advertising contracts on each is a nearly impossible task.

For this reason, most advertisers work through **ad networks,** which act as brokers for advertisers and websites. Ad networks pool hundreds or even thousands of Web pages together and facilitate advertising across these pages. The advantage is that this allows advertisers to gain maximum exposure by covering even the smaller sites. The drawback is that such advertising is more difficult to monitor. Each site must be watched for traffic and content, which creates problems when trying to calculate costs. A few Web masters have been known to try to cheat the system by artificially increasing the number of page requests. So, as with any new medium, caution is always the watchword.

The Global Impact of the Internet

The United States overwhelmingly outspends the rest of the world in Internet advertising. U.S. Web ad expenditures in 2001 topped $34 billion, while Europe came in second with $24 billion and Asia/Pacific third at $9 billion (see Exhibit 17–9).[41]

Currently, the United States enjoys fairly heavy international Web traffic, caused mostly by a lack of telephone and Internet infrastructure and websites overseas. In Europe, online penetration was less than 4 percent in 1996. International websites also tend to remain primitive in design and function compared to U.S. competitors, which are strongly consumer-oriented. Furthermore, the international appeal of U.S. brands, especially companies such as Coca-Cola and Disney, is strong.[42]

But as the Internet increasingly becomes a household word, the content of websites for local businesses overseas will also grow. Already Yahoo! has staked an early claim by servicing Japan, Germany, France, Norway, Sweden, Denmark, and Korea in their native languages. And while today most international Web surfers are proficient in English, this can be expected to change. As local online markets grow, so will the number of non-English-speaking users.

Exhibit 17–9

Online ad spending ($ millions).

Region	2001
Africa	$ 175.5
Asia and Pacific	9,189.5
Europe	24,092.5
Latin America	1,788.4
Middle East	556.0
Canada	981.1
U.S.	34,167.8
Total worldwide spending	70,950.8

With the growth of an overseas online market, we can anticipate that American companies will try harder to cater to the native population.[43] Expanding their horizons to encompass the whole world will be the key to businesses' success in the twenty-first century.

Other Interactive Media

In addition to the Internet, advertisers now also use other new media vehicles, such as CD-ROMs, kiosks, and interactive TV. While they are not major media forms, they do warrant some brief discussion.

CD-ROM Catalogs and Magazines

Virtually every new personal computer today comes equipped with **CD-ROM** (compact disk-read only memory) capabilities, and the CD is the fastest-growing segment of the software industry. The benefit of this technology is storage space; a high concentration of data, combined with full-motion video and high-quality audio, can be stored on one disk.

Marketers like the CD-ROM format because of its high quality and versatility. In fact, CompuServe, which already publishes a monthly magazine for its customers, is enhancing its online electronic mall with sound and video and mailing it as a bimonthly CD magazine. A number of its advertisers are participating. One of them, *Chef's Catalog,* included video clips about the creation of cookware and the proper way to carve a turkey.[44] The CD-ROM is also being used as a sound and video catalog that can be connected to its source online and used to make transactions.[45]

Kiosks

The immense storage capacity of the CD makes it an ideal medium for saving the detailed information housed in stand-alone sales and information **kiosks.** In fact, kiosks were used for voter education during the 1994 national elections in South Africa. The project used video messages from 19 political parties, plus text, graphics, and sound—recorded in 11 languages—to detail information for the largely illiterate electorate on why, where, and how to vote. The kiosks made the information available 24 hours a day even in remote areas. Over a three-month period, the information in the 30 kiosks was regularly updated, and more than a million people used them. The experiment was so successful that the South African government put two of the kiosks in museums to commemorate part of the country's history.[46]

Kiosks are used around the globe for many purposes. The Singapore Postal Service has an award-winning, computerized vending kiosk that allows customers to pay utility bills; buy postcards, stamps, and envelopes; and get government information. The architectural firm Szabo International in Irvine, California, uses an elegant custom-built kiosk in its offices for impressive presentations of the firm's capabilities. BVR Group, the firm that developed Szabo's kiosk, won a gold medal for its creativity.[47]

Interactive TV

Imagine you're watching *Will & Grace* and a spot for State Farm Insurance appears. You remember you're not happy with your current insurance carrier. You pick up your remote control and click it on a box in the corner of the screen: "For more information." A menu appears. You click on "Auto insurance," and a multimedia presentation begins. At various prompts, you click your remote to get more information. At the end you request the location of a State Farm agent. The directions appear from a PC printer attached to your TV. Then it's back to *Will & Grace.*[48]

Although this rosy scenario fills the dreams of many advertisers, the reality is not nearly so encouraging. **Interactive TV** is powered by digital video recorders (DVRs, sometimes also called *personal video recorders*). In 2003, interactive TV, provided by companies such as TiVo and DirecTV, reached 3.2 million U.S. households.[49] TiVo subscribers take full advantage of their commercial-skipping powers, zooming past three-quarters of advertisements in programs they have recorded.[50]

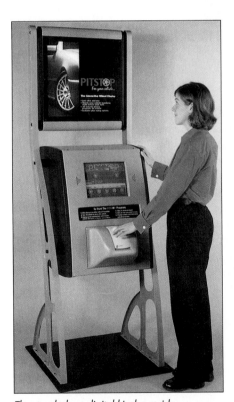

The stand-alone digital kiosk provides businesses and municipal organizations with a new technology for communication and advertising. Kiosks today are used for a variety of purposes, ranging from the sale of train tickets to distribution of coupons to information about tourist attractions.

Exhibit 17–10

Responses of 55 national advertisers when asked "If large numbers of consumers could skip commercials while watching television, which of the following forms of advertising would you spend more on?"

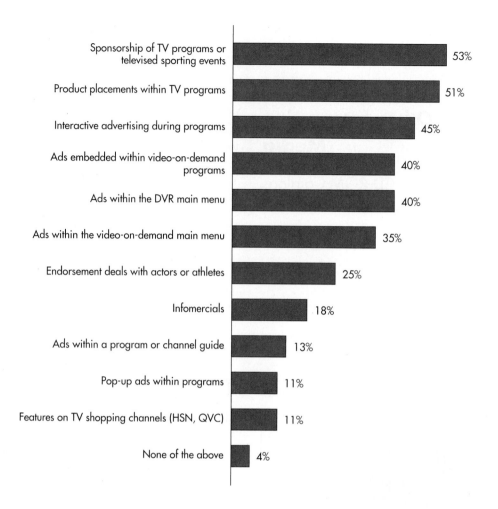

Sponsorship of TV programs or televised sporting events	53%
Product placements within TV programs	51%
Interactive advertising during programs	45%
Ads embedded within video-on-demand programs	40%
Ads within the DVR main menu	40%
Ads within the video-on-demand main menu	35%
Endorsement deals with actors or athletes	25%
Infomercials	18%
Ads within a program or channel guide	13%
Pop-up ads within programs	11%
Features on TV shopping channels (HSN, QVC)	11%
None of the above	4%

Experts predict that 6 million households will be interactive TV subscribers by the end of 2004, and that within a decade, interactive TV will be as common as cable is today. Accordingly, advertisers like Coca-Cola, Pfizer, and Chrysler are scrambling to innovate and adapt to the new medium, which compels them to reach consumers with advertising vehicles other than the traditional 30-second commercial. In particular, television advertisers are working to increase program sponsorship and product placement. Forrester Research asked television advertising executives how they might cope in a DVR-saturated environment. Exhibit 17–10 shows how television advertising might differ. Other forms of advertising, like TiVo's "Showcase" feature, allow subscribers to access entertaining, long-format ads. For example, Best Buy sponsored a Rolling Stones concert segment in order to advertise the group's new live DVD boxed set.[51] For the moment, however, because the percentage of interactive TV households remains so low, most advertisers are simply repackaging existing TV or Internet spots for the interactive TV format rather than investing in developing unique content.

Direct-Mail Advertising: The Addressable Medium

All forms of advertising sent directly to prospects through a government, private, or electronic mail delivery service are called **direct-mail advertising.** In dollars spent, direct mail is the third-ranked advertising medium today, surpassed only by newspapers and TV.

Both large and small companies use direct mail. New firms usually use direct mail as their first advertising medium. The reason is clear: Of all media, direct-mail advertising offers the straightest line to the desired customer. Decades of mailboxes stuffed with catalogs, credit card offers, and music club packets have made

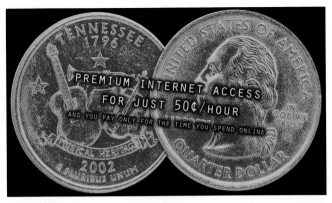

Aristotle.net worked with Conversant Marketing to send metallic ShipShapes in the form of two Tennessee state quarters to 27,000 potential clients in Memphis. To test the response rate of the eye-catching but more expensive ShipShapes, the company also sent traditional four-sided mailers to another 27,000 addresses on its Memphis mailing list.

today's advertising-weary consumers harder to reach, though. How does direct mail continue to generate return on investment (ROI) in such a market?

In 2003, the United States Postal Service approved **Customized MarketMail (CMM),** a new class of mail that gives direct-mail advertisers the opportunity to truly innovate. The new regulations allow for pieces of mail of almost any shape, within certain dimensions, to be sent without an envelope. No longer limited to rectangles, direct mail can now take more novel, eye-catching forms. From simple geometric shapes, like circles, to more curious and bizarre shapes, like Zambonis (used by First Tennessee Bank to promote a checking account associated with the local Predators hockey team), CMM stands out in a sea of mail that might otherwise go directly from the mailbox to the trash.[52]

CMM is the brainchild of Tom Becker, who for three years lobbied the USPS to authorize direct marketers to think outside the envelope. Becker is the president of ShipShapes, a company that is patenting a plastic coating that it specially developed for CMM items. ShipShapes are resilient enough to withstand the stress of being processed and delivered by the Postal Service; they are waterproof and can be stuffed into mailboxes because they bend without creasing. On the eve of the August 2003 introduction of CMM, ShipShapes was in a unique position because no other company had the resources to create durable envelope-less direct mail.[53]

But the new marketing method itself needed to be promoted. Both Ship-Shapes and the USPS needed a well-known third party to further introduce their services. With the help of Chicago public relations firm Porter Novelli, Becker arranged a media blitz to accompany the launch of CMM. Looking among its clients for an established brand to pair with the fledgling venture, Porter Novelli turned to Krispy Kreme doughnuts. Erica Swerdlow of Porter Novelli said, "We wanted third parties that could serve as endorsements as to how great customized mail marketing was going to be and, more specifically, how ShipShapes were the great example of what you can do with CMM."[54]

A 10,000-piece pilot mailing was sent to Orange County, California, residents who lived within three miles of a Krispy Kreme shop. The ShipShape of choice for the promotion was that of an open box of doughnuts, with a coupon on the back offering a second dozen doughnuts for a dime. The results? An astounding 11 percent of recipients, five times the usual response rate for similar direct-mail offers, flooded the area's three Krispy Kreme outlets. The marketing manager for the Los Angeles–area franchisee, Amy Inabinet, said, "This was a fun, new offer that we hadn't done before. We believe that the irregular shape of the Krispy Kreme Customized MarketMail direct-mail piece, coupled with the high-quality image of our Original Glazed doughnuts, made for very excited customers and employees and led to the very high response rates that we witnessed with this test mailing."[55]

By working directly with an Associated Press reporter, ShipShapes ensured that its Krispy Kreme success story was picked up by 550 newspapers. Porter Novelli also created a video news release in order to tap into television newscasts. The CMM pioneer itself was soon being contacted by an average of 50 prospective clients per day.[56]

The next step was an intense business-to-business campaign. Citing the extraordinary response rate of the pilot mailing, ShipShapes worked to convince direct mailers that its product's high visibility would translate into a greater ROI. Over three weeks in October 2003, ShipShapes used CMM to send over 45,000 pieces of its work to direct-mail advertisers. The targeted companies received each of three different designs, striking cutouts of dancers adapted from Lois Greenfield's photography, with tag lines like "Bare your imagination," "If you've got it, flaunt it," and "Don't cover your concepts, let the whole world see what you've got." Response rate for the B2B campaign was almost 5 percent, with approximately 2,250 requests for information.[57]

In 2004, the USPS expanded the range of possibilities for CMM. Advertisers can now attach magnets or clips to CMM, adding even more punch to their efforts and increasing the chance that recipients will save and display the eye-candy mailers. Other small objects can also be affixed, like compact disks or casino tokens. According to Becker, "By attaching important consumer information, promotional items and samples to direct mail pieces, advertisers and marketers can increase their response rates and drive more sales leads."[58]

CMM is not without its limitations. The die-cut pieces are more expensive to manufacture and send (ranging from $1 to $3 each for ShipShape) than traditional direct mail. Each set of customized mailers must be boxed and shipped to the postal sorting station for the destination area. The postage rate is also higher—57.4 cents for regular customers or 46 cents for nonprofits, about four times the cost to send a basic postcard—because each piece must be canceled by hand rather than being automatically postmarked by sorting machines.[59] For these reasons, CMM will likely generate the greatest ROI for advertisers with well-established, high-value products and streamlined mailing lists.

Growth of Direct Mail

Direct methods of advertising and selling grew astronomically in the last decade. Robert Coen of McCann Erickson Worldwide estimates that national advertisers spent more than $48 billion on direct mail in 2003, more than 20 percent of all the ad dollars spent in the United States.[60]

Direct mail is successful for two reasons. First, it meets the needs of today's fast lifestyles. Families have less time, so shopping by mail is convenient. Second, it's the most effective medium for generating immediate results.

Marketers are expanding their profits by stuffing monthly credit card statements with tempting mail-order offers. Today's leading mail-order products include insurance and financial services, department-store merchandise, and the other products and services listed in Exhibit 17–11.

Types of Direct-Mail Advertising

Direct-mail advertising comes in a variety of formats, from handwritten postcards to dimensional mailings like ShipShapes. The message can be one sentence or dozens of pages. And within

Exhibit 17–11

Top 10 catalog companies (2004).

Rank	Company	2003 sales ($ millions)	Market segment
1	Dell	$35,227.0	Computers, consumer electronics
2	International Business Machines Corp.	7,489.2	Computers
3	Corporate Express North America	4,456.7	Office and facility supplies
4	Boise Cascade Corp.	4,025.1	Office products
5	Office Depot	3,965.3	Office products
6	Staples	3,700.0	Office products
7	Fisher Scientific International	3,564.4	Scientific, medical, and lab supplies
8	Henry Schein	3,353.8	Dental, medical, and veterinary supplies
9	United Stationers	2,890.0	Wholesale office, janitorial, and computer supplies
10	CDW	2,741.0	Computers

each format—from tiny coupon to thick catalog or box—the creative options are infinite. In addition to the dimensional direct-mail category are the following:

E-mail, as mentioned earlier, is one of the newest tools in direct marketing and is best used for customer retention and relationship management. It is most effective when the marketer first seeks *permission* to mail. In other words, advertisers should always give people the opportunity to opt in and to opt out of their e-mail programs. For new business acquisition, the best use is in a viral marketing campaign—otherwise it will probably be perceived as spam.

Sales letters, the most common direct-mail format, are often mailed with brochures, price lists, or reply cards and envelopes. **Postcards** are used to announce sales, offer discounts, or generate customer traffic. National postal services regulate formats and dimensions. Some advertisers use a double postcard, enabling them to send both an advertising message and a perforated reply card. A recipient who wants the product or service tears off the reply card and mails it back to the advertiser. To encourage response, some advertisers use **business reply mail** so the recipient can respond without paying postage. The advertiser needs a special first-class postal permit and must print the number on the face of the return card or envelope. On receiving a response, the advertiser pays postage plus a handling fee of a few cents. "Postage-free" incentives usually increase response rates.

Folders and **brochures** are usually printed in multiple colors with photos or other illustrations on good paper stock that reproduces printed images well. **Broadsides** are larger than folders and are sometimes used as window displays or wall posters in stores. They fold to a compact size to fit in a mailbag.

Self-mailers are any form of direct mail that can travel without an envelope. Usually folded and secured by a staple or seal, they have special blank spaces for the prospect's name and address to be written, stenciled, or labeled.

Statement stuffers are ads enclosed in monthly customer statements from department stores, banks, oil companies, and the like. To order, customers write in their credit-card number and sign the reply card.

House organs are publications produced by associations or business organizations—for example, stockholder reports, newsletters, consumer magazines, and dealer publications.

Catalogs are reference books that list, describe, and often picture the products sold by a manufacturer, wholesaler, jobber, or retailer. With more high-income families shopping at home, specialized catalogs are becoming very popular. Some mail-order companies prosper with specialized approaches, like outdoor clothing and equipment (L.L. Bean), electronic gadgets (Sharper Image), or gourmet foods (Sutton Place Gourmet).

Catalogs are big business. The industry was hit hard by the recent recession, but all indicators point to a recovery that began in 2003. Direct Media Catalog Tracker keeps tabs on circulation by counting how many catalogs hit its mailbox each month. In April 2004, it received 415 consumer catalogs, 19 percent more than the same month in 2003.[61] Wider circulation, when combined with cleaner, tighter address lists, helped 70 of 100 industry leaders post revenue increases in 2003.[62] Certain trends emerge among the top catalog marketers (see Exhibit 17–11). For instance, three of the top ten companies are computer vendors or resellers (Dell, IBM, and CDW, respectively), and the remainder sell office, business, or technical supplies.

Using Direct Mail in the Media Mix

Direct mail is an efficient, effective, and economical medium for sales and business promotion (see the Checklist, "The Pros and Cons of Direct-Mail Advertising"). That's why it's used by a wide variety of companies, charity and service organizations, and individuals. Direct mail can increase the effectiveness of ads in other media. Publishers Clearinghouse uses TV spots to alert viewers to the impending arrival of its direct-mail sweepstakes promotions.

The Pros and Cons of Direct-Mail Advertising

Pros

____ **Selectivity.** Direct mail helps advertisers communicate directly with the people most likely to buy. Computerized mailing lists group people by occupation, region or state, income, and other characteristics.

____ **Intensive coverage and extensive reach.** Everyone has a mailbox. With direct mail, an advertiser can reach 100 percent of the homes in a given area.

____ **Flexibility.** Direct-mail advertising can be uniquely creative, limited only by the advertiser's ingenuity and budget and postal regulations. Advertisers can produce direct-mail pieces fast and distribute them quickly.

____ **Control.** Preprinted direct-mail pieces enable an advertiser to control circulation and reproduction quality.

____ **Personal impact.** Advertisers can personalize direct mail to the needs, wants, and whims of specific audiences without offending other prospects or customers.

____ **Exclusivity.** There are no distractions from competitive ads.

____ **Response.** Direct mail achieves the highest response of any advertising medium. About 15 percent of the responses arrive within the first week, so the advertiser can quickly judge the campaign's success.

____ **Testability.** Direct mail is good for testing prospect reactions to product acceptability, pricing, offers, copy approaches, sales literature, and so on.

Cons

____ **High cost per exposure.** Direct mail has the highest cost per exposure of any major medium, about 14 times as much as most magazine and newspaper advertising.

____ **Delivery problems.** The mass media offer precise delivery times, but the postal service makes no delivery commitments on third-class mail. And up to 10 percent of mailings may be undeliverable because people move.

____ **Lack of content support.** Direct mail must capture and hold the reader's attention without the support of editorial or entertainment content.

____ **Selectivity problems.** Effective direct mail depends on correctly identifying the target audience and obtaining a good list. Some groups of prospects, such as physicians, are so saturated with direct mail they ignore it.

____ **Negative attitudes.** Many consumers think of direct mail as junk mail and automatically throw it away. They may also believe it's too difficult to return merchandise purchased by mail.

____ **Environmental concerns.** Some consumers see direct mail as landfill fodder. Some direct marketers (Eddie Bauer, L.L. Bean) print parts of their catalogs on recycled paper, and now new de-inking facilities will make more catalogs recyclable.

____ **Anti-spam laws.** The CAN-SPAM Act and similar laws impose many requirements, making it more difficult for marketers to electronically send prospective clients unsolicited marketing materials.

Direct mail has two main drawbacks: cost and the "junk mail" image, both of which are almost inescapable. No other medium (except personal selling and consumer targeting on the Internet) has such a high cost per thousand. For this reason, many small advertisers participate in cooperative mailings with companies such as ADVO, which serves most major U.S. cities. ADVO mails an envelope containing a coupon for each participating company to targeted zip codes.

Some large advertisers don't send unsolicited mail. To locate prospects, they use other direct-response media. Then they use direct mail to respond to inquiries. They save money by mailing only to qualified prospects, and by sending higher-quality materials, they build their image and improve their chances of establishing a worthwhile relationship.

Buying Direct-Mail Advertising

Direct-mail advertising has three basic costs: list acquisition, creative production, and distribution.

Acquiring Direct-Mail Lists

The heart of any direct-mail program is the mailing list. Each list actually defines a market segment. Direct-mail advertisers use three types of lists: *house, mail-response,* and *compiled.*

House lists The company's relational database of current, recent, and long-past customers as well as future prospects comprises the **house list** for direct-mail programs. Because customers are its most important asset, every company should focus sufficient resources on developing a rich database of customer and prospect information and profiles. There are several ways a company can build its own house list, from offering credit plans to sending useful information to exchanging names with other businesses with similar customer profiles.

Consumer product companies like General Electric gather customer data by enclosing an owner registration form with their products. On the mail-in form, purchasers give their name, address, phone number, birth date, occupation, income range, credit card preferences, home ownership status, and number of children. They also indicate their hobbies and interests (such as golf, foreign travel, photography, or bowling). Companies use this information for their own mailings and sell it to other direct-mail advertisers.

Mail-response lists   The advertiser's second most important prospects are people who respond to direct-mail pieces from other companies—especially those with complementary products or services. **Mail-response lists** are the house lists of other direct-mail advertisers, and they can be rented with a wide variety of demographic breakdowns.

Compiled lists   The most readily available lists are those that some entity compiles for a different reason and then rents or sells—for example, lists of car owners, new-home purchasers, business owners, and so on. **Compiled lists** typically offer the lowest response rate, so experts suggest using numerous sources, merging them on computer with mail-response and house lists, and then purging them of duplicate names.[63]

Direct-mail lists can be bought or rented. Purchased lists can be used without limit; rented lists may be used for a single mailing only. List owners plant decoy names in the list to be sure renters don't use it more than once.

Some list owners pay a **list broker** a commission (usually 20 percent) to handle the rental details. The advertiser, in turn, benefits from the broker's knowledge of list quality without having to pay more than the rental cost.

Lists can be brokered or exchanged with list houses or other noncompetitive companies. And they can be tailored to reflect customer location (zip code); demographics such as age, income, and credit card ownership; or psychographic characteristics such as personality and lifestyle. The SRDS *Direct Mail List Rates and Data* comes in two volumes, *Consumer Lists* and *Business Lists,* and contains more than 48,000 list selections in hundreds of classifications (see Exhibit 17–12).

The quality of mailing lists varies enormously. The wrong list can have out-of-date addresses and names of people who live too far away, don't use the product advertised, and can't afford it anyway. Mailing list prices vary according to quality. Rental rates average about $55 per thousand names (or about $50 for 5,000 e-mail addresses) but can be as little as $35 per thousand or as much as $400 per thousand. About half of all catalog companies rent their address lists to other direct mailers; in 2004, revenue from list rental accounted for an average of 2 percent of these companies' total revenues.[64] The more stringent the advertiser's selection criteria, the more expensive the list. An extra $10 per thousand is often well worth the savings in mailers and postage that would otherwise be wasted.

The average mailing list changes more than 40 percent a year as people relocate, change jobs, get married, or die. So mailing lists must be continually updated (*cleaned*) to be sure they're current and correct. Advertisers can also test the validity and accuracy of a given list. They rent or buy every *n*th name and send a mailer to that person. If the results are favorable, they purchase additional names, usually in lots of 1,000.

Production and Handling

To create a direct-mail package, the advertiser may use in-house staff, an ad agency, or a freelance designer and writer. Some agencies specialize in direct mail.

The direct-mail piece normally goes through the same production process as any other print piece. The size and shape of the mailing package, as well as the type, illustrations, and colors, all affect printing costs. Special features such as simulated

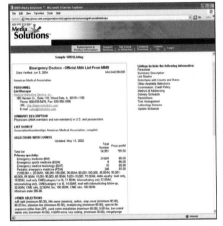

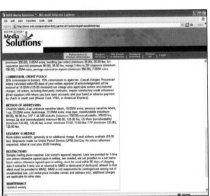

Exhibit 17–12

Typical listing from Direct Mail List Rates and Data, *published by Standard Rate & Data Service.*

Developing Effective Direct-Mail Packages

Good direct-mail campaigns help build relationships between advertisers and customers. As with an ad, the effectiveness of a direct-mail campaign relies strongly on both its message and its overall appearance.

Shaping the Message

When Air France wanted to reach valued customers, its agency, Wunderman Cato Johnson, New York, created the direct-mail pieces shown here. The strategy was to emphasize an upscale design style with the *Paris Bistro Cooking* book and *Savoir Faire* newsletter to make the recipient feel like a truly valued Air France customer.

To develop the message element in direct mail, experts suggest several techniques: stress the benefits; repeat your offer more than once; offer an incentive; offer a guarantee; don't be afraid of long copy; don't write copy that is over the reader's head; and give the customer more than one option for responding.

This elegant, three-dimensional mailing is part of a series providing positive recognition to valued Air France customers while maintaining the airline's upscale image. The target market received a personalized cover letter, a monthly newsletter, a travel survey, and a book, *Paris Bistro Cooking*. Air France received a substantial response, including dozens of thank-you notes.

Integrating the Message with the Direct-Mail Pieces

Creating direct mail involves fitting the message with the key physical components of the direct-mail package. As discussed in Chapter 13, the five steps of the creative pyramid (attention, interest, credibility, desire, and action) may be guidelines for forming the message. Next, this information must be incorporated into all the components of the direct-mail package: the mailing envelope, the sales letter, the color piece or brochure, and the response device.

Paris Bistro Cooking and *Savoir Faire* attract *attention* with their large type and color. The sales letter's color logo and signature catch the recipient's eye and keep his or her *interest* on the letter and its contents.

The specifics within the letter and the matching travel survey card build *credibility* by providing data useful in the purchase decision. Details include the features and benefits of the product, the deadline and value of the offer, and instructions the recipient should follow.

The cookbook features images suggesting how the airline puts the recipient in touch with the elegance of life, whetting the recipient's *desire* to purchase the product.

In the last step, the postage-free business reply card as well as telephone and fax numbers and URL make it easy for the recipient to take *action* to buy the product.

Some Secrets of Direct Mail

Research has revealed countless direct-mail techniques that improve response rates: indent type and set it flush left with a ragged right edge; avoid printing in reverse type; list dollars saved in your offer rather than percentages; use the word *you* in text; provide a reason for sale pricing (almost any will do); and do not paste labels over old addresses—print new materials.

Laboratory Applications

1. Locate a direct-mail package that has the four components common to most mailings and list how the elements of the creative pyramid are integrated throughout the components.

2. Review the copywriting in your direct-mail package and identify how many of the techniques mentioned in this Ad Lab are used or could be improved.

---

blue-ink signatures, cardboard pop-ups, and die-cutting (the cutting of paper stock into an unusual shape) add to the cost. But the larger the printing volume, or *run,* the lower the printing cost per unit (see Ad Lab 17–B, "Developing Effective Direct-Mail Packages").

Remaining production and handling tasks can be done by a local **letter shop** (or *mailing house*), or the advertiser can do them internally. On a cost-per-thousand basis, letter shops stuff and seal envelopes, affix labels, calculate postage, and sort, tie, and stack the mailers. Some shops also offer creative services. If the advertiser is using third-class bulk mail, the letter shop separates mailers by zip code and ties them into bundles to qualify for low bulk rates. Then the letter shop delivers the mailers to the post office.

Distribution

Distribution costs are based chiefly on the weight of the mailer and the delivery method. U.S. advertisers can use the U.S. Postal Service, air freight, or private delivery services like UPS and FedEx. The most common, the U.S. Postal Service, offers several types of delivery (for more postal information, see RL 17–1 in the Reference Library on the *Contemporary Advertising* CD). Direct-mail advertising is most effective when it arrives on Tuesdays, Wednesdays, and Thursdays.

Chapter Summary

The digital interactive media, which include online database services, the Internet and the World Wide Web, CD-ROM catalogs, magazines, kiosks, and interactive television, represent a revolution in the making. From an advertising standpoint, these media offer an opportunity to develop customer relationships rather than volume. These media are still in flux, but they're growing at an exponential rate and offer an array of challenges and opportunities for advertising creativity.

The commercialization of the Internet really began with the commercial online services that offered a large subscriber base to potential advertisers. However, the Internet itself dwarfed the online services in potential since it reached so many people around the globe. Once Web browser software became available, it made the Internet user-friendly to noncomputer specialists.

Similarly, search engines made sites on the World Wide Web available to PC users with just the click of a mouse. When people began migrating to the Web, so did advertisers. The first banner ad was sold by *Hotwired* magazine.

Web users tend to be upscale, college-educated men and women. This is an ideal target, especially for business-to-business advertisers. This group is rapidly broadening, which will make the Web even more attractive to many mainline advertisers. People currently access the Net through Internet service providers, cable modems, and satellites. The most common, though, is dial-up modem through an ISP.

The most common types of Net advertising are banners, buttons, sponsorships, interstitials, and classifieds. Like all media, the Internet has many advantages and disadvantages.

Most Internet advertising is sold by CPM. Some, though, is sold by click-through or results. In some cases, marketers conducting commerce on the Net take a commission on what is sold.

Direct mail attracts nearly 20 percent of all ad dollars. While it has historically been the most expensive major medium on a cost-per-exposure basis, it has also always been the most effective in terms of tangible results. Marketers like direct mail for its accountability. There are many types of direct-mail advertising, from catalogs and brochures to statement stuffers.

One of the great features of direct mail is that it can increase the effectiveness of ads in other media. However, direct mail has many drawbacks too—primarily its cost and the junk-mail image.

The two most important things that affect direct-mail success are the mailing list and the creativity used. The direct-mail piece normally goes through the same production process as any other print piece. The size and shape of the mailing package, as well as the type, illustrations, and colors, all affect printing costs.

Important Terms

ad networks, *564*

ad impression, *559*

affiliate marketing program, *562*

banner, *554*

broadband, *552*

broadside, *569*

brochure, *569*

business reply mail, *569*

button, *554*

cable modem, *553*

catalog, *569*

CD-ROM, *565*

classified ad website, *556*

click rate, *559*

click-throughs, *562*

compiled lists, *571*

cookies, *560*

Customized MarketMail (CMM), *567*

customer retention and relationship management (CRM), *556*

digital interactive media, *540*

digital subscriber line (DSL), *553*

DirecPC, *553*

direct-mail advertising, *566*

e-mail, *569*

e-mail advertising, *556*

folder, *569*

house list, *570*

house organ, *569*

interactive TV, *565*

Internet, *543*

Internet service provider (ISP), *543*

interstitial, *555*

keyword, *562*

kiosk, *565*

landing page, *554*

letter shop, *572*

list broker, *571*

mail-response lists, *571*

MSN TV, *553*

narrowband, *552*

natural search engine optimization, *556*

pay per click advertising (PPC), *556*

postcard, *569*

rich mail, *555*

rich-media advertising, *554*

sales letter, *569*

search engine, *544*

self-mailer, *569*

spam, *556*

sponsorship, *555*

statement stuffer, *569*

viral marketing, *557*

Web browser, *543*

Web page, *543, 554*

website, *545*

World Wide Web (WWW), *543*

Review Questions

1. How did the Internet evolve to its present status as an advertising medium?
2. Which companies on the Internet receive the greatest amount of advertising revenue? Why?
3. What are the different ways of advertising online?
4. What are cookies, and what are they used for?
5. What are the different ways Web publishers charge for advertising?
6. How would you describe the advantages the Internet offers advertisers over traditional media?
7. How does audience measurement on the Web differ from that for traditional media?
8. What is the importance of the new interactive media to small advertisers?

9. How could you use direct mail in an integrated marketing communications program? Give an example.
10. What factors have the greatest influence on the success of a direct-mail campaign?
11. **The Advertising Experience**
    Despite its junk-mail image, direct mail requires a great deal of creativity. Jones Educational Services, which provides GMAT, GRE, and MGAT preparation, has agreed that a direct-mail campaign may be the best way to increase its market share. Create a campaign like the one that Porter Novelli created for Krispy Kreme.

Exploring the Internet

The Internet exercises for Chapter 17 address the following areas related to the chapter: Internet advertising (Exercises 1 and 3) and direct mail (Exercise 2).

1. **Internet Advertising**
   Advertising banners on the Internet are akin to outdoor billboards and fill the information superhighway with advertising messages, corporate signage, and hyperlinks. But, as is the case with all new media, the future of ad banners is uncertain. The only thing that is certain is that they will exist—in one form or another. Many advertisers are unsure about putting their advertising dollars toward cyberspace, but companies like DoubleClick (www.doubleclick.com) are flourishing as they introduce new and better ways of managing Web advertising—helping advertisers to feel more confident about the ad programs they place.

   Visit the following advertising-related sites on the Internet and discover more about this fast-changing segment of the advertising industry. Then answer the questions that follow.

   - AdForce www.adforce.com
   - ChannelSeven.com www.channelseven.com
   - Classifieds 2000 www.classifieds2000.com
   - DoubleClick www.doubleclick.com
   - eBusiness Association (eBA) www.ebizassociation.org
   - I/PRO www.ipro.com
   - Interactive Advertising Bureau (IAB) www.iab.net
   - Internet Advertising Resource Guide www.admedia.org
   - Jupiter Research www.jup.com

   a. What group sponsors the site and what is the organization's purpose?
   b. What is the size/scope of the organization?
   c. Who is the intended audience(s) of the website?
   d. What services does the organization offer Web advertisers?

2. **Direct Mail**
   Direct-mail advertising is one of the advertiser's best tools to execute highly targeted relationship-building communications. Take a few moments to familiarize yourself further with this side of the advertising business. Browse the direct-mail-related websites below and then answer the questions that follow.

   - Advo, Inc. www.advo.com
   - Alamo Direct www.alamodirect.com
   - American List Counsel www.amlist.com
   - Catalyst Direct Marketing www.catalystdm.com
   - Direct Mail Express www.dmenet.com
   - Direct Marketing Association www.the-dma.org
   - L.I.S.T. Incorporated www.l-i-s-t.com
   - Mailing and Fulfillment Service Association (MFSA) www.mfsanet.org
   - PostMaster Direct Response www.postmasterdirect.com
   - Response Mail Express www.responsemail.com
   - United States Postal Service www.usps.com

   a. What company or group sponsors the site?
   b. What is the organization's purpose?
   c. Who makes up the organization's membership? Its constituency?
   d. What benefit does the organization provide individual members and the advertising community?

3. **Designing a Banner Ad**
   X-Scream magazine, which is dedicated to extreme sports of all kinds, would like to dedicate some of its advertising budget to banner ads. Taking into account the target market this magazine would have, find three websites its consumers might visit, and design a banner ad that would motivate them to learn more about (and subscribe to) the magazine.

Chapter 18

Using Out-of-Home, Exhibitive, and Supplementary Media

Objectives

TO PRESENT THE FACTORS ADVERTISERS CONSIDER when evaluating various out-of-home, exhibitive, and supplementary media. Many advertisers use these media to either complement or replace print and electronic media, so it's important to understand how advertisers buy these media and the advantages and disadvantages of each.

After studying this chapter, you will be able to:

- **Discuss** the pros and cons of outdoor advertising.

- **Explain** how to measure exposure to outdoor media.

- **Describe** the types of standard outdoor advertising structures.

- **Detail** the various options available in transit advertising.

- **Identify** the influences on the cost of transit and other out-of-home media.

- **Discuss** the importance of exhibitive media in a company's marketing mix.

- **Explain** the issues advertisers face when considering a change in packaging.

- **Identify** several types of supplementary media.

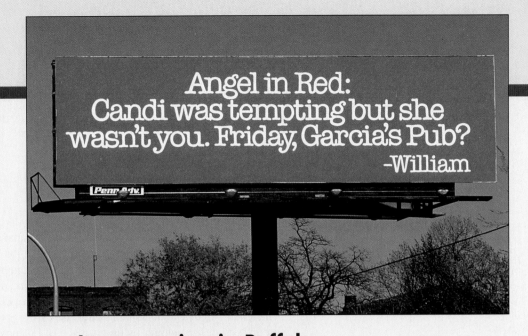

It was spring in Buffalo, and love was in the air. One Monday morning, as people were driving to work, they suddenly noticed a big new billboard. In large white letters against a siren-red background, it displayed a very personal message: ■   Angel in Red: Saw You at Garcia's Irish Pub.   ■   Love to meet you.—William.   ■   For the next nine weeks, commuters discovered a new message every Monday morning, each more romantic—and more desperate—than the last. "Angel in Red: Still waiting. Garcia's Pub. Friday?—William." "Angel in Red: I'm going broke with these billboards. Garcia's . . . Please!—William."   ■   People started going to Garcia's to see if they could spot Angel, or meet William. Soon a board appeared authored by Frankie warning William that his angel was out of bounds. William responded with a board saying: "Angel in Red: Frankie be damned! I'd risk it all to meet you at Garcia's." Women started calling the local billboard company to see how they could get to meet romantic William.   ■   The story became the talk of the town. And for nine weeks, nobody caught on, not even the employees at Garcia's.   ■   Finally, the board everyone was waiting for appeared: "Dear William: I must be crazy. Garcia's, Friday, 8:30.—Angel."   ■   That night the place was jammed. Garcia's had to hire two models to play William and Angel. Yes, William finally found his angel, and they danced to (what else?) "Lady in Red."   ■   The final board appeared the next week. "Angel: Thanks for Friday at Garcia's. I'm in heaven.—Love, William."   ■   The campaign was the brainchild of Crowley Webb & Associates, the ad agency next door to Garcia's. The owner of Garcia's was nervous about a new restaurant chain's plans to open a pub on the lakefront. So he hired Crowley Webb to come up with something really "way out"—for under $20,000. ■ The agency demonstrated to Garcia's (and the world) that with a little imagination, outdoor advertising is an ideal medium for achieving local reach, frequency, and continuity on a very limited budget.[1] ■

Out-of-Home Media

Media that reach prospects outside their homes—like outdoor advertising, bus and taxicab advertising, subway posters, and terminal advertising—are part of the broad category of **out-of-home media** (see Exhibit 18–1). Today, there are more than 30 different types of out-of-home media, generating $5.5 billion in revenues in 2003.[2] The most common are *on-premise signs,* which promote goods and services, or identify a place of business, on the property where the sign is located.[3] The golden arches at McDonald's franchises are a good example. On-premise signs are important for helping us find a place of business, but they don't provide any kind of market coverage, and they aren't an organized medium like, for instance, the standardized outdoor advertising business.

In the past three chapters, we've looked at the traditional mass media forms as well as some of the interesting new media vehicles that have burst upon the advertising scene in recent years. Now, to round out our discussion of advertising media, we'll present in this last chapter some of the other vehicles that advertisers use today.

We'll start with the last major media category: the organized out-of-home media. These include standardized outdoor advertising and transit advertising. We'll also briefly discuss some other out-of-home vehicles that are gaining in popularity: mobile billboards, electronic signs and displays, and even the ads that are now cropping up on phone booths and parking meters.

Next we'll discuss a category we call *exhibitive media,* which includes product packaging and trade shows and exhibits. Finally, we'll examine some of the media that advertisers typically consider supplementary to their other advertising activities—things like promotional products (specialty advertising), directories, and Yellow Pages—as well as some of the emerging media that are beginning to gain advertiser interest.

Exhibit 18–1

Breakdown of out-of-home media.

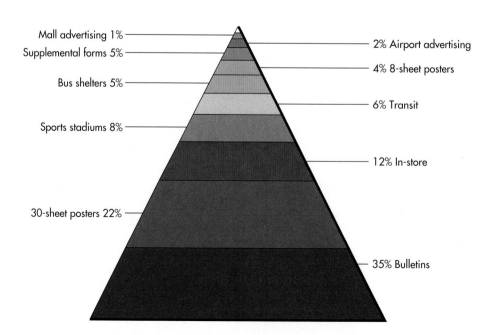

Mall advertising 1%
Supplemental forms 5%
Bus shelters 5%
Sports stadiums 8%
30-sheet posters 22%

2% Airport advertising
4% 8-sheet posters
6% Transit
12% In-store
35% Bulletins

One of the most common forms of out-of-home advertising is the billboard. Compared to other major media, billboards offer the lowest cost per thousand. This creative example for the Museum of Flight (www.museumof flight.com) is actually a painted bulletin with a 3-D extension added—the take-off ramp for the boy and his wagon.

Outdoor Advertising

As a national and global medium, outdoor advertising has achieved great success. It was probably the first advertising medium ever used, dating back more than 5,000 years to when hieroglyphics on obelisks directed travelers. In the Middle Ages, bill posting was an accepted form of advertising in Europe. And in the nineteenth century, it evolved into a serious art form, thanks to the poster paintings of both Manet and Toulouse-Lautrec.[4]

Today, from Africa to Asia to Europe to South America, both local and global marketers use outdoor media for the same reasons as Garcia's Irish Pub: to communicate a succinct message or image in the local language to a mass audience quickly and frequently at the lowest cost per thousand of any major medium.

In 2003, U.S. advertisers spent a total of $5.5 billion in standardized outdoor advertising, a 5 percent increase over 2002 figures.[5] This growth is expected to continue as advertisers seek alternatives to the declining audiences and ad clutter of other mass media forms. Now that TV viewers can choose from more than 50 channels, it has become increasingly difficult for national advertisers to tell their story to mass audiences. But there's still one medium that can carry their message 24 hours a day, seven days a week, day and night, without interruption. It's never turned off, zipped, zapped, put aside, or left unopened. And it's big. That's outdoor. For that reason, some experts refer to billboards as the *last* mass medium.[6]

Outdoor advertising may be used for a variety of purposes. For example, nothing beats outdoor as a directional medium for motorists. But in an IMC program, outdoor also greatly enhances awareness of or reinforces the advertiser's core message with high frequency at a very reasonable cost.

Standardization of the Outdoor Advertising Business

Standardized outdoor advertising uses scientifically located structures to deliver an advertiser's message to markets around the world.

In the United States, there are approximately 390,000 outdoor ad structures owned and maintained by some 3,000 outdoor advertising companies, known as *plants*.[7] Plant operators find suitable locations (usually concentrated in commercial and business areas), lease or buy the property, acquire the necessary legal permits, erect the structures in conformance with local building codes, contract with advertisers for poster rentals, and post the panels or paint the bulletins. Plant operators also maintain the outdoor structures and keep surrounding areas clean and attractive.

The Pros and Cons of Outdoor Advertising

The Pros

____ **Accessibility.** Outdoor carries the message 24 hours per day and cannot be fast-forwarded, put aside, zapped, or turned off.

____ **Reach.** For the same dollars, outdoor delivers a reach of 86.4 percent compared with spot TV (76.5 percent), radio (72.3 percent), and newspaper (72.2 percent) for the same target audience in the same city. The audience is mostly young, educated, affluent, and mobile—an attractive target to many national advertisers.

____ **Frequency.** Nine out of 10 people reached with a 100 GRP showing receive an average of 29 impressions each over a 30-day period.

____ **Geographic flexibility.** Outdoor advertisers can place their advertising where they want it nationally, regionally, or locally in more than 9,000 markets across North America.

____ **Demographic flexibility.** Messages can be concentrated in areas frequented or traversed by young people, upper-income people, or people of specific ethnic backgrounds. With computerization, it's possible to characterize outdoor audiences by age, sex, income, and lifestyle down to the block level.

____ **Cost.** Outdoor offers the lowest cost per exposure of any major advertising medium. Rates vary depending on market size and intensity, but the GRP system makes cost comparisons possible from market to market.

____ **Impact.** Because advertisers can build up GRPs very fast, outdoor is the ideal medium for those with a short, simple, and authoritative message.

____ **Creative flexibility.** Outdoor offers a large display and the spectacular features of lights, animation, and brilliant color. New fiber optics, giant video screens, and backlit display technologies offer more creative options.

____ **Location.** Outdoor can target consumers by activity, reaching shoppers on their way to the store, businesspeople on their way to work, or travelers on their way to the airport, thereby influencing shoppers just before they make a purchase decision.

The Cons

____ **Fleeting message.** Customers pass quickly, so outdoor advertising must intrude to be effective. The design and copy must tell a story briefly and crisply, and the words must sell.

____ **Environmental influence.** Outdoor messages are influenced by their environment. Placement in a run-down area can detract from a product's image.

____ **Audience measurement.** Audience demographics are difficult to measure. Not every passerby sees or reads the ad, so some media buyers distrust reach estimates.

____ **Control.** Unlike print and broadcast ads, it's hard to physically inspect each outdoor poster panel.

____ **Planning and costs.** Outdoor messages usually require six to eight weeks of lead time for printing and posting. High initial preparation cost may discourage local use. And for national advertisers, buying outdoor is complex. As many as 30 companies may sell ad space in a single market.

____ **Availability of locations.** Outdoor is so popular that demand now exceeds supply.

____ **Visual pollution.** Some people object to outdoor advertising as visual pollution. They have a negative reaction to advertisers who use it.

The plant operator may have its own art staff to supply creative services for local advertisers; ad agencies usually do the creative work for national advertisers. The biggest outdoor advertisers are traditionally in the entertainment and amusement category (see Exhibit 18–2). The next largest category is local retail. Typically, the smaller the market, the larger the percentage of local advertisers.

Types of Outdoor Advertising

To buy outdoor advertising effectively, the media planner must understand its advantages and disadvantages and the types of structures available (see the Checklist, "The Pros and Cons of Outdoor Advertising"). Standardized structures come in three basic forms: *bulletins, 30-sheet poster panels*, and *eight-sheet posters*. For extra impact, some companies may use the nonstandard *spectacular*.

Exhibit 18–2

Outdoor advertising expenditures, 2003 (ranked by total spending).

Rank	Industry categories	2003 ($ millions)
1	Automotive	$339.4
2	Retail	291.3
3	Airlines, hotels, car rental	264.4
4	Movies, media, advertising	230.6
5	Restaurants and fast food	206.2
6	Insurance and real estate	195.5
7	Financial services	192.9
8	Beer, wine, and liquor	156.4
9	Telecommunications	107.1
10	Government, politics, and organizations	99.0

How to Use Type and Color in Outdoor Advertising

Outdoor advertising is generally viewed from 100 to 500 feet away by people in motion. So it must be simple, brief, and easy to discern. Large illustrations, bold colors, simple backgrounds, clear product identification, and easy-to-read lettering are essential for consumer comprehension.

Type Weight and Spacing

The recommended maximum for outdoor copy is seven words. Bold typefaces appear blurred and thin ones seem faded. Ornate typefaces are too complicated. Simple sans serifs are the most effective. Spacing between letters and words (kerning) should be separated to reduce confusion.

Color Contrast and Value

In outdoor advertising, a full range of colors can be vividly and faithfully reproduced. A huge poster or bulletin alive with brilliant reds, greens, yellows, and blues produces an effect unmatched by any other medium.

In choosing colors for outdoor, the designer should seek high contrast in both hue (the identity of the color, such as red, green, yellow) and value (the color's lightness or darkness) to make it more readable. Contrasting colors work well at outdoor-viewing distances; colors lacking contrast in value blend together and obscure the message.

The color wheel illustrates the need for contrast in both hue and value. For example, green and red are opposite each other on the wheel (dashed line) and are therefore complementary colors. They contrast well in hues—but when their values are similar, they can create an annoying visual vibration. The same is true of a blue and orange combination.

Blue and green, and orange and red, are especially poor combinations to use because they are generally so similar in both hue and value.

Yellow and violet (dissimilar in both hue and value) provide a strong, effective contrast for outdoor. White goes well with any dark-value color, while black is good with colors of light value.

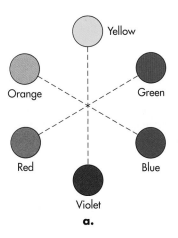

a.

Most readable	Least readable
Upper & Lower Case	ALL UPPER CASE
Regular Kerning	Tight Kerning
Bold Face	Light Face
Uniform Thicknesses	**Too Thick & Thin**

b.

c.

Color Impact

Among the color combinations shown below, legibility ranges from best in combination 1 (upper left) to poorest in combination 18 (lower right).

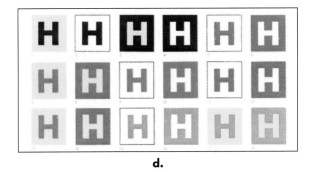

d.

Laboratory Applications

1. Which outdoor ads in this chapter use color the most effectively? Explain.

2. What outdoor ads have you seen that don't use color effectively? How can they be improved?

Bulletins

Where traffic is heavy and visibility is good, advertisers find that large **bulletin structures** work best, especially for long-term use. Bulletins measure 14 by 48 feet, plus any extensions, and may carry either painted or printed messages. They are created in sections in the plant's shop and then brought to the site, where they are assembled and hung on the billboard structure.

Painted displays are normally lighted and are repainted several times each year (color is very important for readability; see Ad Lab 18–A). Some bulletins are three-dimensional or embellished by extensions (or cutouts) that stretch beyond the frames of the structure. Variations include cutout letters, backlighting, moving messages, and electronic time and temperature units called jump clocks.

This ad for Dulux Paint beautifully underscores the blossoming flowers in these trees. Using existing surroundings to accent an ad is a creative and memorable strategy, and in this case earned a Gold Lion at Cannes.

Painted bulletins are very costly, but some advertisers overcome this expense by rotating them to different choice locations in the market every 60 or 90 days. Over time, this gives the impression of wider coverage than the advertiser is actually paying for. As Garcia's Pub found out, the dominating effect of bulletins frequently make them well worth the extra cost—especially in small markets.

Poster Panels

The **30-sheet poster panel** (*standard billboard*) is less costly per unit and is the basic outdoor advertising structure. A poster consists of blank panels with a standardized size and border. Its message is first printed at a lithography or screen plant on large sheets of paper, then mounted by hand on the panel.

Poster sizes are referred to in terms of *sheets*. The poster sheets are mounted on a board with a total surface of 12 by 25 feet and usually change every 30 days.

Some local advertisers get high-quality outdoor advertising at reduced cost by using **stock posters.** These ready-made, 30-sheet posters are available in any quantity and often feature the work of first-class artists and lithographers. Local florists, dairies, banks, or bakeries simply place their name in the appropriate spot.

Eight-Sheet Posters

Manufacturers of grocery products, as well as many local advertisers, use smaller poster sizes. Called **eight-sheet posters** (or *junior panels*), these offer a 5- by 11-foot printing area on a panel surface 6 feet high by 12 feet wide. They are typically concentrated in urban areas, where they can reach pedestrian as well as vehicular traffic. In an integrated marketing communications campaign, they are also an excellent medium for coverage close to the point of purchase.

Spectaculars

Times Square in New York is well known for its **spectaculars**—giant electronic signs that incorporate movement, color, and flashy graphics to grab attention in high-traffic areas. Spectaculars are very expensive to produce and are found primarily in the world's largest cities, such as Tokyo, London, Atlanta, Los Angeles, and, of course, Las Vegas (see the Portfolio Review, "Out-of-Home Advertising").

Buying Outdoor Advertising

Advertisers use outdoor advertising for a variety of purposes. For example, to introduce a new product or announce a change in package design, an advertiser might want to saturate the market. Outdoor advertising makes broad coverage possible—overnight. For a small portion of its total media budget, for example, Saturn was able to buy 400 billboards and dominate the outdoor medium in the important California market, contributing significantly to the success of the car's introduction. California is the state with the most import car owners, Saturn's key competitive target.[8]

The basic unit of sale for billboards, or posters, is *100 gross rating points daily,* or a **100 showing.** One rating point equals 1 percent of a particular market's population. Buying

Spectaculars are expensive, elaborate animated signs found primarily in the heart of large cities. They incorporate movement, color, and flashy graphics to grab attention in high-traffic areas.

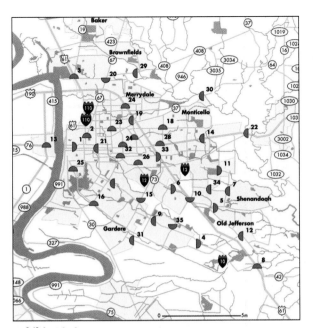

Exhibit 18–3

Billboard locations in Baton Rouge that achieve at least 100 GRPs daily when posted for 30 days. The red semicircles indicate which way the boards face. This map displays typical locations for a given 100 showing coverage.

100 gross rating points does *not* mean the message will appear on 100 posters; it means the message will appear on as many panels as needed to provide a daily exposure theoretically equal to the market's total population. Actually, a showing of 100 gross rating points achieves a *daily* reach of about 88.1 percent of the adults in a market over a 30-day period.[9]

For less saturation, units of sale can be expressed as fractions of the basic unit, such as 75, 50, or 25 gross rating points. If a showing provides 750,000 total impression opportunities daily in a market with a population of 1 million, it delivers 75 GRPs daily. Over a period of 30 days, the showing would earn 2,250 GRPs (30 × 75).

Location, Location, Location

As in real estate, location is everything in outdoor advertising. Advertisers that want more saturation can increase the number of posters or purchase better locations to achieve 200 or 300 GRPs per day. The map in Exhibit 18–3 shows the billboard locations in Baton Rouge, Louisiana, that together would total 100 or more GRPs per day. To achieve a 100 showing in Baton Rouge, Lamar Outdoor Advertising would place 30-sheet posters along all major traffic arteries, facing in both directions. Rates vary considerably from market to market due to variations in property rentals, labor costs, and market size. As Exhibit 18–4 shows, locations in larger markets with high traffic volume have higher rates. However, as a rule of thumb, a standard billboard costs around $500 per month. At that rate, billboards still offer the lowest cost per thousand (an average of $1.45 for 30 weekly GRPs) of any major mass medium.[10]

(continued on page 589)

Exhibit 18–4

Monthly rates for standard 30-sheet posters (approximately 12 by 25 feet) in selected metropolitan markets. Lamar Outdoor Advertising, 2004.

Market	Adult population	25 daily GRPs		50 daily GRPs		100 daily GRPs		Average cost for 100 daily GRPs
		Number	Cost	Number	Cost	Number	Cost	
Baton Rouge metro area	405,500	10	$ 6,700	20	$12,900	40	$23,100	$578
Boise	183,800	4	2,768	7	4,844	13	8,993	692
Buffalo metro area	787,800	24	18,890	48	36,675	96	63,505	662
Cincinnati metro area	1,159,100	23	15,129	46	29,598	92	57,340	623
Chicago suburbs	1,180,246	28	19,063	55	36,815	111	69,428	625
Las Vegas metro area	1,216,850	10	6,000	18	10,260	37*	19,973*	535*
Los Angeles (North County)	525,140	12	6,000	24	12,000	48	24,000	500
Omaha	575,000	8	4,600	17	9,520	33	17,655	535
Pittsburgh metro area	1,983,500	42	42,735	84	78,540	168	143,220	853
Savannah metro area	244,500	6	3,990	11	7,315	21	13,965	665

Note: Costs are for space only, based on a 30-day posting period; they do not include production.

*Approximation based on 75 GRPs.

As the oldest medium on Earth, outdoor advertising benefits from its inherent nature as a "sign" as well as the modern features of graphic design and technology. In fact, thanks to technology, advertisers can do things in outdoor today they couldn't have dreamed of just a few years ago. Plus, no other medium is this big—commanding attention from motorists and pedestrians 24 hours a day, seven days a week at a fraction of the cost of other media. However, outdoor is limited in what it can say. For normal outdoor structures on the highway, seven words is the rule-of-thumb. That places an additional burden on the nonverbal (artistic) aspects of the ad, and this definitely challenges the creative muscle of every advertiser's ad agency.

■ Study the ads in this portfolio to see how big, strategic ideas get translated into outstanding outdoor or transit advertising. Then consider why the advertiser chose this particular medium. Was outdoor or transit the right choice for this advertiser? Why? Or why not? Could the same concept be used in other media? How?

Out-of-Home Advertising

This poster, which blends photography with computer animation, won a Bronze Lion at Cannes. The disadvantage of an ad like this is that some may find it offensive; on the other hand, few will forget it.

When mounting a billboard campaign, successful advertisers keep copy to a minimum. This ad for Electrolux vacuums won a Gold Lion at Cannes for its simply stated, yet highly expressive, message.

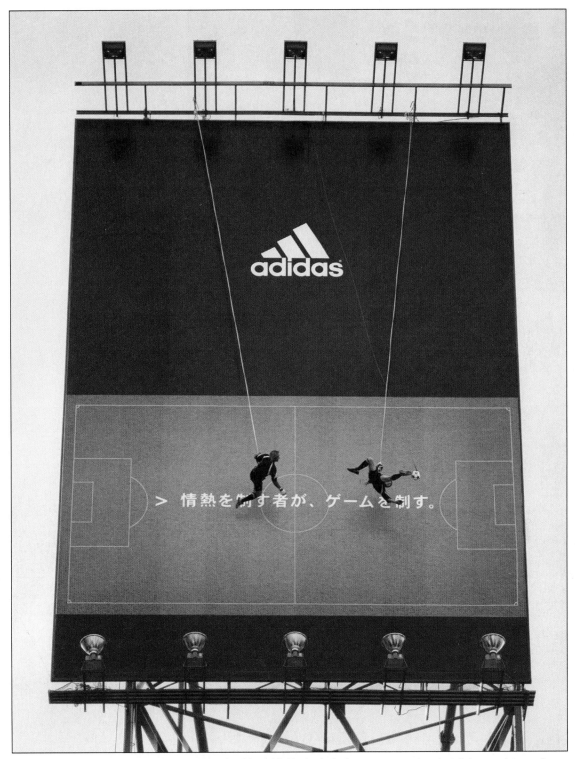

In the future, holograms will be able to take the role of these life-like football players. For now, though, Adidas is at the top of its game in this winning ad, which received a Gold Lion at Cannes.

This ad for Thompson Lab ingeniously employs another, more familiar logo, making both more memorable in the process. What may initially appear to be a mistake is quickly understood to be a deliberate omission. Moreover, viewers may be more likely to eye this billboard carefully, a natural reaction when encountering a presumed error. The smart alliance between form and content earned this ad a Bronze Lion at Cannes.

Motorists are reminded to drive carefully with this billboard for Diario Noticias. To help differentiate itself from other nearby billboards, this billboard takes advantage of a nearby light post by incorporating it in the ad. How well do you think this approach will work?

Amusing, unusual ads in unexpected places pique the viewer's interest and can be especially effective. This campaign, a Bronze Lion winner at Cannes, features cutout figures being blown away by air conditioning.

Unique and resourceful use of transit advertising is on display in this Bronze Lion award-winning bus design from the National Geographic Channel. The clever illusion created by the opening and closing of the bus doors is a concept that was sure to get people talking.

587

This life-like cutout poster of gorgeous hitchhikers immediately catches a driver's attention. Why do you think Nashua (www.nashua.com) chose this approach? What are the pros and cons of this kind of guerrilla advertising?

(continued from page 583)

Technology in Outdoor Advertising

In the past it was always a problem for a media buyer in New York to adequately supervise the posting of outdoor boards in Peoria, Illinois. A buyer can't just jump on a plane and travel to all the cities where the client's boards are posted to verify the value of the locations. Fortunately, though, new technology has helped solve this dilemma and has thus made outdoor an even more attractive medium to national advertisers. Today, outdoor companies can use sophisticated **global positioning systems (GPS)** to give the exact latitude and longitude of particular boards using satellite technology. Media buyers, equipped with sophisticated new software on their desktop computers, can then integrate this information with demographic market characteristics and traffic counts to determine the best locations for their boards.[11]

Some outdoor companies even provide digitized video of their locations so the buyer can see the actual board and the environment in which it is located. Other new developments include bar coding of materials so they can be tracked, posted, and authenticated, all by computer. Computerized painting on flexible vinyl is another recent breakthrough that guarantees a high-quality, high-resolution, faithful reproduction of the advertiser's message regardless of the market.[12]

One of the most exciting new technologies may change the future of how we "see" outdoor and other out-of-home ads. Hologrex, a Japanese computer software development company, has created a revolutionary program that can produce 3-D images on translucent film. When backlit, the 3-D image is visible to the naked eye, with no need for those stupid glasses. Imagine a bulletin-size structure on the highway, advertising the latest *Jurassic Park* sequel, with a larger-than-life T-Rex coming at you in 3-D. Thrilling possibilities—especially now that they're working on animating these images.

Regulation of Outdoor Advertising

The Highway Beautification Act of 1965 controls outdoor advertising on U.S. interstate highways and other federally subsidized highways. It was enacted partly in response to consumer complaints that outdoor advertising was spoiling the environment. Over 700,000 billboards were removed by 1991, the year Congress banned the construction of new billboards on all scenic portions of interstate highways.[13] Since that time, the image of outdoor advertising has improved dramatically. Today, most people polled say they like billboards, believe they promote business, and find them useful travel information for drivers.[14]

Each state also regulates, administers, and enforces outdoor advertising permit programs through its department of transportation. Some states (Maine, Vermont, Hawaii, and Alaska) prohibit outdoor advertising altogether. Ironically, though, some of these states use outdoor advertising themselves in other states to promote tourism (see the Ethical Issue, "Does Spillover Need Mopping Up?").

Transit Advertising

Back in 1910, Campbell Soup started advertising. The company spent its first $5,000 placing ads on one-third of the buses in New York City for one year. The ads were so successful that after only six months, Campbell enlarged the contract to include all surface vehicles in the city. People started trying more Campbell's and soon sales were up 100 percent. For the next 12 years, transit advertising was the only medium Campbell employed. Today, Campbell is still a major user of transit advertising.

Transit advertising is a category of out-of-home media that includes bus and taxicab advertising as well as posters on transit shelters, terminals, and subways. Although transit is not considered a major medium by most advertising

Does Spillover Need Mopping Up?

While numerous laws and self-regulatory efforts have banished products like tobacco and hard liquor from the airwaves, it is virtually impossible to keep minors from being exposed to such advertising due to the *spillover* nature of some media. The ethical issues involved with spillover media are complex, including the kind of advertising appeals used to target audiences.

Take outdoor advertising, for example. It is the most public mass medium. It cannot be turned off like television, radio, or the Internet, and it's displayed 24 hours a day for all to see—even children.

The trend in outdoor advertising today is toward eye-catching, sexually explicit ads, seen especially in high urban areas. Most outdoor advertising regulations have focused on the *location* of billboards, not the *content*. The Outdoor Advertising Association of America's (OAAA) Code of Principles says that they "support the right to reject advertising that is misleading, offensive, or otherwise incompatible with community standards." But it is unknown how often this clause is invoked. Communities, therefore, have taken it upon themselves to regulate the placement and content of outdoor advertising, rather than relying on self-regulation by the advertising industry. In 1998, for example, the Los Angeles City Council passed an ordinance that prohibited alcoholic beverage advertising on virtually all publicly visible sites, even store windows. The OAAA and other local Los Angeles trade association members filed a federal civil rights action, claiming that the ordinance violates the right to free speech.

As technology advances, so do the venues for advertising. Advertisers have found ways to work around billboard restrictions. Taxicabs and buses have carried ads for years; however, now appearing on Boston cabs are electronic billboards that have the ability to change their message minute by minute—depending on a few desired variables. Using a satellite feed and wireless Internet links, color messages change depending on time of day and location. Different neighborhoods will see different ads and, if appropriate, even different languages. The taxi's location is monitored by an Internet link to a satellite tracking system. This new technology is inexpensive for advertisers and may become a common feature on taxicabs across America. However, this raises legal and ethical questions. Should mobile billboards be subjected to the same restrictions as stationary billboards? Neighborhoods and schools may theoretically be protected from unwanted advertising, but can concerned parents protect their children from viewing advertising that travels on taxis?

---

practitioners, standardization, better research, more statistical data, and measured circulation have made transit advertising more attractive to national advertisers. National marketers of designer apparel and movies, for example, are two of the many categories of advertisers spending dramatically more in this medium, replacing the traditional transit advertising leaders such as petroleum products, financial services, and proprietary medicines.[15]

Transit advertising is especially suitable for reaching middle- to lower-income urban consumers and providing supplemental coverage of these groups. Patrick Media and Gannett Outdoor Group are using innovative marketing strategies to highlight both outdoor boards and transit ads in Hispanic communities, catering to marketers' increasing desire to tap into the $240 billion Hispanic market. Today, marketers like Coke, Pepsi, and Modelo Beer spend more than $20 million a year on out-of-home ads aimed at Hispanic consumers.[16]

Transit advertising is equally popular with local advertisers. Retailers can expand their reach inexpensively and often receive co-op support from national marketers, which thrive on the local exposure[17] (see the Checklist, "The Pros and Cons of Transit Advertising").

Types of Transit Advertising

Transit advertising targets the millions of people who use commercial transportation (buses, subways, elevated trains, commuter trains, trolleys, and airlines), plus pedestrians and car passengers, with a variety of formats: transit shelters; station, platform, and terminal posters; inside cards and outside posters on buses; and taxi exteriors.

Transit Shelters

In cities with mass-transit systems, advertisers can buy space on bus shelters and on the backs of bus-stop seats. **Transit shelter advertising** is a relatively new out-of-home form enjoying great success. It reaches virtually everyone who is outdoors: auto passengers, pedestrians, bus riders, motorcyclists, bicyclists, and more. It is extremely inexpensive and available in many communities that restrict billboard advertising in business or residential areas. In fact, shelter advertising is sometimes the only form of outdoor advertising permitted. It's also an excellent complement to outdoor posters and bulletins, enabling total market coverage in a comprehensive outdoor program.

Spillover also reaches children in other media vehicles besides out-of-home. The movies, for example, consistently show people smoking. And if the smoker is a celebrity, an impressionable child might interpret that as an endorsement. In a study conducted by Dartmouth Medical School, researchers concluded that actor endorsements of tobacco brands jumped tenfold in the 1990s. The study also found that 87 percent of popular movies contain tobacco use and about one-third display identifiable brand-name logos. Minors make up a large percentage of moviegoers and through movies they may be getting more exposure to smoking endorsements than in real life. Young people who look up to sport stars and movie celebrities may be vulnerable to intentional and unintentional endorsements. Benedict Carey of the *Los Angeles Times* calls today's movies "almost as smoke-laden as the stock car racing circuit."

Many people feel that ads are not to blame for the rise of teen sexual activity and tobacco and alcohol use. Others feel that advertisers have a greater responsibility to separate youth from the adult world of unhealthy and explicit activity. Regardless of who is right, advertisers, agencies, and media companies must be sensitive to public opinion and seek creative solutions to protect impressionable children. Otherwise, the industry will risk severe restriction and regulation for having failed to responsibly and conscientiously assert firm ethical standards itself.

Questions

1. Do you believe the goal of protecting children justifies banning advertising for legal products? Which products specifically?

2. Should ads in spillover media be censored for sexually explicit content? If so, who should the censors be and what specifically should they prohibit?

3. What alternatives might be available to fight teenage smoking, drinking, and sexual promiscuity besides banning advertising for legal adult products?

Sources: "Los Angeles Alcoholic Beverage Ban Statement," Outdoor Advertising Association of America, September 30, 1999 (retrieved from www.oaaa.org, April 2001); Benedict Carey, "Cigarettes Are Doing Big Box Office," *Los Angeles Times*, January 8, 2001; OAAA Code of Principles (retrieved from www.oaaa.org/government); Jon P. Nelson, "Advertising Bans in the United States," May 21, 2004 (retrieved from http://econ.la.psu.edu/papers/adbans_critical.pdf); "Tobacco Menace," Consumer-Voice.org (retrieved from www.consumer-voice.org/tobacco/tobacco3.htm); "Beer Advertising Facts," Beer Institute (retrieved from www.beerinstitute.org/pdfs/beeradfacts.pdf); David Goetz, "Liquor Industry Gets Stricter on Advertising," *The Courier-Journal*, September 10, 2003 (retrieved from www.courier-journal.com/business); "Framework Convention on Tobacco Control," Health Canada, October 2002 (retrieved from www.hc-sc.gc.ca/english/media/releases/2002/2002_66bk.htm).

Terminal Posters

In many bus, subway, and commuter train stations, space is sold for one-, two-, and three-sheet **terminal posters.** Major train and airline terminals offer such special advertising forms as floor displays, island showcases, illuminated cards, dioramas (3-D scenes), and clocks with special lighting and moving messages.

In Paris, Nike made a splash at the French Open tennis tournament even though a competitor had locked up advertising rights within the stadium. Nike covered the city by buying space on some 2,500 buses during the tournament. As the coup de grace, it bought up every bit of signage space at the Porte d'Auteuil metro (subway) station close to the stadium and turned it into a Nike gallery of terminal posters featuring famous tennis players from around the world.[18]

Inside and Outside Cards and Posters

The **inside card** is placed in a wall rack above the vehicle windows. Cost-conscious advertisers print both sides of the card so it can be reversed to change the message, saving on paper and shipping charges. Inside **car-end posters** (in bulkhead positions) are usually larger than inside cards, but sizes vary. The end and side positions carry premium rates.

Outdoor advertising doesn't consist of billboards only. Customers entering the parking lot to fetch their cars are met with this inventive ad for the Fiat, which employs photographic adhesives to create a lifelike image. Can you imagine the effect this might have on a person whose car is in fact in need of work? The ingenuity of this ad won it a Bronze Lion at Cannes.

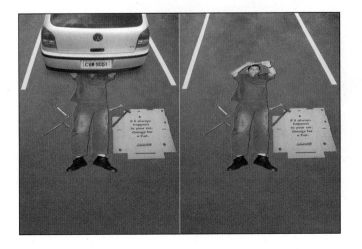

Checklist

The Pros and Cons of Transit Advertising

The Pros

____ **Long exposure.** The average transit ride is 25 minutes.

____ **Repetitive value.** Many people take the same routes day after day.

____ **Eagerly read messages.** Riders get bored, so readership is high and ad recall averages 55 percent.

____ **Low cost.** Transit ads cost less than any other medium.

____ **Creative flexibility.** Special constructions and color effects are available at relatively low cost.

____ **Need satisfying.** Transit can target the needs of riders—with ads for cool drinks in summer, for example. Food ads do well as evening riders contemplate dinner.

____ **Environmentally sensitive.** As social pressure to use public transportation increases, transit is well positioned as a medium of the future.

The Cons

____ **Status.** Transit lacks the status of the major advertising media, like print and broadcast.

____ **Crowded environment.** Rush-hour crowding limits the opportunity and ease of reading. The vehicle itself, if dirty, may tarnish the product's image.

____ **Selectivity.** Transit reaches a nonselective audience, which may not meet the needs of some advertisers.

____ **Clutter.** Cards are so numerous and look so similar they may be confusing or hard to remember.

____ **Location.** With outlying shopping malls, fewer shoppers make trips downtown.

____ **Creative restrictions.** Although transit cards may carry longer messages than billboards, copy is still limited.

Outside posters are printed on high-grade cardboard and often varnished for weather resistance. The most widely used outside posters are on the side, rear, and front of a bus. (See RL 18–1 in the Reference Library on the *Contemporary Advertising* CD for common sizes and placement of inside cards and outside transit posters.)

Advertisers may also buy space on **taxicab exteriors,** generally for periods of 30 days, to display internally illuminated, two-sided posters positioned on the roofs. Some advertising also appears on the doors or rear of taxicabs. In some major areas, sponsors can buy cards mounted on the trunks. In Southern California, advertisers can rent cards mounted on the tops of cabs that travel throughout Los Angeles, Orange, and San Diego counties, serving major airports and traveling the busiest freeways in the country. Costing from $110 to $130 per month per cab, this is a very cost-effective way to reach the mobile public.

Buying Transit Advertising

The unit of purchase is a **showing,** also known as a *run* or *service*. A **full showing** (or *No. 100 showing*) means that one card will appear in each vehicle in the system. Space may also be purchased as a *half* (No. 50) or *quarter* (No. 25) *showing*.

Rates are usually quoted for 30-day showings, with discounts for 3-, 6-, 9-, and 12-month contracts. Advertisers supply the cards at their own expense, but the transit company can help with design and production.

Cost depends on the length and saturation of the showing and the size of the space. Rates vary extensively, depending primarily on the size of the transit system. Advertisers get rates for specific markets from local transit companies and the Transit Advertising Association's *TAA Rate Directory of Transit Advertising*.

The Transit Advertising Association is the national trade organization and promotion arm of the industry. It performs research and supplies industry data on the number of vehicles, trends, and rider demographics. TAA members represent 80 percent of the transit advertising volume in the United States and Canada.

The headline in this clever poster campaign says, "Doesn't hurt at all." It's for a competitively priced health insurance plan in Hong Kong.

Special Inside Buys

In some cities, advertisers gain complete domination by buying the **basic bus**—all the inside space on a group of buses. For an extra charge, pads of business reply cards or coupons (called **take-ones**) can be affixed to interior ads for passengers to request more detailed information, send in application blanks, or receive some other benefit.

Special Outside Buys

Some transit companies offer **bus-o-rama signs,** jumbo full-color transparencies backlighted by fluorescent tubes and running the length of the bus. A bus has two bus-o-rama positions, one on each side. A single advertiser may also buy a **total bus**—all the exterior space, including the front, rear, sides, and top.

For years, New York subways have been running **brand trains,** which include all the subway cars in a particular corridor. However, with the July 2004 opening of its monorail system, the city of Las Vegas has taken the concept further. The glitz of the city's strip extends to its public transportation: Each of the nine monorail trains and seven stations has a corporate sponsor, and many feature elaborate **immersive advertising** themes. City officials banked on the monorail system, which is entirely funded by passenger fares instead of tax dollars, to generate at least $6.5 million annually in advertising revenue. However, with the help of ad agency Promethean Partners, ad revenues are now expected to be at least three times that amount. Consider the deal that the city struck with Nextel, estimated at $50 million. The company has signed on for a 12-year sponsorship of one train and the system's "crown jewel," the main station at the Las Vegas Convention Center, which more than 1 million annual visitors are expected to pass through each year.[19] Nextel is even paying construction costs for the station, which is adjacent to company's largest retail venture yet, the full-service, interactive Nextel Pavilion and Theater. Motorola, Bacardi, Coca-Cola, and General Motors are also negotiating train and station sponsorship deals.

Clever out-of-home buys can give public exposure and cut through advertising clutter in a spectacular way. The Firm, a workout studio in Minneapolis, came up with this creative way to get attention and people's hearts racing.

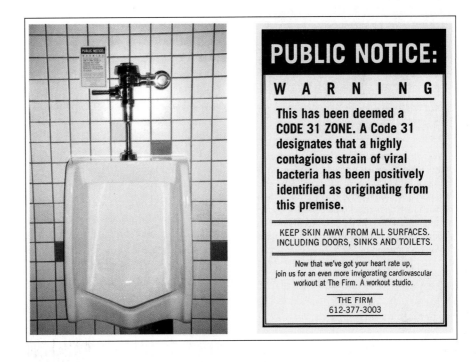

Other Out-of-Home Media

As mentioned earlier, there are many forms of out-of-home media. Some are so new that they are still unproven. However, several seem to be gaining in popularity, and they demonstrate how far advertisers will go to get their messages seen by the consuming public.

Mobile Billboards

The **mobile billboard,** a cross between traditional billboards and transit advertising, was conceived as advertising on the sides of tractor-trailer trucks. Today in some large cities, specially designed flatbed trucks carry long billboards up and down busy thoroughfares. Local routes for mobile ads are also available on delivery trucks in San Francisco, Los Angeles, and Seattle.

Electronic Signs and Display Panels

Electronic signs display text and graphic messages much like the big screens in sports stadiums. The signs transmit commercial messages to retail stores, where shoppers see them. The stores pay nothing for the signs and receive 25 percent of the advertising revenue. In Montreal, Telecite used its new visual communication network (VCN) technology to install electronic display panels on subway cars. Advertisers got a powerful, inexpensive, and flexible medium with a large, captive audience; the transit authority got a modern, self-financed emergency and public information system; and passengers got something to watch while they ride.[20] Telecite is negotiating with numerous U.S. and European cities to install the systems in their subway and metro cars.

Parking Meters and Public Phones

Thanks to a couple of enterprising companies, American Parking Meter Advertising and American Telephone Advertising (ATA), marketers can now advertise on parking meters and public phones. ATA offers 20 market segments, such as hotels, restaurants, airports, college campuses, and convenience stores.

Exhibitive Media

Some media are designed specifically to help bring customers eyeball to eyeball with the product—often at the point of sale or close to it. These **exhibitive media** include *product packaging* and *trade-show booths and exhibits.* When successful, the synergy of combining exhibitive media with other media can improve product or brand awareness by as much as 500 percent.[21]

Product Packaging

In 1996, U.S. companies spent some $95 billion on packaging (as much as they spent on media advertising).[22] Since upward of 70 percent of all buying decisions are made at the point of purchase, packages play a major role in both advertising and selling. And in the world of integrated marketing communications, the package is not only the last "ad" a consumer sees before purchasing the product, it is the only "ad" the consumer sees when using the product. So it is more than just another *planned message.* Packaging influences the *product message* as well, since (as we discussed in Chapter 6) it is often an intrinsic aspect of the basic product concept.

Packaging encompasses the physical appearance of the container and includes design, color, shape, labeling, and materials. Packaging serves marketers in four major ways: protection, preservation, information, and promotion.[23] Although the protection and preservation aspects reduce the costly effects of damage, pilferage, and spoilage, the importance of packaging as an informational and promotional tool cannot be underestimated. An attractive package can create an immediate relationship with the customer, influence in-store shopping decisions, help set the product apart from competitors, and inform customers of the product's features and benefits.

Designers consider three factors: the package's stand-out appeal, how it communicates verbally and nonverbally, and the prestige or image desired.

Consumers respond to packaging intuitively, so packaging design can be as important as advertising in building a product's brand image. Packaging establishes or reinforces the brand's personality at the point of sale. So if status is the goal, the

Packaging is an extremely important medium since it typically serves as the last advertising a consumer sees before taking the product home. Plus, package design plays a major role in how the quality of the product is perceived. Good packaging can often make or break the deal for a consumer. This packaging was created in both English and Russian by WPF Depot in Moscow.

package designer must consider what consumers regard as prestigious. This is especially important for so-called nonrational products—cosmetics and perfumes, sports accessories, confection gifts, and certain luxury products—in which fantasy, impulsiveness, or mystique may overrule rational choice.

To sell products off the shelf, packages may use shape, color, size, interesting visuals, or even texture to deliver a marketing message, give product information, and indicate application. After they are purchased, packages continue promoting the product in the home, reinforcing the brand's image, so they should open and close with minimal effort and be easy to handle.

Buying packaging includes two major phases: *concept* and *production*. The *conceptual process* involves input from five major groups: consumers, manufacturers, marketing intermediaries, consumer advocacy groups, and government agencies.[24] The conflicting concerns of these groups strongly influence the nature and the cost of packaging (see Exhibit 18–5).

Environmental Issues in Packaging

As manufacturers continue to produce environmentally safe packaging, the marketer's cost of materials rises. And what some consumers expect from *green packaging* is not necessarily what manufacturers traditionally offer or what marketing intermediaries prefer to use.[25]

With the public's growing concern for the environment, especially in international markets, recyclable tin-coated steel and aluminum packages are enjoying a resurgence in popularity. Because European countries are so densely populated, their regulations requiring environmentally friendly packaging are far more stringent than in North America. Marketers need to take this into consideration since such regulations add to the cost of doing business overseas.

Government Impact on Packaging

Government agencies also affect package design. The Food and Drug Administration (FDA), for example, and the Nutrition Labeling and Education Act of 1990

Exhibit 18–5

Expectations and concerns in packaging development.

Consumers	Manufacturers	Marketing intermediaries (retailers/ wholesalers)	Consumer advocacy groups	Government agencies
Ease (to handle and store)	Sturdiness	Sturdiness (of case and packages)	Package safe to:	Free of deception
Convenience	Suppleness	Convenience (of removal)	– handle	Free of harmful effects to ecology
List of ingredients	Attractiveness	Tamper proof	– use	Biodegradable
Instructions	Safety (to users and for the product)	Identifiable	Environmentally safe (biodegradability, etc.)	Free of health hazards
Life of product	Cost of:	Safety (to users and for the product)	Package free of health hazards	All-around safety
Disposal method	– materials	Ease of:	Self-informative	– Safe to handle
Toll-free phone number for emergencies	– fabrication	– storage	– List of ingredients	– Safe to use
Performance guarantees	– labor	– shelving stacking	– Instructions	Labeled properly
Safety guarantees	– inventory	– package stacking	– Disposal method	– List of ingredients
Environmental safety (biodegradability)	– shipping	– inventory (by computer)	– Toll-free phone number for emergencies	– Nutritional facts with guidelines
Reusable	– storage	Room for price	– Warranties	Expiration date for certain products
Recyclable	Need to change	Stickers	– Expiration date	Recyclable
	Lighter weight (with safety)		Recyclable	Adherence to federal and local regulations
	Tamper proof		Adherence to federal and local regulations	
	Package size (promotion space versus materials cost and environmental safety)			
	Availability of materials			

There are many different types of packaging available. In this very creative example for Hollywood Video, Sandstrom Design came up with tins of peanuts with names that are reminiscent of famous movie titles.

(which went into effect in 1994) imposed stricter labeling requirements for nutrition and health products. And sometimes a state's packaging requirements differ from the federal government's, adding even more complexity for manufacturers.

Package Manufacturing

Packages may come in many forms: wrappers, cartons, boxes, crates, cans, bottles, jars, tubes, barrels, drums, and pallets. And they may be constructed of many materials, from paper and steel ("tin" cans) to wood, glass, and burlap. Newer packaging materials include plastic-coated papers, ceramics, metal foils, and even straw. Improvements in packaging include amber-green glass bottles that protect the contents from light damage and heavy-duty, gray computer-disk jackets that reflect heat and protect the disk. The plastic film pouch for food products has become a substitute for tin cans and is more flexible, light, and compact. For pharmaceutical products, consumers prefer plastic containers.[26]

The second phase of packaging, the *production process,* may require the use of many packaging specialists: experts in package engineering (box designers, packaging materials consultants, and specialists in equipment configuration); graphic artists (designers, production/computer artists, illustrators, and photographers); label producers (printers and label manufacturers); die-cutters for custom packages; and package warehousing companies (wholesalers of prefabricated packages and package manufacturers). (See RL 18–2: The Packaging Production Process, in the Reference Library on the *Contemporary Advertising* CD.)

Ad agencies are not usually involved in packaging decisions. This is typically the realm of specialists. However, it's not uncommon for an agency to be consulted on the design of labels and packages, and some may even prepare the copy that goes on them. In an IMC program, the agency can be very helpful in coordinating this work with the overall theme of the ad campaign.

Generally, the package's design should be kept simple for three reasons: Typical packaging materials (such as corrugated cardboard) cannot support high-resolution printing, intricate folding and die-cutting can be very expensive, and packaging that requires exact folding and fitting often creates excessive assembly costs and leads to structural challenges that most cost-effective packaging materials cannot support.[27]

When Should a Package Be Changed?

There are many reasons to change a package: product alteration or improvement, substitution in packaging materials, competitive pressure, environmental concerns, changes in legislation, or the need to increase brand recognition.[28]

Advertisers spend millions researching and promoting new images. And packages have to reflect a contemporary brand image consistent with constantly changing consumer perceptions and desires. However, marketers should always exercise caution. Designers often change packaging very gradually to avoid confusing consumers.

Trade-Show Booths and Exhibits

Every major industry sponsors annual **trade shows**—exhibitions where manufacturers, dealers, and buyers get together for demonstrations and discussion. More than 9,000 industrial, scientific, and medical shows are held in the United States each year, and many companies exhibit at more than one show. Trade shows are

This trade show booth for Shiseido uses projection technology to put subtle images of the cosmetic company's packages on the wall. With upscale cosmetics, the goal is lightness, naturalness, purity, and radiance. Note the use of lighting, colors, and seeming transparency to achieve those same qualities in the booth.

also very important for global marketers, because they may be the only place where an advertiser can meet the company's major international prospects at one time. Moreover, some of the world's largest trade shows (the Paris Air Show, for example) are held overseas.

The construction of trade-show **booths** and **exhibits** has become a major factor in sales promotion plans. To stop traffic, a booth must be simple and attractive and have good lighting and a large visual. It should also provide a comfortable atmosphere to promote conversation between salespeople and prospects. Many regular trade-show exhibitors use state-of-the-art technology, such as holograms, fiber optics, and interactive computer systems, to communicate product features quickly and dramatically.

When establishing an exhibit booth program, managers should consider planning, budgeting, promotion, people, and productivity.[29]

Planning

Planning pivots on four major areas: the budget, the image of the company or brand, the frequency of the shows, and the flexibility of booth configuration.[30] In planning the actual exhibits or trade-show booths, advertisers need to consider numerous factors: size and location of space; desired image or impression of the exhibit; complexities of shipping, installation, and dismantling; number of products to be displayed; need for storage and distribution of literature; use of preshow advertising and promotion; and the cost of all these factors.

Budgeting

Trade shows are expensive, and costs have increased substantially in the last decade. A large company may spend $1 million or more on a booth for one trade show. With staffers' travel, living, and salary expenses added to booth costs and

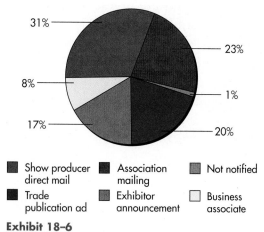

- ■ Show producer direct mail
- ■ Trade publication ad
- ■ Association mailing
- ■ Exhibitor announcement
- ■ Not notified
- □ Business associate

Exhibit 18–6

How do customers learn about trade shows?

preshow promotion, the cost per visitor reached rises to more than \$185.[31] Despite the expense, trade shows can still be a cost-effective way to reach sales prospects.

Budgeting for trade shows and a booth may require an extensive review of more than 60 factors (see RL 18–3: Trade-Show Budgeting Checklist, in the Reference Library on the *Contemporary Advertising* CD).

Promotion

To build traffic for a trade-show booth or exhibit, marketers send out personal invitations, conduct direct-mail campaigns, place ads in trade publications, issue news releases, and perform telemarketing. The pie chart in Exhibit 18–6 portrays how customers typically learn about the trade shows they attend.[32]

At the show itself, activities at the booth and promotional materials (handouts, brochures, giveaway specialty items, raffles) can stimulate customer interest and improve product exposure. 3M's Telcomm Products Division mailed 6,000 potential show attendees a Pony Express theme folder that invited them to pick up a trail map at the booth. The map guided the visitors (Pony Express riders) through a series of stations shared by seven product groups within the huge booth. Once the visitors' maps had been stamped at each station, they were given a "pay envelope" containing replicas of 1850 coins and vouchers redeemable for merchandise awards.[33]

People

The company representatives staffing the booth personify the kind of service the customer can expect to receive. They should be articulate, people-oriented, enthusiastic, knowledgeable about the product, and empathetic listeners.[34]

The primary goal of a trade-show booth is to meet with qualified prospects face to face. However, research shows that 58 percent of the people visiting a booth will not wait more than one minute to meet a representative (see Exhibit 18–7). Ideally, 80 percent of the salesperson's time should be spent listening and 20 percent talking.[35]

Productivity

A company's trade-show effort may be wasted if prospects' names are not collected and organized properly. Each lead should be evaluated as to the prospect's readiness to receive another contact (A = now; B = 2 weeks; C = 6 months; D = never).[36] The resulting lead list is the link to future sales and augments the company's prospect database.

Supplementary Media

Many promotional media are difficult to classify because they are tailored to individual needs. Such supplementary media include specialty advertising, directories and Yellow Pages, and a variety of emerging alternative media vehicles.

Specialty Advertising

The Promotional Products Association International (PPAI) defines an **advertising specialty** as a promotional product, usually imprinted with an advertiser's name, message, or logo, that is distributed free as part of a marketing communications program.[37] Today, nearly every business uses advertising specialties of some sort. As many as 15,000 different specialty items, ranging from coffee mugs to ballpoint pens, key chains, and T-shirts, represent an annual volume of more than \$6 billion.[38]

An advertising specialty is different from a premium. **Premiums** are also promotional products; they are typically more valuable and usually bear no advertising mes-

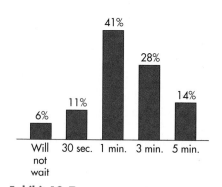

Exhibit 18–7

How long a visitor will wait for a sales rep at a trade-show booth.

Fossil Watches (www.fossil.com) used this specialty packaging as a gift to consumers. The container is modeled after automotive oil cans and is reusable. This novelty gift is more useful and appealing than the typical key chain or pencil. The text proclaims the quality and style of the watch that can be found inside and serves as both a reminder to the customer and an ad for others who see it.

sage. However, to get a premium, recipients must buy a product, send in a coupon, witness a demonstration, or perform some other action advantageous to the advertiser. An advertising specialty, on the other hand, is always given *free* as a goodwill item. Some specialty items may be kept for years and serve as continuous, friendly reminders of the advertiser's business. Companies often spend substantial sums for goodwill items to promote customer referrals. In fact, some studies show that recipients of advertising specialties are typically better referrers than nonrecipients.[39]

Consumer Specialties

Consumers associate the quality of a specialty item with the organization providing it, so companies tend to lean toward more expensive gifts. Items costing $3 to $5 have become the norm, as opposed to cheap key rings and pencils. Specialties work best when they are integrated into a broader marketing program or service strategy. For some businesses, like banks and savings and loans, the government regulates the value of gifts they can give.

Business-to-Business Specialties

In the business-to-business arena, companies use more structured specialty promotions to improve their goodwill standing over competitors. In one case, including an ad specialty with a thank-you letter improved customer attitude by 34 percent compared to sending a thank-you letter alone. At the same time, customers' general feelings about the company and its sales reps improved 52 percent.[40]

In one test, a group of realtors received a $1.49 ballpoint pen imprinted with a mortgage company's name, a second group received a $10 sports bag (also imprinted), and a third group got nothing. In a follow-up questionnaire, Realtors who received nothing were least inclined to recommend the product, but both the sports bag and ballpoint groups responded equally positively. Evidently, gift recipients felt obliged to reciprocate, but the value of the gift was not crucial. So the $1.49 pen was the better return on investment.[41]

Inappropriate specialty items can backfire no matter what the cost. A recipient may perceive an overly expensive gift as a form of bribery, yet a cheap trinket could make a quality-conscious business look cheap. Finally, marketers should realize that the value and nature of gifts may raise ethical issues.

Directories and Yellow Pages

Thousands of **directories** are published each year by phone companies, trade associations, industrial groups, and others. They mainly serve as locators, buying guides, and mailing lists, but they also carry advertising aimed at specialized fields. When Yellow Pages advertising is combined with other media, reach increases significantly, as illustrated in Exhibit 18–8. In Yellow Pages ads, content is most important. The ad should tell people *how* to make the purchase, not why. As with most advertising media, the larger the ad, the more attention it attracts.[42]

The United States has about 6,000 local telephone directories with a combined circulation of 350 million. Since deregulation of the phone industry and the 1984 breakup of AT&T, the Yellow Pages business has boomed, with ad revenues reaching over $14 billion in 2004.[43] In fact, the Yellow Pages is now the fourth-largest medium, ahead of radio, magazines, and outdoor. The five largest publishers (see

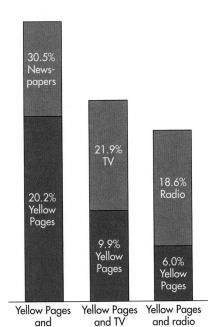

Exhibit 18–8

Overall advertising reach from media combinations. When Yellow Pages advertising is used in conjunction with other media, reach increases significantly.

Exhibit 18–9

Top Yellow Pages directory publishers by revenue, 2003.

Rank	Publisher	Revenues ($ billions)
1	SBC Communications	$4.478
2	Verizon Communications	4.114
3	BellSouth Corp.	1.906
4	Dex Media (formerly QWest Dex)	1.631
5	Yellow Book USA (Yell Group)	1.023

Exhibit 18–9) account for more than 90 percent of the industry's revenues.[44] However, competition is possible because the Yellow Pages name and walking fingers logo are not trademarked. Some 250 independent publishers produce Yellow Pages directories, and market share for these companies is steadily increasing.

Stiff competition has forced phone and directory companies to differentiate their Yellow Pages with more user-friendly directories containing supplemental general-interest information. Techniques being used include

- An alphabetical index grouping related headings beneath a consumer description of the product.
- A brand-name index listing the Yellow Pages heading where a specific brand can be found.
- A subject index that groups headings by broad areas, such as Automotive; Entertainment and Leisure; Health and Well-Being; Just for Kids; and Pets.
- Pages with local maps and information on parks, events, community services, transportation, and shopping.
- Free interactive voice services ("audiotext") that link the telephone with a host computer to allow the easy retrieval of information.

In addition, highly specialized directories aim at particular audiences, such as the Chinese-language Yellow Pages in San Francisco and the Paginas Amarillas in the border states.

Yellow Pages are often the sole advertising medium for local businesses, and nearly 85 percent of Yellow Pages revenue is derived from local advertisers.[45] But Yellow Pages directories can be an important medium for national advertisers, too. For example, U-Haul spends more than $20 million a year on Yellow Pages ads. The Yellow Pages Publishers Association created the BrandSell program for national packaged-goods advertisers whose products have no specific Yellow Pages heading. BrandSell enables a toothpaste manufacturer, say, to advertise under the "Dentists" heading and a telephone calling-card company to advertise in the "Airlines" section.

A growing number of publishers now offer a "ride-along" program that lets regional and national marketers deliver coupons and product samples along with the white and Yellow Pages directories. The ride-along program now reaches about 75 percent of the top 300 markets, resulting in a potential audience of 60 million households.[46]

Emerging Media

As traditional advertising media become more expensive and audiences become more fragmented, many advertisers seek new ways to reach their customers. Several types of alternative media are potentially viable options.

Videotapes

People rent millions of videos every week. However, as we discussed in Chapter 16, commercials on movie videos are controversial and have not achieved much success. In a less intrusive approach, ads are placed on the videocassette boxes. A third type of video advertising is the **video brochure,** which advertisers produce and mail to customers and prospects.

Cinema Advertising

Advertising in movie theaters (**cinema advertising**) is a growing but controversial practice. Some audiences boo and hiss during commercials, but studies show that 77 percent of viewers recall theater ads the following day, compared with 20 percent for TV ads.[47] Cinema advertising grew to a $315 million industry in 2003, up 48 percent from 2002.[48] Nonetheless, some movie theater chains prohibit filmed advertising for fear of offending their audience. Walt Disney Studios no longer allows U.S. theaters to run commercials before any of its movies.

Product placement is an increasingly popular way to advertise consumer products. In a recent James Bond movie, Die Another Day, *the international superspy races around in a DB5, one of Aston Martin's latest sassy automobiles. Car companies typically donate the cars used and also pay a hefty fee to have their products showcased.*

Product Placement

Another way to reach movie and television audiences is to pay a fee to have the product written into the movie or program. Such **product placement** is becoming more common—and more controversial. Notice the number of identifiable products in the next movie you see.

Increasingly, product placement in the multibillion dollar movie industry has become an important advertising medium. By getting their brands appearances, and sometimes roles, in movies, companies benefit from the association with top films and big-name actors. Nokia has had great success with this technique: Its phones were so prominent in the 1999 film *The Matrix* that 31 percent of moviegoers thought that characters in 2003's *The Matrix Reloaded* sequel were still using Nokia phones, when in fact they had switched to Samsung.[49]

Constantly fretting about viewers' newfound ability to avoid commercials by using TiVo, advertisers are also embedding their products more frequently in television programs. Ford and Coca-Cola both had high-profile presences on *American Idol*—judges drank from red cups with the Coca-Cola logo and contestants performed in Ford vehicles—is but one example in the emerging "brand casting" trend, worth an estimated $300 million in 2003.[50]

However, controversy surrounds some product placement categories. In response to severe new laws prohibiting most forms of tobacco advertising, the Canadian Tobacco Manufacturers' Council withdrew all product placements in films, videotapes, TV programs, and computer games.

ATMs

These days it seems you can't travel one city block without running into the omnipresent automated teller machine (ATM), a fact that marketers are well aware of. With so many thousands of money devices in service, it's only natural that the captive audience of this medium be targeted for creative promotional tactics.

Fleet Financial Group has capitalized on ATM technology by printing retailer coupons on the back of ATM receipts, the other piece of paper that customers receive from the machines. The coupons, which were initially redeemable at Bruegger's Bagels, Firestone, Great Cuts, Oil Doctor, and Pizza Hut, originated in Massachusetts and provided advertising that customers were likely to carry around in their wallets or cars.

Marketers are quickly filling every space where advertisements might be seen by an unsuspecting customer. From blimps to video game placements to parking meters, advertisers go where consumers congregate. Today, we can even find short video clip ads played on selected ATMs across the country.

The newest ATM innovation, developed by Electronic Data Systems Corp., puts full-motion video ads on the machine's screen as customers wait for their transaction to be processed. The 15-second ads, which debuted in 7-Eleven stores in San Diego, replace the "Transaction being processed" or "Please wait" messages that appeared on the screen. The original ads promoted Fox Searchlight Pictures' films *The Ice Storm* and *The Full Monty*.

Other promotions run through ATM machines include a MasterCard International and Coca-Cola USA collaboration on the "Coca-Cola incredible summer," in which customers could win cash instantly by using a special disposable ATM card.

Chapter Summary

Media that reach prospects outside their homes are called out-of-home media. They include outdoor advertising, transit advertising, and exotica like electronic signs and parking meters. Of the major advertising media, outdoor advertising is the least expensive per message delivered. It also offers other attractive features: instant broad coverage (reach), very high frequency, great flexibility, and high impact. Drawbacks include the limits of brief messages, long lead times, high initial preparation costs, and the difficulty of physically inspecting each billboard.

The standardized outdoor advertising industry consists of about 3,000 local and regional plant operators. National advertising makes up the bulk of outdoor business. The three most common forms of outdoor advertising structures are the 30-sheet poster, the eight-sheet poster, and the bulletin. A form of outdoor available in some cities is the spectacular, an expensive electronic display. The basic unit of sale for outdoor advertising is the 100 showing, or 100 GRPs, which means the message will appear on enough panels to provide a daily exposure equal to the market's total population.

Transit advertising includes transit shelters; station, platform, and terminal posters; inside cards and outside posters on buses; and taxi exteriors. This medium offers high reach, frequency, exposure, and attention values at very low cost. It gives long exposure to the advertiser's message and offers repetitive value and geographic flexibility. In addition, advertisers have a wide choice in the size of space used.

But transit advertising does not cover some segments of society. Also, it reaches a nonselective audience, it lacks prestige, and copy is still somewhat limited.

Other out-of-home media include mobile billboards, electronic signs and display panels, parking meters, and public phones.

Exhibitive media include product packaging and trade-show booths and exhibits. These media are designed to help bring consumers or business customers eyeball to eyeball with the product, often at the point of sale or close to it.

Supplementary media include specialty advertising, Yellow Pages directories, and emerging media like videotapes, movie theaters, product placements, and ATMs. Product placement includes films, videos, computer games, and the Internet. The advantage of film is that it creates brand association with top movies and actors.

ATMs provide several means of exposure, from printed ads on receipts to full-motion video to promotionals like ATM-card cash giveaways. Because most Americans today use ATMs, they offer a high frequency of exposure.

Important Terms

advertising specialty, *598*

basic bus, *593*

booth, *597*

brand trains, *593*

bulletin structure, *581*

bus-o-rama sign, *593*

car-end poster, *591*

cinema advertising, *600*

directories, *599*

eight-sheet poster, *582*

electronic sign, *594*

exhibit, *597*

exhibitive media, *594*

full showing, *592*

global positioning system (GPS), *589*

immersive advertising, *593*

inside card, *591*

mobile billboard, *594*

100 showing, *582*

out-of-home media, *578*

outside poster, *592*

packaging, *594*

premium, *598*

product placement, *601*

showing, *592*

spectaculars, *582*

standardized outdoor advertising, *579*

stock poster, *582*

take-ones, *593*

taxicab exterior, *592*

terminal poster, *591*

30-sheet poster panel, *582*

total bus, *593*

trade show, *596*

transit advertising, *589*

transit shelter advertising, *590*

video brochure, *600*

Review Questions

1. What is the difference between out-of-home media and outdoor advertising?
2. Why is outdoor advertising sometimes referred to as the last mass medium?
3. Which advertising objectives are the outdoor media most suitable for?
4. Is outdoor an effective advertising medium for a local political candidate? Why?
5. How do gross rating points for outdoor media differ from GRPs for electronic media?
6. What are the principal categories of transit advertising?
7. What is a brand train and what advantages does it offer over less expensive forms of transit advertising?
8. Which are the exhibitive media and why are they called that?
9. What is the principal benefit of trade shows and exhibitions?
10. How does specialty advertising differ from premiums? How could a local computer store use these media, and which would be better for the store to use?
11. **The Advertising Experience**

    Upshaw Books, the largest independent bookstore in the area, wants to advertise on billboards along the area's main commuter route. Create a series of three standard billboards that would grab commuters' attention and motivate them to visit the store.

Exploring the Internet

The Internet exercises for Chapter 18 address the following areas covered throughout the chapter: outdoor advertising (Exercise 1) and specialty advertising (Exercises 2 and 3).

1. **Outdoor Advertising**

   As you have learned in this chapter, out-of-home advertising and communication have been a mainstay in consumers' lives for quite some time. The outdoor advertising industry certainly makes up the largest portion of such advertising.

   Although often overlooked in advertising and media decision making, outdoor can have a powerful effect as a supplemental medium to broader print or broadcast campaigns. Now, find out more about this side of the advertising business by visiting five of the websites for the outdoor advertising organizations below and answer the questions that follow.

   - Burkhart Advertising www.burkhartadv.com
   - Edwards Outdoor www.edwards1.com
   - Eight-Sheet Outdoor Association www.eightsheet.com
   - Eller Media www.ellermedia.com
   - Gallop & Gallop Advertising www.gallop.ca
   - Lamar Outdoor Advertising www.lamar.com
   - Outdoor Advertising Association of America, Inc. (OAAA) www.oaaa.org
   - Poster Publicity www.posterpublicity.com
   - *Sign Business* magazine www.nbm.com/signbusiness
   - *SignCraft* magazine www.signcraft.com
   - Steen Outdoor Systems www.steen.com
   - Wilkins Media Company www.outdoor-ad.com

   a. What organization sponsors the site? Who is the intended audience(s)?
   b. What is the purpose of the site? Does it succeed? Why?
   c. What services (if any) does the organization provide advertisers?
   d. How important do you feel this organization is to outdoor advertising today and in the future? Why?

2. **Specialty Advertising**

   Promotional specialty items are, perhaps, one of the oldest forms of media. Though consumers do not always think of these items as "advertising," they most certainly are—being clearly composed, nonpersonal communications by an identified sponsor. Many organizations and firms are involved in specialty advertising and the industry is still growing today. Peruse some of the websites below and learn more about the products, processes, and promotional power of specialty ad items. Then answer the questions that follow.

   - ADCOLOR, Inc. www.logomall.com/adcolorinc
   - BCG Creations www.bcgcreations.com
   - Bells Advertising www.bells.com
   - Corporate Graphics, Inc. www.wearables.com
   - Cowan Graphics Inc. www.cowan.ca
   - Image Pointe www.imagepointe.com
   - LogoZ www.logoz.com
   - PromoMart www.promomart.com
   - PROMO'S www.coolgifts.com
   - Promotional Product Association International (PPAI) www.ppa.org
   - Promotions Online www.promosonline.com
   - S-N-T Graphics www.sntgraphics.com

   a. What is the focus of the organization sponsoring this site?
   b. Who is the intended audience of the site?
   c. What services (if any) does the organization offer?
   d. What is your overall impression of the organization and its work? Explain?

3. **Integrating Specialty Items into the Ad Mix**

   It seems that every insurance agency distributes pens, calendars, or keychains. Henderson Insurance Agency wants to add a more novel specialty item to its mix in order to remind regular customers of Henderson's extended line of services. Visit the sites in Exercise 2 for ideas about items Henderson could distribute. Note which sites had the best ideas and decide which specialty items Henderson should opt for. How should the insurance agency distribute these items?

Epilogue

Re-Positioning a Brand
MasterCard's "Priceless" Campaign

One of the riskiest endeavors in marketing and advertising is to relaunch a product from scratch. It takes a long time—and a lot of money—to develop a clear position for a brand, and major changes to the brand concept may confuse consumers and result in weakened brand equity. This is especially true when the brand in question is a global giant, universally recognized and used almost everywhere that people spend money.

So why, in 1997, did MasterCard abandon its existing campaign and issue a call to dozens of top agencies to help conceive of a way to overhaul the venerable MasterCard brand? And what made the eventual winner, the "Priceless" campaign developed by McCann-Erickson Worldwide, such a dramatic success?

In the pages that follow, you'll see how everything we've studied—from the most basic truths about consumers to the most complex media strategies—can come together to make a runaway hit, in which a big idea, based on consumer insights, electrifies a brand and provides a boost for all its constituencies. You'll also see how such a campaign can be executed around the world and take the idea to the next level through integrated marketing communications. In short, you'll see how to translate theory into practice: from ideas to the bottom line.

A Universal Emotional Chord

The scene is immediately familiar—a father and son arriving at the ballpark for an afternoon baseball game—but the narrative device is not. As the crew-cut, all-American boy hands his ticket to the usher, a voice-over accompanied by white lettering superimposed on the screen announces, "Two tickets: $28." Next we see the boy holding two large boxes of popcorn and the voice-over and lettering (super) continue: "Two hot dogs, two popcorns, and two sodas: $18."

The male voice-over is warm and comforting; the soft musical soundtrack of piano and classical guitar equally so; the production values are top quality, giving this scene as much emotional force as an Oscar-winning movie. But why the "shopping list" of costs? Within 10 seconds, the viewer is hooked, needing to know where this is going. But the mystery continues as the father and son make their way toward their seats: "One autographed baseball: $45."

Finally, the pair takes their seats, and we see the father gesturing at the field, to explain some aspect of the game that is getting underway. The voice-over and super continue: "Real conversation with 11-year old son: Priceless."

Boom!

The emotional connection—dangled temptingly throughout the commercial—is finally made with the viewer. But a subtle message has also gotten across: All of those everyday purchases—the tickets, the concessions, and the autographed ball—have somehow added up to this memorable and traditional bonding experience between a father and son. And then, the new tagline puts it all together: "There are some things money can't buy—for everything else there's MasterCard."

The emotional connection between a father and a son is dramatized in MasterCard's spot inaugurating its new "Priceless" campaign.

A Marriage of Analytic Research and Creative Execution

With the launch of this new campaign, and its subsequent global rollout, McCann-Erickson started the process of rebuilding a gold standard brand in the minds of consumers everywhere.

The remarkable "Priceless" MasterCard campaign has been an enormous success because it resonates with consumers, and it's dead on target strategically. It is consistent with contemporary values and provides a positive message—something truly refreshing for a credit card company—in a format that's familiar. Every spot expresses an underlying concept that is immediately recognizable to everybody. It is eminently executable. And it translates into any culture around the world, for every nation has its own local "Priceless" stories. If you don't look too closely it might seem easy, like a stroke of astounding good luck—one of those rare moments when a whole campaign is born from a single moment of insight that is legendary to advertising executives. But it took more than luck. A lot more.

This is the story of how McCann-Erickson Worldwide and MasterCard used sophisticated proprietary techniques to reposition MasterCard within the credit card category, giving the brand a completely new face and a meaningful, likeable point of difference in an incredibly competitive environment. It started with McCann conducting painstaking research, performing meticulous analysis, and then developing some big creative ideas, all aimed at helping MasterCard reclaim its position as the world's leading credit card. Their work shows how the commitment to research, which we discussed in Part Two, combined with the high standard in creative development and production values we studied in Part Four, helped MasterCard launch an historic, award-winning global campaign.

A Search for New Direction

In March 1997, MasterCard put its advertising account into review. The one thing everybody in the company could agree on was that MasterCard—one of the most recognized brands in the world—needed a makeover. While successful past marketing efforts had made MasterCard a ubiquitous presence in the United States and around the world, the brand now needed a new identity and one that could endure, guiding the company into the next millennium. Nick Utton, then MasterCard's chief marketing officer, assembled a core group that represented the best minds in the global research, marketing, and advertising departments to evaluate new ideas from a variety of world-class advertising agencies.

Every agency MasterCard invited to join the pitch relished the opportunity to participate. It's not every day that a brand as well known and universally recognized as MasterCard decides to undergo such an overhaul. But what sort of overhaul? Where did they want to go with this brand and what was the problem with where they were already?

Though MasterCard management provided volumes of information on the brand to every agency, the most insightful observation was made by Utton himself: "The challenge is to revitalize a brand that is emotionally bankrupt." As Matt Weiss, SVP/group account director at McCann, put it at the time, "It was the third card in the wallet, behind Visa and American Express. Visa, the main competitor, was firmly entrenched as the top credit card with its worldly, 'Everywhere You Want to Be' campaign. Our challenge was to find a way to bring emotional aspiration back to the MasterCard brand." The current campaign, "Smart Money," developed by another agency, simply wasn't resonating with customers.

"The problem wasn't just with consumers," explains Elisa Romm, VP U.S. advertising at MasterCard. MasterCard is an association that supports more than 30,000 member banks across the country, and these banks needed to become excited again about the brand. "The members looked to MasterCard to support them and they were very concerned about finding a consistent direction that could have a lasting impact with consumers. We needed a new, enduring campaign to energize consumers and member banks. We needed to demonstrate consistency, along with superior strategy and execution."

The company needed a big idea to bring the member banks together and lift their spirits. It was no small challenge—and the image of a major worldwide company was hanging in the balance.

McCann-Erickson believed they could meet this challenge. "We considered it a travesty that Visa was *it* and MasterCard was just another card, even though you could use your MasterCard wherever you could use your Visa—and actually in more places around the world," explains Eric Einhorn, EVP and marketing director of McCann-Erickson World Group. To discover why this situation existed, McCann turned to its proprietary brand planning process, a comprehensive arsenal of services and tools developed over many years of experience implementing campaigns for companies like Coca-Cola, Microsoft, and L'Oréal.

McCann's "Selling Strategy"

McCann-Erickson Worldwide's Selling Strategy™ would provide the roadmap for developing the MasterCard campaign. The Selling Strategy is a service that is single-mindedly focused on generating brand-building ideas—ideas that attract customers, develop corporate and brand franchises, and create market dominance for McCann's clients. The McCann Selling Strategy uncovers the motivations of conceptual target audiences and results in a strategic concept that pinpoints a unique "selling idea."

According to Matt Weiss, "the Selling Strategy is a discipline to be pursued with passion—it's a way of thinking and a way of working meant to encourage greater strategic focus, consumer insight, and creative depth, resulting in advertising that sells." In today's fast-paced and diversified global marketplace, a comprehensive brand campaign needs to be both consistent enough to be immediately recognizable and readily identified with the brand, and yet flexible enough to appeal to

donation at animal shelter:
$50

collar, bowl and food:
$32

shots at the vet:
$85

your first dog:
priceless

We'll help you take good care of your new best friend. Get 25% off all your visits to participating vets with petassure.com when you join through MasterCard Exclusives Online.℠ For more information, go to mastercard.com

there are some things money can't buy. *MasterCard* for everything else there's MasterCard.®

In advertising lore, dogs and kids are always sure winners for pulling at the heartstrings of the audience. Many of the MasterCard ads successfully use emotional moments that, in our memories, become "priceless."

different target consumer groups and fit into different media formats, whether they be print, electronic, or interactive.

The Selling Strategy begins with the Brand Footprint™, which seeks to find where the brand is in the marketplace and in consumers' minds, why it is there, where it should be, and how it will get there. This process of mapping the brand footprint of MasterCard and its competitors would allow McCann to discover areas that MasterCard's brand could grow into and inhabit naturally, without a forced appearance that might alienate consumers or be confused with the brand footprints of its competitors.

The Brand Footprint is more than a concept—as McCann's proprietary technique, it takes the form of a specific model. As a tool to map out the space a brand occupies, it identifies and defines a group of three personality characteristics and three descriptors that the brand stands for in the mind of the consumer. We'll see examples below, when we turn to the application of the Selling Strategy to the MasterCard pitch.

Once they'd identified MasterCard's current Brand Footprint and those of its competitors, McCann moved on to the task of developing a new prescribed brand positioning, "the most basic of all strategic statements about the brand." This internal statement grows out of the Brand Footprint and, in turn, inspires the creative brief, the group of concepts that summarizes the planning process. The creative brief addresses several issues: what the advertising is going to do; what insights about the target consumer the advertising will connect with; and what the target consumers will think and feel about the brand. The creative brief serves as the stimulus for the selling idea—the bridge between the communications strategy and the creative execution of the campaign.

The first thing the Selling Strategy calls for is information—lots of it.

Researching the Industry and a Lot More

McCann's management understood the challenge that lay before them. "We knew we had to come up with a campaign that had breakthrough ability—a campaign that could endure," explains Matt Weiss. They began by teaming up with MasterCard for a comprehensive research and information-gathering program that would give them as much data as possible to help discover and understand MasterCard's Brand Footprint.

"We started with a review of where MasterCard was," explains Weiss. They reviewed their annual reports, payment industry overview/situation analyses, strategic marketing overviews, market research highlights, global issues, and Nielsen reports, the comprehensive positioning for the current advertising concept. They did content audits of MasterCard's business and consumer advertising, and they reviewed the competitive landscape in great detail.

Next, they conducted secondary data analysis: Simmons and MRI Double-base's credit card usage data, and the Yankelovich Monitor and Roper Reports of credit card and financial services attitudes and behavior.

Many agencies might stop there. But McCann always relies extensively on primary research where they talk directly to consumers. The agency conducted 28 focus groups, 24 one-on-one personal interviews, and 250 telephone interviews among credit card users. And while they learned a lot about attitudes toward MasterCard and its competitors and some preliminary campaign ideas, they went much further. To fully understand the psychic space that MasterCard did—and could—inhabit, McCann conducted wide-ranging sociological surveys that helped them understand the feelings and emotions behind the brand category.

Finding the Sweet Spot

This process of mapping the brand against its available "brand-scape" was a crucial step in the journey toward an executable and winning campaign. Studying consumer perceptions of MasterCard's principal competitors, McCann determined the Brand Footprint for American Express included the three personality characteristics

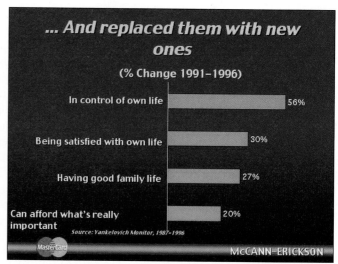

McCann-Erickson's research discovered that important changes had taken place in consumer attitudes during the last decade.

of "Membership," "The Business Life," and "The Charge Card." Its three descriptors were "Professional," "Worldly," and "Responsible." Visa's Brand Footprint was not so different. The personality characteristics were "Everywhere," "The High Life," and "The Credit Card," and its descriptors were "Sociable," "Stylish," and "On-the-Go." MasterCard's Brand Footprint, on the other hand, was very different. Its personality characteristics were "Everyday," "Ordinary Life," and "Generic"; its descriptors were "Unassuming," "Unpretentious," and "Practical."

MasterCard's existing Brand Footprint was, in McCann's estimation, neutral. As a rule, this is not a good place for a brand to be. But there was an up side. MasterCard had an opportunity to use that neutrality to create a new, more powerful and relevant brand positioning that reflected contemporary attitudes about not only credit cards and spending, but about much more far-reaching and important themes like success, and the current normative underpinning of value itself—to turn a neutral brand footprint into a powerful and meaningful space.

Here was the key that eventually unlocked the Big Idea: American Express and Visa were rooted in dated values that harkened back to the materialistic 1980s. They'd maintained their popularity for years, but the social and cultural terrain had subtly evolved, and they hadn't changed with them. MasterCard was actually in a better starting place to take advantage of this shift in values. By going beyond the obvious questions and research methods, McCann learned that in just one decade, Americans had radically altered the symbols they associated with success and accomplishment. Gone were the days when designer clothes, prestigious stores, luxury hotels, expensive cars—and prestigious credit cards—were the badges of success. By 1997, the new signs of success were control of one's own life, personal satisfaction, good family relationships, and the ability to afford those things one considers important.

"We found that consumers had some feelings about MasterCard as the card for regular people, while Visa and American Express had a more exclusive, worldly appeal," says Joyce King Thomas, EVP deputy creative director at McCann. In an industry based on spending money, that might seem like a negative, but McCann saw it as a potential positive. With American Express and Visa inhabiting somewhat dated brand spaces, MasterCard's current brand image gave them an opportunity to claim a fresh, new, and more contemporary brand territory, closer to today's consumption ideals than their main competitors. "We decided to give value to those everyday situations and emotions, the little things that add up to the big things in life," explains Thomas.

McCann also learned that along with these new attitudes about spending, consumers were feeling more and more responsible about themselves as users of credit cards. In one study, a surprising majority of 82 percent felt their unpaid credit card balance was "necessary and justified." McCann identified a MasterCard "sweet spot" born of the new consumer values coupled with the emerging credit card mind-set and dubbed it "Good Spenders."

McCann had found the Brand Footprint for MasterCard, the truth of what the brand stood for in the minds of consumers. More important, they'd found insight into where it could grow: They could use this "sweet spot," the overlap of new values combined with an adjustment in attitudes toward credit cards, to define a re-energized, re-positioned, prescribed Brand Footprint for MasterCard. "Good spenders use credit cards to acquire the things that are important to them—the things that enrich their everyday lives," explains Nat Puccio, McCann's EVP, strategic planning director. This new mind-set was in sharp contrast to that of MasterCard's competitors. With this realization—that MasterCard's core brand values were closer to today's credit card consumption ideals than Visa or American Express—what had been a liability yesterday was suddenly a strength. Now, they had to figure out how to demonstrate this to MasterCard and then to leverage it with the public.

Moving from the Brand Footprint to an Executable Campaign

As the day for the pitch presentation grew closer, Puccio and his team came up with a brilliant way of differentiating MasterCard's footprint from the competitors. Alongside two identical photographs of a large-screen TV, they put an image of a Visa card under one and a MasterCard under another. Under the Visa symbol, they put the words, "The Super Bowl is going to look great on that large-screen TV"; under the MasterCard, "We really need a family entertainment center." With a single, deft touch, McCann found a way to demonstrate how different values and spending attitudes could add up to the *same* purchase.

To further the point, they added another page to the presentation, with two identical images of a skier and the two credit cards. Under the Visa card were the words, "I haven't been to that hot new ski resort yet"; under the MasterCard, "I should really take a moment to relax and recharge from all this stress." The message was clear: These new spending attitudes provided a new justification for the same purchases previously associated with consumption-oriented lifestyles. Consequently, that opened up a whole new space for the MasterCard brand.

Next, McCann developed the Selling Idea, "The Best Way to Pay for Everything That Matters." This wasn't the tagline, but a precise strategic articulation of what they wanted the advertising to express. With "The Best Way to Pay for Everything That Matters," McCann's planners had synthesized all of their painstaking research into an idea so simple that it would make what followed look effortless.

Next came the moment of inspiration. Jonathan Cranin, McCann's chief creative officer for North America, Europe, Africa, and the Middle East, was actually in the shower one morning, mulling over the fruits of the agency's research, when the line popped into his head, "There are some things money can't buy. For everything else there's MasterCard." From there, everything fell into place with amazing speed. Joyce King Thomas and creative director partner Jeroen Bours quickly came up with the shopping list approach that was expressed in the baseball spot. This would become the hallmark of the whole campaign.

camera for voyage you didn't get to take in 1964:
$250

engraved compass for voyage that fell through in 1972:
$122

bottle of wine for voyage you had to cancel in 1985:
$65

setting sail:
priceless

Don't know your port from starboard? We'll give you a free skipper for your voyage when you use your MasterCard® to charter a Sunsail Yacht. (Or a free yacht upgrade if you're an old sea dog). So come sign up with MasterCard Exclusives Online™ at mastercard.com

there are some things money can't buy. **MasterCard** for everything else there's MasterCard.™

McCann's Selling Idea—"The Best Way to Pay for Everything That Matters"—provided the rationale for all the ads in the "Priceless" campaign.

McCann wasn't pitching an advertising campaign: They were pitching an idea. And it was such a powerful idea that they needed to come up with a special way to present it. Bours came up with the inspiration of making giant blue velvet storybooks and a large wooden box to house them all. "We put a big cover over the box, and when we pulled the cover off, the client actually gasped," reports Thomas. MasterCard's Debra Coughlin, SVP, global brand building, remembers the moment—and the gasp—well. "One of my colleagues literally did gasp. They'd caught lightning in a bottle."

Matt Weiss remembers overhearing MasterCard officials in the halls immediately after the pitch. "They were ecstatic, talking about how we'd 'struck gold.' It was amazing."

Implementing the Campaign

The first spot, shot by Tony Kaye, a world-renowned director, was the father/son baseball story described earlier. It first aired in Game Three of the 1997 World Series. Other spots were quick to follow. Each story was different and unique, but the structure was consistent: a family prepares to pose for a photo; the voice-over (always supplied by actor Billy Crudup) supplies the costs of the camera and new clothes, arriving at "Five Generations in One Photograph: Priceless." In another, a young woman prepares herself meticulously for an evening out, until we're told, "Look on Old Boyfriend's Face at High School Reunion: Priceless." In still another, two golfers have a day at the course, ending with, "A Hole in One, with a Witness: Priceless."

The results of the campaign were instant and dramatic. Consumers responded immediately, with higher levels of advertising empathy and likeability toward the

All the little purchases paid for with a MasterCard add up to one memorable moment that's so big, so important, it's priceless—in this case, the look on the old boyfriend's face.

Every golfer knows the emotional value of a hole-in-one—priceless. The same is true for advertising people. A campaign like "Priceless" is so good and has such long legs that it can run for years. It is the advertising equivalent of a hole-in-one—with lots of witnesses.

TITLE: "MOTHER/DAUGHTER"   LENGTH: 30 SECONDS

(MUSIC UNDER)
ANNCR VO: Plane tickets to
the town where she was born:

$1,200.

Train to the house where
she grew up:

$63.

Pints at the pub where she
met your father.

$8.

Finally understanding

where your mother was
coming from:

Priceless.

There are some things
money can't buy:

For everything else there's
Platinum MasterCard.

Accepted all over,

even pubs in Ireland.

(MUSIC OUT)

*Consumers liked the Priceless campaign, and that translated into greater
likeability for the brand. The advertising industry liked it, too, showering
the campaign with a slew of awards.*

brand. Member banks commented on the insights embodied in the campaign and how it would improve perceptions of the brand. Importantly, neither MasterCard nor McCann lost sight of the "rational" side of the brand positioning—that MasterCard is accepted everywhere.

Employees cheered the campaign. When MasterCard first launched "Priceless," they previewed the campaign for the employees, presenting the entire strategy and lineup of commercials and discussing the underlying intentions and goals of the campaign. They also gave employees a gift to commemorate the launch, a Tiffany picture frame with "Celebrating a priceless moment" inscribed on the frame.

"Initiatives like this helped bring everybody on board in a cooperative manner," says Larry Flanagan, chief marketing officer. "It really paid off when we were able to get our employees to understand that they were an important part of the branding process."

Production companies began to call, begging to do new spots. Famous Irish director Jim Sheridan (whose credits include *My Left Foot* and *In the Name of the Father*) shot a "Priceless" ad in which a mother takes her daughter to visit Ireland. And McCann won a slew of industry honors for the campaign. These included the "Good" award from Advertising Women of New York; a Gold Effie, presented by the American Marketing Association in recognition of powerful creative work that works in the marketplace—based on actual business results; and a Gold and Grand AME, as well as EuroEffies, for global effectiveness and creativity. "Priceless" was named "Best New Campaign of the Year" in 1997 by Frohlinger's Market Report; the campaign was a Cannes Finalist; more than a dozen executions have been named among the "Best Spots of the Month" by *AdWeek* magazine; the print work won an Addy; and so on.

In 2002, MasterCard won the inaugural Gold Effie for Sustained Success—given to the most effective campaign over the course of three years. By 2004, the campaign won a total of three Effies and eight AMEs (which stands for Advertising Marketing Effectiveness).

And in what may be the surest sign of the campaign's success, it thoroughly entered the popular consciousness. People looked forward to the new spots and talked about them around the water cooler in the office. It soon became a part of the cultural vernacular. Another sign of success was when the format and line were spoofed and lampooned by top comedians, including Jay Leno (on a remarkable five separate occasions), David Letterman, *Saturday Night Live, Talk Soup,* Gannett Newspapers, NBC's *Will and Grace,* MTV, VH1, *The Simpsons,* and many popular Internet sites. The millions of dollars worth of free exposure that the campaign received on television and in print was due primarily to the real appeal of the campaign. But also at work here was a parallel and deft public relations campaign by MasterCard that used publicity to build up anticipation before every major new spot. The company understood the value of high profile spoofs and encouraged them.

The Next Step: Integrated Marketing

Now that the campaign was such a hit, there were new challenges. The first was integrating the positioning idea across all of MasterCard's different communications channels. Larry Flanagan developed an integration model that had the "Priceless" concept at the center, with all positioning and marketing activities supporting the

Many of the ad concepts were adapted to fit international markets. In less than a decade, MasterCard has completely redeveloped and rejuvenated their image, and the "Priceless" campaign has become part of our popular culture. For the 2004 Oscars telecast, McCann developed the epic "Dog Trilogy" in grand Hollywood style.

Part One: "Lost Dog"

VO: film and dog food for Badger in the Redwoods: $10
Super: film and dog food: $10

VO: bandana for lost dog in Napa Valley: $3
Super: bandana: $3

VO: dog bone in Fresno: $7
Super: dog bone: $7
VO/Super: forgetting you're far from home: priceless

VO: there are some things money can't buy.
VO: for your journey there's MasterCard.

Part Two: "On the Road"

VO: water for a lost dog in the Mojave: $2
Super: water: $2

VO: rhinestone collar in Vegas: $40
Super: rhinestone collar: $40

VO: meatloaf special in Arizona: $8
Super: meatloaf special: $8

VO/Super: Feeling at home when you're only halfway there: priceless

VO: there are some things money can't buy.
VO: for your journey there's MasterCard.

center. While MasterCard developed sponsorships with Major League Baseball, the PGA, and the National Hockey League, McCann created new spots to promote them—and the concept applied easily to every new venture.

The MasterCard All-Century Team

In numerous ways, MasterCard integrated "Priceless" across the whole marketing mix. For example, in 1999, the company wanted to increase the efficiency and impact of its number one sponsorship property, Major League Baseball. With McCann's help, MasterCard created a fully integrated program—the MasterCard All-Century Team—that used the "Priceless" campaign to add dimension to the brand and appeal to those consumers who followed baseball.

Consumer research indicated MasterCard cardholders had a strong affinity toward Major League Baseball. This "love of the game" ran deep and often found its way into family life. Fathers, for example, clearly remembered taking their sons to their first "big league" game—the basic premise of the very first "Priceless" spot. Moms often talked of the "good quality" times shared at the ballpark. McCann found that consumers wanted to experience the game frequently and were positively predisposed to brands that had a strong association with Major League Baseball.

For MasterCard, this presented a huge opportunity. The positioning, as demonstrated by the "Priceless" campaign, was founded on the premise of "what matters" in everyday life. To this target, Major League Baseball mattered greatly. Thus, the positioning—The Best Way to Pay for Everything That Matters—was ultimately used

Part Three: "Home"

VO: chew toy for lost dog in Colorado: $5

Super: chew toy: $5

VO: silk doggy bed for trip across Kansas: $200

Super: silk doggy bed: $200

VO: bubble bath in Jefferson City: $15 (dog at pet groomer)

Super: bubble bath: $15

VO: coming home after a long trip: priceless

Super: coming home: priceless

VO: there are some things money can't buy.

VO: for your journey there's MasterCard.

to form the link between the brand (MasterCard), the sponsorship partner (Major League Baseball), and the consumer (the MasterCard/Major League Baseball fan). The strategic positioning became: "MasterCard. The card at the heart of Major League Baseball," and the implementation was the wildly popular MasterCard All-Century Team, something that truly mattered to baseball fans. Without such a strong and flexible positioning to work from, it wouldn't have been such a runaway success.

By 2003, "Priceless" had gone from being an advertising campaign that lived primarily within the traditional realm of TV and print to a truly integrated global platform encompassing event sponsorship, sales promotion, and public relations activities and spanning a myriad of communication vehicles including radio, the Internet, point-of-sale (POS), and direct mail.

Harnessing the "Priceless" Potential for a Global Campaign

The next challenge was to use the "Priceless" umbrella to solve MasterCard's fractured global marketing problems. Before "Priceless," MasterCard—which was a truly global product—was using some 16 agencies in Europe and Asia alone, generating a message that was inconsistent and scattered around the world.

Debra Coughlin recalls her hope at the very start of the pitch process that "our new agency would be able to deliver and execute a truly global idea." Given MasterCard's image problems at the time, many of her colleagues thought she was reaching too far. But nobody forgot her global vision, and "Priceless" proved the perfect vehicle. Rather than simply imposing this new campaign on all of MasterCard's international partners, though, MasterCard insisted that McCann pitch for the international business, region by region. "As a result, there is a true buy-in of the idea, a shared pride of ownership," explains Coughlin. The success of MasterCard's and McCann's global partnership has helped change attitudes about the potential for global marketing campaigns.

By 2004, the "Priceless" campaign was running in some 96 countries and 47 languages outside the United States. In fact, it is now the largest singular campaign in the world. The creative use of film footage allowed MasterCard to maximize its global budget: In some cases, the ads translate directly with only the language changed. Others are altered slightly to fit the new market, and some spots are now conceived and executed with dual markets in mind. McCann has facilitated this global usage by creating an extranet that allows any MasterCard or McCann office anywhere in the world to view and download the latest TV, radio, or print ad.

Once again, it's the quick-grasp appeal of "Priceless" that has energized the global rollout. McCann and MasterCard captured the spirit of the Japanese market by adapting the baseball spot to one where a father and son go fishing; in Korea they go hiking. For Australia, the baseball footage—that focuses on the grandstands with only a late, brief cut of the game itself—was used with the reference altered to cricket. The successful "Cardboard box" spot, in which a baby ignores a list of popular toys bought over the Internet to play with the box they came in, has been rolled out with minor alterations through Latin America and Asia.

And it's not a unidirectional push: Ads conceived and executed in other countries have caught on in America. "That's the true hallmark of a successful global campaign, when every region is getting in on the creative process," says Larry Flanagan. A popular spot made in France, in which a mother and daughter shop, cook, and catch up, was adapted successfully for the United States. Stories about world travel have to be adapted for the markets where they're set. A Canadian hockey piece has been used in Norway. The list goes on, demonstrating how "Priceless" has struck a truly universal chord—with MasterCard as the beneficiary of this worldwide responsiveness. By 2003, McCann had created over 200 different "Priceless" ads in all—and there was no end in sight.

MasterCard's integrated marketing strategy has also been a part of the global rollout. "Twice a year all of our top marketing people from around the world get together to share best practices and experiences," explains Coughlin. From these meetings comes a solid global platform for all of MasterCard's marketing activities, including their many sponsorships. Soccer—"football" to most of the world—has been a crucial global sponsorship. It starts with the World Cup and moves to many other soccer championships and teams.

A Textbook Case

As one of the most recognizable campaigns in the world, "Priceless has become an icon in a very short time," says former MasterCard marketer Jim Accomando. "As an ad campaign, it's as good as any I've seen." Campaigns like "Priceless" suggest a kind of magical creativity that seems impossible to harness. But as we've seen throughout this book, that magic *can* be harnessed, with the right mix of rigorous marketing research and analytical techniques, a focused partnership between agency and client, and a devotion to creative excellence.

Result? In 2003, for the first time in the history of the category, MasterCard surpassed Visa for the most credit cards in circulation.

A strategically relevant campaign that resonates with people around the world pays untold dividends. Priceless!

Appendix A

Marketing Plan Outline

Date:
Company Name:
Brand or Service:

Encapsulation, for executive review, of entire marketing plan in no more than two or three pages.

I. Executive Summary
    A. Summary of situation analysis
    B. Summary of marketing objectives
    C. Summary of marketing strategies
    D. Budget summary

Complete statement of where the organization is today and how it got there. See Checklist: Situation Analysis (RL 8–1).

II. Situation Analysis
    A. The industry
        1. Definition of industry and company business
        2. History of industry

What business the organization is in and characteristics of the industry as a whole. Information available from industry trade publications, trade association newsletters, consumer business press, Department of Commerce publications.

            a. Technological advances
            b. Trends
        3. Growth patterns within industry
            a. Demand curve
            b. Per capita consumption
            c. Growth potential
        4. Characteristics of industry
            a. Distribution patterns and traditional channels
            b. Regulation and control within industry
            c. Typical promotional activity
            d. Geographical characteristics
            e. Profit patterns

All relevant information on the company and its capabilities, opportunities, and/or problems. Information may be found in annual reports, sales records, warranty card records, customer correspondence, sales staff reports.

    B. The company
        1. Brief history
        2. Scope of business
        3. Current size, growth, profitability
        4. Reputation
        5. Competence in various areas
            a. Strengths
            b. Weaknesses

Complete description and all relevant information on the product/service mix, sales, and the strengths and weaknesses therein. See sales literature, sales reports, dealer correspondence, and so on.

    C. The product/service
        1. The product story
            a. Development and history
            b. Stage of product life cycle
               (1) Introduction
               (2) Growth
               (3) Maturity
               (4) Decline
            c. Quality factors
            d. Design considerations

   e. Goods classification
    (1) Consumer or industrial good
    (2) Durable or nondurable good or service
    (3) Convenience, shopping, or specialty good
    (4) Package good, hard good, soft good, service
   f. Packaging
   g. Price structure
   h. Uses
    (1) Primary
    (2) Secondary
    (3) Potential
   i. Image and reputation
   j. Product/service strengths
   k. Product/service weaknesses
  2. Product sales features
   a. Differentiating factors
    (1) Perceptible, imperceptible, or induced
    (2) Exclusive or nonexclusive
   b. Position in mind of customer
   c. Advantages and disadvantages (customer perception)
  3. Product research and development
   a. Technological breakthroughs
   b. Improvements planned
   c. Technical or service problems
  4. Sales history
   a. Sales and cost of sales
    (1) By product/service
    (2) By model
    (3) By territory
    (4) By market
   b. Profit history for same factors
  5. Share of market
   a. Industry sales by market
   b. Market share in dollars and units
   c. Market potential and trends
 D. The market
  1. Definition and location of market
   a. Identified market segments
    (1) Past
    (2) Potential
   b. Market needs, desires
   c. Characteristics of market
    (1) Geographic
    (2) Demographic
    (3) Psychographic
    (4) Behavioral
   d. Typical buying patterns
    (1) Purchase patterns
    (2) Heavy users/light users
    (3) Frequency of purchase
   e. Buying influences on market
  2. Definition of our customers
   a. Present, past, and future
   b. Characteristics
    (1) Shared characteristics with rest of market
    (2) Characteristics unique to our customers

All relevant information about the people or organizations that comprise the current and prospective market for the firm's offerings. See market research reports, consumer/business press, trade publications, Census of Manufacturers, trade association reports.

   c. What they like about us or our product
   d. What they don't like
  3. Consumer appeals
   a. Past advertising appeals
    (1) What has worked
    (2) What has not worked and why
   b. Possible future appeals
  4. Results of research studies about market and customers

E. The competition
  1. Identification of competitors
   a. Primary competitors
   b. Secondary competitors
   c. Product/service descriptions
   d. Growth and size of competitors
   e. Share of market held by competitors
  2. Strengths of competition
   a. Product quality
   b. Sales features
   c. Price, distribution, promotion
  3. Weaknesses of competition
   a. Product features
   b. Consumer attitude
   c. Price, distribution, promotion
  4. Marketing activities of competition
   a. Product positioning
   b. Pricing strategies
   c. Distribution
   d. Sales force
   e. Advertising, publicity
   f. Estimated budgets

F. Distribution strategies
  1. Type of distribution network used
   a. History of development
   b. Trends
  2. Evaluation of how distribution is accomplished
  3. Description and evaluation with channel members
  4. Promotional relationship with channel members
   a. Trade advertising and allowances
   b. Co-op advertising
   c. Use of promotion by dealer or middlemen
   d. Point-of-purchase displays, literature
   e. Dealer incentive programs.
  5. Strengths/weaknesses of distribution systems
  6. Opportunities/threats related to distribution

G. Pricing policies
  1. Price history
   a. Trends
   b. Affordability
   c. Competition
  2. Price objectives and strategies in past
   a. Management attitudes
   b. Buyer attitudes
   c. Channel attitudes
  3. Opportunities/threats related to pricing

Complete information about the competition, the competitive environment, and the opportunities or challenges presented by current or prospective competitors. See SEC Form 10-Ks, consumer/business press articles, Moody's Industrial Manual, Standard & Poor's reports, Dun & Bradstreet report, Thomas Register of American Corporations.

Complete discussion of how the firm's products/services are distributed and sold, what channels are available, and characteristics of channel members. See dealer and distributor correspondence, sales staff reports, advertising reports, trade publication articles.

Background and rationale for firm's pricing policies and strategies, discussion of alternative options. Study sales reports, channel-member correspondence, customer correspondence, competitive information.

All relevant data concerning the firm's personal sales efforts and effectiveness as well as complete discussion of the firm's use of advertising, public relations, and sales promotion programs. Examine sales reports, advertising reports, articles in Advertising Age, Marketing Communications, and so on, in-house data on advertising, sales, and training.

Enumeration of environmental factors that may be beyond the firm's immediate control but affect the firm's business efforts. See government reports and announcements, consumer/business press, trade association articles.

Recitation of relevant attitudes and directives of management as they pertain to the firm's marketing and advertising efforts. Information available from corporate business plan, management interviews, internal memos and directives.

Enumeration or summary of problems considered most serious to the firm's marketing success.

Summary of those opportunities which offer the greatest potential for the firm's success. What general and specific needs the firm seeks to satisfy. Determine through study of situation analysis factors and management discussions and interviews.

Organization sales goals defined for whole company or for individual products by target market, by geographic territory, by department, or by some other category. Must be specific and realistic based on study of company capabilities, funding, and objectives.

H. Communication strategies
  1. Past promotion policy
     a. Personal versus nonpersonal selling
        (1) Use of sales force
        (2) Use of advertising, public relations, sales promotion
     b. Successes and failures of past policy
  2. Sales force
     a. Size
     b. Scope
     c. Ability/training
     d. Cost per sale
  3. Advertising programs
     a. Successes and failures
     b. Strategies, themes, campaigns, media employed
     c. Appeals, positionings, and so on
     d. Expenditures
        (1) Past budgets
        (2) Method of allocation
        (3) Competitor budgets
        (4) Trend
  4. Opportunities/threats related to communications
I. Environmental factors
  1. Economy
     a. Current economic status
     b. Business outlook and economic forecasts
  2. Political situation
  3. Societal concerns
  4. Technological influences
J. Corporate objectives and strategies
  1. Profitability
     a. Sales revenue
     b. Cost reductions
  2. Return on investment
  3. Stock price
  4. Shareholder equity
  5. Community image
  6. New product development
  7. Technological leadership
  8. Mergers and/or acquisitions
  9. Overall corporate mission
K. Potential marketing problems
L. Potential marketing opportunities
III. Marketing Objectives
A. Market need objectives
  1. Market need-satisfying objectives
  2. Community need-satisfying objectives
  3. Corporate need-satisfying objectives
B. Sales target objectives
  1. Sales volume
     a. Dollars
     b. Units
     c. Territories
     d. Markets
  2. Share of market
  3. Distribution expansion
  4. Other

The method(s) by which the organization plans to achieve the objectives enumerated above.

A general description of the type of marketing strategy the organization intends to employ.

A detailed description of the marketing mix(es) the firm intends to use to achieve its objectives.

IV. Marketing Strategy
- A. General marketing strategy
  1. Positioning strategy
  2. Product differentiation strategy
  3. Price/quality differentiation strategy
  4. Mission marketing strategy
- B. Specific market strategies
  1. Target market A
     - *a.* Product
     - *b.* Price
     - *c.* Distribution
     - *d.* Communication
       - (1) Personal selling
       - (2) Advertising
       - (3) Direct marketing
       - (4) Sales promotion
       - (5) Public relations
  2. Target market B
     - *a.* Product
     - *b.* Price
     - *c.* Distribution
     - *d.* Communication
       - (1) Personal selling
       - (2) Advertising
       - (3) Direct marketing
       - (4) Sales promotion
       - (5) Public relations

The detailed tactical plans for implementing each of the elements of the firm's marketing mix.

V. Action Programs (Tactics)
- A. Product plans
- B. Pricing plans
- C. Distribution plans
- D. Communication plans
  1. Sales plan
  2. Advertising plan
  3. Direct marketing plan
  4. Sales promotion plan
  5. Public relations plan
- E. Mission marketing plan
- F. Interactivity plan

Description of the methods the firm will use to review, evaluate, and control its progress toward the achievement of its marketing objectives.

VI. Measurement, Review, and Control
- A. Organizational structure
- B. Methodology for review and evaluation
- C. Interactivity monitoring

Determination of the amount of money needed to conduct the marketing effort, the rationale for that budget, and the allocation to various functions.

VII. Marketing Budget
- A. Method of allocation
- B. Enumeration of marketing costs by division
  1. New product research
  2. Marketing research
  3. Sales expenses
  4. Advertising, direct marketing, sales promotion, public relations

Details of information, secondary data, or research conducted to develop information discussed in the marketing plan.

VIII. Appendixes
- A. Sales reports
- B. Reports of market research studies
- C. Reprints of journal or magazine articles
- D. Other supporting documents

Appendix B

Advertising Plan Outline

Date:
Company (Brand/Service) Name:

Brief encapsulation, for executive review, of entire advertising plan in no more than two or three pages.

I. Executive Summary
 A. Premises—summary of information presented in marketing plan
 B. Summary of advertising objectives
 C. Summary of advertising strategy
 D. Budget summary

Condensed review of pertinent elements presented in the marketing plan.

II. Situation Analysis
 A. Company's (or product's) current marketing situation
  1. Business or industry information
  2. Description of company, product, or service
   a. Stage of product life cycle
   b. Goods classification
   c. Competitive or market positioning
  3. General description of market(s) served
  4. Sales history and share of market
  5. Description of consumer purchase process
  6. Methods of distribution
  7. Pricing strategies employed
  8. Implications of any marketing research
  9. Communications history
 B. Target market description
  1. Market segments identified
  2. Primary market
  3. Secondary markets
  4. Market characteristics
   a. Geographic
   b. Demographic
   c. Psychographic
   d. Behavioral
 C. Marketing objectives
  1. Need-satisfying objectives
  2. Long- and short-term sales target objectives
 D. Marketing mix for each target market—summarized from marketing plan
  1. Product
  2. Price
  3. Distribution
  4. Communication
 E. Intended role of advertising in the communications mix
 F. Miscellaneous information not included above

Analysis and statement of what the advertising is expected to accomplish—see Checklist: Developing Advertising Objectives (RL 8–3).

III. Advertising Objectives
  A. Primary or selective demand
  B. Direct action or indirect action
  C. Objectives stated in terms of:
    1. Advertising pyramid
    2. Purchase behavior
    3. Other
  D. Quantified expression of objectives
    1. Specific quantities or percentages
    2. Length of time for achievement of objectives
    3. Other possible measurements
      a. Inquiries
      b. Increased order size
      c. Morale building
      d. Other

Intended blend of the creative mix for the company as a whole, for each product, or for each target market.

IV. Advertising (Creative) Strategy
  A. Product concept—how the advertising will present the product in terms of:
    1. Product or market positioning
    2. Product differentiation
    3. Life cycle
    4. Classification, packaging, branding
    5. Kim-Lord grid purchase-decision position
      a. High/low think involvement
      b. High/low feel involvement
  B. Target audience—the specific people the advertising will address
    1. Detailed description of target audiences
      a. Relationship of target audience to target market
      b. Prospective buying influences
      c. Benefits sought/advertising appeals
      d. Demographics
      e. Psychographics
      f. Behavioristics
    2. Prioritization of target audiences
      a. Primary
      b. Secondary
      c. Supplementary

The strategy for selecting the various media vehicles that will communicate the advertising message to the target audience—see Chapters 8, 12–14.

  C. Communications media
    1. Definition of media objectives
      a. Reach
      b. Frequency
      c. Gross rating points
      d. Continuity/flighting/pulsing
    2. Determination of which media reach the target audience best
      a. Traditional mass media
        (1) Radio
        (2) Television
        (3) Newspapers
        (4) Magazines
        (5) Outdoor
      b. Other media
        (1) Direct mail
        (2) Interactive/digital media
        (3) Publicity

        c. Supplemental media
          (1) Trade shows
          (2) Sales promotion devices
          (3) Other media
          (4) Off-the-wall media
   3. Availability of media relative to purchase patterns
   4. Potential for communication effectiveness
   5. Cost considerations
        a. Size/mechanical considerations of message units
        b. Cost efficiency of media plan against target audiences
        c. Production costs
   6. Relevance to other elements of creative mix
   7. Scope of media plan
   8. Exposure/attention/motivation values of intended media vehicles

What the company wants to say and how it wants to say it, verbally and nonverbally—see Chapters 10–11.

D. Advertising message
   1. Copy elements
        a. Advertising appeals
        b. Copy platform
        c. Key consumer benefits
        d. Benefit supports or reinforcements
        e. Product personality or image
   2. Art elements
        a. Visual appeals
          (1) In ads and commercials
          (2) In packaging
          (3) In point-of-purchase and sales materials
         b. Art platform
          (1) Layout
          (2) Design
          (3) Illustration style
   3. Production elements
        a. Mechanical considerations in producing ads
          (1) Color
          (2) Size
          (3) Style
        b. Production values sought
          (1) Typography
          (2) Printing
          (3) Color reproduction
          (4) Photography/illustration
          (5) Paper
          (6) Electronic effects
          (7) Animation
          (8) Film or videotape
          (9) Sound effects
         (10) Music

The amount of money to be allocated to advertising and the intended method of allocation—Chapters 7, 17.

V. The Advertising Budget
  A. Impact of marketing situation on method of allocation
   1. New or old product
   2. Primary demand curve for product class
   3. Competitive situation
   4. Marketing objectives and strategy
   5. Profit or growth considerations
   6. Relationship of advertising to sales and profits
   7. Empirical experience

B. Method of allocation
    1. Percentage of sales or profit
    2. Share of market
    3. Objective/task method
    4. Unit of sale
    5. Competitive parity

VI. Testing and Evaluation

The research techniques that will be used to create the advertising and evaluate its effectiveness—see Chapter 7.

A. Advertising research conducted
    1. Strategy determination
    2. Concept development
B. Pretesting and posttesting
    1. Elements tested
        a. Markets
        b. Motives
        c. Messages
        d. Media
        e. Budgeting
        f. Scheduling
    2. Methodology
        a. Central location tests
        b. Sales experiments
        c. Physiological testing
        d. Aided recall tests
        e. Unaided recall tests
        f. Attitude tests
        g. Inquiry tests
        h. Sales tests
        i. Other
    3. Cost of testing

Important Terms

AAAA See *American Association of Advertising Agencies.*

AAF See *American Advertising Federation.*

ABC See *Audit Bureau of Circulations.*

account executive (AE) The liaison between the agency and the client. The account executive is responsible both for managing all the agency's services for the benefit of the client and for representing the agency's point of view to the client.

account planning A hybrid discipline that bridges the gap between traditional research, account management, and creative direction whereby agency people represent the view of the consumer in order to better define and plan the client's advertising program.

action advertising Advertising intended to bring about immediate action on the part of the reader or viewer.

action programs See *tactics.*

actual consumers The people in the real world who comprise an ad's target audience. They are the people to whom the sponsor's message is ultimately directed.

ad networks The Internet equivalent of a media rep firm, *ad networks* act as brokers for advertisers and websites. Ad networks pool hundreds or even thousands of Web pages together and facilitate advertising across these pages, thereby allowing advertisers to gain maximum exposure by covering even the small sites.

ad request An opportunity to deliver an advertising element to a website visitor.

advertising The structured and composed nonpersonal communication of information, usually paid for and usually persuasive in nature, about products (goods and services) or ideas by identified sponsors through various media.

advertising agency An independent organization of creative people and businesspeople who specialize in developing and preparing advertising plans, advertisements, and other promotional tools for advertisers. The agency also arranges for or contracts for purchase of space and time in various media.

advertising allowance Either a percentage of gross purchases or a flat fee paid to the retailer for advertising the manufacturer's product.

advertising impression A possible exposure of the advertising message to one audience member; see *opportunity to see (OTS).*

advertising message An element of the creative mix comprising what the company plans to say in its advertisements and how it plans to say it—verbally or nonverbally.

advertising plan The plan that directs the company's advertising effort. A natural outgrowth of the marketing plan, it analyzes the sit-uation, sets advertising objectives, and lays out a specific strategy from which ads and campaigns are created.

advertising research The systematic gathering and analysis of information specifically to facilitate the development or evaluation of advertising strategies, ads and commercials, and media campaigns.

advertising response curve Studies of this indicate that incremental response to advertising actually diminishes—rather than builds—with repeated exposure.

advertising specialty A promotional product, usually imprinted with an advertiser's name, message, or logo, that is distributed free as part of a marketing communications program.

advertising strategy The methodology advertisers use to achieve their advertising objectives. The strategy is determined by the particular creative mix of advertising elements the advertiser selects, namely: target audience; product concept; communications media; and advertising message. Also called the *creative mix.*

advertising strategy research Used to help define the product concept or to assist in the selection of target markets, advertising messages, or media vehicles.

advertorial An ad that is half advertising, half editorial, aimed at swaying public opinion rather than selling products.

advocacy advertising Advertising used to communicate an organization's views on issues that affect society or business.

affidavit of performance A signed and notarized form sent by a television station to an advertiser or agency indicating what spots ran and when. It is the station's legal proof that the advertiser got what was paid for.

affiliate marketing program A contractual advertising program, often used in e-commerce, under which a seller pays a manufacturer, marketer, or other business a percentage of the sale price of an item sold. This payment is compensation for services or cooperation in making the sale. For example, a site devoted to music reviews may have a banner link to an online music retailer. When consumers use that link to buy music, the music seller pays the owner of the music review site a percentage of the sale as consideration for the banner link.

affirmative disclosure Advertisers must make known their product's limitations or deficiencies.

agricultural advertising See *farm advertising.*

ambush marketing A promotional strategy utilized by nonsponsors to capitalize on the popularity or prestige of an event or property by giving the false impression that they are sponsors, such as by buying up all the billboard space around an athletic stadium. Often employed by the competitors of the property's official sponsor.

IT

American Advertising Federation (AAF) A nationwide association of advertising people. The AAF helped to establish the Federal Trade Commission, and its early "vigilance" committees were the forerunners of the Better Business Bureaus.

American Association of Advertising Agencies (AAAA) The national organization of the advertising business. It has members throughout the United States and controls agency practices by denying membership to any agency judged unethical.

ANA See *Association of National Advertisers.*

analog proof See *Chromalin proof.*

animatic A rough television commercial produced by photographing storyboard sketches on a film strip or video with the audio portion synchronized on tape. It is used primarily for testing purposes.

animation The use of cartoons, puppet characters, or demonstrations of inanimate characters come to life in television commercials; often used for communicating difficult messages or for reaching specialized markets, such as children.

answer print The final print of a filmed commercial, along with all the required optical effects and titles, used for review and approval before duplicating.

aperture The opening in a camera that determines the amount of light that reaches the film or videotape.

art The whole visual presentation of a commercial or advertisement—the body language of an ad. Art also refers to the style of photography or illustration employed, the way color is used, and the arrangement of elements in an ad so that they relate to one another in size and proportion.

art direction The act or process of managing the visual presentation of an ad or commercial.

art director Along with graphic designers and production artists, determines how the ad's verbal and visual symbols will fit together.

art studio Company that designs and produces artwork and illustrations for advertisements, brochures, and other communication devices.

Artist role A role in the creative process that experiments and plays with a variety of approaches, looking for an original idea.

Association of National Advertisers (ANA) An organization composed of 400 major manufacturing and service companies that are clients of member agencies of the AAAA. These companies, which are pledged to uphold the ANA code of advertising ethics, work with the ANA through a joint Committee for Improvement of Advertising Content.

attention value A consideration in selecting media based on the degree of attention paid to ads in particular media by those exposed to them. Attention value relates to the advertising message and copy just as much as to the medium.

attitude The acquired mental position—positive or negative—regarding some idea or object.

attitude test A type of posttest that usually seeks to measure the effectiveness of an advertising campaign in creating a favorable image for a company, its brand, or its products.

audience The total number of people exposed to a particular medium.

audience composition The distribution of an audience into demographic or other categories.

audience objectives Definitions of the specific types of people the advertiser wants to reach.

audience share The percentage of homes with TV sets in use (HUT) tuned to a specific program.

audio The sound portion of a commercial. Also, the right side of a script for a television commercial, indicating spoken copy, sound effects, and music.

audio console In a sound studio control room, the board that channels sound to the appropriate recording devices and that blends both live and prerecorded sounds for immediate or delayed broadcast.

audiovisual materials Slides, films, filmstrips, and videocassettes that may be used for training, sales, or public relations activities.

Audit Bureau of Circulations (ABC) An organization supported by advertising agencies, advertisers, and publishers that verifies circulation and other marketing data on newspapers and magazines for the benefit of its members.

author In Stern's communication model, a copywriter, an art director, or a creative group at the agency that is commissioned by the sponsor to create advertising messages.

autobiographical messages A style of advertising that utilizes the first person "I" to tell a story to the audience, "You."

automated teller machine (ATM) Automated machines that dispense cash to bank customers. ATMs are now used to display full-motion video ads while the transaction is processed.

avails An abbreviated term referring to the TV time slots that are *available* to an advertiser.

average quarter-hour audience (AQH persons) A radio term referring to the average number of people who are listening to a specific station for at least 5 minutes during a 15-minute period of any given daypart.

average quarter-hour rating The average quarter-hour persons estimate expressed as a percentage of the estimated population.

average quarter-hour share The radio station's audience (AQH persons) expressed as a percentage of the total radio listening audience in the area.

awareness advertising Advertising that attempts to build the image of a product or familiarity with the name and package.

Ayer No. 1 See *poster-style format.*

banner Little billboards of various sizes that pop up when a visitor lands on a particular Web page.

barter syndication Marketing of first-run television programs to local stations free or for a reduced rate because some of the ad space has been presold to national advertisers.

base art The first image on an artboard on which an overlay may be placed.

baseband A type of digital data transmission in which each wire carries only one signal, or channel, at a time.

basic bus In transit advertising, all the inside space on a group of buses, which thereby gives the advertiser complete domination.

behavioristic segmentation Method of determining market segments by grouping consumers into product-related groups based on their purchase behavior.

benefit headline Type of headline that makes a direct promise to the reader.

benefits The particular product attributes offered to customers, such as high quality, low price, status, speed, sex appeal, good taste, and so on.

benefit segmentation Method of segmenting consumers based on the benefits being sought.

Better Business Bureau (BBB) A business-monitoring organization funded by dues from more than 100,000 member companies. It operates primarily at the local level to protect consumers against fraudulent and deceptive advertising.

big idea The flash of creative insight—the bold advertising initiative—that captures the essence of the strategy in an imaginative, involving way and brings the subject to life to make the reader stop, look, and listen.

billboards See *30-sheet poster panel.*

bleeds Colors, type, or visuals that run all the way to the edge of the page.

blinking A scheduling technique in which the advertiser floods the airwaves for one day on both cable and network channels to make it virtually impossible to miss the ads.

blueline A proof created by shining light through the negatives and exposing a light-sensitive paper that turns from white to blue; it helps reveal scratches and flaws in the negatives.

board See *audio console.*

body copy The text of an advertisement that tells the complete story and attempts to close the sale. It is a logical continuation of the headline and subheads and is usually set in a smaller type size than headlines or subheads.

boldface Heavier type.

booths At trade shows, a major factor in sales promotion plans. To stop traffic, it must be simple and attractive and have good lighting and a large visual.

bottom-up marketing The opposite of standard, top-down marketing planning, bottom-up marketing focuses on one specific tactic and develops it into an overall strategy.

brainstorming A process in which two or more people get together to generate new ideas; often a source of sudden inspiration.

brand That combination of name, words, symbols, or design that identifies the product and its source and distinguishes it from competing products—the fundamental differentiating device for all products.

brand development index (BDI) The percentage of a brand's total sales in an area divided by the total population in the area; it indicates the sales potential of a particular brand in a specific market area.

brand equity The totality of what consumers, distributors, dealers, and competitors feel and think about a brand over an extended period of time; in short, it is the value of the brand's capital.

branding A marketing function that identifies products and their source and differentiates them from all other products.

brand interest An individual's openness or curiosity about a brand.

brand loyalty The consumer's conscious or unconscious decision—expressed through intention or behavior—to repurchase a brand continually. This occurs because the consumer perceives that the brand has the right product features, image, quality, or relationship at the right price.

brand manager The individual within the advertiser's company who is assigned the authority and responsibility for the successful marketing of a particular brand.

brand trains An advertising program under which all the advertising in and on a train is from a single advertiser. This advertising concept was first used in subway trains in New York City and is being used on the Las Vegas monorail.

broadband A type of digital data transmission that enables a single wire to carry multiple signals simultaneously.

broadcast TV Television sent over airwaves as opposed to over cables.

broadside A form of direct-mail advertisement, larger than a folder and sometimes used as a window display or wall poster in stores. It can be folded to a compact size and fitted into a mailer.

brochures Sales materials printed on heavier paper and featuring color photographs, illustrations, typography. See also *folders.*

budget buildup method See *objective/task method.*

bulk discounts Newspapers offer advertisers decreasing rates (calculated by multiplying the number of inches by the cost per inch) as they use more inches.

bulletin boards An internal public relations means for announcing new equipment, meetings, promotions, new products, construction plans, and recreation news.

bulletin structures A type of outdoor advertising meant for long-term use and works best where traffic is heavy and visibility is good. They carry printed or painted messages, are created in sections, and are brought to the site where they are assembled and hung on the billboard structure.

bursting A media scheduling method for promoting high-ticket items that require careful consideration, such as running the same commercial every half-hour on the same network in prime time.

business advertising Advertising directed at people who buy or specify goods and services for business use. Also called *business-to-business advertising.*

business magazines The largest category of magazines, they target business readers and include: *trade publications* for retailers, wholesalers, and other distributors; *industrial magazines* for businesspeople involved in manufacturing and services; and *professional journals* for lawyers, physicians, architects, and other professionals.

business markets Organizations that buy natural resources, component products, and services that they resell, use to conduct their business, or use to manufacture another product.

business reply mail A type of mail that enables the recipient of direct-mail advertising to respond without paying postage.

business-to-business (B2B) advertising See *business advertising.*

business-to-business agency Represents clients that market products to other businesses; also called high-tech agency.

bus-o-rama sign In transit advertising, a jumbo roof sign, which is actually a full-color transparency backlighted by fluorescent tubes, running the length of the bus.

button In Internet advertising, buttons are small versions of a banner and sometimes look like an icon, and they usually provide a link to an advertiser's home page. Because buttons take up less space than banners, they also cost less.

buyback allowance A manufacturer's offer to pay for an old product so that it will be taken off the shelf to make room for a new product.

cable modem A system of connecting with the Internet that offers high-speed data transfer direct to the computer. Only available from those cable TV companies that offer one of the new cable-modem services such as Roadrunner or @Home.

cable TV Television signals carried to households by cable and paid by subscription.

camera-ready art A finished ad that is ready for the printer's camera to shoot—to make negatives or plates—according to the publication's specifications.

car-end posters Transit advertisements of varying sizes, positioned in the bulkhead.

CARU See *Children's Advertising Review Unit.*

casting brief A detailed, written description of the characters' personalities to serve as guides in casting sessions when actors audition for the roles.

catalogs Reference books mailed to prospective customers that list, describe, and often picture the products sold by a manufacturer, wholesaler, jobber, or retailer.

category development index (CDI) The percent of a product category's total U.S. sales in an area divided by the percent of total U.S. population in the area.

CD-ROM Acronym for compact disk-read only memory; computer storage disk that offers a large amount of storage space and a high concentration of data, combined with full-motion video and high-quality audio.

cease-and-desist order May be issued by the FTC if an advertiser won't sign a consent decree; prohibits further use of an ad.

centers of influence Customers, prospective customers, or opinion leaders whose opinions and actions are respected by others.

centralized advertising department A staff of employees, usually located at corporate headquarters, responsible for all the organization's advertising. The department is often structured by product, advertising subfunction, end user, media, or geography.

central location test A type of pretest in which videotapes of test commercials are shown to respondents on a one-to-one basis, usually in shopping center locations.

central route to persuasion One of two ways researchers Petty, Cacioppo, and Schumann theorize that marketers can persuade consumers. When consumers have a high level of involvement with the product or the message, they are motivated to pay attention to the central, product-related information in an ad, such as product attributes and benefits, or demonstrations of positive functional or psychological consequences; see *elaboration likelihood model.*

cents-off promotion A short-term reduction in the price of a product designed to induce trial and usage. Cents-off promotions take various forms, including basic cents-off packages, one-cent sales, free offers, and box-top refunds.

channel Any medium through which an encoded message is sent to a receiver, including oral communication, print media, television, and the Internet.

channels of distribution See *distribution channels.*

character-count method A method of copy casting in which an actual count is made of the number of characters in the copy.

Children's Advertising Review Unit (CARU) This entity, created by the Council of Better Business Bureaus, provides a general advisory service for advertisers, agencies, children, parents, and educators.

Chromalin proof This proof uses a series of four very thin plastic sheets pressed together; each layer's light-sensitive emulsion turns one of the process colors when exposed to certain wavelengths of light.

cinema advertising Advertising in movie theaters.

cinematographer A motion picture photographer.

circulation A statistical measure of a print medium's audience; includes subscription and vendor sales and primary and secondary readership.

circulation audit Thorough analysis of circulation procedures, distribution outlets, and other distribution factors by a company such as the Audit Bureau of Circulations (ABC).

circus layout A layout style filled with multiple illustrations, oversized type, reverse blocks, tilts, or other gimmicks to bring an ad alive and make it interesting.

classified ads Newspaper, magazine, and now Internet advertisements usually arranged under subheads that describe the class of goods or the need the ads seek to satisfy. Rates are based on the number of lines the ad occupies. Most employment, housing, and automotive advertising is in the form of classified advertising.

classified advertising Used to locate and recruit new employees, offer services, or sell or lease new and used merchandise.

Classified Advertising Network of New York (CANNY) A statewide affiliation of daily newspapers that enables advertisers to place classified ads in daily newspapers throughout the state easily and inexpensively.

classified ad website Websites that specialize in providing classified advertisements, often provided for free. Many classified ad websites are supported by ad banners of other advertisers.

classified display ads Ads that run in the classified section of the newspaper but have larger-size type, photos, art borders, abundant white space, and sometimes color.

clearance advertising A type of local advertising designed to make room for new product lines or new models or to get rid of slow-moving product lines, floor samples, broken or distressed merchandise, or items that are no longer in season.

click rate In Internet advertising, the number of "clicks" on an advertisement divided by the number of ad requests. A method by which marketers can measure the frequency with which users try to obtain additional information about a product by clicking on an advertisement. Also called *click-through rate.*

click-through A term used in reference to when a World Wide Web user clicks on an ad banner to visit the advertiser's site. Some Web publishers charge advertisers according to the number of click-throughs on a given ad banner.

close That part of an advertisement or commercial that asks customers to do something and tells them how to do it—the action step in the ad's copy.

closing date A publication's final deadline for supplying printing material for an advertisement.

clutter tests Method of pretesting in which commercials are grouped with noncompetitive control commercials and shown to prospective customers to measure their effectiveness in gaining attention, increasing brand awareness and comprehension, and causing attitude shifts.

cognition The point of awareness and comprehension of a stimulus.

cognitive dissonance   See *theory of cognitive dissonance.*

cognitive theory   An approach that views learning as a mental process of memory, thinking, and the rational application of knowledge to practical problem solving.

collateral material   All the accessory nonmedia advertising materials prepared by manufacturers to help dealers sell a product— booklets, catalogs, brochures, films, trade-show exhibits, sales kits, and so on.

color key   A color proof that is a less-expensive form of the Chromalin, with thicker plastic sheets that can be lifted up.

color separations   Four separate continuous-tone negatives produced by photographing artwork through color filters that eliminate all the colors but one. The negatives are used to make four printing plates—one each for yellow, magenta, cyan, and black—for reproducing the color artwork.

color strip   Samples of eye shadow, blush, lipstick, and other makeup inserted into magazines.

column inch   The basic unit by which publishers bill for advertising. It is one vertical inch of a column. Until 1984, the column width in newspapers varied greatly. In 1984, the industry introduced the standard advertising unit (SAU) system, which standardized newspaper column width, page sizes, and ad sizes. Today, most newspapers—and virtually all dailies—have converted to the SAU system. A SAU column inch is 2-1/16 inches wide by 1 inch deep.

combination offers   A sales promotion device in which two related products are packaged together at a special price, such as a razor and a package of blades. Sometimes a combination offer may be used to introduce a new product by tying its purchase to an established product at a special price.

combination rates   Special newspaper advertising rates offered for placing a given ad in (1) morning and evening editions of the same newspaper; (2) two or more newspapers owned by the same publisher; or (3) two or more newspapers affiliated in a syndicate or newspaper group.

combo layout   A layout style that combines two or more other layout types to make an ad look more interesting.

command headline   A type of headline that orders the reader to do something.

communication element   Includes all marketing-related communications between the seller and the buyer.

communications media   An element of the creative mix, comprising the various methods or vehicles that will be used to transmit the advertiser's message.

communications mix   A variety of marketing communications tools, grouped into personal and nonpersonal selling activities.

community involvement   A local public relations activity in which companies sponsor or participate in a local activity or supply a location for an event.

company conventions and dealer meetings   Events held by manufacturers to introduce new products, sales promotion programs, or advertising campaigns.

comparative advertising   Advertising that claims superiority to competitors in some aspect.

compiled list   A type of direct-mail list that has been compiled by another source, such as lists of automobile owners, new home purchasers, business owners, union members, and so forth. It is the most readily available type of list but offers the lowest response expectation.

comprehensive layout   A facsimile of a finished ad with copy set in type and pasted into position along with proposed illustrations. The "comp" is prepared so the advertiser can gauge the effect of the final ad.

conceptualization   See *visualization.*

conditioning theory   The theory that learning is a trial-and-error process. Also called *stimulus-response theory.*

consent decree   A document advertisers sign, without admitting any wrongdoing, in which they agree to stop objectionable advertising.

consumer advertising   Advertising directed at the ultimate consumer of the product, or at the person who will buy the product for someone else's personal use.

consumer advocates   Individuals and groups who actively work to protect consumer rights often by investigating advertising complaints received from the public and those that grow out of their own research.

consumer behavior   The activities, actions, and influences of people who purchase and use goods and services to satisfy their personal or household needs and wants.

consumer decision process   The series of steps a consumer goes through in deciding to make a purchase.

consumer information networks   Organizations that help develop state, regional, and local consumer organizations and work with national, regional, county, and municipal consumer groups. Examples include the Consumer Federation of America (CFA), the National Council of Senior Citizens, and the National Consumer League.

consumerism   Social action designed to dramatize the rights of the buying public.

consumer magazines   Information- or entertainment-oriented periodicals directed toward people who buy products for their own consumption.

consumer sales promotions   Marketing, advertising, and sales promotion activities aimed at inducing trial, purchase, and repurchase by the consumer. Also called *pull strategy.*

consumers, consumer market   People who buy products and services for their own, or someone else's, personal use.

contest   A sales promotion device for creating consumer involvement in which prizes are offered based on the skill of the entrants.

continuity   The duration of an advertising message or campaign over a given period of time.

continuous schedule   A method of scheduling media in which advertising runs steadily with little variation.

continuous tone   Normal photographic paper produces images in black and white with shades of gray in between.

contract rate   A special rate for newspaper advertising usually offered to local advertisers who sign an annual contract for frequent or bulk-space purchases.

controlled circulation   A free publication mailed to a select list of individuals the publisher feels are in a unique position to influence the purchase of advertised products.

control room   In a recording studio, the place where the producer, director, and sound engineer sit, monitoring and controlling all the sounds generated in the sound studio.

cookies   Small pieces of information that get stored in a computer's Web browser when one loads certain websites. Cookies keep track of whether a certain user has ever visited a specific site and allows the site to give users different information according to whether or not they are repeat visitors.

cooperative (co-op) advertising The sharing of advertising costs by the manufacturer and the distributor or retailer. The manufacturer may repay 50 or 100 percent of the dealer's advertising costs or some other amount based on sales. See also *horizontal cooperative advertising, vertical cooperative advertising.*

copy The words that make up the headline and message of an advertisement or commercial.

copy cast To forecast the total block of space the type in an ad will occupy in relation to the typeface's letter size and proportions.

copy-heavy layout A layout style used when the advertiser has a lot to say and visuals won't say it. Typically, a large dominant headline will run above or below the copy or even be framed by it.

copy points Copywriting themes in a product's advertising.

copyright An exclusive right granted by the Copyright Act to authors and artists to protect their original work from being plagiarized, sold, or used by another without their express consent.

copywriters People who create the words and concepts for ads and commercials.

corporate advertising The broad area of nonproduct advertising aimed specifically at enhancing a company's image and increasing lagging awareness.

corporate identity advertising Advertising a corporation creates to familiarize the public with its name, logos, trademarks, or corporate signatures, especially after any of these elements are changed.

corporate objectives Goals of the company stated in terms of profit or return on investment. Objectives may also be stated in terms of net worth, earnings ratios, growth, or corporate reputation.

corrective advertising May be required by the FTC for a period of time to explain and correct offending ads.

cost efficiency The cost of reaching the target audience through a particular medium as opposed to the cost of reaching the medium's total circulation.

cost per rating point (CPP) A simple computation used by media buyers to determine which broadcast programs are the most efficient in relation to the target audience. The CPP is determined by dividing the cost of the show by the show's expected rating against the target audience.

cost per thousand (CPM) A common term describing the cost of reaching 1,000 people in a medium's audience. It is used by media planners to compare the cost of various media vehicles.

coupon A certificate with a stated value that is presented to a retail store for a price reduction on a specified item.

cover date The date printed on the cover of a publication.

cover paper Paper used on soft book covers, direct-mail pieces, and brochure covers that are thicker, tougher, and more durable than text paper.

cover position Advertising space on the front inside, back inside, and back cover pages of a publication which is usually sold at a premium price.

CPM See *cost per thousand.*

creative boutique An organization of creative specialists (such as art directors, designers, and copywriters) who work for advertisers and occasionally advertising agencies to develop creative concepts, advertising messages, and specialized art. A boutique performs only the creative work.

creative brief A written statement that serves as the creative team's guide for writing and producing an ad. It describes the most important issues that should be considered in the development of the ad (the who, why, what, where, and when), including a definition and description of the target audience; the rational and emotional appeals to be used; the product features that will satisfy the customer's needs; the style, approach, or tone that will be used in the copy; and, generally, what the copy will say.

creative director Heads a creative team of agency copywriters and artists that is assigned to a client's business; is ultimately responsible for the creative product—the form the final ad takes.

creative mix Those advertising elements the company controls to achieve its advertising objectives, including the target audience, the product concept, the communications media, and the advertising message. See also *advertising strategy.*

creative process The step-by-step procedure used to discover original ideas and reorganize existing concepts in new ways.

creative pyramid A five-step model to help the creative team convert advertising strategy and the big idea into the actual physical ad or commercial. The five elements are: attention, interest, credibility, desire, and action.

creatives The people who work in the creative department, regardless of their specialty.

creativity Involves combining two or more previously unconnected objects or ideas into something new.

crisis management A company's plan for handling news and public relations during crises.

culture A homogeneous group's whole set of beliefs, attitudes, and ways of doing things, typically handed down from generation to generation.

cume persons The total number of different people listening to a radio station for at least one 15-minute segment over the course of a given week, day, or daypart.

cume rating The estimated number of cume persons expressed as a percentage of the total market population.

current customers People who have already bought something from a business and who may buy it regularly.

customer lifetime value (LTV) The total sales or profit value of a customer to a marketer over the course of that customer's lifetime.

customers The people or organizations who consume goods and services. See also *centers of influence, current customers,* and *prospective customers.*

custom magazine Magazine-length ads that look like regular magazines but are created by advertisers. They are sold at newsstands and produced by the same companies that publish traditional magazines.

customer retention and relationship management (CRM) A promotional program that focuses on existing clients rather than prospecting for new clients. Due to negative reaction to spam (unsolicited e-mail), e-mail programs are often focused on customer retention and relationship management (CRM) rather than prospecting.

Customized MarketMail (CMM) A class of mail, introduced by the United States Postal Service in 2003, that allows direct-mail advertisers to send pieces in unusual shapes without envelopes.

CYMK printing See *four-color process.*

daily newspapers   Often called *dailies,* these newspapers are published at least five times a week, in either morning or evening editions.

data access   Characteristic of a database that enables marketers to manipulate, analyze, and rank all the information they possess in order to make better marketing decisions.

database   The corporate memory of all important customer information: name and address, telephone number, NAIC code (if a business firm), source of inquiry, cost of inquiry, history of purchases, and so on. It should record every transaction across all points of contact with both channel members and customers.

database marketing   Tracking and analyzing the purchasing patterns of specific customers in a computer database and then targeting advertising to their needs.

data management   The process of gathering, consolidating, updating, and enhancing the information about customers and prospects that resides in a company's database.

daypart mix   A media scheduling strategy based on the TV usage levels reported by the rating services.

decentralized system   The establishment of advertising departments by products or brands or in various divisions, subsidiaries, countries, regions, or other categories that suit the firm's needs, which operate with a major degree of independence.

deceptive advertising   According to the FTC, any ad in which there is a misrepresentation, omission, or other practice that can mislead a significant number of reasonable consumers to their detriment.

decline stage   The stage in the product life cycle when sales begin to decline due to obsolescence, new technology, or changing consumer tastes.

decoding   The interpretation of a message by the receiver.

demarketing   Term coined during energy shortage of the 1970s and 1980s when advertising was used to slow the demand for products.

demographic editions   Magazines that reach readers who share a demographic trait, such as age, income level, or professional status.

demographic segmentation   Based on a population's statistical characteristics such as sex, age, ethnicity, education, occupation, income, or other quantifiable factors.

demographics   The statistical characteristics of the population.

demonstration   A type of TV commercial in which the product is shown in use.

departmental system   The organization of an ad agency into departments based on function: account services, creative services, marketing services, and administration.

design   Visual pattern or composition of artistic elements chosen and structured by the graphic artist.

designated market areas (DMA)   The geographical areas in which TV stations attract most of their viewers.

development stage   In the agency-client relationship, the honeymoon period when both agency and client are at the peak of their optimism and are most eager to quickly develop a mutually profitable mechanism for working together.

device copy   Advertising copy that relies on wordplay, humor, poetry, rhymes, great exaggeration, gags, and other tricks or gimmicks.

dialogue/monologue copy   A type of body copy in which the characters illustrated in the advertisement do the selling in their own words either through a quasi-testimonial technique or through a comic strip panel.

digital interactive media   Electronic channels of communication—including online databases, the Internet, CD-ROMs, and stand-alone kiosks—with which the audience can participate actively and immediately.

digital media   Channels of communication that join the logic of multimedia formats with the electronic system capabilities and controls of modern telephone, television, and computer technologies.

digital proof   A prepress proof that uses inkjet technology and offers fairly accurate reliability as well as lower cost and faster turnaround time. Also called an *Iris.*

digital subscriber line (DSL)   Technology that transforms a traditional telephone line into a high-speed digital link to provide homes and small businesses with always-on, broadband Internet access.

digital video effects (DVE) unit   In video, special-effects equipment for manipulating graphics on the screen to produce fades, wipes, zooms, rotations, and so on.

DirecPC   Satellite-based system to connect with the Internet that offers very fast downloading—faster even than cable—but is still very expensive and requires a dial-up modem and separate phone line for sending material.

direct distribution   The method of marketing in which the manufacturer sells directly to customers without the use of retailers.

direct-mail advertising   All forms of advertising sent directly to prospective customers without using one of the commercial media forms.

direct marketing   A system of marketing in which companies build their own database of customers and use a variety of media to communicate with them directly such as through ads and catalogs.

director   The director supervises preproduction, production, and postproduction of radio and television commercials.

directories   Listings, often in booklet form, that serve as locators, buying guides, and mailing lists.

direct questioning   A method of pretesting designed to elicit a full range of responses to the advertising. It is especially effective for testing alternative advertisements in the early stages of development.

direct-response advertising   An advertising message that asks the reader, listener, or viewer to provide feedback straight to the sender. Direct-response advertising can take the form of direct mail, or it can use a wide range of other media, from matchbook covers or magazines to radio, TV, or billboards.

direct sales strategy   Strategy where representatives sell to customers directly at home or work rather than through a retail establishment or other intermediary.

direct selling   Face-to-face selling away from a fixed retail location. Usually refers to a method of marketing consumer goods—everything from encyclopedias and insurance to cosmetics and nutritional products.

display advertising   Type of newspaper advertising that includes copy, illustrations or photographs, headlines, coupons, and other visual components.

display allowances   Fees paid to retailers to make room for and set up manufacturers' displays.

display type   A style of typeface used in advertising that is larger and heavier than normal text type. Display type is often used in headlines, subheads, logos, and addresses, and for emphasis.

distribution channel   The network of all the firms and individuals that take title, or assist in taking title, to the product as it moves from the producer to the consumer.

distribution element How and where customers will buy a company's product; either direct or indirect distribution.

distribution objectives Where, when, and how advertising should appear.

diverting Purchasing large quantities of an item at a regional promotional discount and shipping portions to areas of the country where the discount isn't being offered.

DMA See *designated market areas.*

donut When writing a jingle, a hole left for spoken copy.

drama message One of the three literary forms of advertising messages in which the characters act out events directly in front of an imagined empathetic audience.

drive times Radio use Monday through Friday at 6–10 A.M. and 3–7 P.M.

DSL See *digital subscriber line.*

dubs Duplicates of radio commercials made from the master tape and sent to stations for broadcast.

dummy A three-dimensional, hand-made layout of a brochure or other multipage advertising piece put together, page for page, just like the finished product will eventually appear.

dupes Copies of a finished television commercial that are delivered to the networks or TV stations for airing.

earned rate A discount applied retroactively as the volume of advertising increases through the year.

effective frequency The average number of times a person must see or hear a message before it becomes effective.

effective reach Term used to describe the quality of exposure. It measures the number or percentage of the audience who receive enough exposures for the message to truly be received.

eight-sheet-foot posters A type of outdoor advertising offering a 5-foot by 11-foot printing area on a panel surface 6 feet tall by 12 feet wide.

Elaboration Likelihood Model A theory of how persuasion occurs due to promotion communication. Psychologists Petty, Cacioppo, and Schumann theorize that the method of persuasion depends on the consumer's level of involvement with the product and the message. When consumers have a higher level of involvement with the product or the message, they will tend to comprehend product-related information, such as product attributes and benefits or demonstrations, at deeper, more elaborate levels. This can lead to product beliefs, positive brand attitudes, and purchase intention. On the other hand, people who have low involvement with the product or the message have little or no reason to pay attention to it or to comprehend the central message of the ad. As a result, direct persuasion is also low, and consumers form few if any brand beliefs, attitudes, or purchase intentions. However, these consumers might attend to some peripheral aspects of the ad or commercial—say, the pictures in the ad or the actors in a commercial—for their entertainment value. And whatever they feel or think about these peripheral, nonproduct aspects might integrate into a positive attitude toward the ad. See also *central route to persuasion* and *peripheral route to persuasion.*

electronic couponing In supermarkets, the use of frequent-shopper cards that automatically credit cardholders with coupon discounts when they check out. Also using touch-screen videos at the point of purchase, instant-print discounts, rebates, and offers to try new brands.

electronic media Radio and television, which may be transmitted electronically through wires or broadcast through the air.

electronic production The process of converting a script or storyboard into a finished commercial for use on radio, TV, or digital media.

electronic sign Large displays that provide text and graphic messages, similar to those found in sports stadiums.

e-mail advertising Has become one of the fastest growing and most effective ways to provide direct mail.

emotional appeals Marketing appeals that are directed at the consumer's psychological, social, or symbolic needs.

empirical research method A method of allocating funds for advertising that uses experimentation to determine the best level of advertising expenditure. By running a series of tests in different markets with different budgets, companies determine the most efficient level of expenditure.

endcap promotion A merchandising method that uses special displays on shelving at the end of aisles in a store. Endcap promotions usually highlight sale merchandise or new products. Such promotions are often one part of a large promotion program that includes coupons, discounts, or other enticements.

encoding Translating an idea or message into words, symbols, and illustrations.

endorsement See *testimonial.*

entertainment The second largest area of sponsorship, which includes things like concert tours, attractions, and theme parks.

environments Surroundings that can affect the purchase decision.

equipment-based service A service business that relies mainly on the use of specialized equipment.

ethical advertising Doing what the advertiser and the advertiser's peers believe is morally right in a given situation.

evaluation of alternatives Choosing among brands, sizes, styles, and colors.

evaluative criteria The standards a consumer uses for judging the features and benefits of alternative products.

evoked set The particular group of alternative goods or services a consumer considers when making a buying decision.

exchange The trading of one thing of value for another thing of value.

exclusive distribution The strategy of limiting the number of wholesalers or retailers who can sell a product in order to gain a prestige image, maintain premium prices, or protect other dealers in a geographic region.

exhibitive media Media designed specifically to help bring customers eyeball to eyeball with the product. These media include product packaging and trade show booths and exhibits.

exhibits A marketing or public relations approach that involves preparing displays that tell about an organization or its products; exhibits may be used at fairs, colleges and universities, or trade shows.

experimental method A method of scientific investigation in which a researcher alters the stimulus received by a test group or groups and compares the results with those of a control group that did not receive the altered stimulus.

exploratory research See *informal research.*

Explorer role A role in the creative process that searches for new information, paying attention to unusual patterns.

exposure value   The value of a medium determined by how well it exposes an ad to the target audience. In other words, how many people an ad "sees" rather than the other way around.

fact-based thinking   A style of thinking that tends to fragment concepts into components and to analyze situations to discover the one best solution.

family brand   The marketing of various products under the same umbrella name.

farm advertising   Advertising directed to farmers as businesspeople and to others in the agricultural business. Also called *agricultural advertising.*

farm publications   Magazines directed to farmers and their families or to companies that manufacture or sell agricultural equipment, supplies, and services.

FCC   See *Federal Communications Commission.*

FDA   See *Food and Drug Administration.*

feature article   Soft news about companies, products, or services that may be written by a PR person, the publication's staff, or a third party.

Federal Communications Commission (FCC)   Federal regulatory body with jurisdiction over radio, television, telephone, and telegraph industries. Through its licensing authority, the FCC has indirect control over broadcast advertising.

Federal Trade Commission (FTC)   The major federal regulator of advertising used to promote products sold in interstate commerce.

fee-commission combination   A pricing system in which an advertising agency charges the client a basic monthly fee for its services and also retains any media commissions earned.

feedback   A message that acknowledges or responds to an initial message.

first-run syndication   Programs produced specifically for the syndication market.

five Ms   The elements of the media mix that include markets, money, media, mechanics, and methodology.

flat rate   A standard newspaper advertising rate with no discount allowance for large or repeated space buys.

flats   Opaque plastic sheets that film negatives are mounted on in perfect registration; light passes through only where lines and dots are to appear on the printing plate.

flighting   An intermittent media scheduling pattern in which periods of advertising are alternated with periods of no advertising at all.

focus group   A qualitative method of research in which four or more people, typical of the target market, are invited to a group session to discuss the product, the service, or the marketing situation for an hour or more.

folders   Large, heavy-stock fliers, often folded and sent out as self-mailers.

font   A uniquely designed set of capital, small capital, and lowercase letters, usually including numerals and punctuation marks.

Food and Drug Administration (FDA)   Federal agency that has authority over the labeling, packaging, and branding of packaged foods and therapeutic devices.

foreign media   The local media of each country used by advertisers for campaigns targeted to consumers or businesses within a single country.

formal research   Collecting primary data directly from the marketplace using qualitative or quantitative methods.

forward buying   A retailer's stocking up on a product when it is discounted and buying smaller amounts when it is at list price.

four-color process   The method for printing color advertisements with tonal values, such as photographs and paintings. This process is based on the principle that all colors can be printed by combining the three primary colors—yellow, magenta (red), and cyan (blue)—plus black (which provides greater detail and density as well as shades of gray).

four Ps   See *marketing mix.*

fragrance strips   Perfume samples included in sealed inserts in magazines.

franchising   A type of vertical marketing system in which dealers pay a fee to operate under the guidelines and direction of the manufacturer.

freestanding inserts (FSIs)   Coupons distributed through inserts in newspapers.

frequency   The number of times the same person or household is exposed to a vehicle in a specified time span. Across a total audience, frequency is calculated as the average number of times individuals or homes are exposed to the vehicle.

frequency discounts   In newspapers, advertisers earn this discount by running an ad repeatedly in a specific time period.

FTC   See *Federal Trade Commission.*

full position   In newspaper advertising, the preferred position near the top of a page or on the top of a column next to reading matter. It is usually surrounded by editorial text and may cost the advertiser 25 to 50 percent more than ROP rates.

full-service advertising agency   An agency equipped to serve its clients in all areas of communication and promotion. Its advertising services include planning, creating, and producing advertisements as well as performing research and media selection services. Nonadvertising functions include producing sales promotion materials, publicity articles, annual reports, trade show exhibits, and sales training materials.

full showing   A unit of purchase in transit advertising where one card will appear in each vehicle in the system.

game   A sales promotion activity in which prizes are offered based on chance. The big marketing advantage of games is that customers must make repeat visits to the dealer to continue playing.

gatefold   A magazine cover or page extended and folded over to fit into the magazine. The gatefold may be a fraction of a page or two or more pages, and it is always sold at a premium.

general consumer agency   An agency that represents the widest variety of accounts, but it concentrates on companies that make goods purchased chiefly by consumers.

geodemographic segmentation   Combining demographics with geographic segmentation to select target markets in advertising.

geographic editions   Magazines that target geographic markets and have different rates for ads.

geographic segmentation   A method of segmenting markets by geographic regions based on the shared characteristics, needs, or wants of people within the region.

global advertising   Advertising used by companies that market their products, goods, or services throughout various countries around the world with messages that remain consistent.

global marketers   Multinationals that use a standardized approach to marketing and advertising in all countries.

global positioning system (GPS)   New satellite-based system whereby outdoor advertising companies give their customers the exact latitude and longitude of particular boards. Media buyers, equipped with sophisticated new software on their desktop computers, can then integrate this information with demographic market characteristics and traffic counts to determine the best locations for their boards without ever leaving the office.

goods   Tangible products such as suits, soap, and soft drinks.

government markets   Governmental bodies that buy products for the successful coordination of municipal, state, federal, or other government activities.

gross impressions   The total of all the audiences delivered by a media plan.

gross rating points (GRPs)   The total audience delivery or weight of a specific media schedule. It is computed by dividing the total number of impressions by the size of the target population and multiplying by 100, or by multiplying the reach, expressed as a percentage of the population, by the average frequency. In television, gross rating points are the total rating points achieved by a particular media schedule over a specific period. For example, a weekly schedule of five commercials with an average household rating of 20 would yield 100 GRPs. In outdoor advertising, a 100 gross rating point showing (also called a number 100 showing) covers a market fully by reaching 9 out of 10 adults daily over a 30-day period.

group system   System in which an ad agency is divided into a number of little agencies or groups, each composed of an account supervisor, account executives, copywriters, art directors, a media director, and any other specialists required to meet the needs of the particular clients being served by the group.

growth stage   The period in a product life cycle that is marked by market expansion as more and more customers make their first purchases while others are already making their second and third purchases.

GRPs   See *gross rating points.*

guaranteed circulation   The number of copies of a magazine that the publisher expects to sell. If this figure is not reached, the publisher must give a refund to advertisers.

habit   An acquired or developed behavior pattern that has become nearly or completely involuntary.

halftone plate   Plate that prints dots, the combination of which, when printed, produces an optical illusion of shading as in a photograph.

halftone screen   A glass or plastic screen, crisscrossed with fine black lines at right angles like a window screen, which breaks continuous-tone artwork into dots so that it can be reproduced.

halo effect   In ad pretesting, the fact that consumers are likely to rate the one or two ads that make the best first impression as the highest in all categories.

headline   The words in the leading position of an advertisement—the words that will be read first or that are positioned to draw the most attention.

hidden differences   Imperceptible but existing differences that may greatly affect the desirability of a product.

hierarchy of needs   Maslow's theory that the lower biological or survival needs are dominant in human behavior and must be satisfied before higher, socially acquired needs become meaningful.

home page   In Internet advertising, an advertiser's virtual storefront or gateway to more specific information about the company and its products.

hook   The part of a jingle that sticks in your memory.

horizontal cooperative advertising   Joint advertising effort of related businesses (car dealers, realtors, etc.) to create traffic for their type of business.

horizontal publications   Business publications targeted at people with particular job functions that cut across industry lines, such as *Purchasing* magazine.

households using TV (HUT)   The percentage of homes in a given area that have one or more TV sets tuned on at any particular time. If 1,000 TV sets are in the survey area and 500 are turned on, the HUT figure is 50 percent.

house list   A company's most important and valuable direct-mail list, which may contain current, recent, and long-past customers or future prospects.

house organs   Internal and external publications produced by business organizations, including stockholder reports, newsletters, consumer magazines, and dealer publications. Most are produced by a company's advertising or public relations department or by its agency.

icon   A pictorial image that represents an idea or thing.

ideas   Economic, political, religious, or social viewpoints that advertising may attempt to sell.

illustrators   The artists who paint, sketch, or draw the pictures we see in advertising.

image advertising   Type of advertising intended to create a particular perception of the company or personality for the brand.

imagery transfer   When advertisers run a schedule on TV and then convert the audio portion to radio commercials, fully 75 percent of consumers replay the video in their minds when they hear the radio spot.

immersive advertising   Proprietary technique developed by Neopets.com for integrating an advertiser's products or services into the website experience.

implied consumers   The consumers who are addressed by the ad's persona. They are not real, but rather imagined by the ad's creators to be ideal consumers—acquiescing in whatever beliefs the text requires. They are, in effect, part of the drama of the ad.

incentive system   A form of compensation in which the agency shares in the client's success when a campaign attains specific, agreed-upon goals.

independent production house   Supplier company that specializes in film or video production or both.

independent research company   Research firms that work outside of an agency. They may come in all sizes and specialties, and they employ staff statisticians, field interviewers, and computer programmers, as well as analysts with degrees in psychology, sociology, and marketing.

independent shopping guide   Weekly local ad vehicles that may or may not contain editorial matter. They can be segmented into highly select market areas.

in-depth interview An intensive interview technique that uses carefully planned but loosely structured questions to probe respondents' deeper feelings.

individual brand Assigning a unique name to each product a manufacturer produces.

induced differences Distinguishing characteristics of products effected through unique branding, packaging, distribution, merchandising, and advertising.

industrial age A historical period covering approximately the first seventy years of the twentieth century. This period was marked by tremendous growth and maturation of the U.S. industrial base. It saw the development of new, often inexpensive brands of the luxury and convenience goods we now classify as consumer packaged goods.

industrializing age The period of time from the mid-1700s through the end of World War I when manufacturers were principally concerned with production.

industrial markets Individuals or companies that buy products needed for the production of other goods or services such as plant equipment and telephone systems.

infomercial A long TV commercial that gives consumers detailed information about a product or service; see also *program-length advertisement.*

informal research The second step in the research process, designed to explore a problem by reviewing secondary data and interviewing a few key people with the most information to share. Also called *exploratory research.*

informational motives The negatively originated motives, such as problem removal or problem avoidance, that are the most common energizers of consumer behavior.

in-house agency Agency wholly owned by an advertiser and set up and staffed to do all the work of an independent full-service agency.

in kind The donation of goods and services as payment for some service such as a sponsorship.

inquiry test A form of test in which consumer responses to an ad for information or free samples are tabulated.

insert An ad or brochure which the advertiser prints and ships to the publisher for insertion into a magazine or newspaper.

insertion order A form submitted to a newspaper or magazine when an advertiser wants to run an advertisement. This form states the date(s) on which the ad is to run, its size, the requested position, and the rate.

inside card A transit advertisement, normally 11 by 28 inches, placed in a wall rack above the windows of a bus.

institutional advertising A type of advertising that attempts to obtain favorable attention for the business as a whole, not for a specific product or service the store or business sells. The effects of institutional advertising are intended to be long term rather than short range.

institutional copy A type of body copy in which the advertiser tries to sell an idea or the merits of the organization or service rather than the sales features of a particular product.

in-store sampling The handing out of free product samples to passing shoppers.

integrated commercial A straight radio announcement, usually delivered by one person, woven into a show or tailored to a given program to avoid any perceptible interruption.

integrated marketing communications (IMC) The process of building and reinforcing mutually profitable relationships with employees, customers, other stakeholders, and the general public by developing and coordinating a strategic communications program that enables them to make constructive contact with the company/brand through a variety of media.

intellectual property Something produced by the mind, such as original works of authorship including literary, dramatic, musical, artistic, and certain other "intellectual" works, which may be legally protected by copyright, patent, or trademark.

intensive distribution A distribution strategy based on making the product available to consumers at every possible location so that consumers can buy with a minimum of effort.

intensive techniques Qualitative research aimed at probing the deepest feelings, attitudes, and beliefs of respondents through direct questioning. Typical methods include in-depth interviews and focus groups.

interactive agency An advertising agency that specializes in the creation of ads for a digital interactive medium such as Web pages, CD-ROMs, or electronic kiosks.

interactive TV A personal audience venue where people can personally guide TV programming through a remote control box while watching TV.

interconnects Groups of cable systems joined together for advertising purposes.

interior paragraphs Text within the body copy of an ad where the credibility and desire steps of the message are presented.

international advertising Advertising aimed at foreign markets.

international agency An advertising agency that has offices or affiliates in major communication centers around the world and can help its clients market internationally or globally.

international media Media serving several countries, usually without change, available to an international audience.

international structure Organization of companies with foreign marketing divisions, typically decentralized and responsible for their own product lines, marketing operations, and profits.

Internet A worldwide network of computer systems that facilitates global electronic communications via e-mail, the World Wide Web, ftp, and other data protocol.

Internet service provider (ISP) Companies which offer consumer and business access to the Internet.

interpersonal influences Social influences on the consumer decision-making process, including family, society, and cultural environment.

interstitial Animated screens, often advertisements, which pop up momentarily as the computer searches for and downloads information for a requested Web page. Also known as *splash pages.*

interview See *in-depth interview.*

introductory phase The initial phase of the product life cycle (also called the *pioneering phase*) when a new product is introduced, costs are highest, and profits are lowest.

inventory Commercial time for advertisers.

island half A half-page of magazine space that is surrounded on two or more sides by editorial matter. This type of ad is designed to dominate a page and is therefore sold at a premium price.

italic A style of printing type with letters that generally slant to the right.

jingle A musical commercial, usually sung with the sales message in the verse.

job jacket In the preproduction phase, a place to store the various pieces of artwork and ideas that will be generated throughout the process.

Judge role A role in the creative process that evaluates the results of experimentation and decides which approach is more practical.

junior unit A large magazine advertisement (60 percent of the page) placed in the middle of a page and surrounded by editorial matter.

kerning The measurement of the space between individual letters of text.

keyword A single word that a user inputs into an Internet search engine to request information that is similar in subject matter to that word. Advertisers may buy keywords from search engines so that their advertisements appear when a user inputs the purchased word.

kicker A subhead that appears above the headline.

kiosks Interactive computers in a stand-alone cabinet that make information available 24 hours a day even in remote areas.

layout An orderly formation of all the parts of an advertisement. In print, it refers to the arrangement of the headline, subheads, visuals, copy, picture captions, trademarks, slogans, and signature. In television, it refers to the placement of characters, props, scenery, and product elements, the location and angle of the camera, and the use of lighting. See also *design*.

leading The measurement of the space between separate lines of text (pronounced *ledding*).

lead-in paragraph In print ads, a bridge between the headlines, the subheads, and the sales ideas presented in the text. It transfers reader interest to product interest.

learning A relatively permanent change in thought processes or behavior that occurs as a result of reinforced experience.

letter shop A firm that stuffs envelopes, affixes labels, calculates postage, sorts pieces into stacks or bundles, and otherwise prepares items for mailing.

licensed brands Brand names that other companies can buy the right to use.

lifestyle technique Type of commercial in which the user is presented rather than the product. Typically used by clothing and soft drink advertisers to affiliate their brands with the trendy lifestyles of their consumers.

lifetime customer value (LTCV) A measurement of a consumer's economic value to a company over the course of his or her entire lifetime which comes from developing lasting relationships.

limen Our threshold of perception.

line film The product of a photograph shot with orthographic film which yields a high-contrast black-and-white image with no gray tones.

line plate A printing plate used to produce black-and-white artwork from line film

linkage media In direct marketing, media that help prospects and customers link up with a company.

list broker An intermediary who handles rental of mailing lists for list owners on a commission basis.

live action The basic production technique in television that portrays real people and settings, as opposed to animation.

lobbying Informing government officials and persuading them to support or thwart administrative action or legislation in the interests of some client.

local advertising Advertising by businesses within a city or county directed toward customers within the same geographical area.

local agency Advertising agencies that specialize in creating advertising for local businesses.

local city magazine Most major U.S. cities have one of these publications. Typical readership is upscale, professional people interested in local arts, fashion, and business.

local time Radio spots purchased by a local advertiser.

location Shooting away from the studio. Location shooting adds realism but can also be a technical and logistical nightmare, often adding cost and many other potential problems.

logotype Special design of the advertiser's name (or product name) that appears in all advertisements. Also called a signature cut, it is like a trademark because it gives the advertiser individuality and provides quick recognition at the point of purchase.

long-term macro arguments Criticisms of advertising that focus on the social or environmental impact of marketing.

loss-leader advertising Advertising that promotes drastically discounted goods to create an impression of storewide low prices and thereby increase traffic in the store. Loss-leader merchandise may be offered at or below retailer cost in order to encourage the sales of more profitable merchandise.

lot Acreage outside a studio that is shielded from stray, off-site sounds.

Magazine Publishers Association (MPA) A trade group made up of more than 230 publishers who represent 1,200 magazines. It compiles circulation figures on ABC member magazines and promotes greater and more effective use of magazine advertising.

mail-response list A type of direct-mail list, composed of people who have responded to the direct-mail solicitations of other companies, especially those whose efforts are complementary to the advertiser's.

maintenance stage In the client-agency relationship, the day-to-day interaction that, when successful, may go on for years.

makegoods TV spots that are aired to compensate for spots that were missed or run incorrectly.

management (account) supervisors Managers who supervise account executives and who report to the agency's director of account services.

mandatories The address, phone number, Web address, etc., that the advertiser usually insists be included within an ad to give the consumer adequate information.

market A group of potential customers who share a common interest, need, or desire; who can use the offered good or service to some advantage; and who can afford or are willing to pay the purchase price. Also, an element of the media mix referring to the various targets of a media plan.

marketer Any person or organization that has products, services, or ideas to sell.

marketing The process of planning and executing the conception, pricing, promotion, and distribution of ideas, goods, and services to create exchanges that satisfy the perceived needs, wants, and objectives of individuals and organizations.

marketing communications   The various efforts and tools companies use to initiate and maintain communication with customers and prospects, including solicitation letters, newspaper ads, event sponsorships, publicity, telemarketing, statement stuffers, and coupons, to mention just a few.

marketing information system (MIS)   A set of procedures for generating an orderly flow of pertinent information for use in making market decisions.

marketing mix   Four elements, called the 4Ps (product, price, place, and promotion), that every company has the option of adding, subtracting, or modifying in order to create a desired marketing strategy.

marketing objectives   Goals of the marketing effort that may be expressed in terms of the needs of specific target markets and specific sales objectives.

marketing plan   The plan that directs the company's marketing effort. First, it assembles all the pertinent facts about the organization, the markets it serves, and its products, services, customers, and competition. Second, it forces the functional managers within the company to work together—product development, production, selling, advertising, credit, transportation—to focus efficiently on the customer. Third, it sets goals and objectives to be attained within specified periods of time and lays out the precise strategies that will be used to achieve them.

marketing public relations (MPR)   The use of public relations activities as a marketing tool.

marketing research   The systematic gathering, recording, and analysis of information to help managers make marketing decisions.

marketing strategy   The statement of how the company is going to accomplish its marketing objectives. The strategy is the total directional thrust of the company, that is, the how-to of the marketing plan, and is determined by the particular blend of the marketing mix elements (the 4 Ps) which the company can control.

market prep corporate advertising   Corporate advertising that is used to set the company up for future sales; it simultaneously communicates messages about the products and the company.

market segmentation   Strategy of identifying groups of people or organizations with certain shared needs and characteristics within the broad markets for consumer or business products and aggregating these groups into larger market segments according to their mutual interest in the product's utility.

markup   A source of agency income gained by adding some amount to a supplier's bill, usually 17.65 percent.

mass audience venue   One category of digital media based on audience size, where hundreds of people are in the live audience and millions more are watching at home.

mass media   Print or broadcast media that reach very large audiences. Mass media include radio, television, newspapers, magazines, and billboards.

master tape   The final recording of a radio commercial, with all the music, sound, and vocals mixed, from which dubs (duplicates) are recorded and sent to radio stations for broadcast.

maturity stage   That point in the product life cycle when the market has become saturated with products, the number of new customers has dwindled, and competition is most intense.

mechanical   The set type and illustrations or photographs pasted into the exact position in which they will appear in the final ad. Also called a *pasteup,* this is then used as the basis for the next step in the reproduction process.

mechanics   One of the five Ms of the media mix; dealing creatively with the available advertising media options.

media   A plural form of *medium,* referring to communications vehicles paid to present an advertisement to its target audience. Most often used to refer to radio and television networks, stations that have news reporters, and publications that carry news and advertising.

media buyer   Person responsible for negotiating and contracting the purchase of advertisement space and time in various media.

media-buying service   An organization that specializes in purchasing and packaging radio and television time.

media classes   Broad media categories of electronic, print, outdoor, and direct mail.

media commission   Compensation paid by a medium to recognized advertising agencies, usually 15 percent ($16 \frac{2}{3}$ percent for outdoor), for advertising placed with it.

Mediamark Research, Inc. (MRI)   MRI conducts personal interviews to determine readership patterns, reports the audience and demographics for leading magazines and newspapers, and publishes annual studies on markets and decision makers.

media planning   The process that directs advertising messages to the right people in the right place at the right time.

media research   The systematic gathering and analysis of information on the reach and effectiveness of media vehicles.

media subclasses   Smaller divisions of media classes, such as radio, TV, magazines, newspapers, and so on.

media units   Specific units of advertising in each type of medium, such as half-page magazine ads, 30-second spots, and so on.

media vehicles   Particular media programs or publications.

medium   An instrument or communications vehicle that carries or helps transfer a message from the sender to the receiver. Plural is media. See also *media.*

mental files   Stored memories in the consumer's mind.

merchandise   Synonymous with *product concept* when used in reference to the 5Ms of advertising testing.

message   In oral communication, the idea formulated and encoded by the source and sent to the receiver.

message strategy   The specific determination of what a company wants to say and how it wants to say it. The elements of the message strategy include verbal, nonverbal, and technical components; also called *rationale.*

message weight   The total size of the audience for a set of ads or an entire campaign.

meta ad   An advertisement displayed on the results page of a search, specific to the searched term.

methodology   The overall strategy of selecting and scheduling media vehicles to achieve the desired reach, frequency, and continuity objectives.

mixed interlock   The edited version of a filmed television commercial mixed with the finished sound track. Used for initial review and approval prior to being duplicated for airing.

mixed-media approach   Using a combination of advertising media vehicles in a single advertising campaign.

mnemonic device   A gimmick used to dramatize the product benefit and make it memorable, such as the Imperial Margarine crown or the Avon doorbell.

mobile billboard A cross between traditional billboards and transit advertising; some specially designed flatbed trucks carry long billboards up and down busy thoroughfares.

Mondrian grid layout A layout style that uses a series of vertical and horizontal lines, rectangles, and squares within a predetermined grid to give geometric proportion to an ad.

money In media planning, one of the five elements in the media mix.

montage layout Similar to the circus layout, the montage layout brings multiple illustrations together and arranges them by superimposing or overlapping them to make a single composition.

motivation The underlying drives that stem from the conscious or unconscious needs of the consumer and contribute to the individual consumer's purchasing actions.

motivation value A consideration in selecting media based on the medium's ability to motivate people to act. Positive factors include prestige, good quality reproduction, timeliness, and editorial relevance.

motives Emotions, desires, physiological needs, or similar impulses that may incite consumers to action.

MPA See *Magazine Publishers Association.*

MSN TV A service offered by Microsoft that allows individuals to access Internet services (such as e-mail and traditional Web pages) using special hardware and a typical television set instead of a computer.

multimedia presentation Presenting information or entertainment using several communications media simultaneously.

multinational corporations Corporations operating and investing throughout many countries and making decisions based on availabilities worldwide.

musical commercial See *jingle.*

musical logo A jingle that becomes associated with a product or company through consistent use.

NAD See *National Advertising Division.*

NAICS See *North American Industry Classification System.*

NARB See *National Advertising Review Board.*

NARC See *National Advertising Review Council.*

narrative copy A type of body copy that tells a story. It sets up a problem and then creates a solution using the particular sales features of the product or service as the key to the solution.

narrative message Advertising in which a third person tells a story about others to an imagined audience.

narrowband A type of digital data transmission in which wires carry only one signal (channel) at a time. Examples of narrowband transmission include many telephone calls and most transmissions between computers and peripheral devices such as printers.

national advertisers Companies which advertise in several geographic regions or throughout the country.

national advertising Advertising used by companies that market their products, goods, or services in several geographic regions or throughout the country.

National Advertising Division (NAD) The National Advertising Division of the Council of Better Business Bureaus. It investigates and monitors advertising industry practices.

National Advertising Review Board (NARB) A five-member panel, composed of three advertisers, one agency representative, and one layperson, selected to review decisions of the NAD.

National Advertising Review Council (NARC) An organization founded by the Council of Better Business Bureaus and various advertising industry groups to promote and enforce standards of truth, accuracy, taste, morality, and social responsibility in advertising.

national agency Advertising agencies that produce and place the quality of advertising suitable for national campaigns.

national brands Product brands that are marketed in several regions of the country.

national magazines Magazines that are distributed throughout a country.

national rate A newspaper advertising rate that is higher, attributed to the added costs of serving national advertisers.

needs The basic, often instinctive, human forces that motivate us to do something.

need-satisfying objectives A marketing objective that shifts management's view of the organization from a producer of products or services to a satisfier of target market needs.

negatively originated motives Consumer purchase and usage based on problem removal or problem avoidance. To relieve such feelings, consumers actively seek a new or replacement product.

network marketing A method of direct distribution in which individuals act as independent distributors for a manufacturer or private-label marketer.

networks Any of the national television or radio broadcasting chains or companies such as ABC, CBS, NBC, or Fox. Networks offer the large advertiser convenience and efficiency because the message can be broadcast simultaneously throughout the country.

news/information headline A type of headline that includes many of the "how-to" headlines as well as headlines that seek to gain identification for their sponsors by announcing some news or providing some promise of information.

Newspaper Association of America (NAA) The promotional arm of the American Newspaper Publishers Association and the nation's newspaper industry.

Newspaper Space Bank (NSB) An online database service through which advertisers can buy canceled, unsold, or remnant space in major market newspapers at deeply discounted rates after normal closings.

news release A typewritten sheet of information (usually $8\frac{1}{2}$ by 11 inches) issued to print and broadcast outlets to generate publicity or shed light on a subject of interest. Also called *press release.*

NLEA See *Nutritional Labeling and Education Act.*

noise The sender's advertising message competing daily with hundreds of other commercial and noncommercial messages.

noncommercial advertising Advertising sponsored by or for a charitable institution, civic group, religious order, political organization, or some other nonprofit group to stimulate donations, persuade people to vote one way or another, or bring attention to social causes.

nonpersonal communication Marketing activities that use some medium as an intermediary for communication, including advertising, direct marketing, public relations, collateral materials, and sales promotion.

nonpersonal influences Factors influencing the consumer decision-making process that are often out of the consumer's control, such as time, place, and environment.

nonpersonal selling All selling activities that use some medium as an intermediary for communication, including advertising, public relations, sales promotion, and collateral materials.

nonprobability samples Research samples that do not provide every unit in the population with an equal chance of being included. As a result, there is no guarantee that the sample will be representative.

nonproduct advertising Advertising designed to sell ideas or a philosophy rather than products or services.

nonproduct facts Product claims not about the brand but about the consumer or the social context in which the consumer uses the brand.

nonverbal Communication other than through the use of words, normally visual.

North American Industry Classification System (NAICS) codes Method used by the U.S. Department of Commerce to classify all businesses. The NAICS codes are based on broad industry groups, subgroups, and detailed groups of firms in similar lines of business.

Nutritional Labeling and Education Act (NLEA) A 1994 congressional law setting stringent legal definitions for terms such as fresh, light, low fat, and reduced calorie; setting standard serving sizes; and requiring labels to show food value for one serving alongside the total recommended daily value as established by the National Research Council.

objectives See *marketing objectives.*

objective/task method A method of determining advertising allocations, also referred to as the *budget-buildup method,* that defines objectives and how advertising is to be used to accomplish them. It has three steps: defining the objectives, determining strategy, and estimating the cost.

observation method A method of research used when researchers actually monitor people's actions.

off-network syndication The availability of programs that originally appeared on networks to individual stations for rebroadcast.

on camera Actually seen by the camera, as an announcer, a spokesperson, or actor playing out a scene.

100 showing The basic unit of sale for billboards or posters is 100 gross rating points daily. One rating point equals 1 percent of a particular market's population.

on-sale date The date a magazine is actually issued.

open rate The highest rate for a one-time insertion in a newspaper.

opinion leader Someone whose beliefs or attitudes are respected by people who share an interest in some specific activity.

opinion sampling A form of public relations research in which consumers provide feedback via interviews, toll-free phone lines, focus groups, and similar methods.

opportunities to see (OTS) A possible exposure of an advertising message to one audience member. Also called an *advertising impression.* Effective frequency is considered to be three or more opportunities-to-see over a four-week period; but no magic number works for every commercial and every product.

organizational buyers People who purchase products and services for use in business and government.

orthographic film A high-contrast photographic film yielding only black-and-white images, no gray tones.

outdoor advertising An out-of-home medium in the form of billboards.

out-of-home media Media such as outdoor advertising (billboards) and transit advertising (bus and car cards) that reach prospects outside their homes.

outside posters The variety of transit advertisements appearing on the outside of buses, including king size, queen size, traveling display, rear of bus, and front of bus.

overlay On a pasteup, a piece of clear plastic containing a second image from which a second printing plate can be made for color printing.

packaging The container for a product—encompassing the physical appearance of the container and including the design, color, shape, labeling, and materials used.

paid circulation The total number of copies of an average issue of a newspaper or magazine that is distributed through subscriptions and newsstand sales.

PANTONE Matching System® (PMS) A collection of colors that are premixed according to a formula and given a specific color number. PANTONE® swatch books feature over 100 colors in solid and screened blocks printed on different paper finishes.

participation basis The basis on which most network television advertising is sold, with advertisers buying 30- or 60-second segments within the program. This allows the advertiser to spread out the budget and makes it easier to get in and out of a program without a long-term commitment.

pasteup See *mechanical.*

patent A grant made by the government that confers upon the creator of an invention the sole right to make, use, and sell that invention for a set period of time.

people-based service A service that relies on the talents and skills of individuals rather than on highly technical or specialized equipment.

percentage-of-sales method A method of advertising budget allocation based on a percentage of the previous year's sales, the anticipated sales for the next year, or a combination of the two.

perceptible differences Differences between products that are visibly apparent to the consumer.

perception Our personalized way of sensing and comprehending stimuli.

perceptual screens The physiological or psychological perceptual filters that messages must pass through.

peripheral route to persuasion One of two ways researchers Petty, Cacioppo, and Schumann theorize that marketers can persuade consumers. People who have low involvement with the product or message have little or no reason to pay attention to it or to comprehend the central message of the ad. However, these consumers might attend to some peripheral aspects of an ad or commercial for their entertainment value. Whatever they feel or think about these peripheral, nonproduct aspects might integrate into a positive attitude toward the ad. At some later date, these ad-related meanings could be activated to form some brand attitude or purchase intention. Typical of advertising for many everyday low-involvement purchases such as many consumer packaged goods: soap, cereal, toothpaste, and chewing gum. See also *elaboration likelihood model.*

persona A real or imaginary spokesperson who lends some voice or tone to an advertisement or commercial.

personal audience venue A category of digital media based on audience size; where one person in front of a personal computer can receive multimedia information.

personal communication Marketing activities that include all person-to-person contact with customers.

personal processes The three internal, human operations—perception, learning, and motivation—that govern the way consumers discern raw data (stimuli) and translate them into feelings, thoughts, beliefs, and actions.

personal selling A sales method based on person-to-person contact, such as by a salesperson at a retail establishment or by a telephone solicitor.

persuasion A change in thought process or behavior that occurs when the change in belief, attitude, or behavioral intention is caused by promotion communication (such as advertising or personal selling).

philanthropy Support for a cause without any commercial incentive.

photographers The artists who use cameras to create visuals for advertisements.

physiological screens The perceptual screens that use the five senses—sight, hearing, touch, taste, and smell—to detect incoming data and measure the dimension and intensity of the physical stimulus.

picture-caption copy A type of body copy in which the story is told through a series of illustrations and captions rather than through the use of a copy block alone.

picture-window layout Layout that employs a single, dominant visual that occupies between 60 and 70 percent of an advertisement's total area. Also known as *poster-style format* or *Ayer No. 1*.

platform licensing A fee paid to original software developers for the special key codes that access multimedia programs on certain computer networks.

point In retailing, the place of business. In typography, the measurement of the size and height of a text character. There are 72 points to an inch.

point-of-purchase (P-O-P) advertising Materials set up at a retail location to build traffic, advertise the product, and promote impulse buying. Materials may include window displays, counter displays, floor and wall displays, streamers, and posters.

polybagging Samples are delivered in plastic bags with the daily newspaper or a monthly magazine.

pop-up ad A three-dimensional magazine ad.

position The way in which a product is ranked in the consumer's mind by the benefits it offers, by the way it is classified or differentiated from the competition, or by its relationship to certain target markets.

positioning strategy An effective way to separate a particular brand from its competitors by associating that brand with a particular set of customer needs.

positively originated motives Consumer's motivation to purchase and use a product based on a positive bonus that the product promises, such as sensory gratification, intellectual stimulation, or social approval.

postcards Cards sent by advertisers to announce sales, offer discounts, or otherwise generate consumer traffic.

posters For public relations purposes, signs that impart product information or other news of interest to consumers, or that are aimed at employee behavior, such as safety, courtesy, or waste reduction.

poster-style format Layout that employs a single, dominant visual that occupies between 60 and 70 percent of an advertisement's total area. Also known as *picture-window layout* and *Ayer No. 1*.

postindustrial age Period of cataclysmic change, starting in about 1980, when people first became truly aware of the sensitivity of the environment in which we live.

postproduction phase The finishing phase in commercial production—the period after recording and shooting when a radio or TV commercial is edited and sweetened with music and sound effects.

postpurchase dissonance See *theory of cognitive dissonance.*

postpurchase evaluation Determining whether a purchase has been a satisfactory or unsatisfactory one.

posttesting Testing the effectiveness of an advertisement after it has been run.

preemption rates Lower TV advertising rate that stations charge when the advertiser agrees to allow the station to sell its time to another advertiser willing to pay a higher rate.

preferred position rate A choice position for a newspaper or magazine ad for which a higher rate is charged.

preindustrial age Period of time between the beginning of written history and roughly the start of the nineteenth century, during which the invention of paper and the printing press and increased literacy gave rise to the first forms of written advertising.

premium An item offered free or at a bargain price to encourage the consumer to buy an advertised product.

prepress phase The process of converting page art and visuals into materials (generally film negatives and color separation) needed for printing.

preprinted inserts Newspaper advertisements printed in advance by the advertiser and then delivered to the newspaper plant to be inserted into a specific edition. Preprints are inserted into the fold of the newspaper and look like a separate, smaller section of the paper.

preproduction phase The period of time before the actual recording or shooting of a commercial—the planning phase in commercial production.

prerelationship stage The initial stage in the client-agency relationship before they officially do business.

presenter commercial A commercial format in which one person or character presents the product and sales message.

press agentry The planning of activities and the staging of events to attract attention to new products or services and to generate publicity about the company or organization that will be of interest to the media.

press kit A package of publicity materials used to give information to the press at staged events such as press conferences or open houses. Also, a package of sales material promoting a specific media vehicle. Also called a *media kit.*

press release See *news release.*

pretesting Testing the effectiveness of an advertisement for gaps or flaws in message content before recommending it to clients, often conducted through focus groups.

price element In the marketing mix, the amount charged for the good or service—including deals, discounts, terms, warranties, and so on. The factors affecting price are market demand, cost of production and distribution, competition, and corporate objectives.

primary circulation The number of people who receive a publication, whether through direct purchase or subscription.

primary data   Research information gained directly from the marketplace.

primary demand   Consumer demand for a whole product category.

primary demand trend   The projection of future consumer demand for a whole product category based on past demand and other market influences.

primary motivation   The pattern of attitudes and activities that help people reinforce, sustain, or modify their social and self-image. An understanding of the primary motivation of individuals helps advertisers promote and sell goods and services.

prime time   Highest level of TV viewing (8 P.M. to 11 P.M. EST).

printer   Business that employs or contracts with highly trained specialists who prepare artwork for reproduction, operate digital scanning machines to make color separations and plates, operate presses and collating machines, and run binderies.

print media   Any commercially published, printed medium, such as newspapers and magazines, that sells advertising space to a variety of advertisers.

print production manager   Manager who oversees the entire production process, including reproduction of visuals in full color, shooting and editing of scenes, precise specification and placement of type, and the checking, approving, duplicating, and shipping of final art, negatives, tape, or film to the communication media.

print production process   The systematic process a layout for an ad or a brochure goes through from concept to final printing. The four major phases are preproduction, production, prepress, and printing and distribution.

privacy rights   Of or pertaining to an individual's right to prohibit personal information from being divulged to the public.

private audience venue   A category of digital media based on audience size; where meetings, conferences, and seminars use computer-driven multimedia presentations to inform, persuade, remind, and entertain people.

private labels   Personalized brands applied by distributors or dealers to products supplied by manufacturers. Private brands are typically sold at lower prices in large retail chain stores.

process   A planned series of actions or methods that take place sequentially, such as developing products, pricing them strategically, making them available to customers through a distribution network, and promoting them through sales and advertising activities.

producer   For electronic media, the person responsible for keeping the project moving smoothly and under budget, while maintaining the required level of quality through every step of the production process.

product   The particular good or service a company sells. See also *product concept.*

product advertising   Advertising intended to promote goods and services; also a functional classification of advertising.

product concept   The consumer's perception of a product as a "bundle" of utilitarian and symbolic values that satisfy functional, social, psychological, and other wants and needs. Also, as an element of the creative mix used by advertisers to develop advertising strategy, it is the bundle of product values the advertiser presents to the consumer.

product element   The most important element of the marketing mix: the good or service being offered and the values associated with it—including the way the product is designed and classified, positioned, branded, and packaged.

production phase   An element of creative strategy. The whole physical process of producing ads and commercials; also the particular phase in the process when the recording and shooting of commercials is done.

product life cycle   Progressive stages in the life of a product—including introduction, growth, maturity, and decline—that affect the way a product is marketed and advertised.

product placement   Paying a fee to have a product included in a movie.

professional advertising   Advertising directed at individuals who are normally licensed to operate under a code of ethics or set of professional standards.

program-length advertisement (PLA)   A long-form television commercial that may run as long as an hour; also called an *infomercial.*

programming format   The genre of music or other programming style that characterizes and differentiates radio stations from each other (i.e., contemporary hit radio, country, rock, etc.).

program rating   The percentage of TV households in an area that are tuned in to a specific program.

projective techniques   In marketing research, asking indirect questions or otherwise involving consumers in a situation where they can express feelings about the problem or product. The purpose is to get an understanding of people's underlying or subconscious feelings, attitudes, opinions, needs, and motives.

proof copy   A copy of the completed advertisement that is used to check for final errors and corrections.

prospective customers   People who are about to make an exchange or are considering it.

provocative headline   A type of headline written to provoke the reader's curiosity so that, to learn more, the reader will read the body copy.

psychographics   The grouping of consumers into market segments on the basis of psychological makeup—values, attitudes, personality, and lifestyle.

psychographic segmentation   Method of defining consumer markets based on psychological variables including values, attitudes, personality, and lifestyle.

psychological screens   The perceptual screens consumers use to evaluate, filter, and personalize information according to subjective standards, primarily emotions and personality.

public affairs   All activities related to the community citizenship of an organization, including dealing with community officials and working with regulatory bodies and legislative groups.

publicity   The generation of news about a person, product, or service that appears in broadcast or print media.

public notices   For a nominal fee, newspapers carry these legal changes in business, personal relationships, public governmental reports, notices by private citizens and organizations, and financial reports.

public relations (PR)   The management function that focuses on the relationships and communications that individuals and organizations have with other groups (called *publics*) for the purpose of creating mutual goodwill. The primary role of public relations is to manage a company's reputation and help build public consent for its enterprises.

public relations activities   Publicity, press agentry, sponsorships, special events, and public relations advertising used to create public awareness and credibility—at low cost—for the firm.

public relations advertising Advertising that attempts to improve a company's relationship with its publics (labor, government, customers, suppliers, etc.).

publics In PR terminology, employees, customers, stockholders, competitors, suppliers, or general population of customers are all considered one of the organization's publics.

puffery Exaggerated, subjective claims that can't be proven true or false such as "the best," "premier," or "the only way to fly."

pull strategy Marketing, advertising, and sales promotion activities aimed at inducing trial purchase and repurchase by consumers.

pulsing Mixing continuity and flighting strategies in media scheduling.

purchase occasion A method of segmenting markets on the basis of *when* consumers buy and use a good or service.

push money (PM) A monetary inducement for retail salespeople to push the sale of particular products. Also called *spiffs.*

push strategy Marketing, advertising, and sales promotion activities aimed at getting products into the dealer pipeline and accelerating sales by offering inducements to dealers, retailers, and salespeople. Inducements might include introductory price allowances, distribution allowances, and advertising dollar allowances to stock the product and set up displays.

qualitative research Research that tries to determine market variables according to unquantifiable criteria such as attitudes, beliefs, and lifestyle.

quantitative research Research that tries to determine market variables according to reliable, hard statistics about specific market conditions or situations.

question headline A type of headline that asks the reader a question.

radio personality A disk jockey or talk show host.

random probability samples A sampling method in which every unit in the population universe is given an equal chance of being selected for the research.

rate base With magazines, the circulation figure on which the publisher bases its rates.

rate card A printed information form listing a publication's advertising rates, mechanical and copy requirements, advertising deadlines, and other information the advertiser needs to know before placing an order.

rating The percentage of homes or individuals exposed to an advertising medium.

rating services These services measure the program audiences of TV and radio stations for advertisers and broadcasters by picking a representative sample of the market and furnishing data on the size and characteristics of the viewers or listeners.

rational appeal Marketing appeals that are directed at the consumer's practical, functional need for the product or service.

rationale See *message strategy.*

reach The total number of *different* people or households exposed to an advertising schedule during a given time, usually four weeks. Reach measures the *unduplicated* extent of audience exposure to a media vehicle and may be expressed either as a percentage of the total market or as a raw number.

readers per copy (RPC) Variable used to determine the total reach of a given print medium. RPC is multiplied by the number of vendor and subscription sales to determine the total audience size.

reading notice A variation of a display ad designed to look like editorial matter. It is sometimes charged at a higher space rate than normal display advertising, and the law requires that the word *advertisement* appear at the top.

rebates Larger cash refunds on items from cars to household appliances.

recall tests Posttesting methods used to determine the extent to which an advertisement and its message have been noticed, read, or watched.

receiver In oral communication, this party decodes the message to understand it and responds by formulating a new idea, encodes it, and sends it back.

recency planning Erwin Ephron's theory that most advertising works by influencing the brand choice of consumers who are ready to buy, suggesting that continuity of advertising is most important.

recruitment advertising A special type of advertising, most frequently found in the classified sections of daily newspapers and typically the responsibility of a personnel department aimed at attracting employment applications.

reference groups People we try to emulate or whose approval concerns us.

regional advertiser Companies that operate in one part of the country and market exclusively to that region.

regional advertising Advertising used by companies that market their products, goods, or services in a limited geographic region.

regional agency Advertising agency that focuses on the production and placement of advertising suitable for regional campaigns.

regional publications Magazines targeted to a specific area of the country, such as the West or the South.

regular price-line advertising A type of retail advertising designed to inform consumers about the services available or the wide selection and quality of merchandise offered at regular prices.

relationship marketing Creating, maintaining, and enhancing long-term relationships with customers and other stakeholders that result in exchanges of information and other things of mutual value.

reliability An important characteristic of research test results. For a test to be reliable, it must be repeatable, producing the same result each time it is administered.

reputation management In public relations, the name of the long-term strategic process to manage the standing of the firm with various publics.

reseller markets Individuals or companies that buy products for the purpose of reselling them.

resellers Businesses that buy products from manufacturers or wholesalers and then resell the merchandise to consumers or other buyers; also called *middlemen.* These businesses do not change or modify the goods before they resell them. Resellers make their profits by selling the goods they buy for more than they paid. The most common examples of resellers are retail stores and catalog retailers. Internet retailers comprise a growing portion of the reseller business segment.

residual fee Payment to the talent if the commercial is extended beyond its initially contracted run.

resources axis A term in the Values and Lifestyles (VALS) typology relating to the range of psychological, physical, demographic, and material capacities that consumers can draw upon. The resource axis includes education, income, self-confidence, health, eagerness to buy, and energy level.

retail advertising   Advertising sponsored by retail stores and businesses.

retainer method   See *straight-fee method.*

reverse knockout   Area within a field of printed color on a page that is free of ink and allows the paper's surface to show.

RFM formula   The RFM formula is a mathematical model that provides marketers with a method to determine the most reliable customers in a company's database, according to Recency, Frequency, and Monetary variables.

rich mail   Technology that allows graphics, video, and audio to be included in an e-mail message.

rich media ads   The graphical animations and ads with audio and video elements that overlay the Web page or even float over the page. Most common types include animated banners, interstitials, superstitials, and rich mail.

roadblocking   Buying simultaneous air time on all four television networks.

ROP advertising rates   Run of paper. A term referring to a newspaper's normal discretionary right to place a given ad on any page or in any position it desires—in other words, where space permits. Most newspapers make an effort to place an ad in the position requested by the advertiser.

rough   Penciled sketch of a proposed design or layout.

run-of-paper   See *ROP advertising rates.*

run of station (ROS)   Leaving placement of radio spots up to the station in order to achieve a lower ad rate.

sale advertising   A type of retail advertising designed to stimulate the movement of particular merchandise or generally increase store traffic by placing the emphasis on special reduced prices.

sales letters   The most common form of direct mail. Sales letters may be typewritten, typeset and printed, printed with a computer insert (such as your name), or fully computer typed.

sales promotion   A direct inducement offering extra incentives all along the marketing route—from manufacturers through distribution channels to customers—to accelerate the movement of the product from the producer to the consumer.

sales promotion department   In larger agencies, a staff to produce dealer ads, window posters, point-of-purchase displays, and dealer sales material.

sales-target objectives   Marketing objectives that relate to a company's sales. They should be specific as to product and market, quantified as to time and amount, and realistic. They may be expressed in terms of total sales volume; sales by product, market segment, or customer type; market share; growth rate of sales volume; or gross profit.

sales test   A useful measure of advertising effectiveness when advertising is the dominant element, or the only variable, in the company's marketing plan. Sales tests are more suited for gauging the effectiveness of campaigns than of individual ads or components of ads.

sample   A portion of the population selected by market researchers to represent the appropriate targeted population. Also, a free trial of a product.

sample unit   The actual individuals chosen to be surveyed or studied.

sampling   Offering consumers a free trial of the product, hoping to convert them to habitual use.

sans serif   A type group that is characterized by a lack of serifs.

SAU   See *standard advertising unit.*

scale   The regular charge for talent and music agreed to in the union contract.

script   Format for radio and television copywriting resembling a two-column list showing dialog and/or visuals.

seal   A type of certification mark offered by such organizations as the Good Housekeeping Institute and Underwriters' Laboratories when a product meets standards established by these institutions. Seals provide an independent, valued endorsement for the advertised product.

search engine   Websites that are devoted to finding and retrieving requested information from the World Wide Web. Because search engines are the gatekeepers to information on the Internet they are extremely popular with advertisers.

secondary data   Information that has previously been collected or published.

secondary (pass-along) readership   The number of people who read a publication in addition to the primary purchasers.

selective demand   Consumer demand for the particular advantages of one brand over another.

selective distribution   Strategy of limiting the distribution of a product to select outlets in order to reduce distribution and promotion costs.

selective perception   The ability of humans to select from the many sensations bombarding their central processing unit those sensations that fit well with their current or previous experiences, needs, desires, attitudes, and beliefs, focusing attention on some things and ignoring others.

self-concept   The images we carry in our minds of the type of person we are and who we desire to be.

self-mailer   Any type of direct-mail piece that can travel by mail without an envelope. Usually folded and secured by a staple or a seal, self-mailers have a special blank space for the prospect's name and address.

serif   The most popular type group that is distinguished by smaller lines or tails called serifs that finish the ends of the main character strokes and by variations in the thickness of the strokes.

services   A bundle of benefits that may or may not be physical, that are temporary in nature, and that come from the completion of a task.

session   The time when the recording and mixing of a radio commercial takes place.

share-of-market/share-of-voice method   A method of allocating advertising funds based on determining the firm's goals for a certain share of the market and then applying a slightly higher percentage of industry advertising dollars to the firm's budget.

short rate   The rate charged to advertisers who, during the year, fail to fulfill the amount of space for which they have contracted. This is computed by determining the difference between the standard rate for the lines run and the discount rate contracted.

short-term manipulative arguments   Criticisms of advertising that focus on the style of advertising (e.g., that it is manipulative or deceptive).

showing A traditional term referring to the relative number of outdoor posters used during a contract period, indicating the intensity of market coverage. For example, a 100 showing provides an even and thorough coverage of the entire market.

signature cut See *logotype*.

Simmons Market Research Bureau (SMRB) A syndicated research organization that publishes magazine readership studies.

situation analysis A factual statement of the organization's current situation and how it got there. It includes relevant facts about the company's history, growth, products and services, sales volume, share of market, competitive status, market served, distribution system, past advertising programs, results of market research studies, company capabilities, and strengths and weaknesses.

slice of life A type of commercial consisting of a dramatization of a real-life situation in which the product is tried and becomes the solution to a problem.

slogan A standard company statement (also called a *tagline* or a *themeline*) for advertisements, salespeople, and company employees. Slogans have two basic purposes: to provide continuity for a campaign and to reduce a key theme or idea to a brief, memorable positioning statement.

slotting allowances Fees that manufacturers pay to retailers for the privilege of obtaining shelf or floor space for a new product.

social classes Traditional divisions in societies by sociologists—upper, upper-middle, lower-middle, and so on—who believed that people in the same social class tended toward similar attitudes, status symbols, and spending patterns.

social responsibility Acting in accordance to what society views as best for the welfare of people in general or for a specific community of people.

source In oral communication, this party formulates the idea, encodes it as a message, and sends it via some channel to the receiver.

spam Unsolicited, mass e-mail advertising for a product or service that is sent by an unknown entity to a purchased mailing list or newsgroup.

special effects Unusual visual effects created for commercials.

special events Scheduled meetings, parties, and demonstrations aimed at creating awareness and understanding for a product or company.

spectaculars Giant electronic signs that usually incorporate movement, color, and flashy graphics to grab the attention of viewers in high-traffic areas.

speculative presentation An agency's presentation of the advertisement it proposes using in the event it is hired. It is usually made at the request of a prospective client and is often not paid for by the client.

speechwriting Function of a public relations practitioner to write speeches for stockholder meetings, conferences, conventions, etc.

spiff See *push money*.

spillover media Foreign media aimed at a national population that are inadvertently received by a substantial number of the consumers in a neighboring country.

split runs A feature of many newspapers (and magazines) that allows advertisers to test the comparative effectiveness of two different advertising approaches by running two different ads of identical size, but different content, in the same or different press runs on the same day.

sponsor The company or organization ultimately responsible for the message and distribution of an advertisement. Although the sponsor is often not the author, the sponsor typically pays for the creation of the ad and its distribution.

sponsorial consumers A group of decision makers at the sponsor's company or organization who decide if an ad will run or not, typically composed of executives and managers who have the responsibility for approving and funding a campaign.

sponsorship The presentation of a radio or TV program, or an event, or even a website by a sole advertiser. The advertiser is often responsible for the program content and the cost of production as well as the advertising. This is generally so costly that single sponsorships are usually limited to TV specials.

spot announcements An individual commercial message run between programs but having no relationship to either. Spots may be sold nationally or locally. They must be purchased by contacting individual stations directly.

spot radio National advertisers' purchase of airtime on individual stations. Buying spot radio affords advertisers great flexibility in their choice of markets, stations, airtime, and copy.

SRDS See *Standard Rate and Data Service*.

stakeholders In relationship marketing, customers, employees, centers of influence, stockholders, the financial community, and the press. Different stakeholders require different types of relationships.

standard advertising unit (SAU) A system of standardized newspaper advertisement sizes that can be accepted by all standard-sized newspapers without consideration of their precise format or page size. This system allows advertisers to prepare one advertisement in a particular size or SAU and place it in various newspapers regardless of the format.

standardized outdoor advertising Specialized system of outdoor advertising structures located scientifically to deliver an advertiser's message to an entire market.

Standard Rate and Data Service (SRDS) A publisher of media information directories that eliminate the necessity for advertisers and their agencies to obtain rate cards for every publication.

standard-size newspaper The standard newspaper size, measuring approximately 22 inches deep and 13 inches wide and is divided into six columns.

statement stuffers Advertisements enclosed in the monthly customer statements mailed by department stores, banks, utilities, or oil companies.

stimulus Physical data that can be received through the senses.

stimulus-response theory Also called conditioning theory. Some stimulus triggers a consumer's need or want, and this in turn creates a need to respond.

stock posters A type of outdoor advertising consisting of ready-made 30-sheet posters, available in any quantity and often featuring the work of first-class artists and lithographers.

storyboard A sheet preprinted with a series of 8 to 20 blank frames in the shape of TV screens, which includes text of the commercial, sound effects, and camera views.

storyboard roughs A rough layout of a television commercial in storyboard form.

straight announcement The oldest type of radio or television commercial, in which an announcer delivers a sales message directly into the microphone or on-camera or does so off-screen while a slide or film is shown on-screen.

straight-fee (retainer) method   A method of compensation for ad agency services in which a straight fee, or *retainer*, is based on a cost-plus-fixed-fees formula. Under this system, the agency estimates the amount of personnel time required by the client, determines the cost of that personnel, and multiplies by some factor.

straight-sell copy   A type of body copy in which the text immediately explains or develops the headline and visual in a straightforward attempt to sell the product.

stripping   Assembling line and halftone negatives into one single negative, which is then used to produce a combination plate.

subculture   A segment within a culture that shares a set of meanings, values, or activities that differ in certain respects from those of the overall culture.

subhead   Secondary headline in advertisements that may appear above or below the headline or in the text of the ad. Subheads are usually set in a type size smaller than the headline but larger than the body copy or text type size. They may also appear in boldface type or in a different ink color.

subliminal advertising   Advertisements with messages (often sexual) supposedly embedded in illustrations just below the threshold of perception.

substantiation   Evidence that backs up cited survey findings or scientific studies that the FTC may request from a suspected advertising violator.

Sunday supplement   A newspaper-distributed Sunday magazine. Sunday supplements are distinct from other sections of the newspaper since they are printed by rotogravure on smoother paper stock.

supers   Words superimposed on the picture in a television commercial.

suppliers   People and organizations that assist both advertisers and agencies in the preparation of advertising materials, such as photography, illustration, printing, and production.

survey   A basic method of quantitative research. To get people's opinions, surveys may be conducted in person, by mail, on the telephone, or via the Internet.

sweepstakes   A sales promotion activity in which prizes are offered based on a chance drawing of entrants' names. The purpose is to encourage consumption of the product by creating consumer involvement.

SWOT analysis   An acronym for internal *strengths* and *weaknesses* and external *opportunities* and *threats*, which represent the four categories used by advertising managers when reviewing a marketing plan. The SWOT analysis briefly restates the company's current situation, reviews the target market segments, itemizes the long- and short-term marketing objectives, and cites decisions regarding market positioning and the marketing mix.

syndication   See *barter syndication, first-run syndication, off-network syndication.*

synergy   An effect achieved when the sum of the parts is greater than that expected from simply adding together the individual components.

tabloid newspaper   A newspaper size generally about half as deep as a standard-sized newspaper; it is usually about 14 inches deep and 11 inches wide.

tactics   The precise details of a company's marketing strategy that determine the specific short-term actions that will be used to achieve its marketing objectives.

tagline   See *slogan.*

take-ones   In transit advertising, pads of business reply cards or coupons, affixed to interior advertisements for an extra charge, that allow passengers to request more detailed information, send in application blanks, or receive some other product benefit.

talent   The actors in commercials.

target audience   The specific group of individuals to whom the advertising message is directed.

target market   The market segment or group within the market segment toward which all marketing activities will be directed.

target marketing process   The sequence of activities aimed at assessing various market segments, designating certain ones as the focus of marketing activities, and designing marketing mixes to communicate with and make sales to these targets.

taxicab exteriors   In transit advertising, internally illuminated, two-sided posters positioned on the roofs of taxis. Some advertising also appears on the doors or rear.

tearsheets   The printed ad cut out and sent by the publisher to the advertiser as a proof of the ad's print quality and that it was published.

technical   One of the three components of message strategy, it refers to the preferred execution approach and mechanical outcome including budget and scheduling limitations

telemarketing   Selling products and services by using the telephone to contact prospective customers.

telephone sales   See *telemarketing.*

Teleprompter   A two-way mirror mounted on the front of a studio video camera that reflects moving text to be read by the speaker being taped.

television households (TVHH)   Households with TV sets.

terminal posters   One-sheet, two-sheet, and three-sheet posters in many bus, subway, and commuter train stations as well as in major train and airline terminals. They are usually custom designed and include such attention getters as floor displays, island showcases, illuminated signs, dioramas (three-dimensional scenes), and clocks with special lighting and moving messages.

termination stage   The ending of a client-agency relationship.

testimonial   The use of satisfied customers and celebrities to endorse a product in advertising.

test market   An isolated geographic area used to introduce and test the effectiveness of a product, ad campaign, or promotional campaign, prior to a national rollout.

text   See *body copy.*

text paper   Range of less expensive papers that are lightweight. More porous versions are used in printing newspapers and finer, glossier versions are used for quality printed materials like magazines and brochures.

text type   The smaller type used in the body copy of an advertisement.

themeline   See *slogan.*

theory of cognitive dissonance   The theory that people try to justify their behavior by reducing the degree to which their impressions or beliefs are inconsistent with reality.

30-sheet poster panel The basic outdoor advertising structure; it consists of blank panels with a standardized size and border. Its message is first printed on large sheets of paper and then mounted by hand on the panel.

3-D ads Magazine ads requiring the use of 3-D glasses.

thumbnail A rough, rapidly produced pencil sketch that is used for trying out ideas.

top-down marketing The traditional planning process with four main elements: situation analysis, marketing objectives, marketing strategy, and tactics or action programs.

total audience The total number of homes reached by some portion of a TV program. This figure is normally broken down to determine the distribution of audience into demographic categories.

total audience plan (TAP) A radio advertising package rate that guarantees a certain percentage of spots in the better dayparts.

total bus A special transit advertising buy that covers the entire exterior of a bus, including the front, rear, sides, and top.

trade advertising The advertising of goods and services to middlemen to stimulate wholesalers and retailers to buy goods for resale to their customers or for use in their own businesses.

trade concentration More products being sold by fewer retailers.

trade deals Short-term dealer discounts on the cost of a product or other dollar inducements to sell a product.

trademark Any word, name, symbol, device, or any combination thereof adopted and used by manufacturers or merchants to identify their goods and distinguish them from those manufactured or sold by others.

trade promotions See *push strategy*.

trade shows Exhibitions where manufacturers, dealers, and buyers of an industry's products can get together for demonstrations and discussion; expose new products, literature, and samples to customers; and meet potential new dealers for their products.

transformational motives Positively originated motives that promise to "transform" the consumer through sensory gratification, intellectual stimulation, and social approval. Also called *reward motives*.

transit advertising An out-of-home medium that actually includes three separate media forms: inside cards; outside posters; and station, platform, and terminal posters.

transit shelter advertising A newer form of out-of-home media, where advertisers can buy space on bus shelters and on the backs of bus-stop seats.

transnational (global) markets Consumer, business, and government markets located in foreign countries.

trap Where, in the printing process, one color overlays the edge of another to keep the paper from showing through.

trial close In ad copy, requests for the order that are made before the close in the ad.

TV households (TVHH) The number of households in a market area that own television sets.

type families Related typefaces in which the basic design remains the same but in which variations occur in the proportion, weight, and slant of the characters. Variations commonly include light, medium, bold, extra bold, condensed, extended, and italic.

typography The art of selecting, setting, and arranging type.

UHF (ultrahigh frequency) Television channels 14 through 83; about half of the U.S. commercial TV stations are UHF.

unfair advertising According to the FTC, advertising that causes a consumer to be "unjustifiably injured" or that violates public policy.

Universal Product Code (UPC) An identifying series of vertical bars with a 12-digit number that adorns every consumer packaged good.

universe An entire target population.

usage rates The extent to which consumers use a product: light, medium, or heavy.

user status Six categories into which consumers can be placed, which reflect varying degrees of loyalties to certain brands and products. The categories are *sole users, semisole users, discount users, aware nontriers, trial/rejectors,* and *repertoire users*.

U.S. Patent and Trademark Office Bureau within the U.S. Department of Commerce that registers and protects patents and trademarks.

utility A product's ability to provide both symbolic or psychological want satisfaction and functional satisfaction. A product's problem-solving potential may include form, time, place, or possession utility.

validity An important characteristic of a research test. For a test to be valid, it must reflect the true status of the market.

value The ratio of perceived benefits to the price of the product.

value-based thinking A style of thinking where decisions are based on intuition, values, and ethical judgments.

venue marketing A form of sponsorship that links a sponsor to a physical site such as a stadium, arena, auditorium, or racetrack.

verbal Words, written or spoken.

vertical cooperative advertising Co-op advertising in which the manufacturer provides the ad and pays a percentage of the cost of placement.

vertical marketing system (VMS) A centrally programmed and managed system that supplies or otherwise serves a group of stores or other businesses.

vertical publications Business publications aimed at people within a specific industry; for example, Restaurants & Institutions.

VHF (very high frequency) Television channels 2 through 13; about half of the U.S. commercial TV stations are VHF.

video brochure A type of video advertising which advertises the product and is mailed to customers and prospects.

video news release (VNR) A news or feature story prepared in video form and offered free to TV stations.

viral marketing The Internet version of word-of-mouth advertising e-mail.

visualization The creative point in advertising where the search for the "big idea" takes place. It includes the task of analyzing the problem, assembling any and all pertinent information, and developing some verbal or visual concept of how to communicate what needs to be said.

visuals All of the picture elements that are placed into an advertisement.

voice-over In television advertising, the spoken copy or dialogue delivered by an announcer who is not seen but whose voice is heard.

volume discount   Discounts given to advertisers for purchasing print space or broadcast time in bulk quantities.

volume segmentation   Defining consumers as light, medium, or heavy users of products.

wants   Needs learned during a person's lifetime.

Warrior role   A role in the creative process that overcomes excuses, idea killers, setbacks, and obstacles to bring a creative concept to realization.

Web browser   Computer program that provides computer users with a graphical interface to the Internet.

Web design house   Art/computer studios that employ specialists who understand the intricacies of HTML and Java programming languages and can design ads and Internet Web pages that are both effective and cost efficient.

Web page   A single page out of an online publication of the World Wide Web, known as a website. Websites are made up of one or more Web pages and allow individuals or companies to provide information and services with the public through the Internet.

website   On the Internet, a place where a company or organization is located.

weekly newspapers   Newspapers that are published once a week and characteristically serve readers in small urban or suburban areas or farm communities with exclusive emphasis on local news and advertising.

word-count method   A method of copy casting in which all the words in the copy are counted and then divided by the number of words per square inch that can be set in a particular type style and size, as given in a standard table.

work print   The first visual portion of a filmed commercial assembled without the extra effects or dissolves, titles, or supers. At this time, scenes may be substituted, music and sound effects added, or other changes made.

World Wide Web (WWW)   One section of the Internet where advertisers use online services as an advertising medium.

writing paper   Form of plain, lightweight paper commonly used for printing fliers and for letterhead.

End Notes

Chapter One

1. www.altoids.com.
2. Ibid.
3. Altoids case study.
4. Ibid.
5. www.altoids.com.
6. Altoids case study.
7. "Advertising: The Way Great Brands Get to Be Great Brands" (retrieved from www.aaf.org).
8. R. Craig Endicott, "100 Leading National Advertisers," *Advertising Age,* special report, June 28, 2004, pp. S1–S21.
9. "Advertising: The Way Great Brands Get to Be Great Brands."
10. John McDonough, "FCB: From One-Man Fiefdom to Global Power-house," *Advertising Age,* Commemorative Section: "FCB at 120," December 13, 1993, p. F4.
11. Communication process adapted from J. Paul Peter and Jerry C. Olsen, *Understanding Consumer Behavior* (Burr Ridge, IL: Richard D. Irwin, 1994), p. 184.
12. Barbara B. Stern, "A Revised Communication Model for Advertising: Multiple Dimensions of the Source, the Message, and the Recipient," *Journal of Advertising,* June 1994, pp. 5–15.
13. Adapted from American Marketing Association definition of marketing: *Dictionary of Marketing Terms,* 2nd ed., Peter D. Bennett, ed. (New York: American Marketing Association, 1995).
14. Tom Duncan and Sandra Moriarty, *Driving Brand Value* (New York: McGraw-Hill, 1997), pp. 69–94.

Chapter Two

1. www.kodak.com.
2. Ibid.
3. Ibid.
4. Ibid.
5. Ibid.
6. Roland Marchand, *Creating the Corporate Soul* (Berkeley: University of California Press, 1985), pp. 48–49; Roland Marchand, *Advertising the American Dream* (Berkeley: University of California Press, 1985), p. 5.
7. William M. O'Barr, *Culture and the Ad,* excerpted at www2.uwsuper.edu/hps/mjohnson/intro/obarr.htm.
8. www.kodak.com.
9. John McDonough, "FCB: From One-Man Fiefdom to Global Power-house," *Advertising Age,* Commemorative Section: "FCB at 120," December 13, 1993, p. F4.
10. Some material in this section has been adapted from Hugh M. Cannon, *Course Packet for Advertising Management,* Fall 1996, Wayne State University.

11. William O'Barr, address to the Council on Advertising History, Duke University, March 12, 1993, reported in *Advertising in America: Using Its Past, Enriching Its Future* (Washington, DC: Center for Advertising History of the National Museum of American History, 1994), p. 6.
12. Leonard L. Bartlett, "Three Giants—Leo Burnett, David Ogilvy, William Bernbach: An Exploration of the Impact of the Founders' Written Communications on the Destinies of Their Advertising Agencies," paper presented to the annual meeting of the Association for Education in Journalism and Mass Communication, Kansas City, August 13, 1993.
13. Marcel Bleustein-Blanchet, *La Rage de Convaincre* (Paris: Editions Robert Laffont, 1970), pp. 307–10, 375; Jean-Marc Schwarz, "A Brief History of Ad Time," *Adweek,* February 14, 1994, p. 46.
14. Schwarz, "A Brief History of Ad Time."
15. Ibid.
16. Ibid.
17. Ibid.
18. Cannon, *Course Packet for Advertising Management.*
19. Warren Berger, "Chaos on Madison Avenue," *Los Angeles Times Magazine,* June 5, 1994, p. 14.
20. William F. Arens and Jack J. Whidden, "La Publicité aux Etats-Unis: Les Symptômes et les Stratégies d'une Industrie Surpeuplée," *L'Industrie de la Publicité au Québec* (Montreal: Le Publicité Club de Montréal, 1992), pp. 383–84.
21. Berger, "Chaos on Madison Avenue," pp. 12, 14.
22. Bob Coen, "Bob Coen's Insider's Report," December 2002, McCann-Erickson WorldGroup, www.universalmccann.com/ourview.html.
23. Judann Pollock, "Marketing Put on Hold," *Advertising Age,* September 17, 2001, pp. 1, 25.
24. Coen, "Bob Coen's Insider's Report."
25. R. Craig Endicott, "100 Leading National Advertisers," *Advertising Age,* special report, June 28, 2004, pp. S1–S21.
26. Tom Cuniff, "The Second Creative Revolution," *Advertising Age,* December 6, 1993, p. 22.
27. Coen, "Bob Coen's Insider's Report."
28. M. H. Moore, "Global Ad Trends Set Stage for '94," *Adweek,* January 3, 1994, p. 13.
29. John McManus, "Cable Proves It's Media's Live Wire," *Advertising Age,* November 26, 1990, p. S6; "Media & Measurement Technologies (Part 1)," *Direct Marketing,* March 1991, pp. 21–27, 79.
30. Tobi Elkin, "Analysts Predict iTV Growth in 2002," December 10, 2001, www.adage.com.
31. Clinton Wilder, "Interactive Ads," *Information Week,* October 3, 1994, p. 25.
32. Tom Cuniff, "The Second Creative Revolution," *Advertising Age,* December 6, 1993, p. 22.

33. Brad Lynch, address to the Council on Advertising History, Duke University, March 12, 1993, reported in *Advertising in America: Using Its Past, Enriching Its Future* (Washington, DC: Center for Advertising History of the National Museum of American History, 1994), p. 3.

Chapter Three

1. Sean Collins, "Quarterly Concern: The Boycott of Abercrombie & Fitch," *Disinformation* online, July 29, 2001, www.disinfo.com/archive/pages/dossier/id1439/pag1.

2. Quoted in Collins, "Quarterly Concern."

3. "National Coalition Requests Written Statement from Abercrombie & Fitch before Calling off Boycott," *National Coalition for the Protection of Children and Families Online,* December 10, 2003, http://php.eos.net/nationalcoalition/index.phtml.

4. John O'Toole, *The Trouble with Advertising* (New York: Times Books, 1985), pp. 7–14.

5. Marcel Bleustein-Blanchet, *La Rage de Convaincre* (Paris: Editions Robert Laffont, 1970), p. 25.

6. Ernest Dichter, *Handbook of Consumer Motivations* (New York: McGraw-Hill, 1964), pp. 6, 422–31.

7. Richard E. Kihlstrom and Michael H. Riordan, "Advertising as a Signal," *Journal of Political Economy,* June 1984, pp. 427–50.

8. Ivan Preston, *The Tangled Web They Weave* (Madison: University of Wisconsin Press, 1994), pp. 94–95.

9. John Kenneth Galbraith, "Economics and Advertising: Exercise in Denial," *Advertising Age,* November 9, 1988, pp. 80–84.

10. Fabiana Giacomotti, "European Marketers Keep Up Ad Budgets," *Adweek,* January 24, 1994, pp. 16–17.

11. Michael Schudson, *Advertising, The Uneasy Persuasion: Its Dubious Impact on American Society* (New York: Basic Books, 1984).

12. Ivan Preston, "A New Conception of Deceptiveness," paper presented to the Advertising Division of the Association for Education in Journalism and Mass Communication, August 12, 1993.

13. Ibid.

14. "Pizza Hut Files Suit against Pizza Rival," *Advertising Age,* August 13, 1998; "Papa John's Ordered to Move 'Better' Slogan," *Advertising Age,* January 5, 2000 (retrieved from http://adage.com).

15. Barry Newman, "An Ad Professor Huffs against Puffs, but It's a Quixotic Enterprise," *The Wall Street Journal,* January 24, 2003, pp. A1, A9.

16. Preston, *The Tangled Web They Weave,* pp. 185–98.

17. Stuart C. Rogers, "Subliminal Advertising: Grand Scam of the 20th Century," paper presented to the Annual Conference of the American Academy of Advertising, April 10, 1994.

18. Ibid.; Martha Rogers and Kirk H. Smith, "Public Perceptions of Subliminal Advertising," *Journal of Advertising Research,* March/April 1993, p. 10.

19. Andrew Jaffe, "Advertiser, Regulate Thyself," *Adweek,* August 2, 1993, p. 38.

20. Ibid.

21. Preston, *The Tangled Web They Weave,* p. 164.

22. Kevin Downey, "TV Ad Clutter Worsens, and Buyers Grouse," *Media Life Magazine,* February 15, 2002 (retrieved from www.medialifemagazine.com).

23. Joe Flint, "Meredith Cuts 'Clutter' and Boosts Ratings," *The Wall Street Journal,* January 4, 2000, p. B8.

24. "The Public and Broadcasting," FCC Mass Media Bureau, June 1999 (retrieved from www.fcc.gov/mb/audio/includes/45-public_and_broadcasting.htm).

25. "French May Get Second Break," *Advertising Age International,* October 11, 1993, p. I-6.

26. Laurie Freeman, "Ad Group Balks at Rule Change," *Advertising Age International,* October 11, 1993, p. I-6.

27. Shelly Garcia, "What's Wrong with Being Politically Correct?" *Adweek,* November 15, 1993, p. 62.

28. Adrienne Ward, "What Role Do Ads Play in Racial Tension?" *Advertising Age,* August 10, 1992, pp. 1, 35.

29. Joy Dietrich, "Women Reach High," *Advertising Age International,* January 1, 2000; quoted in Genaro C. Armas, "Women Gaining in Workplace," *Advocate,* Baton Rouge, LA, April 24, 2000 (retrieved from Lexis-Nexis Academic Universe).

30. U.S. Census Bureau, *Statistical Abstract of the United States: 2001* (Washington, DC: U.S. Department of Commerce, 2001; retrieved from www.census.gov).

31. John B. Ford and Michael S. LaTour, "Differing Reactions to Female Role Portrayals in Advertising," *Journal of Advertising Research,* September/October 1993, pp. 43–52.

32. Michael L. Klassen, Cynthia R. Jasper, and Anne M. Schwartz, "Men and Women: Images of their Relationships in Magazine Advertisements," *Journal of Advertising Research,* March/April 1993, pp. 30–39.

33. "Revealing Abercrombie Catalog Sparks a Boycott," *The Cincinnati Enquirer,* June 26, 2001 (retrieved from www.enquirer.com/editions/2001/06/26/tem_revealing.htm).

34. Mark Schone, "Rubbered Out," *Adweek,* July 18, 1994, p. 22.

35. Laurel Wentz and Geoffrey Lee Martin, "Cheaply Made Gore Scores," *Advertising Age,* July 4, 1994, p. 38.

36. Matt Warren, "Are You Ready for This?" *The Scotsman,* Edinburgh (UK), October 6, 2000, p. 9 (retrieved from Lexis-Nexis Academic Universe).

37. Gary Levin, "More Nudity, but Less Sex," *Advertising Age,* November 8, 1993, p. 37.

38. Caity Olson, "Ad Boycott Concern Is Real," *Advertising Age,* June 13, 1994, p. 3.

39. Preston, "A New Conception of Deceptiveness."

40. Robert W. McChesney, *Corporate Media and the Threat to Democracy* (New York: Seven Stories Press, 1997), p. 23.

41. Preston, *The Tangled Web They Weave,* pp. 94, 127–31.

42. James Maxeiner and Peter Schotthoffer, eds., *Advertising Law in Europe and North America* (Deventer, The Netherlands: Kluwer Law and Taxation Publishers, 1992), p. v; Rein Rijkens, *European Advertising Strategies* (London: Cassell, 1992), pp. 201–2.

43. Keith Boyfield, "Business Europe: When Advertising Is against the Law," *The Wall Street Journal, European edition,* March 6, 2000, p. 11 (retrieved from Lexis-Nexis Academic Universe).

44. Tobacco Advertising and Promotion Act 2002, January 2003 (retrieved from www.hmso.gov.uk/acts/acts2002/20020036.htm).

45. Raf Casert, "EU Approves Ban on Tobacco Advertising," Associated Press, December 3, 2002 (retrieved from www.aef.com/06/news/data/2002/2206).

46. Karly Preslmayer, "Austria," in Maxeiner and Schotthoffer, eds., *Advertising Law in Europe and North America.*

47. Peter Schotthoffer, "European Community," in Maxeiner and Schotthoffer, eds., *Advertising Law in Europe and North America,* p. 89.

48. "Last Minute News: Singapore Condemns Ads with Harmful Values," *Advertising Age,* August 29, 1994, p. 42.

49. "Regulation Briefs: Costa Rica May Soften Pre-clearance Rules," *Advertising Age International,* April 18, 1994, p. I4.

50. "Last Minute News: China Accepts Taiwanese Ads, after 45-Year Ban," *Advertising Age,* September 5, 1994, p. 38; Sally D. Goll, "Chinese Officials Attempt to Ban False Ad Claims," *The Wall Street Journal,* February 25, 1995, pp. B1, B9.

51. James R. Maxeiner, "United States," in Maxeiner and Schotthoffer, eds., *Advertising Law in Europe and North America,* p. 321; see also *Virginia State Board of Pharmacy* v. *Virginia Citizens Consumer Council,* 425 U.S. 748 (1976).

52. See *Central Hudson Gas & Electric Corp.* v. *Public Service Commission of New York,* 447 U.S. 557 (1980).

53. Kartik Pashupati, "The Camel Controversy: Same Beast, Different Viewpoints," paper presented to the annual conference of the Association for Education in Journalism and Mass Communication, Kansas City, MO, August 11, 1993; Maxeiner, "United States," pp. 321–22.

54. Steven W. Colford, "Big Win for Commercial Speech," *Advertising Age,* March 29, 1993, pp. 1, 47.

55. "Tobacco Settlement Agreement at a Glance," National Association of Attorneys General website: (www.naag.org), October 2000.

56. John Malmo, "Restricting Commercial Speech Isn't Justifiable," *The Commercial Appeal,* Memphis, TN, July 5, 1999, p. B3; John Malmo, "Banning Tobacco Ads Spells Monopoly," *The Commercial Appeal,* Memphis, TN, August 9, 1999, p. B4 (retrieved from ProQuest).

57. *Self-Regulatory Guidelines for Children's Advertising,* The Children's Advertising Review Unit (CARU), Copyright 2000 Council of Better Business Bureaus (retrieved from http://216.46.241.4/advertising/caruguid.asp); "CARU Issues Breakthrough Advertising Guidelines to Protect Children on the Internet," Better Business Bureau Press Release, April 21, 1997 (retrieved from www.caru.org/guidelines/index.asp).

58. "A Spoonful of Sugar: Television Food Advertising Aimed at Children: An International Comparative Survey," Consumers International.

59. "Online Privacy—It's Time for Rules in Wonderland," *Business Week,* March 20, 2000, p. 85.

60. http://news.cnet.com/news/0-1005-200-2572324.html.

61. FTC on the Web, July 2000, Federal Trade Commission (retrieved from http://adage.com).

62. http://news.cnet.com/news/0-1005-200-2572324.html.

63. Ibid.

64. "Online Privacy—It's Time for Rules in Wonderland."

65. www.ftc.gov/os/2000/07/onlineprofiling.htm.

66. Eric Gross and Susan Vogt, "Canada," in Maxeiner and Schotthoffer, eds., *Advertising Law in Europe and North America,* pp. 39, 41.

67. Federal Trade Commission, "Vision, Mission, and Goals," 1997.

68. Minette E. Drumwright, "Ethical Issues in Advertising and Sales Promotion," in N. Craig Smith and John A. Quelch, eds., *Ethics in Marketing* (Burr Ridge, IL: Richard D. Irwin, 1993), p. 610.

69. Ann Carrns, "FTC Settles with Office Depot, Buy.com, Value America over 'Low Cost' PC Ads," *The Wall Street Journal,* June 30, 2000, p. B4.

70. "Exxon Settles FTC Charges; Ground-Breaking Educational Ad Campaign Ordered," FTC news release, June 24, 1997.

71. David Riggle, "Say What You Mean, Mean What You Say," *In Business,* May/June 1990, pp. 50–51.

72. Dean Keith Fueroghne, *But the People in Legal Said . . .* (Burr Ridge, IL: Professional Publishing, 1989), p. 14.

73. Christy Fisher, "How Congress Broke Unfair Ad Impasse," *Advertising Age,* August 22, 1994, p. 34.

74. "Editorial: A Fair FTC Pact?" *Advertising Age,* March 21, 1994, p. 22.

75. "Arizona Trade Association Agrees to Settle FTC Charges It Urged Members to Restrain Competitive Advertising," FTC News Release, February 25, 1994 (retrieved from www.ftc.gov/opa/predawn/F95/azautodealers.htm).

76. "Comparative Advertising," *ADLAW,* copyright 2000 Hall Dickler Kent Goldstein & Wood (retrieved from www.adlaw.com/rc/handbk/rf comparative.html).

77. "Crackdown on Testimonials," *The Wall Street Journal,* July 13, 1993, p. B7.

78. Drumwright, "Ethical Issues in Advertising and Sales Promotion," pp. 615–16.

79. Ira Teinowitz, "Doan's Decision Sets Precedent for Corrective Ads," *Advertising Age,* September 4, 2000, p. 57.

80. Gross and Vogt, "Canada," pp. 50, 67.

81. "The Food and Drug Administration: An Overview," www.eduneering.com/fda/courses/fdatour/welcome.html.

82. "The Growing Brouhaha over Drug Advertisements," *The New York Times,* May 14, 1989, p. F8.

83. "FDA to Review Standards for All Direct-to-Consumer Rx Drug Promotion," FDA news release, August 8, 1997.

84. "FDA Seeks Rx for Drug Ads; New Policy Delays Process," *Newsday* (Nassau and Suffolk edition), December 5, 2002.

85. Steven W. Colford, "Labels Lose the Fat," *Advertising Age,* June 10, 1991, pp. 3, 54; Steven W. Colford and Julie Liesse, "FDA Label Plans under Attack," *Advertising Age,* February 24, 1992, pp. 1, 50; John E. Calfee, "FDA's Ugly Package: Proposed Label Rules Call for Vast Changes," *Advertising Age,* March 16, 1992, p. 25; Pauline M. Ippolito and Alan D. Mathios, "New Food Labeling Regulations and the Flow of Nutrition Information to Consumers," *Journal of Public Policy & Marketing,* Fall 1993, pp. 188–205.

86. John Carey, "The FDA Is Swinging a Sufficiently Large Two-by-Four," *Business Week,* May 27, 1991, p. 44; Steven W. Colford, "FDA Getting Tougher: Seizure of Citrus Hill Is Signal to Marketers," *Advertising Age,* April 29, 1991, pp. 1, 53.

87. Joe Mandese, "Regulation," *Advertising Age,* November 30, 1992, p. 23.

88. "The Experts Speak Out," *TV Guide,* August 22, 1992, p. 19.

89. U.S. Constitution, Article 1, Section 8.

90. U.S. Copyright Office, Library of Congress, 1997.

91. Wayne E. Green, "Lawyers Give Deceptive Trade-Statutes New Day in Court, Wider Interpretations," *The Wall Street Journal,* January 24, 1990, p. B1.

92. Howard Schlossberg, "Marketers Say State Laws Hurt Their 'Green' Efforts," *Marketing News,* November 11, 1991, pp. 8–9.

93. Frank Phillips, "Mass. in Court to Defend Curbs on Tobacco Ads," *The Boston Globe,* April 7, 2000, p. A1; Gaylord Shaw, "Smoking Ads a Smoldering Issue: High Court May Review City's Ban on Tobacco Displays," *Newsday,* Long Island, NY, March 18, 2000, p. A31.

94. E. J. Gong, "Fraud Complaints on the Rise, Reports D.A.," *Los Angeles Times,* February 13, 1994, p. B1.

95. "Closet Factory to Pay Penalty for Misleading Advertising," Orange County District Attorney press release, June 24, 2002.

96. Maxeiner, "United States," p. 321.

97. Ibid.

98. Felix H. Kent, "Control of Ads by Private Sector," *New York Law Journal,* December 27, 1985; reprinted in Kent and Stone, eds., *Legal and Business Aspects of the Advertising Industry,* 1986, pp. 20–79.

99. "NAD Pilots Successful Resolution Between Neil Cooper and Avirex," Better Business Bureau News Release, August 11, 2000 (retrieved from www.nadreview.org/casereports.asp).

100. Maxeiner, "United States," p. 321; NAD Case Report, National Advertising Division, Council of Better Business Bureaus, January 21, 1991.

101. Public Relations Department, KLBJ, Austin, TX, 1991.

102. Public Relations Department, KDWB, Minneapolis/St. Paul, MN, 1991.

103. Public Relations Department, KSDO, San Diego, CA, 1991.

104. Kevin Goldman, "From Witches to Anorexics, Critical Eyes Scrutinize Ads for Political Correctness," *The Wall Street Journal,* May 19, 1994, p. B1.

105. Garcia, "What's Wrong with Being Politically Correct?" p. 62.

106. Ibid.

107. Jaffe, "Advertiser, Regulate Thyself," p. 38.

108. Federal Trade Commission, 1991.

Chapter Four

1. www.bajagrill.com.

2. Jim Rowe, "Integrated Marketing Tips? Study Retail Trade," *Advertising Age,* April 4, 1994, p. 32.

3. Henry A. Laskey, J. A. F. Nicholls, and Sydney Roslow, "The Enigma of Cooperative Advertising," *Journal of Business and Industrial Marketing,* vol. 8, no. 2 (1993), pp. 70–79.

4. Riccardo A. Davis, "Retailers Open Doors Wide for Co-op," *Advertising Age,* August 1, 1994, p. 30.

5. Tobi Elkin, "Intel Set to Revamp $800 Million War Chest," *Advertising Age,* November 8, 1999, p. 1 (retrieved from http://webgate.sdsu.edu).

6. R. Craig Endicott, "100 Leading National Advertisers," *Advertising Age,* special report, June 28, 2004, p. S2 (retrieved from www.adage.com).

7. "100 Leading National Advertisers," *Advertising Age,* September 28, 1999 (retrieved from http://adage.com).

8. *Standard Directory of Advertisers* (New Providence, NJ: National Register Publishing Company, 2000), p. 616.

9. William O. Bearden, Thomas N. Ingram, and Raymond W. LaForge, *Marketing Principles & Perspectives* (Burr Ridge, IL: Richard D. Irwin, 1995), p. 96.

10. www.pg.com.

11. R. Craig Endicott, "100 Leading National Advertisers."

12. Alan Mitchell, "P&G Drops Old Job Tags in Rejig," *Marketing* (UK), October 14, 1993, p. 4.

13. Aelita G. B. Martinsons and Maris G. Martinsons, "In Search of Structural Excellence," *Leadership & Organization Development Journal,* vol. 15, no. 2 (1994), pp. 24–28.

14. Jennifer Lawrence, "Thinning Ranks at P&G," *Advertising Age,* September 13, 1993, p. 2.

15. E. Jerome McCarthy and William D. Perreault Jr., *Basic Marketing,* 11th ed. (Burr Ridge, IL: Richard D. Irwin, 1993), p. 593.

16. "U.S. Firms with the Biggest Foreign Revenues," *Forbes,* July 23, 1990, p. 362.

17. Eric N. Berkowitz, Roger A. Kerin, Steven W. Hartley, and William Rudelius, *Marketing,* 3rd ed. (Burr Ridge, IL: Richard D. Irwin, 1992), p. 609.

18. Anne Cooper, "Cosmetics: Changing Looks for Changing Attitudes," *Adweek,* February 22, 1993, pp. 30–36.

19. James E. Ellis, "Why Overseas? 'Cause That's Where the Sales Are," *BusinessWeek,* January 10, 1994, p. 63; "How CAA Bottled Coca-Cola," *Fortune,* November 15, 1993, p. 156; Deborah Hauss, "Global Communications Come of Age," *Public Relations Journal,* August 1993, pp. 22–23; Sally Solo, "How to Listen to Consumers," *Fortune,* January 11, 1993, pp. 77–78; Jennifer Lawrence, "Delta Gears Up for Global Fight," *Advertising Age,* August 19, 1991, pp. 3, 44; Charles Hennessy, "Globaldegook," *BusinessLondon,* March 1990, p. 131; Raymond Serafin, "W. B. Doner Hits a Gusher," *Advertising Age,* June 6, 1988, p. 43.

20. Jim Patterson, "Viewpoint: Global Communication Requires a Global Understanding," *Adweek,* October 31, 1994, p. 46; "Efficacy of Global Ad Prospects Is Questioned in Firm's Survey," *The Wall Street Journal,* September 13, 1984, p. 29.

21. Patterson, "Viewpoint: Global Communication Requires a Global Understanding."

22. Martinsons and Martinsons, "In Search of Structural Excellence."

23. Frederick R. Gamble, *What Advertising Agencies Are—What They Do and How They Do It,* 7th ed. (New York: American Association of Advertising Agencies, 1970), p. 4.

24. "Brands on Trial," *Adweek,* May 24, 1993, pp. 24–31.

25. Melanie Wells, "The Interactive Edge—Part II: Desperately Seeking the Super Highway," *Advertising Age,* August 22, 1994, pp. 14–19.

26. Jennifer Gilbert, "Gotham Gathers Interactive under Hinkaty," *Advertising Age,* July 31, 2000, p. 42 (retrieved from http://webgate.sdsu.edu).

27. *Standard Directory of Advertisers,* pp. 245–46.

28. "Casting a Broader Net," *The Washington Post,* August 17, 2002 (retrieved from http://pqasb.pqarchiver.com/washingtonpost/search.html).

29. Beth Snyder, "True North Unites Modem, Poppe into Digital Force," *Advertising Age,* May 1998 (retrieved from Articles & Opinions, http://adage.com); Kate Maddox, "Agency Pitch Heats Up Camp Interactive Show," *Advertising Age,* August 1998 (retrieved from Articles & Opinions, http://adage.com); "Think New Ideas Takes AnswerThink Moniker," *Advertising Age,* April 3, 2000 (retrieved from Interactive Daily, http://adage.com).

30. "Inside the AAAA," *Fact Sheet,* American Association of Advertising Agencies, August 15, 2000 (retrieved from www.aaaa.org/inside/about_us.html).

31. Kevin Goldman, "IBM—Account Fight Lifts Planner Profile," *The Wall Street Journal,* October 26, 1993, p. B8.

32. Nancy D. Holt, "Workspaces/A Look at Where People Work," *The Wall Street Journal,* January 22, 2003, p. B6.

33. Sally Goll Beatty, "Leo Burnett Group to Decentralize U.S. Operations," *The Wall Street Journal,* September 17, 1997, p. B10; Sally Goll Beatty, "Leo Burnett to Offer Small-Agency Style," *The Wall Street Journal,* September 18, 1997, p. B4; Dottie Enrico, "Ad Agency Ready for a New Day," *USA Today,* September 19, 1997, p. 5B.

34. Alison Fahey, "Agencies Look to Shape Up, Slim Down," *Adweek,* August 16, 1993, p. 4.

35. William F. Arens and Jack J. Whidden, "La Publicité aux Etats-Unis: Les Symptômes et les Stratégies d'une Industrie Surpleuplée," *L'Industrie de la Publicité au Québec* (Montreal: Le Publicité-Club de Montréal, 1992), pp. 383–84.

36. Jon Lafayette and Cleveland Horton, "Shops to Clients: Pay Up—4A's Members Call for an End to Free Services," *Advertising Age,* March 19, 1990, pp. 1, 66.

37. Andrew Jaffe, "Has Leo Burnett Come to the End of the 'Free Overservice' Era?" *Adweek,* December 6, 1993, p. 46; Melanie Wells and Laurel Wentz, "Coke Trims Commissions," *Advertising Age,* January 31, 1994, p. 2.

38. John Micklethwait, "Cut the Ribbon," *The Economist,* June 9, 1990, pp. S16–S17; Tom Eisenhart, "Guaranteed Results' Plan May Suit Business Marketers," *Business Marketing,* July 1990, p. 32; Jim Kirk, "Miller Sets Free Rates," *Adweek,* January 24, 1994, p. 4.

39. James R. Willis, Jr., "Winning New Business: An Analysis of Advertising Agency Activities," *Journal of Advertising Research,* September/October 1992, pp. 10–16.

40. Andrew Jaffe, "The Fine Art of Keeping Clients Happy while Chasing New Business," *Adweek,* May 9, 1994, p. 38.

41. Melanie Wells, "Courtship by Consultant," *Advertising Age,* January 31, 1994, pp. 10–11; "Accounts on the Move," *Advertising Age,* June 2, 1997 (retrieved from http://adage.com); "H&R Block Review Down to 3," *Advertising Age,* May 17, 2000 (retrieved from Daily Deadline, http://adage.com); "Monster, L.L. Bean Open Account Review," *Advertising Age,* July 12, 2000 (retrieved from Daily Deadline, http://adage.com); "Deutsch Tunes in $70 mil DirecTV Account," *Advertising Age,* August 18, 2000 (retrieved from Daily Deadline, http://adage.com).

42. Thorolf Helgesen, "Advertising Awards and Advertising Agency Performance," *Journal of Advertising Research,* July/August 1994, pp. 43–53.

43. Daniel B. Wackman, Charles T. Salmon, and Caryn C. Salmon, "Developing an Advertising Agency-Client Relationship," *Journal of Advertising Research,* December 1986/January 1987, pp. 21–28.

44. Kevin Goldman, "FCB Bumps Ayer as AT&T's Top Agency," *The Wall Street Journal,* November 22, 1994, p. B8.

45. Kevin Goldman, "Ties That Bind Agency, Client Unravel," *The Wall Street Journal,* November 16, 1994, p. B6.

46. Yumiko Ono, "Apple Picks TBWA," *The Wall Street Journal,* August 11, 1997, p. B3.

47. Paul C. Katz, "Getting the Most of Your Advertising Dollars: How to Select and Evaluate an Ad Agency," *Bottomline,* March 1987, pp. 35–38.

48. Steven Raye, "Agencies, Clients: It's Mutual Contribution for Mutual Gain," *Brandweek,* September 12, 1994, p. 20; Ed Moser, "Inside Information," *Adweek,* January 24, 1994, p. 22; Mat Toor, "Fear and Favour in Adland," *Marketing* (UK), November 15, 1990, pp. 30–32.

49. Paul C. N. Mitchell, Harold Cataquet, and Stephen Hague, "Establishing the Causes of Disaffection in Agency-Client Relations," *Journal of Advertising Research,* March/April 1992, pp. 41–48.

50. Isabelle T. D. Szmigin, "Managing Quality in Business-to-Business Services," *European Journal of Marketing,* vol. 27, no. 1 (1993), pp. 5–21.

51. Ron Jackson, "If You Hire a Vendor, You Get a Vendor Mindset," *Marketing News,* April 25, 1991, pp. 13–14.

52. Steven A. Meyerowitz, "Ad Agency Conflicts: The Law and Common Sense," *Business Marketing,* June 1987, p. 16.

53. Andrew Jaffe, "For Agencies, Conflict Taboo Seems Strong as Ever," *Adweek,* January 24, 1994, p. 46.

54. Betsy Sharkey, "New Suit," *Adweek,* June 20, 1994, p. 20.

55. U.S. Census Bureau, *Statistical Abstract of the United States,* § 24, "Information and Communications," p. 8, 2003, www.census.gov/prod/2004pubs/03statab/inforcomm.pdf.

56. "Circulation Data," The New York Times Company online, www.nytco.com/inverstors-nyt-circulation.html.

57. www.magazine.org.

58. U.S. Census Bureau, *Statistical Abstract of the United States,* § 24, p. 14.

59. Sean Savage, "For Firms on Network, Net Gains Can Be Great," *ComputerLink,* Knight-Ridder News Service, November 29, 1994, pp. 3–4.

60. Amy Dockser Markus, "Advertising Breezes along the Nile River with Signs for Sale," *The Wall Street Journal,* July 18, 1997, p. A1.

Chapter Five

1. Monica Soto, "Internet Grocery Company Fails to Deliver," *Dow Jones Publications Library,* May 7, 2001.

2. Matthew A. Debellis, "VCs Patronize HomeGrocer.com," *Red Herring* online, November 3, 1999 (retrieved from www.redherring.com).

3. Monica Soto, "HomeGrocer Fortunes Steadily Decline after Merger with Rival," *Dow Jones Publications Library,* May 6, 2001.

4. Ibid.

5. "HomeGrocer/Webvan Group: Deceased," *Seattle Dot Economy.* Discussion group, February 22, 2002 (retrieved from http://pub86.ezboard.com/bseattledoteconomy).

6. Nancy J. Kim, "HomeGrocer to Unveil Ad Blitz," *Puget Sound Business Journal,* June 11, 1999 (retrieved from http://seattle.bizjournals.com/seattle).

7. E. Jerome McCarthy and William D. Perreault Jr., *Basic Marketing: A Global-Managerial Approach,* 11th ed. (Burr Ridge, IL: Richard D. Irwin, 1993), pp. 5–6; Eric N. Berkowitz, Roger A. Kerin, Steven W. Hartley, and William Rudelius, *Marketing,* 3rd ed. (Burr Ridge, IL: Richard D. Irwin, 1992), p. 27.

8. Kathryn Kranhold, "Ford Woos 'Echo Boomers' with Live TV," *The Wall Street Journal,* August 13, 1999, p. B8.

9. James J. Kellaris, Anthony D. Cox, and Dena Cox, "The Effect of Background Music on Ad Processing: A Contingency Explanation," *Journal of Marketing,* October 1993, pp. 114–25.

10. William O. Bearden, Thomas N. Ingram, and Raymond W. LaForge, *Marketing Principles and Perspectives,* 2nd ed. (Burr Ridge, IL: Irwin/McGraw-Hill, 1997) p. 49.

11. Chart #729, U.S. Census Bureau, *Statistical Abstract of the United States: 1999,* 119th ed. (Washington, DC: U.S. Department of Commerce, 1999).

12. Chart #872, U.S. Census Bureau, *Statistical Abstract of the United States: 1999.*

13. Chart #862, U.S. Census Bureau, *Statistical Abstract of the United States: 1999.*

14. Bearden et al., *Marketing Principles and Perspectives,* p. 99.

15. S. Kent Stephan and Barry L. Tannenholz, "The Real Reason for Brand Switching," *Advertising Age,* June 13, 1994, p. 31.

16. "Ad Nauseum," *Advertising Age,* July 10, 2000.

17. Kellaris, Cox, and Cox, "The Effect of Background Music on Ad Processing," p. 123.

18. Alice Z. Cuneo, "Dockers Takes a Sexier Approach in New Ad Push," *Advertising Age,* January 19, 1999, p. 8.

19. Michael J. McCarthy, "Mind Probe—What Makes an Ad Memorable? Recent Brain Research Yields Surprising Answers," *The Wall Street Journal,* March 22, 1991, p. B3.

20. Al Ries and Jack Trout, *Positioning: The Battle for Your Mind,* rev. ed. (New York: McGraw-Hill, 1986), pp. 30–32.

21. Stephan and Tannenholz, "The Real Reason for Brand Switching."

22. J. Paul Peter and Jerry C. Olson, *Consumer Behavior and Marketing Strategy,* 4th ed. (Burr Ridge, IL: Richard D. Irwin, 1996), p. 554.

23. R. E. Petty, J. T. Cacioppo, and D. Schumann, "Central and Peripheral Routes to Advertising Effectiveness: The Moderating Role of Involvement," *Journal of Consumer Research,* vol. 10, no. 2 (1983), pp. 135–46.

24. This section and the model are adapted from Peter and Olson, *Consumer Behavior and Marketing Strategy,* pp. 554–55.

25. Ibid., pp. 556–57.

26. Yumiko Ono, "Overcoming the Stigma of Dishwashers in Japan," *The Wall Street Journal,* May 19, 2000, p. B2.

27. Karen A. Machleit, Chris T. Allen, and Thomas J. Madden, "The Mature Brand and Brand Interest: An Alternative Consequence of Ad-Evoked Affect," *Journal of Marketing,* October 1993, pp. 72–82.

28. Ibid.

29. Peter and Olson, *Consumer Behavior and Marketing Strategy,* p. 513.

30. Ken Dychtwald and Greg Gable, "Portrait of a Changing Consumer," *Business Horizons,* January/February 1990, pp. 62–74; Larry Light, "Trust Marketing: The Brand Relationship Marketing Mandate for the 90s," address to the American Association of Advertising Agencies annual meeting, Laguna Niguel, CA, April 23, 1993.

31. Colin McDonald, "Point of View: The Key Is to Understand Consumer Response," *Journal of Advertising Research,* September/October 1993, pp. 63–69.

32. McCarthy and Perreault, *Basic Marketing,* p. 204.

33. Vanessa O'Connell, "Nabisco Portrays Cookies as Boost to Women's Self-Esteem," *The Wall Street Journal,* July 10, 1998, p. B7.

34. John R. Rossiter and Larry Percy, *Advertising Communications and Promotion Management,* 2nd ed. (New York: McGraw-Hill, 1997), pp. 120–22.

35. Ibid., p. 121.

36. Ken Bryson and Lynne M. Casper, "Current Population Reports, Household and Family Characteristics: March 1997 and March 1998," U.S. Bureau of the Census; Laura Zinn, "Move Over, Boomers, the Busters Are Here—And They're Angry," *BusinessWeek,* December 14, 1992, pp. 74–82; Jeffrey Zaslow, "Children's Search for Values Leading to Shopping Malls," *The Wall Street Journal,* March 13, 1987.

37. "The Worth of the Cool: Asking Teenagers to Identify the Coolest Brands," *Adweek,* May 9, 1994, p. 18.

38. Greg Farrell, "Star Search," *Adweek,* December 6, 1993, p. 26.

39. Wayne Friedman, "Jordan the Star Athlete Retires, Jordan the Brand Comes to Life," *Advertising Age,* January 18, 1999, p. 3.

40. McCarthy and Perreault, *Basic Marketing,* p. 131; Peter and Olson, *Consumer Behavior and Marketing Strategy,* p. 368.

41. Carolyn A. Lin, "Cultural Differences in Message Strategies: A Comparison between American and Japanese TV Commercials," *Journal of Advertising Research,* July/August 1993, pp. 40–48.

42. Ibid.

43. Ibid.

44. Peter and Olson, *Consumer Behavior and Marketing Strategy,* p. 413.

45. U.S. Census Bureau, *Statistical Abstract of the United States: 2001* (Washington, DC: U.S. Department of Commerce, 2001), Table 15.

46. www.adage.com.

47. Rebecca Purto, "Global Psychographics," *American Demographics,* December 1990, p. 8.

48. The classic studies on cognitive dissonance were initiated by Leon Festinger, *A Theory of Cognitive Dissonance* (Evanston, IL: Row, Peterson, 1957), p. 83; for more recent views, see Hugh Murray, "Advertising's Effect on Sales—Proven or Just Assumed?" *International Journal of Advertising* (UK), vol. 5, no. 1 (1986), pp. 15–36; Delbert Hawkins, Roger Best, and Kenneth Coney, *Consumer Behavior,* 7th ed. (Burr Ridge, IL: McGraw-Hill/Irwin, 1998), pp. 609–10; Ronald E. Milliman and Phillip J. Decker, "The Use of Post-Purchase Communication to Reduce Dissonance and Improve Direct Marketing Effectiveness," *Journal of Business Communication,* Spring 1990, pp. 159–70.

49. Larry Light, "Advertising's Role in Building Brand Equity," speech to annual meeting of the American Association of Advertising Agencies, April 21, 1993.

Chapter Six

1. Gregg Cebrzynski, "Hardee's: Thickburger Ads Help Chain Beef Up Same-Store Sales," *Nation's Restaurant News,* August 4, 2003 (retrieved from www.findarticles.com, August 1, 2004).

2. Bruce Horovitz, "Fast-Food Battle Escalates into Whopper of a Price War," *USA Today,* December 2, 2002 (retrieved from www.usatoday.com, August 1, 2004).

3. Hardee's, Inc., press release, "Hardee's Breaks Rank from Competition," January 21, 2003 (retrieved from www.hardees.com, July 31, 2004).

4. Hardee's, Inc., press release, "New Hardee's Thickburger Commercial Features Mark McGwire," April 13, 2004 (retrieved from www.hardees.com, July 30, 2004).

5. American Family Association Online (retrieved from www.afa.net/activism/IssueDetail.asp?id=134, accessed November 10, 2004).

6. Hardee's, Inc., press release, "Hardee's Introduces the Lettuce-Wrapped Low Carb Thickburger," December 15, 2003 (retrieved from www.hardees.com, July 30, 2004); Dave Marino-Nachison, "The Health of Hardee's," *The Motley Fool,* June 23, 2004 (retrieved from www.fool.com, July 29, 2004).

7. S. Kent Stephan and Barry L. Tannenholz, "The Real Reason for Brand Switching," *Advertising Age,* June 13, 1994, p. 31, and "Six Categories That Hold Elusive Consumers," *Advertising Age,* June 20, 1994, p. 32.

8. Quoted in Al Stewart, "Edgy Ads, Burgers Drive CKE," *Orange County Business Journal* 27, no. 30 (July 26, 2004): 5.

9. "Descriptive Materials for the VALS2 Segmentation System," *Values and Lifestyles Program* (Menlo Park, CA: SRI International, 1989).

10. Nancy Ten Kate, "Squeaky Clean Teens," *American Demographics,* January 1995.

11. "Weather or Not to Sell," *Personal Selling Power,* September 1994, p. 79.

12. Joel S. Dubow, "Occasion-Based vs. User-Based Benefit Segmentation: A Case Study," *Journal of Advertising Research,* March/April 1992, pp. 11–18.

13. "Hispanic Media and Marketing Factoids," Association of Hispanic Advertising Agencies Media Room (retrieved from www.ahaa.org/media/Finalfacts03.htm, August 23, 2004).

14. Leon E. Wynter, "Business and Race: JCPenney Launches Diahann Carroll Line," *The Wall Street Journal,* July 2, 1997, p. B1.

15. Jennifer Foote, "Shhh, It's a Secret: Buick Discovers Untapped Market of Mature Singles," *Chicago Tribune,* May 5, 1994, sec. 6, p. 4.

16. Jean Halliday, "The Coming Generation Y Car-Buying Boom: And How Population Racial Shifts Impact Auto Advertising," *AdAge.Com* (retrieved from www.adage.com/news.cms?newsId=35462, July 15, 2002).

17. Eric Schlosser, "Meat & Potatoes," *Rolling Stone* 800 (November 26, 1998); accessed November 9, 2004, via EBSCO.

18. Eric Schlosser, "The True Cost of America's Diet," *Rolling Stone* 794 (September 3, 1998); accessed November 9, 2004, via EBSCO.

19. Kathleen Barnes, "Changing Demographics: Middle Class," *Advertising Age International,* October 17, 1994, pp. I-11, I-16.

20. Kevin Goldman, "U.S. Brands Trail Japanese in China Study," *The Wall Street Journal,* February 16, 1995, p. B8.

21. Guy Chazan, "Marketers Race to Woo Russians," *The Wall Street Journal,* February 5, 2003, p. B4.

22. Henry Assael and David F. Poltrack, "Can Demographic Profiles of Heavy Users Serve as a Surrogate for Purchase Behavior in Selecting TV Programs?" *Journal of Advertising Research,* January/February 1994, p. 11.

23. Emanuel H. Demby, "Psychographics Revisited: The Birth of a Technique," *Marketing Research: A Magazine of Management & Applications,* Spring 1994, pp. 26–29.

24. SRI Consulting Business Intelligence, "Welcome to VALS" (www.sri-bi.com/vals).

25. Ibid.

26. Ibid.

27. Judith Waldrop, "Markets with Attitude," *American Demographics,* July 1994, pp. 22–32.

28. SRI Consulting Business Intelligence, "VALS Links Global Strategies to Local Efforts through GeoVALS" (www.sri-bi.com/vals/geovals.shtml); SRI Consulting Business Intelligence, "Japan-Vals" (www.sri-bi.com/vals/jvals.shtml).

29. For an excellent discussion of the major psychographic studies used around the world, see Marieke De Mooij, *Advertising Worldwide,* 2nd ed. (Hertfordshire, UK: Prentice Hall International Ltd., 1994), pp. 165–90.

30. "Re-Mapping the World of Consumers," special advertising section by Roper Starch Worldwide, *American Demographics,* October 2000 (www.demographics.com).

31. Lewis C. Winters, "International Psychographics," *Marketing Research: A Magazine of Management & Application,* September 1992, pp. 48–49.

32. James Hutton, "A Theoretical Framework for the Study of Brand Equity and a Test of Brand Sensitivity in an Organizational Buying Context," dissertation, University of Texas, Austin, 1993.

33. William D. Perreault Jr. and E. Jerome McCarthy, *Basic Marketing,* 12th ed. (Burr Ridge, IL: Irwin, 1996), p. 261.

34. *New Data for a New Economy,* U.S. Bureau of the Census, Economic Classification Policy Committee (Washington, DC: U.S. Department of Commerce, 1998).

35. U.S. Bureau of the Census, *Statistical Abstract of the United States: 1999,* 119th ed. (Washington, DC: U.S. Department of Commerce, 1999), pp. 741–42, 744.

36. Michael Schrage, "Think Big," *Adweek,* October 11, 1993, p. 25.

37. Perreault and McCarthy, *Basic Marketing,* pp. 48–49, 91–112.

38. Walter van Waterschoot and Christophe Van den Bulte, "The 4P Classification of the Marketing Mix Revisited," *Journal of Marketing,* October 1992, pp. 83–93.

39. The now widely popularized conceptual model of the 4Ps was developed by E. J. McCarthy, *Basic Marketing* (Homewood, IL: Richard D. Irwin, 1960); the usage of the marketing mix derived from Neil H. Borden, "The Concept of the Marketing Mix," *Journal of Advertising Research,* June 1964, p. 27.

40. Perreault and McCarthy, *Basic Marketing,* pp. 310–21.

41. "Use of Cellular Phones Trends Upward, Survey Shows," press release, Decision Analyst, Inc., July 24, 1998; Matthew Klein, "More Callers Unleashed," *Forecast,* September 1998 (www.demographics.com).

42. Brian Wansink, "Making Old Brands New," *American Demographics,* December 1997 (www.demographics.com).

43. Adapted from William O. Bearden, Thomas N. Ingram, and Raymond W. LaForge, *Marketing: Principles & Perspectives* (Burr Ridge, IL: Irwin, 1995), pp. 211–13; and from Philip Kotler and Gary Armstrong, *Principles of Marketing* (Englewood Cliffs, NJ: Prentice Hall, 1994), pp. 640–43.

44. Hank Seiden, *Advertising Pure and Simple, The New Edition* (New York: AMACOM, 1990), p. 11.

45. Pat Sabena, "Tough Market for New Products Requires Partnership," *Marketing Review,* June 1996, pp. 12–13.

46. Adrienne Ward Fawcett, "In Glut of New Products, 'Different' Becomes Key," *Advertising Age,* December 13, 1993, p. 28.

47. Seiden, *Advertising Pure and Simple,* pp. 23–30; Robert Pritikin, *Pritikin's Testament* (Englewood Cliffs, NJ: Prentice Hall, 1991), pp. 25–33.

48. "On the Pavement, 'Corporate Graffiti' to Sell Fruit Juice," *The New York Times,* May 19, 2002.

49. Haim Oren, "Branding Financial Services Helps Consumers Find Order in Chaos," *Marketing News,* March 29, 1993, p. 6.

50. Frank Bilorsky, "Grocers Labels Offer a New Kind of Branding," *Rochester Democrat and Chronicle,* July 11, 2004 (www.rochesterdandc.com).

51. "The Best Global Brands; *BusinessWeek* and Interbrand Tell You What They're Worth," *BusinessWeek* Special Report, August 5, 2002 (retrieved from www.businessweek.com).

52. "Billion Dollar Brand," *Financial Times,* July 17, 2000 (retrieved from http://news.fr.com).

53. C. Manly Molpus, "Brands Follow New Shopping Patterns," *Advertising Age,* February 14, 1994, p. 22.

54. Stephan and Tannenholz, "The Real Reason for Brand Switching," p. 31.

55. Annetta Miller, "The Millenial Mind-Set," *American Demographics,* January 1999 (www.demographics.com/publications/AD/99_ad/9901_ad/ad990102a.htm).

56. Larry Light, "Brand Loyalty Marketing Key to Enduring Growth," *Advertising Age,* October 3, 1994, p. 20.

47. Andrew Jaffe, "A Compass Point Out of Dead Calm: 'Brand Stewardship,'" *Adweek,* February 7, 1994, p. 38.

58. Linda Trent, "Color Can Affect Success of Products," *Marketing News,* July 5, 1993, p. 4.

59. Shlomo Kalish, "A New Product Adoption Model with Price, Advertising, and Uncertainty," *Management Science,* December 1985, pp. 1569–85.

60. Raymond Serafin, "Brands in Demand—BMW: From Yuppie-Mobile to Smart Car of the '90s," *Advertising Age,* October 3, 1994, p. S2.

61. Perreault and McCarthy, *Basic Marketing,* p. 16.

62. "The ABCs of Franchising," International Franchising Association (retrieved from www.franchisingworld.com).

63. van Waterschoot and Van den Bulte, "The 4P Classification of the Marketing Mix Revisited," p. 89.

64. www.subway.com.

65. Lori Francisco, "Key Contenders," *Entrepreneur International,* March 1999 (retrieved from www.entrepreneur.com/Magazines/MA_SegArticle/0,1539,230050——1-,00.html).

66. Jim Emerson, "Levi Strauss in the Early Stages of Shift to Database Marketing," *DM News,* December 7, 1992, pp. 1–2; Lisa Benenson, "Bull's-Eye Marketing," *Success,* January/February 1993, pp. 43–48.

67. Al Ries and Laura Ries, *The Fall of Advertising and the Rise of PR* (New York: HarperBusiness, 2002), pp. 8–12.

68. van Waterschoot and Van den Bulte, "The 4P Classification of the Marketing Mix Revisited," p. 89.

69. Carol Angrisani, "The Road to Redemption," *Brandmarketing,* July 2000 (retrieved from http://web.lexis-nexis.com/univers).

70. van Waterschoot and Van den Bulte, "The 4P Classification of the Marketing Mix Revisited," pp. 89–90.

Chapter Seven

1. John Martin, "Playing for Keeps: How to Build a Lasting Partnership," *Agency,* Summer 1997, pp. 16–18.

2. Beth Rilee-Kelley, personal interview, November 1997.

3. Martin, "Playing for Keeps," p. 18; Rilee-Kelley interview.

4. Media kits: www.businessweek.com and www.forbes.com, October 2000; Chad Rubel, "Some Cute Super Spots Now Just a Memory," *Marketing News,* March 13, 1995, p. 15.

5. William D. Perreault Jr. and E. Jerome McCarthy, *Basic Marketing,* 12th ed. (Burr Ridge, IL: Richard D. Irwin, 1996), p. 155.

6. "Top 50 Research Organizations," American Marketing Association online (retrieved from www.data.marketingpower.com, August 22, 2004).

7. David G. Bakken, "Measure for Measure," *Marketing Tools,* premier issue, 1994, p. 14.

8. Brian Ottum, "Focus Groups and New Product Development," *Marketing News,* June 3, 1996, p. H26.

9. Ibid., pp. 14–15.

10. Don Peppers and Martha Rogers, "Welcome to the 1:1 Future," *Marketing Tools,* premier issue, 1994, p. 4.

11. Bakken, "Measure for Measure," p. 15.

12. Rilee-Kelley interview.

13. Jerry W. Thomas, "Media Advertising Is an Unfulfilled Promise," *Marketing News,* September 23, 1996, p. 28.

14. Ibid.

15. Stuart Agres, "How Great Brands Got to Be That Way," adapted from a speech to the Advertising Research Foundation, April 7, 1997 (retrieved from www.warc.com, November 22, 2004); Cathy Taylor, "Brand Asset Valuator Turned toward Media," *Adweek,* July 11, 1994, p. 14.

16. Kathryn Kranhold, "Agencies Boost Research to Spot Consumer Views," *The Asian Wall Street Journal,* March 10, 2000, p. 6.

17. Story adapted from "Cheese, Please!" *American Demographics,* March 2000, pp. S6–S8. (Copyright Primedia Intertec March 2000.)

18. Ibid.

19. Pat Sloan, "DDB Boosts Planning by Hiring Brit Expert," *Advertising Age,* September 21, 1992, pp. 3, 53.

20. Rilee-Kelley interview.

21. "Quick Reliable Test Marketing Is a Virtual Reality," *Marketing Tools,* premier issue, 1994, p. 22.

22. Thomas, "Media Advertising Is an Unfulfilled Promise," pp. 28, 32.

23. Perreault and McCarthy, *Basic Marketing,* p. 153.

24. Jack Honomichl, "Research Cultures Are Different in Mexico, Canada," *Marketing News,* May 10, 1993, pp. 12, 13.

25. Paul Conner, "Defining the 'Decision Purpose' of Research," *Marketing News,* September 23, 1996, p. 18.

26. Michael L. Garee and Thomas R. Schori, "Focus Groups Illuminate Quantitative Research," *Marketing News,* September 23, 1996, p. 41.

27. Robert West, Schering Canada, personal interview, May 17, 1993.

28. William Weylock, "Focus: Hocus Pocus?" *Marketing Tools,* July/August 1994, pp. 12–16; Thomas L. Greenbaum, "Focus Groups Can Play a Part in Evaluating Ad Copy," *Marketing News,* September 13, 1993, pp. 24–25.

29. Pat Sloan and Julie Liesse, "New Agency Weapon to Win Clients: Research," *Advertising Age,* August 30, 1993, p. 37.

30. Gloria F. Mazzella, "Show-and-Tell Focus Groups Reveal Core Boomer Values," *Marketing News,* September 23, 1996, p. 9.

31. Jack Honomichl, "The Honomichl 50," *Marketing News,* June 10, 2002, p. H2; Don E. Schultz, Stanley I. Tannenbaum, and Robert F. Lauterborn, *Integrated Marketing Communications: Putting It Together and Making It Work* (Lincolnwood, IL: NTC Business Books, 1993), pp. 149–50.

32. Leah Rickard, "Helping Put Data in Focus," *Advertising Age,* July 11, 1994, p. 18.

33. François Descarie, director, Impact Research, personal interview, May 17, 1993.

34. Richard Gibson, "Marketers' Mantra: Reap More with Less," *The Wall Street Journal,* March 22, 1991, p. B1.

35. Karen A. Machleit, Chris T. Allen, and Thomas J. Madden, "The Mature Brand and Brand Interest: An Alternative Consequence of Ad-Evoked Affect," *Journal of Marketing,* October 1993, pp. 72–82.

36. Pamela L. Alreck and Robert B. Settle, *The Survey Research Handbook,* 2nd ed. (Burr Ridge, IL: Richard D. Irwin, 1995), pp. 56–59.

37. Ibid., p. 40.

38. Perreault and McCarthy, *Basic Marketing,* p. 173.

39. Alreck and Settle, *The Survey Research Handbook,* pp. 88–90.

40. MINITAB software for IBM-PC, for Microsoft Windows, and for academic use in an inexpensive student edition through Addison-Wesley Publishing Co., Reading, MA.

41. George S. Fabian, panelist, "Globalization: Challenges for Marketing and Research," *Marketing Review,* February 1993, p. 23.

42. Maureen R. Marston, panelist, "Globalization: Challenges for Marketing and Research," pp. 20–21.

43. Suzanne Bidlake, "Nestlé Builds Database in Asia with Direct Mail," *Advertising Age International,* January 1998, p. 34.

44. Michael Brizz, "How to Learn What Japanese Buyers Really Want," *Business Marketing,* January 1987, p. 72.

45. Simon Chadwick, panelist, "Globalization: Challenges for Marketing and Research," p. 18.

46. Thomas L. Greenbaum, "Understanding Focus Group Research Abroad," *Marketing News,* June 3, 1996, pp. H14, H36.

47. Marston, "Globalization," p. 24.

48. Ibid.

49. Deborah Szynal, "Big Bytes," *Marketing News,* March 18, 2002, p. 3.

Chapter Eight

1. Undated promo sheet and letter from BBDO-NY (1995).

2. Theresa Howard, "Brand Builders: Being True to Dew," *Brandweek,* April 24, 2000, p. 28.

3. Ibid., p. 30.

4. Ibid.

5. Hillary Chura, "Code Red Soft Drink Sales Explode," *Advertising Age,* August 27, 2001, p. 1; Hillary Chura, "Identifying a Demographic Sweet Spot," November 12, 2001 (retrieved from www.adage.com).

6. William O. Bearden, Thomas N. Ingram, and Raymond W. LaForge, *Marketing Principles & Perspectives,* 2nd. ed. (Burr Ridge, IL: Richard D. Irwin, 1998), pp. 75–76.

7. *Advertising Age,* Ad Age Dataplace—September 27, 1999: "Top 10 Soft Drink Brands" (retrieved from www.adage.com/dataplace/archives/dp364.html).

8. "Market Analysis—Defining the Market," Tutor2u, retrieved from www.tutor2u.net/business/marketing, February 26, 2003).

9. Greg Farrell, "Dew Poses Real Pepsi Challenge to Coke Ads for Soft-Drink Brand Gain in Teen Popularity," *USA Today,* July 10, 2000, p. B2.

10. "Saturn SC1 and the Young, College-Educated Import Intenders," 1993 Case Study, NSAC: AAF College World Series of Advertising, pp. 2, 11, 23.

11. Kate MacArthur and Hillary Chura, "Urban Youth," *Advertising Age,* September 4, 2000, pp. 16–17.

12. Private interview with Scott Moffitt, Director of Marketing, Pepsi-Cola Company, December 2000.

13. Automation Marketing Strategies, "The Art of Market Positioning," *Strategic Advantage Newsletter,* January 2000 (retrieved from www.automationmarketing.com, February 2003).

14. Ernest Martin, "Target Marketing: Summary and Unit Learning Outcomes," Course Syllabus CADV 213 (retrieved from www.campbell.edu/faculty/martine/index.htm, February 26, 2003).

15. Raju Narisetti, "Xerox Aims to Imprint High-Tech Image," *The Wall Street Journal,* October 6, 1998, p. B8.

16. Farrell, "Dew Poses Real Pepsi Challenge to Coke," p. B2.

17. Adapted from Al Ries and Jack Trout, *Bottom-Up Marketing* (New York: McGraw-Hill, 1989), p. 8.

18. Frederick E. Webster Jr., "Executing the New Marketing Concept," *Marketing Management* 3, no. 1 (1994), pp. 8–16.

19. Philip Kotler and Gary Armstrong, *Principles of Marketing* (Englewood Cliffs, NJ: Prentice Hall, 1994), p. 560; Don E. Schultz, Stanley I. Tannenbaum, and Robert F. Lauterborn, *Integrated Marketing Communications: Putting It Together & Making It Work* (Lincolnwood, IL: NTC Business Books, 1993), p. 52.

20. Frederick E. Webster Jr., "Defining the New Marketing Concept (Part I)," *Marketing Management* 2, no. 4 (1994), pp. 22–31.

21. Frederick E. Webster Jr., "The Changing Role of Marketing in the Corporation," *Journal of Marketing,* October 1992, pp. 1–17, 22–31.

22. Ibid.

23. Ibid.

24. Kotler and Armstrong, *Principles of Marketing,* p. 559.

25. Ibid., p. 560.

26. Stan Rapp and Thomas L. Collins, "Nestlé Banks on Databases," *Advertising Age,* October 25, 1993, pp. 16, S–7.

27. Denison Hatch, "The Media Mix: How to Reach the Right Person with the Right Message in the Right Environment," *Target Marketing,* July 1994, pp. 8–10; and Kenneth Wylie, "Direct Response: Database Development Shows Strong Growth as Shops Gain 16.9% in U.S.," *Advertising Age,* July 12, 1993, p. S8.

28. Gary Levin, "Wunderman: 'Personalized' Marketing Will Gain Dominance," *Advertising Age,* October 25, 1993, p. S1.

29. Kotler and Armstrong, *Principles of Marketing,* p. 560.

30. Glen Nowak and Joseph Phelps, "Conceptualizing the Integrated Marketing Communications Phenomenon: An Examination of Its Impact on Advertising Practices and Its Implications for Advertising Research," *Journal of Current Issues and Research in Advertising,* Spring 1994, pp. 49–66.

31. Thomas R. Duncan and Sandra E. Moriarty, *Driving Brand Value: Using Integrated Marketing to Manage Stakeholder Relationships* (New York: McGraw-Hill, 1997), p. 42.

32. Adapted from Kotler and Armstrong, *Principles of Marketing,* pp. 560–61.

33. Arthur M. Hughes, "Can This Relationship Work?" *Marketing Tools,* July/August 1994, p. 4.

34. Hillary Chura and Kate MacArthur, "Flat Colas Anxiously Watch Gen Yers Switch," *Advertising Age,* September 25, 2000; and Howard, "Brand Builders," p. 30.

35. Kotler and Armstrong, *Principles of Marketing,* p. 561.

36. Schultz, Tannenbaum, and Lauterborn, *Integrated Marketing Communications,* p. 52.

37. Lou Wolter, "Superficiality, Ambiguity Threaten IMC's Implementation and Future," *Marketing News,* September 13, 1993, p. 21.

38. Regis McKenna, "Marketing Is Everything," *Harvard Business Review,* January/February 1991, p. 65.

39. Tom Duncan, "Integrated Marketing? It's Synergy," *Advertising Age,* March 8, 1993, p. 22.

40. Duncan and Moriarty, *Driving Brand Value,* pp. 3–6.

41. Karlene Lukovitz, "Get Ready for One-on-One Marketing," *Folio: The Magazine for Magazine Management,* October 1, 1991, pp. 64–70.

42. Don E. Schultz, "Four Basic Rules Lay Groundwork for Integration," *Marketing News,* August 16, 1993, p. 5.

43. Ibid.

44. William F. Arens and Jack J. Whidden, "La Publicité aux Etats-Unis, 1992; Les Symptomes et les Stratégies d'une Industrie Surpeuplée," *L'industrie de la Publicité au Québec 1991–1992* (Montreal: Le Publicité-Club de Montréal, October 1992), pp. 365–99.

45. Regis McKenna, "Marketing in an Age of Diversity," *Harvard Business Review,* September/October 1988, p. 88; Schultz, Tannenbaum, and Lauterborn, *Integrated Marketing Communications,* p. 21.

46. Duncan and Moriarty, *Driving Brand Value,* pp. 78–90.

47. Ibid., p. 90.

48. Adapted from Tom Duncan, "A Macro Model of Integrated Marketing Communication," paper presented to the annual conference of the American Academy of Advertising, Norfolk, VA, March 23–24, 1995, pp. 7–10.

49. Don E. Schultz, "The Next Step in IMC?" *Marketing News,* August 15, 1994, pp. 8–9.

50. Rapp and Collins, "Nestlé Banks on Databases," pp. 16, S7.

51. Don E. Schultz, "Trying to Determine ROI for IMC," *Marketing News,* January 3, 1994, p. 18; Don E. Schultz, "Spreadsheet Approach to Measuring ROI for IMC," *Marketing News,* February 28, 1994, p. 12; and Matthew P. Gonring, "Putting Integrated Marketing Communications to Work Today," *Public Relations Quarterly,* Fall 1994, p. 45.

52. Don E. Schultz, "Integration Helps You Plan Communications from Outside-In," *Marketing News,* March 15, 1993, p. 12.

53. McKenna, "Marketing Is Everything."

54. Schultz, Tannenbaum, and Lauterborn, *Integrated Marketing Communications,* pp. 55–6.

55. Paul Wang and Don E. Schultz, "Measuring the Return on Investment for Advertising and Other Forms of Marketing Communication, Using an Integrated Marketing Communications Planning Approach," paper presented at the annual conference of the Association for Education in Journalism and Mass Communication, Kansas City, August 13, 1993.

56. Schultz, Tannenbaum, and Lauterborn, *Integrated Marketing Communications,* p. 58.

57. Wayne Henderson, "The IMC Scale: A Tool for Evaluating IMC Usage," *Integrated Marketing Communications Research Journal,* vol. 3, no. 1 (Spring 1997), pp. 11–17.

58. Ibid; Cyndee Miller, "Everyone Loves 'IMC,' but . . . ," *Marketing News,* August 16, 1993, pp. 1, 6.

59. Don E. Schultz and Paul Wang, "Real World Results," *Marketing Tools,* premier issue, May 1994, pp. 40–47.

60. Ibid.

61. Don E. Schultz, "Integrated Marketing Communications: A Competitive Weapon in Today's Marketplace," *Marketing Review,* July 1993, pp. 10–11, 29.

62. Ned Anschuetz, "Point of View: Building Brand Popularity: The Myth of Segmenting to Brand Success," *Journal of Advertising Research,* January/February 1997, pp. 63–66.

63. Sally Beatty, "Two GM Divisions Try to Create Different Images for Their Trucks," *The Wall Street Journal,* October 14, 1998, p. B8.

64. Chung K. Kim and Kenneth R. Lord, "A New FCB Grid and Its Strategic Implications for Advertising," in *Proceedings of the Annual Conference of the Administrative Sciences Association of Canada* (Marketing), Tony Schellinck, ed. (Niagara Falls, Ontario: Administrative Sciences Association of Canada, 1991), pp. 51–60.

65. Johan C. Yssel and Mark W. Walchle, "Using the FCB Grid to Write Advertising Strategy," paper presented to the Annual Conference of the Association for Education in Journalism and Mass Communication, 1992.

66. Howard, "Brand Builders," p. 30.

67. Ibid., p. 31; Kate MacArthur, "Mountain Dew: Dawn Hudson," *Advertising Age,* June 26, 2000, p. 27.

68. Howard, "Brand Builders," p. 31.

69. Farrell, "Dew Poses Real Pepsi Challenge to Coke."

70. Ibid.

71. Gregg Ambach and Mike Hess, "Measuring Long-Term Effects in Marketing," *Marketing Research: A Magazine of Management and Applications,* American Marketing Association, Summer 2000, pp. 23–30.

72. Robert D. Buzzell and Frederick D. Wiersema, "Successful Share-Building Strategies," *Harvard Business Review,* January/February 1981, p. 135; Siva K. Balasubramanian and V. Kumar, "Analyzing Variations in Advertising and Promotional Expenditures: Key Correlated in Consumer, Industrial, and Service Markets," *Journal of Marketing,* April 1990, pp. 57–68.

73. Bernard Ryan Jr., *Advertising in a Recession: The Best Defense Is a Good Offense* (New York: American Association of Advertising Agencies, 1991), pp. 13–29; Priscilla C. Brown, "Surviving with a Splash," *Business Marketing,* January 1991, p. 14; Edmund O. Lawler, "A Window of Opportunity," *Business Marketing,* January 1991, p. 16; Rebecca Colwell Quarles, "Marketing Research Turns Recession into Business Opportunity," *Marketing News,* January 7, 1991, pp. 27, 29.

74. Fabiana Giacomotti, "European Marketers Keep Up Ad Budgets," *Adweek,* January 24, 1994, pp. 16–17.

75. Leo Bogart, *Strategy in Advertising,* 2nd ed. (Chicago: Crain Books, 1984), pp. 45–47.

76. John Philip Jones, "Ad Spending: Maintaining Market Share," *Harvard Business Review,* January/February 1990, pp. 38–42; James C. Schroer, "Ad Spending: Growing Market Share," *Harvard Business Review,* January/February 1990, pp. 44–49.

77. Peter Breen, "Seeds of Change," *Promo Sourcebook Supplement,* Copyright 2000, INTERTEC, p. 18 (retrieved from www.lexisnexis.com).

78. Ambach and Hess, "Measuring Long-Term Effects in Marketing."

Chapter Nine

1. Sony story adapted from Eric Schmuckler, "Best Campaign Spending $1 Million or Less (Tie): Media Edge/Y&R," *Mediaweek,* June 19, 2000, pp. S50–S54.

2. Merecedes M. Cardona, "Media Mavens: 'Great People Leader Ensures Y & R Unit Consolidation Works: Beth Gordon," *Advertising Age,* September 15, 1997 (retrieved from www.adage.com, November 22, 2004).

3. Craig R. Endicott, "60th Annual Agency Report," *Advertising Age,* April 19, 2004, p. S14.

4. Laurie Freeman, "Experience Worth More than Byte," *Advertising Age,* July 23, 1996, p. S15.

5. Julie Liesse, "Inside Burnett's Vaunted Buying Machine," *Advertising Age,* July 25, 1994, p. S6.

6. Yumiko Ono, "Cordiant Puts Hamilton in Key U.S. Post," *Advertising Age,* July 18, 1997, p. B2.

7. Stephanie Thompson, "Universal McCann Gets $150 Million Nestlé Account," *AdAge.com,* April 12, 2002; Richard Linnett and Jack Neff,

"Mindshare Wins $600 Million Gillette Media Account," *AdAge.com*, September 26, 2002 (retrieved from www.adage.com).

8. Jon Lafayette, "Agency Media Staffs Gain Clout," *Advertising Age*, March 4, 1991, p. 12; Peter J. Danaher and Roland T. Rust, "Determining the Optimal Level of Media Spending," *Journal of Advertising Research*, January/February 1994, p. 28.

9. "Business: Hi Ho, Hi Ho, Down the Data Mine We Go," *The Economist*, August 23, 1997, pp. 47–48.

10. Tom Duncan and Sandra Moriarty, *Driving Brand Value* (New York: McGraw-Hill, 1997), p. 100.

11. Veronis Suhler Stevenson, 16th Annual Communications Industry Forecast, August 5, 2002 (retrieved from www.veronissuhler.com).

12. "The Phenomenon behind *American Idol*," Nielsen Media Research, May 21, 2003 (retrieved from www.nielsenmedia.com/newsreleases/2003/AmericanIdol_052203.htm).

13. Wayne Friedman, "Discovery Pitches Ad Convergence," *Advertising Age*, March 2000 (retrieved from www.adage.com, December 2000).

14. Rick Klein and Jeff Jensen, "GM's Huge Pact Raises Olympics Bar," *Advertising Age*, August 4, 1997, p. 6.

15. Dorothy Giobbe, "Newspapers Urged to Be More Creative," *Editor & Publisher*, July 2, 1994, p. 38.

16. Christina Merrill, "Media Rising," *Adweek*, November 9, 1998 (retrieved from http://members.adweek.com/archive).

17. Joe Mandese, "Boost for Media Buyers," *Advertising Age*, March 7, 1994, p. 47.

18. Winston Fletcher, "Independents May Have Had Their Day: Media Buying Is Returning to the Full-Service Fold, But This Time Only at Arm's Length," *Financial Times*, July 27, 1999, p. 15.

19. Christina Merrill, "Media Agencies: What's in a Name? Lots!" *Adweek*, August 24, 1998 (retrieved from http://members.adweek.com/archive).

20. "World's Top Media Specialist Companies," *AdAge.com* Data Center, April 21, 2003 (retrieved from www.adage.com).

21. Liesse, "Inside Burnett's Vaunted Buying Machine," p. S6.

22. Don E. Schultz, Stanley I. Tannenbaum, and Robert F. Lauterborn, *Integrated Marketing Communications: Putting It Together & Making It Work* (Lincolnwood, IL: NTC Business Books, 1993), pp. 81–82, 108.

23. Adapted from Donald W. Jugenheimer, Arnold M. Barban, and Peter B. Turk, *Advertising Media: Strategy and Tactics* (Dubuque, IA: Brown & Benchmark, 1992), p. 131.

24. Ibid., pp. 131–33.

25. Jim Surmanek, *Introduction to Advertising Media: Research, Planning, and Buying* (Chicago: NTC Business Books, 1993), p. 54.

26. Shula Bigman, "First, Let's Find Out How Media Works: Making Media Accountable Means Creating New Tools," *Advertising Age*, October 5, 1998, p. 40.

27. Adapted from Surmanek, *Introduction to Advertising Media*, p. 106.

28. Jugenheimer, Barban, and Turk, *Advertising Media: Strategy and Tactics*, p. 135.

29. Joe Mandese, "Revisiting Ad Reach, Frequency," *Advertising Age*, November 27, 1995, p. 46.

30. George B. Murray and John G. Jenkins, "The Concept of 'Effective Reach' in Advertising," *Journal of Advertising Research* 32, no. 3, 1992, pp. 34–44.

31. John Philip Jones, *When Ads Work: New Proof That Advertising Triggers Sales* (New York: Simon & Schuster/Lexington Books, 1995); Colin McDonald, "From 'Frequency' to 'Continuity'—Is It a New Dawn?" *Journal of Advertising Research*, July/August 1997, p. 21.

32. Hugh M. Cannon and Edward A. Riordan, "Effective Reach and Frequency: Does It Really Make Sense?" *Journal of Advertising Research*, March/April 1994, pp. 19–28.

33. Ibid., pp. 27–28; John Philip Jones, "What Does Effective Frequency Mean in 1997?" *Journal of Advertising Research*, July/August 1997, pp. 14–20.

34. Kenneth A. Longman, "If Not Effective Frequency, Then What?" *Journal of Advertising Research*, July/August 1997, pp. 44–50; Hugh M. Cannon, John D. Leckenby, and Avery Abernethy, "Overcoming the Media Planning Paradox: From (In)Effective to Optimal Reach and Frequency," *Proceedings of the 1996 Conference of the American Academy of Advertising*, pp. 34–39.

35. Erwin Ephron, "Recency Planning," *Journal of Advertising Research*, July/August 1997, pp. 61–64.

36. Laurie Freeman, "Added Theories Drive Need for Client Solutions," *Advertising Age*, August 4, 1997, p. S18.

37. Schultz, Tannenbaum, and Lauterborn, *Integrated Marketing Communications: Putting It Together & Making It Work*, pp. 116–22, 132–33; Julie Liesse, "Buying by the Numbers? Hardly," *Advertising Age*, July 25, 1994, p. S16.

38. "European Adspend Forecasts," World Advertising Research Center, October 15, 2002 (www.warc.com).

39. Joe Mandese, "Cultures Clash as 'Optimizers' Sort Out U.S. Media," *Advertising Age*, August 4, 1997, p. S2.

40. Rein Rijkens, *European Advertising Strategies* (London: Cassell, 1992), pp. 86–87.

41. Special Report: Best Media Plan Competition, "Guerrilla Tactics Get Panasonic Noticed," *Strategy* (Canada), March 27, 2000, p. BMP10.

42. Todd Pruzan, "Global Media: Distribution Slows, but Rates Climb," *Advertising Age International*, January 16, 1995, p. I19.

43. Neil Kelliher, "Magazine Media Planning for 'Effectiveness': Getting the People Back into the Process," *Journal of Consumer Marketing*, Summer 1990, pp. 47–55.

44. Kenneth Longman, *Advertising* (New York: Harcourt Brace Jovanovich, 1971), pp. 211–12.

45. Kevin Goldman, "With Vietnam Embargo Lifted, Agencies Gear Up for Business," *The Wall Street Journal*, February 7, 1994, p. B8.

46. "The Power of Partnership," NBC Marketing Supplement, *Advertising Age*, November 16, 1992, p. 13.

47. Kevin Goldman, "Digital Warms Couch Potatoes with Only-on-Sunday TV Ads," *The Wall Street Journal*, November 22, 1994, p. B8.

48. Telmar website, July 2004 (www.telmar.com).

49. Interactive Market Systems website, December 2000 (www.imsusa.com/products-applications.html).

Chapter Ten

1. "Dell Kicks Off Back-to-School Season with a '$50,000-a-Day Giveaway,'" July 2, 2002 (retrieved from www.dell.com).

2. Ibid.

3. "Dell's Back-to-School Sweepstakes Takes to the Skies," August 1, 2002 (retrieved from www.dell.com).

4. "Dell's 'BMW-a-Day Giveaway' Puts Customers in Driver's Seat," August 29, 2002 (retrieved from www.dell.com).

5. "Dell Says Making Customers No. 1 Accounts for Return to Global Market-Share Leadership," October 17, 2002 (retrieved from www.dell.com).

6. "Dell at a Glance" (retrieved from www.dell.com).

7. Todd Wasserman, "Grand Marketer; The 'Dude' You May Not Know; One of the Few Firms to Survive the Tech Crash; Dell Won Over Consumer Market with a Savvy Business Model and Its Ads' Unlikely Teen Hero," October 14, 2002 (retrieved from www.lexis-nexus.com).

8. The 2002 *Fortune* 500 (retrieved from www.fortune.com).

9. Wasserman, "Grand Marketer."

10. "Dell Launches New Consumer Advertising Campaign," September 22, 1999 (retrieved from www.dell.com).

11. Shelly Solheim, "Dell Reclaims PC Crown," April 16, 2004 (retrieved from www.eweek.com, August 7, 2004).

12. "Sony Tops the List in Annual 'Best Brands' Survey for Fifth Consecutive Year," *The Harris Poll 50,* July 7, 2004 (retrieved from www.harrisinteractive.com/harris_poll/index.asp?PID=479, August 12, 2004).

13. "1999 Economic Impact: U.S. Direct Marketing Today," The WEFA Group and The Direct Marketing Association, 2000 (retrieved from www.the-dma.org, December 2000).

14. Joan Throckmorton, "We Are Interactive—Repeat—We Are Interactive," *Direct,* November 1997.

15. Ray Schultz, "Wunderman at 75," *Direct,* February 15, 1996.

16. Bob Stone, *Successful Direct Marketing Methods,* 4th ed. (Chicago: NTC Business Books, 1988), p. 3.

17. "Civilian Labor Force and Participation Rates with Projections: 1980 to 2008," *Statistical Abstract of the United States: 2001,* Table 568 (Washington DC: U.S. Census Bureau, 2001).

18. Direct Marketing Association, "2003 Direct Marketing Sales Estimated to Hit 1.7 Trillion," October 13, 2003 (retrieved from www.the-dma.org, August 7, 2004).

19. "Civilian Labor Force and Participation Rates with Projects: 1980 to 2008," The WEFA Group and The Direct Marketing Association, 2002 (retrieved from www.the-dma.org).

20. "Economic Impact: U.S. Direct Marketing Today Executive Summary; International Direct Marketing Expenditures in All Markets (Ranked by Level of 2001 Forecast)" (retrieved from www.the-dma.org).

21. Addressing Technology website, 2003 (www.addressing.fr).

22. Peppers and Rogers Group, *Marketing 1 to 1* (www.m1to1.com/success_stories).

23. Nicholas G. Poulos, "Customer Loyalty and the Marketing Database," *Direct Marketing,* July 1996, pp. 33–34.

24. Rob Jackson, "Database Doctor," *Direct,* January 9, 1996 (www.mediacentral.com).

25. Stone, *Successful Direct Marketing Methods,* pp. 29–33.

26. Jackson, "Database Doctor."

27. Thomas E. Caruso, "Kotler: Future Marketers Will Focus on Customer Data Base to Compete Globally," *Marketing News,* June 8, 1992, pp. 21–22.

28. Seth Godin, "GUEST COLUMNIST: Permission Key to Successful Marketing," *Advertising Age,* November 1997 (http://adage.com).

29. Poulos, "Customer Loyalty and the Marketing Database," pp. 32–35.

30. Mollie Neal, "Marketers Looking Ahead in Chicago," *Direct Marketing,* March 1993, pp. 9–11.

31. Robert A. Peterson and Thomas R. Wotruba, "What Is Direct Selling?—Definition, Perspectives, and Research Agenda," *Journal of Personal Selling and Sales Management,* 16, no. 4 (Fall 1996), pp. 1–16.

32. "Economic Impact: U.S. Direct & Interactive Marketing Today Executive Summary 2002."

33. Cyndee Miller, "Telemarketing Cited as Chief Form of Direct Marketing," *Marketing News,* p. 6.

34. "Brief History of Toll-Free Numbers" (retrieved from www.tollfreenumbers.com, August 7, 2004).

35. "Economic Impact: U.S. Direct & Interactive Marketing Today Executive Summary 2002."

36. "The Catalog Age 100: Ranking 1–50," *Catalog Age,* August 1, 2003 (retrieved from www.catalogagemag.com).

37. Laura Bird, "Beyond Mail Order: Catalogs Now Sell Image, Advice," *The Wall Street Journal,* July 29, 1997, pp. B1, 2.

38. Personal Interview with Tom Campanaro, President, Total Gym Inc., December 2000.

39. "Consumer Spending Shows Electronic Retailing Shopper as Loyal, Satisfied, and Likely to Return for More Purchases," Electronic Retailing Association press release, June 9, 2004 (retrieved from www.retailing.org, August 8, 2004).

40. Nancy Colton Webster, "Radio Tuning in to Direct Response," *Advertising Age,* October 10, 1994, pp. S14, S15.

41. Murray Raphel, "Meet One of America's Top Salespeople," *Direct Marketing,* March 1994, p. 31.

42. Adapted from Barton A. Weitz, Stephen B. Castleberry, and John F. Tanner Jr., *Selling: Building Partnerships* (Burr Ridge, IL: Richard D. Irwin, Inc., 1992), p. 5.

43. Edwin Klewer, Robert Shaffer, and Bonnie Binnig, "Sales Is an Investment, Attrition an Expense," *Journal of Health Care Marketing,* September 1995, p. 12.

44. "Excerpt: Under the Radar," *Brandweek,* December 8, 1997 (http://members.adweek.com/archive/adweek/current/brandweek).

45. Peter Breen, "Seeds of Change," *Promo Sourcebook Supplement,* October 2000, p. 18.

46. Larry Light, "Trustmarketing: The Brand Relationship Marketing Mandate for the 90s," address to American Association of Advertising Agencies annual meeting, Laguna Niguel, CA, April 23, 1993.

47. Magid M. Abraham and Leonard M. Lodish, "Getting the Most Out of Advertising and Promotion," *Harvard Business Review,* May/June 1990, p. 51.

48. Light, "Trustmarketing."

49. Larry Light, "At the Center of It All Is the Brand," *Advertising Age,* March 29, 1993, p. 22.

50. Federal Trade Commission, *Report of the Federal Trade Commission Workshop on Slotting Allowances and Other Marketing Practices in the Grocery Industry,* February 2001, p. 69.

51. Robert A. Skitol, "FTC Spices Up Debate over Slotting Fees and the Robinson-Patman Act with Its McCormick Action," March 13 2000, American Antitrust Institute FTC: Watch #540 (retrieved from www.antitrustinstitute.org, August 8, 2004).

52. *The Point of Purchase Advertising Industry Fact Book* (Washington, DC: POPAI, 1997), p. 51.

53. Kelly Shermach, "Study: Most Shoppers Notice P-O-P Material," *Marketing News,* January 1995, pp. 27.

54. *The Point of Purchase Advertising Industry Fact Book,* p. 39.

55. Kelly Shermach, "Great Strides Made in P-O-P Technology," *Marketing News,* January 2, 1995, pp. 8–9.

56. Angela Lawson, "The End of the Line," June 18, 2004 (retrieved from www.kioskmarketplace.com, August 8, 2004).

57. Kathleen M. Joyce, "Fast Clip," *Promo Magazine,* April 1, 2003; "CPG Coupon Volume on the Rise: NCH Study," *Promo Magazine,* April 11, 2003 (retrieved from http://promomagazine.com).

58. The 16th Annual Survey of Promotional Practices, Donnelley Marketing Inc., 1994.

59. "About Us," Catalina Marketing (retrieved from www.catalinamarketing.com/our_advantage/index.html, August 8, 2004).

60. Bruce Crumley, "Multipoints Adds Up for Quick Burger," *Advertising Age,* November 29, 1993, p. 14.

61. Stephanie Moore, "Rebate Madness: How to Defend Yourself against Ruthless Rebate Scams" (retrieved from www.consumeraffairs.com, August 8, 2004).

62. Lorraine Calvacca, "Polybagging Products to Pick Up Customers," *Folio: The Magazine for Magazine Management,* January 1993, p. 26.

Chapter Eleven

1. www.benjerry.com (retrieved August 4, 2004).

2. Ibid.

3. Ben & Jerry's Homemade, Inc., press release, "Fight Global Warming with Ice Cream, Music and Activism: Dave Matthews Band, Ben & Jerry's

and Environmental Leaders Launch One Sweet Whirled Campaign," April 2, 2002 (retrieved from www.benjerry.com, August 5, 2004).

4. Ben & Jerry's Homemade, Inc., press release, "Ben & Jerry's Announces Environmentally Friendly Packaging Innovation: Company Offers to Share ECO-Pint Information," February 22, 1999 (retrieved from www.benjerry.com, August 5, 2004).

5. Ben & Jerry's Homemade, Inc., press release, "Turn It Up to Cool It Down! This Earth Day, Ben & Jerry's Introduces Thermoacoustic Refrigeration—An Environmentally Friendly Way to Chill Out," April 15, 2004 (retrieved from www.benjerry.com, August 5, 2004).

6. Ben & Jerry's Homemade, Inc., press release, "Happiness Is . . . Free Ice Cream! Ben & Jerry's Celebrates 25th Annual Free Cone Day," April 22, 2003 (retrieved from www.benjerry.com, August 5, 2004).

7. Ben & Jerry's Homemade, Inc., press release, "Ben & Jerry's and Unilever to Join Forces," April 12, 2000 (retrieved from www.benjerry.com, August 5, 2004).

8. Jim Osborne, "Getting Full Value from Public Relations," *Public Relations Journal,* October/November 1994, p. 64.

9. CSPI Newsroom, "Ben & Jerry's Fudging the Truth, Says CSPI: Nothing 'All-Natural' about Ingredients," July 30, 2002 (retrieved from www.cspinet.org/new/200207301.html, August 8, 2004).

10. Ben & Jerry's Homemade, Inc., press release, "Ben & Jerry's Response to CSPI Concerns," July 31, 2002 (retrieved from www.benjerry.com, August 8, 2004).

11. Ben & Jerry's Homemade, Inc., press release, "Ben & Jerry's Voluntarily Initiates the Recall of Pints of Karamel Sutra Ice Cream with Code 02/14/04," March 28, 2003 (retrieved from www.benjerry.com, August 8, 2004).

12. Sandra Moriarty, "PR and IMC: The Benefits of Integration," *Public Relations Quarterly,* Fall 1994, pp. 38–44.

13. Publisher's Statement, *Inside PR,* March 1993, p. 3.

14. Thomas L. Harris, "PR Gets Personal," *Direct Marketing,* April 1994, pp. 29–32.

15. Al Ries and Laura Ries, *The 22 Immutable Laws of Branding* (New York: HarperCollins, 1998), pp. 25–31.

16. "Coke Faces Struggle in Europe Recovery, Goldman Report Says," *The Wall Street Journal,* July 28, 1999, p. B5.

17. Ibid.

18. Bill Patterson, "Crisis Impact on Reputation Management," *Public Relations Journal,* November 1993, p. 48.

19. Ben White, "Stewart's Legal Problems Hurt Firm," *Washington Post,* August 4, 2004, p. E01 (retrieved from www.washingtonpost.com/wp-dyn/articles/A38202-2004Aug3.html).

20. Dennis L. Wilcox, *Public Relations Strategies and Tactics* (New York: HarperCollins, 1994), p. 381.

21. "What's Your Best Marketing Tool?" *Public Relations Journal,* February 1994, p. 12.

22. Adapted from Stephanie Gruner, "Event Marketing: Making the Most of Sponsorship Dollars," *Inc.,* August 1996, p. 88.

23. IEG FAQ: "What Is Sponsorship?" IEG Network 1998 (www.sponsorship.com).

24. Ibid.

25. "IEG Sponsorship Report, "Sponsorship Spending in North America," 2003 (www.sponsorship.com/learn/northamericaspending.asp); IEG Sponsorship Report, "Sponsorship Spending Worldwide," 2003 (www.sponsorship.com/learn/worldwidespending.asp).

26. "Telco Ericsson Calls on James Bond, Volleyball," *Advertising Age,* June 1997 (www.adage.com).

27. "Let Sponsors Do Their Thing," *Advertising Age,* May 23, 1996 (www.adage.com).

28. "Impact of Sponsored Events Cited," *Advertising Age,* December 9, 1997 (www.adage.com).

29. Thomas R. Duncan and Sandra E. Moriarty, *Driving Brand Value: Using Integrated Marketing to Manage Stakeholder Relationships* (New York: McGraw-Hill, 1997), p. 203.

30. Ibid.

31. Ibid.; Terry G. Vavra, *Aftermarketing: How to Keep Customers for Life Through Relationship Marketing* (Burr Ridge, IL: Irwin Professional Publishing, 1992), p. 190.

32. Vavra, *Aftermarketing,* p. 192.

33. "Assertions," *IEG Sponsorship Report* (www.sponsorship.com); Ron Lemasters, Jr., "Sponsorship in NASCAR Breeds Fan Loyalty," Turner Sports Interactive, July 7, 2004 (www.nascar.com/2004/news/business/07/07/sponsor_nascar).

34. Vavra, *Aftermarketing,* p. 192.

35. "Where the Dollars Go," *IEG Sponsorship Report 2003,* (www.sponsorship.com/learn/wheredollarsgo.asp).

36. Ibid.

37. Jonathan Bond and Richard Kirshenbaum, *Under the Radar: Talking to Today's Cynical Consumers* (New York: John Wiley and Sons, 1998), p. 63.

38. Melanie Wells, "Going for Nagano Gold; Nagano's Remoteness Challenges Marketers," *USA Today,* February 6, 1998, p. 1B.

39. Boaz Herzog, "Let the Ads Begin," *The Oregonian,* August 13, 2004, p. B01.

40. Eric Prisbell, "Summer Camps without Counselors: Shoe Companies Rule Hoops Scene," *Washington Post,* July 26, 2004, p. D01.

41. Junu Bryan Kim, "Most Sponsorships Waste Money: Exec," *Advertising Age,* June 21, 1993, pp. S2, S4.

42. "California, L.A. a Contender to Host Next Summer's X Games," *Los Angeles Times,* October 11, 2002 (www.proquest.com).

43. Lesa Ukman, "Assertions," *IEG Sponsorship Report,* February 23, 1998 (www.sponsorship.com).

44. "Soccer Sponsorship Grows Rapidly in Argentina," *Advertising Age,* September 9, 1997 (www.adage.com).

45. "Get Ready for the Bangalore Braves," *Advertising Age,* December 3, 1997 (www.adage.com).

46. Vans Warped Tour '04 (www.warpedtour.com/attractions.html).

47. Lesa Ukman, "Assertions," *IEG Sponsorship Report,* November 3, 1997 (www.sponsorship.com).

48. Wilcox, *Public Relations Strategies and Tactics,* p. 384.

49. Lesa Ukman, "Assertions," *IEG Sponsorship Report,* November 3, 1997 (www.sponsorship.com).

50. David Lister and Colin Brown, "Arts World Takes Sides with Tobacco Kings," *Independent* (UK), June 30, 1997, p. 3.

51. John Karolefski, "The Sport of Naming," Brand Channel.com, May 13, 2002 (www.brandchannel.com).

52. Paul Stanley, "Sponsownership: Sponsorships Will Become Standard for Events," *Potentials in Marketing,* June 1990, p. 64.

53. "Nabisco's Cornnuts Sponsors Skaters Association Pro Tour," e-sports! PR Sportswire, December 1, 2000 (retrieved from www.e-sports.com, December 30, 2000).

54. Lesa Ukman, "Assertions," *IEG Sponsorship Report,* January 26, 1998 (www.sponsorship.com).

55. Vavra, *Aftermarketing,* p. 191.

56. "Corporate Advertising/Phase II, An Expanded Study of Corporate Advertising Effectiveness," conducted for *Time* magazine by Yankelovich, Skelly & White, undated.

Chapter Twelve

1. Gary Levin, "VitroRobertson Lets Success Do the Talking," *Advertising Age,* August 29, 1994, p. 29; Ken Mendelbaum, "I Wish I'd Done That Ad," for Magazine Publishers of America, *Adweek,* September 19,

1994, p. 29; private correspondence and interviews with Taylor Guitar and VitroRobertson, February 1995.

2. Adapted from interviews and private correspondence with Hugh G. Cannon, Wayne State University, 1997.

3. Adapted from Bruce Bendinger, *The Copy Workshop Workbook* (Chicago: The Copy Workshop, 1993), pp. 128–47.

4. Hank Seiden, *Advertising Pure and Simple* (New York: AMACOM, 1990), pp. 23–340.

5. Nancy A. Mitchell, Diane M. Badzinski, and Donna R. Pawlowski, "The Use of Metaphors as Vivid Stimuli to Enhance Comprehension and Recall of Print Advertisements," in Karen Whitehill King, ed., *Proceedings of the 1994 Conference of the American Academy of Advertising* (Athens, GA: Henry W. Grady College of Journalism and Mass Communication, the University of Georgia, 1994), p. 199.

6. Ibid.

7. Sandra Moriarty and Shay Sayre, "An Interpretive Study of Visual Cues in Advertising," paper presented to the annual convention of the Association for Education in Journalism and Mass Communication, Montreal, August 1992, p. 5.

8. Sal Randazzo, *The Mythmakers: How Advertisers Apply the Power of Classic Myths and Symbols to Create Modern Day Legends* (Chicago: Probus Publishing, 1995), pp. 28–51.

9. Barry A. Hollander, "Infomation Graphics and the Bandwagon Effect: Does the Visual Display of Opinion Aid in Persuasion?" paper presented to the annual convention of the Association for Education in Journalism and Mass Communication, Montreal, August 1992, p. 21.

10. Kevin Goldman, "Nike, H-P Gamble on New Sales Pitches," *The Wall Street Journal,* April 8, 1994, p. B8.

11. J. P. Guilford, "Traits of Personality," in *Creativity and Its Cultivation* (New York: Harper, 1959).

12. Allen F. Harrison and Robert M. Bramson, *The Art of Thinking* (New York: Berkley Books, 1984), pp. 5–18, 182.

13. Roger von Oech, *A Whack on the Side of the Head* (New York: Warner Books, 1990), pp. 35–37.

14. Anthony Alessandra, James Cathcart, and Phillip Wexler, *Selling by Objectives* (Englewood Cliffs, NJ: Prentice Hall, 1988), pp. 31–56.

15. Harrison and Bramson, *The Art of Thinking,* pp. 26, 34, 181.

16. Ibid.

17. Goldman, "Nike, H-P Gamble on New Sales Pitches," p. B5.

18. Roger von Oech, *A Kick in the Seat of the Pants* (New York: Harper-Perennial, 1986), p. 12.

19. Adapted with permission from ibid., pp. 24–53.

20. John O'Toole, *The Trouble with Advertising,* 2nd ed. (New York: Random House, 1985), p. 132; Fred Danzig, "The Big Idea," *Advertising Age,* November 9, 1988, pp. 16, 138–40.

21. O'Toole, *The Trouble with Advertising,* pp. 132–33.

22. Adapted with permission from von Oech, *A Kick in the Seat of the Pants,* pp. 55–87.

23. Bob Garfield, "Lovestruck Praying Mantis Is Hooked on Fila," *Advertising Age,* February 13, 1995, p. 3.

24. Von Oech, *A Whack on the Side of the Head,* p. 6.

25. Ibid., pp. 108–43.

26. Kevin Goldman, "Leap Partnership Touts All-Creative Shop," *The Wall Street Journal,* December 23, 1993, p. B3.

27. William D. Perreault Jr. and E. Jerome McCarthy, *Basic Marketing,* 14th ed. (Burr Ridge, IL: Richard D. Irwin, 2002), p. 467.

28. Adapted with permission from von Oech, *A Kick in the Seat of the Pants,* pp. 89–111.

29. Kevin Goldman, "The Message, Clever as It May Be, Is Lost in a Number of High-Profile Campaigns," *The Wall Street Journal,* July 27, 1993, pp. B1, B8.

30. Adapted with permission from von Oech, *A Kick in the Seat of the Pants,* pp. 15–16.

31. Bendinger, *The Copy Workshop Workbook,* pp. 170–74.

32. David Ogilvy, *Ogilvy on Advertising* (New York: Random House, 1985), pp. 17–18.

Chapter Thirteen

1. U.S FTC and Synovate Research, *Identity Theft Survey Report* (September 2003), 4-7, accessed October 28, 2004, at www.ftc.gov/os/2003/09/synovatereport.pdf.

2. U.S. FTC, *Overview of the Identity Theft Program* (September 2003), 8, accessed October 28, 2004, at www.ftc.gov/os/2003/09/timelinereport.pdf.

3. Quoted in Eleftheria Parpis, "Campaign of the Year: Citibank," *Adweek* 45, no. 6 (February 9, 2004): 30, accessed October 28, 2004, at www.proquest.com.

4. Ibid.

5. Mae Anderson, "Creative Best Spots: April," *Adweek* 45, no. 20 (May 17, 2004): 26–27, accessed October 28, 2004, at www.proquest.com. See also Lance Ulanoff, "Opting into Identity Theft," *PC Magazine* online (July 21, 2004), accessed October 29, 2004, at www.pcmag.com.

6. Sue Chastain, ed., "Types of Graphics Software, Part 3," About.com, October 5, 1999, http://graphicssoft.about.com/library/weekly/aa051099.htm.

7. Jeremy Sindair, "Why I Think It's Time for a New Kind of Advertising," *Campaign* (UK), September 8, 2000 (retrieved from Lexis-Nexis Academic Universe http://web.lexis-nexis.com/universe/printdoc, January 2001).

8. Glenn Mohrman and Jeffrey E. Scott, "Truth(s) in Advertising? Part II," *Medical Marketing & Media,* October 1, 1988, pp. 28–32.

9. A. Jerome Jeweler and Bonnie L. Drewniany, *Creative Strategy in Advertising* (Belmont, CA: Wadsworth Publishing, 1998), p. 139.

10. Roy Paul Nelson, *The Design of Advertising* (Dubuque, IA: Brown & Benchmark, 1994), p. 107; J. Douglas Johnson, *Advertising Today* (Chicago: Science Research Associates, 1978).

11. John O'Toole, *The Trouble with Advertising,* 2nd ed. (New York: Random House, 1985), p. 149.

12. Axel Andersson and Denison Hatch, "How to Create Headlines That Get Results," *Target Marketing,* March 1994, pp. 28–35.

13. Murray Raphel and Neil Raphel, "A New Look at Newspaper Ads," *Progressive Grocer,* November 1993, pp. 13–14; David Ogilvy, *Ogilvy on Advertising* (New York: Random House, 1985), pp. 88–89.

14. Philip Ward Burton, *Advertising Copywriting,* 6th ed. (Lincolnwood, IL: NTC Business Books, 1991), pp. 65–66, 70.

15. Nelson, *The Design of Advertising,* p. 91.

16. Jeweler and Drewniany, *Creative Strategy in Advertising,* p. 115; Burton, *Advertising Copywriting,* p. 188; Julia M. Collins, "Image and Advertising," *Harvard Business Review,* January/February 1989, pp. 93–97.

17. Neil Raphel and Murray Raphel, "Rules to Advertise By," *Progressive Grocer,* December 1993, pp. 13–14; Murray Raphel, "How to Get Ahead in Direct Mail," *Direct Marketing,* January 1990, pp. 30–32, 52.

18. Jay Conrad Levinson, *Guerrilla Advertising* (Boston: Houghton Mifflin, 1994), p. 168.

19. Ogilvy, *Ogilvy on Advertising,* p. 71.

20. Raphel and Raphel, "A New Look at Newspaper Ads," pp. 13–14.

21. James H. Leigh, "The Use of Figures of Speech in Print Ad Headlines," *Journal of Advertising Research,* June 1994, pp. 17–33.

22. Ogilvy, *Ogilvy on Advertising,* pp. 10–11.

23. Andersson and Hatch, "How to Create Headlines That Get Results," pp. 28–35.

24. Burton, *Advertising Copywriting*, p. 54; Arthur J. Kover and William J. James, "When Do Advertising 'Power Words' Work? An Examination of Congruence and Satiation," *Journal of Advertising Research*, July/August 1993, pp. 32–38.

25. Burton, *Advertising Copywriting*, p. 58.

26. Raphel and Raphel, "A New Look at Newspaper Ads," pp. 13–14.

27. Burton, *Advertising Copywriting*, p. 54.

28. Ibid., p. 65; Andersson and Hatch, "How to Create Headlines That Get Results," pp. 28–35.

29. Bruce Bendinger, *The Copy Workshop Workbook* (Chicago: The Copy Workshop, 1993), p. 177.

30. Burton, *Advertising Copywriting*, p. 12.

31. Raphel and Raphel, "Rules to Advertise By," pp. 13–14.

32. Bendinger, *The Copy Workshop Workbook*, p. 192.

33. Burton, *Advertising Copywriting*, p. 74.

34. Ogilvy, *Ogilvy on Advertising*, p. 119.

35. Burton, *Advertising Copywriting*, p. 79.

36. Leigh, "The Use of Figures of Speech in Print Ad Headlines," pp. 17–33.

37. Burton, *Advertising Copywriting*, p. 90; Marjorie Zieff-Finn, "It's No Laughing Matter," *Direct Marketing*, September 1992, pp. 38–40.

38. O'Toole, *The Trouble with Advertising*, p. 149.

39. Joanne Lipman, "It's It and That's a Shame: Why Are Some Slogans Losers?" *The Wall Street Journal*, July 16, 1993, pp. A1, A4.

40. Levinson, *Guerrilla Advertising*, p. 203; Burton, *Advertising Copywriting*, pp. 221–22.

41. Herschell Gordon Lewis, "Radio Copywriting—Not as Easy as You May Think," *Direct Marketing*, July 1992, pp. 17–18.

42. Adapted with permission from Bob Garfield, "The Best Ad Missed the Boat to Cannes," *Advertising Age*, June 23, 1997, p. 29.

43. Ogilvy, *Ogilvy on Advertising*, p. 109.

44. Ibid., pp. 103–13.

45. Bendinger, *The Copy Workshop Workbook*, p. 284.

46. Ibid., p. 250.

47. "Corporate Advertising Study," Burson-Marsteller, October 13, 2003, www.efluentials.com/documents/pr_101303.pdf.

48. John Morkes and Jakob Nielsen, "Concise, SCANNABLE, and Objective: How to Write for the Web," 1997 (www.useit.com/papers/web writing/writing.html).

49. Reid Goldsborough, "Text Demands Respect on the Web; Viewpoint: Looks Do Count, But an Honest Presentation Matters More," *Advertising Age*, July 31, 2000, p. 44.

50. Richard N. Weltz, "How Do You Say, 'Ooops!'" *Business Marketing*, October 1990, pp. 52–53.

51. Lennie Copeland, "Foreign Markets: Not for the Amateur," *Business Marketing*, July 1984, pp. 112–18.

52. John Freiralds, "Navigating the Minefields of Multilingual Marketing," *Pharmaceutical Executive*, September 1994, pp. 74–78.

Chapter Fourteen

1. Saatchi & Saatchi Los Angeles and Toyota Motor Sales, personal correspondence and interviews, January 2001.

2. Susan and Gregory Pyros, "Success Depends on Organization & Planning," *Computer Pictures*, January/February 1994, p. 31.

3. Personal interview, Lorraine Alper Kramer, Saatchi & Saatchi Los Angeles, January 2001.

4. "Argentinian Ad Industry Rocked by New 10.5% Tax," *Advertising Age*, August 1996 (www.adage.com).

5. Wayne Robinson, *How'd They Design and Print That?* (Cincinnati: North Light Books, 1991), p. 6.

6. "Paper Costs Rise," *American Printer*, February 1995, p. 11.

7. "AAAA Survey Finds 8 Percent Hike in Cost to Produce 30-Second TV Commercials," ICom, October 14, 2002 (retrieved from www.icommag.com/november-2002/november-page-1b.html, August 26, 2004).

8. Cleveland Horton, "Spots: Cheaper Is More Effective," *Advertising Age*, July 4, 1994, p. 6.

9. Kenneth Roman and Jane Maas, *How to Advertise* (New York: St. Martin's Press, 1992), pp. 26–28; Miner Raymond, "How to Cut Commercial Production Costs without Anyone Knowing You've Done It," *Sales & Marketing Management in Canada*, December 1987, pp. 20–22; "Marketing Guide 19: Advertising Production," *Marketing* (UK), February 7, 1991, pp. 21–24.

10. "Multimedia on Wheels," *Multimedia Today* 2, no. 4 (1994), pp. 44–49.

11. Button Pushers: Ordering Kiosks Boost Sales and Speed of Service but Don't Necessarily Cut Labor Costs," *Chain Leader* 9, no. 1 (January 2004), p. 54 (retrieved from www.lexisnexis.com, August 26, 2004).

12. Scott Banerjee and Ed Christman, "Players Race to Place Kiosks," Billboard.com, July 11, 2004 (retrieved from www.lexisnexis.com, August 26, 2004); "Best Buy Enhances the Image of Digital Kiosks," *Retail Merchandiser*, August 1, 2004 (retrieved from www.lexisnexis.com, August 26, 2004).

13. Personal interview, Dean Van Eimeren, Saatchi & Saatchi Los Angeles, April 2001, p. 51.

14. Ibid., January 2001.

15. PANTONE® is a registered trademark of PANTONE, Inc.

16. Kathleen Lewis, "Printing: Teach Your Boss a Lesson," *In-House Graphics*, February 1990, p. 89.

17. Dave Zwang, "Proof of What? (New Technologies in Proofing Operations)," *American Printer*, October 1, 1996, pp. 40–44.

18. Jonathan Bond and Richard Kirshenbaum, *Under the Radar: Talking to Today's Cynical Consumer* (New York: John Wiley & Sons, 1998), p. 154.

19. Andrew Olds, "Creativity-Production: The Generalists," *Advertising Age*, January 1, 1990, pp. S26–S29, S31.

20. Adapted from Greg Hofman, "Splash Graphics That Say 'Gotcha,'" *Step-by-Step Graphics*, May/June 1991, p. 40.

21. David Ogilvy, *Ogilvy on Advertising* (New York: Random House, 1985), pp. 113–16.

22. Tom Cuniff, "The Second Creative Revolution," *Advertising Age*, December 6, 1993, p. 22.

23. Kate Fitzgerald, "Budget, New Media Issues on Front Burner," *Advertising Age*, April 4, 1994, p. 26.

Chapter Fifteen

1. National Institutes of Health.

2. "Milk Mustache Campaign Moves into Second Phase," *DQA Quest*, August 1996.

3. Laura Bird, "'Custom' Magazines Stir Credibility Issues," *The Wall Street Journal*, February 14, 1994, p. B10.

4. Stephanie Thompson and Jack Neff, "Covering All the Bases: Kraft Expands Circ for *Food & Family*; Targeted Title May Cut into Print Spending," *Advertising Age*, November 11, 2002, p. 41 (retrieved from www.lexis-nexis.com).

5. "Magazines by Circulation for 6 Mos. Ended 12/31/2002," AdAge.com Data Center (retrieved from www.adage.com, March 2003).

6. Patrick M. Reilly and Ernest Beck, "Publishers Often Pad Circulation Figures," *The Wall Street Journal*, September 30, 1997, p. B12.

7. Shu-Fen Li, John C. Schweitzer, and Benjamin J. Bates, "Effectiveness of Trade Magazine Advertising," paper presented to the annual conference of the Association for Education in Journalism and Mass Communication, Montreal, Quebec, August 1992.

8. Gene Willhoft, "Is 'Added Value' Valuable?" *Advertising Age*, March 1, 1993, p. 18.

9. Stephen M. Blacker, "Magazines' Role in Promotion," *Advertising Age,* June 30, 1994, p. 32.

10. Answers: *Car & Driver* is $113.79 CPM, *Car & Driver* media kit (www.caranddriver.com); *Road & Track* is $114.33 CPM, *Road & Track* media kit (www.roadandtrack.com).

11. Lisa I. Fried, "New Rules Liven Up the Rate-Card Game," *Advertising Age,* October 24, 1994, p. S8.

12. "CorePrint 2.2 Stewardship," COREMedia Systems, Inc. (retrieved from www.coremedia-systems.com, April 16, 2001); "STRATA's Media Buying," STRATA Marketing Inc. (retrieved from www.stratag.com, April 16, 2001); rate data from *SRDS Consumer Magazine Advertising Source* 85, no. 4 (April 2003).

13. Joyce Rutter Kaye, *Print Casebooks 10/The Best in Advertising,* 1994–95 ed. (Rockville, MD: RC Publications, 1994), pp. 63–65; Tony Case, "Getting Personal," *Editor & Publisher,* February 1, 1992, pp. 16, 31; Ann Cooper, "Creatives: Magazines—Believers in the Power of Print," *Adweek* (Eastern ed.), April 12, 1993, pp. 34–39.

14. "Facts about Newspapers," Newspaper Association of America (retrieved from www.naa.org/info/facts04, October 8, 2004).

15. Ibid.

16. Ibid.

17. Ronald Redfern, "What Readers Want from Newspapers," *Advertising Age,* January 23, 1995, p. 25.

18. "Facts about Newspapers."

19. "Newspaper Cirbulation Volume," Newspaper Association of America (retrieved from www.naa.org, October 8, 2004).

20. "General Facts on *Parade*" (retrieved from www.parade.com/mediarelations, October 9, 2004).

21. "Top 100 Daily Newspapers in the United States," Infoplease Arts & Entertainment Almanac (retrieved from www.infoplease.com/ipea, October 8, 2004).

22. *Newspaper Rate Differentials* (New York: American Association of Advertising Agencies, 1990); Christy Fisher, "NAA Readies National Ad-Buy Plan," *Advertising Age,* March 1, 1993, p. 12.

23. "Facts about Newspapers."

24. John Flinn, "State of the National Buy," *Adweek,* June 26, 1995, p. 56.

25. Christy Fisher, "Chrysler's One-Stop Ad Buys Boost Ailing Newspapers," *Advertising Age,* March 7, 1994, p. 49.

26. Dorothy Giobbe, "One Order/One Bill System Gets a Dress Rehearsal," *Editor & Publisher,* March 12, 1994, pp. 26, 46.

27. Fisher, "Chrysler's One-Stop Ad Buys Boost Ailing Newspapers," p. 49; ibid.

28. Joe Mandese and Scott Donaton, "Wells Rich Tests 4A's Liability Clause," *Advertising Age,* April 22, 1991, pp. 1, 40; Willie Vogt, "Defining Payment Liability," *AgriMarketing,* May 1992, pp. 42–43.

29. Sally D. Goll, "Ignoring the Masses, Avenue Magazine Launches an Edition for China's Elite," *The Wall Street Journal,* September 28, 1994, p. B1.

30. Stephen Barr, "Moving Ahead," *Adweek,* January 31, 1994, p. 26.

Chapter Sixteen

1. Paula Mergenhagen. "How 'Got Milk?' Got Sales," *American Demographics,* September 1996.

2. Ibid.

3. "TV Basics: Television—Top Ad Medium" (retrieved from www.tvb.org, March 23, 2003).

4. "U.S. Advertising Expenditures—All Media," Newspaper Association of America (retrieved from www.naa.org, August 26, 2004).

5. "TV Basics: Commercial Television Stations" (retrieved from www.tvb.org, August 26, 2004).

6. "TV Basics: Reach-Broadcast vs. Cable" (retrieved from www.tvb.org, August 26, 2004).

7. "Time Spent Viewing—Households," Television Bureau of Advertising, Inc. (retrieved from www.tvb.org, April 11, 2001); "Time Spent Viewing—Persons," Television Bureau of Advertising, Inc. (retrieved from www.tvb.org, April 11, 2001); "Consumer Media Usage," Television Bureau of Advertising, Inc. (retrieved from www.tvb.org, April 11, 2001).

8. "TV Basics: Channels—Receivable vs. Viewed," Television Bureau of Advertising, Inc. (retrieved from www.tvb.org, August 26, 2004).

9. "Ad-Supported Cable Networks" (retrieved from www.cabletvadbureau.com, March 23, 2003).

10. "Media Comparisons Study 2003," TVB Research Central (retrieved from www.tvb.org/mediacomparisons, October 11, 2004).

11. "Time Spent Viewing by TV Source in Hrs:Mins per Week (2000/01)" (retrieved from www.cabletvadbureau.com, March 24, 2003).

12. "Basic Cable—Biggest Gains," *Cable Advertising,* CableSCAN, a division of Tapscan, Inc., December 1997 (www.cableads.com); *Marketer's Guide to Media,* Fall/Winter 1992–93, p. 50.

13. "Advertising Revenues Will Reach over $14 Billion in 2002" (retrieved from www.cabletvadbureau.com, March 24, 2003).

14. "TV Basics: Channels—Receivable vs. Viewed."

15. Thomas R. Duncan and Sandra E. Moriarty, *Driving Brand Value: Using Integrated Marketing to Manage Stakeholder Relationships* (New York: McGraw-Hill, 1997), pp. 101–2.

16. Ibid.

17. Eric Schmuckler, "Betting on a Sure Thing," *MediaWeek,* January 23, 1995, pp. 18–20; Steve Coe, "UPN Beats . . . Everybody," *Broadcasting & Cable,* January 23, 1995, pp. 4, 10; T. L. Stanley, "Network Branding," *Brandweek,* January 9, 1995, pp. 30–32; Ronald Grover, "Are Paramount and Warner Looney Tunes?" *BusinessWeek,* January 9, 1995, p. 46; David Tobenkin, "New Players Get Ready to Roll," *Broadcasting & Cable,* January 2, 1995, pp. 30–33.

18. Michael Freeman, "Lucie Salhany," *Mediaweek,* January 23, 1995, pp. 34–35; Eric Schmuckler, "New Network Ready to Roll," *MediaWeek,* October 10, 1994, p. 3; Eric Schmuckler, "Media Outlook '95: Network TV," *Adweek,* September 19, 1994, pp. S8–S12.

19. "How Cable Stacks up against the Competition," Cabletelevision Advertising Bureau (retrieved from www.cabletvadbureau.com, August 26, 2004).

20. Kathy Haley, "Spot TV Is Power Tool," *The Power of Spot TV,* supplement to *Advertising Age,* September 29, 1993, p. T3.

21. "National Sales Reps Are Key to the Spot TV Mix," *The Power of Spot TV,* supplement to *Advertising Age,* September 23, 1992, pp. T10, T12.

22. Haley, "Spot TV Is Power Tool," p. T3; Kathy Haley, "Reps Zero In on Advertiser Goals," *The Power of Spot TV,* supplement to *Advertising Age,* September 29, 1993, p. T6.

23. Michael Burgi, "Welcome to the 500 Club," p. 45; Christopher Stern, "Advertisers Hear Promise of Smooth Spot Cable Buys," *Broadcasting & Cable,* April 26, 1993, pp. 56, 58.

24. R. Craig Endicott, "100 Leading National Advertisers," *Advertising Age,* June 28, 2004, p. S21.

25. "What Is Syndication?" *1994 Guide to Advertiser-Supported Syndication,* supplement to *Advertising Age* (New York: Advertiser Syndicated Television Association, 1994), p. A6; David Tobenkin, "Action Escalates for Syndicators," *Broadcasting & Cable,* August 29, 1994, pp. 29–35.

26. "Syndication Showcase," *Broadcasting & Cable,* January 24, 1994, pp. 82–86.

27. Kathy Haley, "The Infomercial Begins a New Era as a Marketing Tool for Top Brands," *Advertising Age,* January 25, 1993, p. M3.

28. Nancy Coltun Webster, "Marketers Look to Cable for Direct-Response Ads," *Advertising Age Special Report: Cable TV,* December 8, 1997, p. S8.

29. Jim Cooper, "Long-Form Ad Used in Contract Dispute," *Broadcasting & Cable,* May 24, 1993, p. 71.

30. Kevin Goldman, "CBS to Push Videotaping of Infomercials," *The Wall Street Journal,* November 15, 1993, p. B7.

31. Ibid.; Tom Burke, "Program-Length Commercials Can Bring These Six Benefits to a Major Brand Campaign," *Advertising Age,* January 25, 1993, p. M5.

32. Webster, "Marketers Look to Cable for Direct-Response Ads."

33. "1999 U.S. Advertising Volume," *Advertising Age* (retrieved from www.adage.com, April 10, 2001); Nielsen Media Research (retrieved from www.nielsenmedia.com, April 10, 2000).

34. Jack Honomichl, "Top 25 Global Firms Earn $6.1 Billion in Revenue," *Marketing News,* August 18, 1997, p. H2; Nielsen Media Research, (retrieved from www.nielsenmedia.com, May 2001); "Media Measured" (retrieved from www.nielsenmedia.com/monitor-plus, October 12, 2004).

35. Bill Carter, "Television: A Monopoly Once More, Nielsen Is Still Unloved," *The New York Times,* September 7, 1992, p. 19; Jim Cooper, "Arbitron Exit Sparks Concern about Lack of Competition," *Broadcasting & Cable,* October 25, 1993, p. 45.

36. Jane Hall, "Company Town: Networks Give Nielsen a Low Rating; Television: Calling the Firm's Method Inaccurate and Antiquated, NBC, CBS and ABC Are Investing in the Test of an Alternate System," home edition, *Los Angeles Times,* May 24, 1996, p. D4.

37. Tracey M. Dooms, "Nielsen Comes under Fire; TV Networks Say Research Firm Hasn't Kept Pace with Today's Viewers," *Indianapolis Business Journal,* March 3, 1997, p. 17A (2).

38. Will Workman, "ADcom's Cable Meter: A Revolution in the Making," *Cable World,* March 17, 1997 (www.mediacentral.com).

39. Ibid.

40. Kevin Goldman, "CBS Pays Price for Losing Bet on Ratings," *The Wall Street Journal,* November 30, 1993, p. B4; Kevin Goldman, "CBS Again Must Offer Make-Good Ads," *The Wall Street Journal,* October 27, 1994, p. B6; Kevin Goldman, "'Scarlett' Make-Goods," *The Wall Street Journal,* November 21, 1994, p. B8.

41. Kevin Goldman, "Cable-TV Ads Fight Satellite Dish Threat," *The Wall Street Journal,* February 6, 1995, p. B8.

42. Joanne Lipman, "Video Renters Watch the Ads, Zapping Conventional Wisdom," *The Wall Street Journal,* April 28, 1989, p. B1.

43. Wei-Na Lee and Helen Katz, "New Media, New Messages: An Initial Inquiry into Audience Reactions to Advertising on Videocassettes," *Journal of Advertising Research,* January/February 1993, pp. 74–85.

44. *Radio Marketing Guide & Fact Book For Advertisers 2000–2001 Edition,* Radio Advertising Bureau, p. 5, 6, 9 (retrieved from www.rab.com, April 11, 2001).

45. "Radio Is Cost-Effective," *1997 Radio Marketing Guide and Fact Book for Advertisers.*

46. "Radio's Personalities Help Find Snapple's Sales Targets," *The Power of Radio,* special advertising supplement to *Advertising Age,* October 18, 1993, p. R3.

47. "Media Comparisons," *1997 Radio Marketing Guide and Fact Book for Advertisers; Imagery Transfer Study* (New York: Network Radio Association, 1993).

48. Ibid.; *Media Facts: The Complete Guide to Maximizing Your Advertising* (New York: Radio Advertising Bureau, 1994), pp. 8–9.

49. "Maximize Your Marketing Message with Radio," *1997 Radio Marketing Guide and Fact Book for Advertisers; Radio Marketing Guide and Factbook for Advertisers: 1993–1994,* pp. 29–33.

50. "There's a Radio Format for Everybody," *1997 Radio Marketing Guide and Fact Book for Advertisers.*

51. *Network Radio: Targeting the National Consumer,* supplement to *Advertising Age,* September 6, 1993, pp. R2, R4; *Marketer's Guide to Media,* Fall/Winter 1992–93, pp. 69–70.

52. Janet Stilson, "Radio Scraps for Its Ad Share," *Advertising Age,* February 2, 2004, p. 22 (retrieved from www.lexisnexis.com, October 12, 2004).

53. Scott MacDonald, "Cable, Satellite TV Fuel Top 100," from "100 Leading Media Companies," *Advertising Age,* August 25, 2004, p. S2 (retrieved from www.lexisnexis.com, October 12, 2004).

54. Ibid.

Chapter Seventeen

1. Meeting with Rik Kinney and Stephanie Yost Cameron at NeoPets office in Glendale, California, March 25, 2003; "NeoPets Online Presskit" (retrieved from http://info.neopets.com/presskit, September 2, 2004).

2. Thom Forbes, "Ads in Cyberspace: Light Your Beacon, but Don't Get Flamed," *Agency,* Winter 1995, p. 32.

3. "December Shopping Up from Last Year in Spite of Rough Economy, According to the Forrester Research Online Retail Index," January 24, 2002 (retrieved from www.forrester.com).

4. Janis Mara, "Slow, Steady Ad Growth Predicted for 2004," *ClickZ News,* December 30, 2003 (retrieved from www.clickz.com/news/article.php/3293681, September 2, 2004).

5. "eMarketer: Worldwide B2B Revenues to Pass One Trillion," April 1, 2003 (retrieved from www.nua.com/surveys).

6. Kevin Goldman, "Shopping Comes to Cyberspace with Launch of On-Line Catalogs," *The Wall Street Journal,* November 18, 1994, p. B7.

7. "Web Characterization," Online Computer Library Center, Inc., Office of Research (retrieved from http://wcp.ock.org, September 2, 2004).

8. "Top 25 Websites for October Announced," *Relevant Knowledge,* 1997 (www.relevantknowledge.com); "Media Metrix Top 50 US Web & Digital Media Properties for November 2000" (http://us.mediametrix.com).

9. "Media Metrix Top 50 U.S. Web & Digital Media Properties for April 2004" (retrieved from www.comscore.com, September 2, 2004).

10. "How Many Online?" Nua Internet Surveys, September 2002 (retrieved from www.nua.com/surveys/how_many_online/n_america.html); "United States: Average Web Usage, July 2004," Nielsen//NetRatings (retrieved from www.nielsen-netratings.com, September 3, 2004).

11. "Countries with Highest Internet Penetration Rate," Internet World Stats, September 1, 2004 (retrieved from www.internetworldstats.com, September 3, 2004).

12. Mary Kuntz, "Burma Shave Signs on the I-Way," *BusinessWeek* via America Online, April 17, 1995.

13. Marissa Gluck, "Online Advertising through 2005: Flourishing in the Dot-com Decline," Vision Report, Jupiter Research, August 16, 2000 (retrieved January 2001 from www.jup.com); "IAB Advertising ABC's," Internet Advertising Bureau, 1997 (www.iab.net); Kate Fitzgerald, "Debate Grows over Net Data," *Advertising Age,* March 15, 2004 (retrieved from www.adage.com, September 3, 2004).

14. Susannah Fox, principal researcher, *Older Americans and the Internet,* Pew Internet and American Life Project, pp. 2–3, March 25, 2004 (retrieved from www.pewinternet.org/pdfs/PIP_Seniors_Online_2004.pdf, September 1, 2004).

15. Tom Spooner, principal researcher, *Internet Use by Region in the United States,* Pew Internet and American Life Project, August 27, 2003 (retrieved from www.pewinternet.org/pdfs/PIP_Regional_Report_Aug_2003.pdf, September 1, 2004).

16. U.S. Census Bureau, "Table No. 1156 Internet Access and Usage and Online Service Usage: 2003," *Statistical Abstract of the U.S. 2003,* p. 735 (retrieved from www.census.gov/prod/2004pubs/03statab/inforcomm.pdf, September 1, 2004).

17. Ibid.

18. Tobi Elkin and Jack Neff, "Dove Soap Study Documents Branding Impact of Online Ads: Analyzed a Six-Week Integrated Campaign," Ad Age.com, February 20, 2002 (retrieved from www.adage.com/news).

19. "Baseband Transmission," *Webopedia* (retrieved January 2001 from http://webopedia.internet.com).

20. "Broadband Transmission," *Webopedia* (retrieved January 2001 from http://webopedia.internet.com).

21. Greg Holden, "DSL vs. Cable: The Truth about Cable," CNET Internet (retrieved January 2001 from www.cnet.com).

22. Greg Holden, "DSL vs. Cable: The Straight Dope about DSL," CNET Internet (retrieved January 2001 from www.cnet.com).

23. "DSL Beats Cable Modem in Prime-Time Internet Performance Duel," press release from Keynote Systems, May 17, 1999 (retrieved January 2001 from www.keynote.com/news/announcements/pr051799.html).

24. Holden, "DSL vs. Cable: The Straight Dope about DSL."

25. Craig Crossman, "Computer Column," Knight Ridder Tribune Business News, October 6, 2004, p. 1 (retrieved from www.proquest.com, October 15, 2004).

26. Tobi Elkin, "51% of US Online Time Now Broadband," AdAge.com, March 5, 2002 (retrieved from www.adage.com/news); "Broadband Access Grows 59 Percent, while Narrowband Use Declines, According to Nielsen//NetRatings," Nielsen//NetRatings press release, January 15, 2003 (retrieved from www.nielsennetratings.com); "U.S. Broadband Connections Reach Critical Mass," Nielsen//NetRatings press release, August 18, 2004 (retrieved from www.nielsennetratings.com/pr/pr_040818.pdf, September 3, 2004).

27. Jane Black, "Where the Online Ad News is Good," Business Week Online, January 17, 2002 (retrieved from www.businessweek.com/bwdaily).

28. Netlingo Dictionary, 1997 (www.netlingo.com).

29. Samantha Yaffe, "Are Marketers Undervaluing the Internet?" *Strategy*, March 8, 2004, p. 1 (retrieved from www.lexis-nexis.com, September 3, 2004).

30. "IAB Announces Final Interactive Universal Ad Package," Interactive Advertising Bureau Press Release, April 28, 2003 (retrieved from http://www.iab.net/news).

31. Stefanie Olsen, "Bigger Web Ads Endorsed by Industry," C/NET News.com, December 11, 2002 (retrieved from http://news.com.com).

32. Macromedia website (www.macromedia.com/resources/richmedia).

33. Charles Waltner, "Going Beyond the Banner with Web Ads," *Advertising Age*, March 4, 1996, p. 22.

34. Claudia Kuehl, "Spam's Good Twin If E-mail Is Done Just Right, People Will Want to Receive It. Really," The DMA Interactive, Library White Papers, May 2000 (retrieved January 2001 from www.the-dma.org/library/whitepapers/spamsgoodtwin.shtml).

35. Bart Lazar, "CAN-SPAM Creates Quandary, Opportunities," *Marketing News*, June 15, 2004 (retrieved from www.lexis-nexis.com, September 1, 2004); William Jackson, "FTC Files First CAN-SPAM Cases," *Newsbytes*, April 29, 2004 (retrieved from www.lexis-nexis.com, September 1, 2004).

36. David Gikandi, "Find and Keep: Sticky and Viral Site Marketing," *Web Developer's Journal*, Internet.com (retrieved January 2001 from www.webdevelopersjournal.com).

37. Amanda Beeler, "Word-of-Mouth Pitches Mutate into New Forms on the Internet," *Advertising Age*, April 2000 (retrieved January 2001 from www.adage.com).

38. Michael Krantz, "Style in America: Modemocracy in Action," *Adweek*, November 7, 1994, pp. 28–31.

39. "Metrics and Methodology," The Media Measurement Task Force, Internet Advertising Bureau, September 15, 1997.

40. Kate Maddox, "ANA Study Finds Marketers Triple Net Ad Budgets," *Advertising Age*, May 1998 (retrieved from www.adage.com).

41. "United States," Ad Age Dataplace (retrieved from http://adage, June 2001).

42. Ibid.

43. Ibid.

44. Alicia Orr, "The Lowdown on High Tech," *Target Marketing,"* January 1995, pp. 8–10.

45. Ibid.

46. "Kiosks Bring Out the Vote," *New Media*, August 1994, p. 32.

47. "New Media Envision Multimedia Awards," *New Media*, August 1994, pp. S16, S19.

48. Orr, "The Lowdown on High Tech."

49. Dinesh C. Sharma, "Study: DVR Adoption on the Rise," CNET News.com, March 30, 2004 (retrieved from http://news.com.com/Study+DVR+adoption+on+the+rise/2100-1041_3-5182035.html?tag=nl, October 14, 2004).

50. Ann M. Mack, "Ad-justment," *Adweek* 45, no. 35 (September 20, 2004), pp. 28–31 (retrieved from www.proquest.com, October 14, 2004).

51. Ibid.

52. Andrew K. Macris (www.macrisdirect.com/directmail.html).

53. Jen Adams, "Broad PR Initiative Is Key in Delivering ShipShape Launch," *PR Week*, May 31, 2004 (retrieved from www.lexis-nexis.com, September 1, 2004).

54. Quoted in ibid.

55. Quoted in "Customized MarketMail Testimonials: The Krispy Kreme Doughnut Company" (retrieved from www.usps.com/customizedmarketmail/testimonials.htm, September 1, 2004).

56. Adams, "Broad PR Initiative Is Key in Delivering ShipShape Launch."

57. "Customized MarketMail Testimonials: ShipShapes."

58. "ShipShapes First to Take Advantage of USPS Changes Allowing Direct Mail Attachments," *PR Newswire*, June 28, 2004 (retrieved from www.lexis-nexis.com, September 1, 2004).

59. "Quick Service Guide 660 Standard Mail Customized MarketMail," USPS, July 2004 (retrieved from http://pe.usps.gov/text/qsg/q660.htm).

60. R. Craig Endicott, "100 Leading National Advertisers," *Advertising Age*, June 28, 2004.

61. Sherry Chiger, "More, More, More," *Catalog Age* 21, no. 7 (July 2004), p. 15 (retrieved from www.proquest.com, October 14, 2004).

62. Sherry Chiger, "Looking Up: The *Catalog Age* 100," *Catalog Age* 21, no. 9 (August 2004) (retrieved from www.proquest.com, October 14, 2004).

63. Robert H. Hallowell III, "The Selling Points of Direct Mail," *Trusts & Estates*, December 1994, pp. 39–41.

64. Sherry Chiger, "Benchmark 2004: Lists," *Catalog Age* 21, no. 8 (August 1, 2004) pp. 34–38 (retrieved from www.proquest.com, October 15, 2004).

Chapter Eighteen

1. Mary Yeung, *Print Casebooks 9: The Best in Advertising* (Rockville, MD: R. C. Publications, 1991), pp. 19–20.

2. "Facts and Figures," Outdoor Advertising Association of America, Inc. (retrieved from www.oaaa.org, October 8, 2004).

3. "Introduce Yourself to Outdoor Advertising," Outdoor Advertising Association of America, Inc. (retrieved from www.oaaa.org, October 8, 2004).

4. *Billboard Basics* (New York: Outdoor Advertising Association of America, 1994), p. 5.

5. www.oaaa.org (retrieved October 8, 2004).

6. Mary Jo Haskey, "The Last Mass Medium," *Mediaweek*, December 6, 1993, p. 17.

7. Ibid., pp. 11, 21; Kevin Goldman, "Billboards Gain Respect as Spending Increases," *The Wall Street Journal*, June 27, 1994, p. B5.

8. Riccardo A. Davis, "Apparel, Movies Orchestrate an Outdoor Rebirth," *Advertising Age*, November 22, 1993, p. S2.

9. Institute of Outdoor Advertising, press release, 1991.

10. "Facts and Figures," OAAA about Outdoor (retrieved from www.oaaa. org/outdoor/facts/cpmcomparison.asp, October 11, 2004).

11. "Technology Standards," Outdoor Advertising Association of America, 1997 (www.oaaa.org/Tech).

12. Ibid.

13. Cyndee Miller, "Outdoor Advertising Weathers Repeated Attempts to Kill It," *Marketing News,* March 16, 1992, pp. 1, 9; *Billboard Basics,* pp. 15–16.

14. "Surveys Show Americans Like Their Billboards," Outdoor Advertising Association of America, 1997 (www.oaaa.org).

15. Davis, "Apparel, Movies Orchestrate an Outdoor Rebirth," p. S1.

16. Joan Brightman, "Signs of the Times," *Marketing Tools,* July/August 1995; Riccardo A. Davis, "Patrick Media Eyes Hispanics," *Advertising Age,* January 17, 1994, p. 27.

17. Riccardo A. Davis, "Retailers Open Doors Wide for Co-op," *Advertising Age,* August 1, 1994, p. 30.

18. "Advertising That Imitates Art," *Adweek,* June 20, 1994, p. 18.

19. Fara Warner, "DKNY Takes Upscale Ads Underground," *The Wall Street Journal,* October 6, 1994, p. B4; "Nextel, Las Vegas Link Brands in Monorail Deal," *Los Angeles Times,* November 17, 2003 (retrieved from www.lvmonorail.com/about_01_news_detail.asp, September 9, 2004).

20. James Ferrier, "Spotlight on Technology—Telecite," *Advertising Age,* November 22, 1993, p. SS10.

21. *The Point of Purchase Advertising Industry Fact Book* (Englewood, NJ: Point of Purchase Advertising Institute, 1992), p. 51.

22. "Industry Relations; Westpack '97: The World's Fair of Packaging National Manufacturing Week," Material Handling Equipment Distributors Online, 1997 (www.mheda.org).

23. W. Wossen Kassaye and Dharmendra Verma, "Balancing Traditional Packaging Functions with the New 'Green' Packaging Concerns," *SAM Advanced Management Journal,* Autumn 1992, pp. 15–23.

24. Ibid.

25. Ibid.

26. Chris Baum, "10th Annual Packaging Consumer Survey 1994: Consumers Want It All—And Now," *Packaging,* August 1994, pp. 40–43.

27. Wayne Robinson, *How'd They Design and Print That?* (Cincinnati, OH: North Light Books, 1991), pp. 74–75.

28. Kassaye and Verma, "Balancing Traditional Packaging Functions with the New 'Green' Packaging Concerns."

29. Susan A. Friedmann, *Exhibiting at Trade Shows* (Menlo Park, CA: Crisp Publications, 1992), p. V.

30. Ibid., p. 16.

31. Helen Berman, "The Advertising/Trade Show Partnership," *Folio: The Magazine for Magazine Management,* May 1, 1995, pp. 44–47.

32. Friedmann, *Exhibiting at Trade Shows,* p. 24.

33. Ibid., pp. 34–39.

34. Ibid., p. 44.

35. Ibid., pp. 70–71.

36. Ibid., p. 90.

37. "Promotional Products Fact Sheet," Promotional Products Association International, Irving, TX, 1995.

38. "1993 Estimate of Promotional Products Distributor Sales," Promotional Products Association International, Irving, TX, 1994.

39. *Promote Customer Referrals with Promotional Products* (Irving, TX: Promotional Products Association International, 1994).

40. *How Specialty Advertising Affects Goodwill* (Irving, TX: Specialty Advertising Association International, 1993).

41. Avraham Shama and Jack K. Thompson, "Promotion Gifts: Help or Hindrance?" *Mortgage Banking,* February 1989, pp. 49–51.

42. *Yellow Pages Industry Facts Booklet,* 1994–95 edition (Troy, MI: Yellow Pages Publishers Association, 1994), p. 32.

43. "Independent Yellow Pages Publishers' Revenues to Increase 16.7% to $2.8 Billion in 2004," *PR Newswire,* July 19, 2004 (retrieved from www.lexisnexis.com, September 9, 2004).

44. "100 Leading Media Companies," *Advertising Age* Special Report, August 23, 2004, p. S7.

45. Bradley Johnson, "Yellow-Pages Deals Red Hot as Telecom Industry Regroups," *Advertising Age,* January 6, 2003 (retrieved from www.proquest.com, May 12, 2003).

46. Randall Crosby, "Is Ride-Along the Right Track?" *Link,* February 1995, pp. 17–23.

47. Kevin Goldman, "Capital Cities Builds New Media Sales Unit," *The Wall Street Journal,* January 24, 1994, p. B7.

48. Nicole Sperling, "Cinema Advertising Exhibits Growth," *The Hollywood Reporter,* June 14, 2004 (retrieved from www.lexisnexis.com, September 9, 2004).

49. Emma Hall, "Young Consumers Receptive to Movie Product Placement," *Advertising Age,* March 29, 2004 (retrieved from www.lexisnexis.com, September 9, 2004).

50. Michael McCarthy, "Also Starring (Your Product Name Here)," *USA Today,* August 12, 2004 (retrieved from www.lexisnexis.com, September 9, 2004).

Credits and **Acknowledgments**

Part One

p. 3, Reprinted with permission of the AAF.

Chapter 1

Photos/Ads

p. 5, Used with permission of Callard & Bowser-Souchard, Inc.; Agency: Leo Burnett/Chicago. **p. 7,** Courtesy International Advertising Festival Ltd. **p. 9,** Courtesy International Olympic Committee. **p. 11 all,** Courtesy International Advertising Festival Ltd. **p. 13,** Courtesy International Advertising Festival Ltd. **p. 16,** Courtesy International Advertising Festival Ltd. **p. 17 left,** Courtesy Palmer Jarvis DDB/Vancouver. **p. 17 right,** Courtesy Rational Therapeutic Cancer Evaluation Center. **p. 19,** Courtesy Saatchi & Saatchi/Singapore. **p. 20–23 all,** Used with permission of Callard & Bowser-Souchard, Inc.; Agency: Leo Burnett/Chicago.

Exhibits/Checklists/Ad Labs

Exhibit 1–2: "A Revised Communication Model for Advertising," *Journal of Advertising* 23 (2): 1–15.

Chapter 2

Photos/Ads

p. 29, Stock Montage, Inc. **p. 35,** Colonial Williamsburg Foundation. **p. 36,** Courtesy of The Coca-Cola Company. **p. 37 top,** Courtesy of The Coca-Cola Company. **p. 37 bottom,** Coolstock.com Advertising Archives. **p. 38 both,** Coolstock.com Advertising Archives. **p. 39 top,** Coolstock.com Advertising Archives. **p. 39 bottom,** Courtesy of The Coca-Cola Company. **p. 42,** Stock Montage, Inc. **p. 43,** Courtesy NW Ayer Agency. **p. 44,** Property of AT&T Archives. Reprinted with permission of AT&T. **p. 45 left and right,** These ads have been copyrighted and are reproduced with the permission of Volkswagen of America. **p. 46,** Courtesy International Advertising Festival Ltd. **p. 47 top,** Courtesy Bates Delvico. **p. 47 bottom,** Courtesy Team One Advertising/El Segundo, California; Photographer: Scott Downing. **p. 48,** Courtesy The Coca-Cola Company. **p. 49,** www.pbs.org/nova. **p. 51,** Courtesy Eisner Communications/Baltimore; Art Director: Mark Rosica; Photographer: Ron Simrod; Creative Director: Steve Etzie.

Exhibits/Checklists/Ad Labs

Exhibit 2–1: Adapted from www.kodak.com, "Milestones—Chronology." **Exhibit 2–4:** Top 10 global marketers. Adapted with permission from "Top 100 Global Marketers," *Advertising Age,* November 10, 2003; and "100 Leading National Advertisers," *Advertising Age,* June 28, 2004. Copyright Crain Communications, Inc. All rights reserved. **Ad Lab 2–A:** What Kills Bugs Dead? Adapted with permission from *Advertising Age,* December 13, 1993. Copyright Crain Communications, Inc. All rights reserved.

Chapter 3

Photos/Ads

p. 55, © Tim Boyle/Getty Images. **p. 57,** Concept: O. Toscanni. Courtesy of United Colors of Benetton. **p. 60,** Courtesy International Advertising Festival Ltd. **p. 61,** Courtesy DocuSystems. **p. 63 top,** Courtesy International Advertising Festival Ltd. **p. 63 bottom,** Stock Montage, Inc. **p. 64,** Courtesy Devito Verdi. **p. 66,** Courtesy The Ritz-Carlton Hotel Company; Agency: Sawyer Riley Compton/Atlanta; Creative Director: Bart Cleveland; Art Director: Tammy Anderson/Rick Bryson; Copywriter: Al Jackson; Account Team: Andrea Brooks/Alison Simmons; Photographer: Jim Erickson. **p. 67,** Courtesy Adworks, Inc. **p. 68,** Courtesy Saturn Corporation. **p. 69,** Courtesy Kadu Surfwear: Paul Bennell; Copywriter: Ben Nott; Photographer: Simon Howsant. **p. 71 top,** Courtesy DDB Needham/ New York. **p. 71 bottom,** Courtesy CLM/BBDO Paris. **p. 77 top,** Courtesy BBDO/Helsinki. **p. 77 bottom,** www.gala-marketlaw.com. **p. 81,** Courtesy Meyer & Wallis. **p. 82 both,** Courtesy Hewlett-Packard/Canada; Agency: Publicis Hal Riney. Client: Richard Cram. **p. 83,** © The Procter & Gamble Company. Used by permission. **p. 84 both,** Courtesy Pfizer Animal Health. **p. 86,** Courtesy The Coca-Cola Company. **p. 89,** Courtesy Heat-N-Glo.

Exhibits/Checklists/Ad Labs

Exhibit 3–1: Per capita ad spending around the world. Adapted with permission from "Advertising Industry Profile," Datamonitor, 2003. **Exhibit 3–4:** Children's Advertising Review Unit guidelines. Adapted with permission from "Self-Regulatory Guidelines for Children's Advertising: Principles," accessed at www.caru.org/guidelines/index.asp. **Ad Lab 3–C:** Sources: "Editorial vs. Advertorial," *Steel Kaleidoscopes,* June 4, 2004, accessed at http://Steelkaleidoscopes.typepad.com/steel_kaleidoscopes/); McMellon, Charles, "Will He? Or Won't He? A dilemma for a media supervisor," case study exchange, Hofstra University, January 7, 2004, accessed at www.aejmc.net/advertising/case/clairol.htm; and Mullin, Bill. "Magazine Advertising Content vs. Placement," *Marketing Electronic Products,* January 2003, accessed at http://elecprodz.com/mep/mep0103.pdf. **Exhibit 3–5:** AAAA comparative advertising guidelines. Used with permission from American Association of Advertising Agencies. **Exhibit 3–6:** Advertising Principles of American Business of the American Advertising Federation (AAF). Used with permission from AAF.

Chapter 4

Photos/Ads

p. 97, Courtesy Honda North America; Agency: Muse Cordero Chen/San Francisco. **p. 99 top,** Courtesy Rubio's Baja Grill. **p. 99 bottom,** Courtesy Butler, Shine & Stern/Sausalito. **p. 101,** Agency: Kirshenbaum Bond & Partners; Art Directors: Marta Ibarrondo and Lubna Abu-osba; Copywriter: Karen Dunbar. **p. 104,** Courtesy Siddall, Matsu & Coughter; Copywriter:

Navid Neale. **p. 105,** Courtesy of Dunkin' Donuts, Inc. and Hill, Holliday, Connors, Cosmopulos, Inc. **p. 108,** Courtesy Leo Burnett/Copenhagen. **p. 109,** Courtesy Mad Dogs & Englishmen; Writer: Deacon Webster; Art Director: Nick Cohen. **p. 112,** Courtesy Financial Times. **p. 114,** Courtesy International Advertising Festival Ltd. **p. 116,** Courtesy Honda North America; Agency: Muse Cordero Chen; Photo by: John Thoeming. **p. 118 both,** Courtesy Callison Architecture, Inc. **p. 120,** Concept: O. Toscani; Courtesy of United Colors of Benetton. **p. 121,** Courtesy of Fallon McElligott. **p. 127 all,** Courtesy of Kinetic Interactive (Singapore) PTE LTD—(www.kinetic.com). **p. 129 top,** Courtesy International Advertising Festival Ltd. **p. 129 bottom,** "Eat Mor Chikin" and "Chick-fil-A" are registered trademarks of Chick-fil-A, Inc. **p. 130,** Courtesy International Expeditions; Agency: Slaughter Hanson; Creative Director: Terry Slaughter; Art Director: Pat Powell; Photographer: Frans Lanting/Geoff Knight; Illustrators: Doug Benson/David Webb; Copywriter: Dave Smith.

Exhibits/Checklists/Ad Labs

Exhibit 4–2: Co-op dollars as a percent of ad budget. **Exhibit 4–3:** Top 10 Advertisers in the United States. Adapted with permission from R. Craig Endicott, "100 Leading National Advertisers," *Advertising Age,* June 28, 2004: S2, Copyright Crain Communications, Inc. All rights reserved. **Ad Lab 4–B:** Top 10 U.S. cities by billings. Adapted from "Agency report 2002," Advertising Age online, April 22, 2002, accessed at www.adage.com. World's top 10 advertising organizations; Top 10 U.S. agency brands. Adapted from R. Craig Endicott, "Agency Report," *Advertising Age,* April 19, 2004: S2. All used with permission and copyright Crain Communications, Inc., 2002 and 2004. All rights reserved. **Exhibit 4–8:** Top media companies in 2002. Adapted with permission from Scott MacDonald, "100 Leading Media Companies," *Advertising Age,* August 18, 2003. Copyright Crain Communications, Inc., 2003. All rights reserved. **Checklist:** Agency Review: Adapted with permission from March 30, 1981, issue of *Crain's Chicago Business.* Copyright Crain Communications, Inc., 1981. All rights reserved. **Checklist:** Ways to be a Better Client. Adapted from Kenneth Roman and Jane Maas, *How to Advertise* (New York: St. Martin's Press, MacMillan & Co., Ltd, 1976), 151–56.

Part Two
p. 135, Courtesy International Advertising Festival Ltd.

Chapter 5

p. 140, Courtesy International Advertising Festival Ltd. **p. 141,** Courtesy Audi of America, Inc.; Agency: McKinney & Silver/Raleigh. **p. 142,** By Fallon-McElligott/Rolling Stone. **p. 143,** © 2003. Land Rover North America, Inc. **p. 144,** Courtesy International Advertising Festival Ltd. **p. 145,** Courtesy Tibor Nemeth. **p. 150,** Courtesy International Advertising Festival Ltd. **p. 153,** Courtesy Stride Rite Corporation. **p. 154,** Courtesy Southwest Airlines; Agency: GSD&M/Austin. **p. 155,** PORSCHE, BOXSTER, the Porsche Crest are registered trademarks and the distinctive shapes of Porsche automobiles are trademarks of Dr. Ing. h.c.F Porsche AG. Used with permission of Porsche Cars North America, Inc. Copyrighted by Porsche Cars North America, Inc. **p. 156,** Courtesy of BDDP-GGT Advertising/London. **p. 157,** Courtesy Hewlett-Packard Company; Agency: Goodby, Silverstein & Partners/San Francisco. **p. 160,** Courtesy A.T. Cross Company. **p. 161 top,** Ogilvy & Mather/Singapore. **p. 161 bottom,** Army Reserves Materials courtesy of the U.S. Government, as represented by the Secretary of the Army. **p. 163,** Courtesy Leonard/Monahan Providence. **p. 164,** Courtesy Jenn-Air; Agency: Leo Burnett.

Exhibits/Checklists/Ad Labs

Exhibit 5–4: Rossiter, John R., and Larry Percy, *Advertising Communications and Promotion Management,* 2nd ed. (McGraw-Hill, 1997). Reprinted with permission from the McGraw-Hill Companies. **Exhibit 5–6:** Rossiter and Percy. **Exhibit 5–7:** Equifax National Decision Systems.

Chapter 6

Photos/Ads

p. 169, The Atlanta-Constitution Journal. **p. 171 top,** Courtesy Hardee's. **p. 171 bottom,** Courtesy David Yang. **p. 172,** Courtesy Crate & Barrel. **p. 173,** Courtesy Columbia Sportswear Company. **p. 176,** Courtesy International Advertising Festival Ltd. **p. 178,** Courtesy Adidas America, Inc. **p. 180,** Courtesy International Advertising Festival Ltd. **p. 182,** Courtesy Sybase, Inc. **p. 184,** Courtesy TBWA Hunt Lascaris/Capetown, South Africa. **p. 185,** Courtesy Braun, Inc. **p. 187,** Made by Telestar Interactive Corporation/Cincinnati, OH. **p. 189,** Courtesy BBDO/Toronto. **p. 190,** © M. Hruby. **p. 191,** Courtesy International Advertising Festival Ltd. **p. 192 top,** Courtesy Smith Eyewear. **p. 192 bottom,** Courtesy International Advertising Festival Ltd. **p. 196,** © 1995–2001 FedEx. All Rights Reserved. **p. 197 top,** Courtesy Hewlett-Packard Company; Agency: Goodby, Silverstein & Partners/San Francisco. **p. 197 bottom,** Courtesy International Advertising Festival Ltd. **p. 199,** Courtesy Catalina Marketing.

Exhibits/Checklists/Ad Labs

Exhibit 6–1: Methods for segmenting consumer markets. Data used with permission from Mediamark Research, Inc., 2000. **Exhibit 6–3:** Estimated annual ad spending in U.S. Hispanic market. Adapted with permission from "Hispanic Fact Pact," *Advertising Age* Supplement 2004: 23, accessed at www.adage.com. Copyright Crain Communications, Inc., 2004. **Exhibit 6–5:** The VALS (Values and Lifestyles) classification system. VALS2: Used with permission SRI International. **Ad Lab 6–A:** Market Segmentation: A Dog of A Job. Used with permission from Michael Reinemer, "It's a Dog's Life, and It's Time to Cash in on Trend," *Advertising Age* 65, no. 42 (October 3, 1994): 20. Copyright Crain Communications, Inc., 1994. **Exhibit 6–8:** Value of states' manufactured products. Adapted from U.S. Department of Commerce, Bureau of the Census, Census of Manufacturers, Area Statistics (Washington D.C.: Government Printing Office, 1995). **Exhibit 6–9:** Claritas MicroVision system Chicago map. Equifax National Decision Systems, 1993. **Exhibit 6–10:** Product life cycle curve. Adapted from Ben M. Ennis, *Marketing Principles* (Santa Monica, CA: Goodyear Publishing, 1980), 351. **Exhibit 6–12:** Reprinted with permission from the March 13, 1997 issue of *Advertising Age.* Copyright, Crain Communications, Inc., 1997. **Exhibit 6–13:** World's most valuable brands. Adapted with permission from "The World's 10 Most Valuable Brands," *BusinessWeek* 3958 (August 4, 2003), accessed at www.businessweek.com. **Exhibit 6–14:** Adapted from Elwood S. Buffa and Barbara A. Pletcher, *Understanding Business Today* (Burr Ridge, IL: Richard D. Irwin, 1980), 37. **Ad Labs 6–B, 6–C, and 6–D:** Starbucks and the 4Ps. Sources: Diane Brady et al., "Cult Brands," *BusinessWeek* 3958 (August 9, 2004): 58; Starbucks "Annual Report 2004," part I; "Corporate Social Responsibility Annual Report 2003"; and "Timeline and History," all accessed at www.starbucks.com/aboutus/.

Chapter 7

Photos/Ads

p. 205, Courtesy Healthtex; Agency: The Martin Agency. **p. 207,** © 2002 Nielsen//NetRatings. **p. 208,** Courtesy Healthtex; Agency: The Martin Agency. **p. 210,** Courtesy Healthtex; Agency: The Martin Agency. **p. 212,** Courtesy Bissel. **p. 215,** www.edgar-online.com. **p. 218,** Courtesy Nordhaus Research, Inc./Southfield, MI. **p. 220,** Courtesy Envirosell, Inc. **p. 222,** TABASCO®, the TABASCO® diamond logo and the TABASCO® bottle design are trademarks exclusively of McIlhenny Co., Avery Island, LA. 70513. **p. 223,** Courtesy Roper Starch Worldwide, Inc. and Sara Lee Corporation. **p. 229 both,** Courtesy International Advertising Festival Ltd.

Exhibits/Checklists/Ad Labs

Exhibit 7–1: Top 10 research companies. Adapted with permission from "Top 50 U.S. Research Organizations," American Marketing Association, accessed at www.data.marketingpower.com/live/content19312.php. **Exhibit 7–2:** Categories of research. Adapted with permission from Edmund J. Faison, *Advertising: A Behavioral Approach for Managers* (New York: John Wiley, 1980), 664. **Exhibit 7–8:** The reliability/validity diagram. Adapted from Pamela Alreck and Robert Settle, *The Survey Research Handbook* (Burr Ridge, IL: McGraw-Hill/Irwin, 1995), 32. **Checklist:** Developing an Effective Questionnaire. Adapted from Don E. Schultz and Dennis G. Martin, *Strategic Advertising Campaigns* (Chicago: Crain Books, 1979).

Chapter 8

Photos/Ads

p. 233, Courtesy Pepsi Cola Company. **p. 236,** Courtesy Pepsi Cola Company. **p. 237,** Courtesy of Vince the Mover. **p. 239,** Courtesy International Advertising Festival Ltd. **p. 241,** Agency: The Richards Group; Art Director: Jim Baldwin; Writer: Mike Renfro. **p. 242,** Courtesy CIT Group, Inc. **p. 243 both,** Courtesy British Airways. **p. 244,** Agency: J. Walter Thompson/New York; Client: Diamond Trading Company; Creative Directors: Chris D'Rozario and Ed Evangelista; Art Director: Phil Kelly; Copy Writer: Erik Izo; Photographer: Steve Hellerstein. **p. 249,** Concept: O. Toscani. Courtesy of United Colors of Benetton. **p. 250,** Courtesy International Advertising Festival Ltd. **p. 251,** Courtesy of Oneida, Ltd. **p. 253,** Courtesy TAM Airlines; Agency: DM9DDB; Copywriter: Manir Fadel; Art Director: Mariana Sa; Creative Director: Jader Rossetto, Pedro Cappeletti & Erh Ray; Photographer: Manolo Moran. **p. 254,** Courtesy Pepsi Cola Company. **p. 255,** Courtesy of Seattle Chocolate Company. **p. 256 top,** Courtesy International Advertising Festival Ltd. **p. 256 bottom,** Courtesy Milko/Romson—Sweden. **p. 257 top,** Courtesy International Advertising Festival Ltd. **p. 257 bottom,** Courtesy Black Rocket. **p. 258 top,** Courtesy HVAC. **p. 258 bottom,** Courtesy Friends of Boston's Homeless. **p. 259,** School: The Creative Circus; Copy Writer: Dave Laskarzewski.

Exhibits/Checklists/Ad Labs

Ad Lab 8–A: The Strategy of Marketing Warfare. Adapted from Al Ries and Jack Trout, *Marketing Warfare* (New York: McGraw-Hill, 1986). **Exhibit 8–3:** Relationship levels. Adapted from Philip Kotler and Gary Armstrong, *Principles of Marketing* (Englewood Cliffs, NJ: Prentice-Hall, 1994), 561. **Exhibit 8–7:** Wang-Schulz IMC planning model. Adapted from Don E. Schultz and Stanley Tannenbaum, and Robert Lauderborn, *Integrated Marketing Communications* (Lincolnwood, IL: NTC Business Books, 1993). **Exhibit 8–9:** Marketing feedback loop. Used with permission from *Marketing Tools* magazine. Copyright 1994. **Exhibit 8–11:** The Kim-Lord grid. Used with permission from Chung K. Kim and Kenneth R. Lord, "A New FCB Grid and Its Strategic Implications for Advertising," in *Proceedings of the Annual Conference of the Administrative Sciences Association of Canada (Marketing)*, ed. Tony Schellinck, 51–60 (Niagara Falls, Ontario, Administrative Sciences Association of Canada, 1991). **Ad Lab 8–B:** The Economic Effect of Advertising on Sales. Adapted from William J. Baumol and Alan S. Blinder, *Economics: Principles and Policy*, 3rd ed. (New York: Harcourt Brace Jovanovich, 1985), 386. **Exhibit 8–12:** Advertising expenditures by the top 15 advertisers. Used with permission from R. Craig Endicott, "100 Leading National Advertisers," *Advertising Age*, June 28, 2004: S2–S10. Copyright, Crain Communications, Inc., 2004.

Chapter 9

Photos/Ads

p. 267, Courtesy of Sony Electronics, Inc. **p. 270,** Courtesy BMW Canada Inc. ~ Mini; Agency: Taxi; Creative Director: Zak Mroueh; Copywriter: Michael Clowater; Art Director: Lance Martin. **p. 271,** Courtesy International Advertising Festival Ltd. **p. 272 left,** Agency: Mires Design Incorporated; Park Bench/Illustrator: Tracy Sabin; Designer: Jose Serrano. **p. 272 right,** Courtesy Woody Wilson, Tony DiPreta, Mort Walker, Dean Young, Stan

Drake; Designer: Jose Serrano. **p. 273,** Courtesy International Advertising Festival Ltd. **p. 279,** Courtesy International Advertising Festival Ltd. **p. 285,** Courtesy Kinko's, Inc. **p. 287,** The Advertising Practice/London. **p. 289,** Courtesy Fujitsu Computer Products of America, Inc. **p. 291,** Courtesy Godiva Chocolatier, Inc. **p. 293,** www.marketingcentral.com. **p. 297,** Telmar Flowmaster, www.us.telmar.com. **p. 298,** Courtesy SRDS.

Exhibits/Checklists/Ad Labs

Exhibit 9–1: U.S. ad spending by medium. Adapted with permission from "Total U.S. Spending by Media," *Advertising Age FactPack* 2004, accessed at www.adage.com. Copyright, Crain Communications, 2004. **Ad Lab 9–A:** Off-the-Wall Media. Sources: Elise Allen, "Outdoor Advertising," accessed at http://outdooradvertising.articleinsider.com/; Johnny Duncan, "Take It Outside . . . Current Trends in Out-of-Home Signage," accessed at www.signindustry.com; Sangita Joshi, "The Great Outdoors," *Business Line Internet Edition,* March 4, 2004, accessed at www.thehindubusinessline.com; and Jenny Schnetzer, "Outdoor Advertising: Big, Bold and Brassy," accessed at www.signweb.com/outdoor/cont/outdoor.html. **Exhibit 9–2:** Time spent with media. Used with permission from *Communications Industry Forecast,* Veronis Suhler Stevenson, 350 Park Avenue, New York, NY, Aug. 2002. **Exhibit 9–3:** Media powerhouses. Adapted with permission from Craig R. Endicott, "60th Annual Agency Report," *Advertising Age,* April 19, 2004: S-14. Copyright, Crain Communications, 2004. **Exhibit 9–6:** A media planner's toolbox. Adapted from Jack J. Sissors and Lincoln Bumba, *Advertising Media Planning,* 4th ed. (Lincolnwood, IL: NTC Business Books, a division of NTC Publishing Group, 1993), 9. **Exhibit 9–9:** Random combination table. Reprinted with permission of the McGraw-Hill Companies, from Jim Surmanek, *Introduction to Advertising Media Research: Planning and Buying* (Lincolnwood, IL: NTC Business Books, 1993), 119. **Exhibit 9–12:** BDI/CDI grid. Adapted from Sissors and Bumba, *Advertising Media Planning.* **Exhibit 9–13:** Top 10 countries outside the U.S. by billings. Reprinted with permission from *Advertising Age FactPack 2003,* accessed at www.adage.com. Copyright, Crain Communications, 2003. **Checklist:** International Media Planning. Adapted from Directories International, Inc. **Exhibit 9–14:** Effect of size and color. Adapted from "How is Advertising Readership Influenced by Ad Size and Color?" *Cahners Advertising Research Report* 105.1B, accessed at www.cahnerscarr.com/PDF/105.1B.pdf; and "Is Advertising Readership Affected by Ad Size?" *Cahners Advertising Research Report* 110.1C, accessed at http://www.cahnerscarr.com/PDF/110.1C.pdf.

Part Three

p. 303, Courtesy International Advertising Festival Ltd.

Chapter 10

Photos/Ads

p. 305, © 2003 Dell Computer Corp. All Rights Reserved. **p. 307,** © 2003 Dell Computer Corp. All Rights Reserved. **p. 308,** Courtesy International Advertising Festival Ltd. **p. 309,** Courtesy International Advertising Festival Ltd. **p. 310,** © 2002. American Express. **p. 314,** Courtesy Microsoft Corporation, **p. 315,** © Charles Gupton/CORBIS. **p. 316 top,** © Lands' End, Inc. Used with permission. **p. 316 bottom,** © 2003 Dell Computer Corp. All Rights Reserved. **p. 317,** Courtesy Total Gym. **p. 319 all,** Courtesy Orbitz. **p. 320,** Custom Medical Stock Photo. **p. 321,** © Photo Disc Blue. **p. 322,** Courtesy International Advertising Festival Ltd. **p. 323,** Courtesy Tri-Arc Beverage Group. **p. 326,** Courtesy Carmichael Lynch Advertising. **p. 327,** Ziggy Kluzny/Gamma Liaison. **p. 328,** Courtesy Nokia Americas. **p. 330 top,** Courtesy Campbell Soup Company. **p. 330 bottom,** Photo by John Saller. **p. 332 both,** Courtesy Gold's Gym.

Exhibits/Checklists/Ad Labs

Exhibit 10–1: Largest Direct Response Agencies. Adapted with permission from "The Direct Marketing Association Annual Direct Response Agency

Report for 2001," accessed at www.the-dma.org. **Exhibit 10–2:** RFM analysis of accounts. Adapted from Bob Stone, *Successful Direct Marketing Methods,* 6th ed. (New York: McGraw-Hill/Contemporary Books, 1996). **Exhibit 10–3:** Top 10 catalog companies. Adapted with permission from "The 2003 Top 100 U.S. Catalogers," accessed at www.catalogagemag.com/ar/marketing_catalog_age_ranking/. **Exhibit 10–4:** Who watches (and buys from) infomercials. Adapted with permission from "2003 Consumer Expenditure Study (Summary)," Electronic Retailing Association, accessed at www.retailing.org. **Checklist:** Creating Effective Sales Promotion: Copyright 2002 Sales Promotion Services, Inc. **Exhibit 10–6:** Effects of techniques for changing consumer behavior. Used with permission from "Study: Some Promotions Change Consumer Behavior," *Marketing News,* October 15, 1990: 12.

Chapter 11

Photos/Ads

p. 337, © M. Hruby. **p. 339 top,** Courtesy Crain's New York Business Goldsmith/Jeffrey, Inc. **p. 339 bottom,** Tara Flanagan. **p. 342,** Kevin Maney, "Kodak, Intel Put Heads Together," *USA Today,* May 1, 1998. Copyright 1998 USA TODAY. Reprinted with permission. **p. 346,** Courtesy Butler, Shine & Stern. **p. 347,** Courtesy Gateway, Inc. **p. 350,** Courtesy Panasonic. **p. 353,** Courtesy DGWB Advertising & Communications. **p. 355,** Courtesy Campbell Soup Company. **p. 356,** H. Howe/Allsport. **p. 358,** Courtesy NASA. **p. 360 top,** Courtesy Rainey Kelly Campbell Roalfe/Y&R/London. **p. 360 bottom,** Courtesy TAXI & Cossette Media. **p. 361 top,** Courtesy L.L.Bean, Inc. **p. 361 bottom,** Courtesy International Advertising Festival Ltd. **p. 362 top,** Courtesy International Advertising Festival Ltd. **p. 362 bottom,** Courtesy Neogama BBH/Sao Paulo. **p. 363 top,** Courtesy International Advertising Festival Ltd. **p. 363 bottom,** Courtesy International Advertising Festival Ltd.

Exhibits/Checklists/Ad Labs

Exhibit 11–1: 2004 public relations industry benchmarks. Data from Kathy Cripps, "Benchmark Data Reflects a Renewed Optimism in PR," *PRweek,* July 26, 2004: 5, accessed at www.proquest.com. **Ad Lab 11–A:** "Green" Advertising. This article was first published in *The Journal of Sustainable Product Design,* April 1998. Copyright 1998 J. Ottman Consulting, Inc. Sources: FTC, April 1999, retrieved from www.ftc.gov/opa/1999/9904/green.htm; 1999 Environment News Service, retrieved from http://ens.lycos.com/ens/apr99/1999L-04-11g.html; Green Seal, retrieved from www.greenseal.org/; Scientific Certification Systems, retrieved from www.scs1.com/; SPINE, 1999, retrieved from www.globalspine.com; Sierra Club California Legislative Alert, no. 97-2, May 9, 1997; and Jacquelyn Ottman and Virginia Terry, "Green Marketing and Eco-Innovation: Strategic Marketing of Greener Products," retrieved from www.greenmarketing.com/articles/JSP1Apr98.html, April 2001. **Exhibit 11–2:** Annual Sponsorship Spending. Adapted with permission from "Where the Dollars Go," *IEG Sponsorship Report 2003,* accessed at www.sponsorship.com. **Exhibit 11–3:** U.S. companies spending more than $50 million on event sponsorship. Adapted with permission from "Sponsorship Spending to Increase 8.7 Percent in 2004," *IEG Sponsorship Report* 22, no. 24 (December 2003): 4. **Checklist:** How to Select Events for Sponsorship. From Terry G. Vavra, *Aftermarketing: How to Keep Customers for Life Through Relationship Marketing* (Burr Ridge, IL: Irwin Professional Publishing, 1992). **Ad Lab 11–B:** David Ogilvy Talks About Corporate Advertising. Sources: Judann Dagnoll, "Ogilvy at 80," *Advertising Age,* November 4, 1991: 1, 53; David Ogilvy, *Ogilvy on Advertising* (New York: Crown Publishers, 1985), 117–26; and David Ogilvy, "We Sell, Or Else," *A.N.A./The Advertiser,* Summer 1992: 21–25.

Part Four

p. 369, Courtesy International Advertising Festival Ltd.

Chapter 12

Photos/Ads

p. 371, Ad Agency: Franklin Stoorza; Creative Directors: John Vitro, John Robertson; Art Director: John Vitro; Copywriter: John Robertson; Photographers: Art Wolfe, Marshall Harrington. **p. 373,** Courtesy Lowe Worldwide. **p. 374,** Agency: Frank Stoorza; Creative Directors: John Vitro, John Robertson; Art Director: John Vitro; Copywriter: John Robertson; Photographer: Art Wolfe. **p. 375,** Courtesy of California Department of Health Services. **p. 378,** Courtesy Beast/Hong Kong. **p. 379,** Courtesy International Advertising Festival Ltd. **p. 382,** Courtesy International Advertising Festival Ltd. **p. 383,** Courtesy Pepsi-Cola Company. **p. 384,** Courtesy Kelliher Samets Volk. **p. 387,** Courtesy International Advertising Festival Ltd. **p. 388,** Agency: Frank Stoorza; Creative Directors: John Vitro, John Robertson; Art Director: John Vitro; Copywriter: John Robertson; Photographers: Art Wolfe, Marshall Harrington. **p. 389 top,** Courtesy Volkswagen of America; Agency: Arnold Worldwide, Inc. **p. 389 bottom,** Courtesy Giovanni, FCB; Creative Director: Aaron Sutton; Art Director: Marcelo Pallotta; Copywriter: Aaron Sutton. **p. 393,** Courtesy K2 Skis. **p. 395,** Courtesy International Advertising Festival Ltd. **p. 398 both,** Courtesy International Advertising Festival Ltd. **p. 399 top left,** Courtesy International Advertising Festival Ltd. **p. 399 top right,** Courtesy Covenant House; Agency: Taxi; Creative Director Zak Mroueh, Paul Lavoie; Copywriter: Terry Drummond; Art Director: Alan Madill. **p. 399 bottom left,** Courtesy Berkshire Blanket; Art Director: Brian Gross; Copywriter: Alec Beckett; Agency: Nail Communications. **p. 400 top,** Courtesy International Advertising Festival Ltd. **p. 400 bottom,** Courtesy Toyota of Australia. **p. 401 top,** Courtesy International Advertising Festival Ltd. **p. 401 bottom,** Courtesy Leo Burnett Publicidade LTDA.

Exhibits/Checklists/Ad Labs

Exhibit 12–3: Leo Burnett Global Product Committee's rating scale. From Eirmalasare Bani, "Advertising Malaysian Style," *Adtimes Interactive,* February 7, 2001, accessed at http://adtimes.nstp.com.my/archive/, December 17, 2004. **Ad Lab 12–C:** The Creative Gymnasium. Exercises reprinted with permission from Roger von Oech and George Willet, *A Kick in the Seat of the Pants* (HarperCollins, 1986). Copyright 1986 by Roger von Oech.

Chapter 13

Photos/Ads

p. 405 both, Courtesy Cit Group, Inc. **p. 407 top,** Courtesy Ogilvy & Mather/Capetown. **p. 407 bottom,** Courtesy Cit Group, Inc. **p. 412 both,** Courtesy Tom Michael, Market Design/Encinitas, CA. **p. 413 all,** Courtesy Tom Michael, Market Design/Encinitas, CA. **p. 414 both,** Courtesy Tom Michael, Market Design/Encinitas, CA. **p. 415,** Courtesy Ogilvy & Mather Advertising/Bangalore, India. **p. 416,** Courtesy International Advertising Festival Ltd. **p. 417,** Courtesy The Allstate Insurance Company. **p. 419,** Courtesy International Advertising Festival Ltd. **p. 420,** Courtesy International Advertising Festival Ltd. **p. 421,** Courtesy International Advertising Festival Ltd. **p. 423,** Courtesy International Advertising Festival Ltd. **p. 425,** Courtesy McCann-Erickson Worldwide. **p. 426,** Courtesy Ford Motor Company. **p. 429,** Jack in the Box, Inc. **p. 430,** Courtesy MasterCard. **p. 434 both,** Courtesy Korean Air; Agency: Ogilvy & Mather/Hong Kong. **p. 435 both,** The Jupiter Drawing Room/Capetown.

Exhibits/Checklists/Ad Labs

Checklist: Writing Effective Copy. Sources: David L. Malickson and John W. Nason, *Advertising: How to Write the Kind that Works* (Charles Scribner's Sons, 1982), 74; Jay Conrad Levinson, *Guerilla Advertising* (New York: Houghton Mifflin, 1994), 174–75; Neil Raphael and Murray Raphel, "Rules to Advertise By," *Progressive Grocer,* December 1993: 13–14; William H. Motes et al., "Language, Sentence, and Structural Variations in Print Advertising," *Journal of Advertising Research,* September/October 1992: 63–77; and

"Copy Chaser Criteria," *Business Marketing,* January 1991: 33. **Checklist:** Creating Effective Radio Commercials. Source: Peter Hochstein, "Ten Rules for Making Better Radio Commercials," *Viewpoint III,* 1981. **Checklist:** Creating Effective TV Commercials. Sources: Bruce Bendinger, *The Copy Workshop* (Chicago: The Copy Workshop, 1993), 286–92; and David Ogilvy, *Ogilvy on Advertising* (New York: Random House, 1985). **Exhibit 13–3:** The Execution Spectrum. Developed by Hank Seiden. **Ad Lab 13–B:** Creative Ways to Sell on Radio. Adapted from Wallace A. Ross and Bob Landers, "Commercial Categories," in *Radio Plays the Plaza* (New York: The Radio Advertising Bureau, 1969).

Chapter 14

Photos/Ads
p. 439, Courtesy Saatchi & Saatchi/Los Angeles. **p. 440,** Courtesy Saatchi & Saatchi/Los Angeles. **p. 444,** Courtesy International Advertising Festival Ltd. **p. 449 both,** © M. Hruby. **p. 450 top,** Courtesy Elena Ramirez. **p. 450 bottom,** © M. Hruby. **p. 455–459 all,** Courtesy Saatchi & Saatchi/Los Angeles. **p. 461,** Digital Vision/Getty Images. **p. 463 all,** Courtesy Saatchi & Saatchi/Los Angeles. **p. 464 all,** © 2003. The New York Times. **p. 467,** Courtesy Saatchi & Saatchi/Los Angeles. **p. 470,** Courtesy Saatchi & Saatchi/Los Angeles.

Exhibits/Checklists/Ad Labs
Exhibit 14–2: Average cost to produce a TV commercial. Adapted from "AAAA Survey Finds Eight Percent Hike In Cost To Produce 30-Second TV Commercials," ICom, October 14, 2002, accessed at www.icommag.com/november-2002/november-page-1b.html, August 26, 2004. **Exhibit 14–6:** The production processes for film and videotape. Adapted from William M. Wellbacher, *Advertising* (Free Press, 1962), 273. Copyright Macmillan Publishing Co., Inc.

Part Five
p. 477, Courtesy International Advertising Festival Ltd

Chapter 15

Photos/Ads
p. 479, Courtesy National Fluid Milk Processor Promotion Board; Agency: Bozell Worldwide. **p. 484,** Courtesy International Advertising Festival Ltd. **p. 485,** Courtesy Chicago Magazine **p. 486 top,** Courtesy Saatchi & Saatchi/Hong Kong. **p. 486 bottom,** Courtesy Young & Rubicam/Saó Paulo. **p. 487 both,** Courtesy International Advertising Festival Ltd. **p. 488,** Courtesy Loeffler Ketchum Mountjoy/Charlotte. **p. 489 both,** Courtesy International Advertising Festival Ltd **p. 491,** Reprinted with permission from the February 10, 2003 issue of Advertising Age. Copyright, Crain Communications Inc. 2003. **p. 494,** Agency: Mad Dog & Englishman; Writer: Mikal Reich; Art Directors: Carol Holsinger, Gina Fortunato, David Cook; Creative Directors: Nick Cohen & David Cook. **p. 496,** Courtesy BBDO/Atlanta; Creative Director Lee Dayvault. **p. 497,** Courtesy David & Goliath. **p. 499,** Courtesy SRDS. **p. 501,** Reprinted with permission of the Newspaper Association of America. **p. 504,** Courtesy International Advertising Festival Ltd **p. 505,** © 2006 Newspaper Association of America.

Exhibits/Checklists/Ad Labs
Exhibit 15–1: Top 10 magazine advertisers. Adapted with permission from R. Craig Endicott, "100 Leading National Advertisers," *Advertising Age,* June 28, 2004: S-20. Copyright Crain Communications, Inc., 2004. **Exhibit 15–2:** An ad's position on the page influences its effectiveness. Adapted with permission from Magazine Publishers Association, *Magazine Newsletter of Research* 8, no.1. **Exhibit 15–3:** Advertisers benefit from selecting regional editions. Map courtesy of the Reader's Digest Association. **Exhibit 15–4:** Advertising costs for U.S. consumer magazines. Fall 2004 data courtesy of

SRDS. **Exhibit 15–5:** Top 10 newspaper advertisers. Adapted with permission of R. Craig Endicott, "100 Leading National Advertisers," *Advertising Age,* June 28, 2004: S-20. Copyright Crain Communications, Inc., 2004. **Exhibit 15–6:** International consumer magazine paid circulation. U.S. data courtesy of SRDS.

Chapter 16

Photos/Ads
p. 509 all, Courtesy California Milk Processor Board. **p. 516,** Courtesy International Advertising Ltd. **p. 520 all,** Courtesy International Advertising Festival Ltd. **p. 522–523,** Reprinted courtesy of Nielsen Media Research. **p. 532,** BDDP, Mancebo, Kaye. **p. 535,** Courtesy Agency: The Richards Group/Dallas; Client: Motel 6.

Exhibits/Checklists/Ad Labs
Exhibit 16–1: Top 10 network TV advertisers in the United States (2003). Adapted with permission from R. Craig Endicott, "100 Leading National Advertisers," *Advertising Age,* June 28, 2004: S-20. Copyright Crain Communications, Inc., 2004. **Exhibit 16–2:** Major cable TV networks. Adapted with permission from "Cable Network Profiles," Cable Television Advertising Bureau, 2004, accessed at www.onetvworld.org. **Exhibit 16–3:** TV is the most authoritative, influential, and persuasive advertising medium. Adapted with permission from "Media Comparisons Study 2003," TVB Research Central, accessed at www.tvb.org/mediacomparisons/. **Checklist:** The Pros and Cons of Broadcast TV Advertising. Source: "Marketing Tips: Electronic Media," Old Dominion University, accessed at www.odu.edu/ao/universitymarketing/electronic_media.html. **Exhibit 16–4:** Cable households are more likely to purchase goods and services. Adapted from "Cable HHs More Likely To Purchase Goods And Services Than Non-Cable HHs," Cabletelevision Advertising Bureau, accessed at www.oneworldtv.org. **Exhibit 16–5:** Top 10 cable network advertisers. Adapted with permission from R. Craig Endicott, "100 Leading National Advertisers," S-20. **Exhibit 16–6:** Where does all the money go? Adapted with permission from R. Craig Endicott, "100 Leading National Advertisers," S-21. **Exhibit 16–7:** Advertising cost per 30-second spot. Adapted with permission from Richard Linnet, "TV Show with Highest-Priced Ads: 'Friends,'" AdAge.com, September 15, 2003, accessed at www.adage.com/news.cms?newsId=38720. Copyright Crain Communications, Inc., 2003. **Exhibit 16–9:** Syndication viewing shares. Data courtesy of Nielsen Media Research, Copyright 1997. **Ad Lab 16–A:** Where Do Those Infamous TV Ratings Come From? Nielsen people meter: Reprinted courtesy of Nielsen Media Research. **Exhibit 16–10:** Market data courtesy of Nielsen Media Research, 1995. **Exhibit 16–11:** Daily and weekly reach of radio. Adapted from *Radio Marketing Guide & Fact Book for Advertisers, 2000–2001 Edition,* Radio Advertising Bureau, p. 8, accessed at www.rab.com. **Exhibit 16–12:** Radio station programming. Adapted with permission from R. Craig Endicott, "100 Leading National Advertisers," S-20. **Exhibit 16–13:** Radio mini-networks. Adapted from "Percentage of Total Station Programming Each Format Type," *M Street Journal,* February 1993. **Exhibit 16–14:** Top 10 national spot radio advertisers. Adapted with permission from R. Craig Endicott, "100 Leading National Advertisers," S-20.

Chapter 17

Photos/Ads
p. 539, Courtesy Neopets. **p. 541,** www.barnesandnoble.com. **p. 544 top,** www.animal.discovery.com. **p. 547 all,** Courtesy International Advertising Festival Ltd. **p. 548 bottom,** Courtesy International Advertising Festival Ltd. **p. 549 top,** Dentsu East Japan, Inc. **p. 551,** www.adcritic.com. **p. 555,** Alma BBDO/Saó Paulo. **p. 559,** © comScore Media Metrix. **p. 564,** www.ebay.com. **p. 565,** Courtesy Frank Mayer & Assoc., Inc. **p. 567 both,** Courtesy Conversant Marketing. **p. 571 both,** Courtesy SRDS. **p. 572,** Courtesy Air France USA; Agency: Wunderman Cato Johnson.

Exhibits/Checklists/Ad Labs

Exhibit 17–1: U.S. online advertising spending. Adapted with permission from Emarketer, "Ad Spending in the U.S.: Online & Offline," August 2004, accessed at www.emarketer.com/Report.aspx?ad_spend_aug04. **Exhibit 17–2:** Top 25 most visited websites. "Media Metrix Top 50 U.S. Web and Digital Media Properties for April 2004" (retrieved from www.comscore.com). **Exhibit 17–3:** Number of people online. Table adapted from "World Internet Usage and Population Statistics," Internet World Stats, September 1, 2004, accessed at www.internetworldstats.com/stats.htm. **Exhibits 17–4 and 17–5:** Household income composition and Internet use. Data from U.S. Census Bureau, "Table No. 1156: Internet Access and Usage and Online Service Usage: 2003," Statistical Abstract of the U.S. 2003, accessed at www.census.gov/prod/2004pubs/03statab/inforcomm.pdf. **Exhibit 17–6:** Percent of Internet ad revenues by type of advertising. "Internet Ad Revenues by Advertising Vehicle," *IAB Internet Advertising Revenue Report* (April 2004), 10, accessed at http://iab.net/resources/ad_revenue.asp. **Ad Lab 17–A:** Internet Ratings: The Next Frontier. Sources used with permission and accessed at www.adage.com: Kate Fitzgerald, "Debate grows over Net data," *Advertising Age,* March 15, 2004; Randall Rothenberg, "Understanding the Audience Knowability Paradox," *Advertising Age,* June 20, 2004; "Ad Buyers, Sellers Rip Online Audience Data Accuracy," *Advertising Age,* November 3, 2003; and "Old-Line Marketers Drive New Surge in Online Advertising," *Advertising Age,* March 15, 2004. Copyright Crain Communications, Inc., 2003 and 2004. **Exhibit 17–7:** Top 10 Internet advertisers. Adapted with permission from R. Craig Endicott, "100 Leading National Advertisers," *Advertising Age,* June 28, 2004: S-20. Copyright Crain Communications, Inc., 2004. **Exhibit 17–9:** Online ad spending. Adapted with permission from Laurel Wentz, "Global marketers spend $71 billion," accessed at www.adage.com. Copyright Crain Communications, 2001. **Exhibit 17–10:** Responses of 55 national advertisers. Adapted with permission of Forrester Research, September 8, 2004 (accessed October 14, 2004, at www.forrester.com. **Exhibit 17–11:** Top 10 catalog companies. Adapted with permission from Sherry Chiger, "Looking Up: The Catalog Age 100," *Catalog Age* 21, no. 9 (August 15, 2004), accessed at www.proquest.com.

Chapter 18

Photos/Ads

p. 577, Client: Garcia's Irish Pub; Agency: Crowley/Webb & Associates; Account Executive: Joseph Crowley, Bart Tschamler; Copywriter/Creative Director: Paul Cotter; Art Director: Jean Schweikhard; Media Director: Richard Spears. **p. 579,** Courtesy Wong Doody/Seattle. **p. 582 top,** Courtesy International Advertising Festival Ltd. **p. 582 bottom,** Nawrocki Stock Pho-

tos. **p. 584 both,** Courtesy International Advertising Festival Ltd. **p. 585,** Courtesy International Advertising Festival Ltd. **p. 586 top,** Courtesy International Advertising Festival Ltd. **p. 586 bottom,** Agency: FCB Portugal; Creative Director: Edson Athayde; Copywriter: Sandro Porto; Art Director: José Carlos Silva; Photographer: Picto (Francisco Prata). **p. 587 all,** Courtesy International Advertising Festival Ltd. **p. 588 both,** Courtesy Nashua. **p. 591,** Courtesy International Advertising Festival Ltd. **p. 592,** J. Walter Thompson/Hong Kong. **p. 593,** Courtesy The Firm. **p. 594,** Courtesy International Advertising Festival Ltd. **p. 596,** Courtesy Sandstrom Design. **p. 599,** Courtesy of Authentic Fossil. **p. 601,** Photo by Dave Hogan/Getty Images. **p. 602,** © Photo Disc.

Exhibits/Checklists/Ad Labs

Exhibit 18–1: Breakdown of out-of-home media. Outdoor Services, Division of Western Media, New York, NY. **Checklist:** The Pros and Cons of Outdoor Advertising. Outdoor Advertising: Guide to Out-of-Home, Gannett Outdoor Network, U.S., 1992, p.21; and Yellow Pages Industry Fact Book, 1990–1995 Edition (Troy, MI: Yellow Pages Publishers Association, 1994). **Exhibit 18–2:** Outdoor advertising expenditures. Adapted with permission from R. Craig Endicott, "100 Leading National Advertisers," *Advertising Age,* June 28, 2004: S-21. Copyright Crain Communications, Inc., 2004. **Ad Lab 18–A:** Type and Color in Outdoor Advertising: Outdoor Advertising Association of America, 1995. **Exhibit 18–3:** Billboard locations Courtesy Gannett Outdoor of Southern California. **Exhibit 18–4:** Monthly rates for standard 30-sheet posters. October 2004 Data courtesy of Lamar Outdoor Advertising, accessed at www.lamaroutdoor.com/main/rates/. **Exhibit 18–5:** Expectations and concerns in packaging development. W. Wossen Kassaye and Dharmendra Verma, "Balancing Traditional Packaging Functions with the New Green Packaging Concerns," SAM Advanced Management Journal, Autumn 1992, pp. 15-23. **Exhibit 18–6:** How do customers learn about trade shows? Trade Show Bureau, Denver, Colorado. **Exhibit 18–7:** How long a visitor will wait. Allen Konopacki, Incomm Research. **Exhibit 18–8:** Overall advertising reach from media combinations. Reprinted with permission of Yellow Pages Publishers Association (YPPA). **Exhibit 18–9:** Top Yellow Pages directory publishers. Adapted with permission from "100 Leading Media Companies," *Advertising Age* Special Report, August 23, 2004: S-7. Copyright Crain Communications, Inc., 2004.

Epilogue

Photos/Ads

p. 605–613, Courtesy MasterCard.

Company Index